MOON HANDBOOKS®

ARIZONA

NINTH EDITION

BILL WEIR

AVALON TRAVEL

ARIZONA
NEVADA
UTAH
COLORADO
NEW MEXICO
CALIFORNIA
Caliente
Enterprise
Cedar City
Panguitch
Dixie National Forest
Capitol Reef National Park
Monticello
Manti-Lasal National Forest
Blanding
Cortez
Bryce Canyon National Park
Glen Canyon National Recreation Area
Zion National Park
Hurricane
St George
Kanab
Fredonia
Kaibab Indian Res
Pipe Spring National Monument
Paiute Indian Reservation
Mesquite
Moapa River Indian Reservation
Rainbow Bridge National Monument
San Juan River
Lake Powell
MONUMENT VALLEY
Page
Navajo National Monument
Kayenta
Shiprock
Navajo Indian Reservation
Tsaile
Chinle
Canyon de Chelly National Monument
Kaibab National Forest
Grand Canyon National Park
Grand Canyon-Parashant National Monument
Las Vegas
Lake Mead
Havasupai Indian Reservation
Grand Canyon Village
Tuba City
Hopi Indian Reservation
Polacca
Ganado
Navajo
Fort Defiance
Window Rock
Gallup
Boulder City
Lake Mead National Recreation Area
Colorado River
Kaibab National Forest
Hualapai Indian Reservation
Dolan Springs
Wupatki National Monument
Sunset Crater Volcano National Monument
Lake Mohave
Seligman
Kingman
Williams
Flagstaff
Walnut Canyon National Monument
Petrified Forest National Park
Zuni Pueblo
Laughlin
Bullhead City
Fort Mohave Indian Reservation
Needles
Prescott National Forest
Chino Valley
Sedona
Cottonwood
Winslow
Coconino National Forest
Holbrook
Camp Verde
Prescott
Sitgreaves National Forest
Snowflake
Taylor
St Johns
Springerville
Lake Havasu City
Chemehuevi Indian Reservation
Payson
Show Low

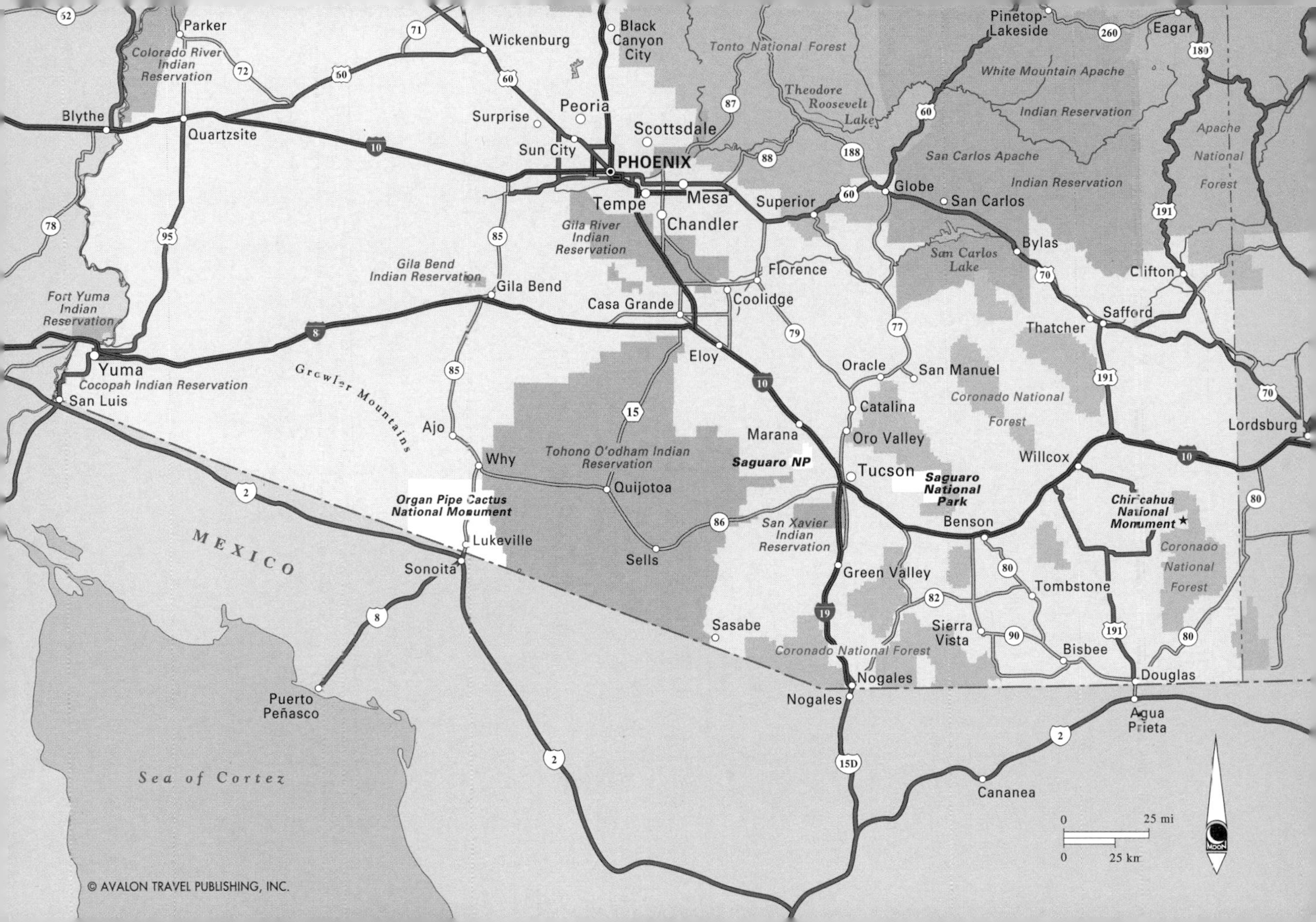

PHOENIX
Parker
Wickenburg
Black Canyon City
Pinetop-Lakeside
Eagar
Colorado River Indian Reservation
Tonto National Forest
White Mountain Apache Indian Reservation
Theodore Roosevelt Lake
Apache National Forest
Blythe
Quartzsite
Surprise
Peoria
Scottsdale
Sun City
San Carlos Apache Indian Reservation
Globe
San Carlos
Tempe
Mesa
Superior
Chandler
Gila River Indian Reservation
Bylas
San Carlos Lake
Gila Bend Indian Reservation
Florence
Clifton
Gila Bend
Coolidge
Fort Yuma Indian Reservation
Casa Grande
Safford
Thatcher
Yuma
Eloy
Oracle
San Manuel
Cocopah Indian Reservation
San Luis
Growler Mountains
Coronado National Forest
Catalina
Ajo
Marana
Oro Valley
Lordsburg
Why
Tohono O'odham Indian Reservation
Saguaro NP
Tucson
Willcox
Saguaro National Park
Organ Pipe Cactus National Monument
Quijotoa
Chiricahua National Monument
Benson
San Xavier Indian Reservation
MEXICO
Lukeville
Sells
Sonoita
Green Valley
Tombstone
Sasabe
Sierra Vista
Bisbee
Nogales
Douglas
Puerto Peñasco
Agua Prieta
Sea of Cortez
Cananea
0
25 mi
0
25 km
MOON
© AVALON TRAVEL PUBLISHING, INC.

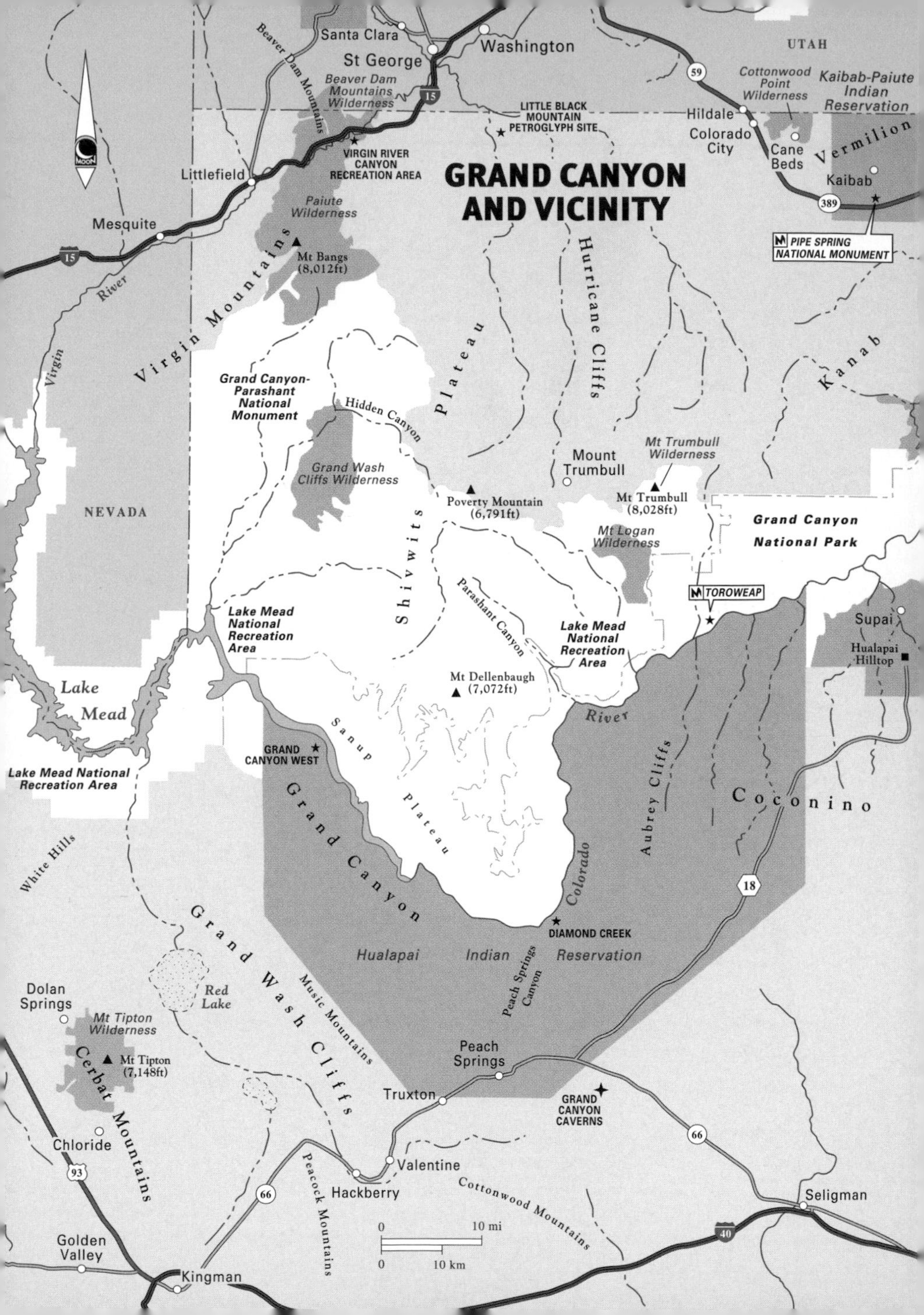
GRAND CANYON AND VICINITY
MOON
UTAH
NEVADA
Santa Clara
Washington
St George
Beaver Dam Mountains
Beaver Dam Mountains Wilderness
15
59
Cottonwood Point Wilderness
Kaibab-Paiute Indian Reservation
LITTLE BLACK MOUNTAIN PETROGLYPH SITE
Hildale
Colorado City
Cane Beds
Vermilion
Kaibab
389
VIRGIN RIVER CANYON RECREATION AREA
Littlefield
Paiute Wilderness
Mesquite
Mt Bangs (8,012ft)
PIPE SPRING NATIONAL MONUMENT
Virgin River
Virgin Mountains
Hurricane Cliffs
Plateau
Kanab
Grand Canyon-Parashant National Monument
Hidden Canyon
Grand Wash Cliffs Wilderness
Mount Trumbull
Mt Trumbull Wilderness
Poverty Mountain (6,791ft)
Mt Trumbull (8,028ft)
Shivwits
Mt Logan Wilderness
Grand Canyon National Park
TOROWEAP
Parashant Canyon
Lake Mead National Recreation Area
Supai
Hualapai Hilltop
Lake Mead
Mt Dellenbaugh (7,072ft)
River
GRAND CANYON WEST
Sanup Plateau
Lake Mead National Recreation Area
Grand Canyon
Aubrey Cliffs
Coconino
Colorado
18
White Hills
DIAMOND CREEK
Grand Wash Cliffs
Hualapai Indian Reservation
Peach Springs Canyon
Music Mountains
Red Lake
Dolan Springs
Mt Tipton Wilderness
Mt Tipton (7,148ft)
Cerbat Mountains
Peach Springs
Truxton
GRAND CANYON CAVERNS
66
Chloride
Valentine
Hackberry
93
Peacock Mountains
Cottonwood Mountains
Seligman
40
0 10 mi
0 10 km
Golden Valley
Kingman

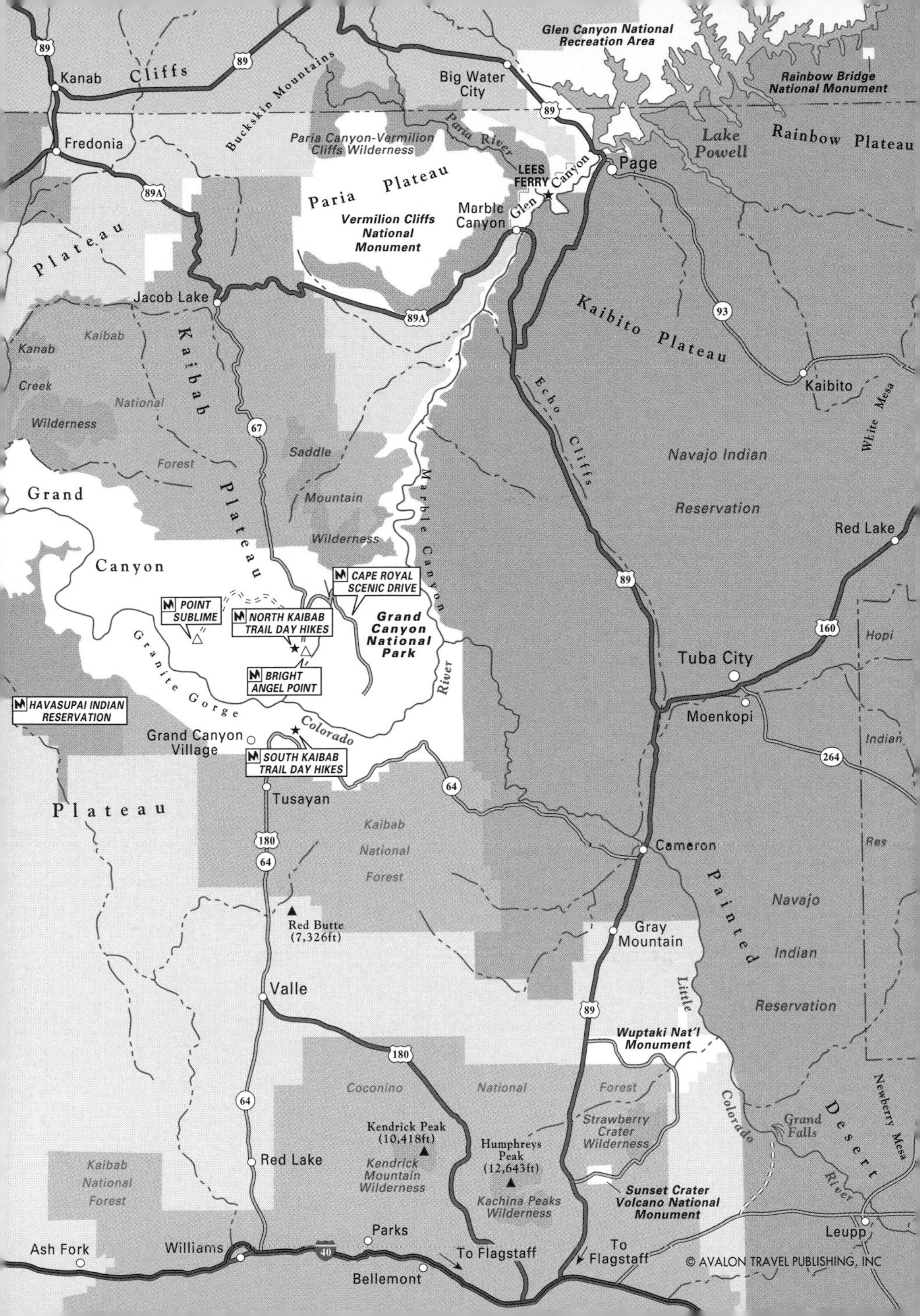

Glen Canyon National Recreation Area
Rainbow Bridge National Monument
Kanab
Cliffs
Big Water City
Buckskin Mountains
Fredonia
Paria Canyon-Vermilion Cliffs Wilderness
Paria River
Lake Powell
Rainbow Plateau
Page
Paria Plateau
LEES FERRY
Glen Canyon
Marble Canyon
Vermilion Cliffs National Monument
Plateau
Jacob Lake
Kaibito Plateau
Kaibab
Kanab Creek Wilderness
National
Kaibab Plateau
Kaibito
Echo Cliffs
White Mesa
Saddle Mountain Wilderness
Forest
Navajo Indian Reservation
Grand Canyon
Marble Canyon
Red Lake
CAPE ROYAL SCENIC DRIVE
POINT SUBLIME
NORTH KAIBAB TRAIL DAY HIKES
Grand Canyon National Park
Hopi
Granite Gorge
BRIGHT ANGEL POINT
River
Tuba City
HAVASUPAI INDIAN RESERVATION
Moenkopi
Colorado
Grand Canyon Village
Indian
SOUTH KAIBAB TRAIL DAY HIKES
Tusayan
Plateau
Kaibab National Forest
Cameron
Res
Painted
Navajo Indian Reservation
Red Butte (7,326ft)
Gray Mountain
Valle
Little Colorado River
Wuptaki Nat'l Monument
Coconino National Forest
Desert
Newberry Mesa
Strawberry Crater Wilderness
Grand Falls
Kendrick Peak (10,418ft)
Humphreys Peak (12,643ft)
Red Lake
Kendrick Mountain Wilderness
Kaibab National Forest
Kachina Peaks Wilderness
Sunset Crater Volcano National Monument
Parks
Leupp
Ash Fork
Williams
To Flagstaff
To Flagstaff
Bellemont
© AVALON TRAVEL PUBLISHING, INC
89
89A
67
93
160
264
64
180
40

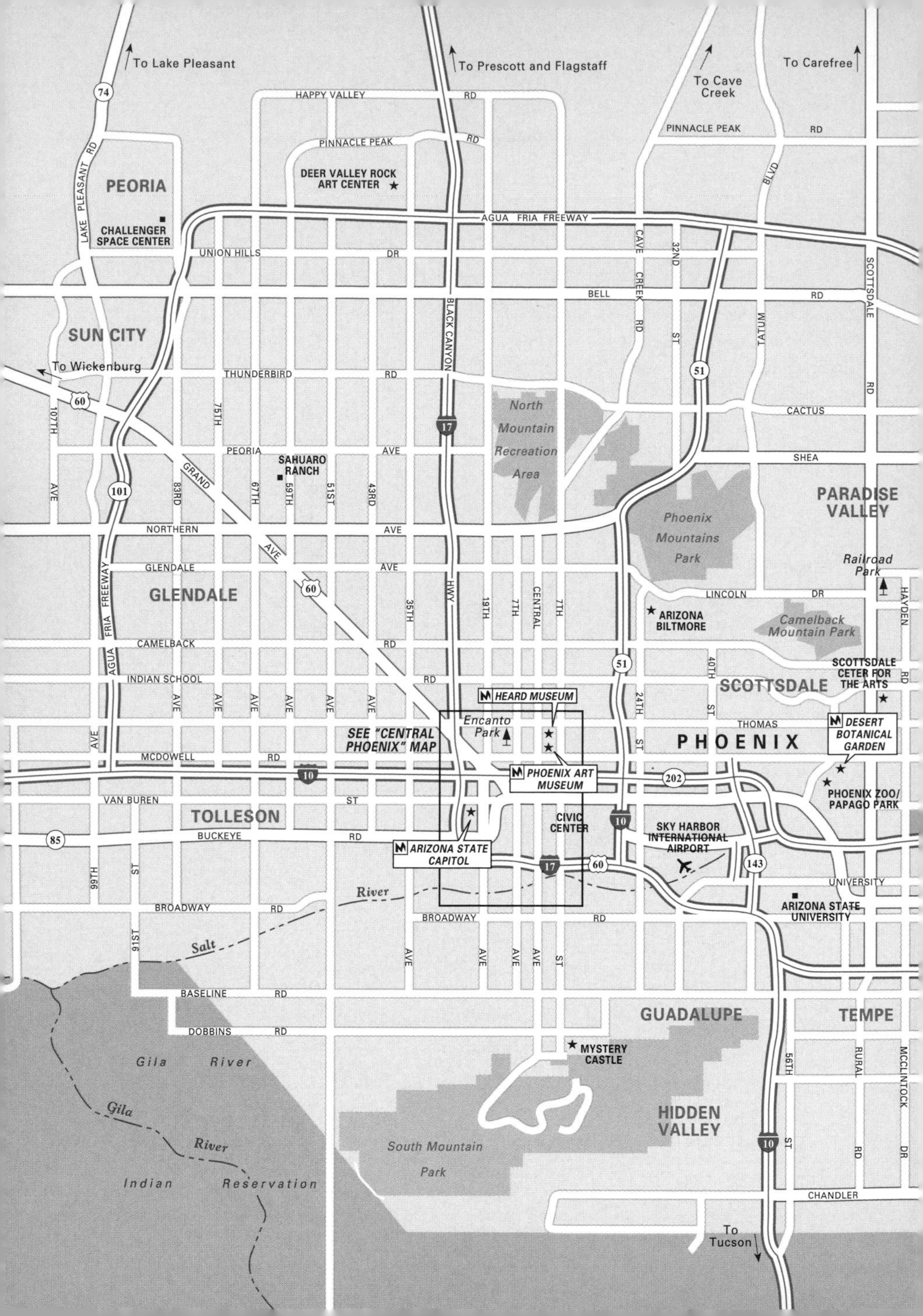
To Lake Pleasant
To Prescott and Flagstaff
To Cave Creek
To Carefree
74
HAPPY VALLEY RD
PINNACLE PEAK RD
PINNACLE PEAK RD
DEER VALLEY ROCK ART CENTER
PEORIA
LAKE PLEASANT RD
CHALLENGER SPACE CENTER
AGUA FRIA FREEWAY
UNION HILLS DR
CAVE CREEK RD
32ND ST
BLVD
TATUM
SCOTTSDALE RD
BELL RD
SUN CITY
To Wickenburg
60
THUNDERBIRD RD
51
BLACK CANYON HWY
17
North Mountain Recreation Area
CACTUS
SHEA
107TH AVE
75TH
PEORIA AVE
SAHUARO RANCH
GRAND AVE
101
83RD
67TH
59TH
51ST
43RD
PARADISE VALLEY
NORTHERN AVE
Phoenix Mountains Park
GLENDALE AVE
Railroad Park
GLENDALE
AGUA FRIA FREEWAY
35TH
19TH
7TH
CENTRAL
7TH
LINCOLN DR
HAYDEN
ARIZONA BILTMORE
Camelback Mountain Park
CAMELBACK RD
51
40TH ST
SCOTTSDALE CETER FOR THE ARTS
INDIAN SCHOOL RD
SCOTTSDALE
HEARD MUSEUM
24TH ST
Encanto Park
SEE "CENTRAL PHOENIX" MAP
THOMAS
PHOENIX
DESERT BOTANICAL GARDEN
MCDOWELL RD
10
PHOENIX ART MUSEUM
202
PHOENIX ZOO/ PAPAGO PARK
VAN BUREN ST
TOLLESON
CIVIC CENTER
SKY HARBOR INTERNATIONAL AIRPORT
85
BUCKEYE RD
ARIZONA STATE CAPITOL
17
60
143
99TH
91ST ST
River
UNIVERSITY
ARIZONA STATE UNIVERSITY
BROADWAY RD
BROADWAY RD
Salt
BASELINE RD
DOBBINS RD
GUADALUPE
TEMPE
MYSTERY CASTLE
Gila River
Gila River
Indian Reservation
South Mountain Park
HIDDEN VALLEY
56TH ST
RURAL RD
MCCLINTOCK DR
10
CHANDLER
To Tucson

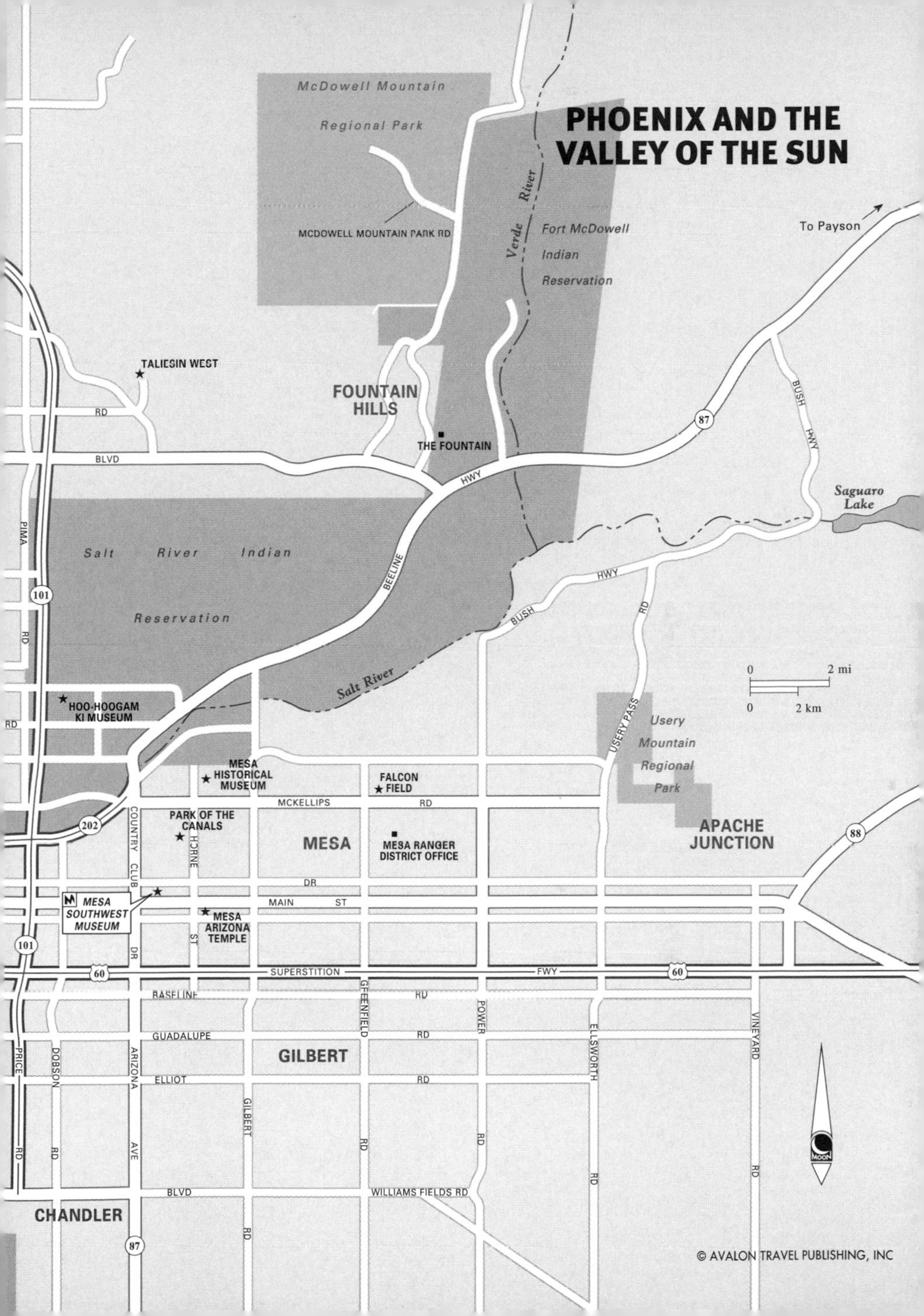
PHOENIX AND THE VALLEY OF THE SUN
McDowell Mountain Regional Park
MCDOWELL MOUNTAIN PARK RD
Verde River
Fort McDowell Indian Reservation
To Payson
TALIESIN WEST
FOUNTAIN HILLS
THE FOUNTAIN
RD
BLVD
HWY
87
BUSH HWY
Saguaro Lake
PIMA RD
101
Salt River Indian Reservation
BEELINE
BUSH HWY
RD
Salt River
0 2 mi
0 2 km
HOO-HOOGAM KI MUSEUM
RD
USERY PASS
Usery Mountain Regional Park
MESA HISTORICAL MUSEUM
FALCON FIELD
MCKELLIPS RD
PARK OF THE CANALS
202
COUNTRY CLUB DR
HORNE ST
MESA
MESA RANGER DISTRICT OFFICE
APACHE JUNCTION
88
DR
MESA SOUTHWEST MUSEUM
MAIN ST
MESA ARIZONA TEMPLE
60
SUPERSTITION FWY
BASELINE RD
GREENFIELD RD
POWER
ELLSWORTH RD
VINEYARD RD
GUADALUPE RD
GILBERT
DOBSON RD
ARIZONA AVE
PRICE RD
ELLIOT RD
GILBERT RD
BLVD
WILLIAMS FIELDS RD
CHANDLER
© AVALON TRAVEL PUBLISHING, INC

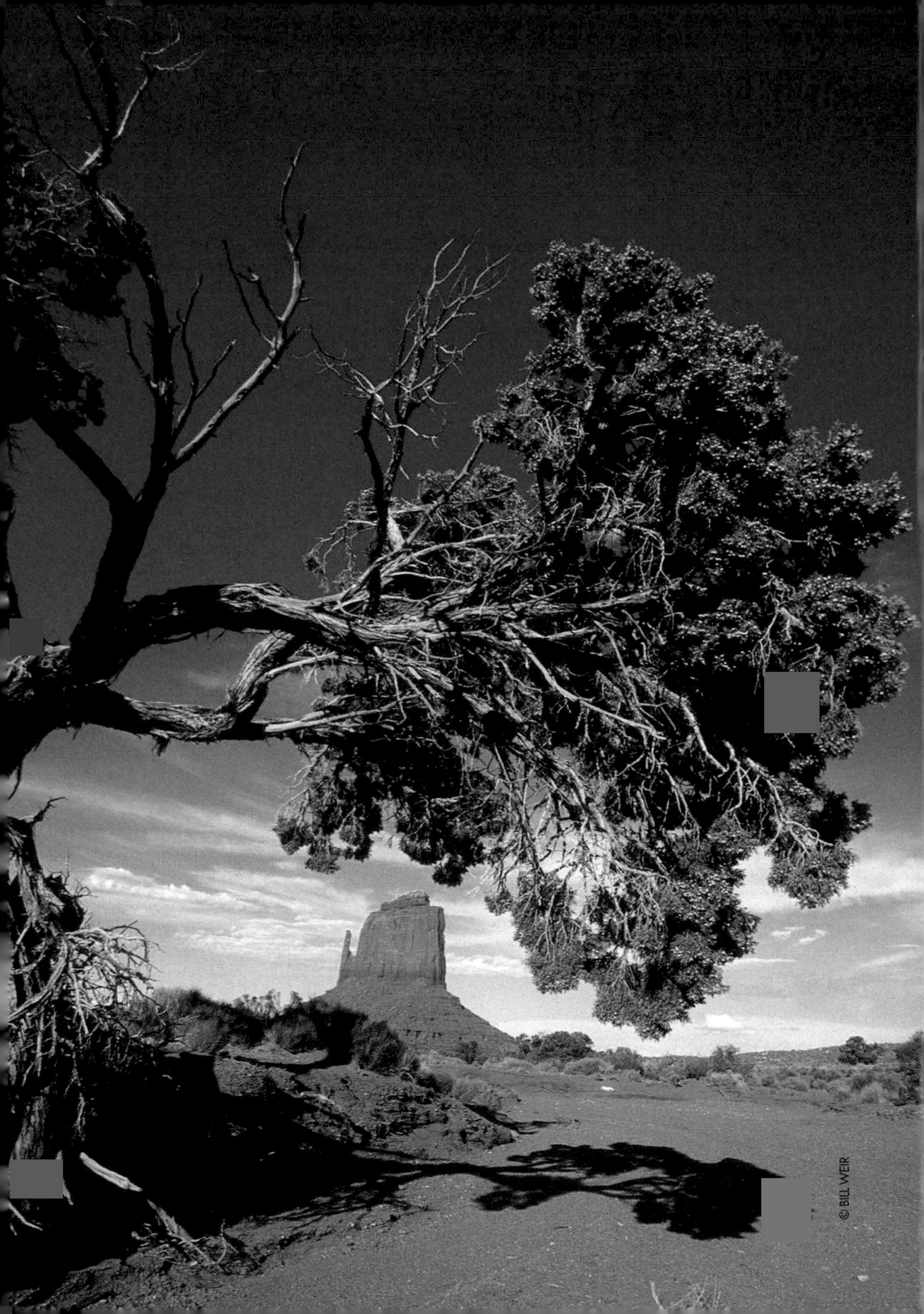
© BILL WEIR

CONTENTS

Discover Arizona

Explore Arizona

Know Arizona

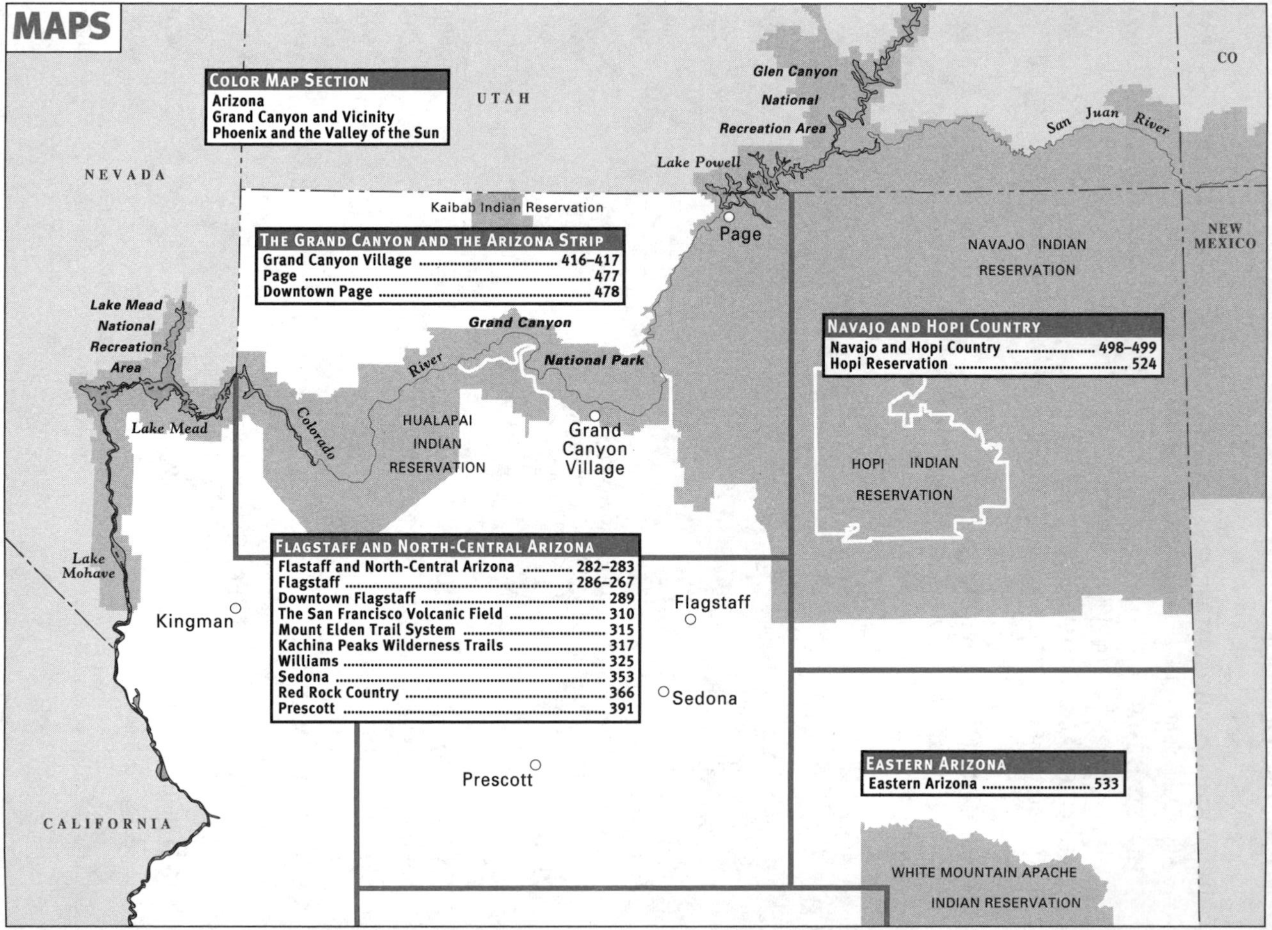
MAPS
COLOR MAP SECTION
Arizona
Grand Canyon and Vicinity
Phoenix and the Valley of the Sun
THE GRAND CANYON AND THE ARIZONA STRIP
Grand Canyon Village 416–417
Page 477
Downtown Page 478
NAVAJO AND HOPI COUNTRY
Navajo and Hopi Country 498–499
Hopi Reservation 524
FLAGSTAFF AND NORTH-CENTRAL ARIZONA
Flastaff and North-Central Arizona 282–283
Flagstaff 286–267
Downtown Flagstaff 289
The San Francisco Volcanic Field 310
Mount Elden Trail System 315
Kachina Peaks Wilderness Trails 317
Williams 325
Sedona 353
Red Rock Country 366
Prescott 391
EASTERN ARIZONA
Eastern Arizona 533
UTAH
NEVADA
CO
NEW MEXICO
CALIFORNIA
Glen Canyon National Recreation Area
Lake Powell
San Juan River
Page
Kaibab Indian Reservation
NAVAJO INDIAN RESERVATION
HOPI INDIAN RESERVATION
Lake Mead National Recreation Area
Lake Mead
Grand Canyon
National Park
Colorado
River
HUALAPAI INDIAN RESERVATION
Grand Canyon Village
Lake Mohave
Kingman
Flagstaff
Sedona
Prescott
WHITE MOUNTAIN APACHE INDIAN RESERVATION

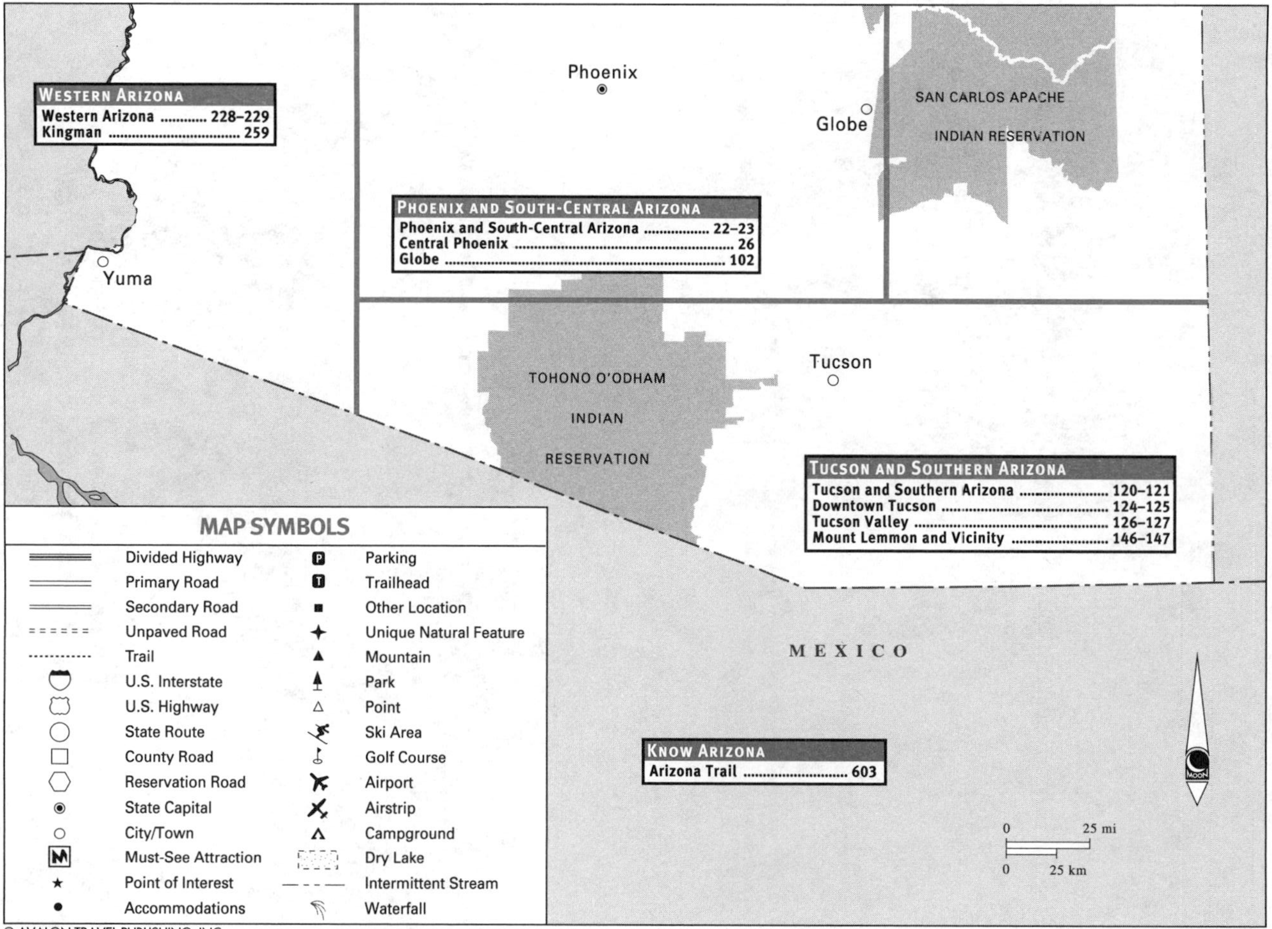

WESTERN ARIZONA
Western Arizona 228–229
Kingman 259
Yuma
Phoenix
Globe
SAN CARLOS APACHE
INDIAN RESERVATION
PHOENIX AND SOUTH-CENTRAL ARIZONA
Phoenix and South-Central Arizona 22–23
Central Phoenix 26
Globe 102
TOHONO O'ODHAM
INDIAN
RESERVATION
Tucson
TUCSON AND SOUTHERN ARIZONA
Tucson and Southern Arizona 120–121
Downtown Tucson 124–125
Tucson Valley 126–127
Mount Lemmon and Vicinity 146–147
MEXICO
KNOW ARIZONA
Arizona Trail 603
0
25 mi
0
25 km
MAP SYMBOLS
Divided Highway
Primary Road
Secondary Road
Unpaved Road
Trail
U.S. Interstate
U.S. Highway
State Route
County Road
Reservation Road
State Capital
City/Town
Must-See Attraction
Point of Interest
Accommodations
Parking
Trailhead
Other Location
Unique Natural Feature
Mountain
Park
Point
Ski Area
Golf Course
Airport
Airstrip
Campground
Dry Lake
Intermittent Stream
Waterfall

Discover Arizona

ARIZONA
THE GRAND CANYON STATE
WELCOMES YOU

© BILL WEIR

Arizona's diversity and beauty still surprise and awe visitors. The popular image of barren wastes under a burning sun dates back more than a hundred years, when most early travelers kept to the south, avoiding potentially hostile tribes farther north. Hollywood perpetuated the stereotype, preferring to play out dramas across rippled sand dunes beneath soaring rock spires, rather than in flower-filled meadows. Yet the northern and eastern parts of the state have extensive coniferous forests and rushing mountain streams. Even desert areas can be astonishingly verdant, as both winter and summer rains refresh the Sonoran Desert, supporting towering saguaro and a host of other striking and adaptable plants.

Although not on the ocean, Arizona has a shoreline hundreds of miles long! The placid waters of the Colorado River form the western shore providing countless boating and fishing opportunities. Rugged cliffs inhabited by desert bighorn sheep rise above the river in Black Canyon just below Hoover Dam, and in Topock Gorge, above Lake Havasu. You can venture into these canyons in canoes and other small craft because the lower Colorado River has no rapids. Two of the nation's largest reservoirs—Lake Mead and Lake Powell—lie in the northern part of the state, where their dark-blue waters contrast starkly with the surrounding desert. Each has a very different setting: Lake Mead is in more open and mostly volcanic country, while Lake Powell lies deep in canyons of gracefully curved sandstone. Countless coves along both reservoirs offer quiet corners to explore. Between the two lakes, the Grand Canyon slices nearly a vertical mile into the geologic layer cake of the Colorado Plateau. You'll be impressed by the immensity and complexity of this majestic wonder as you watch the patterns and soft colors of the rock layers change during the day and into the golden sunset. Hidden wonders reveal themselves as you venture on trails or on a river trip into the depths.

Movements deep underground have uplifted much of northern Arizona into lofty plateaus. Here you'll see hundreds of well-preserved volcanoes, now quiet, which once blasted magma into the air. The starkly beautiful cinder cones and lava flows at Sunset Crater Volcano National Monument, northeast of Flagstaff, look as if they had just cooled yesterday. Farther south in the state, shifting and faulting of rock layers created rugged mountain ranges. "Sky islands," the most spectacular of these, rise from the desert and provide cool-climate homes for rare species of plants and wildlife. Paved roads lead up some of the sky islands and all have great hiking possibilities. In winter, you can soak up the desert warmth in the morning and play in the snow atop a mountain in the afternoon. Mt. Lemmon, in the Santa Catalinas just north of Tucson, has the nation's southernmost ski area. All this churning of the earth's surface has resulted in a great range of climates and vegetation zones—you can find ideal conditions somewhere in any season. The forested uplands offer delightful conditions in summer, the plains and rocky hills of the desert provide spring-like weather in winter, and almost every area enjoys a pleasant climate in spring and autumn. Elevations within this varied land extend from just 70 feet above sea level where the Colorado River enters Mexico to 12,633 feet atop Humphrey's Peak, a weathered stratovolcano in the north.

Native Americans know this land well, and some can trace their clans back thousands of years through legends and rock art. Tribes across Arizona represent many cultural traditions. You can explore their beautiful lands and perhaps get an insight into their beliefs. In northeastern Arizona, the Navajo have the largest population of all the tribes in the United States and a vast reservation renowned for its scenic splendor. The Hopi, surrounded by Navajo lands, have villages and traditions that date back more than one thousand years.

Arizona's cities provide a sophisticated art and entertainment scene, though never far from the natural world. You'll find the most varied cultural offerings, nightlife, and sporting events in the two largest metropolitan areas of Phoenix and Tucson. Arizona State University in the greater Phoenix area and the University of Arizona in Tucson add much to the energy of each place. Similarly, Northern Arizona University up north in Flagstaff makes this mountain town a far livelier place than its population figure would suggest. When you feel like getting away from it all, the many resorts let you do just that. You'll find most of them in the Phoenix and Tucson areas, where you can rest beside a pool in a beautifully landscaped setting, spend the day on an immaculate golf course, or ride your horse amidst saguaro-studded hills.

WHEN TO GO

Come any time of year! You'll always find regions with a pleasant climate. Grand Canyon National Park and most other major attractions stay open year-round. The seasons do have a big influence on the Great Outdoors, however, so it's worth planning your travels to take the best advantage of the state's attractions.

SUMMER

In the high country of the north and east, this is a wonderful time to enjoy pine-scented breezes on a hike, out on the water, or on a scenic drive. Mountain towns put on many festivals, concerts, and rodeos.

The deserts turn into an oven, so you probably won't linger in them, but air-conditioning makes life pleasant even here, and you may wish to take in some of the top sights in cities such as Phoenix and Tucson. If you'd like to stretch your legs, early mornings can be pleasant for short excursions into the desert. At the Grand Canyon, the Inner Gorge becomes too hot for hiking, but the upper and rim trails offer fine scenery and the likelihood of a cool breeze, especially on the North Rim. Irregular thunderstorms arrive in late summer, adding refreshing coolness to the air at the higher elevations and miserable humidity to the desert. Plants sprout new greenery and some burst into flower.

AUTUMN

Nearly the entire state enjoys warm and dry weather, though hot temperatures can linger into October at the lowest elevations, and the possibility of snow gradually increases on the plateaus and mountains. Aspens turn to gold in the high country in late September and early October, followed by colorful displays of oaks, cottonwoods, and other deciduous plants in canyons lower down.

WINTER

Desert dwellers enjoy wonderful springlike weather for most of this season. It's also a fine time for exploring the rugged mountain ranges of the south and west, where you're likely to come across ghost towns, prehistoric rock art, and other reminders of the past. Flocks of "snowbirds," mostly retirees, leave their frosty northern homes for the sun in Arizona's luxurious resorts or out in remote desert locales. Phoenix, Tucson, and the other valley communities put on many events during the cooler months.

You can also enjoy travels in the high country, as weather tends to be bright and sunny even in midwinter. Keep an ear out for weather forecasts, because passing storms can make driving difficult for a few days. Only a handful of highways close for the entire winter, most notably Highway 67 to Bright Angel Point on the Grand Canyon's North Rim. Gentle rains—snow in the mountains—arrive now and then.

SPRING

The warmth and flowers arrive as early as February in the low deserts and gradually work their way up to the higher mountains by May. The desert country blooms with wildflowers in early spring, the choice time to visit. Each year's floral display depends on both the amount and timing of rains the preceding winter. By April, when the saguaro and other large cacti bloom, the snowbirds have long gone and locals start up their air conditioners. The mountains shake off most of their remaining snow and experience warm, dry days.

fall Aspens outside of Flagstaff

WHAT TO TAKE

Comfortable walking shoes should be at the top of your list—Arizona has many wonderful day hikes and strolls! Also check that you have a hat and sunscreen.

Arizonans tend to dress informally. You're unlikely to need a tie or an evening gown, and "business casual" will do fine at most upscale restaurants. A warm jacket or sweater will often be handy in the evenings, as the dry air quickly cools after sundown. Winter gear will keep you comfortable on travels in the high country, when temperatures can drop well below freezing.

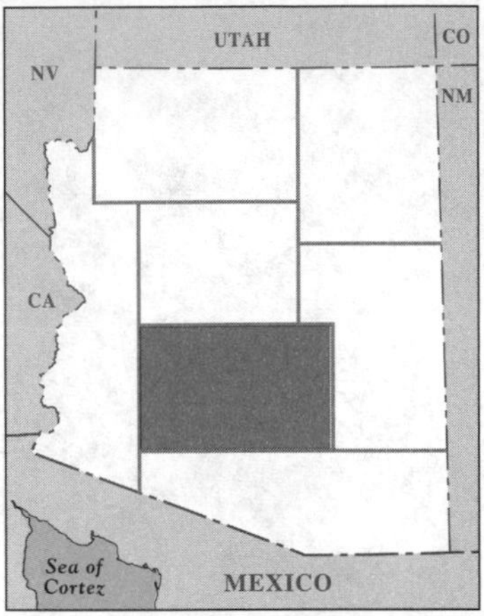

PHOENIX AND SOUTH-CENTRAL ARIZONA

Phoenix, Arizona's largest city, sprawls along with its neighboring urban areas for mile after mile across the aptly named "Valley of the Sun." You could spend weeks taking in the dozens of museums here, of which the Heard with its superb Native American exhibits is the most famous. The greater Phoenix area also gives you a chance to get close to nature at the Desert Botanical Garden, Phoenix Zoo, Wildlife World Zoo, and a variety of large parks. You can explore the art world at the Phoenix Art Museum, at Arizona State University's collections, and at galleries in Scottsdale's Old Town and nearby Fifth Avenue. The range of musical and theatrical performances at numerous venues has something for everyone. Annual events peak in the cooler months, when you can take in excitement at the Heard Museum's Native American shows in Phoenix or the Parada del Sol's rodeos and parade in Scottsdale. Major league sports teams provide thrills at impressive stadiums. Rugged mountain ranges and large wilderness areas begin just beyond the urban area. Attractions outside the Phoenix area include the Superstition Wilderness, famed for its lost gold mines, the twisting Apache Trail scenic drive, Florence and other Wild West towns, the giant prehistoric building at Casa Grande Ruins National Monument, and rafting in the Salt River Canyon Wilderness.

TUCSON AND SOUTHERN ARIZONA

Tucson may be number two in size among the state's cities, but you'd never know it from the excellent array of museums, art venues, and happenings. The "Old Pueblo," as it's also known, has a heritage going back to Spanish times, which you can still sense in the historic districts. You could begin at the Tucson Museum of Art and Historic Block, which provides a great introduction to the city's art and culture as well as a starting point for walks to nearby historic sites. You'll find more culture and science just east of downtown at the University of Arizona. Tucson's calendar of music, theater, and sports competes well with that of the Phoenix area. As Tucson also lies in the low desert, most major annual events take place in winter and early spring; February sees the enormous Tucson Gem and Mineral Show, which attracts rock

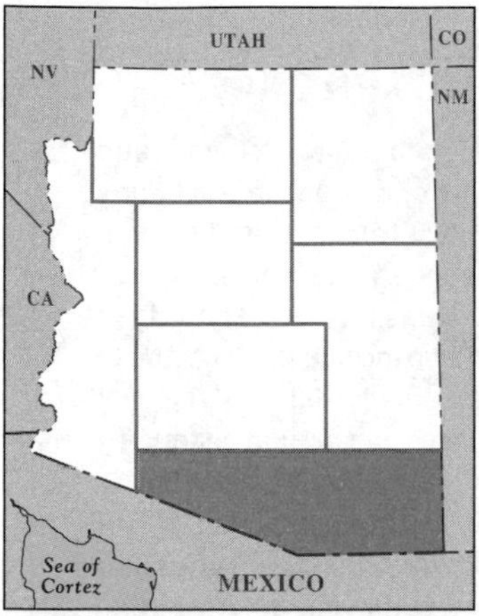

hounds from all over the world, and La Fiesta de los Vaqueros with a horse-drawn parade and rodeo action. Great day trips lead out of town in every direction. The area's top sight, the Arizona-Sonora Desert Museum, lies just west of Tucson with wildlife and flora of the Sonoran Desert. Down in the extreme southeast corner of the state, best done as a multi-day trip from Tucson, you can encounter the Wild West at Tombstone, head underground into the Copper Queen mine in the picturesque town of Bisbee, wander among strange-looking rock spires at Chiricahua National Monument, and visit the vast and colorful chambers of Kartchner Caverns State Park.

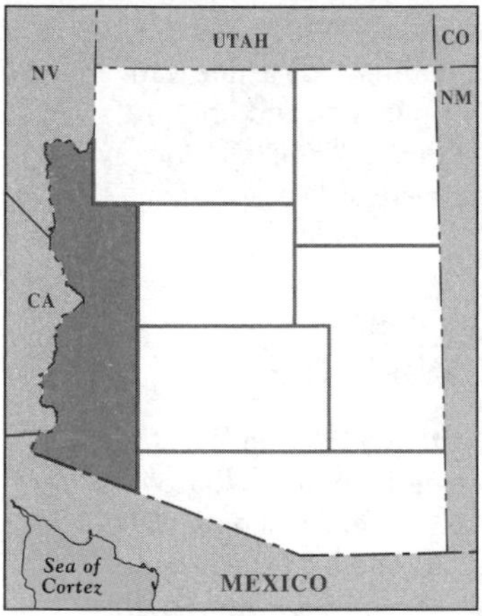

WESTERN ARIZONA

Arizona's "west coast" contains both water—the Colorado River and its chain of reservoirs—and the waterless, extremely arid mountain ranges and valleys with rugged scenery, remote ghost towns, challenging back-road drives, and seldom-visited wilderness areas. Yuma, in the south, preserves its river-boating history and Arizona's first territorial prison in two state parks. Lake Havasu City, farther up the Colorado River, has the most unusual piece of history—London Bridge! Kingman, a railroad town in the north, commemorates its mining and Route 66 history in two fine museums. All three cities put on a series of entertaining events, but it's the tiny community of Quartzsite with the most amazing spectacle—the Quartzsite Pow Wow Gem and Mineral Show, which along with many smaller events, attracts about a million people to the desert. Native American tribes live and farm along the lower Colorado River; you can learn about them in cultural centers near Yuma and Parker. Wetlands in a series of national wildlife refuges attract huge numbers of Canada geese and other birds that winter here or stop by on migrations.

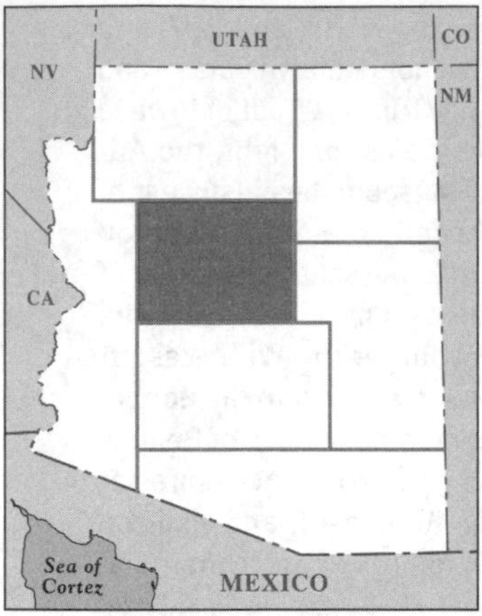

FLAGSTAFF AND NORTH-CENTRAL ARIZONA

Flagstaff's invigorating mountain climate and surrounding natural wonders make it a handy base for lovers of the outdoors. Grand Canyon National Park, five national monuments, and half a dozen wilderness areas lie just a short drive away. Attractions in town include the Museum of Northern Arizona's excellent exhibits of regional Native American cultures and natural history. To the south, you can drop into Oak Creek Canyon on a spectacular scenic drive that leads to Sedona's magical Red Rock Country of buttes and canyons. Continuing south, you can drive up to Jerome, an old copper mining town that just barely hangs on to the steep hillside, and continue over Mingus Mountain to Prescott, Arizona's first capital. Festivals fill the region's calendar during the warmer months and include Native American shows at Flagstaff's Museum of Northern Arizona and Prescott's Frontier Days big parade and the "World's Oldest Rodeo." You'll find many places to shop for Native American and Southwestern art, such as in Sedona's recreated Mexican village of Tlaquepaque.

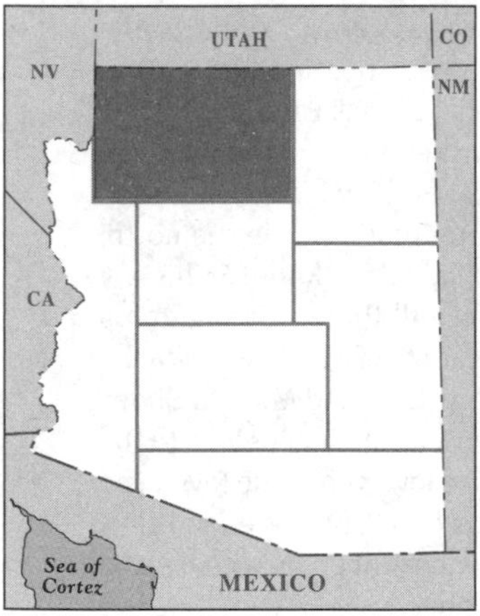

THE GRAND CANYON AND THE ARIZONA STRIP

The Grand Canyon rightfully tops most visitors' lists. You'll take in awe-inspiring panoramas from easily accessible overlooks and on walks along the rims. To get to know the Canyon better, head down a trail into the Inner Canyon. For the experience of a lifetime, arrange a river-rafting trip through the Canyon on the Colorado River. Try to visit both rims if you can; the higher and more remote North Rim offers perspectives quite unlike the South Rim. High elevations on the North Rim, however, limit road access from mid-May until some time in autumn. The Havasupai tribe's famed canyon of majestic waterfalls and pools of blue-green waters below the South Rim have no road access, but you can arrange to ride a mule or horse if you'd rather not hike in. A bit farther west, the Hualapai tribe has an unpaved scenic drive all the way to the bottom of the Grand Canyon; other roads lead out to impressive viewpoints of the lower Grand Canyon. Adventurous travelers can explore wilderness areas and Grand Canyon viewpoints on the Arizona Strip along undeveloped areas of the North Rim.

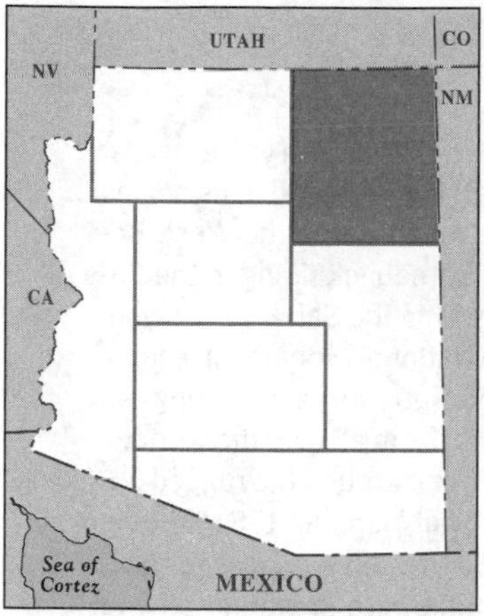

NAVAJO AND HOPI COUNTRY

Although very different from each other, the Navajo and Hopi tribes still follow traditional ways of life. You can get a glimpse of their lives on your travels and on visits to tribal museums. You're sure to be enchanted by the region's otherworldly landscapes of vast treeless plateaus, soaring buttes, and sheer-walled canyons. Two national monuments—Navajo and Canyon de Chelly—enclose well-preserved prehistoric cliff dwellings within canyons of exceptional beauty. Monument Valley Navajo Tribal Park also has many signs of early cultures along with iconic landscapes of soaring pinnacles and buttes. The Hopi village of Old Oraibi may be the oldest continually inhabited settlement in the country. Also try to visit Walpi, where you can learn about the Hopi way of life on guided tours. With luck, you may be able to witness Hopi dances, usually held on weekends. Both tribes produce appealing artwork and crafts, which can be purchased directly from the families at roadside stalls or in Hopi villages.

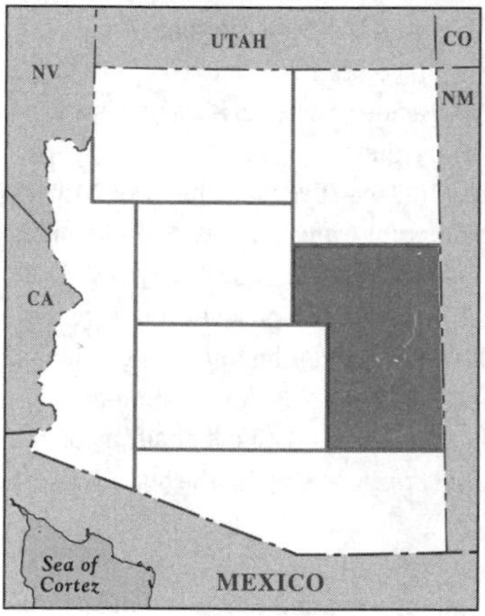

EASTERN ARIZONA

Cool forests, alpine meadows, and rushing streams of the White Mountains and surrounding high country offer a refreshing contrast to surrounding deserts. In summer you can enjoy hiking, fishing, and boating. When the snow flies, Sunrise Park Resort Ski Area provides many downhill runs and some cross-country skiing. The White Mountain and San Carlos Apache tribes have adjoining reservations in this scenic region, and both offer cultural centers and recreation areas. The Coronado Trail, a wildly twisting highway between Clifton and Springerville, is one of the state's best scenic drives. North of the White Mountains, the forests gradually fade away to the Painted Desert, home of Petrified Forest National Park and its extensive deposits of colorful fossilized wood. South of the White Mountains, rugged hills drop to the Gila River Valley. Here you can drive up the Swift Trail into the Pinaleno Mountains, a sky island that soars almost 8,000 feet above the surrounding desert. To the west, a perennial creek flows through the heart of Aravaipa Canyon Wilderness, a popular hiking area.

Apache Trail Loop

Phoenix and the Valley of the Sun seem to vanish instantly when you turn east on the Apache Trail and into the canyons of the Salt River. Here begins begins a 200-mile loop through some of the most rugged country in the West. Besides the wild scenery, you can enjoy hiking and horseback riding in the Superstition Wilderness, boating on a chain of lakes within the Salt River Canyon, stepping inside prehistoric cliff dwellings in Tonto National Monument, seeing copper-mining operations near Globe, Miami, and Superior, and visiting the Boyce Thompson Arboretum—a collection of plants from all over the world.

Allow at least six hours plus stops to drive this circuit around the rugged Superstition Mountains, taking AZ 88, "The Apache Trail," and AZ 188 to Globe, then returning to Apache Junction via US 60/70. The drive is possible in a day, but best over two or more days. Avoid coming here in summer if you can, as the weather then will be very hot.

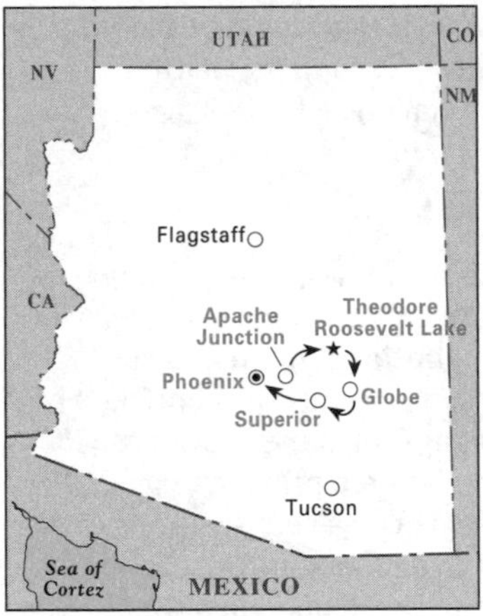

ONE DAY

The trail begins from Apache Junction at the east edge of the Phoenix area. To get started, follow the Superstition Freeway/US 60 east to Apache Junction, then turn north on Idaho Road (exit 11) to the Apache Trail. The Apache Trail, also signed as AZ 88, has a long unpaved section and a steep grade, not suitable for large RVs or trailers. When you start down the trail, once used as a raiding route, you'll see the towering peaks of the Superstition Mountains on the right, and Four Peaks, a southern extension of the Mazatzals, on the left across the Salt River Canyon. About 3.5 miles from the start, you can stop at Superstition Mountain Museum on the right and at Goldfield Ghost Town, another mile on the left, to learn about the mysterious lost gold mines rumored to lie within the Superstitions. A mile farther on the right, you can detour to Lost Dutchman State Park with a fine network of hiking trails and an excellent campground.

The Apache Trail then twists and turns for 20 miles through an incredibly rugged landscape with many viewpoints until you reach Theodore Roosevelt Lake. Turn south here on AZ 188 past several recreation areas on the lake. Two prehistoric cliff dwellings, high on the hillside in Tonto National Monument, overlook the lake. Globe, a bit over halfway on the loop, is the best place to stop for the night.

TWO DAYS

Old copper mines surround Globe and the nearby town of Miami. Highway US 60 ascends west over rugged mountains and drops into Devils Canyon and Superior, another old copper mining town. Just beyond Superior, an amazing variety of plants and wildlife dwells in Boyce Thompson Arboretum State Park. A short and fast drive west on US 60 returns you all too quickly to the hectic pace of greater Phoenix.

Mogollon Rim and Red Rocks Loop

Sheer cliffs of the Mogollon Rim drop into an expanse of forested hills southeast of Flagstaff. The rim's streams, lakes, and cool ponderosa forests attract the most visitors in summer, but you can enjoy the beautiful views and the canyon scenery any time of year. Without major detours, the loop can be done in a long day or explored further over two days.

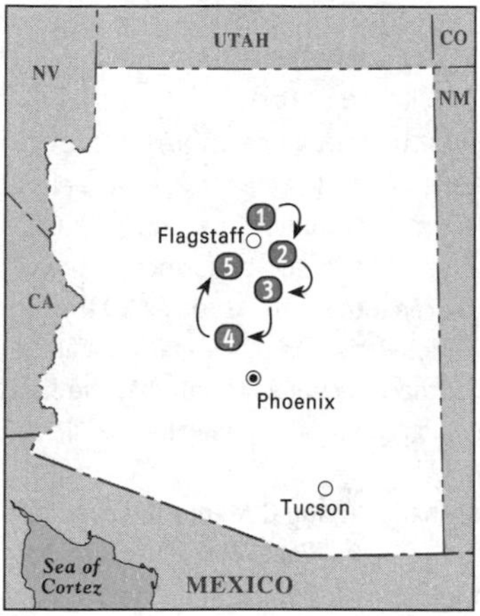

ONE DAY

From (1) Flagstaff, head southeast on Lake Mary Road/County 3 past the grassy shores of Lower and Upper Lake Mary. (2) Mormon Lake, a bit farther, would be the state's largest natural lake if it weren't totally dry so often! After a pleasant forest drive of 55 miles—watch for elk and deer—turn right 12 miles on AZ 87, then turn right 31 miles on AZ 260 to (3) Camp Verde.

In town, you can experience 19th-century army life at Fort Verde State Historic Park. Montezuma Castle National Monument, just north of Camp Verde, contains a five-story prehistoric cliff dwelling that so impressed early visitors that they assumed the great Aztec ruler must have built it. Continue north 11 miles via I-17 to see (4) Montezuma Well, a spring-fed lake with traces of ancient pueblos. Another short drive up I-17 brings you to the gateway of (5) Sedona's famous Red Rock Country. Follow AZ 179 for 15 miles into town past wondrous rock formations, then continue north on AZ 89A beneath the beautifully sculptured walls of Oak Creek Canyon. After the climb out of the canyon you'll be back on the Mogollon Rim to continue through the ponderosa pines back to Flagstaff, 27 miles from Sedona.

TWO DAYS

With an extra day, you can explore more of the Mogollon Rim by turning east from AZ 87 on unpaved Forest Road 300 along the rim; cars can often negotiate this road in dry weather. You'll pass viewpoints, campgrounds, and fishing lakes on the way to AZ 260, where you can retrace your route or take AZ 260 west to Payson, then continue north on AZ 87 and west on AZ 260 to Camp Verde.

For an adventurous back-road loop, best done with a high-clearance vehicle, take AZ 87 to the village of Strawberry, northwest of Payson, and turn west on Fossil Creek Road. The pavement soon gives out and the road drops steeply to Fossil Creek with great panoramas of the rim country. Towering trees, flowers, and swimming holes surround Fossil Springs, a popular hiking destination up the canyon. After crossing the bridge over Fossil Creek, the road winds through rugged and remote hill country before emerging on AZ 260 just east of Camp Verde.

Cochise Trail Loop

History and natural beauty intertwine in the southeastern corner of Arizona where the spirit of Cochise (a Chiricahua Apache chief of the 1800s) still seems to pervade the landscapes. Tucson is the logical starting point for this weeklong drive, which tourist offices call the "Cochise Trail". Any time of year can be good for a visit and all of the towns mentioned have accommodations and dining for stops along the way.

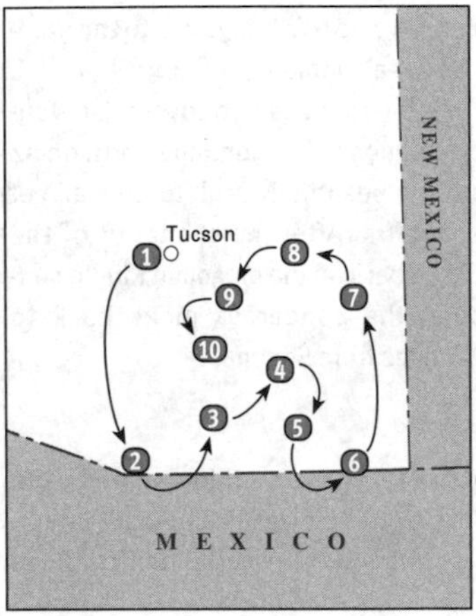

Tucson to Nogales

From (1) Tucson, attractions along the drive south on I-19 to (2) Nogales include the 18th-century Spanish Mission San Xavier del Bac just south of the city, an authentic underground missile silo complex at Green Valley, birding and hiking in Madera Canyon to the east, and experiencing early Spanish history at Tubac Presidio State Historic Park and Tumacacori National Historic Park.

Sierra Vista and the Huachuca Mountains

Turn northeast from Nogales on AZ 82 through picturesque hill country to Patagonia, a good place to see birds and other wildlife in a Nature Conservancy preserve. At Sonoita, a bit farther northeast on AZ 82, you can turn southeast on AZ 83 toward Coronado National Memorial, a scenic area at the south end of the Huachuca Mountains; the first 30 miles are mostly paved, followed by 18 miles of gravel road.

From Coronado National Memorial, turn left on AZ 92 to (3) Sierra Vista. Along the way you can detour into the Huachuca Mountains at Carr Canyon on a scenic drive high up the slopes or turn up to Ramsey Canyon, famous for hummingbirds and other wildlife at another Nature Conservancy preserve. Fort Huachuca, just west of downtown Sierra Vista, dates back to 1877 and is Arizona's only fort to remain in use since the Indian wars; a good museum here illustrates the life of the soldiers, their families, and the Indian scouts.

Tombstone and the Wild West

Head east via Charleston Road or AZ 82 across the San Pedro Riparian National Conservation Area, which has nature trails and several historic sites, to (4) Tombstone, an authentic town from the Wild West. Exhibits in Tombstone Courthouse State Historic Park provide a fine introduction to the colorful events that took place here.

Bisbee and the Copper Queen Mine

A short drive south on AZ 80 across the Mule Mountains leads to (5) Bisbee, a copper mining town with many appealing old buildings tucked in the bottom of canyons; you can ride deep underground on a tour of the Copper Queen Mine. The old smelter town of (6) Douglas to the east via AZ 80 also has notable architecture, including the Gadsden Hotel, whose soaring columns and a Tiffany stained-glass mural decorate the spacious lobby.

Chiricahua National Monument and Willcox

Turn north on US 191, then head east on AZ 181 for (7) Chiricahua National Monument, a geologic wonderland of pinnacles and curious rock features. Or, if you'd like the adventure of driving an unpaved mountain road, take AZ 80 northeast from Douglas, continue a few miles into New Mexico, turn left to Portal and Cave Creek Canyon, where the pavement ends, then continue over Onion Saddle and down Pinery Canyon to the monument entrance.

From Chiricahua National Monument, take AZ 181 and AZ 186 northwest to (8) Willcox and I-10, perhaps with a detour to the ruins of an old army fort at Fort Bowie National Historic Site. At Willcox, you might enjoy a stop at the Rex Allen Cowboy Museum in the historic old downtown.

Kartchner Caverns and Benson

On the way back west to Tucson via I-10, between Willcox and (9) Benson, seek out the outstanding Amerind Foundation Museum of Native American cultures. And finally, one of the top sights of the region, (10) Kartchner Caverns State Park offers two tours in an exceptionally pretty living cave a short drive west of Benson and 9 miles south of I-10.

Grand Canyon Loop

This grand tour goes completely around the Canyon via both rims and has lots of side trip possibilities; allow about a week. You can drive it any time of year, though expect high temperatures at Lees Ferry and Lake Mead National Recreation Area in summer, and closure of the North Rim's Bright Angel Point area in winter and spring. Starting points could be Flagstaff (as used here) Page, St. George, Las Vegas, or Kingman.

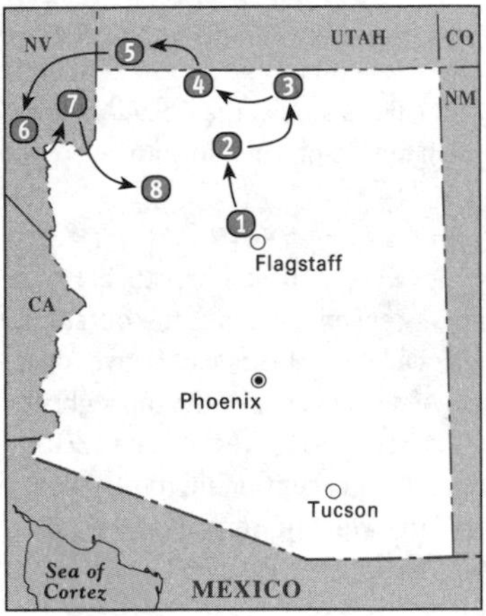

Flagstaff to the South Rim

In addition to offering a good base for this loop, (1) Flagstaff features great hiking and some good museums. Consider visits to the nearby Walnut Canyon, Sunset Crater Volcano, and Wupatki National Monuments. From Flagstaff, take US 180 and AZ 64 northwest to Grand Canyon National Park. Highlights include (2) Grand Canyon Village, Hermit Road, Desert View Drive and on the South Rim.

North Rim

From Grand Canyon Village, follow AZ 64 east to US 89 and turn north one mile on US 89 to Cameron Trading Post, a good place for a lunch break or shopping. Continue north on US 89, then turn northwest on US 89A to Navajo Bridge across the Colorado River above the Grand Canyon. (3) Lees Ferry nearby has two historic districts to explore. Continue west on US 89A and turn south on AZ 67 to the Grand Canyon's North Rim. Highlights include Bright Angel Point and Cape Royal Scenic Drive. If you're ready for a long drive on unpaved roads, Toroweap Overlook, farther west on the Grand Canyon's North Rim, has a stunning view and remains open all year.

Former trail guide T.L. Brown hams it up between two limestone walls in the Grand Canyon.

© COURTESY OF THE FLAGSTAFF CONVENTION AND VISITORS BUREAU

Walnut Canyon

St. George

North of the Grand Canyon, return to US 89A and continue west to (4) Fredonia. Turn west here on AZ 389 for Pipe Spring National Monument, where you can learn about pioneer ranchers and the local Paiute tribe. AZ 389 and UT 59 will take you farther west to I-15 and (5) St. George, Utah.

Kingman

From St. George, continue on I-15 through the scenic Virgin River and enter Nevada. Here you have the option of continuing on I-15 into dazzling (6) Las Vegas or turning south on Hwy. 169 to Overton and (7) Lake Mead. Paved highways 169, 167, 147, and 166 parallel the shore of Lake Mead with fine views of rugged mountains and the dark blue lake. Just before you reach US 93, you'll pass the visitor center for Lake Mead National Recreation Area on your left. Turn four miles on US 93 to admire the engineering marvel of Hoover Dam and see exhibits in its spacious visitor center. Continuing on US 93, you'll be back in Arizona and on your way to Kingman.

Kingman lies on the longest remaining section of Route 66, which will take you on a journey into America's motoring past. Two excellent museums downtown interpret the region's mining, railroad, and Route 66 history. Instead of heading back to Flagstaff on I-40, turn northeast from Kingman on Route 66 through lonely country and small towns. On the way you'll pass the Hackberry General Store (Route 66 memorabilia) and Grand Canyon Caverns. If you're feeling adventurous, and are willing to drive some dirt roads, detour off Route 66 on the (8) Hualapai Indian Reservation to the western Grand Canyon viewpoints at Grand Canyon West or drive all the way down into the Canyon on Diamond Creek Road. You can also hike into the Shangri La of Havasu Canyon with its waterfalls and travertine pools on the Havasupai Indian Reservation. Route 66 ends east of Seligman, where I-40 will take you up into the ponderosa pine forests and on past Williams to Flagstaff.

Navajo and Hopi Lands Loop

A drive of about one week will take you around the scenic and cultural highlights of Arizona's northeast corner. The region is accessible year-round, but in winter you may wish to avoid mountain roads such as Indian 12 near the New Mexico border. Flagstaff makes a good starting point, or you could follow your map west from Page or the Grand Canyon National Park's South or North Rims.

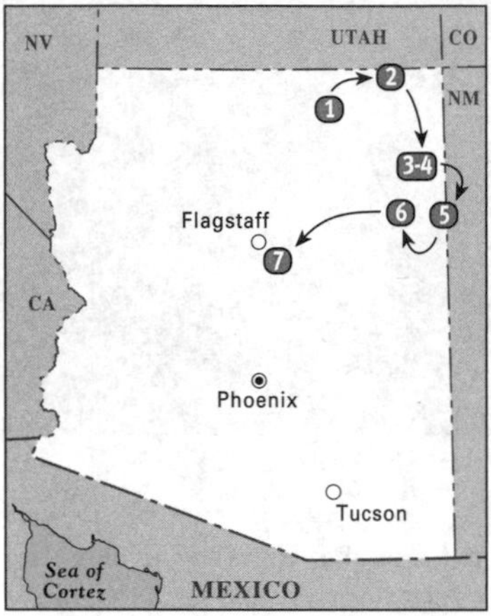

DAY 1

Navajo National Monument's scenery and large prehistoric cliff dwellings provide a fine introduction to the northern Navajo lands; it's 136 miles northeast of Flagstaff via US 89, US 160, and AZ 564. Hikers can arrange to descend to nearby Betatakin Ruin or the more distant but better preserved Keet Seel Ruin. Navajo National Monument has two campgrounds, but travelers can continue to Kayenta if they prefer a motel.

DAY 2

A 59-mile drive farther northeast on US 160 and US 163 takes you to the dramatic buttes and spires of **Monument Valley.** On your own, you can take a self-guided driving tour in the heart of the valley or go on a self-guided hike around West Mitten. Guides at the visitor center offer more extensive tours by 4WD, horseback, or hiking. Monument Valley has two campgrounds and an astronomically-priced motel, but Kayenta's motels are just a short drive away

DAYS 3–4

Canyon de Chelly National Monument, a highlight for many visitors, lies in the eastern Navajo Nation; it's a 112-mile journey southeast from Monument Valley via US 163, US 160, Indian 59, US 191, and Indian 7. Two canyons, both with many Navajo farms and ancient cliff dwellings, can be enjoyed from viewpoints, on hikes, and on a variety of 4WD and horseback tours.

DAY 5

From Canyon de Chelly National Monument, you could turn northeast 20 miles to **Tsaile** on Indian 64 and stop at Diné College's tribal museum. From Tsaile, Indian Route 12 winds 53 miles south through ponderosa pine forests to the Navajo Nation's capital of **Window Rock,** which also has a fine museum.

DAY 6

Turn west 28 miles on AZ 264 to Ganado and the **Hubbell Trading Post National Historic Site,** a 19th-century trading post that's still in business;

descent into Canyon del Muerto in Canyon de Chelly

you'll see exceptional Native American work in the trading post and on tours of Hubbell's house.

Continuing west 54 miles on AZ 264, you'll enter Hopi country and arrive at Polacca below **First Mesa;** follow the sign for First Mesa Village to Sichomovi at the top of the mesa and the well-preserved traditional village of Walpi. Guided walking tours take you through Walpi and explain the history and culture of the Hopi; you'll have a chance to purchase crafts from the villagers. Over on **Second Mesa,** 13 miles farther west on AZ 264, stop at the Hopi Cultural Center for the museum, restaurant, and the reservation's only motel. Finally, nine miles farther west on AZ 264, you come to **Third Mesa,** site of Old Oraibi, which may be the oldest continually inhabited community in the United States.

DAY 7

From Third Mesa, you can continue west 50 miles on AZ 264 to Tuba City and another 75 miles south to Flagstaff via US 160 and US 89; alternately, there's a shortcut from Kykotsmovi (below Third Mesa) back to Flagstaff via Leupp Road, which is just 88 miles.

Coronado Trail and Salt River Canyon Loop

The Coronado Trail roughly follows the path of the Spanish explorer, Francisco Vásquez de Coronado, on his search for gold and fame. This drive in the mountainous heart of eastern Arizona takes several days. In winter, snows may close the middle of the Coronado Trail, so you'll need to check weather forecasts then.

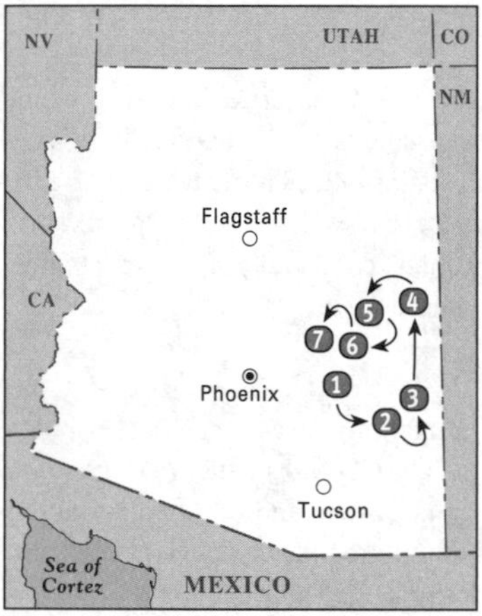

Safford

Start from (1) Globe, which lies just a few hours east of the Phoenix area. U.S. 70 crosses the San Carlos Indian Reservation, where you can stop at the Apache Cultural Center, then enters the broad valley and cotton fields of the Gila River. (2) Safford, the largest town in the region, is a good place to stay overnight; use it as a base to explore the nearby Aravaipa Wilderness or to take the Mount Graham Drive high into the Pinaleno Mountiains.

Below the Mogollon Rim

Continuing to (3) Clifton, you can take US 191 or try the more scenic but unpaved Black Hills Back Country Byway, best driven with a high-clearance vehicle. In the old mining town of Clifton, set deep in a canyon of the San Francisco River, turn up Chase Creek Street to admire the old buildings and see the Greenlee County Historical Society Museum. Just north of Clifton, the Coronado Trail (US 191) begins the first of its countless climbs and twists, winding past the modern town of Morenci and the huge open-pit copper mine. Soon you'll be in the forested mountains with many back roads, hiking trails, and campgrounds. Stock up on gas and supplies in Clifton or Morenci, the last towns until Alpine.

Atop the Mogollon Rim

Near the halfway point 68 miles north of Clifton, you ascend the Mogollon Rim; Blue Vista Overlook here has a wonderful panorama. The Coronado Trail ends at the twin towns of (4) Springerville and Eagar. Tours leave from downtown Springerville to Casa Malpais, an unusual prehistoric pueblo.

Salt River Canyon

Turn west on AZ 260 through beautiful alpine country to (5) Hon-Dah on the White Mountain Apache Indian Reservation; along the way you'll pass turnoffs for the resort village of Greer and the ski area at Sunrise. A store at Hon-Dah provides recreation information and permits if you'd like to camp or explore the area. Turn south on AZ 73 past the town of Whiteriver to (6) Fort Apache which has an excellent tribal museum and some well-preserved 19th-century buildings; ask here about visiting Kinishba, a large prehistoric pueblo nearby. Continue on AZ 73 to its end at US 60, then turn south for the immense (7) Salt River Canyon and fine mountain scenery on the way back to Globe.

Explore Arizona

Phoenix and South-Central Arizona

Though you'll rarely see the name on a map, you'll frequently hear people call the greater Phoenix area the "Valley of the Sun," a name that accurately reflects the area's pleasant winters and its average of 300 sunny days per year. More than half the state's population lives here, and large numbers of visitors arrive in the cooler months to play in the posh resorts or join fellow "snowbirds" in vast RV parks. Phoenix and its surrounding cities have some of the state's best museums, entertainment, golf courses, resorts, and dining. When you're ready to hit the trail, several city parks have small peaks to climb in the midst of the Valley.

Urban sophistication fades away quickly once you reach the edge of town, and you can soon be in ruggedly picturesque mountain ranges with great opportunities for scenic drives, four-wheeling, hiking, mountain biking, and horseback riding. The mountains in this region aren't

© BILL WEIR

Must-Sees

Look for to find the sights and activities you can't miss and for the best dining and lodging.

The **Arizona State Capitol** has been beautifully restored to appear as it did in 1912, when Arizona attained statehood. Inside, you can explore the old legislative chambers, governor's office, and other offices. Exhibits illustrate aspects of Arizona's history (page 27).

Phoenix Art Museum will take you to many lands and times with its wide-ranging collections. Major visiting shows also appear in the spacious galleries (page 30).

Heard Museum offers outstanding exhibits about Southwestern Native American cultures. You'll get a feel for tribal values and lifestyles and see the very best crafts and art (page 31).

Wildlife World Zoo holds Arizona's largest collection of exotic wildlife, including the big-game animals of Africa, white tigers from Asia, all five of the world's ostrich species, and even some penguins. The birds alone are worth a trip—some of them are exhibited nowhere else (page 35).

Desert Botanical Garden shows off the beauty of desert flora on well-designed walking paths. You'll learn what makes a cactus a cactus and how we can live in harmony with the desert (page 37).

Mesa Southwest Museum takes you into the region's past with a replica of a Spanish mission, a prehistoric Hohokam village, a dinosaur mountain inhabited by animated beasts, and astronomy exhibits about the beginning of time. It's great for families—there's a lot to see and do for both kids and adults (page 57).

Desert Caballeros Western Museum in Wickenburg captures the Old West through art, a re-created street scene, dioramas, and a Native American room. You'll see paintings and sculpture by top Western artists (page 88).

Tonto National Monument protects two well-preserved cliff dwellings built by the prehistoric Salado. The museum displays their polychrome pottery, stone tools, and finely woven cotton cloth (page 100).

Boyce Thompson Arboretum State Park features Arizona's largest and most diverse botanical garden. Trails loop through Sonoran, Chihuahuan, and Australian areas and a variety of gardens. A pond and a perennial stream make this a great spot for watching birds and other wildlife (page 108).

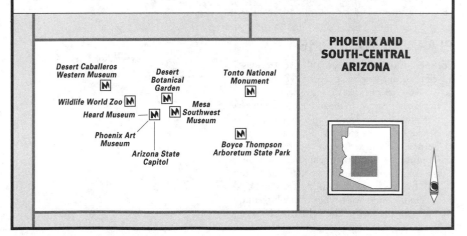

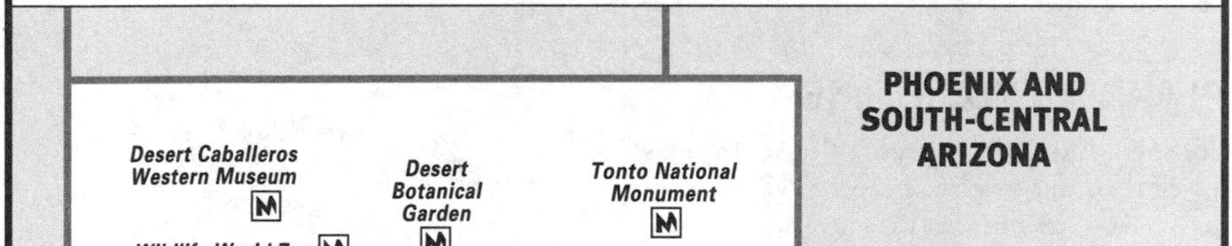

particularly high—most summit elevations range from 3,000 to 8,000 feet. But what they lack in size they make up for in challenging terrain. The major ranges—Bradshaw, Mazatzal, Sierra Ancha, Superstition, and Pinal—all with good hiking and wilderness—lie north and east of Phoenix. To the south and west you'll find a very different sort of country—the often harsh desert most people associate with Arizona. In this region, small, craggy ranges break through plains of rock and sand, springs and streams rarely flow, and only hardy desert plants and wildlife survive. Adventurous travelers can explore such places as Woolsey, Signal Peak and Sierra Estrella Wildernesses, and the Sonoran Desert and Ironwood National Monuments.

Outlying towns in the region make good day or overnight trips. Wickenburg, 58 miles northwest of Phoenix, has many reminders of the Old West, as well as a fine regional museum, great horseback country, guest ranches, and the well-preserved ghost town at Vulture Mine, where a gold rush started in the 1860s. Florence, 60 miles southeast of Phoenix, is another 1860s town with two good historical museums. Nearby Casa Grande Ruins National Monument contains a far older settlement from prehistoric times with a mysterious four-story adobe building. The scenic Apache Trail loop east of the Valley of the Sun takes in not only the incredibly rugged scenery of the Salt River Canyon, but also the historic copper-mining towns of Globe, Miami, and Superior.

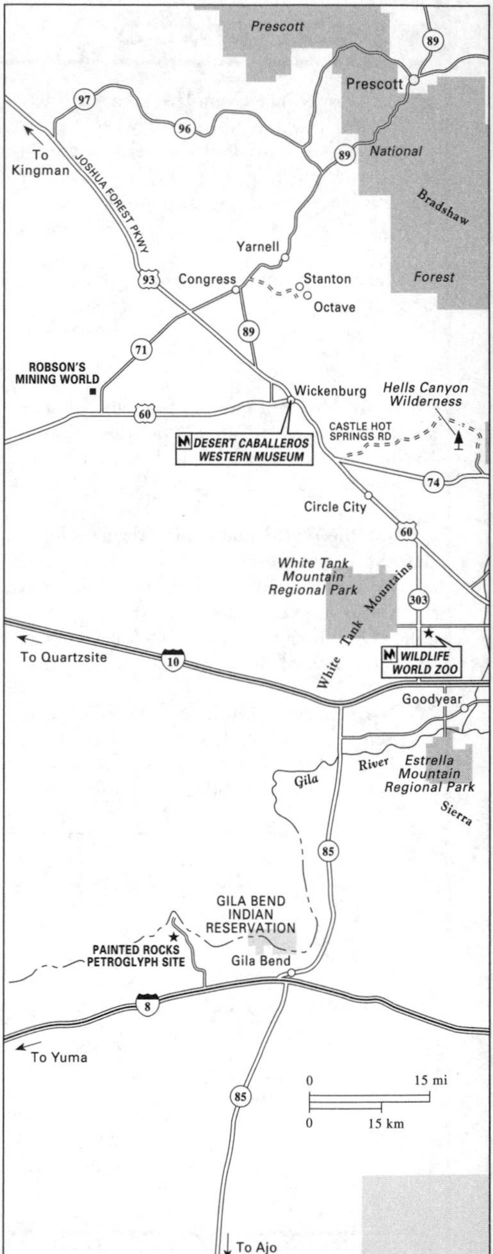

PLANNING YOUR TIME

Phoenix makes the best base to travel from as it's close to most sights; freeways will quickly take you out to other places. There's a lot to see, so you might first take in the top sights and then scan through descriptions of others to see which catch your fancy. The Heard Museum, just north of downtown Phoenix, tops most visitors' lists because of the beautifully presented exhibits on Native American history, culture, crafts, and art. If you'd like to see more art, the nearby Phoenix Art Museum offers wide-ranging exhibits and frequent major shows. The delightful Desert Botanical Garden on the east side of the city

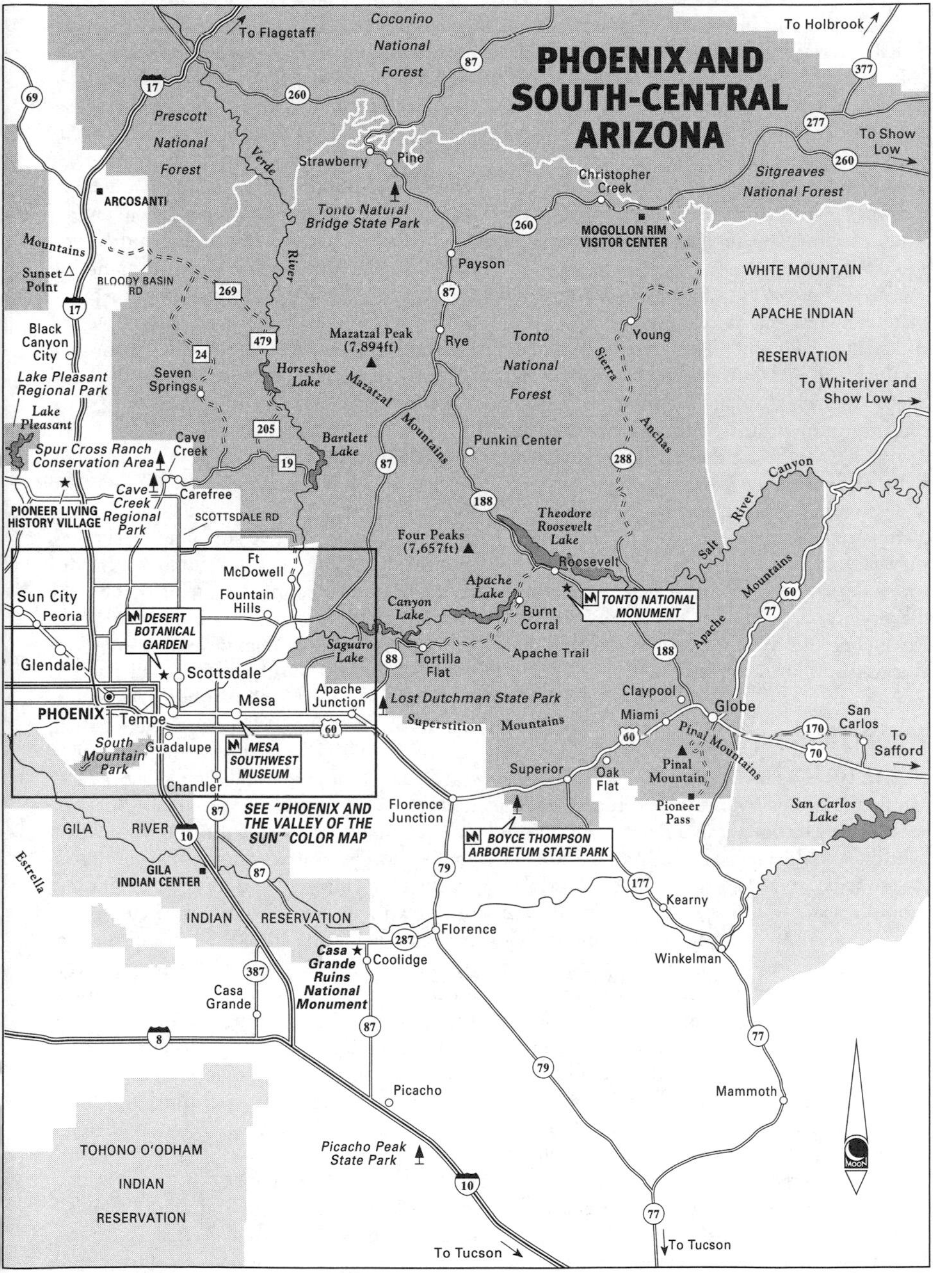
PHOENIX AND SOUTH-CENTRAL ARIZONA
To Flagstaff
Coconino National Forest
To Holbrook
Prescott National Forest
Verde River
Strawberry
Pine
To Show Low
Christopher Creek
Sitgreaves National Forest
ARCOSANTI
Tonto Natural Bridge State Park
MOGOLLON RIM VISITOR CENTER
Mountains
Sunset Point
BLOODY BASIN RD
Payson
WHITE MOUNTAIN APACHE INDIAN RESERVATION
Black Canyon City
Mazatzal Peak (7,894ft)
Rye
Tonto National Forest
Young
Sierra Anchas
Seven Springs
Horseshoe Lake
Mazatzal Mountains
To Whiteriver and Show Low
Lake Pleasant Regional Park
Lake Pleasant
Cave Creek
Bartlett Lake
Punkin Center
Spur Cross Ranch Conservation Area
Salt River Canyon
Carefree
Cave Creek Regional Park
PIONEER LIVING HISTORY VILLAGE
SCOTTSDALE RD
Theodore Roosevelt Lake
Four Peaks (7,657ft)
Ft McDowell
Roosevelt
Fountain Hills
Apache Lake
TONTO NATIONAL MONUMENT
Apache Mountains
Sun City
Peoria
DESERT BOTANICAL GARDEN
Canyon Lake
Burnt Corral
Saguaro Lake
Tortilla Flat
Apache Trail
Glendale
Scottsdale
Claypool
Apache Junction
Lost Dutchman State Park
PHOENIX
Tempe
Mesa
Miami
Globe
San Carlos
Superstition Mountains
Pinal Mountains
To Safford
South Mountain Park
Guadalupe
MESA SOUTHWEST MUSEUM
Superior
Oak Flat
Pinal Mountain
Chandler
Florence Junction
Pioneer Pass
San Carlos Lake
SEE "PHOENIX AND THE VALLEY OF THE SUN" COLOR MAP
GILA RIVER INDIAN RESERVATION
BOYCE THOMPSON ARBORETUM STATE PARK
Estrella
GILA INDIAN CENTER
Kearny
Florence
Casa Grande Ruins National Monument
Coolidge
Winkelman
Casa Grande
Picacho
Mammoth
TOHONO O'ODHAM INDIAN RESERVATION
Picacho Peak State Park
To Tucson
To Tucson

introduces local and exotic flora of the desert and includes many informative displays. Arizona State University, southeast of Phoenix, adds to the cultural energy to the area with art and science collections as well as entertainment venues.

The local bus service can take you to nearly all points of interest, but is best used only for short distances; you'll save a lot of time by driving your own vehicle. No matter how you travel, it's worth a little planning and phoning ahead, especially to avoid the rush hours.

The season will be a major consideration in planning your visit. Since most of south-central Arizona lies below 4,500 feet, temperatures stay on the warm side. In winter you'll enjoy spring-like weather while people in the north are digging out from snowstorms. Spring and autumn also bring fine weather, and these are good seasons to be outdoors in the higher country. From May to September, the sun turns the desert into a giant oven with highs often topping 100°F! Annual rainfall varies from about 5 inches in the lowest desert to more than 20 inches in the highest mountains, arriving as gentle rains between December and March or spectacular thunderstorms from July to September.

HISTORY

Prehistoric Tribes

Nomadic groups roamed across the region in seasonal cycles for thousands of years before learning to cultivate the land. Around 200–300 B.C., a tribe we know as the Hohokam settled in the Gila and Salt River valleys. They may have had the most sophisticated ancient culture that ever developed north of Mexico. Industrious agriculturalists, the Hohokam dug more than 300 miles of irrigation canals in the Salt River Valley alone. The larger canals measured more than 15 feet wide and 10 feet deep. Using water from the canals, the Hohokam grew corn—the staple of their diet—as well as beans and squash. They also hunted game and gathered wild plants.

For most of their history the Hohokam lived in pit houses built of brush and mud over shallow pits. Later, some built rectangular adobe houses. Larger towns had houses by the hundreds and ball courts—large walled fields likely made for games played with hard rubber balls. The Hohokam made pottery, clay figurines, stone bowls, shell jewelry, paint palettes, and cotton cloth. At their peak around A.D. 1100, Hohokam settlements contained a population of between 50,000 and 100,000. The civilization disappeared by about A.D. 1450; much mystery surrounds its origin and demise. The Pima, who likely descended from these people, described their predecessors as Hohokam—a word meaning "all used up" or "departed." Today you can see Hohokam artifacts and two of their most impressive ruins at Pueblo Grande Museum in Phoenix and at Casa Grande National Monument about 50 miles to the southeast.

Anglos Arrive

Spanish and early American explorers overlooked the area. It wasn't until after the Civil War that stories of gold attracted streams of fortune hunters into this wild land. Pinal and Tonto Apache discouraged outsiders, but in September 1865, the army arrived to build Camp McDowell. Ranching and businesses soon followed.

Jack Swilling, a prospector who had served on both sides in the Civil War, first took advantage of the Salt River Valley's farming potential. In 1867, he formed a company with $400, eight mules, and 16 former miners to dig out the Hohokam canals. By the summer of 1868, the group had harvested their first crops of wheat and barley. Their success attracted 30 more farmers the following year, and soon the beginnings of a town appeared. Swilling predicted that a new city would rise from the ruins of the Hohokam civilization, just as the mythical phoenix arose from its own ashes. Surveyors laid out Phoenix in 1870, marking off lots selling for $20–140 apiece. The early settlers had little wood, so they built with adobe. The results looked, according to some accounts, much like an ancient Hohokam village.

Phoenix Comes of Age

With increasing prosperity and a nearby railroad line, residents built ornate Victorian houses, planted trees, put in sidewalks, and opened an icehouse. Soon Phoenix resembled a town transplanted from the Midwest.

By 1889 the town had enough energy and political muscle to wrest the state capital from Prescott. Not even 20 years old, Phoenix had established itself as the business, political, and agricultural center of the territory. Roosevelt Dam, dedicated by Theodore Roosevelt in 1911, ensured water for continued growth. With the glamorous West now safe, Easterners flocked to dude ranches where they could dress like cowboys, ride the range, and eat mesquite-grilled steaks.

World War II brought new industry and an increased military presence. Growth has been frantic ever since, helped by the development of air-conditioning, which makes the desert summer bearable. Though major manufacturing and service industries now dominate the economy of south-central Arizona, agriculture remains important. Area farmers raise crops of citrus, cotton, melons, sugar beets, and vegetables.

Phoenix

Hub of the sprawling Valley of the Sun, Phoenix has a larger population, bigger businesses, and greater clout than any other city in Arizona. Here state laws are made and big corporate deals signed. A Western sense of informality and leisure slows the pace a bit, making for a relaxed style that's quickly picked up by the hordes of newcomers flocking to the city. Phoenix is the sixth-largest city in the country and one of the fastest growing. The city proper holds more than 1.3 million residents, while a similar number inhabit the surrounding area. Many retired people live in the Valley of the Sun, and whole towns are planned just for them. A negative aspect to the area's development is that smoke from industry and the many cars has created a serious air pollution problem, something not historically associated with the blue skies of Arizona.

Downtown Phoenix sits in the heart of the Valley. Here you'll find the State Capitol, Phoenix Civic Plaza, Heritage and Science Park, America West Arena, Bank One Ballpark, and many offices. Streets running east–west in the downtown take the names of U.S. presidents—Van Buren, Monroe, Adams, Washington, Jefferson, and others; Washington Street divides city addresses between north and south. A newer downtown, or "midtown," extends one mile north on Central Avenue. Along this strip you'll see the Phoenix Central Library, Phoenix Art Museum, Phoenix Theatre, Heard Museum, and still more office buildings. The Camelback Road corridor in northeast Phoenix between 24th and 44th Streets holds some of the city's best restaurants and shops, along with many corporate offices.

Central Avenue divides both downtown and midtown into west and east halves. Parallel roads west of Central are designated as Avenues, those east as Streets. (Grand Avenue, however, angles northwest from downtown across this grid on its way to Wickenburg.) In finding Valley addresses, it helps to remember that odd-numbered addresses line the south and east sides of roads.

DOWNTOWN

Downtown, also dubbed "Copper Square," has become an increasingly exciting place with museums, restaurants, entertainment venues, stadiums, and shopping centers. The **Greater Phoenix Convention & Visitors Bureau** (50 N. 2nd St., 602/254-6500 or 877/225-5749, 8 A.M.–5 P.M. Mon.–Fri.) provides much helpful information at its central location; you can park at 15-minute meters in front or in nearby lots.

In addition to the metered street parking downtown, you'll find many indoor and outdoor parking lots. Usually it's easy to find a space, but if a special event is taking place, costs will soar and you may have to do some hunting.

Arizona Center, at Third and Van Buren Streets, offers an oasis of palms, waterfalls, and pools with a variety of restaurants and specialty shops, a 24-screen movie theater, and some night spots. Two blocks south you'll find the oldest and the newest in Phoenix—Heritage Square

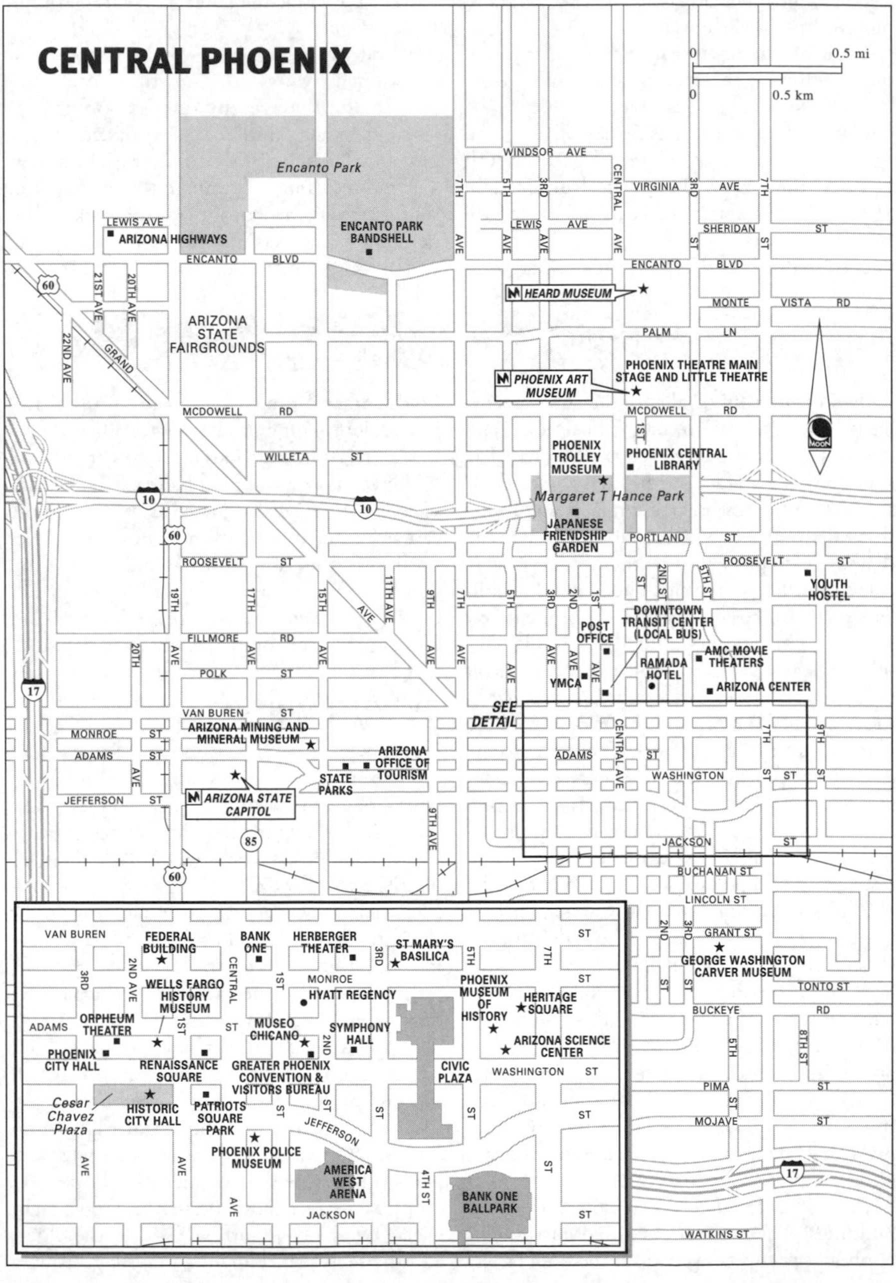

CENTRAL PHOENIX

0.5 mi

0.5 km

Encanto Park

WINDSOR AVE

VIRGINIA AVE

LEWIS AVE
ARIZONA HIGHWAYS

ENCANTO PARK
BANDSHELL

LEWIS AVE

SHERIDAN ST

ENCANTO BLVD

ENCANTO BLVD

MONTE VISTA RD

ARIZONA
STATE
FAIRGROUNDS

HEARD MUSEUM

PALM LN

PHOENIX THEATRE MAIN
STAGE AND LITTLE THEATRE

PHOENIX ART
MUSEUM

MCDOWELL RD

MCDOWELL RD

WILLETA ST

PHOENIX
TROLLEY
MUSEUM

PHOENIX CENTRAL
LIBRARY

Margaret T Hance Park

JAPANESE
FRIENDSHIP
GARDEN

PORTLAND ST

ROOSEVELT ST

ROOSEVELT ST

YOUTH
HOSTEL

FILLMORE RD

DOWNTOWN
TRANSIT CENTER
(LOCAL BUS)

POST
OFFICE

AMC MOVIE
THEATERS

POLK ST

RAMADA
HOTEL

YMCA

ARIZONA CENTER

VAN BUREN ST

MONROE ST

ARIZONA MINING AND
MINERAL MUSEUM

SEE
DETAIL

ADAMS ST

ARIZONA
OFFICE OF
TOURISM

ADAMS ST

WASHINGTON ST

JEFFERSON ST

STATE
PARKS

ARIZONA STATE
CAPITOL

JACKSON ST

BUCHANAN ST

LINCOLN ST

VAN BUREN

FEDERAL
BUILDING

BANK
ONE

HERBERGER
THEATER

ST MARY'S
BASILICA

GRANT ST

GEORGE WASHINGTON
CARVER MUSEUM

WELLS FARGO
HISTORY
MUSEUM

MONROE ST

HYATT REGENCY

PHOENIX
MUSEUM
OF
HISTORY

HERITAGE
SQUARE

TONTO ST

ORPHEUM
THEATER

ADAMS

MUSEO
CHICANO

SYMPHONY
HALL

BUCKEYE RD

ARIZONA SCIENCE
CENTER

PHOENIX
CITY HALL

RENAISSANCE
SQUARE

GREATER PHOENIX
CONVENTION &
VISITORS BUREAU

CIVIC
PLAZA

WASHINGTON ST

PIMA ST

Cesar
Chavez
Plaza

HISTORIC
CITY HALL

PATRIOTS
SQUARE
PARK

JEFFERSON

MOJAVE ST

PHOENIX POLICE
MUSEUM

AMERICA
WEST
ARENA

BANK ONE
BALLPARK

JACKSON ST

ST

WATKINS ST

© AVALON TRAVEL PUBLISHING, INC.

and Science Park, home of the 1895 Rosson House, Phoenix Museum of History, and Arizona Science Center. Continue two blocks farther south and you'll be at the huge Bank One Ballpark with its retractable roof. Turn west two blocks and you'll reach America West Arena, another major sports center. Other attractions in the heart of downtown include Symphony Hall, Herberger Theater, and the Orpheum Theater—a 1929 Spanish Baroque Revival building restored to its original elegance. Look west down Washington Street and you'll see the copper dome of the old state capitol, where much of Arizona's past has played out.

Arizona State Capitol

With its winged figure of Victory atop a shiny copper dome, the old state capitol dates from 1900, a dozen years before statehood. The Arizona Legislature outgrew this structure in 1960 and moved into adjacent new quarters. The old capitol then became a museum (1700 W. Washington St., 602/542-4675, 8 A.M.–5 P.M. Mon.–Fri., except on state holidays, free), carefully restored to look as it did when Arizona became a state in 1912. The Senate and House chambers and other rooms contain period furnishings, historical photos, and tales of frontier days. A lifelike statue of former governor George W. P. Hunt sits behind his desk in the old governor's office. Permanent and changing exhibits occupy four levels; at the top one you can look through the dome's skylight at the Victory, which turns with the wind. On the lowest floor, a memorial room of the battleship USS *Arizona* displays the ship's silver service, photos of the crews, a scale model, a piece of the superstructure, and other memorabilia of the ship sunk at Pearl Harbor in 1941. A gift shop, also on the lowest floor, sells Arizona books and souvenirs.

You can join free guided tours at 10 A.M. and 2 P.M.; groups of 12 or more must schedule tours in advance. To dig deeper into the state's past, drop into the research library, Room 300, where you'll see the 1930s murals *Pageant of Arizona Progress* by Jay Datus. You can view many historic photos from the archives on the capitol's website, azcapitol.lib.az.us, and you can see what the legislature is up to at www.azleg.state.az.us.

Free parking is available in front of the capitol at Wesley Bolin Memorial Plaza; turn in from Adams Street. The Plaza features many commemorative monuments and an anchor and signal mast from the USS *Arizona.*

Arizona Mining and Mineral Museum

In this large collection, you'll see examples of the minerals that drew many prospectors to Arizona. Specimens of copper minerals—azurite, malachite, chrysocolla, cuprite, and chalcanthite—sparkle in brilliant hues. Fluorescent lights make otherwise undistinguished-looking minerals glow in bright colors. Lapidary exhibits display the art of gem cutting and polishing, while old mining tools, lamps, assay kits, photos, and models reveal how miners worked. A cave exhibit illustrates how wondrous features formed deep in the earth. Fossils trace the evolution of life beginning with cyanobacteria more than a billion years old. Step outside to see the diminutive Arizona Copper Co. locomotive, a headframe, and a stamp mill; the mural on the museum's outside back wall makes a great background for photos. The Rose Mofford Collection, an eclectic assemblage of mementos from Arizona's first woman governor, is in a separate gallery.

The museum staff can tell you of upcoming lapidary and jewelry classes, family programs, and rock and mineral shows (most are held during the winter), as well as put you in touch with local rock shops and clubs. A gift shop sells specimens, gold pans, handcrafted jewelry, and an excellent selection of rockhounding books. Look for the museum's unusual Moorish architecture on the corner of W. Washington Street and 15th Avenue (1502 W. Washington St., 602/255-3791, 8 A.M.–5 P.M. Mon.–Fri., 11 A.M.–4 P.M. Sat., closed Sun. and state holidays, $2 ages 18 and up, www.admmr.state.az.us); parking is available behind the museum.

Wells Fargo History Museum

An 1868 Concord coach forms the centerpiece of this Old West collection (Adams St., between 1st and 2nd Aves., 602/378-1852,

9 A.M.–5 P.M. Mon.–Fri., free). You can experience a re-created Wells Fargo office, admire gold nuggets from Wickenburg, see antique guns, and take in the Western art gallery. It's in the high-rise Wells Fargo building.

Phoenix Police Museum

This small museum (101 S. Central Ave. and Jefferson St., 602/534-7278, 9 A.M.–3 P.M. Mon., Wed., and Fri., except holidays, free) presents the challenges and stories of men and women who have served over the years. You'll learn of Phoenix's first marshal, Henry Garfias, and his difficult job of dealing with lawless elements in the 1880s. Police equipment shows the many changes in communications and transportation over the decades. A memorial room honors those who have lost their lives or suffered injuries while answering the call of duty.

Museo Chicano

Vibrant art of Latin America showcases Chicano and Mexican culture in the galleries (147 E. Adams St., 602/257-5536, 10 A.M.–4 P.M. Tues.–Sat., $2 adults, $1 students and seniors). Each exhibit changes several times a year. A gift shop offers colorful art and crafts, including prints, posters, cards, jewelry, books, and videos.

Arizona Center

Shade trees, fountains, and waterfalls provide a pleasant respite from busy city life at this dining, entertainment, and shopping complex (Van Buren St. between 3rd and 5th Sts., www.arizonacenter.com). A variety of restaurants—many with both indoor and outdoor seating—offer seafood, Mexican, Italian, or Southwestern cuisine. An AMC 24-screen movie theater (602/956-4262) and a few nightspots provide entertainment. Parking is available just to the north in the same block; enter from Fillmore or 5th Street. Businesses will validate your parking stub.

St. Mary's Basilica

Catholic residents built an adobe church here in 1881 and finished the present Mission Revival–style basilica in 1914 (E. Monroe St. between 3rd and 4th Sts., 602/354-2100, 10 A.M.–2 P.M. Mon.–Fri. and during liturgies, free). The interior of the basilica contains beautiful art and symbolism in a peaceful setting. You can purchase *An Historical Guide to the Sacred Art of St. Mary's Basilica* next door at the church office, on the corner of Third and Monroe Streets.

Heritage and Science Park

Museums and historic buildings in this park downtown at Fifth and Monroe Streets reflect Phoenix's past, present, and future. You can step inside most of the historic houses and visit two large museums nearby—Phoenix Museum of History and the Arizona Science Center. Two garages offer parking—on the northwest corner of the park (enter from Fifth or Monroe St.) and south across Washington Street (RVs and tall vehicles must park here); bring your ticket into a museum for validation.

Heritage Square

The Victorian-style, 1895 **Rosson House** (602/262-5029 recording or 262-5071 office, www.rossonhousemuseum.org, noon–3:30 P.M. Sun., 10 A.M.–3:30 P.M. Wed.–Sat., call for hours in Aug., $4 adults, $3 seniors, $1 children 6–12) stands tall on the north side of Heritage Square. Meticulous restoration has returned the structure—once one of Phoenix's most elegant houses—to its original grand appearance. Guided tours tell about its construction and former residents. Buy tickets at the Burgess Carriage House next door.

The Burgess Carriage House has a Colonial Williamsburg–style rarely seen this far west. Originally located at Second and Taylor, this was the first of two structures moved to Heritage Square. A second carriage house (c. 1900) at the site is now an education center. The Lath Pavilion dates from 1980 but is typical of early Phoenix architecture.

The other buildings on Heritage Square also represent early Phoenix. The Duplex (1923) now contains offices; you can drop into the city office on the left for more information about the historic buildings. The Stevens House (1901) holds the **Arizona Doll and Toy Museum** (602/253-9337, noon–4 P.M. Sun., 10 A.M.–4 P.M. Tues.–

Sat., closed Mon. and Aug., $3 adults, $1 children 3–12). Beside it, the Stevens-Haustgen House (1901) is currently closed. Next, the Bouvier-Teeter House (1899) offers the **Teeter House Tea Room** (602/252-4682, www.theteeterhouse.com, closed Mon.), serving tea and lunch; on Friday and Saturday evenings October–June you can enjoy light dinners with live jazz. The Silva House next door dates from 1900 and now has fine dining and a cooking school of the **Ruby Beet Gourmet Restaurant** (602/258-8700, Thurs.–Sat evenings by reservation). Baird Machine Shop (1929) houses the popular **Pizzeria Bianco** (602/258-8300, open Tues.–Sun. for dinner), which creates pizza and salads. The 1909 Thomas House next door is home to Bar Bianco, which serves wine, beer, and appetizers.

Phoenix Museum of History

Permanent and changing exhibits illustrate important milestones in the development of Phoenix (105 N. 5th St. in Heritage and Science Park, 602/253-2734, www.pmoh.org, 10 A.M.–5 P.M. Tues.–Sat., $5 adults, $3.50 students/AAA/military/seniors 65+, $2.50 ages 7–12). Wandering through the many sections, you'll follow the lives of local citizens from the arrival of the entrepreneurial settlers to modern times. Exhibits illustrate the harsh living conditions of the town's early years and the delight of residents when they could replace primitive adobe houses with ones of brick and timber. The displays then relate how the populace, having produced a thriving city, looked back and romanticized the West. Artifacts enliven replicas of Hancock's general store and other period rooms. You may see such curiosities as an 1883 steam engine that powered one of the world's first motorcycles—a high wheeler! Interactive displays scattered through the museum will entertain the kids. Visiting shows provide additional perspectives. Walk along the entry hall to see a steam locomotive from early mining operations and a lineup of old printing presses. A small library is available if you'd like to delve deeper into the city's early history. The museum store offers books, crafts, and souvenirs for all ages.

Arizona Science Center

"Have fun with science," suggests the Center (600 E. Washington St. in Heritage and Science Park, 602/716-2000, www.azscience.org, 10 A.M.–5 P.M. daily except Thanksgiving and Christmas, $9 adults, $7 children 3–12 and seniors 62+). And its 300 or so different hands-on exhibits do make scientific exploration exciting! Both children and adults will find the projects challenging and fun. (Mornings, though, can be very busy with school kids.) A Play Space will entertain the age four and under set. New and improved exhibits continually appear, such as All About You (the workings of mind and body), Networks (finding out how things interlink), Fab Lab (exploring the nature of forces and movement), and The World Around You (studying earth sciences and aerospace). The experiments you try may be as simple as a test of perception or as complex as working the controls of an actual helicopter. Staff present demonstrations during the day. Radio hams at station W7ASC (www.w7asc.org) will let you have the microphone to "work" other hams. Art exhibits and visiting exhibitions reveal beautiful and fascinating aspects of science. A planetarium will take you from the skies of Arizona to the mysteries of the universe. A giant-screen theater (similar to Imax) shows impressive movies. The interactive fountain, Water Works, may put on a show for you. Awesome Atom's Science Store, an intriguing gift shop, and a small food court round out the facilities.

Bank One Ballpark

Baseball fans will enjoy the 75-minute tour of this amazing stadium that combines features of an old-fashioned ballpark with the latest technologies. Your guide will tell of exploits by Mark McGuire and other hitters, along with technical details such as how the retractable roof operates. You'll see the poolside "seating" beside right field, hall of fame exhibits, and party rooms, and you'll visit the Arizona Diamondbacks dugout. Tours start at the ticket windows on the west side of the stadium (401 E. Jefferson St., 602/514-8400 advance purchase or 602/462-6799 information, www.bankoneballpark.com,

Mon.–Sat., call for times and recommended reservations, $6 adult, $4 senior 60+ and children 7–12, $2 ages 3–6).

George Washington Carver Museum & Cultural Center

The Phoenix Union Colored High School (415 E. Grant St., 2 blocks south of Bank One Ballpark, 602/254-7516, www.gwcm.org, 10 A.M.–3 P.M. Mon.–Fri. and the third Sat., $3 adult, $2.50 seniors 60+, $2 youth 6–12, $1 kids 3–5), built in 1926 as Arizona's first Black high school and later named in honor of the scientist, now has exhibits that relate the lives, challenges, and triumphs of Phoenix's African-American community. You'll get a sense of what it was like for the Black pioneers and later generations. Galleries tell of individuals prominent locally and nationally, student experiences, sports achievements, military heroes, and religious roots. Art and visiting exhibits appear too. A library specializes in African-American subjects. The sculpture garden contains *That Which Might Have Been, Birmingham 1963,* a memorial to four girls killed in a bombing in Alabama.

CENTRAL AVENUE CORRIDOR

Japanese Friendship Garden and Margaret T. Hance Park

The East comes to Phoenix at this garden and its Musoan (Dream for the Future) Tea House (south side of Margaret T. Hance Park, 602/256-3204, http://phoenix.gov/parks/jfg.html, 10 A.M.–4 P.M. Sat., Oct.–May, $1). Phoenix's Japanese sister city, Himeji, assisted in the design. Visitors leave their troubles at the gate to experience the simplicity and beauty of nature. October–May you can participate in an authentic Japanese tea ceremony on the second Saturday by reservation.

Margaret T. Hance Park runs in a long, grassy strip (actually atop the Papago Freeway tunnel) south of Phoenix Central Library and Culver Street. The park holds scattered monuments to Phoenix's eight sister cities, including a huge bronze panda sculpture from Chengdu, China, at the park's east end. Parking is plentiful off Culver Street, west of Central Avenue.

Phoenix Trolley Museum

From 1887 to 1948, streetcars rattled down the city streets to almost anywhere you'd want to go. Car No. 116 now rolls again on a short section of track at the museum (1218 N. Central Ave., 602/254-0307 or 277-6627, www.phoenixtrolley.com, Sat. by appointment December–early May). Turn west on Culver Street just north of the Margaret T. Hance Park bridge.

Phoenix Art Museum

The nearly 17,000 works of art in this wide-ranging collection will take you to many different times and places (1625 N. Central Ave., 602/257-1222 recording or 602/257-1880, www.phxart.org, 10 A.M.–5 P.M. Tues.–Sun., until 9 P.M. Thurs., closed Mon. and major holidays, $9 adults, $7 students 18+ and seniors 65+, $3 children 6–17, free on Thurs.). European galleries illustrate important themes and styles as far back as the Renaissance. Works in the American galleries span the years from Colonial times to about 1900 and include Western landscapes and bronzes. The Art of Our Time Gallery presents pieces from the modern and contemporary collection. Latin American art reveals the traditions and mixing of Spanish Colonial and indigenous forces up to the present. The exceptional Asian collection reflects the heritage of China, Japan, Tibet, and Southeast Asia over the centuries. Exhibits of fashion design emphasize American trends of the 20th century but also include pieces by European designers. You'll marvel at the details of the famous Thorne Miniature Rooms, which re-create in intricate detail historic interiors of Europe and America at a scale of 1:12. Two large halls host major shows and you'll often find other visiting exhibits too.

You can check for presentations at the video theater or borrow an audio guide for additional background. Scheduled tours offer an in-depth look at exhibitions and collections. Talks, art classes, and other special programs for adults and children take place regularly. The Art Research Library holds more than 40,000 books, monographs, and other material; call for hours. Kids discover art projects and some touchable pieces in the ArtWorks Gallery. The Museum Store sells art, jewelry, crafts, apparel, cards, posters, and books. A café serves creative light meals during museum hours. (You don't have to pay museum admission if you're just visiting the store or café.)

The museum forms a large courtyard with the Phoenix Theatre's Main Stage and Little Theatre at the northeast corner of Central Avenue and McDowell Road. Free parking is available around the museum and in designated spaces across Coronado Road to the north. Some exhibits may have a different fee and hours.

Heard Museum

This world-famous collection introduces regional Native American groups and reveals insights into many aspects of their cultures (2301 N. Central Ave. between McDowell and Thomas, 602/252-8848 recording or 602/252-8840, www.heard.org, 9:30 A.M.–5 P.M. daily except major holidays, $7 adults, $6 seniors 65+, $3 ages 4–12). You'll not only see some of the finest tribal art from prehistoric times to the present, but also gain an appreciation of how the Native peoples relate to their lands, stories, and family and spiritual values. Native people talk about their feelings in the video *Our Voices, Our Land,* complete with beautiful photography and Native music. Displays of superb Native American jewelry—mostly from Navajo, Hopi, and Zuni artisans—show artistic skill and development of styles. Notable exhibits have included a collection of nearly 250 kachina dolls (illustrating the complexity of the Hopi pantheon), the worlds of Arizona's 21 federally recognized tribes, and the boarding school system that has been feared, hated, endured, and loved by Native American children. Other permanent and changing exhibit galleries hold large collections of Southwest pottery, weavings, basketry, and fine art, including contemporary Native American pieces.

The Spanish Colonial–style museum itself has a long history, and, in one of the original

COURTESY OF THE THE HEARD MUSEUM

Native Americans at Phoenix Indian School in 1900; from the exhibit "Remembering Our Indian School Days" at the Heard Museum

galleries, you can get a feel for how the collection looked on opening day in 1929 and how it has grown over the decades. Along the way you'll also pass through attractive courtyards graced with fountains, native flora, and sculpture.

Docents offer guided tours daily, and you can rent an audio tour. For deeper research, visit the extensive library. The museum's outstanding shop and bookstore sells authentic Native American arts and crafts, plus a fine selection of regional books; there's a children's corner too. Arcadia Farms at the Heard café offers a light breakfast and lunch each day inside or in a courtyard.

Major annual events to watch for include the World Championship Hoop Dance the first weekend in February, the Guild Indian Fair & Market the first weekend in March, the Spanish Market (Hispanic artists) the second weekend in November, and the Celebration of Basketweaving and Native Foods Festival the first weekend in December.

NORTH OF DOWNTOWN

Steele Indian School Park

When the final graduating class of 19 Native American students walked across the stage of Memorial Hall to receive their high school diplomas in 1990, the school's 99-year history came to a close. A Circle of Life pathway now encircles Memorial Hall and two other old school buildings. As you walk past 28 interpretive columns, you can read about the students and how they—and the school—changed over the years. Turn south from the Circle on a footbridge across Garden Pond to see a sunken garden of desert flora. A larger lake and grassy acres lie north of the Circle of Life with picnic tables, playground, and basketball and volleyball courts. The park (602/495-0739) is also a fine place for a stroll; turn north on 3rd Street from Indian School Road and continue to the last parking lot.

The Medical Museum

Exhibits in the Phoenix Baptist Hospital and Medical Center (2000 W. Bethany Home Rd., 602/249-0212, 8 A.M.–8 P.M. daily, free) display antique medical and pharmaceutical artifacts, including rare drug jars, doctors' medical bags, and quack medicine items. Look for them in the lobby and on each floor by the elevator. The hospital is at the northwest corner of Bethany Home Road and 19th Avenue.

Shemer Art Center

Housed in a historic residence surrounded by sculpture, Shemer Art Center features works of Arizona artists and craftspeople. A new show comes about once a month. Galleries close between shows, so it's best to call before coming out. The center also hosts art classes for adults and children. Leaflets describe the history and features of the Santa Fe Mission–style house and surrounding Arcadia District. The Center (5005 E. Camelback Rd., 602/262-4727, www.phoenix.gov/parks/shemer.html, 10 A.M.–5 P.M. Mon.–Fri., until 9 P.M. Tues., 9 A.M.–1 P.M. Sat., donations welcome) is near Camelback Mountain at the southeast corner of E. Camelback Road and Arcadia Drive (enter from Arcadia).

Plotkin Judaica Museum

This collection at Temple Beth Israel (10460 N. 56th St. at Shea Blvd., 480/951-0323, 10 A.M.–3 P.M. Tues.–Fri., and Fri. after evening services, $3) illustrates Jewish heritage and displays ancient artifacts from the Holy Land.

Deer Valley Rock Art Center

Prehistoric tribes chipped more than 1,500 petroglyphs into the rock at this site in the Hedgpeth Hills (I-17 Deer Valley Road Exit 215B, then west 2.5 miles, keep right at the signed fork, 623/582-8007, www.asu.edu/clas/anthropology/dvrac, $5 adults, $3 seniors and students, $2 children 6–12). Scholars believe that prehistoric tribes created the images over several periods between about 5000 B.C. and A.D. 1400. Interpretive displays in the visitor center help you gain an appreciation for the rock art from the perspectives of researchers, Native Americans, physical scientists, and archaeologists. An easy quarter-mile trail leads to viewpoints where you can see many of the petroglyphs in their natural settings. (The three boulders at trail marker #2, however, come from another location.) Bring or rent binoculars from the visitor center to get a better look at the rock art. Signs along the wheelchair-accessible path identify local desert plants.

Kids can go on a scavenger hunt, make their own rock art, and practice drawing. Special events include field trips, lectures, workshops, and children's programs. The Glyph Shop sells attractive Southwestern gifts, jewelry, and books. The trail and gift shop close half an hour earlier than the museum. Guided tours go at 1 P.M. on Tuesdays and Thursdays and at 10 A.M. on Saturdays, October–April; they can also be arranged with advance notice. The museum is open noon–5 P.M. Sunday and 9 A.M.–5 P.M. Tuesday–Saturday, October–April; noon–5 P.M. Sunday, 8 A.M.–2 P.M. Tuesday–Friday, and 7 A.M.–5 P.M. Saturday, May–September.

Pioneer Living History Village

Set among rocky desert foothills about 30 miles north of downtown Phoenix, this historical village brings the territorial times back to life. You'll see how residents lived from the mid-1800s to statehood in 1912. The nearly complete little town has a school, church, sheriff's office, bank, blacksmith shop, carpenter shop, opera house, ranch, cabins, and houses—including the John Sears house, one of the first frame houses in Phoenix. Farm animals live in pens at the ranch complex. Many of the 26 or so authentic buildings have been brought here from other sites; others have been reconstructed from old photos or plans.

This collection emphasizes historical accuracy, setting it apart from "Wild West towns" based more on Hollywood fiction than on fact. The community celebrates Statehood Day on the weekend nearest its—and the state's—birthday of February 14. A Bluegrass Festival plays in February. The Gunfighters' Rendezvous brings blazing action in late March or early April. Melodrama and other productions occasionally appear in the opera house; call or check the website for times (I-17 Pioneer Road Exit 225, 623/465-1052, www.pioneer-arizona.com, 9 A.M.–5 P.M. Wed.–Sun., to 3 P.M. June–Sept., $7 adults, $6 seniors 60+, $5 students, $4 children 3–5).

early 1890s Victorian House, Pioneer Living History Village

Pioneer Restaurant (623/465-1821) serves up American food with a choice of indoor or patio seating for breakfast weekends and for lunch and dinner Wednesday–Monday. The magnificent bar has a colorful history.

Agua Fria National Monument

Like many desert rivers, the Agua Fria largely flows underground, popping up here and there along its course. Cottonwoods and willows add splashes of green. Herds of pronghorn roam the grasslands. Prehistoric pueblo ruins perch atop mesas and near the riverbanks. The monument protects 71,100 acres of the river area just to the east of I-17, about 60 miles north of downtown Phoenix. I-17 Badger Springs Exit 256 provides easy access—head one mile southeast from the exit on a dirt road to the parking area, then follow a trail one mile down Badger Spring Wash to the river. Shallow pools and water-sculpted rocks lie in a picturesque little canyon here; look for petroglyphs near the confluence. Most other hiking is cross-country.

Of the many prehistoric sites, **Pueblo la Plata** atop Perry Mesa is one of the largest, with 80–120 rooms, dating from about 1200–1450. If you have a high-clearance vehicle and dry roads, head east 8.5 miles on unpaved Bloody Basin Road from I-17 Exit 259, then turn north 1.5 miles.

The monument lacks facilities. Leave-no-trace camping is permitted except within 200 feet of water. The Bureau of Land Management's Phoenix Field Office (21605 N. 7th Ave., Phoenix, AZ 85027, 623/580-5500, www.az.blm.gov) looks after the area.

WEST OF DOWNTOWN

Downtown Glendale Sights

Besides the shopping for antiques and crafts that attract many visitors, you can tour several unusual museums. **Glendale Visitor Center** (5800 W. Glenn Dr., Ste 140, 623/930-4500 or 877/800-2601, www.visitglendale.com, 10 A.M.–5 P.M. Mon.–Sat.) makes a fine place to start. Turn north one block on 58th Avenue from Glendale Avenue; there's lots of free parking.

Head east across the street for **The Bead Museum** (5754 W. Glenn Dr., 623/931-2737, www.beadmuseumaz.org, 11 A.M.–4 P.M. Sun., 10A.M.–5 P.M. Mon.–Sat., to 8 P.M. Thurs., $4 adult, $2 children). Beautiful examples illustrate the long history and diversity of beads from around the world. The museum shop sells beads and supplies.

Fans of country-western singer Marty Robbins will enjoy a visit to the **Marty Robbins Glendale Exhibit** (5804 W. Myrtle Ave., 623/847-7047, www.friendsofmartyrobbins.org, 10 A.M.–5 P.M. Tues.–Sat., check for summer hours, donations welcome). It's two blocks north of Glendale Visitor Center in the Historic Catlin Court District.

Life doesn't get much sweeter than at the **Cerreta Candy Company** factory (5345 W. Glendale Ave., 623/930-9000, www.cerreta.com, 8 A.M.–6 P.M. Mon.–Sat., free). Monday–Thursday is best to see the candy-making; call for times of free tours.

Ever pet a water puppy? **The Katydid Insect Museum** features hands-on experiences with docile reptiles, amphibians, arthropods, and insects. Kids—and many adults—love it. The museum is in a little shopping center at the northeast corner of 51st Avenue and Bethany Home Road (5060 W. Bethany Home Rd. #7, 623/931-8718, www.insectmuseum.com, 11A.M.–4 P.M. Mon.–Fri., also noon–4 P.M. Sat., Oct.–Feb., $4 adult, $3 student and senior, $2 ages 7–11, $1 kids 3–6).

Historic Sahuaro Ranch

A visit here will take you back to a time when orchards and ranches dotted the Valley. You can step inside the 1887 adobe house—the first permanent building at the ranch—and take a tour of the luxurious 1895 main house. Nearby to the north, the 1899 foreman's house has a gift shop, and the 1891 fruit-packing shed now contains art and historical exhibits. A stroll around the grounds offers views of the historic citrus orchards, date palms, olive groves, and a large rose garden. Peacocks and other fowl strut about. You can take a self-guided audio tour of the grounds and the Xeriscape Botanical Garden just to the north; pick up an audio wand from the gift shop or Glendale Public Library, which has longer hours. The garden surrounds the library parking area. Buildings on the ranch are open noon–4 P.M. Sunday, 10 A.M.–2 P.M. Wednesday–Friday, and 10 A.M.–4 P.M. Saturday; they close in summer. Grounds are open 6 A.M.–sunset daily year-round. There's a small fee for a half-hour tour of the main house. From downtown Glendale, head north about 2.5 miles on 59th Avenue; the entrance is on the left between Olive and Peoria Avenues (9802 N. 59th Ave., 623/930-4200, www.sahuaroranch.org, free).

Challenger Space Center

Journey into space on a two-hour simulated team mission or take in the exhibits, space videos, and astronomy programs at this gleaming center (21170 N. 83rd Ave. in Peoria, 623/322-2001, www.azchallenger.org, 9 A.M.–4 P.M. Mon.–Fri., 10 A.M.–4 P.M. Sat.). Admission for exhibits costs $6 adults, $4 seniors/student; missions require reservations and are open to the public only a few days per week ($17.50 adults, $15 children). A six-story mural by Robert McCall surrounds you in the central rotunda, and you'll see other space art in the corridors. Docents use models and other exhibits to explain features of space exploration on tours of the facility. The modest number of exhibits may not be enough to make your visit worthwhile, however; they're probably best thought of as a bonus to participating in a mission. A gift shop sells space-related items. To reach the Center, turn west from the 101 Loop (Agua Fria Fwy.) at the Union Hills Exit, then turn north on 83rd Avenue. The distinctive white-metal structure will be on your left. The excellent website lists programs, exhibits, and future plans.

Wildlife World Zoo

Begun in 1974 as a breeding farm for rare and endangered species, this zoo opened to the public 10 years later and today houses Arizona's largest collection of exotic wildlife. You'll meet the patas monkey, fastest of all primates, which can run doglike across the ground at 35 miles per hour. Larger animals include the scimitar-horned oryx, dama gazelle, addax (an antelope of the Sahara Desert), rhino, tapir, zebra, giraffe, camel, kangaroo, and white tiger. The zoo's impressive bird collection displays pheasants, toucans, cockatoos, macaws, curassows, ostriches (all five of the world's species), and some birds exhibited nowhere else in the country. A large, walk-in African aviary contains Abdim's storks and other unusual birds. Penguins from South Africa keep their cool. Additional creatures live in the small mammal, reptile, and aquarium exhibits. Wildlife Encounters shows and feedings take place several times daily. A Safari Train takes visitors on a narrated excursion past animals of Africa. The Australian boat ride wends its way around an island inhabited by wildlife from Down Under. A skyride offers a bird's-eye view of the zoo. Children enjoy meeting domestic animals in a petting area and taking a spin on the carousel.

From Phoenix, head west 18 miles on I-10 to Cotton Lane/303 Loop (Exit 124), then turn north 6 miles to Northern Avenue. From the northern Valley, it's fastest to take the 101 Loop to Northern Avenue, then follow Northern west eight miles (16501 W. Northern Ave., 623/935-9453, www.wildlifeworld.com, 9 A.M.–5 P.M. daily year-round, $14 adults, $6 children 3–12).

West Valley Art Museum

You'll experience a lot of variety in both the local and visiting exhibits at this fine museum (northwest of Phoenix at 17420 N. Avenue of the Arts, 623/972-0635, www.wvam.org, 10 A.M.–4 P.M. Tues.–Sun., closed Mon. and holidays, $7 adult and $2 students). Shows change every month or two. At 4 P.M. on Tuesdays, except in summer, you can attend Artful Afternoon, an art or music presentation. The Museum Gift Store sells some unique items. Classic Café serves Italian and American lunches. The museum is on the north side of Bell Road between Sun City and Sun City West; turn in on Avenue of the Arts/114th Avenue. Call or check the website for exhibits, programs, and art classes.

SOUTH OF DOWNTOWN

Mystery Castle

Boyce Luther Gulley always dreamed of building his own castle (800 E. Mineral Rd., 602/268-1581, 11 A.M.–4 P.M. Thurs.–Sun., closed July–Sept., $5 adults, $2 children 6–15). One fine day in 1930 he disappeared, leaving his wife and daughter behind. His whereabouts remained unknown until his death in 1945, when both Gulley and his castle were identified. Gulley's daughter, Mary Lou, now presides over the castle. She and assistants lead tours through the main house (decorated with Native American baskets and rugs), the caretaker's room (with its Stairway to the Rainbow), the Saguaro Room (built around a saguaro skeleton), the wedding chapel (with a Grand Canyon North Rim fireplace), and the Dug Out bar. Everything from Stutz-Bearcat wheels to discarded bricks went into the imaginative and whimsical architecture.

The castle is seven miles south of downtown Phoenix near the entrance to South Mountain Park. Drive south on Central Avenue, turn left on Mineral Road, and continue eight blocks. Alternatively, you can drive south on 7th Street to its end at Mineral Road, then turn left and proceed one block.

EAST OF DOWNTOWN

Pueblo Grande Museum and Archaeology Park

Excellent exhibits depict how life may have been for the Hohokam. Archaeologists have learned much about this ancient society by studying the plant and animal remains, artifacts, and burial sites uncovered at this large site. They know, for example, that the average Hohokam man stood five feet four inches tall, weighed 130–140 pounds, and had a 40-year life span. Many of the artifacts, along with a platform mound bearing what appear to be solstice markings, suggest that the Hohokam had a rich ceremonial culture.

A short video introduces the site and its former inhabitants, and a giant map shows the tribe's intricate canal system—one of the greatest engineering feats of prehistoric America. Tools, decorated ceramics, jewelry, and other finds show how skillfully the Hohokam lived in the desert and what crops they grew. The gallery's shows change about twice yearly and spotlight archaeology, Southwest cultures, or contemporary Native American arts. A children's area invites hands-on exploration of archaeology.

After looking at the indoor exhibits (1–4:45 P.M. Sun., 9 A.M.–4:45 P.M. Mon.–Sat., $2 adults, $1.50 seniors 55+, $1 children 6–17, free on Sun.), you'll better appreciate the ruins outside. Signs along a two-thirds-mile paved trail describe features of Pueblo Grande's construction and excavations. The Hohokam began construction of the platform mound at Pueblo Grande about A.D. 1150 on a terrace overlooking the Salt River. From the top of the mound you can see an oval depression thought to be a ball court; a trail leads over to it for a closer look. On the way to the ball court, you'll pass a reconstructed adobe compound and a pit-house cluster with furnished interiors. You can borrow a copy of *Desert Plants of Pueblo Grande* to identify species along the trails.

The museum sponsors events, tours, and hikes for both children and adults; staff also have information on other Southwest activities and places to visit. A research library can be used by appointment. On the second full weekend in December, Native Americans present entertainment, arts and crafts, and food at the Annual Indian Market, held at the Activity Center in South Mountain Park.

The museum store sells Native American jewelry and other crafts, children's items, and books, including the excellent *Desert Farmers at the River's Edge: The Hohokam and Pueblo Grande.* Picnic tables lie outside near the museum entrance (5 mi. east of downtown at 4619 E. Washington St., 602/495-0900 recording or 602/495-0901, www.pueblogrande.com).

Arizona Military Museum

The collection traces Arizona's military history—and where its soldiers have fought—from Spanish days to the present. Maps, photos, weapons, uniforms, and other memorabilia represent each period. During World War II, the adobe museum building served as part of a prison camp detaining German submariners. A model depicts the daring "Great Escape" on December 23, 1944, of 25 German officers and sailors. (They were all recaptured.) One hall features a well-armed UH-1M helicopter that was shot down three times in Vietnam. An outdoor exhibit displays vehicles and artillery that range in date from World War I to the latest Iraq conflict. A library holds many books and some videos on military history.

The museum is part of the Arizona National Guard complex about seven miles east of downtown. Turn in at the main gate on McDowell Road and look for the large Arizona Military Academy building (northeast corner of E. McDowell Rd. and 52nd St., 602/267-2676, 1–4 P.M. Thurs. and Sat.–Sun., donations needed).

Desert Botanical Garden

If you're curious about all those strange cacti and other plants so abundant in the deserts of Arizona, this is the place to learn about them (1201 N. Galvin Pkwy. in Papago Park, .5 mi. north of Phoenix Zoo, 480/941-1225, www.dbg.org, 8 A.M.–8 P.M. daily Oct.–April and 7 A.M.–8 P.M. daily May–Sept., $9 adults, $8 seniors 60+, $5 students, $4 ages 3–12). A stroll through the extensive gardens will show how much life and beauty the desert holds.

The one-third-mile-loop Desert Discovery Trail winds past thousands of plants, including more than half the cactus species in the world. You can determine what it takes for a plant to be a cactus in the Cactus House and find out about other succulents in the Succulent House. Short trails branching off highlight other aspects of desert life: the Plants and People of the Sonoran Desert Trail shows how early inhabitants met their needs with the desert's resources; the Sonoran Desert Nature Trail has fine views and tells of the plants and animals here; the Center for Desert Living Trail features demonstration gardens, landscaping, and the Desert House to illustrate how we can live in harmony with the desert. Desert House, an actual residence, has many design features that conserve water and energy; exhibit rooms (9 A.M.–5 P.M. daily) beside the house illustrate techniques of living in the desert and show a video of the house under construction. The one-third-mile Desert Wildflower Trail begins near the Garden Shop and loops past wildflowers from the four deserts of the United States; interpretive signs explain how wildflowers and pollinators interact.

All of the trails have plant identification signs and have been graded for wheelchair access. If you arrive in spring, you'll see many plants in bloom. Lighting on the main trail and late closing hours allow for the unusual experience of strolling through the desert at night, though it's necessary to come during the day to read the plant labels and to take the side trails. Inexpensive booklets offer more information on the trails and Desert House. Sculpture exhibits in the garden change every 6–8 months.

A Garden Activities Hotline (480/481-8134) fills you in on the garden's many docent tours, special events, classes, and workshops. During March and April the hotline reports where you can view Arizona wildflowers. Major events include the Butterfly Pavilion (hundreds of butterflies enclosed in a garden habitat) mid-March–mid-May, Las Noches de las Luminarias (over 6,000 luminarias plus music and food) throughout the month of December, concerts (varied programs) on Sundays in spring and autumn, jazz concerts on Friday evenings in late spring and summer, and landscape plant sales in mid-March and mid-October. Arcadia Farm's Patio Café serves breakfast and lunch. The Garden Shop (9 A.M.–5 P.M. daily) offers natural history books, gift items, and cactus and succulent specimens.

Phoenix Zoo

More than 1,300 animals from Arizona and all over the world inhabit 125 acres of rolling hills and lakes at the Phoenix Zoo (455 N. Galvin Pkwy. in Papago Park, 602/273-1341, www.phoenixzoo.org, 9 A.M.–5 P.M. daily Sept.–May and 7 A.M.–4 P.M. daily June–Aug., $12 adults, $9 seniors 60+, $5 children 3–12 with adult). You'll see pronghorn from Arizona, oryx from the Arabian Desert, orangutans from Southeast Asia, baboons from Africa, and spectacled bears from South America, among many others. Breeding programs have increased populations of such endangered creatures as the Arabian oryx, on the brink of extinction when brought to the zoo in 1963, and the chacoan peccary, thought to be extinct until rediscovered in 1972 in its native Paraguay.

The zoo uses moats and steep inclines instead

© BILL WEIR

A goat surveys his domain at Harmony Farm in the Phoenix Zoo.

of cages, where possible, to provide the animals with an open and natural setting. Native habitats re-create tropical rainforest, desert mountains, savanna, wetlands, and temperate woodlands, so each animal feels at home. "Behavioral enrichment programs" make life more interesting for the animals: Wildlife may have to forage for hidden food or chase and catch their dinner. The Arizona Trail section reveals many rarely seen mammals, birds, and reptiles, including some surprisingly beautiful rattlesnakes. Special free programs include animal encounters, storytellers, and zookeeper talks. Kids have playgrounds and lots of things to do; on the Children's Trail, they can feel sculptures of wildlife, pet tame animals in Harmony Farm, and walk through a wallaby habitat. The narrated Safari Train ($2 all day) will save you some walking. In the hot months it's best to come early to see the animals when they're most active. The zoo's gift shop offers books, posters, clothing, and toys. Snack bars sell light meals and fast food. More than two million lights decorate the grounds for ZooLights in the evenings from late November to the beginning of January; call for hours.

Hall of Flame

In the old days the position of volunteer firefighter carried great prestige. Men eagerly joined the local fire brigade, which also served as a social club. Firefighters competed in drills and marched in parades alongside their glistening machines. Here at the Hall of Flame (opposite Papago Park at 6101 E. Van Buren St., 602/275-3473, www.hallofflame.org, noon–4 P.M. Sun., 9 A.M.–5 P.M. Mon.–Sat., $5.50 adults, $4.50 seniors 62+, $3 students 6–17), you'll see what may be the world's largest display of fire-fighting gear. The pieces, many works of art in themselves, come from all over the world.

The first gallery contains hand- and horse-drawn pumpers, hose carriers, and hook-and-ladder wagons from the 18th and 19th centuries. A second gallery displays antique motorized fire trucks. The third and fourth galleries feature historic fire-alarm systems (including the world's first computerized dispatch system), a fire-safety exhibit, and additional fire trucks. Photo and print collections on the walls show firefighters past and present. The National Firefighting Hall of Heroes honors firefighters who lost their lives.

Another gallery explores the world of the wildland firefighter—smokejumpers, hotshots, helitacks, air tankers, engine crews, and ground crews. You'll see a replica of a 1930s lookout cabin, interactive exhibits, and videos of firefighters in action.

The theater screens videos about steam fire engines, great fires, and the people who fight fires. A gift shop sells souvenirs.

Salt River Project History Center

Exhibits by the Salt River Project illustrate the Hohokam life and canal system, then tell of the construction of Theodore Roosevelt Dam and other endeavors that tamed the Salt and Verde Rivers (1521 N. Project Dr., near the Hall of Flame, 602/236-2723, 9 A.M.–4 P.M. Mon.–Fri., free).

Arizona Historical Society Museum

This spacious museum (1300 N. College Ave. and Weber Dr. near southeast corner of Papago Park, 480/929-0292, www.arizonahistoricalsociety.org, noon–4 P.M. Sun., 10 A.M.–4 P.M. Tues.–Sat., $5 adult, $4 student and senior, free for kids under 12, free for everyone on the first Sat.) portrays central Arizona's modern history—the dynamic transformations of the 20th century—with some 19th-century background. As you walk into the courtyard, you're greeted by the sound of rushing water. The dolomite blocks, generator, and freight wagon here come from the early days of Roosevelt Dam; exhibits nearby and inside illustrate how the dam made possible the Valley's agricultural and industrial development. A wide-screen video introduces the people and geography that influenced this region.

Head upstairs to see territorial Arizona come to life in the exhibit Natives and Newcomers: Foundations of Central Arizona. Enter the 20th century with Growing Arizona: Just Add Water, presented as a state fair. Continue into Views from the Home Front, about the time leading up to World War II and the exciting and challenging war years, told from the perspectives of men and women in the military, civilians supporting the war effort, Japanese-American relocatees, and German and Italian prisoners of war. You'll then enter Desert Cities, which illustrates the rapid development of the Valley of the Sun in the postwar era and where it could go in the future.

Downstairs, the Wallace & Ladmo galleries—a favorite with Arizona baby boomers—tells the story of two zany actors who hosted the longest-running live television show in history. Nearby, a large hall hosts changing exhibits. You can detour along the Historymakers Hall and Wall to learn about people who have helped make the state what it is today. Photo displays and videos in *Routes: A Moving Experience* tell the story of what travel was once like for Arizonans. Kids will like the museum's many projects and interactive exhibits. Other offerings include a research library (check for hours), gift shop, guided tours (by appointment), and special programs.

From Phoenix, you can take the 202 Loop (Red Mountain Fwy.), exit north on Scottsdale Road, then turn left on Curry Road or Weber Drive to College Avenue. Alternatively, you can head east on Van Buren Street, turn left on Curry Road, then left on College Avenue; if coming on Washington Street, continue east (it becomes Curry Rd.), then turn left on College Avenue. From Tempe, head north on Mill Avenue, turn right on Curry Road, and left on College Avenue, or head north on Rural Road (becomes Scottsdale Rd.) and turn left on Curry Road or Weber Drive. From Scottsdale, head south on 68th Street (which becomes College Ave.) or you can go south on Scottsdale Road and turn right on Weber Drive.

ACCOMMODATIONS

Nowhere else in Arizona will you find such a wide selection of accommodations at such a wide range of prices—from basic motels to posh luxury resorts. Expect higher prices in the cooler months, especially in early spring when the numbers of snowbirds and other vacationers peak. On the other hand, resorts can be bargains in summer—prices may plummet more than 50 percent when the mercury soars. Seasonal savings decrease with lower-priced accommodations. Rates fluctuate not only through the year, but also during the day if rooms are slow or quick to fill! You may get better rates by calling ahead for a reservation or by arriving in the morning. Always ask for discounts; seniors and members of AARP or AAA often get a lower price, and some places give a "super saver" rate to everyone else. Business hotels often have a lower weekend rate, while some motels charge extra then. Except at small bed and breakfast places, you'll have to pay a tax of about 12 percent on room rates.

Most all national chains are represented here—many in several locations. Check motel and resort listings in the free *Official Visitors Guide* published by the Greater Phoenix Convention and Visitors Bureau. Prices below reflect approximate winter rates. Categories are based on double occupancy.

Reservation Services

The sheer number of hotels and resorts in the

Valley may seem overwhelming. Tourist offices give advice, and you can check the Internet travel sites. For bed and breakfast accommodations, try ***Mi Casa Su Casa*** (P.O. Box 950, Tempe, AZ 85280, 480/990-0682 or 800/456-0682, www.azres.com) and **Arizona Trails Reservation Service** (P.O. Box 18998, Fountain Hills, AZ 85269, 480/837-4284 or 888/799-4284, www.arizonatrails.com).

Hostel

Metcalf House Hostel (1026 N. 9th St. between Portland and Roosevelt Sts., 602/254-9803, www.phxhostel.com, closed Aug., $15) offers shared rooms—separate men's and women's—that make a good choice for lowest-budget travelers.

Rarely full, the hostel is open on a first-come, first-served basis with check-in 4–10 P.M. A three-night-stay limit may apply if the hostel is crowded. Facilities include a kitchen, washer and dryer, and info-packed bulletin boards. As the only Hostelling International–affiliated place in Arizona, the hostel sells memberships and gives out the annual HI directory. The hostel is in a run-down residential area, one mile northeast of downtown. Parking is on the street. You can walk or take a city bus to many Phoenix sights from here.

Under $50

A central place for both men and women is the **Downtown YMCA** (350 N. First Ave., 602/253-6181, $20 s per night or $99 s per week, no reservations taken). Rooms—all singles—have bathrooms down the hall. For a small extra fee, you can use the pool, weight room, racquetball and basketball courts, running track, sauna, and hot tub.

Downtown Motels: You can't get much closer to the heart of downtown than **Budget Inn** (424 W. Van Buren St., 602/257-8331, $45 d) and **Budget Lodge Motel** (402 W. Van Buren St., 602/254-7247, $35 d), which has a pool. A bit farther west is **Desert Sun Hotel** (1325 Grand Ave., 602/258-8971 or 800/227-0301, $35 d) with a pool and restaurant. South two miles, **E-Z 8 Motel** (1820 S. 7th St., 602/254-9787 or 800/655-3465, $40 s, $45 d) has a pool, hot tub, and restaurant.

$50–100

Downtown: Econo Lodge Inn and Suites (202 E. McDowell Rd., 602/258-6911 or 800/776-5560, $79 d room, $99 d suite w/kitchenette) provides a pool and hot tub at a great location near the Phoenix Art and Heard Museums.

East of Downtown/Airport: This area is handy for Valley sights as well as the airport, but don't expect much charm. Nearly all have a pool. The less expensive places in this region include the independent **Pyramid Inn** (3307 E. Van Buren St., 602/275-3691, $45 s, $50 d) and **Phoenix Sunrise Motel** (3644 E. Van Buren St., 602/275-7661, $45 s, $53 d).

Popular chains include **Howard Johnson Phoenix** (124 S. 24th St., 602/220-0044, $60–80 d), **Travelodge Suites** (3101 N. 32nd St., 602/956-4900 or 800/950-1688, $79–119 d all with kitchenettes), **Days Inn Airport** (3333 E. Van Buren St., 602/244-8244 or 800/329-7466, $79 s, $89 d), **Super 8 Phoenix Airport** (3401 E. Van Buren St., 602/244-1627 or 800/800-8000, $50–89 d), and **Ramada Limited Airport North** (4120 E. Van Buren St., 602/275-5746 or 800/272-6232, $50–80 d).

$100–150

Downtown: The 1928 **San Carlos Hotel** (202 N. Central Ave., 602/253-4121, www.hotelsancarlos.com, $129–225 s, $139–235 d) features antique-filled rooms and suites where Hollywood stars once stayed. The seven-story hotel emphasizes fine service and old-fashioned charm with modern facilities. In the heart of the city, it also offers a restaurant, café, Irish pub, rooftop pool, and sundeck.

Best Western Central Phoenix Inn (1100 N. Central Ave., 602/252-2100, $139 d) provides a great location with a restaurant, business center, fitness center, sauna, pool, and hot tub; 8th-floor suites ($199) feature views of the Valley. **Ramada Inn Downtown Phoenix** (401 N. 1st St., 602/258-3411 or 800/272-6232, $99–159 d) has a pool and restaurant in a very central location.

East of Downtown/Airport: Holiday Inn Select East (4300 E. Washington St., 602/273-7778 or 800/465-4329, $99–145 d) offers a restaurant, pool, hot tub, and fitness center.

$150 and up

Downtown: Two hotels in the heart of downtown appeal especially to businesspeople and convention-goers. The 24-story **Hyatt Regency** (122 N. 2nd St. at Adams St., 602/252-1234 or 800/233-1234, $195–265 d) features modern rooms and suites in Southwest colors, a spectacular atrium lobby, the revolving Compass Restaurant, a rooftop pool, exercise room, and a hot tub. The 19-story **Wyndham Hotel Phoenix** (50 E. Adams St. at 1st St., 602/333-0000 or 800/996-3426, $130–205 d) has a restaurant, pool, fitness center, and business center.

Biltmore Area of Northeast Phoenix: Walking into the vast atrium of **Embassy Suites** (2630 E. Camelback Rd., 602/955-3992 or 800/362-2779, $199–239 d) you might think you're in a tropical paradise. All suites have two rooms, wet bar, and dining area, and guests have use of the fitness center, pool, and hot tub.

Resorts

Phoenix's grand old resort, the **Arizona Biltmore & Spa** offers a wonderful combination of atmosphere, location, and luxury in a 39-acre oasis northeast of downtown (2400 E. Missouri Ave. at 24th St., 602/955-6600 or 800/950-0086, www.arizonabiltmore.com, $395–600 room and $685–1,800 d suite Jan. 1–May 22, $195–275 room and $325–885 d suite May 23–Sept. 26, $340–550 room and $550–1,495 d suite Sept. 27–Dec. 31). Frank Lloyd Wright's influence shows in the hotel's stained glass, geometric designs, and interplay of light and shadow. Amenities include Wright's Restaurant, Biltmore Grill & Patio, two 18-hole golf courses, a putting course, eight pools, a 92-foot water slide, two whirlpools, seven lighted tennis courts, a health spa/athletic club, and the Kids Korral offering children's activities. The hotel is also convenient to good hiking and mountain biking in the nearby Phoenix Mountains Park and Recreation Area.

Also in north Phoenix, **Pointe Hilton Resort at Squaw Peak** (7677 N. 16th St., 602/997-2626 or 800/876-4683 reservations, www.pointehilton.com, $299–399 suites and $600 casitas Oct.–May, $79–119 suites and $169 casitas June–Sept.) features suites and larger, more secluded one- and two-bedroom casitas on 27 acres near Phoenix Mountains Park and Recreation Area. Lush landscaping surrounds the Spanish-style buildings. The waterfalls, seven swimming pools, 130-foot water slide, and tubing river will make a splash with the aquatic set. Kids will enjoy these as well as the game room and activities offered especially for them. The resort also provides four lighted tennis courts, Tocasierra Spa & Salon, and a fitness center. Guests enjoy golf privileges at Hilton's Tapatio Cliffs, four miles away. Dining choices include Aunt Chilada's (Mexican), Hole-in-the-Wall (Western steakhouse), and the elegant Lantana Grille (American/Southwestern).

Pronounced "tapa-TEE-oh," the **Pointe Hilton Resort at Tapatio Cliffs** (11111 N. 7th St., 602/866-7500 or 800/876-4683 reservations, www.pointehilton.com, $189–389 mid-Jan.–mid-May, $89–159 mid-May–mid-Sept., and $109–189 mid-Sept.–mid-Jan.) offers two-room suites, a business center, an 18-hole golf course, two lighted tennis courts, hiking and mountain biking in the nearby North Mountain Recreation Area, seven swimming pools, a 138-foot water slide, and Tocaloma Spa & Salon. You can dine at the Different Pointe of View (French-Italian-Mediterranean) and enjoy its stunning view, or at more informal restaurants.

The **Wigwam Resort** is 17 miles west of central Phoenix in Litchfield Park; head north 2.5 miles from the I-10 Litchfield Road Exit 128 (300 Wigwam Blvd., 623/935-3811 or 800/327-0396, www.wigwamresort.com, $365–425 casita and $425–535 casita suite Jan.–May, $199–239 d casita and $239–329 casita suite June–Sept., $309–359 casita and $359–459 d casita suite Oct.–Dec.). The Southwestern-style resort has a history dating back to 1929 and a reputation for superb golf on its three 18-hole courses. Besides the fairways, guests enjoy fine dining in the Arizona Kitchen (Southwestern cuisine), nine tennis courts (six lighted), two swimming pools, and a fitness center. A spa is planned for September 2005.

CAMPGROUNDS AND RV PARKS

Many Valley RV parks cater to retired people, who come in the cooler months to spend as long as seven months under the Arizona sun. Guests enjoy an active social life then, including many craft and sport programs. Families won't fit in well at such places, but the parks listed here do accept children unless otherwise noted. RVers will find the largest selection of places to stay in Mesa and Apache Junction; the tourist offices there have lists of RV parks.

North of Phoenix

For **Covered Wagon RV Park** (6540 N. Black Canyon Hwy., 602/242-2500, $18 tents, $21–36 RVs), take the I-17 Glendale Exit and go south a half mile on the west frontage road. To reach **North Phoenix RV Park** (2550 W. Louise Dr., 623/581-3969, $25 RV w/hookups), take the I-17 Deer Valley Road Exit, go west one block to 26th Avenue, then turn right. **Pioneer RV Park** (just off I-17 Pioneer Road Exit 225, 623/465-8000 or 800/658-5895, $27 RV w/hookups) sits in the desert near Pioneer Arizona Living History Museum (not affiliated), about 30 miles north of downtown Phoenix. **Black Canyon City KOA** (I-17 Exit 242, then north on the east frontage road, 623/374-5318 or 800/562-5314, $19 tents, $28–31 RV w/hookups, $37 cabins) lies about 48 miles north of downtown with a pool, hot tub, and other amenities.

Lake Pleasant County Park (about 30 miles northwest of Phoenix), **Cave Creek Regional Park** (about 30 miles north of Phoenix), and **McDowell Mountain Regional Park** (15 miles northeast of Scottsdale) all feature developed campgrounds with showers and hookups. (See the *Sports and Recreation* section for details and directions.)

West of Phoenix

Destiny RV Resort (416 N. Citrus Rd., about 25 miles west of downtown Phoenix, 623/853-0537 or 888/667-2454, $30–36 RV with hookups) is in Goodyear; take I-10 Exit 124, go south on Cotton Lane to Van Buren Street, then turn right to Citrus Road.

White Tank Mountain Regional Park (about 25 miles northwest of downtown Phoenix) offers tent and RV camping with showers in a scenic desert setting. **Estrella Mountain Regional Park** (about 25 miles southwest of downtown Phoenix) has plenty of room for basic camping (water but no showers) plus a few RV sites with hookups. (See the *Sports and Recreation* section for details and directions.)

FOOD

Phoenix and the Valley hold an amazing number of restaurants. You'll find many restaurant reviews and listings in the free weeklies *New Times* (www.phoenixnewtimes.com), *The Rep* (www.azcentral.com), and *Get Out* (www.getoutaz.com).

The more expensive places suggest making reservations and may have a dress code. The following list offers highlights and typical examples of the dining scene. You'll rarely be far from an American, Mexican, or Asian eatery, and nearly all of the resorts offer at least one elegant restaurant. All of the following have a smoke-free room or confine smoking to the bar. Prices refer to the cost of dinner entrées; lunch specials generally cost less.

American, Western, and Southwestern

You'll glide high above the city at **The Compass** (122 N. 2nd St., 602/440-3166, Sun. brunch and dinner, Mon.–Sat. lunch and dinner, $24–40), the Hyatt Regency's 24th-floor revolving restaurant. There's also a cocktail lounge on the same floor.

Sam's Café (455 N. 3rd St. in the Arizona Center., 602/252-3545, daily lunch and dinner, $8–20) creates Southwest flavors in steak, chicken, tuna, quesadillas, tacos, and other specialties; you can dine indoors or on the patio, which overlooks fountains and a garden. Another branch is in northeast Phoenix at the Biltmore Fashion Park (northeast corner of E. Camelback Rd. and 24th St., 602/954-7100).

Durants (2611 N. Central Ave., 602/264-

5967, Mon.–Fri. lunch, daily dinner, $18–35) has been serving steaks, prime rib, chicken, and seafood for 50 years. **Morton's of Chicago** (2501 E. Camelback Rd. in The Esplanade, 602/955-9577, nightly dinner, $20–34) is a link in the famous steakhouse chain. **Stockyards Restaurant** (5001 E. Washington St., 602/273-7378, Mon.–Fri. lunch, daily dinner, $11–30) features beef with some seafood, chicken, and pork options in an 1890s setting.

Different Pointe of View (11111 N. 7th St. and Thunderbird Rd., 602/866-6350, www.differentpointeofview.com, nightly dinner, closed Sun.–Mon. in summer, $26–48) in the Pointe Hilton Resort at Tapatio Cliffs, presents sophisticated French-Italian-Mediterranean dining with a dazzling view of Phoenix. Jazz musicians play Wednesday–Saturday. The Chef's Tasting Menu includes wine pairings from the award-winning wine cellar.

Vincent Guerithault on Camelback (3930 E. Camelback Rd., 602/224-0225, weekdays lunch and nightly dinner, closed Sun.–Mon. in summer, $18–32) prepares imaginative Southwestern cuisine with first-rate service. **Wright's** (Missouri Ave. and 24th St. in the Arizona Biltmore Resort, 602/954-2507, daily dinner, $27–31) also has excellent service and presents contemporary American cuisine in a Frank Lloyd Wright–style decor. Patio and wine cellar dining are available too.

Mrs. White's Golden Rule Café (downtown at 808 E. Jefferson St., 602/262-9256, Mon.–Fri. lunch, $9) has real Southern cookin' and plenty of it. The menu written on the wall lists such favorites as fried chicken, pork chops, catfish, and a vegetable plate with a sampling of every kind of veggie in the kitchen. After filling up on soul food, you simply tell the cashier, perhaps Mrs. White herself, what you had—that's the golden rule.

Green Leaf Café (4426 N. 19th Ave., 602/265-5992, Mon.–Sat. lunch and Tues.–Sat. dinner, $10–17) specializes in vegetarian food and also offers chicken and fish options. **Katz** (5144 N. Central Ave., 602/277-8814, about $7) fixes deli food for breakfast and lunch daily. **Miracle Mile** (9 Park Central Mall, 602/277-4783, Mon.–Sat. breakfast and lunch, about $6) is a kosher-style cafeteria serving good portions of excellent food.

Seafood

At **The Fish Market** (1720 E. Camelback Rd., 602/277-3474, daily lunch and dinner, most $12–21), the informal restaurant downstairs features mesquite-grilled fish and New England–style seafood. The upstairs Top of the Market room offers elegant dining with an exhibition kitchen (daily dinner only, most $16–30). You can also drop by the downstairs oyster bar, sushi bar, and fresh-fish sales counter.

Steamers (24th St. and Camelback Rd. in Biltmore Fashion Park, 602/956-3631, daily lunch and dinner, $19–68, about $24) prepares seafood and some steak and chicken items.

Mexican and Latin American

Matador Restaurant (125 E. Adams St., 602/254-7563, $8–23) specializes in Mexican, but offers American and a few Greek items as well. It's one of the few downtown places open daily for breakfast, lunch, and dinner.

Aunt Chilada's (daily lunch and dinner, $10–18) has a century-old, general-store ambience. It's across from Pointe Hilton Resort at Squaw Peak (7330 N. Dreamy Draw Dr., 602/944-1286) and in Pointe Hilton Resort at South Mountain (2021 W. Baseline Rd., 602/431-6470).

Eliana's (1627 N. 24th St., 602/225-2925, Tues.–Sun. lunch and dinner, $8–10) offers home-cooked Salvadoran food. **Havana Café** (4225 E. Camelback Rd., 602/952-1991, Mon.–Sat. lunch, nightly dinner, most $10–18) will give you a taste of Cuban, Spanish, and South American foods.

La Parrilla Suiza (two locations: 3508 W. Peoria Ave., 602/978-8334; 13001 N. Tatum Blvd., 602/996-6479; both daily lunch and dinner, $6–10) prepares authentic Mexico City food, including vegetarian specials. **San Carlos Bay** (1901 E. McDowell Rd., 602/340-0892, daily lunch and dinner, $11–16) specializes in Mexican seafood.

French

Sophisticated yet fun, **Coup des Tartes** (4626 N. 16th St., 602/212-1082, Tues.–Sat. for dinner, $17–25) serves eclectic French and other cuisines in a small house. Bring your own wine ($8 corkage fee).

Christopher's Fermier Brasserie (2584 E. Camelback Rd. in Biltmore Fashion Park, 602/522-2344, www.fermier.com, daily lunch and dinner, $17–28) goes the extra distance to please its customers. The menu includes truffle-infused steaks, foie gras, smoked salmon, a seafood platter, cheese plates, and tasting menus (dinner only). You can choose from 100 wines by the glass. A three-course brunch is offered on weekends. You have a choice of indoor, patio, and bar seating.

Italian

Lombardi's Romagna Mia (455 N. 3rd St. in the Arizona Center, 602/257-8323, daily lunch and dinner, $10–19) is known for its seafood as well as pasta, pizza, rib-eye, veal, and chicken dishes. Patio seating overlooks a garden and fountains.

Avanti's (2728 E. Thomas Rd., 602/956-0900, Mon.–Fri. lunch, nightly dinner, $17–32) offers a varied menu, including Italian cuisine.

Pronto Ristorante (3950 E. Campbell Ave., 602/956-4049, Mon.–Fri. lunch, nightly dinner, $12–19) serves regional Italian cuisine in a wood-paneled dining area decorated with antique clocks and musical instruments. **Tomaso's** (3225 E. Camelback Rd., 602/956-0836, Mon.–Fri. lunch, nightly dinner, $12–30) prepares northern and central Italian and some Sicilian offerings.

Pizzeria Bianco (623 E. Adams St. in Heritage Square, 602/258-8300, Tues.–Sun. dinner, $9–13) has creative pizzas, salads, and antipasti in a historic brick building. Bar Bianco next door serves wine, beer, and appetizers. **California Pizza Kitchen** (24th St. and Camelback Rd. in the Biltmore Fashion Park, 602/553-8382, daily lunch and dinner, $8–12) prepares gourmet pizza along with pasta, soups, and salads. **Our Gang Pizza & Café** (9832 N. 7th St., 602/870-4122, Tues.–Sun. dinner, $7–17) serves great Italian food in a New York atmosphere.

Greek

Greekfest (1940 E. Camelback Rd., 602/265-2990, Mon.–Sat. lunch and dinner, $10–25) serves tasty food in elegant surroundings.

Middle Eastern

The owner of **Mediterranean House** (1588 E. Bethany Home Rd., 602/248-8460, Mon.–Fri. lunch, Mon.–Sat. dinner, $8–15) has an Israeli and Yemeni background.

Indian

In east Phoenix, the popular **Indian Delhi Palace** (5104 E. McDowell Rd., 602/244-8181, daily lunch and dinner) offers a large selection of flavorful vegetarian and meat dishes from north India. Options include a great-value lunch buffet ($7), entrées ($6–14), and set dinners ($14–18). Adjacent shops offer Indian clothing and a selection of South Asian sweets, snacks, and groceries.

In north Phoenix, **Delhi Palace** (16842 N. 7th St. at Bell Rd., 602/942-4224, daily lunch and dinner) prepares excellent vegetarian and non-vegetarian food in tandoori and other north-Indian styles, with an inexpensive lunch buffet ($6), entrées ($7–13), and set dinners ($12–14).

Chinese

The **Chinese Cultural Center,** a modern Chinatown with distinctive architecture, offers four restaurants, a large oriental supermarket, and some specialty shops. Look for the tile roofs at 668 N. 44th Street on the west side between Van Buren and McDowell Streets, just south from Exit 2 of the 202 Loop.

Ichi Ban Sushi Buffet (Chinese Cultural Center, 602/286-0040, closed Mon., $14 lunch, $21 dinner, less for kids) offers an amazing variety and quality of Japanese and Chinese food—all served buffet style—including sushi, seafood and meat dishes, soups, and salads. It's an oriental splurge and reasonably priced for what you get. **Szechwan Palace** (Chinese Cultural Center, 602/685-0888, daily lunch and dinner, $7–11, some seafood is higher) fixes flavorful dishes, including kung pao and Szechwan styles in its long menu of seafood, meat, and vegetable dishes. **Lao Ching Hing** (Chinese Cultural Center, 602/286-6168, daily lunch and dinner, most $8–13) specializes in Shanghai cuisine, with other popular and authentic styles too; the Peking duck ($27) must be ordered 24 hours in advance. **Sampan Seafood Restaurant** (Chinese Cultural

Center, 602/286-9888, daily lunch and dinner, $7–30) has a nautical setting for its mostly Cantonese and some Mandarin cuisine. Tanks hold live fish, lobster, and crab for many of the menu options, so you know that you're getting them fresh. You can also order vegetable and meat items, including Peking duck and kung pao chicken, or choose from the hot pot menu. There's a lunch buffet option on weekdays. Also in the Chinese Cultural Center, **99 Ranch Market** has a large selection of Oriental groceries, a deli, and a bakery.

Vegetarian House (3239 E. Indian School Rd., 602/264-3480, Tues.–Sat. lunch and dinner, $6–10) is fun to try for its long, varied, and strictly vegetarian menu. Chefs offer mock-seafood and -meat dishes as well as tofu and vegetable choices. According to the menu, "To eat vegetarian food often will be beneficial to your health, remove miscellaneous matters from your body, and help enhance happiness and wisdom." The Suma Ching Hai International Association runs the restaurant and sells books and videos on its teachings; you can also buy meatless ingredients.

Gourmet House of Hong Kong (1438 E. McDowell Rd., 602/253-4859, daily lunch and dinner, $7–20) offers more than 300 entrées and dinners from many corners of China! Specialties include live lobster and Peking duck. Don't be put off by the plain exterior and decor.

China Doll (3336 N. Seventh Ave. at Osborn Rd., 602/264-0538, daily lunch and dinner, $7–10, seafood is higher) offers a large selection of Cantonese specialties, including lunchtime dim sum. The shrimp in garlic sauce is a favorite.

Golden Phoenix (6048 N. 16th St., 602/263-8049, Sun.–Fri. lunch, daily dinner, $6–8) serves good Mandarin, Cantonese, and Szechwan styles.

At **Great Wall Cuisine** (5057 N. 35th Ave., 602/973-1112, daily lunch and dinner, $6–20) lunch-time dim sum will come to you—just wave over a cart operator when something good catches your eye. Dinners are from the regular menu.

Thai

Thai Rama (1221 W. Camelback Rd., 602/285-1123, Mon.–Fri. lunch, daily dinner, $7–10) offers inexpensive northern Thai food on a varied menu.

Vietnamese

Pho Bang (1702 W. Camelback Rd., 602/433-9440, daily lunch and dinner, $4–17) has great food, including some do-it-yourself grills. **Tu Do** (7828 N. 19th Ave., just south of Northern Ave., 602/864-6759, daily lunch and dinner, $4–16) is a good choice in the north Valley.

Japanese

The chefs at **Ayako of Tokyo** (2564 E. Camelback Rd. in Biltmore Fashion Park, 602/955-7007, Mon.–Fri. lunch, nightly dinner, $12–36) offer teppanyaki tabletop cooking, tempura, and a sushi bar.

Tempe

When the enterprising merchant Charles Trumbull Hayden arrived here in 1871 to set up a trading post, he liked this spot on the south bank of the Salt River because it was the safest place to cross with his freight wagons. Hayden also found it a great location for his flour mill and ferry service.

Darrel Duppa came over from Phoenix to visit Hayden's ferry one day, and remarked that the Salt River Valley reminded him of the Vale of Tempe between Mt. Olympus and Mt. Ossa in Thessaly, Greece. Hayden liked the name and, eventually, it stuck.

Farmers settled in Tempe (tem-PEE) to raise livestock, establish a dairy, and grow a variety of crops. In 1885 the Territorial Legislature established nearby Arizona State Teachers College, now Arizona State University (ASU) and one of the largest schools in the country. Sandwiched between Phoenix to the west and Mesa to the east, Tempe (pop. 163,000) lies just south of Scottsdale.

Downtown Tempe offers more than 140 cafés, restaurants, nightspots, bookstores, and specialty shops along and just off Mill Avenue. Brick-paved sidewalks shaded by trees invite a stroll.

The Tempe Convention & Visitors Bureau at 51 W. 3rd Street can fill you in on local events and services.

Many of Tempe's original buildings have survived. Charles Hayden's home at 1st Street and Mill Avenue dates from the early 1870s and is now Monti's La Casa Vieja Restaurant. His flour mill (rebuilt in 1918 after a fire) and the 1951 grain elevator stand across Mill Avenue. Other notable historic structures downtown include the 1888 Hackett House/Tempe Bakery (now a gift shop) at 95 W. 4th Street, the 1899 Hotel Casa Loma (now a restaurant and offices) at 398 S. Mill Avenue, the Laird and Dines Building at 501 S. Mill Avenue, and the Tempe Hardware Building at 520 S. Mill Avenue. Architecture that would have surprised the pioneers lies to the east—the upside-down glass-and-steel pyramid city hall at 31 E. 5th Street and an Arab-styled mosque at 6th and Forest Streets.

Parking and Getting Around

The parking garage at Hayden Square is a good bet downtown; the nearby Visitors Bureau and other area businesses will validate your parking. Enter the garage by turning west one block on 3rd or 5th Streets from Mill Avenue. You can also park in the metered spaces in front of the Visitors Bureau.

Parking is tight on the ASU campus, but you can use metered parking spaces (one hour maximum) or several pay lots; visitors parking is well marked. Most of the central campus is closed to motor traffic. Valley Metro (602/253-5000) connects the university with Tempe and the rest of the Valley. The free FLASH bus services make loops Monday–Friday around campus and downtown. Cyclists will find marked bike lanes. Both motorists and pedestrians need to be on the lookout for bicycle riders, especially at night when they may zip down streets and sidewalks without lights. The Visitors Bureau provides bus and cycling maps.

SIGHTS

Tempe Historical Museum

This attractive museum (809 E. Southern Ave. at Rural Rd., 480/350-5125 recording or 480/350-5100, www.tempe.gov/museum, 1–5 P.M. Sun., 10 A.M.–5 P.M. Mon.–Thurs. and Sat., closed Fri. and major holidays, donations welcome) covers many aspects of Tempe. The large main gallery presents history as an ongoing process, from a Hohokam archaeological dig reconstruction to the present time. Exhibits include many historical photos, an interactive model of the Salt River and canals, a fire station, and video programs. You can also explore the research reading room and the gift shop.

Niels Petersen House

Built in 1892, this late Victorian Queen Anne–style house (1414 W. Southern Ave. at Priest Dr., 480/350-5151, 480/350-5100 group tours, 10 A.M.–2 P.M. Tues.–Thurs. and Sat., last tour at 1:30 P.M., donations welcome) used a clever ventilation system to keep the interior livable in summer. You can tour the interior, restored to its 1930s bungalow appearance, and learn how Niels Petersen contributed to Tempe's early growth. Outside, a small park offers picnic tables and a playground.

Tempe Town Lake

A two-mile section of the barren gravel riverbed of the Salt River just north of Tempe has been transformed into a lake with parks on each shore. Inflatable dams hold the water in, which arrives via a canal. Visitors can bring their own nonmotorized boats, rent one, or take a tour, but there's no swimming. Free outdoor concerts take place Sunday evenings in spring. Tempe Beach Park on the south shore offers picnic tables and playgrounds. Rio Lago Cruise (480/517-4050, www.riolagocruise.com) runs tours and rents a variety of small boats.

Hayden (Tempe) Butte

A short stiff climb will take you from downtown to the rocky summit for a panorama of Tempe and beyond. Interpretive signs describe some plants and history. The trail begins on the butte's south side near the junction of 5th Street and College Avenue beside Sun Devil Stadium.

Guadalupe

A bit of old Mexico lies just beyond southwest Tempe. Yaqui and Mexican-Americans offer restaurants, fruit stands, bakeries, and craft shops in this small, slightly run-down community. Most of the shopping is along Avenida del Yaqui (Priest Dr.) between Guadalupe and Baseline Roads. The large white Yaqui Temple and Our Lady of Guadalupe Church can be seen one block west.

ARIZONA STATE UNIVERSITY

When the Arizona Legislature founded ASU in 1885, classes met in a four-room, red-brick structure set on 20 acres of cow pasture. Today, broad lawns, stately palms, and flowering subtropical trees grace the 700-acre main campus of Arizona's largest university. Growth has been spectacular in recent decades; the school now has more than 47,000 students and an instructional and research faculty of about 1,800. About 7,100 students attend the 300-acre ASU West campus in Phoenix, while another 3,100 students take classes at the ASU East campus in Mesa. Undergraduates can choose from 87 majors, master's degrees are available in 95 subjects, and doctorates in 48.

Attractions on campus include the striking Gammage Auditorium, art galleries, and a variety of museums. The landscaped grounds offer pleasant walking among many different exotic and native trees, plus some unique sculptures and architecture. You can learn about points of interest and the campuswide arboretum from free maps and pamphlets available at ASU's visitors center. Additional exhibits described in the brochures, but not listed below, may interest you, too. Activity slows down a bit in summer—it's *hot*—but most of the galleries and museums stay open, except as noted.

The domed **visitors center** (826 E. Apache Blvd. and Rural Rd., 480/965-0100, 8:15 A.M.–4:45 P.M. Mon.–Fri.) has free parking; you can pick up Arizona tourist literature here, too; there's talk of the visitors center moving to a different location, so you should call first. **Campus tours** (480/965-2604) start at the Student Services Building at 10:45 A.M. and 2 P.M. Monday–Friday, and last 50–60 minutes. ASU's website www.asu.edu lists exhibits, libraries, events, and has some enormous databases. The university sponsors two FM radio stations, **KBAQ** with classical music at 89.5 MHz and **KJZZ** featuring jazz and National Public Radio at 91.5 MHz.

ASU Art Museum at Nelson Fine Arts Center

Art and architecture intertwine on the west side of campus (southeast corner of Mill Ave. and 10th St., 480/965-2787, http://asuartmuseum.asu.edu, 10 A.M.–5 P.M. Wed.–Sat., 10 A.M.–9 P.M. Tues. except in summer, closed Sun.–Mon. and major holidays, free). The American Gallery traces themes from early portraiture to landscapes and abstract art. Other exhibit spaces usually host contemporary art. You can also explore sculpture on several outdoor terraces. A gift shop sells a variety of unique crafts.

Architect Antoine Predock designed the Center to provide a "village-like aggregation of buildings" housing the arts. Aspects of the existing campus and the Southwest can be seen in the choice of materials, forms, and colors. Light coming in from skylights reflects off surfaces a total of 10 times before illuminating the artwork—a process meant to disperse the harmful qualities of daylight. In addition to the museum, the Center is home to the Galvin Playhouse and University Dance Laboratory. You can park in front at the meters or in the nearby visitors parking lot.

Ceramics Research Center

ASU Art Museum's ceramic collection (north across 10th St. from the Nelson Fine Arts Center, 480/965-2787, 10 A.M.–5 P.M. Tues.–Sat., free) will amaze you with its diversity, beauty, and whimsy. Rotating exhibits may show pots by noted Native American artists, lifelike figures, abstract forms, and perhaps a bit of bawdy playfulness.

Step Gallery

Undergraduates stage shows in this little gallery (480/965-3468, noon–5 P.M. Mon.–Thurs., noon–3 P.M. Fri., closed in summer, free) just north of the Ceramics Research Center, but you have to walk around to the north-side entrance.

Harry Wood Gallery

Here you can peruse exhibitions of paintings, photography, or sculpture by Master of Fine Arts candidates (School of Arts building, 480/965-3468, 9 A.M.–5 P.M. Mon.–Thurs., 9 A.M. to 3 P.M. Fri., free).

Gallery of Design

You can see some of the latest techniques here, illustrated by drawings and scale models (south side of the Architecture and Environmental Design building, 480/965-6384, 8 A.M.–5 P.M. Mon.–Fri., free). The building also holds the Howe Library of Architecture.

Northlight Gallery

This gallery features historic and contemporary photographic exhibits (Matthews Hall, 480/965-6517, 12:30–4:30 P.M. Sun., 10:30 A.M.–4 P.M. Mon.–Thurs., closed in summer, free).

Museum of Anthropology

The collection illustrates prehistoric Hohokam and modern Native American cultures, archaeological techniques, and concepts of anthropology (Anthropology Building, 480/965-6213, 11 A.M.–3 P.M. Mon.–Fri., summer hours 10 A.M.–2 P.M. Mon.–Fri., free).

Hayden Library

The university's main library (480/965-6164, www.asu.edu/lib/hayden) houses the Arizona, Chicano, and East Asian special collections, along with the Labriola National American Indian Data Center and government documents. Staff can also tell you of specialized libraries at other campus locations. Computers provide access to library holdings and the Internet. Head up to the 4th floor to see the Luhrs Gallery exhibitions of historic photos in the hallways. The library is open from early morning to late at night, with shorter hours for the special collections and during summer and academic breaks.

Memorial Union

The university's social center offers more than a dozen places to eat. Students and visitors relax downstairs in a lounge or patio, go bowling, or play a game of billiards. Staff at the main floor information desk (480/965-5728) can tell you about the latest concerts, theater performances, art shows, and sporting events. It's open daily from early morning to late at night with shorter hours in summer and breaks.

Computing Commons Gallery

Intriguing technology-generated artwork appears in five or six shows annually (Computing Commons building, 480/965-3609, 10 A.M.–4 P.M. Mon.–Fri., free).

ASU Bookstore

Offerings include general-interest books, textbooks, supplies, maps, and Sun Devils souvenirs (480/965-4170, http://bookstore.asu.edu).

Life Sciences Center

Meet the university's live rattlesnakes—perhaps all 18 of Arizona's subspecies—plus Gila monsters and non-venomous snakes in hallway exhibits (Life Sciences Center, A Wing, 480/965-3369, 8 A.M.–5 P.M. Mon.–Fri., free).

Center for Meteorite Studies

See visitors from outer space (Room C-139 and adjacent hallways, Physical Sciences building, C Wing, 8:30 A.M.–4 P.M. Mon.–Fri., free).

Geology Museum

Here in the F Wing of the Physical Sciences building (480/965-7065, about 9 A.M.–12:30 P.M. Mon.–Fri., free), you can check the six-story Foucault pendulum to see if the Earth is still spinning, or watch the earthquake map to learn what's shaking. Exhibits illustrate geologic processes and identify rocks, minerals, and fossils.

ASU Planetarium

Gaze up at star shows in ASU's Planetarium (Physical Sciences building, F Wing, 480/965-6891, http://phyastweb.la.asu.edu/planetarium, small charge).

Daniel E. Noble Science Library

The nearby science and engineering departments have their collections here (480/965-7607, www.asu.edu/lib/noble, open morning to late at night). You can look up collections or browse the Internet on computers. Inventors check to see if they're first with a bright new idea in the U.S. Patents & Trademark Depository Library. Hikers plan trips using the map collection (3rd level, 480/965-3582, 8 A.M.–8 P.M. Mon.–Thurs., 8 A.M.–5 P.M. Fri.).

Gammage Auditorium

You'll see this circular structure, commemorating a former ASU president, on the southwest corner of campus (480/965-4050 tours, 480/965-3434 box office, www.asugammage.com). Dedicated in 1964, the 3,000-seat auditorium was the last major building designed by Frank Lloyd Wright. Broadway plays and many cultural offerings take place on its stage. Free half-hour tours are offered (Mon.–Fri. 1–3:30 P.M. Oct. 1–mid-May), unless the auditorium is in use; call the day before to get on a tour. The auditorium, set into a curve where Apache Boulevard meets Mill Avenue, is easy to spot.

Sports

The university has fielded some top teams. You can see their trophies, clippings, and photos at the **ASU Sports Hall of Fame** (in the circular corridor of the Wells Fargo Arena, 8 A.M.–5 P.M. Mon.–Fri.). The giant 74,000-seat Sun Devil Stadium hosts football games, and the 14,000-seat Wells Fargo Arena serves ASU's basketball squads. Baseball plays in the 8,000-seat Packard Stadium. Buy tickets to games in front of the Sun Devil stadium at the Sun Devils Athletic Ticket Office (480/965-2381, www.thesundevils.com) or at the event.

ACCOMMODATIONS

$50–100

University Motel (902 S. Mill Ave., 480/966-7221, $40–45 s, $45–55 d) features a pool and a handy location for downtown and ASU. **Hideaway Lodge Motel** (1461 E. Apache Blvd., 480/829-8829, $45 d and up) offers a pool and some kitchenettes east of ASU. **Econo Lodge of Tempe** (2101 E. Apache Blvd., 480/966-5832, 800/207-1317, $59–69 s, $69–79 d) has a pool about two miles east of ASU. **Motel 6** (513 W. Broadway Rd., 480/967-8696 or 800/466-8356, $44–50 s, $50–56 d) includes a pool about a mile southwest of downtown and ASU. **Tempe Travelodge** (1005 E. Apache Blvd., 480/968-7871 or 800/578-7878, $69–89 d) has two pools just east of ASU. Also nearby with pool and hot tub are **Super 8** (1020 E. Apache Blvd., 480/967-8891 or 800/800-8000, $69–75 d) and **Days Inn** (1221 E. Apache Blvd., 480/968-7793 or 800/329-7466, $60–69 d).

$100–150

Holiday Inn (915 E. Apache Blvd., 480/968-3451 or 800/465-4329, $99–109 d) has a pool, hot tub, and Ducks Restaurant & Sports Lounge just southeast of ASU. **Country Suites by Carlson** (1660 W. Elliot Rd., 480/345-8585 or 800/456-4000, $90 d studio, $110 d suite) is in the far southwestern part of town convenient to I-10. Guests have a pool, hot tub, and nearby fitness center.

$150 and up

Tempe Mission Palms (60 E. 5th St., 480/894-1400 or 800/547-8705, www.missionpalms.com, $155 d and up) features a very central location close to both ASU and downtown with a restaurant, pool, exercise room, tennis courts, and business center. Towering seven floors just south across from ASU, **Twin Palms Hotel** (225 E. Apache Blvd., 480/967-9431 or 800/367-0835, www.twinpalmshotel.com, $95–159 d) offers guests a pool and use of ASU recreation facilities.

Courtyard by Marriott (601 Ash Ave., 480/966-2800 or 800/321-2211, $149–179 d) provides a pool, hot tub, fitness center, and business center near downtown and ASU. **Fiesta Inn** (2100 S. Priest Dr., 480/967-1441 or 800/528-6481, $179 s, $189 d) provides a pool, hot tub, exercise room, tennis courts, and business center in southwestern Tempe.

RV Parks

Three places lie about one mile east of the ASU campus: Families can pull in at **Apache Palms RV Park** (1836 E. Apache Blvd., 480/966-7399, www.apachepalmsrvpark.com, $22–$29 RV w/hookups), which offers a pool and hot tub. Adults stay at **Tempe Travel Trailer Villa** (1831 E. Apache Blvd., 480/968-1411, $24 RV w/hookups) and **Green Acres RV Park III** (1890 E. Apache Blvd., 480/829-0106, $20 RV w/hookups).

FOOD

American

Monti's La Casa Vieja (1 W. Rio Salado Pkwy., 480/967-7594, www.montis.com, daily lunch and dinner, $8–29) specializes in steaks for an appreciative crowd. Other meats, pasta, and seafood fill out the menu. The restaurant occupies the large, rambling 1871 Charles Hayden house near the corner of Mill Avenue and 1st Street in the north end of downtown.

At **House of Tricks** (114 E. 7th St., 480/968-1114, www.houseoftricks.com, Mon.–Sat. lunch and dinner, $17–29), chef-owners Robert and Robin Trick offer contemporary American eclectic cuisine.

Gentle Strength Cooperative (234 W. University Dr., 480/968-4831, Sun. brunch, daily lunch, and Mon.–Sat. dinner, $6–14) fixes tasty and healthy vegetarian food in their little café. The natural foods store is open 9 A.M.–9 P.M. daily. **Pita Jungle** (1250 E. Apache Blvd., 480/804-0234, daily breakfast, lunch, and dinner, $4–13) serves up tasty poultry, seafood, and veggie versions of hot and cold pitas, regular and sizzling salads, and pizza.

Greek

My Big Fat Greek Restaurant (525 S. Mill Ave., 480/966-5883, daily lunch and dinner, $7–16) dishes up gyro, souvlaki, mousaka, pasta, and other traditional foods.

Middle Eastern

Close to ASU and downtown, **Phoenicia Café** (616 S. Forest Ave. at 7th St., 480/967-8009, daily lunch and dinner, $3–19) offers tasty Middle Eastern food, including vegetarian or meat pita boats. **Tasty Kabob** (1250 E. Apache Blvd., 480/966-0260, Tues.–Sun. lunch and dinner, $8–16) brings flavors of the Persian Empire to the Valley.

Haji-Baba (1513 E. Apache Blvd., 480/894-1905, daily lunch and dinner, Sun. to go, $5–10) prepares excellent and inexpensive Middle Eastern meals. You can also shop here for groceries, magazines, and music from the region.

Indian

Delhi Palace (933 E. University Ave., 480/921-2200, daily lunch and dinner, $7–14) prepares excellent vegetarian and nonvegetarian food in tandoori and other northern Indian styles. The lunch buffet is a great value and has extras such as free masala (spiced) tea and a selection of sweets. The dinner menu offers entrées and set meals.

Chinese

P.F. Chang's China Bistro (740 S. Mill Ave. at University Dr., 480/731-4600, daily lunch and dinner, $6–14) combines a menu reflecting many regions of China with American comforts—you can have coffee, wine, or dessert with your meal.

Vietnamese

Saigon Healthy Deli (820 S. Mill Ave. at University, 480/967-4199, Mon.–Sat. lunch and dinner, $4–6) is a simple café offering a good selection of both meat and vegetarian dishes at bargain prices.

Korean

Korean Garden (1324 S. Rural Rd., 480/967-1133, Mon.–Fri. lunch and Mon.–Sat. dinner, $14–19) offers authentic food in a pleasant environment.

Scottsdale

Chaplain Winfield Scott, Scottsdale's first resident, fell in love with the Valley when he homesteaded here in the 1880s. During his frequent travels, he promoted the land as "unequaled in greater fertility or richer promise." A small close-knit community soon formed at Brown Avenue and Main Street.

Today the little village has grown up—215,000 people now live here. Scottsdale, once billed as The West's Most Western Town, boasts innumerable porch-fronted shops selling Western and Native American art, international art, crafts, and Western clothing. Both residents and visitors enjoy the top-notch specialty shops, art galleries, cultural events, resort hotels, restaurants, nightlife, and beautiful landscaping. Scottsdale, just east of Phoenix and just north of Tempe, makes an excellent base for a stay in the Valley if you can afford the premium prices. More than 25 resort and day spas cater to their guests.

The Civic Center Mall area downtown makes a good starting or resting place with its fountains, sculpture, and flowers. The Scottsdale Historical Museum, Scottsdale Center for the Arts, Museum of Contemporary Art, and a large library surround the central plaza. Shoppers need only cross Brown Avenue on the west to visit Old Town Scottsdale's shops and restaurants. Many of the galleries stay open late and offer artists' demonstrations for the Scottsdale Art-Walk (480/990-3939, www.scottsdalegalleries.com, 7–9 P.M. Thurs. year-round). Scottsdale welcomes you with lots of free parking.

Scottsdale Trolley (480/421-1004, www.scottsdaletrolley.com, Mon.–Sat., mid-Nov.–late May) provides a free service connecting Old Town Scottsdale with nearby Marshall Way, Fifth Avenue, Galleria Corporate Center, and Scottsdale Fashion Square.

DOWNTOWN

Scottsdale Historical Museum (The Little Red Schoolhouse)

Scottsdale was so small when this schoolhouse opened in 1909 that all the town's children could fit into its two classrooms. From the 1920s up to the 1950s, Mexican agricultural workers used the building as a schoolhouse and community center. Today, photos and artifacts in the Little Red Schoolhouse (7333 Scottsdale Mall in Civic Center complex, 480/945-4499, www.scottsdalemuseum.com, noon–4 P.M. Sun., 10 A.M.–5 P.M. Wed.–Sat., closed July–Aug., free) remind us of the town's past. Located near the center of the original Scottsdale, just east of the intersection of Brown Avenue and Main Street, the schoolhouse makes a good place to begin a tour of the modern city. You can pick up a self-guided walking-tour map of Old Town Scottsdale at the schoolhouse.

House of Broadcasting

Old photos and news clippings illustrate stories of radio and television broadcasting in Arizona (upstairs in Santa Fe West at 7150 E. Fifth Ave., just west of Scottsdale Rd., 10 A.M.–6 P.M. daily). You'll learn about personalities who appeared over the years and see vintage equipment.

Scottsdale Center for the Arts and Museum of Contemporary Art

Galleries of contemporary art, an 800-seat performing arts theater, a cinema, and an outdoor amphitheater occupy the two large buildings of this facility (7380 E. 2nd St. in Civic Center complex, two blocks east of Scottsdale Rd. and two blocks south of Indian School Rd., 480/994-2787, www.scottsdalearts.org, $7 adults, $5 students, free for ages 15 and under, free on Thurs.). It's open noon–5 P.M. Sunday, 10 A.M.–5 P.M. Tuesday–Saturday, until 8 P.M. Thursday; in summer it's closed Monday and Tuesday and doesn't open until noon on Wednesday; call for extended hours in winter. Each building has a museum store, where you'll likely find items related to current exhibits.

McCormick-Stillman Railroad Park

Rail buffs of all ages hop on a five-twelfths-scale train for a ride around this park's grassy acres (7301

E. Indian Bend Rd., just east of Scottsdale Rd. and 1.7 miles west of the 101 Loop, 480/312-2312, www.therailroadpark.com). The train rides and a 1950 carousel operate daily from 10 A.M. to between 5:30 and 7:30 P.M., September–May, depending on the month; call for summer hours. Stroll over to the Mogul-type Baldwin steam engine and the two historic railway cars behind it (11 A.M.–4 P.M. Wed.–Sun., Oct.–May); one has served several U.S. presidents. The Merci Train boxcar on display nearby brought gifts from France after World War II. Stillman Station, a replica, sells tickets and souvenirs. One of two historic railway stations houses a hobby shop and the other offers snacks, as does a Southern Pacific caboose. On Sunday afternoons you can see live steamers and visit several model railroad clubs, each running a different scale train. Other attractions in the park include playgrounds, a small xeriscape arboretum, and reservable picnic ramadas.

NORTH OF DOWNTOWN

Cosanti

Italian-born Paolo Soleri first came to Scottsdale in 1947 to study architecture with Frank Lloyd Wright. In 1956 Soleri started the Cosanti Foundation (6433 E. Doubletree Ranch Rd. in Paradise Valley, look for Soleri sign on south side of street, 480/948-6145, www.arcosanti.org, 11 A.M.–5 P.M. Sun., 9 A.M.–5 P.M. Mon.–Sat., donations welcome) to design energy- and space-efficient cities. At Cosanti you can see some of Soleri's unique structures and learn about his ideas for making the world a better place. The gallery/gift shop sells books, a video, drawings, sculpture, and Soleri's famous windbells. You can often see the pouring of bronze to make bells 10 A.M.–noon on weekdays. From central Scottsdale, go north five miles on Scottsdale Road, then turn left on Doubletree Ranch Road and continue one mile. You can also visit Soleri's town-in-the-making, Arcosanti, 65 miles north of Phoenix.

Rawhide Western Town & Steakhouse

This replica of an 1880s Old West town (call for location, 480/502-5600 or 800/527-1880, www.rawhide.com, 5–10 P.M. daily all year, extended to 11 A.M.–10 P.M. on Fri.–Sun., Oct.–May) invites you in for some fun and food. Pistol Packin Paula and other characters regularly enliven the scene. Rough Riders stage stunt action shows in the Six Gun Theater. A haunted hotel and Lost Dutchman's Mine provide additional thrills. Or take a ride on a stagecoach, train, burro, or camel. Kids may also have a hard time passing up the petting ranch, shooting gallery, ice cream parlor, and candy store. A photo emporium lets you pose in period costumes. Shops sell a variety of Western-themed goods. Rawhide Steakhouse and the Sundown Cookout offer food and entertainment. Admission and Main Street activities are free; you pay for the attractions and shows with carnival-style tickets. Rawhide will be moving to a new location around late 2005, so you'll need to call or check the website for the current address.

Heard Museum North

This satellite of the Heard in el Pedregal Festival Marketplace hosts two shows annually, and has a good gift shop (34505 N. Scottsdale Rd. at Carefree Hwy., 480/488-9817, noon–5 P.M. Sun., 10 A.M.–5:30 P.M., Mon.–Sat., to 5 P.M. in summer, $3 adults, free 12 and under).

Cave Creek and Carefree

The adjacent towns of Cave Creek and Carefree lie in the foothills about 25 miles northwest of downtown Scottsdale and 30 miles north of downtown Phoenix. They fit well into a scenic drive between northern Scottsdale and northern Phoenix. Cave Creek has a good historical museum and Carefree features one of the world's largest sundials. You'll also find many art galleries and several restaurants. The Carefree/Cave Creek Chamber of Commerce (748 Easy St., 480/488-3381, 9 A.M.–4 P.M. Mon.–Fri., www.carefree-cavecreek.com), along with the sundial and many shops, is near the southeast corner of Tom Darlington and Cave Creek Roads. Maricopa County parks and the Tonto National Forest have scenic areas to explore nearby.

To reach Cave Creek and Carefree from Scottsdale, follow Scottsdale Road (turns into Tom

Darlington) north to its end. From Phoenix, drive north on Cave Creek Road, or take I-17 north to Carefree Highway/Highway 74 (Exit 223), and head east 10.2 miles.

Cave Creek Museum (corner of Skyline Dr. and Basin Rd., 480/488-2764, www.cavecreek-museum.org, 1–4:30 P.M. Wed.–Sun., Oct.–May, $3 adult, $2 students and seniors 55+, free for kids under 12) offers a look at the region's past. The Archaeology Wing holds a fine collection of pottery, baskets, and other crafts from prehistoric and modern times. The Pioneer Wing displays aspects of early mining, ranching, and home life. Changing exhibits fill the central hall. Walk out back to see an early 1920s tubercular cabin and a small church. There's a well-preserved mining arrastre (primitive tool to grind ore) in front. A gift shop offers books and crafts of Native Americans and the Southwest. To get here, turn east on Skyline Drive or south on Basin Road from Cave Creek Road in Cave Creek.

EAST OF DOWNTOWN

Taliesin West

Considered one of renowned architect Frank Lloyd Wright's greatest masterpieces, Taliesin West (12621 Frank Lloyd Wright Blvd., 480/860-8810 recording or 480/860 2700 ext. 494 or 495, www.franklloydwright.org, closed Tues.–Wed. July–Aug.) began in 1937 as a winter home for Wright's school of architecture. The apprentices lived in tents and simple shelters on the property, and today, more than 60 years later, they still do. Wright didn't just design buildings according to plan, he let them "grow" from the inside out. He used a similar method for training his student architects, encouraging them to grow and develop far beyond facts and formulas. Nature inspired many of Wright's ideas, which still look contemporary. You'll see how his walls ". . . define and differentiate, but never confine or obliterate."

Although Wright died in 1959, the Frank Lloyd Wright School of Architecture and Taliesin-trained architects carry on his high standards here. Most students stay 3–5 years, living and working closely with one another and the faculty. Tour guides or (occasionally) apprentices lead a variety of walking tours through the complex.

The one-hour Panorama tour ($18 adults, $16 seniors and students, $5 children 4–12) introduces Wright's architectural ideas and takes you through several of the buildings as well as the attractive grounds. Tours depart frequently every day. On the 90-minute Insights tour ($22.50 adults, $20 seniors and students, $15 children 4–12), you'll also visit Wright's dramatic Garden Room and his newly opened living quarters wing. Tours run frequently every day. Desert Walks tours ($20; discount if taken with the Panorama or Insights tour) introduce you to the Sonoran Desert that so inspired Wright. They last 90 minutes and run every morning, weather permitting; reservations are requested. The Night Lights on the Desert tour ($25) lets you experience the drama of the buildings and grounds on Friday evenings from early March through summer.

On the two-hour Apprentice Shelter tour ($30), an apprentice will take you to the individually designed structures in the desert. Tours go only on Saturdays early December–mid-April; reservations are requested. In-depth Behind the Scenes tours ($45) last about three hours and provide the most personal experience. Associates—some who actually worked with Wright—give presentations on life and architecture at Taliesin West as you make an extensive tour of the buildings. These tours operate only a few days a week, so reservations are requested.

In summer, tours tend to be less expensive and run less frequently. At any time of year, it's a good idea to call ahead and check the current schedule. There's a remarkable selection of related books, videos, prints, and gift items in the visitors center.

Northeast of Scottsdale, Taliesin West is set on 600 acres in the western foothills of the McDowell Mountains. From central Scottsdale, you can go north 7 miles on the 101 Loop (Pima Fwy.) to Cactus Road Exit 40, head east 2.8 miles on Cactus Road to the junction with Frank Lloyd Wright Boulevard, then continue 1 mile farther on Taliesin Drive. From the north or west, you can take the 101 Loop, exit east on Frank Lloyd Wright Boulevard, and turn left at the Cactus Road junction. From the east, take Shea Boulevard, turn north on 114th Street/ Frank Lloyd Wright Boulevard, then turn right at the Cactus Road junction.

Fountain Hills

One of the world's highest artificial fountains shoots as high as 560 feet into the air in this community 18 miles northeast of Scottsdale. A display takes place daily on the hour, 10 A.M.–9 P.M., and is lit up at night. The surrounding park is a fine place for a picnic or stroll. From Scottsdale, go north 6 miles on the 101 Loop (Pima Fwy.) or Scottsdale Road, turn east 12 miles on Shea Boulevard, then turn north 2.5 miles on Saguaro Boulevard. **Fountain Hills Chamber of Commerce** (16837 E. Palisades Blvd., 480/837-1654, www.fountainhillschamber.com, 8 A.M.–5 P.M. Mon.–Fri., 10A.M.–3 P.M.Sat.–Sun.) is one block off Saguaro Boulevard.

Exhibits at the **River of Time Museum** (12901 N. La Montana Blvd., 480/837-2612, www.riveroftimemuseum.org, 1–4 P.M. Wed.–Sun. in the cooler months, call for summer hours, $3 adult, $2 seniors, $1 kids 2–12) begin with a poem, then go on to illustrate the local history from prehistoric times to the founding of Fountain Hills (by the same two-man team that started Lake Havasu City). You'll learn of pioneer ranchers—and the soldiers of Fort McDowell who protected them 1865–1890—and the life-giving waterways of the area. A monstrous amethyst crystal cluster comes from a mine high on Four Peaks. Displays also tell about the Yavapai tribe who now live nearby on the Fort McDowell Reservation. Changing exhibits appear, and there's a gift shop. From Scottsdale, you can head east on Shea Boulevard, turn left on Palisades Boulevard, then turn right on La Montana Boulevard. You can also head northeast on Highway 87 from Mesa, turn left on Shea Boulevard, turn right on Saguaro Boulevard, then left on El Lago Boulevard.

Hoo-hoogam Ki Museum

Pima and Maricopa on the Salt River Indian Reservation exhibit baskets, pottery, historic photos, and other artifacts just east of Scottsdale at this museum (10005 E. Osborn Rd. on the southeast corner with Longmore Rd., 480/850-8190, 9:30 A.M.–4:30 P.M. Mon.–Fri., closed on tribal and major American holidays, donations welcome). The museum building incorporates adobe, desert plants, and stone in a traditional "sandwich-style" construction. A gift shop sells crafts from many tribes, and a kitchen in back serves breakfast and lunch weekdays on a patio. From Phoenix or Scottsdale, you can head east on Thomas Road and turn north on Longmore Road or head east on Indian School Road and turn south on Longmore Road.

ACCOMMODATIONS

$50–100

Downtown Area: Motel 6 Scottsdale (6848 E. Camelback Rd. at 69th St., 480/946-2280 or 800/466-8356, $50–70 s, $56–76 d) has a pool; shopping and sights lie close at hand. **Ramada Limited Scottsdale** (6935 E. 5th Ave., 480/994-9461 or 800/528-7396, call for rates) offers a pool, fitness center, and a central location. **Rodeway Inn** (7110 E. Indian School Rd., 480/946-3456 or 800/228-2000, $89–110 d) provides a pool, hot tub, and a business center.

$100–150

Downtown Area: Days Inn Scottsdale Fashion Square Resort (4710 N. Scottsdale Rd., 480/947-5411 or 800/325-2525, $104 d) offers a pool, hot tub, and tennis next to Scottsdale Fashion Square shopping.

North of Downtown: Comfort Inn Scottsdale (7350 E. Gold Dust Ave., one block east of Scottsdale Rd., 480/596-6559 or 888/296-9776, $109 d) provides a pool, hot tub, and exercise room; it's great value for this part of the Valley.

South of Downtown: Hospitality Suite Resort Scottsdale (409 N. Scottsdale Rd., 480/949-5115 or 800/445-5115, www.hospitalitysuites.com, $69–89 d studio, $89–119 d suite) features a restaurant, kitchens, three pools, a whirlpool tub, and lighted tennis and basketball courts.

$150–200

Downtown Area: The stylish **James Hotel** (7353 E. Indian School Rd., 480/994-9203 or

866/505-2637, www.jameshotels.com, $145 s, $155 d and up) puts you in the heart of downtown Scottsdale next to shopping and the Civic Center complex. Guests enjoy an Italian restaurant, two pools, hot tub, fitness center, tennis, pillow-top mattresses, 42-inch plasma TVs, and, of course, high-speed Internet.

Resorts

The Phoenician (6000 E. Camelback Rd., 480/941-8200 or 800/888-8234, www.thephoenician.com, $395–725 Jan.–May, $179–355 June–Sept. 12, and $395–585 Sept. 13th–Dec., incredibly luxurious suites are also available) spreads across 250 landscaped acres at the base of Camelback Mountain. The Valley's most lavish resort, it has been rated one of the top 10 in the world. Fountains, pools, and waterfalls grace the grounds, which also hold a 27-hole golf course, nine pools, a 165-foot water slide, and a tennis garden with 11 lighted courts. Other attractions include nine dining areas, afternoon tea, a mineral water/juice bar in the spa, poolside snacks, and an ice cream parlor. The Center for Well Being offers a fitness center, spa treatments, and a beauty salon. Kids will love the water and the Funicians Club activities.

Camelback Inn, A JW Marriott Resort & Spa (5402 E. Lincoln Dr., 480/948-1700 or 800/242-2635, www.camelbackinn.com, $399–529 casitas and $700–2000 suites Jan.–May, $129–199 casitas and $350–750 suites June–mid-Sept., and $199–299 casitas and $600–1500 suites mid-Sept.–Dec.) opened in 1936 and became Marriott's first resort in 1967. It features pueblo-styled casitas and suites, some with private sundecks or pools. Dining options include the Chaparral restaurant for continental fine dining, the Navajo Room for Southwestern cuisine, and four other restaurants and cafés. Guests play at two 18-hole golf courses, six lighted tennis courts, three pools, whirlpools, and a large spa/fitness center.

The Boulders (34631 N. Tom Darlington Dr., 16 miles north of downtown Scottsdale, 480/488-9009 or 800/553-1717, www.wyndhamboulders.com, $349–699 casitas and $549–1100 pueblo villas Sept.–May, $149–225 casitas and $299–630 pueblo villas June–Aug.) has a picturesque setting among natural rock formations. Dining options include the formal Latilla Room for American cuisine, the Palo Verde for Southwestern food, and Boulders Country Club for meat and seafood. Known as a premier golf and spa resort, The Boulders offers two 18-hole golf courses, a driving range, four pools, eight tennis courts, jogging and hiking trails, and the Golden Door Spa, which has a fitness center. Individual casitas and pueblo villas fit in with the natural terrain and offer fully stocked minibars, patios or balconies, and wood-burning fireplaces. The resort is in Carefree, one-third mile north of el Pedregal and the Scottsdale Road–Carefree Highway junction.

FOOD

American

In Old Town Scottsdale, **Arcadia Farms Café** (7014 E. 1st Ave., 480/941-5665, www.arcadiafarmscafe.com, daily lunch, $9–13) creates fancy sandwiches, salads, and desserts; there's a choice of indoor or patio seating. The nearby **Sugar Bowl** (4005 N. Scottsdale Rd. at 1st Ave., 480/946-0051, daily lunch and dinner, $4–8) offers myriad tempting treats for sweet tooths in an old-fashioned ice-cream parlor, plus home-style meals. The **Original Pancake House** (6840 E. Camelback Rd., next to Motel 6, 480/946-4902, 7 A.M.–2 P.M. daily, $5.50–9) serves some of the best breakfasts in the Valley.

Western

Don & Charlie's (7501 E. Camelback Rd., 480/990-0900, nightly dinner, $14–38) features top-notch steak and barbecue; baseball memorabilia decorate the walls.

Pinnacle Peak Patio (10426 E. Jomax at Alma School Rd., 480/585-1599, www.pppatio.com, Sun. lunch, daily dinner, $15–33) serves mesquite-broiled steaks, ribs, and chicken in a strictly cowboy atmosphere—if you wear a tie inside, it'll be snipped off and added to the large collection hanging from the rafters. Musicians play country tunes nightly. There's a dance floor and you can sit indoors or outdoors. It's in the foothills of the McDowell Mountains about 20 miles northeast of Scottsdale; take Pima Road north, turn east on Happy Valley Road, then north on Alma School Road.

French

Voltaire (8340 E. McDonald Dr., 480/948-1005, Mon.–Sat. dinner, call for hours June–July, closed Aug.–mid-Sept., $19–26) is known for its friendly atmosphere and superb food, such as veal marsala, duck, and sandabs.

Italian

Mancuso's (6166 N. Scottsdale Rd. in the Borgata Shopping Center, 480/948-9988, www.mancusosrestaurant.com, nightly dinner, $16–29) prepares outstanding northern Italian and continental cuisine from family recipes, including cabernet and roasted garlic gnocchi, chicken marsala, and seafood provençal. You'll feel like a guest in a castle.

La Locanda (10201 N. Scottsdale Rd., south of Shea Blvd., 480/998-2822, nightly dinner, $14–26) serves highly rated northern Italian food, such as osso buco dei navigli, a chianti-glazed veal shank, and risotti alla boscaiola with porcini mushrooms, vegetables, parmigiano, and white truffle oil.

Spanish and Mediterranean

Ibiza Café (4400 N. Scottsdale Rd., 480/421-2492, www.ibizacafe.com, Tues.–Sat. lunch and dinner, $10–20) offers indoor and patio seating for tapas, paella, and a variety of Mediterranean cuisines, including North African specialties.

Marquesa (7575 E. Princess Dr. in the Fairmont Scottsdale Princess, 480/585-4848, Wed.–Sat. dinner, Sunday brunch Nov.–June, $25–40) serves fine cuisine from Catalonia and the Basque region in an elegant Spanish-colonial setting.

Mexican

Los Olivos (7328 E. 2nd St. in Old Town, 480/946-2256, and at 15544 N. Pima Rd., 480/596-9787, www.losolivosrestaurant.com, daily lunch and dinner, $9–14) has offered fine food in Scottsdale since 1949. Folk art fills the colorful interior.

Carlsbad Tavern (3313 N. Hayden Rd., just south of Old Town Scottsdale, 480/970-8164, www.carlsbadtavern.com, daily lunch and dinner, $13–21) offers a New Mexican menu in a casual restaurant/bar setting with a patio. Highlights include chipotle barbecued baby back ribs, pecan wood–grilled fish, and crab poblanos with red bell cream sauce.

In north Scottsdale, **Havana Café** (6245 E. Bell Rd., 480/991-1496, Mon.–Sat. lunch and nightly for dinner, $10–29) will give you a taste of Cuban, Spanish, and other Latin American foods, such as paella, tapas, arroz con pollo, and mariscos con salsa verde.

Indian

Jewel of the Crown (7373 Scottsdale Mall near Scottsdale Center for the Arts, 480/949-8000, Wed.–Sun. lunch, nightly dinner, $10–14) prepares both vegetarian and meat dishes in tandoori and other north Indian styles. Diners can also order a *thali* (set meal) for lunch ($9) or dinner ($20–23).

Chinese

Restaurant Hapa (6204 N. Scottsdale Rd., 480/998-8220, www.restauranthapa.com, Mon.–Sat. dinner, $24–36) presents superb Asian-fusion cuisine, such as caramelized Chinese mustard beef tenderloin, miso-marinated Chilean sea bass, and trio of Maine lobster. Another option is the $85 tasting menu.

China Gate (7820 E. McDowell Rd., 480/946-0720, daily lunch and dinner, $8–13) is a Valley favorite with good Mandarin, Szechuan, and Hunan food available from the menu and buffet.

Thai

In Old Town Scottsdale, **Mallee's on Main** (7131 E. Main St., 480/947-6042, www.maleeson-main.com, Mon.–Sat. lunch, daily dinner, $11–18) fixes many tempting dishes of gourmet Thai food.

Japanese

RA Sushi Bar & Restaurant (3815 N. Scottsdale Rd. and 1st St. in Old Town Scottsdale, 480/990-9256, Mon.–Fri. lunch, nightly dinner, $10–18) offers a long list of sushi items at its bar and a selection of noodle, meat, and fish entrées such as the popular apple, salmon, and yaki soba.

Korean

Korean Restaurant (1414 N. Scottsdale Rd., 480/994-5995, Mon.–Fri. lunch, daily dinner, $8–15) serves flavorful *bulkogi* (barbecued beef) and other specialties; try the tangy kimchee (marinated vegetables).

Mesa

In March 1877, when a group of 84 Mormon settlers arrived here, they found a desert landscape with only thin strips of vegetation lining the Salt River. The eager families immediately began rebuilding the old Hohokam irrigation canals, hoping to make the desert green and start a prosperous new life under the warm Arizona sun. Because the land reminded them of a tabletop, they named the settlement Mesa. From the tiny adobe fort used by pioneers in the first years, Mesa has grown into Arizona's third-largest city, with a population approaching half a million. More people arrive in winter to enjoy the sunny climate, the lakes, and the Superstition Mountains. Mesa, bordered by Tempe and Apache Junction, lies 15 miles east of Phoenix.

SIGHTS

Mesa Southwest Museum

Exciting exhibits take you from the beginning of time to the modern era (53 N. Macdonald St., 480/644-2230, http://mesasouthwestmuseum.com, 1–5 P.M. Sun., 10 A.M.–5 P.M. Tues.–Sat., $6 ages 13–54, $5 seniors and students, $3 ages 3–12). Turn right in the lobby to enter the Tunnel of Time to see meteorites and exhibits about the universe. Next, the Hall of Minerals has some beautiful specimens along with illustrations of how rocks formed. You'll come out at Dinosaur Mountain, a towering rock face inhabited by lifelike animated beasts. Pictures, fossils, and realistic models trace the development of early life. Families can detour into the Desert Discovery Zone to check out the hands-on exhibits and projects. Skeletons in Dinosaur Hall represent over 20 species, including a giant, plant-eating Camarasaurus. Continuing to the upper gallery, you'll have another perspective of Dinosaur Mountain, see a gallery of impressive Arizona Highways photos, and view Sonoran Desert exhibits. On entering the Paleo-Indian room, you'll pass archaeologic displays and a skeleton of a mammoth. A re-created Hohokam village just beyond looks like it's still inhabited. A gallery of Mesoamerican art contains figurines and other ceramics.

You'll feel the Spanish presence on entering a replica of Guevavi Mission (1701–1774), the first one built in Arizona. A short side trip leads to a grim territorial jail. Continue to the courtyard outside where you can see a mine replica and try some gold panning. Back inside you can enter the tunnel of the Lost Dutchman Mine and discover some of its facts and mysteries. The historic displays end with an entertaining Arizona and the Movies room. Several changing galleries and a theater room host a variety of shows about the Southwest and beyond.

A gift shop sells books and souvenirs. Staff can tell you about Mesa Grande Ruins, a nearby Hohokam platform mound excavation that can be visited by appointment. The museum is downtown on the corner with W. 1st Street; from the Superstition Freeway/U.S. Highway 60, turn north on Country Club Drive, then right on 1st Street.

Sirrine House

Joel Sirrine built this Queen Anne Victorian-style house (downtown at 160 N. Center St., 480/644-2760, 10 A.M.–5 P.M. Sat., 1–5 P.M. Sun., Oct.–late March, free) in 1896 with a wraparound porch. It's one of the finest surviving homes from Mesa's early years, and contains period antiques from the early 20th century. Look for the 1906 washing machine.

Mesa Arts Center

Scheduled to open in 2005, this impressive complex of glass walls and spacious galleries will house galleries, theaters, studios, classrooms, and offices. You'll see exhibits by the Mesa Contemporary Arts collection, plus visiting shows. The performing arts will include a wide variety of concerts and plays. The Center is downtown at the southeast corner of Main and Center Streets (1 E. Main St., 480/644-5285, www.mesaarts.com).

Arizona Museum for Youth

Children view art exhibits and participate in art projects presented just for them (downtown at 35 N. Robson St., 480/644-2467, www.arizonamuseumforyouth.com, $3.50 ages 1 and up). The main gallery will appeal to ages 5–12, while ArtVille entertains younger kids. Workshops and classes also have fun things to do. The museum is open 1–5 P.M. Tuesday–Friday and 9 A.M.–5 P.M. Saturday–Sunday; summer hours (Memorial Day–Labor Day) run 9 A.M.–5 P.M. Tuesday–Sunday; exhibits change three times a year.

Mesa Arizona Temple

Rising from beautifully landscaped gardens just east of downtown, this temple of the Church of Jesus Christ of Latter-day Saints (Mormons) rates as Mesa's most notable landmark. Workers completed the structure, based on classical Greek architecture, in 1927. Friezes at the top four corners of the exterior represent the gathering of church members from different regions of the world; brochures at the visitor center explain each of the eight scenes and the temple's history.

Marriages and other sacred ceremonies take place inside the temple, so it's not open for tours, but you're welcome to wander among the exotic plants in the gardens and view exhibits in the nearby visitor center (525 E. Main St., 480/964-7164, 9 A.M.–9 P.M. daily, but 10 A.M.–10 P.M. in Dec., free). Personalized tours in the visitor center begin at the *Christus,* a ten-foot statue of Italian marble, and present the basic doctrines of the church. You can explore further with interactive exhibits or online at www.lds.org.

Special events at the temple include the Easter Pageant during the week preceding Easter and the display of Christmas lights (600,000 of them!) that brighten the grounds from late November through December. Also during the Christmas holidays are 30-minute musical programs at 7 P.M. nightly.

Trace your family roots at the **Mesa Regional Family History Center** (41 S. Hobson, 480/964-1200, www.mesarfhc.org, 9 A.M.–5 P.M. Mon. and Sat., 9 A.M.–9 P.M. Tues.–Fri., free), located across the street from the temple grounds. An introductory video and tour will help you get started.

Mesa Historical Museum

This remarkable collection (2345 N. Horne in north Mesa, 480/835-7358, www.mesaaz.org, 10 A.M.–4 P.M. Tues.–Sat., Sept.–May, then 9 A.M.–1 P.M. Tues.–Sat. in summer, free) of pioneer memorabilia in the 1913 Lehi School tells the stories of settlers and later citizens who contributed to the now flourishing city. Each of the many rooms has a different theme. You'll find antique furnishings, school exhibits, a sports hall of fame, personal histories, old photos, and changing exhibits. A video about Mesa's history provides a good introduction. Outside in front, you can see replicas of Fort Utah (the area's first pioneer building) and Mesa's first schoolhouse. Antique farm machinery rests in the side yard and around back. Auditorium murals, shown on request, depict Southwest history. A gift shop has books and crafts.

On the way, you may wish to stop at **Park of the Canals** (1710 N. Horne St., free) to view three ancient Hohokam canals that pioneers dug out and used in 1878. The park also has picnic tables, a playground, and a small desert botanical garden.

Arizona Wing CAF Museum

The World War II B-17G bomber *Sentimental Journey* stands out as the centerpiece of a vintage aircraft collection (northeast corner of Greenfield and McKellips Rds. at Falcon Field, enter from Greenfield, 480/924-1940, www.arizonawingcaf.org, 10 A.M.–4 P.M. daily, $5 adults, $2 ages 6–14). The B-17G and other aircraft may be open for tours, or you may be lucky enough to see one roar down the runway and take off into the skies. Even more exciting is a ride in one! Call to check

© BILL WEIR

Sentimental Journey B-17G of the Arizona Wing CAF Museum taxis in.

on the flying schedule. Other World War II planes in the collection include a B-25J Mitchell bomber that flew missions out of Corsica, a C-45 transport, and a SNJ trainer. The hangars also house visiting aircraft, photo exhibits, engines, and displays of radio, navigation, and gunnery equipment. The museum hosts special aviation programs at the Annual Veterans Day Fly-in and Community Expo the weekend prior to Veterans Day. You can see warbirds in flight and in ground displays.

Chandler Historical Museum

Historical exhibits at this museum (178 E. Commonwealth Ave. in downtown Chandler, 480/782-2717, 11 A.M.–4 P.M. Tues.–Sun., donations welcome) display Native American artifacts and memorabilia of pioneer life and early agriculture. You'll learn about Dr. Alexander J. Chandler (1859–1950), who pioneered irrigation here, opened the nearby San Marcos Hotel, and founded the town named for him.

The museum is just east of A. J. Chandler Park. To get there from Mesa, head south on Country Club Drive (AZ 87), which becomes Arizona Avenue and is the main street through Chandler. Go east one block on Buffalo Street (look for City Complex sign), south one block on Arizona Place, then east one block on Commonwealth Avenue.

Arizona Railway Museum

Railroad enthusiasts have preserved a 1906 steam locomotive and a wide variety of other historic rolling stock (399 N. Delaware and Erie Sts. in Chandler, 480/821-1108, www.azrymuseum.org, noon–4 P.M. Sat.–Sun. Labor Day–Memorial Day weekends, donations welcome). You may be able to enter some of the Pullman cars and a caboose. The museum, which resembles an early Southwest railroad depot, holds a 1950s Traffic Control Center (push the button to see it work) and railroad memorabilia.

Gilbert Historical Museum

In the small agricultural town of Gilbert, south of Mesa and east of Chandler, exhibits in eight rooms of the 1913 Gilbert Grammar School tell the town's story from prehistory to the present (10 S. Gilbert Rd., enter from Elliot Rd., 480/926-1577, 9 A.M.–4 P.M. Tues., Thurs., and Sat., donations appreciated). A lineup of antique farm machinery sits outside.

ACCOMMODATIONS

Under $50

Motel 6 (630 W. Main St., 480/969-8111, 800/466-8356, $30–40 s, $36–46 d) has a pool.

$50–100

The **Mesa Downtown Motel** (22 S. Country Club Dr., 480/964-5694, $60 d) offers a pool. **Quality Inn Royal-Mesa** (951 W. Main St., 480/833-1231 or 800/333-5501, $60–90 d) offers a pool, sauna, hot tub, and exercise room.

Days Inn East Mesa (5531 E. Main St., 480/981-8111 or 800/329-7466, $50–80 s, $60–90 d) includes a pool and hot tub. **Windemere Hotel** (5750 E. Main St., 480/985-3600 or 800/888-3561, $79–109 d) has a restaurant, pool, and hot tub. **Super 8** (6733 E. Main St., 480/981-6181 or 800/800-8000, $59 s, $65 d) also has a pool and hot tub.

$100 and up

The **Phoenix Marriott Mesa** (200 N. Centennial Way, off Main between Center and Mesa, 480/898-8300, call for rates) has a restaurant, business center, pool, hot tub, and an exercise room. East of downtown, **Country Inn & Suites by Carlson** (6650 E. Superstition Springs Blvd., 480/641-8000 or 800/456-4000, $139 d room, $149 d suite) offers a pool, hot tub, and exercise room. **Hilton Phoenix East/Mesa** (1011 W. Holmes Ave. 480/833-5555 or 800/544-5866, $129–159 d room or $159–189 d suite) has a restaurant, business center, pool, hot tub, and fitness center; it's in the southwestern part of town, near the Alma School Road Exit from Superstition Freeway.

South of downtown, **Hampton Inn Mesa** (1563 S. Gilbert Rd., 480/926-3600 or 800/426-7866, $109–119 d) offers a pool and hot tub. **Holiday Inn Hotel & Suites** (1600 S. Country Club Rd., 480/964-7000 or 800/465-4329, $119–129 d room, $139–149 d suite) features a restaurant, pool, hot tub, and fitness room.

Resorts

The rustic **Saguaro Lake Ranch Resort** (13020 Bush Hwy., 480/984-2194, www.saguarolakeranch.com) is in a beautiful setting overlooking the Salt River below Saguaro Lake. Guests enjoy dining in the main lodge, a swimming pool, and hiking and riding trails. Staff can arrange horseback riding in winter, kayaking and tubing the Salt River in summer, and mountain biking and jeep tours year-round. Bed and breakfast rates are $95 s, $125 d December 15–May 31, and $80 s, $100 d the rest of the year. The American Plan with room and three meals runs $160 s, $270 d, but isn't offered in summer.

Arizona Golf Resort (425 S. Power Rd., 480/832-3202 or 800/528-8282, www.azgolfresort.com, $129–159 d rooms, $169–189 d suites, $298–368 two-bedroom suites) features an 18-hole golf course, conference center, fitness center, large pool, hot tubs, and outdoor barbecues. The central location is north from the Superstition Freeway's Power Road exit.

Best Western Dobson Ranch Inn (1666 S. Dobson Rd., 480/831-7000 or 800/528-1356, www.dobsonranchinn.com, $125 d rooms, $140–185 d suites) offers a continental restaurant, buffet breakfast, large pool, hot tubs, and a fitness center on 10 acres, centrally located just south from the Superstition Freeway's Dobson Road exit.

CAMPGROUNDS AND RV PARKS

Green Acres I (2052 W. Main St., 480/964-5058, $20–24 RV w/hookups) is an adult park four miles west of downtown Mesa. **Goodlife RV Resort** (3403 E. Main St., 480/832-4990 or 800/999/4990, $32 RV w/hookups) has more than 1,100 spaces designed for people 55 and over; guests have a pool, hot tubs, and many seasonal activities. Farther out, **Mesa Regal RV Resort** (4700 E. Main St., 480/830-2821 or 800/845-4752, $30 RV w/hookups) also provides a pool, hot tub, exercise room, and wintertime programs for guests 55 and over. **Usery Mountain Regional Park,** 12 miles northeast of downtown Mesa, has a campground with hookups and showers in a very scenic setting.

Apache Junction

Lost Dutchman State Park (6 miles northeast

from U.S. 60/89 on AZ 88, 480/982-4485, $12 tent or RV, $20 w/electric) has a spectacular setting in the foothills of the Superstition Mountains with hiking trails, interpretive programs, and showers. Both tents and RVs are also welcome at **Mesa–Apache Jct. KOA** (1540 S. Tomahawk Rd., 1 mile north from Superstition Fwy. Exit 197, 480/982-4015 or 800/562-3404, $20 tent, $25–27 RV w/hookups), which has a store, pool, hot tub, and showers. **Rock Shadows RV Resort** (600 S. Idaho Rd., 480/982-0450 or 800/521-7096, www.rockshadows.com, $26 RV w/hookups) provides a pool, hot tubs, and seasonal programs for seniors 55 and over.

FOOD

American

The Landmark Restaurant (809 W. Main St., 480/962-4652, daily lunch and dinner, on Sun. the dinner menu is served all day, $11.50–25) draws customers for favorites such as prime rib, New York steak, pot roast, and pork chops. Its Salad Room, one of the Valley's best salad bars, has over 100 items.

Ripe Tomato Café (745 W. Baseline Rd., 480/892-4340, daily breakfast and lunch, prices average about $6) is famous for its tasty omelets, pancakes, burgers, chimichangas, and other fare served in generous quantities. **Aloha Kitchen** (2950 S. Alma School Rd., 480/897-2451, Tues.–Sun. lunch and dinner, most about $6–7) is a casual café with Hawaiian flavors.

Western

In south Mesa, **Rockin' R Ranch** (6136 E. Baseline Rd., 480/832-1539, www.rockinr.net, call for reservations and times, $25 adults, $23 seniors 65+, and $15 kids 3–12) dishes up barbecued beef or chicken with 'taters, beans, biscuits, and coffee. After dinner the wranglers entertain with Western music and humor.

Barleen's Arizona Opry (2275 Old West Hwy. in Apache Junction, 480/982-7991, www.azopry.com, $21 adult, $15 children 12 and under) presents dinner and a lively country music show during its November–April season. **Mining Camp** (4 miles northeast of Apache Junction on AZ 88, then 1 mile right at the sign, 480/982-3181, daily dinner and Sun. lunch, Oct.–June, $18–20 adults, discounts for children, seniors, and cash payment) offers great Western grub, much of it all-you-can-eat, served family style in a replica of an old mining camp's cook shanty. It's a great place for the kids. You have a choice of steak, barbequed ribs, chicken, or vegetarian entrees.

Mexican

Mata's (932 E. Main St., 480/964-7881, Tues.–Sun. lunch and dinner, $6–10) is a family restaurant known for its chimichangas, chile rellenos, tacos, flautas, and strawberry burros. **Rancho de Tia Rosa** (3129 E. McKellips Rd., 480/659-8787, Tues.–Sat. lunch and dinner, $5–12) features Baja coastal cuisine, a great selection of salsas, and a beautiful garden patio.

Italian

Anzio Landing Italian Restaurant (2613 N. Thunderbird Cir., 480/832-1188, www.anziolanding.com, Mon.–Sat. lunch and dinner, $16–24) has a great reputation for northern and southern Italian food. It's on the north side of Falcon Field near the corner of Higley and McDowell Roads.

Organ Stop Pizza (1149 E. Southern Ave., 480/813-5700, www.organstoppizza.com, nightly dinner, $5–16) serves pizza and pasta to the sounds of a huge Wurlitzer organ. It's a fun spot for all ages. Look for the unusual building near the southwest corner of Southern Avenue and Stapely Drive, just north of the Superstition Freeway. (See the *Entertainment and Events* section for more details.)

German

Zur-Kate (4815 E. Main St., 480/830-4244, Mon.–Sat. lunch and dinner, call for summer schedule, $6–11) serves hearty schnitzels and wursts along with beers from the Old Country. Musicians play German tunes on weekends.

Chinese

Hong Kong Gourmet (1744 W. Main St., 480/835-1966, daily lunch and dinner, about

$9) prepares a wide variety of styles for buffet or à la carte dining.

Japanese

Ichi Ban (2015 S. Alma School Rd., 480/777-8433, Mon.–Fri. lunch, daily dinner, $12–35) creates elegant cuisine and offers a sushi bar.

Thai

Pink Pepper (1941 W. Guadalupe Rd. and Dobson, 480/839-9009, Mon.–Sat. lunch, daily dinner, $8–13) offers an extensive menu of flavorful meat, seafood, and vegetarian items.

Entertainment and Events

EVENTS

Concerts, festivals, shows, and other special events happen nearly every day in the Valley. The Arizona Office of Tourism publishes a comprehensive event-listing that's available at local tourist offices and online at www.arizonaguide.com. In Phoenix, you can stop by the Greater Phoenix Convention & Visitors Bureau at 50 N. 2nd Street or call the Visitor Information Line (602/252-5588, www.visitphoenix.com).

January

Celebrations continue around the **Tostitos Fiesta Bowl** (www.tostitosfiestabowl.com), which kicks off the year on or near January 1; Super Bowl XLII will take place here in 2008. **Glendale Glitters Holiday Light Display** concludes mid-month with a display of lighted hot-air balloons. Competitors put their best stock forward during the **Arizona Stock Livestock Show and Rodeo** in late December and early January. Top PGA golfers compete in the **FBR Phoenix Open.** The **Scottsdale Celebration of Fine Art** (www.celebrateart.com) brings together more than 100 artists, many of whom can be seen at work, at Scottsdale Road and the 101 Loop from mid-January to late March. In late January or early February, the **Parada del Sol** in Scottsdale features the world's longest horse-drawn parade and a big rodeo.

February

Scottsdale Celebration of Fine Art continues. The Heard Museum (www.heard.org) sponsors fast-paced competition among Native Americans in the **World Championship Hoop Dance Contest** on the first weekend. **Glendale Chocolate Affaire** celebrates sweetness and romance along with entertainment, arts, and crafts. The horsey set enjoys Scottsdale's **Arabian Horse Show** at WestWorld (www.scottsdaleaz.gov/westworld), which hosts many other horse shows and sales through the year. Native Americans celebrate in the **O'odham Tash Indian Pow Wow** near the city of Casa Grande, 45 miles south of Phoenix, with a parade, rodeo, dances, and crowning of the O'odham queen. Fountain Hills hosts the **Great Fair,** featuring a hot-air balloon race, 5K and 10K runs, and the Southwest Arts and Crafts Show. **Lost Dutchman Days and Rodeo** presents a parade, rodeo, and bluegrass festival in Apache Junction.

Step back to the 16th century for the **Arizona Renaissance Festival** (www.royalfaires.com) when a vast site southeast of Apache Junction becomes a medieval playground of tournament jousting, theater, crafts, food, and costumed performers; it begins early in the month and runs to late March on each weekend and Presidents' Day. **VNSA Used Book Sale** (www.vnsabooksale.org) sponsored by the Volunteer Nonprofit Service Association, presents a huge selection on the second weekend at the Arizona State Fairgrounds; proceeds go to charities. **Arizona Scottish Highland Games and Clan Gathering** (www.arizonascots.com) brings out the pipes and drums along with athletic competitions, food, and games at Mesa Community College (northeast corner of Dobson and U.S. 60).

March

The **Arizona Renaissance Festival** and the **Scottsdale Celebration of Fine Art** continue.

THE ARIZONA RENAISSANCE FESTIVAL

For eight consecutive weekends each February and March, a merry town comes to life on the east side of the Valley of the Sun. Modern cares fade away as one walks through the gate into a 16th-century world of magicians, storytellers, comics, jugglers, and musicians. Entertainers on a dozen stages provide amusement for audiences throughout the day, and you'll meet many costumed actors engaged in song, dance, or other festivities elsewhere in the 30-acre park. You're welcome to dress up too, and there's a costume-rental shop just inside the entrance. The emphasis is on fun—and joining in the nonstop activities. Artisans demonstrate glass blowing, weaving, pottery, armor making, and other skills as you watch. Kids have many games of skill and chance. Jousting knights, dressed in armor and mounted on powerful horses, battle each other three times a day in the King's Arena, with the last match a "joust to the death."

Even in a full eight-hour day, you cannot see everything. An early start helps, and you can ask staff which shows are not to be missed. Actors in some of the stage shows toss out risqué humor, but the program schedule lets you know which ones these are! Kitchens turn out such offerings as turkey drumsticks, steak on a stake, stews, and pizza. Pastries and chocolates may tempt you, too. Or you can splurge on the Pleasure Feast, a two-hour dinner with lively entertainment, for $80 including festival admission; reservations are recommended.

The festival runs rain or shine, 10 A.M.–6 P.M. on Saturday and Sunday, plus Presidents' Day, from early February to late March. Entry fees are $18 adults, $15 seniors 60 and over, $8 kids 5–12. Also budget some money for meals (no outside food is allowed) and tips for the performers. Call 520/463-2700 or check www.royalfaires.com for days and times. From Phoenix, take the Superstition Freeway (U.S. 60) east past Apache Junction and the Gold Canyon Resort to the festival village, which will be on your right. If you're driving from Tucson, either follow the Pinal Pioneer Parkway (AZ 79) or take I-10, to Highways 87, 287, and 79 to Florence Junction, then continue northwest seven miles.

COURTESY OF THE ARIZONA RENAISSANCE FESTIVAL

© BILL WEIR

Luke Day at Luke Air Force Base

The **Heard Museum Guild Indian Fair and Market** (www.heard.org) brings nearly 500 Native American artists to show and demonstrate their work, along with entertainment, food, and children's activities, on the first weekend. Baseball's **Cactus League** plays spring training games at many stadiums in the Valley. **Scottsdale Arts Festival** celebrates with juried craft booths, music, food, and children's activities. Old Town Tempe's **Spring Festival of the Arts** features work by some of the Southwest's best artists and craftspeople, along with food treats and live performances on Mill Avenue. Chandler hosts the annual **Ostrich Festival** with ostrich races and arts and crafts booths. Bright colors, speedy jets, and vintage aircraft fill the sky during the **Thunderbird Balloon & Air Classic** (www.thunderbirdballoonandairclassic.com) at Glendale Airport. The Mesa Arizona Temple puts on an **Easter Pageant** during the week preceding Easter. **Luke Day** features a big air show with the U.S. Air Force's Thunderbirds aerial demonstration team, the U.S. Army's Golden Knights parachute team, civilian plane acrobatics, and ground displays; the event doesn't happen every year but it's worth seeing when it does; it may run in April.

April

Mesa Arizona Temple's **Easter Pageant** runs during the week preceding Easter. **Maricopa County Fair** (www.maricopacountyfair.org) features entertainment, rides, and agricultural exhibits at the Arizona State Fairgrounds in Phoenix. The **Paradise Valley Jazz Party** (www.paradisevalleyjazz.com) draws top talent. **Arizona Book Festival** (www.azbookfestival.org) is the place to meet authors—both local and nationally known—and listen to their experiences. **Sunday on Central** is a huge street fair with entertainment, community booths, and food on Central Avenue. **Glendale Jazz and Blues Festival** plays in Murphy Park in downtown Glendale.

The **Yaqui Indian Easter Celebration** begins on Ash Wednesday and continues every Friday until Holy Week, then Wednesday to Easter Sunday. Dancers wear special masks and costumes in a re-enactment of the crucifixion. The ceremonies, believed to be nearly 300 years old, symbolize the battle between good and evil. The Yaqui community sponsors the celebration at the Church Plaza between Iglesia and San Angelo roads in Guadalupe, southeast of Phoenix (480/730-3080 town hall).

May

Mexican music, dancing, and food mark **Cinco de Mayo,** the anniversary of Mexico's 1862 expulsion of the French; it's celebrated on the weekend nearest May 5.

June–September

It's hot! Valley residents head for the nearest swimming pool or drive to the high country. Those who stay enjoy programs of musicals, plays, and concerts held at various locations. **July 4th Fireworks** explode in the night skies at Wesley Bolin Plaza in front of the state capitol and in Glendale. **Fiesta Glendale** celebrates Hispanic culture in downtown Glendale.

October

The **Arizona State Fair** (www.azstatefair.com) in Phoenix features exhibits of the state's best in agriculture, livestock, and home crafts, along with concerts, rides, and games. The Phoenix Art Museum (www.phxart.org) puts on the **Cowboy Artists of America Sale & Exhibition.**

November

Murphy Park in downtown Glendale glows under a canopy of half a million lights in the **Glendale Glitters Holiday Light Display** from the day after Thanksgiving until mid-January. The Arizona Wing CAF Museum in Mesa hosts the **Annual Veterans Day Fly-in and Community Expo** the weekend prior to Veterans Day, where you can see warbirds both roaring overhead and parked in ground displays. The museum also features special aviation programs for the event.

December

Holiday celebrations include **Festival of Lights** (a festival and electric light parade in downtown Phoenix), **Glendale Glitters Holiday Light Display,** Heritage Square's **Victorian Holiday,** the Desert Botanical Garden's **Noche de las Luminarias,** the Phoenix Zoo's **ZooLights,** and the Mesa Arizona Temple's **Christmas Lights** (600,000 of them, late Nov.–Dec.). On the first weekend, **Celebration of Basketweaving** attracts skilled Native American artisans to the Heard Museum (www.heard.org). Tempe's Old Town hosts the **Fall Festival of the Arts** to exhibit the work of local and visiting artists, along with food, music, dance, and children's entertainment. On the second full weekend, Native Americans present entertainment, arts and crafts, and food in the **Annual Indian Market,** sponsored by the Pueblo Grande Museum (www.pueblogrande.com) and held at the Activity Center in South Mountain Park. **Tostitos Fiesta Bowl** (www.tostitosfiestabowl.com) activities in late December include an impressive parade, the National Band Championship, and sports events, all leading up to the big game on or near New Year's Day.

MOVIES, THEATER, AND CONCERTS

To find out what's happening in the Valley, call the Visitor Information Line (602/252-5588). Newspapers all review the entertainment scene, especially the free weekly *New Times* (www.phoenixnewtimes.com), the *Rep* (www.azcentral.com), and *Get Out* (www.getoutaz.com).

Movie Theaters

AMC (602/956-4262) has a—count 'em—30-screen theater in the Deer Valley area at the southwest corner of I-17 and Loop 101, as well as 24-screen theaters downtown at Arizona Center and at Awatukee (I-10 and Ray Rd.), and 14 screens in Phoenix (Esplanade at 24th St. and Camelback Rd.) and in Glendale (75th Ave. and Bell Rd).

Giant-screen movies, some in 3D, play at **Arizona Mills Imax** (Arizona Mills in Tempe, near the junction of I-10 and Superstition Fwy., 480/897-4629, www.imax.com/tempe) and at **Arizona Science Center** (600 E. Washington St. in Heritage and Science Park, downtown Phoenix, 602/716-2000, www.azscience.org).

Phoenix

Arizona Theatre Company (Herberger Theater Center, 222 E. Monroe St., 602/256-6995 Arizona Theatre Company box office or 602/252-8497 Herberger Theater box office, www.arizonatheatre.org) performs classic and contemporary plays and some musicals September–May.

Phoenix Theatre (100 E. McDowell Rd., 602/254-2151, www.phxtheatre.org) opened in 1920 and has run continuously, longer than any other theater in the country. The Main Stage hosts large-scale productions, while the Cookie Company entertains children at the neighboring Little Theatre. Both venues form a courtyard with the Phoenix Art Museum on the northeast corner of Central Avenue and McDowell Road.

Phoenix Symphony (225 E. Adams St., 602/495-1999 or 800/776-9080, www.phoenixsymphony.org) offers a variety of concerts during its September–May season, when the music resounds at Symphony Hall in downtown Phoenix and at Scottsdale Center for the Arts. **Ballet Arizona** (602/381-1096 or 888/322-5538 box office, 602/381-0184 office, www.balletaz.org) productions run October–May downtown at the Orpheum and at Symphony Hall. **Arizona Opera** (602/266-7464, www.azopera.com) presents productions October–April at Symphony Hall.

Herberger Theater Center (222 E. Monroe St., 602/254-7399, www.herbergertheater.org) hosts many Broadway- and off-Broadway-style events; the Lunch-Time Theater one-act plays usually take place midday Tuesday–Thursday year-round. The **Orpheum Theatre** (203 W. Adams St., 602/262-7272) opened in 1929 to great acclaim with an ornate sandstone facade and luxurious interior. It's now restored and hosts a variety of cultural events. You can tour the theatre on Mondays unless there's an event; call 602/534-4874 for times.

Dodge Theatre (400 W. Washington St., 602/379-2888, www.dodgetheatre.com) offers Broadway shows, big-name entertainers, and other events downtown. The **Cricket Pavilion** (2121 N. 83rd Ave., 602/254-7200, www.cricketpavilion.com) hosts major music events in an open-air 20,000-seat amphitheater in far western Phoenix, .5 miles north of I-10 on 83rd Avenue. **Celebrity Theatre** (440 N. 32nd St., 602/267-1600, www.celebritytheatre.com) brings in top names performing a wide spectrum of popular music.

The city of Phoenix (602/261-8993 or 602/261-8991), presents free **Coffeehouse Concerts** on Wednesday evenings year-round at the clubhouse in Encanto Park.

Scottsdale

Scottsdale Center for the Arts (7380 E. 2nd St., 480/994-2787, www.scottsdalearts.org) sponsors diverse musical and theatrical offerings and contemporary art exhibits; the Center is one block south of Indian School Road and two blocks east of Scottsdale Road. **Kerr Cultural Center** (near Rose Lane off 6110 N. Scottsdale Rd., south of the Borgata, 480/596-2660, www.asukerr.com) offers musical ensembles and theatrical productions all year in a charming adobe recital hall; art exhibits (8:30 A.M.–5 P.M. Mon.–Fri.) change each month.

Tempe

On the ASU campus, **Gammage Center for the Performing Arts** (480/965-3434, www.asugammage.com) presents a varied program of theater, concerts, and dance in a distinctive rotunda.

Mesa

Organ Stop Pizza (1149 E. Southern Ave., 480/813-5700, www.organstoppizza.com) has good pizza, but it's the sounds of the mighty Wurlitzer that draw the crowds. This amazing instrument has four manuals, 276 keys, 798 stops and controls, and over 5,500 pipes! The tallest pipe measures 36 feet and weighs nearly a ton. The organ includes two pianos, a variety of percussion, and some amusing special effects. Organists play requests, which can include anything from a Scott Joplin rag to a Bach cantata. The theater-like interior offers seating on a balcony as well as on the main floor. Admission is free and the pizza and pasta inexpensive. Open nightly for dinner. From Superstition Freeway Exit 181, turn north one long block on Stapley Drive, turn left on Southern Avenue, then left to the parking.

Sun City

ASU Sundome Center for the Performing Arts (19403 R.H. Johnson Blvd., north of Bell Rd., in Sun City West, 623/975-1900, www.asusundome.com) frequently hosts big-name performers in a 7,000-seat facility, said to be the world's largest single-level theater, during the September–May season.

NIGHTLIFE

The Valley moves to many different beats. Check out the free weekly papers for what's playing: *New Times* (www.phoenixnewtimes.com), the *Rep* (www.azcentral.com), and *Get Out* (www.getoutaz.com).

Country-Western

The music gets enthusiastic couples onto the dance floors of **Mr. Lucky's** (in Phoenix at 3660 Grand Ave., two blocks north of Indian School Rd., 602/246-0686, www.mrluckys.com).

Comedy

Tempe Improv (in Tempe at 930 E. University Dr., 480/921-9877, www.tempeimprov.com) showcases top talent.

Jazz

Swing to the music at **A League of Our Own** (in Phoenix at 40 E. Camelback Rd., 602/265-2354), a jazz supper club with fine dining and live music. It's on the northeast corner of Camelback Road and Central Avenue.

Blues

Hear cool sounds in Phoenix at **The Rhythm Room** (1019 E. Indian School Rd., 602/265-4842, www.rythymroom.com) and **Char's Has the Blues** (4631 N. 7th Ave., 602/230-0205, www.charshastheblues.com). Also contact the **Phoenix Blues Society** (602/252-0599, www.phoenixblues.org).

Latin and Flamenco

Move to the beat at **Pepin** in Scottsdale (7363 Scottsdale Mall, 480/990-9026, www.pepin-restaurant.com).

Rock

For alternative and unusual performances in Phoenix, check out **Modified Arts** (407 E. Roosevelt St., 602/462-5516, www.modified.org) and the **Mason Jar** (2303 E. Indian School Rd., 602/954-0455, www.masonjarlive.com).

Sports Bars

Majerle's Sports Grill in Phoenix (24 N. 2nd St., 602/253-9004) attracts the downtown crowd.

Pubs

George & Dragon English Restaurant & Pub (in Phoenix at 4240 N. Central Ave., two blocks north of Indian School Rd., 602/241-0018, daily lunch and dinner) creates authentic English pub food such as steak and kidney pie, fish and chips, and Cornish pasties, and keeps more than a dozen brews on tap.

Seamus McCaffrey's Irish Pub & Restaurant in downtown Phoenix (18 W. Monroe St., 602/253-6081, daily lunch and dinner) serves Guinness and traditional foods. Irish musicians often perform on Friday and Saturday. It's next door to the San Carlos Hotel.

Casinos

Fort McDowell Casino (800/843-3678, www.fortmcdowellcasino.com) is in the northeastern part of the Valley at Highway 87 and Fort McDowell Road. **Harrah's Phoenix Ak-Chin Casino** (480/802-5000, 800/427-7247, www.harrahs.com) is 25 miles south of Phoenix near the town of Maricopa; take I-10 Queen Creek Road Exit 164 and head southeast 17 miles.

SHOPPING

Glittering department stores and boutiques display the latest in fashion. Or you can visit rustic, porch-fronted shops and be outfitted in Western duds from boots to bolo ties. Western and Native American art make distinctive gifts. Anglo and Hispanic artists recall the frontier days in painting and sculpture, while Native American artists reveal their heritage in arts and crafts. Mexican import shops represent skilled craftspeople from south of the border.

Old Town Scottsdale

Arts, crafts, clothing, and restaurants—many with

an Old West theme—abound in the area centered around Main Street just west of Scottsdale's Civic Center Mall. You'll also find an outlet for Arizona Highways (7235 E. 1st Ave.), whose publications feature beautiful photography and excellent writing. Many galleries open Thursday evenings for the **Scottsdale ArtWalk** (www.scottsdalegalleries.com), which presents exhibitions, demonstrations, and entertainment 7–9 P.M. year-round.

Scottsdale Trolley (480/421-1004, www.scottsdaletrolley.com) provides a free service connecting Old Town Scottsdale with nearby Marshall Way, Fifth Avenue, Galleria Corporate Center, and Scottsdale Fashion Square; services run daily except Sunday from mid-November to the end of May. You can park for free at many downtown locations.

Fifth Avenue Shops and Marshall Way Arts District

Shops and galleries here, several blocks north of Old Town Scottsdale, feature diverse offerings, including contemporary, Western, and Native American art. Fifth Avenue Shops begin just west of Scottsdale Road. Marshall Way Arts District extends two blocks south from Fifth Avenue.

The Borgata

This elegant shopping center (6166 N. Scottsdale Rd., 2 miles north of Old Town Scottsdale, 480/998-1822) is modeled after the Tuscan village of San Gimignano, complete with cobblestone paths, courtyards, and medieval towers and archways.

Glendale—"Arizona's Antique-Shopping Capital"

Glendale, the fourth largest city in Arizona, lies northwest of downtown Phoenix; take I-17 Glendale Exit 205 and go west five miles or head northwest on Grand Avenue/U.S. Highway 60. For information on sights, shopping, and events, drop by the centrally located **Glendale Visitor Center** (5800 W. Glenn Dr., Ste. 140, 623/930-4500 or 877/800-2601, www.visitglendale.com, 10 A.M.–5 P.M. Mon.–Sat.); it's one block north on 58th Avenue from Glendale Avenue. There's lots of free parking.

Downtown Glendale's **Old Towne Shopping District,** centered on Glendale and 58th Avenues, offers a host of antique stores and other specialty shops. Murphy Park here hosts a Saturday crafts market 9 A.M.–4 P.M. from November to mid-April.

The **Historic Catlin Court Shops** hold more treasures for shoppers just two blocks north. Visitors with a sweet tooth won't want to miss **Cerreta Candy Company** (5345 W. Glendale Ave., 623/930-9000, www.cerreta.com, closed Sun.).

Other Shopping Malls

Metrocenter (exit west at Dunlap or Peoria Aves. from I-17 in north Phoenix, 602/997-2641) is *big*—five major department stores, more than 200 specialty shops and eateries, and a 14-screen movie theater; you'll find hotels, restaurants, an amusement park, and two movie theaters nearby. **Biltmore Fashion Park** (Camelback Rd. and 24th St. in Phoenix, 602/955-8400, www.shopbiltmore.com) features about a dozen restaurants and 60 luxury stores, including Saks Fifth Avenue, Polo/Ralph Lauren, and Gucci.

Scottsdale Fashion Square (7014 E. Camelback Rd. at Scottsdale Rd., 480/941-2140) has four major department stores, about 150 specialty stores, a food court, five full-service restaurants, and two cinemas. **El Pedregal Festival Marketplace at the Boulders** (34505 N. Scottsdale Rd., 480/488-1072, www.elpedregal.com) features boutique shopping in a Moroccan festival–style marketplace with 35 restaurants, galleries, and shops, including an exhibit gallery and a shop of the Heard Museum. Two miles north of el Pedregal in Carefree, shops in **Spanish Village** (Tom Darlington Dr. and Cave Creek Rd., 480/488-0350) offer Western and Native American art and crafts in a relaxed atmosphere. **Superstition Springs Center** (6555 E. Southern Ave. in Mesa, 480/396-2570) has five department stores, over 120 specialty stores, an eight-screen cinema, and a 36-horse carousel.

Outlet Malls

Arizona Mills (480/491-7300, www.arizonamills.com) brings "Shoppertainment" to the Valley with many factory and specialty shops, a

24-screen theater, Imax theater, games arcade, and a food court. Two information desks offer Arizona tourist literature as well as a map of Arizona Mills. It's in Tempe at the southeast corner of the Superstition Freeway (U.S. 60) and I-10; head east from I-10 on Baseline Road or south from the Superstition Freeway on Priest Drive.

North of the Valley, **Outlets at New River** (4250 W. Anthem Way, 623/465-9500) sells many big-name brands at bargain prices in more than 80 stores, and there's a food court. Head 15 miles north of Bell Road on I-17 to Anthem Way Exit 229.

Outdoor Supplies

REI offers two co-op stores in the Valley. Both stock an excellent selection of gear for hiking, backpacking, bicycling, river-running, downhill skiing, cross-country skiing, and other sports; rentals are available too. Experts give regular free presentations on outdoor adventures and skills; call or check www.rei.com for the schedules. Optional lifetime memberships, available for a small fee, pay dividends of about 10 percent of all purchases at the end of each year. The Tempe REI (1405 W. Southern Ave., 480/967-5494) is across from the Niels Peterson house. In Paradise Valley, REI (12634 N. Paradise Village Pkwy. W., 602/996-5400) lies one long block north of Cactus Road, across the street from Paradise Valley Mall. **Arizona Hiking Shack** (11649 N. Cave Creek Rd., a quarter mile south of Cactus Rd. in north Phoenix, 602/944-7723) also has a fine array of outdoor gear and rentals.

Native American Music

Drumbeat Indian Arts (4143 N. 16th St. in Phoenix, 602/266-4823) stocks hundreds of different Native American music titles from many American tribes.

Books and Maps

The Book Store (4230 N. 7th Ave., 602/279-3910) has many used books and one of the best selections of magazines in the state. **Bent Cover Bookstore** (12428 N. 28th Dr., 1 block west of I-17, just north of the Cactus Rd. Exit, 602/942-3778) offers used hardbacks and paperbacks. **Arizona Book Gallery** (4717 E. Indian School Rd., 602/263-8353) stocks a large selection of used books.

Guidon Books (7117 Main St., 480/945-8811) in Old Town Scottsdale specializes in Western Americana with both new and out-of-print books. **Changing Hands** (6428 S. McClintock Dr. #101 on the southwest corner with Guadalupe, 480/730-0205) in Tempe carries a large selection of new and used books. **Book Gallery** (50 W. Main St., 480/835-0757) in downtown Mesa has a great selection of books on art, music, philosophy, and Latin America, as well as fiction. Shopping malls house the popular book chains.

For maps of Arizona and the world, along with regional and international travel books, drop by **A Wide World of Maps** (in Phoenix at 2626 W. Indian School Rd., 602/279-2323; in Mesa at 1444 W. Southern Ave., 480/844-1134 or 800/279-7654, www.maps4u.com).

Sports and Recreation

Valleyites take their sports seriously and enjoy the many recreational facilities in the area. You can play golf, tennis, or racquetball, go horseback riding, jump in the pool, tube the Salt River, and even surf. The **Phoenix Parks and Recreation Department** (602/262-6861, www.phoenix.gov/parks) sponsors some excellent parks and a variety of educational and recreation programs for children, adults, and seniors. Large county parks ring the Valley, providing additional opportunities to enjoy nature; contact the **Maricopa County Parks and Recreation Department** (602/506-2930, www.maricopa.gov). The book *Day Hikes and Trail Rides In and Around Phoenix* by Roger and Ethel Freeman offers detailed trail descriptions for hikers and equestrians.

SPORTS

Professional Sports

The **Arizona Diamondbacks** (Bank One Ballpark, 401 E. Jefferson St., 602/514-8400 or 888/777-4664 ticket office, 602/462-6500 general information, www.azdiamondbacks.com) play major-league baseball in their spacious home. The NBA's **Phoenix Suns** (America West Arena, 201 E. Jefferson St., 602/379-7867, www.suns.com) play professional basketball. **Phoenix Mercury** (602/252-9622, www.wnba.com/mercury) WNBA basketball players compete at America West Arena. The NFL's **Arizona Cardinals** (602/379-0102 or 800/999-1402 ticket office, www.azcardinals.com) play home football games at Arizona State University's Sun Devil Stadium in Tempe.

The **Phoenix Coyotes** (480/563-7825 or 888/255-7825, www.phoenixcoyotes.com) play NHL ice hockey October–April at Glendale Arena near the intersection of the 101 Loop and Glendale Avenue. The **FBR Phoenix Open** (480/870-4431, www.phoenixopen.com) attracts big-name professional golfers each January to the Tournament Players Club in Scottsdale.

College Sports

The Arizona State University **Sun Devils** (ASU campus in Tempe, 480/965-2381, www.thesundevils.com) battle opponents in an active program of football, baseball, basketball, swimming, gymnastics, archery, and other sports.

Motor Sports

Engines roar as cars strain for the finish line February–November at **Manzanita Speedway** (35th Ave. and W. Broadway, 602/276-7575, www.manzanitaspeedway.com). **Phoenix International Raceway** (707 S. 115th Ave., 602/252-3833, www.phoenixraceway.com) schedules major events. **Firebird International Raceway** (602/268-0200, www.firebirdraceway.com) offers land and water racing at a professional NHRA drag strip and a 120-acre water-sports lake 12 miles southeast of Phoenix off I-10 at Exit 162A.

At the Races

Dogs run at **Phoenix Greyhound Park** (3801 E. Washington at 40th St., 602/273-7181, www.phoenixgreyhoundpark.com) at 7:30 P.M. daily year-round; stay cool in the air-conditioned grandstands and clubhouse. In Apache Junction, **Apache Greyhound Park** (2551 W. Apache Trail, 480/982-2371) runs events at 1 P.M. Wednesday and Friday–Sunday, from late November to early April; off-track betting is offered daily year-round.

Thoroughbreds and quarter horses race at **Turf Paradise** (1501 W. Bell Rd. and 19th Ave., 602/942-1101, www.turfparadise.com) from late September to mid-May, usually Friday–Tuesday, with simulcast racing on other days.

RECREATION

Amusement Parks

In Phoenix, **Speedway Indoor Kart Racing Center** (2425 S. 21st St., 602/275-5278, www.speedwayraceway.com) offers excitement 365 days a year. **Castles-n-Coasters** (9455 N. Metro Pkwy.

THE CACTUS LEAGUE: SPRING TRAINING UNDER THE SUN

The 12 major-league baseball teams known as the Cactus League currently warm up for the season in spring training camps under Arizona's blue skies. For fans who enjoy watching players practice and play exhibition games in Valley of the Sun or Tucson stadiums, the time is one of welcoming back their teams after a long winter. Low ticket prices and the many new or renovated stadiums add to the pleasure of watching the teams begin their play. Admission prices run $5–24 depending on venue and seating. The action takes place in March, with the possibility of some games at the end of February and beginning of April.

You can get the schedules and venue information for all of the teams from the Mesa Convention & Visitor's Bureau (120 N. Center, Mesa, AZ 85201, 480/827-4700 or 800/283-6372, www.visitmesa.com, 8 A.M.–5 P.M. Mon.– Fri.). Staff will mail or fax you the information, or you can get it from the website.

Sports sections of the *Arizona Republic,* the *Tribune,* the *Arizona Daily Star,* and other newspapers will have the latest spring-training write-ups and schedules.

Teams and Venues

The **Anaheim Angels** play ball at Tempe Diablo Stadium, 2200 W. Alameda Drive in Tempe (it's off 48th St., 1 mile south of I-10 Exit 153).

The **Arizona Diamondbacks** compete at Tucson Electric Park, 2500 E. Ajo Way in Tucson (take I-10 Kino Parkway Exit 263 and turn east on Ajo Way).

The **Chicago Cubs** are at Hohokam Park Stadium, 1235 N. Center Street in Mesa, 1.5 miles north of downtown.

The **Chicago White Sox** play at Tucson Electric Park, 2500 E. Ajo Way in Tucson (take I-10 Kino Parkway Exit 263 and turn east on Ajo Way).

The **Colorado Rockies** swing at Hi Corbett Field in Randolph Park, east of downtown Tucson at 3400 E. Camino Campestre (take the I-10 Broadway/Congress Exit 258 and go east 4 miles).

The **Kansas City Royals** preside at Surprise Stadium, 158501 N. Bullard Avenue northwest of Phoenix in Surprise (head west on Bell Rd. from the 101 Loop/Agua Fria Fwy. or east on Bell Rd. from the 303 Loop/Estrella Fwy.).

The **Milwaukee Brewers** play at Maryvale Baseball Park, 3600 N. 51st Avenue in west Phoenix (take I-10 51st Ave. Exit 139 and go north 1.5 miles, the park is on the left just before Indian School Rd., or take I-17 Indian School Exit 202 and head west 4.5 miles on Indian School Rd.).

The **Oakland Athletics** practice at Phoenix Municipal Stadium on the south side of Papago Park, 5999 E. Van Buren Street in east Phoenix (from the 202 Loop/Red Mountain Fwy. eastbound, take the Van Buren St. exit and go 1 mile east on Van Buren St.; westbound take the Priest Dr. Exit and go 1 mile north on Priest Dr.).

The **San Diego Padres** converge at Peoria Stadium, 16101 N. 83rd Avenue, northwest of Phoenix in Peoria (take I-17 Bell Rd. Exit 212, go west 8 miles on Bell, then left on 83rd Ave.).

The **San Francisco Giants** play at Scottsdale Stadium, 7408 E. Osborn Road in downtown Scottsdale (stadium is on the northeast corner of Osborn and Civic Center Plaza, half a mile east of Scottsdale Rd.).

The **Seattle Mariners** sail at the Peoria Stadium, 16101 N. 83rd Avenue, northwest of Phoenix in Peoria (take I-17 Bell Rd. Exit 212, go west 8 miles on Bell, then left on 83rd Ave.).

The **Texas Rangers** ride at Surprise Stadium, 158501 N. Bullard Avenue northwest of Phoenix in Surprise (head west on Bell Rd. from the 101 Loop/Agua Fria Fwy. or east on Bell Rd. from the 303 Loop/Estrella Fwy.).

East, 602/997-7575, www.castlesncoasters.com) thrills with a double-loop coaster and other rides, along with minigolf and arcade games. It's on the south side of Metrocenter; turn west from I-17 at the Dunlap Exit.

Fiddlesticks Family Fun Park (in Tempe at 1155 W. Elliot Rd., 480/961-0800; in Scottsdale at 8800 E. Indian Bend Rd., 480/951-6060, www.fiddlesticksaz.com) has go-carts, bumper boats, minigolf, and other games. **CrackerJax** in Scottsdale (16001 N. Scottsdale Rd., 480/998-2800, www.crackerjax.com) gives you a driving range, batting cages, volleyball, minigolf, go-carts, and bumper boats.

Golf and Tennis

Both are extremely popular in the Valley. Enthusiasts spend entire vacations at resorts offering top-notch facilities and professional instructors. Four Phoenix city parks have golf courses and many offer tennis courts, as well as two tennis centers. Newsstands and tourist offices provide many free publications and brochures of public and private golf courses.

Swimming

Phoenix alone offers 28 public pools (602/534-7946 swim line, www.phoenix.gov/parks, or see the Yellow Pages under "Swimming Pools"). If you're looking for waves and water slides, try these places:

Kiwanis Recreation Center (in Tempe at 6111 S. All-America Way, 480/350-5201) features an indoor wave pool with spiral slide (closed Dec.), gym, and tennis and volleyball courts at the southeast corner of the large Kiwanis Park, reached by Mill Avenue between Baseline and Guadalupe Roads.

Big Surf (in northern Tempe at 1500 N. McClintock Dr., south of McKellips Rd., 480/947-7873) has artificial waves 3–5 feet high that come crashing onto the beach. You can rent rafts and for added thrills, try the water slides. Small children can play in a shallow pool. The season runs daily between Memorial Day and Labor Day weekends.

Golfland-Sunsplash (in Mesa at 155 W. Hampton Ave., 480/834-8318) offers a wave pool and 10 water slides for fun and excitement, plus rental rafts, three 18-hole miniature golf courses, video games, bumper boats, Indy race cars, and other amusements; the action is one block north on Country Club Drive from the Superstition Freeway, then right on Hampton.

Waterworld Safari (in Glendale at 4243 W. Pinnacle Peak Rd., 623/581-1947) contains a wave pool, water slide, and the Lazy River to cool you off; shallow pools cater to small children. The park is open between Memorial Day and Labor Day weekends. From downtown Phoenix take I-17 north 17 miles to Pinnacle Peak Road, then go west 2 miles on Pinnacle Peak Road.

Tubing Down the Lower Salt River

Cool off in the summer on a leisurely float down the Salt River east of Mesa. **Salt River Recreation** (1320 N. Bush Hwy., 480/984-3305, www.saltrivertubing.com) rents innertubes and provides a shuttle bus back to the put-in point for $12 per person or $9 for just a shuttle pass. The season runs May–September, weather and water permitting. The shuttle bus serves four points along the river, with a choice of floats lasting from 90 minutes to a half day. Below Granite Reef Dam, the Salt is a river no more—the water is channeled into canals, leaving only a dry riverbed downstream. From the east edge of Mesa, take Bush Highway north to the Salt River.

An extra tube will carry your cooler of cold drinks, but don't bring glass containers. Weekends often see large crowds, and the Salt becomes one big party. Wear tennis shoes to protect your feet when walking in the river. Life jackets are a good idea—a necessity with children. Don't tie your tubes together; rather, lock your feet into each other's tubes.

Canoeists can enjoy the trip from spring through autumn (there's no flow in winter). You can beat the summer tubing crowds by starting at sunup. If you'd like to float down in a raft, contact **Desert Voyagers** (480/998-7238, www.desertvoyagers.com); trips go year-round and can be combined with a jeep tour.

Horseback Riding

The Phoenix area offers miles of scenic trails

suitable for horses. Many of the stables can arrange lessons, breakfast rides, steak cookouts, hayrides, overnight trips, and boarding. Riding season runs from about October to May, and reservations are advised.

For trips into South Mountain Park, contact **Ponderosa Stables** (just outside the park entrance at 10215 S. Central Ave., 602/268-1261, www.arizona-horses.com). In Tempe near Papago Park, you can go with **Papago Riding Stable** (400 N. Scottsdale Rd., turn in at Club Rio, 480/966-9793). In Cave Creek, ride with **MacDonald's Ranch** (26540 N. Scottsdale Rd., 480/585-0239, www.macdonaldsranch.com).

For guided hourly horseback rides in the nearby Goldfield Mountains and overnight pack trips into the wild Superstition Mountains and other desert areas, see **OK Corral** (480/982-4040, www.okcorrals.com). There's an RV park here, too. At the beginning of the Apache Trail, turn north five miles on Idaho Road, go east one mile on McKellips Road, then turn left at the sign.

Ben Avery Shooting Facility

Shooters and archers can practice at this fine facility run by Arizona Game and Fish (west off I-17 Carefree Hwy. Exit 223, 26 miles north of downtown Phoenix, 623/582-8313 rifle and pistol range, 602/287-1019 Black Canyon Trap and Skeet Club, www.basfaz.com). The range operates 7 A.M.–dark Wednesday–Sunday; check for trap and skeet range hours. Users also enjoy picnicking and camping.

CITY PARKS

City parks offer everything from a gentle stroll to challenging mountain hiking, as well as many recreation facilities. Tourist offices may have brochures, and you can contact the main Parks, Recreation, and Library Department office (Phoenix City Hall, 200 W. Washington St., 16th Fl., Phoenix, AZ 85003, 602/262-6861, www.phoenix.gov/parks, 8 A.M.–5 P.M. Mon.–Fri.). City parks have free admission; they're for day use only.

Encanto Park

This 222-acre oasis (2 miles northwest of downtown Phoenix at N. 15th Ave. and Encanto Blvd., 602/261-8991) of lakes and trees features picnic areas and many recreation facilities. The southern section has tennis, racquetball, volleyball, basketball, a swimming pool, playgrounds, and picnic areas. Free **Coffeehouse Concerts** entertain on Wednesday evenings year-round at the clubhouse. You can check out sports equipment from the Recreation Building south of the swimming pool; parking is off 15th Avenue south of Encanto Boulevard.

The family amusement park **Enchanted Island** (602/254-2020) offers a carousel, train, and other rides on weekends and some weekdays. Parking is north of Encanto Boulevard between 7th and 15th Avenues. The northern section of Encanto has a clubhouse for special events (check the bulletin board or call 602/261-8993), picnic areas, playgrounds, a small lake with boat rentals (602/254-1520), an urban fishing program, and a golf driving range; parking is off 15th Avenue north of Encanto Boulevard. Two golf courses lie farther north: an 18-hole course at 2775 N. 15th Avenue (602/253-3963); and a 9-hole course—excellent for beginners—at 2300 N. 17th Avenue (602/262-6870).

Papago Park

Once designated a national monument because of its desert flora and Native American history, this large park (602/256-3220) on the east edge of Phoenix offers numerous attractions, such as the Phoenix Zoo, Desert Botanical Gardens, Arizona Historical Society Museum, an 18-hole golf course, Phoenix Municipal Stadium, and a baseball field. Enter Papago Park from Galvin Parkway, which runs between McDowell Road and Van Buren Street/Mill Avenue.

The park also has a recreation area with picnicking, easy hiking, a bike trail, and small lakes where children 15 and under may fish without a license. Hole in the Rock provides a scenic window onto Phoenix; you can hike up into it on a short trail. Continue to road's end for the short walk to the white-tiled pyramid tomb of George W. P. Hunt, seven times governor of Arizona.

The recreation area is east off Galvin Parkway; turn in at the zoo entrance, then turn left. You'll find softball and baseball diamonds and an archery range in the northeast corner of the park near 62nd and Oak Streets.

Phoenix Mountains Park & Recreation Area

Piestewa Peak crowns a group of desert hills in the Phoenix Mountains, nine miles northeast of downtown Phoenix. Formerly known as Squaw Peak, it honors a Hopi servicewoman who died in the 2003 Iraq war; you'll see both names used. The park (602/262-7901) offers some great hiking trails as well as picnic areas with water and shaded tables. Saguaro cactus, palo verde, creosote bush, and barrel and cholla cactus thrive on the rocky hillsides. Turn onto Squaw Peak Drive from Lincoln Drive between 22nd and 23rd Streets.

Summit Trail #300 climbs to the top of 2,608-foot Piestewa Peak in 1.2 miles one-way with a 1,200-foot elevation gain. You'll enjoy a superb panorama and lots of company—it's probably Phoenix's most popular trail. The path has steep sections, but it's well graded and easy to follow. On Sunday the peak hosts a remarkable crowd of teenagers, families, joggers wearing headsets—all puffing along. No dogs or bicycles allowed, though. In the warmer months, be sure to carry water and get an early start.

Freedom (Circumference) Trail #302 makes a scenic 3.7-mile loop—it's one of Phoenix's best hikes. In some of the beautiful valleys you may forget that you're in the middle of an urban area. The trail climbs two saddles, so you'll get a good workout and gain 720 feet at the highest saddle, where you'll meet the Summit Trail, 488 feet below the top. To reach the Circumference Trail, either take Summit Trail #300 to the saddle or drive to the end of the park road and take the trail signed #302. Note that dogs cannot go on the Summit Trail section.

Piestewa Peak Nature Trail #304 and a section of Trail #302 make a 1.5-mile loop from the end of the road. Signs identify some plants, but the beautiful desert scenery will be the main attraction; you'll cross two passes with views and a 180-foot elevation gain.

Camelback Mountain Trail/ Echo Canyon Recreation Area

The steep, rough **Camelback Mountain Trail** to

© BILL WEIR

view east from the summit of Camelback Mountain

the 2,704-foot summit will challenge kids and a lot of adults, yet most seem to make it to enjoy the spectacular views. The adventure starts on the northwest side of the mountain in Echo Canyon Recreation Area (602/262-4837). In .3 miles you'll reach a minor ridge. Continue up along the base of 200-foot cliffs to the Camel's Neck, from which additional steep climbing takes you to the summit, 1.2 miles one-way total and a 1,264-foot elevation gain. On a clear day you can take in countless aspects of the vast Valley; you won't need a map to identify the edge of the Salt River Indian Reservation to the east—it's the line where the city ends and irrigated fields begin. For a much easier walk, there's a short trail to Robby's Rock, a popular area with rock climbers. Beautiful rock formations provide a bonus for either hike. Carry at least a quart of water on the summit trail; it's a good idea to get a very early start in summer and avoid the trail after rain, when it becomes slippery.

From Phoenix, head north on 44th Street, which curves east and becomes McDonald Drive, then turn right (south) on E. Echo Canyon Parkway just 200 feet past the Tatum Boulevard junction. The Recreation Area has water but no restrooms or other facilities. On weekends and holidays, you'll either be lucky or wait a long time to snag a parking space.

Cholla Trail, approximately 1.5 miles one-way, climbs 1,200 feet in elevation from a trailhead at about 6200 E. Cholla Lane; the first section is easy, then the going becomes very steep. Some parking is available along the west side of Invergordon (64th St.).

North Mountain Recreation Area

This desert park (10600 N. 7th St., 602/262-7901) features many family and group ramadas along a loop road, plus a playground and basketball and volleyball courts. The easy **Penny Howe Barrier-Free Trail #40** has interpretive signs about plants along its one-third-mile loop; the trail starts from the northwest corner of the Havasupai parking lot. For a workout, many locals head up **North Mountain Trail #44** from Maricopa Picnic Area at the north end of the road loop; it climbs to a road that leads to the summit (2,104 ft.). You can make a loop by taking Trail #44A to the left of the towers and southeast along ridges to the Quechan Picnic Area on the southwest part of the loop road. The hike is about 1.6 miles long (round-trip or the loop) with an elevation gain of 614 feet.

Christiansen Trail #100 offers more areas to explore for hikers, cyclists, and horseback riders. You can start from a trailhead opposite the Pointe Hilton at Tapatio Cliffs, 1.4 miles north of the North Mountain entrance on 7th Street; the trail leads west to Shaw Butte and southeast to Piestewa Peak in the Phoenix Mountain Preserve. Altogether, the easy-to-moderate trail is 10.7 miles one-way, with elevations ranging from 1,290 to 2,080 feet; many other trails loop off it. The west trailhead is on the north side of Mountain View Park at 7th Avenue and Cheryl Drive. East trailheads are at Dreamy Draw Recreation Area, 40th Street (south from Shea), and Tatum Boulevard (opposite Tomahawk Dr.).

South Mountain Park

The world's largest city park, South Mountain encompasses 16,500 acres of desert mountain country. A paved road winds to the top for great views of the Valley. On the way you'll pass several picnic areas and trailheads. Hikers, equestrians, and mountain bikers can explore 58 miles of trails in the backcountry. A park map shows roads, facilities, lookouts, and trails; pick one up outside the ranger station or at the visitor center. A stable just outside the park's entrance offers trail rides, and there's an equestrian area inside the park. An activity center on the left just inside the entrance hosts special events. The Environmental Education Center (on the left just inside the gate, 602/534-6324, 9 A.M.– P.M. Tues.–Sun.) offers maps, literature, some exhibits, and picnic area reservations. A short nature trail nearby introduces the desert's flora and fauna. South Mountain Park lies seven miles south of downtown Phoenix on Central Avenue.

After the ranger station, roads branch off on both sides to covered picnicking areas, some of which can be reserved. San Juan Road forks right two miles inside the park, leading four miles through a valley to a trailhead and a low overlook of Phoenix. Take the Summit Road left at the fork to reach the heights. The road climbs to Telegraph Pass, then on past several lookouts on the left, of which Dobbin's has the best views of the Valley. Continue to the end of TV Towers Road for panoramas to the south from Gila Valley Overlook.

The 18 trails, many of which form loops, present a range of lengths and challenges. Besides the views, you may spot prehistoric petroglyphs. **National Trail** extends the length of the park, climbing from low elevations at each end to high ridges in 14.3 miles one-way; it's not recommended for equestrians. Hidden Valley, a popular half-day trip through a landscape of giant granite boulders and stately saguaros, is 3.5 miles round-trip via National Trail. To reach the trailhead, go two miles past the park entrance gate, turn left onto Summit Road and follow it four miles (keeping right past the turnoffs for two lookout points), then stay left at the next fork to Buena Vista Lookout. The first quarter mile of trail follows a ridge east with good views before gently dropping into a valley. After a mile or so, some large slick rocks must be negotiated before entering wide, bowl-shaped Hidden Valley. Near the lower end of the little valley, you'll pass through a natural tunnel about 50 feet long. This makes a good turnaround point, or you can explore more of the valley and surrounding hills. In summer carry extra water and avoid the heat of the day.

MARICOPA COUNTY PARKS

These scenic areas ring the Valley with picnicking, hiking trails, mountain-biking tracks, equestrian facilities, and campgrounds. Interpretive programs take place at all of the parks; call or check the website for the schedule. Leashed pets can come along on the trails and in the campgrounds. The main office (411 N. Central Ave., Phoenix, AZ 85004, 602/506-2930, www.maricopa.gov/parks, 8 A.M.–5 P.M. Mon.–Fri.) in downtown Phoenix provides excellent maps and brochures, though staff may not have first-hand knowledge of all areas. You can usually reach individual park offices seven days a week, though staff will all be out on patrol at times. The entry fee of $5 per vehicle ($1/cyclist) is credited toward camping fees of $10, or $18 if the site has electricity. Estrella and Lake Pleasant also offer free primitive camping that's included with your $5 entry fee and is good until 1 P.M. the next day. Only groups can reserve sites; campgrounds have a 14-day stay limit. A variety of annual day-use passes can be purchased. Weekends in the cool season, especially in early spring, see the most visitors; you'll find more solitude on a weekday visit. Few people come in summer, and sections of parks may close.

Estrella Mountain Regional Park

Spanish explorers named the range Estrella (Star) after the pattern of deeply carved canyons radiating from the jagged summits. This 19,840-acre recreation area (14805 W. Vineyard Ave., Goodyear, AZ 85338, 623/932-3811, www.maricopa.gov/parks, $5/vehicle) southwest of Phoenix offers picnicking, camping, many miles of trails, a rodeo arena, and a golf course. **Estrella Mountain Golf Course** (in the northwest corner of the park, 623/932-3714) has 18 holes, a pro shop, and a snack bar.

The huge, grassy picnic area has playgrounds and covered picnic tables. It's also popular with groups, who can rent picnic ramadas, the two ball fields, an amphitheater, and the rodeo arena; they can also arrange camping. You may catch a rodeo or horse show at the rodeo arena. Families and individuals can camp in the grassy area (no showers or established sites) at no additional charge or stay in the tiny RV section ($18 w/hookups). Entry to the park includes primitive camping (good until 1 P.M. the next day). From Phoenix, head west about 20 miles on I-10 to Estrella Parkway Exit 126, go south about 5 miles on Estrella Parkway, then turn left on Vineyard Avenue just after the Gila River bridge; the golf course entrance is on the right after half a mile, the main park entrance is just beyond, and the Estrella Competitive Track entrance is a few miles farther east.

The rocky foothills of the range provide a scenic backdrop for the trails, all of which form loops. **Gila Trail,** the easiest walk, is a half-mile, barrier-free loop that begins near the grassy area; for a longer stroll, you can continue on the 1.7-mile **Baseline Trail** loop. The main group of trails starts from two trailheads south near the rodeo arena; hikers, mountain bikers, and equestrians have many options; the shortest loop begins at the west trailhead and climbs over a ridge with good views in 3.9 miles, or you could continue on other trails for as long as 19 miles without retracing your steps.

Estrella Mountain Competitive Track appeals to mountain bikers, runners, and equestrians looking for a challenge; it has a 1.6-mile Junior Loop for beginners, a 9.5-mile Long Loop, and a 4.7-mile Technical Loop (experts only); slow users yield to fast ones on these one-way loops, which have a separate entrance east of the main park gate.

The Estrella summits in the park have no roads or trails—they're as rough and forbidding as when the Spanish explorers passed by! Climbing them can be hazardous. You must obtain a permit for off-trail travel or for camping in the backcountry.

White Tank Mountain Regional Park

Inviting trails here wind back into the White Tank Mountains on the west side of the Valley (P.O. Box 91, Waddell, AZ 85335, 623/935-2505, www.maricopa.gov/parks/, $5/vehicle). Infrequent flash floods have roared down the canyons, scouring out depressions (tanks) in the white granite, giving the park its name. Elevations range from 1,402 feet at the park entrance to 4,083 feet on the highest peak. Archaeologists have identified seven Hohokam village sites and numerous petroglyphs. The county's largest park at about 30,000 acres, it offers picnic areas (some with covered tables), group ramadas, family and group campgrounds, and interconnecting trails. A visitors center, on the right after you enter the park, provides information, maps, a few exhibits, and a gift shop. The family campground ($10/night) and one of the group campgrounds have showers but no dump station; a few sites have hookups for $18. Campers can watch the vast spread of lights coming on across the Valley at sunset, then admire the golden glow of the mountains at sunrise.

To reach the park from Phoenix, head west on I-10 to Cotton Lane/Loop 303 Exit 124, go north 7 miles to Olive Avenue, then west 4.5 miles. From the north Valley, take the 101 Loop to Olive Avenue, then turn west.

Hiking trails range from two short, barrier-free trails to rugged all-day loops high into the hills. Backcountry campers must register first. The popular **Waterfall Trail** leads to pools and a seasonal waterfall deep in a box canyon; it's a cool spot even in summer. Petroglyphs cover some of the big boulders along the way. The first .4 miles to Petroglyph Plaza has barrier-free access, then it's another .5 miles to the waterfall for a round-trip of 1.8 miles. **Black Rock Trail** offers two options: a .5-mile, barrier-free interpretive loop and a 1.3-mile loop. A short connector trail links Black Rock Trail's 1.3-mile loop with Petroglyph Plaza on the Waterfall Trail.

For a longer hike, consider one of the four interconnecting trails that lead deep into the range. **Ford Canyon Trail** in the north starts out with gentle grades, then becomes rougher and meets the upper ends of the other three trails; it's 5.6–7.9 miles one-way, depending on where you start. **Mesquite Canyon Trail** climbs steadily with good views over the Valley, crosses over a ridge, enters its namesake, then continues up some steep sections with loose rock underfoot to the head of the canyon in 3.3–4.1 miles one-way, depending on which trailhead you use. Willow Springs, at the site of a former ranch outpost, is a popular destination near the upper end of **Willow Canyon Trail,** reached from either Mesquite Canyon or Ford Canyon Trails; a hike via Mesquite Canyon Trail from the Ramada Road trailhead to Willow Springs and back is seven miles round-trip and takes about four hours, or you could make it an all-day excursion by looping back on one of the other trails. **Goat Camp Trail** in the south offers the greatest challenge as well as good views; it begins at Black Canyon Drive near the entrance station, enters the canyon, and climbs high ridges before ending at a junction with Ford Canyon and Mesquite Canyon trails in 6.3 miles one-way.

Mountain bikers and other fast users head for the **Sonoran Loop Competitive Track** in the north of the park. The many loop possibilities range from 2.5 miles (suitable for beginners) to 6.9 miles; experts can tackle the 1-mile-long technical segment. Equestrians have a staging area but only short sections to ride, as most trails get too rough higher up. **White Tanks Riding Stables** (623/935-7455) will take you out on the trails; look for the sign on the right just before the park entrance.

Lake Pleasant Regional Park

On the west shore of this large reservoir just northwest of the Valley, the park (41835 N. Castle Hot Springs Rd., Morristown, AZ 85342, 928/501-1710, www.maricopa.gov/parks/, $5/vehicle plus $2/watercraft) offers year-round camping, picnicking, boating, and fishing. It sits among saguaro-studded hills with a backdrop of the rugged Bradshaw Mountains. Fishing and camping draw visitors during the cooler months, and boaters stream in to cool off in summer. The lake's open waters provide excellent conditions for sailing. Anglers seek out largemouth bass, white bass, catfish, bluegill, sunfish, and crappie. Jet-ski races, sailing regattas, and fishing tournaments take place annually. Few people come to the lake for hiking, but you can follow Pipeline Canyon Trail, two miles one-way, between the north and south recreation areas. A few short trails begin near the visitor center.

Completion of New Waddell Dam in 1993 raised the lake level to about 1,700 feet with a maximum surface area of about 10,000 acres. The lake level peaks in March and April, then drops 100 feet or so by September or October of each year as the water goes out to irrigate desert farms. Eagles nest in the Agua Fria River arm in the northeast from mid-December to mid-June; no visitors may enter while they're there.

Take the main entrance for Lake Pleasant Visitor Center, which has information, a great panorama of the lake, exhibits, and a gift shop. On the way you'll pass turnoffs for picnic areas, two campgrounds, and a 10-lane boat ramp. In summer a concession near the boat ramp offers boat rentals. Desert Tortoise Campground has showers and sites for both tenters ($10) and RVers ($18 with water and electricity); a dump station is near the turnoff. Roadrunner Campground ($18), close to the visitor center, provides showers and water/electric hookups. Groups can reserve campsites and day-use areas. Primitive camping is possible for both vehicles and boaters along the lakeshore; there's no additional charge for this.

Turn in at the north entrance for picnic areas, shoreline camping, and a four-lane boat ramp. Unpaved back roads from Castle Hot Springs Road farther north lead to the northernmost reaches of the lake, though you'll still need to pay the park entry fees.

The park is about 30 miles northwest of Phoenix; take I-17 north to Highway 74 (Exit 223), go west 11.5 miles on Highway 74, turn north 2.2 miles on Castle Hot Springs Road, then turn right into the park. The north entrance is three miles farther north on Castle Hot Springs Road. To reach Lake Pleasant from Sun City, head north 15 miles on 99th Avenue to Highway 74 and follow signs.

Vicinity of Lake Pleasant

Pleasant Harbor (928/501-5253 or 800/475-3272) marina and RV resort on the east shore provides RV sites ($28–33 w/hookups), a convenience store, game room, horseshoe pits, volleyball, showers, laundry, pool, and hot tub. The full-service marina (602/977-7377, www.azmarinas.com) offers a ship's store and rentals of jet-skis and fishing, ski, and patio boats. **Desert Princess II** (623/815-2628, www.desertprincess2.com), an 1880s Mississippi riverboat replica, heads out on lunch or dinner cruises many days year-round. Follow directions to Lake Pleasant Regional Park, but turn north at the sign before crossing the Agua Fria riverbed and continue 2.2 miles. A $6 entry fee is collected for each vehicle and watercraft; additional watercraft cost $2 each.

Castle Hot Springs Road makes a scenic loop in the mountains northwest of the lake. It's largely unpaved and best suited for high-clearance vehicles. Along the way you'll see attractive grounds of the former Castle Hot Springs Resort, now closed to the public. Turn north from Highway 74 near Lake Pleasant Regional Park or north from Highway 74 or U.S. Highway 60 near Morristown.

Hells Canyon Wilderness protects rugged mountains northeast of the lake. The easiest access, which you'll probably need directions and a map to find, lies off Castle Hot Springs Road. The BLM Phoenix Field Office (623/580-5500, www.az.blm.gov) has information on this area as well as the 50-mile-long **Black Canyon Trail,** located east of the lake.

Cave Creek Regional Park

In the north Valley, just west of the town of Cave Creek, this park (37019 N. Lava Lane, Cave Creek, AZ 85331, 623/465-0431, www.maricopa.gov/parks, $5/vehicle) nestles in picturesque rocky hills. Turn left after the entrance for the family campground, which has showers and water/electric hookups for $18; there's a dump station near the entrance. Groups can reserve a separate campground and picnic ramadas. From the Carefree Highway between I-17 and Cave Creek Road, turn north 1.6 miles on 32nd Street.

The popular **Go John Trail** makes a 4.8-mile loop around a 3,060-foot peak—the park's highest—from the day-use area. A pass on the west side of the loop has great views of the Valley to the south and forested mountains to the north; it's just one mile round-trip and offers a quick workout. **Overton Trail** to the west connects with the Go John to make a 3- or 6-mile loop. **Slate Trail** also begins from the day-use area, but heads southeast to the park boundary in 3.2 miles round-trip, returning the same way. **Flume Trail** branches off 1 mile along Slate and continues 1.5 miles one-way to the southeast corner of the park. The easy **Clay Mine Trail** begins at the family campground, climbs a bit to a white clay deposit, then continues to the Overton Trail in .8 miles one-way. Be aware that the several mine shafts in the park are dangerous—and illegal—to enter.

Equestrians enjoy the park and have a horse staging area just south of the day-use area. There's a rodeo arena in the southwest corner of the park; look for the sign on 32nd Street before the park entrance. If you don't have your own steed, you can go with **Cave Creek Trailrides** (623/742-6700 or 877/942-6700), on the left before the day-use area.

Spur Cross Ranch Conservation Area

This primitive park—famed for its beautiful Sonoran Desert uplands and prehistoric Ho-

© BILL WEIR

A naturalist-led hike winds up the trail to Elephant Head in Spur Cross Ranch Conservation Area, north of Cave Creek.

hokam sites—lies in scenic hills northeast of Cave Creek Regional Park. The Conservation Area (480/488-6601, www.maricopa.gov/parks, $3/person) had its grand opening in January 2004. Currently you can explore three trails, and more are in the works. Guided hikes go to riparian and archaeological sites not otherwise open to the public; call or check the website for the schedule. There's no camping allowed in the Conservation Area, but you could camp in the Tonto National Forest to the north.

Spur Cross Trail (open to hikers, mountain bikers, and equestrians) follows an old road north 1.2 miles to Cave Creek, a popular spot for families to splash in the shallow water; the road continues about 2 miles into the Tonto National Forest and connects with the Cave Creek Trail system. The **SR Trail** branches to the northwest near the beginning of Spur Cross Trail and follows an old road 1.4 miles. At its end, you can continue on **Elephant Mountain Trail,** a rugged

2.9-mile (one-way) route that climbs over a pass and descends to the south boundary of the Conservation Area; these last two trails are for hikers and equestrians only. You can make a fine 5.8-mile loop with trails in the national forest: follow SR Trail to its end, turn north half a mile into national forest land to a trail junction, turn east via Page and Limestone Springs to Cave Creek, then follow the creek downstream and continue south on Spur Cross Trail back to the trailhead.

To reach the Conservation Area, follow Cave Creek Road into the town of Cave Creek, then turn north 4.3 miles on Spur Cross Road (the last 1.3 miles are unpaved). Two stables near the Conservation Area offer trail rides.

McDowell Mountain Regional Park

You'll enjoy beautiful vistas at this park (P.O. Box 18415, Fountain Hills, AZ 85269, 480/471-0173, www.maricopa.gov/parks, $5/vehicle) near the eastern McDowells, 15 miles northeast of Scottsdale. A wide variety of desert plants grows at the 1,550- to 3,100-foot elevations, though two-thirds of the 21,000-acre park burned in the lightning-caused Rio Fire of July 1995. You can compare areas and see how the desert has recovered. From 1870 to 1890, the Stoneman Military Road ran through the park, connecting nearby Fort McDowell with Fort Whipple near Prescott. Today, 40.5 miles of recreation trails and 14.1 miles of competitive trails wind through the foothills and lower slopes, though not up the McDowells themselves.

Two picnic areas with playgrounds lie about six miles down the main park road. The family campground has showers and water/electric hookups for $18; an overflow area may be available if the campground is full. There's also a dump station. Groups can reserve picnic ramadas and camping areas. Take Shea Boulevard from Scottsdale (or AZ 87 from Mesa) to Fountain Hills, then turn north on Palisades Boulevard, Fountain Hills Boulevard, or Saguaro Boulevard (passes near the fountain), all of which join and become McDowell Mountain Road. Entrance is on the east side of the park, four miles beyond Fountain Hills.

Nursery Tank Trail (no bikes or horses) offers an easy, barrier-free stroll to an old stock pond with a good view east to the Mazatzals; you may see wildlife here, especially early or late in the day; it's a half mile out and back. The popular and gentle **North Trail** (no horses) loops 2.9 miles through an unburned area with interpretive signs. The 1.2-mile **Lousley Hill Trail** loop (hikers only) offers good panoramas of the McDowells, Mazatzals, Four Peaks, and Superstitions. These trails begin near the day-use areas near the end of the park road.

The 15.4-mile loop **Pemberton Trail** is too long for most hikers, but will give mountain bikers and horses a good workout. Several interconnecting trails offer a variety of shorter loops with the Pemberton from the campground (hikers can park just outside the entrance at the Wagner Trailhead, near the main kiosk and telephone) or Trailhead Staging Area. One of these, the **Scenic Trail,** makes a 4.4-mile loop via a wash (too sandy for most bikers) and a ridge. For a short, .5-mile round-trip hike with a 360-degree panorama, you can head up the **Hilltop Trail** (hikers only) from the Trailhead Staging Area.

McDowell Competitive Track, on your left just after entering the park, offers interconnected loops for mountain bikers, runners, and trotting horses: a 3-mile Sport Loop, an 8.2-mile Long Loop, and the challenging 2.9-mile Technical Loop. Slower users yield to faster on these one-way loops.

Usery Mountain Regional Park

Visitors enjoy this scenic setting with picnicking, trails, camping, abundant wildlife, and fantastic sunsets over the Valley. About 12 miles northeast of downtown Mesa, the park (3939 N. Usery Pass Rd., #190, Mesa, AZ 85207, 480/984-0032, www.maricopa.gov/parks, $5/vehicle) includes more than 3,500 acres of Sonoran Desert with elevations from 1,700 to 2,750 feet. It takes its name from Usery Mountain in the northwest corner. King Usery, whose name the mountain bears, was a cattleman who had difficulty staying on the right side of the law; he lived in the area in the late 1800s. Mexican and Basque shepherds still herd flocks across Usery Pass in the spring and autumn.

Picnic areas offer shaded tables. Kids can frolic

in the playgrounds. The family campground has showers and water/electric hookups for $18. If it's full, you can stay in overflow sites (no hookups) for $10. Tenters have a separate area that they can use anytime for $10. A dump station is near the campground entrance. Groups can reserve their own campground and picnic areas. Equestrians have a horse-staging area. From the Superstition Freeway (U.S. 60), turn north on Ellsworth Road, which becomes Usery Pass Road; the park entrance is on the right. The road continues over the pass with good views and descends to the Lower Salt River Recreation Area.

The park has trails to suit almost everyone. For an easy stroll, try the barrier-free **Merkle Memorial Trail**—a 0.9-mile loop around a rocky hill in the picnic area. **Vista Trail,** with a 90-foot climb, follows a ridge .5 miles between the north and south ends of the Merkle loop. The popular **Wind Cave Trail** climbs 800 feet in 1.5 miles one-way to shallow caves in the cliffs of Pass Mountain. The trail, for hikers only, offers views all along the way. Volcanic ash formed these light-colored cliffs of tuff, which are capped by a layer of basalt. Hikers, skilled mountain bikers, and equestrians can follow **Pass Mountain Trail,** a very scenic 7.1-mile loop around Pass Mountain; going clockwise works best as you'll be going down instead of up a steep 500-foot grade. A network of trails in the southern area of the park, such as the 2.9-mile loop **Blevins Trail,** crosses gentle terrain—good for beginner mountain bikers; several other loops branch off it for longer trips.

Archers can practice at a range near the entrance station. The **Usery Mountain Shooting Range** of the Rio Salado Sportsman's Club (480/984-9610) is one-third mile north of the park entrance.

TONTO NATIONAL FOREST RECREATION AREAS

The Salt and Verde Rivers bring greenery and water sports to the northeast corner of the Valley.

Lower Salt River Recreation Areas

The Salt's final run below Saguaro Lake offers a glimpse of what the riparian life of the Valley looked like before the coming of modern irrigation canals. Visitors come to enjoy tubing in the Salt during the warm months, camping in winter (Oct. 15–April 15 only), and fishing and picnicking year-round. Recreation areas have vault toilets but no drinking water; day use is free, campers pay $6.

The Bush Highway connects the area with Mesa to the south and Highway 87 to the north. If coming from Mesa, you'll first reach the turnoff for **Phon D. Sutton Recreation Area;** it's 1.2 miles in and has lots of parking for RVs. The **Lower Salt River Nature Trail,** an easy 2.3-mile loop, begins at the downstream end of Phon D. Sutton, follows the shore downstream, turns inland through cottonwood and mesquite woodlands, then returns via some desert uplands; signs tell of life here and the changes that settlement has brought.

Coon Bluff Recreation Area is one mile east on Bush Highway past the Sutton turnoff, then one mile in. Picnic tables under the trees overlook the river. This is an especially good spot for tent camping.

Goldfield Recreation Area is 1.3 miles past the Coon Bluff turnoff, then 1.3 miles in. Tube rental and the shuttle-bus center are near the turnoff. Usery Pass Road ends at this junction; turn south for Usery Mountain Recreation Area and good views back to the Salt River Valley.

You'll find three recreation areas near where the Bush Highway crosses the Salt on Blue Point Bridge, 2.5 miles east of the Goldfield turnoff: **Pebble Beach** is southeast of the bridge, **Blue Point** is northeast of the bridge, and **Sheep Crossing** is northwest of the bridge. Another two miles east takes you to **Water Users Recreation Area** and some impressive canyon scenery; a short trail leads to the river. All of these have a $4/vehicle day-use fee. Continue up a hill on the Bush Highway to the turnoff for Saguaro Lake.

Saguaro Lake

The scenery, fishing, and boating on Saguaro Lake attract people year-round. The 10-mile-long, 1,100-acre lake within Tonto National Forest is the last in the chain of lakes on the Salt River and the closest to Phoenix. Anglers catch largemouth and yellow bass, channel catfish, bluegill, and walleye. **Lakeshore Restaurant** (480/984-5311) serves breakfast and lunch daily and dinner Wednesday–Sunday, either indoors or out on the patio (great views). **Saguaro Lake Marina** (480/986-5546 marina, 480/986-0969 rentals) offers boating supplies and rentals of fishing, patio, and ski boats.

The adjacent **Saguaro del Norte** area provides day-use boat ramps, picnic areas with shaded tables, and Saguaro Lake Vista Trail, but no water; $4/vehicle and $2/boat. **Butcher Jones Recreation Area** offers a picnic area and hiking along the northern lakeshore, but no boat ramp; $4/vehicle day use. **Butcher Jones Trail** follows the shore—the first quarter mile is paved for wheelchair fishing access—and crosses a ridge (115-foot climb) to Burro Cove in 2.5 miles one-way. The road to Butcher Jones turns off the Bush Highway one mile north of the marina. Picnic and boating areas almost always fill up on Sunday and sometimes on Saturday from mid-spring to mid-summer; try to arrive by early morning. Only boaters can reach **Bagley Flat Campground,** about four miles from the marina; it has tables and pit toilets, but no water or fee. Dispersed camping is also permitted, but again, you'll need a boat.

To reach Saguaro Lake, take the Bush Highway or Highway 87 from eastern Mesa. The **Mesa Ranger District Office** of the Tonto National Forest (5140 E. Ingram St., Mesa, AZ 85205, 480/610-3300, 8 A.M.–4:30 P.M. Mon.–Fri.) stocks recreation information for the Saguaro Lake, lower Salt River, Superstitions, and Four Peaks areas. You can also contact the main Tonto office (2324 E. McDowell Rd., Phoenix, AZ 85006, 602/225-5200, 8 A.M.–4:30 P.M. Mon.–Fri.).

Bartlett and Horseshoe Reservoirs

These lakes on the Verde River offer fine scenery and outdoor recreation, including fishing for largemouth bass, catfish, crappie, bluegill, and carp. Horseshoe also supports endangered razorback sucker and Colorado pikeminnow, which must be returned to the water. At each reservoir, you'll need to pay day-use fees at vending machines of $4 per vehicle and $2 per boat, but there's no additional charge for camping. For more information, contact the **Cave Creek Ranger Station** (40202 N. Cave Creek Rd., Scottsdale, AZ 85262, 480/595-3300, 8 A.M.–5 P.M. Mon.–Fri., www.fs.fed.us/r3/tonto). You'll pass the ranger station on the left just after turning toward the reservoirs from Cave Creek Road.

From the town of Cave Creek, go east seven miles on Cave Creek Road, turn right and drive six miles on Forest Road 205, then continue eight miles on Forest Road 19 to the lake. These roads are paved and make a great scenic drive, especially on weekdays when traffic is light.

The main road to Bartlett ends at **Jojoba Boating Site,** which has a paved boat ramp. A sign says that RV camping is permitted here from October 31 to May 1. The nearby sheriff's office is staffed on summer weekends and has an emergency phone. **Jojoba Trail** begins on the north side of the parking area and winds north about one mile through granite boulders and desert plants. The Mazatzal Mountains soar into the sky across the lake. **Bartlett Lake Marina** (602/316-3378, www.bartlettlake.com), just south of Jojoba Boating Site, provides two convenience stores, pontoon boat rentals, wet and dry storage, auto and boat fuel, and bait and tackle year-round. Continue south 2.1 miles past the marina turnoff on an unpaved road through boulder-strewn hills for Riverside Campground (vault toilets but no drinking water) below the dam.

North Lake Road (Forest Road 459) leads to recreation areas on the lake; the turnoff from the main road is half a mile before Jojoba Boating Site. In .6 miles you'll reach the entrance for **Rattlesnake Cove Recreation Site,** a day-use area with water, shaded tables, grills, restrooms, and fishing pier. Pavement ends in another 2.5 miles at **Yellow Cliffs Boating Site,** which has a paved boat ramp, water, and restrooms. Primitive camping is just beyond at S. B. Cove. The road ends .7 miles farther on at Bartlett Flat, popular with boaters and campers; outhouses are the only facilities.

Horseshoe Lake, upstream from Bartlett, offers a quieter experience. The road is unpaved and facilities are very basic. Personal watercraft and water-skiing are not permitted, and there's a 15 mph speed limit. Follow directions toward Bartlett, but turn left on unpaved Forest Road 205 and follow it for 10 miles all the way to the dam. You can stay on the Verde River at **Mesquite Recreation Site,** which has tables, grills, and outhouses in a mesquite grove; the turnoff is 8.2 miles in on your right. **Horseshoe Campground** offers similar facilities near the river 1.5 miles farther north. Catfish Point nearby has river access just below the dam; you can hand-launch boats here. Canoeists enjoy the eight miles of river between Horseshoe and Bartlett; for information on flow and lake levels, call the Salt River Project (602/236-5929). A few shaded picnic tables overlook the lake near road's end. The boat ramp here is paved, but narrow and usable only at higher lake levels. Visitors pay the same daily fees as at Bartlett, $4 per vehicle and $2 per boat.

Sears-Kay Ruin

About 900 years ago, the Hohokam built this hilltop village as one of a series between the Valley and the mountains to the north. A one-mile loop trail climbs to the 40-room pueblo and its main plaza, laboriously constructed with a retaining wall. On top, you'll enjoy a great view of Weaver's Needle in the Superstitions, Four Peaks, the fountain in Fountain Hills, and many hills to the north. The trailhead has a few covered picnic tables for day use only; no water or fee. Follow Cave Creek Road east from Carefree, turn left (north) 2.6 miles on Forest Road 24 at the Bartlett Lake junction (the last one-third mile of Forest Road 24 is gravel), then turn right at the sign.

Mistress Mine

A bit farther north of the Sears-Kay Ruin, you can stop on the left to visit a rock shop and see a little museum near the old mine shaft (480/488-0842, www.ccmistressmine.com); the owner also offers tours and cabin and teepee accommodations. Open 9 A.M.–6 P.M. daily in the cooler months, then weekends in summer.

Seven Springs and CCC Campgrounds

Large sycamore and ash trees provide shade for these two adjacent campgrounds ($4/vehicle) among hills of the Tonto National Forest, north of the Valley. Sites have picnic tables and pit toilets but no drinking water. From the town of Cave Creek go seven miles east on Cave Creek Road to a junction, then keep left on Forest Road 24. It becomes dirt after 2.3 miles, then it's another 11 miles of scenic, winding road to the two campgrounds. **Cave Creek Campground,** a mile farther, is a group-fee area requiring reservations from the Cave Creek Ranger Station. The **Cave Creek Trail System** offers about 30 miles of trails for hikers, horseback riders, and mountain bikers. The Cave Creek Ranger Station (480/595-3300, www.fs.fed.us/r3/tonto) has recreation information for this area.

Bloody Basin Road

Drivers with high-clearance vehicles can leave the crowds behind on this 60-mile scenic back road through the Tonto National Forest. The road connects Carefree/Cave Creek with I-17 Exit 259 (Bloody Basin/Crown King). You'll enjoy views of the Mazatzals, rugged high-desert hill country, and wooded canyons. In Bloody Basin, 26 miles from I-17, a very bumpy side road goes southeast 12 miles to the Verde River and Sheep Bridge, where hikers can head into the Mazatzal Wilderness. Primitive camping is possible almost anywhere in Tonto National Forest, or you can stop at Seven Springs or CCC Campgrounds near the south end of Bloody Basin Road. Follow directions to Seven Springs Campground, then continue north on Forest Road 24.

Information and Services

TOURIST OFFICES

Greater Phoenix Convention & Visitors Bureau (50 N. 2nd St., Phoenix, AZ 85004, 602/254-6500 or 877/225-5749, www.visitphoenix.com, 8 A.M.–5 P.M. Mon.–Fri.) has a free *Official Visitors Guide* and many brochures downtown. You can park at 15-minute meters in front. For Valley event news and other services, call the Visitor Information Line (602/252-5588). The Visitors Bureau maintains a branch office in Biltmore Fashion Park (24th St. and Camelback Rd., open daily during shopping center hours).

Scottsdale Convention & Visitors Bureau (4343 N. Scottsdale Rd., Suite 170, Scottsdale, AZ 85251, 480/421-1004 or 800/782-1117, www.scottsdalecvb.com, 8:30 A.M.–6 P.M. Mon.–Fri.) is in Galleria Corporate Center on the east side of Scottsdale Road, about halfway between Camelback and Indian School Roads; it's on the free trolley route. Staff also provide information at the concierge desk of the nearby Scottsdale Fashion Square (1–6 P.M. Tues.–Sat., Sept.–May, then 11 A.M.–4 P.M. Tues.–Sat. in summer).

Tempe Convention and Visitors Bureau (51 W. 3rd St., Suite 105, Tempe, AZ 85281, 480/894-8158 or 800/283-6734, www.tempecvb.com, 8:30 A.M.–5 P.M. Mon.–Fri.) is off Mill Avenue at Hayden Square in Old Town Tempe.

Mesa Convention & Visitors Bureau (120 N. Center, Mesa, AZ 85201, 480/827-4700 or 800/283-6372, www.mesacvb.com, 8 A.M.–5 P.M. Mon.–Fri.) has a central location downtown.

Carefree/Cave Creek Chamber of Commerce (748 Easy St., P.O. Box 734, Carefree, AZ 85377, 480/488-3381, www.carefree-cavecreek.com, 9 A.M.–4 P.M. Mon.–Fri.) is in Carefree near the southeast corner of Tom Darlington and Cave Creek Roads in the north Valley.

Apache Junction Chamber of Commerce (567 W. Apache Trail, Apache Junction, AZ 85220, 480/982-3141 or 800/252-3141, www.apachejunctioncoc.com, 8 A.M.–5 P.M. Mon.–Fri. and, except in summer, 9 A.M.–2 P.M. Sat.) is in the far east side of the Valley.

Fountain Hills Chamber of Commerce (16837 E. Palisades Blvd., P.O. Box 17598, Fountain Hills, AZ 85269-7598, 480/837-1654, www.fountainhillschamber.com, 8 A.M.–5 P.M. Mon.–Fri., 10A.M.–3 P.M. Sat.–Sun.) is one block off Saguaro Boulevard in the northeast Valley.

Glendale Visitor Center (5800 W. Glenn Dr., Suite 140., Glendale, AZ 85301, 623/930-4500 or 877/800-2601, www.visitglendale.com, 10 A.M.–5 P.M. Mon.–Sat.) is in the northwest Valley.

The **Arizona Office of Tourism** (1110 W. Washington Street, Suite 155, Phoenix, Arizona 85007, 602/364-3700 or 866/891-3640, fax 602/364-3702, www.arizonaguide.com, 8 A.M.–5 P.M. Mon.–Fri.) offers information on every region of the state. You can find most of the literature at other tourist offices, but this one has the best selection. It's in a modern building behind the 1893 Evans House. The excellent website has travel tips, event listings, trip-planning ideas, foreign-language sections, and links to many chamber of commerce sites; the Kid's Zone entices the younger set to learn Arizona history.

Arizona Public Lands Information Center

The center's helpful staff (call for location, 602/417-9300, www.publiclands.org, 8:30 A.M.–4:30 P.M. Mon.–Fri.) should be able to meet all your needs for recreation information and permits on federal and state lands in Arizona. You can ask questions and purchase books on scenic drives, camping, hiking, mountain biking, off-highway trails, river running, regional history, Native Americans, natural history, travel, and other topics. Maps on hand include those of Arizona's national forests and BLM lands, plus topographic, city, and state; custom topographic and land-use maps are available too. The Center sells fishing and hunting licenses, national and state park passes, national forest recreation permits, and state trust permits. You can order publications and permits directly at 800/986-1151 or az_plic@blm.gov.

Tonto National Forest

The Tonto's 2.9 million acres include deep canyons, soaring peaks, and gentle hills north and east of the Valley. The Supervisor's Office (2324 E. McDowell Rd., Phoenix, AZ 85006, 602/225-5200, www.fs.fed.us/r3/tonto, 8 A.M.–4:30 P.M. Mon.–Fri.) has general information, or you can contact one of the Tonto's districts. Frequent visitors to recreation areas in the Tonto can save money with the **Tonto Golden Passport Upgrade Decal.** It covers entry fees—but not campgrounds or marinas—in the Cave Creek, Mesa, and Roosevelt districts; contact the supervisor's or district offices for details.

The **Cave Creek Ranger District** (40202 N. Cave Creek Rd., Scottsdale, AZ 85262, 480/595-3300, 8 A.M.–5 P.M. Mon.–Fri.) includes Bartlett and Horseshoe Lakes, the Cave Creek Trail System, and other areas north of the Valley. From Carefree, head northeast on Cave Creek Road, turn right on Bartlett Lake Road, then it's on your left.

The **Mesa Ranger District** (5140 E. Ingram St., south of Falcon Field, Mesa, AZ 85205, 480/610-3300, 8 A.M.–4:30 P.M. Mon.–Fri.) covers Saguaro Lake, lower Salt River, Superstitions, Four Peaks, and other areas east of the Valley.

Bureau of Land Management

The Phoenix Field Office (21605 N. 7th Ave., south of Deer Valley Rd., Phoenix, AZ 85027, 623/580-5500, www.az.blm.gov, 7:30 A.M.–4:15 P.M. Mon.–Fri.) provides information on BLM areas in most of central and northern Arizona.

Arizona State Parks

The main office (1300 W. Washington St., Phoenix, AZ 85007, 602/542-4174 or 800/285-3703, fax 602/542-4188, www.azstateparks.com, 8 A.M.–5 P.M. Mon.–Fri.) provides outdoor recreation information for the entire state, as well as for all of the state parks; there's a gift shop, too. Free visitor parking is in back.

Arizona Game and Fish

The main office (2221 W. Greenway Rd., Phoenix, AZ 85023, 602/942-3000, www.azgfd.com, 8 A.M.–5 P.M. Mon.–Fri.) has information and sells licenses for fishing, hunting, and boat registration; you can also learn about off-highway vehicle travel. The office for central Arizona is in Mesa (7200 E. University Dr., Mesa, AZ 85027, 480/981-9400).

LIBRARIES

The massive **Phoenix Central Library** (1221 N. Central Ave., 602/262-4636, www.phoenixlibrary.org, noon–9 P.M. Sun., 9 A.M.–9 P.M. Mon.–Thurs., 9 A.M.–6 P.M. Fri.–Sat.), two blocks south of McDowell Road, looks like a giant glass-and-metal cube. Once inside the five-story atrium, you'll have much to explore in the spacious facility. A map lists what's on each floor and describes some of the unusual design features of the building. The Friends Place near the entrance sells gift items and surplus books. First floor has fiction, foreign languages, and children's books. Second floor houses periodicals, Internet computers, and a copy center. The Arizona Room (closed Mon. and Fri.) on the fourth floor has great reading on the state's history, travel, and natural life; this is the place to pore over maps and books about lost-mine legends before setting off on your own treasure hunt! You'll need an appointment to see the Rare Book Collection, located across from the Arizona Room. Nonfiction hangs out on the fifth floor, claimed to be the largest reading room in North America. See the website or the blue pages in the phone book under "Phoenix Libraries" for information on the 12 branches scattered around town.

The **State Capitol** has a research library (1700 W. Washington, Rm. 300, 602/542-3701, www.lib.az.us, 8 A.M.–5 P.M. Mon.–Fri.) filled with Arizona history, maps, state documents, federal documents, and genealogy.

Scottsdale Public Library (3839 Civic Center Blvd., 480/994-2474, http://library.ci.scottsdale.az.us, 1–5 P.M. Sun., 9 A.M.–9 P.M. Mon.–Thurs., 10 A.M.–6 P.M. Fri.–Sat.) is in the Civic Center complex downtown.

Tempe Public Library (3500 S. Rural Rd., 480/350-5555 recording, 480/350-5511 reference, www.tempe.gov/library, noon–5:30 P.M. Sun., 9 A.M.–9 P.M. Mon.–Thurs., 9 A.M.–5:30 P.M. Fri.–Sat.) sits next to the Tempe Historical Museum at the southwest corner with Southern

Avenue. (See the *Arizona State University* section for descriptions of the two largest libraries there.)

Mesa Public Library (64 E. 1st St., 480/644-3100 recording, 480/644-2207 reference, www.mesalibrary.org), downtown, is open 1:30–5:30 P.M. Sunday, and 9:30 A.M.–9 P.M. Monday–Saturday, but closes at 5:30 P.M. Friday and Saturday.

Apache Junction Public Library (1177 N. Idaho Rd., 480/474-8555, www.ajpl.org, 9 A.M.–5 P.M. Mon., Wed., Fri., and Sat., 9 A.M.–8 P.M. Tues. and Thurs.) is north of the city hall complex.

NEWSPAPERS

The *Arizona Republic* (www.azfamily.com) comes out every morning and features a big Sunday edition; the paper also does a free weekly entertainment guide, the *Rep.* The *Tribune* (www.eastvalleytribune.com) serves the east Valley and publishes a free Valley-wide weekly paper, *Get Out* (www.getoutaz.com). The free weekly *New Times* (www.phoenixnewtimes.com) presents hard-hitting journalism, local news, and extensive entertainment coverage. Newsstands and tourist offices can be treasure-troves of free information on golf, tennis, bicycling, running, New Age, and many other topics.

SERVICES

You can find **post offices** in downtown Phoenix (522 N. Central Ave.), Scottsdale (7242 E. Osborn Rd.), Tempe (500 S. Mill Ave. and 1962 E. Apache Blvd.), and Mesa (135 N. Center). For postal information or to get the address of the post office nearest you, call 800/275-8777 or check www.usps.com. General Delivery mail can be sent to the Rio Salado Station (1441 E. Buckeye Rd.); address it with your name, General Delivery, Phoenix, AZ 85034.

American Express (Biltmore Fashion Park, 2508 E. Camelback Rd., 602/468-1199) handles currency exchange.

Need a doctor? **Maricopa County Medical Society** (602/252-2844, 8 A.M.–5 P.M. weekdays) will refer you to one.

GETTING THERE

Air

Commercial flights land at Phoenix Sky Harbor Airport (602/273-3300, www.phxskyharbor.com), just three miles east of downtown Phoenix. International flights serve Mexico, Canada, and Europe. The busy airport is well organized but you'll have to do some walking. The west entrance off 24th Street and I-10/Papago Freeway is closer to downtown. The east entrance off 44th Street and Hohokam Expressway/143 serves Scottsdale, Tempe, and other east Valley areas. Sky Harbor has three separate terminals, each with an information desk, connected by a free 24-hour shuttle bus. Free telephones near the baggage claims link to many Valley hotels and motels. You'll see art and aviation exhibits in the terminals; ask at an information booth for current shows and locations.

"Where's Terminal 1?" you may ask. Well, just as major-league sports teams retire jersey numbers of famous players, so did the airport with its original terminal, used 1952–1990!

Taxis waiting outside charge widely varying fares—shop around. **SuperShuttle** (602/244-9000 or 800/331-3565) provides door-to-door service from homes and hotels to or from the airport; on arrival at Sky Harbor, step outside any of the terminals to locate a representative; for a ride to the airport, call 24–48 hours in advance; fares start at $6–12 for downtown and increase with distance. **Valley Metro** buses (602/253-5000) are the cheapest way into town; they leave the airport about every 30 minutes (every hour on Sun.) from early morning to late evening.

Long-Distance Bus

The **Greyhound** bus terminal (2115 E. Buckeye Rd. near 24th St., 602/389-4200 or 800/231-2222, www.greyhound.com) is east of downtown near the airport. You'll find other Greyhound stations in northwest Phoenix, Tempe, Mesa, Chandler, and Tolleson.

Buses of **White Mountain Passenger Lines** (319 S. 24th St., 602/275-4245 or 866/255-4819, www.wmlines.com) head from Phoenix to the cool pines of the Mogollon Rim with stops at Mesa (Greyhound depot, 1423 S.

Country Club Dr., 480/834-3360), Payson, Heber, Snowflake, and Show Low. Another route serves Globe and Pinetop–Lakeside; services run in each direction twice daily weekdays and once on Saturday; the main office (928/537-4539) is in Show Low.

Train

Amtrak (401 W. Harrison St. and 4th Ave. in downtown Phoenix, 800/872-7245, www.amtrak.com) trains no longer stop in the Valley. Connecting buses will take you to the Sunset Limited/Texas Eagle, which runs three eastbound and three westbound departures each week across southern Arizona, or to the Southwest Chief, which runs both east and west daily across the northern part of the state.

GETTING AROUND

Car Rentals

The Valley moves on wheels; if you need some, check the Yellow Pages or the Visitors Bureau's *Official Visitors Guide.* Rental companies offer many different plans; most maintain offices at the airport or make free pickups. You can rent RVs too.

Local Bus

Valley Metro (602/253-5000, www.valleymetro.org) will take you around the Valley, visiting parks, shopping areas, most of the sights, and the airport—all for just $1.25 ($1.75 express); transfers are free when requested upon boarding. All-day passes cost $3.60; you can purchase them at the downtown terminal at Van Buren Street and Central Avenue. The *Bus Book* available free at the terminal, many tourist offices, and online has maps and timetables. In the downtown area you can ride Valley Metro's **Downtown Area Shuttle** (DASH) on weekdays for free.

Tours

The Valley of the Sun features many tour operators. Drop by one of the Visitors Bureau offices for the latest brochures and *Official Visitors Guide* listings. The Sunday *Arizona Republic* travel section advertises deals within the state and beyond.

The **Gray Line** (1243 S. 7th St., Phoenix, AZ 85034, 602/495-9100 or 800/732-0327, www.graylinearizona.com) runs tours of the Phoenix area including the Heard Museum (4 hours), Sedona/Oak Creek Canyon (9 hours), Nogales (10 hours), and the Grand Canyon (14 hours); two-day trips visit the Grand Canyon, and longer excursions roll to other areas of the Southwest.

Grand Canyon Airlines (866/235-9422, www.grandcanyonairlines.com) offers a variety of one-day tours to the Grand Canyon from the Scottsdale airport.

Wickenburg and Vicinity

WICKENBURG

You still get a sense of the Old West in easygoing Wickenburg, where Western-style buildings line the downtown streets. Picturesque rocky hills all around invite exploration on foot or horseback. Local guest ranches will put you in the saddle and even let you join the cowboys to work the cattle. Not surprisingly, the town has a good selection of shops specializing in Western apparel, Western art, Native American arts and crafts, and antiques.

Wickenburg's pleasantly cool and sunny weather lasts from November to May. Summers at the town's 2,100-foot elevation can get very hot; average highs in July run 103° F.

You'll find most of the places to stay and eat along the two highways that meet in the center, where U.S. Highway 93 (Tegner St.) turns north from U.S. Highway 60 (Wickenburg Way). The chamber of commerce makes a good place to start a visit; follow signs for Tourist Info. Besides information on sights and services of the area, you can pick up a map of a historic walking tour that begins here. Wickenburg is 58 miles northwest of Phoenix via U.S. Highway 60 (Grand Ave.), but the less congested route via I-17 and Highway 74 past Lake Pleasant is quicker and easier. A bypass planned for 2007 will route U.S. Highway 93 traffic east of downtown Wickenburg.

Henry Wickenburg had roamed the hills of Arizona for a year in search of gold before striking it rich at the Vulture Mine in 1863. According to one legend, he noticed the shiny nuggets when reaching down to pick up a vulture he'd shot; others claim he glimpsed the gold while picking up a rock to throw at his burro. Either way, Wickenburg set off a frenzied gold rush.

The Vulture Mine lacked the water needed for processing, so miners hauled the ore 14 miles northeast to the Hassayampa River. In just a few years, the town that grew up around the mills became Arizona's third-largest city. It missed becoming the territorial capital in 1866 by only two votes.

Prospectors discovered other gold deposits in the Wickenburg area until more than 80 mines operated at the height of the gold rush. A bit of gold fever lingers today, still drawing prospectors into the backcountry. Mining for gold and other minerals continues on a small scale.

Desert Caballeros Western Museum

This excellent downtown museum (21 N. Frontier St., 928/684-2272 or 684-7075, www.westernmuseum.org, noon–4 P.M. Sun., 10 A.M.–5 P.M. Mon.–Sat., $6 adults, $4.50 seniors 60+, $1 youth 6–16) presents many facets of Western art, culture, and history. A large art gallery features outstanding paintings and sculpture by Remington, Russell, and other inspired artists. The Native American Room displays a varied collection of prehistoric and modern crafts, including kachina dolls, pottery, baskets, and stone tools. Precious stones and minerals glitter in the Mineral Room. Temporary exhibits delve into intriguing topics.

Dioramas illustrate the history of the Vulture Mine and the early mining community. Downstairs you'll step into a street scene and period rooms that show how Wickenburg actually looked. Outside, walk over to a small park behind the museum to see *Thanks for the Rain,* a bronze sculpture by Joe Beeler. The museum store sells crafts and books.

Old Jail Tree

The town lacked a jail in the early days, so prisoners were shackled to this old mesquite tree. The tree stands behind the Circle-K store at the highway junction downtown.

Hassayampa River

Normally you'll see just a dry streambed through town. The river's Apache name means "river that runs upside down," because its waters flow beneath the sandy surface. A wishing well and sign at the west end of the highway bridge relate the legend that anyone drinking from the stream will never tell the truth again. See for yourself!

Hassayampa River Preserve

The river pops out of the ground along a five-mile section of riverbed below town, watering lush vegetation. The Goodding willow–Fremont cottonwood forest along the banks is one of the rarest forest types in North America. Spring-fed Palm Lake attracts many waterfowl not normally seen in the desert. Visitors have counted more than 280 species of birds, including zone-tailed and black hawks that fly up from Mexico to nest. The preserve, managed by the Arizona chapter of the Nature Conservancy, provides a sanctuary for these hawks and other wildlife. You can enjoy quiet walks through the natural settings, reflecting on the fact that of Arizona's streamside habitats existing a century ago, only 5–10 percent exist today. Hassayampa River Preserve lies three miles southeast of Wickenburg on U.S. Highway 60 near Milepost 114.

Check in at the visitor center (928/684-2772, www.nature.org/arizona, 8 A.M.–5 P.M. Wed.–Sun., but only Fri.–Sun. in summer, $5, $3 members) to pick up trail information and to see exhibits. The four-room adobe core of the visitor center, built in the 1860s, has served as ranch, stagecoach way station, and one of Arizona's first guest ranches. A network of trails begins near the visitor center and wanders along the riverbank, through the woodlands, around Palm Lake, and up to a viewpoint. The preserve offers guided nature walks on the last Saturday of each month; call for time and reservations.

Entertainment and Events

Saguaro Theater (176 E. Wickenburg Way, 928/684-7189) screens current films. **Rodeos** provide excitement at 2 P.M. each Sunday from the first Sunday in December to the first Sunday in February at Bowman Arena; head east on Wickenburg Way across the Hassayampa bridge, turn left on Jack Burden Road, then turn right one mile on Constellation Road.

Gold Rush Days celebrates Wickenburg's Western heritage with a shootout, parade, rodeo, concerts, "mellerdramas," a gold-panning contest, and other activities on the second full weekend in February. **July 4th** brings fireworks and a watermelon feed. **Fiesta Septiembre,** on the first Saturday of September, celebrates Hispanic culture with dances and music in the park behind Desert Caballeros Western Museum. The **Wickenburg Bluegrass Festival** brings foot-tapping music and dancing to town on the second full weekend in November. A **Cowboy Poets Gathering** on the first full weekend in December presents the rich heritage of those who work the range. The **Christmas Light Parade** brightens the evening on the second Friday in December.

Recreation

Coffinger Park offers picnicking, a swimming pool, tennis courts, and a ball field off N. Tegner Street, just across the Sols Wash bridge. **Sunset Park,** four miles west of town on U.S. Highway 60, has picnicking, tennis courts, a basketball court, and ball fields. Play golf year-round at the 9-hole **Wickenburg Country Club** course (2 miles west on U.S. 60, then north on Country Club Rd., 928/684-2011) or the 18-hole course at **Los Caballeros Golf Club** (3.5 miles west on U.S. 60, then south 2 miles on Vulture Mine Rd., 928/684-2704).

Guest Ranches

Kay El Bar Ranch (P.O. Box 2480, Wickenburg, AZ 85358, 928/684-7593 or 800/684-7583, www.kayelbar.com, mid-Oct.–early May) has been around so long it's on the National Register of Historic Places. It began as a cattle ranch in the early 1900s, then became a dude ranch in 1926. The adobe lodge and casitas help create a Western experience for guests—never more than 24—who ride, receive riding instruction, hike a scenic trail, enjoy the pool and hot tub, and have family-style meals and cookouts. Rates include all meals, riding, and ranch facilities: $185 s, $325 d in lodge rooms or Casa Monterey, $370 d in Casa Grande with a fireplace and sitting area, or $700 for four in Homestead House, a two-bedroom cottage with fireplace and living room; weekly rates are available too. From downtown, head 1.7 miles northwest on U.S. Highway 93 and turn right on Rincon Road, then follow signs 1.5 miles.

Flying E Guest Ranch (2801 W. Wickenburg Way, Wickenburg, AZ 85390, 928/684-2690 or 888/684-2650, www.flyingeranch.com, Nov. 1–April 30, $150–205 s, $240–305 d) still works cattle. It has an informal atmosphere where guests can ride, play tennis, enjoy family-style meals, work out in the fitness room, or relax around the pool and hot tub. To get to the ranch go four miles west on U.S. Highway 60, then one mile south.

Rancho de los Caballeros (1551 S. Vulture Mine Rd., Wickenburg, AZ 85390, 928/684-5484 or 800/684-5030, www.sunc.com, early Oct.–early May) is the largest and most elegant of the group. Guests enjoy horseback riding, an 18-hole golf course, pool, tennis, trap and skeet, hot-air balloon rides, children's activities, and fine dining. Rates are $198–374 s, $316–499 d in high season (Feb.–April); $178–299 s, $271–399 d in low season (Oct.–Jan. and May). From Wickenburg, go 3.5 miles west on U.S. Highway 60, then turn left (south) 2 miles.

Williams Family Ranch (P.O. Box 3855, Wickenburg, AZ 85358, 928/308-0589, www.williamsfamilyranch.com) offers the experience of a working cattle ranch in a remote area along the Hassayampa River, 16 miles northeast of Wickenburg. Guests can come out just for the day to ride (four-person minimum), but a visit of at least 3–5 days is recommended, especially if you'd like to try your hand with the cattle. Guests stay in a bunkhouse and dine family-style in the main ranch house. Rates with accommodations, meals, riding, and transportation from Wickenburg are $125 s, $230 d ($795/week s, $1,550/week d). The season runs September–early June.

Rancho Casitas (56550 Rancho Casitas Rd., Wickenburg, AZ 85390, 928/684-2628, Oct.–May, $550 s, $650 d and up) provides comfortable accommodations with kitchens, patios, pool, and hot tub in a hilltop setting five miles north of town. No meals or activities are available but you can bring your own horse. There's a one-week minimum stay.

Motels and Hotels

Under $50: Of the older motels west of downtown, your best bet is the **Westerner Motel** (680 W. Wickenburg Way, 928/684-2493, $37 d) with a pool.

$50–100: Look for the palms and old wagons outside the restored motor court **Legends West** (1.5 miles east of downtown on U.S. 60, 928/684-8833, $65 s, $70 d including tax); each room has its own Old West or Victorian theme. **AmericInn** (850 E. Wickenburg Way, 928/684-5461 or 800/634-3444, $64–100 d) provides modern rooms with a Southwest decor, along with the Willows Restaurant, a pool, and a hot tub. **Best Western Rancho Grande** (293 E. Wickenburg Way, 928/684-5445 or 800/854-7235, $71 s, $74 d and up) was known as the Palm Court back in 1946, when it became one of the first motels in the Best Western group; you can stay in the restored Southwestern-style rooms or in newer and larger rooms, some with kitchenettes; guests enjoy a pool and hot tub.

Turn north downtown for the Santa Fe–style **Los Viajeros Inn** (1000 N. Tegner, 928/684-7099 or 800/915-9795, $55 s, $58 d), whose rooms have a patio or balcony; Denny's Restaurant is next door. Across the road is the Western-themed **Super 8 Motel** (975 N. Tegner, 928/684-0808 or 800/800-8000, $60 s, $65 d).

For bed and breakfast in a house several blocks off W. Wickenburg Way, contact **Owl Tree Inn** (928/684-1197) at least one day in advance; two rooms ($75 d and $100 d) have shared bath and one ($125 d) has a private bath.

Campgrounds

Horspitality RV Park and Boarding Stable (2 miles southeast on U.S. 60, 928/684-2519) is the only place to offer sites for both tents ($15) and RVs ($15–26 w/hookups); amenities include showers, winter activities, and a stable for your horse. The adult **Desert Cypress Trailer Ranch** (610 Jack Burden Rd., 928/684-2153, $25 RV w/hookups and showers) is across the Hassayampa bridge from downtown, then left after McDonalds. Self-contained rigs (no tents) can stay just northeast of town at **Constellation Park,** where sites cost only $5 but have no water or facilities; from downtown head east on Wickenburg Way across the Hassayampa bridge, turn left on Jack Burden Road, then turn right one mile on Constellation Road.

Another possibility for both tents and RVs is camping out in the desert. Avoid washes and be sure you're on public land; you'll need a permit if camping on state trust land.

Food

For good American fare, join the locals at the **Cowboy Café** (445 N. Tegner St., 928/684-2807, daily breakfast, lunch, and dinner). **Chicken Noodle Café** (2021 W. Wickenburg Way in West Plaza Shopping Center, 928/684-2294, Mon.–Sat. breakfast, lunch, and dinner) serves American favorites in a homey atmosphere. Named after Alice in Wonderland's floppy-eared rabbit, **The March Hare** (170 W. Wickenburg Way, 928/684-0223, Tues.–Sat. lunch) serves quiche and other tasty light fare in a historic house; it's a small place, so reservations are recommended.

Qorri's (651 W. Wickenburg Way, 928/684-2002, Wed.–Mon. dinner) features fine dining in an elegant setting for steak, seafood, chicken, and pasta dishes. The rib eye is a favorite at **Charley's Steak House** (1187 W. Wickenburg Way, 928/684-2413, closed Tues.–Sat. lunch and dinner), which also serves other cuts, seafood, and chicken dishes. **Rancho de los Caballeros** (1551 S. Vulture Mine Rd., 928/684-5484, daily) offers fine buffets and à la carte items to the public by reservation.

House Berlin (169 E. Wickenburg Way, 928/684-5044, Wed.–Sun. lunch, and Tues.–Sun. dinner) specializes in hearty German fare such as sauerbraten, schnitzel, roulade (cabbage roll), and hefty sandwiches. The informal

Sangini's (107 E. Wickenburg Way, 928/684-7828, daily lunch and dinner) offers such specialties as eggplant parmesan, chicken marsala, linguini with clam sauce, and Sangini's signature rib eye, as well as pizza selections, sandwiches, and burgers. You can find good Mexican food at **Anita's Cocina** (57 N. Valentine, 928/684-5777, daily lunch and dinner) around the corner from the Gold Nugget Restaurant off E. Wickenburg Way. **Sizzling Wok** (621 W. Wickenburg Way, 928/684-3977, daily lunch and dinner) offers a wide variety of Chinese cuisine. Look for supermarkets and other stores at **Bashas' Frontier Center** on N. Tegner Street and at **West Plaza Shopping Center** on W. Wickenburg Way at the west edge of town.

Information and Services

The friendly **Wickenburg Chamber of Commerce** (216 N. Frontier St., Wickenburg, AZ 85390, 928/684-5479 or 800/942-5242, www.outwickenburgway.com) is in the 1895 railroad depot one block west of N. Tegner Street. Hours are 10 A.M.–2 P.M. Sunday, 9 A.M.–5 P.M. Monday–Friday, and 10 A.M.–3 P.M. Saturday except until 2 P.M. June–September. The Chamber of Commerce can tell you about companies offering backcountry driving tours and trail rides, but there's no local or long-distance bus service.

The **public library** (164 E. Apache St., 928/684-2665, 8 A.M.–7 P.M. Mon.–Fri., 8 A.M.–noon Sat.) is one block north of Wickenburg Way and just west of the river. The **post office** (2030 W. Wickenburg Way, 928/684-2138) is in West Plaza. **Wickenburg Regional Medical Center** (520 Rose Lane, 928/684-5421) is .8 miles north on Tegner Street from the highway junction.

VICINITY OF WICKENBURG

Vulture Mine

At rest now, the Vulture Mine (602/859-2743, $7 adults, $6 seniors 62+, and $5 children 6–12) saw a lot of activity from the time of Henry Wickenburg's discovery in 1863 until wartime priorities shut it down in 1942. Today you have the opportunity to stroll through the remarkably well-preserved ghost town. Gold and silver still lie in underground veins and may be mined again.

The self-guided, quarter-mile loop stays on the surface past the assay office, glory hole, headframe and main shaft (more than 2,000 feet deep), blacksmith shop, ball mill, power plant, apartment houses, mess hall, and other structures. Be sure to keep to the marked trail—some areas and buildings are dangerous to enter—and wear sturdy shoes. It's open 8 A.M.–4 P.M. daily mid-September–early May, then 8 A.M.–4 P.M. Friday–Sunday early May–June, but is closed July–mid-September. Groups can schedule tours. From Wickenburg, head west 2.5 miles on Wickenburg Way, then turn south 12 miles on paved Vulture Mine Road; the mine is on your right.

Robson's Arizona Mining World

The Nella-Meda Mine (928/685-2609, www.robsonsminingworld.com, 10 A.M.–4 P.M. weekdays and 9 A.M.–5 P.M. weekends Oct.–April, $5 adults, $4.50 seniors, free for children under 10, gold panning $8 extra) is a reconstructed ghost town with about 30 buildings, including an antique print shop, blacksmith shop, saloon, general store, and miners' cabins. Miners dug gold ore here from the early 1900s until WWII, and there's evidence that the Spanish worked the site much earlier. A self-guided walking-tour map explains the use and history of many of the buildings and the pieces of machinery in what's claimed to be the world's largest collection of antique mining equipment. You can step inside the buildings, which are opened on request. Hikers enjoy a scenic walk up a nearby canyon to natural pools at Black Tanks, where prehistoric tribes left behind petroglyphs and holes in the streambed; it's about three miles round-trip and a bit rugged in the upper part.

A bed and breakfast has rooms ($70–80 d) and suites ($90–175 d). The restaurant serves breakfast and lunch, and you can arrange dinners (steak, chicken, or fish) and cowboy cookouts by reservation. From Wickenburg, head west 25 miles on U.S. Highway 60, turn north 4 miles on Highway 71, then turn west 1.6 miles at the sign. The mailing address is P.O. Box 3465, Wickenburg, AZ 85358.

© BILL WEIR

On a tour, you can step inside these reconstructed old buildings at Robson's Mining World.

Stanton

Originally called Antelope Station, this settlement began in 1863 when prospectors found placer gold in Antelope Creek. Five years later, the population reached 3,500. The gold began to play out by the early 1900s, and Stanton started fading away. The stage stop, hotel, and opera house survive from the old days. Members of the Lost Dutchman Mining Association now own the site, where they continue the tradition of gold mining in Antelope Creek as a hobby. Ask permission to look around Stanton; no charge, though you can make a donation.

From Wickenburg follow Highway 89 north 18 miles, 2 miles past Congress, then turn right 6.5 miles on a graded dirt road at the sign for Stanton. Along the road you'll see old shacks, mine tailings, rusting machinery, and some new operations, as well as a large dairy. After entering Stanton, turn left through the Lost Dutchman's Mining Association gate. The main road continues another mile to the site of Octave (there's a No Trespassing sign), then becomes too rough for cars. On Rich Hill, between Stanton and Octave, prospectors reportedly picked up gold nuggets the size of potatoes, just lying on the ground.

Drivers with high-clearance vehicles can turn left just past Stanton and climb five miles up the valley past more mining operations to Highway 89 at the top of Yarnell Hill. (The road comes out just north of St. Mary's Catholic Church.) It's fun to search out some of the old gold mines and ghost towns surrounding Wickenburg. Caution is needed on these dirt roads; get local advice on conditions and avoid traveling after heavy rains.

Yarnell Hill Lookout

Southbound travelers can stop at a pullout for a sweeping view of the desert and distant mountains below. The lookout lies 25 miles north of Wickenburg and a half mile south of Yarnell on Highway 89. Northbound travelers don't have access to this stop.

Shrine of St. Joseph

A short trail with steps climbs past statues and plaques depicting the Stations of the Cross. Giant granite boulders weathered out of the hillside add to the beauty of the spot; donations welcome. Turn west one-half mile at the sign in central Yarnell.

Yarnell and Peeples Valley

Yarnell offers the **Oak Park Motel & RV Park** (928/427-6383, $46 s, $51 d, $20 RV w/hookups, $12 tent with showers), and several cafés. The **Yarnell–Peeples Valley Chamber of Commerce** (928/427-6582) can tell you about the area.

Joshua Forest

Joshua trees *(Yucca brevifolia)* line U.S. Highway 93 for 18 miles between Mileposts 180 and 162. You'll see the first ones about 22 miles northwest of Wickenburg. Large clusters of pale-green flowers appear from early February to early April.

Burro Creek Recreation Site

If you're driving between Wickenburg and Kingman, you'll pass this picturesque spot. A perennial stream flows through a scenic canyon area (elev. 1,960 ft.), feeding deep blue pools and lush greenery in the desert. Open all year, it's a great place to take a break from the long drive on U.S. Highway 93; day use is free. Visitors enjoy camping, picnicking, birding, swimming, hiking, four-wheeling, and rockhounding for agates and Apache tears. A cactus garden and interpretive signs introduce life of the desert. Hikers can head up the creekbed if the water isn't too high—the creek extends some 40 miles upstream and goes through the heart of **Burro Creek Wilderness;** downstream is private land. The campground ($10/night) has drinking water, flush toilets, and a dump station, but no showers. For information and group campsite ($30) reservations, contact the Kingman Field Office of the BLM (2475 Beverly Ave., Kingman, AZ 86401, 928/692-4400, www.az.blm.gov). Head northwest 63 miles from Wickenburg on U.S. Highway 93 or southeast 65 miles from Kingman on I-40 and U.S. Highway 93, then turn west 1.3 miles at the sign. An overlook on the west side of the highway near the bridge provides a fine panorama of the area.

The Apache Trail

Driving east through Phoenix, Tempe, Mesa, and Apache Junction, you might think the city will never end. But as soon as you head east on Highway 88 from Apache Junction, the shopping centers, gas stations, and hamburger stands fade away, and you're left with just the desert, lakes, and mountains.

The Tonto National Forest (www.fs.fed.us/r3/tonto) offices provide recreation information for the Apache Trail and many of the places of interest along it, such as the Superstition Wilderness and Roosevelt Lake. The **Supervisor's Office** (2324 E. McDowell Rd., Phoenix, AZ 85006, 602/225-5200, 8 A.M.–4:30 P.M. Mon.–Fri.) covers the entire Tonto National Forest. You're more likely to reach people with first-hand experience at the **Mesa Ranger District Office** (5140 E. Ingram St., Mesa, AZ 85205, 480/610-3300, 8 A.M.–4:30 P.M. Mon.–Fri.) for the western Apache Trail and the Superstition and Four Peaks Wilderness Areas and the **Tonto Basin Ranger District Office** (HC 02, Box 4800, Roosevelt, AZ 85545, 928/467-3200, 7:45 A.M.–4:30 P.M. daily) for the eastern Apache Trail and Roosevelt Lake area.

SUPERSTITION WILDERNESS

Some of the Southwest's best desert hikes wind through the canyons and mountains of this 160,200-acre wilderness. It lies south of the Salt River Canyon and Apache Trail, about 40 miles east of Phoenix. Elevations range from about 2,000 feet along the west boundary to over 6,000 feet in the eastern uplands. Desert vegetation dominates, but a few pockets of ponderosa pine hang onto the highest slopes. Wildflowers may put on colorful extravaganzas in early spring and following summer rains.

Gold Fever

Legends tell of Don Miguel Peralta discovering fantastic amounts of gold somewhere in the

Superstitions in 1845. He and most of his miners, however, met their deaths at the hands of Apache and took the location of Peralta's Sombrero Mine to their graves. At least one member of Peralta's party survived the massacre, the stories go, and some 30 years later revealed the location of the mine to a German immigrant, Jacob Waltz. Locally known as The Dutchman, Waltz worked the mine without ever revealing its location. Those who tried to follow him into the Superstitions either became lost in the maze of canyons or were found murdered. The power of the Lost Dutchman legends has intensified since the prospector's death in 1891.

The stories about Jacob Waltz and his Lost Dutchman Mine may be just tall tales. Despite the efforts of thousands of gold-crazed prospectors, no major finds have ever been confirmed. Geologists studying the mountains say that they are remnants of volcanic calderas, an unlikely source of rich veins of precious metal. Perhaps the crafty Dutchman worked as a fence for gold thieves employed in the Vulture Mine near Wickenburg. Miners stealing nuggets wouldn't be able to sell their loot in Wickenburg, so Waltz may have run a gold-laundering operation by caching the Vulture gold in the Superstitions. If so, he still has a lot of people fooled, even after 100 years!

Climate

Spring and autumn bring the most pleasant weather for a visit to the Superstitions. Winter is often fine at lower elevations, though snow and cold hit the higher areas. Summer (May–Oct.) gets unbearably hot. Temperatures can exceed 115°F in the shade—and there's precious little of that. You can venture into the Superstitions in the summer on a crack-of-dawn journey, then be out by late morning when the heat hits. Carry plenty of water, especially in summer when springs and creeks dry up.

Hiking

The 12 trailheads and 180 miles of trail offer all kinds of possibilities. Because they're so close to Phoenix, the Superstitions get unusually heavy traffic for a wilderness area. The west half, especially near the Peralta and First Water trailheads, receives the most visitors. You're more likely to see javelina, desert mule deer, mountain lion, black bear, and other wildlife in the eastern part of the range. You don't need a permit to hike or camp in the Superstitions; just leave the area as you found it and limit groups to 15 people and stays to 14 days. Horses are allowed, but bring feed, as grazing is prohibited. Laws protect the wilderness from prospecting involving surface disturbance, so no one can file new claims. For additional information, check with the Forest Service offices and take a look at guidebooks such as *Hikers Guide to the Superstition Wilderness* by Jack Carlson and Elizabeth Stewart.

FOUR PEAKS WILDERNESS

This wilderness area covers 60,743 acres in the southern Mazatzal Mountains, located north across the Salt River Canyon from the Superstition Mountains. Four Peaks—visible over a large section of central Arizona—have long been a major landmark. From their deeply incised lower slopes along Canyon Lake at an elevation of 1,600 feet, the mountains top off at Browns Peak, northernmost of the four, at 7,657 feet.

Vegetation ranges from saguaro cactus at the base to ponderosa pine, Douglas fir, and aspen near the top. Javelina, deer, black bear, mountain lion, and smaller animals inhabit the slopes. Arizona's highest concentration of black bear live here; wise campers use bear canisters or hang food out of reach at night. Trailheads can be reached from Highway 87 on the west (northeast of Mesa) and from Highway 188 on the east (northwest of Roosevelt Dam). Lone Pine Saddle Trailhead is the most popular, though the 6,500-foot elevation can get snow in winter; access is easiest from the Roosevelt Lake side, but a high-clearance vehicle is still needed. A huge fire in 1996, caused by two careless campers near Lone Pine Saddle, burned 61,000 acres, though all trails have reopened.

APACHE JUNCTION TO THEODORE ROOSEVELT DAM

Once a raiding route for Apache, the Apache Trail (AZ 88) still has a primitive and imposing character. It twists and climbs as it tries to find a way through the rugged land. Jagged ridges, towering cliffs, and the desert itself inspire awe among travelers. Much of the Apache Trail, now designated a National Scenic Byway, is graded dirt. Due to narrow bridges and blind curves, the road isn't recommended for large trailers or large RVs. From the Phoenix area, take the Superstition Freeway or other roads east to Apache Junction and follow signs for Highway 88.

Horsin' Around

OK Corral (480/982-4040, www.okcorrals.com) offers hourly guided horseback rides into the nearby Goldfield Mountains and day and overnight trips in the Superstitions. RV sites cost $25 w/hookups. At the beginning of the Apache Trail, turn north five miles on Idaho Road, turn east one mile on McKellips Road, then turn left at the sign.

Superstition Mountain Museum

Exhibits (480/983-4888, www.superstitionmountainmuseum.org, 9 A.M.–4 P.M. daily, $4 adults, $3 seniors 55+, $2 youth 6–17) introduce the region's geology, wildlife, prehistoric tribes, prospectors, miners, cowboys, and military. You'll learn about the Lost Dutchman Mine and have an opportunity to decode maps of it. A lecture series runs January–March. The gift shop offers a great selection of Southwestern books, jewelry, and crafts; you can also pick up tourist literature on the area. Outside, you can admire massive limestone blocks of Roosevelt Dam and a 20-stamp mill. Stagecoach rides go December–mid-April. The museum is about 3.5 miles down the Apache Trail on your right, 1 mile before Goldfield Ghost Town.

Goldfield Ghost Town and Mine Tours

The original mining camp of Goldfield boomed in the mid-1890s with the discovery of gold. Its population peaked at 5,000 before drifting away after mining yields dwindled in 1915. Nothing remains of the tent and adobe buildings, and the actual mine is too dangerous to enter, but you can see a lot of history and artifacts in today's reconstruction on the site (Mile 4.5 along the Trail).

Goldfield Ghost Town (480/983-0333, www.goldfieldghosttown.com, about 10 A.M.–5 P.M. daily) features many activities and exhibits. Admission is free—you just pay for the attractions that interest you. Things slow down in summer when some businesses may go to shorter hours or close weekdays.

Outdoor exhibits among the weathered buildings include an authentic headframe, hoists, ore cars, a five-stamp mill, and miners' tools. In the re-created **underground mine** ($6 adults, $3 children 6–12), modeled after the nearby Mammoth Mine—one of the world's richest until closed by flooding—a guide takes you on a 25-minute tour and explains how miners tunneled and worked in the stope. A nearby shop offers gold panning and gold nugget jewelry.

Superstition Scenic Railroad (daily Nov.–May, Thurs.–Sun. June–Oct.) rolls down its narrow-gauge tracks with a narrated tour of the history and geology of the Goldfield area. Up on the hill, **Goldfield Superstition Museum** displays old photos, a Lost Dutchman Hunter Hall of Fame, a mineral collection, and an 1886 Brunswick bar that served Goldfield miners. A bit farther up the street, you can climb the stairs to the **Bordello Museum** (10 A.M.–5 P.M. Fri.–Sun.), where the women will explain how lonely miners of bygone years found companionship. A church at the end of the lane has Sunday services and hosts weddings. Other attractions at Goldfield include a live reptile exhibit, horseback and carriage rides (both closed in summer), and a photo studio. Gunslingers shoot up the town Friday–Sunday from January to April. You can shop for Western duds, crafts, jewelry, rocks, and sweets.

Apache Trail Tours (480/982-7661, www.apachetrailtours.com) offers year-round Jeep and hiking trips along the Apache Trail and in the Superstition and Four Peaks mountains.

If you'd like to stay the night in the ghost town, **Goldfield Boarding House** (480/983-0333) offers old-style rooms. If you get a hankerin' for some grub, **Mammoth Steakhouse and Saloon** (480/983-6402) serves lunch and dinner daily but lacks a nonsmoking area; bands entertain some nights. A bakery down the street prepares breakfasts and lunches.

The best place for dinner is the nearby **Mining Camp Restaurant** (480/982-3181) with Western fare in a replica of an old mining camp's cook shanty. It's open daily October–June for dinner and Sunday for lunch ($18–20 adults, discounts for children, seniors, and cash payment; reservations recommended). From Goldfield, head .2 miles back toward Apache Junction, then turn left 1 mile at the sign.

Lost Dutchman State Park

At Mile 5.4, the park (480/982-4485, $6/vehicle day use) offers picnicking, day hiking, and camping at the base of the Superstition Mountains. Staff present interpretive programs October–April, including evening talks (usually Fri.) and guided hikes (usually Sat.). The **Native Plant Trail** loop near the park entrance identifies desert plants on a paved and wheelchair-accessible path. Longer trails loop onto the slopes of the adjacent Superstition Mountains in the Tonto National Forest; ask for a map at the ranger station. **Treasure Loop Trail** has views and a variety of desert plants along its 2.4-mile length. Connecting trails allow for a variety of other loops too, and extend north to First Water Road and south and east to Hieroglyphic Canyon and Peralta Trailhead. **Siphon Draw Trail** climbs into the high country, 3.2 miles round-trip, to a basin at an elevation of 3,100 feet; adventurous hikers can continue up a rough route to the Flatiron (4,862 ft.), a five-hour, five-mile total round-trip.

Individual campsites ($12/vehicle no hookups, $20 w/electricity) are first-come, first-served; only groups can reserve areas. Showers and a dump station are included. The popular campground may fill January–mid-April, so plan to arrive early then.

First Water Trailhead

Just down the highway from the state park you'll enter Tonto National Forest and come to the turnoff for First Water Trailhead, three miles in on the right. It's a popular starting point for hikes in the Superstition Wilderness. Parking runs $4 a day or free with a golden passport or National Parks Pass with hologram.

Different Points of View

At Mile 7.8, **Needle Vista Viewpoint** provides a good look at Weaver's Needle in the Superstitions. The Lost Dutchman Mine is said to lie in the shadow of this striking 4,535-foot pinnacle, which still beckons to gold seekers. The pinnacle's name honors frontier scout Pauline Weaver. Local Apache had a different appellation for it, relating to a certain part of a stallion's anatomy.

Farther down the highway you'll come to **Canyon Lake Vista Point** at Mile 12.5. The series of lakes along the Salt River provides fishing and boating for visitors and precious water for Phoenix. Past the viewpoint, the road sweeps down from the heights to the lakeshore.

Canyon Lake

Mormon Flat Dam, completed in 1925, created this reservoir. Anglers have hooked largemouth and yellow bass, trout, catfish, bluegill, carp, walleye, and crappie. During the busy mid-spring–mid-summer season, Sunday crowds sometimes fill all available parking places in the Canyon Lake area; try to arrive early then.

Acacia Picnic Site (at Mile 14.5) offers swimming at a gravel beach and fishing, $4 per vehicle. Nearby **Palo Verde Boating Site** (Mile 14.7) has a boat ramp and restrooms but no picnic tables, $4 per vehicle and $2 per watercraft. **Boulder Recreation Site** (Mile 14.9) provides a swimming beach, picnic tables, and wheelchair-accessible fishing; $4 per vehicle.

At Mile 15.2, you'll come to **Canyon Lake Marina** (602/944-6504) with a campground, restaurant, boat tours, fishing supplies, and boat rentals and storage. **Laguna Beach Campground** offers year-round lakeshore sites for picnicking ($15), tent camping ($18), and RV camping ($20 dry, $30 w/hookups), showers included. **Lakeside Restaurant & Cantina** (480/288-8290) features steak, chicken, and seafood; open for breakfast weekends, lunch daily, and dinner Friday–Sunday with indoor seating and patio tables overlooking the lake. The ***Dolly Steamboat*** (480/827-9144, www.dollysteamboat.com) takes visitors on scenic 90-minute narrated cruises daily at noon and 2 P.M. Tues.–Sun.; lunch and dinner cruises go some days and require reservations; the vessel's double decks have both indoor and outdoor seating.

Boulder Canyon Trail #103 begins across the highway from the marina and climbs up a ridge to spectacular views of the Superstitions and Canyon Lake area. The trail continues on through La Barge and Boulder Canyons, linking with several other trails in the Superstition Wilderness.

Only boaters can access **the Point** camping area; it's on the left, three miles upstream from the marina. Continuing down the highway, you'll soon come to **Laguna Boating Site** (Mile 15.5), $4 per vehicle and $2 per watercraft.

Tortilla Flat and Vicinity

Tortilla Flat (480/984-1776, www.tortillaflataz.com) is just a tiny community (pop. 6), but it's the only one along this section of road (Mile 17.3). The faded Western-style buildings—including a café, post office, country store, and curio shop—look as though they're from a movie set. Old mining and farming relics lie around. A hungry pioneer, who perceived the surrounding rock outcrops as stacks of tortillas, reportedly gave the place its name. The country store has an ice cream parlor—try a scoop of prickly pear. The café, wallpapered with dollar bills, serves American and Mexican meals.

Tortilla Campground (elev. 1,752 ft.) across the highway is popular with RVers thanks to the large spaces (RVs up to 40 ft.) and water and sewer hookups; electric hookups may be available at some sites. Cost is $12 per night and there's usually room. One section has been designated a quiet area (no generators) for tenters and solar-powered RVs. Summer temperatures get hot by mid-April in this canyon setting, so the campground closes May–September. Note that the gate closes from sunset to sunrise.

Continuing down the highway, you'll reach the end of the pavement at Mile 23.0 and the beginning of 22 miles of graded dirt road to Roosevelt Dam. A mile farther, **Tortilla Trailhead** for the Superstition Wilderness is on the right.

Fish Creek Hill to Apache Lake

At Mile 24.9, **Fish Creek Hill Scenic Vista** on the left is well worth a stop and has a restroom. The paved path leads to overlooks of rugged canyons, and there's a very good chance of seeing desert bighorn sheep. Four Peaks rises to the north.

The descent down Fish Creek Hill provides a thrill, especially for the driver, who must negotiate sharp bends as the road traverses a cliff face and drops 1,500 feet in three miles. Fish Creek, near the bottom, is said to have native Gila chub and Gila topminnow. Hikers can head up Fish Creek Canyon.

At Mile 30.6 on the right, Forest Road 212 goes three bumpy miles to **Reavis Trailhead.** Reavis Ranch Trail #109 climbs into ponderosa pine forests near Reavis Ranch in the eastern part of the Superstition Wilderness. Elisha Reavis lived a hermit's life on his ranch from 1872 until his death in 1896.

At Mile 32.4, **Apache Lake Vista** provides views of the lake in the canyon below. Held back by Horse Mesa Dam, Apache Lake reaches nearly to Roosevelt Lake—a distance of 17 miles. Turn left here 1.3 miles for **Apache Lake Marina and Resort** (928/467-2511, www.apachelake.com). The motel offers rooms ($65–75 d) and suites with kitchens ($80–90 d). RV sites go for $20, and include hookups and showers. Tenters can camp in shoreline areas for just $5. Day use at the resort also costs $5. The restaurant (daily breakfast, lunch, and dinner) features steak, chicken, and seafood among other American and some Mexican items. Other amenities include a swimming beach, store with fishing and camping supplies, boat ramp, fishing- and pontoon-boat rentals, car and boat fuel, and boat storage. Anglers can catch smallmouth and largemouth bass, trout, yellow bass, catfish, sunfish, and walleye. Officers staff the **Maricopa County Sheriff Aid Station** (928/467-2619) at the lake on weekends and holidays.

At Mile 34.5, unpaved Forest Road 250 leads down one mile to **Davis Wash** on the lake; this undeveloped area has outhouses and costs $4 per vehicle for day use or camping, and $2 per watercraft. The riparian vegetation here grows on a floodplain surrounded by desert hillsides.

The turnoff may have no sign; look for it between Mileposts 231 and 232.

At Mile 39.5 (Milepost 236) you'll pass the sign for **Burnt Corral Recreation Site,** which lies one-third mile to the left on a paved road. Mesquite trees shade the picnicking and camping sites on the shore of Apache Lake at an elevation of 2,060 feet. Visitors enjoy the delightful setting and well-spaced sites in addition to a beach, drinking water, fish-cleaning station, and paved boat ramp. Day use is $4 per vehicle and $2 per watercraft. Camping costs $10 for a single space (up to two vehicles) and $15 for a double. Sites tend to fill on most weekends except in winter. Dispersed camping is possible along the shore at the adjacent **Lower Burnt Corral,** but this area is a floodplain; turn left through the gate just past the fee station.

At Mile 40.2, **Upper Burnt Corral** offers a primitive lakeshore area in a small cove; drive .7 miles on the Apache Trail beyond the Burnt Corral junction, then turn left half a mile on unpaved Forest Road 52, which may have no sign.

Three Mile Wash is another primitive area a bit farther up the lake at Mile 42.3; the unmarked turnoff is at a bend of the Apache Trail near Milepost 239. A bumpy dirt road leads .2 miles down to the lake in a floodplain area. These undeveloped sites have a fee of $4 per vehicle and $2 per watercraft for day or overnight use. Outhouses are the only facilities, but you can get water at Burnt Corral.

From Three Mile Wash, the Apache Trail begins a climb through Apache Lake Gorge to Roosevelt Dam. You can enjoy the views at Theodore Roosevelt Dam Interpretive Overlook—which also has restrooms—near Milepost 241 before the dam and at Inspiration Point Interpretive Overlook near Milepost 242 after the dam.

Theodore Roosevelt Dam

An engineering feat in its day, the 284-foot-high structure is still the world's highest masonry dam. The arduous task of cutting and placing the stone blocks lasted from 1903 to 1911, when President Teddy Roosevelt motored over the Apache Trail for the dedication ceremony. By the late 20th century, engineers worried that the original dam couldn't survive a moderate earthquake or a massive flood, so a new concrete dam was built over the old structure. It now towers 77 feet higher than before and raises the operating high-water level by 15 feet. A graceful arched suspension bridge spans the lake just above the dam.

THEODORE ROOSEVELT LAKE

Fed by Tonto Creek from the north and the Salt River from the east, the reservoir stretches 23 miles long and as much as 2 miles wide. With approximately 19,199 surface acres when full, it's the largest of the four Salt River lakes. Summers at Roosevelt's 2,151-foot elevation are as hot as those in the Valley, but water-skiing and boating attract many visitors. Anglers enjoy the rest of the year. Known as a good bass and crappie lake, Roosevelt also contains catfish and sunfish.

Great Basin Canada geese take up residence during the winter at Bermuda Flat on the north arm. Part of this area is closed to the public November 15–February 15, but you can view the geese from the highway.

Information

Staff at the **Tonto Basin Ranger District office** (HC 02, Box 4800, Roosevelt, AZ 85545, 928/467-3200, www.fs.fed.us/r3/tonto, 7:45 A.M.–4:30 P.M. daily) in Roosevelt, 1.3 miles southeast of the dam on Highway 188, can tell you about area facilities, fishing, hiking, camping, and boating. The exhibit room has displays of wildlife and illustrates the Tonto Basin's prehistoric Hohokam and Salado and historic Apache residents. A video and exhibits chronicle Theodore Roosevelt Dam's construction and its 1990s modifications. You can purchase annual passes for the Roosevelt Lake recreation sites as well as regional books and maps. A few picnic tables are outside.

Recreation Areas

Fluctuating lake levels determine which boat ramps and recreation sites will be open, so it's a good idea to check with the Tonto Basin Ranger District office before coming out. The Forest Service offers developed campgrounds, primitive camping areas, and boat ramps along the west shore. Camp hosts can be found at the developed and some primitive camping areas except in summer. Daily fees run $10 single (up to two vehicles) and $15 double for the developed campgrounds, $4 for day or overnight use of primitive areas, and $2 per watercraft. You'll find fish-cleaning stations at Grapevine, Cholla, and Windy Hill. A dump station is on Highway 188 opposite the Cholla Recreation Site.

Horses are welcome at **Frazier Campground** and adjacent **Frazier Group Campground** (reserve through the Tonto Basin Ranger District office); sites have water but no showers. A path for equestrians and hikers goes under the highway and connects with Frazier Trailhead for trips to the Arizona Trail and Superstitions. **Cottonwood Cove Picnic Site,** just before the campgrounds, has free day use. From Roosevelt, drive .3 miles southeast on Highway 188 across the bridge, then turn left.

Cholla Recreation Site (5.8 miles northwest of Roosevelt) and **Windy Hill Recreation Site** (2.5 miles southeast of Roosevelt, then north 2 miles on a paved road) have campgrounds with water, solar showers, boat ramps, and playgrounds, but no hookups; both also offer long-term camping—up to six months—from October to March. **Blevins Picnic Site** in Windy Hill Recreation Site is free. **Grapevine Group Site** (5.5 miles southeast of Roosevelt, then north 2.5 miles) has paved roads, a boat ramp, and showers; reserve through the Tonto Basin Ranger District office. Grapevine Wash (open gate on left just before the Grapevine Group Site) is a primitive camping area.

Vineyard Picnic Area, 3.5 miles northwest of Roosevelt on Highway 188, has free day use. Primitive camping areas include Grapevine Wash, Bachelor Cove (5.1 miles northwest of Roosevelt), Cholla Bay (5.6 miles northwest of Roosevelt), and Bermuda Flat (about 8 miles northwest of Roosevelt, but closed Nov. 15–Feb. 15 for the Canada geese).

If you'd like more solitude and don't mind driving on unpaved roads, you can head over to the east side of the lake via the A-Cross Road; this dry-weather route runs between Highway 188 at the north end of the lake (a ford over Tonto Creek may be too high at times) and the Young Road (AZ 288). Salome (SAL-oh-may) Creek in the south end of Salome Wilderness cuts through a narrow canyon, a challenging route for experienced canyoneers, accessible from A-Cross Trailhead.

Diversion Dam Recreation Area, on the Salt River just above its entrance to Roosevelt Lake, offers several access points for river runners who can launch canoes and rafts below the dam. People also come for birding, fishing, and playing in the water. The recreation area has toilets but no drinking water or charge. From the Highway 188–Highway 288 junction 14 miles southeast of the dam and 15 miles northwest of Globe, turn north 4 miles on Highway 288, then turn left on Forest Road 465. Across the river, **Diversion Dam Recreation Area** offers picnic tables under the mesquite and a viewpoint of the diversion dam, completed in 1906; a sign explains the importance that the dam and Roosevelt Power Canal had during construction of Roosevelt Dam. The turnoff is on the left, 1.5 miles farther north on Highway 288 and across the Salt River Bridge; the Tonto Basin Ranger District office has a map.

Services

Roosevelt Marina (in Roosevelt beside the turnoff for Tonto Basin Ranger District office, 928/467-2245, www.azmarinas.com) has a primitive campground ($6 plus $2/watercraft), boat rentals (fishing and pontoon), wet and dry boat storage, a paved boat ramp, a snack bar, gasoline for boats, and a store; it may close Monday–Thursday. **Lakeview Mobile Home Park** across the highway (928/467-2203) has RV spaces with hookups for $26.

Spring Creek RV Park & Motel (8.4 miles southeast of Roosevelt and .6 miles northwest of the Roosevelt Lake Resort turnoff, 928/467-2888, www.rooseveltlake.com) offers rooms at $45 d ($65 d with kitchen), RV sites at $20 with hookups, and a nine-hole golf course. The nearby restaurant, open daily for lunch and dinner, lacks a nonsmoking area. **Spring Creek Store** sells groceries, gasoline, and camping and fishing supplies. **Roosevelt Post Office** lies across the highway.

Roosevelt Lake Resort (928/467-2276) is 9 miles southeast of Roosevelt (or 17 miles northwest of Globe), then east .6 miles. Rooms cost $30 s, $35 d; cabins have kitchens (bring your own cookware) and run $35 s, $40 d. Expect to pay more on summer weekends. The restaurant—which fails to provide a nonsmoking area—serves breakfast, lunch, and dinner daily, though it doesn't open until 10 A.M. on weekdays. **Rock House Grocery** (5.5 miles north on AZ 288/Young Hwy., 928/467-2484) offers provisions, gasoline, and a trailer park (usually full).

In Punkin Center, a village 20 miles northwest of Roosevelt off Highway 188, you can stay at **Punkin Center Lodge** (928/479-2229); rates for up to four people run $39 ($52 kitchenette). Next door, the **Steakhouse** (928/479-2627) is open most days for lunch and dinner; there's live entertainment on Friday and Saturday. RV parks are nearby.

TONTO NATIONAL MONUMENT

Two well-preserved cliff dwellings constructed by the prehistoric Salado overlook the blue waters of Roosevelt Lake. The Salado lived in this part of the Salt River Valley about A.D. 1150–1450. Skillful farmers, they dug irrigation canals to water their corn, squash, beans, grain amaranth, and cotton. They also roamed the desert hills for cactus fruits, mesquite beans, deer, pronghorn, and many other wild foods. Crafts included beautiful polychrome pottery and intricately woven cotton cloth.

At first they built small, scattered pueblos along the river, but about A.D. 1250 some Salado began living on more defensible ridge tops. From 1300 until their departure soon after 1400, part of the population moved into caves like those in the monument.

Exhibits (HC 02, Box 4602, Roosevelt, AZ 85545, 928/467-2241, www.nps.gov/tont, 8 A.M.–5 P.M. daily except Dec. 25, $3/person age 16 and up) illustrate how the Salado lived and what we know of their history. Stone tools, pottery, cotton cloth, and other artifacts reveal their artistic talents. You can watch a video introduction and shop for books and maps. A nature trail near the visitors center identifies desert plants. The visitors center is south 1 mile off Highway 188, 1.8 miles southeast of Roosevelt, and 24 miles northwest of Globe. A picnic area with water is on the left, halfway in from the highway to the visitors center. If you're driving the Apache Trail Loop, this is the halfway point in time; Apache Junction is about three hours away.

The self-guided trail on the hillside above and behind the visitors center leads up to the **Lower Cliff Dwelling.** Originally the cave contained 19 rooms, with another 12 in the annex outside, but those exposed to the weather have worn away. Allow one hour for the trip, on which you'll climb 350 feet on a paved path; the trail closes at 4 P.M.

The **Upper Cliff Dwelling,** reached by a different trail, is about twice the size of the Lower, but it's farther away and requires advance planning. You can visit the Upper Cliff Dwelling only on ranger-guided tours, which are conducted November–April; call or write to check on days and times. The free tours last about three hours and involve a three-mile round-trip hike with an elevation gain of 600 feet.

SALT RIVER CANYON WILDERNESS

The Salt River dances through 51 miles of lively white water from the U.S. Highway 60 bridge north of Globe down to the Highway 288 bridge near Roosevelt Lake. Boaters can raft or kayak on 1- or 2-day trips on the upper section or run the entire stretch in 3–5 days. Midweek travel gives the best chance for solitude, especially in the upper section. Only experienced river-runners should attempt this wild water, as several rapids through the twisting canyons have a rating of Class IV. The bigger rapids have earned names such as Baptism, Maytag Chute, Reforma, Overboard, Cliff Hanger, and Wakeup.

Rafting companies supply skilled crew and all the equipment so that anyone in good health can go through. Trips use paddle rafts (everyone participates in paddling), oar boats (only the guide rows), and combinations of the two. The companies request several weeks' advance notice on all the trips. Contact the Globe Ranger Dis-

COURTESY OF THE NATIONAL PARK SERVICE

one of two cliff dwellings at Tonto National Monument

trict office (7680 S. Six Shooter Canyon Rd., Globe, AZ 85501, 928/402-6200) for a list of current rafting outfits.

The Forest Service requires visitor groups to be no more than 15, to use suitable nonmotorized craft, and to practice no-trace camping. Large rafts over 15 feet can be too unwieldy; open canoes will swamp. Because the Salt has become very popular, all river users must use a fire pan, carry out all non-burnable trash, and pack out all human solid waste.

Flow levels depend on the winter snowpack, so springtime affords the best chance of sufficient water. The liveliest rapids (Class III–IV) most commonly occur mid-March–early April, and the weather is usually reliable after late March. Bridge-to-bridge trips depend on water level—fast flows in early season (March and April) make it a three-day float; lower flows later in the season (May or June) make for four- or five-day trips. The Salt River Project has a recording of flow rates (602/236-5929), or you can check the USGS website at http://az.water.usgs.gov/. Generally for the Salt River, 750 cfs is considered low water and 4,000 cfs or above is high water.

Permits

Rafting companies take care of the needed permits for their trips. Private parties must plan well ahead. You'll need a tribal permit along the upper stretch, because part of the south shore belongs to the San Carlos Apache tribe and the north shore to the White Mountain Apache, who issue the permits; permits won't be required if you start from Horseshoe Bend and maybe from Gleason Flat (check). The store near the U.S. Highway 60 bridge and other outlets on the reservation sell tribal permits, which are easily obtained. For information on the tribal permits, contact the Hon-Dah Ski and Sport Shop (928/369-7669) or the White Mountain Game & Fish Dept. (P.O. Box 220, White River, AZ 85941, 928/338-4385). The Forest Service requires a permit March 1–May 15 for the wilderness section between Gleason Flat and Roosevelt Lake. Since demand far exceeds available dates, permits are issued by a lottery system; contact the Globe Ranger District office (928/402-6200). Both the Globe Ranger District and Phoenix Supervisors (602/225-5200) offices have a detailed booklet on the Upper Salt River.

GLOBE

Tucked into a narrow valley between the Apache Mountains to the northeast and the Pinal Mountains to the south and west, Globe is a handy stopping place for travelers. The town's 3,500-foot elevation provides a pleasant climate most of the year. Though its times of glory as a big copper-mining center have long passed, Globe still has a lot of character. On a drive down Broad Street you can visit its museum, view ruins of the Old Dominion Copper Mine, and see many buildings dating from the early 1900s.

The chamber of commerce, also on Broad Street, offers a leaflet, *Walking Tour of Historic Downtown Globe,* that details the history of these old structures. You can also pick up a *Globe–Miami Drive Yourself Highway Mine Tour* leaflet describing six mines, historic and modern, visible from U.S. Highway 60 in the Globe and Miami areas; none of the mine sites is open to the public. Antique, craft, and gift shops abound in Globe and Miami; the chamber has a list.

In 1875, prospectors struck silver in the hills of the western part of the San Carlos Apache Indian Reservation. The most remarkable find, a globe-shaped silver nugget, reportedly had the rough outlines of the continents scarred on its surface. Miners set up camp on the east bank of Pinal Creek, but their presence, and the government's taking back of reservation lands here, didn't go over well with the Apache, who regularly menaced the camp until Geronimo's surrender in 1886.

The silver began to give out after only four years, but by then rich copper deposits had been discovered beneath the silver lodes. The Old Dominion Copper Company moved in, and during the early 1900s its copper mine ranked as one of the greatest in the world. Globe prospered too—the town's 50 restaurants and saloons operated around the clock and about 150 sporting women worked out of little shacks along N. Broad Street. George W. P. Hunt arrived in 1881 as a young man and became a leading merchant and banker before going on to serve as Arizona's first governor. Labor troubles and declining yields began to eat into mining profits, and the Depression shut

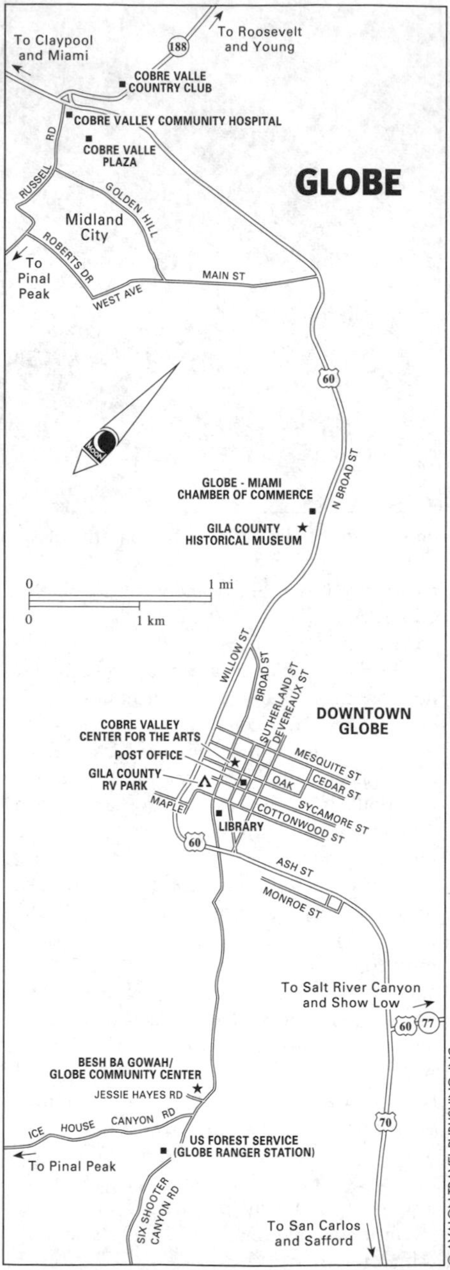

down the Old Dominion completely in 1931. Copper mining shifted to nearby Miami, leaving Globe as a quiet county seat.

Gila County Historical Museum

This varied collection (1330 N. Broad St., 928/425-7385, 10 A.M.–4 P.M. Mon.–Fri., 11 A.M.–3 P.M. Sat., donations welcome) illustrates the area's Native American, pioneer, ranching, and mining history. The Indian Room displays prehistoric pottery and some fine modern baskets. Period exhibits—mine superintendent's office, ranch room, printing shop, and Governor Hunt's bedroom—recall life in early Globe. The museum building, which dates from 1914, served as the company's mine rescue station for many years. It's next door to the chamber of commerce and opposite the Old Dominion Copper Co. Mine.

Cobre Valley Center for the Arts

Local artists banded together to open an art gallery (101 N. Broad St., 928/425-0884, noon–4P.M. Sun., 10 A.M.–5 P.M. Mon.–Fri., 10 A.M.–4 P.M. Sat., free) in the old Gila County Courthouse, built in 1906–1907. The imposing old building stands downtown at the corner of Broad and Oak Streets; wheelchair access is on Oak Street. A theater upstairs hosts performances by the Copper Cities Community Players. Go downstairs to see works of the stained-glass studio, the craft guild shop, and a scrapbooking shop. A gift shop sells colorful art and crafts.

Besh Ba Gowah

Archaeologists count 200 rooms at this pueblo, built and inhabited between A.D. 1225 and 1450, at a time when Salado villages lined both sides of Pinal Creek. An earlier village of pit houses associated with the Hohokam stood on this site about A.D. 600–1150. Exposed to the elements, Besh Ba Gowah has been weathered more than the Tonto National Monument cliff dwellings, but its extensive foundations and few remaining walls testify to its original size. The name Besh Ba Gowah comes from an Apache word meaning "metal camp."

The museum (928/425-0320, 9 A.M.–5 P.M. daily, $3 ages 12+, $2 seniors) offers an introductory video, displays of pottery and other Salado artifacts, a scale model of the village as it might have looked in 1325, a small research library, and a gift shop. Follow the self-guided trail through the ruins—some restored, some only stabilized, some still unexcavated. Baskets, pots, ladders, and other implements in the restored rooms appear as if the Salado had just departed.

Besh Ba Gowah is 1.5 miles south of downtown Globe; follow S. Broad Street to the sign, turn right across the bridge, curve left on Jesse Hayes Road 1 mile, make a sharp right up to Globe Community Center, and follow signs around to the far side of the ruin. The adjacent park offers covered picnic tables, ball fields, and a summertime swimming pool. An ethnobotanical garden next to the ruin entrance contains crops once grown by the Salado. Globe Botanical Garden, on the hillside below, is reached by a trail from the ethnobotanical garden or from parking off Jesse Hayes Road.

Round Mountain Park

The conical hill on the northeast side of town offers hiking, views, and picnicking. Four interconnecting trails provide a way to the top (a 426-foot climb) in loops of 1.7, 2.4, or 3 miles. From downtown, head east on Ash Street, then turn left (north) .6 miles on South Street, just past the Comfort Inn.

Pinal Peak

A dirt road winds up the timber-clad slopes to the summit at 7,812 feet. Weather permitting, you'll enjoy great views, hiking, picnicking, and two of the coolest campgrounds in the Tonto National Forest.

For the 18-mile drive from Globe, follow S. Broad Street, turn right across the bridge, curve left on Jesse Hayes Road to the junction of Ice House Canyon and Six Shooter Canyon Roads, turn right 2.5 miles on Ice House Canyon Road, turn right 3 miles on Kellner Canyon Road/Forest Road 55 (pavement ends), then left 12.5 miles on Forest Road 651 to the summit. An alternative approach follows Russell Road from U.S. Highway 60 (opposite the AZ 188 turnoff); keep right on Russell Road at a fork .3 miles in and continue south on what becomes Forest Road 55. Pavement ends 2.3 miles from U.S. Highway 60 and the road climbs up to the junction of Forest Road 651 in another 3.4 miles.

In summer, you can drive all the way to the top of Signal Peak, the highest point; at other times you must walk the last bit. Ice House Canyon, Six Shooter, Telephone, Kellner Canyon, Squaw Spring, Bobtail Ridge, and Mill Creek Trails climb steeply from the valleys below. The Globe Ranger District office has trail descriptions and maps.

Entertainment and Events

Globe Theatre (141 N. Broad St., 928/425-5581) screens current movies downtown. **Gila County Gem & Mineral Show** sparkles in late January. **Historic Home & Building Tour,** accompanied by the **Antique and Quilt Show,** takes place on Presidents Day weekend in February. **Gila County Championship Rodeo** shakes up March. Miners compete in hand drilling and other skills at Miami in the **Mining Country Boomtown Spree** in April. **Cinco de Mayo** brings entertainment and food to the Saturday nearest May 5th. The **Gold-N-Oldies Car Show** gleams in May. **Fourth of July Fireworks** enliven midsummer. The **Gila County Fair** entertains in September. **Horse races** run in late September and early October. **Apache *Jii* (Day) Celebration** on the third Saturday in October honors the nearby San Carlos Apache community with dances, crafts, and food by Apache and other Native American groups. **San Carlos Veterans Parade, Fair, & Rodeo** takes place 19 miles east on the San Carlos Apache Indian Reservation on Veterans Day weekend in November. **Christmas Light Parade** on the second Saturday of December and **Festival of Lights** at Besh Ba Gowah on the Sunday before Christmas add to holiday cheer.

Recreation

Globe Community Center has a swimming pool, picnic areas, and ball fields 1.5 miles south of downtown Globe; follow S. Broad Street, turn right across the bridge, curve left on Jesse Hayes Street 1 mile, then make a sharp right at the sign.

Cobre Valle Country Club (just north on AZ 188, 928/473-2542) is open to the public with a nine-hole golf course and tennis and racquetball courts. **Best Western Apache Gold Hotel & Casino** (928/475-7600 or 800/272-2438, www.apachegold.com) offers an 18-hole golf course seven miles east of Globe on U.S. Highway 70.

Accommodations

You'll find a good selection of independent and chain motels along U.S. Highway 60 north of downtown (N. Broad and Willow Sts.) and east of downtown (E. Ash St.). The older places are generally fine and offer great deals.

Under $50: If coming from the north you'll pass **Belle-Aire Motel** (1600 N. Broad St., 928/425-4406, $25 s, $30 d), **Economy Inn** (1105 N. Broad St., 928/425-5736, $30 s, $33 d) with a pool, **Willow Motel** (792 N. Willow St., 928/425-9491, $25s, $28 d), **El Rey Motel** (1201 E. Ash St., 928/425-4427, $24 s, $31 d), **El Rancho Motel** (1300 E. Ash St., 928/425-5757, $25 s, $32 d), and **Motel 6** (1699 E. Ash St., 928/425-5741 or 800/466-8356, $40 s, $46 d) with a pool and hot tub.

$50–100: Starting from the north, choices include the **Travelodge** (2119 W. Hwy. 60, 928/425-7008 or 800/215-4034, $58.50 d) with good mountain views, **Super 8 Motel** (637 E. Ash St., 928/425-7124 or 800/800-8000, $55 d) with a pool, **Comfort Inn** (1515 South St. at E. Ash St., 928/425-7575 or 800/228-5150, $59–69 d weekday, $79–89 d weekend) with a pool and hot tub, and **Days Inn** (1630 E. Ash St., 928/425-5500, 800/329-7466, $55 d) with a pool and hot tub. Seven miles east on U.S. Highway 70, the **Best Western Apache Gold Hotel & Casino** (928/475-7600 or 800/272-2438, $59 d weekdays, $79 d Fri.–Sat., $99–109 d Jacuzzi room) offers restaurants (all smoking), golf, pool, hot tub, and a sauna.

For a bed and breakfast inn downtown, contact **Noftsger Hill Inn** (425 North St., 928/425-2260 or 877/780-2479, www.noftsgerhillinn.com, $65–90 d) in a 1907 schoolhouse and **Cedar**

Hill B&B (175 E. Cedar St., 928/425-7530, www.cedarhill.biz, $60 d B&B or $70–80 apartment). South of downtown, **The Hideaway** (7719 Ice House Canyon Rd., 928/402-0454 or 888/692-3369) offers bed and breakfast for $55 d and apartments without breakfast for $55–95.

Campgrounds

Gila County RV Park (300 S. Pine St., 928/425-4653 or 800/436-8083) has dry sites for tents ($5) or RVs ($8) and hookup sites ($20) in a handy downtown location. No showers, but there's a batting range. Take the Maple Street Exit from U.S. Highway 60.

Tent campers and small RVs can head south to one of the Tonto National Forest campgrounds in the Pinal Mountains. The Globe Ranger District office (928/402-6200) provides recreation information and sells the Tonto Forest map. All campgrounds are free, but you need to bring your own water. **Sulphide del Rey** (elev. 4,500 ft.) is 10 miles southwest of Globe via Jesse Hayes Road, Ice House Canyon Road, Kellner Canyon Road/Forest Road 55, and Forest Road 651; open all year. **Lower Pinal** and **Upper Pinal** (elev. 7,500 ft.), accessible April–December, are about 4.5 miles past Sulphide del Rey. There are also Forest Service sites at **Pioneer Pass** (elev. 6,000 ft.), nine miles south via Jesse Hayes Road and Ice House Canyon Road/Forest Road 112, accessible May–November; the upper site has horse corrals. **Jones Water Campground** (elev. 4,500 ft.) offers sites in oaks and cottonwoods 15 miles northeast of town on U.S. Highway 60. **Timber Camp** nestles in the cool pines at an elevation of 6,000 feet, 27 miles northeast of town on U.S. Highway 60; a group site can be reserved with Globe Ranger District (928/402-6200). **Oak Flat** (elev. 4,200 ft.) offers year-round camping west on U.S. Highway 60 near Superior.

Food

For a family café that serves breakfast, lunch, and dinner daily, try **Judy's Cook House** (Cobre Valley Plaza on the west side of town, 928/425-5366) or **Country Kitchen** (1505 E. Ash St. on the east side of town, 928/425-2137). **Java Junction** (102 E. Cedar and Broad Sts., 928/402-8926, closed Sun.) offers a selection of coffees, sandwiches, and desserts downtown. Nearby, **Kelly's Broad Street Brewery** (190 Broad St., 928/425-3313, Tues.–Sat. dinner) serves up steaks, barbeque ribs, chicken, pork chops, fish, and pasta dishes along with brews; a sports bar is in the basement.

Locals love Mexican food, and you'll find some great places. **Libby's El Rey Café** (999 N. Broad St., 928/425-2054, Tues.–Sat. lunch and dinner) serves up simple but satisfying traditional Mexican food in a family-run business that's been going since the 1940s. **La Luz del Dia Restaurant and Bakery** (304 N. Broad St., 928/425-8400, Mon.–Sat. lunch and dinner) is a tiny place for breakfast and lunch downtown. **Chalo's Casa de Reynoso** (902 E. Ash St., 928/425-0515, daily lunch and dinner) is renowned for chili dishes, especially the green chili con carne and the carne adovada (spicy pork burrito with red chili sauce). For a choice of Italian, American, and some Mexican dishes, it's **Joe's Broad Street Grill** (247 S. Broad St., 928/425-4707, Mon.–Sat. breakfast and lunch, Thurs.–Fri. dinner); favorites include the spinach and mozzarella scramble, pasta primavera, cheesecakes, and cobblers. **Guayos on the Trail** (1.2 miles north on AZ 188, 928/425-9969, Wed.–Mon. lunch and dinner) features carne asada (topped with green chilies and cheese) and other steaks plus chimichangas and other popular Mexican dishes.

China Taste Buffet (338 E. Ash St., 928/402-8448, daily lunch and dinner) prepares oriental flavors in a variety of styles with a choice of buffet or à la carte.

Information and Services

The very helpful **Globe-Miami Chamber of Commerce** (1360 N. Broad St., Globe, AZ 85501, 928/425-4495 or 800/804-5623, www.globemiamichamber.com) has lots of local and statewide travel information. Free leaflets describe Globe and Miami historic walking tours and a highway driving tour with views of six local mines. Open 8 A.M.–5 P.M. Monday–Friday and, from October to April, also 10 A.M.–4 P.M. Saturday and Sunday.

The **Globe Ranger District** office (7680 S.

Six Shooter Canyon Rd., Globe, AZ 85501, 928/402-6200, www.fs.fed.us/r3/tonto, 7:45 A.M.–4:30 P.M. Mon.–Fri.) provides details on camping, backcountry drives, an off-highway vehicle area, and hiking trails (which tend to be steep). It's two miles southeast of downtown; follow S. Broad Street to the sign, turn right across the bridge, curve left on Jesse Hayes Road and continue straight on Six Shooter Canyon Road.

Globe Public Library (339 S. Broad St., 928/425-6111, closed Sun.) is downtown, as is the main **post office** (101 S. Hill and Sycamore Sts., 928/425-2381). **Cobre Valley Community Hospital** (928/425-3261) is just south of the U.S. Highway 60–Highway 188 junction on the northwest side of town.

Getting There and Around

Greyhound (1666 E. Ash St., 928/425-2301) offers a couple of westbound and eastbound buses daily.

WINKELMAN AND THE COPPER BASIN

Copper mining and smelting continue on a large scale in several areas near the town of Winkelman, between Globe and Tucson on Highway 77. Mountain and desert scenery provide the biggest attractions for visitors; Highway 77 between Winkelman and Globe follows a beautiful section of the Gila River just north of Winkelman and winds through the Mescal Mountains. Highway 177 between Winkelman and Superior also crosses rugged mountains, and you can stop at an overlook of ASARCO's **Ray Mine,** a vast open-pit copper mine. **White Canyon Wilderness** is west of Highway 177 via some rough roads; contact the BLM's Phoenix Field Office (602/580-5500) for information on this area. **Aravaipa Canyon Wilderness** has a western trailhead off Highway 77 south of Winkelman. Note that even day-hikers must obtain a permit to visit here; contact the BLM office in Safford (928/348-4400).

© BILL WEIR

Gila River float trip above Winkelman

Winkelman and Vicinity

Smelter smokestacks tower over this community and its twin, Hayden. A park beside the Gila River offers picnicking and camping amid giant cottonwood trees; turn in at the Highway 77–Highway 177 junction.

GLOBE TO APACHE JUNCTION

Miami and Claypool

A strange landscape greets you on the approach to these two towns west of Globe. Many-tiered terraces of barren, buff-colored mine tailings and dark slag dumps dominate the view. Miami and Claypool stretch along Bloody Tanks Wash, named for a massacre of Apache in 1864 by a band of whites and allied Maricopa Indians. Developers arrived in 1907 to lay out a town site named after Miami, Ohio. Giant copper-ore reduction plants built by the Miami Copper and Inspiration Companies resulted in the nickname "Concentrator City." Miami (www.miamiaz.org) has had its ups and downs since, following the rise and fall in copper prices, but production continues.

The town has many historic buildings, some now restored as antique and craft shops. Follow signs for the Business District one block north to Sullivan Street. At its west end, you'll see the 1923 Greek revival–style Bullion Plaza School, now a museum (roughly 11 A.M.–3 P.M. Fri.–Sat.) about the people of Miami.

Delvan's Drawing Room (55 Chisholm Ave., 928/473-9045, www.miamiaz.org/BED) offers three rooms with shared bath and an apartment in a restored miners' boarding house. Rooms cost $45 s, $55 d (add $10 on Fri.–Sat.); apartments run $80–125 depending on day and number of people. From Sullivan Street in downtown Miami, turn one block north on Chisholm. **Guayo's El Rey Café** (716 Sullivan St., 928/473-9960, closed Wed.) is the local favorite for Mexican and American food.

Miami to Superior

U.S. Highway 60 climbs over jagged mountains between these two towns. Six miles west of Miami you'll see the vast open-pit Pinto Valley copper mine. The road continues climbing to the small community of Top of the World, then descends into Devils Canyon. **Oak Flat Campground** (elev. 4,200 feet, open all year, no water or fee) lies in more open country nearby; turn south a half mile on Magma Mine Road at the sign near Milepost 231. West of Oak Flat, the highway drops through scenic, steep-walled Queen Creek Canyon to Superior.

Superior

The opening of the rich Silver King Mine in 1875, followed by development of the Silver Queen, brought streams of fortune hunters into this mineral-laden region. As at Globe, miners found rich deposits of copper when the surface silver began to play out. Superior lies just west of scenic Queen Creek Canyon in a valley surrounded by rugged mountains.

North of town you'll see the high smokestack of an idle smelter and extensive tailings from the Magma Copper Mine, where shafts plunge nearly 5,000 feet down. The mine was closed at press time, though exploration continues. Perlite is mined and processed in the area.

All travelers' facilities lie along U.S. Highway 60, which bypasses downtown. Buckboard City has the **World's Smallest Museum** (520/689-5800, www.worldssmallestmuseum.com, 8 A.M.–2 P.M. daily, donation), which packs local, natural, and cultural history into a tiny building. **El Portal Motel** (520/689-2886, $35 s, $40 d) has basic rooms. **Superior RV Park** (520/689-0115) offers a quiet spot for adults just west of town with tent sites ($8), RV sites ($17 w/hookups), coin showers, laundry, and a dump station. **Casa Denogean** (closed Mon.) serves Mexican and American food for lunch and dinner; it's the only one of several restaurants to provide smoke-free dining. Nearby on U.S. Highway 60 you'll find a rest area, and across the highway, a park with a red caboose and picnic tables.

Main Street in downtown Superior practically looks like a ghost town—paint peels from the closed shops. **Bob Jones Museum,** named after Arizona's sixth governor and housed in his former home, has a small historical collection at Main and Neary; it's occasionally open.

Boyce Thompson Arboretum State Park

You can see more than 3,200 different desert plants here in Arizona's oldest (1920s) and largest (323 acres) botanical garden (U.S. 60, 3 miles west of Superior, 520/689-2811, http://arboretum.ag.arizona.edu, 8 A.M.–5 P.M. daily except Dec. 25, $6 adults, $3 children 5–12). Exotic species from around the world thrive alongside native Sonoran Desert plants. Short trails lead through Sonoran and Chihuahuan desert areas, a cactus garden, riparian areas, an Australian forest, and herb and rose gardens. Buy or borrow the booklet for the Main Trail, a scenic 1.5-mile loop in Queen Creek Canyon; handouts offer additional information on many of the other trails and gardens. Most of these trails branch off from the first part of the Main Trail, so you don't have to walk far to see the highlights. Much of the trail system is wheelchair-accessible. The Curandero/Sonoran Desert Trail describes traditional herbal medicines of the Sonoran Desert. (*Curanderos* are healers in traditional Mexican culture.) Greenhouses contain cacti and succulents that might not otherwise survive winter cold at this 2,400-foot elevation. The Smith Interpretive Center, between the display greenhouses, has exhibits on plants and local history. A Demonstration Garden offers tips and examples of water-efficient landscaping design.

More than 200 bird and 72 terrestrial species have been seen in the area. Ayer Lake and Queen Creek on the Main Trail are good places to watch for them; you may see endangered Gila topminnow and desert pupfish in the lake. Nearby Picket Post Mountain (4,400 ft.) soars above the gardens. A heliograph station, equipped with mirrors to flash the rays of the sun, operated atop the peak during the Apache wars. No developed trails go to the summit and there's no access from the arboretum.

The visitors center offers some exhibits and a gift shop with snacks, books, prints, posters, and seed packets. You can also purchase cactus, other succulents, trees, shrubs, ground cover, and herbs. The cooling-tower exhibit at the visitors center creates a cool microclimate; its 30-foot tower functions as a giant evaporative cooler.

Scheduled events include an **Arid Land Plant Show** on the first weekend in April and a **Fall Landscaping Festival.** A picnic area near the parking lot is available to visitors. Today the University of Arizona, the State Parks Board, and the nonprofit Arboretum Corporation manage the arboretum.

Florence Junction

Turn south 16 miles on Highway 79 at this junction for the town of Florence, home to McFarland State Historic Park and the Pinal County Historical Museum, or continue on U.S. Highway 60 for Apache Junction and the Valley of the Sun.

Peralta Trailhead

One of the most popular trailheads for the Superstition Wilderness lies off U.S. Highway 60 about nine miles northwest of Florence Junction, or eight miles southeast of Apache Junction. Follow graded-dirt Forest Road 77 in for seven miles, $4 per day parking or free with a golden passport or National Parks Pass with hologram.

Three very scenic trails branch off into the wilderness here, including **Peralta Trail #102,** which goes up Peralta Canyon to Fremont Saddle, where you get a great view of Weaver's Needle. It's four miles round-trip and a 1,400-foot climb to the pass; carry water and avoid the heat of a summer day. Peralta Trail continues down the other side past the base of Weaver's Needle, connecting with other trails in the Superstitions.

Phoenix to Tucson

On the drive between Phoenix and Tucson you'll cross desert plains with views of the Superstitions, Picacho Peak, Santa Catalina Mountains, and other rugged ranges. Desert plants along the roadside sometimes bloom in blazes of bright color in spring. Several spots are worth a visit, whether you take the old Pinal Pioneer Parkway (AZ 79) or the speedier I-10.

FLORENCE

Florence, one of the oldest white settlements in Arizona, dates back to the arrival of Levi Ruggles in 1866. Ruggles noted a safe ford on the nearby Gila River, and saw potential for farming. The town site that he laid out soon became a trade center and stage stop for surrounding army camps. Some people advocated Florence as the Arizona territorial capital, but the town had to settle for designation as the Pinal County seat. The first county courthouse went up in 1878, and is now open as McFarland State Historic Park. The second county courthouse, completed in 1891 with an ornate cupola, stands as Florence's chief landmark. Funds ran out before the clock could be installed in the cupola, so workers fixed the hands permanently at 11:44!

Not everybody comes to Florence by choice—the Arizona State Prison sits at the edge of town. Convicts completed the prison in 1909, replacing the territorial prison at Yuma. Inmates now number over 12,000—more than double the number of townspeople.

Florence has two museums and more than 150 historic buildings listed with the national register. Old porch-fronted shops along Main Street invite a stroll and perhaps a look inside. You can learn about the structures and their history from a leaflet available at the visitor centers and museums.

Pinal County Historical Museum

This diverse collection (715 S. Main St., 520/868-4382, noon–4 P.M. Sun., 11 A.M.–4 P.M. Tues.–Sat., closed July 15–Aug. 31, donations welcome) portrays the area's long history. Native American pottery, baskets, and stone tools come from prehistoric and modern tribes of the area. An 1880s horse-drawn brougham and an 1884 Victorian grand piano reveal early pioneer elegance. Tools, mining gear, household items, and clothing exhibits portray the life of the early settlers. News clippings and memorabilia commemorate the tragic death of silent-screen hero Tom Mix, killed in a car accident nearby. The prison exhibits are sobering: hangman's nooses framing photos of their victims, a hanging board, gas-chamber chair, and massive prison registers from Yuma and Florence. A research library has a state prison archive and additional information on local history. Outdoor exhibits include farming and mining machinery, a blacksmith shop, and a homesteader shack. Main Street Park, across from the museum, has picnic tables.

McFarland State Historic Park

This adobe building (near the north end of Main St. at Ruggles St., 520/868-5216, 8 A.M.–5 P.M. Thurs.–Mon., $3 adults, $1 ages 7–13) served as Pinal County's first courthouse, sheriff's office, and jail 1878–1891, then functioned for 50 years as the county hospital. You can step into the courtroom and county clerk's office, both restored to their original appearance. Other rooms have exhibits about the lives and personalities of Florence's pioneers—including the town's heroes and villains—and detail construction of the town's hospital and courthouse. Photos show the Florence P.O.W. camp through which 13,000 Italian and German prisoners passed 1942–1945. You'll also learn about Ernest McFarland (1894–1984), who began his political career in 1925 as Pinal county attorney, then rose to serve as U.S. senator, Arizona governor, and chief justice of the State Supreme Court. A city park just to the north offers shaded tables, playground, ball fields, and a pond.

Poston's Butte

Charles Poston explored and mined in what is

now Arizona from 1853 to 1861, but his greatest achievement was successfully lobbying in Washington, D.C., for a territorial government in 1863. Poston went on to become the first superintendent of Indian affairs in Arizona and one of the first Arizona delegates to Congress.

His congressional term finished, Poston traveled to India and became a fire worshipper. Upon returning to Arizona in 1878, he built a continuous fire—a sort of temple of the sun—atop a hill, naming it Parsee Hill. The flames died out several months later, ending a project that disbelievers mocked as "Poston's Folly." Poston lies buried in a pyramid-shaped tomb on the summit of the hill, renamed Poston's Butte, northwest of Florence across the Gila River.

A trail—steep with some loose rock—leads to the top. If you'd like some exercise and views from the butte, drive north a bit over a mile from downtown on Highway 79, cross the Gila River bridge and continue .1 miles, turn left (near Milepost 136) 1.3 miles on the Hunt Highway, then turn right onto an unpaved road leading under the railroad tracks. Depending on your vehicle, you may wish to park here and walk. After the underpass, park on the left and walk half a mile (one-way) on the track up the hillside; elevation gain is about 300 feet. It's possible to reach the summit with a 4WD vehicle, but the way is very bumpy.

Box Canyon

Volcanic rock walls of this beautiful canyon enclose desert plants and an intermittent stream. It's a delightful place for exploring. Loose sand and gravel can trap cars, so you should have 4WD. From Florence, drive north on Highway 79 across the Gila River bridge and continue .3 miles, then turn right 14 miles on a dirt road (before the railroad tracks). On the way in you'll parallel the Gila River past fields, an orchard, and, at 9.4 miles, the Ashurst-Hayden Diversion Dam. The road curves northeast, crosses some washes (cars may have trouble here), and enters Box Canyon. Some drivers manage to get all the way through the canyon in another 13 miles and come out on Highway 79 or U.S. Highway 60 to the north, though this route requires difficult four-wheeling.

St. Anthony's Greek Orthodox Monastery

The main church and four chapels rise above beautifully landscaped gardens about 10 miles southeast of Florence. Father Ephraim, a spiritual leader from Mt. Athos in Greece, chose the spot for its serenity and isolation from the distractions of the world. Since its founding in July 1995, the monastery (520/868-3188, www.stanthonysmonastery.org) has grown to shelter about 40 monks who follow a rigorous schedule of work and prayer, including praying while working. Visitors interested in the monastery and its religion may drop by for a visit 10:30 A.M.–4 P.M. daily. Modest dress is important: Men should wear long pants and long-sleeved shirts, women need to wear skirts well below the knees, long-sleeved shirts, and a head covering such as a scarf; clothing may be available to borrow. Come to the gatehouse/bookstore, just inside the entrance, and someone will show you around. From Highway 79 just south of Milepost 124, turn east 2.5 miles on paved Paisano Road.

Tom Mix Monument

October 12, 1940, was a sad day for fans of movie hero Tom Mix. Speeding north from Tucson in his big Cord, he lost control of the car and rolled it over in a ditch (subsequently renamed Tom Mix Wash) and was killed. A roadside monument, topped by a riderless horse, marks the spot, 17 miles south of Florence on Highway 79, between Mileposts 115 and 116. A rest area here has picnic tables.

Events

The **Tour of Historic Florence** visits private and public buildings on the second weekend in February; you can walk or take a shuttle. **Pinal County Fair** brings fun and exhibits to the town of Casa Grande from the last Wednesday in March through the following Sunday. Fireworks go off for the **July 4 Festivities.** The **Junior Parada** on Thanksgiving weekend celebrates with a rodeo, parade, entertainment, and food.

Shopping

The **Prison Outlet** (northeast corner of Butte

Ave. and AZ 79, 520/868-3014, 9 A.M.–5 P.M. Fri.–Mon., then daily in Dec.) sells arts and crafts produced by the inmates.

Accommodations and Campgrounds

On the east side of town at the junction of Highways 79 and 287, **Blue Mist Motel** (40 S. Pinal Pkwy., 520/868-5875, $40 s, $55–65 d) has a pool. **Taylor's Bed & Breakfast Inn** (321 N. Bailey St., 520/868-3497, $55 d shared bath, $75 d private bath), in one of Florence's 19th-century buildings downtown, contains many antiques. The owner can arrange horseback and 4WD tours.

Rancho Sonora Inn & RV Park (5.2 miles south of town on AZ 79 at Milepost 128, 520/868-8000 or 800/205-6817, www.ranchosonora.com) offers a Southwestern atmosphere in the adobe buildings of a 1930's guest ranch. Courtyard rooms cost $89 d, one-bedroom cottages are $125 d, and two-bedroom cottages run $175 d, with lower prices in summer; amenities include a pool and hot tub. The pleasant campground ($18 tent, $22 RV w/hookups) has showers and a clubhouse, also with lower rates off-season.

Desert Garden RV Park (5 miles south on AZ 79, 520/868-3800 or 888/868-4888, www.desertgardensrvpark.com, $13–18 RV w/hookups) has an attractive desert setting amid saguaro. Guests also enjoy a clubhouse, craft room, wood shop, exercise room, and planned wintertime activities. Long-term sites are available too; reservations are recommended December–March.

Food

Old Pueblo Restaurant (505 S. Main St., 520/868-4784, Tues.–Sun. breakfast, lunch, and dinner) offers American and Mexican food. **L&B Inn** (695 S. Main St., 520/868-9981, daily breakfast, lunch, and dinner, no dinner on Sun.) has a similar menu plus a courtyard and waterfall in back. **Tea & Coffee Emporium** (110 N. Main St., 520/868-5748, Mon.–Sat. lunch) is a teahouse in the Florence General Store. For Italian dining, try **A&M Pizza** (445 W. AZ 287, 520/868-0170, daily lunch and dinner), which prepares pasta, chicken, and seafood dishes as well as pizza and subs.

Information and Services

Operated by the Greater Florence Chamber of Commerce, **Florence Visitor Center** (291 Baily St., P.O. Box 929, Florence, AZ 85232, 520/868-9433 or 800/437-9433, www.florenceaz.org) offers lots of information on local history and sights as well as places farther afield in Arizona; some books are sold. The visitor center is in an 1890 brick commercial building one block east on 8th Street from N. Main. Hours run 9 A.M.–4 P.M. Monday–Saturday, October–April, then 10 A.M.–4 P.M. Monday–Friday in summer.

One block south and east from the courthouse, the **Pinal County Visitor Center** (330 E. Butte Ave./AZ 287, P.O. Box 967, Florence, AZ 85232, 520/868-4331 or 800/557-4331, http://co.pinal.az.us/visitorcenter) will also help you with local and state travel. It's open 9 A.M.–4 P.M. Monday–Friday and 9 A.M.–2 P.M. Saturday.

The **post office** is on N. Main Street across from the state park. **Florence Community Library** (520/868-9471) is open daily near the high school; turn off S. Main Street at the sign, one block south of the Pinal County Historical Museum.

CASA GRANDE RUINS NATIONAL MONUMENT

Arizona's biggest and most perplexing prehistoric building contains 11 rooms and rises four stories above an earthen platform. An estimated 3,000 tons of mud went into the rectangular structure, whose walls range in thickness from 4.5 feet at the base to 1.8 feet near the top. Workers hauled 600 roof beams from at least 60 miles away. The monument (1100 Ruins Dr., Coolidge, AZ 85228, 520/723-3172, www.nps.gov/cagr, 8 A.M.–5 P.M. daily, $2/person, maximum $4/vehicle) is one mile north of downtown Coolidge off Highway 87. The ruins shouldn't be confused with the modern town of Casa Grande, which is about 20 miles away.

Hohokam, who had farmed the Gila Valley since about 200–300 B.C., built Casa Grande around A.D. 1350. This is the only structure of its type still standing. Archaeologists don't know the purpose of Casa Grande, but some speculate that it was used for astronomical observations to set dates for ceremonies and crop planting; certain holes in the walls appear to line up with the sun at the summer solstice and possibly with the moon during certain lunar events. By about 1450, after just a few generations of use, the Hohokam abandoned Casa Grande along with all their other villages. The Jesuit priest Eusebio Kino recorded the site in 1694, giving it the Spanish name for "great house." It became the first archaeological site to receive federal protection, in 1892.

You can also explore smaller structures and a wall that surround the main building. Walk across the parking lot and picnic area to a viewing platform to see the ball court. Off to the north lie ruins of Compound B with two platform mounds; they're not normally open to the public.

At the monument's visitors center, exhibits introduce you to the Hohokam and their irrigation canals, farming tools, jewelry, and ball courts. You'll learn some of the theories that account for their disappearance. Models show how the Great House may have looked. Rangers lead tours of Casa Grande, or you can set off on the self-guided trail. Signs identify cactus and other desert plants. The visitors center sells books on Arizona's tribes, settlers, and natural history. The picnic area offers shaded tables.

Coolidge

Two small museums encourage a detour east off the highway onto the quiet streets of this small town. **Golden Era Museum** (297 W. Central Ave., 520/723-5044 or 480/948-9570, 11 A.M.–5 P.M. Sat.–Sun., Jan.–May, $5 adults, $2 kids 12 and under) will take you down memory lane with its huge collection of antique toys, dolls, Lionel trains, and model planes, plus some antique and classic cars. The **Coolidge Museum** (161 W. Harding Ave., 520/723-3588 or 723-5436, 1–5 P.M. Sun., Sept.–June) tells the town's story in the original justice of the peace/jail building; an exhibit room out back and an early farmhouse have more displays. From the highway, go east on Central Avenue, turn right (south) two blocks on Main Street, then turn left on Harding Avenue.

Travelers will find two motels on the north side of town and two adult RV parks on the south side along the main highway, Highway 87/Arizona Boulevard. **Coolidge Chamber of Commerce** (320 W. Central Ave., Coolidge, AZ 85228, 520/723-3009, www.coolidgeaz.org, 8 A.M.–5 P.M. Mon.–Fri.) offers local info beside a city park.

Blackwater Trading Post and Museum

Drop in to this old-style trading post (520/723-5516, daily, donations welcome) to see fine Hohokam pottery, baskets by Tohono O'odham and Pima, and artifacts of other Southwestern tribes. You can shop for Native American jewelry and crafts. It's on the north side of Highway 87; head west 4.3 miles from the Highway 287–87 junction or, from I-10, you can go east 9 miles on Highways 387 and 87.

GILA INDIAN CENTER

This cultural center (480/963-3981, www.gilaindiancenter.com, 8 A.M.–5 P.M. daily, donations welcome) on the Gila River Reservation makes a fine break from freeway driving. From I-10 Exit 175, go west half a mile on Casa Blanca Road; the exit is 26 miles southeast of Phoenix and 85 miles northwest of Tucson.

About 12,000 Pima and Maricopa live on the 387,000-acre reservation, which was founded in 1859. A museum displays artifacts of the tribes and interprets local history. Photo exhibits include Snaketown, a 200-acre Hohokam site, and the 1942–1945 Gila River Internment Center that held Japanese-Americans. Crafts in the gift shop include pottery of Maricopa and New Mexican tribes, Tohono O'odham baskets, Hopi kachina dolls, and Navajo rugs. Jewelry, paintings, and prints come from many tribes. An inexpensive restaurant offers fry bread and some Mexican and American items for breakfast and lunch daily.

Outside, Heritage Park contains traditional structures of the Hohokam, Pima, Maricopa, Tohono O'odham, and Apache tribes; a booklet available at the gift shop describes each group. Native American craft demonstrations and performances take place for the Anniversary Celebration (third weekend in March) and during the Thanksgiving Celebration (weekend following Thanksgiving).

CASA GRANDE

Winter visitors have discovered Casa Grande, formerly a small, sleepy agricultural town. Nobody had planned a town here—it was just a spot where the railway stopped laying tracks in the summer heat of 1879. Shipping agents then dropped off agricultural and mining supplies beside the track. When the tracks continued on to Yuma, people stayed and the population grew to 500 by 1882, but the national mining slump in the 1890s caused Casa Grande to dwindle to just a mercantile store, a saloon, and two small businesses. Agriculture became the mainstay, with livestock, vegetables, alfalfa, wheat, barley, citrus, and cotton contributing to the local economy. Today the town prospers with manufacturing and the 10,000–15,000 winter visitors, as well as the crops. Casa Grande's population has now passed 28,000.

Casa Grande Valley Historical Museum

The museum (110 W. Florence Blvd., 520/836-2223, www.cgvhs.org, 1–5 P.M. Mon.–Sat., Sept. 15–May 15, $3 age 17+) takes you back to the days of the early tribes and pioneers. You'll view period rooms and learn about area mining. Step outside to see the 1934 Southside Colored Grammar School, agricultural gear, and a building with additional exhibits. Kids will like the three vintage fire engines. The collection and a gift shop are downtown behind a 1927 stone former church.

Casa Grande Art Museum

This small gallery (319 W. 3rd. St., 520/836-3377, 1–4 P.M. Wed.–Thurs. and Sat.–Sun., Oct.–May) offers a chance to enjoy paintings, sculpture, photographic displays, and ceramics as well as an outdoor sculpture garden. Most work is for sale. Exhibits change about once a month. It's one block south and west from the historical museum.

Accommodations

The **Francisco Grande Resort and Golf Resort** (5 miles west of downtown at 26000 Gila Bend Hwy., 520/836-6444 or 800/237-4238, www.franciscogrande.com) offers accommodations with an 18-hole golf course, pool, hot tub, tennis, and restaurant. Motels, restaurants, and many RV parks lie scattered around town and near I-10.

Information and Services

The friendly **Greater Casa Grande Chamber of Commerce** (575 N. Marshall St., Casa Grande, AZ 85222, 520/836-2125 or 800/916-1515, www.casagrandechamber.org, 9 A.M.–5 P.M. Mon.–Fri.) has a central location; turn south from Florence Boulevard at the Dairy Queen.

Shoppers enjoy **Outlets at Casa Grande** (formerly Tanger Factory Outlet Center), which holds more than four dozen shops at I-10 Exit 198. **Casa Grande Regional Medical Center** (1800 E. Florence Blvd., 520/426-6300, www.casagrande-hospital.com) is the local hospital.

PICACHO PEAK STATE PARK

Picacho Peak has long served as a landmark for tribal groups, Spanish explorers, American frontiersmen, and modern-day motorists. Visitors to the park (520/466-3183, $6/vehicle day use) enjoy hiking, picnicking, and camping in the splendid setting. Saguaro and other plants of the Sonoran Desert thrive on the rocky hillsides, and Mexican gold poppies can blanket the hillsides in spring after a wet winter. Take I-10 Exit 219 (70 miles southeast of Phoenix and 40 miles northwest of Tucson) and follow signs a half mile.

The campgrounds, with showers and a dump station, cost $12 for nonhookup sites, $20 with electric hookups; no reservations are taken, but it's uncommon for all sites to fill. Groups can reserve picnic, tent camping, and RV areas.

Monuments near the flagpole commemorate the Battle of Picacho Pass (where I-10 now runs) and the building of a road by the Mormon Battalion. The Battle of Picacho Pass—the most significant conflict of the Civil War this far west—took place on April 15, 1862. Confederate forces killed Lieutenant James Barrett, leader of the Union detachment, and two privates. Aware that Union reinforcements would soon arrive, the Confederates retreated back down the Butterfield Road to Tucson.

Hiking Trails

Hunter Trail climbs 1,500 feet to the summit of 3,374-foot Picacho Peak, a tilted remnant of ancient lava flows. This rugged four-mile round-trip requires 4–5 hours. (For a shorter but still strenuous hike, also with expansive views, take the Hunter Trail just as far as the saddle, a 2-mile round-trip of 1.5 hours.) Be careful on the backside where the trail crosses some loose rock; posts and cables provide handholds in the rougher spots. **Sunset Vista Trail** traverses the back of the peak in a 6.2-mile round-trip to the summit; it has fewer hikers and a more secluded setting as I-10 is out of view most of the way. Good shoes, plenty of water, and sun protection will help make an enjoyable and successful climb on either of these trails. If you hike up one trail and down the other, you'll have to arrange a shuttle or walk the 2.2 miles between the two trailheads to get back to your car.

Calloway Trail is an easier climb to a low pass between Bugler's and Picacho peaks, 1.5 miles round-trip, requiring an hour. A half-mile-loop **nature trail** introduces desert plants; you can begin from Memorial Plaza near the contact station or from the hookup campground. Rangers offer trail maps.

Civil War in the Southwest

This large-scale reenactment takes place on the second weekend in March. Infantry and cavalry fight three historic engagements to commemorate two battles that took place in New Mexico plus the Battle of Picacho Pass. Smoke spreads over the desert as the crack of rifles and roar of cannons echo off the hillsides. In calmer moments between the conflicts, you can visit the encampments of each side and see how the soldiers and civilians lived.

Phoenix to Yuma

GILA BEND

The town of Gila Bend (pop. 2,000) sits near the Gila River 68 miles southwest of Phoenix. Father Kino, who came through here in 1699, found a prosperous Maricopa village with irrigated fields yielding two harvests annually. The Butterfield stagecoach first rolled through in the early 1850s, and a town later grew up around its station. Today Gila Bend serves as an agricultural center and a travelers' stop. Surrounding farms raise cotton, wheat, barley, and other crops. San Lucy, a Tohono O'odham village, lies just north of town.

Hop off I-8 on the Business Loop through town for the seven motels, a few RV parks, and a variety of restaurants. A tourist information sign on the Business Loop will direct you to the **Gila Bend Museum and Tourist Center** (644 W. Pima St. or P.O. Drawer A, Gila Bend, AZ 85337, 928/683-2002, 8 A.M.–4 P.M. daily), which offers historical exhibits and travel information. The **public library** and a city park are two blocks north of the Business Loop at 202 N. Euclid.

Painted Rocks Petroglyph Site

Prehistoric travelers left hundreds—perhaps thousands—of designs on the boulders of a small hill northwest of Gila Bend. A caretaker tried to count the pieces of artwork on just one boulder, then gave up saying he "wasn't drunk enough." You'll recognize the human figures, deer, pronghorn, snakes, and other life. Other designs remain a mystery, though at least one "calendar" has been found to mark winter and summer solstices. The rock art will fade away if people touch it, so avoid contact and make sure that the kids don't climb on the rocks! The BLM's Phoenix Field Office manages the site and provides shaded tables for picnics and a campground. You'll need to bring water. Day use costs $2, camping $4. A paved road leads to the entrance. Take I-8 Painted Rock Dam Road Exit 102 (13 miles west of Gila Bend) and follow it north 12 miles, then turn left .5 miles on Painted Rock Road.

WILDERNESS AREAS

You don't have to travel far to go from the biggest city in Arizona to some of the state's loneliest

A "sun dagger" crosses this petroglyph at midday during the winter solstice.

landscapes! Adventurous travelers discover pristine animal and plant communities, plus signs of prehistoric villages and trade routes. A few trails lead into some wildernesses, while others require challenging cross-country hiking. Most access roads will daunt ordinary cars—you'll need a high-clearance vehicle to get close. The BLM's Phoenix Field Office looks after these areas.

Woolsey Peak and Signal Mountain Wilderness Areas

Although less than 40 miles southwest of Phoenix, these adjoining wildernesses see few visitors. They protect part of the Gila Bend Mountains and take their names from their respective highest summits—3,271-foot Woolsey Peak and 2,182-foot Signal Peak. The open desert below the weathered volcanic peaks offers many cross-country hiking possibilities. You can also hike across Woolsey Peak Wilderness on an eight-mile former road that has trailheads at both ends. Both wildernesses can be reached on a vehicle road that runs between them.

Access is easiest from the Phoenix side, but you'll need a high-clearance vehicle: Head south 5.5 miles on Highway 85 from I-10 Exit 112, follow old Highway 80 west and south 14 miles via Hassayampa, turn west 5.5 miles on Agua Caliente Road (pavement ends), then turn southwest on an unmarked road at a bend. After four miles you'll see a sign identifying Signal Mountain Wilderness on the right, then in another three miles, a sign identifying Woolsey Peak Wilderness on the left. The trailhead for the hike across Woolsey Peak Wilderness is near Woolsey Spring; look for an unmarked track to the left at a wide spot in Woolsey Wash. You can also get here from the east edge of Gila Bend by heading north 25.2 miles on old Highway 80 to Agua Caliente Road (between Mileposts 25 and 26), then following the same directions.

A 4WD vehicle is recommended if you continue southwest on the road between the two wildernesses. At the T-junction where it finally ends, turn right (west) 1.3 miles, then right (northwest) 3.4 miles at the next T-junction and continue to Saddle Road (Milepost 35) at a third T-junction. Here you can turn north toward I-10 and Phoenix or south 10.8 miles to Rocky Point Road (turn left 12.6 miles for Painted Rocks Petroglyph Site) and I-8 west of Gila Bend. Note that some maps show roads across the Gila River just below Painted Rock Dam, but these washed out long ago; you have to detour via Saddle Road.

Sonoran Desert National Monument

Arizona's newest monument, designated in 2001, contains three wilderness areas within its nearly 500,000 acres. Located about 60 miles southwest of Phoenix, it can be reached from I-10 in the north or off I-8 near Gila Bend in the south. As the name suggests, the monument protects fine examples of Sonoran Desert plant and animal communities, including desert bighorn sheep. Early travelers crossed the Maricopa Mountains on a shortcut known as the Forty-Mile Desert between Maricopa and Gila Bend, saving 80 miles over following the Gila River.

Butterfield Pass takes its name from the stage service that used this mountain route 1858–1861. You can still cross the pass with a 4WD vehicle and a good map. Today this road divides the North and South Maricopa Mountains Wildernesses. Over to the southeast lies the smaller Table Top Wilderness, named for its highest peak. Hikers can follow trails in the wilderness areas, including a trail to the summit of Table Top Mountain. Note that part of the southern monument lies within the Barry M. Goldwater Air Force Range, so you'll need the same permit and clearance as for Cabeza Prieta National Wildlife Refuge to visit this section.

Tucson and Southern Arizona

Tucson (TOO-sawn), with a metropolitan population of more than 900,000, may be second in size among Arizona's cities, but it's a favorite for residents and visitors who appreciate the history, culture, and recreation of the "Old Pueblo." It's far older than Phoenix, and a strong sense of history pervades the entire region; you'll see many reminders of the Spanish legacy while exploring the historic districts in town. This heritage extends south of Tucson at Mission San Xavier del Bac, Tubac Presidio State Historic Park, and at the mission ruins of Tumacacori National Historical Park. In the southeastern corner of Arizona, you may feel the presence of the great chief Cochise, who once led the Chiricahua Apache without ever losing a battle. Later Apache did lose their fights, and you can learn about them and the troops they fought at a fine museum in Fort Huachuca. The Old West lives on as well in the dozens of abandoned mining camps, on the ranches where cowboys still work huge herds, and at the OK Corral in Tombstone where the Earps and Doc Holliday shot it out with the Clantons. Allow

Must-Sees

Look for M to find the sights and activities you can't miss and M for the best dining and lodging.

M Tucson Museum of Art and Historic Block includes several of Tucson's oldest adobe houses, now restored with historical and art exhibits, along with a spacious exhibit hall. Highlights include works from Pre-Columbian, Spanish colonial, Latin American folk art, Western, modern, and contemporary collections. Visiting shows appear as well (page 123).

M Arizona Historical Society Museum re-creates Arizona's history with very imaginative exhibits (page 130).

M Arizona-Sonora Desert Museum uses highly realistic enclosures to display the wildlife and flora of the Sonoran Desert. You're likely to see such elusive animals as desert bighorn sheep, black bear, jaguar, javelina, and river otter. Walk-in aviaries let you get close to hummingbirds and other birds. This is Tucson's top must-see! (page 134).

M Catalina Highway/Sky Island Scenic Byway sweeps you from the Sonoran Desert to cool aspen and fir forests atop one of Arizona's "sky islands." The paved highway begins from the north edge of Tucson and climbs past viewpoints, picnic areas, campgrounds, hiking trails, and the nation's southernmost ski area (page 145).

M Sabino Canyon's creek flows year-round, creating a lush oasis beneath towering canyon walls. A shuttle tram provides easy access (page 149).

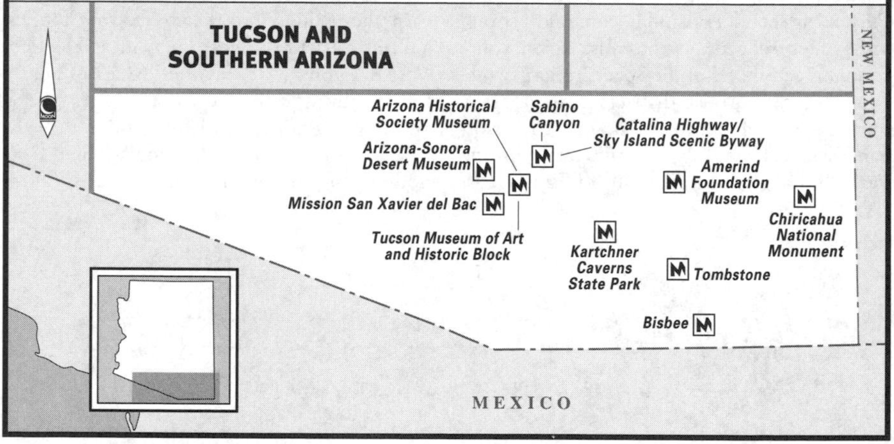

time to explore southern Arizona. It's a big land with many attractions.

PLANNING YOUR TIME

On a short visit, you'll probably find it most convenient to base yourself in Tucson, which has many attractions and good public transportation. The Arizona-Sonora Desert Museum just west of town tops most visitors' lists as a "must see." It's an outstanding collection of native wildlife and flora in a lovely setting. Tucson's long history invites exploration of the Tucson Museum of Art and Historic Block and surrounding neighborhoods. Your imagination will take flight among the more than 250 historic aircraft at the Pima Air & Space Museum—the largest private collection in the country. If you'd like to stretch your legs and enjoy nature, head in almost any direction! The stream-fed Sabino and Bear Canyons in the Santa Catalinas to the north offer hikes among lush vegetation and soaring rock walls. Or you can

Mission San Xavier del Bac, full of wonderful folk art, has served the Tohono O'odham Indians since the days of the Spanish in the late 1700s. A small museum highlights the church's history (page 165).

Tombstone, "the town too tough to die," is straight out of the Old West. Daily shows reenact the OK Corral gunfight and other violence that took place here. You can stroll the boardwalks, enter the old saloons, head over to Boot Hill, and even get your own epitaph. Exhibits in the 1881 Bird Cage Theatre and the 1882 courthouse shed light on the momentous events and everyday life of early Tombstone (page 189).

Bisbee, tucked deep in canyons of the Mule Mountains, became a wealthy town in the early 1900s from its copper mines. A stroll along its narrow, winding streets will turn up many fine examples of solid commercial buildings and fanciful Victorian houses. You can take a ride inside the Copper Queen Mine—the most famous of all—and see how the miners did their work (page 194).

KARTCHNER CAVERNS STATE PARK

the Big Room in Kartchner Caverns State Park

Chiricahua National Monument contains fanciful rock features that have weathered from the volcanic rock. You can see these on a scenic drive and on a network of hiking trails (page 206).

Amerind Foundation Museum, secluded among the boulders of Texas Canyon, displays exceptional archaeological and ethnographic exhibits on American Indian cultures (page 212).

Kartchner Caverns State Park offers two tours in a living cave full of almost every type of cave feature known (page 216).

drive higher into these mountains for panoramas, hiking, camping, and the nation's southernmost ski area. Saguaro National Park has two units—west and east of Tucson—with splendid trails and scenic drives among the towering saguaro. The Santa Ritas to the south include the highest summit in the area—9,453-foot Mt. Wrightson—and, on a peak just to the south, the telescopes of Whipple Observatory.

The southeastern corner of Arizona, which you can tour either on trips of one or more days, holds some of the state's most atmospheric historic sites, such as the picturesque Spanish mission ruins at Tumacacori National Historical Park, the neat rows of 19th-century buildings at Fort Huachuca that date from the Indian Wars, the copper-mining town of Bisbee with its elegant early 20th-century buildings packed into narrow canyons, and the Old West town of Tombstone famed for it boisterous past. "Sky islands" poke up in this region with abundant wildlife and exceptional birding opportunities, such as

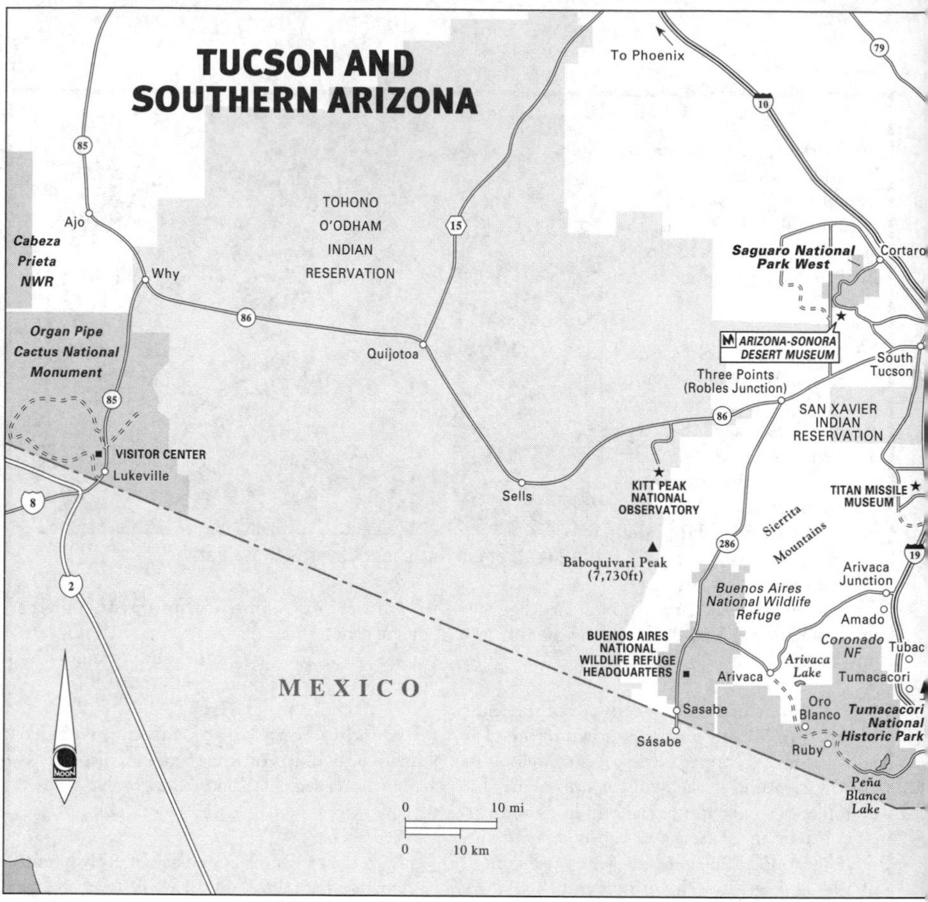

in Ramsey Canyon of the Huachuca Mountains. The maze of whimsical rock features farther east at Chiricahua National Monument enchants visitors on trails and the scenic drive.

Southwest of Tucson, you'll see the white domes of some of the more than two dozen telescopes atop Kitt Peak, which has a paved road to the top, a visitors center, and guided and self-guided tours. Farther west, you'll see desert flora in Organ Pipe Cactus National Monument that grows nowhere else in the country.

Astonishing varieties of birds, animals, and plants find niches in southern Arizona's rugged topography. Some species, such as the whiskered senita cactus and the colorful trogon bird, have migrated north from Mexico and are rarely seen elsewhere in the United States. The combination of clear, dry air and the many mountain ranges provides excellent observing conditions for astronomers. It's said that more astronomers live within a 50-mile radius of Tucson than in all the rest of the world! As you head farther into the southeastern corner of Arizona, elevations and precipitation rise enough to support grasslands.

Summers are warm in Tucson and surrounding desert areas, but not as hot as in Phoenix or Yuma. Temperatures peak in June and July with highs generally near 98°F and lows near 70°F. Even in

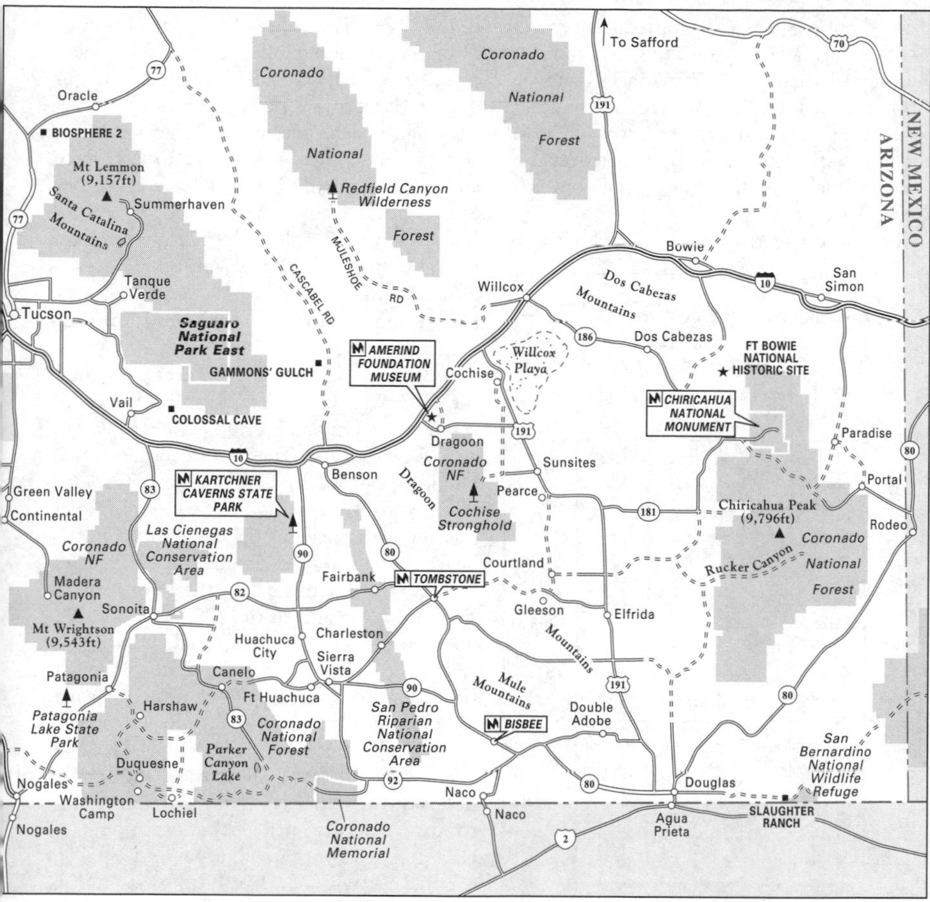

Southern Arizona

the depths of winter, you'll often enjoy springlike weather, with average highs in the mid-60s and lows in the upper 30s. Of the 11 or so inches of annual rainfall, over half falls in the July–September rainy season. Four ranges—the Santa Catalinas, Santa Ritas, Huachucas, and Chiricahuas—have peaks over 9,000 feet and offer delightful weather in summer and deep snow during the winter.

HISTORY

The Early Farming Culture tilled the soil of the Tucson Basin as far back as 2000 B.C. and appears to have been the first group in the Southwest to have villages, canal systems, pottery, bow and arrow, and trade routes. These people lived in pit houses, some of which were very large and likely had ceremonial functions. About A.D. 150 this group gave way to the Hohokam, who continued farming the river valleys until breaking up as a culture sometime around 1400. It's likely that some of the Hohokam survived to become the ancestors of today's Akimel O'odham and Tohono O'odham tribes.

The first Spanish visitors found an Akimel O'odham village, Stjuk-shon (*stjuk* means "dark mountain" and *shon* is "foot of"), at the base of Sentinel Peak, the hill with the large *A* now painted on it. Spaniards adopted the name as "Tucson" when laying out the Presidio of San Agustín del Tucson in 1775. Attacks by roving Apache made fortifications necessary, so adobe walls 12 feet high and 750 feet long enclosed the new settlement. Mexico inherited Tucson from Spain after the 1821 revolution, but little changed except the flag.

Tucson joined the United States with the Gadsden Purchase in June 1854, but 21 months of boundary-marking and bureaucratic delays passed before the arrival of American officialdom in the form of the army's First Dragoons. Although Apache continued to menace settlers and travelers, Americans began to arrive in force, and the Butterfield Overland Stagecoach soon opened service to Tucson. To cope with the desert climate, Anglos adopted much of the food, building techniques, and other customs of the Mexicans. You'll see the results of these practices, as well as of Anglo-Mexican intermarriage, in Tucson's cultural mix.

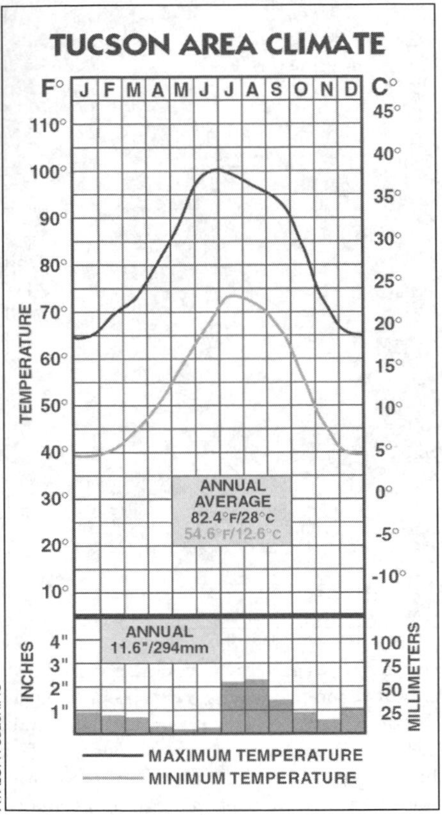

AVALON PUBLISHING

When U.S. army troops headed east to fight in the Civil War, Confederate cavalry under the command of Captain Sherrod Hunter came west and easily captured Tucson in February 1862. Union troops led by Colonel James Carleton marched in from California two months later, clashing with the Confederates at Picacho Pass, on the Butterfield Road about 42 miles northwest of Tucson. After this battle, the most westerly significant skirmish of the Civil War, the outnumbered Confederates retreated.

Tucson's Wild West years continued after the Civil War, and men rarely ventured unarmed onto the dusty streets. Still, the town prospered, serving as the territorial capital 1867–1877. By 1880, when the first train rolled in, the population had grown to over 7,000. The Arizona Territorial University opened its doors in 1891 on land donated by a saloonkeeper and a pair of gamblers. Davis-Monthan Field brought Tucson into the aviation age and became an important training base during World War II. Many of the airmen and others passing through the city during those hectic years returned to settle here. With new postwar industries and the growth of tourism, the Old Pueblo has boomed ever since.

Tucson

Though the Old Pueblo, as it's known locally, is modern and lively, Tucson's Old West heritage will surprise you. Tucson has some of the finest cultural offerings in Arizona—a large university, historic sites, fine museums, and a great variety of restaurants and nightlife. Yet you can actually see most of the city's downtown sights by walking.

Tucson lies in a broad valley of the Sonoran Desert at an elevation of 2,400 feet. The mountains ringing Tucson offer splendid scenery and great hiking. In just minutes, you can get out of the city to enjoy a range of vegetation and climate zones equivalent to traveling from Mexico to Canada!

DOWNTOWN WALKING TOUR

Northern Section

The historical walking tour provides a look at the Spanish, Mexican, and Anglo legacies of Tucson. Tucson Museum of Art and Historic Block—the biggest attraction on the walk—makes a convenient place to start. It doesn't open until 10 A.M. (noon on Sun.), so you may wish to visit at the end of your walk. You can park in the museum's lot west across Main Avenue (enter from Paseo Redondo), the underground lot south across Alameda Street, the multilevel lot just to the east, or the large outdoor lot two blocks north along Court Avenue.

You're sure to find many delightful pieces at the **Tucson Museum of Art and Historic Block** (140 N. Main Ave., 520/624-2333, www.tucsonarts.com, noon–4 P.M. Sun., 10 A.M.–4 P.M. Mon.–Sat. except closed Mon. in summer, $5 adults, $4 seniors 60+, $2 students 13+, free for children 12 and under, free for everyone on Sun.). Exhibits of the Americas span the centuries from Pre-Columbian artifacts and Spanish colonial paintings and furnishings, to Latin American folk art and works by Western, modern, and contemporary artists. Special exhibits appear frequently. Docents lead tours of the collections daily except Mondays.

The Plaza of the Pioneers and adjoining courtyards provide a space for fiestas, concerts, markets, or just relaxing. Café à la C'Art here serves creative sandwiches and salads for lunch Monday–Friday. The research library (10 A.M.–3 P.M. Mon.–Fri.) is east of the main museum building. The Tucson Museum of Art School offers a variety of noncredit classes for children and adults on creating and appreciating art.

Just inside the main entranceway at 140 N. Main Avenue, turn left to enter the **Stevens/Duffield House,** part of which dates from 1856. It now houses the Palice Pavilion/Art of the Americas with colorful exhibits of Pre-Columbian, Spanish colonial, and folk art.

Next door, across the main entranceway from the Stevens/Duffield House, you can step into the **Edward Nye Fish House,** built by a rich

Southern Arizona

RÍO NUEVO PROJECTS

Ever since urban renewal projects in the late 1960s and early 1970s wiped out old neighborhoods and two Spanish-era plazas, downtown Tucson has suffered a split personality. Even worse, the I-10 freeway cut off the city from the Santa Cruz River that gave it birth.

The Río Nuevo projects aim to heal the rift by providing downtown with new cultural, housing, and shopping opportunities. A historic/cultural area west across the river will have a reconstructed San Agustín Mission complex, history museums, a regional visitors center, and a cultural plaza. Back on the east side of the river, a new science center and town square will join a renovated Tucson Convention Center. Downtown's Congress Street will become an arts and entertainment district, including a renovation of the historic Fox and Rialto theaters. You can follow progress of the projects at 520/791-5580 or www.rio-nuevo.org.

businessman in 1868 with 15-foot ceilings and solid adobe walls more than 2.5 feet thick. The rooms display high-quality pieces from the Goodman Pavilion of Western Art, mostly from the Southwest. Edward Fish was a good friend of Hiram Sanford Stevens, and much of Tucson's early social life centered on their houses.

Head northeast across the Plaza of the Pioneers to see **La Casa Cordova,** built of adobe in about 1848 and one of the oldest houses in the area. Period rooms reflect life in the 1800s, and historic exhibits relate the story of the Tucson presidio. From November to March you can enjoy *El Nacimiento*—more than 400 hand-painted terracotta figurines that form a tableau illustrating biblical scenes and traditional Mexican life. The **Romero House** north of La Casa Cordova dates from the 1860s and was modified many times. The Tucson Museum of Art School now uses it for ceramics classes.

The main museum building's spacious galleries host modern and contemporary art; a gently descending ramp takes you from the main floor down to additional exhibit spaces on the lower level. A large museum shop off the lobby sells creative art and crafts.

You can walk around to the street side of the Stevens/Duffield House and continue north to the **Corbett House** next door. Come inside to see the beautiful arts and crafts furnishings on a self-guided tour. This restored mission revival–bungalow represents a middle-class house of the early 1900s. J. Knox Corbett came to Arizona to recover from tuberculosis in 1880 and built this house in 1906–1907. He became a successful businessman and served 23 years as the Tucson postmaster.

Follow Main Avenue north to the corner with Washington Street, where a sign marks the site of the original presidio wall's northwest corner. Across Washington is the **Sam Hughes House,** now a series of garden apartments. Hughes came to Tucson for his health in 1858 and became an important businessman and developer in early Tucson. He moved into this house with his bride in 1864, expanding it considerably over the years to accommodate their 15 children. Hughes and

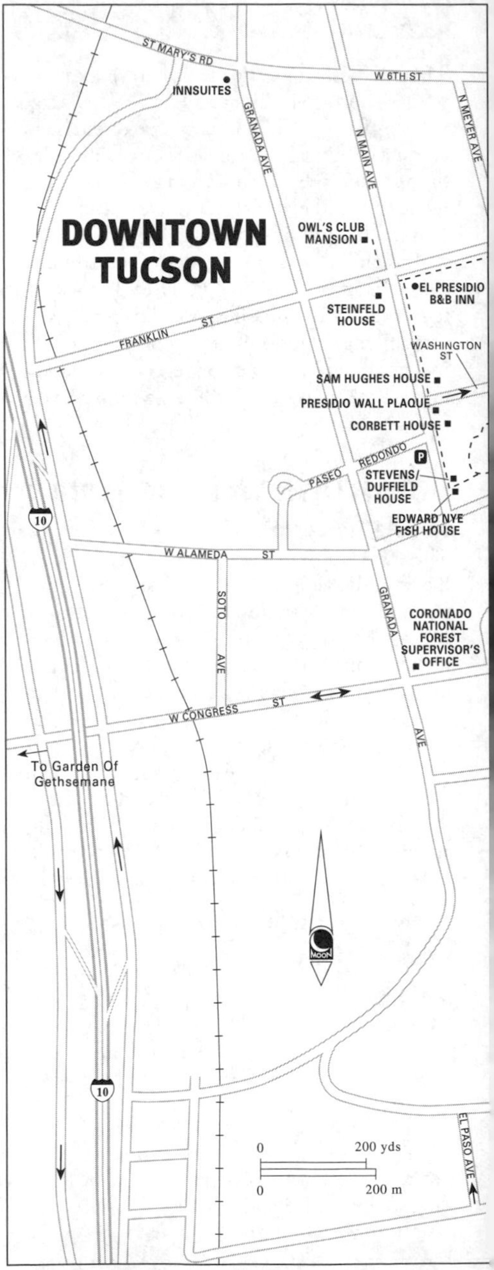

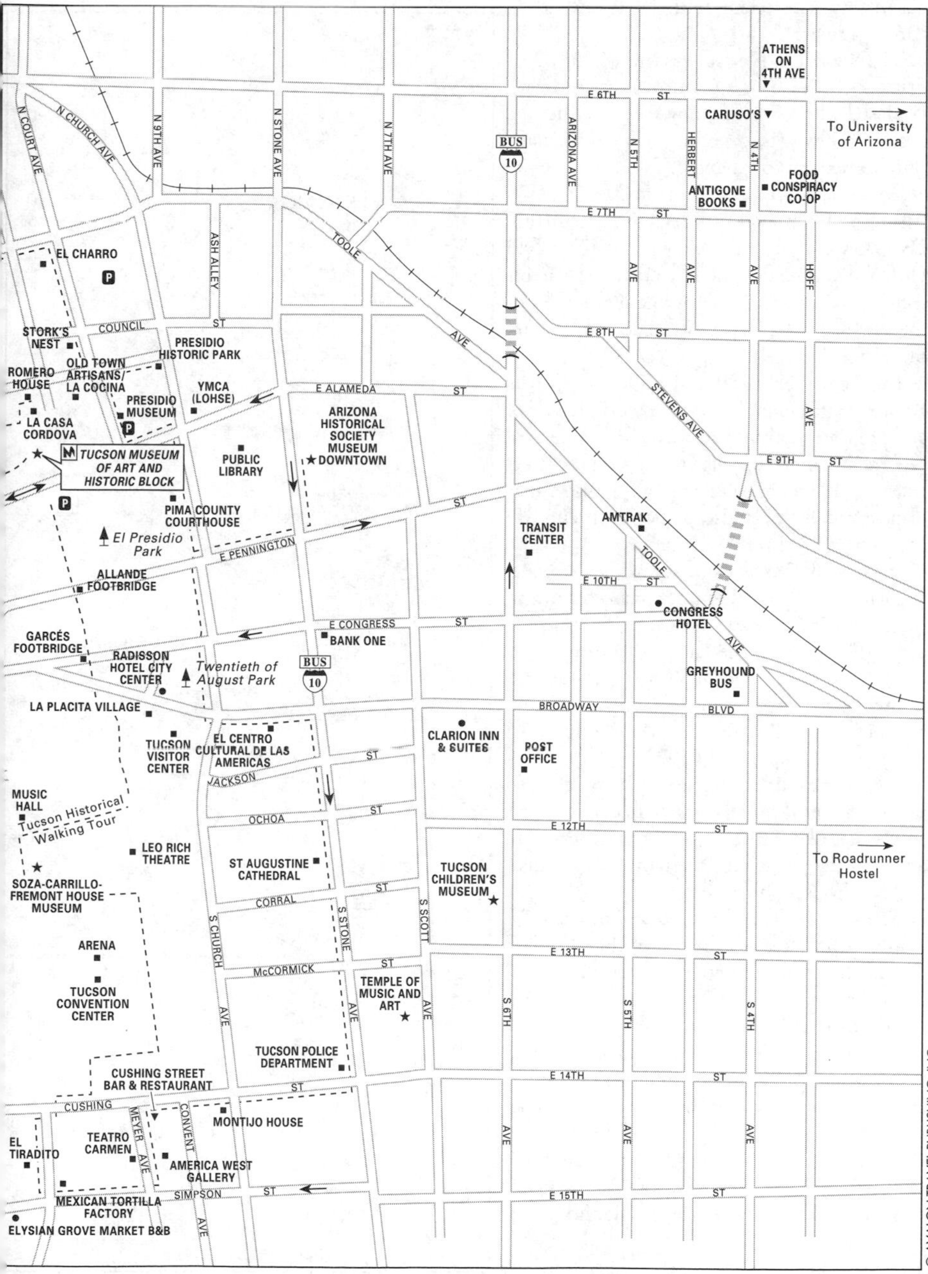

Southern Arizona

his wife lived to celebrate their 50th wedding anniversary here.

The **Steinfeld House** was built in 1900 of brick and stucco in a California mission revival–style. Its residents enjoyed one of Tucson's first bathtubs with piped-in water. The mansion has been restored for use as offices.

Continue north across Franklin Street to #378 (the second house on your left) to see the 1902 **Owl's Club Mansion,** which, like the Steinfeld House, had been designed by noted local architect Henry Trost for use by the gentlemen of the Owl's Club. The exterior reflects an ornate mission revival style.

Built between 1889 and 1896, the **Julius Kruttschnitt House** blends the Mexican style of adobe construction and a *zaguan* (a central breezeway connecting the entrance on the street side with a patio in back) with an Anglo-American verandah and landscaped yards. It's now El Presidio Bed & Breakfast Inn.

If you walk two blocks east to Court Avenue, you'll find the house built by French stonemason Jules le Flein, now **El Charro Café.** Le Flein came to Tucson in the late 1800s to remodel the St. Augustine Cathedral. In 1900 he built this house for his family, using volcanic stone from Sentinel Peak. His daughter, Monica, founded the Mexican restaurant in 1922.

One block south is the **Stork's Nest,** so called because it served as Tucson's first maternity ward. It was first recorded after the fire of 1883 as an adobe dwelling with attached ramada. The building now houses offices.

You may wish to detour one block east on Washington Street to the site of the presidio's northeast corner; a new park will have a reconstruction of the wall, tower, and commandante's office.

Returning to Court Avenue and continuing south, you'll pass an adobe building on the left that will house a Presidio Museum. On the other side of Court Avenue, you may wish to drop in at the arts and crafts shops of **Old Town Artisans** (520/623-6024 or 800/782-8072, www.oldtownartisans.com, daily except major holidays). The shops, in an 1800s adobe building with saguaro-rib ceilings, display lively sculptures,

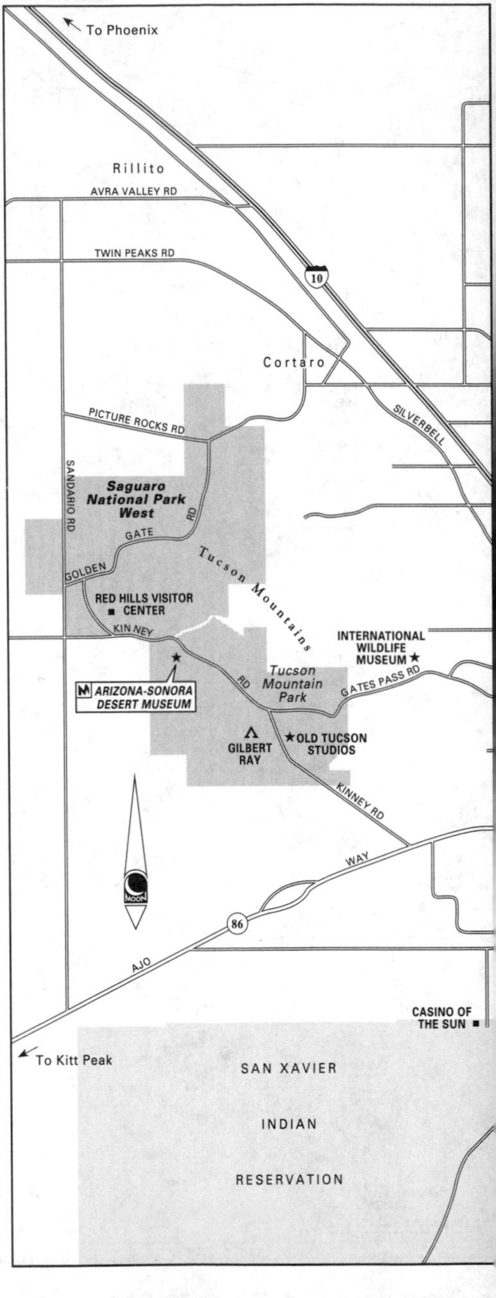

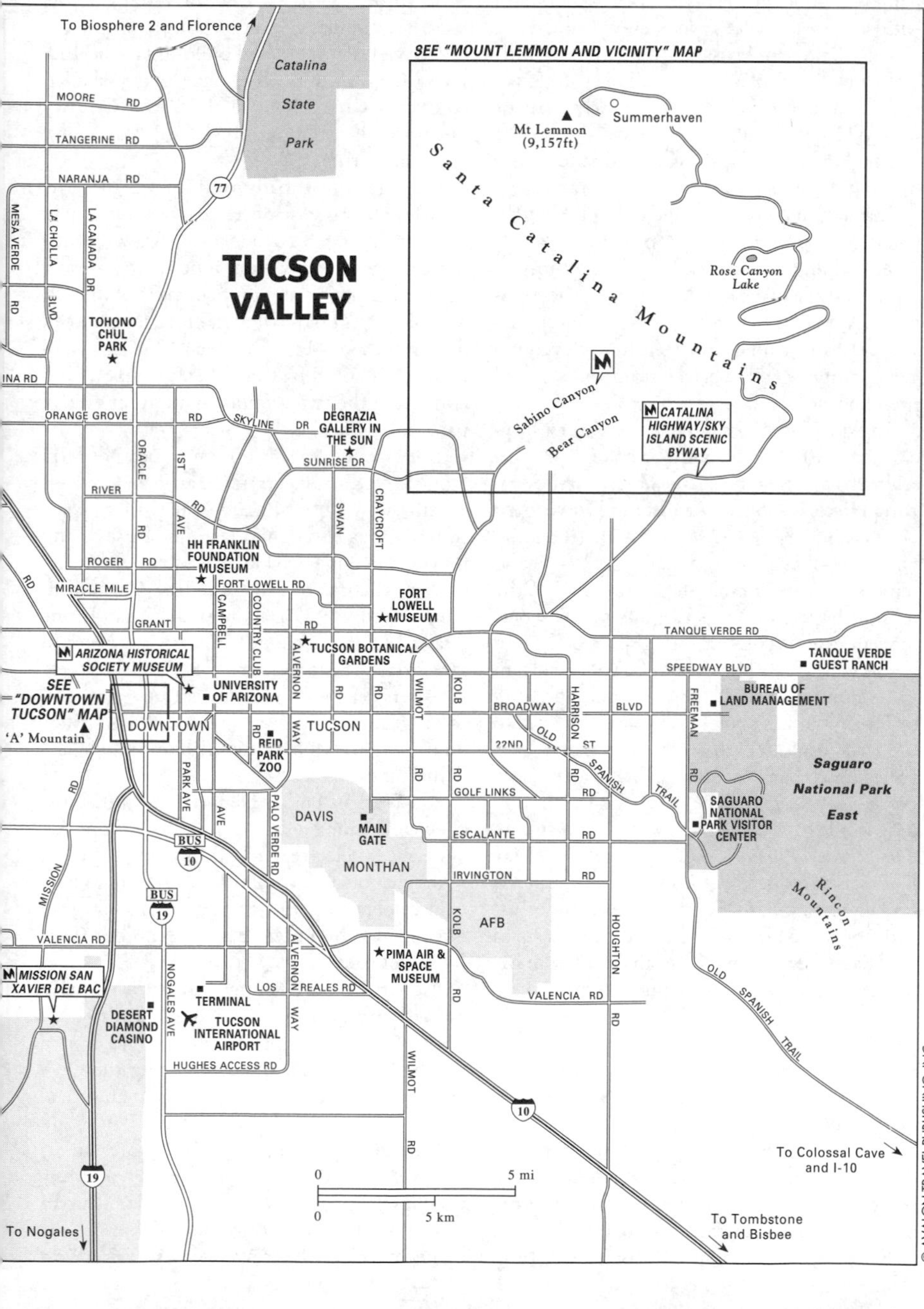
TUCSON VALLEY
To Biosphere 2 and Florence
Catalina State Park
SEE "MOUNT LEMMON AND VICINITY" MAP
Mt Lemmon (9,157ft)
Summerhaven
Santa Catalina Mountains
Rose Canyon Lake
Sabino Canyon
Bear Canyon
CATALINA HIGHWAY/SKY ISLAND SCENIC BYWAY
MOORE RD
TANGERINE RD
NARANJA RD
MESA VERDE RD
LA CHOLLA BLVD
LA CANADA DR
TOHONO CHUL PARK
INA RD
ORANGE GROVE RD
SKYLINE DR
DEGRAZIA GALLERY IN THE SUN
SUNRISE DR
ORACLE RD
1ST AVE
RIVER RD
SWAN
CRAYCROFT
HH FRANKLIN FOUNDATION MUSEUM
ROGER RD
MIRACLE MILE
FORT LOWELL RD
FORT LOWELL MUSEUM
CAMPBELL
COUNTRY CLUB
GRANT RD
TUCSON BOTANICAL GARDENS
TANQUE VERDE RD
TANQUE VERDE GUEST RANCH
ARIZONA HISTORICAL SOCIETY MUSEUM
SPEEDWAY BLVD
SEE "DOWNTOWN TUCSON" MAP
UNIVERSITY OF ARIZONA
'A' Mountain
DOWNTOWN
TUCSON
REID PARK ZOO
ALVERNON WAY
WILMOT RD
KOLB RD
HARRISON RD
FREEMAN RD
BROADWAY BLVD
BUREAU OF LAND MANAGEMENT
22ND ST
OLD SPANISH TRAIL
Saguaro National Park East
SAGUARO NATIONAL PARK VISITOR CENTER
GOLF LINKS RD
ESCALANTE RD
IRVINGTON RD
PARK AVE
PALO VERDE RD
DAVIS MONTHAN AFB
MAIN GATE
Rincon Mountains
MISSION RD
BUS 10
BUS 19
VALENCIA RD
HOUGHTON RD
PIMA AIR & SPACE MUSEUM
MISSION SAN XAVIER DEL BAC
LOS REALES RD
TERMINAL
DESERT DIAMOND CASINO
NOGALES AVE
TUCSON INTERNATIONAL AIRPORT
HUGHES ACCESS RD
10
19
77
0 5 mi
0 5 km
To Colossal Cave and I-10
To Tombstone and Bisbee
To Nogales
© AVALON TRAVEL PUBLISHING, INC.

Southern Arizona

paintings, prints, and crafts by Southwestern and Mexican artists—worth a look even if you're not buying. **Saguaro Artisans** offers more handicrafts north across Washington Street. If you're ready for a break, **La Cocina Restaurant** (520/622-0351, daily lunch) serves a variety of dishes along with soups, salads, and sandwiches on a patio or indoors at Old Town Artisans.

Turning left on Alameda and right on Church, you come to **Pima County Courthouse,** a colorful building constructed in 1928 in a mix of Southwest, Spanish, and Moorish architectural styles. A small exhibit open weekdays in the Assessor/Treasurer office (turn left from the courtyard) contains adobe bricks from the original presidio wall.

To experience more of the city's history, head east across Church and Stone Avenues, passing a sculpture courtyard beside the library, to the **Arizona Historical Society Museum Downtown** (140 N. Stone Ave., 520/770-1473, 10 A.M.–4 P.M. Mon.–Fri., $3 adult, $2 students 12–18 and seniors 60+, free for all on the first Fri. of the month) beside the Wells Fargo Bank. The permanent exhibit History in the Heart of Tucson begins with a large photo of the town taken from "A" Mountain in 1880, then illustrates the story of Tucson from its origins as a Spanish presidio to modern times. A theater screens videos. One gallery hosts changing exhibits. Wells Fargo Bank, next door at 150 N. Stone Avenue, is worth stepping inside to see the dramatic 122-foot mural, *The Legend of the Seven Cities of Cibola* by Jay Datus; ask a bank teller for a brochure about the mural. You can also see some Wells Fargo historical exhibits in the back; the bank is open weekdays. Free parking is available behind in the bank's parking garage off Alameda Street.

Southern Section

Strolling two blocks south on Church Avenue, you'll reach the small **Twentieth of August Park,** dominated by an equestrian statue of General Francisco "Pancho" Villa, the Mexican revolutionary. Originally part of the Plaza de la Mesilla, the park's name commemorates the founding date of the Tucson presidio on August 20, 1775.

For a break or to obtain tourist information, you can turn in to **La Placita Village** across Broadway Boulevard. Signs point the way between the brightly colored buildings to the Tucson Visitor Center, which faces a tree-shaded courtyard with cafés and the **Pima County Sports Hall of Fame** (10 A.M.–2 P.M. Mon., Wed., and Fri.).

Head east on Broadway Boulevard for the **Charles O. Brown House,** now occupied by El Centro Cultural de Las Americas. Brown owned the Congress Hall Saloon, a popular watering hole and gambling spot for politicians of the day. The oldest part of the house, on Jackson Street, dates from about 1858. Between 1868 and 1888 Brown built on Broadway (then Camp St.) and connected the two sections with an attractive patio and garden.

You may enjoy a side trip one block north on Stone to see Tucson's first skyscraper, an attractive 10-story tower of brick and stone with a handsome lobby. The structure now houses Bank One. Continuing two blocks south on Stone Avenue, you come to **St. Augustine Cathedral,** constructed in 1896. Its impressive sandstone facade, fashioned after the Cathedral of Querétaro in Mexico, was added in the late 1920s, as were the stained-glass windows. A bronze statue of St. Augustine stands watch above the doorway. Southwestern symbols mix with traditional elements on the facade.

The **Tucson Police Department,** in a large concrete building two blocks south on Stone Avenue, has police-related exhibits in its lobby; highlights include a collection of antique law-enforcement equipment and a submachine gun once owned by Public Enemy Number One, John Dillinger.

Turn right on Cushing Street to **Montijo House,** which preserves the name of the well-known Mexican ranching family that once owned it. The house was completed during the Civil War, then remodeled in the 1890s in an ornate Victorian style.

Cushing Street Bar & Grill features an attractive 1880s decor with beautiful wood furnishings. Joseph Ferrin lived here and operated a general store about 100 years ago. Around the corner at 373 S. Meyer Avenue is **America West**

© BILL WEIR

St. Augustine Cathedral

Gallery (520/623-4091, 10 A.M.–4 P.M. Mon.–Fri.) with exotic antiques and primitive art gathered from many countries. The gallery is in a 19th-century adobe row house; enter from the back. **Teatro Carmen** across the street hosted many Spanish-language productions after its opening in 1915. Around the corner on Main Avenue is a traditional **Mexican flour tortilla factory** (closed Sun.); pick up fresh tortillas or just watch them being made, but you'll have to be early as workers finish by late morning.

El Tiradito, or Wishing Shrine, commemorates a tragic love triangle. The story has many versions, but one account tells of a love affair between young Juan Olivera and his mother-in-law. Juan was caught and killed by his father-in-law on this spot in 1880. Because of his sins, the dead Juan could not be laid in consecrated ground, and so he was buried where he fell. The pious lit candles and prayed for his soul at the site. Later, parents came to pray for their errant daughters. The custom then developed that anyone could light a candle on the grave and make any kind of wish. If the candle burns to its base, the wish will be granted. The shrine is said to be the only one in North America dedicated to a sinner. If it's lunchtime, you may wish to drop into the attractive Mexican café El Minuto just to the north.

Follow the sidewalk around the Exhibit Hall and Arena of the Tucson Convention Center. Back in the early 1900s, you would be walking along Gay Street past the adobe cribs of Tucson's red-light district! Follow the map and signs to the **Sosa-Carrillo-Frémont House Museum** (151 S. Granada Ave., 520/622-0956, 10 A.M.–4 P.M. Wed.–Sat., $3 adult, $2 students 12–18 and seniors 60+), constructed in about 1880 by the Carrillo family on land purchased from the Sosas. The adobe building, saved in 1969 when surrounding houses were torn down, takes one of its names from the fifth territorial governor, John C. Frémont, who rented it in 1881. Inside the restored rooms, you can imagine the life of a wealthy Tucson family in the 1880s. A self-guided tour explains the architectural features of the house. Be sure to look up at the five different types of ceiling used: saguaro rib, ocotillo, cane, painted cloth (looks like plaster), and redwood. Changing exhibits appear in one room. A gift shop sells history books. Staff lead two-hour guided tours of El Presidio Historic District on Saturday mornings, November–March for $10; call for reservations and times. If driving to the museum, you can park in front (free for museum visitors).

As you leave the Frémont House, turn right and walk up the steps alongside the Music Hall into an oasis of gardens, trees, and fountains. The small building ahead to the east is the Leo Rich Theatre. Turn left and walk through **La Placita Village.** Continue on to the **Garcés Footbridge** across Congress Street, then the **Allande Footbridge** across Pennington Street to **El Presidio Park.** These modern bridges honor early Spaniards. Francisco Garcés, an explorer and Franciscan priest, was the first missionary to visit the Akimel O'odham village at the base of Sentinel Peak. Pedro Allande, first resident commander of the Tucson presidio, once led a spirited defense against 600 warring Apache. Despite a severe leg wound, he continued to direct his 20 presidial soldiers, eventually saving the settlement.

At El Presidio Park, you'll be standing where Spanish soldiers drilled and held holiday fiestas at Plaza de las Armas in the original presidio 200 years ago. The park offers a quiet spot to rest and enjoy the sculptures and fountains. The **Tucson Museum of Art and Historic Block** is just a short walk away and marks the end of your journey.

DOWNTOWN TO THE UNIVERSITY OF ARIZONA

Tucson Children's Museum

Full of things to do, this museum (200 S. 6th Ave., 520/792-9985, www.tucsonchildrensmuseum.org, noon–5 P.M. Sun., 10 A.M.–5 P.M. Tues.–Sat., closed Mon. except some holidays, $3.50 children 2–16, $5.50 adults, $4.50 seniors) is in the historic 1901 Carnegie Library building between 12th and 13th Streets. The exhibits have been designed especially for kids ages 2–11, who must be with an adult at all times. Children have fun exploring the world, conducting scientific experiments, learning about different careers, discovering new cultures, and getting behind the wheel of a real fire truck. Wee World offers a play area for the four and under set. A gift shop sells souvenirs. Special activities take place on some days and you can rent a room for a birthday party.

Fourth Avenue

The Bohemian heart of Tucson lies along this street located between downtown and the university. Ethnic cafés, restaurants, galleries, and thrift shops line both sides from University Boulevard south to 9th Street. **Old Pueblo Trolley** (520/792-1802, www.oldpueblotrolley.org) runs antique electric streetcars along 4th Avenue and University Boulevard on Friday evenings, Saturday afternoons and evenings, and Sunday afternoons. You can learn more about 4th Avenue, the March and December street fairs, and other activities from the local merchant's association (520/624-5004, www.fourthavenue.org).

The Postal History Foundation

An ornate 100-year-old postal counter from Naco, Arizona, and rotating exhibits greet you upon entering the main building. A philatelic counter offers a large variety of current stamps along with other postal services (except money orders). Stamp enthusiasts can delve into the large research library just to the north, which also has Civil War exhibits. The foundation (just west of the university at 920 N. 1st Ave., 520/623-6652, www.postalhistoryfoundation.org, 8 A.M.–3 P.M. Mon.–Fri., philatelic counter closes a half hour earlier, donations welcome) actively promotes postal research and education. Free parking is available in back.

Arizona Historical Society Museum

Imaginative exhibits take you through Arizona's Spanish, Mexican, Mountain Men, Territorial, and Early Statehood eras (just west of the University of Arizona at 949 E. 2nd St., 520/628-5774, www.arizonahistoricalsociety.org, 10 A.M.–4 P.M. Mon.–Sat., $5 adults, $4 students 12–18 and seniors 60+). Period rooms, artifacts, and photos bring the state's history to life. Temporary exhibits and special programs interpret additional aspects of the past. In the early-1900s copper-mine exhibit, a favorite of visitors, you walk through a realistic mine complete with sound effects, emerging at a giant stamp mill and other processing machinery. Panels tell of miners' social lives, work, and labor troubles. Brightly colored minerals on display show off the state's underground wealth and beauty.

Also take a look at the museum's front: Stonemason Jules le Flein created this sandstone facade in 1883 for Arizona's first Roman Catholic cathedral, which was demolished in 1936. A museum shop provides a fine selection of books and crafts. Kids will enjoy exploring many of the exhibits and doing some projects designed just for them. You can delve into the Arizona Historical Society's extensive document and photo collection in the research library, which is open until 3 P.M. Monday–Friday and 1 P.M. on Saturday. You can park for free at the Arizona Historical Society spaces in the parking garage one block west on 2nd Street; pick up a parking pass at the museum information desk.

UNIVERSITY OF ARIZONA

In 1885, the 13th Territorial Legislature awarded Tucson $25,000 to establish Arizona's first university. Most townspeople didn't think much of the idea; they wanted the territorial capital (awarded to Prescott) or at least the territorial insane asylum (awarded to Phoenix). It was left to a handful of determined citizens to get the school built. The walls went up after a saloonkeeper and two gamblers donated the land, but money ran out before the roof was finished. A federal loan completed the structure, and the university opened in 1891. The sole building, today known as Old Main, contained the classrooms, library, offices, and dorms.

Six faculty taught 32 students the first year, nearly all in the Preparatory School because, like many other states at the time, Arizona suffered from a lack of secondary schools. The university has since expanded to 34,000 students with a faculty and staff of about 12,000. Its 14 colleges and eight schools offer 131 undergraduate, 138 master's, and 95 doctoral degree programs.

Visitors enjoy several excellent museums, Flandrau Planetarium, theater and concert performances, and sporting events. Campus grounds also serve as an arboretum; you can find out about the collections from brochures at the Visitor Center or online at http://arboretum.arizona.edu. FM stations offer public-radio programs with classical music (KUAT 90.5) and jazz (KUAZ 89.1).

The campus (520/621-2211 switchboard, www.arizona.edu) lies about a mile east of downtown. Parking is tight—look for metered street spaces or signs directing you to visitor lots; you can pick up a parking map at the Visitor Center and at http://parking.arizona.edu. Note that campus buildings number their floors beginning with the basement level, so the entry level is often the second floor. Free shuttle buses make loops around campus on weekdays, and Sun Tran offers good bus connections to other parts of Tucson.

Visitor Center and Tours

The campus visitor center (845 E. University Blvd. Suite 145, 520/621-5130, 8 A.M.–5 P.M. Mon.–Fri., to 4 P.M. in summer) was in a temporary location at press time, so you may wish to call for its location. Drop by for free maps, literature, and listings of U of A events.

The **Visitor Information Program** (520/884-7516) offers 90-minute walking tours; reservations are required. Prospective students and parents will be interested in the 60- to 90-minute **campus walking tours** (520/621-3641) that leave from the Nugent Building.

Arizona State Museum

This is a great place to learn about Arizona's Native American peoples. Founded in 1893, the museum (E. University Blvd. and N. Park Ave. in the southwest part of campus, 520/621-6302, www.statemuseum.arizona.edu, noon–5 P.M. Sun., 10 A.M.–5 P.M. Mon.–Sat., $3) houses an extensive collection of artifacts from prehistoric, historic, and contemporary tribes. The exceptional Paths of Life: American Indians of the Southwest exhibit explores the cultural traditions and current lifestyles of 10 native peoples of Arizona and Northern Mexico. Major temporary exhibits appear as well.

The museum shop sells books and a good selection of tribal arts and crafts. To learn more, you can head upstairs to the museum's library of books on archaeology and anthropology. In February, you can enjoy demonstrations, dancing, storytelling, and traditional foods at the Southwest Indian Art Fair.

Museum of Art

The diverse collection here spans the years from the Renaissance to the present (near Park Ave. and Speedway Blvd., 520/621-7567, http://artmuseum.arizona.edu, donations welcome). It's open 9 A.M.–5 P.M. Tuesday–Friday and noon–4 P.M. Saturday and Sunday mid-August–mid-May, then 10 A.M.–3:30 P.M. Tuesday–Friday and noon–4 P.M. Saturday and Sunday the rest of the year. A highlight of the permanent Kress Collection, the late-15th-century Retablo of Ciudad Rodrigo has 26 panels from a cathedral in

making tortillas at a Tucson museum

© BILL WEIR

west-central Spain. Hispano-Flemish artists used fine brushwork and brilliant colors to tell the Christian story. Other works in the Kress Collection present a variety of European artists from the 14th–19th centuries. Modern and contemporary art appear in changing exhibits in the downstairs galleries and some of the spaces upstairs. Audrey Flack's 1977 pop-art painting *Marilyn* above the staircase is a favorite of visitors. A small gift shop sells books, magazines, posters, and cards. The museum is on the east side of campus; you can use the Park Avenue Garage, north of Speedway Boulevard, and take the pedestrian underpass.

Center for Creative Photography

Drop in to view exhibits of photographs by Richard Avedon, Ansel Adams, Paul Strand, and other famous artists. The center (just southeast of the Museum of Art, 520/621-7968, www.creativephotography.org, 9 A.M.–5 P.M. Mon.–Fri., noon–5 P.M. Sat.–Sun., donations welcome) holds some 60,000 prints by more than 2,000 photographers, plus an archive of manuscripts, photography materials, and artifacts. With prior notice, you can arrange to see original works of your choice in the Print Viewing Room. Binders at the center and on the website list collections and artists. An extensive photography library lies across the lobby from the exhibition gallery. There's also a small gift shop. Staff can direct you to other photographic exhibits in town.

Student Union

This spacious complex in the center of campus is a good place to meet students and learn what's going on. The main level has an information desk (520/621-7755, www.union.arizona.edu), post office, and copy shop. You'll find a huge selection of places to eat, including an inexpensive Italian cafeteria south of the bookstore and a buffet restaurant on the level above. Gallagher Theatre shows popular movies. The USS Arizona Lounge displays photographs, a model, and artifacts from the battleship *Arizona,* destroyed at Pearl Harbor on December 7, 1941. Union Gallery upstairs hosts changing exhibits, but is closed Sundays and in summer. In the basement, the Cellar often jumps to live music during lunch hour. The nearby Games Room provides pocket billiards, table tennis, and other games.

The attractive bookstore (520/621-2428, www.uofabookstores.com) in the west building of the Student Union offers a fine selection of general reading matter, plus University of Arizona Press titles, regional books, school supplies, and University of Arizona clothing. Head downstairs for textbooks and a computer store.

Flandrau Science Center and Planetarium

Flandrau (North Cherry Ave. and University Blvd., 520/621-7827, www.flandrau.org, $3 adults, $2 children 3–13) offers engaging science exhibits for visitors of all ages. You can explore visiting shows and the permanent astronomy displays, or head downstairs to see the Mineral Museum's beautiful specimens. Kids have their own projects to do. A gift shop sells books, posters, and astronomy souvenirs. Hours run 1–5 P.M. Sunday, 9 A.M.–5 P.M. Monday–Saturday, and 7–9 P.M. Thursday–Saturday.

Free public viewings of the stars, planets, and galaxies use the center's 16-inch telescope (7–10 P.M. Wed.–Sat., Sept.–March and 8–10 P.M. Wed.–Sat., April–Aug.). Inside the planetarium theater, amateur stargazers can experience dynamic and entertaining programs on astronomy, Native American sky lore, and wonders of the universe. Call or check the website for show times and topics. Planetarium shows ($5.50 adult, $4.50 seniors, $4 children 3–13, no entry for tots under 3) include admission to the exhibits.

Some parking is available on the northeast side of the building. Flandrau may move to a new site in 2008 as part of the Rio Nuevo projects.

Library

With about eight million items and access to more than 1,600 databases, the university offers serious research possibilities. The Main Library (520/621-6441, www.library.arizona.edu, long hours during main terms) has an information desk, periodicals, and a reference section on the second floor (main entrance). Government documents are up on the 3rd floor. The map collection and copy center are downstairs, as is the Information Commons, which open out onto a subterranean courtyard. The public can use computers in the Information Commons, but university people have priority.

Special Collections has a separate entrance in front of the Main Library. Step inside to see some exhibits. Other specialized libraries on campus include Science-Engineering, Architecture, Center for Creative Photography, Music, and Oriental Studies.

Hall of Champions

See photos of Wildcat teams and players 1897–present at this glass-walled gallery (520/626-3263, http://arizonaathletics.com, 9 A.M.–5 P.M. Mon.–Fri. and noon–5 P.M. Sat.) on the upper level of the north side of McKale Memorial Center. The ticket office and a sports shop are on the south side, where you'll also find parking on the street.

The History of Pharmacy Museum

Exhibits in the College of Pharmacy building (4 blocks north of the main campus at Warren Ave. and Mabel St., 520/626-1427, www.pharmacy.arizona.edu, 8 A.M.–5 P.M. Mon.–Fri., free) trace the history of Arizona pharmaceuticals with drugstore paraphernalia, old-time cure-alls, and antique medicine bottles. Pick up a self-guided tour booklet at the Dean's Office on the 3rd floor. Look for displays near the elevators on the 1st–4th floors and off the hallway between the 3rd-floor elevator and the Dean's Office. A visitor parking lot is at Martin and Mabel.

WEST OF DOWNTOWN

Garden of Gethsemane

While lying wounded on a World War I battlefield, Felix Lucero made a vow to dedicate his life, if he lived, to the creation of religious statues. He kept the vow and his life-size sculptures of the Last Supper and other subjects can be seen at the northeast corner of W. Congress Street and Bonita Avenue, just west of I-10 (open daily, free).

"A" Mountain

You can't miss this small peak just west of downtown. In earlier days soldiers used it as a lookout point for hostile Indians, which explains its original name, Sentinel Peak. The giant *A* dates from October 23, 1915, when the local university football team beat Pomona College with a score of 7–3; jubilant sports fans immediately headed out to paint the *A*. The painting became a tradition, and every year freshmen whitewash the giant letter—and themselves—for all to see.

To enjoy the panorama from the top of the peak, drive west .6 miles on Congress Street to just before it ends, then turn left on Cuesta, which becomes Sentinel Peak Road. The road loops around the summit; there's a large parking area on the west side, from which the summit is a short walk up.

International Wildlife Museum

More than 400 kinds of mounted wildlife from all over the world illustrate the wondrous diversity of life (4800 W. Gates Pass Rd., 520/617-1439, www.thewildlifemuseum.org, 9 A.M.–5 P.M. Mon.–Fri., to 6 P.M. Sat.–Sun., $7 adults, $5.50 students 13–17/military/seniors 62+, $2.50 children 6–12). Many creatures appear in naturalistic habitat dioramas. Informative exhibits tell about animal behavior, evolution, and how conservation programs work. The insect collection contains dazzling butterflies, bizarre beetles, and camouflaged stick insects. You'll see rare birds of paradise from Papua New Guinea and the extinct passenger pigeon from the United States. Big game from Africa and Asia will impress you with their size. Wild sheep and goats from many lands pose on the steep slopes of a 30-foot mountain. Arizona creatures "inhabit" both nocturnal and diurnal settings. And finally, daunting recreations of an Irish elk and a woolly mammoth show prehistoric life.

A theater screens wildlife movies on the hour. Kids can feel horns, furs, teeth, and skulls and try the interactive computers and other projects. The gift shop will interest small folks, too. A snack bar is open most days. From I-10 or downtown Tucson, head west five miles on Speedway Boulevard and look for the large fort-like building on your right. This section of road is fine for large vehicles and trailers.

Tucson Mountain Park

Rugged mountains in this park just eight miles west of town cover over 17,000 acres. Attractions include the Arizona-Sonora Desert Museum, Old Tucson Studios, picnic areas, hiking trails, and Gilbert Ray Campground. Saguaro National Park provides additional scenic backcountry just to the north. The campground and area attractions may have a map of the park. Unless you're driving a big rig, the best route in is Gates Pass Road, reached from Tucson by driving west on Speedway Boulevard. Gates Pass has a great view and is a fine place to watch the sunset. RVs over 25 feet or vehicles with trailers should take Ajo Way and Kinney Road from I-19 Exit 99.

Old Tucson Studios

The West has been won many, many times at Old Tucson! This famous movie location re-creates Tucson of the 1860s with weathered adobe or frontier buildings, board sidewalks, and dusty streets. It began back in 1939 as the setting for the Columbia Pictures film *Arizona.* Since then, more than 350 movie and video projects have been filmed here, including *Dirty Dingus Magee, Rio Lobo, Death of a Gunfighter,* and *Young Guns II.* Directors have shot such well-known TV shows as *Gunsmoke* and *Little House on the Prairie* here as well.

Today, adults and kids enjoy a wide variety of shows and rides. A miniature train chugs around Old Tucson on a narrated excursion, providing a good introduction. Stunt people wearing period clothing stage blazing gunfights at several locations. Step into the Grand Palace Saloon for uproarious entertainment. Rosa's plays movie clips of past cowboy action filmed here. The Iron Door Mine, stagecoach, carousel, old-time car, and trail rides provide additional excitement. You'll find food at several eateries, a sweet shop, and an ice cream parlor. You may bring a picnic (no alcohol). Pets on leash are welcome. Drive west on Speedway Boulevard/Gates Pass Road (not suited for large rigs) or take Ajo Way and Kinney Road. Admission includes all activities and shows except for gold panning, which is $1 extra (12 miles west of Tucson in Tucson Mountain Park, 520/883-0100, www.oldtucson.com, open at 10 A.M. daily, closing time depends on the season, $15.79 adults, $14.20 seniors and Pima County residents, $9.98 children ages 4–11).

You can also visit **Mescal,** a late 1800s movie set 40 miles southeast of Tucson, on some days; call Old Tucson or check its website for details.

Arizona-Sonora Desert Museum

This world-famous living museum (14 miles west of downtown in Tucson Mountain Park, 520/883-2702, www.desertmuseum.org, 8:30 A.M.–5 P.M. daily Oct.–Feb. and 7:30 A.M.–5 P.M. daily March–Sept.) gives you a look into the life of animals and plants native to the Sonoran Desert of Arizona, the Mexican state of Sonora, and the Gulf of California region. Mountain lions, bighorn sheep, javelinas, and over 300 other types of animals as well as 1,200 species of plants live in nearly natural surroundings. The superb setting looks across the Avra Valley to Baboquivari Peak (7,730 ft.), sacred to the O'odham tribe, and Kitt Peak (6,875 ft.), site of important astronomical observatories. Admission costs $12 for adults, $4 children ages 6–12 November–April, then $9 adults, $2 ages 6–12 May–October.

You could begin with a quick stop at the orientation area to see the day's event schedule, tour times, and what flowers are in bloom. The path into the Earth Sciences section leads underground through a realistic limestone cave, then opens up to a gallery with exhibits that illustrate the formation of the Earth and how it has changed up to the present time. A mineral

a juvenile Harris hawk in the Raptor Free Flight program

room displays exquisite specimens. Back outside, you can visit the realms of the mountain lion, black bear, and Mexican wolf. Cat Canyon has several elusive species, which you should be able to spot from one of the vantage points above and below. A detour down the half-mile Desert Loop Trail winds past the homes of javelina and coyote. The Riparian Corridor contains a desert oasis with pools inhabited by frolicking otters, beavers, and endangered fish, all of which you can observe through underwater panels. Nearby, desert bighorn sheep stand majestically in their mountainside habitat. Try to spot the birds in the walk-in aviaries—not as easy as you'd expect, as many desert birds blend in well with their surroundings. The Life Underground exhibit takes you below the surface to observe wildlife in their burrows. Other exhibits let you meet rattlesnakes, Gila monsters, scorpions, and other desert dwellers face to face. You'll find desert flora well represented and labeled throughout the museum grounds. Side paths lead to cactus and pollination gardens.

Bring a sun hat and good walking shoes—there's a lot to see. Animals tend to more active in the morning, which is a good time to visit. You'll have many opportunities to meet docents and see their presentations. Try to take in the Raptor Free Flight program (Nov.–April), when trainers demonstrate behavior and flying skills of raptors such as owls and hawks.

An art gallery offers visiting shows. The excellent gift shop sells Native American arts, natural history books, and Southwestern crafts. At lunch time you have a choice of self-serve or fine-dining restaurants, both with indoor and patio tables. A coffee bar and a snack bar provide refreshment too. The museum has a picnic area near the southwest side of the parking lot, and you'll see signs for two picnic areas just to the east in Tucson Mountain Park.

On "Summer Saturdays," the museum stays open until 9 or 10 P.M. so visitors can enjoy the evenings. Take Speedway Boulevard west across Gates Pass or, if you have a large RV or trailer-rig, come via Ajo Way and Kinney Road. No pets permitted.

Saguaro National Park West

The Tucson Mountains District of Saguaro National Park contains vigorous stands of saguaro cactus, as well as an abundance of other desert life. Stop at the **Red Hills Visitor Center** (520/733-5158, www.nps.gov/sagu, 9 A.M.–5 P.M. daily) to view exhibits and a video about the Sonoran Desert. Staff answer questions and provide handouts on the park and its hiking trails. A bookstore has a fine selection of regional and natural history titles. Naturalists offer walks and talks daily October–April. To get here from Tucson, continue two miles past the Arizona-Sonora Desert Museum. If coming from Phoenix, take I-10 Avra Valley Road Exit 242 and follow signs 13 miles.

The six-mile **Bajada Loop Drive** winds through scenic countryside with two picnic areas and several trailheads along the way; it's a graded dirt road with a one-way section. The drive and other unpaved roads in the park close from sunset to 6 A.M. The visitors center sells an interpretive guide.

SAGUARO

These adaptable cacti have a shallow root system to soak up even the slightest rains; "rain hairs" on the roots can grow within a few hours to take up even more moisture. Saguaro *(Carnegiea gigantea)* require about 25 years to grow just two feet and need protective shade. Arms don't appear until the plant is about 75 years old. Old-timers may live more than 200 years and reach 50 feet in height. Creamy white blossoms, the state flower, appear in early May. The fruit, which matures in midsummer, resembles a flower with shiny black seeds surrounded by a bright red shell.

The park has about 40 miles of trails with many interesting loop possibilities. A map available at the visitors center shows trails, trailheads, and distances. The short paved **Cactus Garden Trail** beside the visitor center introduces the unique saguaro and other plants of the Sonoran Desert. **Javelina Wash Trail** makes a short loop behind the visitors center. **Desert Discovery Nature Trail** interprets desert ecology, plants, and wildlife on an easy paved half-mile loop; the trailhead is .9 miles northwest of the visitors center. **Valley View Overlook Trail** begins .2 miles past the start of the one-way section of the Bajada Loop Drive and climbs to a fine panorama; signs tell of plant and animal life on the .8-mile round-trip. Farther along the loop drive, you can take a short detour to Signal Hill picnic area, then climb the easy half-mile round-trip **Signal Hill Petroglyphs Trail.** You'll see intriguing spirals and other rock art from the trail and at the summit. Interpretive signs tell of the peoples who have come through this land. Desert varnish wears off easily, so it's important not to touch the petroglyphs or let kids climb on the boulders.

Hikers climb the summit of **Wasson Peak** (elev. 4,687 ft.), the highest in the Tucson Mountains, from several trailheads. King Canyon Trail provides the shortest way to the top in seven miles round-trip with an elevation gain of about 1,900 feet. It begins across Kinney Road from the Arizona-Sonora Desert Museum and goes northeast in a gradual .9-mile climb to Mam-a-Gah picnic area; the path steepens to a moderate grade for the next 1.4 miles to a ridge with views of the Catalinas, then switchbacks .9 miles to the Hugh Norris Trail, on which you turn right .3 miles to the summit. Coming down, you can make a loop by following the Hugh Norris Trail 1.9 miles past the King Canyon Trail junction, down a set of switchbacks, and along a ridge, left 1 mile down the Sendero Esperanza Trail to the workings of the abandoned Gould Mine, then right 1.1 miles on the Gould Mine Trail back to the King Canyon Trailhead.

Ironwood Forest National Monument

This beautiful area of the Sonoran Desert northwest of Tucson will appeal to nature lovers who shun blacktop and other developments. You won't find any marked trails, visitors center, or campgrounds here. The monument's 129,000 acres protects bighorn sheep, saguaro, ironwood, and other desert life. You can find many cross-country hiking and some four-wheeling adventures. Little has been published on this relatively new monument, which is administered by the BLM office in Tucson (520/258-7200, www.az.blm.gov/ironwood/ironwood.htm).

High-clearance vehicles work best on the main roads; you'll need 4WD on some side roads. Three routes lead into the monument, so you can make a loop. From Tucson and the south, take paved Avra Valley Road (I-10 Exit 242) 19.9 miles, then turn left on unpaved Silverbell Road before the entrance to a large mine. On the northeast side of the monument, a road from Marana (I-10 Exit 236) passes north of aptly named Ragged Top (elev. 3,907 ft.), whose lower slopes make a fine area to explore; bighorn sheep inhabit the steep upper reaches. Farther north, you can take Sasco Road (I-10 Red Rock Exit 226); pavement ends after 3.6 miles and you'll see ruins of Sasco ghost town in another 3.2 miles. All three roads meet near Ragged Top at a junction 13 miles from Avra Valley Road, 17 miles from Marana, and 13 miles from Red Rock.

West Silver Bell Mountains offer another fine place to explore; turn west at the unmarked four-way junction on Silverbell Road, 5.4 miles south of the three-way junction or 7.5 miles from the

IRONWOOD

A member of the pea family *(Leguminosae)*, the ironwood *(Olneya tesota)* can be distinguished by its smooth, light-gray bark on branches and young trees, becoming darker and fissured with age. The largest trees reach 30 feet in height and 1.5 feet in diameter. Pink and purple to white flowers, measuring about half an inch across, appear in May and June, followed by beanlike pods. The seeds must pass through the digestive tract of birds or small animals before germination. Bighorn sheep browse the compound leaves despite the small needles at the base of each leaf pair. As its name suggests, the wood is one of the world's heaviest, weighing in at 66 pounds per cubic foot. Native Americans used it to fashion arrow shafts. Citrus farmers eye it as an indicator of a frost-free zone.

Avra Valley Road turnoff. You'll know you're on the correct road when Silverbell Cemetery appears after 100 yards; it's one of the few remnants of Silverbell and Silver Bell ghost towns. Curve left just beyond the cemetery and take a right turn after .5 miles; this road makes a loop of about 2 miles (keep left at road forks); you can explore side roads along the way or head off on cross-country hikes.

NORTH OF DOWNTOWN

T-Rex Museum

Kids have lots of hands-on exhibits and projects to explore as they learn about early life on our planet and that most famous of all dinosaurs—*Tyrannosaurus rex* (1202 N. Main Ave., 520/792-2884, www.trexmuseum.org, noon–5 P.M. Sun., 10 A.M.–5 P.M. Tues.–Sat., $2 age 1+). You and your youngsters can feel casts of actual dinosaur skin, teeth, claws, eggs, and bones. Reconstructed T-rex babies and an outline of a full-grown one show just how big they got! The displays begin with the early life forms on the sea floor and progress through the ages of dinosaurs, showing how they evolved. Projects along the way include puzzles, games, fossil digs, and an art corner. Gift shops sell fossils and dinosaur-related items. From Speedway Boulevard, turn north one block on Main Avenue, then turn right on Helen Street; entrance is on the left.

Tucson Botanical Gardens

You'll enjoy a visit to experience many different types of gardens, as well as to see beautiful flora (2150 N. Alvernon Way, 520/326-9686, www tucsonbotanical.org, 8:30 A.M.–4:30 P.M. daily, $5 adults, $2.50 children 6–12). The oldest areas have lush plantings of mostly Mediterranean and Asian species popular with Tucson gardeners in the 1930s, '40s, and '50s. As you progress through the gardens, you'll come across more modern types better suited for the region's arid climate. Collections include tropical plants in the greenhouse, a cactus and succulent garden, Tucson Basin natives, small trees for landscaping, and low-water-use ornamentals. Signs in the Backyard Bird Garden provide helpful tips on how to best attract birdlife. The Native American Crops Garden includes plants used by Tohono O'odham and other tribes for food, medicines, and basket making.

Children have their own garden to explore, and they will also like the Sensory Garden that invites visitors to smell, touch, listen, look, or just be curious. A small art gallery near the entrance has changing exhibitions. Staff offer tours, workshops, and classes. Special events include spring and autumn plant sales. A gift shop sells books, seeds, food items, jewelry, and crafts. The gardens are about six miles northeast of downtown and just south of Grant Road.

Fort Lowell Museum

U.S. army troops chasing troublesome Apache in the 1860s needed a base. So they built Camp Lowell on the outskirts of Tucson in 1866 and named it in honor of an officer killed in the Civil War. The camp moved to its present site in 1873 and became a fort in 1879. Patrolling, guarding, and offensive operations kept it a busy place during the Geronimo campaigns, which ended with the Apache leader's surrender in September 1886. With the Indian wars finally over, the army abandoned the fort in 1891.

The commanding officer's quarters and nearby kitchen building have been reconstructed as a museum (Fort Lowell Park, 2900 N. Craycroft Rd., 520/885-3832, 10 A.M.–4 P.M. Wed.–Sat., $3 adults, $2 students 12–18 and seniors 60+). Inside the quarters you'll find a period room, a model of the fort, army equipment, and many photos with the stories of officers, enlisted men, wives, children, and Apache scouts. The kitchen has some excavated artifacts and exhibits about life of the enlisted men. The adobe house across the street is an original officer's quarters. Martha Summerhayes stayed here in 1886 with her husband, a regimental quartermaster, and later wrote of her experiences in *Vanished Arizona* (see *Suggested Reading*). Currently the house is a private residence and closed to the public. Signs with maps lead around the park to an equestrian statue and ruins of the adobe hospital and other buildings. In early February, **La Reunión de El Fuerte** presents cavalry drills, music, and self-guided tours to historic sites in Fort Lowell Park and the surrounding community, including places not normally open to the public. The museum, just south of the Craycroft Road–Fort Lowell Road junction, is about eight miles northeast of downtown. Fort Lowell Park (520/791-4873) also has picnicking, reservable ramadas, a playground, pool, and ball fields.

H. H. Franklin Foundation Museum

This unusual museum (3420 N. Vine Ave., 520/326-8038, www.franklincar.org, Oct. 15–late May, call for hours, $5 suggested donation) specializes in the Franklin, a luxury car produced from 1902 until the financial woes of the Depression ended work in 1934. Gleaming antique cars reveal the elegance and amazing engineering of a time gone by. Franklin innovations included air-cooled engines, the first auto assembly line for luxury cars, extensive use of die-cast aluminum parts to save weight and improve fuel efficiency, and one of the first starter/generators. The 20 or so Franklins here illustrate the evolution of the auto during these years. The cars still run and appear in regional auto shows. The museum is between E. Fort Lowell and E. Prince Roads, about two miles north of the University of Arizona.

De Grazia Gallery in the Sun

A work of art in itself, the adobe gallery (6300 N. Swan Rd., 520/299-9191 or 800/545-2185, wwwdegrazia.org, 10 A.M.–4 P.M. daily, free) blends into the desert. You enter through a gate patterned after the one at Yuma Territorial Prison, then pass through a short mine tunnel.

Ettore "Ted" De Grazia, born in the Arizona mining district of Morenci, became fascinated at an early age by the desert colors and cultures of the Southwest. In a short video, he narrates the story of his life and work. He earned fame for his paintings, but created ceramics, sculpture, and jewelry and wrote books as well. Since his death in 1982, the gallery has continued as a museum. The many exhibit rooms illustrate his varied interests, themes, and techniques. A gift shop sells his prints, sculpture, and books.

De Grazia built Mission in the Sun, the adobe chapel outside to the west, as his first project on this site in the early 1950s. He dedicated it to Our Lady of Guadalupe, patron saint of Mexico. You can step inside to see the murals and seating illuminated by the open sky. Local artists display work nearby in the Little Gallery from November to April. From downtown, head east four miles on Broadway Boulevard to Swan Road, then turn north six miles; the gallery is on the right just before Skyline Drive.

Tohono Chul Park

You'll enjoy natural desert beauty at this 49-acre park (7366 N. Paseo del Norte, 520/742-6455, www.tohonochulpark.org, 8 A.M.–5 P.M. daily and you can stay until sunset), (Exhibit House and greenhouse 9 A.M.–5 P.M. daily, $5 adult, $4 seniors 62+, $3 students with valid ID, $2 kids 5–12, first Tues. free for everyone) whose name means Desert Corner in the Tohono O'odham language. Nature trails wind past about 1000 plant species from the Southwest and northern Mexico. Signs identify plants, describe life in the desert, and illustrate some of the many bird species that you may see. Javelina, desert tortoise, collared lizard, chuckwalla, ground squirrel, desert cottontail, and black-tailed jackrabbit also inhabit the park. Wildflower plots display dazzling colors in spring.

© BILL WEIR

DeGrazia's Mission in the Sun

The Hummingbird Garden, near the Tea Room, buzzes with activity when in bloom. Riparian areas have examples of water-loving plants and attract birds. The Demonstration Garden provides ideas for landscaping. You can learn how the Santa Catalina Mountains formed—and see rocks from more than two dozen geologic formations—at the Geology Wall. Crops in the Ethnobotanical Garden represent those used by Native peoples or European settlers for food, fiber, medicine, or dyes. Garden for Children encourages youngsters to explore the natural world; gift shops sell a booklet with additional projects and games. Art shows in the charming Exhibit House change every 6–8 weeks. A small gallery (closed Sun.) at the Desert Discovery Education Center exhibits Native American works. Staff lead a wide variety of tours, lectures, and concerts; call for times.

The Tea Room's (520/797-1222, 8 A.M.–5 P.M. daily) indoor and outdoor areas offer a pleasant place for breakfast, lunch, and afternoon tea. You can picnic at one of the tables in the southeastern section of the park. Three museum shops sell handcrafts and books, including a guide to the park. The Greenhouse sells plants requiring little water. From the junction of Ina and Oracle Roads in northwest Tucson, head west on Ina and turn north at the first stoplight. No pets, please.

Catalina State Park

In the western foothills of the Catalinas 14 miles north of downtown Tucson, this 5,500-acre park (11570 N. Oracle Rd./Hwy. 77, 520/628-5798, $6/vehicle for day use) offers picnicking, camping, birding, hiking, and horseback riding. All of the trails feature mountain views and a chance to see desert birds, other animals, and wildflowers. Staff lead guided hikes, bird walks, and wildflower walks October–April. Hikers can walk easy loops within the park, explore nearby canyons, or climb all the way to the top of Mt. Lemmon. The ranger station offers free trail maps of the park area and a bird list and sells detailed topo maps of the Catalinas.

The .75-mile **Romero Ruin Interpretive Trail** climbs a low ridge and makes a loop through a Hohokam village site and the ruins of Francisco

NORTH OF TUCSON

Biosphere 2 Center

You're welcome to take a peek into this unusual compound 30 miles north of Tucson and to learn how it has contributed toward understanding Biosphere 1—our planet Earth (520/838-6200, www.bio2.com, 9 A.M.–4 P.M. daily except Thanksgiving and Christmas, grounds close about 5:30 P.M., $19.95 adults, $17.95 seniors 62+, $12.95 youth 6–12). Technicians keep watch over the computers, which operate the life-support system for the more than 3,000 species of plants and animals inhabiting the five biomes (self-sustaining communities of living organisms). The marvelous "space frame" architecture—no internal pillars are used—encloses tropical rainforest (the largest and highest section), desert, savanna, marsh, and a one-million-gallon ocean.

Construction began in 1986 as a daring experiment to determine whether a sealed mini-world could sustain life over an extended period. On September 26, 1991, the first crew of Biospherians—four men and four women—stepped through an airlock to be sealed in for a two-year "voyage." They had to struggle at times, combating lower-than-expected crop yields and declining oxygen levels, but managed to complete their two years. Columbia University scientists, who had been invited to help solve the mystery of the low oxygen levels (caused by microorganisms in the soil), stepped in to manage Biosphere 2 from 1996 to 2003. Studies investigated the interaction of plants, carbon dioxide, water, and pests; the relationship between coral reefs and the atmosphere; and the effect of global warming on ecosystems. No crews have been sealed inside since the first missions in 1991–1994, but the option hasn't been ruled out for the future.

Begin at the visitors center, where you can view a short introductory video. Guided tours of about 75 minutes take you inside the amazing structure of Biosphere 2 itself—the world's largest greenhouse, up to 91 feet high and enclosing 3.15 acres. In the Biosphere 2 Habitat, you'll see the living and working quarters of the Biospherians—the well-equipped kitchen, dining room, an apartment, and computer center. Then you'll enter several of the biomes and enjoy a bird's-eye view of the ocean. Next the tour enters the bowels of Biosphere 2—the Technosphere, where two acres of machinery provide the climate and rainfall for the plant and animal communities above. The tour route then follows an underground tunnel into one of the massive "lungs" designed to compensate for changing air pressures.

After the tour, you can explore additional areas on your own. The ocean-viewing gallery gives you a window into the underwater world of corals and tropical fish. Back at the Biosphere 2 Habitat, head downstairs into the old animal bay and some former recreation and work areas to see exhibits that interpret the facts and mysteries of the Earth's climate and how we're finding ways to counteract global warming and air pollution. There's a snack bar and gift shop, but no facilities for picnics or pets

The Center is about a 45-minute drive from Tucson or a two-hour drive from Phoenix. From Tucson, head north 25 miles on Oracle Road/Highway 79 to Oracle Junction, turn northeast 5.5 miles on Highway 77 to the sign (between Mileposts 96 and 97), then turn south 2.8 miles to visitor parking. The best route from the Phoenix area is via Florence and Highway 79 to Oracle Junction. Alternatively, you can take I-10 to the Ina Road Exit, go east on Ina Road to Oracle Road/Highway 79, then north to Oracle Junction.

Oracle

This small town lies at an elevation of 4,514 feet in the northern foothills of the Catalinas, 37 miles from Tucson. American Avenue—the main road through Oracle—makes a loop off Highway 77; look for the Business District sign.

Acadia Ranch Museum (825 Mt. Lemmon Rd., 520/896-9609, www.oraclehistoricalsociety.org) has some historic exhibits and a reading room in an 1880 adobe ranch house that later expanded to become a boardinghouse, then a sanitarium. It's usually open Saturdays 1–5 P.M. (except major holidays), possibly on Sundays, and by appointment. Look for it just south of Mt. Lemmon Road near American Avenue in the town center.

Residents celebrate **Oracle Oaks Festival** in April with a parade, car show, and carnival. Oracle also has a few places to stay, restaurants, and a library. **Peppersauce Campground** ($10, 520/749-8700, open year-round) in the Coronado National Forest is 8.4 miles southeast on Mt. Lemmon Road/Forest Road 38.

Oracle State Park, Center for Environmental Education

Set on nearly 4,000 acres of rolling hills in the Santa Catalina foothills, this park (PO Box 700, Oracle, Hwy. 85623, 520/896-2425, 7 A.M.–5 P.M. daily except Dec. 25, $6/vehicle, $1/individual for nonmotorized travel) offers fine scenery and a chance to see wildlife. Picnic tables nestle under the oaks. About 15 miles of trails—including a 7-mile segment of the Arizona Trail—loop through oak woodlands, grasslands, chaparral, and picturesque granite boulders at elevations ranging 3,500–4,622 feet. All of the trails offer panoramas of surrounding mountains and valleys as well. Three short hiking trails begin near the Kannally Ranch House: **Nature Trail Loop** (1.2 miles), **Windy Ridge Trail Loop** (0.9 mile), and **Bellota Trail Loop** (0.75 mile); these last two are foot travel only and are closed to pets. For the best views and a good workout, with some steep sections, take **Granite Overlook Trail** to the park's highest point—4,622 feet with about a 200-foot elevation change; it's 1.2 miles round-trip (out and back) or it can be done as a 1.8-mile loop; begin from Oak Woodland Area, the first picnic area on your right from the main entrance. These and other trails interconnect for loops of seven miles or more including the Arizona Trail segment. Mountain bikers can follow several trails for a variety of loops. Equestrians should use the Cherry Valley entrance on the west side of the park, at the start of a network of trails especially for them; there's also access to the Arizona Trail.

The park's 5 P.M. closing allows wildlife to have some time unhindered by human presence. Staff offer tours of the Mediterranean revival–style Kannally Ranch House, built in 1929-1933, at 10 A.M. and 2 P.M. weekends and holidays. Groups can reserve a day-use area, rent the house for events, and arrange house tours.

From Tucson or Phoenix, drive to Oracle Junction, then follow Highway 77 northeast for 9 miles (to just past Milepost 100), turn right 2.5 miles on American Avenue through Oracle's business district, turn right at the sign and follow Mt. Lemmon Road 1 mile, then make a left into the main park entrance; the park road ends 1.3 miles farther at the Kannally Ranch House and park office (staffed irregular hours). For the Cherry Valley entrance, stay on American Avenue for 3.5 miles, then turn right at the sign. If you're coming from Mammoth, follow American Avenue for .3 miles and turn left at the sign.

Romero's mid-19th-century ranch. The one-mile **Nature Trail** loop has interpretive signs about desert life. The **Birding Trail** offers good opportunities for sightings on its one-mile loop. These first three loops are open to foot travel only, but the 2.3-mile **Canyon Loop Trail** can be used by hikers, cyclists, and equestrians.

Romero Canyon Trail and **Sutherland Trail** head east deep into the Catalinas. The trails narrow and steepen where they leave the state park and enter Pusch Ridge Wilderness and the Bighorn Sheep Management Area. At this point, cyclists and dogs—both prohibited in the Wilderness—have to turn back. The trails also become too rough for most equestrians. In spring, the creek in Romero Canyon and its tributary Montrose Canyon will be running and have small waterfalls. Natural pools along the lower part of the popular Romero Canyon Trail make good day-hike destinations. Montrose Pools lie a short, steep descent off Romero Canyon Trail just 1.1 miles up. Romero Pools, 2.8 miles one-way with a 900-foot elevation gain, can be deep enough for swimming. The Romero Canyon and Sutherland Trails meet the Mt. Lemmon Trail that leads to the summit (14 strenuous miles one-way) and other destinations. Sabino Canyon is about 17 strenuous miles away via Romero Canyon Trail and the 6,000-foot Romero Pass.

Equestrians especially like the **Fifty-Year Trail,** though hikers and mountain bikers enjoy it, too; the six-mile (one-way) trail heads northeast from the Equestrian Center across rolling foothills to connect with Sutherland and other trails in the National Forest. Hikers, equestrians, and experienced mountain bikers can do a challenging loop of about nine miles on Fifty-Year, a trail link, and Sutherland Trail.

The campground fee of $12 with no hookups or $19 with electricity and water includes showers and a dump station. There's usually room, even in the busy January–April season, thanks to a recent campground expansion. Only groups can reserve areas. Your horse is welcome to stay at the Equestrian Center, in which case you would camp here. Special events include an Easter sunrise service and a Solar Expo in May.

EAST OF DOWNTOWN

Reid Park Zoo

You'll meet wildlife from the far reaches of the world here (Randolph Way, 520/791-4022 recording or 520/791-5064, www.tucsonzoo.org, 9 A.M.–4 P.M., daily, $5 adults, $4 seniors 62+, $2 children 2–14). Landscaping and plants add beauty and provide a natural setting for the different habitats. Tigers from Asia prowl their territory just inside the entrance on the left. Beyond lie many of the famous African animals, such as a white rhino, a pair of lions, mandrills, giraffes, and zebras. A polar bear seems quite content as its insulating fur protects it from Tucson's heat, and there's a big swimming pool at hand (with an underwater viewing window). The South American loop winds through jungle foliage past piranhas, a spectacled bear, llamas, fat capybaras (world's largest rodent), sleek jaguars, long-limbed gibbons, and other wonderful creatures. Many of the zoo's birds, some in two walk-in aviaries, display spectacular plumage and colors. Zoo staff breed anteaters and other rare animals and participate in a species survival plan. Reid Park, which also has picnic and ball fields, lies 3.5 miles east of downtown. Turn north on Randolph Way at the light on 22nd Street, midway between Country Club Road and Alvernon Way.

Pima Air & Space Museum

You'll experience the dramatic advances in aviation technology over the past 100 years at the nation's largest private collection (6000 E. Valencia Rd., 520/574-0462, www.pimaair.org, 9 A.M.–5 P.M. daily, slightly shorter hours for some exhibits, $9.75 adults, $8.75 seniors 62+ and active military, $6 ages 7–12). More than 250 historic aircraft—and extensive exhibits about the people who flew them—fill six large buildings and spread outside across the museum's 75 acres. The first hangar that you enter has a full-scale replica of the Wright brothers' 1903 *Wright Flyer* along with some unique planes and helicopters. A motion simulator takes off for exciting rides. Outside, you can see several VIP aircraft and tour the VC-118A/DC-6A presidential plane used by Kennedy and Johnson. A handful of civilian airliners are on display, but it's the military planes that will most impress you with their history, size, and diversity. Fighters show developments from World War II models to early jets, through the F-100 series, to some current models; there's also a lineup of Migs. Huge transports, three B-52 bombers, many helicopters, and a speedy SR-71 Blackbird stand at rest. The Space Exploratorium & Challenger Learning Center traces the journey into outer space with full-size mockups of Robert Goddard's 1926 liquid-fuel rocket, an X-15, and Mercury and Apollo capsules along with models, rocket engines, planetary spacecraft, and a space video; school kids participate in space missions, which staff explain on free tours. The Arizona Aviation Hall of Fame next door recounts the contributions of state aviators; in the back you can marvel at the complexity of piston, jet, and rocket engines in Thrust: the Engine Gallery. Famous aircraft of WWII fill three hangars, where you'll see gleaming B-17G, B-24, and B-29 bombers, plus many other famous planes and a few early helicopters. The 390th Memorial Museum, home of the B-17G, displays photos of crews along with some of their stories; a diorama and video show aerial dramas.

Free walking tours take you around to some of the most famous exhibits. Tram tours ($4) provide a great introduction to the museum and save shoe leather. A gift shop sells aircraft models, books, and posters. There's an inexpensive snack bar. Researchers can make an appointment to use the library. Combination tickets for the museum, Titan Missile Museum, and AMARC tours save money. The museum is about 12 miles southeast of downtown. Take I-10 southeast to Valencia Road Exit 267, then drive east two miles on Valencia Road.

Davis-Monthan Air Force Base and AMARC Tours

Charles Lindbergh dedicated Davis-Monthan in 1927 as the country's first municipal airport. Crews of B-17 bombers and other aircraft trained here during World War II. Today, pilots learn to fly combat and electronic reconnaissance aircraft.

A tenant at the base, AMARC (Aerospace Maintenance and Regeneration Center), stores a staggering number of surplus planes—more than 5,000. The great variety of fighters, transports, and bombers extends across 2,600 acres. You can see them on scheduled bus tours ($6) that depart Monday–Friday from Pima Air & Space Museum; reservations are recommended in the cooler months.

Saguaro National Park East

Many huge saguaros grow here in the foothills of the Rincon Mountains, about 16 miles east of downtown. Just inside the park entrance, the **visitor center** (3693 S. Old Spanish Trail, 520/733-5153, www.nps.gov/sagu, 9 A.M.–5 P.M. daily, $6/vehicle, $3 bicyclists or foot travelers) houses exhibits describing desert geology, ecology, flora, and fauna. A 15-minute program shown every half-hour illustrates the biotic communities of the park and the influence of the encroaching city. Naturalists offer special programs and walks, especially during the cooler months. Staff have books, maps, and hiking information.

Outside, the **Cactus Garden** displays a variety of labeled desert plants. **Cactus Forest Drive,** an eight-mile paved road open 7 A.M.–sunset, begins near the visitors center and winds through the foothills of the Rincon Mountains with many fine views. After you've driven about 2.2 miles along this one-way route, you'll come to the turnoff for **Mica View Picnic Area** on the left. Another .3 miles past the turnoff, look for the **Desert Ecology Trail.** On this paved quarter-mile trail, you'll learn how plants and animals cope with the environment.

Freeman Homestead Nature Trail begins on the right, 200 yards down the spur road to Javelina Picnic Area. The trail makes a one-mile loop past huge saguaro and along a wash filled with mesquite; interpretive signs describe homesteading in the desert. **Javelina Picnic Area** has some shaded picnic tables.

Cactus Forest Trail System offers about 40 miles of interconnecting trails with many loop possibilities in the desert hills; ask for a trail brochure at the visitors center. Mountain bikers particularly enjoy the system's namesake, the 2.5-mile one-way **Cactus Forest Trail** through the heart of the cactus forest between the north and south sides of the drive; it's wide and heavily used, shared by hikers, cyclists, and equestrians. Hiking trails north of Cactus Forest Drive follow gentle terrain and can be reached from several trailheads on the north side of the drive. For more rugged and scenic country, try the trails east of Garwood Trail. Douglas Spring Trailhead at the east end of Speedway Boulevard is the closest access point for this area. **Bridal Wreath Falls** is a good destination during runoff; follow **Douglas Spring Trail** 2.5 miles in, then turn right .3 miles at the sign to the falls. Hikers must keep to the trails if below an elevation of 4,500 feet to protect fragile desert soils and vegetation.

Backpackers can explore more of the park's 128 miles of trails. **Tanque Verde Ridge Trail** begins near the Javelina Picnic Area and climbs into the rugged **Saguaro Wilderness** of the Rincon Mountains. The trail continues with lots of ups and downs to Mica Mountain, at 8,666 feet the highest peak in the wilderness and 17.5 miles one-way. Several other trailheads provide access to Mica Mountain, though hiking distances are also too far for day trips. Spring and autumn are the best seasons for a visit as the wilderness is especially dry and unforgiving in the heat of summer, and winter can bring snow. A permit ($6/site/night) from the visitors center is needed for backcountry camping, which is permitted only at designated sites. Carry water (1 gallon/day) and topo maps.

Colossal Cave Mountain Park

Tour guides lead you deep underground to the large formations in this dry limestone cave (520/647-7275 cave tours or 520/647-7121 ranch, www.colossalcave.com, $3/car, $2/motorcycle, $1/bicycle). The park is open 9 A.M.–5 P.M. daily (until 6 P.M. Sun. and holidays) mid-September–mid-March, then 8 A.M.–6 P.M. daily (until 7 P.M. Sun. and holidays) mid-March–mid-September. You'll learn about the cave's history and geology, but not where outlaws hid their $60,000 in gold! The tour ($7.50 adults, $4 children 6–10) covers a half-mile and requires a great deal of stair climbing—a total of 363 steps—at a leisurely pace. The cave stays a comfortable 70°F year-round. Tours last 45–55 minutes and leave frequently; you can usually get in within a half hour. Ladder Tours operate some days by reservation; you'll don a hard hat and follow the guide to areas off the normal tour route. A snack bar and gift shop await outside the entrance. Civilian Conservation Corps workers laid the cave's flagstone pathways and constructed the buildings outside in the mid-1930s.

Other caves lie within the 2,400-acre park, too. La Tetera (Spanish for Teakettle), named for the plume of steam that first gave away its location, contained bones of extinct camels and horses. Further exploration revealed a large room filled with richly colored features and a dazzling crystal-covered floor, which blocked progress, as the discoverers didn't wish to trample it. The cave will be reserved for scientific research in the future, but you may see photos of it.

While in the park, you can visit **La Posta Quemada,** a working ranch that dates back to the 1870s. It offers a museum, hiking, horseback riding (520/647-3450), a research library, and a café. Exhibits illustrate the cave's formation, animals, and prehistoric artifacts. Historical displays relate the ranch's history. The park also offers picnic areas and a playground. You can camp one night only in the picnic areas at no extra charge, but you'll need to arrive in the park before closing time.

Colossal Cave Mountain Park lies 22 miles southeast of downtown Tucson. Take I-10 east to Vail-Wentworth Exit 279, then go 7 miles north; or take the Old Spanish Trail to Saguaro National Monument East, then go 12 miles south.

Redington Pass

The bumpy, unpaved Redington Road offers a scenic "back door" to the eastern Tucson Valley. You'll enjoy panoramas of Tucson as the road winds up to the high-desert Redington Pass, which connects the Santa Catalinas and the Rincons; side roads lead to trailheads for the Arizona Trail and other paths into the mountain ranges.

From Tucson, head east on Tanque Verde Road; pavement runs out 2.7 miles past the Wentworth Road junction, then it's 9 miles to the pass via Redington Road. On the east side, the road gradually descends 17.5 miles from the pass into the San Pedro Valley, where you can turn north to San Manuel (17 miles) or south to Gammon's Gulch (30 miles) and Benson (42 miles) on partly paved roads.

SANTA CATALINA MOUNTAINS

The Santa Catalinas, crowned by 9,157-foot Mt. Lemmon, rise in ragged ridges from the north edge of Tucson to cool forests atop the higher slopes. A paved road, the Catalina Highway/Sky Island Scenic Byway, winds high into the mountains past many vistas and recreation areas. Down below, a tram ride or easy walk takes you into Sabino Canyon, an oasis of greenery beneath rock walls dotted with saguaro cactus. Catalina State Park offers trails and vistas beneath the imposing western face of the Catalinas.

Be aware that mountain lions live in the mountains and canyons! To reduce the danger of attack, hikers should pair up and keep children close at hand.

Hikers can choose among trails totaling over 150 miles in length and ranging from easy strolls to extremely difficult climbs. Much of the hiking lies within the **Pusch Ridge Wilderness,** which protects most of the western part of the range. Hikers in the wilderness must heed special regulations to protect the desert bighorn sheep by not going more than 400 feet off trail from January 1 to April 30, not bringing in dogs (service animals are OK), and by limiting group size to 15 for day use and 6 for camping. The *Santa Catalina Mountains* topo map shows the main trails, distances, and trailheads; it's sold at Forest Service offices and hiking stores. Volunteers and foresters of the Santa Catalina Ranger District office provide information on the Santa Catalinas at the Sabino Canyon Visitor Center (5700 N. Sabino Canyon Rd., Tucson, AZ 85750, 520/749-8700, www.fs.fed.us/r3/coronado/scrd, 8 A.M.–4:30 P.M. Mon.–Fri., 8:30 A.M.–4:30 P.M. Sat.–Sun.)

History

In 1697, the tireless Jesuit priest Eusebio Francisco Kino visited a Tohono O'odham village near what's now Tucson. He may have been the first to name it, and the high ranges to the north and east, Santa Catarina. Spanish prospectors found gold in Cañada del Oro, and they also reportedly mined gold in the Mine with the Iron Door and silver in La Esmeralda, both lost mines lying somewhere in the range. Raiding Apache discouraged mining until the late 1870s, when Anglo gold seekers began placer operations in Cañada del Oro, tunneling into the hillsides. This canyon and most of the other mining areas lie in the northern part of the mountains.

Mt. Lemmon honors botanist Sara Lemmon, who, with her husband John, discovered many species of plants on an 1881 expedition to the summit. As trails into the mountains improved, the citizens of Tucson headed to the hills more often for the cool air and scenery. The highway to the top, built largely by federal prisoners, opened in 1951.

Catalina Highway/ Sky Island Scenic Byway

In just an hour, this 40-mile scenic drive from Tucson leaves the saguaro, palo verde, and cholla behind, passes through woodlands of oak, juniper, and pinyon, enters ponderosa pine forests at about 7,000 feet, then fir and aspen on the cool, north-facing slopes above 8,000 feet. Meadows bloom with wildflowers in spring and summer. Superb panoramas and fanciful rock pinnacles line much of the drive. Up on top, you'll enjoy camping, picnicking, and hiking in the warmer months, skiing in winter. The many vista points and picnic areas along the way offer places to stop but you'll need to bring water. *Be sure to fill up with gas before leaving Tucson,* as none is available on the Catalina Highway. It's also a good idea to check for road closures due to construction or storms. For highway construction information, call 520/751-9405; for a weather forecast, call 520/537-7510.

The drive begins from the northeast corner of Tucson; head east on Tanque Verde Road, then turn left on the Catalina Highway. After 4.3 miles, you'll enter the Coronado National Forest and the start of the highway's mileposts. If driving, keep an eye out for cyclists who enjoy the challenging ride. Unless you're going straight through to Summerhaven or Ski Valley, you'll need a recreation pass from the Forest Service for use of any roadside parking areas, picnic or camping areas, restrooms, trailheads, or vista points. Travel will be free with a National Parks Pass if it has a hologram or if you have one of the Golden Eagle, Age, or Access passes; otherwise entry is $5 per day, $10 per week, or $20 per year per vehicle. The recreation passes also include same-day visits to Sabino and Madera Canyons. Passes can be purchased from a booth at Mile 5.1 on the Catalina Highway, the entry booth at Sabino Canyon, as well as from Sabino Canyon Visitor Center, Palisades Visitor Center, and some other vendors. Cyclists don't need a pass.

Mile 2.6: Babad Do'ag, the first marked vista point, is on the right. The Tohono O'odham name means Frog Mountain, which the Santa Catalinas resemble when viewed from the south. All of Tucson Valley lies at your feet from this 3,450-foot perch.

Mile 4.3: The highway climbs north between the rugged cliffs of Molino Canyon to **Molino Canyon Vista** on your right. Two short trails, one paved for wheelchair access, lead to viewpoints of the canyon; the seasonal creek below cascades into pools. Look for the transformation of plants as the Sonoran Desert begins to give way to oaks and grasslands.

Mile 5.7: Molino Basin, on the left, is the first campground on the drive and 18 miles from downtown Tucson. Summers get hot at the 4,370-foot elevation, so it's open only from late October to the end of April. You'll need to bring drinking water; cost is $10 per vehicle for picnicking and camping, though three picnic areas outside the campground are free. Groups can reserve a large ramada for day use or camping with the district office. Hikers can head north or south on the Arizona Trail.

Mile 7.4: Prison Camp Road, on the left, leads to **Gordon Hirabayashi Recreation Site.** Either picnicking or camping costs $10 per vehicle, but you need to bring drinking water. A trailhead on the left just inside the gate and another at

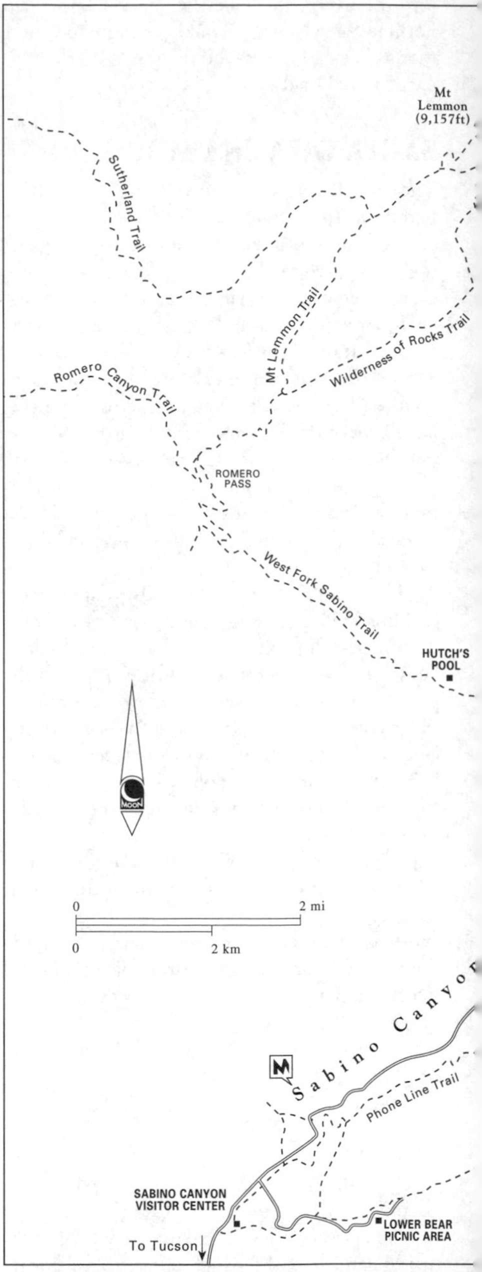

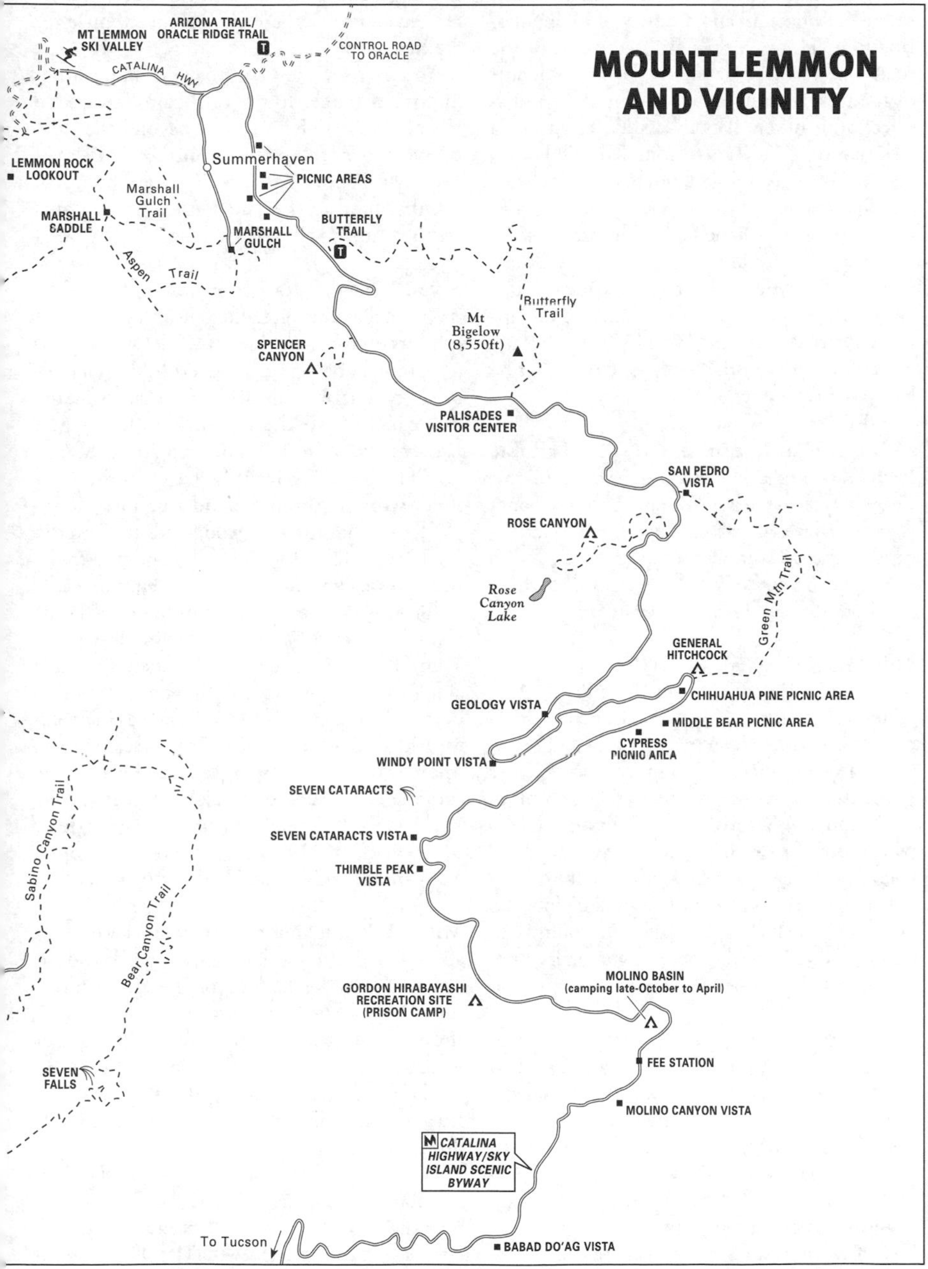
MOUNT LEMMON AND VICINITY
MT LEMMON SKI VALLEY
ARIZONA TRAIL/ ORACLE RIDGE TRAIL
CONTROL ROAD TO ORACLE
CATALINA HWY
LEMMON ROCK LOOKOUT
Summerhaven
PICNIC AREAS
Marshall Gulch Trail
MARSHALL SADDLE
MARSHALL GULCH
BUTTERFLY TRAIL
Aspen Trail
Butterfly Trail
Mt Bigelow (8,550ft)
SPENCER CANYON
PALISADES VISITOR CENTER
SAN PEDRO VISTA
ROSE CANYON
Rose Canyon Lake
Green Mtn Trail
GENERAL HITCHCOCK
CHIHUAHUA PINE PICNIC AREA
GEOLOGY VISTA
MIDDLE BEAR PICNIC AREA
CYPRESS PICNIC AREA
WINDY POINT VISTA
SEVEN CATARACTS
SEVEN CATARACTS VISTA
THIMBLE PEAK VISTA
Sabino Canyon Trail
Bear Canyon Trail
GORDON HIRABAYASHI RECREATION SITE (PRISON CAMP)
MOLINO BASIN (camping late-October to April)
FEE STATION
SEVEN FALLS
MOLINO CANYON VISTA
CATALINA HIGHWAY/SKY ISLAND SCENIC BYWAY
To Tucson
BABAD DO'AG VISTA

the end of the road, one-third mile in, give access to the Arizona Trail and a variety of hiking destinations. Horse corrals are at the end of the road. You'll see foundations and other remnants of the prison camp established in 1930s; prisoners built much of the Catalina Highway, a task that took 18 years to complete. The camp later housed juvenile offenders until it closed and the buildings were razed in the mid-1970s. Interpretive signs tell the story of the camp and its people. The present name honors Gordon Hirabayashi, who challenged the constitutionality of internment and curfew imposed on Japanese-Americans during World War II; the case went all the way to the Supreme Court, but he lost and had to serve a sentence here.

Mile 8.6: In another mile, you'll pass **Thimble Peak Vista** on the left with fine views west across Bear Canyon—the largest drainage of the Santa Catalinas. **Seven Cataracts Vista,** 0.6 mile farther on the left, takes in a series of cascades. (Note that these are different from Seven Falls, which are about 4 miles down Bear Canyon.)

Mile 11.5: Cypress and Middle Bear Picnic Areas on the right, then Chihuahua Pine Picnic Area on the left lie tucked in the forest. **General Hitchcock Campground,** on the right at Mile 12, was closed at press time; check with the visitors center to see if it has reopened. In another two miles you'll come to **Windy Point Vista** on the left, which provides sweeping panoramas of the Rincons, Santa Ritas, southern foothills of the Catalinas, and the Tucson Valley. The granite pinnacles here attract rock climbers and camera buffs. **Geology Vista,** a bit farther on the right, offers more pinnacles and good views to the east and southeast.

Mile 17: Rose Canyon Lake lies at an elevation of 7,200 feet amid ponderosa pines; turn left. Its seven acres offer trout fishing and a half-mile lakeside trail, but no swimming or boating. The nearby campground, 33 miles from downtown Tucson, is open from Easter weekend to the end of October and has drinking water, interpretive programs, and a $15 per vehicle fee; you can reserve sites and a group picnicking ramada at 877/444-6777, www.reserveusa.com. Day use runs $5 per vehicle for parking at the lake or picnicking.

You can see the Galiuros and many other mountain ranges to the east from **San Pedro Vista,** on the right 0.4 miles beyond the Rose Canyon turnoff. **Green Mountain Trail** connects San Pedro Vista with General Hitchcock Campground to the south. Allow three hours for the four-mile (one-way) hike.

Mile 19.9: Palisades Visitor Center, on the left, is open depending on staffing. Inside, you can see exhibits on the many life zones that you're passing through; books and maps are sold. At a trailhead one-quarter mile before the visitors center, you can hike to the top of 8,550-foot **Mt. Bigelow,** a 1.5-mile round-trip climb of 600 feet. The **Butterfly Trail** also begins at this trailhead, winding through ponderosa pine, Douglas fir, and juniper-oak woodlands to Butterfly Trailhead (Mile 22.8), 5.7 miles one-way to the northwest; allow 4–5 hours between trailheads.

Groups can reserve nearby Showers Point Campground (877/444-6777, www.reserveusa.com). Primitive camping (no facilities) is possible along Mt. Bigelow Road on the right, 1.1 miles beyond Palisades Visitor Center, and at Incinerator Ridge; these areas receive heavy use, however. **Spencer Canyon Campground** ($12/vehicle camping, $5/vehicle day use), on the left at Mile 21.7, offers cool mountain air at an elevation of 8,000 feet; it's 38 miles from Tucson, open May–mid-October, and has drinking water.

Mile 22.7: One mile farther, at an elevation of about 8,000 feet, you'll pass Sykes Knob and Inspiration Rock Picnic Areas on the left, then Box Elder, Alder, and Loma Linda Picnic Areas on the right. **Aspen Vista Point,** on the right at Mile 23 between Sykes Knob and Inspiration Rock Picnic Areas, overlooks the San Pedro Valley and many hills beyond; a copper mine is visible in the valley.

Control Road (Forest Road 38), on the right half a mile past Loma Linda and one-third mile before the Ski Valley turnoff, offers an adventure for drivers with high-clearance vehicles. The unpaved road bounces steeply down the northeast side of the Catalinas, past Oracle Ridge Mine to Peppersauce Campground. The 21 miles to the campground takes about two hours, then the road continues another 8 miles to Oracle. The first nine miles is especially steep and rough—4WD might be handy. Cars may be able to make it one-third mile down the Control Road to a trailhead for the Arizona Trail/Oracle Ridge Trail #1, which winds north down to Oracle in 12.5 miles one-way. Winter snow usually closes the road.

Mile 25: You'll come to a highway junction; turn right 1.5 miles to Ski Valley or continue straight a quarter mile for the village of Summerhaven. The Aspen Forest Fire devastated **Summerhaven** in the summer of 2003, and the community will take years to rebuild. At press time only one café, the general store, and the post office were in business. **Mt. Lemmon Café** (520/576-1234, daily breakfast in summer and lunch year-round) specializes in Pennsylvania Dutch cooking and pies, with a large patio as well as indoor seating. The post office is next door.

A half mile beyond Summerhaven, you'll reach **Marshall Gulch Picnic Area** on the left. (A gate blocks the road in winter, when you'll have to park outside and walk the last bit.) A sign for Aspen Trail #93, Marshall Saddle 2.5, marks the start of the 3.8-mile **Aspen Loop Trail,** which is open about May–October. The trail climbs through an area burned in the Aspen Fire. At Marshall Saddle, turn right down Marshall Gulch and walk 1.3 miles back to the picnic area.

The southernmost ski area in the United States, **Mount Lemmon Ski Valley** (520/576-1400 ski conditions, 520/885-1181 business office, 520/547-7510 Pima County Sheriff's road condition hotline), sweeps winter skiers and summer visitors from 8,200 to 9,157 feet on a double chairlift. During the ski season, about mid-December–mid-April, skiers have a choice of 21 runs, including "bunny slopes" for beginners. Lift tickets cost $35 per day ($30 half day) for adults, $16 ($14 half day) for children 12 and under. After the ski season, you can take the Skyride ($9 adults, $5 children 4–12) up to enjoy the views and cool forests. The ski area has a rental shop, snack bar, fudge shop, and a gift shop near the lifts. The large decks provide the venue for an Oktoberfest with a German band, dancing, beer, and food on the last two weekends of September and the first two weekends of October. **Iron Door Restaurant** (across the highway with indoor and outdoor seating, Sat.–Sun. breakfast, daily lunch) is renowned for its chili and cornbread.

A hiking trail, open about May–October, goes from the bottom of the ski lift, through fir and aspen forests, to the summit in 1.5 miles one-way. It's unmarked, so ask someone to point out the start. You could also take the Skyride up and walk down.

An all-weather forest road continues past Mt. Lemmon Ski Valley to an infrared observatory near the top of Mt. Lemmon. Except in winter, you may be able to drive 1.7 miles up the road to a trailhead for Mt. Lemmon Trail and other high-country walks. The observatory area is gated.

Peppersauce Campground lies in a shallow canyon of the northeastern foothills at an elevation of 4,700 feet. Large sycamore and walnut trees shade the sites, which have water and cost $10 per vehicle for camping or day use year-round. If all spaces are taken, seek dispersed camping along Forest Road 29 starting opposite the campground entrance. Groups can reserve an area through the district office. From Oracle, head southeast 8.4 miles on Mount Lemmon Road/Forest Road 38.

Peppersauce Cave is an undeveloped limestone cavern 2.2 miles past the campground turnoff on the road from Oracle. Despite the road warning sign, you can usually negotiate this stretch in a car and reach the one-lane bridge, where you'll find parking. Walk about 300 feet up the wash, then bear right along the second well-trod path to the cave entrance. Take at least two flashlights per person and expect to do some crawling in muddy passageways.

Sabino Canyon

Sabino Creek, deep in the southern foothills of the Santa Catalina Mountains, begins its journey on the slopes of Mt. Lemmon, bouncing down through the canyon and supporting the lush greenery and trees in which deer, javelina, coyotes, bobcats, mountain lions, birds, and other animals find food and shelter.

At the entrance to the canyon, **Sabino Canyon Visitor Center** (520/749-8700, www.fs.fed.us/r3/coronado, 8 A.M.–4:30 P.M. Mon.–Fri., 8:30 A.M.–4:30 P.M. Sat.–Sun.) has exhibits, scheduled nature walks, and sales of books and maps. The self-guided, accessible **Bajada Nature Trail** identifies desert plants on a loop behind the visitors center. The parking fee charged here also covers the Catalina Highway ($5/day, $10/week, or $20/year per vehicle, unless you have a National Parks Pass w/hologram or one of the Golden passes). Sabino Canyon lies 13 miles northeast of downtown Tucson. Take Tanque Verde Road to Sabino Canyon Road, then turn north and drive 4.5 miles to the canyon entrance. An early arrival will beat the crowds. No pets, glass containers, or alcohol are permitted in the canyon.

A road winds up through Sabino Canyon for 3.8 miles, crossing the creek many times. Visitors enjoy birding, picnicking, hiking, swimming, and horseback riding. Private motor vehicles are prohibited beyond the visitors center, but you can take a shuttle tram up the canyon. Bicycles may not enter on Wednesday and Saturday and 9 A.M.–5 P.M. the rest of the week.

The **shuttle** leaves the visitors center every half hour 9 A.M.–4:30 P.M. daily (4 P.M. summer weekdays); fares are $7.50 adults, $3.50 ages 3–12. Call 520/749-2861 (recording) or visit www.sabinocanyon.com to check schedules. The narrated ride lasts 45–50 minutes round-trip; you can get on and off as often as you choose at any of the nine stops.

The Forest Service provides picnic areas and restrooms, though you'll find drinking water only at the visitors center and the first two stops. Visitors can bring a picnic and spend all day relaxing by the water. Groups can reserve either of the Cactus Ramadas one-quarter mile from the visitors center; contact the district office. Camping is not allowed in the canyon; backpackers must hike at least a quarter mile in from trailheads before setting up camp.

Hikers have a choice of many destinations at the last stop, Stop 9: back to the visitors center via the **Phone Line Trail** high on the east slopes of Sabino Canyon (5.5 miles one-way), to lower Bear Canyon via Seven Falls (12 miles one-way), up the West Fork of Sabino Canyon to Hutch's Pool (8.2 miles round-trip), or to Mt. Lemmon's summit (13 hard miles one-way).

Enjoy the special magic of Sabino Canyon on a **moonlight ride** (520/749-2327) during full-moon evenings April–June and September–November. Fees are the same as the daytime shuttles, but reservations and prepayment are required.

Bear Canyon

This beautiful desert canyon east of Sabino features Tucson's most popular hiking destination—Seven Falls, a series of waterfalls, each with a pool at its base. Some of the pools are large enough for swimming, a great way to cool off in the warmer months, though pools can completely dry up at times.

To reach the falls, you can either hike from the visitors center or take the Bear Canyon shuttle for the first 1.5 miles. Bear Canyon Trail begins just south of the Sabino Canyon Visitor Center, crosses some rolling foothills to Bear Canyon (1.5 miles one-way), then turns up the canyon to Seven Falls (3.8 miles total, one-way). The trail continues 4.3 miles to connect with other trails in the Catalinas. On the hike to Seven Falls you'll cross the creek seven times, make a gentle climb onto the east hillside, then descend to the falls. The water-polished rock surrounding the pools requires care in walking, as it's very slippery. Allow about 4.5 hours for the round-trip or 3.5 hours from the Bear Canyon shuttle terminus; elevation change is 650 feet. Picnic tables nestle beside Bear Creek and at Bear Canyon Overlook along the way.

Those who wish to skip the first 1.5 miles of hiking can pick up the shuttle bus at the visitors center for the short ride east to Bear Canyon; the canyon scenery doesn't begin until you leave the road, so there's no point in taking this shuttle unless you plan on hiking. The shuttle (no narration, $3 adults, $1 ages 3–12) leaves the visitors center every hour on the hour, daily 9 A.M.–4 P.M. Bicyclists may not ride into Bear Canyon because it lies in Pusch Ridge Wilderness, but

Seven Falls, cascading from pool to pool, is one of the prettiest spots in the Catalinas.

they may take the road to the mouth of the canyon and continue on foot.

ENTERTAINMENT

You'll find club, movie, and concert listings in the *Tucson Weekly* (www.tucsonweekly.com), free at newsstands, and in the entertainment sections of the *Arizona Daily Star* (www.azstarnet.com) and *Tucson Citizen* (www.tucsoncitizen.com).

Nightlife

Club Congress (311 E. Congress St., 520/622-8848, www.hotelcongress.com) presents local and national artists on Friday, then DJ music or bands the rest of the week. The action, mostly for ages 21 and up, takes place downtown in the Hotel Congress. **Berky's Bar** (5769 E. Speedway Blvd., 520/296-1981) has the blues with some rock-and-roll nightly. **Chicago Bar** (5954 E. Speedway Blvd., 520/748-8169) moves to sounds of reggae, blues, and rock nightly. **O'Malley's** (247 N. 4th Ave., 520/623-8600) is a popular bar downtown with live music (mostly 1980s and 1990s) on Thursday and Saturday.

Musicians play Latin-jazz favorites Monday–Wednesday and mariachi Thursday–Sunday in the evenings at **La Fuente Restaurant** (1749 N. Oracle Rd., 520/623-8659), where you can dine on Mexican or sit at the lounge. For jokes, it's **Laffs Comedy Caffé** (2900 E. Broadway Blvd., 520/323-8669, www.laffscomedycaffe.com) Tuesday–Saturday.

Movies

Loft Cinema (3233 E. Speedway Blvd., 520/795-7777, www.loftcinema.com) screens independent and foreign films. See local papers or online listings for other area theaters.

Theater and Concerts

The **University of Arizona** (520/621-1162, www.arts.arizona.edu Fine Arts box office; 520/621-3341, www.uapresents.org Centennial Hall) presents theater productions, music concerts, and big-name performers on campus.

Many performances take place at the **Tucson Convention Center** (520/791-4101, www.ci.tucson.az.us/tcc), including **Ballet Arizona** (888/322-5538, www.balletaz.org, Oct.–May), the **Tucson Symphony** (520/882-8585, www.tucsonsymphony.org, Sept.–May), the **Arizona Opera** (520/293-4336, www.azopera.org, Oct.–April), and **Arizona Friends of Chamber Music** (520/577-3769.www.arizonachambermusic.org, Oct.–April).

Pima Community College's Center for the Arts (2202 W. Anklam Rd., 520/206-6986) offers a large variety of theatrical and musical performances produced not only by the college but by many of the area's cultural organizations. The college's facilities include Proscenium Theatre, Black Box Theatre, Recital Hall, and a small art gallery just west of downtown (head west on 6th St., which turns into St. Mary's Rd., then into Anklam Rd.).

The professional **Arizona Theatre Company** (330 S. Scott Ave., 520/622-2823, www.arizonatheatre.org, Sept.–May) presents a series of plays at the 1927 Temple of Music and Art, which also has an art gallery upstairs; the box office and art gallery are open 10 A.M.–6 P.M. Monday–Friday. The experimental **Invisible Theatre** (1400 N. 1st Ave. at Drachman St., 520/882-9721, www.invisibletheatre.com, Sept.–June) offers performances one mile northeast of downtown. For hilarious family entertainment, take in an old-fashioned melodrama at the **Gaslight Theatre** (7010 E. Broadway Blvd., 520/886-9428, www.gaslighttheatre.com, Tues.–Sun. year-round) on the southwest corner of Broadway Boulevard and Kolb Road, eight miles east of downtown.

Casinos

Local tribes provide 24-hour gambling, but don't expect nonsmoking areas. The Tohono O'odham's **Desert Diamond Casino** (520/294-7777 or 866/332-9467, www.desertdiamondcasino.com) has two locations south of town: 7350 S. Old Nogales Highway one mile south of Valencia Road and the new casino just east of I-19 Pima Mine Road Exit 80. The Pascua Yaqui tribe runs two casinos on the southwest edge of town off W. Valencia Road (west from I-19 Exit 95): the **Casino of the Sun** (7406 S. Camino de Oeste, 520/883-1700 or 800/344-9435, www.casinosun.com) and **Casino del Sol** (5655 W. Valencia Rd., 520/838-6506).

Events

Something's happening nearly every day in the cooler months! Check with the Metropolitan Tucson Convention & Visitors Bureau (520/624-1817 or 800/638-8350, www.visittucson.org) and its *Tucson Official Visitors Guide* for what's coming up.

January: Tucson Quilt Show takes place mid-month. **Southern Arizona Square and Round Dance and Clogging Festival** attracts more than 3,000 dancers.

February: The giant **Tucson Gem, Mineral, and Fossil Showcase** features more than 25 shows over a two-week period beginning in late January and climaxing with the three-day **Tucson Gem and Mineral Show** (www.tgms.org), which has museum exhibits and hundreds of dealers. The **Tohono O'odham All-Indian Rodeo and Fair** features a rodeo, parade, singing, dancing, crafts, and food—usually on the first weekend—near Sells, 58 miles southwest of Tucson. **La Reunión de El Fuerte** in the Old Fort Lowell Neighborhood presents cavalry drills, band music, and self-guided tours to historic sites in Fort Lowell Park and the surrounding community, including places not normally open to the public.

Cowboys and cowgirls get together for a big rodeo and a colorful nonmotorized parade in **La Fiesta de los Vaqueros** (www.tucsonrodeo.com) on the last full week of the month, with rodeo action on Thursday. At Arizona State Museum's **Southwest Indian Art Fair** (www.statemuseum.arizona.edu), Native Americans offer demonstrations, dancing, storytelling, and traditional foods. Bluegrass musicians play in the **Old Time Fiddler's Contest.** Top golf players compete in the PGA's **Chrysler Classic of Tucson** (www.tucson.pgatour.com) at Omni Tucson National Golf Resort & Spa.

March: Baseball fans anticipate the month-long **Spring Training** by the major-league Arizona Diamondbacks and White Sox teams at Tucson Electric Park (520/434-1000) and the Colorado Rockies at Hi Corbett Field (520/327-9467). Rifles and cannon roar during the **Civil War in the Southwest** (www.azstateparks.com), as soldiers in period dress reenact three Civil War battles that took place in the Southwest at Picacho Peak State Park, 41 miles northwest on I-10.

Equestrians display their hunter/jumper skills in the **Arizona Winter Festival Horse Show** (www.swfair.com). A **St. Patrick's Day Parade and Festival** celebrates Irish heritage on or near the 17th. **Wa:k Pow Wow** attracts Southwestern Native American groups to Mission San Xavier for traditional and modern singing and dancing. Women golfers play in the **Welch's/Fry's LPGA Golf Championship** (www.tucsonlpga.com). The **4th Avenue Street Fair** (www.fourthavenue.org) brings artists, craftspeople, entertainers, and food to N. 4th Avenue between University and 8th Streets; the fest repeats in December. During the Easter season, Yoeme (Yaqui) Indians of Pascua Village in Tucson stage the **Yaqui Lenten Ceremonies,** a passion play; masked dancers perform a ceremony that's a mixture of Catholic and tribal ritual depicting the forces of good overcoming those of evil. **"Simon Peter" Passion Play** (www.simonpeterproductions.org) is a three-hour Easter pageant during the week preceding Easter.

April: During **Spring Fling** (http://uaspringfling.com), university students stage a huge carnival featuring rides, games, and food. The **Pima County Fair** (www.swfair.com) offers circus events, concerts, carnival rides and games, exhibits, and livestock shows at the Pima County Fairgrounds. The **Tucson International Mariachi Conference** (www.tucsonmariachi.org) presents concerts, a parade, art exhibits, and a golf tournament.

May: The Latino community celebrates **Cinco de Mayo** on or near May 5 with art, music, dances, and food.

June: The African-American community rejoices with entertainment, food, fashion, and crafts in the **Juneteenth Festival,** held midmonth in honor of the day that slaves got word of the Emancipation Proclamation—June 19, 1865.

July: Parades, picnics, and fireworks commemorate **Independence Day** on July 4.

August: Fiesta de San Agustín (www.tucsonfestival.org) marks the birthday of Tucson's patron saint and the founding of El Presidio de San Agustín de Tucson with music, dancing, and food.

September: The **Mexican Independence Day Celebration** is a traditional Mexican fiesta with music, folkloric dancers, arts, and food. **Oktoberfest** brings German music, food, and beer to Mt. Lemmon Ski Valley on the last two weekends.

October: Oktoberfest at Mt. Lemmon Ski Valley continues on the first two weekends. Experience Tucson's ethnic diversity in art, music, dance, and food during **Tucson Meet Yourself** (www.tucsonfestival.org).

November: Thousands of bicyclists challenge the clock and one another in **El Tour de Tucson** (www.pbaa.com) on the Saturday before Thanksgiving.

December: Luminaria Nights (www.tucsonbotanical.org) brightens Tucson Botanical Gardens with entertainment and 20,000 luminarias on the first two weekends. The **4th Avenue Street Fair** (www.fourthavenue.org) brings artists, craftspeople, entertainers, and food outdoors to N. 4th Avenue between University and 8th Streets. **Winterhaven Festival of the Lights** has designated walk-through and drive-through nights for the holidays in this community northeast of downtown.

SHOPPING

Fourth Avenue

The section of 4th Avenue between 4th and 7th Streets has many ethnic restaurants and a variety of craft, thrift, and antique shops. Big street fairs take place here in late March and early December. **Food Conspiracy Co-op** (412 N. 4th Ave. between 6th and 7th Sts., 520/624-4821) has been selling organic and bulk foods since 1971. **Old Pueblo Trolley** (520/792-1802, www.oldpueblotrolley.org) runs a historic trolley Friday–Sunday along 4th Avenue and University Boulevard. You can find out more about 4th Avenue activities and businesses from the local merchant's association (520/624-5004, www.fourthavenue.org).

Shopping Centers

Tucson has four giant malls, all enclosed, air-conditioned, and open daily with department stores, specialty shops, restaurants, and movie theaters (either inside or adjacent).

Tucson Mall (4500 N. Oracle and Wetmore Rds., 4.5 miles north of downtown, 520/293-7330) is one of the largest in the state, with more than 200 stores. **Foothills Mall** (7401 N. La Cholla Blvd. and W. Ina Rd., 10 miles north of downtown, 520/219-0650) includes outlet stores. **El Con Mall** (3601 E. Broadway Blvd., 520/795-9958) is three miles east of downtown between Country Club Road and Alvernon Way. **Park Place** (5870 E. Broadway Blvd., 520/748-1222) is six miles east of downtown between Craycroft and Wilmot Roads.

Art Galleries

Be sure to see **De Grazia Gallery in the Sun,** northeast of downtown. **Etherton Gallery** (upstairs at 135 S. 6th Ave., 520/624-7370, www.ethertongallery.com, Tues.–Sat.) displays top contemporary art along with contemporary and historic photo exhibitions. Head upstairs in the 1927 Temple of Music and Art for shows in the **Temple Gallery** (330 Scott Ave., 10 A.M.–6 P.M. Mon.–Fri.). **Old Town Artisans** (186 N. Meyer Ave., 520/623-6024 or 800/782-8072, www.oldtownartisans.com) offers a large selection of crafts and art produced by local, Native American, Mexican, and international artists in the downtown El Presidio district, near the Tucson Museum of Art. The Visitors Bureau has many listings for arts, crafts, and antiques in its *Tucson Official Visitors Guide.*

Bookstores

Bookman's Used Books (1930 E. Grant Rd. at Campbell, 520/325-5767; at 6230 E. Speedway Blvd., 520/748-9555; and at 3733 W. Ina Rd., 520/579-0303) claims to be Arizona's largest used-book store, with some music, video, software, games, and new titles too. You'll find huge selections of new books at **Borders Books & Music** (4235 N. Oracle Rd., 520/292-1331; in Park Place at 5870 E. Broadway Blvd., 520/584-0111).

Audubon Nature Shop (300 E. University Blvd., 520/629-0510, closed Sun.) offers books on nature and birdwatching along with binoculars and other supplies. **Antigone Books** (411 N. 4th Ave., 520/792-3715) has a good general selection, plus many books by and about women. The **University of Arizona Bookstore** (in the west building of the Student Union, 520/621-2428, www.uofabookstores.com) sells Arizona and Southwest books, University of Arizona Press titles, U of A clothing, and student supplies, along with a fine selection of general reading material. Textbooks and a computer store are downstairs.

Outdoor Supplies and Maps

For hiking, camping, and climbing gear, try **Summit Hut** (5045 E. Speedway Blvd. at Rosemont, 520/325-1554; 605 E. Wetmore Rd. at 1st Ave., www.summithut.com) or the three stores of **Popular Outdoor Outfitters** (2820 N. Campbell Ave. and Glenn, 520/326-2520; 6315 E. Broadway Blvd. and Wilmot, 520/290-1644; 6314 N. Oracle Rd. and Orange Grove, 520/575-1044, www.popularoutdooroutfitters.com).

Cactus

B&B Cactus Farm (11550 E. Speedway Blvd., 520/721-4687, closed Sun–Mon.), on the east edge of town, sells a great variety of cacti and succulents, from tiny potted arrangements to huge saguaro. Also in far eastern Tucson, **Tanque Verde Greenhouses** (10810 E. Tanque Verde Rd., 520/749-4414, closed Sun.) has thousands of cacti of many sizes from many lands.

SPORTS AND RECREATION

Spectator Sports

The University of Arizona **Wildcat** teams compete in football, basketball, baseball, tennis, swimming, track and field, and other sports during the school year. For ticket information call the McKale Center (520/621-2287 or 800/452-2287, www.arizonaathletics.com). The **Tucson Sidewinders** play minor-league baseball from early April to early September at Tucson Electric Park (2500 E. Ajo Way, 520/434-1021, www.tucsonsidewinders.com). **Spring training** in March brings the major-league baseball teams Arizona Diamondbacks and Chicago White Sox to the Tucson Electric Park (2500 E. Ajo Way, 520/434-1000) and the Colorado Rockies to Hi Corbett Field (520/327-9467).

Greyhounds hit the track evenings year-round at **Tucson Greyhound Park** (4th Ave. at E. 36th St., 520/884-7576, www.tucdogtrak.com) in South Tucson. Stock cars (mostly) roar toward the finish line at **Tucson Raceway Park** (520/762-9200, www.tucsonracewaypark.com) on most Saturday nights from March to November; take the I-10 Rita Road Exit 273, turn south, make the first left, and follow signs.

Reid Park

This spacious green park in the middle of Tucson has a zoo, Hi Corbett baseball field, a soccer field, rose garden, lakes, and picnic areas. The park is three miles east of downtown; turn north on Randolph Way from 22nd Street. **Tucson City Parks and Recreation** (900 S. Randolph Way, 520/791-4873, www.ci.tucson.az.us/parksandrec) offers information on facilities and programs centered at Reid and other parks.

Lohse YMCA

This downtown center (60 W. Alameda, 520/623-5200, www.tucsonymca.com) has a covered outdoor pool, fitness center, racquetball/handball courts, indoor track, sauna, and whirlpool; it offers fitness classes and other programs. You can purchase a one-day pass ($10 adult) or an annual membership. There's a county parking garage above the center.

Swimming

Tucson Parks and Recreation Aquatics Dept. (520/791-4245, www.ci.tucson.az.us/parksandrec) maintains 21 swimming pools, about a third of which stay open year-round. Look up addresses and phone numbers in the telephone book under "Tucson City Government."

You can also swim year-round in the covered outdoor pool at Lohse YMCA and in the outdoor pool at University of Arizona's McKale Center (520/621-2599).

Tennis

Randolph Tennis Center (50 S. Alvernon Way, 520/791-4896, www.randolphtenniscenter.com) offers 25 lighted tennis courts, instruction, and a pro shop, as well as 10 lighted racquetball courts. It's just south of E. Broadway, three miles east of downtown.

Golf

The city of Tucson (520/791-4336) has five 18-hole courses. The *Tucson Official Visitors Guide* and the Yellow Pages have listings for the many private and resort clubs in town.

Horseback Riding

The countryside surrounding Tucson offers some fine riding. Stables may close in summer or stay open only early and late in the day. **El Conquistador Stables** (10000 N. Oracle Rd., 520/742-4200) and **Pusch Ridge Stables** (13700 N. Oracle Rd., 520/825-1664) offer rides year-round in the Santa Catalina foothills about 13 miles north of downtown. **Cocoraque Ranch Horse Rides** (6255 N. Diamond Hills Lane, 520/682-8594, www.cocoraque.com) leads rides and other activities on a working cattle ranch west of the Arizona-Sonora Desert Museum. **Colossal Cave Mountain Park Stables** (16721 E. Old Spanish Trail, 520/647-3450) has a variety of rides in the Rincon Mountain foothills east of town.

Southern Arizona Hiking Club

About 2,000 members belong to this active group, which organizes about 50–60 hikes monthly that range from easy to challenging. The club schedules day hikes, backpacks, climbs, river trips, ski tours, and snowshoe trips. Members also promote conservation and build trails. Visitors are welcome on hikes. Contact the club for membership information by sending a self-addressed, stamped envelope to P.O. Box 32257, Tucson, AZ 85751. You can also call 520/751-4513 for recorded information or check the website www.sahcinfo.org.

Skiing

At **Mt. Lemmon Ski Valley** (576-1400 recording or 520/885-1181 business office) in the Santa Catalina Mountains you can enjoy downhill skiing during the mid-December–mid-April season. The longest run is three-quarters of a mile, dropping from 9,150 to 8,200 feet through fir and aspen forests.

ACCOMMODATIONS

Tucson has more than 100 hotels, motels, bed and breakfasts, and resorts—near the freeway, downtown, at the airport, near the university, and scattered around the valley. Good hunting grounds for older, less expensive motels lie on the zigzag Business Route north along Stone Avenue from Speedway Boulevard, west on Drachman Street, north along Oracle Road, then finally west on Miracle Mile to I-10 Exit 255. You'll find some better independents along this route, too, as well as some inexpensive chain motels. Look for lodging listings in the free *Tucson Official Visitors Guide* distributed by the Tucson Convention and Visitors Bureau.

Prices rise during the cooler months, especially during February and March when the weather and popular events, such as the Gem and Mineral Show and Fiesta de los Vaqueros, draw huge numbers of visitors. Reservations will come in handy then. Also, take the motel prices with a grain of salt—prices fluctuate with demand. The rates listed below reflect those in the spring high season; they'll go higher during the Gem and Mineral Show and lower in the warmer months. Add about 9.5 percent tax to rates at all accommodations except perhaps the smallest bed and breakfasts.

Bed-and-Breakfasts

Downtown and University: The **Adobe Rose Inn** (940 N. Olsen Ave., 520/318-4644 or 800/328-4122, www.aroseinn.com, $95–165 d winter, $75–125 d summer) offers a 1933 adobe with Southwestern furnishings, pool, and a hot tub in a quiet historic neighborhood. **Catalina Park Inn** (309 E. 1st St., 520/792-4541 or 800/792-4885, www.catalinaparkinn.com, $136–166 d, less in shoulder seasons, closed June–Aug.) is in a 1927 house with beautiful interiors. **Peppertrees Bed & Breakfast Inn** (724 E. University Blvd., 520/622-7167 or 800/348-5763, www.peppertreesinn.com, $125–195 d, less in summer) has rooms in four houses just two blocks from the University of Arizona's main entrance; one of the owners is a pastry chef! **El Presidio Bed and Breakfast Inn** (297 N. Main Ave., 520/623-6151 or 800/349-6151, $105–135 d, less off-season) is in an 1880s adobe house in El Presidio Historic District. Mexican folk art and antiques fill the **Elysian Grove Market Bed & Breakfast Inn** (400 W. Simpson St., 520/628-1522, www.elysiangrove.com, $85 d, closed June–Sept.) in the Barrio Historico district, just south of the Tucson Convention Center; the two-bedroom suites have fireplaces and a shared kitchen in a 1920s adobe building that began as a corner store.

East Tucson Valley: SunCatcher Bed & Breakfast (105 N. Avenida Javelina, 520/885-0883 or 877/775-8355, www.thesuncatcher.com, $120–185 d) sits on five acres at the east edge of Tucson near Saguaro National Park; the decor of each room evokes one of the ethnic groups of the American West.

West Tucson Valley: Courtyards, fountains, and archways of the **Casa Tierra Adobe B&B Inn** (11155 W. Calle Pima, 520/578-3058 or 866/254-0006, www.casatierratucson.com, $150–325 d, closed June 15–Aug. 15) will remind you of Mexican haciendas; guests enjoy hot tubs and star gazing with the provided telescopes in the desert 15 miles west of town.

Hostels

Roadrunner Hostel (346 E. 12th St., 520/628-4709, www.roadrunnerhostel.com) is a 1900 adobe house in the downtown Amory Park district. Amenities include big-screen TV, free Internet computers, air conditioning, a kitchen, laundry, and no curfew. Beds run $18 a night and $110 a week; a private room is $38 d per night and $230 d per week. The hostel is just a short walk from the bus and train stations or you can call for a free pickup; transportation cost from the airport is $10.

Hotel Congress has a hostel as well as regular rooms downtown.

Historic Downtown Hotels

In the heart of downtown, **Hotel Congress** (311 E. Congress St., 520/622-8848 or 800/722-8848, www.hotelcongress.com) opened in 1919 to serve passengers of the Southern Pacific Railroad. It's a short walk from the Amtrak, Greyhound, and local bus stations. All of the rooms have 1930s decor and furnishings—you'll get a radio and an old-fashioned telephone—along with a bath or shower; rates run $59 s, $69 d January–April, then decrease to about $39 s, $49 d June–August (only evaporative cooling). The hotel also has a **youth hostel** ($20/bunk with hostel or student card, otherwise $25), café, and a nightclub (expect some noise in the rooms).

Under $50

Downtown: Along the frontage road just west of I-10 you'll find the usual **Motel 6** (960 S. Freeway, I-10 Congress St. Exit 258, then south on the west frontage road, 520/628-1339 or 800/466-8356, $40–50 s, $46–56 d) with a pool.

North of Downtown: On Stone Avenue, there's the **Flamingo Hotel** (1300 N. Stone Ave., 520/770-1910 or 800/300-3533, $45–69 d) offering a pool, hot tub, and some kitchenettes. On Drachman Street, you can't miss the huge sign for **Tucson Inn Motor Hotel** (127 W. Drachman St., 520/624-8531 or 800/627-2041, $29 s, $32 d) with a pool. In the next block you'll find **Copper Cactus Inn** (225 W. Drachman St., 520/622-7411, $30 s, $40 d) and **Frontier Motel** (227 W. Drachman St., 520/798-3005, $35 d), both with pool and kitchenettes.

Oracle Road possibilities include **Quail Inn** 1650 N. Oracle Rd., 520/622-8757, $30 s, $35 d), **Oasis Motel** (1701 N. Oracle Rd., 520/622-2808, $27 s, $32 d) with pool and kitchenettes, and **Highland Tower Motel** (1919 N. Oracle Rd., 520/791-3057, $30 s, $35 d) with a pool and kitchenettes.

Miracle Milers include **Terrace Motel** (631 W. Miracle Mile, 520/624-8248, $30 s, $35 d) and **Wayward Winds Lodge** (707 W. Miracle Mile, 520/791-7526, $30 s, $33 d), both with pool and kitchenettes.

South of Downtown and Airport: The south side of town isn't much to look at, but you'll be close to I-10 and the airport. Bargain hunters can find good deals just north of Exit 261 and along the old Benson Highway, which parallels the south side of I-10 between Exits 261 and 267. Many of the old motels along here offer low weekly rates as well, and will more likely have vacancies than places closer to downtown. Just north of I-10 6th Avenue Exit 261 are the **Econo Lodge** (3020 S. 6th Ave., 520/623-5881 or 800/553-2666, $40 s, $45 d) with a pool and hot tub and **Budget Inn** (3033 S. 6th Ave., 520/884-1470, $30 d and up).

Just south of I-10 Exit 261, turn east on the frontage road for the **Lazy 8 Motel** (314 E. Benson Hwy., 520/622-3336 or 888/800-8805, $37 s, $43 d) with a pool. Motels east along the Benson Highway between I-10 Exits 262 and 267 include the **Redwood Lodge** (3315 E. Benson Hwy., 520/294-3802, $35 d) with a pool and weekly kitchenettes.

$50–100

Downtown: A series of motels line the frontage road just west of I-10 and include **The Pueblo Inn** (350 S. Freeway, I-10 Congress St. Exit 258, then south on the west frontage road, 520/622-6611 or 800/551-1466, $89 d) offering a restaurant, pool, hot tub, and fitness center.

North of Downtown: On Stone Avenue you'll find **University Inn** (950 N. Stone Ave., 520/791-7503 or 800/233-8466, $39–49 s, $49–55 d and up) with a pool and **Super 8** (1248 N. Stone Ave., 520/622-6446 or 800/800-8000, $45 s, $55 d) with a pool. Around on Drachman Street, **Best Western Executive Inn** (333 Drachman St., 520/791-7551 or 800/255-3371, $89–129 d) has a restaurant and pool. **Arizona University Plaza** (1601 N. Oracle Rd., 520/740-0123 or 866/882-7661, $49–69 d) encloses a six-acre courtyard; guests have a restaurant, bar, pool, and exercise room. Georgia O'Keeffe created the cow's skull logo of the **Ghost Ranch Lodge** (801 W. Miracle Mile, 520/791-7565 or 800/456-7565, www.ghostranchlodge.com, $80–96 s, $86–104 d and up), which opened in 1941; the rooms, kitchenettes, cottages, and suites spread across eight acres of gardens with a pool and hot tub.

East of Downtown: At the **Smugglers Inn** (6350 E. Speedway Blvd., 520/296-3292 or 800/525-8852, www.smugglersinn.com, $89–189 d), guests enjoy beautifully landscaped grounds, a restaurant, pool, and hot tub.

South of Downtown and Airport: Moving up to the newer motels, choices include **Quality Inn** (1025 E. Benson Hwy., 520/623-7792 or 800/424-6423, $49–79 d) with a pool and hot tub.

$100–150

Downtown: InnSuites Hotel & Resort (475 N. Granada Ave., 520/622-3000 or 800/842-4242, $100 d) includes a restaurant, breakfast buffet, business center, pool, spa, and fitness center on 11 acres between downtown and I-10. **Clarion Inn & Suites** (88 E. Broadway Blvd., 520/622-4000 or 800/424-6423, $114 d) features the excellent Mexican Café Poca Cosa, a buffet breakfast, pool, spa, sauna, fitness center, and a business center in the heart of downtown.

North of Downtown: Best Western Royal Inn (1015 N. Stone Ave., 520/622-8871 or

800/528-1234, $109 d room, $129 d suite) has a pool and hot tub.

South of Downtown and Airport: The group of hotels just north of the airport includes the **Clarion Hotel Airport** (6801 S. Tucson Blvd., 520/746-3932 or 800/526-0550, $99–139 d) with a restaurant, pool, hot tub, fitness center, and business center.

$150 and Up

Downtown: Radisson Hotel City Center (181 W. Broadway Blvd., 520/624-8711 or 800/333-3333, $169 d) has a restaurant, business center, pool, and fitness room close to everything downtown.

East of Downtown: Just a block from the university, **Tucson Marriott University Park** (880 E. 2nd St., 520/792-4100 or 800/228-9290, $184 d) features a nine-story atrium and some rooms especially set up for the business traveler; amenities include a restaurant, pool, whirlpool, sauna, fitness center, and business center. The romantic **Lodge on the Desert** (306 N. Alvernon Way, 520/325-3366 or 800/456-5634, www.lodgeonthedesert.com, $189–269 d) provides a hacienda atmosphere, fireplaces in some units, restaurant, and a pool. **Doubletree Hotel at Reid Park** (445 S. Alvernon Way, 520/881-4200 or 800/222-8733, $149–289 d) has two restaurants, golf (across the street), pool, spa, tennis, exercise room, and business center.

South of Downtown and Airport: Embassy Suites Tucson Airport (7051 S. Tucson Blvd., 520/573-0700 or 800/362-2779, $199 d) includes a restaurant, pool, hot tub, and exercise room.

Guest Ranches

The Tucson area features one of the world's largest concentrations of guest ranches, where you can enjoy Western hospitality and activities as well as high-quality accommodations and food. Popular activities include horseback riding, swimming, tennis, hiking, birding, socializing, and just relaxing.

Tanque Verde Guest Ranch (14301 E. Speedway, Tucson, AZ 85748, 520/296-6275 or 800/234-3833, www.tanqueverderanch.com) lies in the foothills of the Rincon Mountains 10 miles east of Tucson. The luxurious ranch dates from the 1880s and offers a host of amenities and activities, including horseback riding, indoor and outdoor pools, a whirlpool tub and saunas, an exercise room, five tennis courts, and nature walks. Guests feast on the dining room's buffets and on cookouts. Prices include meals, riding, and ranch activities. Daily rates during the peak season (Dec. 16–April 30) are $300–380 s, $360–550 d; summer rates (May–Sept.) drop to $235–320 s, $290–405 d; autumn (Oct.–Dec. 15) runs $255–330 s, $305–435 d.

Lazy K Bar Guest Ranch (8401 N. Scenic Dr., Tucson, AZ 85743, 520/744-3050 or 800/321-7018, www.lazykbar.com) is an informal family ranch 16 miles northwest of downtown at the foot of the Tucson Mountains, next to Saguaro National Park West. Guests enjoy horseback riding, a swimming pool, whirlpool tub, volleyball, basketball, hiking, and family-style meals. Inclusive rates run $225 s, $340 d during the December–April peak season, less other months. A three-day minimum stay is requested. The ranch closes in July and August.

White Stallion Ranch (9251 W. Twin Peaks Rd., Tucson, AZ 85743, 520/297-0252 or 888/977-2624, www.wsranch.com) sprawls over 3,000 acres some 17 miles northwest of Tucson. The ranch offers horseback riding, a pool, hot tub, two tennis courts, nature trails, and varied ranch activities. Breakfast, buffet lunch, and family-style dinner are included in the rates of $184 s, $288–422 d December 19–April 30, then slightly less in autumn and May; there's a four-night minimum in winter. The ranch closes June–August.

Rancho de la Osa Guest Ranch (P.O. Box 1, Sasabe, AZ 85633, 520/823-4257 or 800/872-6240, www.ranchodelaosa.com) dates back 250 years to a Spanish land grant; it's 66 miles southwest of Tucson near the Mexican border. Guests will enjoy horseback riding, a pool, hot tub, birding, hiking, biking, and lots of peace and quiet. The adobe buildings feature artwork and colorful Mexican-inspired decor. The dining room serves gourmet Southwestern cuisine. Inclusive rates are $250–350 s, $350–440 d September–May, then $225–350 s, $330–430 d in summer. There's a three-night minimum stay and weekly rates are available.

Resorts

Just northeast of the University of Arizona, **Arizona Inn** (2200 E. Elm St., Tucson, AZ 85719, 520/325-1541 or 800/933-1093, www.arizona-inn.com) opened in 1930 and continues to combine old Arizona elegance with modern luxury. The peaceful 14 acres offer gardens, a pool, sauna, fitness center, two clay tennis courts, and croquet—you may forget that you're in the middle of Tucson! The restaurant serves contemporary cuisine with international flavors. High season rates (Jan.–April) run about $265–339 d for a room and $340 d and up for a suite; by summer, rates have dropped to $139–194 s, $154–194 d for a room and $249–299 d for a suite.

The health-and-fitness vacation resort **Canyon Ranch** (8600 E. Rockcliff Rd., Tucson, AZ 85750, 520/749-9000 or 800/742-9000, www.canyon-ranch.com) provides an active program of exercise classes, tennis, racquetball, swimming, hiking, biking, yoga, and meditation. Chefs prepare healthy gourmet meals from natural ingredients; no alcohol is served. The 70-acre grounds lie northeast of town near Sabino Canyon. There's a four-night minimum stay during the high season, though the resort recommends a seven-day visit. A seven-night package between September and June goes for $5,530 s, $9,020 d with meals and an allowance for services.

Omni Tucson National Golf Resort & Spa (2727 W. Club Dr., Tucson, AZ 85742, 520/297-2271 or 800/278-5880, www.tucsonnational.com) spreads across 650 acres at the base of the Catalinas on the northwest side of the city. The Tucson home of the PGA, the resort features a 27-hole golf course, lakes, full-service spa services, an exercise room, four tennis courts, two pools, volleyball, basketball, and fine dining. In high season, rates are about $319–389 d, decreasing by summer to $139–199 d.

On the north edge of town next to the Catalinas, the **Westin La Paloma Resort and Spa** (3800 E. Sunrise Dr., Tucson, AZ 85718, 520/742-6000 or 800/228-3000, www.westin.com/lapaloma) features a 27-hole golf course, health center, many tennis courts, racquetball courts, two giant pools, a water slide, and a selection of restaurants. The high-season (Jan.–late May) rate is $229–359 d, autumn (early Sept. –Dec.) goes for $199–339 d, and summer (late May–early Sept.) runs $99–169 d.

Nestled in the foothills of the Catalinas north of the city, **Loews Ventana Canyon Resort** (7000 North Resort Dr., Tucson, AZ 85750, 520/299-2020 or 800/234-5117, www.loews-hotels.com) offers 93 acres with a natural waterfall, two 18-hole golf courses, eight lighted tennis courts, two swimming pools, a hot tub, health club, and several restaurants. Rates vary widely depending on the view and range $195–425 d in the February–late-May season, $99–239 d in the late-May–early-September summer season, and $179–359 d in the early-September–January shoulder season.

Westward Look Resort (245 E. Ina Rd., Tucson, AZ 85704, 520/297-1151 or 800/722-2500, www.westwardlook.com) began in 1929 as a dude ranch and now rates as one of the area's best value resorts. It's on 80 acres near the north edge of town beneath the Catalinas. Guests enjoy eight tennis courts, three pools, three hot tubs, a jogging trail, fitness center, aerobics, massage therapy, volleyball, and basketball. Diners sample continental cuisine in the Gold Room. High season (Jan.–March) rates run $329–369 d; summer rates drop to $119–159 d.

Campgrounds and RV Parks

All of the following welcome families, except as noted. Both tenters and RVers will find especially scenic settings at Catalina State Park, in the Coronado National Forest, and at Gilbert Ray Campground. Seniors have many RV parks catering just to them with recreation facilities and activities. The *Tucson Official Visitors Guide* and the Yellow Pages list other RV parks and campgrounds.

Catalina State Park (12 miles north of Tucson on Oracle Road/Hwy. 77, 520/628-5798, $12 no hookups, $19 w/electric and water) offers campsites with showers and a dump station in the foothills of the Santa Catalinas. You and your horse can camp in the equestrian center.

Several Coronado National Forest campgrounds

(520/749-8700) line the Catalina Highway, beginning with **Molino Basin,** 18 miles from Tucson (see the *Santa Catalina Mountains* section for details).

Gilbert Ray Campground (McCain Loop Rd. in Tucson Mountain Park, 520/883-4200, $10 tent, $20 RV w/electric) has a desert setting, eight miles west of town; cars can take Speedway Boulevard (I-10 Exit 257) west over Gates Pass, but large rigs should follow Ajo Way and Kinney Road. The campground has a dump station but no showers. The first marked turnoff from Kinney Road is 2 miles before the Arizona-Sonora Desert Museum, and the second turnoff is .9 miles after the museum.

Desert Trails RV Park (3551 S. San Joaquin Rd., 520/883-8340, $21 RV w/hookups) is just south of Tucson Mountain Park off Ajo Highway. It's an adult park, but children are welcome in summer when the adjacent Water World is open. **Prince of Tucson RV Park** (3501 N. Freeway, 520/887-3501 or 800/955-3501, $26 RV w/hookups) has a swimming pool, hot tub, and recreation room. It's four miles northwest of downtown on the west side of I-10 off Prince Road Exit 254.

Tratel Tucson RV Park (2070 W. Fort Lowell Rd., 520/888-5401, www.tra-tel.com, $19 RV w/hookups) in the north part of town caters mainly to seniors and offers a pool and recreation room. Take I-10 Prince Road Exit 254, then go a half mile south on the west frontage road. **Whispering Palms RV Trailer Park** (3445 N. Romero Rd., 520/888-2500 or 800/266-8577, $18.23 tent, $23.57 RV w/hookups) offers a pool, shuffleboard court, and recreation hall. From I-10 Prince Road Exit 254, head east, then south on Romero.

Crazy Horse RV Campground (6660 S. Craycroft Rd., 520/574-0157 or 800/279-6279, www.crazyhorserv.com, $21.70 tent or RV) has a pool and recreation room. It's southeast of downtown; take I-10 Exit 268, then drive a quarter mile north on Craycroft. **Cactus Country RV Resort** (10195 S. Houghton Rd., 520/574-3000 or 800/777-8799, $16.50 tent, $27 RV w/hookups) welcomes seniors and families with a pool, hot tub, and organized winter activities. It's 16 miles southeast of downtown off I-10; take Exit 275, then go .2 miles north.

Seniors can enjoy a wide range of recreation and entertainment programs at large RV resorts such as **Rincon Country West RV Resort** (4555 S. Mission Rd., 4 miles south of Tucson off I-19 Ajo Way Exit 99, 520/294-5608 or 800/782-7275, $33 RV w/hookups), **Western Way RV Resort** (3100 S. Kinney Rd., west from 1-19 Ajo Way Exit 99, 520/578-1715 or 800/292-8616, $32 RV w/hookups), and **Voyager RV Resort** (8701 S. Kolb Rd., just south of I-10 Kolb Road Exit 270, 520/574-5000 or 800/424-9191, $42.96 RV w/hookups).

FOOD

Diners give especially high marks to Tucson's Mexican food, and you'll find many other flavors from around the world too. The more expensive places may have a dress code; ask when making reservations. The price ranges are for dinner entrées.

American, Southwestern, and Continental

The elegant dining room at **Arizona Inn** (2 miles northeast of downtown at 2200 E. Elm St., between Campbell and Tucson Blvd., 520/325-1541, daily breakfast, lunch, and dinner and Sunday brunch, $21–32) serves contemporary cuisine with international flavors. There's a tasting menu available for dinner. You can dine indoors or poolside.

The **Gold Room** (245 E. Ina Rd., 520/297-0134, ext. 413, daily breakfast, lunch, and dinner, $21–33) serves excellent Southwest/continental food along with fine service and a sweeping view of the city. It's at the Westward Look Resort, nine miles north of downtown.

In the Westin La Paloma, **Janos** (3770 E. Sunrise Dr., 520/615-6100, www.janos.com, Mon.–Sat. dinner, $20–45, with more expensive tasting menus) prepares exceptionally good and creative New Southwestern cuisine with influences from France, the Mediterranean, and Asia.

The Latin Caribbean grill **J Bar** next door serves the same excellent food in a casual setting for only $14–20; address, telephone, and days open are the same as Janos.

Kingfisher (northeast of downtown at 2564 E. Grant Rd., 520/323-7739, Mon.–Fri. lunch, daily dinner, most $14–25) has an extensive seafood menu plus some meat and vegetarian items. A late-night menu is offered after 10 P.M.

La Cocina Restaurant (Old Town Artisans at 201 N. Court, 520/622-0351, daily lunch, $7–13) serves Southwestern and a variety of other dishes, along with soups, salads, and sandwiches on the patio and indoors.

Cushing Street Bar & Restaurant (198 W. Cushing St. at Meyer, just south of the Tucson Convention Center, 520/622-7984, Tues.–Sat. lunch and dinner, $9–21) offers a variety of American, Mexican, and pasta dishes in an attractive 1880s setting with a patio out back. The former general store is in the historic Barrio Viejo.

Little Anthony's Diner (7010 E. Broadway Blvd., 520/296-0456, daily lunch and dinner, $5–14) gives you many choices of burgers, sandwiches, chicken dishes, and deserts in a 1950s setting—enjoyable for kids of all ages. The menu advertises blue-plate specials "just like Mom's." Grandma Tony's Pizza is available here too, for dine in or takeout. Located behind the Gaslight Theatre on the southwest corner of E. Broadway Boulevard and Kolb Road, eight miles east of downtown.

Steak Houses

Jonathan's Tucson Cork (8 miles northeast of downtown at 6320 E. Tanque Verde Rd., 520/296-1631, daily dinner, $14–35) rates as one of the best steakhouses in Tucson. It also serves ostrich, buffalo, chicken, seafood, and prime rib.

Pinnacle Peak Steakhouse (south of Grant Rd. at 6541 E. Tanque Verde Rd., 520/296-0911, nightly dinner, $8–17 adults, $4–7 children) is a family-style steakhouse with a cowboy atmosphere. If you wear a tie here, make it a cheap one as it will join the thousands of severed ties that decorate the ceilings! No reservations taken, but you can avoid the crowds by arriving early. A train ride, carousel, shooting gallery, and evening stunt shows provide entertainment. The restaurant, along with the Dakota Café (lighter fare, lunch and dinner daily) and shops are in Trail Dust Town, a re-created Old West town eight miles northeast of downtown.

Vegetarian

Oasis Vegetarian Eatery & Food Co. (375 S. Stone Ave., 520/884-1616, Sun. brunch and Mon.–Sat. lunch and dinner, $4–10) features home-made veggie burgers and a long list of sandwiches and salads.

Govinda's Natural Food Buffet (711 E. Blacklidge Dr., east off 1st Avenue between Glenn and Fort Lowell, 520/792-0630, Sun. brunch, Wed.–Sat. lunch, Tues.–Sat. dinner, $8 lunch buffet, $9 brunch/dinner buffet, lower children's and salad bar prices) offers a flavorful menu with indoor and patio dining. Tuesday is East Indian night and Thursday is vegan. You can join the Hare Krishna community for a Sunday Feast and Festival with chanting, meditation, discussion, and a meal on Sunday 5:30–8 P.M.

Mexican

Poca Cosa (downtown at 88 E. Broadway, 520/622-6400, Mon.–Sat. lunch and dinner, $13–18) prepares traditional Mexican cuisine in the dining room of the Clarion Hotel.

El Charro (311 N. Court Ave., 520/622-1922, daily lunch and dinner, $6–16) has been a popular dining spot for Sonoran and other styles since 1922. A second El Charro is in El Mercado (6310 E. Broadway Blvd., 520/745-1922). Both offer patio and indoor areas.

El Minuto (354 S. Main Ave., 520/882-4145, daily lunch and dinner, $7–13) prepares Mexican favorites in a little café with a patio. It's just south across Cushing Street from the Tucson Convention Center.

La Fuente Restaurant (north of downtown at 1749 N. Oracle Rd., 520/623-8659, www.lafuenterestaurant.com, daily lunch and dinner, closed Mon. in summer, $10–23) has a very attractive garden setting for fine dining with choices of meat, seafood, and vegetarian food. Lunches feature a tostada-taco bar Monday–Thursday and a buffet on Friday. On Sundays you can enjoy a champagne brunch. Musicians serenade diners every evening and during the Sunday brunch with Latin jazz Monday–Wednesday and mariachi Thursday–Sunday.

La Parrilla Suiza (5602 East Speedway Blvd., 1 block east of Craycroft, 520/747-4838; 2720 North Oracle Rd., 1 block south of Glenn, 520/624-4300; daily lunch and dinner, $8–19) specializes in the cuisine of Mexico City, with many grilled items.

French

Le Rendez-Vous (6 miles northeast of downtown at 3844 E. Fort Lowell Rd., 520/323-7373, Tues.–Fri. lunch, Tues.–Sun. dinner, $19–36, also prix fixe options) offers fine French food in a formal setting.

Italian

Caruso's (just east of downtown at 434 N. 4th Ave., 520/624-5765, Tues.–Sun. dinner, $7–10) serves southern Italian cooking in a Tucson institution dating back to the 1930s. **Vivace Restaurant** (4310 N. Campbell Ave., 520/795-7221, Mon.–Sat. lunch and dinner, $18–26) prepares top-rated northern Italian cuisine.

Mediterranean

Athens on 4th Avenue (500 N. 4th Ave., 520/624-6886, Mon.–Sat. dinner, $10.50–20) presents Greek cuisine prepared with many imported ingredients; there's also patio dining. It's half a mile from downtown near the northeast corner of 4th Avenue and 6th Street; look for the sign.

Evangelo's (6 miles west of downtown at 4405 W. Speedway Blvd., 520/624-8946, daily lunch and dinner, $15–21) has a fine reputation as one of the best restaurants in town, with a wide selection of entrées and an extensive wine list.

Indian

Gandhi (150 W. Fort Lowell, north of downtown and just west of Stone Ave., 520/292-1738, daily lunch and dinner, $6–11) prepares seafood, meats, and vegetarian food in tandoori and other north Indian styles. Lunch has a buffet option.

New Delhi Palace (6 miles east of downtown at 6751 E. Broadway Blvd., 520/296-8585, daily lunch and dinner, $7–14) offers north Indian cuisine, including tandoori. There's a lunchtime buffet here too.

Chinese

Gee Garden (4 miles northeast of downtown at 1145 N. Alvernon Way and Speedway Blvd., 520/325-5353, daily lunch and dinner, $8–20) serves Cantonese food; you can order dim sum for lunch. **Lotus Garden** (6 miles northeast of downtown at 5975 E. Speedway Blvd., 520/298-3351, daily lunch and dinner, $9–15) features a long menu of Cantonese and Szechuan specialties.

Japanese

Shogun (north of downtown at 5036 N. Oracle Rd. in River Village Center, 520/888-6646, daily lunch and dinner, $10–15) has attractive decor with a choice of tables or tatami booths. There's a sushi bar too.

Thai

China-Thai Cuisine (7 miles northeast of downtown at 6502 E. Tanque Verde Rd., 520/885-6860, daily lunch and dinner, $8–14) cooks tasty Thai, Mandarin, and Szechwan food.

Pubs

Frog and Firkin (874 E. University Blvd., 520/623-7507, www.frogandfirkin.com) serves up pub fare, pizza, and brews in an English-style pub one block west of the university. **Gentle Ben's Brewing Company** (865 E. University Blvd., 520/624-4177, www.gentlebens.com) has a choice of seven brews and good food one block west of the university.

The Home Plate Sports Pub (4880 E. 22nd St., 520/745-8446) features batting cages as well as a variety of food and drinks southeast of downtown.

INFORMATION AND SERVICES

Tourist Office

The very helpful folks at **Metropolitan Tucson Convention & Visitors Bureau** provide the excellent *Tucson Official Visitors Guide* and many brochures of area sights and services;

you can find them downtown in the Visitor Center (110 S. Church Ave., Ste. 7199, 520/624-1817 or 800/638-8350, fax 520/884-7804, www.visittucson.org, 8 A.M.–5 P.M. Mon.–Fri., 9 A.M.–4 P.M. Sat.–Sun.). Mailing address is 100 S. Church Ave., Tucson, AZ 85701. You can pick up the visitor guide outside when the office is closed. Parking is at 30-minute meters on Church Avenue in front or in a garage across the street.

Coronado National Forest

The **Supervisor's Office** (300 W. Congress St., Tucson, AZ 85701, 520/670-4552, www.fs.fed.us/r3/coronado, 8 A.M.–4:30 P.M. Mon.–Fri.) contains general information on all the districts in the Coronado, including many of the most scenic areas in southeastern Arizona. It's downtown in room 6A on the 6th floor of the Federal Building.

For specific information on the Santa Catalinas' campgrounds, trails, and backcountry regions, contact the **Santa Catalina Ranger District office** (5700 N. Sabino Canyon Rd., Tucson, AZ 85750, 520/749-8700, www.fs.fed.us/r3/coronado/scrd, 8 A.M.–4:30 P.M. Mon.–Fri., 8:30 A.M.–4:30 P.M. Sat.–Sun.) in the Sabino Canyon Visitor Center.

Bureau of Land Management

For recreational opportunities on land administered by the BLM in southeastern Arizona, including the Ironwood Forest National Monument, Las Cienegas National Conservation Area, San Pedro, and middle Gila River areas, contact the Tucson office (12661 E. Broadway, Tucson, AZ 85748, 520/722-4289, www.az.blm.gov, 8 A.M.–4 P.M. Mon.–Fri.). It's *way* out of town next to Saguaro National Park East.

Mexican Consulate

The Consulado de Mexico (553 S. Stone Ave., Tucson, AZ 85701, 520/882-5595 or 520/882-5596, 8 A.M.–2 P.M. Mon.–Fri.) has information for visiting and driving in Mexico. Some tourist literature may be available too. It's just south of downtown in an 1860s building between 16th and 17th Streets.

Libraries

The **City of Tucson Main Library** (101 N. Stone Ave., 520/791-4393 or 520/791-4010 Infoline, www.lib.ci.tucson.az.us) is downtown between Pennington and Alameda; look for a large white and gray marble building. It's open 9 A.M.–8 P.M. Monday–Wednesday, 9 A.M.–6 P.M. Thursday, 9 A.M.–5 P.M. Friday, 10 A.M.–5 P.M. Saturday, and 1–5 P.M. Sunday. You can park in the underground garage, two hours free with validation; enter from Alameda. The library has about 20 branches.

University of Arizona libraries (520/621-6441, www.library.arizona.edu, hours vary with seasons) are open to the public and include some outstanding collections.

Newspapers

The *Arizona Daily Star* (www.azstarnet.com) comes out each morning, including Sunday. The *Tucson Citizen* (www.tucsoncitizen.com) appears Monday–Saturday in the afternoon. The lively pages of the *Tucson Weekly* (www.tucsonweekly.com) report on most everything that's happening in Tucson, along with feature articles and restaurant listings; check the website for the annual Best of Tucson reviews. It's free at newsstands.

Services

The **main post office** (1501 S. Cherrybell Stravenue, Tucson, AZ 85726, 520/388-5043 or 800/275-8777) is 2.5 miles southeast of downtown; you can have General Delivery mail sent to you here. The downtown branch is at 141 S. 6th Avenue.

Banks no longer provide a foreign exchange service unless you have an account, but ATMs are widespread and accept foreign cards. **Pima County Medical Society** (520/795-7985, 8:30 A.M.–4:30 P.M. Mon.–Fri.) will refer you to any sort of doctor you might need.

GETTING THERE AND AROUND

Air

Tucson International Airport (520/573-8000, www.tucsonairport.org) is 8.5 miles south of downtown. About 10 airlines touch down here with nonstop service to at least 10 cities in the

United States, as well as to Hermosillo in Mexico. Information counters at both ends of the airport have brochures. Sun Tran (bus #6, 11, and 25), airport shuttles, and taxis connect the airport with downtown. **Arizona Stagecoach** (520/889-1000, www.azstagecoach.com) provides 24-hour shuttle service between the airport and your destination in the Tucson and Green Valley areas; call 24 hours in advance.

Arizona Shuttle Service (5350 E. Speedway Blvd., 520/795-6771, www.arizonashuttle.com) connects Tucson with Sky Harbor Airport in Phoenix.

Long-Distance Bus

Greyhound (2 S. 4th Ave. at E. Broadway, 800/231-2222 fares and schedules or 520/792-3475 local terminal, www.greyhound.com) offers daily service to many cities from its terminal downtown; it's open 24 hours and has lockers and a coffee shop. **Crucero** (520/792-3475) connects the Greyhound terminal with Nogales; some buses continue past Nogales into Mexico.

Train

Amtrak (400 E. Toole Ave. downtown, 800/872-7245, www.amtrak.com) schedules three eastbound and three westbound departures every week on the Sunset Limited/Texas Eagle. The train connects Los Angeles with Chicago (Texas Eagle) and Orlando (Sunset Limited), splitting or joining in Texas.

Local Bus

Sun Tran (520/792-9222, www.suntran.com) takes you to the parks, sights, and shopping areas of the city and to the airport for only $1, exact change only. Transfers are free; ask the driver before you pay your fare. Drivers also sell a $2 day pass. Buses congregate downtown at the Ronstadt Transit Center on the corner of Congress Street and 6th Avenue; the Transit Center, Visitors Bureau, and website have free schedules.

Old Pueblo Trolley (520/792-1802, www.oldpueblotrolley.org) runs historic trolleys along 4th Avenue and University Boulevard on Friday evening, Saturday afternoon and evening, and Sunday afternoon.

Tours

Gray Line Tours (181 W. Broadway Blvd., P.O. Box 1991, Tucson, AZ 85702, 520/622-8811 or 800/276-1528, www.graylinearizona.com) offers day-trips of the city (Barrio Historico, Old Town Artisans, and San Xavier; 3.5 hours), Arizona-Sonora Desert Museum/San Xavier (4 hours), Old Tucson (4 hours), Tombstone (8 hours), Bisbee (8 hours), and the Grand Canyon (3 days).

Great Western Tours (520/572-1660, www.gwtours.net) heads out on a City of Tucson tour (3 hours) and goes to many other destinations in the city and southern Arizona. **Trail Dust Adventures Jeep Tours** (520/747-0323, www.traildustadventures.com) shows you scenery and petroglyphs on a private jeep trail near Tucson.

Chandelle Tours (520/577-1824 or 800/242-6335, www.chandelletours.com) runs ATV trips around Tucson and other areas of the state.

For hot-air balloon flights in the Tucson area, call **Fleur de Tucson Balloon Tours** (520/529-1025, www.fleurdetucson.net), **Balloon America** (520/299-7744, www.balloonrideusa.com), or **Thunderbird Adventures** (520/544-4500, www.thunderbirdadventures.com).

Tucson to Mexico

Mexico lies at the end of a short drive south from Tucson via I-19, just 63 miles or 100 km—all signs on I-19 are in metric. Except for the speed limits, that is—the Highway Patrol doesn't want motorists feigning confusion at the sight of 120 kph signs!

You'll follow the Santa Cruz River Valley, one of the first areas in Arizona colonized by the Spanish. The Jesuit priest Eusebio Francisco Kino began mission work at Guévavi and Tumacacori in 1691, then moved to San Xavier and other sites. Livestock, new crops, and the new religion introduced by Father Kino and later padres greatly changed the lives of the local tribes. You may wish to stop at some of the many historic and scenic sights on the way. Some fine resorts, guest ranches, and inns lie along the route.

MISSION SAN XAVIER DEL BAC

This gleaming white church (10 miles south of downtown Tucson, 520/294-2624, www.sanxaviermission.org, 7 A.M.–5 P.M. daily, donations welcome) rises from the desert as a testimonial to the faith of early Spanish missionaries and the Tohono O'odham Indians. One of the finest pieces of Spanish colonial architecture in the United States, its beauty has given rise to the name White Dove of the Desert. Padre Kino first visited the site in 1692, and a chapel went up in 1700. The church's name honors Kino's patron saint. The village name of Bac or *Wa:k* means "where the water comes out of the ground."

The mission often lacked a resident priest and suffered many difficulties during its early years. Revolts in 1734 and 1751 caused serious damage. Raiding Apache harassed residents and stole livestock. The oldest surviving part of the mission dates from 1757–1763, when the Jesuit Father Alonso Espinosa built a large, flat-roofed adobe church. This structure was later moved and butted up against the east bell tower of the present church, and it is now part of the south wing of the mission.

Franciscan missionaries began construction of the present church, a marvelous example of Mexican folk baroque architecture, in 1783. Shortage of materials and skilled artisans resulted in the folksy character of the building. Workers painted the main altar to resemble marble and the dadoes to look like glazed tiles. With few fine fabrics on hand, painters simply depicted curtains on the walls. A bit of mystery surrounds the church. No one knows for sure who designed it. Legends give various reasons for the unfinished state of the east bell tower and other parts, but records state that friars ran short of construction funds.

You're welcome to step inside the church and admire the many paintings, statues, and embellishments. A statue of St. Francis Xavier above the altar, ordered from Mexico in 1759, predates the church and is the most famous of the 50 or so statues inside. Above him stands the Virgin of the Immaculate Conception; highest of all is a figure representing the Catholic God. Another figure of St. Francis Xavier reclines in the west alcove where it is much venerated. You can take flash photos unless a service is in progress, though you shouldn't photograph worshippers. The church is still a spiritual center for the Tohono O'odham. Masses take place daily; call or check the website for times.

The **mission museum** (about 9 A.M.–4 P.M. daily, donations welcome) introduces the people of Wa:k and the Spanish missionaries, then gives the church's history with architectural plans, photos, religious art, priests' vestments, and furnishings; a video illustrates how the artwork has been brought back to life in a major restoration project. A gift shop on the east side sells religious and Southwest souvenirs, regional books, and some Native American crafts. To the west stands a former mortuary chapel where two early Franciscan friars lie buried. The small hill to the east features a replica of the Grotto of Lourdes.

San Xavier Plaza across from the mission includes the Wa:k Snack Shop (Mexican, Native American, and American food) and shops selling crafts of Tohono O'odham, Zuni, Hopi, Navajo,

Saint Antonio, Mission San Xavier del Bac

© BILL WEIR

and other tribes. Tohono O'odham set up food stalls outside, especially on Sunday and religious holidays. Major celebrations are the two-day Feast of St. Francis of Assisi on October 4 and the three-day Feast of St. Francis Xavier on December 3. In March, usually on the second weekend, the Wa:k Pow Wow attracts Southwestern Native American groups to San Xavier Mission for traditional and modern singing and dancing. Take I-19 south to Exit 92 and follow signs west and north 1.2 miles.

GREEN VALLEY

Green Valley, populated almost entirely by seniors, nestles in rolling hills overlooking the Santa Cruz Valley, 25 miles south of Tucson.

Asarco Mineral Discovery Center and Mine Tours

This museum (just west of I-19 Pima Mine Rd. Exit 80, 520/625-7513 recording or 520/625-8233 tour reservations, www.mineraldiscovery.com, 9 A.M.–5 P.M. Tues.–Sat., free) illustrates the fascinating processes of copper mining and refining. Video programs and exhibits show each step of the operations. Mineral displays have beautiful specimens of copper ore. Outdoor exhibits include massive haul trucks, an early 20th-century mine headframe, and other historic mine equipment. A gift shop offers excellent Southwestern crafts, many made of copper, along with regional books. Arizona tourist literature is available too. You can enjoy your lunch at a picnic area.

Tours (9:30 A.M.–3:30 P.M. Tues.–Sat., $6 adults, $5 seniors 62+, $4 ages 5–12) take you up past terraced white hills to view the giant Mission Mine. Your guide will point out and explain features of the operation, which is able to make a profit with an ore averaging only .6 percent copper. The pit is a quarter mile deep and up to two miles across, and miners will continue digging at least another 700 feet down. Giant shovels load the huge trucks, some of which can carry 320 tons of earth. With luck, you may get to see a mine blast. The tour goes inside a mill, where machinery grinds and concentrates the ore in several stages to achieve a 28 percent copper content, ready for shipment to smelters elsewhere. Tours are wheelchair accessible and depart from the Mineral Discovery Center; only large groups need to make reservations.

Titan Missile Museum

You may think that you're trespassing on a top-secret military installation—official Air Force vehicles, a helicopter, giant antenna, and refueling equipment look ready for action. But this once-top-secret facility has thrown open its heavy doors to the public. Only this site, in use 1963–1982, has been preserved (I-19 Duval Mine Rd. Exit 69, then west .6 miles, 520/625-7736, www.pimaair.org, 1-hour tours depart 9 A.M.–4 P.M. daily, $8.50 adults, $6.50 seniors and military, $5 ages 7–12). After a look at the antennas, fueling equipment, rocket engines, and missile door on the surface, you'll descend to the subterranean chambers and make your way past security gates and a pair of blast doors to the control room. Here your guide will demon-

COLD WAR DEFUSED—THE TITAN MISSILE MUSEUM

When the SALT treaty called for the deactivation of the 54 Titan missiles buried deep below the ground in Arizona, Kansas, and Arkansas, the people at Pima Air and Space Museum asked that one site remain open for public tours. After complex international negotiations, the request was granted. And so today the Green Valley complex of the 390th Strategic Missile Wing has been declassified and opened to the public.

Here you can watch a tape of an Air Force crew going to work, prepared for a command that fortunately never came. Had they launched their nuclear missile, in less than an hour its 440,000 pounds of thrust could have taken it from its blastproof Arizona silo to a target 8,000 miles away.

You can sit behind the consoles where two officers once waited for the command that would tell them to use two sets of keys in two combination locks to retrieve launch codes that would incinerate millions of people. The hardened command center is mounted on springs to withstand anything but a direct hit. You'll pass through a pair of 6,000-pound blast doors to approach the missile itself—110 feet tall and weighing 170 tons when fully fueled and ready to fly.

strate the launch sequence. Then you'll walk down a 200-foot tunnel for a close look at the awesome Titan II missile.

It's best to call for reservations, though walk-ins can usually get on the next tour. An elevator allows access for people unable to climb the stairs. The visitors center has a cold war timeline, missile warhead housing, and equipment used by technicians. A gift shop sells souvenirs.

Accommodations

Holiday Inn Express (I-19 Duval Mine Rd. Exit 69, then south on the west frontage road, 520/625-0900 or 800/465-4329, $105 d) offers an indoor pool and spa. **Green Valley Best Western** (111 S. La Cañada Dr., 520/625-2250 or 800/344-1441, about $100 d, less in summer) has the Lavender Restaurant, pool, and a hot tub; take I-19 Exit 65, turn west on Esperanza, then south on La Cañada.

Food

For superb French-American dining, try **Lavender Restaurant** (111 S. La Cañada Dr., 520/648-0205, daily breakfast, lunch, and dinner, brunch Sun., $11–23) in the Green Valley Best Western; entrées include the popular crab meat–sea scallop duo and the roasted half duckling. You'll find seven more restaurants in the adjacent Green Valley Mall, just west of I-19 Esperanza Boulevard Exit 65, including Mexican at **La Placita** (90 W. Esperanza Blvd., 520/625-2111) and Chinese at **China View** (101 S. La Cañada Dr., 520/648-3848, closed Sun.). Desert Diamond Casino, just east of I-19 Pima Mine Rd. Exit 80, offers fine dining in the **Agave Restaurant** (520/393-2720, daily lunch and dinner); there's a buffet restaurant too.

Information

Green Valley Chamber of Commerce (270 W. Continental Rd., P.O. Box 566, Green Valley, AZ 85622, 520/625-7575 or 800/858-5872, www.greenvalleychamber.com, 9 A.M.–5 P.M. Mon.–Fri., 9 A.M.–3 P.M. Sat.) provides both local and statewide information. From I-19 Continental Exit 63, head west, then turn right at the tourist information sign just past the Continental Shopping Plaza.

SANTA RITA MOUNTAINS

Mount Wrightson tops the range at 9,453 feet with some of the best mountain scenery and views in the Tucson area. The forests and perennial creek of Madera Canyon on the northern slope attract many species of birds and other wildlife. A network of trails, some wheelchair accessible, wind along the creek or climb to lofty vistas in the canyon.

The Nogales Ranger District of the Coronado

National Forest (just north of Nogales, 520/281-2296, www.fs.fed.us/r3/coronado) has maps and trail descriptions. You can also obtain information at Santa Rita Lodge's gift shop in Madera Canyon, at some trailheads, and from the Supervisor's Office in Tucson (520/670-4552). *Tucson Hiking Guide,* by Betty Leavengood, contains detailed trail descriptions and maps. *Santa Rita Mountains, Arizona—A Trail and Recreation Map* covers the entire range with trail names and distances.

Madera Canyon

Birdwatchers flock here to see abundant and unusual wildlife, of which the coppery-tailed elegant trogon bird *(Trogon elegans)* is the star attraction. During summer this colorful, parrotlike bird flies in from Mexico to nest in tall trees in the canyon bottoms. More than 200 other bird species have been spotted in Madera Canyon, including 13 species of hummingbirds. Mid-March–mid-September is the best time for birdwatching. Bear, deer, mountain lion, coatimundi, and javelina also share the spring-fed canyon.

Madera Canyon is an easy 38-mile drive south from Tucson on paved roads, which stay open all year. Head south on I-19 to Continental Exit 63, then exit to the east and follow signs 11.5 miles. You'll go past pecan orchards in the Santa Cruz Valley, then mesquite, ocotillo, and cacti of the desert before reaching forests of juniper, oak, and pine in Madera Canyon. The road gently climbs through the canyon about two miles before ending at Mt. Wrightson Picnic Area. Entry is $5 per day or $20 per year unless you have one of the Golden passes or a National Parks pass with a hologram.

From **Proctor Parking Area,** on the right at the entrance to the canyon (elev. 4,400 ft.), a paved path (wheelchair accessible) with interpretive signs heads upstream in a .8-mile loop. Benches along the way offer places for rest and contemplation. A crumbling adobe wall of White House Ruins lies just off the trail. A narrow trail continues upstream to trailheads at White House Picnic Area in .75 miles, Madera Picnic Area in 1.2 miles, Santa Rita Lodge in 1.4 miles, the Amphitheater in 1.7 miles, and trail's end at Roundup Picnic Area in 4.4 miles one-way.

White House Picnic Area, on the right a bit beyond Proctor Parking Area, offers tables in a woodland and an easy .4-mile paved loop trail that's wheelchair accessible. **Madera Picnic Area,** about halfway up Madera Canyon at Milepost 12, has tables in the forest on both sides of the road at an elevation of 4,820 feet. At a loop at road's end, **Mt. Wrightson Picnic Area** (elev. 5,400 ft.) offers tables under the trees and trailheads for the Nature, Old Baldy, Super, and Vault Mine Trails. The **Nature Trail** has interpretive signs and some good views of the canyon as it descends 2.7 miles one-way to the Amphitheater trailhead; elevation change is 510 feet. You could also continue on trails down as far as Proctor Parking Area in 4.4 miles total one-way, with a 1,000-foot elevation drop.

Bog Springs-Kent Spring Loop Trail

One of Madera Canyon's prettiest hikes begins from Madera Picnic Area. The moderate 5.8-mile trail has an elevation gain of 1,600 feet with fine views of the Santa Ritas, Madera Canyon, and far across the Santa Cruz Valley. Three springs along the way usually have water (treat before drinking) that attracts birds and other wildlife and supports large sycamore trees. The path climbs gently .7 miles from the east side of the picnic area to the start of the loop; turn left for Bog Springs, another .8 miles. The trail steepens to its highest point just before Kent Spring (elev. 6,620), 1.2 miles farther. The way then follows an old jeep road, steeply downhill at first, to Sylvester Spring in .5 miles, swings over into another seasonal drainage, curves back to the start of the loop in 1.9 miles, and back to the picnic area in .7 miles. You can save a bit of hiking by starting from the trailhead at Bog Springs Campground, but there's no hiker parking here—you'd have to pay the campground fee. It's also possible to access the loop on the new Four Springs Trail from the Amphitheater trailhead.

Mt. Wrightson Trails

On a clear day at the top, you'll see most of southeastern Arizona and well into Mexico. Don't climb if thunderstorms threaten—another good reason to get an early start in summer. Usually May–November offers the best hiking. Pines begin to appear at trailhead elevations, then become more numerous higher up. Douglas fir and aspen groves thrive in protected areas. Only hardy trees hang onto the wind-blasted ridges. Mount Wrightson, along with most of the highest mountains, lies within the **Mount Wrightson Wilderness.**

Two trails to the summit start from Madera Canyon's Mt. Wrightson Picnic Area (elev. 5,400 ft.). **Super Trail** has a relatively gentle grade, but the trail is long (16.2 miles round-trip) and offers little shade. **Old Baldy Trail** is steeper and shorter (10.8 miles round-trip) with lots of shade. Many hikers go up one trail and descend the other on a figure-eight loop. The trails cross at Josephine Saddle (elev. 7,250 ft.), southwest of the peak, then meet again at Baldy Saddle (elev. 8,800 ft.) just below the peak's north face. From here it's just .9 miles more to the summit. Both trails lie mostly in the wilderness, where mountain bikes are prohibited.

Hikers with a high-clearance 4WD vehicle can reach **Gardner Canyon Trail** on the east side of the Santa Ritas. This trail is slightly shorter with a bit less climb than the ascent from Madera Canyon. From Tucson, head east about 21 miles on I-10 to Exit 281, turn south about 21 miles on Highway 83, then turn west about 11 miles on Gardner Canyon Road (Forest Road 92). You'll pass Apache Springs Ranch and trailheads for the Arizona Trail before reaching the Gardner Canyon Trailhead at road's end. The last several miles have several creek fords and hill climbs that can be rough. At the trailhead (elev. 6,070 ft.), follow Gardner Canyon Trail #143 3 miles to the Super Trail, which curves around to Baldy Saddle in another .8 miles, then continue .9 miles on Old Baldy Trail to the summit.

The new **Four Springs Trail** begins at the Amphitheater trailhead, then climbs steeply to the ridge-top **Orange Trail** north of Mt. Wrightson. You could do a loop with these and either the Super or Old Baldy trails.

Elephant Head Mountain Bike Route

Mountain bikers can follow a very technical and scenic series of back roads and trails between the entrance of Madera Canyon (begin at Proctor Parking Area) and a junction .75 miles past the Whipple Observatory visitor center. Elevations range 3,600–4,600 feet, and the trail is rated "most difficult." It's 10 miles one-way and best done in the cooler months.

Accommodations and Campgrounds

All of the lodges have an idyllic streamside setting. **Santa Rita Lodge** (520/625-8746, www.santaritalodge.com) offers 12 rental units with kitchenettes for $83–98 d February–May, $60–93 d June–January, with discounts for long stays. The lodge's gift shop and website are handy sources for local information. The lodge organizes **bird walks** March–August that last about four hours; call for reservations. **Madera Kubo** (.4 miles past Santa Rita Lodge on the left, 520/625-2908, www.maderakubo.com, $75 d year-round) rents four cabins and has a gift shop. **Chuparosa Inn** (a bit farther up on the right, 520/393-7370, www.chuparosainn.com, $110 d room, $130 d suite year-round) has three bed and breakfast rooms.

Bog Springs Campground (elev. 5,600 feet, $10 camping, $5 day use) is open all year with water; some sites can accommodate rigs to 22 feet. Turn left at Madera Picnic Area and go half a mile.

Whipple Observatory

The Smithsonian Institution studies the heavens with a variety of telescopes on Mt. Hopkins in the Santa Ritas. A visitor center (520/670-5707, http://cfa-www.harvard.edu/flwo, 8:30 A.M.–4:30 P.M. Mon.–Fri. except federal holidays) at the base of the mountain offers seasonal tours to several telescopes atop the summit and year-round astronomy exhibits.

From mid-March to November, six-hour tours of the observatory depart from the visitor center. Call up to four weeks in advance—especially early in the season—for the schedule (generally Mon., Wed., and Fri.; $7 adults, $2.50 children 6–12; no children under 6), directions, and required reservations. The tour begins with a short video presentation at 9 A.M., followed by a narrated bus ride high into the mountains. It's great to let the experienced driver tackle the narrow,

the Cosmic Ray telescope, Whipple Observatory

winding mountain road, stopping at a 10-meter-diameter reflector designed for gamma ray studies and at other telescopes along the way. The famous MMT, one of the world's largest telescopes, has a 6.5-meter mirror inside a 4.5-story housing that weighs 550 tons and turns with the telescope. At each stop, your guide discusses astronomy and local history and points out distant summits. The outstanding views are almost as good as those from nearby Mt. Wrightson. You may be able to pick out the Guillermo Haro Astrophysical Observatory 56 miles south-southeast in Mexico. The tour takes a midday break atop Mt. Hopkins for a picnic (bring your own lunch). Be prepared for temperatures 15–20°F cooler than in the valley, possible summer showers, and the thin air at Mt. Hopkins's 8,550-foot summit.

Whipple Picnic Area near the visitors center is open daily all year with a nature trail, picnic tables, grills, and restrooms. You can drive up the Mt. Hopkins Road on your own for views and a few undeveloped spots for picnicking or camping; a gate 7.5 miles past the visitor center blocks the remaining 5 miles to the top, though you can walk on this road.

The visitor center is 43 miles south of Tucson and 38 miles north of Nogales. From Tucson, head south on I-19 to Canoa Exit 56, go south 3 miles along the east frontage road, east 1.5 miles on Elephant Head Road, then southeast 6.5 miles on Mt. Hopkins Road; all of these are paved. From Nogales, you can take I-19 Amado Exit 48, go north 2 miles on the east frontage road, then turn east on Elephant Head Road.

Northern Areas of the Santa Rita Mountains

Though little visited, the north side has ghost towns, shady canyons, and towering rocky summits. Back-road enthusiasts can seek out Helvetia's adobe ruin, mine workings, and cemetery; this copper mining center came to life in the 1890s and died in the 1920s. It's easily reached from Sahuarita or Green Valley, but you'll need a good map, as there are no signs for the ruin or cemetery. Scenic drives across the Santa Ritas include the fairly easy Box Canyon Road (Forest

Road 62) and the challenging Lopez Pass road (4WD needed). You can reach this region from I-19 on the west or Highway 83 on the east.

Eastern Areas of the Santa Rita Mountains

The back roads on the eastern side of the Santa Ritas offer scenic drives and mountain biking too. Hikers can access the Arizona Trail or head off on other trails into the heights of the range. **Kentucky Camp,** a well-preserved ghost town, dates from 1904 when the Santa Rita Water and Mining Company started construction of a placer gold mine; financial woes the following year ended the dreams. Volunteers have restored the adobe hotel/office, assay office, and two cabins. You can rent one of the cabins for $75 a day; contact the Nogales Ranger Station (520/281-2296) for reservations. To get here, take Highway 83 south 21 miles from I-10 (or north 4 miles from Sonoita) to unpaved Gardner Canyon Road/Forest Road 92; follow it west .75 miles, turn right on Forest Road 163 and continue 4.3 miles to the gate, then walk a quarter-mile to Kentucky Camp. Cautiously driven cars may be able to do the trip. The gate is often open on Saturday and can be opened on request (call the Nogales Ranger Station) for people who have difficulty walking.

Cave of the Bells attracts experienced spelunkers to see a variety of minerals and an underground lake inside. This undeveloped "wild" cave lies in East Sawmill Canyon off Gardner Canyon Road. Obtain gate key and directions from the Forest Service's Nogales Ranger District office north of Nogales or the supervisor's office in Tucson.

AMADO TO ARIVACA AND THE BUENOS AIRES NATIONAL WILDLIFE REFUGE

Amado and Vicinity

Rex Ranch (east from I-19 Exit 48 or 42, 520/398-2914 or 800/547-2696, www.rexranch.com, $125 d and up Oct.–May, less off-season) enjoys a quiet and scenic location ideal for relaxation. It's also popular with groups and families. Guests can use the full-service spa facilities, go horseback riding, mountain biking, or bird-watching, and play golf at a nearby course. A fine-dining restaurant serves European and Southwestern cuisine.

Amado Territory Inn Bed & Breakfast (just east off I-19 Exit 48, 520/398-8684 or 888/398-8684, www.amado-territory-inn.com, $120–135 d Nov.–June, $95–105 d July–Oct.) offers rooms with views of the Santa Ritas and a restful atmosphere; rooms have no TVs or telephones, and children under 12 are not permitted. **Amado Café** (520/398-9211, closed Sun. evening and Mon.) next door prepares Southwestern and Mediterranean food for lunch and dinner. Galleries nearby include Blackstar, which mines opal locally and sets the stones in jewelry. To the north in the Amado Territory grounds, **Kristofer's** (520/625-0331) prepares gourmet sandwiches and wraps for lunch, then fine dining for dinner.

Two RV parks offer overnight and long-term spaces about two miles south on the east frontage road off I-19 Exits 46 or 42. **Mountain View RV Ranch** (520/398-9401, $15 no hookups, $21.21 w/hookups including tax) has basic sites for tents and RVs along with a pool and showers. **De Anza Trails RV Resort** (520/398-8628, $25 RV w/hookups) next door offers a pool, hot tub, and showers.

Two atmospheric restaurants lie just west of I-19 Exit 48. You'll see how the **Longhorn Grill** (520/398-3955, daily lunch and dinner) got its name! The horns originally served as a movie set. Inside, the menu includes meat, fish, pasta, and pizza dishes. Across the street, the **Cow Palace** (520/398-2201, daily breakfast, lunch, and dinner) serves up cowboy, Mexican, and Italian food in a Western setting.

Arivaca

A paved road winds southwest 23 miles across the desert hills from I-19 Exit 48 to this little village of about 1,500 people. Birders and other nature lovers come to see wildlife at the nearby springs of the Buenos Aires National Wildlife Refuge. You can also get here on paved roads via Highway 286 from the west or on the very scenic but twisting 36-mile Ruby Road (AZ 289/Forest

Road 39, partly dirt) through the Coronado National Forest. Downtown Arivaca has a store/gas station, post office, and a library. A small refuge visitors center next to the Arivaca Mercantile is open irregular hours.

Arivaca Lake

This 90-acre reservoir with its cottonwood- and willow-lined shoreline attracts anglers, who catch largemouth bass, bluegill, and catfish while enjoying the solitude here. Facilities are minimal—just parking areas, a boat ramp, and outhouses. Single electric motors can be used.

The easiest way in is from Amado (I-19 Exit 48, 37 miles south of Tucson) to the village of Arivaca, 20 miles. From Arivaca head southeast 5 miles on paved Forest Road 39, then turn left 2.3 unpaved miles to the lake.

The other route follows the Ruby Road; head west 10 miles from I-19 Exit 12 on Highway 289 to just before Peña Blanca Lake, then continue west 21 miles on unpaved Forest Road 39, turning right after 2.3 miles. This slow but scenic route winds through the Atascosa Mountains on dirt roads—usually passable by cautiously driven cars—past the ghost towns of Ruby (fenced off; call 520/744-4471 to arrange a visit) and Oro Blanco.

Buenos Aires National Wildlife Refuge

Located about 60 miles southwest of Tucson, this former ranch now provides a habitat for over 300 species of birds, including the masked bobwhite that was reintroduced here. You have a good chance of seeing pronghorn, mule deer, coyote, and javelina along refuge roads. With luck, you might spot a mountain lion, coatimundi, ringtailed cat, badger, desert tortoise, or Gila monster. Grazing over the past 100-plus years damaged the grasslands, which are now being restored with controlled burns. Riparian lands, added later to the refuge, attract both wildlife and visitors. The refuge brochure contains a map, an introduction to the resident wildlife, and advice on visits; it's available at refuge visitors centers and some tourist offices. Call or check the website for a schedule of tours and workshops.

Refuge headquarters (P.O. Box 109, Sasabe, AZ 86633, 502/823-4251, http://southwest.fws.gov, 7 A.M.–4 P.M. daily) lies in the southern part of the refuge with information and a few exhibits. Pronghorn Drive begins just south of the headquarters and loops 10 miles across open grassland with sweeping views of the Altar Valley; it's passable for cars in dry weather. Aguirre Lake, just north of the headquarters, has water and birds only after plentiful rain. Most back roads in the refuge require 4WD, especially after rains. Mountain bikers can make many loop trips. You can camp at any of the more than 100 primitive sites along the back roads; no permit is needed, but you must stay at a designated site.

From Tucson, the fastest way heads west 21 miles on Highway 86 to Robles Junction, turns south 38 miles on Highway 286 to the headquarters turnoff (between Mileposts 7 and 8), then turns east 3 miles on a paved road to the headquarters. The more scenic route goes via the tiny town of Arivaca and refuge riparian areas: Drive 33 miles south on I-19 to Arivaca Junction, turn southwest 32 miles via Arivaca to Highway 286, then turn south about 4 miles to the headquarters turnoff.

Just east of Arivaca, seven springs rise from the desert valley at **Arivaca Cienega.** A boardwalk trail leads out to Willow Pond and marshlands, popular for birdwatching, in a 1.3-mile loop. **Arivaca Creek** pops up above ground two miles west of Arivaca and supports towering Fremont cottonwood trees, lush vegetation, birds, and other wildlife. A trail makes a figure-eight loop of about one mile. For great views of the area, branch off on the **Mustang Trail,** which leads to the top of El Cerro in five miles round-trip, with the last section rough and on loose rock. You'll need a hat, sturdy shoes, and water, as there's no shade.

Guided tours visit Brown Canyon, a sycamore-lined creek in the Baboquivari Mountains in the northwest corner of the refuge; it's too fragile for public access otherwise.

Sasabe

This sleepy adobe village on the Arizona side of the border has a store and a nearby guest ranch. The larger Mexican town of Sasabe has about

1,000 inhabitants and lies a mile south of the border. It serves as a ranching center but lacks tourist shops. Besides running cattle, local people export mesquite firewood and adobe bricks. The border is open daily, but few travelers cross into Mexico here; there's no source for vehicle permits or insurance, and the 60-mile stretch of dirt road heading south from the border is rough. The excellent Rancho de la Osa Guest Ranch makes a great getaway just a few miles from Sasabe; visitors should call first. (See the description in the *Tucson Guest Ranches* section.)

TUBAC

After the Pima Indian Revolt in 1751, the Spanish decided to protect their missions and settlers in this remote region, so they built Tubac Presidio, the first European settlement in what's now Arizona. When the Spanish departed in 1776, garrisons of Pima Indians and later Mexicans provided some security, yet Apache raids and political turmoil in following decades often made life unbearable at times. Tubac's citizens had to flee repeatedly.

By the time the United States took over after the 1854 Gadsden Purchase, Tubac had decayed into a pile of crumbling adobe ruins. Prospectors and adventure-seekers, fired by tales of old Spanish mines, soon poured in. They hit rich mineral deposits, and by 1859 Tubac had become a boomtown with Arizona's first newspaper, the *Weekly Arizonan.* The Civil War brought the good times to an end when the troops guarding the town headed east to fight the Confederacy. Apache once again raided the settlement, and the inhabitants once again had to seek safer locales. Tubac recovered after the Civil War, but the boom days were finished.

Much later, when an art school opened in 1948, Tubac began a slow transformation into an artists' colony. Today you can explore about 100 studios and galleries displaying modern jewelry, ceramics, fountains, woodcarvings, prints, batiks, paintings, and other works. During the week-long **Tubac Festival of the Arts** in February, residents and visiting artists celebrate with exhibitions, demonstrations, and food. Tubac lies 45 miles south of Tucson off I-19 Exit 34.

Tubac Center of the Arts

This gallery (Plaza Road, near the entrance to Tubac, 520/398-2371, www.TubacArts.org, 1–4:30 P.M. Sun., 10 A.M.–4:30 P.M. Tues.–Sat. early Sept.–mid-May, $2 suggested donation) displays excellent work by local, regional, and national artists. Most works are for sale and there's a gift shop. A Performing Arts program offers a variety of presentations. Both adults and children can attend workshops; kids also have a summer program.

Tubac Presidio State Historic Park

This park (520/398-2252, 8 A.M.–5 P.M. daily, $3 ages 14+, $1 ages 7–13), on the site of the Spanish presidio, displays Tubac's history. A short video in the visitors center provides an introduction. Continue outside and descend stairs to see the original foundation and wall in an underground excavation. Next, in the museum, models illustrate how the presidio appeared in the early years. Exhibits illustrate the lives of the people who were here during the prehistoric, Spanish, Mexican, and American periods. You'll see the printing press used for Arizona's first newspaper and a reproduction of the first issue, dated March 3, 1859. The schoolhouse adjacent to the visitors center dates from 1885; it's a successor to Arizona's first school, which was built in 1789. You can also visit St. Ann's Church, just outside the park; it was rebuilt in the 1920s as the latest in a series of churches built on the site since the early 1700s. The state park itself is historic because it's Arizona's first, established in 1959.

Living History Programs (1–4 P.M. Sun. Oct.–March) portray the Spanish colonial period's crafts, food, traditional medicine, and religion. In October, on the weekend closest to the 23rd, the park hosts **Anza Days Cultural Celebration** that commemorates the 1775 departure from Tubac of the de Anza expedition; you can enjoy reenactments, historic craft demonstrations, entertainment, and local foods.

From the gateway to Tubac, turn right .3 miles on Tubac Road to the park entrance. A mesquite-shaded picnic area lies south across the street from the park.

Juan Bautista de Anza National Historic Trail

You can hike a 4.5-mile section of trail once used by the Spanish to secure a route to the west coast. Tubac Presidio Captain Juan Bautista de Anza led 240 colonists in 1775–1776 to what would become San Francisco in northern California. You can start at either Tubac Presidio State Historic Park (south side of the state park's parking lot) or Tumacacori National Historical Park. From either trailhead, you will cross the Santa Cruz River after 1.25 miles, but the river can be too high to cross safely at times. There's excellent birding, and the state park visitors center has a bird list. Hikers should carry plenty of water, especially in hot weather, and keep on the trail, as it crosses private land.

Shopping

Tubac's many galleries sell outstanding art and crafts. Pick up a map at many businesses or just wander down the lanes. **La Paloma de Tubac** (just east of the state park, 520/398-9231) offers a huge selection of folk art and crafts from Mexico, Central America, and South America. **Tortuga Books** has a great regional and general offering in front of the Mercado de Baca.

Accommodations and Campgrounds

Tubac Country Inn (corner of 13 Burruel St. and Plaza, 520/398-3178, www.tubaccountryinn.com, $85–155 d) has five suites with continental breakfast. **Secret Garden Inn Bed & Breakfast** (520/398-9371, $105 d) offers two rooms with continental breakfast down a little lane north of the state park.

Tubac Golf Resort (1 mile north of Tubac, 520/398-2211 or 800/848-7893, www.tubacgolfresort.com) offers posada rooms ($140–175 d), casitas ($175–190 d), and hacienda suites ($195–265 d) along with an 18-hole golf course, tennis court, pool, and a hot tub; prices are lower in the warmer months. The dining room serves American and continental food daily for breakfast, lunch, and dinner. It's off the I-19 east frontage road between I-19 Exit 40 and Tubac.

Tubac Trailer Tether (Burruel St., 520/398-2111, $19 RV w/hookups) offers spaces in town.

Food

Tosh's Hacienda de Tubac (corner of Camino Otero and Burruel St., 520/398-3008, daily lunch and dinner, closed Mon.–Tues. in summer) serves Southwestern and Mexican cuisine indoors or on the patio. Cross the footbridge in the Mercado de Baca for **Shelby's Bistro** (520/398-8075, daily lunch, Wed.–Sat. dinner) offers a lunch menu of sandwiches, salads, pasta, and pizza plus additional meat and seafood dishes for dinner; you have a choice of patio and indoor seating.

Information

Tubac–Santa Cruz Visitor Center (4 Plaza Rd., 520/398-0007, www.toursantacruz.com, 9 A.M.–4 P.M. Mon.–Fri., 10 A.M.–4 P.M. Sat.–Sun.) is on your left as you enter Tubac. **Tubac Chamber of Commerce** (P.O. Box 1866, Tubac, AZ 85646, 520/398-2704, www.tubacaz.com) also provides local information. The **Tubac Historical Society** has a research library and gift shop north of the state park, but it's open only 1–4 P.M. Thursday–Sunday from October to May.

TUMACACORI NATIONAL HISTORICAL PARK

This massive adobe ruin evokes visions of Spanish missionaries and devout Indian followers. Father Kino first visited the Pima village of Tumacacori in 1691, saying Mass under a brush shelter. Kino's successors continued the missionary work, teaching, converting, and farming, but construction didn't begin on the present church until 1800.

Franciscan Father Narciso Gutierrez, determined to build a church as splendid as San Xavier del Bac, supervised the construction. Work went slowly, and although never quite finished, the building was in use by 1822. Then the fledgling Mexican government restricted funds for missionary work and began to evict all foreign missionaries. Tumacacori's last resident priest, Father Ramon Liberos of Spain, had to leave in 1828.

Indians continued to care for the church and received occasional visits by missionaries from Mexico, but raiding Apache made life hard. The last devout Indians finally gave up in 1848, packing the church furnishings and moving to San Xavier del Bac.

Tumacacori fell into ruins before receiving protection as a national monument in 1908, then as a national historical park in 1990. Today, a museum (48 miles south of Tucson near I-19 Exit 29, just 3 miles south of Tubac on the east frontage road, 520/398-2341, www.nps.gov/tuma, 8 A.M.–5 P.M. daily, $3/person age 17+) recalls the mission life of the Indians and Spanish with an introductory video, historical and architectural exhibits, and some of the mission's original *santos* (wooden statues of saints). An interpretive booklet for the self-guided tour relates details of the church, circular mortuary chapel, graveyard, storeroom, and other structures. Staff offer scheduled tours September–June and on request. Herbs, flowers, shade trees, and other plants grace the Patio Garden. Craft demonstrations take place weekends September–June. **Tumacacori Fiesta** features Native American dances, crafts, and food on the first weekend in December. You can have a picnic, but no camping is permitted. The visitors center has a good selection of regional books.

Two other early Spanish mission ruins belong to the park—Guevavi (started in 1701 and abandoned in 1776) and Calabazas (founded in the 1750s and faded away in the 1800s). You can visit them only on guided tours that run monthly October–April.

Tumacacori Restaurant (across the street from the mission, 520/398-9038, closed Mon.) serves Greek and Mexican food for lunch and dinner.

PEÑA BLANCA LAKE AND VICINITY

The light-colored bluffs overlooking this 52-acre lake inspired the name, Spanish for White Rock. It's at an elevation of 4,000 feet in scenic hills 16 miles northwest of Nogales. Anglers come to catch bass, bluegill, crappie, catfish, and rainbow trout (Nov.–March). Mercury in the lake water may require catch and release for the warm-water fish, but trout might be OK. The lake has a boat ramp and a trail around the shore. Take I-19 Ruby Road Exit 12 and drive west 11 miles on paved Highway 289. Upper and Lower Thumb Rock Picnic Areas are just before road's end.

White Rock Campground is in Peña Blanca Canyon upstream from the lake; sites cost $5 and are open year-round but lack water; trailers to 22 feet are OK. Turn left .1 miles onto Forest Road 39 at Milepost 10, 1 mile before the lake; a smaller section of the campground is .1 miles down the road to the lake from the junction.

Forest Road 39 continues west from the lake area through canyons and mountains with some great scenery. The road is slow, bumpy, and unpaved within the national forest, so allow plenty of time. Trails and back roads branch off for further exploration. It's about 21 miles from the Highway 289 turnoff to the Arivaca Lake turnoff, where pavement begins, then another 5 miles to the town of Arivaca. The Nogales Ranger District office (520/281-2296, www.fs.fed.us/r3/coronado) north of Nogales has maps and recreation information.

Atascosa Lookout Trail #100

The path climbs steeply from 4,700 feet through desert vegetation, oaks, juniper, and pinyon pine to the summit at 6,255 feet. Allow a half day for the six-mile round-trip; see the 7.5-minute Ruby topo map. The trailhead is five miles west of Peña Blanca Lake on unpaved Forest Road 39. Look for a parking area on the south side of the road; the unmarked trailhead is on the north side. From the top, you can see mountain ranges in Mexico to the south, Peña Blanca Lake and Nogales to the east, the Santa Ritas and Rincons to the northeast, the Santa Catalinas to the north, and the Baboquivaris to the west. You can hike year-round except after snowstorms.

Sycamore Canyon Trail #40

Plants and wildlife rarely found elsewhere in the United States live in the scenic canyon. The trail crosses both the **Goodding Research Natural Area,** named for a prominent Arizona botanist, and the **Pajarita Wilderness.** The trail is rough in spots but you can follow it downstream all the way to the Mexican border, a distance of 5.3 miles one-way. The first 1.3 miles is easy walking, then boulder-hopping and wading are necessary.

Toward the end, the canyon opens up and you'll see saguaro on the slopes. A barbed-wire fence marks the Mexican border. No camping is allowed along the trail.

The trailhead is about 10 miles west of Peña Blanca Lake on Forest Road 39, then left a quarter mile on Forest Road 218 to Hank and Yank Historical Site. These adobe ruins were part of a ranch started in the 1880s by two former army scouts.

Hiking in Sycamore Canyon is good all year. Elevation ranges from 4,000 feet at the trailhead to 3,500 feet at the border. Depending on how far you go, the hike can be an easy two-hour stroll for the first mile or so, or a long (10-hour) 10.6-mile round-trip day hike all the way to Mexico; see the Ruby topo map. At the border, you have the options of retracing your steps or heading east four miles along Border Trail #45 to a trailhead on Forest Road 39A.

NOGALES

The twin cities of Nogales, astride the U.S.–Mexican border, are truly international. Many visitors come for shopping, and the Mexico side of Nogales offers a huge selection of handicrafts. You'll also find good restaurants and serenading mariachi bands south of the border.

History

Native Americans used Nogales Pass for at least 2,000 years on migration and trade routes. The Hohokam came through on their way to the Gulf of California to collect shells prized as bracelet and necklace material. Pima, possibly descended from the Hohokam, settled and traveled in the Santa Cruz River Valley and Nogales area after A.D. 1500. During the Spanish era, missionaries, soldiers, ranchers, and prospectors also passed through. Apache used the pass on raiding forays well into the 1800s. Traders on the Guaymas–Tucson route knew the spot as Los Nogales (Spanish for The Walnuts). A survey team marked the international boundary line here in 1855, one year after the Gadsden Purchase.

The twin cities got their start in 1880, when Juan José Vásquez established a roadhouse on the Mexican side, and some months later Jacob Isaacson set up a trading post on the American side. The first railroad line to cross the border between the United States and Mexico came through in October 1882, and Nogales prospered with trade, silver mining, and ranching.

When Pancho Villa threatened Nogales in 1916, the worried U.S. Army established Camp Little on the edge of town. Relations between the two halves of Nogales remained good despite the political turmoil in Mexico, and Camp Little closed in 1933. Tourists discovered Nogales in the 1940s, and tourism, along with trade, keeps the border busy today.

Sights

Artifacts and old photos of the **Pimeria Alta Historical Society Museum** (Grand Ave. and Crawford St., 520/287-4621, 10 A.M.–4 P.M. Wed.–Sun. depending on staffing, donations welcome) illustrate the long and colorful history of southern Arizona and northern Sonora. An attraction in itself, the mission-style building dates to 1914 and housed the Nogales City Hall and police and fire departments. You can see the old jail, hand-powered water pump, law office, and other exhibits. The society's research library and archives offer a wealth of books on regional history as well as an extensive collection of historic photographs.

The 1904 former **Santa Cruz County Courthouse,** a square granite structure with a shiny aluminum dome, presides on the hillside to the northeast. You can visit the Cowbelles and Arizona Rangers museums inside 10 A.M.–4 P.M. on Saturdays.

Local artists display their work in the **Hilltop Art Gallery** (Hilltop Dr., 520/287-5515, noon–4:30 P.M. daily Sept.–May, free). From Grand Avenue, turn west on Ellis Street, right on Marina Street, then right following signs.

Events

The Mexican side hosts a big parade and entertainment for **Cinco de Mayo** (during the week or so leading up to May 5), **Independence Day** (Sept. 16), and **Revolution Day** (Nov. 20).

Baseball players drop into the Arizona side of

town for **spring training** in March. Patagonia Lake State Park hosts a **Mariachi Festival,** also in March. Fireworks celebrate the American **Independence Day** on July 4. **Santa Cruz County Fair** puts on a rodeo, fiddlers' competition, rooster-crowing contest, and agricultural exhibits in Sonoita on the last weekend in September. Arizonans have a **Christmas Parade** on the first Saturday in December.

Shopping

Most visitors to Ambos Nogales (Both Nogales) find it easier to park on the American side near the border (about $4 all day) and set off on foot. This saves delays in crossing the border by car and finding parking spots in Mexico.

Mexican craftspeople turn out an astonishing array of products, from saddles to Tiffany-style lampshades. Because a day's wages in Mexico comes close to an hour's wages in the United States, most crafts are real bargains. Be sure to shop around and politely request a discount before laying out any cash, even in the large, fixed-price stores. Most salespeople speak English, and you don't need pesos, as dollars and major credit cards are happily accepted.

Popular buys include chess sets of carved onyx, clay reproductions of Mayan art, painted vases, embroidered clothing, glassware, hand-tooled leather pieces, wool blankets, and woodcarvings. Pharmacies line the streets too, but staff may not be knowledgeable; you'll need a prescription to bring drugs back to the United States. Some items are very unpopular with U.S. Customs: guns and ammunition, fireworks, illegal drugs, switchblades, most meat products, and sea-turtle products. Adults can bring back other goods totaling US$400, including one quart of liquor every 31 days. Also, be careful not to bring guns into Mexico.

No permit is needed for U.S. or Canadian citizens to walk or drive across the border for visits in Nogales of 72 hours or less. Visitors from other countries should check with a Mexican consulate for entry requirements; they should also see U.S. Immigration about re-entry before stepping across. The Consulado de Mexico (571 N. Grand Ave., 520/287-2521) is in Nogales, Arizona.

Recreation

You'll find a public **swimming pool** and **tennis courts** near the War Memorial Park on Madison Street. Another pool is in Fleisher Park farther north on Hohokam Drive.

Golfers can play at three 18-hole courses, each with a restaurant, in the area: **Palo Duro Creek Golf Club** (in the northwest part of town at 2690 N. Country Club Dr., 520/761-4394), **Rio Rico Golf Course** (12 miles north of downtown at 1410 Rio Rico Dr., near I-19 Exit 17, 520/281-8567 or 800/288-4746), and **Kino Springs Country Club** (6 miles northeast on AZ 82, then right on Kino Springs Dr., 520/287-8701).

Accommodations

The winter rates listed here tend to go down in summer.

Under $50: El Dorado Motel (884 N. Grand Ave., 520/287-4611, $40 d) has just the basics. **Motel 6** (141 W. Mariposa Rd. at Grand Ave., 520/281-2951 or 800/466-8356, $37 s, $43 d) has a pool.

$50–100: Super 8 Motel (547 W. Mariposa Rd., west of I-19 Exit 4, 520/281-2242 or 800/800-8000, $45 s, $55 d) offers a pool and hot tub. **Holiday Inn Express** (850 W. Shell and Mariposa Rds., 520/281-0123 or 877/232-3630, $85 s, $90 d) also includes a pool and hot tub. **Americana Motor Hotel** (639 N. Grand Ave., 520/287-7211 or 800/874-8079, $60 s, $70 d) has a pool. **Best Western Siesta Motel** (673 N. Grand Ave., 520/287-4671 or 888/215-4783, $55 d) provides a pool and hot tub.

Over $100: Rio Rico Resort and Country Club (12 miles north of town near I-19 Exit 17, 520/281-1901 or 800/288-4746, www.riori-coresort.com, $139 d room, $175 d suite Jan.–April) features an 18-hole golf course, tennis, pool, hot tub, and horseback riding.

About 18 hotels lie on the Mexican side of the border; check with tourist offices for a map and suggestions.

Campgrounds

Mi Casa RV Park (2901 N. Grand Ave., 520/281-1150, $15.40 RV w/hookups) is 4.5 miles north of the border and has showers.

Food

Many restaurants line Grand Avenue on the Arizona side. **China Star Restaurant** (272 W. Mariposa Rd. in Mariposa Shopping Mall, 520/281-0633) serves popular Chinese dishes. **Zulas Papachoris'** (982 N. Grand Ave., 520/287-2892) features steak, seafood, Mexican, and Greek food. **Las Vigas Steak Ranch** (180 Loma St. at Fiesta Market off Arroyo Blvd., 520/287-6641, closed Mon.) has great Mexican food as well as steaks. **Bella Mia Ristorante** (204 W. Mariposa Rd. #6, 520/761-3535) serves up Italian antipasto, pasta, seafood, and meat dishes.

San Cayetano Dining Room (Rio Rico Resort, 12 miles north of downtown off I-19 Exit 17, 520/281-1901 or 800/288-4746) offers Southwestern fine dining daily for breakfast, lunch, and dinner.

Many restaurants in Mexico have English menus and all accept U.S. dollars. **La Roca,** partially carved out of the rock cliff, attracts visitors for the good food, gaily decorated dining rooms, and strolling musicians. Chefs offer steak, shrimp, fish, chicken, chimichangas, enchiladas, and other Mexican fare in the $9–20 range. It lacks a nonsmoking area, however. Look for the sign to the left a couple of blocks south of the border.

Information and Services

The **Nogales–Santa Cruz Chamber of Commerce** (123 Kino Park, Nogales, AZ 85621, 520/287-3685, www.nogaleschamber.com, 8 A.M.–5 P.M. Mon.–Fri.) is very helpful with information on both the local area and travel into Mexico. A video program presents a visual tour of Santa Cruz County sights, plus information on crossing the border and visiting Mexico. When entering Nogales from the north on Grand Avenue, turn right on the street just past the Patagonia Road interchange (AZ 82). The Mexicans have a **tourist office** just south of the Grand Avenue border crossing.

The **Nogales Ranger District** office (5 miles north of downtown at 303 Old Tucson Rd., Nogales, AZ 85621, 520/281-2296, www.fs.fed.us/r3/coronado, 8 A.M.–4:30 P.M. Mon.–Fri.) has recreation information for the Santa Ritas and Peña Blanca areas; take I-19 Ruby Road Exit 12, turn south .4 miles on the east frontage road, then left .1 mile on Old Tucson Road.

Nogales, Arizona, has a **public library** (518 N. Grand Ave., 520/287-3343, closed Sun.). The **post office** lies just east of the border station. **Carondelet Holy Cross Hospital** (1171 W. Target Range Rd., 520/287-2771) is on the west side of town.

Getting There and Around

Autobuses Crucero (35 N. Terrace Ave., 2 blocks from the border, 520/287-5628) goes north to Tucson and south to Hermosillo and other cities in Mexico. On the Mexican side, buses offer extensive routes at low cost, but you'll have to take a taxi to the station.

PATAGONIA AND VICINITY

The rolling hills of grass and woodlands surrounding Patagonia make up some of the state's finest cattle and horse land. Patagonia, 19 miles northeast of Nogales, lies on the alternate route to Tucson. Many people like to make a loop from Tucson by driving through Sonoita and Patagonia in one direction (I-10, Hwys. 83 and 82) and the Santa Cruz Valley (I-19) in the other.

The long, grassy park in the middle of town has some tables and the yellow, circa 1900 Patagonia Depot of the New Mexico and Arizona Railroad; trains stopped running here in 1962, and the depot now contains city offices. Also in the park, the Patagonia Butterfly Garden attracts resident and migrant butterflies from May to early October. Nearby Richardson Park has a playground.

Patagonia–Sonoita Creek Preserve

The Nature Conservancy looks after more than 750 acres along Sonoita Creek in this preserve (P.O. Box 815, Patagonia, AZ 85624, 520/394-2400, http://nature.org, 7:30 A.M., except 6:30 A.M. April–Sept., to 4 P.M. Wed.–Sun., 7-day entry pass costs $5, $3 members). Year-round water and a variety of habitats attract many birds, with about 300 species identified. White-tailed deer, coatimundi, javelina, bobcat, and other animals live in the thickets and woods. Four native fish species, including the endangered Gila topminnow, swim in the creek. The splendid cottonwood-willow riparian forest contains Fremont cottonwoods that tower more than 100 feet. About 2.5 miles of trails make loops near the creek; wheelchairs can follow one loop. The 3.5-mile loop Geoffrey Platts Memorial Trail climbs into the juniper and oak uplands on the other side of the road; you'll have good views and a chance to see resident wildlife; the trailhead is .6 miles before the visitors center.

The public is welcome to visit, but no picnicking, camping, or pets are allowed. The visitors center isn't always staffed, but you can see the outdoor exhibits and pick up a trail map and bird list. Nature walks begin here at 9 A.M. on Saturday year-round; no reservation needed. Check with the preserve for other walks and programs. Visitors during the summer monsoon season should apply insect repellent to keep off chiggers.

To reach the preserve from Highway 82 in Patagonia, turn northwest two blocks on 4th Avenue, then turn left 1.5 miles on Pennsylvania Avenue. The pavement ends and you'll have to drive across the creekbed—don't cross if you can't see the bottom. Continue to the visitors center for parking and trailheads. You can also take the back way by continuing on the dirt road two miles to Highway 82 at an unsigned junction between Mileposts 16 and 17, but the creek ford is likely to be deeper here.

Hummingbird feeders attract up to 11 species at **Paton's Birder's Haven,** a private residence adjacent to the preserve; it's the first house on the left just past the creekbed crossing. Park outside the gate, though drivers with mobility problems can park inside.

Ghost Towns

Decaying houses, piles of rubble, cemeteries, and old mine shafts mark deserted mining camps in the Patagonia Mountains to the south. You'll need the topo or Forest Service maps to find these old sites. In a 45-mile loop drive, you can visit Harshaw, Mowry, Washington Camp, and Duquesne. You can also drive east to the Huachuca Mountains, Parker Canyon Lake, or Coronado National Memorial on back roads. Most are dirt and should be avoided if it has recently rained or snowed.

Patagonia is a good place to start a drive to these sites. Turn beside the post office or head east on McKeown Avenue on the Harshaw Road. You'll pass a trailhead for the Arizona Trail in 2.7 miles. After 5.8 miles from Patagonia, turn right (pavement ends) and continue 1.8 miles to Harshaw, marked by a sign, a decaying house on the left, and the cemetery—worth seeing for its pioneer history—to the right. The road continues to the other sites. Mountain bikers also enjoy touring these scenic back roads.

Patagonia Lake State Park

Centered on a 265-acre reservoir, the park (520/287-6965, $7/vehicle day use) offers families and water sports enthusiasts an enjoyable place to picnic, camp, boat, and fish. Anglers catch largemouth bass, crappie, sunfish, bluegill, catfish, and, in winter, rainbow trout. Mesquite trees and some pines provide shade. Facilities include day-use areas, two wheelchair-accessible fishing docks, campground loops ($15/vehicle no hookups, $22/vehicle camping w/water and electric), showers, two boat ramps, a dump station, and a fish-cleaning station. A store sells groceries and camping supplies. The marina supplies fishing gear and rents canoes, pedal boats, and fishing boats (you can row or bring your own motor).

At an elevation of 3,750 feet, the park stays open all year; March–October tends to get busy, when the campground (first-come, first-served) often fills by Friday afternoon; it's a good idea to call ahead. Picnic areas also fill up on summer weekends. Groups can reserve a ramada for day use. Boaters may camp at primitive sites around the lake and on islands. The west half of the lake is open for waterskiing and personal watercraft Monday–Friday from May 1 to September 30 and daily the rest of the year; the east half of the lake is a no-wake area. Swim at Boulder Beach (no lifeguard).

The visitors center offers natural history exhibits, videos, a tiny library, and children's projects; you can pick up a bird list and find out about recent sightings. Birding walks and boat tours go some days; call for the schedule or drop by the visitors center to sign up. **Sonoita Creek Trail** begins at the east end of the hookup campground and winds to the mouth of Sonoita Creek, 1.2 miles round-trip. **Sonoita Creek State Natural Area,** northwest of the state park, holds about 5,000 acres of riparian, grassland, and woodland habitats; trails here are being planned.

From Patagonia, head southwest 7 miles on Highway 82, then turn right 4 miles on a paved road; from Nogales, go 12 miles northeast on Highway 82, then turn left 4 miles. The park gate is closed 10 P.M.–4 A.M.

Entertainment

If you're up to some music and dancing on a weekend, drop by the smoke-free **La Misión de San Miguel** (335 McKeown Ave., 520/394-0123, www.lamisionpatagonia.com). The 1915 adobe building looks like an old Spanish mission from the outside. Inside, you're greeted by a fountain and two St. Michaels—one a traditional statue and the other a painting depicting him as a Native American. And yes, those carved wooden temple doors inside really did come from India! Farther in, a brightly painted tropical forest mural contrasts with a 60-foot mural of the Four Horsemen of the Apocalypse. The beautiful 30-foot bar was made here of rare parota wood from Mexico. Bands play Friday and Saturday nights, then Sunday is usually an open-mic night.

Antiques and hunting trophies adorn the interior of the 1937 **Wagon Wheel Saloon** (Naugle and 4th Aves.), "Patagonia's Original Cowboy Bar."

Accommodations and Campgrounds

The **Stage Stop Inn** (303 W. McKeown, 520/394-2211 or 800/923-2211, $50 s, $60 d, $80 d kitchenette, $99 or $129 for a suite) has a restaurant and pool in the middle of Patagonia. Several small inns offer places to stay in and near town; check with Mariposa Books visitor information desk or its website for details.

Circle Z Ranch (4 miles southwest of Patagonia, 520/394-2525 or 888/854-2525, www.circlez.com) features horseback riding, swimming, hiking, birding, and tennis during the November 1–May 15 season. Inclusive rates for adults (age 16+) run $1,025–1,600 per week, or you can choose from weekend and weekday specials.

Patagonia RV Park (.7 miles south on the road to Harshaw, 520/394-2491, $10 tents, $22 RV w/hookups) has showers.

Food

The **Stage Stop Inn's** restaurant (303 W. McKeown, 520/394-2211, daily breakfast, lunch, and dinner, plus Sun. brunch) serves Mexican and American food with a choice of indoor or patio seating. Nearby, the **Gathering Ground** (319 McKeown Ave., 520/394-2097, daily breakfast and lunch) bakes tempting breads and pastries as well as offering sandwiches, quiches, ice cream, and coffees.

Velvet Elvis Pizza Company (292 Naugle Ave./AZ 82, 520/394-2102, Thurs.–Sun. lunch and dinner) offers gourmet pizza, plus chicken and rib dishes, soups, and organic salads. **Red's Real Pit Barbecue** (436 Naugle Ave., 520/394-0284, Fri.–Sun. lunch, Fri.–Mon. dinner) serves up Texas-style barbecue.

Information and Services

Mariposa Books (436 Naugle Ave., 520/394-9186) offers both a bookstore and a **tourist information desk** (520/394-0060 or 888/794-0060, www.patagoniaaz.com); closed Tuesday. Look for a quilt shop and art galleries on McKeown Avenue; another gallery is on Naugle Avenue. The **post office** is on the northeast side of town.

SONOITA AND VICINITY

This little crossroads town is at the junction of Highway 82 and Highway 83 in gently rolling grasslands. Parker Canyon Lake lies 30 miles to the south and east on Highway 83. Near the junction, you'll find restaurants, shops, gas stations, and a post office.

Accommodations and Food

The **Sonoita Inn** (520/455-5935, www.sonoitainn.com) offers spacious rooms—each named for a local ranch—with views of rolling hills. The rustic yet elegant Western decor and the high-ceilinged common area with a fireplace make this an exceptionally pleasant place to stay; it's expensive, however, at $125 d downstairs and $140 d upstairs, but all rooms drop to $89 d mid-June–mid-August.

For a tiny town, Sonoita offers very good restaurants. At the highway junction, **The Steak Out Restaurant & Saloon** (520/455-5205, Sat.–Sun. lunch and daily dinner) has a great selection of steaks along with chicken, ribs, and fish.

Café Sonoita (half a mile east of the highway junction, 520/455-5278, Fri.–Sat. lunch and Wed.–Sat. dinner) typically offers beef, quail, chicken, seafood, and pasta on its chalkboard menu; its long wine list includes some local labels. **Grasslands, A Natural Foods Café** (south on AZ 83, around the corner from the highway junction, 520/455-4770, Wed.–Sun., breakfast and lunch, only Fri.–Sun. in summer) provides a pleasant alternative to the usual café scene. You can also buy baked goods, preserves, and local wines here.

Las Cienegas National Conservation Area

The landscape of much of Arizona changed drastically in the late 1800s, when extensive grazing by domestic cattle severely depleted native grasses. Livestock still graze in this area—as they have for 300 years—but they're now controlled. As a result, the grass has recovered and stands as high as six feet. The 15 inches of annual rainfall supports some of the best examples of native grassland in the state. Within the 45,000 acres of the conservation area you'll also find large cottonwood trees lining the banks of perennial Cienega Creek, oaks and junipers clinging to the hills, and mesquite trees scattered throughout the range.

The public lands in the conservation area, previously known as the Empire-Cienega Resource Conservation Area, are open to individual visitors and campers without permits, but group activities do require one. There are no paved roads, campgrounds, or picnic areas within the conservation area. Visitors enjoy birding, wildlife (keep an eye out for pronghorn), hiking, horseback riding, bicycling, hunting, and no-facility camping (limited to 14 days). Campfires are allowed, but only dead wood lying on the ground may be collected. For more information and road conditions, call the BLM office in Tucson (520/722-4289).

You can enter the conservation area on the west from Highway 83 between Mileposts 39 and 40, 6.4 miles north of Sonoita, and follow Empire Ranch Road past Empire Ranch (on the left 3 miles in from the highway) to Cienega Creek and other destinations. From the south, you can enter on South Road off Highway 82 between Mileposts 36 and 37, about four miles east of Sonoita; this road ends at some corrals just east of Empire Ranch. Together, these roads make a scenic 11-mile loop that may be passable by cars in dry weather; both are marked as EC-900.

Parker Canyon Lake

This 130-acre fishing lake west of the Huachucas is a rarity in a land of little surface water. Trout are stocked in the cooler months to join the year-round population of bass, northern pike, bluegill, sunfish, and catfish. The water also attracts many birds and other wildlife, which you can see from a 4.5-mile hiking trail that goes around the lake. The **Arizona Trail** reaches Mile 20 from the Mexican border near the lake.

Lakeview Campground (elev. 5,400 feet, $10 camping or day use) is open all year with drinking water but no showers or hookups. Groups can reserve nearby **Rock Bluff** for day use or camping with the Sierra Vista Ranger District office (520/378-0311).

A **marina** (520/455-5847, closed Wed. March–Oct. and Tues.–Thurs. in winter) provides groceries, fishing supplies, licenses, boat ramp, and boat rentals. You can rent a rowboat or a boat with electric motor, but you need to bring your own battery or gas motor (8 hp limit).

Parker Canyon Lake lies 30 miles south of Sonoita at the end of Highway 83; 4 miles are gravel but eventually will be paved. You can also come on gravel roads from Coronado National Memorial or Nogales. All of these routes pass through highly scenic forest and ranch country.

The Cochise Trail

Chief of the Chiricahua Apache, Cochise earned great respect from whites and Indians alike for his integrity and leadership skills; he never lost a battle. Even though he waged war against Anglo troops and settlers from 1861 to 1872, government officials named Arizona's southeast corner Cochise County in his honor in 1881. Many historic sites of the Old West lie along a 206-mile loop—the Cochise Trail—through this varied country.

FORT HUACHUCA AND SIERRA VISTA

When raiding Apache threatened settlers and travelers in the San Pedro Valley in 1877, the army set up a temporary camp near the Huachuca (wa-CHOO-ka) Mountains. In 1886, Fort Huachuca became the advance headquarters for the campaign against Geronimo. Although the army later closed more than 50 forts and camps in the territory, it retained Huachuca to deal with outlaws and renegade Indians near the Mexican border. World Wars I and II and the Korean War saw new duties for the fort; finally, in 1954, it began its current task of testing electronics and communications gear and serving as an information center and intelligence school. Except during rough weather, you'll see an aerostat tethered high above the fort scanning for low-flying smugglers' planes. It also serves as a weather vane. The website http://huachuca-www.army.mil tells of some of the projects at the post.

Sierra Vista (pop. 30,000), the largest and fastest-growing community in Cochise County, includes Fort Huachuca (pop. 10,000). It lies on the east side of the Huachuca Mountains at an elevation of 4,623 feet and makes a handy base for exploring the surrounding region.

When driving toward Sierra Vista, you have a choice of taking the bypass route across the north or going downtown on Fry Boulevard. You'll find nearly all motels, restaurants, shopping, and other visitor services on or near this busy street.

Fort Huachuca Museum

The Old West comes alive as you walk by life-size figures of the fort's soldiers, scouts, officers, and wives. Each has a story to tell. Exhibits begin in the main building with experiences of chasing renegade Apache during the fort's early days, then progress to the World War II years. Head upstairs to see the Black Military Experience in the American West display. Nearby exhibits show how soldiers, officers, and Apache scouts helped tame the frontier. Period rooms portray family life. You'll get a feel for how tough life in the army could be, yet why many army people developed a fondness for Fort Huachuca. A gift shop sells history, hiking, and regional books as well as souvenirs. The Annex across the street displays additional exhibits arranged chronologically around a campfire scene. Barracks and administrative buildings from the 1880s line the nearby parade ground outside. A sign on the south side of the main museum building gives the dates and functions of the old buildings.

The two museum buildings (520/533-3898, 9 A.M.–4 P.M. Mon.–Fri., 1–4 P.M. Sat.–Sun., $2 suggested donation) lie on either side of Hungerford (at Grierson), about 2.5 miles in from the main gate in Sierra Vista; you'll need to follow signs carefully.

Army Intelligence Museum

Follow signs a short way down Hungerford from the Fort Huachuca Museum to see exhibits on intelligence history and the equipment used to crack the other side's secrets. Life-size figures show intelligence pioneers and personnel at work. The collection even has some aircraft used for spying, as well as radios and cryptography gear. Videos can be seen on request. Open the same hours as the Fort Huachuca Museum.

Henry F. Hauser Museum

This small rotating collection (8 A.M.–5 P.M. Mon.–Fri.) portrays the history of Sierra Vista and the San Pedro River Valley. It's in the Ethel H. Berger Center, across the parking lot from the Visitors Bureau.

Cowboys at the Parker Ranch in San Rafael Valley, ca. 1910.

Events

The Visitors Bureau maintains a listing of regional happenings and a Special Events Hotline (520/459-3868).

Athletes age 50 and up compete in the **Senior Games** in January. The all-women pro rodeo **Sierra Stampede** rides in January on the weekend before Martin Luther King, Jr. Day. Performers portray the West during the **Cochise Cowboy Poetry & Music Gathering** (www.cowboypoets.com) on the first full Friday–Sunday in February. **Festival of the Southwest** in early May features music, arts, and crafts of the Southwest. Fireworks light the sky during the **4th of July** celebration.

Oktoberfest, in September, creates a German atmosphere with oompah bands, food, crafts, dancing, and song. The **Fun Festival** in September brings a big carnival, concerts, food, and crafts to Fort Huachuca. **Art in the Park,** on the first weekend of October, attracts artists and craftspeople from all over the Southwest. Custom and antique cars shine for **Cars in the Park** on the second Saturday of October. Balloons take to the air for the **Festival of Color** on the fourth weekend of October. **Festival of the Trees** adds to holiday spirit in the Mall at Sierra Vista at the end of November and beginning of December. The **Christmas Parade** marches on the first Saturday of December. You can enjoy holiday decorations and history in the **Tour of Officers' Homes** at Fort Huachuca on the first Sunday of December.

Shopping and Services

The **Mall at Sierra Vista** has department stores on Highway 92, 1.8 miles south of Fry Boulevard. **Hastings** (3758 E. Fry Blvd., 520/459-8130) offers regional books as well as general reading, on the southwest corner of Fry Boulevard and Highway 92. **San Pedro House Books & Gifts** (520/508-4445) has an excellent selection of regional and natural history books, seven miles east of town on Highway 90. You can pick up outdoor supplies at **Big Five** on the southeast corner of Fry Boulevard and Highway 92, and at **Wal-Mart** a couple of blocks farther north.

Recreation

Veterans Memorial Park (3105 E. Fry Blvd., 520/458-7922) offers picnic tables, a playground, basketball court, horseshoe pits, and an aquatic center (520/417-4800). **Buffalo Corral Riding Stables** (520/533-5220) has rides and instruction at Fort Huachuca. Play golf year-round at Fort Huachuca's 18-hole **Mountain View Golf Course** (Buffalo Soldier Trail and Willcox Dr., 520/533-7092).

Accommodations

Inns and Bed & Breakfasts: Highly recommended, these places south of town let you get close to nature in the Huachucas or near the San Pedro River. All attract birders as well as hikers and people who enjoy beautiful surroundings.

Nestled under the trees and managed by the Nature Conservancy, **Ramsey Canyon Inn Bed & Breakfast** (520/378-3010, www.ramseycanyoninn.com) lies just below Ramsey Canyon Preserve. Rooms with breakfast and private bath cost $130–150 d and apartments with kitchens but no breakfast run $150–225 d. Guests enjoy homemade pie in the afternoon. Head six miles south of Sierra Vista on Highway 92, then turn west four miles up Ramsey Canyon Road.

Beatty's Guest Ranch & Orchard (2173 E. Miller Canyon Rd., 520/378-2728, www.BeattysGuestRanch.com) has a stunning setting on 10 acres of apple orchard, forest, and ponds below Miller Peak. The 5,800-foot elevation makes this one of the coolest places to stay in the area. Hummingbirds arrive in great numbers during the warmer months—15 species have been counted here. Drop by the website for birding and hiking information. Two large apartments ($80–95 d) and a 1911 cabin ($110 d) stay open year-round. Three small cabins, a short hike up in the woods, have solar lighting and composting toilets; they're open April–September and cost $50–95 s, $65–95 d. All units have kitchens. A campground ($20) has tent spaces and a shower; no fires. Small RVs can park, but there aren't any hookups. The little store sells local produce, snacks, and birding books. Drive about nine miles south of town on Highway 92, then turn west three miles up Miller Canyon Road.

San Pedro River Inn (8326 S. Hereford Rd., 520/366-5532, www.sanpedroriverinn.com, $105 d and up), 17 miles southeast of town, offers four adobe houses with 1–3 bedrooms, all with kitchens. Your horse can stay in the stables. Two ponds attract waterfowl, and the San Pedro River is just a short stroll away.

Also near the river, **Casa de San Pedro** (8933 S. Yell Lane in Hereford, 520/366-1300 or 888/257-2050, www.bedandbirds.com, $119–149 d) has a peaceful setting on 10 acres. Guests enjoy birdwatching, gourmet breakfasts, a pool, and a hot tub. From Sierra Vista, go south on Highway 92, east on Hereford Road, south on Palominas Road, then east on Waters Road.

Under $50: Choices include **Western Motel** (43 W. Fry Blvd., 520/458-4303, $38 s, $42 d) with some kitchenettes, **Bella Vista Motel** (1101 E. Fry Blvd., 520/458-6737, $32 s, $38 d) with a pool and kitchenettes, and **Motel 6** (1551 E. Fry Blvd., 520/459-5035 or 800/466-8356, $37 s, $43 d) with a pool.

$50–100: Gateway Studio Suites (203 S. Garden Ave. near the fort's main gate, 520/458-5555 or 877/443-6200, $65 s, $75 d) features minisuites, all with kitchenettes, plus an exercise room, pool, and hot tub. **Super 8 Motel** (100 Fab Ave., 520/459-5380 or 800/800-8000, $50 s, $55 d) has a pool. **Sierra Suites** (391 E. Fry. Blvd., 520/459-4221, $69 s, $79 d, $99 d suite) offers a fitness room, pool, and hot tub. **Best Western Mission Inn** (3460 E. Fry Blvd., 520/458-8500 or 877/937-8386, $66.50 s, $72.50 d) has a pool. **Fairfield Inn & Suites** (3855 El Mercado Loop, 520/439-5900, $79 d room or $89 d suite) provides an exercise room, pool, and hot tub; it's on the north side of the Mall at Sierra Vista off Highway 92. **Windemere Hotel & Conference Center** (2047 S. Hwy. 92, 520/459-5900 or 800/825-4656, www.windemerehotel.com, $139 d but can drop as low as $59 d on weekends) provides meeting rooms, a restaurant, pool, hot tub, fitness-center privileges, and full breakfast; it's across Highway 92 from the Mall at Sierra Vista.

Campgrounds

Pueblo del Sol RV Resort (3400 Resort Dr., 520/378-0213 or 888/551-1432, www.pdsrvresort.com, $31 RV w/hookups) offers many activities and amenities for seniors; head south on Highway 92, turn left on Canyon de Flores, then left on Resort Drive. **Sierra Vista Mobile Home Village** (733 S. Deer Creek Lane, 2 miles east on AZ 90/Bisbee Rd., 520/459-1690 or 800/955-7606, $25.50 RV w/hookups) accepts families. **Tombstone Territories RV Park** (2111 E. Hwy. 82 in Huachuca City, 520/457-2584 or 877/316-6714, $25.50 RV w/hookups) also accepts families.

Tenters have just a few options, all outside of town, notably Carr Canyon Road and Beatty's Guest Ranch & Orchard. San Pedro Riparian National Conservation Area has walk-in camping.

Food

You'll find a platoon of eateries on Fry Boulevard, plus several popular spots south on Highway 92. **Mesquite Tree** (Hwy. 92, 520/378-2758, www.mesquitetreerestaurant.com, Tues.–Sun. dinner) serves up steak, prime rib, fish, shrimp, and Italian dishes at the turnoff for Carr Canyon, seven miles south of downtown; favorites include the stuffed filet mignon and the Vargas ribeye (smothered with green chili, cheese, and enchilada sauce); reservations are recommended.

A favorite spot with local collectors of classic cars, **The Diner** (3500 Canyon de Flores off S. Hwy. 92, 520/378-1958, weekends breakfast, daily lunch and dinner) brings back memories with its American comfort food, stainless-steel exterior, vinyl booths, and '50s decor. **Caffe O Le** (400 E. Fry Blvd., 520/458-6261) draws in the locals for good food at bargain prices; it's especially popular for breakfast. South-of-the-border flavors inhabit **La Casita Mexican Restaurant & Cantina** (465 E. Fry Blvd., 520/458-2376).

Sierra Vista's many Asian restaurants have been credited in part to wives from overseas who married army personnel. For Chinese, try **Golden China Restaurant** (220 W. Fry Blvd., 520/458-8588) or the **Golden Phoenix** (1173 E. Fry Blvd., 520/459-4717, closed Mon.). Enjoy Japanese cuisine at **Tanuki Sushi Bar & Garden** (1221 E. Fry Blvd., 520/459-6853, closed Sun.). For fine Vietnamese food, there's the **Peacock** (80 S. Carmichael Ave. near the west end of Fry Blvd., 520/459-0095, closed Mon.). You'll find supermarkets in the shopping centers along Fry Boulevard.

Information

Sierra Vista Convention & Visitors Bureau (3020 E. Tacoma St., 520/417-6960 or 800/288-3861, www.visitsierravista.com, 8 A.M.–5 P.M. Mon.–Fri., 9 A.M.–4 P.M. Sat.) offers information about the sights and services of the region. Its mailing address is 1011 N. Coronado Drive, Sierra Vista, AZ 85635. You can purchase books and maps here for local hiking and birding. It's in the northeastern part of town near the library; follow signs north one mile on Moorman Avenue/Coronado Drive from Fry Boulevard, or south one block on Coronado Drive from the Highway 90 bypass, then turn east on Tacoma.

Sierra Vista Ranger Station (5990 S. Hwy. 92, Hereford, AZ 85615, 520/378-0311, www.fs.fed.us/r3/coronado, 8 A.M.–4:30 P.M. Mon.–Fri.) provides recreation information for national forest lands in the Huachuca and Whetstone Mountains and sells maps and books. It's 6.5 miles south of downtown Sierra Vista, midway between the Ramsey Canyon and Carr Canyon turnoffs.

The **BLM San Pedro Project Office** (1763 Paseo San Luis, Sierra Vista, AZ 85635, 520/439-6400, www.az.blm.gov, 8 A.M.–4 P.M. Mon.–Fri.) has information on the San Pedro Riparian National Conservation Area. The office is on the east side of town; from Fry Boulevard, turn south one mile on Highway 92, left one block on Snyder Boulevard, then right about a block on Paseo San Luis.

Sierra Vista Public Library (2600 E. Tacoma St., 520/458-4225) is open daily in the northeastern part of town—turn north on Moorman Avenue/Coronado Drive from Fry Boulevard, then right on Tacoma; Friends Bookstore sells bargain books.

The **post office** (2300 E. Fry Blvd., 520/458-2540) is opposite the turnoff for the library and Visitors Bureau. **Sierra Vista Regional Health Center** (300 El Camino Real, 520/458-4641 or 800/880-0088) is a block east then south from the post office.

HUACHUCA MOUNTAINS

The Huachucas, south of Sierra Vista, present many hiking possibilities and some very scenic drives. Trails climb from all sides of the range to Miller Peak Wilderness, which contains much of the high country between Coronado National Memorial and Fort Huachuca.

Huachuca and Garden Canyons

Each of these canyons offers a scenic drive, good birding, picnic areas, and trailheads from which you can hike into the Huachuca Mountains and south to the Miller Peak Wilderness. The oldest part of Fort Huachuca lies near the mouth of **Huachuca Canyon.** From the intersection of Hungerford and Grierson Avenues at the Fort Huachuca Museum, head southwest .6 miles on Grierson, then turn left .1 miles on Hines Road to the canyon entrance. Sycamore, oaks, pines, and junipers shade the canyon floor as you follow the gravel road past several picnic areas in another two miles. The road then becomes too rough for cars, but high-clearance vehicles can continue a bit farther. You may, however, prefer to walk and listen to the sounds of birds and the gurgling creek. Picnic areas are free and don't require a permit.

Garden Canyon lies farther south on the east side of the Huachucas. If you're driving in from the main gate toward the Fort Huachuca Museum, you'll see a sign two miles in for Garden Canyon. Head south five miles, following signs, past the Fort Huachuca Sportsmen's Center, firing ranges, and an aerostat site to a group picnic area at the mouth of the canyon. A kiosk here has information on the canyon and its history and bird life. Garden Canyon's picnic areas require a permit and fee. You'll pass a few more picnic areas in the thickly wooded canyon along the next 1.2 miles to where pavement ends. Depending on road conditions you may be able to continue driving several more miles or you can walk or mountain bike. A pictograph site is 3.3 miles from the group picnic area. The Fort Huachuca Museum's gift shop sells a guidebook and map for hiking in the Huachucas.

Arizona Folklore Preserve

Dolan Ellis, Arizona's Official State Balladeer and an original member of the New Christy Minstrels, organizes highly enjoyable programs of acoustic and folk entertainment. The shows run at 2 P.M. weekends and are very popular—you'll need to make reservations at 520/378-6165 or www.arizonafolklore.com. The delightful theater has a beautiful setting along Ramsey Creek. Head 3.5 miles up Ramsey Canyon Road from Highway 92; the turnoff is 6 miles south of Sierra Vista.

Ramsey Canyon Preserve

The Nature Conservancy operates this 300-acre sanctuary for hummingbirds and other wildlife (520/378-2785, http://nature.org/Arizona, $5, $3 members and Cochise County residents, free for kids under 16 and everyone on the first Sat.). Up to 14 species of hummers congregate here from spring to early autumn. Butterflies also appear in the warmer months. A year-round stream and a wide range of elevations provide habitats for many other kinds of creatures as well, including white-tailed deer, coati, javelina, black bear, and turkey. The Hamburg Trail goes through the preserve one mile, then continues a short way to an overlook (6,380 ft.) in the Coronado National Forest. Guided nature walks depart at 9 A.M. on Tuesday, Thursday, and Saturday March–October. The Ramsey Canyon bird observation area, Hamburg Trail, and visitors center are open 8 A.M.–5 P.M. daily March–October, then 9 A.M.–5 P.M. the rest of the year.

Begin at the visitors center, where a gift shop sells hiking maps and an excellent selection of natural history and regional books. The Preserve can be crowded mid-March–September; groups should call ahead. The parking area has an 18-foot vehicle-length limit and cannot accommodate RVs or trailers. No pets, smoking, picnicking, or camping, please. From the turnoff on Highway 92, six miles south of Sierra Vista, head west four miles up Ramsey Canyon Road.

Carr Canyon Road

This scenic road ascends 7.8 miles up the east slopes of the range to the cool pine forests at over 7,000 feet. You'll enjoy spectacular views over the San Pedro Valley and distant mountains at overlooks along the way. Cautiously driven cars can do the trip if the road is dry; no vehicles over 20 feet or trailers over 12 feet long are allowed. Snow may close the road in winter.

The turnoff from Highway 92 is seven miles south of downtown Sierra Vista between Mileposts 328 and 329. Pavement ends after 1.5 miles where Forest Road 368 continues to the heights. A picnic area and trailhead are 1.8 miles in. At 2.4 miles, look on the left for Carr House (9 A.M.–4 P.M. Sat.–Sun. May–Oct.), which has exhibits and a nature trail.

About 6.5 miles in, **Reef Townsite Campground** (7,150 ft.) lies at the site of a former mining camp. It has a $10 picnicking/camping fee, but may not have water. The nearby Reef Group Area can be reserved for day use. **Reef Historic Trail** makes a .7-mile loop from the far end of the campground; signs point out mine and mill sites and relate their history. Prospectors filed claims here in 1893, then mined gold and silver until about WWI. Large mills processed the ore, but operations never proved very profitable. Some tungsten and quartz were mined later, but all operations ceased by the end of the 1950s. The trail descends several hundred feet and affords fine views of the Huachuca Mountains and its canyons. For longer hikes, start at the trailhead opposite the entrance to the campground, where **Old Sawmill Trail** climbs to Carr Peak Trail, which in turn leads to Carr Peak (3 miles), Crest Trail #103 (3.5 miles), and Miller Peak (6.5 miles).

Ramsey Vista Campground (7,200 ft.), 1.3 miles farther at the end of the road and near the wilderness boundary, has a $10 picnicking/camping fee but no water. From the trailhead just before the campground, **Carr Peak Trail #107** heads up to Carr Peak (2.75 miles) and connects with Comfort Spring Trail #109 (.25 miles) and other destinations; another trailhead lies at the far end of the campground. There's no charge for trailhead parking outside the campgrounds, though donations are accepted. Contact the Sierra Vista Ranger Station (520/378-0311, www.fs.fed.us/r3/coronado) of the Coronado National Forest for information on exploring the Huachucas; the office is on Highway 92 just half a mile north of the Carr Canyon Road turnoff.

Our Lady of the Sierras Shrine

This peaceful spot high on a hillside offers space for reflection amid grand views of the Huachucas and the San Pedro Valley. A stone pathway winds up a hillside past the Stations of the Cross. You can step inside the stone chapel to see its art. A 75-foot Celtic cross and 32-foot statue of the Madonna stand nearby. The shrine is open 9 A.M.–sunset daily with free admission; call 520/378-2950 or surf to www.ourladyofthesierras.org for more information. Head south about 12 miles on Highway 92, turn right (between Mileposts 333 and 334) on Stone Ridge, which curves to the west and becomes Prince Placer Road; you'll see the entrance on the left .7 miles from Highway 92.

Miller Peak Wilderness

High summits surrounded by sheer cliffs and deep canyons distinguish this rugged area of 20,190 acres in the Huachuca Mountains. Elevations range from 5,200 to 9,466 feet at the top of Miller Peak. Trails wind up the slopes from the east off Ash Canyon, Miller Canyon, Carr Canyon, and Ramsey Canyon Roads, from the south at Montezuma Pass in Coronado National Memorial, and from the west via Oversite, Ida, Bear, and Sunnyside Canyons. The 11.5-mile Crest Trail between Montezuma Pass and Fort Huachuca ties all of the trails together. Although the long climbs are challenging, the mountains offer outstanding views and chances to see birds and other wildlife. The Sierra Vista Ranger Station has descriptions of trails and sells maps and a hiking book for the Huachucas.

CORONADO NATIONAL MEMORIAL

Francisco Vásquez de Coronado marched through this area in 1540 in search of the mythical Seven Cities of Cíbola. Although his backers judged the quest a failure, Coronado led the first major European expedition into the American Southwest, and the names of both this park and the adjacent national forest honor him.

Coronado National Memorial (520/366-5515, www.nps.gov/coro, 9 A.M.–5 P.M. daily except Thanksgiving and Dec. 25, free) offers hiking and a scenic drive in the Huachuca Mountains just north of the Mexican border. You'll experience the grasslands and woodlands typical of "sky islands" in the region and have a good chance to see birds and other wildlife. The visitors center has an information desk, bookstore, and exhibits on the area's history, plants, and wildlife. A video introduces Coronado and the memorial, and other videos can be seen on request.

Outside, a nature walk identifies local flora. There's a picnic area in an oak grove across the road. The turnoff for Coronado National Memorial lies about midway between Sierra Vista and Bisbee on Highway 92. Turn west 4.7 miles on Coronado Memorial Drive to the visitors center and another 3.2 miles and 1,345 feet higher for Montezuma Pass; the last 2 miles are unpaved and not suited for vehicles or trailers over 24 feet. You can also take very scenic back roads—mostly dirt or gravel—from Patagonia or Nogales. Snowstorms occasionally close the pass in winter. Although the memorial closes at night, the road remains open 24 hours. There's no place to camp here. Pets can go only on the Crest Trail to Miller Peak Wilderness.

Coronado Cave Trail

This 1.5-mile round-trip trail winds up the hillside behind the visitors center to a limestone cave with some formations; the first quarter mile is gentle, followed by a steep half mile with some stone steps to the cave entrance; elevation gain is 470 feet. The cave is about 600 feet long, 70 feet wide, and up to 20 feet high, with some short crawl ways. All cave visitors must obtain the required free permit first and carry a flashlight (sold at the visitors center). A spare flashlight is recommended, and essential for solo travelers. To preserve the cave's environment, no food, candles, flares, or lanterns should be brought in. Visitors are asked not to disturb wildlife, such as the several species of bats that inhabit the cave at times.

Montezuma Pass and Hiking

Outstanding views of Arizona and Mexico stretch to the horizon from the top of 6,864-foot Coronado Peak, reached by the .8-mile round-trip **Coronado Peak Trail** south from Montezuma Pass. The path ascends 290 feet with many benches for resting. Signs along the way describe Coronado's expedition in his own words, along with accounts by his men and later historians. In .1 miles, you'll reach the turnoff for **Joe's Canyon Trail** (3.1 miles one-way), which connects Montezuma Pass with the visitors center in the valley below; elevation change is 1,345 feet.

Arizona Trail

The southernmost section of this trail begins at the Mexican border. There's no access from the Mexican side, so hikers begin by taking Joe's Canyon Trail southwest 2.1 miles from the visitors center or southeast 1 mile from Montezuma Pass, then following Yaqui Ridge Trail south 1 mile to International Border Monument #102. From here the Arizona Trail leads generally northward across the state to Utah.

You can reach Miller Peak (9,466 ft.), the highest point in the Huachuca Mountains, by hiking 5.3 miles (one-way) on the **Crest/Arizona Trail** north from Montezuma Pass. With a car shuttle, you could continue down from the summit into Miller Canyon in 11.6 miles. Mountain bikers may not ride trails in the memorial or wilderness, but they have many options in the Coronado National Forest to the west.

SAN PEDRO RIPARIAN NATIONAL CONSERVATION AREA

The San Pedro River, though only a trickle at times, nourishes willows, cottonwoods, and other streamside vegetation. It's one of the last undammed rivers in the Southwest. Residents of this choice wildlife habitat—one of the richest in the United States—include more than 400 bird species, 82 mammal species, and 45 reptile and amphibian species. From its beginning in the grasslands of Sonora, Mexico, the river flows north 140 miles to join the Gila River near Winkelman.

The San Pedro Riparian National Conservation Area, run by the BLM, is 1–3 miles wide and stretches for 36 miles from the Mexican border to near St. David. Visitors enjoy birdwatching, nature walks, and historic sites. Hikers, horseback riders, and mountain bikers may use the backcountry trails, but motorized vehicles are prohibited. Special firearms restrictions apply.

Information

You can usually find volunteers daily at Fairbank (520/457-3395) and San Pedro House (520/508-4445), though the people here may know only their immediate area. For more information, contact the **BLM's San Pedro Project Office** (1763 Paseo San Luis, Sierra Vista, AZ 85635, 520/439-6400, www.az.blm.gov, 8 A.M.–4 P.M. Mon.–Fri.).

Fairbank

This ghost town beside the San Pedro River began life in 1881 with construction of a railroad. Nearby mines, mills, and booming Tombstone generated a lot of freight and passenger traffic for the depot. An adobe commercial building (1883), home (1885), schoolhouse (1920), and other structures still stand, and interpretive panels give their histories. Volunteers and the BLM look after the site; there's usually someone here to answer your questions. Fairbank is on the north side of Highway 82, just east of the San Pedro River bridge.

Birders find good opportunities near the river. Hikers and mountain bikers can set off on abandoned roads to the north and south. The site of Grand Central Mill lies an easy 1.5 miles north, where foundations display fine stonework. Contention Mill site and town are four miles north of Fairbank, but you'll need a map, as the way isn't marked. You could also detour across the river to Terranate.

Presidio Santa Cruz de Terranate

Visitors can experience some of the isolation of this unsuccessful outpost of Spain. In 1775, the Irish mercenary Colonel Hugo O'Conor led construction of the fort to extend and protect the northern reaches of New Spain. Apache raids, however, prevented the raising of crops, robbed supply parties, and killed two captains and more than 80 soldiers. By 1780, after less than five years of use, the Spanish abandoned the site. A few weathered adobe walls from the chapel and commandant's quarters still stand, along with stone foundations of the walls and other structures. An interpretive trail within the presidio tells of the fortifications and what life may have been like here.

You must hike in, following an easy, well-marked trail that winds 1.2 miles across the desert to the site overlooking the San Pedro River. To reach the trailhead, take Highway 82 to Milepost 60, 1.2 miles west of Fairbank, then turn north 1.8 miles on gravel Ironhorse (Kellar) Road. Hikers could extend their trip by continuing north along and across the river to Contention; it's also possible to reach this area from Fairbank via Grand Central Mill. A map, available free from the BLM, will be needed for explorations beyond Terranate.

San Pedro House and Trails

Birdwatchers come here to take advantage of the excellent sighting possibilities. Friends of the San Pedro River runs a bookstore/gift shop in San Pedro House (520/508-4445, 9:30 A.M.–4:30 P.M. daily) with a large selection of regional and natural-history books; you can also obtain BLM handouts on the San Pedro National Conservation Area. Pick up a brochure for an easy interpretive loop of about one mile from the San Pedro House to the forested riverbanks and a pond. Other trails branch off to give you a longer hike. **San Pedro Trail** is planned to be 30 miles long; currently you can follow it south 8 miles to Hereford Road and north 3.6 miles to Escapule Road.

Murray Springs Clovis Site

Scientists have unearthed bones of extinct mammoths, bison, horses, camels, and dire wolf here along with stone weapons and tools used by the Clovis culture to kill and butcher the animals 8,000–11,000 years ago. A one-third-mile interpretive trail loops through the site; interpretive panels have photos of bones and tools found and illustrations of how the Clovis people may have hunted. Signs identify desert plants along the trail and describe their medicinal uses. From Sierra Vista head east 3.8 miles on Highway 90, turn left 1.2 miles on Moson Road, then right .4 miles at the sign; or you can take Charleston Road from Sierra Vista or Tombstone and turn south 1.8 miles on Moson Road, then left to the site. Lehner Mammoth Kill Site, farther south in the National Conservation Area, has also yielded bone and Clovis projectile points, but there is little to see and access is difficult.

Camping

Primitive walk-in camping (no facilities, $2/person/night) is permitted one mile or more from trailheads; note that parking at some trailheads closes in the evening. No car camping is allowed in the National Conservation Area.

TOMBSTONE

When prospector Ed Schieffelin headed out this way in March of 1877, friends told him the only thing he'd find among the Apache and rattlesnakes would be his own tombstone. But he set out anyway, alone, and staked a silver claim, proclaiming it Tombstone. When Ed struck it rich at an adjacent site, his brother Al said, "You're a lucky cuss." And the Lucky Cuss Mine became one of Arizona's richest. Other claims bore such descriptive names as Contention, Tough Nut, and Goodenough.

The town incorporated in 1879 and contained as many as 10,000 souls just five years later. It was said that saloons and gambling halls accounted for two of every three buildings in the business district. The famous OK Corral gunfight took place here in 1881—and historians still debate the details. The town's riches attracted many crooks and Apaches, who, along with political corruption, gave the region considerable notoriety. Shootings and hangings in the 1880s kept Boothill Graveyard busy. Fires nearly wiped out Tombstone on two occasions, but flooding of the mines by 1886 came close to driving the final nail in the town's coffin. Still, Tombstone, "the town too tough to die," managed to survive, and now attracts throngs of visitors seeking the Wild West. You'll experience both the authentic history of Tombstone and pistol-packing entertainment! The downtown section of Allen Street—Tombstone's heart—now has a more authentic atmosphere since it has been closed to motor vehicles.

Tombstone Courthouse State Historic Park

Drop by the 1882 red-brick courthouse (3rd and Toughnut Sts., 520/457-3311, 8 A.M.–5 P.M. daily, $4 adults, $1 ages 7–13) to find out what life was like for the people of early Tombstone. The venerable building, abandoned in 1931 when the county seat moved to Bisbee, has been restored and now houses a museum of artifacts and photos of the old days. The courtroom, lawyer's office, and assay office look ready for business. Exhibits introduce the Native Americans, prospectors, sheriffs, ranchers, and the famous gunfight of October 26, 1881. Mining exhibits show how miners dug and assayed their ore. An old bar, faro table, and roulette wheel illustrate how many miners lost their underground riches. Women probably did more to tame the town than the marshals and sheriffs; you'll learn about some of them and see exhibits on family life. A gift shop offers books and videos about Tombstone's history. Researchers can make an appointment to delve into the extensive historic archives.

Gunfights

Guns blaze and bodies hit the dust in staged gunfights and barroom brawls. The Visitor Information Center has the day's schedule. The action takes place most days at three sites. The **Boothill Gunslingers** (Allen St. between 3rd and 4th Sts., 520/457-3643) reenact the OK Corral gunfight and other events. **Six Gun City** (5th and Toughnut Sts., 520/457-3827) presents a lively musical show in a series of acts depicting actual Tombstone events. **Tombstone Cowboys** (4th and Toughnut Sts., 520/457-9153) promise "hysterically correct" entertainment in a series of action-packed gunfights at the Helldorado. Each Sunday afternoon, one of the local groups puts on another show. All events have a small admission fee or request a donation.

The OK Corral and Historama

The Earp brothers and Doc Holliday shot it out with the Clanton cowboys on this site in October 1881. Markers and life-size figures show how it all happened—or at least one version of the story. Other sights to see include the studio (reconstructed) and photos of Camilius S. Fly, old stables, carriages, a hearse, and even a red-light-district shack. Visitors can "walk where they fell" 9 A.M.–5 P.M. daily (520/457-3456, www.ok-corral.com). Package tickets for $7.50 (children under 6 free) include the OK Corral, the 2 P.M. gunfight show, Historama, and a copy of the *Epitaph*; without the gunfight it's $5.50. Located on Allen Street between 3rd and 4th Streets.

The 25-minute Historama show re-creates the major events of Tombstone with movies and animated figures. Presentations take place 9:30 A.M.–4:30 P.M. (last show) daily next door to the OK Corral entrance.

Crystal Palace Saloon

Built in 1879, this watering hole and gambling house offered an elegant setting for patrons in early Tombstone. As many as five bartenders stood on duty to serve thirsty customers round the clock. The clientele has changed over the years, but the saloon still serves up drinks and hosts live music. The interior has been accurately restored. It's in the center of town at 5th and Allen Streets.

Big Nose Kate's Saloon

This large and colorful cowboy bar began life as the Grand Hotel in 1881. There's lots of stuff to see on the walls in the bar room, but perhaps the most unusual feature is the downstairs shaft. Working in the hotel by day, an employee dug in secret at night from his room to prospect in the mineshafts under Tombstone. It's on Allen Street between 5th and 6th Streets.

Stagecoach and Wagon Rides

Hop on a stage or wagon for a narrated tour of Tombstone's colorful past. The horse-drawn vehicles depart frequently from near Big Nose Kate's Saloon on Allen Street downtown. Rides last about 15 minutes and cost $5 for adults, $4 senior 55+, and $3 children 4–15.

Tombstone *Epitaph*

As one story goes, the town's newspaper got its name when its founder, John P. Clum, took the stagecoach home from Tucson and asked passengers for appropriate suggestions. Ed Schieffelin happened to be on board, and he replied, "Well, I christened the district Tombstone; you should have no trouble furnishing the *Epitaph*." Clum started the *Epitaph* in 1880 and it's still in business. You can visit the office (9:30 A.M.–5 P.M. daily, free) to see the original press and other printing exhibits and to pick up your own *Epitaph*. It's on 5th Street around the corner from the Crystal Palace Saloon.

Bird Cage Theatre

This 1881 dance hall, gambling house, saloon, brothel, and theater provided the finest and most expensive entertainment of the day. During its first eight years, the doors never closed. Prostitutes scouted for customers from the 14 cribs overlooking the hall. The hit song "She's Only a Bird in a Gilded Cage" may have given the place its name. Or, as reported by the *Arizona Star* of

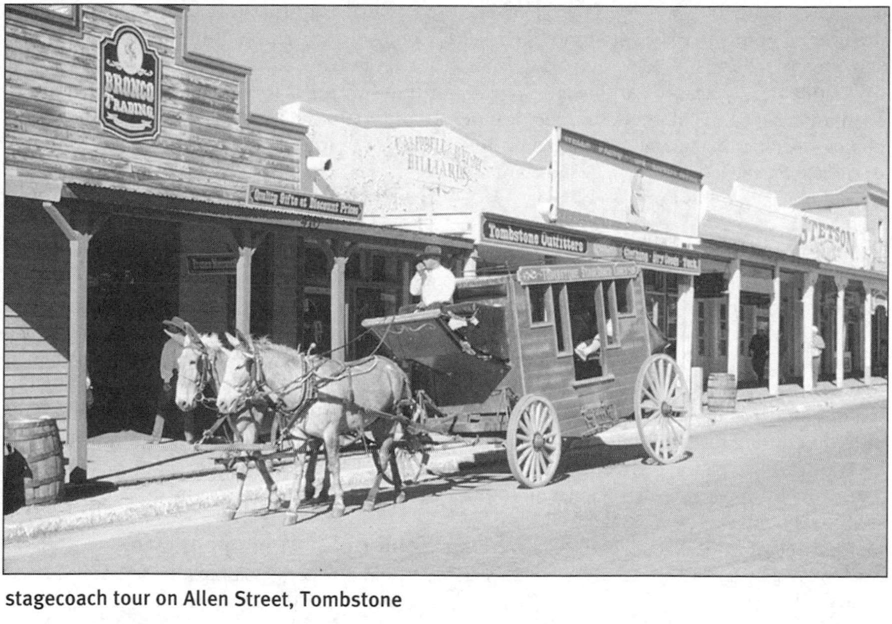

© BILL WEIR

stagecoach tour on Allen Street, Tombstone

August 18, 1882, the Bird Cage may have been so named because it had so many doves in it.

A self-guided tour winds through the theater, below the cribs, and past rare circus posters and gambling tables (Allen and 6th Sts., 520/457-3421, 8 A.M.–6 P.M. daily, $6 adults, $5.50 seniors 60+, $5 youth 8–18, $17 families). See if you can find some of the estimated 140 bullet holes in the walls and ceiling. A back room has the hearse that carried all but six residents on their last ride to Boothill. Downstairs, you can imagine life at the bar, at gambling tables, and in the bordello rooms. An 1881 City License here signed by Wyatt Earp allows the Bird Cage to operate a "House of Ill Fame." Many old photos and prints—some copies of which are for sale in the gift shop—show notable prostitutes and other characters. The exceptionally well-preserved building closed in late 1889 and remained boarded up for 45 years. When it reopened as a museum, everything inside was still there.

Tombstone Western Heritage Museum

A vast array of personal items, including some owned by Virgil and Wyatt Earp, gives a look into the lives of people in old Tombstone (Fremont and 6th Sts., 520/457-3800, 9 A.M.–5 P.M. Monday–Saturday, 12:30 P.M.–5 P.M. Sunday, $5 adult, $3 youth 12–18). Exhibits also include historic photos, documents, guns, ghost town relics, bottle collections, and a craps table. The museum's antique shop next door is worth a look too.

Pioneer Home Museum

While most of the early houses of miners and their families have been remodeled over the years, this one has been remarkably preserved (804 E. Fremont St., 520/457-3853, open on request, donations appreciated). It's little changed since Cornish miner Frank Garland and his wife Julia moved in during the late 1800s. Inside you can see the furnished parlor, bedroom, and kitchen. The former dining room has photos of Tombstone's distinguished citizens, along with a band uniform and other belongings of the Garlands. A blacksmith shop and a 1921 Chevy delivery truck lie in the backyard.

Rose Tree Museum

A rose root sent from Scotland to comfort a homesick bride in the spring of 1885 has grown to cover an amazing 8,700 square feet. The rose tree, believed to be the world's largest and listed in the *Guinness Book of Records,* is a Lady Banksia. Its sweet-scented white blossoms usually appear in early April. Rooms exhibit many historic photos and a collection of antique furnishings belonging to a pioneer who arrived by wagon in 1880 (4th and Toughnut Sts., 9 A.M.–5 P.M. daily, $3 adults, free for kids under 14). A gift shop sells new and used books.

Schieffelin Hall

Major theatrical companies of the day performed in this 1881 adobe building, claimed to be the largest adobe in the United States. John Sullivan and his company of boxers gave exhibitions here. Now restored, the hall once again hosts theater companies; upcoming events will be posted here and at the Visitor Information Center. Otherwise, it's usually closed to the public. It's on the corner of Fremont and 4th Streets.

St. Paul's Episcopal Church

Completed in 1882, St. Paul's is the oldest standing Protestant church in Arizona. Inside you can admire the original stained glass, two ship's lamps, and the sturdy adobe walls. It's open daily at the corner of 3rd and Safford Streets.

Boothill Graveyard

Here lie the losers of the OK Corral shootout, hanging/lynching victims, assorted gunslingers, and Dutch Annie, a widely admired prostitute. As the graveyard's name suggests, a lot of those who ended up here died violent deaths. Many of the estimated 300 graves are marked and have much to say about life in old Tombstone. Boothill (7:30 A.M.–6 P.M. daily, donations welcome) lies just off Highway 80 on the north edge of town. Enter through the Boot Hill Gift Shop, which sells an informative self-guided tour booklet.

Schieffelin Monument

The old prospector's last request was to be buried on top of the granite hills three miles west of town. He specified that "a monument such as prospectors build when locating a mining claim be built over my grave . . . under no circumstances do I want to be buried in a graveyard or cemetery." Head west 2.3 miles on Allen Street to see this lonely spot.

Nearby Ghost Towns

Ghost-town enthusiasts can explore remnants of former mining towns in the area. **Gleeson,** 18 miles east of Tombstone on a graded gravel road, flourished around a copper mine from 1909 until the 1930s. Operations ended in 1955. You can see ruins of the jail, cemetery, school, adobe hospital, and other buildings. Mine tailings and machinery rest on the hillside.

Courtland, now occupied solely by ghosts, lies one mile east and three miles north of Gleeson on good gravel roads. A jail and numerous foundations remain. Watch out for open mine shafts in the area.

Jimmie Pearce found gold in 1894 at the site of **Pearce,** nine miles north of Courtland. The Commonwealth Mine here was a success, and the town's population reached 1,500 before the mine closed in the 1930s. Reminders of the past include the old store, cemetery, post office, Pearce Church, abandoned houses, and Commonwealth Mine ruins. You can also reach Pearce from I-10; take Exit 331 and head south 22 miles on U.S. Highway 191.

Entertainment and Events

Shootouts take place every day throughout the year when weather permits. The Crystal Palace and Big Nose Kate's Saloon often provide live Western music.

Helldorado Days, Tombstone's biggest celebration, features three days of shootouts, parades, dances, and other lively entertainment on the third full weekend of October. Smaller-scale festivities include **Territorial Days** in March, the **Rose Festival** in April, **Wyatt Earp Days** on Memorial Day weekend, **Family-Style 4th of July, Western Film Festival & Book Exposition** (www.tombstonewesternfilm.com) on July 4 weekend, **Vigilante Days** on the second full weekend in August, **Rendezvous of the Gunfighters** on Labor Day weekend, **Tombstone Western Music Festival** with entertainment and street dances in November on Veterans' Day weekend, and the **Clanton Gang Reunion,** also in November.

Shopping

The many shops along Allen Street sell Old West souvenirs, clothing, jewelry, art, and crafts. You can dress in period costumes at old-time photo studios. **Tombstone Art Gallery** displays and sells varied local art and crafts on Allen Street next to the Visitor Information Center. **Tombstone Old West Books** has a fine selection at the corner of Allen and 4th Streets.

Accommodations

Bed and Breakfasts: All offer guests a chance to spend the night in a piece of history. The **Tombstone Boarding House** (108 N. 4th St., 520/457-3716 or 877/225-1319, www.tombstoneboardinghouse.com, $59–79 s, $69–89 d) has an old-fashioned ambiance with modern comforts in two 1880 adobe houses; rooms all have private baths and entrances. The owner also offers an excellent restaurant. Nearby, **Marie's Engaging Bed & Breakfast** (101 N. Fourth and Safford Sts., 520/457-3831 or 877/457-3831, www.mariesbandb.com, $65 s, $70–80 d including tax) is in a 1906 adobe; rooms have shared bath.

The Wild Rose Inn (101 N. 3rd St., 520/457-3844 or 866/457-3844, www.wildroseinnbandb.com, $79–89 d, $109 d with private bath) is a 1904 country Victorian house. **The Buford House** (113 E. Safford and 2nd Sts., 520/457-3969, bufordhousebandb@aol.com, $75–100 d) is an 1880 adobe with five guest rooms; each has a different theme and two include private bath. The **Silver Nugget** puts you right over the action of Allen Street across from the Bird Cage (520/457-9223, $64–79 d); the four rooms (two have private bath) share a balcony and include a continental breakfast.

Motels and Hotels: Trail Riders Motel and Mini-RV Park (corner of Fremont and 7th Sts., 520/457-3573 or 800/574-0417, $40 s, $50 d, $20 RV w/hookups) has a pool and hot tub.

Other options in the heart of town include the **Larian Motel** (410 E. Fremont St., 520/457-2272, www.tombstonemotels.com, $39–49 s, $45–59 d), **Tombstone Motel** (5th and Fremont Sts., 520/457-3478 or 888/455-3478, $60–70 d), and **Adobe Lodge** (5th and Fremont Sts., 520/457-2241 or 888/457-2241, $55 s, $65 d and up, suites are available too).

Tombstone Sagebrush Inn (4th St., 520/457-2311, $49–119 d, the more expensive have spas and kitchens) has a pool and a quiet location two blocks north of Fremont Street; weekly and monthly rates are also available. The **Best Western Lookout Lodge** (801 N. AZ 80, 520/457-2223 or 877/652-6772, www.tombstone1880.biz, $85–95 d) has a great view, breakfast, and a pool just north of town on Highway 80. Just beyond, **Holiday Inn Express** (1001 N. AZ 80, 520/457-9507, $98–119 d) also has fine views along with breakfast, pool, and a hot tub.

Campgrounds

Wells Fargo RV Park (3rd and Fremont Sts., 520/457-3966, $25 tent or RV w/hookups including tax) features a central location with showers, laundry, Internet access, and some of the cleanest restrooms in Arizona. **Stampede RV Ranch** (201 W. Allen St., 520/457-3738, $20 RV w/hookups) provides showers and laundry. **Trail Riders Motel and Mini-RV Park** (corner of Fremont and 7th Sts., 520/457-3573 or 800/574-0417, $20 RV w/hookups) has a pool and hot tub.

Tombstone RV Park & Resort (1 mile north of downtown on AZ 80, 520/457-3829 or 800/348-3829, $20 tent or RV no hookups, $24 RV w/hookups, $38 cabin) has a rural setting with a pool, showers, laundry, and store.

Food

Not surprisingly, most restaurants in town feature Western or Mexican decor and food. For a romantic dining spot, try Tombstone Boarding House's **Lamplight Room** (108 N. 4th St., 520/457-3716) with a choice of two menus, traditional American nightly for dinner (reservations recommended) or Mexican daily for lunch and dinner.

Longhorn Restaurant (5th and Allen Sts., 520/457-3405, daily breakfast, lunch, and dinner) offers Mexican, American, and a few Italian items; stained-glass images show old Tombstone scenes. Serving customers since 1882, **Nellie Cashman Restaurant** (5th and Toughnut Sts., 520/457-2212, daily breakfast, lunch, and dinner) offers American and a few pasta dishes; you can read about the remarkable Irish lass who founded the restaurant and see her photos here. The **OK Café** (Allen and 3rd Sts., 520/457-3980, daily) is popular for breakfast and lunch. **Tombstone Coffee & Tea Co.** (414 Allen St. 520/437-3045) will fix you up with beverages and pizza.

Tombstone lacks a supermarket, though you can pick up items at the Tombstone General Store on Allen Street (between 5th and 6th Sts.) and the Circle-K on Highway 80 north of downtown.

Information and Services

The **Visitor Information Center** (4th and Allen Sts., P.O. Box 1314, Tombstone, AZ 85638, 520/457-3929, www.cityoftombstone.com, 10 A.M.–4 P.M. daily) will fill you in on local action. You can also obtain information next door at the **Tombstone Chamber of Commerce** (4th St., P.O. Box 995, Tombstone, AZ 85638, 520/457-9317 or 888/457-3929, www.tombstone.org, 9 A.M.–5 P.M. Mon.–Fri.). The **websites** www.tombstoneweb.com and www.tombstone1880.com also provide background on Tombstone and links to local businesses.

Tombstone City Library (4th and Toughnut Sts., 520/457-3612, 8 A.M.–noon and 1–5 P.M. Mon.–Fri.) in Tombstone's 1903 railway station offers many regional books in its Southwestern collection and has Internet computers. The **post office** is on the west side of town at Safford and Haskell Streets. A small **city park** sits on the corner of Allen and 3rd Streets.

BISBEE

Squeezed into Mule Pass Gulch of the Mule Mountains, the old mining town Bisbee has a lot of character. A tiny mining camp in 1877, Bisbee grew into a solid and wealthy town by 1910. The side canyon Brewery Gulch held more than 50 saloons in the early 1900s, earning a reputation as the best drinking and entertainment venue in the territory. Many of the fine commercial buildings and Victorian houses built in the boom years still stand. Bisbee's riches, mostly copper ore, came from underground chambers and giant surface pits. It's 24 miles south of Tombstone and 95 miles southeast of Tucson.

History

The story of Bisbee began over 100 million years ago, when a giant mass of molten rock deep in the earth's crust expelled great quantities of steam and hot water. The mineral-rich solutions slowly worked their way upward, replacing the overlying limestone rock with rich copper ores. Three hundred different minerals, many in bright hues, have been identified here.

While looking for silver in 1875, Hugh Jones noticed mineral deposits, but, annoyed to find only copper, he soon left. Two years later, Jack Dunn, an army scout, also found ore. He couldn't leave his army duties to go prospecting, so he and his partners made a deal with George Warren to establish a claim and share the profits. Warren, a tough old prospector and heavy drinker, lost Dunn's grubstake in a saloon while on his way to the Mule Mountains, then quickly found new backers—Dunn and his partners not among them—and filed claims. Two years later he recklessly put his share on a wager that he could outrun a man on horseback, losing everything. Warren died penniless, but his image endures as the miner on the State Seal of Arizona. The suburb south of downtown Bisbee also honors him.

New electrical industries needed copper, and investors took a keen interest in Warren's camp. Judge DeWitt Bisbee and a group of San Francisco businessmen bought the Copper Queen Mine in 1880, though the judge never did visit the mining community named for him. From the east, Dr. James Douglas of the Phelps Dodge Company came to Arizona, buying property near the Copper Queen. After the two companies discovered that the richest ores lay on the property boundary, they decided to merge rather than fight it out in court.

Soon a smelter filled the valley with smoke and the clatter of machinery. Streets were paved and substantial buildings went up. Labor troubles between newly formed unions and mine management culminated in the infamous Bisbee Deportation in July 1917, when deputies herded more than 1,000 striking miners at gunpoint into boxcars and shipped them out of the state. Working conditions improved in the following years, but Bisbee's economic life rolled with copper prices. The giant Lavender Pit closed in 1974, and underground mining ended the following year. The district had provided more than eight billion pounds of copper from 40 mines. Although mining has ended, a huge amount of ore still lies underground.

The town didn't dry up and blow away when the mines closed, however. People liked it here—the climate (elev. 5,300 ft.), the scenery, the character. Bisbee has become a popular destination for many visitors, artists, and retired people. The city consists of the historic district downtown and the communities of Lowell, Warren, and San Jose.

Walking Bisbee

The twisting streets offer some great walking and photographing possibilities. Main Street, Brewery Gulch, and other downtown areas have well-preserved commercial buildings. Side streets lead past old residences. Two churches are worth a visit, the 1903 Covenant Presbyterian Church with its slender steeple at 19 Howell Avenue (next to the Copper Queen Hotel) and the 1915–1917 St. Patrick's Roman Catholic Church with its 27 stained-glass windows (turn off Tombstone Canyon at the *Iron Man* statue). You can learn the history of the many early-1900s buildings in town with the chamber of commerce's *Bisbee Walking Tours* pamphlet. If you'd like some *real* exercise, ask for a map of the Thousand Step Stair Climb route—actually 1,034 steps! Parking can be a challenge in town—another good reason to get around on foot—but with a little patience you'll find a space.

Bisbee Mining and Historical Museum

Step into the 1895 former Phelps Dodge General Office Building to experience the remarkable history of Bisbee's people and mining (Copper Queen Plaza downtown, 520/432-7071, www.bisbeemuseum.org, 10 A.M.–4 P.M. daily, $4 adults, $3.50 seniors, $1 ages 4–16). The exhibit *Bisbee: Urban Outpost on the Frontier* illustrates the city's remarkable transition from a remote mining camp to a bustling city complete with trolleys and other modern conveniences. Also on the main floor, the former General Manager's Office still commands respect with its wood-paneled elegance. Changing exhibits and a research library lie just beyond. Continue upstairs for *Digging In: Bisbee's Mining Heritage,* which tells the copper story from the Bisbee perspective. You'll see how miners worked in underground and pit mines. Mineral specimens and a reconstructed crystal cave show the bright colors and beautiful forms found deep within the earth.

Queen Mine Tour

Don a hard hat, lamp, and yellow slicker for a ride deep underground on a mine car. A guide—himself a miner—will issue the equipment and lead you through the mine. He'll explain history, drilling tools, blasting methods, ore loading, and other mining features in the stope (work area) and tunnels. The mine operated for more than 60 years before shutting down in 1943. Its seven levels have 143 miles of passageways; the whole district boasts over 2,000 miles. The tour is highly recommended.

Bring a sweater or jacket as it's cold inside (47°F). There are some steps to the stope area but the rest of the walking is level. The 60- to 75-minute tour leaves at 9 A.M., 10:30 A.M., noon, 2 P.M., and 3:30 P.M. daily and costs $12 for adults, $5 youth 4–15. Reservations (520/432-2071 or 866/432-2071) are a good idea in the busy January–May season and anytime for groups. Buy tickets at the Queen Mine Building just south of downtown across Highway 80.

COURTESY OF THE BISBEE MINING AND HISTORICAL MUSEUM

mule pulling an ore wagon in the Copper Queen Mine, circa 1910

Surface Tour

A guide recounts the mining history and stories of the area; stops include the Lavender Open Pit and points of interest in downtown Bisbee. Tours last about 60–75 minutes and leave the Queen Mine Building daily at 10:30 A.M., noon, 2 P.M., and 3:30 P.M. for $7.

Lavender Open Pit

A total of 380 million tons of ore and waste has been scooped out of this giant hole, which you can peer into from a parking area off U.S. Highway 80, one mile south of downtown. Surface mining began only in 1951.

Bisbee Restoration Association Museum

Drop in to see old photos, mining gear, clothing, and household items of Bisbee's early residents (downtown at 37 Main St., about 10 A.M.–3 P.M., may close for lunch and on Sun.–Mon., free).

Muheim Heritage House

On tours through this restored and furnished 1902 Victorian dwelling at 207 Youngblood Hill, you'll see how a prominent family lived early in the 20th century. The house (520/432-7698, usually 10 A.M.–4 P.M. Fri.–Tues., but call to check, $2 adults, free for children) is a pleasant walk up Brewery Gulch; continue past Youngblood Hill to stairs that lead up the hillside to the house. If driving, take either the easier Brewery Avenue or the very narrow OK Street to Youngblood Hill, which is not suitable for RVs or trailers.

Miracle Hill

For views of town and surrounding hills, climb to this pilgrimage site above Brewery Gulch. A man with failing eyesight once asked permission from land owner Joseph Muheim for permission to erect a cross here. When the man's eyesight dramatically improved, people began constructing shrines and continue to do so—you may even see a Tibetan one. At the upper end of OK Street, look for a well-worn path, probably unmarked, and follow it to the 5,850-foot summit, also known as Grotto Hill or Youngblood Hill; generally take the uphill branches where the trail forks. The round-trip is about an hour with a 450-foot elevation gain. There's no parking at the trailhead, so you'll need to leave your vehicle back in town.

Entertainment and Events

Contact the chamber of commerce to find out what's playing in town. **Center for the Arts** (94 Main St., 520/432-6065 or 888/432-6065, www.thedeepblueC.net) puts on plays, art exhibits, concerts, and other performances.

Chocolate Tasting at Bisbee Library draws aficionados on the Saturday closest to Valentine's Day in February. **Spring Arts Festival** welcomes the season in March. **Copper Classic Car Show** usually runs the second weekend in April. **La Vuelta de Bisbee** is a major bicycle stage race on the last weekend of April. You can enjoy flowers and landscaping on the **Bisbee Garden Tour** on the Saturday before Mother's Day in May.

Arizona's oldest **July 4th Celebration and Parade** includes fireworks, entertainment, coaster races, and miners' contests. **Brewery Gulch Daze** brings music and other entertainment on the day before Labor Day in September. **Fiber Arts Festival** weaves workshops with fashion shows on the second weekend of October. Competitors and noncompetitors get a real workout on the 1,034 steps of the **Thousand Step Stair Climb** on the third weekend of October. The **Festival of Lights** on the Friday following Thanksgiving and the **Historic Home Tour** on the weekend following Thanksgiving mark the start of the holiday season.

Shopping

Bisbee's mines have yielded turquoise and other beautiful copper minerals, available at **Minerals & More** (24 Brewery Ave., 520/432-3065, www.rockdoc1.com) and other shops downtown. Jewelry stores, including **Bisbee Blue** at the Lavender Pit overlook, offer stones set in silver as well as loose and rough stones. Art shops downtown display paintings, ceramics, and other work by local artists.

More than a dozen antique stores line Bisbee's streets; **On Consignment** on the traffic circle south of downtown is the largest. **Atalanta's Music & Books** (38 Main St., 520/432-9976) sells regional books among its varied offerings. The **Farmers Market** runs May–October and offers music and crafts as well as local produce at Vista Park in Warren District, 1.4 miles down Bisbee Road from the traffic circle.

Recreation

Arizona's oldest, the **Turquoise Valley Golf Course** (520/432-3091) has 18 holes, a restaurant open daily for breakfast and lunch, and an RV park. The clubhouse dates to 1936 when built as a WPA project. It's on the edge of Naco, 9.5 miles southwest of downtown Bisbee.

Accommodations

Bisbee has a large selection of accommodations, especially inns and bed and breakfasts. The chamber of commerce has a list.

Under $50: Jonquil Motel (317 Tombstone Canyon, 520/432-7371, $40 s, $45 d) lies a short stroll from downtown.

$50–100: You can really spread out in the spacious accommodations at **Canyon Rose Suites** (27 Subway and Shearer Sts., 520/432-5098 or 866/296-7673, www.canyonrose.com, $95–200 d depending on size). Each unit in the 1905 building has hardwood floors, a high ceiling, full kitchen, and a private bath. The four-story **Copper Queen Hotel** (11 Howell Ave., 520/432-2216, www.copperqueen.com, $70–160 d) dates to 1902, when built by the Copper Queen Mining Company. Rooms—no two alike—differ in size and features, but all have old-fashioned decor and private bath. The elegant hotel has a saloon, dining room, and swimming pool. It's downtown behind the Mining and Historical Museum. The restored 1917 **LaMore Hotel** (45 OK St., 520/432-5131 or 888/432-5131, www.hotellamore.com, $60 d shared bath,

© BILL WEIR

Picturesque old buildings crowd lower Brewery Gulch.

$75–85 d private bath) overlooks Brewery Gulch and includes continental breakfast.

Bisbee Grand Hotel (61 Main St., 520/432-5900 or 800/421-1909, www.bisbeegrandhotel.com, $75–150 d) provides a romantic getaway in a 1906 building restored with a Victorian motif; rooms and suites all have private bath. A Southwestern breakfast is included, and a Western saloon and billiard room lie downstairs. **Main Street Inn** (26 Main St., 520/432-1202 or 800/467-5237, www.mainstreetinn.net, $85–110 d room, $125–195 d suite) dates back to 1888; it provides a continental breakfast.

The **Inn at Castle Rock** (112 Tombstone Canyon, 520/432-4449 or 800/566-4449, www.theinn.org, $60–80 s, $62–92 d) has a large hillside garden, fish ponds, and a full breakfast; each room has a different theme. Farther up the canyon and with good views, **School House Inn Bed & Breakfast** (818 Tombstone Canyon, 520/432-2996 or 800/537-4333, $65–95 d) offers rooms and a full breakfast in a 1918 school.

South of downtown in the Warren District, you can stay in the 1906 **Calumet & Arizona Guest House** (608 Powell St. and Cole Ave., 520/432-4815, www.calumetaz.com, $45–65 s, $60–80 d), built by the chief clerk of the Calumet & Arizona Mining Company and later used as a guest house for company officials. Two of the six rooms have private bath and one room features an attached spa tub. The hosts provide flexible check-in times, a guest kitchen, Internet access, and a full breakfast that you order from a menu.

Five miles southwest of downtown Bisbee, **Best Value Inn & Suites** (1372 Hwy. 92, 520/432-2293, $55–125 d) offers kitchenettes and an RV park. Six miles southwest of downtown, **San Jose Lodge** (1002 Naco Hwy., 520/432-5761, $65–125 d) has kitchenettes, a swimming pool, an RV park, and a Mexican-American restaurant.

Campgrounds

Queen Mine RV Park (520/432-5006) features great views across the highway from downtown; take the road to Copper Queen Mine Tours and continue a short way up the hill. RVers can stay for $16 without hookups, $21 with hookups;

tenters can pitch for $15 on the gravel sites; rates include tax. Guests have showers and a laundry.

Shady Dell RV Park (1 Douglas Rd., behind the Chevron station near the traffic circle, 520/432-3567) has sites for tents or RVs without hookups ($10) and RVs with hookups ($15), as well as showers and a laundry. Vintage trailers in one section of the park offer a trip back in time; their beautifully restored interiors have cooking facilities; some trailers have toilets, but showers are in the bathhouse; rates run $35–75 depending on size; weekly rates are offered too; reservations required. The tiny Dot's Diner serves breakfast and lunch Thursday–Monday. **Turquoise Valley Golf Course** (on the edge of Naco, 9.5 miles southwest of downtown Bisbee, 520/432-3091, $17.50 w/hookups) has an RV park with showers.

If you'd like to be out in the countryside, stay at **Double Adobe Campground & Recreational Ranch** (Double Adobe Rd., 520/364-4000 or 800/694-4242, www.doubleadobe.com, $10 tent and dry RV spaces, $15 RV w/hookups). The park has showers, laundry, Internet connection, recreation room, hiking, stables, and a trap range. Breakfast is available daily except Monday November–April. Take Highway 80 east 4.3 miles toward Douglas, then turn left 4.3 miles.

Two motels southwest of town offer RV spaces: **Best Value Inn & Suites** (5 miles from Bisbee at 1372 Hwy. 92, 520/432-2293, $15 RV w/hookups) and **San Jose Lodge and RV Park** (6 miles from Bisbee at 1002 Naco Hwy., 520/432-5761, $15 RV w/hookups), which has a pool and a Mexican-American restaurant.

Food

Café Roka (35 Main St., 520/432-5153, www.caferoka.com, Wed.–Sat. dinner, also Sun. in winter and spring) prepares excellent contemporary Italian cuisine. You'll likely spot the signature roasted half duck (with a sauce of cranberry, honey, and merlot) on the menu, plus some new and rotating items. Four-course dinners include entrée, soup, salad, and sorbet.

The **Copper Queen Hotel's** restaurant (520/432-2216, daily breakfast, lunch, and dinner) offers continental and American cuisine. Nearby in the Copper Queen Plaza on Main Street, you'll find the **Bisbee Grill** (520/432-6788, daily lunch and dinner), serving Southwestern cuisine of pasta, steak, fajitas, chicken, and shrimp. In the same building, **Bisbee Coffee Co.** (520/432-7879) has javas, sandwiches, baked goods, and ice cream to keep customers energized from morning to evening.

The **Brewery Steakhouse** (15 Brewery Ave., 520/432-3317, daily dinner), downstairs in the 1905 Muheim Block, fixes sandwiches and salads for lunch, then steak, ribs, chicken, pasta, and seafood for dinner. Check out the original interior of the **Stock Exchange Bar** upstairs, where the Bisbee Stock Exchange conducted operations from 1919.

Café Cornucopia (14 Main St., 520/432-4820) is a handy lunch spot for quiches, sandwiches, salads, soups, and baked goodies. For a quick snack at lunchtime, turn in at **Peddler's Alley Café** (17 Main St.) for a meatloaf sundae (topped with mashed potatoes and gravy), hot dogs, tofu dogs, sandwiches, and ice cream. **El Zarape Café** (46 Main St., 520/432-5031, Mon.–Sat. breakfast and lunch) cooks up Mexican and American food. The cheerful **Big Sky Café** (203 Tombstone Canyon opposite the *Iron Man* statue, 520/432-5025, closed Mon.) serves healthy breakfasts and lunches; changing art exhibits decorate the dining room.

For good American food served in an authentic 1957 Valentine Diner, head south to **Dot's Diner** (1 Douglas Rd., 520/432-2046, Thurs.–Mon. breakfast and lunch) in the Shady Dell RV Park behind the Chevron station near the traffic circle; it's a small place where you'll meet the locals and visitors. Pies are a big hit here, especially the Bisbeeberry, a tasty mix of blackberries and raspberries.

Rosa's Little Italy (Warren Plaza, #7 Bisbee Rd., 520/432-1331, Wed.–Fri. lunch, Wed.–Sun. dinner) offers great Italian food south in the Warren district. The lunch menu lists pastas, hearty sandwiches, and salads. Dinner lays out the full menu of veal, chicken, seafood, and pasta, including many vegetarian items. You can bring your own wine. From the traffic circle south of Bisbee, turn south .8 miles on Bisbee Road.

Bisbee Food Co-op is a natural-foods grocery and deli in Lowell Plaza; head south past the Lavender Pit, then turn right at the sign. **Safeway** supermarket is five miles south and west from downtown at the Naco turnoff.

Information and Services

The very helpful **Bisbee Chamber of Commerce & Visitor Center** (1 Main St., P.O. Box BA, Bisbee, AZ 85603, 520/432-5421 or 866/224-7233, www.bisbeearizona.com, 9 A.M.–5 P.M. Mon.–Fri., 10 A.M.–4 P.M. Sat.–Sun.) is in the heart of downtown at the 1902 Arizona Bank building; ask for the self-guided tour leaflet.

The **post office** (520/432-2052) and the **city library** (520/432-4232) are at 6 Main Street in downtown Bisbee; both close on Sunday. **Bisbee Internet Café** (8 Brewery Ave., 520/432-5766, www.bisbeeinternetcafe.com) provides inexpensive broadband along with coffee and snacks. **Copper Queen Community Hospital** (Bisbee Rd. and Cole Ave., 520/432-5383) is three miles south of downtown in the Warren district.

Tours

A trolley of the **Warren–Bisbee Railway** (520/940-7212, www.bisbeetrolley.com) offers a narrated tour of the Bisbee area from the Copper Queen Plaza downtown. **Lavender Jeep Tours** (520/432-5369) takes you into places you'd probably never discover on your own. **Southeastern Arizona Bird Observatory** (520/432-1388, www.sabo.com) has a field station in the Mule Mountains and offers bird walks, tours, and workshops.

Vicinity of Bisbee

Arizona Cactus & Succulent Research Inc. (8 miles south of Bisbee near the Mexico border, 520/432-7040, www.arizonacactus.com, sunrise–sunset daily, donations welcome) offers free tours and cuttings. The nonprofit organization promotes knowledge and landscaping uses of cacti and other desert plants through the tours, a newsletter, and a research library. You can purchase books in the gift shop. Most of the plants you'll see belong to the surrounding Chihuahuan Desert and are well adapted to the cold, dry climate at the 4,780-foot elevation here. From downtown Bisbee, head south 1.5 miles on Highway 80 to the traffic circle, continue south on Bisbee Road another 1.5 miles through Warren, turn right 4 miles on Arizona Street and follow signs to the Border Road; turn left .7 miles on the Border Road, then turn left on Cactus Lane and right on Mulberry Lane to the garden. The Bisbee Visitor Center has a brochure with a map.

The sleepy Mexican border town of **Naco** is just 10 miles south of downtown Bisbee. There's little to see or do here; the Mexican side is much like rural communities of interior Mexico. The downtown has a few restaurants and pharmacies, but no craft shops. To walk across the border, follow signs for Naco, Arizona, and turn left on Towner Avenue to its end, where you can park.

DOUGLAS

In 1900, finding Bisbee's smelter too small and inconvenient to handle ores from recently purchased mines in Mexico, the Phelps Dodge Company, began looking for a new smelter site in Sulphur Springs Valley. They chose this spot and named the new town for Dr. James Douglas, president of the company.

In the early 20th century, Douglas and its sister town in Mexico, **Agua Prieta,** saw their share of excitement. Mexican government troops battled it out in Agua Prieta with revolutionaries Captain "Red" Lopez in 1911 and Pancho Villa in 1915. Pancho Villa even made threats against the town of Douglas before eventually retreating. An international airport—part of its runway in the United States and part in Mexico—opened here in 1928.

The fortunes of both Douglas and Agua Prieta rose and fell with the price of copper. The prettiest sight in Douglas, some residents used to say, was the billowing steam and smoke from the giant copper smelter just west of town. The busy ore-processing plant meant jobs.

Smokestacks of the Phelps Dodge smelter puffed their last in January 1987, but the two cities have diversified with other industries. American companies operate manufacturing plants in Agua Prieta under the "twin plant" concept, using Mexico's inexpensive labor to assemble American products. With these new opportunities, Agua Prieta's population has mushroomed to about 150,000, eclipsing that of Douglas's approximately 17,500.

Historic Architecture

Many fine early-20th-century commercial buildings line downtown streets. Church Square, two blocks east of the Gadsden Hotel, earned fame in the 1930 *Ripley's Believe It or Not* as the only city block in the world with a church on each corner; it's between 10th and 11th Streets and D and E Avenues. These old churches and the buildings in the adjacent Douglas Residential District (7th to 12th Sts. and E to Carmelita Aves.) are fine examples of period architecture.

The beaux arts classic revival–style railroad depot, used from 1913 until the end of passenger service in 1961, has been restored to its former elegance; you're welcome to step inside the rotunda and see the stained-glass ceiling. The depot is a couple of blocks north of the chamber of commerce and now serves as the police station, so it's always open.

Douglas/Williams House Museum

Jimmy "Rawhide" Douglas—who later built the house that's now a museum for Jerome State Historic Park—constructed this house in 1908 when he was working for his dad, Dr. James Douglas, at Phelps Dodge Company. The redwood house (10th St. and D Ave., across from Church Square, 520/364-7370, 1–4 P.M. Tues.–Thurs. and Sat., donations welcome) now holds exhibits on regional history, including photos showing the early town and smelter operation.

Douglas Art Association Gallery

You'll find changing exhibits of local art inside the town's first public building—a 1901 hall that has served as town hall, church, school, and library. A gift shop sells handicrafts. The Gallery (625 10th St., 520/364-6410, 10 A.M.–4 P.M. daily Sept.–May, 1–4 P.M. daily June–Aug., free) is next door to the post office, two blocks west of the museum.

Events

The **Cinco de Mayo** festivities have horse races between American and Mexican riders on the weekend before May 5. The **July 4 Celebration** includes entertainment, a parade, car show, games, dances, and fireworks at Veterans Park. The **Labor Day Golf Tournament** in September has been running longer than any other invitational golf tournament in the state. **Douglas Fiestas Celebration** in mid-September honors Mexican independence with ballet folklorico, mariachis, a talent show, games, and food at Veterans Park. **Cochise County Fair** presents intercollegiate rodeo, livestock exhibits, carnival, and other entertainment on the third weekend of September at Cochise County Fairgrounds on Leslie Canyon Road. The **Christmas Light Parade** is an evening event of lighted floats held the last Saturday of November.

Shopping

Shops in the first six blocks across the border in Agua Prieta sell Mexican crafts, but on a much smaller scale than in Nogales. Merchants generally have a competitive fixed price, so bargaining isn't as common as in other border towns. U.S. dollars will be welcome. There's a parking lot near the border; drive south on Pan American Avenue, then turn left one block on 1st Avenue, the last street before the border station. The Douglas Chamber of Commerce offers advice and a map for Agua Prieta.

Recreation

Veterans Park (Dolores Ave. and 6th St.) offers picnic tables, playground, outdoor pool, tennis, basketball, and ball fields. **Douglas Golf & Social Club** (off Leslie Canyon Rd., 520/364-3722) features 18 holes north of town.

Accommodations

The massive five-story **Gadsden Hotel** (1046 G Ave., 520/364-4481, www.hotelgadsden.com, $50–70 d rooms, $80–100 d suites.) dominates downtown Douglas. Built in 1907 and rebuilt in 1928, the hotel calls itself "the last of the grand hotels." The lobby features massive faux-marble columns decorated with 14-karat gold leaf supporting a vaulted ceiling with stained-glass panels. A Tiffany stained-glass mural 42 feet long decorates one wall of the mezzanine, reached by an Italian white marble staircase. If you'd rather ride up, hop in the old-fashioned manual elevator. Over 200 authentic cattle brands embellish the walls of the Saddle and Spur Tavern, just off the lobby. A restaurant serves American and Mexican food.

Motel 6 (111 16th St., 520/364-2457 or 800/466-8356, $36 s, $42 d) is just west of downtown. The **Travelers Motel** (19th St., 520/364-8434, $35 s, $38 d) and the nearby **Border Motel** (1725 A Ave., 520/364-8491, $32 s, $35 d) each have a pool.

Price Canyon Ranch (P.O. Box 1065, Douglas, AZ 85608, 520/558-2383 or 800/727-0065, www.pricecanyon.com) offers horseback riding in the scenic Chiricahuas with the option of joining the cowboys in working the cattle. Guests also enjoy birding, hiking, and the swimming pool. The rates of $150 per adult and $75 ages 12–15 give you comfortable rooms, family-style meals, and riding. The ranch, open year-round at an elevation of 5,600 feet, is 37 miles northeast of Douglas on Highway 80, then west 7.5 miles on Price Canyon Road between Mileposts 400 and 401.

Campgrounds

Saddle Gap RV Park (AZ 80 and Washington Ave. on the northeast edge of town, 520/364-5824) has RV sites for $12 with hookups, but no showers. **Douglas Golf & Social Club** (AZ 80 and Leslie Canyon Rd. on the north side of town, 520/364-3722) charges $15 for RV sites with hookups, but usually needs advance reservations.

Double Adobe Campground & Recreational Ranch (520/364-4000 or 800/694-4242, www.doubleadobe.com, $10 tent or RV no hookups, $15 RV w/hookups) offers grassy sites and shade trees on 240 acres; guests have access to showers, laundry, hiking, Internet, recreation room, stables, and a trap range. Breakfast is available daily except Monday November–April. Head north 7.4 miles on U.S. Highway 191 from the west side of Douglas, then turn left (west) 9.8 miles on Double Adobe Road. (The road makes a jog to the south after the store at Double Adobe; follow signs for Bisbee.)

Food

El Conquistador Dining Room in the Gadsden Hotel (1046 G Ave., 520/364-4481, daily breakfast, lunch, and dinner) serves Mexican-American food. **Grand Café** (nearby at 1119 G Ave., 520/364-2344, Mon.–Sat. lunch and dinner) has great Mexican-American food. **Las Nubes Steak House** (515 Pan American Ave., 520/364-4936, nightly dinner) prepares steak, seafood, and Mexican dishes. **Lai-Lai Restaurant** (1341 F Ave., 520/364-8898, daily lunch and dinner) offers a variety of Chinese cuisines.

Safeway supermarket (90 5th St.) is near the border just west from Pan American Drive. **Food City** (1300 San Antonio Dr.) is east of downtown.

Information and Services

Staff at the **Douglas Visitor Center** (1125 Pan American Ave., Douglas, AZ 85607, 520/364-2478 or 888/315-9999, www.douglaschamber.com, 8 A.M.–5 P.M. Mon.–Fri., 8 A.M.–1 P.M. Sat.) provide maps, brochures, and advice on both Arizonan and Mexican travel.

The **Douglas Ranger Station** (3081 N. Leslie Canyon Rd., Douglas, AZ 85607, 520/364-3468, www.fs.fed.us/r3/coronado, 7:30 A.M.–4:30 P.M. Mon.–Fri.) provides Coronado National Forest information on camping, hiking, and the back roads in the Chiricahua and Dragoon Mountains. From Highway 80 just north of downtown, turn north on Leslie Canyon Road, then take the first right.

The **public library** (560 E. 10th St. at F Ave., 520/364-3851) is open daily. The 1917 beaux arts–style **post office** sits on the corner of 10th Street and F Avenue downtown. **Southeast Arizona Medical Center** (520/364-7931) is four miles west of town on Highway 80, then north at the sign.

VICINITY OF DOUGLAS

Douglas Wildlife Zoo

Drop in to see parrots, peacocks, emus, deer, lemurs, apes, and other creatures from near and distant lands. The collection (520/364-2515, 10 A.M.–5 P.M. daily to 4 P.M. on Sun., closed major holidays, $3 adults, $2 children 3–12) got its start as a place for propagation of exotic animals and birds. From Douglas, head west 3 miles on Highway 80 (between Mileposts 362 and 363), then turn north 1.7 miles on Plantation Road.

Slaughter Ranch

John Slaughter (1842–1922), a former Texas Ranger, wandered into southeast Arizona in 1884 and bought a lease to the 73,240-acre San Bernardino Ranch. Today it's the last survivor of Arizona's great 19th-century cattle ranches (520/558-2474, www.vtc.net/~sranch, 10 A.M.–3 P.M. Wed.–Sun., $5 adults, free under age 14).

Long before Slaughter developed the vast spread, the springs here had attracted Opata Indian farmers, Apache, Spanish, Mexicans, and Americans. Slaughter shipped 10,000 head of cattle one year and employed up to 500 people, including 200 Chinese vegetable farmers. His 1890s house and other structures have been restored to show ranch life in territorial Arizona at the turn of the 20th century.

A self-guided tour leaflet given out at the visitor center describes the buildings and grounds. The house contains period furniture, photo exhibits of Slaughter's colorful career—including two terms as sheriff of Tombstone—and stories about the area's long history. Longhorn cattle, a breed brought in by Slaughter, graze in a nearby field. The pond, containing endangered native fish and surrounded by grass and cottonwoods, offers a pleasant spot for a picnic. A trail near the pond climbs the hill to ruins of a U.S. Army post used during the time of Mexican civil unrest in 1911–1923; you can see far to the south into Mexico and to the east across the San Bernardino National Wildlife Refuge.

From Douglas, head east on 15th Street to the edge of town, then continue 15 miles on the graded dirt Geronimo Trail to the ranch turnoff, marked by a memorial to the Mormon Battalion. No dogs, please.

San Bernardino National Wildlife Refuge

At this 2,330-acre refuge, springs and ponds attract more than 270 species of birds, as well as mule deer, javelina, mountain lions, bobcats, and other wildlife. The waters support endangered Yaqui chub, Yaqui topminnow, Yaqui catfish, and beautiful shiner. Elevations range 3,720–3,920 feet. Old roads and trails lead to ponds and wetlands with excellent birding. The entrance is three-quarters of a mile past the Slaughter Ranch turnoff. Open daily during daylight hours.

Leslie Canyon National Wildlife Refuge, on the south end of the Swisshelm Mountains, protects endangered fish and a rare velvet ash-cottonwood-black willow gallery forest. You can reach it on Leslie Canyon Road; lands south of the road are closed to the public, but you can visit areas north of the road.

San Bernardino and Leslie Canyon National Wildlife Refuges headquarters (7628 N. Hwy. 191, P.O. Box 3509, Douglas, AZ 85607, 520/364-2104, http://southwest.fws.gov/refuges/arizona/sanb.html, 8 A.M.–4 P.M. Mon.–Fri.) are 11 miles north of Douglas; turn east 1 mile on the paved road about a quarter-mile past Milepost 11 on U.S. Highway 191.

CHIRICAHUA MOUNTAINS

Rising from dry grasslands, the Chiricahua (chee-ree-KAH-wah) Mountains hold a wonderland of rock formations, spectacular views, diverse plant and animal life, and a variety of hiking trails. The name may come from the Opata Indian Chiguicagui, meaning Mountain of the Wild Turkeys. Volcanic rock, fractured by slow uplift of the region, has eroded into strangely shaped forms. Weathering of softer rock at the base of some columns creates the appearance of giant boulders balanced delicately on pedestals.

The Chiricahuas harbor a unique mix of Sierra Madrean and Southwestern flora and fauna. Birders come to view coppery-tailed elegant trogons, hummingbirds, and many other species. But bears live here, too, so take care with storing food; forest service signs list necessary precautions.

Chiricahua National Monument offers the

most spectacular erosional features, a scenic drive, many trails, and a visitor center. Chiricahua Wilderness, to the south, protects the highest summits of the range, including 9,796-foot Chiricahua Peak. A narrow mountain road crosses the range from near the entrance of the national monument on the west side to Portal on the east side; it's not recommended for trailers and is sometimes closed by snow in winter. Be sure to fill up with gas before coming out to the Chiricahuas, as there are no supplies here. Douglas Ranger Station (3081 N. Leslie Canyon Rd., Douglas, AZ 85607, 520/364-3468, www.fs.fed.us/r3/coronado, 7:30 A.M.–4:30 P.M. Mon.–Fri.) has information on the Coronado National Forest lands.

Hiking

Forest trails in the Chiricahua Mountains total about 111 miles. The Rattlesnake Fire in 1994 burned more than 25,000 acres on the west side of the wilderness, and dead trees continue to fall across trails. No permits are needed for backpacking or hiking, but South Fork and Rustler Park have $3 parking fees. Topographic maps, such as the Chiricahua Mountains Trail and Recreation (scale 1:62,500), show trail locations and lengths; look for them at Tucson hiking stores, some Forest Service offices, and Chiricahua National Monument. The Coronado National Forest (Douglas Ranger District) map shows trails but lacks contour lines and fine detail.

Rucker Canyon

Four routes lead to Rucker Creek and its pretty canyon on the southwest side of the Chiricahuas; they're unpaved but usually OK for cautiously driven cars in dry weather. From Douglas you can head north on Leslie Canyon Road from the Douglas Ranger Station and cross the Swisshelm Mountains into Leslie Canyon National Wildlife Refuge (lands south of the road are closed to the public); after about 30 miles you'll reach Rucker Canyon Road—continue another 7 miles to the canyon. Tex Canyon Road is another scenic route; 29 miles northeast of Douglas it turns off Highway 80 and crosses a gentle pass into Rucker Canyon in another 16 miles. You can also take Rucker Canyon Road from U.S. Highway 191, a 22-mile drive one-way, or reach the canyon via the Kukkendall Cut Off from Highway 181 near Chiricahua National Monument, a 20-mile drive one-way.

Campgrounds usually stay open all year with water available April–November; sites have a charge of $10 for camping or $5 for day use. You'll first come to **Camp Rucker Group Use Area** (5,600 ft.) on the left in a desert grassland with scattered oaks and junipers; you can stay here if no group has reserved it. (Groups can make reservations with the Douglas Ranger Station.) In another 3.3 miles, **Cypress Campground** (6,000 ft.) on the left sits beside the creek in a forest of Arizona cypress, oaks, and pines. **Bathtub Campground** (6,300 ft.) is .4 miles farther on the left on a shelf overlooking the creek. A trail below the dam leads to the "bathtubs," depressions carved in the bedrock by the creek. You have to park at the edge of the campground, so it's suitable only for tenters. Rucker Lake nearby has completely filled in with sediment and the campground once here is closed. **Rucker Forest Camp** (6,500 ft.) sits beside the creek at the end of the road, .3 miles beyond Bathtub, in a dense forest of oaks, junipers, and pines. **Rucker Canyon Trail #222** and **Raspberry Ridge Trail #228** climb into the Chiricahua Wilderness from here.

The U.S. Army set up a supply depot in 1878 for Indian scouts who patrolled the region on the lookout for hostile Apache. Originally named Camp Supply, it later became **Camp Rucker** to honor an officer who drowned while trying to save another man during a flash flood. The camp saw use until Geronimo's surrender in 1886, when it became part of a ranch. You can visit this remnant of the Old West and walk an interpretive trail past the adobe bakery, still in good condition, and the large ruin of the commissary with its stone cellar. From the junction of Forest Roads 74 and 74E near Camp Rucker Group Use Area, head east .7 miles on Forest Road 74 and look for a gate in the fence on the left; park outside the gate, walk in about .1 miles, then turn left past the barn to the site.

Turkey Creek Canyon

West Turkey Creek Campground (5,900 ft.)

and **Sycamore Campground** (6,200 ft.) lie along Turkey Creek on the west side of the Chiricahuas in a densely wooded canyon of sycamores, pines, oaks, and junipers. Sites have tables and grills but no drinking water or fee; the season is about March–November. From the 90-degree bend in Highway 181 east of Sunizona and south of the Chiricahua National Monument turnoff, head east on unpaved Turkey Creek Road. Tall pines appear among the oaks and junipers after 7 miles and you'll enter the national forest in another mile; West Turkey Campground is on the left just .1 miles farther and Sycamore is 1.5 miles past that on the left. You'll also pass several trailheads in the national forest that connect to the heights.

Sunglow Ranch (520/824-3334 or 866/786-4569, www.sunglowranch.com) provides year-round accommodation, gourmet meals, birding, hiking, a fishing pond, and astronomy programs on nearly 400 acres that stretch across to the Coronado National Forest. You can bring your horse, too. Rates include breakfast, afternoon tea, and a four-course dinner. One-room casitas run $139 s, $201.50 d; two-room casitas feature a living room and fireplace for $189 s, $251.50 d; and the two-bedroom apartments have kitchens for $299 d, $62.50 each additional person. The restaurant serves breakfast, lunch, and dinner to the public by reservation. The ranch is about 15 miles south of Chiricahua National Monument; follow Turkey Creek Road 4.3 miles from Highway 181, then turn right 1 mile.

Rustler Park Area

A scenic mountain road crosses the range through Pinery Canyon on the west near Chiricahua National Monument to Onion Saddle (7,600 ft.) and continues east to Cave Creek Canyon and Portal. The road is narrow, bumpy, and mostly unpaved, but may be passable by car for cautious drivers. Trailers and RVs over 28 feet aren't permitted. Snow and fallen trees can close the road at times December–April. From just outside the entrance of Chiricahua National Monument, take Pinery Canyon Road, which enters the national forest after 3.8 miles; you'll see many undeveloped camping spots along the next 3 miles before the grade steepens. **Pinery Canyon Campground** is tucked under tall pines and Douglas fir on the left, 9.8 miles from the start of the road; it has just four sites (no water or fee) and is difficult to spot if you're coming from below. The road tops out at Onion Saddle, 11.5 miles from Highway 181. If you're coming up from Cave Creek Canyon on the east side, the driving distance from Portal to the saddle is 13 miles with some great panoramas along the way.

A side road from Onion Saddle climbs south along a ridge to **Rustler Park Campground** (8,400 ft.) in pines and Douglas fir. Sites (may be closed in winter, $10 camping, $5 day use, $3 trailhead parking) usually have water April–November, and steel boxes to protect your food from bears.

Hikers at Rustler Park have the advantage of starting from the highest trailhead in the Chiricahuas. The **Crest Trail #270** winds south over the gently undulating summit ridge of the Chiricahuas to Chiricahua Peak (9,796 ft.), the highest point in the range, in 10.5 miles round-trip. Trees, however, block the view from the top! **Centrella Point** (9,320 ft.) has a spectacular vantage point overlooking Cave Creek Canyon and far beyond; follow the Crest Trail south to just inside the wilderness boundary, 2.5 miles one-way, then turn left 1.9 miles one-way on the Centrella Trail #334. **Fly Peak** (9,666 ft.) is an easy half-mile one-way jaunt from the wilderness boundary and has some views through the trees. Many other trails branch off the Crest Trail along ridges or down into canyons. Springs lie just off the Crest Trail but can dry up in drought years.

Cave Creek Canyon

Although remote, Cave Creek Canyon on the east side of the Chiricahuas has spectacular rock features, excellent birding, and paved road access that make it a favorite with visitors. You can get here by taking Highway 80 northeast from Douglas for 51 miles or Highway 80 south from I-10 for 28 miles, then turning west to the village of Portal at the mouth of the canyon. The road continues up along Cave Creek beneath vertical rock walls past campgrounds, vista points, and hiking trails. The Forest Service operates **Cave Creek Visitor Information Center** (1.9

miles upcanyon from Portal, 520/558-2221, about 9 A.M.–4:30 P.M. Thurs.–Mon. early April–Labor Day). **Cave Creek Nature Trail** makes a short loop across the road. For a bird's-eye view of the region, determined hikers ascend **Silver Peak Trail #280,** a strenuous climb of 3,000 feet over 4.6 miles one-way to the 7,975-foot summit; the trailhead is just upcanyon from the information center. Bring a hat and lots of water—there's little shade—and avoid the trail if thunderstorms threaten.

Idlewilde Campground (5,000 ft., $10 camping, $5 day use) lies on the left across a bridge .4 miles upcanyon from the information center; sycamores, oaks, junipers, and pines provide shade. The season runs April–November, and water is available. **Stewart Campground** (5,100 ft., $10 camping, $5 day use) is another .3 miles up on the left with the same types of trees; it has drinking water from April–November. On the left .4 miles farther, look for **Cathedral Vista** parking; an easy 200-yard walk takes you to a stunning 360-degree panorama of the canyon and the Chiricahuas.

Continue .2 miles upcanyon and turn left on unpaved South Fork Road for a pretty drive up this side canyon and creek to **South Fork Picnic Area** and trailhead at road's end, 1.3 miles in; there's a $3 parking fee. **South Fork Trail** leads up the wooded canyon with some creek fords. Maple Camp, 1.6 miles one-way, is a popular destination for birders; the trail continues up into the high country.

Back on the main road and .2 miles upcanyon, turn right across a ford for **Sunny Flat Campground** (5,200 ft.), which despite its name is shaded by sycamores, oaks, junipers, and pines. There's year-round drinking water and fees run $10 for camping, $5 for day use. A trail begins near the end of the campground and follows the creek downstream about a mile to the information center.

Pavement runs out 1.7 miles farther up Cave Creek Canyon at the Southwestern Research Center of the American Museum of Natural History; staff occasionally offer public programs, which the information center should know about. Turn left just past the research center for **John Hands Campground** (5,600 ft.) one mile in, and **Herb Martyr Campground** (5,800 ft.) 2.2 miles up at the end of the unpaved road; oaks and junipers shade these campgrounds near Cave Creek; they're open all year, and have no drinking water or fee. If you look up on the cliffs above to the west, you may see Winn Falls making a 400-foot plunge; **Greenhouse Trail #248** climbs up for a closer view. Experienced cavers will enjoy a visit to **Crystal Cave.** A key is needed to get inside; contact the Douglas Ranger Station for access details. The cave is closed April 15–August 31 to protect bats and other life inside.

Portal

This small community lies on the east side of the Chiricahuas just below the mouth of Cave Creek Canyon. **Portal Peak Lodge** (520/558-2223, $65 s and $75 d) offers rooms year-round, a tiny café with American and Mexican food (daily breakfast, lunch, and dinner), and a store which also has groceries and some regional books. Continue 1.5 miles west into the canyon for **Cave Creek Ranch** (520/558-2334, www.cavecreekranch.com, $85–140 d), which has a gorgeous setting beside the creek. The owners are bird enthusiasts, as are 95 percent of the guests here. All of the lodge rooms and cabins have kitchens. No meals are served, nor are there trail rides.

CHIRICAHUA NATIONAL MONUMENT

In 1924, President Calvin Coolidge signed a bill making the most scenic part of the mountains a national monument. The entrance is 70 miles north of Douglas, 36 miles southeast of Willcox, and 120 miles east of Tucson. Rigs longer than 29 feet may not head up the drive or enter the campground, but may park in the paved lot near Faraway Ranch. The entrance station collects a fee of $5 per person age 17+; those 16 and under get in free.

The Chiricahuas are best appreciated on foot, whether on short nature trails or extended hikes. Many species of birds can be seen, from grassland inhabitants near the monument entrance to mountain dwellers at the top. Rangers advise you to pace yourself, allowing for the altitude and rough terrain, and to carry water on longer trips. Thunderstorms often strike in July and August; if caught, stay low and avoid exposed areas. Watch for rattlesnakes—summer is their most active season, though they also slither about in spring and autumn.

You can hike any time of year, but conditions are usually ideal March–May and October–November. Snow sometimes blocks trails December–February. Monument trails are for day-hikes only, and no permit is needed. Camping is restricted to the campground near the visitor center. Horseback riding is permitted in the monument, but rangers like to be told when horses are brought in; horse trailers should be parked at the Faraway Ranch parking lot. Dogs are not permitted on any trails except the Faraway Trail, and they must be leashed at all times within the monument.

Maps sold at the visitor center include Chiricahua topo maps, a geologic map, and a Coronado National Forest map. The **hikers' shuttle** will take you up Bonita Canyon Drive to the high country daily at 8:30 A.M., so that you can walk trails downhill back to the visitor center.

Visitor Center

Exhibits (520/824-3560, www.nps.gov/chir, 8 A.M.–4:30 P.M. daily) illustrate area geology, ecology, and wildlife, as well as the lifestyles of the Chiricahua Apache, early ranchers, and the Civilian Conservation Corps. A video introduces the monument and its sightseeing possibilities. Rangers can answer questions and advise on road and hiking conditions. Campfire programs run mid-March–mid-September, and other naturalist programs may be scheduled too. You can purchase books, prints, posters, videos, maps, and other items.

Bonita Canyon Drive

This six-mile paved mountain road from the visitor center climbs through Bonita Canyon to Massai Point (6,870 ft.), where you'll encounter sweeping views of the rock features and distant valleys and mountains. A wheelchair-accessible path leads up to the little geology exhibit building for the best panorama. Look north for the profile of Cochise Head. Interpretive signs on **Massai Point Nature Trail,** a quarter mile one-way, explain how this wonderland of rocks formed and describe some of the plants found here; the trail also passes some great viewpoints. Winter storms can close the road, but snowplows clear it soon afterward.

Hiking Trails

The free monument brochure includes a map outlining all trails. **Faraway Meadow Trail** is an easy 1.2-mile walk between Faraway Ranch and the visitor center. The path winds through lush vegetation watered by a small seasonal stream, a good place for bird watching. A short side trail leads to the campground.

The most impressive scenery awaits hikers on the Echo Canyon Loop and Heart of Rocks trails. **Echo Canyon Trail** winds through spectacular rock formations in a 3.5-mile loop; begin from Echo Canyon parking area or Massai Point trailheads, both near the end of Bonita Canyon Drive. **Heart of Rocks Trail** passes famous rock formations—Punch and Judy, Duck on a Rock, Big Balanced Rock, and others—on a seven-mile out-and-back trip from Massai Point. With a half day, you can make a nine-mile loop by returning on the **Sarah Deming** and **Echo Canyon** trails. **Inspiration Point** is a one-mile round-trip excursion off Heart of Rocks Trail with views over the whole length of Rhyolite Canyon.

You can also hike all the way down to the visitor center via **Rhyolite Canyon Trail,** 4.1 miles one-way from Echo Canyon parking area or 6 miles one-way from Massai Point trailhead. **Sugarloaf Mountain** (7,310 ft.) is the highest peak in the monument, with an excellent panorama of Arizona, New Mexico, and the Chiricahuas, including the eroded remnants of the volcano that was the source of the rock layers; the 1.8-mile round-trip begins from the Sugarloaf trailhead. **Natural Bridge Trail,** from the lower part of Bonita Canyon Drive, offers pleasant but less spectacular hiking to a small rock bridge—actually a fallen rock column—2.4 miles from the road.

Faraway Ranch

Members of the Erickson family lived on this ranch for 91 years before its purchase in 1979

© BILL WEIR

Lillian Riggs accommodated guests at the Faraway Ranch for many years. Now you can go inside on a tour with a Park Service ranger.

by the National Park Service. Rangers lead tours through the old ranch house most days, offering tales of the family, ranch life, and the surrounding region. You're also welcome to visit the grounds on your own during daylight hours; signs and a small exhibit building relate stories about the ranch and the people who lived here. Trails continue another quarter mile to the 1880 Stafford Cabin, one of the oldest in the state.

Faraway Ranch is 1.5 miles west of the visitors center by road, then a quarter mile in on foot, or you can take the 1.2-mile Faraway Meadow Trail from the visitors center or campground.

Campgrounds and Services

Picnic areas lie along the main road at several locations—see the map given you at the entry booth. The first one, Bonita Creek Picnic Area, is on the left just .3 miles inside the monument; the last one is at Massai Point at the end of the Bonita Canyon Drive.

Bonita Campground, a half mile past the visitors center, is open year-round with water and costs $12 (no hookups or showers); sites can accommodate trailers or RVs to 29 feet. The campground often fills by mid-day March–early May; only the group site can be reserved. Dispersed camping outside the monument is another possibility; you can drive up Pinery Canyon Road 3.8 miles to the Coronado National Forest, then look for a likely spot in the next 3 miles; no water, facilities, or charge. Pinery Canyon Road begins just outside the monument entrance.

Willcox, 36 miles north of the monument, offers the nearest motels as well as restaurants, stores, and RV parks. Sunizona, 27 miles west of the monument, has the nearest gas, RV park, and cafés. Sunsites, 38 miles west of the monument, has RV parks and cafés.

FORT BOWIE NATIONAL HISTORIC SITE

When the Butterfield Stagecoach line began to carry mail and passengers from Missouri to California in 1858, the company built a station near a spring at Apache Pass. Although it was in the middle of Indian country, Cochise and his Chiricahua Apache allowed the station and stage to operate unhindered. All this changed two and a half years later when Cochise was falsely accused of kidnapping and theft. Troops used treachery to seize Cochise, but the chief knifed through the tent he was held in and escaped. Both sides executed hostages, and the war was on. Cochise and his band tried to kill or drive off all white people from the region. Unfortunately for white settlers, many army troops left Arizona at this time to fight in the Civil War in the east.

On July 15, 1862, Brigadier General James Carleton and his California Column were on their way to meet the threat posed by the Confederate invasion of New Mexico when Indians attacked an advance detachment under the command of Captain Thomas Roberts at Apache Pass. Roberts fended them off, but suggested to Carleton the need for a fort. The first Fort Bowie (BOO-ee) went up within a month. Raids continued until 1872, when Cochise made peace with the army in exchange for reservation land.

Troubles for the Chiricahua Apache began two years later when Cochise died. Bad management by the Indian Bureau, the government's taking back much of the reservation, and a fractured tribal leadership left many Apache angry. In 1881, Apache warriors such as the wily Geronimo began leading a new series of raids in the United States and Mexico. Army cavalry and scouts from Fort Bowie and other posts then rode forth to fight the elusive Indians. Geronimo's small band was the last to surrender, five years later, ending Arizona's Indian wars. The army finally abandoned the fort on October 17, 1894.

Visiting the Fort

Only evocative ruins remain of what was once a major trade route and military post (520/847-2500, www.nps.gov/fobo, trails open sunrise–sunset daily, visitors center open 8 A.M.–4:30 P.M. daily, free). To preserve the historic setting, a hiking trail brings visitors to the fort. The three-mile round-trip is easy with an elevation gain of only 180 feet, but one should consider the 5,000-foot elevation and the summer heat. Good walking shoes, a hat, and water will add to your enjoyment of the trip. You could also bring a picnic and use tables near the visitors center. Shaded benches along the trail allow for a rest or some reflection. Signs tell of historic events in the area and identify sites such as the stage-station ruin, the post cemetery, a ruin believed to have been the Chiricahua Apache Indian Agency, the Battle of Apache Pass site, a reconstructed Apache camp, and Apache Spring. You'll learn a lot of the area's history on the way, and you'll enjoy the mountain views and a variety of wildflowers and other plants. Just before the main fort, you can head up to the ruins of the first Fort Bowie on a quarter-mile round-trip side trail; this site proved too small and was replaced in 1868–1869 by new buildings on a more spacious site to the east. Signs identify the many ruins of the second Fort Bowie, which operated for 26 years. An optional return trail from the visitors center takes you to a ridge top with a panorama of the fort and surrounding countryside without adding extra distance. No camping is permitted. Dogs may come along if leashed.

The visitors center has many old photos that show how the fort looked in its heyday. Exhibits also display uniforms, a mountain howitzer, guns, Apache crafts, and excavated artifacts. You can purchase books on the Apache, U.S. Army, and natural history. The visitors center has a water fountain and restrooms. Call for access for travelers with disabilities.

Modern highways bypass the area. From the town of Bowie (I-10 Exits 362 or 366), drive 12.5 miles south on Apache Pass Road, of which the last .8 miles is gravel; parking is on the right, trailhead on the left. You can also drive over Apache Pass on an unpaved section of Apache Pass Road from Highway 186. Head southeast 22 miles from Willcox or northwest 14 miles from Chiricahua National Monument to the turnoff between Mileposts 350 and 351 on Highway 186, then turn east 8 miles on Apache Pass Road. In bad weather, Apache Pass Road can become slippery and is not recommended.

WILLCOX

Just off I-10, Willcox (pop. 3,825) is a convenient base for visiting the scenic and historic sights of the area. The town got its start in 1880 as a construction camp for the Southern Pacific

Railroad, then became a supply and shipping point for local ranchers. Agriculture continues to be the town's most important industry, with ostriches, apples, peaches, cherries, grapes, pecans, and pistachios now supplementing the mainstays of cattle, cotton, and small grains. Many orchards let customers pick their own fruit during the July–October season. The chamber of commerce has a list with directions; most lie 15–20 miles north on Fort Grant Road. The chamber also has a walking-tour leaflet of the historic downtown and information on local birding opportunities.

Willcox has three exits off I-10 that lead to the downtown museums and historic buildings. The middle one, Exit 340, is close to the Willcox Visitor Center and the newer motels. To reach downtown from here, turn south on Rex Allen Drive, right on Haskell Avenue, then left on Maley Street. Haskell Avenue/Business I-10, where you'll find the older motels, connects Exit 336 on the west side of town with Exit 344 on the east; turn south at the light on Maley Street for the museums.

Rex Allen Arizona Cowboy Museum

Rex Allen (1920–1999) grew up singing and playing the guitar on a homestead near Willcox. His musical skills led him to the recording industry, then into movies. *Arizona Cowboy,* released in 1950, was the first of his 19 films. He also starred in the TV series *Frontier Doctor* and provided the narration for some Disney productions.

Inside the museum (150 N. Railroad Ave., 520/384-4583 or 877/234-4111, 10 A.M.–4 P.M. daily, $2 individual, $3 couple, $5 family), you'll see photos and movie posters of Rex Allen, guitars, saddles, sequined cowboy suits, and a buggy used in *Frontier Doctor.* Music by Rex Allen or his son, Rex Allen, Jr., plays in the background. You can sit and watch videos of Rex Allen battling the bad guys in action-packed westerns. The Willcox Cowboy Hall of Fame in the back honors local ranchers and displays photos of life on the range. A gift shop sells music, movie videos, and souvenirs. The park across the street has some tables, a statue of Rex Allen and memorials to him and his movie star horse, Koko.

The early 1890s adobe museum building housed a saloon from 1897 until Prohibition in 1919, when a grocery store took over. You'll see other historic structures nearby, such as the 1881 adobe **Willcox Commercial** store, the oldest one in Arizona still in use in its original location. Geronimo used to shop for his sugar here! The 1935 art deco **Willcox Rex Allen Theater** hosted early performances by Rex Allen and Roy Rogers; today it screens first-run movies on weekends.

Chiricahua Regional Museum & Research Center

Drop in to learn about Cochise and his Chiricahua Apache tribe, early mining and ranching, and the history of the town (127 E. Maley St., between Railroad and Haskell Aves., 520/384-3971; 10 A.M.–4 P.M. Mon.–Sat., $2 adult, $3 couple, $4 family). Staff also work at tracing genealogy of local pioneers.

Southern Pacific Depot

Built in 1880 when the railroad first arrived, the busy depot became the town's business and social center for ranchers, miners, and traders. It expanded in 1882 and 1915 and has now been beautifully restored (Mon.–Fri. 8 A.M.–4:30 P.M., free). Step into the lobby to see railroad artifacts and exhibits about pioneer life. A video by Rex Allen, Sr. tells how the building was saved. It's just west of Maley Street on Railroad Avenue—Willcox's main street in the old days.

Events

Wings Over Willcox celebrates the birds with tours and lectures on the third weekend in January. **Rex Allen Days** honors Arizona's "Mr. Cowboy" on the first Friday–Sunday of October with a rodeo, parade, Western music, street dance, cowboy poetry, Rex Allen movies, and a carnival.

Recreation

Keillor Park has picnic tables, a playground, outdoor pool, and tennis courts; from I-10 Exit 340, take Rex Allen Drive south one block toward downtown, then turn right one block on Bisbee Avenue. **Twin Lakes Golf Course** (1000 S. Rex Allen Jr. Rd., 520/384-2720) has a nine-hole course south of downtown off Maley Street/Highway 186.

Accommodations

Under $50: For the independents, head down the old highway/Business I-10. From north to south are the **Desert Breeze Motel** (556 N. Haskell Ave., 520/384-4636, $25 s, $29 d) with kitchenettes, **Motel 8** (331 N. Haskell Ave., 520/384-3270, $32 s, $40 d) with a pool, **Arizona Sunset Motel** (340 S. Haskell Ave., 520/384-4177, $30 s, $35 d incl. tax) with kitchenettes, **Sands Motel** (400 S. Haskell Ave., 520/384-3501, $20 s, $30 d), **Royal Western Lodge** (590 S. Haskell Ave., 520/384-2266, $34 d), and **Desert Inn of Willcox** (704 S. Haskell Ave., 520/384-3577, $34 s, $40 d incl. tax) with a pool. **Motel 6** (921 N. Bisbee Ave., 520/384-2201 or 800/466-8356, $30 s, $36 d), just south of I-10 Exit 340, has a pool.

$50–100: Just south of I-10 Exit 340 you'll find **Best Western Plaza Inn** (1100 W. Rex Allen Dr., 520/384-3556 or 800/262-2645, $70 d), with breakfast, restaurant, and a pool, and **Days Inn** (724 N. Bisbee Ave., 520/384-4222 or 800/329-7466, $47 s, $54 d), also with a pool. Just to the north of I-10 Exit 340 is the **Super 8 Motel** (1500 W. Fort Grand Rd., 520/384-0888 or 800/800-8000, $46 s, $50 d), featuring an indoor pool and spa.

Campgrounds

Magic Circle RV Park (just north of I-10 Exit 340, then left, 520/384-3212, $18 tent, $25 RV w/hookups incl. tax) welcomes both RVs and tenters with a pool and showers. **Grande Vista Mobile/RV Park** (711 N. Prescott, 520/384-4002, $12 tents, $17.55 RV w/hookups) is south of I-10 Exit 340. **Lifestyle RV Resort** (622 N. Haskell Ave., 520/384-3303, $13 tent, $20 RV w/hookups) features a restaurant (closed Sun.), indoor pool and spa, exercise room, and showers. **Sagebrush Mobile/RV Park** (200 W. Lewis St. off S. Haskell Ave. behind the Desert Rose Café, 520/384-2872, $15 RV w/hookups) is on the south edge of town. **Fort Willcox RV Park** (1765 S. Haskell Ave., 520/384-4986, $5.30 tent, $7.42 RV dry site, $15.85 RV w/hookups incl. tax), near I-10 Exit 336 south of town, has showers.

Food

The **Desert Rose Café** (706 S. Haskell Ave., 520/384-0514, Mon.–Sat. breakfast, lunch, and dinner; Sun. breakfast and lunch buffet only) features a long menu of sandwiches, chicken, fish, shrimp, pasta, and steak plus a wine list. You'll also find some places to eat near I-10 Exit 340 and several interesting eateries along Railroad Avenue near the Rex Allen Arizona Cowboy Museum.

Safeway is just south of Exit 340, then right a block on Bisbee Avenue. The **IGA** supermarket is a block farther south on Rex Allen Drive.

Information and Services

The **Willcox Chamber of Commerce** (in the Cochise Visitors Center, 520/384-2272 or 800/200-2272, www.willcoxchamber.com, 9 A.M.–5 P.M. Mon.–Sat., 10 A.M.–2 P.M. Sun.) has the scoop on sights, services, and events of the area; you can purchase regional books and gift items. Take I-10 Exit 340 (AZ 186) north, then turn right a half-mile on Circle I Road. **Stouts Cider Mill** near the visitors center sells products from local apple orchards daily.

The **public library** (207 W. Maley St. and Curtis Ave., 520/384-4271, ext. 503) and the nearby **post office** (200 S. Curtis Ave. and Grant St.) are downtown; both close on Sunday. **Northern Cochise Community Hospital** (901 W. Rex Allen Dr., 520/384-3541) is south of I-10 Exit 340.

VICINITY OF WILLCOX

Frontier Relics

Orville Mickens has packed this small museum (look to see if the gate is open or call 520/384-3481, 9 A.M.–5 P.M. Mon.–Sat.) with historical artifacts from Fort Bowie and other areas of the Southwest; he'll also show you his big 1950 Cadillac. The museum is in Dos Cabezas, about 14 miles southeast of Willcox on Highway 186, on the way to Chiricahua National Monument.

Willcox Playa

This giant lake bed south of Willcox is visible from I-10 and covers 50–60 square miles. The playa is usually dry, but after heavy rains it becomes a shallow lake. You may see mirages on the surface in summer. As many as 10,000 sandhill cranes and smaller numbers of ducks and geese winter here from October to about late February. Private land makes access difficult, but you can visit Cochise Lake (just past Twin Lakes Golf Course) on the northeast side of the playa, the Arizona Fish & Game Reserve on the southwest side near Kansas Settlement Road, and wetlands of the Apache Station Wildlife Area on the west side just north of the power plant off U.S. Highway 191. The Willcox Chamber of Commerce has information and directions for these sites.

Cochise Stronghold Canyon

Set in a beautiful wooded area of towering pinnacles and great jumbles of boulders in the Dragoon Mountains, 30 miles southwest of Willcox, this canyon once provided a refuge for the Chiricahua Apache. During the 15 years that the great Apache chief Cochise and about 250 warriors hid out here, no white person was safe in the valleys below. Cochise—never defeated in battle—agreed to peace in 1872 only when the federal government promised land for his tribe. The mountains take their name from the Third U.S. Cavalry Dragoons.

Today the mountains offer picnicking, hiking trails, birding, and camping. The first-come, first-served campground in an oak grove has year-round water and costs $3 for day use or $10 for an overnight stay; it can fill on weekends in spring and autumn. A 400-foot paved loop trail here has interpretive signs about the Chiricahua Apache. A bit farther along the campground loop, the self-guided **Stronghold Nature Trail** crosses a footbridge and identifies some of the many plants found here; the .4-mile loop also has good views of the rock features that overlook the campground. **Cochise Stronghold Trail** turns off the nature trail and continues up the valley past Cochise Spring and Halfmoon Tank to Stronghold Divide, six miles round-trip. It's also possible to continue down the other side of the range to a trailhead in West Stronghold Canyon, 10 miles round-trip.

Dispersed camping is possible a couple of miles before the campground in Cochise Stronghold Canyon; turn in on Forest Roads 84A or 84B, which connect to form a loop. Equestrians must stay here if camping with their animals. You can also find places to camp on back roads in other parts of the Dragoon Mountains.

A rough but scenic 24-mile drive crosses the southern part of the range at Middlemarch Pass, connecting the ghost town of Pearce with Tombstone to the west. For Cochise Stronghold, take I-10 Exit 331, head southeast on U.S. Highway 191 to the north side of Sunsites, then turn west nine miles on Ironwood Road; the last four miles are unpaved.

Amerind Foundation Museum

Secluded among the boulders of Texas Canyon, the Foundation's Spanish colonial revival buildings include an outstanding museum (520/586-3666, www.amerind.org, 10 A.M.–4 P.M. daily, closed Mon.–Tues. June–Sept. and major holidays, $5 adults, $4 seniors 60+, $3 ages 12–18) with archaeological and ethnographic exhibits of the native peoples of the Americas. Amateur archaeologist William Fulton started the foundation—named from a contraction of *American* and *Indian*—in 1937 to increase the world's knowledge of American Indian cultures. Especially active in research of Southwest and Mexican archaeology, the foundation has amassed an amazing artifact collection, some of which you can see here. Call or check the website for special events held in the cooler months. A museum store sells high-quality Native American artwork, crafts, and books. The Amerind's art gallery displays paintings and sculptures by Native American and other artists of the 19th and 20th centuries; it closes noon–1 P.M.

Take I-10 Dragoon Exit 318 (64 miles east of Tucson between Willcox and Benson), go southeast one mile, turn left at the sign and drive three-quarters of a mile. An inviting picnic area lies nearby.

The Thing

This archetypal tourist trap features a whimsical museum with antique vehicles, wacky woodcarvings, and old wagons, as well as The Thing. (You can decide for yourself whether it's real.) You'll have to fork out one dollar (75 cents children 6–18) to see the exhibits. Yes, there's also a huge gift shop that sells regional souvenirs. Open 6:30 A.M. to 7 or 8 P.M. daily, depending on the season; it's just south off I-10 Exit 322 between Willcox and Benson.

Galiuro Mountains

Rugged and brush-covered, the Galiuro Mountains rise above the desert in two parallel ranges northwest of Willcox. The **Galiuro Wilderness** of the Coronado National Forest protects 76,317 acres of the range. Another 6,600 acres just to the south lies within the BLM's **Redfield Canyon Wilderness.** The remote location and unpaved roads of this little-known range mean that you're likely to have solitude. Because of the rough terrain, hikers stick mostly to the network of 10 trails, which total 95 miles. Note that most streams dry up during late spring and early summer. See the Forest Service and BLM offices in Safford for the latest water, trail, and road conditions. Deer Creek Trailhead, on the northeast side near the end of Forest Road 253, is sometimes accessible by car. From the south, the 4WD Jackson Cabin Road provides the best access, following a corridor through Redfield Canyon Wilderness and ending just south of the Galiuro Wilderness.

The south and west slopes have dense growths of manzanita, live oak, and other brush, with juniper, pinyon, and oak trees higher up. The higher canyons and north-facing slopes support Arizona cypress, ponderosa pine, Chihuahua pine, Mexican white pine, Douglas fir, and some white fir. Sycamore, alder, aspen, and other deciduous trees grow along stream banks. Mule deer, white-tailed deer, black bear, javelina, and mountain lion roam the hillsides and canyons. The old Power's cabin (built 1910), mine shafts, and ore-milling machinery lie along Rattlesnake Canyon. Power's Garden cabin, also in Rattlesnake Canyon, may be open to hikers—check with the Forest Service.

Parts of the two wilderness areas, along with private lands to the south, make up the 49,000-acre **Muleshoe Ranch Cooperative Management Area,** a collaborative effort of the Bureau of Land Management, Coronado National Forest, and the Nature Conservancy. Several perennial streams here support wildlife and lush greenery, so it's a great place for birding and hiking. Elevations range from 4,100 feet at headquarters to 7,600 feet atop Bassett Peak. You're welcome to stop in to see exhibits and visit the gift shop at the Nature Conservancy's headquarters (520/507-5229, http://nature.org/arizona, 8 A.M.–5 P.M. Thurs.–Mon. year-round and possibly daily in spring, $5). You can get a feel for the land on the nearby three-quarter-mile interpretive trail loop that winds through riparian, mesquite bosque, and semidesert grassland habitats. Ask at the headquarters for directions to longer hikes in the area. You can stay at casitas, all with kitchens, for $95–155 d depending on size; they close June–August. There are no facilities for car camping, nor RV parking. Bring all supplies, but you can get water at headquarters. Horses can stay at a corral. Pets won't be welcome in the headquarters-area trails or casitas.

The rugged and extremely scenic **Jackson Cabin Road** continues north from the Nature Conservancy's headquarters. You'll need a high-clearance 4WD vehicle for this adventure. There's no charge, but you must sign in at the information kiosk at the start and practice no-trace ethics; prescribed burns occasionally close the road in summer. The drive passes riparian areas, abandoned ranches, and dramatic vistas beneath the western escarpment of the Galiuros. You'll reach Jackson Cabin at road's end after 14.2 miles and 2.5 hours. You can camp along the road, except for the first 1.5 miles, or stay in the primitive cabin. **West Divide Trail 289** begins near the cabin and heads down Jackson Creek to the narrow red-walled chasm of Redfield Canyon in about a mile one way. The trail turns up Redfield Canyon and reaches **Power's Garden Trail 96** in 12.3 miles total one-way.

To reach the Muleshoe Ranch area, you can take I-10 Wilcox Exit 340, turn south one block, turn right .7 mile on Bisbee Avenue, turn right 14 miles on Airport Road/Cascabel Road, then right 13.5 miles on Muleshoe Road to the headquarters. Pavement gives out soon after you leave Willcox, but the road is passable for cars when dry. It's also possible to take I-10 Benson Exit 306 and follow unpaved Pomerene, Three Links, and Muleshoe Roads. None of these roads should be attempted in wet weather.

BENSON

The Butterfield Stage crossed the San Pedro River nearby in the early 1860s, but the town didn't really get going until the railroad arrived in 1880, filling its saloons with cowboys, miners, Mexicans, and Chinese. Benson, 36 miles southwest of Willcox and 45 miles southeast of Tucson, is quiet now and offers motels, campgrounds, and restaurants for travelers.

San Pedro Valley Arts and Historical Society Museum

Photos and artifacts show life in the early railroad, mining, and ranching days (180 S. San Pedro, 520/586-3070, 10 A.M.–4 P.M. Tues.–Fri. but to 2 P.M. Sat. and May–Sept., closed Aug., free). Outside in back, you can see a 1923 fireless steam engine used by the Apache Powder Company. A gift shop sells local handmade crafts. From 4th Street, the main street through downtown, turn one block south on San Pedro.

Events

Cowpunchers compete in team roping, barrel racing, and other events at the Arena, behind Pardner's RV Park on the west edge of town; ask for the schedule at the Benson Visitor Center. The **Antique Tractor Pull** in early February pits machines against one another in antique (before 1940), classic (1940–1960), garden, and pedal classes. **Territorial Days** on the second weekend of February presents music and other entertainment along with family activities. The **4th of July** celebration features firefighter competitions and fireworks. **Butterfield Overland Stage Day** on the second Saturday of October entertains with a blues concert, parade, and crafts.

Recreation

San Pedro Golf Club (926 N. Madison, 520/586-7888, www.sanpedro.com) is an 18-hole championship facility and restaurant north of town beside the San Pedro River. **Turquoise Hills Family Golf Center** (800 E. Country Club Dr., 520/586-7535, www.turquoisehills.com) offers an 18-hole executive course, a restaurant, and miniature golf near the San Pedro River off Highway 80 south of downtown.

Accommodations

Bed and Breakfast: **Skywatcher's Inn** (520/586-7906, www.skywatchersinn.com, $85 or 119 d room, $175 d suite) offers bed and breakfast accommodations at the Vega-Bray Observatory on a hill overlooking the San Pedro Valley. Astronomy sessions with a variety of telescopes cost $95–130 with up to five adults. The observatory also has a planetarium, classroom, and exhibits. Reservations for rooms and astronomy should be made as much as three months in advance for the popular October–March season.

Under $50: Independents include **Quarter Horse Motel** (800 W. 4th St., 520/586-3371, $38 d) and **Sahara Motel** (1150 S. AZ 80, south of town, 520/586-3611, $35 s, $39 d). **Motel 6** (2 miles west of downtown at I-10/AZ 90 Exit 302, 520/586-0066 or 800/466-8356, $39 s, $45 d), with a pool, is at the turnoff for Kartchner Caverns and Sierra Vista.

$50–100: Days Inn (621 Commerce Dr., just north of I-10, 520/586-3000 or 877/586-3303, $53 d) with a pool, **Super 8 Motel** (855 N. Ocotillo, just north of I-10, 520/586-1530 or 800/800-8000, $50 s, $55 d) with a pool, and **Best Western Quail Hollow Inn** (699 N. Ocotillo, just south of I-10, 520/586-3646 or 800/322-1850, $65 s, $70 d) with a pool and hot tub, all hang out near I-10 Exit 304.

$100 and up: Holiday Inn Express (2 miles west of downtown at I-10/AZ 90 Exit 302, 520/586-8800 or 888/263-2283, $119 s, $99–119 d) offers a pool and fitness center at the turnoff for Kartchner Caverns and Sierra Vista.

Campgrounds

All of these have showers. **KOA Campground** (.5 miles north of I-10 Exit 304, 520/586-3977 or 800/562-6823, $20–22 tent, $25–27 RV w/hookups, $39 d cabin) offers a natural setting away from the highways; guests have a pool, hot tub, game room, and store. **Benson I-10 RV Park** (520/586-4252 or 800/599-0081, $22–24 RV w/hookups) is just north of I-10 Exit 304, then right. **Red Barn RV Park** (520/586-2035, $12.50 tent or RV w/hookups) is just north of I-10 Exit 304, then right past the Benson I-10 RV Park. **Quarter Horse Motel** (800 W. 4th St., 520/586-3371, RV $16 w/hookups) is on the west side of town, as is **Pardner's RV Park** (950 W. 4th St., 520/586-7887, $13 RV w/hookups). **Cochise Terrace RV Resort** (520/586-0600 or 800/495-9005, www.cochise-terrace.com, $28 RV w/hookups) features a pool, hot tub, and many other amenities; it's on the right, one mile south of I-10 Exit 302 on the way to Kartchner Caverns.

Food

Horse Shoe Café (154 E. 4th St., 520/586-3303, daily breakfast, lunch, and dinner) is an old-fashioned place with Western decor serving American and some Mexican items. **Chute-Out Steak House** (161 S. Huachuca St., 520/586-7297, nightly dinner) serves up a variety of steaks plus shrimp, fish, ribs, and chicken. **Galleano's** (601 W. 4th St., 520/586-3523, daily breakfast, lunch, and dinner) serves American standards plus some Italian items. **Beijing Palace** (577 W. 4th St. in the Safeway Shopping Center, 520/586-7140, daily lunch and dinner) specializes in Chinese food. **Magaly's Mexican Restaurant** (675 W. 4th St., 520/5866-2027, closed Sun.) is a simple café with good south-of-the-border food. At the east end of town, **86 Café** (700 E. 4th St., 520/586-3169, closed Sun.) cooks bargain-priced American and Mexican food. You'll also find American favorites at **Country View Restaurant** (600 N. Ocotillo St., just south of I-10 Exit 304) and **Denny's** (825 N. Ocotillo St., just north of the exit).

Information and Services

To learn about sights and services, stop by the central **Benson Visitor Center** (249 E. 4th St., Benson, AZ 85602, 520/586-4293, www.cityofbenson.com, 9 A.M.–5 P.M. Mon.–Sat. year-round, also 10 A.M.–2 P.M. Sun. in winter). The **public library** (300 S. Huachuca St., 520/586-9535, closed Sun.) is two blocks south of 4th Street.

A **city park** lies three blocks north on Patagonia from 4th Street. The **post office** (250 S. Ocotillo St.) is two blocks south of 4th Street. **Benson Hospital** (450 S. Ocotillo St., 520/586-3606) is four blocks south of 4th Street.

Getting There

Amtrak trains (800/872-7245) stop downtown three days a week in each direction on their route across southern Arizona. **Greyhound** buses (680 W. 4th St., 520/586-3388 or 800/231-2222) swing by the Benson Flower Shop.

VICINITY OF BENSON

Singing Wind Bookshop

This unique shop (Singing Wind Rd., 520/586-2425, 9 A.M.–5 P.M. daily including most holidays) on a ranch near Benson carries an excellent selection of regional books and a bit of just about everything else! A children's room has many enchanting books too. Owner Winifred Bundy is a treasure trove of advice about authors and titles. She also organizes three fiestas: music and regional authors on the Sunday preceding Thanksgiving, cowboy and cowgirl poetry on the last Sunday in January, and a literary-themed event on the last Sunday of February. Go north three miles on Ocotillo from downtown (2.5 miles north from I-10 Exit 304), then turn right at the sign and drive a half-mile; there's a gate halfway in.

Gammons's Gulch

Jay Gammons loves old towns so much that when he couldn't buy one, he built his own (520/212-2831, www.gammonsgulch.com, $5 adults, $1 children 12 and under). He carefully assembled the buildings from parts of old ones, along with many antiques, to create a ghost town that appears to come straight out of the Old West. Jay has also been in the movie business—his dad worked as a bodyguard for John Wayne—and the town and props have been used in films. Every item has a story as Jay or an assistant enthusiastically takes you around to the saloon with its 1880s bar (you can order a rootbeer), the sheriff's office, mercantile store, wagon shop, blacksmith shop, assay office, hotel, wheelwright

Jay Gammon plays a tune for visitors in the saloon at Gammon's Gulch.

© BILL WEIR

shop, telegraph office, barbershop, engine house, undertaker's, Chinese laundry, and mine. A nature trail loops through the picturesque desert country nearby.

Call ahead to check the hours and see if you need a reservation. The Gulch is 12 miles north of Benson; from I-10 Exit 306 at the east end of town, head north 11.8 miles on Pomerene and Cascabel Roads (observe speed limits), turn left .2 miles on Rockspring Road, then left to the entrance.

Kartchner Caverns State Park

Discovered in 1974, Kartchner Caverns (P.O. Box 1849, Benson, AZ 85602, 520/586-4100, www.azstateparks.com, 7:30 A.M.–6 P.M. daily, free w/tour reservation, or $5/vehicle up to four people, $2 each additional person or cyclist) became Arizona's 25th state park in 1988. Because of the exceptional care needed to preserve the pristine interior formations and environment during trail construction, the cave didn't open to the public until November 1999. Beautiful limestone formations, softly tinted yellow and red, decorate the living cave system. You'll see magnificent columns up to 58 feet high, delicate "soda straws" (one is a quarter of an inch in diameter and over 21 feet long, but too fragile to be visited), shields, stalactites, stalagmites, and nearly every other type of cave formation.

Begin your visit in the **Discovery Center,** where you can watch a 15-minute video about the exciting discovery of the cave. Exhibits illustrate local geology, cave features, and the web of life inside. Highlights include a replica of the long soda straw and a reproduction of the 80,000-year-old Shasta ground sloth, whose bones were found in the cave. A cut-away cave model shows the layout of the chambers. Even if you're not taking a tour, the Discovery Center makes a worthwhile visit. There's a gift shop and overpriced vending machines, but no restaurant. Outside, you can wander through the hummingbird garden, go for a hike, or have a picnic. The information desk has a bird list.

The park offers two tours, each a half-mile loop: the **Rotunda/Throne Room** (1.5 hours, open year-round; $19 adult, $10 kids 7–13, free under 7) and the **Big Room** (1.75 hours, open Oct. 15–April 15; $23 adult, $13 ages 7–13, no children under 7). A tram takes you from the Discovery Center to the cave entrance, which has protective air locks. Once inside, you'll experience the cave's temperature of 68°F at 99 percent humidity. Guides ask that you not bring cameras, strollers, walkers, or food inside the cave. The paved paths have moderate grades but no steps; wheelchair users should call for advice. Tours depart daily every 20 minutes 8:40 A.M.–4:40 P.M. You can tour both sections of the cave in one day, though this isn't recommended for people with heart problems. Note that the Big Room, which opened to the public only in 2003, closes each summer when bats move in. Try to make reservations for the cave tours as far in advance as possible, though last-minute spots may become available due to cancellations. If you can't get a reservation, try for one of the tickets sold first-come, first-served each morning; call ahead and ask advice on what time you should arrive and get in line. The reservation line (520/586-2283) is open Monday–Friday 8 A.M.–5 P.M. except state holidays.

The 2.4-mile **Foothills Loop Trail** provides an aboveground perspective of the park and takes 2–3 hours; a spur trail leads to a viewpoint, adding a mile and 45 minutes to the round-trip. The 4.2-mile **Guindani Loop Trail** heads deeper into the Whetstone Mountains of the Coronado National Forest. Bring water and wear sturdy shoes for these trails.

The campground offers first-come, first-served sites with electric and water hookups for $22; guests have showers and a dump station. Both tents and RVs are welcome, but everyone should check in before 5:30 P.M. The park is in the Whetstone Mountains just west of Highway 90, 9 miles south of I-10 Exit 302, 11 miles from Benson, 19 miles from Sierra Vista, 28 miles from Tombstone, and 49 miles from Tucson.

St. David

This small town is seven miles south of Benson on the way to Tombstone. Phileman Merrill, an adjutant general of the Mormon Battalion, founded the town of Marcus at springs beside the San Pedro River in 1877; it later took the name of another Mormon (Latter-Day Saint). Holy Trinity Monastery lies 1.5 miles south of town.

Holy Trinity Monastery

This Benedictine monastery on the banks of the San Pedro River welcomes visitors to experience the tranquility and spiritual life here (P.O. Box 298, Saint David, AZ 85630, 520/720-4016, www.holytrinitymonastery.org). The monastery began in 1974 and now houses monks, sisters, and a small group of lay people. The community looks after 150 acres, which includes a pecan orchard, lakes, and riparian and desert areas. You could begin your visit at the Monastery Store (on your left as you enter the grounds), where you can pick up a map, get information, browse the gifts and books, and register for overnight stays. Our Lady of Guadalupe Chapel stands nearby on a low hill. Trinitas Art Gallery & Museum presents historical and religious exhibits, but you may need to call ahead to see them. A library holds spiritual and regional titles. There's also a thrift shop. A 1.3-mile trail loop begins near the RV park and heads over to the San Pedro River with excellent birding opportunities; a second trail branches off partway and loops back in about 1.4 miles. People on retreat can stay in the accommodations, and anyone is welcome to use the RV park, which is first-come, first-served and costs $15 with hookups.

You're invited to participate in the daily schedule, which includes a mid-day prayer at 11:45 A.M. (10:15 A.M. on Sun.) followed by Mass 15 minutes later. Art festivals run on Mother's Day weekend in May and on the second weekend of November. Holy Trinity Monastery is nine miles south of Benson on the way to Tombstone; look for the 74-foot Celtic cross on the west side of Highway 80 between Mileposts 302 and 303.

West of Tucson

TOHONO O'ODHAM INDIAN RESERVATION

The main reservation, a land of dry sandy washes and plains broken here and there by rocky hills or mountains, lies 25 miles west of Tucson on Highway 86. The first white people couldn't believe that humans could live in such wild and parched desert, yet the Tohono O'odham have thrived here for centuries.

Most Tohono O'odham are friendly, but the tribe has shown no interest in tourism. The vast reservation has hardly any visitor facilities and not a single motel, full-service restaurant, tourist office, or tribal museum. Two attractions, in addition to the desert scenery, make a visit worthwhile, the world-famous Kitt Peak Observatory and the Tohono O'odham All-Indian Rodeo and Fair. You'll see Tohono O'odham crafts—primarily basketry—at a store near Milepost 140 between Tucson and the Kitt Peak turnoff and at Kitt Peak's visitors center.

KITT PEAK

Large white domes perched atop the 6,875-foot summit enclose instruments that help unravel the mysteries of the universe. You're welcome to drive up and see the observatory and astronomy exhibits. The telescopes come in many sizes and types, including two that use radio waves. Seven cosmic-ray telescopes were in the works at press time. The Association of Universities for Research in Astronomy (AURA) operates these National Optical Astronomy Observatories for the National Science Foundation.

Visitors Center

Step inside to see videos and exhibits that illustrate the nature of light and the workings of telescopes. The visitors center gift shop sells Tohono O'odham basketry at very good prices, as well as astronomy-related books, posters, videos, and T-shirts. Kitt Peak National Observatory is open 9 A.M.–4 P.M. daily (visitors center to 3:45 P.M.) except New Year's Day, Thanksgiving Day, and December 24–25; $2 suggested donation. During the "monsoon season" of July and August, try to arrive first thing in the morning, as thunderstorms often build up later in the day. No smoking on the grounds, please. Check schedules, basic information, and winter road conditions by calling 520/318-8200 (recording) or 520/318-8726 (visitors center) or by checking www.noao.edu.

The air is cool up here—15–20°F colder than Tucson—so you'll probably need a jacket or sweater. Kitt Peak lies 56 miles southwest of Tucson via Highway 86 and Highway 386. The last 12 miles are on a paved and well-graded mountain road, though winter storms can close it for short periods. Visitors need to come prepared with warm clothing, food, and a full tank of gas—there's no restaurant or store here. On the drive up, 1.5 miles before the visitors center, you'll pass the turnoff for a picnic area in an oak forest.

Tours and Visitor Programs

Pick up a map at the visitors center for the self-guided tour of the grounds that passes some of the most impressive telescopes. Visitors may enter viewing galleries of three telescopes and read signs about the workings of others. Free one-hour tours present more background and details; they leave the visitors center daily at 10 A.M., 11:30 A.M., and 1:30 P.M. Stargazing programs take place nightly using either the 20-inch telescope located directly above the entrance to the visitors center or a 16-incher in a nearby dome. You'll need to make a reservation (not later than 3 P.M. of the same day) and pay $36 ($31 students and seniors). The Advanced Observing Program enables one or two amateur astronomers to use telescope equipment with professional guidance; reservations, a $350 fee (no rainchecks!), and $55 per person for room and board will be needed. The website www.noao.edu and visitors center staff have details of these programs, which run September–June.

The Telescopes

Before Kitt Peak was built, students and women found it almost impossible to secure time at a major telescope; here they have an equal chance. Astronomers use the equipment free of charge, but must learn to be philosophical, sometimes waiting many months only to be clouded out.

Computers control the instruments; CCD (charge-coupled device) image sensors convert light into digital form and store it on computer tape for later analysis. It's rare for an observer to actually look through a telescope these days, and few instruments even feature an eyepiece. Most telescopes at Kitt Peak are designed to maximize their light-gathering power rather than their magnification—so a distant star looks the same size through even the biggest scopes. The McMath-Pierce Solar Telescope, however, produces a 30-inch image of the sun by using mirrors in a slanted 500-foot corridor, about 300 feet of which run belowground. You can go inside to peer up and down the long chamber and see the mirrors. This telescope won an architectural award in 1962, a rare accolade for an observatory.

The 2.1-meter (84-inch) telescope nearby was the first large instrument on Kitt Peak for nighttime observing; a viewing gallery and exhibits are inside. Astronomers use the scope to observe distant stars and galaxies in both the visible and infrared spectra. The Mayall 4-meter (158-inch), one of the world's largest telescopes, resides in an

© BILL WEIR

McMath-Pierce Solar Telescope

18-story building. An elevator takes you to the 10th-floor observation deck, offering panoramic views of southern Arizona and northern Sonora. Spacewatch (www.lpl.arizona.edu/spacewatch), a group at the University of Arizona's Lunar and Planetary Laboratory, explores the solar system for small objects—including Earth-orbit-crossing asteroids—with 1.8-meter (71-inch) and .9-meter (35-inch) telescopes. If you stop at the picnic area, you can get a close look at a giant radio telescope of the Very Long Baseline Array; it's one of 10 spaced between Hawaii and the Caribbean that link to form a single antenna with extremely high resolution; a sign explains how the system works.

SELLS

Sells, the largest town on the Tohono O'odham Reservation, serves as tribal headquarters. The dependable water here has made the place a popular stop for travelers since prehistoric times. Originally known as Indian Oasis, the settlement took its present name in 1918 to honor Indian Commissioner Cato Sells. The town lies 58 miles southwest of Tucson via Highway 86, 20 miles past the turnoff for Kitt Peak. Offices, schools, and a shopping center (**Basha's** supermarket/bakery and a post office) line a business loop just south of the main highway.

Tohono O'odham All-Indian Rodeo and Fair

Tohono O'odham cowboys show off their riding and roping skills in the tribe's big annual event, usually held on the first weekend of February. The Tohono O'odham put on a parade, exhibit crafts, serve Indian fry bread, and perform songs and dances. Obtain the dates from the tribal office in Sells (520/383-2588, ext. 5) or the Visitors Bureau in Tucson (520/632-6024 or 800/638-8350).

Before camping or exploring the backcountry, check to see if you'll need a permit from one of the 11 districts of the reservation; the **Tohono O'odham Tribe Administration** (Sells, AZ 85634, 520/383-2028) can advise you on which district to contact and give you its telephone number. The administration office is in an all-white building with a man-in-the-maze symbol, near schools on the north side of the business loop; enter from the back. Ask about road conditions if you plan to venture off the main highway; dirt roads can become impassable after rains.

ORGAN PIPE CACTUS NATIONAL MONUMENT

The Sonoran Desert puts on its finest show in this remote area of Arizona. Some desert plants, such as the senita cactus and elephant tree, grow only here and in Mexico. The name of Arizona's largest national monument honors the giant organ pipe cactus *(Stenocereus thurberi),* which thrives in this area. In appearance it's similar to the saguaro, though the organ pipe's many branches all radiate from the base.

Animals adapt to the heat by hiding out during the hottest part of the day. They're most active in the morning, evening, and night. Wildlife you might see includes lizards, birds, kangaroo rats, kit foxes, bobcats, javelina, bighorn sheep, and pronghorn. The six species of rattlesnakes are nocturnal during hot weather—a good reason to use a flashlight at night. About 40 species of birds stay year-round; more than 230 others drop in while migrating. Quitobaquito Oasis offers prime birding.

If you're lucky enough to arrive in March or April after a wet winter, you'll see the desert ablaze with flowers in yellow, blue, red, and violet. Annual plants bloom first, as they must quickly germinate and produce seeds before the onslaught of the summer heat. The smaller cacti, such as cholla and prickly pear, come next. And lastly, the big saguaro and organ pipe blossoms appear, peaking in May or June. A wildflower hotline provided by the Desert Botanical Garden (602/754-8134) in Phoenix tells what's happening during the spring.

Summer is the quiet season at the monument, as daytime highs commonly hit 95–105°F. Thunderstorms arrive in late summer, bringing about half the annual 9.5 inches or so of rain. Winters run cool to warm, with occasional gentle rains.

Visitors Center

For an introduction to the highly adaptable plants and wildlife that live here, start at the visitors center (22 miles south of Why, 8 A.M.–5 P.M. daily, 520/387-6849, www.nps.gov/orpi, $5/vehicle). A video presentation gives an overview of the area. Exhibits show plants and animals of the region and the effects of humans on the desert. Just outside, a short paved nature trail

cristate growth on an organ pipe cactus

THE GILA MONSTER

This venomous lizard spends more than 95 percent of its solitary life underground or beneath rocks. In spring, during summer monsoons, and in autumn it comes out to feed on eggs—especially of Gambel quail—and small prey such as birds, young rabbits, and rodents. Fat reserves in the tail see it through the winter. Gila monsters *(Heloderma suspectum)* mate in early summer, then the female lays her eggs in cool, moist soil in arroyos.

Although active during the day and on some warm summer nights, the "monster" is seen by few people. You can recognize it by its beadlike scales in black, yellow, orange, or pink patterns. Adults grow to a length of 18–24 inches and weigh up to two pounds. Each individual keeps to a small range, but the species extends over much of southern and western Arizona in desert foothills. A larger and darker cousin, the Mexican beaded lizard *(Heloderma horridum),* roams farther south in Mexico.

The Gila monster, despite its name, is shy and gentle—it becomes dangerous only when picked up or cornered. If threatened, it fights by clamping down with powerful jaws; venom produced in the lower jaw seeps through grooves in the teeth. The lizard may try to hang on and on while the painful poison works its way into the wound. Methods of loosening the grip include using a stick in the mouth and pushing back, applying a flame under the jaw, immersing the lizard in water, or in desperation, yanking the lizard off by its tail. First aid and a physician will be needed to clean the wound and treat the pain, bleeding, swelling, and lowered blood pressure.

Both common sense and Arizona law protect the Gila monster.

identifies common plants and provides more information on the desert environment.

Rangers can answer your questions and issue camping permits. Staff sell books, prints, and topo maps. Naturalists offer programs during the cooler months at the visitors center, on trails, and at the campground. **Tohono O'odham Day** takes place Saturday on the third weekend in March with craft demonstrations, food, and programs.

Puerto Blanco Scenic Drive

Highlights of this 53-mile loop include Quitobaquito Oasis, Senita Basin's rare desert plants, and a variety of desert environments. A pamphlet suggests things to see at numbered stops; pick one up at the visitors center or at the start of the drive just west of the visitors center. Nearly the entire route is graded dirt designed for slow speeds—allow at least half a day. The first five miles are two-way, followed by a one-way (counterclockwise) section on which you can't turn back. Picnic tables and three interconnected hiking trails invite longer visits. Mountain bikers can ride the drive in either direction, though it's a bit long to do the whole loop. Note that construction of a vehicle barrier along the Mexican border may close the southern part of the drive through 2005.

Red Tanks Tinaja Trail, 1.2 miles round-trip, winds through pretty desert hills to some small natural pools in a wash. It starts 600 feet before Stop 3 (where you park), four miles along the drive. For a longer hike you can continue on interconnecting trails to Senita Basin, to several mine sites, or back to the main campground. **Dripping Springs Mine Trail,** two miles round-trip, climbs gentle slopes with views to a 1918 claim. It begins at Mile 11.9 on the drive; park here or at the Little Continental Divide at Mile 11.5. **Senita Basin Trail** makes a 2.5-mile loop from the end of the spur road to Senita Basin and connects with other trails.

Quitobaquito, one mile off the loop, has a large artificial pond surrounded by tall cottonwoods. The springs lie 100 yards north up a trail. Ducks and other waterfowl—not what you'd expect in the desert—drop in during the spring and autumn. Coots stay here year-round. Father Kino and other early Spanish missionaries and explorers stopped by on their way to the Colorado River. The '49ers headed for the California goldfields came this way, too, favoring a southern route to avoid hostile Indians roaming farther north, but some perished of thirst on the fearsome Camino del Diablo (Devil's Highway) west of here. Don't leave valuables in your parked car because break-ins occur occasionally at Quitobaquito and all along the Mexican border.

Senita Basin, four miles off the loop, is home

to the senita cactus and elephant tree. Similar in appearance to organ pipe cactus, the senita *(Pachycereus schottii)* is distinguished by its gray whiskers that shade the tender growing tips and by having far fewer pleats, typically only four or five. The elephant tree *(Idria columnaris)* looks like the root system of an upside-down tree.

Ajo Mountain Drive

Heading into the more rugged country of the eastern part of the monument, this drive skirts the base of 4,808-foot Mt. Ajo with many spectacular views. Most of the 21-mile gravel loop road is one-way; pick up a pamphlet describing the drive at the visitors center or at the start of the loop, just across the highway from the visitors center; allow at least two hours. Mountain bikers enjoy the loop, which they can ride in either direction.

Estes Canyon–Bull Pasture Trail, off Ajo Mountain Drive, is the most spectacular established trail. The Estes Canyon segment follows the canyon; the Bull Pasture part climbs a ridge. The trails meet and then continue to Bull Pasture, where ranchers once grazed cattle. The entire loop, including the spur trail to Bull Pasture, is 4.1 miles round-trip with some steep sections and loose rock; carry water.

Hiking

Besides the trails along the scenic drives, you have several options near the campground, 1.5 miles from the visitors center. On the 1.2-mile-loop **Desert View Nature Trail,** you'll travel up a wash, then climb onto a ridge with a good panorama. **Victoria Mine Trail,** 4.2 miles round-trip, takes you to a historic mine that produced lead, silver, and gold. You could continue on to **Lost Cabin Mine,** adding 3.8 miles round-trip. Other hiking options begin at the T-junction 1.8 miles along the Victoria Mine Trail: Turn right 1.4 miles for **Senita Basin** and a little loop trail there, branch off to Red Tanks Tinaja, 3.7 miles, or go on to Baker Mine, 5.4 miles (mileages are one-way from the T-junction). Also beginning at the campground are a 1-mile trail encircling the camping area and a 1.3-mile trail to the visitors center. You're also free to hike cross-country in the monument's open terrain. Rangers can help you plan. There's a $5 permit for overnight hikes.

Campgrounds

The 208-site campground near the visitors center is open all year, with room for trailers to 35 feet. There's drinking water but no hookups or showers; sites cost $10 per night. It can fill during the busy season after Christmas to early April, when campers should try to arrive by 11 A.M.

Tenters can leave the asphalt and flush toilets behind to stay at **Alamo Canyon Primitive Campground,** 12.5 miles away near the Ajo Range. This pretty spot also makes a good base for day hikes. You'll need to register first at the visitors center, pay a $6 fee, and bring water. No trailers or RVs permitted.

For motels, stores, gas stations, and restaurants, you must leave the monument. Nearest services are at Lukeville, Arizona (5 miles south), Sonoita, Mexico (2 miles farther), Why (22 miles north), and Ajo (32 miles northwest).

VICINITY OF ORGAN PIPE CACTUS NATIONAL MONUMENT

Lukeville

Just a wide spot on the road next to the Mexican border, Lukeville honors WWI flying ace Frank Luke. Turn left at the sign for **Gringo Pass Motel and Trailer Park** (602/254-9284 Phoenix, $56 s, $65 d room, $11 tent, $15 RV w/hookups), which has showers and laundry; call in summer. Across the highway are a gas station, supermarket, café (American and Mexican food, breakfast, lunch, and dinner daily), laundry, post office, Mexican insurance office, and money exchange. Sonoita's restaurants and shops lie two miles southwest of the Mexican border. Beaches, fishing, and seafood lure many visitors 63 more miles to Puerto Peñasco on the Sea of Cortez. There you'll find seaside motels, restaurants, and trailer parks. A permit is required for travel beyond Sonoita. You can buy Mexican auto insurance on both sides of the border, in Why, and in Ajo.

Why

Why "Why"? Because motorists used to call it "the Y." The tiny community centers on the junction of Highways 85 and 86 north of Organ Pipe Cactus National Monument. The **Why Not Travel Store** downtown offers gas, snacks, groceries, Mexican insurance, and a post office. **Why 85 Deli** next door serves light meals. A gas station across the street provides snacks, groceries, and Mexican insurance.

Coyote Howls II (520/387-5933, $17 RV w/hookups) is just west of the junction. On the east side of town, **Coyote Howls RV Park** (520/387-5209, $8.50) offers simple sites without hookups, but guests have senior activities, coin showers, water, and a dump station. To camp free of charge, you might ask people at Why for suggestions. RVs and tenters use BLM land (no facilities) at Gunsight Wash; it's 1.8 miles south of Why on Highway 85 near Milepost 55; turn right just after the bridge.

AJO

This pleasant small town appears lost in a sea of desert. It's 10 miles northwest of Why and 42 miles south of Gila Bend. The town's name (pronounced AH-ho) may have come from the Tohono O'odham word for paint; Native Americans collected copper minerals here to use in painting their bodies.

Prospectors settled as early as 1854, but Ajo didn't really get going until the dawn of the 20th century, when suitable ore-refining techniques became available. The New Cornelia Copper Company began operation in 1917 and was later bought by Phelps Dodge. Squeezed between low copper prices and high costs, Phelps Dodge shut down the mine and smelter in 1985, but retirees and winter visitors helped soften the blow to the town's economy. Graceful palms and flowering trees surround the Spanish colonial–style plaza and many public buildings downtown. Greenery and trees also decorate the miners' tiny houses.

Sights

The **New Cornelia Open Pit Mine** just south of town ranks as one of the world's largest at 1.5 miles across and 1,100 feet deep. A tiny visitor center at the overlook, usually open daily October–April, has a few exhibits and a copper-mining video. From downtown, turn southwest on La Mina Avenue, then turn right on Indian Village Road and follow signs. Continue a bit farther to **Ajo Historical Museum** (520/387-7105, about noon–4 P.M. daily, Oct.–April) and its diverse collection of mining, mineral, home life, and Native American exhibits. Native American workers once lived in this part of town, and the museum building served as St. Catherine's Indian Mission 1942–1968.

Events

Ajo has a surprising number of community events during the cooler months. Biggest are the **Sonoran Shindig** celebration of wildlife on the third Saturday in February, the **Ajo Historical Home Tour** in late March, the **July 4th Parade,** the **Ajo Great Western Street Fair** on the Saturday before Thanksgiving, and **La Posada** candlelight procession and caroling the Saturday evening before Christmas.

Recreation

Ajo Country Club (520/387-5011) offers a nine-hole golf course and a restaurant open daily for breakfast and lunch. It's seven miles northeast of town via Well and Mead Roads.

Accommodations

The Guest House Inn (520/387-6133, 700 Guest House Rd., www.guesthouseinn.biz, $79 s, $89 d) provides bed and breakfast in an attractive house.

La Siesta Motel (2561 N. Hwy. 85, 520/387-6569) offers three sizes of rooms from $36 s and $46 d, plus a pool, hot tub, and tennis courts. **Marine Motel** (1966 N. Hwy. 85, 520/387-7626, $50–58 d) has a pool. The basic **Copper Sands Motel** (3711 N. Hwy. 85, 520/387-4097, $55–60 d) is the last motel until Gila Bend.

Campgrounds

Shadow Ridge RV Resort (431 N. Hwy. 85, 520/387-5055, $12–14 tent, $24 RV w/hookups) is close to downtown. Farther north are **Ajo**

Heights RV Park (2000 N. Hwy. 85, 520/387-6796, $22 RV w/hookups) and **Belly Acres RV Park** (2030 N. Hwy. 85, 520/387-5767, $18 RV w/hookups). **La Siesta Motel** (2561 N. Hwy. 85, 520/387-6569, $10 tent, $20 RV w/hookups) is a good deal with a pool, hot tub, and tennis courts. **Copper Sands Motel** (3711 N. Hwy. 85, 520/387-4097) has some RV spaces for $15 with hookups. All of Ajo's RV parks except Copper Sands have showers.

Food

The Ajo Lily (downtown plaza, 520/387-7000, daily breakfast, lunch, and dinner) is a Mexican-American-Italian café. **Coyote Bob's Deli** (also on the plaza, 520/387-6434) serves sandwiches, light meals, and ice cream. **Don Juan's** (southwest of the plaza across the highway, 520/387-3100, Thurs.–Tues. breakfast, lunch, and dinner) prepares Mexican-American food.

Head north on the highway for a supermarket, bakeries, and more restaurants. **Pizza Hut** (627 N. 2nd Ave., 520/387-6842) serves lunch (buffet available weekdays) and dinner daily. **Señor Sancho's** (663 N. Hwy. 85, 520/387-6226, daily lunch and dinner) offers Mexican fare. **Bamboo Village** (1810 N. 2nd Ave., 520/387-7536, closed Mon.) features Cantonese cuisine for lunch and dinner.

Information and Services

The **Ajo District Chamber of Commerce** (400 Taladro, Ajo, AZ 85321, 520/387-7742, www.ajochamber.com, 9 A.M.–5 P.M. Mon.–Fri., shorter hours July–Sept.) is on the main highway one block southeast of the plaza.

Si Como No (yes, why not) sells regional books and topo maps as well as gifts and clothing at 207 Taladro, just southeast of the plaza. Many businesses in town advertise Mexican insurance. Ajo's **post office** and **public library** are on the plaza.

CABEZA PRIETA NATIONAL WILDLIFE REFUGE

The 860,000 acres of desert wilderness west of Organ Pipe Cactus National Monument hasn't changed much since white people arrived. The region has no facilities or paved roads. Desert bighorn sheep, for which the refuge was founded in 1939, and the endangered Sonoran pronghorn receive protection here. Wildlife and vegetation resemble those in Organ Pipe Cactus National Monument, but they endure a harsher climate. Cabeza Prieta's annual rainfall averages about nine inches in the east and three inches in the west, with some areas going more than a year without rain. Twelve small mountain ranges rise above the desert floor. The recent severe and extended drought has caused a serious decline in the number of Sonoran pronghorn, so much of the refuge and some adjacent lands may close to public vehicle entry during the fawning season of March 15–July 15.

The Cabeza Prieta National Wildlife Refuge visitors center (1611 N. 2nd Ave., Ajo, AZ 85321, 520/387-6483, http://southwest.fws.gov/refuges/Arizona/cabeza.html, 7:30 A.M.–noon and 1–4:30 P.M. Mon.–Fri.) provides information, permits, wildlife exhibits, and a large selection of video programs.

Routes

Only jeep tracks and remnants of the old Camino del Diablo traverse the landscape. Allow at least two days to cross the refuge on the roads between Ajo and Wellton; distance is 124 miles one-way, 59 miles in the refuge. An alternative connecting route, the Christmas Pass/Tacna Road from I-8, allows a shorter journey. Or you can do a longer trip from Ajo via the Tinajas Altas Mountains and come out at the I-8 Foothills Boulevard exit near Yuma.

If you'd like a taste of Cabeza Prieta, drive to Charlie Bell Pass in the Growler Mountains, just 20 miles (two hours) west of Ajo. High-clearance two-wheel-drive vehicles can make this trip. With luck, you may see pronghorn on the plains and desert bighorn sheep in the mountains. The road ends at the pass, where you can hike down the other side or up into the hills.

You can also approach the refuge from Yuma by heading south from I-8 Foothills Exit 14 or the more frequently used branch south from near I-8 Wellton Exit 30. These sandy roads connect near the Tinajas Altas Mountains, and it's possible to make a loop on them in a long day. A connector road over Cipriano Pass provides another loop option. On the road from I-8 Foothills Exit 14, you can detour to Fortuna ghost town and see where miners dug millions of dollars worth of glittering gold between 1896 and 1904.

Water held a far greater allure for most people crossing the desert, though, and the only reliable source for many miles lay in the nine natural pools of the Tinajas Altas (high tanks). At the lowest pool you'll be standing on the very spot where many Native Americans, Spaniards, and '49ers stood in a life-or-death search for water. Padre Kino passed this way around 1700 and called the pools Agua Escondido (hidden water). The lowest pool is an easy walk from the road. The steep and slippery streambed is dangerous to climb, but you can bypass it by scrambling up the slope to the right and descending to the upper pools; you'll see where people have gone up this unmarked route. The pools aren't marked either, so look for a short track to a parking area on the south side of the I-8 Foothills Exit 14 road just 1.8 miles from its junction with the Wellton Road. Note that there are two branches of the road across the Tinajas Altas here; you want the southern one.

Permits and Precautions

Visitors must obtain a permit for entry, sign a liability release for the military, and carefully follow regulations—it's especially important not to approach any ordinance or other military hardware. You'll need a 4WD vehicle for all but the Charlie Bell Pass road, as anything else will get stuck in the loose sand. Because 93 percent of the refuge is managed as wilderness, vehicles must stay on specified roads. Be aware that Cabeza Prieta's rough roads can be very hard on vehicles. Heavy brush can scratch up vehicle paint ("Arizona pin-striping"), though this isn't a problem if you're just driving to the Tinajas Altas Mountains from the Yuma area. Carry desert travel supplies and at least two days' worth of extra water. Three campsites on the way have tables and grills, but you're not restricted to these.

Be sure to talk with a refuge officer before your trip to find out current conditions, then let someone know your intended route. Illegal aliens have become a major problem in the refuge, and you may encounter them as well as Border Patrol agents; it's not recommended to leave your vehicle out of sight. Summer temperatures can be downright dangerous. A single permit covers both Cabeza Prieta and surrounding military land. Before heading onto military land, you must telephone authorities with your proposed route and dates; if the coast is clear, you'll get permission.

A good map and directions will be valuable—this isn't a region to get lost in! The refuge office provides a map, but the book *Backcountry Adventures: Arizona* by Peter Massey and Jeanne Wilson has detailed road logs with GPS coordinates.

Three other agencies also provide the permit—the BLM's Phoenix Field Office (21605 N. 7th Ave., Phoenix, AZ 85027, 623/580-5500), Luke Air Force Base (Gila Bend Auxiliary Field, Range Operations, Gila Bend, AZ 85337, 520/683-6200), and the U.S. Marine Corps Air Station (Range Management Dept., Box 99160, Yuma, AZ 85369-9160, 928/269-3402).

Western Arizona

Few landlocked states can boast more than 1,000 miles of shoreline! The Colorado River, after its wild run through the Grand Canyon, begins a new life in the western part of the state. Tamed by massive dams and irrigation projects, the Colorado flows placidly toward the Gulf of California. The deep blue waters of the river and its lakes form Arizona's west boundary, separating the state from Nevada and California. Boaters enjoy this recreational paradise, breezing along the surface or seeking quiet backwaters for fishing. Once you step away from the life-giving waters though, you're in desert country—the real desert—where legends abound of Native American tribes, hardy prospectors, determined pioneer families, and even a U.S. Army camel corps. Old mines and ghost towns dot mineral-rich ranges throughout the region.

Yuma in the south is a good place to experience the region's long history of Native American tribes, Spanish explorers, gold miners, and steamboating. London Bridge, farther north in Lake Havasu City, now seems at home under the Arizona sun; you can admire the bronze lampposts and stonework while walking across it. Kingman in the north plays up its mining and Route 66 heritage with two fine museums. Then from Kingman it's an easy drive up the Hualapai Mountains, crowned by Hualapai Peak (8,417 feet), the region's highest summit.

Wildlife refuges along the Colorado River attract large numbers of waterfowl and other birds, especially during the cooler months. Inland, the Kofa National Wildlife Refuge provides a home for desert bighorn sheep, mule deer, desert tortoise, Gambel's quail, and rare native palm trees.

© BILL WEIR

Must-Sees

Look for to find the sights and activities you can't miss and for the best dining and lodging.

Yuma Territorial Prison State Historic Park has a fine museum where you can see photos of inmates and guards and read their stories about life behind bars during the territorial years. Outside, you can wander the cellblocks, climb up the main watchtower, and wander over to the graveyard (page 232).

London Bridge

Kofa National Wildlife Refuge harbors a rare native palm, which you can easily see at the end of a short trail, and desert bighorn sheep, which take some luck and perseverance to spot. An extensive network of 4WD roads leads to old mines and scenic vistas in rugged desert mountains (page 242).

Swansea is probably Arizona's best-preserved ghost town with extensive ruins of a large brick smelter, train depot, company housing, and a store (page 250).

London Bridge, an authentic relic from early-19th-century England, now spans a channel at Lake Havasu City (page 251).

Mohave Museum of History and Arts in Kingman tells the story of northwestern Arizona through a recreated Hualapai wickiup brush shelter, ranching and mining exhibits, and a display on the construction of Hoover Dam. You'll see a special exhibit on native son actor Andy Devine and portraits of all U.S. presidents with their first ladies (page 260).

Route 66 Museum takes you back to the times when a road trip meant adventure. Exhibits illustrate each stage of travel along the 35th parallel from early trade routes and the 19th-century Beale Wagon Road to the Great Depression migrations and, finally, the good times that followed WW II (page 261).

Hoover Dam still stands as one of the world's most amazing engineering accomplishments. A large multilevel visitors center provides a multimedia presentation, many historic photos, and a look inside the cavernous Nevada Power Wing. (page 274).

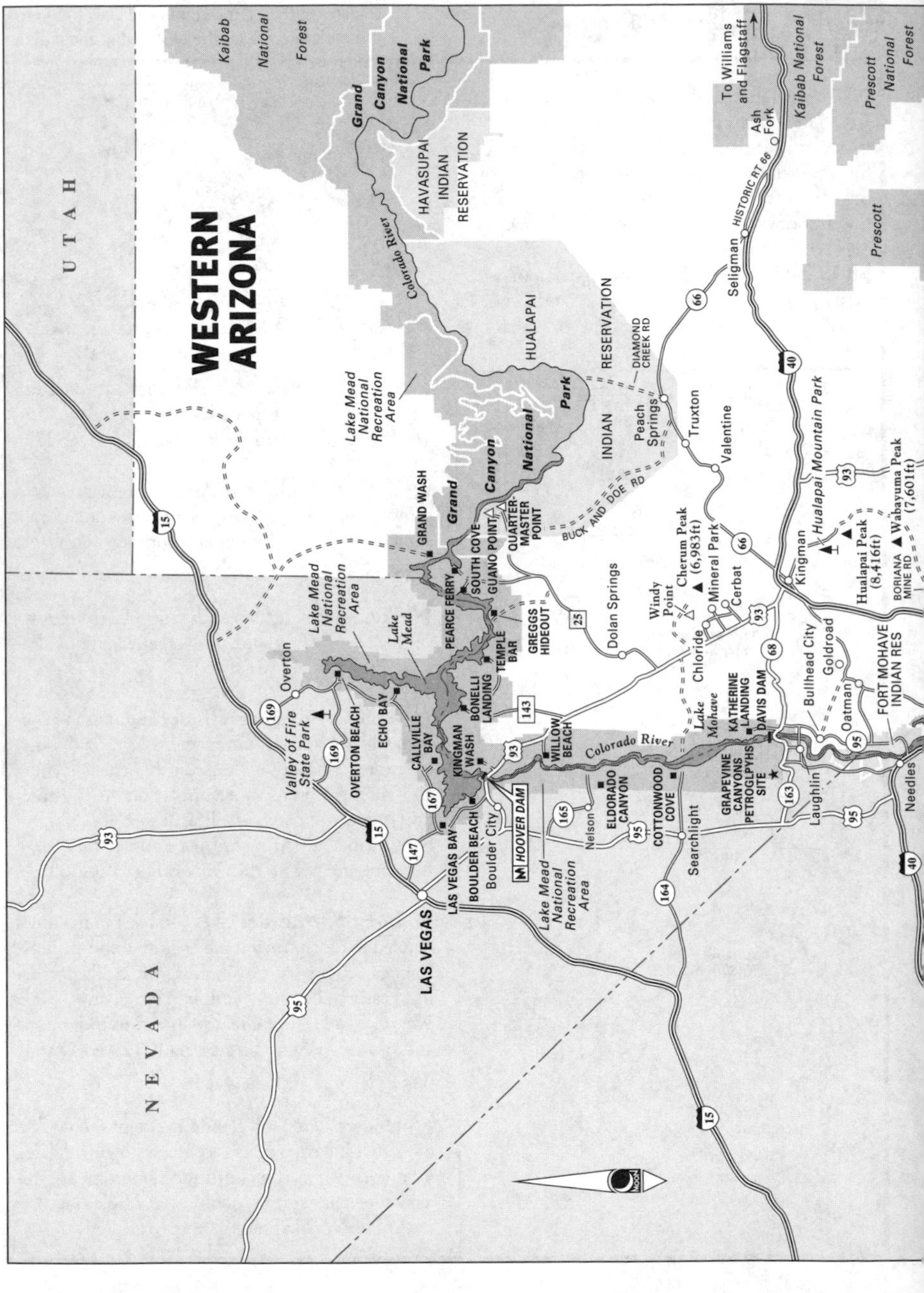
WESTERN ARIZONA
UTAH
NEVADA
Kaibab National Forest
Grand Canyon National Park
HAVASUPAI INDIAN RESERVATION
Colorado River
Lake Mead National Recreation Area
HUALAPAI INDIAN RESERVATION
DIAMOND CREEK RD
Peach Springs
Truxton
Valentine
Seligman
HISTORIC RT 66
Ash Fork
To Williams and Flagstaff
Kaibab National Forest
Prescott National Forest
Prescott
Hualapai Mountain Park
Wabayuma Peak (7,601ft)
Hualapai Peak (8,416ft)
BORIANA MINE RD
Kingman
GRAND WASH
SOUTH COVE
GUANO POINT
QUARTER-MASTER POINT
BUCK AND DOE RD
PEARCE FERRY
GREGGS HIDEOUT
TEMPLE BAR
BONELLI LANDING
Lake Mead
Dolan Springs
Windy Point
Cherum Peak (6,983ft)
Mineral Park
Cerbat
Chloride
Overton
OVERTON BEACH
ECHO BAY
CALLVILLE BAY
KINGMAN WASH
Valley of Fire State Park
LAS VEGAS BAY
BOULDER BEACH
Boulder City
HOOVER DAM
WILLOW BEACH
ELDORADO CANYON
Nelson
COTTONWOOD COVE
Searchlight
Lake Mohave
KATHERINE LANDING
DAVIS DAM
GRAPEVINE CANYONS PETROGLYPHS SITE
Laughlin
Bullhead City
Goldroad
Oatman
FORT MOHAVE INDIAN RES
Needles
LAS VEGAS
15
93
95
147
164
165
167
169
143
25
68
66
40
163
MOON

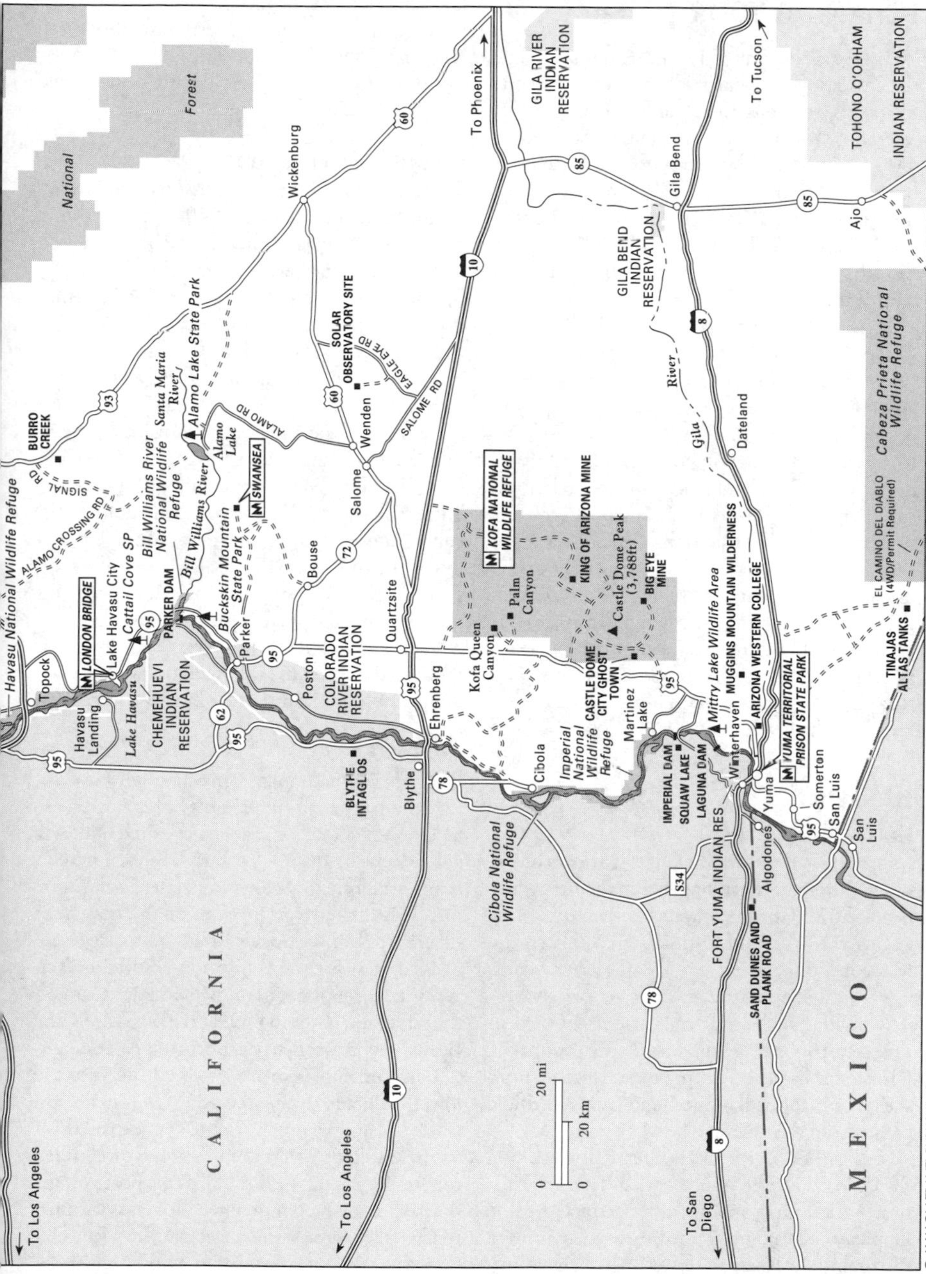
Havasu National Wildlife Refuge
Topock
LONDON BRIDGE
Lake Havasu City
Cattail Cove SP
Havasu Landing
Lake Havasu
CHEMEHUEVI INDIAN RESERVATION
PARKER DAM
Bill Williams River National Wildlife Refuge
Bill Williams River
Buckskin Mountain State Park
Parker
Poston
COLORADO RIVER INDIAN RESERVATION
Quartzsite
Bouse
Salome
SWANSEA
ALAMO CROSSING RD
SIGNAL RD
BURRO CREEK
Alamo Lake
Alamo Lake State Park
Santa Maria River
ALAMO RD
Wenden
SALOME RD
SOLAR OBSERVATORY SITE
EAGLE EYE RD
Wickenburg
National Forest
To Phoenix
GILA RIVER INDIAN RESERVATION
Gila Bend
GILA BEND INDIAN RESERVATION
To Tucson
TOHONO O'ODHAM INDIAN RESERVATION
Ajo
Cabeza Prieta National Wildlife Refuge
EL CAMINO DEL DIABLO (4WD/Permit Required)
TINAJAS ALTAS TANKS
Dateland
Gila River
KOFA NATIONAL WILDLIFE REFUGE
Palm Canyon
Kofa Queen Canyon
KING OF ARIZONA MINE
Castle Dome Peak (3,788ft)
BIG EYE MINE
CASTLE DOME CITY GHOST TOWN
MUGGINS MOUNTAIN WILDERNESS
Mittry Lake Wildlife Area
ARIZONA WESTERN COLLEGE
YUMA TERRITORIAL PRISON STATE PARK
Martinez Lake
Imperial National Wildlife Refuge
Winterhaven
Yuma
Somerton
San Luis
IMPERIAL DAM
SQUAW LAKE
LAGUNA DAM
FORT YUMA INDIAN RES
Algodones
SAND DUNES AND PLANK ROAD
Cibola
Cibola National Wildlife Refuge
Ehrenberg
Blythe
BLYTHE INTAGLIOS
C A L I F O R N I A
M E X I C O
To Los Angeles
To Los Angeles
To San Diego
0 20 mi
0 20 km
© AVALON TRAVEL PUBLISHING, INC.

PLANNING YOUR TIME

Yuma, Lake Havasu City, and Kingman make the best bases to explore this region, or stay in one of the resorts along the Colorado River and its reservoirs. You'll need your own transport, and a 4WD vehicle will be handy for exploring the backcountry and searching out remote ghost towns. You might like to bring or rent a boat as well. Allow a week to take in all the highlights, though many visitors stay for months at a time in winter and early spring.

Western Arizona's star attractions lie outdoors, so the weather will be the biggest factor to consider for your trip. Come in the cooler months to enjoy fishing, prospecting, four-wheeling, and hiking in the desert. This is also the best time to admire the geology, migratory bird flocks, and desert flora. The land bakes under a relentless sun from May to September, and you'll probably wish to either flee or head for the cool waters of the Colorado River and its lakes. Only in the north are the mountains high enough to catch cool breezes in summer, when a drive into the Hualapai Mountains near Kingman has extra appeal. Annual rainfall ranges from less than three inches in the south near Yuma to about 10 inches in the high country.

HISTORY

Native Americans

Indigenous groups lived along the shores of the lower Colorado River long before the first white people arrived. Frequent wars between the tribes, lasting into the mid-19th century, forced the Maricopa to migrate up the Gila River to what is now south-central Arizona. The victorious Mohave, Quechan, and Cocopa tribes—joined in the early 1800s by a nomadic Paiute group, the Chemehuevi—lived simply in brush-and-mud shelters and farmed, hunted, and gathered edible plants from the desert.

Today they have a series of reservations along the Colorado River. Many work at farms or casinos. Agricultural opportunities attracted some Hopi and Navajo from northeastern Arizona to the Colorado River Reservation. Their voluntary resettlement, begun in 1945, came about because the reservation was established to serve "Indians of said river and its tributaries" and because the Colorado River Tribal Council gave the go-ahead.

Spanish Explorations

Spanish explorers made their first tentative forays up the Colorado River in 1540, but they didn't stay. The tireless Jesuit priest Eusebio Francisco Kino explored the lower Colorado in 1700–1702, promoting Christianity and collecting information for the mapmakers of the day.

During the 1760s, fear of Russian expansion down the coast of California caused the Spanish to build settlements there and to open a land route from Mexico. In 1780, Spanish troops and missionaries built two missions on the Colorado River, La Purísima Concepción (opposite today's Yuma) and nearby San Pedro y San Pablo de Bicuner. Abuses by these foreigners infuriated local Quechan Indians, who revolted the following year. They killed Father Francisco Garcés and most of the other male Spaniards and took the women and children as prisoners. Spanish troops ransomed the captives, but made no more attempts to settle along the Colorado River.

Anglos Arrive

Rugged mountain men such as James Ohio Pattie, who later wrote an account of his travels, explored the Colorado River area in search of beaver and adventure during the early 1800s. The U.S Army established Camp Yuma, later Fort Yuma, in 1851 at the river crossing of the Southern Overland Trail (Cooke's Road) to assist those headed west for the California goldfields. Ten years later, troops built Fort Mohave upstream on the Colorado River to protect travelers along the Beale Wagon Road across northern Arizona.

Government surveyors explored much of the lower Colorado during the 1850s, but maps still labeled a large region upstream as "unexplored." It wasn't until 1869 that John Wesley Powell filled the last big gap on the first of his epic boat voyages down the Colorado from Green River, Wyoming, to Callville, Nevada (now under Lake Mead).

Although Spanish miners worked gold deposits in western Arizona before Mexican independence in 1821, large-scale mining in the region didn't begin until the 1860s. Gold discovered in 1858 at Gila City, 20 miles upstream from Yuma, attracted 1,200 miners by 1861. Three years later the gold played out, and a traveler reported, "The promising metropolis of Arizona consisted of three chimneys and a coyote." Prospectors later found many other gold and silver deposits up and down western Arizona, hastening development of the region. Lead-zinc and copper mines opened, too. Most of the old workings lie abandoned now, marked by piles of tailings, foundations, and decaying walls.

Steamboats plied the Colorado River after 1852, providing faster and safer transport than wagon trains. For more than 50 years they served the forts and mining camps along the river. Some of the riverboats stood three decks high and measured more than 140 feet long, yet drew only two feet of water. These giant sternwheelers took on cargo from oceangoing ships at Port Isabel on the Gulf of California, then headed upstream as far as 600 miles. Boat traffic declined when the Southern Pacific Railroad went through Yuma in 1877, and it virtually ended in 1909 with the construction of Laguna Dam.

Yuma

Yuma's rich historical background and sunny, subtropical climate make it an attractive destination. In winter, snowbirds double and even triple the town's year-round population of 83,330. RVs spread across the landscape, filling the many RV parks in town, along the river, and out on the desert. Boaters and anglers explore countless lakes and quiet backwaters on the Colorado River. Date palms, citrus trees, and vegetables on irrigated farmlands add a touch of green. The Mexican border towns of Algodones (8.5 miles southwest) and San Luis (25 miles south) offer colorful shopping.

HISTORY

Yuma's Beginnings

The long recorded history of Yuma begins in 1540, nearly 70 years before the founding of Jamestown, Virginia. Captain Hernando de Alarcón, the first white person to visit the area, led a Spanish naval expedition along the west coast of Mexico and then a short way up the Colorado River. He hoped to meet and resupply Francisco Vásquez de Coronado's expedition to the fabled Seven Cities of Cíbola farther east, but the two groups never met.

While searching for a land route between Mexico and California, Spanish explorers discovered that the best crossing on the lower Colorado River lay just below the mouth of the Gila River. Soldiers and missionaries built a fort and missions here, across from present-day Yuma. Angry Quechan destroyed the settlements during a violent uprising in 1781, ending Spanish domination of Yuma Crossing.

Although small bands of mountain men started drifting through in the early 1800s, little attention was paid to the area until the Mexican War. Kit Carson passed this way in 1829 with a group of trappers, returning in 1846 to guide Colonel Stephen Kearny and 100 soldiers endeavoring to secure former Mexican lands between Santa Fe and San Diego. Colonel Philip Cooke followed with the Mormon Battalion and supply wagons, blazing the first transcontinental road across the Southwest. Crowds of '49ers, seeking gold in the Sierra Nevada of California, pushed westward along Cooke's Road a few years later.

In 1851, the army built Camp Yuma atop a hill on the California side to protect Yuma Crossing from attacks by local tribes. Nearby mining successes, the coming of steamboats, and road improvements encouraged the founding of Colorado City on the Arizona shore in 1854. Residents changed the name to Arizona City in 1858, rebuilt on higher ground after a disastrous 1862 flood, and adopted the present name of Yuma in 1873. Yuma Territorial Prison, the town's first major construction project, went up in 1876. Laguna Dam ended the riverboat era in 1909, but guaranteed water for the fertile desert valleys.

Modern Yuma

Today Yuma ranks as one of Arizona's most important cities and the center of a rich agricultural area. Farmers take advantage of the year-round growing season to raise more than 100 crops. The military has a big presence, and you'll likely see aircraft speeding overhead from the Marine Corps Air Station on the southeast edge of town. The army tests combat vehicles, weapons systems, and other gear at Yuma Proving Grounds, 26 miles north.

Downtown Yuma invites exploration on foot. The Yuma Convention and Visitors Bureau makes a good starting point for a visit to shops and galleries on Main Street. Entertainment spots include Yuma Art Center and Theatre (254 S. Main), Lute's Casino (221 S. Main), and Main Street Cinemas (111 S. Main). To reach the Century House Museum, follow the row of small shops bearing the sign "224 Main Street" to Madison Avenue. A riverside park lies at the north end of Madison. To visit the Yuma Quartermaster Depot, you could follow the Riverside Trail downstream from either the prison or the riverside park; or walk west on 1st Street (not Avenue) from Madison past Yuma City Hall and turn right on 4th Avenue.

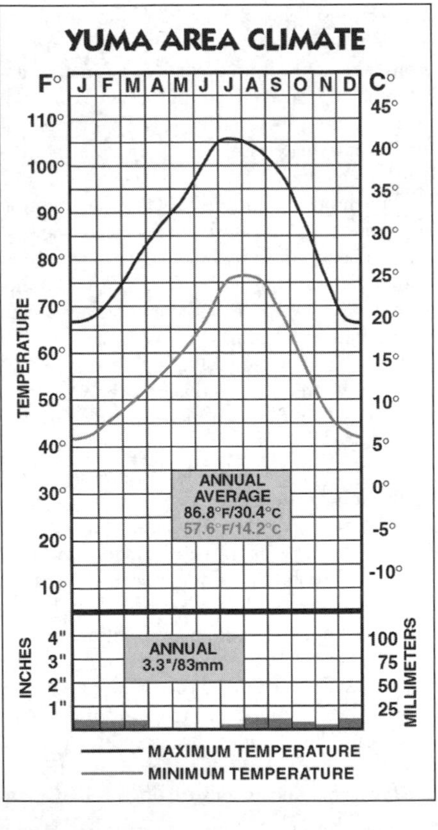

AVALON PUBLISHING

SIGHTS

Yuma Territorial Prison State Historic Park

The old prison (1 Prison Hill Rd., 928/783-4771, 8 A.M.–5 P.M. daily, $4 adults, $2 ages 7–13) has a colorful history. Photos in the museum show the faces of men and women once imprisoned here and of those who guarded them. Stories tell of inmates, guards, riots, and escape attempts. A model shows how the prison originally looked. Outside, you can wander through the cellblocks, climb the main watchtower, and visit the prison graveyard. Staff offer a video program on request and lead winter-time walking tours. Old West reenactors bring pistol-packing action on Sundays October–April and in the Gathering of the Gunfighters on the second weekend of January.

Picnic tables are available on the grounds and in a small park off Prison Hill Road. A gift shop sells books and souvenirs. For additional information about the history of the prison, consult the well-illustrated *Prison Centennial 1876–1976* by Cliff Trafzer and Steve George.

Take Prison Hill Road off Giss Parkway near I-8 Exit 1. You can walk **Riverside Trail** along the shore of the Colorado between here and Yuma Crossing State Historic Park, .9 miles one-way. There's a $1 discount if you visit both state parks in Yuma on the same day.

Yuma Crossing State Historic Park

On a visit to the history-filled buildings (201 N.

YUMA TERRITORIAL PRISON

In 1875 the Territorial Legislature was set to award $25,000 to Phoenix for construction of a major prison. But Yuma's representatives, Jose Maria Redondo and R. B. Kelly, did some fast talking and won the project for their hometown.

The righteous citizens of the territory were fed up with murders, robberies, and other lawless acts on the frontier, and they wanted bad characters behind bars. The niceties of reform and rehabilitation didn't concern them. Yuma, surrounded by hostile deserts and the treacherous currents of the Colorado and Gila Rivers, seemed the ideal spot for a prison.

All prisoners endured searing 120°F summer temperatures; recalcitrant inmates faced the confinement in a Dark Cell. Prisoners themselves built the stone and adobe walls, as money and labor were scarce.

Most of Yuma's convicts were locked away for acts of robbery. Other crimes of the time that could get people to Yuma included seduction, polygamy, adultery, and obstructing a railroad. No executions took place here, though a number of prisoners died trying to escape.

Despite its notoreity today, Yuma in the late 19th century had a reputation as a model prison. It provided benefits and services unknown at other pens of the age; prisoners enjoyed a library, workshop, school, and hospital. Some critics even called it a "country club."

During the 33 years of prison operation, 29 women and about 3,000 men paced the yard and gazed between iron bars. The prison withstood the toughest outlaws of frontier Arizona's wildest years until it outgrew its site and closed in 1909. The remaining 40 prisoners marched in shackles down Prison Hill to a train waiting to take them to a new cage in Florence. High school students in Yuma attended classes at the prison from 1910 to 1914, and even today the Yuma High School sports teams call themselves the Yuma Criminals.

© BILL WEIR

The "hellhole of Arizona" was once considered a model prison.

4th Ave., just before the Colorado River bridge, 928/329-0471, 10 A.M.–5 P.M. daily, $4 adults, $2 ages 7–13) here beside the Colorado River, you'll see how import the site was for past travelers. The army chose this spot for its Yuma Quartermaster Depot after 1865 to supply military posts in the Southwest during the Indian wars. Ships carried cargo to Port Isabel, near the mouth of the Colorado River, where dockworkers transferred goods to river steamers for the trip to Yuma. The oldest buildings have been restored to their mid-1870s appearance, when the depot was at its peak. In the years after, the railroad arrived and greatly reduced waterfront business. The supply depot closed in 1883 and the Signal Corps telegraph office shut down in 1891, but the U.S Weather Service operated here until 1949. Except for the stone reservoir, all structures have walls of adobe, because that was the only material early builders had in abundance.

A 30-minute video in the visitor center illustrates the changes and conflicts brought by Native Americans, Spanish missions, mountain men, the '49ers, and pioneers. A 1909 Model-T Ford rests on a section of plank road once used to cross nearby sand dunes; it represents the last link of the Ocean-to-Ocean Highway that passed through here on the way to San Diego. Historic photos and documents also help to tell the story of Yuma Crossing.

You can look into the restored rooms of the Commanding Officer's Quarters, built in the

1850s and possibly the oldest Anglo house in Arizona. Prints and maps in the 1872 quartermaster depot illustrate life in the army; the telegraph office here looks ready for business. A surviving storehouse holds a collection of wagons and steamboat relics; the 1931 Model-A truck comes from a time when dust-bowl victims passed this way hoping for a new life in California. A 1907 Southern Pacific steam locomotive and a passenger car sit outside. Over in the north end of the corral house, U.S. Bureau of Reclamation Service exhibits tell of the Yuma Project and why a 1,000-foot-long siphon had to be built under the Colorado River to bring river water to the Arizona side. On weekends during winter, members of the Yuma Weavers & Spinners demonstrate their skills in another part of the corral house. Picnic tables lie around the site.

Sanguinetti House Museum

Built in the 1870s and one of Yuma's oldest buildings (240 S. Madison Ave., 928/782-1841, 10 A.M.–4 P.M. Tues.–Sat., $3 adult, $2 youth 12–18 and seniors 60+), it's the former home of influential businessman E. F. Sanguinetti. Exhibits relate the history of Yuma Crossing—the lives of Native Americans, explorers, missionaries, soldiers, miners, riverboat captains, and early settlers. Period rooms and a changing gallery provide additional perspectives. The garden out back harbors flaming bougainvillea and chattering parakeets, colorful parrots, and peacocks.

The 1873 **Adobe Annex** next door sells local crafts and offers an excellent selection of books on regional history, tribes, and gold mining. Farther back, the **Garden Café** serves breakfast and lunch from early October to the end of May on a patio adjacent to the museum gardens; you can browse a gourmet gift shop, too. The Annex and café close on Monday.

Yuma Art Center

Exhibits and theater productions appear downtown (254 S. Main St., 928/329-6607 art exhibits, 928/373-5202 theater, www.yumafinearts.com). The four fine art galleries are open 1–5 P.M. Sunday, 10 A.M.–6 P.M. Tuesday–Saturday ($3 adult, $2.50 seniors, students, and children 6–12).

Yuma Valley Railway

All aboard for a short excursion along a levee of the Colorado River! On weekends October–May, a 1943 diesel-electric locomotive pulls a series of vintage coaches on a round-trip lasting a little over two hours. There'll be entertainment along the way, and a crewmember will tell you about local history, farming, canals, Cocopah land, and other lore. Trips depart at 1 P.M. on Sunday (Oct.–May) and Saturday (Jan.–May); call to check times and to see if dinner or other special rides are offered (downtown near 1st St. and 2nd Ave., 928/783-3456, $17 adults, $16 seniors 55+, and $8 ages 4–12).

Quechan Indian Museum (Fort Yuma)

On the hill just across the Colorado River from Yuma, the museum building dates from 1855 and the days of Camp Yuma. Renamed Fort Yuma in 1861, the site now belongs to the Quechan, who established a museum and tribal

© BILL WEIR

Chief Mechanical Officer Robert Senko at the controls

offices here. Museum exhibits (760/572-0661, 8 A.M.–5 P.M. Mon.–Fri., 10 A.M.–4 P.M. Sat. Arizona time, $1, free for children under 12) illustrate the arrival of the Spanish missionary Father Francisco Garcés, the Quechan Revolt, history of Fort Yuma, and Quechan life. Artifacts include clay figurines, flutes, gourd rattles, headdresses, bows and arrows, and war clubs. No photos allowed.

Note that the museum may close noon–1 P.M. for lunch some days. To reach it, take the 1915 Ocean-to-Ocean Bridge across the river and turn left at the sign; alternatively, head over on I-8 or 4th Avenue to Winterhaven, turn right on S24, and follow signs for the casino. The nearby 1922 St. Thomas Mission occupies the site of Concepción Mission, where Quechan murdered Father Garcés in 1781.

ENTERTAINMENT, EVENTS, AND RECREATION

For the cultural scene, contact the **Yuma Art Center** (928/329-6607 art exhibits, 928/373-5206 theater, www.yumafinearts.com). Take in local color downtown at **Lute's Casino** (221 S. Main St., 928/782-2192), a popular spot to play dominoes, pinball, and pool. The snack bar serves up burgers and tacos. Unfortunately, Lute's doesn't have a nonsmoking area.

Catch movies at **Main Street Cinemas** (111 S. Main St., 928/819-0289), **Plaza Theatres** (1560 S. 4th Ave., 928/782-9292), or **Mandarin Cinemas** (3142 S. Arizona Ave., 928/782-7409).

Both local tribes have smoky casinos. The Quechan offer **Paradise Casino** (across the river, 888/777-4946). The Cocopah have the **Cocopah Casino** (south of town at the junction of U.S. 95 and 15th St., 800/237-5687).

Events

January: Arizona Antique Show, All State Picnic (a big snowbird jamboree), YRMC Tractor Rodeo, and Americana Art & Gem Show.

February: Silver Spur Rodeo and Parade, Yuma Square Dance & Round Dance, Yuma River Daze Air Show at the Marine Corps Air Station (in March some years), and Quechan Pow Wow (in March some years).

March: Midnight at the Oasis Festival (classic car show).

April: Yuma County Fair (in March some years), Yuma Birding & Nature Festival (www.yumabirding.org).

May: Cinco de Mayo Parade & Celebration.

July: July 4th Celebration.

September: Hispanic Heritage Fiesta Night.

October: Oktoberfest and YRMC Western Dance & Barbecue.

November: Children's Festival of the Arts, Quilt & Antique Fair, Colorado River Crossing Balloon Festival, and Día de los Muertos.

December: *Nutcracker* ballet, Christmas Open House on Main Street (parade and tree lighting), and Desert Holiday Arts & Crafts Bazaar.

Recreation

You'll find public **swimming pools** (Yuma Parks and Recreation, 928/783-1284) at Carver on the corner of 5th Street and 13th Avenue, at Kennedy on the corner of 24th Street and Kennedy Lane, and at Marcus on the corner of 5th Street and 5th Avenue. Play **tennis** at **Desert Sun Courts** (near the Convention Center, 35th St. and Ave. A, 928/344-3800). For a round of **golf**, try one of the 12 public courses in the area, such the 18-hole courses at **Arroyo Dunes** (1301 W. 32nd St. and Ave. A, 928/726-8350), **Desert Hills Municipal** (1245 Desert Hills Dr., 928/344-0644), and **Mesa del Sol** (12213 E. Calle del Cid, 928/342-1283). You'll find shooting and archery ranges at **Adair Park** (16 miles northeast of Yuma off U.S. 95, 928/726-0022 Sprague's Sports).

Anglers on the Colorado River and nearby lakes catch largemouth bass, striped bass, channel catfish, tilapia, bluegill, and crappie. Check fishing regulations with **Arizona Game and Fish** (928/342-0091) or **Quechan Indian Fish and Game** in California (760/572-0213). The Visitors Bureau offers fishing information.

ACCOMMODATIONS

Yuma, midway between Phoenix and San Diego, is a popular travelers' stop. You'll find most of the two dozen or so motels along 4th Avenue, which is part of the Business Loop between I-8 and 9. Newer motels form another clus- ɔst off I-8 16th Street Exit 2. Except for the ɔoric hotel, all of places listed below offer ɔools, which you can appreciate much of the year. Rates start around $30 for the independents and $40 for the chains during the peak season of January–March, then drop in summer.

Historic Hotel

The 1917 **Hotel Lee** (390 S. Main St., 928/783-6336, $30 s, $35–90 d) takes you back in time with its antique decor while offering modern amenities such as minifridges, microwaves, TV, and air-conditioning. Some rooms have private baths, but none include a telephone.

Under $50

Independents include **RegaLodge Motel** (344 S. 4th Ave., 928/782-4571, $45 s, $49 d), **El Rancho Motel** (2201 S. 4th Ave., 928/783-4481, $42 s, $47 d), and **Royal Motor Inn** (2941 S. 4th Ave., 928/344-0550 or 800/729-0550, $49 d).

$50–100

Some of these will drop below $50 off-season or if business is slow. **Best Western Coronado Motor Hotel** (233 4th Ave., 928/783-4453 or 877/234-5567, www.bwcoronado.com, $72 s, $79.50 d and up) has a handy location near the downtown sights, plus a restaurant and two pools; the mission revival–style building dates from 1938 and is one of the oldest Best Westerns. Farther south you can look for **Hacienda Motel** (2150 S. 4th Ave., 928/782-4316, $50 s, $58 d), **Yuma Cabana** (2151 S. 4th Ave., 928/783-8311 or 800/874-0811, $52 s, $56 d), **Torch Lite Lodge** (2501 S. 4th Ave., 928/344-1600, $45 d), **Interstate 8 Inn** (2730 S. 4th Ave., 928/726-6110 or 800/821-7465, $60 d), **Desert Grove** (3500 S. 4th Ave., 928/726-1400, $70 d), and **Quality Inn** (711 E. 32nd St., 928/726-4721 or 800/835-1132, $90 d).

Just south off I-8 Exit 2, you'll find the least expensive chains, **Motel 6 Yuma East** (1445 E. 16th St., 928/782-9521 or 800/466-8356, $54 s, $60 d) and nearby **Motel 6 Downtown** (1640 S. Arizona Ave., 928/782-6561 or 800/466-8356, $52 s, $58 d).

$100–150

These and several other top-end motels lie just north of I-8 Exit 2. Rooms of **La Fuente Inn** (1513 E. 16th St., 928/329-1814 or 800/841-1814, www.lafuenteinn.com, $98–109 d) overlook a courtyard with a pool and barbecue grills. The large **Shilo Inn** (1550 S. Castle Dome Ave., 928/782-9511 or 800/222-2244, www.shiloinns.com, $93–103) offers a restaurant, full breakfast buffet, pool, spa, sauna, and fitness center.

Campgrounds

The 175 or so RV parks in and around Yuma cater mostly to retired people. Only a few parks welcome families with children. Similarly, very few places will consider renting tent spaces and then only off-season. Ask the Yuma County Chamber of Commerce for a list of RV parks. Some of the best camping—and the places to go for tenting—lie upstream on the Colorado River.

On the west side of town, **Lucky Park del Sur** (5790 W. 8th St., 928/783-7201, $18 RV w/hookups) has family spaces. **Blue Sky RV** (10247 E. Frontage Rd., 928/342-1444, $25 tent or RV w/hookups) also accepts families and offers showers, a pool, and a hot tub; take I-8 Fortuna Exit 12, then head west a half mile on the south frontage road.

Dateland (65 miles east at I-8 Exit 67, 928/454-2772) offers tent ($13) and RV sites ($16 w/hookups) with showers. The Mexican-American café here is open daily for breakfast, lunch, and dinner; try the tasty date milkshake. Nearby **Oasis RV Park** (928/454-2229) has a more secluded setting with tent ($14) and RV ($20 w/hookups) sites, plus a few rooms for rent. Amenities include showers, a pool, and hiking in the Aztec Hills; continue past Dateland to road's end, turn left two miles, then right at the sign to the entrance.

FOOD

A drive along 4th Avenue will turn up lots of restaurants offering American, Mexican, or Asian food, plus some supermarkets—you can't go hungry here! The following highlights are worth searching out.

American

Julieanna's Patio Café (1951 W. 25th St., 928/317-1961, Mon.–Fri. lunch, Mon.–Sat. dinner, $7–10 lunch and $16–25 dinner) has a romantic garden setting, especially at dinner with flickering candlelight. You can choose patio or indoor seating. The lunch menu lists tempting sandwiches, soups, salads, pizza, meat and seafood entrées, and even a few breakfast items for people who like their eggs in the afternoon. Dinner brings out choices of steaks, prime rib, rack of lamb, chicken, seafood, and pasta; there's a good wine list, too. From 24th Street, turn south one block on 19th Avenue and you'll see the sign.

Birds will serenade you at the **Garden Café** (250 Madison Ave., 928/783-1491, Tues.–Sun. breakfast and lunch, early Oct.–May). Varied choices include sandwiches, quiches, soups, salads, and grilled meats. It's downtown, next door to the aviary and gardens of the Sanguinetti House Museum.

Yuma Landing Restaurant (near downtown at 195 S. 4th Ave., 928/782-7427, daily breakfast, lunch, and dinner, $6–13) has a great choice of sandwiches, steaks, chicken, pork ribs, and seafood, plus some Mexican and pasta items. The restaurant's name commemorates the landing on this site in 1911 of a Wright Model B airplane piloted by Bob Fowler. He continued on his journey from Santa Monica to Miami and became the first person to complete a Pacific to Atlantic flight. Step inside to see photos of the pilot and plane along with many other scenes of early Yuma.

Italian

Villa on the Main (265 Main St., 928/782-2702, Mon.–Sat. lunch, Tues.–Sat. dinner, $13–20) is a simple Italian restaurant downtown offering steak, prime rib, veal, seafood, and pasta dishes. Artwork decorates the walls.

Mexican

For great Mexican food at bargain prices, follow the locals to **Chretin's** (485 S. 15th Ave., 928/782-1291, Mon.–Sat. lunch and dinner, $6.55–11). It started as a dance hall in the 1930s with the wife selling tacos at events. Now diners fill the adobe hall and enjoy the many entrées, such as the machaca (shredded beef or chicken), steaks, and Mexican pizza. The enchilada sauce, available with many dishes, is a hit, as are the margaritas. Expect some noise as families will be out enjoying themselves. Posters, nacho-eating contest results, and Mexican kitsch cover the walls. From 4th Avenue, turn south on 5th Street and look for the sign near 15th Street.

Asian

A pair of stone lions at the entrance set the mood for **Mandarin Palace** (350 E. 32nd St., 928/344-2805, $9–14). Chefs prepare Mandarin and Szechwan cuisine for the à la carte menu and the buffet, both available daily for lunch and dinner. The Friday and Saturday dinner buffets feature steak and seafood as well as the usual large choice of Chinese items.

INFORMATION AND SERVICES

The **Yuma Convention & Visitors Bureau** (377 S. Main St., Yuma, AZ 85364, 928/783-0071 or 800/293-0071, www.visityuma.com) is downtown at the corner of Giss Parkway and Maiden Lane, just off I-8 Exit 1. In the cooler months, it's open 10 A.M.–2 P.M. Sunday, 9 A.M.–6 P.M. Monday–Friday, and 9 A.M.–4 P.M. Saturday; in summer (May–Sept.) the office closes at 5 P.M. on weekdays, 2 P.M. on Saturday, and all day Sunday. The Visitors Bureau publishes a very informative visitors guide with descriptions of sights and listings of practicalities.

The **Kofa National Wildlife Refuge** (downtown at 356 W. First St., Yuma, AZ 85364, 928/783-7861, southwest.fws.gov, 8 A.M.–4:30 P.M. Mon.–Fri.) has information about the Kofa backcountry. Staff at the **BLM's Yuma field office** (2555 E. Gila Ridge Rd., Yuma, AZ 85365, 928/317-3200, yuma.az.blm.gov, 7:45 A.M.–4:30 P.M. Mon.–Fri.) can advise on camping and hiking in much of the region; take I-8 Exit 3, turn south, make a right at the first light, and the office will be on your left. **Arizona Game and Fish** (9140 E. County 10½ St., Yuma, AZ 85365, 928/342-0091, www.azgfd.com, 8 A.M.–5 P.M. Mon.–Fri.) offers information, licenses, and watercraft registration.

The large and attractive **Yuma Library** (350

…ve., 928/782-1871, www.yumalibrary.org) …n 9 A.M.–9 P.M. Monday–Thursday and 9 …–5 P.M. Friday–Saturday; call for the six branch …cations and their hours. Books of regional interest can be purchased at **Barnes & Noble** (819 W. 32nd St., 928/317-1466) and across the street at **Hastings** (501 W. Catalina Dr., 928/344-4614).

Services

The main **post office** (2222 S. 4th Ave., 928/783-2124) is in the south part of town, as is the **Yuma Regional Medical Center** (2400 S. Ave. A, 928/344-2000). **Schuman Insurance Agency** (670 E. 32nd St. #11, 928/726-0300) offers auto insurance and information for drives into Mexico. **Wal-Mart** (2900 S. Pacific Ave., 928/344-0992) and **Big Five Sporting Goods** (505 W. Catalina Dr. near the junction of 4th Ave. and 32nd St., 928/726-2884) sell hiking and camping gear.

TRANSPORTATION

Getting There

Yuma International Airport (2191 E. 32nd St., 928/726-5882, http://yumainternationalairport.com) is conveniently located on the south side of town; the terminal has a restaurant and car rentals. **America West** (800/235-9292, www.americawest.com) offers daily service to Phoenix. **United Express** (800/241-6522, www.united.com) will take you to Los Angeles. Both airlines offer many onward connections.

Greyhound (170 E. 17th Place, 928/783-4403 or 800/231-2222, www.greyhound.com) has bus service several times daily east to Phoenix and Tucson and west to Los Angeles and San Diego. The bus station is off 16th Street behind Staples, two blocks east of 4th Avenue.

Amtrak (281 Gila St., 800/872-7245, www.amtrak.com) runs the Sunset Limited three times a week west to Los Angeles and east to Tucson and beyond.

TourWest Travel (downtown at 333 S. Main St., 928/343-4848) sells both air and Amtrak tickets.

Getting Around

The downtown sights can be covered on foot, but you'll need a car or taxi to go farther afield.

Skim across the Colorado River by jet boat with **Yuma River Tours** (1920 Arizona Ave., between 19th and 20th Sts., 928/783-4400, www.yumarivertours.com). The popular five-hour tour in the Imperial Wildlife Refuge takes in the region's beauty and rich mining history; $56 including lunch, $46 children 4–12. Trips go year-round (10-person minimum); shorter and longer trips can also be arranged. Boats leave from Fisher Landing on Martinez Lake, 36 miles north of Yuma.

The paddlewheel ***Colorado King I*** (1636 S. 4th Ave., 928/782-2412, www.coloradoking.com) will take you out on the river for a narrated three-hour tour. Cruises cost $30 ($20 age 12 and under); with lunch they run $37 ($25 age 12 and under). Trips leave October–May from Fisher's Landing on Martinez Lake.

SIGHTS EAST ALONG I-8

Dome Valley Museum

This collection of hundreds of tractors will enchant any farmer or farmer-at-heart! You'll see many models of the well-known makes, as well as some rare and unusual machines. The streamlined tractors in one shed weren't really built for speed, but for deflecting branches in orchards. Also on display are a 1915 10-ton electric truck, steam tractors, combines and other harvesting equipment, long lineups of pedal tractors and cars, old toys, and three period kitchens. A gift shop sells memorabilia. From Yuma, follow I-8 east and take Dome Valley Exit 21, then continue east 1.4 miles on the north frontage road to the junction with Dome Valley Road. You can also get here from U.S. 95 by following 13 miles of zigzagging farm roads; turn east on Co 3rd Street between Mileposts 40 and 41 (in Wellton 21 miles east of Yuma, 20828 South Dome Valley Rd., 928/785-9081, 10 A.M.–5 P.M. daily Nov.–April 15, $7 adult, $12 couple, and $4 youth 10–17).

Muggins Mountains Wilderness

Reportedly named after a prospector's burro, Muggins Peak (1,424 ft.) towers fortresslike above a rugged landscape. Volcanic eruptions four million years ago left behind the light-colored rhyolite that now forms the jagged peaks and ridges that you see all around. Saguaro, ironwood, and other plants of the Sonoran Desert cling to the rocky slopes. Washes and unsigned trails provide easy access. The 7,640-acre wilderness, managed by the BLM's Yuma field office (928/317-3200), lies only 25 miles east of Yuma.

From Yuma, head east on I-8 to Dome Valley Exit 21 and follow the north frontage road east 1.4 miles. Turn left on Dome Valley Road, which makes a sharp right turn after 1.1 miles and becomes Ave 20 E. You'll reach a four-way stop in another 2.7 miles, where you'll turn right (east) on Co 7th Street. Pavement gives out after a mile (ignore a Closed Road sign here!) and a dirt road continues around a waste transfer facility to the wilderness boundary in another .7 miles. The road then enters a corridor through the wilderness, drops steeply into Muggins Wash, and heads up the wash about two miles. Only high-clearance 4WD vehicles should venture into the wash, and rocky spots may block progress. The wash opens up at a palo verde grove, where an unmarked trail just above the main wash on your right provides easier walking than the gravelly wash. Another trail continues past road's end to a scenic panorama on the pass just east of Muggins Peak. You'll find other trails and washes to explore as well. Navigation is easy if you stay in the Muggins Wash drainage, but be sure to carry water, map, and compass if you go farther afield, such as to hike around Muggins Peak.

El Camino del Diablo

This difficult route across southern Arizona used by the earliest travelers still presents a challenge. You can venture down it with a permit, a high-clearance 4WD vehicle, and supplies for remote desert travel. (See the *Cabeza Prieta National Wildlife Refuge* section for the permit process and some of the travel precautions.)

SIGHTS WEST ALONG I-8

Mexico

Algodones (population 20,000) in Baja California offers the most convenient shopping to Yuma. Just take I-8 west 6.5 miles into California, then turn south 2 miles at the Algodones Road/Andrade Exit. Park in the large lot on the right just before the border, then take a short stroll across the border; a tourist office is on the right just after you cross. Many local craftspeople work with leather; you can see them turning out belts, bags, and saddles in some shops. Other crafts come from all over Mexico—including clothing, blankets, pottery, carved onyx chess sets, glassware, and musical instruments.

U.S. citizens may visit Algodones, San Luis, El Golfo, San Felipe, and Mexicali without formalities for as long as 72 hours. Visitors from countries that require visas for a U.S. visit can usually make a border-town visit without formalities, but check first with U.S. Immigration.

Sand Dunes

Though not typical of the Sonoran Desert, barren sand dunes lie 17 miles west of Yuma. Movie producers have used this "Great American Sahara" for films ranging from *Beau Geste* to *Star Wars.* The Yuma Convention & Visitors Bureau can tell you about recent or current filming.

Rest areas on I-8 in the middle of the dunes provide a place to stop and park, but you cannot go out onto the dunes from here. To do so, take the I-8 Gray's Well Exit (just east of the rest areas), then follow the south frontage road west into the dunes. Dune-buggy drivers like to play here; you'll see a parking area for them at the beginning of the frontage road. Continue 3.2 miles to the site of Gray's Well (you've gone too far if the pavement ends) to see a surviving segment of the **plank road** on the left. From 1914 to 1927, motorists crossed the dunes on a seven-mile road made of these moveable planks until engineers figured out how to build a conventional road through the dunes.

YUMA TO PARKER

Upstream from Yuma, the Colorado River's cool waters support lush greenery along the riverbanks. Backwater lakes, created by silting, provide additional areas to explore. Rugged desert ranges, such as the Trigo Mountains, furnish a scenic backdrop. A rich historical legacy recalls the riverboats and mining towns of the late 19th and early 20th centuries. Parks and wildlife refuges help keep the area in its natural state, though dams have raised the water level and greatly changed the ecology.

A Boating Trail Guide to the Colorado River has canoeing information and maps for the river between Blythe (I-10) and Imperial Dam; it's free at many marinas and parks in the area, or from the California Dept. of Boating and Waterways (2000 Evergreen Street, Ste. 100, Sacramento, CA 95815-3888, 916/263-0784, www.dbw.ca.gov, PDF download available).

Yuma Proving Grounds (YPG)

Driving north on U.S. Highway 95, you can't miss seeing the big guns at the entrance to this facility. The army tests equipment here on the YPG's 1,300 square miles of desert, a greater area than the state of Rhode Island and one of the world's largest military installations. Turn in at the guns (between Mileposts 44 and 45 on U.S. 95) and continue .8 miles to see an outdoor display of armaments on the left. **YPG Heritage Center** (on the main post, 928/328-3394, 10 A.M.–2 P.M. Mon.–Thurs. Nov.–May) has many photos, tank models, and artifacts from WWII to the present. Be sure to check out the monstrous control car of the U.S. Army Overland Train parked nearby. To get here, continue 4.4 miles west past the outdoor display, turn right into the base proper, and continue one block; the museum is in Building 2 on the left. You may need to show ID, vehicle registration, and insurance at the gate. The **Golden Knights** parachute team (928/328-6033 or 328-6533) practices landings on Cox Field in front of the Heritage Center from about mid-January–mid-March. The website www.yuma.army.mil tells about the work done here.

Mittry Lake Wildlife Area and Betty's Kitchen

This natural area offers fishing, boating, picnicking, primitive camping, and wildlife viewing. Laguna Dam, finished in 1909 and the oldest of nine dams along the Colorado River within Arizona, holds back the waters. From Yuma, head east 5.5 miles on U.S. Highway 95, then turn north 9.3 miles on Avenue 7E (pavement ends a half mile before the lake). Turn left at the signed fork for Betty's Kitchen, a day-use area with picnic tables, a fishing pier, and an easy half-mile loop interpretive trail ($5/vehicle). Take the right fork for additional places to fish, including a barrier-free fishing pier after one mile and a boat ramp just beyond. Primitive camping places also line this side of the lake; no water or fee. A 10-day per year stay limit applies. No jet skis or waterskiing allowed. The BLM's Yuma field office (928/317-3200) can answer questions on the area. At 6.3 miles from the fork, the road meets the paved Imperial Dam Road, where you can turn left for Imperial Dam Recreation Area or right to Yuma Proving Grounds and U.S. Highway 95.

Imperial Dam Recreation Area

The Colorado River, 20 miles north on the California side, offers desert walks, fishing, boating, and camping. Cross the river to Winterhaven, California, then turn north on Imperial County Road S-24 and follow signs through the fields. Or, from U.S. Highway 95 in Arizona, turn west six miles at the sign just north of Milepost 44. The **Imperial Dam Long-Term Visitor Area** includes the sites of Quail Hill, Kripple Kreek, Skunk Hollow, Beehive Mesa, and Coyote Ridge, serving self-contained vehicles only (the sites lack improvements). A $140 season pass or a $30 14-day pass is required for any stay during the September 15–April 15 season; at other times, camping is free but limited to stays of 14 days.

South Mesa Recreation Site, also within the Imperial Dam visitor area, offers water, restrooms, and outside showers; the same seasons and fees apply. **Squaw Lake Campground,** at the end of the road, offers water, restrooms, coin showers, paved parking, and two boat ramps; fee is $5 per calendar day (an overnight counts as two days) year-round. An easy two-mile nature trail winds through river vegetation and desert hills from the north end of the parking lot. Contact the BLM's Yuma field office (928/317-3200) for information on these and other recreation areas. **Hidden Shores RV Village** (nearby on the Arizona side and close to Imperial Dam, 928/539-6700, www.hiddenshores.com) has RV sites ($40–60), a restaurant, and a nine-hole executive golf course.

Martinez Lake

Farther upstream on the Arizona side, this lake lies about 35 miles north of Yuma. Go north 24 miles on U.S. Highway 95, then turn left (between Mileposts 46 and 47) and drive 11 miles on Martinez Lake Road. Keep straight near road's end for **Fisher's Landing.** The basic campground here (928/539-9495) offers tent sites ($3 per person) and RV sites ($12 w/hookups), plus coin showers (available to visitors too) and a dump station. A restaurant/saloon (928/782-7049) serves breakfast and lunch daily, but can get smoky. Other services include a store, post office, boat ramp, and marina (boat gas and fishing supplies). The *Colorado King I* and Yuma River Tour boats dock nearby.

Turn right just before Fisher's Landing for **Martinez Lake Resort** (928/783-9589 or 800/876-7004, www.martinezlake.com), which rents rustic cabins and trailers for $95–105 in summer and $65–80 in winter; two- and three-bedroom "party houses" can be rented too. RV sites cost $25 with hookups. A restaurant/cantina, which can get smoky, is open weekends for breakfast and daily for lunch and dinner. The marina rents fishing boats, pontoon boats, canoes, and kayaks, and has boat gas, fishing and picnic supplies, a boat ramp, canoe shuttle service, and a fishing guide service.

Picacho State Recreation Area

This recreation area (P.O. Box 848, Winterhaven, CA 92283, 760/393-3052 Salton Sea SRA, www.picacho.statepark.org) lies on the California side of the river, opposite Imperial Wildlife Refuge. The 7,000-acre park offers a campground with solar showers ($7), boat campgrounds, a boat ramp, store, and hiking. At its peak in 1904, the gold-mining town of Picacho had 2,500 residents; you can explore remnants of the Picacho mill and railroad grade, though the town site lies underwater. From Yuma, cross the river to Winterhaven, California, then turn north on Imperial County Road S-24/Picacho Road and follow signs 25 miles; most of the way is gravel road, normally passable by cars.

Imperial National Wildlife Refuge

Plants and animals of the Colorado River have received protection within this long, narrow refuge since 1941. Birds, especially migratory waterfowl in winter, hang out here. The 30-mile-long refuge includes the river, backwater lakes, ponds, marshland, river-bottom land, and desert, with about 15,000 acres receiving a wilderness designation. Visitors come mostly for fishing, boating, and birding. No camping is permitted in the refuge, but Fisher's Landing and Martinez Lake Resort offer nearby camping, a motel, restaurants, and marinas.

The refuge is about 40 miles north of Yuma; head north 24 miles on U.S. Highway 95, turn left 10 miles on Martinez Lake Road (between Mileposts 46 and 47), then right 4 miles on a gravel road at the sign. The visitors center (P.O. Box 72217, Yuma, AZ 85365, 928/783-3371, southwest.fws.gov) is on the north side of Martinez Lake with maps and information on the refuge. It's open 7:30 A.M.–4 P.M. Monday–Friday, also 9 A.M.–4 P.M. Saturday–Sunday November 15–March 31. A nearby observation tower provides a panorama. Meers Point, .8 miles from the visitors center, offers fishing access, picnic tables, and restrooms.

Four lookout points and a nature trail lie off Red Cloud Mine Road, which turns north one mile before the visitors center. The first lookout point (may not be marked) turns off .7 miles in; the last turns off 3.4 miles in. **Painted Desert Nature Trail** makes a 1.3-mile loop up a winding wash, over a ridge (good views), and down another wash with pretty scenery. You can get a trail leaflet at the trailhead, 2.3 miles in on Red Cloud Mine Road, or at the visitors center. Spring wildflowers bloom in profusion here after a wet winter.

Cibola National Wildlife Refuge

Cibola lies along the Colorado River just upstream from Imperial Refuge. In winter, the refuge hosts 16 duck species, 3 goose species, sandhill cranes, and an occasional swan. Visitors come to see about 700–1,000 sandhill cranes and 6,000–20,000 geese, including 80–85 percent of the Canada geese that winter in Arizona. Best viewing runs mid-November–early February. You can call the refuge for a recording of current bird counts.

The visitors center (Rt. 2, Box 138, Cibola, AZ 85328, 928/857-3253, southwest.fws.gov, 8 A.M.–4:30 P.M. Mon.–Fri.) has an exhibit room, video programs, and wildlife leaflets; volunteers staff the center on Saturday and Sunday November–March. Canada Goose Drive begins near the visitors center and makes a three-mile loop with great opportunities to see wintering waterfowl. A trail, which begins on the right .6 miles in, leads to a loafing pond where birds hang out after feeding. Cibola Lake, at the south end of the refuge, has an overlook at the south end.

You're welcome to hike, boat, or fish on the refuge. No camping is allowed, but you can find private and BLM camping areas along the river near the refuge. Anglers catch largemouth bass, flathead catfish, and channel catfish in Cibola Lake (open March 15–Labor Day) and river channels (open year-round). Power boaters and water skiers must stay in the river's main channel. Cibola Lake is about eight miles south of the visitors center via River and East Riverside Roads; if you continue around to the south shore, there's a bird-viewing area that's available even when the lake is closed.

You can easily reach the refuge headquarters on paved roads from the California side; take the I-10 Neighbours Boulevard Exit (2 miles west of Blythe, California), proceed south 14 miles on Neighbours Boulevard through irrigated fields to Farmers Bridge over the Colorado River, then continue 4 miles farther to the headquarters in Arizona. Drivers with high-clearance vehicles can follow a 32.5-mile backcountry route across the desert on East Cibola Road, between Highway 95 at Milepost 82 and the River Road-Baseline Road junction (four-way stop) 1.2 miles north of the visitors center; signs warn of Primitive Road, but it's normally passable except after storms; navigation can be tricky as not all junctions have signs.

Trigo Mountains Wilderness

Intrepid hikers explore these 30,300 acres of rugged land of mountains and desert washes, located between the Imperial and Cibola refuges and managed by the BLM's Yuma field office (928/317-3200). You may encounter old mines, which are dangerous to enter. A very rough road cuts through a corridor along Clip Wash in the middle of the wilderness, but this is too difficult for stock SUVs; also, the lower wash has such loose gravel that even 4WD vehicles can get stuck! Lopez Wash is a better access point; follow signs for Cibola Lake in Cibola Lake National Wildlife Refuge, then continue past the lake and out of the refuge. Turn left at a road fork marked by a stone cairn .9 miles past the refuge boundary; park at road's end and enter the canyon on foot.

Kofa National Wildlife Refuge

Desert bighorn sheep, desert mule deer, coyote, bobcat, fox, cottontail, and other creatures live in the dry, rugged Castle Dome and Kofa mountain ranges. Gambel's quail scurry into the brush, while falcons and golden eagles soar above. Rare stands of native palm grow in Palm Canyon. The refuge covers 665,400 acres, of which 82 percent has official wilderness designation. For information on the refuge, visit the U.S. Fish & Wildlife Service office (356 W. First St., Yuma, AZ 85364, 928/783-7861, http://southwest.fws.gov).

Gold discovered in 1896 led to development of the King of Arizona Mine, from which the Kofa Mountains took their name. This and some other mining claims remain active today, and they'll have No Entry signs. Castle Dome Peak, in the range just south of the Kofas, serves as a landmark visible from much of Arizona's southwest corner. Two places, accessible by cautiously driven cars from U.S. Highway 95, will give you a feel for the history and beauty of land—Castle Dome City Ghost Town Museum in the south and Palm Canyon farther north.

Castle Dome City Ghost Town tells many stories about people who have lived in this remote desert region (928/920-3062, 10 A.M.–5 P.M. Tues.–Sun., $4.50 adult). Call for information on guided tours of the district and for summer hours. The "town" has a mix of original and reconstructed buildings, all packed with memorabilia and mining gear—there's a lot to see. Castle Dome Mining District contains the world's largest silver-galena deposit, and you can peer down a shaft here. Mining began in 1862 and petered out by 1990. During World War II, the mines produced ore primarily for lead to make bullets. It's said that the Japanese put the site on their target list! The owner has made some surprising discoveries in abandoned mines, such as 1890s Levis and other old clothing perfectly preserved deep underground and now on display. You may have noticed earlier the ruins of Stone Cabin, 52 miles north of Yuma on U.S. Highway 95; an exhibit tells of the remarkable woman, Flora Yarber, who lived there until 1998. Local ores appear in mineral displays and you can purchase specimens. Take the Castle Dome turnoff near Milepost 55 on U.S. Highway 95, 32 miles north of Yuma, then follow signs 10 miles.

A short hike up **Palm Canyon** reveals tall California fan palms *(Washingtonia filifera)* tucked above in a narrow side canyon, lit by sun only at midday. To reach the trailhead, go north 62 miles on U.S. Highway 95 from Yuma (or south 18 miles from Quartzsite) and turn east 7.2 miles on unpaved Palm Canyon Road; the turnoff is between Mileposts 85 and 86. At road's end, follow the trail into Palm Canyon for half a mile and look for towering palms in the cleft on the north side of the main canyon. The trail pretty much ends here, though it's possible to rock-scramble another half mile up the main canyon to a large palmless natural amphitheater. Allow one hour from the trailhead up to the viewpoint in the main canyon and back, or three hours to go all the way to the amphitheater and back. Take care if climbing up to the palms, as you'll cross sheer cliffs and contend with loose rock.

Several roads penetrate the scenic mountains and canyons, but most tend to be rough, passable only by high-clearance 4WD vehicles. Visitors must carry water and all supplies. You're free to camp (14-day limit), but you must stay at least a quarter-mile from water sources; vehicles must be parked within 100 feet of designated roads. Refuge employees can offer suggestions for hikes and backcountry drives. The book *Backcountry Adventures Arizona* by Peter Massey and Jeanne Wilson has detailed driving descriptions.

While visiting Palm Canyon, you may wish to divert into **Kofa Queen Canyon.** The 4WD road, 8.5 miles one-way, turns off opposite the information kiosk about halfway along Palm Canyon Road. Towering cliffs rise on all sides as you enter the canyon; at the wilderness boundary it's possible to continue on foot another .75 miles to a pass at the head of the canyon.

The highly scenic 4WD **Big-Eye Mine Road** winds past old mines near the base of Castle Dome Peak to the cabin and mill of a mine named for an owner who had a glass eye. Ore car tracks still lead out of the main entrance. This may be the best-preserved mine on public land in Arizona, but you need to watch for vertical shafts and unstable structures. The road begins at Marker Post 75, half a mile south of Castle Dome City Ghost Town, and it takes about two hours of driving each way. At road's end, walk along the former road about .75 miles to the cabin, then either continue on the road or take the trail from the upper water tank (good views) to the mine and mill.

A drive the length of the refuge takes at least two days, but there's much to see and do along the way. Starting on Castle Dome Road in the south, you'll soon pass turnoffs for the Big-Eye Mine on the right, then Castle Dome City Ghost Town on the left. The road continues north over McPherson Pass in the Castle Dome Mountains to the broad King Valley. Follow King Valley Road east and north toward North Star Mine (on private land, but you can see it from the road) and a sharp west turn to road's end at nearby Polaris Mine. A former road here continues a mile or so to a picturesque canyon and more mines. To continue the drive through the refuge, backtrack to Marker Post 65, .6 miles south of North Star Mine, and turn east on Engesser Pass Road. The King of Arizona Mine, closed to the public, will soon be visible ahead on the right. Eventually you'll reach Pipeline Road in the far north of the refuge; turn west and you'll come out on U.S. Highway 95 between Mileposts 95 and 96, 10 miles south of Quartzsite.

New Water Mountains Wilderness

These rugged 24,600 acres, looked after by the BLM's Yuma field office (928/317-3200), adjoin the north edge of Kofa National Wildlife Refuge. Black Mesa (3,639 ft.) in the northwest rises 1,200 feet above the Ranegras Plain. Rock spires, cliffs, and canyons offer scenic vistas for the adventurous hikers who make it here. Bighorn sheep can sometimes be spotted. Gold Nugget Road, seven miles east of Quartzsite, provides access to the northwest section of the wilderness from I-10 Exit 26. Ramsey Mine Road reaches the north-central part from U.S. Highway 60.

Quartzsite

Like swallows returning to Capistrano, thousands of snowbirds flock to this tiny desert town every winter. From an estimated 2,000–3,000 summer residents, the population jumps to about one million during the shows and swap meets that peak mid-January–mid-February. It's worth a stop to see this remarkable phenomenon. Quartzsite lies at the junction of I-10 and U.S. Highway 95/Highway 95, 81 miles north of Yuma, 35 miles south of Parker, and 20 miles east of Blythe, California.

Charles Tyson settled here in 1856 and built a fort to fend off Native American attacks. Tyson's Well soon became an important stage stop on the run from Ehrenburg to Prescott. Later it took the name Quartzite, after the rock, but the post office added an *s,* making it Quartzsite.

The 1866–1867 **Tyson's Well Stage Station** (928/927-5229, donation) displays pioneer and mining artifacts, photos, and mineral specimens. An assay office lies out back with more exhibits. The museum is on the south side of the business route one block west of the Highway 95 junction (look for a historical marker sign). It's open November–March; call for hours or just drop by.

Hadji Ali rests under a pyramid-shaped marker in the local cemetery; turn north at the sign from the business route in the west part of town. Ali served as one of several camel drivers with about 80 camels imported by the U.S. Army from the Middle East in 1856–1857. The army hoped the large, hardy beasts would improve transportation and communication in the Southwest deserts. Although the camels showed promise, the army abandoned the experiment during the Civil War. Most of the camels wandered off into the desert, terrorizing stock and wild animals for many years. After the other camel drivers, homesick for their native lands, sailed away, Hadji Ali, whose name soldiers changed to "Hi Jolly," remained in Arizona and took up prospecting.

A handful of motels and restaurants and many RV parks serve passing motorists and the winter community. Most RVers, however, prefer the open freedom of the desert and head for **La Posa Long-Term Visitor Area** just south of town off U.S. Highway 95. La Posa has four sections, with vault toilets and a dump station. Visitors pay a $140 fee for long-term use September 15–April 15; for shorter visits a $30 14-day permit is available. You can camp free (14-day limit) off-season at La Posa and year-round in undeveloped areas such as **Road Runner/Mile Marker 99** 5 miles south of Quartzsite on U.S. Highway 95 and **Hi Jolly/Mile Marker 112** 5.5 miles north of town on Highway 95. The BLM's Yuma field office (928/317-3200) can advise on these recreation areas.

Most restaurants, a post office, and a motel or two lie on the west side of town along the I-10 business route. You'll find many RV parks scattered around town. The giant **Quartzsite gem and mineral shows and swap meets** take place from November to late February. People buy and sell rocks, minerals, gems, lapidary supplies, crafts, antiques, and other treasures. Smaller swap meets are held October–March. You'll find things that you never dreamed of not wanting!

The **Quartzsite Chamber of Commerce** (P.O. Box 85, Quartzsite, AZ 85346, 928/927-5600, www.quartzsitechamber.com) provides visitor information in a trailer one block north of the four-way stop at the west end of Business I-10, just off I-10 Exit 17; you can pick up information outside when the office is closed. The office is usually open 10 A.M.–noon and 1–3 P.M. (to 4 P.M. Jan.–Feb.) Monday–Friday.

Blythe Intaglios

Mysterious geoglyphs—giant human and animal figures on the ground created by prehistoric peoples—occur at several places along the lower

Colorado River Valley. There's little to date or identify the designs, made when dark desert gravel was removed to reveal the light-colored ground underneath. The most accessible are three groups that lie just off U.S. Highway 95, about 15 miles north of the town of Blythe; the turn isn't well marked, so look for the historical marker and turn west on an unpaved road directly opposite; cars need to take it slow. Parking for the first group of human and animal figures is .4 miles in on the right, and a well-preserved human figure is another .4 miles down the road. The largest human figure measures 170.6 feet long, but reaching it requires a .7-mile cross-country hike south across a wash; look for the fenced enclosure before you set off.

From Arizona, take I-10 across the Colorado River to Blythe, which has a good selection of motels and restaurants, and turn north at the U.S. Highway 95 exit. From Parker in the north, you can reach the intaglios via Wilson Road River Crossing/Indian 18 (turn west between Mileposts 29 and 30 on the Ehrenburg–Parker Road).

PARKER AND THE PARKER STRIP

From 1871 to 1908, Parker was nothing but a post office on the Colorado River Indian Reservation. When the railroad came through, the town began to expand, becoming a trading center for the reservation and nearby mining operations. Mining later declined, but agriculture and tourism thrived.

Headgate Rock Dam, finished in 1941 just upstream from Parker, forms Lake Moovalya, which provides water for the irrigation of reservation farmlands. Resorts and parks line Lake Moovalya and both shores of the river, drawing visitors year-round. Better known as the Parker Strip, this 11-mile stretch of scenic waterway begins several miles north of Parker and extends north to Parker Dam. Despite hot summer temperatures—among the nation's highest—many people enjoy the excellent boating and waterskiing Easter–Labor Day. In September the temperature starts to cool and the scene calms. Winter visitors, many retired, enjoy fishing, hunting, hiking, rock hounding, and exploring ghost towns. You can learn more about local history in the **Parker Area Historical Society Museum** downtown (1214 California Ave.), but it's open only short hours a few days a week; ask at the chamber office.

Patria Flats Day-Use Area

This riverside park makes a fine place for a picnic, with shaded tables, restrooms, and boat launch; free. It's on the Parker Strip 6.7 miles north of Parker. **River View Day-Use Area,** a half-mile south, is a small area used by anglers.

La Paz County Park

You'll have lots of room to roam here, as the park (8 miles north of Parker at 7350 Riverside Dr., 928/667-2069, www.lapazcountypark.com) stretches one mile along the Colorado River. Facilities include tent and RV camping with showers, picnicking, swimming beach, boat ramp, playground, tennis, volleyball, softball, basketball, horseshoes, recreation hall, putting green, and dump station. Campers will always find space in the dry area, but hookup sites fill early during summer weekends and October–March. Fees run $2 per person (12 years and over) for day use, $8 per vehicle for dry camping, $12 per vehicle for dry camping with a ramada, and $15 for an RV site with hookups. Only group campgrounds can be reserved. The 18-hole **Emerald Canyon Golf Course** (928/667-3366) lies across the road.

Buckskin Mountain State Park

This scenic park (11 miles north of Parker off Hwy. 95, 928/667-3231) sits on a bend in the river backed by low cliffs. Trees provide welcome shade in summer. Visitors enjoy use of the campground, picnic area, swimming beach, boat ramp, playground, volleyball court, basketball court, horseshoe pit, shuffleboard, and hiking trails. Day use costs $8, but hikers pay only $2 per person for trailhead parking. Campsites go for $20 with showers and water and electric hookups; some sites include sewer hookups for $23. A dump station is available too. Cabana sites ($22) by the river have a covered table and electric hookups only. All camping is first-come,

morning on the Colorado River, Buckskin Mountain State Park

first-served; arrive early in January–March and on summer weekends. You can join interpretive programs and hikes January–April and full moon hikes in summer. An interpretive garden near the ranger station identifies plants of the desert; old mining relics lie nearby. A concession (928/667-3210) runs a café, store, gas dock, and innertube sales/rental; it's closed in winter.

The one-third-mile round-trip **Lightning Bolt Trail** climbs to an overlook from near the ranger station. Also start here for the interpretive **Buckskin Trail** that follows a bridge over the highway, then winds into scenic hills on a one-mile loop; a spur trail halfway leads half a mile farther into the hills to some mines; another trail branches off the mine trail and follows a ridge to an overlook at Interruption Point, adding about a mile round-trip.

River Island State Park

This smaller unit (1.5 miles north of Buckskin Mountain State Park on Hwy. 95, 928/667-3386) offers picnicking, camping, a swimming beach, boat ramp, horseshoe pit, hiking, a reservable group ramada, and an amphitheater. **Wedge Hill Trail** climbs to an overlook in about half a mile round-trip; a trail leaflet tells of wildlife habitats. Interpretive programs run some days January–April. Day use costs $8. Campsites cost $20 and include water and electric hookups and showers. Try to arrive early for summer weekends and during January–March. River Island Market (half mile south of the park, 928/667-2448) offers supplies and tube rentals year-round.

Parker Dam

The world's deepest dam lies about 15 miles upriver from its namesake, the town of Parker. During construction, workers had to dig down 235 feet through the sand and gravel of the riverbed before hitting the bedrock needed to secure the foundation. Today, only the top third of the dam is visible. Lake Havasu, the reservoir behind the dam, has a storage capacity of 211 billion gallons. Pumps transfer one billion gallons a day into the Colorado River Aqueduct for southern California destinations. You can park at both ends of the dam. There's a boat launch at Take-off Point near the dam on the Arizona side. Security restrictions may close the dam to RVs and trucks, and to all traffic at night.

Entertainment and Events

Current movies play on the four screens of **BlueWater CRIT Theaters** (928/669-9222) at the BlueWater Resort & Casino.

Annual events include the off-road-vehicle races **Parker 250** in January and **Parker 425** in February. March is a busy month with **Bluegrass on the River,** a **Water Ski Race,** and **La Paz County Fair.**

BlueWater Resort & Casino sponsors summer regattas. There's a **Great Western Tube Float** in June, **fireworks** on July 4, **Indian Day Celebration** in September, **Parker Rodeo and Parade** in mid-October, **Christmas Lighted Boat Parade** in late November/early December, and the **All Indian Rodeo** in December.

Recreation

Cool off in Parker's public **swimming pool** (1317 9th St., 928/669-5678). Play golf at the 18-hole **Emerald Canyon Golf Course** (8 miles north of Parker, 928-667-3366) across the road from La Paz County Park or at **Havasu Spring's** 9-hole course (16 miles north of Parker, 928-667-3361).

Marinas along the Parker Strip rent boats. Anglers head for the river below Headgate Rock Dam for largemouth and smallmouth bass, striped bass, catfish, crappie, and bluegill. Boaters and water-skiers keep some anglers from Lake Moovalya, but the fish are there. You need reservation fishing permits for lower Lake Moovalya and the Colorado River downstream. Tubers enjoy leisurely trips downriver; a popular ride is the seven-mile, three-hour float from Parker to Big River Park on the California side.

Accommodations in Parker

The motels in town offer convenient places to stay for the night, but they aren't as atmospheric as resorts out along the river. All but Motel 6 have a pool. Rates may go above the following categories on weekends, especially if there's a holiday or special event.

Under $50: From the traffic light at the bend in Highway 95 in the center of town, head southeast toward Quartzsite for the **Kofa Inn** (1700 California Ave., 928/669-2101) or northwest toward the Colorado River bridge for **El Rancho Parker Motel** (709 California Ave., 928/669-2231) and **Motel 6** (604 California Ave., 928/669-2133). Head southwest one block from the junction for **Budget Inn Motel** (912 Agency Rd., 928/669-2566).

$50–100: Best Western Parker Inn (1012 Geronimo Ave., 928/669-6060 or 877/297-6667) is two blocks northeast of the bend in Highway 95.

For a bit of Las Vegas glitz, drive 1.4 miles northwest on Riverside Drive (Hwy. 95) from downtown Parker, then turn left to the huge **BlueWater Resort & Casino** (11300 Resort Dr., 928/669-7000 or 888/243-3360, www.bluewaterfun.com). The complex overlooks the Colorado River and features luxury accommodations, restaurants, three indoor pools with a waterslide, waterfalls, fitness center, movie theater, arcade games, mini golf, and a marina. Rooms cost only $39 d on weekdays, but jump on weekends to $125 d in summer and $79 in winter; suites go for $99–299 depending on day and season. Expect clouds of cigarette smoke in the central gambling area.

Accommodations on the Parker Strip

Both the Arizona and California shores have resorts, RV parks, campgrounds, day-use areas, restaurants, and marinas. You'll also enjoy good views of the river and rugged mountains. Parker Dam Road in California and Highway 95/Business 95 make a 32-mile scenic loop with the bridge at Parker and the road atop Parker Dam to connect the ends. For the Arizona side, head north 4.4 miles on Highway 95 from downtown Parker, then turn in on Riverside Drive at the sign for Business AZ 95. If coming from the north, turn in on the business route near Buckskin Mountain State Park, four miles south of the Parker Dam turnoff.

At the south end of the Parker Strip, five miles north of town, **Arizona Shores Resort Motel** (9388 Riverside Dr., 928/667-2685, $135 d in summer and $65 d in winter) has all kitchenettes and a water-skiing school. Rooms at the small **J.T.'s on the Keys Motel** (8982 Riverside Dr., 928/667-4336, $83 d weekdays,

$99 d Fri.–Sat. in summer, and $45–70 d winter) overlook a courtyard.

Branson's Resort (7.5 miles north of Parker at 7804 Riverside Dr. and Golf Course Dr., 928/667-3346) offers rooms with kitchenettes for $79 d ($91 d Fri.–Sat.) in summer, $55 d in winter. House trailers run $165–450 depending on size and day. Facilities include a boat ramp, docks, and a tiny store. **Castle Rock Shores** (off Hwy. 95, 12 miles north of town between the two state parks, 928/667-2344 or 800/701-1277) rents park models (manufactured houses) for $70–110 depending on size and day; in winter the units are rented by the month. There's a little 10-hole golf course and a marina.

About two miles south of Parker Dam at Holiday Harbor, **Harbour Inn** (4749 Riverside Dr./Hwy. 95, 928/667-2931, $55 d weekdays, $75 Fri.–Sat. in summer, and $49 d the rest of the year) offers large motel rooms with kitchenettes.

Campgrounds

In Parker: Lazy D Mobile Park (1800 15th St., 928/669-8797, $19 w/hookups) offers RV sites with showers in the southwest part of town. **Wheel-er In Resort** (760/665-8487, $20–27.50 tent or RV sites w/hookups) is on the California shore about the same distance from downtown—follow the highway across the Colorado River bridge, then turn left. Guests have use of the showers, boat ramp, dock, putting green, and store. **BlueWater Marine RV Park** (928/669-2433, $23.50 RV w/hookups) sits in a little valley near the Colorado just north of the casino with showers and winter activities.

On the Parker Strip: Branson's Resort (7.5 miles north of Parker at 7804 Riverside Dr., 928/667-3346) provides RV sites with hookups ($21 winter, $32 summer), a boat ramp, docks, and a store. **Red Rock Resort** (6400 Riverside Dr., 928/667-3116) has waterfront sites for tents ($20 summer, $15 winter) and RVs with hookups ($40 summer, $25 winter), with showers, a boat ramp, beach, game room, and a summertime café. At Pierpoint Landing, **Fox's RV Park & Tavern** (6350 Riverside Dr., 928/667-3444, www.foxsresort.com) has RV sites for $30 with hookups. Amenities include the oldest floating restaurant/bar on the river, showers, and a rec room. **Castle Rock Shores** (off Hwy. 95, 12 miles north of town between the two state parks, 928/667-2344 or 800/701-1277) offers sites for tents and RVs at $12.50–20 depending on location and day, plus a small golf course, marina, and store.

On the California shore: The Parker Chamber of Commerce can tell you about the several resorts on the California shore, most of which also offer RV sites. The Bureau of Land Management's Lake Havasu field Office (928/505-1200) oversees two campgrounds along the California side of the river, along with several day-use areas and two off-road-vehicle areas. **Empire Landing,** eight miles from Parker, offers a beach, picnicking, and camping; it should reopen in autumn 2005 after a major renovation. Other BLM recreation sites on the California side of the river include **Rock House Boating Facility** (boat launch and day-use area just south of Empire Landing), **Crossroads** ($4 camping or day-use on the river 1 mile south of Empire Landing, no water), **Bullfrog** ($3 day-use beach and picnic area 2 miles north of Empire Landing), and **Quail Hollow** (day-use picnic and wildlife interpretive area, 4 miles north of Empire Landing and just north of Big Bend Resort).

Food

Sopranos Sports Bar & Grill (621 W. Riverside Dr., 928/669-2403, daily lunch and dinner) prepares Italian cuisine along with American and some Mexican items. **Ruperto's Mexican Food** (800 W. Riverside Dr., 928/669-8420, daily breakfast, lunch, and dinner) is a little café with a drive-through and long hours. **China Garden** (1000 S. Hopi Ave. and Riverside Dr., 928/669-2660, daily lunch and dinner) has popular Chinese items.

BlueWater Resort & Casino (11300 Resort Dr., 928/669-7000 or 888/243-3360) offers the **River Willow** for fine dining nightly, the **Feast** with buffets (breakfast, lunch, and dinner) and a 24-hour menu, and the **River's Edge Cantina** with drinks and light meals.

Parker Strip Grill (10230 Harbor Dr., 928/667-4054, daily lunch and dinner) is a '50s diner near the junction of Highway 95 and the south end of the Parker Strip. **Patty Clearman's Steak House & Bistro** (9218 Lower Moovalya Estate Dr., 928/667-3732, Wed.–Fri. lunch, Wed.–Sun. dinner) serves up steak, seafood, ribs, and chicken near the south end of the strip.

Roadrunner (7000 Riverside Dr., 928/667-4252) features the largest floating restaurant/bar on the river; it's open daily for breakfast (except winter weekdays), lunch, and dinner. **Fox's RV Park & Tavern** (6350 Riverside Dr., 928/667-3444) has the oldest floating restaurant/bar on the river; call for seasonal hours.

Information and Services

The friendly staff at **Parker Chamber of Commerce** (1217 California Ave., Parker, AZ 85344, 928/669-2174, www.parkerareachamberofcommerce.com) will help you find what you're looking for. The office is open 8 A.M.–5 P.M. Monday–Friday (also 10 A.M.–2 P.M. Sat. Oct.–March). The **public library** (1001 Navajo Ave., 928/669-2622) is south of the Highway 95 bend off Agency Road.

The main **post office** (15th St.; 928/669-8179) is on the corner with California Avenue. **Parker Community Hospital** (1200 Mohave Rd., 928/669-9201) is on the south side of town.

Getting Around

Colorado River Buggy Expeditions (928/669-6171 or 916-0838, www.buggytours.com) runs out to Swansea Ghost Town and other scenic destinations in open-sided vehicles October–May. **River Parasail** (928/667-4837, www.riverparasail.com) winches riders out as far as 600 feet from a boat on the Colorado.

FARTHER AFIELD

Colorado River Indian Reservation

Established in 1865, this 268,691-acre reservation lies mostly in Arizona. Inhabitants include Mohave, Chemehuevi, Hopi, and Navajo. Don't expect any picturesque villages—the 6,000-plus residents live in modern houses and work at farms and jobs like everyone else along the Colorado River.

To learn about the tribes and others who've passed this way, visit the **Colorado River Indian Tribes (CRIT) Museum** (928/669-9211, ext. 1335, 8 A.M.–noon and 1–5 P.M. Mon.–Fri., donations welcome) two miles southwest of Parker. You'll see models of traditional shelters, a collection of fine baskets and other crafts, old photos of early reservation life, and exhibits on the Japanese relocation camps. A library houses an extensive collection of books, manuscripts, photographs, and tapes relating to the tribes. A gift shop sells beadwork and other Native American crafts. To reach the museum, head southwest from downtown Parker about 2 miles on Agency Road, or take California Avenue to the south edge of Parker, then turn right 1.8 miles on Mohave Road.

To enjoy a quiet backwater of the Colorado River, stop by **Ahakhav Tribal Preserve** just southwest of Parker. You can picnic, walk through the riparian woodlands, go birding, play in the playground, laze on the beach, rent a canoe, or launch your own nonmotorized craft. Canoe tours are available with advance notice. There's no charge to visit the preserve's 1,253 acres, which are open for day use only. Note that fishing requires a tribal permit (available in Parker) and that alcohol is forbidden. The park office is open 8 A.M.–5 P.M. daily, except in summer when hours change to 6 A.M.–3 P.M. daily. Follow the directions to the CRIT Museum, continue southwest .5 miles on Mohave Road toward Ehrenburg, then turn right 1.3 miles on Rodeo Road to the office; the beach turnoff is .2 miles farther on the right; continue another mile to road's end at the Colorado River.

Poston Memorial Monument marks the area where 17,867 people of Japanese ancestry had to endure confinement in the harsh desert during the hysteria of WWII. Plaques on the monument and a kiosk tell the story of these people who lived in three camps from May 1942 to November 1945. Farmlands have replaced the tarpaper barracks, but an adobe auditorium at Camp I can be seen to the west from the highway; these sites all lie on private land. The memorial stands on the east side of the Parker–Ehrenberg road 13 miles south of the CRIT Museum; look for the broken column just south of Poston.

Swansea

Of the ghost towns near Parker, Swansea is the best preserved, with ruins of a large brick smelter, mine, and more than a dozen buildings. The Clara Consolidated Gold and Copper Mining Company built the smelter in the early 1900s to process its ore locally, instead of sending the stuff to such faraway places as Swansea in Wales. Clara Consolidated closed the smelter in 1912, but other companies continued mining until 1924.

High-clearance vehicles do best, though cautiously driven cars may be able to navigate the dirt roads to the site. From Parker, take Shea Road at the south edge of town and head east about 23 miles to the Four Corners junction, then continue 7.2 miles to Swansea. In this last section you'll cross a pipeline twice, pass through very scenic desert hills, and see a natural arch. From Bouse, 27 miles southeast of Parker, take the road north across the railroad tracks and go 13 miles to Midway (keep left at a fork 3 miles from Bouse). Bear left on the fork at Midway, crossing under power lines after .4 miles, and go northwest 5.7 miles to Four Corners Road junction, then turn right 7.2 miles to Swansea. Obtain local advice and good maps, such as the Swansea 15-minute topo map; BLM and tourist offices may have a brochure on Swansea.

Alamo Lake State Park

This remote desert lake lies on the Bill Williams River at an elevation of 1,200 feet. When Alamo Lake began to fill in the mid-1960s, the flooded cottonwood, mesquite, and paloverde trees became homes for bluegill, sunfish, and tilapia. Hungry largemouth bass and channel catfish then fed on the small fish.

The park (928/669-2088) provides picnic tables, campgrounds with showers and hookups, a group reservation area, boat ramp, and a dump station; costs per vehicle run $5 day use, $10 undeveloped camping sites (chemical toilets), $12 no hookups, and $19–22 with hookups. January–early May is the busiest time, with autumn the next most popular, but the park always has room; groups can reserve a camping area. Fishing draws the most visitors. You can also hike or go bird-watching in the surrounding desert, though there are no designated trails; the ranger station has a bird list.

To get here, drive to Wenden on U.S. Highway 60 (60 miles southeast of Parker and 108 miles northwest of Phoenix), then turn 35 miles north on a paved road at the sign for the park. You'll first come to Cholla Road in the park; turn right for a choice of undeveloped and hookup sites, fish-cleaning station, and paved boat ramp; this area offers closest access to the upper lake and is less likely to be crowded. Continue 1.5 miles on the main road to the ranger station; turn right for the ramada area, developed campgrounds, fish-cleaning station, and paved boat ramp. Or continue straight 1.3 miles at the ranger station to Bill Williams Overlook near the dam for a great overview of the lake and surrounding desert.

Nearby **Wayside Inn** (928/925-3456) offers an RV park ($9.50 dry, $18 w/hookups), a smoky bar/café, a tiny store, and a gas pump. It's about 2 miles off the road to Alamo Lake State Park and about 4.5 miles from the lake itself. Unpaved Alamo/Tres Alamo Road connects Wayside Inn with U.S. Highway 93 (between Mileposts 178 and 179), but you'll need a high-clearance vehicle for the bumpy 30 miles.

Alamo Road

Alamo Road offers a scenic route to the undeveloped north shore of the lake from I-40 Yucca Exit 25 near Kingman. The graded dirt road is 57 miles one-way and can be done in a cautiously driven car. There are no facilities along the way or at the lake. Along the way, adventurous travelers can explore ghost towns, mines, and three wildernesses—Aubrey Peak, Arrastra Mountains, and Rawhide Mountains. You can also reach Alamo Road from U.S. Highway 93 on graded Chicken Springs Road from Wickiup, on Signal Road farther south (just south of U.S. 93 Milepost 132), or on the more mountainous 17 Mile Road (just south of U.S. 93 Milepost 143) that joins Signal Road. Maps show Brown's Crossing above Alamo Lake, but this unsigned 4WD route is subject to loose sand or flooding; you could ask at Wayside Inn about conditions.

McCracken Peak (3,524 ft.) and Mine make a good detour if you have a 4WD vehicle; turn west 4.7 miles at the four-way junction on Alamo Road opposite the turn for Signal Road, 19 miles north of Alamo Lake; the going is bumpy and you may prefer walking the last mile to the summit and the gaping hole of the 19th-century silver mine. Miners transported ore east to Signal near the Big Sandy River for processing. Signal's cemetery and foundations of two mills still exist—you can seek them out by following Signal Road east 5.1 miles from Alamo Road, then turning south (there may be a little sign) about half a mile on an unpaved 4WD road.

Harquahala Mountain National Back Country Byway

This steep 4WD road climbs 3,800 vertical feet in 10.5 miles to the highest point in southwestern Arizona. Weather permitting, you'll have a panorama of seemingly countless mountain ranges rising above the desert floor. The army used the 5,691-foot summit as a heliograph station in the 1800s, but the site is best known for the Smithsonian's solar observatory built in the 1920s, then abandoned after several years in favor of a more accessible location in California. The main building still stands, and interpretive signs tell about the people who lived here. No road existed at the time, so scientists had to climb the steep 5.4-mile one-way Harquahala Pack Trail up the north side of the mountain. Most of the trail lies in the Harquahala Mountains Wilderness; the trailhead (2,320 ft.) is reached on a 4WD road that turns off U.S. Highway 60 13.6 miles southwest of Aguila. Miners later built a road up the south side, completing it to the summit only in 1981. A high-clearance 4WD vehicle is required for this adventure, which can be done in most SUVs. You'll want to use low speeds and be alert to engine overheating on the way up and brake overheating on the way down. The road is open all year except after winter storms.

At the start of the Byway, the BLM's Phoenix Field Office (623/580-5500) provides an information kiosk, a few picnic tables and grills, an outhouse and enough parking for RVs. If coming from the west, you can take U.S. Highway 60 to Salome, turn southeast 26 miles on Salome Road, left 8.5 miles on Eagle Eye Road, then left at the sign. From the Wickenburg area, follow U.S. Highway 60 to Aguila, turn south 18.5 miles on Eagle Eye Road—you'll see how the road got its name—and right at the sign. From Phoenix, you can take I-10 west to Salome Road Exit 81, follow Salome Road northwest 9.6 miles, turn right 8.5 miles on Eagle Eye Road, then left at the sign.

Lake Havasu City

As in other Colorado River towns, fun on the water draws many visitors. Lake Havasu, 45 miles long and 3 miles wide, offers great boating, waterskiing, and sailing. You'll find plenty of boat rentals, boat tours, swimming beaches, tennis, and golf courses. Hikers can stroll the shoreline at English Village or explore Crossman Peak (5,100 ft.) in the Mohave Mountains to the east. Lake Havasu City has a population of about 50,000 and continues to grow rapidly.

SIGHTS

London Bridge

In 1958, the late Robert McCulloch spotted Lake Havasu from the air and decided to build a planned community along its east shore. Lake Havasu City might have become just another ho-hum town if not for a brainstorm by McCulloch and town planner C. V. Wood. They decided to buy London Bridge! Back in England, the 136-year-old bridge was slowly sinking into the Thames. No longer able to handle busy city traffic, the famous London landmark was put up for sale in 1967. McCulloch snapped it up for $2,460,000, then spent more than twice that amount to have 10,276 granite blocks shipped to Long Beach, California, trucked to Lake Havasu City, and painstakingly reassembled. The deal also included ornate lampposts said to have been made from Napoleon's cannons captured at Waterloo in 1815. After three years of construction, the bridge stood in its new home. The Lord Mayor of London graciously came over in October 1971 to preside at the bridge dedication. London Bridge may be one of the stranger sights on the Arizona desert, but it certainly put Lake Havasu City on the map.

More has been added since—an English Village complete with shops, galleries, pub, a double-decker bus, and even bright-red British telephone booths. Nearby London Bridge Resort adds more English atmosphere.

At first, the bridge spanned only dry land. Workers later dug a water channel underneath, cutting off Pittsburgh Point. Now you walk or drive across London Bridge to reach the campgrounds, RV parks, beaches, marina, and other facilities on the new island, still known as Pittsburgh Point.

Lake Havasu Museum of History

This collection (320 London Bridge Rd., 928/854-4938, 1–4 P.M. Tues.–Sat., donation) introduces the region with exhibits on the Chemehuevi tribe, mining and riverboating, Parker Dam, London Bridge, and the development of Lake Havasu City. Displays also illustrate local flora and wildlife. The museum store sells souvenirs. It's next to the Lake Havasu Convention & Visitors Bureau on the west frontage road of Highway 95.

Lake Havasu State Park—Windsor Beach

This park (928/855-2784) occupies about two miles of shoreline north of London Bridge. Visitors enjoy the swimming beaches, picnicking at the shaded tables, boating, fishing, hiking, and camping. Three launch ramps (one just for personal watercraft) serve boaters.

Hikers can stroll along the Mojave Sunset Trail, about 1.5 miles one-way, through desert and riparian habitats; it runs from near the contact station in the north to Windsor 4 day-use area in the south. Halfway along the trail, a botanical garden (also accessible from the park road) demonstrates native and exotic plant landscaping. The park offers interpretive programs some evenings in winter at the main campground. Anglers have a fish-cleaning station. Day use costs $8 per vehicle. Campsites ($19/vehicle) accommodate both tents and RVs, and include showers, electric and water hookups, and a dump station. Groups can reserve a day-use area, but no other reservations are taken. Windsor Beach is 1.5 miles north of London Bridge off London Bridge Road, or turn west off Highway 95 on Industrial Boulevard.

Site Six

In 1943, on what's now the island connected by London Bridge, the military built Lake Havasu Auxiliary Field #6 as an emergency airfield. The lakeside setting soon became popular as an R&R spot, and after the war six servicemen ran a fly-in fishing camp for a while. Today a loop road, paralleled by a bike path, encircles the abandoned runways with some good views of the lake, mountains, and city. Site Six is now a recreation area at the far end of the island with floating fishing piers and a paved boat ramp. Nearby, a one-third-scale lighthouse marks the northwest end of the island.

PRACTICALITIES

Entertainment and Events

For movies, drop in at the 10-screen **Movies Havasu** (180 Swanson Ave., 928/453-7900).

Powerboat regattas run on many weekends throughout the year. **Turquoise Circuit Rodeo Finals** ride in January. Lake Havasu City celebrates **Winterfest** with entertainment and food in February. **Winterblast Fireworks Display** goes off on Presidents Day in February at an annual convention of pyrotechnic professionals. **Havasu Art Guild Juried Spring Show** in March features work of regional artists. The **Blue Water Invitational Boat Regatta** also runs in March. Classic motor vehicles roll into town in April for the **Havasu Happening.**

Anglers compete for the best catches in the **Striper Derby** in May. **Fireworks** light up the sky on July 4. **London Bridge Days** in October celebrates the dedication of the famous structure with a "Grande Parade," contests, games, live entertainment, and food. Antique and classic autos converge for a parade and show in the **Relics and**

Rods Run to the Sun in mid-October. Personal watercraft racers compete in the **Dos Equis World Finals** in October. **Lake Havasu Film Festival** plays in late October/early November.

A **Gem and Mineral Show** sparkles in November. Radio-controlled model airplanes take off in the **London Bridge Seaplane Classic,** also in November. The **Festival of Lights** brightens the holiday season from late November to mid-January with entertainment and more than a million lights in English Village. Watercraft join in the holiday cheer for a **Boat Parade of Lights** on the first weekend December.

Recreation

London Bridge Beach offers swimming and picnicking on the island; cross London Bridge and turn left at the sign. Fido can romp in **Lions Dog Park** just north of London Bridge Beach. **Rotary Park Beach,** south of English Village, offers beaches, covered picnic tables, and ball fields; you can take the shoreline footpath under London Bridge. **Windsor Beach** of Lake Havasu State Park offers beaches, picnic areas, hiking, boat ramps, and camping 1.5 miles north of London Bridge on the mainland. **Ride the Waves Water Park** (100 Park Ave., on Hwy. 95 just southeast of Swanson Ave., 928/453-2687) features an indoor wave pool, a 257 foot water slide, a children's pool, a hot tub, and an outdoor spray park.

London Bridge Golf Club (2400 Club House Dr. off S. Acoma Blvd., 928/855-2719) features two 18-hole courses. **Nautical Inn** (1000 McCulloch Blvd. across London Bridge, 928/855-2131) offers an executive 18-hole course. **Bridgewater Links** (928/855-4777) has a nine-hole executive course adjacent to London Bridge Resort.

Anglers discovered this lake long before any developer. Fishing was good—and still is—for largemouth bass, channel catfish, bluegill, green sunfish, and black crappie. Saltwater striped bass, introduced in the early 1960s, have thrived. Weighing up to 60 pounds, this landlocked fish is now the hottest thing in the lake. The stripers feed in spring and summer below Davis Dam, eating threadfin shad and other fish churned up by water flowing from the turbines. During fall and winter the bass return to the lake and are sought out by thousands of eager anglers. Pick up a local fishing booklet for tips on striper techniques.

Many places in town rent water sports equipment; ask the Visitors Bureau for a list. **Adventure Center** (on the water next to English Village, 928/453-4386) offers parasailing and rents pedal boats, miniboats, and personal watercraft. **Nautical Sports Center** (Nautical Inn on the island, 928/855-7000) offers rentals of kayaks, paddleboats, pontoon boats, ski boats, personal watercraft, and houseboats.

You can also rent boats from **Sandpoint Marina** (14 miles south on the Arizona side, then take the Cattail Cove turnoff, 928/855-0549) and from **Havasu Springs Resort** (20 miles south of town, 928/667-3361). **Park Moabi** (in California off the first I-40 exit, 760/326-3831) offers a campground, swimming beach, putting green, boat ramp, and marina with rentals; day use costs $6 per vehicle, and camping runs $12 ($20 w/hookups) in the main area and $18 ($35 w/hookups) on the riverfront sites.

Accommodations

About two dozen motels and resorts provide a full range of places to stay. The tourist office in English Village (beside London Bridge) and the Visitors Bureau on London Bridge Road will help find the best place for you. Rates go up on Friday and Saturday in summer at many locales and way up during major holidays or events.

$50–100: Lakeview Motel (440 London Bridge Rd., 928/855-3605, $35 s, $45 d) has just the basics. One of the best budget bets, **Bridgeview Motel** (101 London Bridge Rd., 928/855-5559, $40–70 d weekdays, $70–130 d Fri.–Sat.) has a pool. **Motel 6** (111 London Bridge Rd., 928/855-3200 or 800/466-8356, $56 s, $62 d weekdays, $70 s, $76 d Fri.–Sat. in summer, $40 s, $46 d in winter) lacks frills. **Super 8 Motel** (305 London Bridge Rd., 928/855-8844 or 800/800-8000, $46 s, $51 d weekdays, $56 s, $62 d Fri.–Sat.) offers a pool and spa. **Howard Johnson Express Inn & Suites** (335 London Bridge Rd., 928/453-4656 or 800/446-4656, $89 d weekdays, $109 d weekends in summer, then about

$59–69 d in winter) features an indoor pool and spa. **Windsor Inn** (451 London Bridge Rd., 928/855-4135 or 800/245-4135, $40–55 d weekdays, $46–65 d Fri.–Sat.) has some kitchenettes plus a pool and spa. **Havasu Travelodge** (480 London Bridge Rd., 928/680-9202 or 800/578-7878, $60 d summer weekdays and winter, $80 d summer weekends) offers an indoor spa.

Over $100: Close to London Bridge and the water, **London Bridge Resort** (1477 Queen's Bay Rd., 928/855-0888 or 800/624-7939, www.londonbridgeresort.com, $149–189 d weekdays, $209–269 d Fri.–Sat. in summer, $79–159 d winter) features a restaurant, nine-hole executive golf course, tennis, three swimming pools, hot tub, and elegant decor. It's worth stepping inside the lobby to see the world's only replica of the ornate gold state coach. The original, built in 1762, has carried all British monarchs since George III to coronation ceremonies at Westminster Abbey. The one- and two-bedroom units have converted to time-share, but some will be available to rent.

The all-suite boutique hotel **Agave Inn** (on the left just after the bridge at 1420 McCulloch Blvd., 928/854-2833 or 866/854-2833, http://agaveinn.com, $119–299 d weekdays, $139–359 d Fri.–Sat.) offers 17 nonsmoking rooms with a contemporary decor, bridge views, wet bar, and a fitness center.

Nautical Inn Resort & Conference Center (1000 McCulloch Blvd. across London Bridge on the left, 928/855-2141 or 800/892-2141, www.nauticalinn.com, $114–275 d weekdays, $124–375 d weekends in summer, $69–164 d the rest of the year) features waterfront rooms with a balcony or patio, plus a swimming beach, pool and spa, marina, and golf course. The high-rise **Island Inn** (1300 McCulloch Blvd., 928/680-0606 or 800/243-9955, www.havasumotels.com, $65–75 d weekdays and $80–90 d Fri.–Sat. March–Oct., $49–80 d in winter) offers balconies with some rooms, plus a restaurant and an outdoor pool and spa.

Campgrounds

Pleasant camping is available in the two nearby state parks, **Lake Havasu State Park** and **Cattail Cove State Park.** Boaters can choose between many BLM and state park campgrounds, accessible by water only, on the Arizona shore south of town.

On the island a half mile past London Bridge, **Crazy Horse Campground** (1534 Beachcomber Blvd., 928/855-4033, $29 tent or RV w/hookups) provides showers, a dump station, swimming beach, pool, spa, store, boat ramp, and docks; the showers and dump station are also open to the public. Jet skis and personal watercraft can be rented nearby. **Islander RV Resort** (751 Beachcomber Blvd., just past the Nautical Inn, 928/680-2000, www.islanderrvresort.com, $39–54 RV w/hookups) has a swimming beach, two pools, two hot tubs, a boat ramp, docks, and summertime children's activities. Two miles southwest at the far end of the island, **Beachcomber Resort** (601 Beachcomber Blvd., 928/855-2322, $44.31 RV w/hookups and tax) includes a swimming beach, pools, a rec hall, boat ramp, and docks. **Havasu Falls RV Resort** (3493 N. Hwy. 95, 928/764-0050 or 877/843-3255, $30–33 RV w/hookups) overlooks Lake Havasu four miles north of town with a pool and a rec room.

Havasu Landing Resort (760/858-4593 or 800/307-3610, www.havasulanding.com, $10 or $15 tent, $22 or $28 RV w/hookups; higher prices get you closer to the water) lies directly across the lake from Lake Havasu City and is connected to it by a boat shuttle from below Island Mall; amenities include a casino, restaurant, and a swimming beach. **Park Moabi** (on the California side near the I-40 Colorado River bridge, 760/326-3831 park office or 760/326-4777 marina), charges a $6 day-use fee and offers spaces for tents ($10, $12 Fri.–Sun.) and RVs ($18 w/hookups, $20 Fri.–Sun.), along with showers, a boat ramp, a marina with rentals, and a store.

Undeveloped BLM lands used for dispersed camping include **Craggy Wash** north of town past the airport on Highway 95 (turn near Milepost 190 and continue past state trust land) and south of town at **Standard Wash,** which is also an off-road-vehicle area, off Highway 95 between Mileposts 172 and 171.

Food

Bridgewater Café (London Bridge Resort, 928/855-0888, daily breakfast, lunch, and dinner, $9–20) prepares American cuisine. The dinner menu includes steak, prime rib, seafood, and pasta.

Shugrue's (Island Mall, just across London Bridge, 928/453-1400, open daily, lunch entrées $9–13, dinner $17–28) creates impressive entrées such as the 18 oz. del Monaco, Torrington filet, rack of lamb, and garlic-crusted halibut; some tables have great views of the bridge. **Barley Brothers Brewery & Grill** (also in Island Mall and with a great view of the bridge, 928/505-7837, daily lunch and dinner, $8–21) provides diners with a good selection of sandwiches, pizza, pasta, and grilled meats along with brews. **Makai Café** (on the lower level of Island Mall, 928/505-2233, daily breakfast and lunch, $6–9) offers light meals with indoor and patio seating. Several places on McCulloch Boulevard serve American comfort food, such as the **Black Bear Diner** (1900 McCulloch Blvd., 928/855-2013, daily breakfast, lunch, and dinner, $9–13).

For seafood and steak, try the **Captain's Table** (Nautical Inn at 1000 McCulloch Blvd., 928/855-2141, daily breakfast, lunch, and dinner, $14–27). **Juicy's Noodles** (Island Inn, 1300 McCulloch Blvd., 928/680-0883, daily breakfast, lunch, and dinner, $9–19) serves up Italian dishes, steaks, and pizza.

Since 1976 locals have been tucking into Mexican food at **Taco Hacienda** (2200 Mesquite Ave. and Acoma Blvd., 928/855-8932, daily lunch and dinner, $7.50–11) with such favorites as fajitas, chimichangas, Mexican steak, and mix-and-match combos. **Javelina Cantina** (just across the bridge on the left at 1420 McCulloch Blvd., 928/855-8226, daily lunch and dinner, $10–14) offers many flavors of fajitas—steak, chicken, fish, shrimp, or veggie—plus some unusual items like salmon tostada and catfish relleno, along with such favorites as carne asada, fish tacos, and combos; there's patio seating with bridge views.

Safeway and **Bashas'** supermarkets lie off McCulloch Boulevard just east of London Bridge and Highway 95.

Information and Services

Centrally located in English Village near London Bridge, the **Visitors Center** (928/855-5655) is open about 9 A.M.–5 P.M. daily. **Lake Havasu City Convention & Visitors Bureau** (314 London Bridge Rd., Lake Havasu City, AZ 86403, 928/453-3444 or 800/242-8278, www.golakehavasu.com, 8 A.M.–5 P.M. Mon.–Fri.) also has helpful staff and literature. It's several blocks north of English Village, though the entrance is on the Highway 95 frontage road.

The **BLM Lake Havasu field office** (2610 Sweetwater Ave., Lake Havasu City, AZ 86406, 928/505-1200, www.az.blm.gov, 8 A.M.–4:30 P.M. Mon.–Fri.) is in the south part of town near Highway 95 and Acoma Boulevard South, with recreation information and wildlife exhibits.

The **Mohave County Library** (1770 McCulloch Blvd., 928/453-0718) is near the southeast corner of McCulloch and Capri Boulevards; it's open 9 A.M.–5 P.M. Monday–Saturday (to 8 P.M. on Tues. and Thurs.). The main **post office** (1750 McCulloch Blvd., 928/855-2361) is also near the southeast corner of McCulloch and Capri Boulevards. **Hastings Books** (1775 McCulloch Blvd., 928/680-7272) offers books and periodicals. **Wal-Mart** sells outdoor supplies on the west side of Highway 95, two miles north of London Bridge. **Havasu Samaritan Regional Hospital** (101 Civic Center Lane, 928/855-8185) is two blocks north of the traffic circle on McCulloch Boulevard.

Getting There and Around

Air Midwest/America West Express (800/235-9292, www.americawest.com) flies to Phoenix. The airport, off Highway 95 about five miles north of town, offers car rentals.

Several boat tours leave from the shore at English Village. They depart most frequently in the cooler months. The bargain ride crosses the lake to Havasu Landing Resort & Casino on the California shore for only $2 round-trip; departures run roughly hourly from early morning to late night at the dock below Island Mall, across the bridge on your right. **Dixie Belle Cruises** (928/453-6776) will take you out in a paddlewheel replica on a narrated one-hour tour ($13 adults, $7 children 4–12). The same company runs the small *Kon Tiki* boat to Copper Canyon, located on the California side in the southern part of the lake, on one-hour tours ($12 adult, $7 children 12 and under). **Bluewater Jetboat Tours** (928/855-7171 or 888/855-7171, www.coloradoriverjetboattours.com) offers 2.5-hour trips most days upstream into the spectacular Topock Gorge ($35 adults, $32 seniors, and $17.50 youth 10–16); pontoon boats can be rented.

Outback Off-Road Adventures (928/680-6151, www.outbackadventures.us) features educational half-day tours in the Mohave Mountains northeast of town.

VICINITY OF LAKE HAVASU CITY

Cattail Cove State Park

On Lake Havasu 15 miles south of downtown, the park (turn west from Hwy. 95 between Mileposts 167 and 168, 928/855-1223) offers a swimming beach with shaded picnic tables, boat ramp, dock, camping, and hiking. Visitors can learn about the area in the cactus garden and at year-round interpretive programs. Anglers have a fish-cleaning station. Day use runs $8 per vehicle. The campground provides water and electric hookups, showers, and a dump station at a cost of $19 per vehicle. Sites are all first-come, first-served, and tend to fill January–March and on some summer weekends.

Whytes Trail begins near the boat ramp and winds along the shore to the BLM Whytes Retreat boat camp, 1.5 miles one-way. **McKinney Loop Trail** takes an inland route through low desert hills to Whytes Trail in about half a mile; follow the sidewalk along the boat trailer parking area to the trailhead. There's also good walking up the wash from the start of McKinney Loop Trail.

Lake Havasu Boat Campgrounds

Boaters can choose from many state or BLM water-access campgrounds south of Lake Havasu City. Arizona State Parks maintains those between Cattail Cove and Red Rock Cove to the north with a fee of $14 per site. The BLM offers boat camps south of Cattail Cove and north along the coast between Red Rock Cove and near Lake Havasu City; these cost $20 ($10 day use), but you can buy a $50 annual permit. Most boat camps have tables, grills, and outhouses, though none of the sites has drinking water.

Sandpoint Marina & RV Park

Take the Cattail Cove State Park turnoff from Highway 95, then turn right at the sign for this lakeside resort (928/855-0549, www.sandpointresort.com) located on a picturesque peninsula. Amenities include sites for tents or RVs ($30 w/hookups; shore sites are $38), a store, marina (fishing-boat, patio-boat, and See Doo rentals), café (Thurs.–Tues. breakfast, lunch, and dinner), and snowbird activities.

Bill Williams River National Wildlife Refuge

Six thousand acres in the lower 12 miles of Bill Williams River contain the largest surviving cottonwood-willow woodland of the lower Colorado. The office (22 miles south of Lake Havasu City at 60911 Hwy. 95, Parker, AZ 85344, 928/667-4144, southwest.fws.gov, 8 A.M.–4 P.M. Mon.–Fri.) is .8 miles south of the bridge over the Bill Williams River and across from a pumping station. Stop in for wildlife exhibits, lists of refuge birds and other wildlife, and an observation deck. Birders flock to the refuge to see many species year-round—343 at last count. Good places for birding include the marsh behind the refuge office and areas 2, 3.5, and 7 miles up the refuge road. You'll also see butterflies during the warmer months; 34 species flutter about, and 11 of those live only here. Staff run a program to propagate razorback sucker and bonytail chubs, endangered fish native to the Colorado River.

The **Peninsula Trail** is a paved, accessible path out to fishing platforms with interpretive signs, sun shades, and restrooms along the way; it's 1,500 feet one-way and begins near the refuge office. You can also paddle your way through the Bill Williams River estuary; a canoe trail map available at the office shows a suggested route and things to look for. You can launch your craft (no gas motors allowed) behind the office.

A scenic dirt road provides access into the refuge. The turnoff from Highway 95 is .3 miles south of the bridge over the Bill Williams River and a half mile north of the office; look for a sign with a binocular symbol. The first 3.5 miles, usually passable by cars, winds over desert hills with good views of the riparian vegetation below and canyon walls above. Drivers with high-clearance 4WD vehicles can continue upstream another 3.5 miles across many fords and sections of riverbed and return the same way, or they can take Mineral Wash Road and Shea Road about 25 miles to Parker or Swansea ghost town. It's easy to get stuck in a mud hole, so only those experienced at and equipped for water crossings should tackle the road. Reservoir releases upstream may cause flooding that closes the road in the refuge at times.

Havasu Springs Resort

This full-service resort (928/667-3361, www.havasusprings.com) is on Lake Havasu near Parker Dam, 20 miles south of Lake Havasu City. Guests can choose from three motels ($98–115 d summer, $55 d winter), apartments ($140–195 summer, $60–75 winter), and an RV park ($34). Amenities include a restaurant (lunch and dinner daily, breakfast on weekends), nine-hole golf course, swimming beaches, a pool, tennis, boat rentals (fishing and pontoon), a boat ramp, docks, and a store.

HAVASU NATIONAL WILDLIFE REFUGE

The marshes, open water, and adjacent desert of the refuge support many types of birds and animals. The main part of the refuge includes Topock Marsh near Needles, California, and extends southward to just north of Lake Havasu City. Most of the more than 44,371 acres lies in Arizona. In winter, the refuge provides a home for Canada geese, many species of ducks, and other waterfowl.

Boating, fishing, and other water sports are permitted except where marked. No camping is allowed in Mesquite Bay, Topock Gorge, or Topock Marsh. You can boat camp on the Arizona shore below the south entrance to Topock Gorge, except in Mesquite Bay. For a map, bird list, and regulations, visit the Havasu National Wildlife Refuge office (1406 Bailey Ave. or P.O. Box 3009, Needles, CA 92363, 760/326-3853, 8 A.M.–4 P.M. Mon.–Fri.).

Five Mile Landing (928/768-2350) provides a private campground ($7 dry camping for tent or RV) and marina (fishing-boat rentals, slips, and boat ramp) on the east side of Topock Marsh. From I-40 Exit 1, turn north five miles. From Highway 95, 17 miles south of Bullhead City, turn east 8.7 miles on Courtwright Road/County 227, which becomes County 1. **Topock Gorge Marina** (just north of I-40 Exit 1, 928/768-2325) offers a boat dock and gas.

Topock Gorge by Canoe

This is a perfect one-day outing on the cool waters of the Colorado River above Lake Havasu. The usual put-in point is Park Moabi, California, or Topock, Arizona, where I-40 crosses the river. Swift currents speed canoeists down the river without rapids or serious turbulence. Take-out is at Castle Rock on the upper end of Lake Havasu, about seven hours and 17 river miles below. Topock Gorge is part of the Havasu National Wildlife Refuge, where you can spot hundreds of bird species. Look for the mud nests of swallows clinging to the cliffs; herons, ducks, geese, long-billed prospectors, and red-winged blackbirds also visit the canyon. If you're lucky, you may spot a desert bighorn sheep on the steep slopes. Prehistoric petroglyphs cover Picture Rock, a huge dark mass about halfway between Devil's Elbow and Blankenship Bend. Sandy beaches are ideal for a walk or picnic, but no fires or camping are permitted.

Summer temperatures can get uncomfortable, but a hop in the river will cool you off. Bring a hat and sunscreen to protect yourself from the Arizona sun. Other kinds of boats besides canoes can make the trip. Rafts require more time, and powerboat skippers should watch for sandbars. Many other canoe trips are possible; for example, you can start at Needles for a two-day trip or at Bullhead City for a three- or four-day canoe excursion. Topo maps (1:24,000 scale) for the area include Topock (Ariz.–Calif.) and Castle Rock (Calif.–Arizona).

The rugged cliffs of Topock Gorge provide a refuge for desert bighorn sheep and other wildlife.

A Boating Trail Guide to the Colorado River has canoeing information and maps for the river between Davis Dam and Parker Dam; it's free at many marinas and parks in the area, or from the California Department of Boating and Waterways (2000 Evergreen Street, Ste. 100, Sacramento, CA 95815-3888; 916/263-0784, www.dbw.ca.gov; PDF download available).

Jerkwater Canoe & Kayak Co. (928/768-7753 or 800/421-7803, www.jerkwater.com) offers rentals, shuttle service, meals, and bed and breakfast near Topock; staff will set you up for any section of the Colorado between Hoover Dam and Yuma. **WACKO—Western Arizona Canoe & Kayak Outfitters** (928/855-6414 or 888/881-5038, www.azwacko.com) in Lake Havasu City rents canoes and kayaks and provides shuttles.

Kingman

Kingman lies in high-desert country at an elevation of 3,345 feet surrounded by the Cerbat, Hualapai, and Black mountain ranges. Lewis Kingman came through the area in 1880 while surveying a right-of-way for the Atlantic and Pacific Railroad between Albuquerque, New Mexico, and Needles, California. The railroad camp that later bore his name grew into a major mining, ranching, and transportation center for northwestern Arizona. A county election in 1886 required the county seat to move from Mineral Park to Kingman, but residents of Mineral Park balked at turning over county records. Kingmanites, according to one story, then sneaked over to Mineral Park in the dead of night to snatch the records and bring them to Kingman, where they've stayed ever since.

Kingman (area pop. 37,000) lies in the heart of the longest remaining stretch of Route 66—one of the predecessors of today's transcontinental highways. Area businesses play up the Route 66 theme, and there's a good museum in town illustrating travel on the old road. Many motels and restaurants serve motorists on their way across the country on I-40 or U.S. Highway 93. Other visitors

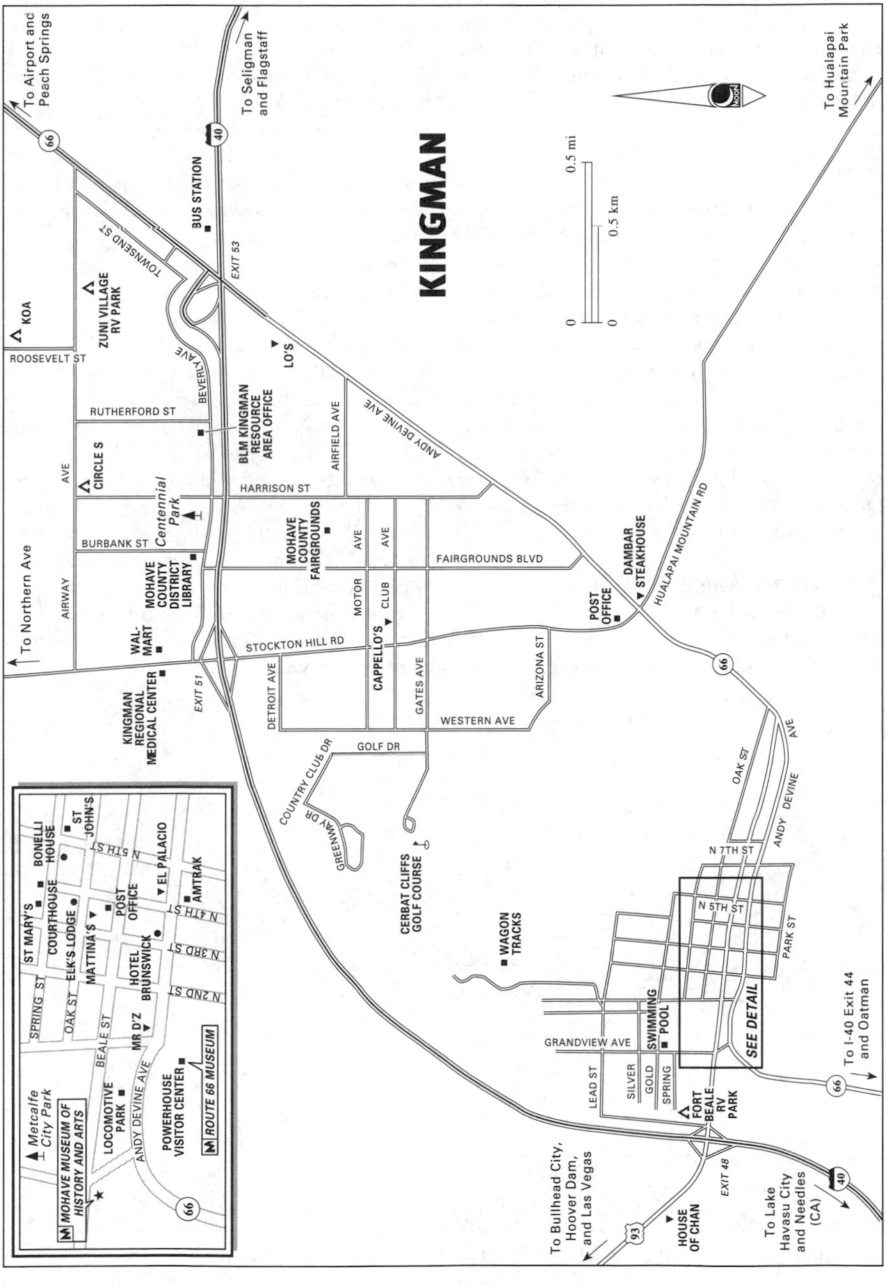

KINGMAN

To Airport and Peach Springs

To Seligman and Flagstaff

To Hualapai Mountain Park

KOA

ZUNI VILLAGE RV PARK

BUS STATION

ROOSEVELT ST

TOWNSEND ST

EXIT 53

LO'S

RUTHERFORD ST

BEVERLY AVE

BLM KINGMAN RESOURCE AREA OFFICE

AIRFIELD AVE

ANDY DEVINE AVE

CIRCLE S

AVE

HARRISON ST

Centennial Park

DAMBAR STEAKHOUSE

HUALAPAI MOUNTAIN RD

BURBANK ST

AVE

AVE

MOHAVE COUNTY FAIRGROUNDS

FAIRGROUNDS BLVD

To Northern Ave

AIRWAY

MOHAVE COUNTY DISTRICT LIBRARY

MOTOR

CLUB

POST OFFICE

WAL-MART

STOCKTON HILL RD

CAPPELLO'S

ARIZONA ST

66

KINGMAN REGIONAL MEDICAL CENTER

EXIT 51

DETROIT AVE

GATES AVE

WESTERN AVE

OAK ST

ANDY DEVINE

AVE

GOLF DR

COUNTRY CLUB DR

GREENWAY DR

CERBAT CLIFFS GOLF COURSE

N 7TH ST

N 5TH ST

PARK ST

SEE DETAIL

WAGON TRACKS

To I-40 Exit 44 and Oatman

Metcalfe City Park

ST MARY'S

BONELLI HOUSE

ST JOHN'S

5TH ST

COURTHOUSE

EL PALACIO

MOHAVE MUSEUM OF HISTORY AND ARTS

SPRING ST

OAK ST

ELK'S LODGE

POST OFFICE

4TH ST

AMTRAK

MATTINA'S

HOTEL BRUNSWICK

N 3RD ST

BEALE ST

MR D'Z

N 2ND ST

LOCOMOTIVE PARK

ANDY DEVINE AVE

POWERHOUSE VISITOR CENTER

ROUTE 66 MUSEUM

66

SWIMMING POOL

GRANDVIEW AVE

LEAD ST

SILVER

GOLD

SPRING

FORT BEALE RV PARK

EXIT 48

66

To Bullhead City, Hoover Dam, and Las Vegas

93

HOUSE OF CHAN

To Lake Havasu City and Needles (CA)

40

0 0.5 mi

0 0.5 km

Western Arizona

© AVALON TRAVEL PUBLISHING, INC.

use the town as a base to explore regional attractions such as the "Mother Road" Route 66, the cool forests of Hualapai Mountain Park, Lake Mead National Recreation Area, and the old mining towns of Oatman and Chloride.

SIGHTS

Historic Downtown

A map available at the town's visitors center provides a brief rundown on many of the old buildings in the historic downtown area. You can tour the early-20th-century Bonelli House or stay in the 1909 Brunswick Hotel, which also has a good restaurant. A few doors down from the Brunswick, Hotel Beale dates from 1899 and was the boyhood home of actor Andy Devine. It currently awaits restoration. The huge steam locomotive across from Powerhouse Visitor Center ran from 1929 to the mid-1950s, when the era of steam ended for the Santa Fe Railroad.

Mohave Museum of History and Arts

The varied collection (400 W. Beale St., 928/753-3195, www.mohavemuseum.org, 9 A.M.–5 P.M. Mon.–Fri. and 1–5 P.M. Sat., closed major holidays, $3 ages 13–59, $2 seniors 60+) offers a fine introduction to the history of northwestern Arizona. Dioramas, murals, and many artifacts show development from prehistoric times to the present. A ranching video tells about life on the range, past and present, in Mohave County. The Hualapai Native American Room contains a full-size wickiup brush shelter, pottery, baskets, and other crafts.

You'll also see paintings, sculpture, and crafts in the art gallery, photos showing construction of Hoover Dam, carved turquoise mined in the Kingman area, portraits of U.S. presidents with their first ladies, and a special exhibit on local-boy-turned-movie-star Andy Devine. The museum even features a pipe organ used in concerts here. Outdoor exhibits display ranching and mining machinery, storefronts, a mine replica, and a 1923 railroad caboose. History buffs can dig into the museum's library. A gift shop sells regional books and Native American crafts. Admission also gets you into the Route 66 Museum. From I-40 Exit 48, turn east .3 miles on Beale Street toward downtown.

COURTESY OF THE MOHAVE MUSEUM OF HISTORY & ARTS #3935

view west on Front Street (now Andy Devine) from 4th Street, 1940–1945

Route 66 Museum

You'll experience the history of travel on the 35th parallel in this museum (upstairs in the Powerhouse Visitor Center at 120 W. Andy Devine, 928/753-9889, daily 9 A.M.–6 P.M., to 5 P.M. in winter, $3 ages 13–59, $2 seniors 60+). The story begins with early trade routes and the Beale Wagon Road, which enabled pioneers to cross the land in "prairie schooners" such as the one on display. An old Chevrolet truck and quotations from John Steinbeck's *Grapes of Wrath* help you understand the tough times along Route 66 during the Great Depression of the 1930s. Storefronts, murals, and a 1950 Studebaker Champion illustrate the good times of the post-war era. Photo exhibits and personal accounts bring the past to life. A small theater shows videos on request.

Bonelli House

This historic house (downtown at 430 E. Spring St. and N. 5th, 928/753-1413, 11 A.M.–3 P.M. Mon.–Fri. except major holidays, donation requested) built of native tufa stone reflects the lifestyle and taste of a prominent Kingman family early in the 20th century. The Bonellis built their house in 1915 using both American and European designs. Thick walls insulate the interior from the temperature extremes of Kingman's desert climate. A member of the Bonelli family lived here until 1973, when the city of Kingman bought the house for restoration as a bicentennial project.

Other Historic Buildings

The former Saint John's United Methodist Church, east across 5th Street from the Bonelli House, dates from 1917; Clark Gable and Carole Lombard got married here in 1939. A block east, you can't miss the commanding 1915 Mohave County Courthouse; unfortunately the old courtroom is normally locked unless in use. A few doors west stands the diminutive 1907 St. Mary's Church; it's now used for Sunday school classes. Turn south one block on 4th Street from the Courthouse to see the 1906 Elks Lodge; the downstairs served as an opera house. South across Oak Street, many early Kingmanites learned their three Rs at the 1896 Little Red Schoolhouse.

Wagon Tracks

Wagons creaking down the hill into Kingman from the 1870s to the early 1900s carved deep ruts in the soft volcanic bedrock. Wagon masters used the evenly spaced holes beside the road for braking or leverage with long poles. Another road bypassed this spot in 1912, leaving the old road in its original condition.

The site lies near a pretty canyon just a short drive from town. From the Mohave Museum of History and Arts, take Grandview Avenue north .4 miles, then turn right and drive .6 miles on Lead Street, which becomes White Cliffs Road. Look for a wooden footbridge on the right, then walk across and follow the path across to the old wagon road.

Camp Beale Loop

If you'd like a scenic walk in the hills, this 3.2-mile loop trail of the Cerbat Foothills Recreation Area will fill the bill. The trail climbs gently up a ridge from 3,640 feet to a well-deserved rest bench 460 hundred feet higher at the top, then returns a different way. Panoramas take in Kingman, the Hualapai Mountains, and surrounding valleys and hills. Head out W. Beale Road/U.S. Highway 93 for .5 miles from I-40 Exit 48 toward Las Vegas, turn right 1.3 miles on Fort Beale Drive, then left .3 miles up a paved lane.

On the drive to the trailhead, you'll pass the remains of historic **Camp Beale Springs.** It's on the left .7 miles up Fort Beale Drive, opposite the sign for Wagon Trail Road. You may need a permit from Kingman's Parks & Recreation Department (3233 Harrison in Centennial Park, 928/757-7919, 8 A.M.–5 P.M. Mon.–Fri.).

If you'd like a longer hike, head northwest on an old road from the ridge-top bench. This is the **Castle Rock Trail,** which reaches a trail junction at the base of its namesake peak (4,634 ft.) in 4.4 miles one-way, where you have the option of ascending it in 1.2 miles round-trip, or continuing west 3.2 miles one-way on the **Badger Trail.** This trail ends at the Badger Trailhead (3,400 ft.), just off U.S. Highway 93 a short way north of the Highway 68 junction; it's accessible only from the northbound lanes.

Kingman Army Air Field Museum

During the darkest hours of World War II, the army hastily constructed a vast training camp northeast of Kingman to prepare gunners, pilots, and copilots for battles in the air. By war's end 35,000 cadets had earned their certificates here. Peacetime saw more than 7,000 bombers—mostly B-17s—make their final flight and land at this airfield to be broken up and melted into aluminum ingots. The museum (Kingman Airport, 928/757-1892, 11 A.M.–3 P.M. Tues.–Sat., donation) tells the stories of the men and women at the base. You'll see their photos, read of their experiences, and examine their equipment. The collection also includes many poignant tales and mementos from combat in World War II, the Korean War, and the Vietnam War. It's in an original 1942 wooden hangar at what's now Kingman's airport. Drive northeast 4.5 miles on Highway 66 from I-40 Exit 53, turn right 1.1 miles into the airport to the four-way stop just before the old control tower, then turn right .5 miles on Flightline Drive to #4540.

PRACTICALITIES

Entertainment and Events

Catch films at **The Movies** (4055 Stockton Hill, 928/757-7985).

Staff at the Powerhouse Visitor Center provide information on local happenings. Classic and antique cars roll into town for the **Route 66 Fun Run Road Rally** in early May. Artists and craftspeople display their work at the **Festival of the Arts** on Mothers' Day weekend in May.

Take in the exhibits and entertainment of the **Mohave County Fair** in mid-September. Kingmanites and visitors celebrate **Andy Devine Days** with a parade, PRCA rodeo, and other festivities in late September or early October. See handmade artistry in the **Kingman Cancer Care Arts and Crafts Fair** on the second weekend in November. The **Caroling Festival and Parade of Lights** add cheer in mid-December.

Recreation

Metcalfe City Park (W. Beale and Grandview Ave.) offers shade trees, picnic tables, and a playground, diagonally opposite the Mohave Museum of History and Arts. You'll find **swimming pools** downtown at the corner of Grandview Avenue and Gold Street (928/753-8155) and in Centennial Park (3333 N. Harrison, 928/757-7910). **Centennial Park** also has tennis and racquetball courts, ball fields, and picnicking.

Golfers play at the 18-hole courses at **Cerbat Cliffs Golf Course** (1001 E. Gates, west off Stockton Hill Rd., 928/753-6593) and 17 miles northeast on Highway 66 at **Valle Vista** (9686 N. Concho Dr., 928/757-8744).

Accommodations

Most of Kingman's motels and restaurants line W. Beale (U.S. 93) and E. Andy Devine (Rte. 66/AZ 66) between I-40 Exits 48 and 53. Travelers have a choice of older, well-kept motels, newer "economy" places, high-standard chains, and one historic hotel. Competition keeps prices low—accommodations are some of the best bargains in the state. Rates tend to go up a bit in summer, when reservations are recommended for weekends, especially during an event. Hualapai Mountain Park offers lodgings too; see Vicinity of Kingman below.

Historic Hotel: The 1909 **Hotel Brunswick** (downtown at 315 E. Andy Devine, 928/718-1800, www.hotel-brunswick.com) has been beautifully restored. Rooms start at $30 d for a small one with bath down the hall and cost $55 d with bath or $85–125 d for a suite. Hubbs Bistro (closed Sun.) offers French and Cajun cuisine for dinner.

Under $50: Many of these post their prices. Motels just off I-40 Exit 48 on the way to Las Vegas include **Knights Inn** (1239 W. Beale, 928/753-2773, $40 s, $45 d) and **Frontier Motel** (1250 W. Beale, 928/753-6171, $25 s, $30 d). If you head toward downtown on W. Beale from Exit 48, you'll soon come to **Motel 6 West** (424 W. Beale, 928/753-9222 or 800/466-8356, $37–40 d) and **Arizona Inn** (411 W. Beale, 928/753-5521, $32–35 d).

Another group lies just east of downtown, and you can get views from some rooms at **El**

Hotel Beale lobby in downtown Kingman

Trovatore Motel (1440 E. Andy Devine, 928/753-6520, $26 d) and **Hill Top Motel** 1901 E. Andy Devine, 928/753-2198, $32–39 s, $32–42 d). The longest string—and greatest concentration of chain motels—lies farther east of downtown along Andy Devine near I-40 Exit 53. Here you'll see such places as **1st Value Inn** (3270 E. Andy Devine, 928/757-7122, $28 s, $32 d), **Silver Queen** (3285 E. Andy Devine, 928/757-4315, $30 s, $33 d), **Motel 6 East** (3351 E. Andy Devine, 928/757-7151 or 800/466-8356, $30 d), **Days Inn East** (3381 E. Andy Devine, 928/757-7337 or 800/329-7666, $33–45 d), and **Super 8** (3401 E. Andy Devine, 928/757-4808 or 800/800-8000, $30–36 s, $36–40 d).

$50–100: The well-known chains hold down this category, and nearly all lie just west off I-40 Exit 53 toward downtown. Choices include **Best Western Kings Inn & Suites** (2930 E. Andy Devine, 928/753-6101 or 800/750-6101, $75 s, $75–79 d and up) with an outdoor pool, indoor spa, and an exercise room; you can upgrade to minisuites or suites.

Campgrounds

All of these stay open year-round. The **Kingman KOA** (928/757-4397 or 800/562-3991, $18 tent or RV no hookups, $25–27 RV w/hookups, $37 cabin) offers a pool, showers, game room, store, and miniature golf. Take I-40 Exit 51, go north half a mile on Stockton Hill Road, turn right one mile on Airway Avenue, then left on Roosevelt to the campground. **Zuni Village RV Park** (2840 Airway Ave., near I-40 Exit 53, 928/692-6202, $16.50 RV w/hookups) has a pool and showers. **Circle S Campground** (2360 Airway, near I-40 Exit 53, 928/757-3235, $12 tents, $17.50 RV w/hookups) also includes a pool and showers.

Fort Beale RV Park (300 Metcalfe Rd. near I-40 Exit 48, 928/753-3355, $25 RV w/hookups) features a pool, showers, and views. **Canyon West RV** (2 miles west of downtown off Rte. 66/Oatman Rd., 928/753-9378, $12 tent, $20 RV w/hookups) offers sites with a shower. **Highway 66 RV Park** (northeast 16 miles down Rte. 66 at Valle Vista, near Milepost 71, 928/757-8878, $20 w/hookups) accepts self-contained RVs only.

Blake Ranch RV Park (18 miles east of Kingman on Blake Ranch Rd., just off I-40

Exit 66, 928/757-3336, $19 tent, $20–22 RV w/hookups) has showers. **Hualapai Mountain Park,** 14 miles southeast of town, offers tent and RV sites in cool pine forests.

Food

Lots of American eateries line the Business Route, and you'll find popular chain and fast-food places near all three I-40 exits. The Route 66 era lives on downtown at the 1950s-style **Mr. D'z Route 66 Diner** (105 E. Andy Devine, 928/718-0066, breakfast, lunch, and dinner daily, $7–12) with American classics on the extensive menu.

Hubbs Bistro (downtown at 315 E. Andy Devine in the Hotel Brunswick, 928/718-1800, dinner Mon.–Sat., $13.50–19) prepares excellent French and Cajun food. Specialties include crayfish étouffée cooked Louisiana style and duck breast Napoleon speared with ginger and baked in a ginger and orange sauce.

When you see the life-size steer on the roof of a western-style building, you've arrived at the **Dambar Steakhouse** (1960 E. Andy Devine and Stockton Hill/Hualapai Mtn. Rds., 928/753-3523, lunch and dinner daily, $9–25). Steaks feature on the menu, which also includes prime rib, chicken, pork, catfish, seafood, and vegetable pasta. There's sawdust on the floor, a saloon, and dining areas decorated with ranch artifacts, mining gear, and Andy Devine memorabilia.

Cappello's (1921 Club Ave., just east off Stockton Hill, 928/718-3300, lunch and dinner daily, $6–29) prepares fine Italian pasta and meat dishes. Staff make their own pasta and pride themselves on their veal and steak dishes. The main dining room has tables and booths around a central fountain; murals and framed paintings decorate the walls.

Mattina's Ristorante Italiano (downtown at 318 Oak St., 928/753-7504, dinner Tues.–Sat., $12–20) has great steaks along with Sicilian flavors of seafood, chicken, and pasta. The owner plays on a mafia theme in naming the dishes, and has photos of Frank Sinatra and his "rat pack" in one dining room and photos of notorious mobsters in another. You can join cooking classes a couple of times a month.

For Mexican food, try **El Palacio** (downtown at 401 E. Andy Devine, 928/718-0018, lunch and dinner daily, $6–13). The menu lists many appetizers and salads as well as such specialties as fajitas and the steak à la diablo—sirloin sautéed in a secret picante hot sauce. You can also choose among the burritos, tostadas, seafood items, egg dishes, and combos. Splashes of bright color add a festive air to the dining room.

Two Chinese-American restaurants at opposite ends of town offer long and varied menus. **House of Chan** (just northwest off I-40 Exit 48 at 960 W. Beale, 928/753-3232, daily lunch and dinner, $5–11.25) features a buffet option for both lunch and dinner. **Lo's Restaurant** (119 Tucker Ave., 928/753-5673, daily lunch and dinner, $5.25–17) is a few blocks west on Andy Devine from I-40 Exit 53—look for the giant sign.

Information and Services

Staff at the **Powerhouse Visitor Center** (downtown at 120 W. Andy Devine or P.O. Box 1150, Kingman, AZ 86402, 928/753-6106 or 866/427-7866, www.kingmantourism.org, daily 9 A.M.–6 P.M., to 5 P.M. in winter) can help you explore this corner of Arizona. The large building—one of Arizona's first reinforced concrete structures—dates from 1907. It also houses a Route 66 museum, photo exhibits, and shops.

Find out about recreation areas and the backcountry near Kingman at the Powerhouse Visitor Center or the **BLM Kingman field office** (2475 Beverly Ave., Kingman, AZ 86401, 928/692-4400, www.az.blm.gov, 7:30 A.M.–4:30 P.M. Mon.–Fri.).

The **Mohave County District Library** (north and east of I-40 Exit 51 at 3269 Burbank St., 928/692-2665, closed Sun.) offers an Arizona collection and Internet access. **Hastings Books** (just south of I-40 Exit 51 at 3153 Stockton Hill Rd., 928/753-1012) has regional titles.

Wal-Mart (just north and east from I-40 Exit 51) sells sporting goods and other supplies. The main **post office** (1901 Johnson, 928/753-2480) is one block north on Stockton Hill Road from Andy Devine, though the downtown branch at 209 N. 4th Street can be more convenient. **Kingman Regional Medical Center** (3269 Stockton Hill Rd., 928/757-2101) is just north of I-40 Exit 51.

Getting There and Around

Buses run by **Greyhound** (3264 E. Andy Devine, 928/757-8400) stop at the tiny station behind McDonald's just east of I-40 Exit 53. **Amtrak** (downtown at the corner of 4th Street and Andy Devine, 800/872-7245) offers daily passenger train service west to Los Angeles and east to Flagstaff, Albuquerque, and beyond. **America West Express** (800/235-9292) flies to Phoenix via Prescott from the airport northeast of town off Highway 66; Hertz rents cars here. **Kingman Area Regional Transit** (928/681-7433) will take you around town.

VICINITY OF KINGMAN

Hualapai Mountain Park

The Hualapai, whose name means Pine Tree Folk, lived in these mountains until the military relocated the tribe northward in the 1870s. Today the 14-mile paved Hualapai Mountain Road takes you up to the park's dense forests, scenic views, hiking trails, picnicking, camping, and rustic cabins. Elevations range from 5,000 to 8,417 feet, attracting wildlife rarely seen elsewhere in northwestern Arizona. Groves of manzanita, scrub and Gambel oak, pinyon and ponderosa pine, white fir, and aspen grow on the slopes. Mule deer, elk, mountain lion, fox, and raccoon roam the forests. Hiking trails wind through the mountains to the summit of Aspen Peak and overlooks on Hayden Peak. Day use costs $5 per vehicle.

Campsites have drinking water, except in winter, but no showers ($10). A small RV area offers hookups for $17. Cabins ($35–75), built for a Civilian Conservation Corps camp in the 1930s, have kitchens and bathrooms. You can visit the park any time of year, though winter snows sometimes require chains or 4WD. The Hualapai Ranger Station (928/757-3859) at the park entrance is open daily 9 A.M.–5 P.M. For information and reservations at the cabins, contact the Mohave County Parks Department (6230 Hualapai Mountain Rd., Kingman, AZ 86401, 928/754-7273 or 877/757-0915, www.mcparks.com, 7 A.M.–3 P.M. daily)

The nearby **Hualapai Mountain Lodge** (in the village of Pine Lake, 928/757-3545) offers a motel, RV park, restaurant, and store. Some of the well-preserved buildings here once belonged to the CCC camp. The motel ($75 d, $110 suite) and restaurant are open Tuesday–Sunday year-round. The restaurant serves breakfast (Sat.–Sun. only), lunch, and dinner. RVs can park for $20 with hookups. From Kingman, drive to the Hualapai Mountain Park, then continue on the paved road .75 miles past the ranger station. Also open all year, **Pine Lake Inn Bed & Breakfast** (928/757-1884, $95 d) is .75 miles farther and overlooks the lake.

The Bureau of Land Management's **Wild Cow Springs Campground** ($5, no water) nestles in a secluded valley of ponderosa pine and Gambel oak at an elevation of 6,200 feet, but you'll need a high-clearance vehicle to get here; the season normally runs May–October. From Hualapai Mountain Park, continue just past the turn for Hualapai Mountain Lodge, then turn right four miles at the sign on a rough unpaved road.

With a high-clearance 4WD vehicle, you can continue high on Hualapai Ridge Road 13.5 miles past the campground to the trailhead for Wabayuma Peak in **Wabayuma Peak Wilderness Area.** From an elevation of 6,047 feet, the trail follows a road at first, then turns west up to a saddle, where you'll head northwest to the 7,601-foot summit and great views; it's three miles one-way; use the 7.5-minute Wabayuma topo map. The rough jeep road continues south, then turns west down the Boriana Mine Road to Yucca at I-40 Exit 25. The drive is slow, taking at least three hours one-way from Wild Cow Springs Campground to I-40, but you'll have great panoramas of the Hualapai Mountains and beyond. The amazing range of vegetation on this drive includes ponderosa pine forests, pinyon pine and juniper woodlands, and chaparral atop the ridges, then saguaro, ocotillo, yucca, and Joshua trees in the desert below. You'll see extensive ruins of the Boriana Mine on the descent.

Hackberry General Store & Visitor Center

For a trip into America's motoring past, stop here on your drive along Route 66 between Kingman

© BILL WEIR

A '57 Corvette stands ready to cruise at the Hackberry General Store & Visitor Center.

and Seligman. A colorful collection (928/769-2605, open daily, free) of Route 66 memorabilia, including a '57 Corvette and other vintage cars and trucks, surrounds the old store. Signs from long ago cover the walls inside and outside. Vintage gas pumps have unbelievable prices, but have long since gone dry. You can shop for Route 66 memorabilia. It's on the north side of Route 66 opposite the Hackberry turnoff, 24 miles northeast of Kingman.

Cerbat

Gold and silver deposits in the Cerbat Mountains, north of present-day Kingman, attracted miners in the late 1860s. They founded the town of Cerbat and worked such mines as the Esmeralda, Golden Gem, and Vanderbilt. Cerbat became the Mohave County seat in 1871 but lost the honor two years later to nearby Mineral Park. By 1912 the Cerbat post office had closed. Still standing are the Golden Gem mill and headframe, structures that rarely survive in other ghost towns. You'll also see stone foundations and ruins of other buildings.

The turnoff for Cerbat lies nine miles northwest of Kingman on U.S. Highway 93 at a historical marker near Milepost 62. Head east .7 miles on a dirt road, turn left and drive .6 miles, then turn right and travel another 2 miles to the site. Keep left when passing a ranch and a group of modern mine buildings just outside old Cerbat. The last .3 miles is too rough for cars.

Mineral Park

During most of the 1870s and 1880s, Mineral Park reigned as the county seat and most important town in the area, losing these distinctions in 1886 to Kingman. By 1912 Mineral Park had lost even its post office. Some tattered cabins, a headframe, mill foundations, and scattered mine shafts survive from the old days. The huge piles of tailings to the south belong to a copper and molybdenum mine that operated 1961–1982. It still contains the world's largest turquoise deposit, which is mined along with decorative rock. The marked turnoff and a historical marker for Mineral Park lie 14 miles northwest of Kingman on U.S. Highway 93, between Mileposts 58 and 59. Turn east 4.3 miles on a paved road, then left .3 miles on a well-used gravel road; the turn is just before the fenced-in modern mine.

Chloride

After discovering silver chloride ore here in the early 1860s, prospectors founded the town—the oldest mining camp in northwestern Arizona. Hualapai warriors made life precarious during Chloride's first years until army troops subdued the tribe. The peak years of 1900–1920 saw 75 mines in operation. Several buildings survive from the town's lengthy mining period, which lasted into the 1940s. A few hundred people, including many retirees and artists, now live here. This friendly town lies 20 miles northwest of Kingman; follow U.S. Highway 93 to the sign between Mileposts 52 and 53, then turn east 3 miles on a paved road.

Historic structures include old miners' shacks, post office, Old Tennessee Saloon, jail, bank, and railroad depot; the cemetery is to the right at the sign as you enter town. It's fun to wander around the historic buildings and check out some of the antique and crafts shops.

Artist Roy Purcell painted giant, brightly colored murals in 1966 and 1975 on cliffs two miles southeast of town. He titled his work *The Journey—Images from an Inward Search for Self.* You can also spot prehistoric petroglyphs across the road from the murals. To get here from Chloride, take Tennessee Avenue (the main road into town) past the post office and Tennessee Mine, then follow signs; the road may be too rough for low-slung cars. With a high-clearance 4WD vehicle, it's possible to continue up the road, which becomes rocky and steep, to a seasonal waterfall in another half mile or all the way up past old mines to the Big Wash Road in the Cerbat Mountains; some of this is private land.

Sheps Miners Inn (Second St., 928/565-4251 or 877/565-4251, www.shepsminersinn.com) offers adobe rooms with private bath and individual entrances at $35–65 d, plus some monthly RV spaces. **Chloride Western RV Park** (on the left as you enter town, 928/565-4492) is open year-round with tent ($7) and RV sites ($10 dry, $13.50 w/hookups), showers, a laundry, and a rec room.

Yesterdays Restaurant at Shep's serves up breakfast, lunch, and dinner daily and often has live music. **DJ's Café & Saloon** and the **Old Tennessee Saloon** serve food too, but can be very smoky. **Mine Shaft Market & Arizona Visitor Center** sells groceries and has a coffee shop. You can have a picnic at the park on Second Street across from Shep's.

Try to be in town at high noon on Saturdays, when blazing action takes place at the Old West set of Cyanide Springs across from Shep's. The **Immortal Gunfighters** perform on the first and third Saturdays of each month, and the all-women Wild Roses of Chloride supply the action on the second and fourth Saturdays (except July and Aug.). Townspeople dress up in old-fashioned clothing on **Old Miners' Day,** the last Saturday and following Sunday in June, for a street dance, games, vaudeville shows, shootouts, and mine tours. Smaller events include a St. Patrick's Day celebration in March, all-town yard sales in May and October, and a car show in October. The **post office,** said to be Arizona's oldest, is at Tennessee Avenue and Second Street.

Mine Shaft Market & Arizona Visitor Center provides tourist information and a historic photo exhibition in the back. You can reach the **Chloride Chamber of Commerce** at P.O. Box 268, Chloride, AZ 86431 or www.chloridearizona.com.

The Cerbat Mountains

Unpaved Big Wash Road twists up to the crest of the Cerbat Mountains, where you can enjoy expansive views, picnicking, camping, and hiking among pinyon pine and chaparral. The road begins near Milepost 51 on U.S. Highway 93, 1.5 miles north of the Chloride junction. It's graded but too steep and winding for RVs or trailers.

Packsaddle Recreation Area lies 9 miles in, and the **Windy Point Recreation Area** entrance is 1.5 miles beyond. Both areas have sites with picnic tables and vault toilets but no water; a $4 camping fee applies at Windy Point, which has a particularly scenic setting among boulders and great views to the west.

Cherum Peak Trail climbs to near the 6,983-foot summit of the peak, second highest in the Cerbats, then it's a short rock scramble up the last 200 feet to the top. This five-mile round-trip hike takes about 3.5 hours. You'll pass through pinyon pine groves and large areas of chaparral, which contains shrub live oak, manzanita, Wrights's silk-tassel, broom snakeweed, skunkbush, New Mexican locust, Gambel oak, and desert ceanothus. Many wildflowers bloom in early summer. The trailhead (elev. about 6,000 ft.) is on the left, two miles past Windy Point. See the 7.5-minute Chloride topo map and the handouts available from the BLM's Kingman field office (928/692-4400, www.az.blm.gov). Only high-clearance 4WD vehicles can negotiate the steep, rough descent to Chloride past the trailhead.

Oatman

The weather-beaten gold-mining town of Oatman nestles in the western foothills of the Black Mountains, 28 miles southwest of Kingman. Elephant's Tooth, the gleaming white quartz pinnacle east of town, beckoned prospectors, who knew that gold and silver often run with quartz. Gold mining began in 1904, attracting hordes of miners and businesspeople. Citizens named the community for the Oatman family, victims of an 1851 Mohave attack.

Oatman prospered, attracting many new businesses including seven hotels, 20 saloons, and even a stock exchange. Area mines produced nearly two million ounces of gold before panning out in the 1930s. The town, which once boasted more than 12,000 citizens, began to fade away and might have disappeared altogether had it not become a travelers' stop on Route 66. Oatman lost its highway traffic in 1952, when engineers rerouted the road to the south. A few hundred citizens hang on today, relying largely on the tourist business. You're almost sure to meet the town's wild burros as they wander the streets looking for handouts. They like carrots but have been known to bite.

Getting here is half the fun if you take old Route 66 from Kingman (west on Andy Devine or I-40 McConnico Exit 44) or from Golden Shores (north of I-40 Topock Exit 1). This section of the old highway, now a National Backcountry Byway, has great scenery at every turn—and there are lots of them! Between Kingman and Oatman you'll cross 3,550-foot Sitgreaves Pass over the Black Mountains; pullouts on each side allow a stop for the views. Near Oatman, you'll pass the Gold Road Mine, which has a long history and now offers underground tours.

Two other roads connect Oatman with the outside world. From Bullhead City and Needles, you can take paved Boundary Cone Road east from Highway 95. A more scenic option—best with a high-clearance vehicle—follows Silver Creek Road into the hills; it turns east off Highway 95 in Bullhead City between Mileposts 246 and 247 (pavement runs out after crossing Bullhead Pkwy.) and joins the Oatman Highway at Milepost 26 between Oatman and the Gold Road Mine.

Many of the town's old buildings survive, and some now house little exhibits, art galleries, and gift shops. Step inside the **Oatman Hotel** (928/768-4408), a two-story adobe structure built in 1902, to peer into the chamber where movie stars Clark Gable and Carole Lombard spent part of their honeymoon in March 1939. Gable liked to visit Oatman, a place where he could get away from the hectic pace of Hollywood and enjoy poker with the miners. The hotel rents basic rooms for $35 d and the Lombard-Gable room for $55. It also serves food and drink, but don't expect luxuries such as a nonsmoking area. Across the street, **Olive Oatman Restaurant & Ice Cream Saloon** serves breakfast, Navajo tacos, and burgers. Musicians often play at both places. RVs can park 11 miles west of town at **Blackstone RV Park** (3299 E. Boundary Cone Rd., 928/768-3303), which has a store. **Oatman Stables** (928/768-3257) shows off the rugged scenery from horseback on one- and two-hour rides at the lower end of town mid-October–mid-May; you can also to head out for a steak dinner by horseback or wagon.

Shootouts take place daily on Main Street. Hilarity reigns on the second Sunday of January in the **Oatman Bed Races.** On July 4, competitors warm up for the **Oatman Sidewalk Egg Fry.** Oatman celebrates **Gold Camp Days** on Labor Day weekend with shootouts, a burro biscuit tossing contest, costume parade, and dancing. Desert flora glitters along Route 66 south of town during the **Christmas Bush Festival.**

For local information, contact the Oatman-Goldroad Chamber of Commerce (PO Box 423,

Oatman, AZ 86433, 928/768-6222, www.oatmangoldroad.com).

Vicinity of Oatman

At **Gold Road Mine** (928/768-1600, www.goldroadmine.com, $12 adult, $6 age 12 and under) you can tour the underground passages where the gold boom started! A guide gives you a hard hat and transports you in a "getman" or other vehicle up to the original entrance. On an easy one-hour walk you'll see the workings and learn about how miners did their job. Longer tours, stagecoach rides (Oct.–mid-April), and trail rides can be arranged by reservation. Head east 2.5 miles from Oatman on Route 66 up into the Black Mountains to between Mileposts 27 and 28.

Mohave and Milltown Railroad Trails follow a seven-mile section of the old railway bed, beginning about five miles southwest of Oatman. Signs at trailheads tell about the railroad's history. Separate trails and trailheads accommodate both off-highway vehicles/equestrians and hikers-bikers. Cautiously driven SUVs can follow the trail. The BLM's Kingman field office (928/692-4400, www.az.blm.gov) has a map and description. From Oatman, head southwest about three miles on Route 66 and turn right two miles at the fork on Boundary Cone Road to Mile 9.25 for the east hiker-biker trailhead at the pullout on your left. For the east vehicle-equestrian trailhead, stay on Route 66 two miles past the fork, then turn right (southwest) half a mile on an unpaved and unmarked road opposite Milepost 21. The west trailhead is a bit trickier to find: Turn east from Highway 95 on Willow Drive near Spirit Mountain Casino, then, after 3 miles, turn left at two consecutive unmarked road forks and continue 1.8 miles.

Dinosphere

This odd structure, looking like a cross between a giant golf ball and a spaceship, stands near Yucca (I-40 Exit 25) between Kingman and the California state line. It has three levels and measures 40 feet in diameter. Lake Havasu Estates built it in 1976 as a restaurant and cocktail lounge for a land development. The company went bankrupt, however, and the white sphere now serves as a private home. It's not open to the public.

Burro Creek Recreation Site

If you're driving U.S. Highway 93 between Kingman and Wickenburg or Phoenix, you'll pass this scenic canyon. A perennial stream feeds deep blue pools and lush greenery in the desert at an elevation of 1,960 feet. Open all year, it's a great place to take a break from the long drive; day use is free. Visitors enjoy camping, picnicking, birding, swimming, hiking, four-wheeling, and rock hounding for agates and Apache tears. A cactus garden and interpretive signs introduce life of the desert. Hikers can head up the creek bed if the water isn't too high—the creek extends some 40 miles upstream and goes through the heart of **Burro Creek Wilderness;** downstream is private land. The campground ($10/night) has drinking water, flush toilets, and a dump station, but no showers. For information and group campsite ($30) reservations, contact the BLM's Kingman field office (2475 Beverly Ave., Kingman, AZ 86401, 928/692-4400, www.az.blm.gov). Head southeast 65 miles from Kingman on I-40 and U.S. Highway 93, or northwest 63 miles from Wickenburg, then turn west 1.3 miles at the sign. An overlook on the west side of the highway near the bridge provides a fine panorama of the area.

Bullhead City and Laughlin

This growing community of more than 35,000 residents lines Highway 95 and the Colorado River for about 10 miles. Gamblers, anglers, and boaters enjoy the river setting, and Lake Mohave's 240 square miles of deep blue water lies six miles north.

Although gold miners had worked prospects nearby, this remote site lay deserted until the 1940s, when construction workers arrived to build Davis Dam upstream. With completion of the dam in 1953, everyone assumed that the construction camp called Bullhead City would disappear. Instead it became a center for outdoor recreation. The "bullhead" rock formation that gave the place its name nearly did disappear—only the "horns" now poke out of the lake.

Bullhead City lies 35 miles west of Kingman via Highway 68 and 25 miles north of Needles, California, on Highway 95. Bright lights of gambling casinos in sister city Laughlin sparkle from across the river in Nevada. South of town, the Colorado River enters Havasu National Wildlife Refuge.

Colorado River Historical Society Museum

Exhibits (928/754-3399, 10 A.M.–4 P.M., Tues.–Sun., closed July–Aug., donations welcome) commemorate local Native Americans, steamboating on the Colorado River, mining, ranching, and dam construction. Photographs and maps show the growth of the Bullhead City/Laughlin area from early beginnings to modern times. A children's room offers activities. Head north .3 miles on Highway 68 from the Laughlin Bridge junction, then turn left.

Arizona Veterns Memorial

In a dramatic setting above the Colorado River, Arizona Veterans Memorial commemorates the 3,000 Arizonans who lost their lives in service for their country during the 20th century. Head south four miles on Highway 95 from the chamber office, then turn west two miles on Riverview Drive and follow signs.

Events

Cloud's Jamboree Rock, Gem, & Mineral Show gleams in January at Laughlin. The dust flies as vehicles compete in **Laughlin Desert Challenge Off-Road Race,** also in January. The **Colorado River Bluegrass Festival** plays in February. **Laughlin River Stampede PRCA Rodeo** gallops in April. Thousands of motorcycle riders rumble into town for the **Harley Run** during April. You can enjoy food and games—but no burro—at the **Burro Barbecue** in Bullhead Community Park in April. In June, Nevadans celebrate **Laughlin River Days** with a boat race. **Fireworks** on July 4 light up the skies over the Colorado River. Cowboys hang on in the **Laughlin Professional Bull Rider Series** in September. Bullhead City throws a community celebration in **Hardyville Days** in October. It's men against beast in **Laughlin Team Roping Finals** in November. Boats glitter in a **Parade of Lights** at Lake Mohave Resort (Katherine Landing) in December.

Recreation

Bullhead Community Park, just north of the chamber of commerce, is a pleasant spot for a picnic overlooking the Colorado River; there's also a playground and boat ramp.

Some of the best Colorado River fishing lies right in front of Bullhead City. The cold and swift waters from Davis Dam harbor large rainbow trout, channel catfish and, during late spring and early summer, giant striped bass weighing 20 pounds and more.

Accommodations and Campgrounds

You have a choice of more than a dozen motels and about a dozen RV parks in Bullhead City, or you can stay across the river at the casinos in Laughlin. Try to make reservations for motels, casinos, and RV parks, especially if you're arriving on a weekend. You can save money at many places by visiting Sunday–Thursday, when casino rooms may drop to as low as $20.

Campgrounds and RV parks stay open year-round, though most RV parks prefer that guests stay a week or longer. Mohave County's **Davis Camp Park** (928/754-7250, 877/757-0915, www.mcparks.com) offers beach sites for tents and RVs ($10 no hookups, $13–16 w/hookups), a picnic area, boat ramps, and showers. Day use is $4, or $7 if pulling a boat trailer. The park is on the west side of Highway 68, .8 miles north of the Laughlin Bridge junction. Katherine Landing, six miles north of Bullhead City on Lake Mohave, has a motel, RV park, and campground.

Food

A variety of restaurants line Highway 95 for many miles. For Italian dining, try **Antonucci's Ristorante** (1751 Hwy. 95, 928/763-8118, Mon.–Sat. lunch and dinner). Enjoy Chinese cuisine at **China Szechuan** (1890 Hwy. 95, 928/763-2610) or **China Panda** (2164 Hwy. 95, 928/763-8899); both are open daily for lunch and dinner. Mexican cuisine is prepared at **El Encanto,** in the north part of town (125 Long Ave. and 7th St., 928/754-5100); **El Palacio** (1884 Hwy. 95, 928/763-2494); and on the water at **Iguana's Mexican River Cantina** (2247 Clearwater Dr., 928/763-9109); all are open daily for lunch and dinner. Casinos on the Nevada side feature enticing menus and prices.

Information and Services

Bullhead Area Chamber of Commerce (1251 Hwy. 95, Bullhead City, AZ 86429, 928/754-4121, www.bullheadchamber.com) is on the south side of Bullhead Community Park, 2.2 miles south of the Laughlin bridge. It's open year-round Monday–Friday 8 A.M.–5 P.M., plus Saturdays October–April. The **public library** (1170 E. Hancock Rd., 928/758-071, closed Sun.) is in south Bullhead City. **Hastings Books** (1985 Hwy. 95, 928/763-0025) offers regional and general-interest titles.

A **post office** (990 Hwy. 95, 928/758-5711) is on the north edge of town. **Western Arizona Regional Medical Center** (2735 Silver Creek Rd., 928/763-2273) is 1.3 miles south of the chamber office on Highway 95, then east on Silver Creek Road.

Getting There and Around

Sun Country (Don Laughlin's Riverside Resort, 800/227-3849, www.riversideresort.com) flies seasonally to many U.S. destinations. The airport is just north of Bullhead City (turn east at the Laughlin Bridge junction) with car rentals, charter flights, and a snack bar.

LAUGHLIN, NEVADA

The casinos on the Nevada side of the river try to attract your business with dazzle, entertainment, lavish food, and lodging deals. Laughlin's casinos have a more casual—some say more friendly—atmosphere than the bigger gambling centers of Las Vegas and Reno. From Bullhead City you can drive across the Colorado River bridge just north of town or take the eight-mile route via Davis Dam farther north. Buses and boats connect the casinos for a small charge.

Standard rooms at the casinos typically run in the low- to mid-$20s Sunday–Thursday, $45–75 Friday–Saturday, and $45–145 on holiday weekends; advance reservations help to secure lower prices. You can call a hotel reservation service at 800/452-8445 (800/4LAUGHLIN) or surf to www.visitlaughlin.com.

Buffets can have long lines—you may wish to avoid those offering specials! Many locals prefer to patronize the town's fine-dining restaurants, which have better service and still offer good prices.

Don Laughlin's Riverside Resort Hotel & Casino (702/298-2535 or 928/763-7070, www.riversideresort.com) features **Don Laughlin's Classic Car Collection** (free) and a six-screen movie theater at the north end of the strip. **Horizon Outlet Center** (1955 S. Casino Dr., 702/298-3003) offers shopping and a nine-screen movie theater. Tour boats head out on short trips near Laughlin and on all-day excursions to Lake Havasu City via Topock Gorge; ask at one of the visitor centers.

Laughlin Visitor Center (1555 S. Casino Dr., Laughlin, NV 89029, 702/298-3321 or 800/452-8445, www.visitlaughlin.com, daily 8 A.M.–4:30 P.M.) is on your right as you enter the strip from Bullhead City; staff offer travel information for Las Vegas, too. Pick up a hotel reservation courtesy phone to find the best lodging deals here or in Las Vegas.

Next door, the **Laughlin Chamber of Commerce** (1585 S. Casino Dr. or P.O. Box 77777, Laughlin, NV 89028, 702/298-2214 or 800/227-5245, www.laughlinchamber.com, 8:30 A.M.–4:30 P.M. Mon.–Fri.) will also help you plan a visit, and can advise on sights and services in the Bullhead City area.

Lake Mead National Recreation Area

The Colorado River forms two long lakes as it winds more than 144 miles through Lake Mead National Recreation Area. From Grand Canyon National Park, the blue waters flow around the extreme northwest corner of Arizona past black volcanic rocks, stark hillsides, and white, sandy beaches. Striking desert scenery and inviting waters make the area a paradise for boaters, anglers, water-skiers, swimmers, and scuba divers. Visitors sometimes sight bighorn sheep on the canyon cliffs and wild burros in the more level areas. Adventurous four-wheelers and hikers can explore the hills and canyons of the wild, seldom-visited country inland.

Some areas have an entry fee unless you have one of the national parks passes; otherwise it's $5 per vehicle ($3 motorcycle, bicycle, or hiker) for a five-day permit. Motorized vessels cost $10 for the first one and $5 for each additional craft for five days; annual permits cost just twice as much.

The National Park Service provides boat ramps, developed campgrounds ($10/night; water but no showers or hookups), and ranger stations at most developed areas. Park Service people and volunteers staff the Alan Bible Visitor Center at the turnoff for Boulder Beach, four miles west of Hoover Dam.

The boating and camping season lasts all year at the lakes. Most people come in summer, and though it's hot, swimmers and water skiers best appreciate the water then. Spring and autumn bring pleasant temperatures both on land and on water. In winter, you wouldn't want to hop in without a wetsuit, though topside temperatures are usually pleasant during the day. Scuba divers find the best conditions in winter (Oct.–April), when visibilities run 20–50 feet versus 10–20 feet in summer.

RECREATION

Boating

To get the most from a visit to Lake Mohave and Lake Mead, you really need a boat, as roads approach the waterline at only a few scattered points. If you don't have your own, marinas offer rentals, from humble fishing craft to luxurious houseboats. Boat tours take in some of the scenery of Lake Mead from near Boulder Beach. You can also glide through Black Canyon below Hoover Dam on a raft tour.

Fishing

Both Lake Mohave and Lake Mead offer excellent fishing year-round for trout, largemouth and striped bass, channel catfish, crappie, and bluegill. Lake Mohave's upper reaches are especially good for rainbow trout. Both lakes offer hot fishing for striped bass—some specimens top 50 pounds. Most marinas sell licenses and tackle. Marinas and ranger stations can advise on the fishing regulations and the best spots to fish. Shore anglers need a license only from the state they're in. If you fish from a boat, you'll need a license from one state and a special-use stamp from the other.

Four-Wheeling

An extensive network of back roads provides access to the lakes as well as scenic hills and canyons. These roads range from easy to challenging and require a high-clearance 4WD vehicle. Ask for the set of free maps that show the approved backcountry roads, which have signs with arrows and numbers. The maps also show locations of primitive campgrounds and indicate whether they have an outhouse. Back-road travelers may camp only in these designated areas. All vehicles in the recreation area must stay on the approved roads or highways.

LAKE MOHAVE

Heading upstream from Bullhead City, you soon arrive at Lake Mohave. Squeezed between hills and canyon walls, the lake seems like a calmer version of the Colorado River. Though 67 miles long, Mohave spans but 4 miles at its widest point. **Davis Dam,** completed in 1953, holds back the waters; visitors can park at an overlook on the dam. At press time, the dam was closed to RVs, trailers, and large trucks.

Katherine Landing

Also known as Katy's Gulch to some folks, Katherine Landing lies six miles north of Bullhead City. A **ranger station/information center** (928/754-3272) near the entrance is open daily 8 A.M.–4 P.M. all year. Staff provide information on interpretive programs, local hikes, the Grapevine Canyon Petroglyphs Site (nearby in Nevada), and back-road drives in the area. Video programs are shown on request and regional books and maps can be purchased. Recreation facilities include a campground ($10), beaches (South Telephone Cove is best), hiking trails, fish-cleaning station, and a lakeside resort. **Lake Mohave Resort** (928/754-3245 or 800/752-9669, www.sevencrown.com) provides a motel ($85–95 d in summer, $35–45 d in winter; add $20 for a kitchenette), house rental ($240), RV park ($18 w/hookups), restaurant (daily breakfast, lunch, and dinner), marina with boat rentals (fishing, ski, patio, and houseboats), store, boat ramp, showers, dump station, and laundry.

For an easy walk with some history, you can hike to **Katherine Mine,** about one mile round-trip. Leave Katherine Landing and turn left .7 miles on the road just past the ranger station, park on the right opposite the turnoff for Telephone Cove, then walk up the wash. You'll see the white tailings all along the way and, where the wash opens up, the foundations and tanks of the mill on your right. The mine produced less than two million dollars of gold and silver between 1900 and 1940, but the mill, built in 1925, continued to process ore from area mines until shut down by the War Production Board in 1943.

Grapevine Canyon Petroglyphs Site and Christmas Tree Pass Road

Large and complex petroglyphs cover boulders on both sides of the mouth of Grapevine Canyon northwest of Bullhead City. From the bridge across the Colorado River, head west 6.3 miles on Highway 163 to near Milepost 13, turn right 1.8 miles on unpaved Christmas Tree Pass Road, then left into Grapevine Canyon Trailhead. Continue west on foot about .3 miles along the easy trail beside Grapevine Wash to the site. Christmas Tree Pass Road offers fine scenery and views as it winds across the desert and up to the pass, about 7.3 miles from Highway 163, then descends to U.S. Highway 95 for a total of 15 miles one-way. The U.S. Highway 95 turnoff is between Mileposts 6 and 7, about 2.2 miles south of Cal-Nev-Ari. You could loop back to Bullhead City or turn north to Cottonwood Cove, Hoover Dam, or Las Vegas. High-clearance vehicles do best on this drive. Camping isn't permitted Lake Mead National Recreation Area, but you could camp on public lands west of the pass.

Cottonwood Cove

This developed area lies about halfway upstream on the main body of water on the Nevada side. If driving, turn off U.S. Highway 95 at Searchlight and go east 14 miles on Highway 164. **Cottonwood Cove Marina** (702/297-1464, www.cottonwoodcoveresort.com) has a motel ($108 d, less in winter), RV park ($19.45–24.45 w/hookups), campground ($10), restaurant, marina with rentals (including houseboats), a boat ramp, and a public swimming beach.

Eldorado Canyon

Northward, the lake narrows at Eldorado Canyon, becoming more like a river. Trout frequent the cold river currents upstream. A paved road (Hwy. 165) approaches Eldorado Canyon from the Nevada side, but there are no facilities.

Willow Beach Harbor

About a dozen river miles below Hoover Dam

you'll reach Willow Beach Harbor (928/767-4747, www.foreverresorts.com) on the Arizona shore, a four-mile paved detour from U.S. Highway 93 from between Mileposts 14 and 15. Facilities include a picnic area, fish-cleaning station, store, boat dock, car and boat fuel, boat ramp, and rentals of ski, fishing, and patio boats. There's no motel or campground here, but boaters can reach nearby campgrounds on the river. A ranger station (928/767-4000) at Willow Beach is open irregularly, as staff are often in the field.

A half mile upstream by road, **Willow Beach National Fish Hatchery** (928/767-3456) raises large numbers of rainbow trout for stocking the lower Colorado River and Lake Mohave. Hatchery staff also study and propagate the endangered razorback sucker and bonytail chub, which are native to the Colorado River. You're welcome to visit the raceways outside daily 7 A.M.–5 P.M. A **Scenic Viewpoint** just off U.S. Highway 93 offers a fine panorama of the Black Canyon area; it's accessible from both directions between Mileposts 12 and 13.

Black Canyon River-Running

A popular float trip for canoes, kayaks, and rafts begins below Hoover Dam, following the swift Colorado beneath the sheer 1,500-foot cliffs of Black Canyon to Willow Beach (12 miles) or Eldorado Canyon (25 miles). A sauna cave and hot springs make enjoyable stops.

Boats can also continue across Lake Mohave to Cottonwood Cove (50 miles) or Katherine Landing (72 miles); this section below Eldorado Canyon isn't recommended for nonmotorized boats April–October because of the prevailing southerly winds. Obtain permission to launch your boat below Hoover Dam at least three weeks and up to six months in advance from Black Canyon/Willow Beach River Adventures (702/293-8204, www.BlackCanyonAdventures.com), which also offers raft tours and can recommend boat rental companies.

Black Canyon/Willow Beach River Adventures (702/294-1414 or 800/455-3490, www.BlackCanyonAdventures.com) rafts the river from Hoover Dam to Willow Beach daily February–November ($73 adults, $70 youth 13–15, and $45 children 5–11). The price includes three hours on the river, lunch, and transportation from the tour office at the Hacienda Hotel near Boulder City; pickup from Las Vegas hotels is available for an extra charge. The rafts are wheelchair accessible.

Arizona Hot Springs Hike

This six-mile round-trip route follows a ruggedly beautiful canyon through layers of volcanic rock to the Colorado River and nearby hot springs. Highly mineralized spring water surfaces in a side canyon at temperatures ranging 113–142°F, which cools to a very pleasant 85–120°F. Rangers warn that the water may contain dangerous amoebas; avoid trouble by keeping your head out of the water.

Allow 4–5 hours for the hike down, time to soak in the hot springs, and the trek back up. The 800-foot descent to the river is gradual, but you'll feel it on the climb out! Hiking isn't recommended in summer, when temperatures can reach hazardous levels. As for any desert hike of this length, bring water (1 gallon per person) and wear a sun hat. Also, be alert for rattlesnakes and flash floods; don't hike if thunderstorms threaten. A map with a description of the hike is available from the visitors center and possibly at a box a short way in on the trail.

From Hoover Dam, drive 4.2 miles southeast on U.S. Highway 93 to a dirt parking area on the right, just south of Milepost 4. The trail goes west and drops into a wash, which deepens dramatically as you enter White Rock Canyon. Look for arches above as you descend the gravelly canyon floor. When you reach the Colorado River, walk a quarter mile downstream along the river and look for signs pointing the way through a narrow defile that leads over to a narrow canyon. Turn up this pretty little canyon, then climb a 20-foot ladder to reach the spring-fed pools. Boaters can pull in at the mouth of this canyon, where there's a campground.

HOOVER DAM

When completed in 1935, this immense concrete structure ranked as one of the world's greatest engineering feats. It remains impressive today, especially when you contemplate the mind-boggling

WINGED FIGURES OF THE REPUBLIC

A statue stands guard on each side of the flag at Hoover Dam. Norwegian-born Oskar J. W. Hansen created them with eagle wings to represent America's construction skills, daring, and readiness to defend its institutions. He explained that the figures express "the immutable calm of intellectual resolution, and the enormous power of trained physical strength, equally enthroned in placid triumph of scientific accomplishment." Hansen also likened the feat of building the dam to construction of the great pyramids of Egypt. The two figures rest on black igneous rock and rise 30 feet; their 5/8-inch-thick shells are made from more than four tons of bronze. The terrazzo floor surrounding the base contains an inlaid star chart that future civilizations can use to determine the date that President Franklin D. Roosevelt dedicated the dam—September 30, 1935.

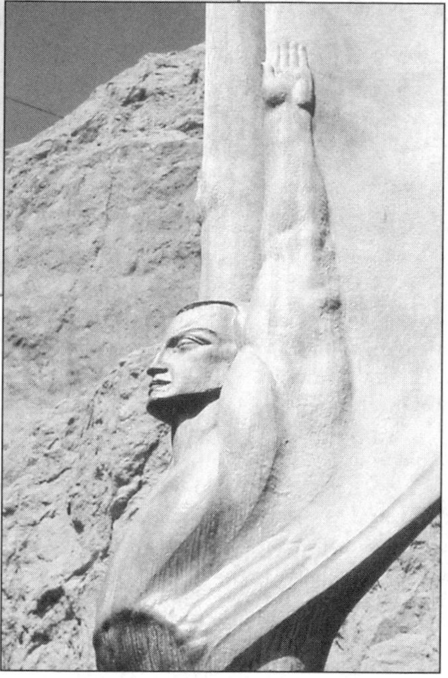

one of the two guardians of Hoover Dam

© BILL WEIR

statistics: The dam contains 3.25 million cubic yards of concrete, rises 726 feet above bedrock, and produces more than four billion kilowatt-hours of energy per year.

With all these numbers coming at you, it's easy to miss the beauty of the dam. Look for the graceful curves, the sculptures of the *Winged Figures of the Republic,* the art deco embellishments, and the terrazzo floor designs. There's a lot to see here—outside on the dam, in the impressive visitors center, and at a viewing gallery of the power plant.

A 1,900-foot bridge under construction will cross the Colorado River about a quarter mile downstream from the dam. This will greatly reduce traffic across the dam, making it a more tranquil place to visit. But until completion in about 2008, you may encounter delays from roadwork; progress can be checked at www.hooverdambypass.org.

Visitor Center

The large visitors center (702/294-3523, www.usbr.gov/lc/hooverdam) on the Nevada side of the dam, offers a multimedia presentation, historic exhibits, a viewing platform, and a look at the generators. It's open daily 9 A.M.–5 P.M. except Thanksgiving and Christmas; admission includes a visit to the powerhouse gallery and costs $10 adults, $8 seniors 62+, and $5 children 7–16; no reservations needed. The easiest parking lies across the road from the visitors center and up the hill a bit. This parking structure—for cars only—will be appreciated in hot weather and by those not wanting to walk far; it costs $5. Several lots across on the Arizona side have parking; the one closest to the dam has a $5 parking fee, while those farther up the hill are free; RVs and vehicles with trailers can park at Lots 11 or 13.

Take the escalator or elevator from in front of the parking structure to the ticket office, theater, and exhibit hall on the lower level. A multimedia program in the theater illustrates construction of the dam. Head down into the dam via elevator for a look at the Nevada Powerplant Wing with its eight turbine generators. The main exhibit gallery, one floor above the theater level, introduces the people who built the dam and how they did it,

COURTESY OF ANDREW PERNICK/BUREAU OF RECLAMATION

The visitor center (left) has a great view of Hoover Dam and Black Canyon.

along with narrations about their experiences. Exhibits also illustrate the plants, wildlife, and other aspects of the region. Continue upstairs to the third level and a viewing platform overlooking the dam and Black Canyon. Your ticket also includes exhibits in the old visitors center across the road.

The High Scaler Café and Hoover Dam Store in the parking structure offer fast food and souvenirs, as does another café and store overlooking the reservoir. Note the bronze *High Scaler* outside the parking structure.

Boulder City, Nevada

Originally built for construction workers of Hoover Dam in the 1930s, the town has an attractive downtown and a good selection of motels and restaurants. It's about eight miles from Hoover Dam; you can take the business route turnoff at the Nevada Welcome Center, then continue to the museum and services downtown.

The **Boulder City/Hoover Dam Museum** (in the Boulder Dam Hotel, 1305 Arizona St., 702/294-1988, www.bcmha.org, 10 A.M.–5 P.M. Mon.–Sat. noon–5 P.M. Sun., $2 adult, $1 children, students, and seniors) will give you a feel for what it was like to be a worker on the dam. Exhibits include a documentary video, 3D displays, interactive projects, photos, and artifacts from the dam's construction days. You'll also find a gift shop.

The 1933 **Boulder Dam Hotel** (1305 Arizona St., 702/293-3510, www.boulderdamhotel.com, $89–159 d) offers restored rooms and suites, an Italian-American restaurant (daily breakfast, lunch, and dinner, $10–25), an art gallery, and other shops. Rates include breakfast and museum admission. The **Boulder City Chamber of Commerce** (465 Nevada Way and Arizona, 702/293-2034, www.bouldercitychamber.com, 9 A.M.–5 P.M. Mon.–Sat.) is across the street from the hotel.

LAKE MEAD

Lake Mead, held back by Hoover Dam, is the largest artificial lake in the United States and holds the equivalent of two years' flow of the Colorado River. Its shape forms a rough Y; one arm of Lake Mead reaches north up the Virgin River, while the longer east arm stretches up the Colorado River into the Grand Canyon. Boaters enjoy lots of room on the 110-mile-long lake, and its countless little beaches and coves provide hideaways for camping and swimming. Large-mouth black bass, striped bass, trout, channel catfish, bluegill, and crappie swim in the waters.

Alan Bible Visitor Center

Four miles west of Hoover Dam on U.S. Highway 93, near the Highway 166 turnoff for Boulder Beach, the Alan Bible Visitor Center (601 Nevada Hwy., Boulder City, NV 89005, 702/293-8990, www.nps.gov/lame, daily 8:30 A.M.–4:30 P.M.) offers National Park Service exhibits introducing Lake Mead National Recreation Area's fishing, boating, wildlife-watching, and desert recreation opportunities.

You can watch a video program shown on request. Staff provide handouts and information on backcountry camping, roads, trails, and interpretive programs. A botanical garden surrounding the visitors center identifies plant communities found throughout the recreation area. Books are for sale, as are nautical charts and topo maps. The visitors center closes on Thanksgiving, Christmas, and New Year's Day.

Historic Railroad Trail

A section of railway bed used during construction of Hoover Dam has become a trail with excellent views of Lake Mead. It's wide and nearly level, easy for both cyclists and hikers. The trailhead and parking are just down the hill from the Alan Bible Visitor Center. You can follow the path 2.7 miles one-way through five tunnels—cool in summer—toward Hoover Dam; eventually the trail will continue down to the dam. The tunnels had been cut oversize to accommodate the huge penstock pipes and other equipment. In the opposite direction from the trailhead, you can head 3.6 miles to Boulder City via the old railroad grade.

Boulder Basin

Above Hoover Dam, the lake opens into the broad Boulder Basin. You'll find campgrounds at Boulder Beach, Las Vegas Bay, and Callville Bay. Most of the facilities like just off Lakeshore Scenic Drive, which begins from U.S. Highway 93 near the Allen Bible Visitor Center. Turn right after 1.2 miles for **East Las Vegas Boat Harbor** (702/565-9111), which has a restaurant, store, boat tours, and marina (fishing-, ski-, and patio-boat rentals). The triple-decked sternwheeler *Desert Princess* (702/293-6180, www.lakemeadcruises.com) leaves from here for a scenic 90-minute trip up the lake to Hoover Dam. The sightseeing excursions ($20) run two or three times a day; on some days you can sign up for a breakfast cruise ($32.50), dinner cruise ($44), or a dinner/dance cruise ($54). Children 2–11 travel at reduced rates except on the dinner/dance cruise.

Boulder Beach, two miles from the visitors center, offers good swimming with picnic sites; the campground ($10) lies on the south side of the beach. RVers can stay nearby in **Lake Mead RV Village** (268 Lakeshore Rd., 702/293-2540, $26–28 w/hookups and showers). **Lake Mead Lodge** (322 Lakeshore Rd., 702/293-2074 or 800/752-9669, www.sevencrown.com, $75–175 d, less in midwinter) lies on the north side of Boulder Beach with lake views. **Lake Mead Marina** (702/293-3484 or 800/752-9669) is half a mile farther north with a restaurant, store, and boat rentals.

You're welcome to drop in and see the trout and exhibits at the **Lake Mead Fish Hatchery** (off Lakeshore Rd., 5.5 miles from the visitors center between Boulder Beach and Las Vegas Bay, 8 A.M.–4 P.M. daily). The Nevada Department of Wildlife raises trout here and sends most of them to Lake Mohave; others go to Lake Mead and scattered locations around southern Nevada. Beyond the fish hatchery, you'll pass several viewpoints, some with shaded tables, overlooking Lake Mead.

Las Vegas Bay has a picnic area and a campground ($10), but low water levels forced the marina to move to East Las Vegas Boat Harbor. **Callville Bay Resort & Marina** (702/565-8958, 800/255-5561 houseboat reservations, www.foreverresorts.com) offers an RV park ($21.50 w/tax and hookups), snack bar, and a marina with boat rentals (ski boats, patio boats, houseboats, and personal watercraft). Two campgrounds in the area cost $10; pay showers are available at the resort.

The undeveloped cove of Kingman Wash on the Arizona shore has been closed to all land access during construction of the Hoover Dam bypass bridge.

Virgin and Temple Basins

Traveling upstream by boat from Boulder Basin you pass through six-mile-long Boulder Canyon, also called the Narrows, before emerging into Virgin and Temple Basins, the largest and most dramatic part of Lake Mead. Rock formations with names such as Napoleon's Tomb, the Haystacks, and the Temple provide scenic landmarks. Many narrow coves snake back into the mountains.

Temple Bar Resort (928/767-3211 or 800/752-9669, www.sevencrown.com), Arizona's only development on Lake Mead, takes its name from a rock monolith across Temple Basin. The resort provides fishing cabins ($55 d), a motel ($80–100 d, $100–115 with kitchenette), an RV park ($18 w/hookups), a restaurant, store, car and boat gas, airstrip, and a marina with boat rentals (ski, fishing, and patio boats and personal watercraft). The restaurant is open daily for breakfast, lunch, and dinner, but lacks a proper nonsmoking section. There's also a park service picnic area and fish-cleaning station near the boat ramp and a campground ($10) farther back in the trees. From Hoover Dam, go southeast 19 miles on U.S. Highway 93 to just south of Milepost 19, then turn left 28 miles on paved Temple Bar Road. A ranger station just before the resort is open occasionally; there's a short hiking trail here.

On the way you can detour north on an unpaved graded road to **Bonelli Landing,** a primitive campground on the Arizona shore of the Virgin Basin. Several 4WD roads branch off Temple Bar Road too, winding across the desert to both lake and inland destinations. Adventurous hikers can take the 4WD back road 130 west to **Mount Wilson Wilderness,** where a former road continues a bit farther, then it's possible to continue cross-country to the summit of Mt. Wilson.

Two resorts lie along the giant Overton Arm, which branches north into the Virgin River. **Echo Bay Resort** (702/394-4000 or 800/752-9669, www.sevencrown.com) features a motel ($98.30–114.35 d w/tax, less in winter), RV park ($19.26 w/tax, hookups, and showers), restaurant, and boat rentals (all types). The Echo Bay area also has a park service campground ($10); campers can use the RV park's showers.

Farther north, **Overton Beach Marina** (702/394-4040) offers an RV park ($19 w/hookups; showers cost extra and are open to the public), snack bar, store, and a marina with boat rentals (fishing, ski, and patio boats and personal watercraft).

Valley of Fire State Park (about 5 miles west of Overton Beach, 702/397-2088) is noted for its impressive rock formations consisting of 150 million-year-old red Jurassic sandstone. The park is open year-round, with visitor center exhibits (daily 8:30 A.M.–4:30 P.M.), two campgrounds ($14 w/showers), picnic areas, and hiking trails. Entry fee is $6 per vehicle, $1 for pedestrians and bicyclists.

You can view Native American artifacts from Pueblo Grande de Nevada at the **Lost City Museum** (13 miles north of Overton Beach, 702/397-2193, daily 8:30 A.M.–4:30 P.M., $3 adults 18–64, $2 seniors) on a hill at the south edge of Overton. Built on an actual Virgin Anasazi site, the adobe museum includes a reconstructed pit house and pueblo, pottery, jewelry, lithic tools, and other artifacts and historic exhibits. Civilian Conservation Corps workers in the 1930s excavated artifacts from many prehistoric sites, some now lost beneath Lake Mead.

Gregg Basin

Upstream, the lake narrows in Virgin Canyon before opening into Gregg Basin, the uppermost large open-water area of Lake Mead. The basin has no campgrounds or resorts; facilities are limited to a picnic area and paved boat ramp at **South Cove** on the Arizona side. By

Lake Mead from the Historic Railroad Trail

car, you reach South Cove by heading south 19 miles on U.S. Highway 93 from Hoover Dam, then turning left 45 miles on a paved road. You'll pass through **Dolan Springs** (www.meadview.info) holding a small motel, RV parks, restaurants, and stores. Joshua trees up to 25 feet tall grow along part of the way; the tree looks like a strange cactus but really belongs to the lily family.

Pearce Ferry, accessible by dirt road off the road to South Cove, offers primitive boat ramps and campsites at the upper end of Lake Mead. Grand Canyon National Park begins just upstream. Low lake levels in 2004 forced a temporary closure.

Grand Wash Bay extends north into Nevada above Iceberg Canyon and lacks any services. You'll need a high-clearance 4WD vehicle and a good map to reach this lonely spot, as much of the road follows sandy washes. Check road conditions and weather forecasts before attempting this route.

Flagstaff and North-Central Arizona

Much of this region lies atop the southern Colorado Plateau, a giant uplifted landmass extending into Utah, Colorado, and New Mexico. As the land rose, vigorous rivers sliced deeply through the rock layers, revealing beautiful forms and colors in countless canyons. Sheer cliffs of the Mogollon Rim mark the south edge of the Colorado Plateau.

While rivers cut down the land, volcanoes shot up. For the last six million years, large and small volcanoes sprouted in the San Francisco Volcanic Field around Flagstaff. The most striking include the San Francisco Peaks, of which Humphrey's Peak at 12,633 feet is Arizona's highest mountain. Sunset Crater, the state's most beautiful volcano, is the youngster of the bunch, last erupting about 800 years ago—just yesterday, geologically speaking. Meteor Crater, east of Flagstaff, formed instantly about 50,000 years ago when a blazing hunk of rock smashed into

Must-Sees

Look for [M] to find the sights and activities you can't miss and [N] for the best dining and lodging.

Museum of Northern Arizona in Flagstaff brings the past to life with geologic, fossil, and archaeology displays, then introduces the Native American cultures of the region. You'll see beautiful crafts and arts of the region from prehistoric to contemporary times (page 288).

Riordan Mansion State Historic Park takes you back to Flagstaff's early years. All of the furnishings are original to the 1904 mansion, and many are in the Arts and Crafts style (page 291).

Walnut Canyon National Monument protects prehistoric cliff dwellings in an exceptionally beautiful little canyon. A trail winds down for a close look at the dwellings (page 306).

Sunset Crater Volcano National Monument has a stark landscape of cinder cones, lava flows, and other volcanic features that look as if they've just cooled. You'll also enjoy views of volcanoes and the Painted Desert from the Scenic Loop between here and Wupatki National Monument (page 309).

Wupatki National Monument provides a close look at a variety of prehistoric pueblos along with a restored ballcourt (page 312).

Tonto Natural Bridge State Park contains an immense travertine bridge that spans a 150-foot wide canyon. Trails lead inside where you can admire the cavelike interior. Springs support lush vegetation and form little waterfalls (page 347).

Oak Creek Canyon has it all—spectacular cliffs, a sparkling creek, dense forests, hiking trails, recreation areas, resorts, and a ribbon of highway through it (page 367).

Montezuma Castle National Monument protects a five-story prehistoric cliff dwelling tucked high in the cliffs. It's amazingly well preserved, though you have to view it from below (page 378).

Jerome clings to a steep hillside above the Verde Valley. Three museums illustrate its fascinating history as a copper-mining town. Not all buildings clung successfully—you can see the former jail that slid across the street and down the hill! (page 386)

Sharlot Hall Museum in Prescott illustrates Native American and pioneer history. You'll see the Governor's Mansion, where territorial Arizona got its start, and many other early buildings (page 392).

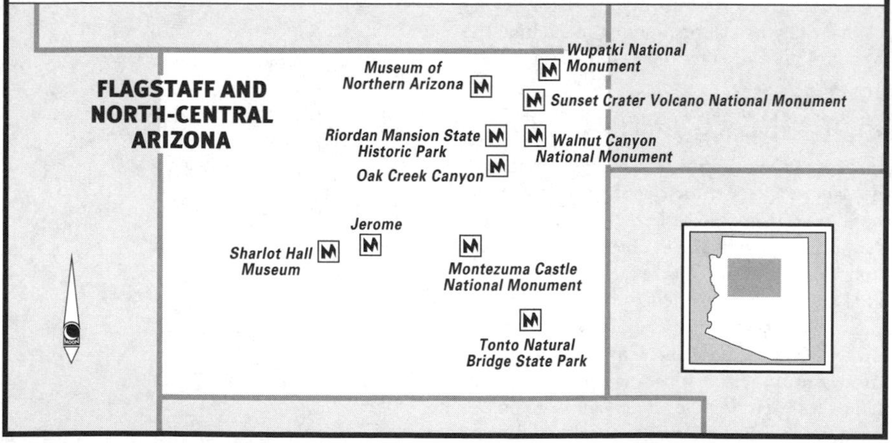

the ground at a tremendous speed; today it's the world's best-preserved impact crater.

With so much natural beauty all around, the outdoors beckons in all seasons! You're sure to enjoy scenic drives, such as the one through Oak Creek Canyon and its wonderfully sculpted and colored cliffs. If you enjoy hiking, you can climb volcanoes and explore mysterious canyons to your heart's content. Anglers enjoy the many lakes on the Colorado Plateau and the streams below it. Then, when the snow flies, skiers zip down the runs on the San Francisco Peaks near Flagstaff, and the shorter runs on Bill Williams Mountain near Williams.

Haunting ruins left by prehistoric peoples offer a peek into the past and some of the most impressive lie within four national monuments: Wupatki north of Flagstaff, Walnut Canyon east of Flagstaff, and Montezuma Castle and Tuzigoot south in the Verde Valley.

Flagstaff, the region's largest city, is worth visiting for its historic downtown, lively university, and the outstanding Museum of Northern Arizona (exhibiting natural history and Native American cultures). Sedona, at the heart of enchanting Red Rock Country, is famous for its inspiring scenery and art galleries. Jerome, high on the steep slopes across the Verde Valley, hangs on to its colorful history as a rough-and-tumble copper-mining town. Farther south, at the base of the rugged Bradshaw Mountains, Prescott's beautiful setting and history as Arizona's first capital delights visitors; highlights include the Sharlot Hall Museum, full of pioneer history.

PLANNING YOUR TIME

Flagstaff provides the greatest range of accommodations and restaurants in the region with the bonus that many motels have bargain prices, except on summer weekends. Sedona offers many luxury bed and breakfasts and resorts that provide memorable experiences if you can afford them, while featuring some of the state's finest dining. Camp Verde and Cottonwood have a modest number of mid-range places that are handy for exploring the Verde Valley, or you can head up to historic Jerome for accomodations

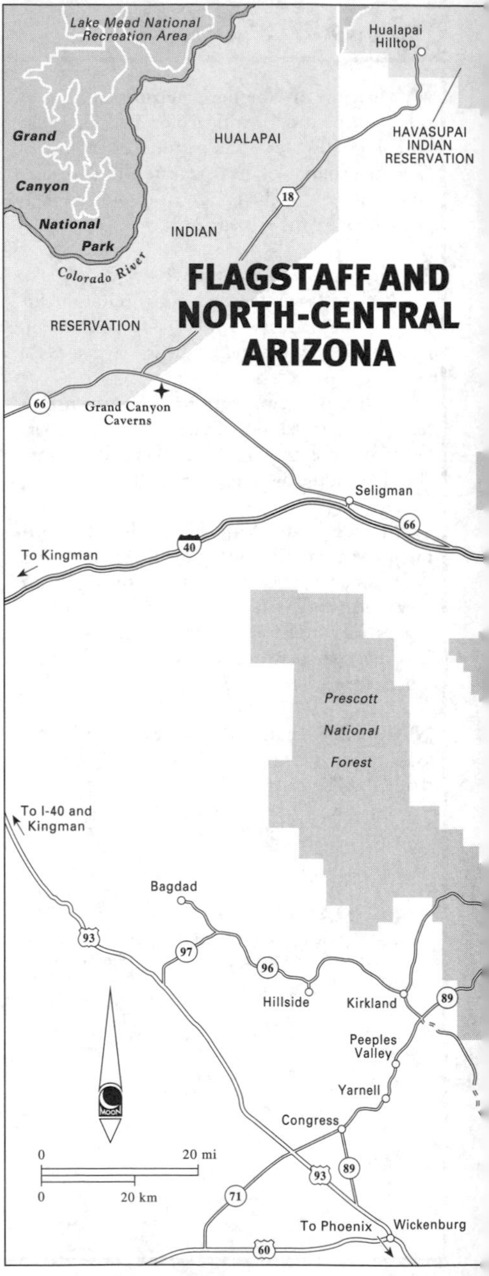

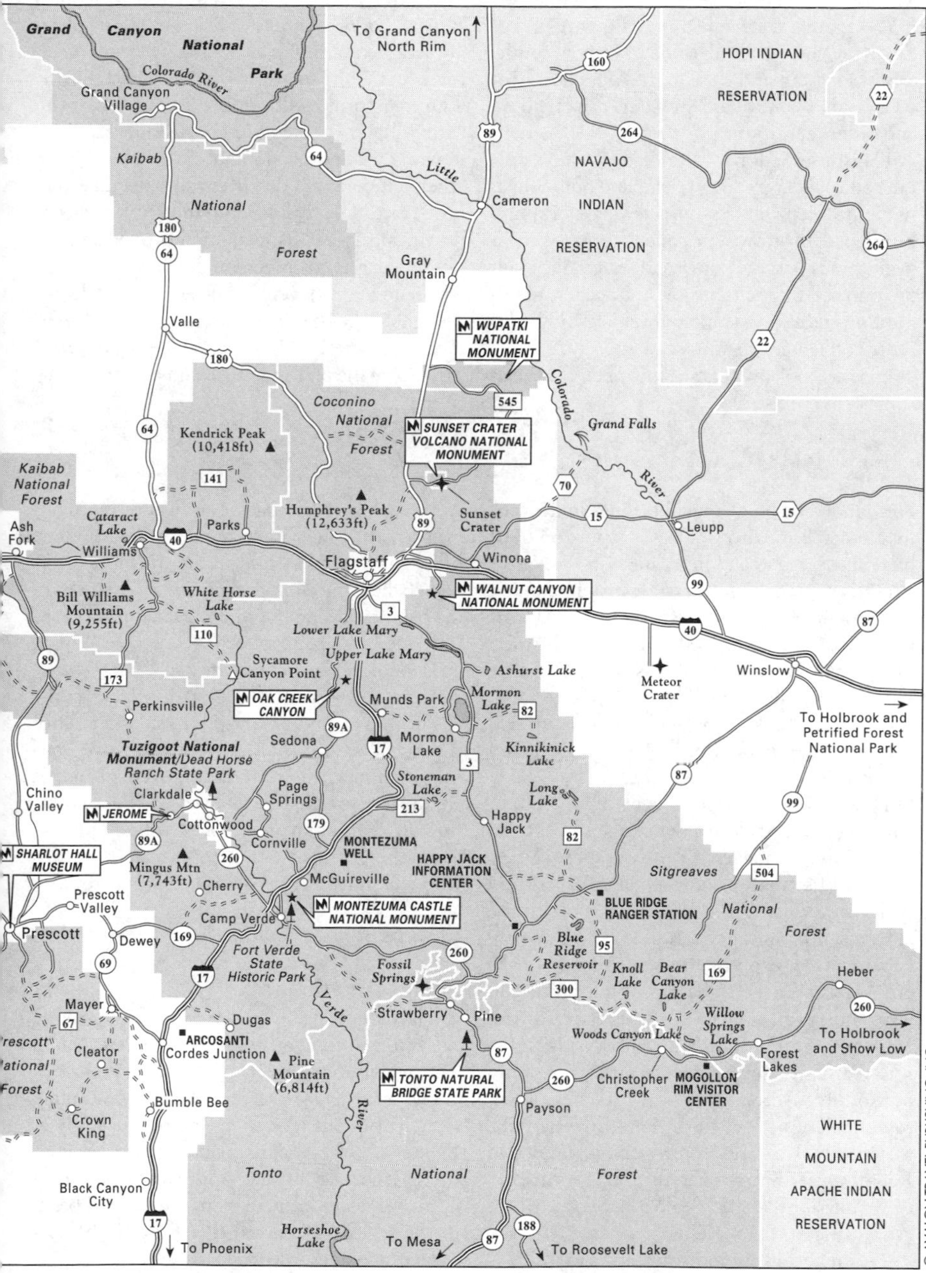

North-Central Arizona

with views and ambiance. Farther south, Prescott is also known for its historic lodging, and offers many choices for fine dining. Payson, southeast of Flagstaff and close to the Mogollon Rim country, is a handy base for scenic drives, hikes, and other recreation.

Flagstaff, Sedona, the Verde Valley, and Prescott each have enough sights and outdoor activities to keep you busy for a few days or more. Historic highway AZ 89A, one of Arizona's most scenic roads, ties these towns together. Although one can use public transport and local tours to get around, having your own vehicle will be far more convenient.

Expect a cool, invigorating mountain climate in Flagstaff and other areas atop the Mogollon Plateau. Spring, summer, and autumn bring pleasant weather to this high country, where temperatures generally peak in the 70s and 80s F. Thunderstorm clouds billow into the air from early July into September, letting loose scattered downpours. Snow and sun battle it out in winter, when temperatures fluctuate widely; you need to be prepared for anything from sub-zero weather to warm, spring-like temperatures. Sedona and the Verde Valley enjoy much milder temperatures in winter and rarely see snow, but summers get hot—though not to the extremes of Arizona's low deserts. Mile-high Prescott has what some people consider to be the perfect four-season climate.

Flagstaff

Surrounded by ponderosa pine forest in the center of northern Arizona, Flagstaff (pop. 63,000) has long served as an important stop for Native Americans, ranchers, and travelers. The older, downtown part of Flagstaff still offers a bit of frontier feeling, expressed in its many historic buildings. Other parts of this small city may seem like endless lines of motels, restaurants, bars, and service stations, but even here one can find reminders of old Route 66 that once linked Flagstaff with the rest of America.

Downtown is an enjoyable place to stroll, to admire the architecture, and perhaps to sample some of the unique restaurants and shops. Many of the old structures have plaques describing their history. To visit the distant past, when the land rose up, volcanoes erupted, and the early tribes arrived, drop by the Museum of Northern Arizona. To learn about the pioneers of 100 years ago, head over to the Pioneer Historical Museum and the Riordan Mansion State Historic Park. To see the current art scene, swing by Northern Arizona University's galleries, downtown galleries, Coconino Center for the Arts, and the Art Barn. For a trip out of this world, visit Lowell Observatory, where astronomers discovered Pluto; or the U.S. Geological Survey, where astrogeologists map celestial bodies.

For the great outdoors, head for the hills—Arizona's highest mountains begin at the northern outskirts of town. In summer, the mountains, hills, and meadows offer pleasant forest walks and challenging climbs. Winter snows transform the countryside into some of the state's best downhill and cross-country skiing areas. As a local guidebook, *Coconino County, the Wonderland of America,* put it in 1916, Flagstaff "offers you the advantages of any city of twice its size; it has, free for the taking, the healthiest and most invigorating of climates; its surrounding scenic beauties will fill one season, May–November, full to overflowing with enjoyment the life of any tourist, vacationist, camper, or out doors man or woman who will but come to commune with nature."

HISTORY

Native Americans

Archaeologists have dated prehistoric sites along the Little Colorado River as far back as 15,000 B.C., when now-extinct species of bison, camel, antelope, and horse roamed the land. Although some tribes engaged in agriculture as early as 2,000 B.C., they maintained a seasonal migration pattern of hunting and gathering. These nomadic groups planted corn, squash, and beans in the spring, continued their travels, then returned to harvest the fields in autumn.

THE MARVELLOUS COUNTRY

In the early 1870s, former Tucson judge Samuel Cozzens traveled east to stir up prospective settlers with a large, well-illustrated book titled *The Marvellous Country; or, Three Years in Arizona and New Mexico, the Apache's Home.* The subtitle expanded upon this theme: *Comprising a Description of this Wonderful Country, Its Immense Mineral Wealth, Its Magnificent Mountain Scenery, the Ruins of Ancient Towns and Cities Found Therein, With a Complete History of the Apache Tribe, and a Description of the Author's Guide Cochise, the Great Apache War Chief, the Whole Interspersed with Strange Events and Adventures.*

Cozzens' book sold well in New England and he gave many talks to eager audiences. With each retelling, his descriptions of Arizona's climate, forests, water, and mineral wealth grew and improved. By 1875, the Arizona Colonization Company, with Cozzens as president, was established in Boston. In February 1876, a group of about 50 men, each with 300 pounds of tools and clothing, set off for Arizona under the auspices of the company. In May a second group embarked for the "marvellous country."

After 90 days of arduous travel, the first group arrived at their destination on the Little Colorado River only to find the land already claimed by Mormons. The group continued west to the San Francisco Peaks and started to build a settlement, dubbed Agassiz. But finding no land suitable for farming or mining, they gave up and left for Prescott and California even before the second group arrived. The second group gave up, too, but not before stripping a pine tree and flying a flag from it to celebrate Independence Day.

From about A.D. 200 to 500 the tribes devoted more time to farming and built clusters of pithouses near their fields. Regional ancestral Puebloan cultures began to form, classified by scientists as the Anasazi of the Colorado Plateau, the Mogollon of the eastern Arizona uplands, and the Hohokam of the desert to the south. A fourth culture, the Sinagua, evolved near present-day Flagstaff between A.D. 900 and 1000 as a blend of the other three groups. The Sinagua (Spanish for "without water") could live here despite the area's dry, volcanic soil.

As these societies developed, the people began to build pueblos above ground—usually on hilltops or in cliff overhangs. By about A.D. 1100 the population reached its peak. Most inhabitants then migrated, abandoning villages and even whole areas. Archaeologists attempt to explain these departures with theories of drought, soil erosion, disease, and raids by the newly arrived Apache. By the 1500s, when Spanish explorers arrived in northern Arizona, the Pueblo tribes had retreated to northeastern Arizona and adjacent New Mexico. Thousands of empty villages remain in the region. Ruins can most easily be seen in the national monuments, but you might discover some while hiking in the backcountry.

Americans Settle In

Beginning in the 1820s, mountain men such as Antoine Leroux became expert trappers and guides in this little-known region between Santa Fe and California. They, and other early travelers, sent out glowing reports of the climate, water, and scenery of the region, but hostile Apache, Navajo, Yavapai, and Paiute discouraged settlement. As a result, the Flagstaff area developed later than much of southern and central Arizona. Captain Lorenzo Sitgreaves brought a surveying expedition across northern Arizona in 1851, prompting Lieutenant Edward Beale and others to build rough wagon roads—but hostile tribes and poor farmland continued to discourage settlers.

Thomas Forsythe McMillan arrived from California with a herd of sheep in 1876 and became Flagstaff's first permanent settler. Other ranchers soon moved into the area, bringing the

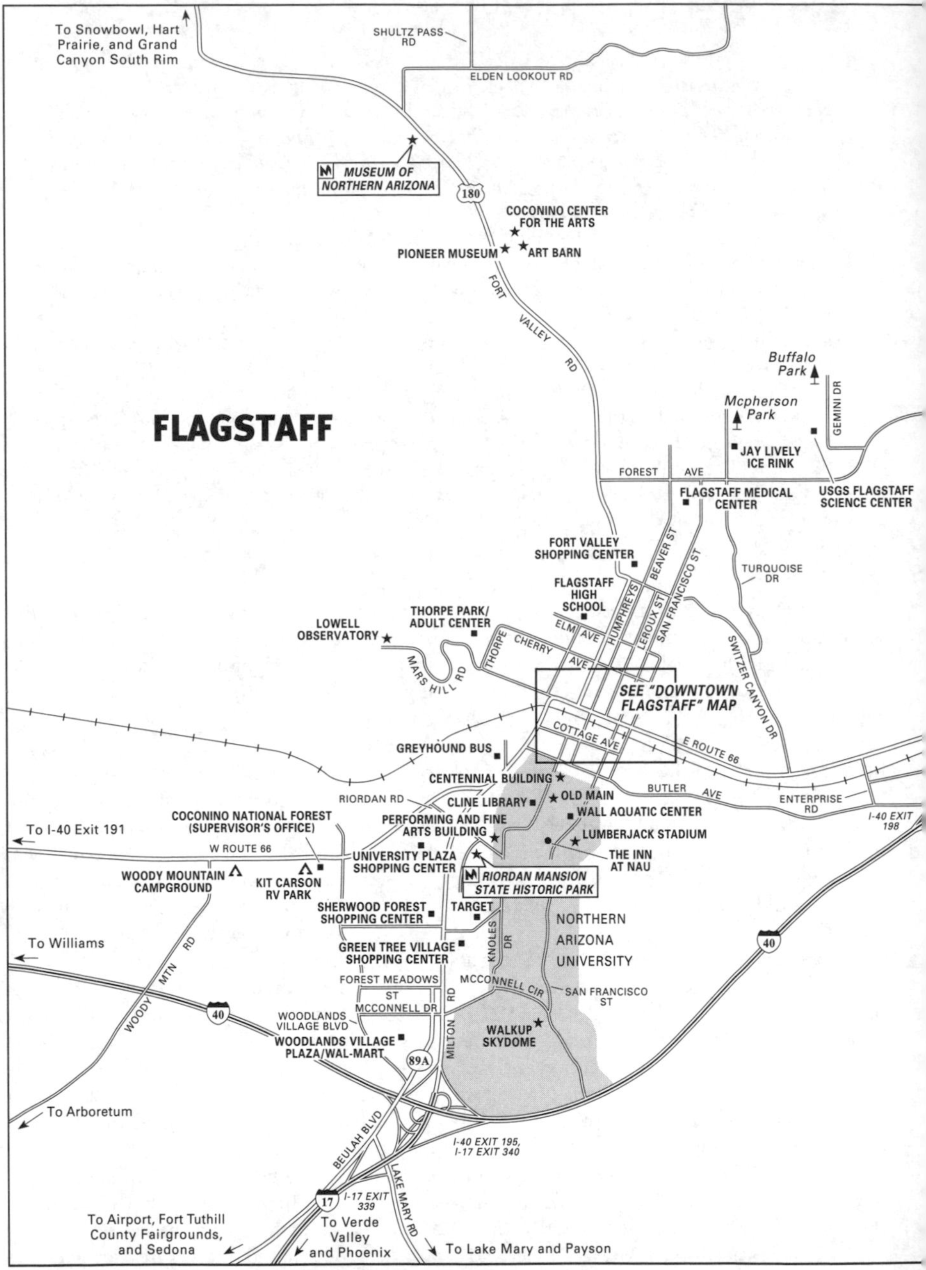
To Snowbowl, Hart Prairie, and Grand Canyon South Rim
SHULTZ PASS RD
ELDEN LOOKOUT RD
MUSEUM OF NORTHERN ARIZONA
180
COCONINO CENTER FOR THE ARTS
PIONEER MUSEUM
ART BARN
FORT VALLEY RD
FLAGSTAFF
Buffalo Park
Mcpherson Park
GEMINI DR
JAY LIVELY ICE RINK
FOREST AVE
FLAGSTAFF MEDICAL CENTER
USGS FLAGSTAFF SCIENCE CENTER
FORT VALLEY SHOPPING CENTER
BEAVER ST
SAN FRANCISCO ST
TURQUOISE DR
FLAGSTAFF HIGH SCHOOL
HUMPHREYS
LEROUX ST
THORPE PARK/ ADULT CENTER
LOWELL OBSERVATORY
ELM AVE
CHERRY AVE
THORPE
MARS HILL RD
SWITZER CANYON DR
SEE "DOWNTOWN FLAGSTAFF" MAP
COTTAGE AVE
E ROUTE 66
GREYHOUND BUS
CENTENNIAL BUILDING
BUTLER AVE
ENTERPRISE RD
RIORDAN RD
CLINE LIBRARY
OLD MAIN
WALL AQUATIC CENTER
I-40 EXIT 198
COCONINO NATIONAL FOREST (SUPERVISOR'S OFFICE)
PERFORMING AND FINE ARTS BUILDING
LUMBERJACK STADIUM
To I-40 Exit 191
W ROUTE 66
UNIVERSITY PLAZA SHOPPING CENTER
THE INN AT NAU
WOODY MOUNTAIN CAMPGROUND
KIT CARSON RV PARK
RIORDAN MANSION STATE HISTORIC PARK
SHERWOOD FOREST SHOPPING CENTER
TARGET
NORTHERN ARIZONA UNIVERSITY
KNOLES DR
To Williams
GREEN TREE VILLAGE SHOPPING CENTER
40
WOODY MTN RD
FOREST MEADOWS ST
MCCONNELL CIR
SAN FRANCISCO ST
MCCONNELL DR
WOODLANDS VILLAGE BLVD
WOODLANDS VILLAGE PLAZA/WAL-MART
MILTON RD
WALKUP SKYDOME
89A
To Arboretum
BEULAH BLVD
I-40 EXIT 195, I-17 EXIT 340
LAKE MARY RD
17
I-17 EXIT 339
To Airport, Fort Tuthill County Fairgrounds, and Sedona
To Verde Valley and Phoenix
To Lake Mary and Payson

North-Central Arizona

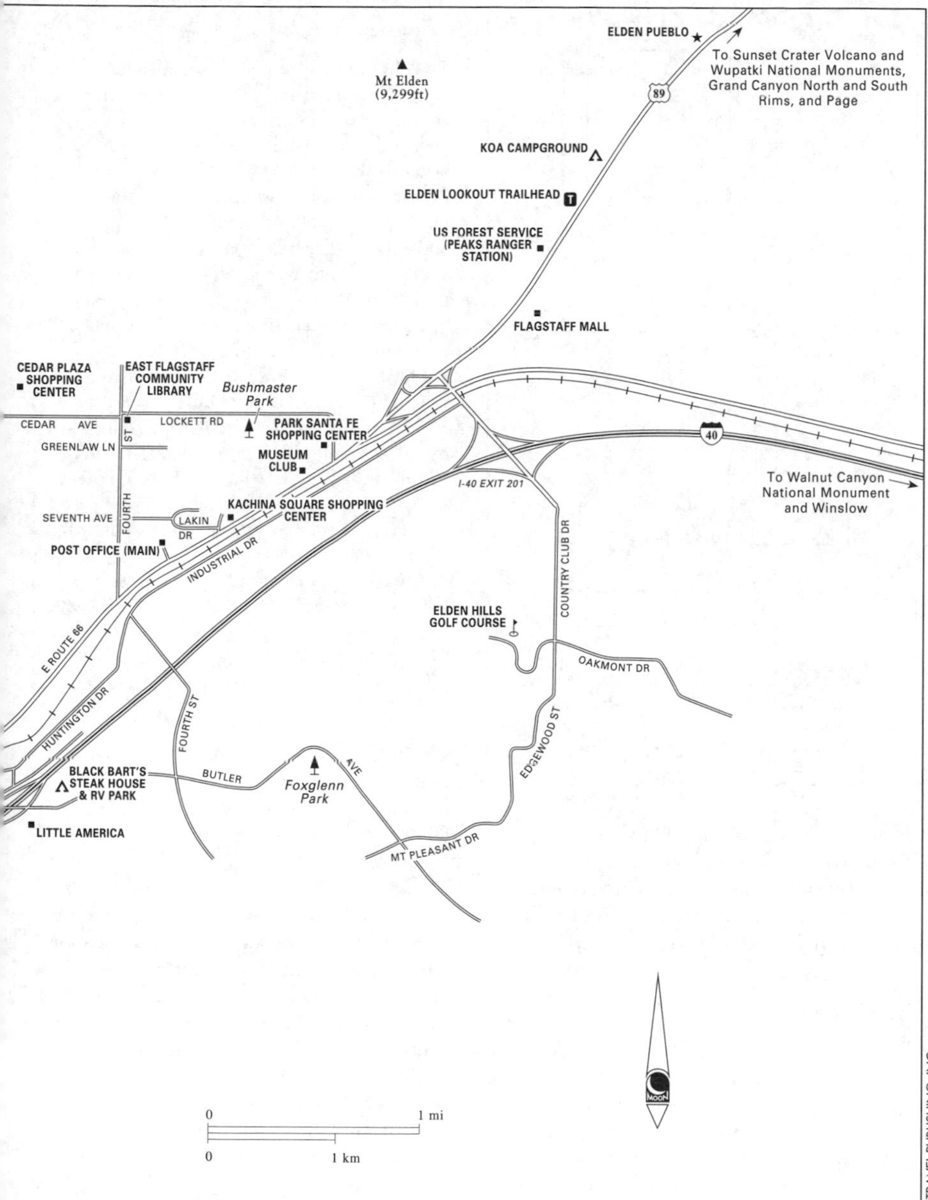
ELDEN PUEBLO
To Sunset Crater Volcano and Wupatki National Monuments, Grand Canyon North and South Rims, and Page
Mt Elden (9,299ft)
89
KOA CAMPGROUND
ELDEN LOOKOUT TRAILHEAD
US FOREST SERVICE (PEAKS RANGER STATION)
FLAGSTAFF MALL
CEDAR PLAZA SHOPPING CENTER
EAST FLAGSTAFF COMMUNITY LIBRARY
Bushmaster Park
CEDAR AVE
LOCKETT RD
PARK SANTA FE SHOPPING CENTER
GREENLAW LN
MUSEUM CLUB
40
I-40 EXIT 201
To Walnut Canyon National Monument and Winslow
SEVENTH AVE
LAKIN DR
KACHINA SQUARE SHOPPING CENTER
FOURTH ST
POST OFFICE (MAIN)
INDUSTRIAL DR
COUNTRY CLUB DR
ELDEN HILLS GOLF COURSE
E ROUTE 66
OAKMONT DR
HUNTINGTON DR
FOURTH ST
EDGEWOOD ST
BUTLER AVE
BLACK BART'S STEAK HOUSE & RV PARK
Foxglenn Park
LITTLE AMERICA
MT PLEASANT DR
MOON
0
1 mi
0
1 km

North-Central Arizona

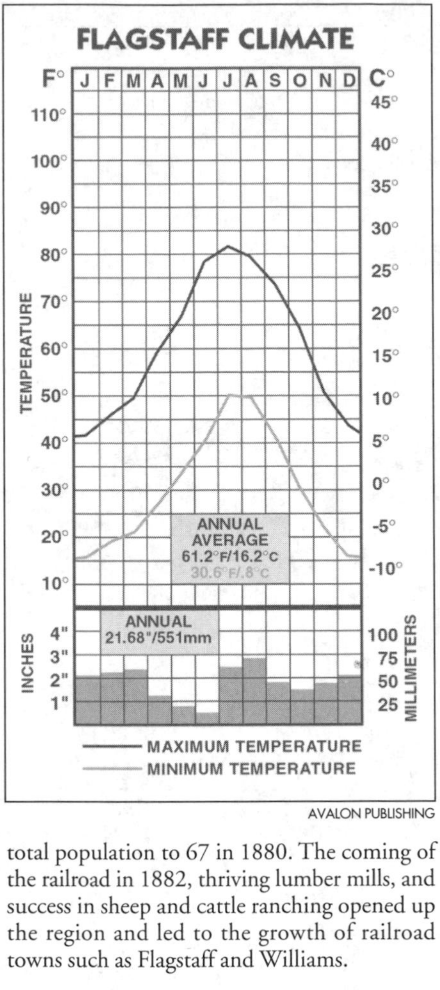

AVALON PUBLISHING

total population to 67 in 1880. The coming of the railroad in 1882, thriving lumber mills, and success in sheep and cattle ranching opened up the region and led to the growth of railroad towns such as Flagstaff and Williams.

SIGHTS

Flagstaff has many free parking spaces along the streets, by the Visitor Center, and in a few lots; these generally have a two-hour limit. Two free all-day lots lie just south of the railroad tracks near the Visitor Center: Turn south on Beaver Street from Route 66, then make the first right; RVs can park in an adjacent lot by turning right on Phoenix Avenue (the next street) then right into the parking area.

FLAGSTAFF'S FLAGPOLES

It's obvious that Flagstaff was named for a flagpole. The question is, which one? The first group of settlers to arrive from Boston claimed to have erected a flagpole in April or May of 1876, before the July 4th celebration held by the second Boston group later that year. The stripped pine tree left by the second group at their Antelope Spring camp may have been the pole that served as the town's namesake. Later travelers referred to the spot as the spring by the flag staff. As the first sheep ranchers settled nearby, the area became known as Flag Staff, then finally Flagstaff.

However, some early settlers regarded a tall tree, trimmed of all branches, at the foot of McMillan Mesa as *the* flagstaff. Others disputed this idea, stating that Lieutenant Edward Beale had delimbed the tree in the 1850s or that it was the work of a later railroad-surveying party. No record actually exists of a flag ever flying from the tree.

At any rate, citizens gathered in the spring of 1881 and chose the name Flagstaff for the settlement. You can visit a memorial near downtown at the Antelope Spring site.

Museum of Northern Arizona

Set beside a little canyon in a ponderosa pine forest three miles northwest on U.S. Highway 180 from downtown, this active museum (3101 N. Fort Valley Rd., 928/774-5213, www.musnaz.org, 9 A.M.–5 P.M. daily, $5 adults, $4 seniors, $3 students with ID, $2 ages 7–17) features excellent displays of the geology, archaeology, anthropology, cultures, and fine art of the Colorado Plateau. The attractive building of dark volcanic stone and tile roofs encloses courtyards filled with native flora. A visit is highly recommended for anyone who wishes to visit the reservations of northern Arizona, to buy Native American crafts, or to better understand the natural history of the Grand Canyon area.

Turn right in the lobby to see the Archaeology Gallery, where a timeline of Native Americans illustrates their stages of development during prehistoric times. Pottery, jewelry, a kiva mural from

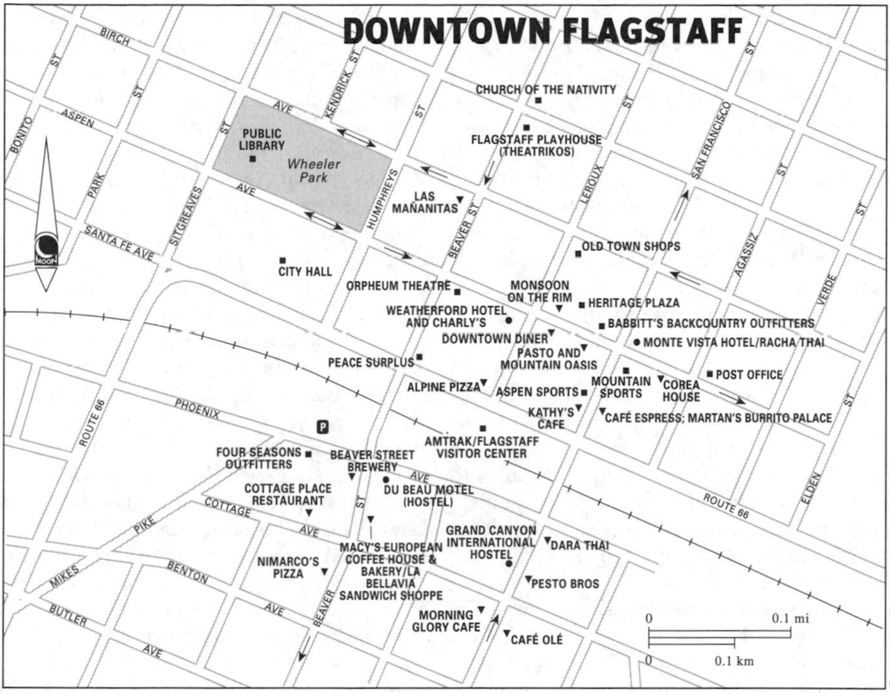

Awatovi, and other beautiful findings show the creativity of these early peoples. Next, the Ethnology Gallery introduces the modern tribes, along with impressive jewelry displays. The Kiva Gallery displays Hopi kachina dolls, textiles, pottery, and a kiva with a contemporary mural. Changing exhibits in other halls always have something new about the land and people of the region. You'll also see a variety of paintings and sculptures by Native American and Southwestern artists. The Babbitt Gallery contains superb prehistoric pottery collections and modern work by tribal artisans.

Popular museum-sponsored events showcase the finest arts and crafts: Hopi Marketplace runs on the weekend nearest July 4th; Navajo Marketplace is on the first weekend in August; Native Artists Marketplace represents Zuni, Pai, and other Colorado Plateau tribes on the first weekend in September; and the Hispanic Festival *Celebrations de la Gente* takes place on the last weekend of October, close to the Day of the Dead. Enduring Creations, a changing sales exhibition of the finest Native American, Hispanic, and Western artwork, runs through the summer.

A bookstore stocks an excellent selection of books, posters, and music related to the region. The museum shop sells high-quality Native American work, including Navajo blankets, Hopi kachina dolls, pottery by several tribes, and jewelry by Navajo, Hopi, and Zuni. Rio de Flag Nature Trail introduces local flora in the little canyon beside the museum; borrow the trail booklet—both adult and children's versions are available—from the ticket desk. To delve deeper into Southwest topics, visit the museum's excellent library (928/774-5211, ext. 256, call for hours) across the highway in the Research Center.

Pioneer Museum

After completion in 1908, this venerable stone building served 30 years as the Coconino County Hospital for the Indigent. Townspeople also knew it as the "poor farm"—because stronger patients grew vegetables in the yard.

Permanent and changing exhibits (2340 N. Fort Valley Rd., 928/774-6272, 9 A.M.–5 P.M. Mon.–Sat., $3 adult, $2 youth 12–18 and seniors 60+) illustrate many aspects of life in Flagstaff's pioneering days. Old photos and artifacts tell the stories of ranchers, timber men, scientists, explorers, and families. A giant stuffed bear greets you on the second floor; slip by the beast to see a restored hospital room and more galleries. Exhibits here may include memorabilia of Percival Lowell and his observatory and the camera gear and photos of Emery Kolb, who came to the Grand Canyon in 1902, set up a photo studio with his brother Ellsworth, and continued showing movies and stills until 1976.

Downstairs, there's a small gift shop. On the last weekend in May or the first weekend in June, the Wool Festival demonstrates shearing and other skills. The Independence Day Festival demonstrates traditional crafts on the weekend nearest July 4. Playthings of the Past marks the winter holiday season.

Outside, you can peer into the restored early-20th-century Ben Doney Cabin, moved here from a site east of town. Old farm machinery and a working blacksmith shop, often in use in summer, lie behind the museum. The powerful 1929 steam locomotive out front once served the logging industry. From downtown, the museum lies on the right just past Sechrist School, about two miles northwest on U.S. Highway 180.

Coconino Center for the Arts and The Art Barn

You can enjoy art at these two facilities a short stroll behind the Pioneer Museum. Coconino Center for the Arts (928/779-2300, www.culturalpartners.org) stages a variety of performances and exhibits through the year. Next door, the Art Barn (928/774-0822) contains a large sales gallery operated by regional artists.

Lowell Observatory

Percival Lowell (1855–1916) founded the observatory in 1894, using his personal fortune to fund a search for signs of intelligent life on Mars. The observatory's early contributions to astronomy included spectrographic photographs by V. M. Slipher that resulted in the discovery of the expanding universe, and Clyde Tombaugh's 1930 discovery of Pluto. Research continues with telescopes here, at Anderson Mesa 12 miles southeast of town, and at other locations.

In the Steele Visitor Center (928/774-2096, www.lowell.edu, $5 adults, $4 university students and seniors 65+, $2 ages 5–17), you can explore the field of astronomy with interactive exhibits and see many examples of instruments used by astronomers over the years. Informative 90-minute tours begin with a multimedia program illustrating the history and work of the observatory; you'll then visit the 24-inch Clark refractor telescope from 1896 used to study Mars and the expanding universe and to map the moon for lunar expeditions. The tour continues to the rotunda, designed as a library by Lowell's wife but completed only in 1916—the year of Lowell's death. Inside you can see the spectrograph used in the discovery of the expanding universe and other historic exhibits, such as the Pluto photographic plates, with the same view Tombaugh enjoyed at the instant he found Pluto. The final stop on the tour visits the specially designed telescope used to discover Pluto. You're free to join and leave the tours as you wish and explore the grounds on your own, but you can see interiors only with the tour guide. A solar viewing program takes place daily if the clouds cooperate; call for the time.

The visitor center is open 9 A.M.–5 P.M. daily March–October and noon–5 P.M. daily the rest of the year, though it's closed Monday and Tuesday in January and February. A bookstore has good reading along with posters and videos. The entry fee includes the guided tours, which depart at 10 A.M., 1 P.M., and 3 P.M. April–October, but only at 1 P.M. and 3 P.M. November–March.

At night, the visitor center reopens for Sky Tonight Programs and viewing through the historic Clark telescope, weather permitting; these run Monday–Saturday in summer, then decrease to Friday and Saturday in midwinter; call to check days and times. The cost is the same as for a daytime visit. The observatory offers many special events through the year, so it's worth calling or looking at the website to see what's coming up.

The observatory sits atop Mars Hill, one mile from downtown; head west on Route 66 and continue straight on Santa Fe Avenue where the business route curves left. In winter the steep road up Mars Hill requires caution and often snow chains.

U.S. Geological Survey Flagstaff Science Center

Spectacular photos, maps, and other exhibits at the Center (2255 N. Gemini Dr., Flagstaff, AZ 86001, 928/556-7000, wwwflag.wr.usgs.gov, 8 A.M.–4:30 P.M. Mon.–Fri., free) illustrate scientific work done here on Earth and beyond. When the facility opened in 1963, staff produced maps of the moon for the Apollo lunar landings. Astronauts received geologic training and tested their equipment here, and geologists from the Center later guided them on the moon. Since then, the Astrogeology Branch has broadened to map and study the planets and other solid bodies of our solar system using data collected from space missions. The geology of the moon and most solid-surfaced planets and their satellites has been mapped in surprising detail. Even cloud-covered Venus gave up many of its secrets through radar images with computer-generated color. Scientists at the Center also investigate and monitor stream flows in the Grand Canyon and water resources on nearby Native American lands. Geologic maps created here help define our landscape and what lies beneath it.

Building 6, the Shoemaker Center for Astrogeology, displays recent color images from spacecraft in *A Walk Through the Solar System* and other hallway exhibits; you can delve deeper into science in the research library. You'll also learn about Eugene M. Shoemaker (1928–1997), who organized and led the Center of Astrogeology. Exhibits in Powell Building 3 focus on the Earth, especially the geology and hydrology of the Grand Canyon region. Dutton Building 4 exhibits cover wide-ranging research in the Southwest and additional planetary exhibits.

Remember that the people working here are normally too busy to show visitors around. Also, don't enter offices or labs unless invited. Groups can arrange tours with advance notice. The Center lies atop McMillan Mesa off Forest Avenue/Cedar Avenue, 1.5 miles northeast of downtown. Nearby Buffalo Park is a good place to go for a walk or hike.

Riordan Mansion State Historic Park

The Riordan brothers Timothy and Michael arrived in Flagstaff during the mid-1880s and eventually took over the Arizona Lumber & Timber Company. Both became involved in the social, business, and political life of early Flagstaff. In 1904, they built a grand mansion just south of downtown. A Rendezvous Room connected the wings occupied by each brother's family. The architect Charles Whittlesey, who also designed El Tovar Hotel on the rim of the Grand Canyon, used a similar rustic style of logs and stonework for the mansion exterior. The brothers christened their joint home Kinlichi, Navajo for Red House.

The park (409 Riordan Rd., 928/779-4395, $6 adults, $2.50 ages 7–13) offers tours of 50–60 minutes in Timothy's side of the house that reveal life in Flagstaff during the early 1900s. All the rooms still display original furnishings, most in the Arts and Crafts style. The wing occupied by Michael's family has exhibits that you can see on your own. You can compare the two sides of the house, which mirror each other.

Open year-round, the visitors center's summer hours (May–Oct.) are 8:30 A.M.–5 P.M. daily; tours depart on the hour with the first one at 9 A.M. and the last at 4 P.M. During the rest of the year, hours are 10:30 A.M.–5 P.M. daily, with the first tour at 11 A.M. and the last at 4 P.M. It's best to phone in advance for tour reservations. There's no charge to see the exhibits in the visitors center or to take the self-guided tour of the grounds. You can picnic under the pines near the parking area. You'll find this piece of historic Flagstaff between S. Milton Road and Northern Arizona University, about a half mile south of downtown; turn east on Riordan Road toward Northern Arizona University from S. Milton Road, then turn right at the sign, opposite Ardrey Auditorium.

Northern Arizona University (NAU)

Flagstaff's character and population owe much to this school, just south of downtown. The university began in 1899 as Northern Arizona Normal School, housed in a vacant reformatory building. Four young women received their diplomas and teaching certificates two years later.

In 1925 the school began offering a four-year Bachelor of Education degree and took the name Northern Arizona State Teachers College. The program broadened over the years to include other degrees, a program in forestry, and graduate studies. In 1966 the institution became a university. NAU's sprawling campus now covers 686 acres, supplemented by the School of Forestry's 4,000-acre laboratory forest. The High Altitude Training Center's programs attract athletic teams from around the world, who come to improve their performance in the thin mountain air.

To learn about NAU services and events, call or visit the **University Union Information Desk** (928/523-4636, www.nau.edu). The university's FM radio station **KNAU** broadcasts classical music and National Public Radio programs at 88.7 MHz.

The 1893 Old Main building, on McMullen Circle in the northern part of campus, houses changing exhibits of the **Old Main Art Gallery** on the second floor and a permanent collection of fine art and furniture in the **Marguerite Hettel Weiss Gallery** on the third floor. Be ready for almost anything in the **Richard E. Beasley Gallery** upstairs in the Fine and Performing Arts building, south on Knoles Drive, where changing shows feature contemporary art. Call 928/523-3471 or check www.nau.edu to find out what's showing at the galleries; they're open Monday–Saturday except between shows.

Northern Arizona University Observatory (928/523-7170), built by the U.S. Air Force as an atmospheric research observatory in the early 1950s, is now an educational tool for university students and the general public. Volunteers, mostly Astronomy Club members, hold an open house most clear Friday nights at 7:30 P.M. with special open nights for astronomical events such as eclipses and occultations. It's off S. San Francisco Street adjacent to a high-rise dormitory and practice field.

Wall Aquatic Center (Franklin Ave. between S. Beaver and S. San Francisco Sts., 928/523-4508), on the north side of campus, contains a large indoor swimming pool that's open to the public. Call or check the Web for the schedule.

Mountain Campus Transit (928/523-5052) connects the northern and southern parts of the main campus; ask someone for the location of the stop nearest you. To park on campus, pick up a visitor's permit from the **Parking Services/Visitor Information** office (928/523-3591, 7:30 A.M.–4:30 P.M. Mon.–Fri.) in the Centennial building at the southwest corner of Dupont Avenue and S. Beaver Street. After hours you can obtain a parking permit from the police office at Lumberjack Stadium off S. San Francisco Street.

The Arboretum

At an elevation of 7,150 feet, the Arboretum (928/774-1441, www.thearb.org, 9 A.M.–5 P.M. daily April 1–Dec. 15, $4 adults, $3 seniors, $1 youth 6–12) is the highest botanical garden in the United States doing horticultural research. Plant researchers study native and non-native flora, including rare and endangered species that thrive in the cool climate of the Flagstaff area. About 2,000 species of plants and trees grow on the 200-acre grounds, despite the short 75-day average growing season. You'll get a great introduction to the flora of the Colorado Plateau here, as well as learn about landscaping and gardening possibilities. The variety of habitats attracts many birds; call for information on birding walks. Summer (June–Sept.) is the best time to visit.

Tours of 45–60 minutes, which begin at 11 A.M. and 1 P.M., introduce ongoing projects and take you through the solar greenhouse and outdoor gardens, which you can also see on your own. Children enjoy exploring a garden based on the Peter Rabbit stories and getting lost in the maze. A nature trail through the ponderosa pine forest has a .6-mile inner loop and a 1-mile outer loop. The visitors center provides exhibits, including mounted specimens of many local species. A gift shop offers books, cards, a bird list, Extension Bulletins (gardening and tree advice), seeds, and gardening supplies.

You can purchase plants at the Summer Plant Sale and Garden Fair in June and through the season. The Summer Sunday Concert series entertains with a varied evening program on the first Sunday of the month June–September. The Penstemon Festival is an open house in July. In autumn, see the website or call to find out where the fall colors are. A Holiday Craft Sale runs on the first Saturday in December.

You're welcome to bring a picnic (tables are available), but no pets. From S. Milton Road in Flagstaff, head west 1.9 miles on Route 66, then turn south 4 miles on Woody Mountain Road.

Elden Pueblo

The resourceful Sinagua tribe lived at this site below Mt. Elden about A.D. 1150. Some of the pueblo, including a large community room, has been excavated. A leaflet explains and illustrates features of the ruin, free and open during daylight hours. From I-40 Exit 201, head north 2.1 miles on U.S. Highway 89 past the Flagstaff Mall and the Peaks Ranger Station and turn at the sign on the left, just before the Camp Townsend–Winona Road.

Scenic Sky Ride

Hop on this chairlift at the Arizona Snowbowl for the most leisurely way to the heights. You'll be swept from 9,500 to 11,500 feet and treated to fantastic views. The Sky Ride (928/779-1951, www.arizonasnowbowl.com, $10 adult, $8 seniors 65–69, $6 kids 6–12) operates 10 A.M.–4 P.M. daily from June 21 through Labor Day, then Friday–Sunday until mid-October, weather permitting. A restaurant serves lunch. To reach the Snowbowl, drive northwest seven miles from downtown on U.S. Highway 180, then turn right seven miles up paved Snowbowl Road.

Although you're not permitted to hike from or to the upper chairlift station, hikers headed for Humphrey's Peak may take the Humphrey's Peak or Weatherford Trails. (The Forest Service closed Agassiz Peak to protect fragile alpine vegetation, including *Senecio franciscanus,* found only on the San Francisco Peaks.)

Spirit Mountain Ranch, "Home of the Sacred White Buffalo"

Owners Jim and Dena Riley feel such a strong bond to these unusual animals that they've developed this small ranch for them 21 miles northwest of Flagstaff (Mile 236.5 on U.S. Highway 180, 928/606-1651, www.sacredwhitebuffalo.org, 8 A.M.–7 P.M. daily spring–summer, call autumn–winter, $5). Only one in ten million buffalo turns out to be white, and you can see six here! DNA testing has confirmed that they are pureblooded buffalo, not a crossbreed. On a visit, you'll learn a lot about these animals and why they're so special to many people.

ENTERTAINMENT AND EVENTS

The free weekly paper ***Flagstaff Live!*** (www.flaglive.com) details the local arts and entertainment scene. **Flagstaff Symphony Orchestra** (928/774-5107, www.flagstaffsymphony.org) performs about eight concerts each season. The play's the thing for **Theatrikos Theatre Company** (11 W. Cherry Ave., 928/774-1662, www.theatrikos.com).

NAU Culture and Sports

Northern Arizona University presents theater, opera, dance, concerts, and a variety of sporting events. For information and tickets, contact **NAU Central Ticket Office** (University Union, 928/523-5661 or 888/520-7214). Professional teams hold summer training camps on NAU's campus: The **Arizona Cardinals** (football) usually come every year, and the **Phoenix Suns** (basketball) and **Phoenix Mercury** (women's basketball) arrive some years.

Nightlife

Something's happening nightly in the **Museum Club** (3404 E. Route 66, 928/526-9434, www.museumclub.com). The huge log structure opened in 1931 as a museum and trading post. Curious motorists sputtering down early Route 66 dropped in to see the thousands of exhibits inside, including such taxidermy oddities as a two-headed calf and a one-eyed lamb along with more conventional animals, Native American artifacts, and a rifle collection. Five years later another entrepreneur converted it into a nightclub to attract the growing crowds of motorists as well as local folk looking for some good music and dancing. Aspiring recording artists traveling cross-country stopped by to perform for appreciative audiences. The Museum Club continues the tradition of fine country music while introducing additional music styles popular with the younger crowd. It's also known as the "The Zoo" because stuffed animals still gaze down from the walls. Wandering through the rustic interior, you'll find photos and news clippings on the walls, a dance floor, and a magnificent late-19th-century bar. *Car and Driver* magazine named it one of the top 10 roadhouses in the nation.

You'll find most of the other nightlife downtown. The venerable **Orpheum Theatre** (15 W. Aspen Ave., 928/556-1580, www.orpheumpresents.com), once Flagstaff's opera house, now hosts bands and special events. Other downtown venues include **Charly's** (23 N. Leroux St., 928/779-1919), **Flagstaff Brewing Co.** (16 E. Route 66, 928/773-1442), **Collin's Irish Pub** (2 N. Leroux St., 928/214-7363), **Mogollon Brewing Co.** (15 N. Agassiz St., 928/773-8950), **The Wine Loft** (17 N. San Francisco St., 928/773-9463), and **Monte Vista Lounge** (100 N. San Francisco St., 928/774-2403). Out east at Little America, **Tiffany Tree Lounge** (2515 E. Butler Ave., 928/779-7979) presents a variety of entertainment by local musicians many nights in a smoke-free setting.

Events

First Friday Artwalk presents artists' demonstrations and book signings each month of the year downtown. All summer, from mid-May to mid-September, Heritage Square downtown hosts free **Music on the Square** each Thursday and **Movies on the Square** (family flicks) each Friday evening.

Major annual festivals include **Flagstaff Winterfest** in February, featuring over 100 events such as skiing competitions, sled-dog races, snow games, and entertainment. In April, the **Northern Arizona Book Festival** draws authors and booklovers for a weekend. From late May to mid-June, **Trappings of the American West** displays outstanding paintings, sculptures, photographs, and saddles and other cowboy gear at the Coconino Center for the Arts.

June activities include **The Great Fiesta del Barrio & Fajita Cook-off** on the second Saturday and **Pine Country Rodeo and Parade** on the third weekend. **Horse races** also run in June. Flagstaff's **Fabulous Fourth Festivities** commemorate July 4th and Flagstaff's founding with a parade, the Fair of Life arts and crafts show, a gem show, historic walks, horse racing, a pioneer festival, barbecue, and fireworks. **Hopi Marketplace,** on the weekend nearest July 4th, brings Hopi artisans and performers to the Museum of Northern Arizona. Also in July, **Arizona Highland Celtic Festival** celebrates the people of Brittany, Cornwall, Ireland, the Isle of Man, Scotland, and Wales with dancing, athletic demonstrations and, of course, bagpiping. **Summerfest/Festival in the Pines** on the first weekend in August features top Southwestern artists for an arts and crafts show. **Navajo Marketplace** celebrates the artistry and culture of the country's largest tribe at the Museum of Northern Arizona on the first full weekend in August.

Native Artists Marketplace presents outstanding works by Zuni, Pai, and other Colorado Plateau tribes on the first weekend in September at the Museum of Northern Arizona. **Coconino County Fair** runs over Labor Day weekend in September as does an arts and crafts show. **Flagstaff Festival of Science** (www.scifest.org) presents talks, demonstrations, and open houses during a 10-day period in late September. The Hispanic Festival ***Celebrations de la Gente*** takes place on the last weekend of October, close to the Day of the Dead, at the Museum of Northern Arizona. Holiday cheer begins around Thanksgiving with the **Pine Cone Festival,** culminating with a giant pine cone descending to ring in the New Year at 10 P.M. and again at midnight. Other December festivities include the **Northern Lights Holiday Parade** and the **Holiday Lights Festival** at Little America.

SHOPPING AND SERVICES

Art Galleries and Native American Crafts

Shops in downtown Flagstaff display a wealth of regional arts and crafts, much of it by Native American artists. You'll see paintings, jewelry,

Navajo rugs, Hopi kachina dolls, pottery, and baskets. The Museum of Northern Arizona and the Art Barn, both northwest of town on U.S. Highway 180, also feature excellent selections of Native American arts and crafts.

The Art Barn

Regional artists and art patrons have banded together to operate this large sales gallery (behind the Pioneer Museum, 928/774-0822, 10 A.M.–6 P.M. Wed.–Sun.). You'll find a great selection of works by both Native American and Anglo artisans, including paintings, sketches, photographs, pottery, jewelry, kachina dolls, Navajo rugs, sand paintings, rock art (petroglyph reproductions), and books. You can also purchase old pawn jewelry. The Art Barn has its own bronze foundry and a frame shop. Prices are right, too, since there's no distributor markup or big advertising budget.

Shopping Mall

Sears, JCPenney, and Dillard's anchor the Flagstaff Mall—the only indoor mall in town—on U.S. Highway 89 just north of I-40 Exit 201.

Bookstores

In a bold modern building with a corner tower, **Barnes & Noble Booksellers** (701 S. Milton Rd., 928/226-8227) offers a large selection of books and music and a little espresso café. **NAU Bookstore** (928/523-4041) on the east side of campus includes many regional and general publications. **Northland Publishing** (2900 N. Fort Valley Rd./U.S. 180, 928/774-5251, www.northlandpub.com, 8 A.M.–5 P.M. Mon.–Fri.) produces outstanding regional and children's books plus some cookbooks and posters; the sales room often has discounted titles. The **Museum of Northern Arizona** (3101 N. Fort Valley Rd., 928/774-5213) offers excellent books on Southwestern Native American cultures, archaeology, and natural history. **Waldenbooks** (Flagstaff Mall, 928/526-5196) stocks good regional and general reading selections. **Crystal Magic** (1 N. San Francisco St., 928/779-2528) downtown features spiritual and New Age titles along with gifts.

For used books, including many regional titles, drop by **Bookman's Used Books** (1520 S. Riordan Ranch St., 928/774-0005), which has 250,000 used books and some new ones as well as music, videos, and games. You can also visit the coffee bar and use the Internet computers. A few doors south, **Hastings** (928/779-1880) sells discounted new books, magazines, music, and videos. **Dragon's Plunder** (217 S. San Francisco St. and Butler Ave., 928/774-1708) has about 30,000 used books. **Starrlight Books** (15 N. Leroux St., 928/774-6813) specializes in modern first editions, rare and antique books, and out-of-print orders.

Outdoor Equipment and Rentals

Outdoor stores, each with a different personality, cluster around downtown. Try **Babbitt's Backcountry Outfitters** (12 E. Aspen Ave., 928/774-4775) and **Aspen Sports** (15 N. San Francisco St., 928/779-1935). South across the tracks, **Four Seasons Outfitters & Guides** (107 W. Phoenix Ave., 928/226-8798, www.fsoutfitters.com) sells and rents gear and leads hikes in the Grand Canyon and Escalante regions. You can often find good deals at **Peace Surplus** (14 W. Route 66, 928/779-4521) and **Popular Outdoor Outfitters** (901 S. Milton Rd., 928/774-0598).

Services

The main **post office** (2400 N. Postal Blvd., Flagstaff, AZ 86004, 928/714-9302) is off E. Route 66; you can have General Delivery mail sent to you here. There's a downtown branch at 104 N. Agassiz Street and one in the NAU Bookstore basement.

If you need medical attention, it's cheaper to go directly to a doctor's office or clinic than to the hospital. You'll find many offices along N. Beaver Street. Walk-in patients are welcome daily at **Concentra Medical Centers** (120 W. Fine Ave. and Humphreys St., 928/773-9695) downtown and at **Walk-In Medical Care** (4215 N. Hwy. 89, 928/527-1920) near the Flagstaff Mall. **Flagstaff Medical Center** (1200 N. Beaver St., 928/779-3366, www.nahealth.com) is the local hospital.

RECREATION

City Parks

Flagstaff Parks & Recreation (211 W. Aspen Ave., 928/779-7690) provides details on facilities and programs. **Thorpe Park,** just west of downtown at 191 N. Thorpe Road, offers picnic tables and playgrounds as well as facilities for baseball, softball, soccer, tennis, basketball, volleyball, racquetball, horseshoes, and disc golf. From downtown, head west on Route 66 and keep straight where the highway curves left, continue west on Santa Fe Avenue five blocks, then turn right one block on Thorpe Road. The adjacent Adult Center (245 N. Thorpe Rd., 928/774-1068) hosts many community activities and clubs. Bark Park, also next to Thorpe Park, is a place for dogs to socialize in two off-leash sections—a larger area for large dogs and a smaller one for pint-size breeds

McPherson Park and the adjacent ice-skating rink (July–April) at **Jay Lively Activity Center** (1650 N. Turquoise Dr., 928/774-1051) lie northeast of downtown; from downtown, you can head north on San Francisco Street, turn right on Forest Avenue, then left on Turquoise Drive. McPherson provides picnic tables under the pines, playground, tennis courts, basketball court, and a horseshoe pit.

Buffalo Park spreads across a large meadow at the base of Mt. Elden with fine views of the San Francisco Peaks. The park has some picnic tables, but it's mainly a place to hit the trail. You can make an easy two-mile loop on the Buffalo Urban Trail, hike up Mt. Elden, or head off on other trails of the Flagstaff Urban Trail System. From downtown, drive north on San Francisco Street, turn right on Forest Avenue, then left on Gemini Drive.

Sawmill Multicultural Art & Nature County Park (703 E. Sawmill Rd., 928/774-5139) features demonstration gardens, a sculpture walk, tile & paint mural walk, playground, and a trailhead for the Rio de Flag area. From E. Butler Avenue, turn south two blocks on Lonetree at the light, then left on Sawmill.

Over on the east side of town, **Bushmaster Park** has picnic tables, playground, tennis, volleyball, basketball, horseshoes, and a skate park. It's at Lockett Road and Alta Vista Drive (turn south from Lockett Road at the sign). **Foxglenn Park** (4200 E. Butler Ave.) offers a fancier skate park along with ballfields, playground, and picnic tables east of I-40 Exit 198.

Flagstaff Urban Trail System (FUTS)

You don't have to go far for a hike, as this trail network goes right through town. It connects the Mt. Elden trails with the Arizona Trail, Walnut Canyon National Monument, and other areas surrounding Flagstaff. Mountain bikers, hikers, joggers, and cross-country skiers use the trails. Flagstaff Parks & Recreation (211 W. Aspen Ave., 928/779-7690) and most outdoor and cycling stores sell a map. Cyclists can check out www.flagstaffbiking.org for additional trail information.

Golf

Continental Country Club (2380 N. Oakmont Dr., 928/527-7997, May–Oct., www.golfflagstaff.com) offers an 18-hole course, driving range, pro shop, and restaurant on the east side of town; turn south from I-40 Exit 201 on Country Club Drive, then right onto Oakmont Drive.

Horseback Riding

The Flagstaff area is great horse country. If you don't have your own steed, local riding stables can provide one; reservations are advised.

The Flying Heart Barn (8400 N. Hwy. 89, 928/526-2788) offers hour-long, half-day, and full-day rides year-round on and near the San Francisco Peaks; head 3.5 miles north on U.S. Highway 89 from I-40 Exit 201. **M Diamond Ranch** (U.S. 180 and Snowbowl Rd., 928/774-4481) leads rides below the Peaks on one-hour trips between Memorial Day and Labor Day weekends; cookouts and hayrides can be arranged with two days' notice.

Downhill Skiing

Arizona Snowbowl (928/779-1951, www.arizonasnowbowl.com), on the San Francisco Peaks, has some of Arizona's best downhill action. Four chair lifts and a towrope provide access to 30

runs/trails ranging from novice to expert. From the top of Agassiz Chairlift, it's two miles and 2,300 feet down. With sufficient snow, the Snowbowl is open for skiing 9 A.M.–4 P.M. daily from mid-December to Easter. Lift tickets cost $42 ($34 afternoons on weekends and holidays; $27 afternoons on weekdays) for adults; $24 for ages 8–12 ($19 afternoons); $22 seniors 65–69; and free for kids seven and younger and for seniors 70 and over.

Hart Prairie Lodge (elev. 9,200 feet) offers a ski school, rentals, repairs and a restaurant. **Ski Lift Lodge** (U.S. 180 opposite the Snow Bowl Road turnoff, 928/774-0729 or 800/472-3599) has rooms and a restaurant. To reach the Snowbowl, drive northwest seven miles from downtown on U.S. Highway 180 to the sign, then turn right seven miles on a paved road, which sometimes requires chains and/or 4WD.

Cross-Country Skiing

Flagstaff Nordic Center (928/779-1951, www.arizonasnowbowl.com) grooms more than 25 miles of trails ranging from beginner to advanced near Hart Prairie and the San Francisco Peaks. The Center provides ski lessons, a beginner package, a snowshoe-only trail, equipment rentals and sales, and a snack bar. Races, clinics, and moonlight tours highlight the calendar. It's open daily from about mid-November until mid-April, as weather permits. Trail passes run $10, free for kids seven and under and seniors 70 and over; snowshoers pay $5. Take U.S. Highway 180 northwest 16 miles from downtown to near Milepost 232.

Wing Mountain Cross-country Ski Trails offers more than 17 miles of marked but ungroomed skiing near the San Francisco Peaks. The rolling meadow and forest country is ideal for ski touring. Head northwest 9.5 miles on U.S. Highway 180, then turn left onto Forest Road 222B, just before Milepost 226, and follow it 1 mile to parking. For road and skiing conditions near the Peaks, check with the Forest Service's Peaks Ranger Station (928/526-0866, www.fs.fed.us/r3/coconino).

The groomed trails of Mormon Lake also attract cross-country skiers. In the village of Mormon Lake, **Mormon Lake Ski Center** (928/354-2240) has 12.4 miles (20 km) of groomed diagonal and skating trails ranging from easy to challenging. It's open daily, snow permitting, with a trail fee of $5 per adult or $15 per family; rentals and instruction are available. Drive 20 miles southeast on Lake Mary Road, then turn right 8 miles on Mormon Lake Loop Road. **Mormon Lake Lodge** (928/354-2227 local or 928/774-0462 Flagstaff) has rooms, cabins, and a café/steakhouse. For Mormon Lake road and ski conditions, call the Forest Service's Mormon Lake Ranger Station (928/556-7474).

Snow Play

To simply frolic in the snow, you can drive out U.S. Highway 180 to Wing Mountain parking or continue northwest seven miles to Crowley Pit on the left near Milepost 233, or to Walker Lake/Kendrick Park Watchable Wildlife Area on the left between Mileposts 235 and 236. Note that the Snowbowl doesn't allow snow play, nor are there parking spots along the Snowbowl Road. Parking along U.S. Highway 180 is permitted only at designated parking areas.

Climbing

Vertical Relief Climbing Center (205 S. San Francisco St., 928/556-9909 or 877/265-5984, www.verticalrelief.com) has indoor walls up to 40 feet high to challenge all ages and abilities. Staff offer a store, instruction, guided outdoor climbs, and local climbing information.

ACCOMMODATIONS

Flagstaff offers a huge number and variety of places to stay. The bed and breakfasts have some of the nicest locations in and near town. Motels congregate in four areas: Most of the independents and some older chain establishments line Route 66 east of downtown; these have the lowest prices, but also the highest noise levels—the busy railroad runs day and night just across the road. Another group of independent and a few chain motels lies just south of downtown on S. Milton Road and adjacent W. Route 66. The newest and largest group of chain motels and hotels lies farther south on Milton Road and nearby streets just before the junction of I-40 and I-17; they're convenient to most of the sights and services yet are well away from the trains. Another group of chain motels clusters near I-40 Exit 198, a couple of miles east of downtown.

Costs fluctuate greatly, with summer weekends the most expensive. If you plan to be in town on Friday and Saturday nights, it's well worth calling ahead to check prices and make reservations. Rates listed below apply in summer but go higher on holiday or special-event periods. Off-season, prices can drop substantially. Winter rates may rise a bit during the ski season and weekends, depending on demand. Many motels list their prices, so you can just turn in where the appearance and price seem most attractive. **Northern Arizona Central Reservations** (928/556-0853 or 800/527-8388, www.flagstaff-rooms.com) provides a free lodging service for some of the more expensive places in Flagstaff and nearby towns.

Bed-and-Breakfasts

The Inn at 410 (410 N. Leroux St., 928/774-0088 or 800/774-2008, www.inn410.com, $145–205 d) offers distinctive guest suites in a restored 1907 craftsman-style bungalow; all have private bath and fireplace, and some a whirlpool tub.

Comfi Cottages of Flagstaff (928/774-0731 or 888/774-0731, www.comficottages.com, $110–145 d, $180–260 for 6–8 guests) has kitchens and provides ingredients for a fix-your-own breakfast at various locations in and near downtown; it's a great choice for families. **Aspen Inn Bed & Breakfast** (218 N. Elden St., 928/773-0295 or 888/999-4110, www.flagstaffbedbreakfast.com, $99 d) provides old-fashioned rooms with private bath in a 1912 house just three blocks east of downtown.

Starlight Pines Bed & Breakfast (3380 E. Lockett Rd., 928/527-1912 or 800/752-1912, www.starlightpinesbb.com, $115–145 d) displays early-20th-century antiques in a recently built Victorian-style house. Tiffany artwork decorates the rooms, all of which have a private bath—most with a claw-foot tub. One room has a wood-burning fireplace and another features a private deck with a view of Mt. Elden.

Rooms and two-bed suites of **The Sled Dog Inn** (10155 Mountainaire Rd., 928/525-6212 or 800/754-0664, www.sleddoginn.com, $110 d–$185 4 people) lie in the woods six miles south of town off I-17 Exit 333; all have private bath, and guests enjoy the hot tub and sauna.

Hostels

For a lively backpacker scene with an international crowd, head south across the train tracks to the Grand Canyon or Du Beau hostels (both under the same management). Each offers free pickup at the Greyhound station, discounts for car rentals, and tours to the Grand Canyon and Sedona. Guests have use of a kitchen, common room, and Internet computers (small fee). There's no need for a hostel card or passport. Call ahead, if possible, to make reservations with a credit card; summer is the busiest time.

Grand Canyon International Hostel (19 S. San Francisco St., 928/779-9421 or 888/442-2696, www.grandcanyonhostel.com) offers dorm beds at $15 ($17 in summer) and double rooms at $30–33 d ($34–37 d in summer) including tax and breakfast. The **Du Beau International Hostel** (nearby at 19 W. Phoenix Ave., 928/774-6731 or 800/398-7112, www.dubeauhostel.com) has dorm spaces at $15 ($17 in summer) and motel rooms for $32–35 d ($36–39 d in summer) including tax and breakfast.

Historic Downtown Hotels

J. W. Weatherford, who came to Flagstaff in 1887 from Texas and stayed 47 years, built the **Weatherford Hotel** (23 N. Leroux St., 928/774-2731, www.weatherfordhotel.com), which was quite elegant in its day, in 1897. Zane Grey wrote *Call of the Canyon* while staying here, describing the hotel as it was in 1918. Weatherford's other projects included a nearby opera house and the Weatherford Road (now a hiking trail in the San Francisco Peaks). Old-fashioned rooms (no TV or phone) cost $60–65 d, but expect some noise from the nightclub and trains. Five of the eight rooms have private bath. Charly's, the hotel's restaurant and pub, serves food and brew downstairs. Musicians often perform foot-tapping bluegrass, jazz, blues, folk, or rock 'n roll Friday and Saturday nights.

The 1927 **Hotel Monte Vista** (100 N. San Francisco St., 928/779-6971 or 800/545-3068, www.hotelmontevista.com) was Flagstaff's grand hotel, where movie stars stayed to film in nearby locations. You can stay in rooms named for those guests, such as the John Wayne, Jane Russell, and Gary Cooper suites ($60–150 d). Rooms with shared bath cost $50 d but are rarely available. The Monte Vista is home to the Racha Thai Restaurant, a lounge, and the Old Post Office Salon & Spa.

Under $50

East of Downtown: East Route 66 features the biggest selection of bargain places. These vary a lot in quality, though you can get an idea from the outside appearance. It's best to check the room before paying. Here's a sampling.

Relax Inn Motel (1500 E. Route 66, 928/779-4469, $28 s, $35 d weekdays, $35 s, $42 d Fri.–Sat.) and **Twilite Motel** (2010 E. Route 66, 928/774-3364, $30 d weekday, $35 d Fri.–Sat.) offer just the basics. **66 Motel** (2100 E. Route 66, 928/774-6403, $22 s, $25 d all week) and **Pinecrest Motel** (2818 E. Route 66, 928/526-1950, $30 s, $35 d weekday, $38 s, $40 d Fri.–Sat.) have some kitchenettes.

South and West of Downtown: Autolodge (1313 S. Milton Rd., 928/774-6621, $38 d weekdays, $49 d Fri.–Sat.) is a good value in this part of town. On Route 66, the **Best Value Inn** (822 W. Route 66, 928/774-1443 or 888/315-2378, $30 s, $35 d weekdays, $39–44 d Fri.–Sat.) has an indoor pool, which closes in winter.

$50–100

East of Downtown: Best Western King's House Motel (1560 E. Route 66, 928/774-7186 or 888/577-7186, $75 d weekdays, $119–135 d Fri.–Sat.) offers a pool. **Best Western Pony Soldier Inn & Suites** (3030 E. Route 66, 928/526-2388 or 800/356-4143, $69–99 d all week) includes an indoor pool, hot tub, and a restaurant.

South and West of Downtown: The Inn at NAU (928/523-1616, www.inn.nau.edu) puts you in the heart of campus with large rooms and fine dining; students operate the facilities under the School of Hotel and Restaurant Management at a cost of $69 d ($99 d in summer) including breakfast; there's no tax.

Basic motels just across the street from NAU include the **Economy Inn** (224 S. Mikes Pike, 928/774-8888, $29 s, $34 d weekdays, $59 s, $64 d Fri.–Sat.) and **Canyon Inn** (500 S. Milton Rd., 928/774-7301 or 888/822-6966, $40 d weekdays, $49–125 d Fri.–Sat.).

Turn west on Route 66 opposite NAU for a variety of motels. **The Travel Inn** (801 W. Route 66, 928/774-3381; $33–36 s, $46–50 d weekdays; $46–50 s, $53–56 d Fri.–Sat.; $60–70 2-bedroom suite) provides a hot tub, sauna, and family suites. Set on a low hill, **Days Inn** (1000 W. Route 66, 928/774-5221 or 800/422-4470, $60–70 d weekdays, $90–110 d Fri.–Sat.) features the largest motel pool in northern Arizona; rooms have views of town or of the central courtyard and pool. The Riordan sawmill stood on this site before it burned down in the 1960s, but the sawmill's stone office still stands across Route 66.

Several chain motels line up near Wal-Mart, just north and west from the interchange of I-40 and I-17. **Motel 6 Woodlands Village** (2745 S. Woodlands Village Blvd., 928/779-3757 or 800/466-8356, $40 s, $46 d weekdays, $50 s, $56 d Fri.–Sat.) has a pool along with the lowest price here.

If you'd like to stay in a three-bedroom log cabin in the forest 22 miles south of town, make a reservation with the Peaks Ranger Station (928/526-0866) for the **Fernow Cabin** (off Woody Mountain Rd., $75–100 up to 8 people).

North of Downtown: On U.S. Highway 180 opposite the Snow Bowl Road turnoff, **Ski Lift Lodge** (6355 N. Fort Valley Rd., 928/774-0729 or 800/472-3599, www.arizonasnowbowl.com, $60 d weekdays, $80 d Fri.–Sat.) has a restaurant, ski packages, and nearby hiking and horseback riding.

Butler Avenue Area: This group of motels just north of I-40 Exit 198 tend to be good value, though the neighborhood lacks character—it looks just like any other interstate area in the country! **Motel 6** (2440 E. Lucky Lane, 928/774-8756 or 800/466-8356; $36 s, $42 d weekdays, $50 s, $56 d Fri.–Sat.) has a pool and the lowest prices here.

$100 and up

East of Downtown: Days Inn East (3601 E. Lockett Rd., 928/527-1477 or 800/329-7466, $80 d weekdays, $119 d Fri.–Sat.) has an indoor pool and hot tub. **Residence Inn by Marriott** (3440 N. Country Club Dr., 928/526-5555 or 800/331-3131) provides kitchens in all units and fireplaces in some and includes a pool, hot tub, and nearby golf at $99–170 d studio or $170–209 two-bedroom every day.

South and West of Downtown: A standout for its distinctive architecture, Southwestern designs, and luxurious furnishings, the **Radisson Woodlands Hotel** (1175 W. Route 66, 928/773-8888 or 877/773-0199 hotel, 800/333-3333 Radisson reservations, $139–169 d) offers rooms and parlor suites along with a pool, indoor and outdoor hot tubs, sauna, and an exercise room.

Embassy Suites Hotel (706 S. Milton Rd., 928/774-4333 or 800/362-1779; $119–129 s, $129–139 d weekdays; $129–139 s, $139–159 d Fri.–Sat.) near NAU has a pool and hot tub. Enjoy the country life at **Arizona Mountain Inn** (4200 Lake Mary Rd., 928/774-8959 or 800/239-5236, www.arizonamountaininn.com, $90 d suites, $115 d and up cabins), about three miles southeast of downtown.

Butler Avenue Area: Set on 500 acres of attractively landscaped grounds and ponderosa forest south of I-40 Exit 198, **Little America** (2515 E. Butler Ave., 928/779-2741 or 800/352-4386, www.flagstaff.littleamerica.com, $119–129 d rooms, $175–275 d suites) offers fine dining, a pool, exercise room, hiking, and a business center.

Campgrounds

These nestle in ponderosa pines; all are open year-round and have showers except as noted.

Kit Carson RV Park (2101 W. Route 66, 928/774-6993, $28 RV w/hookups) is two miles west of downtown between I-40 Exits 191 and 195. **Woody Mountain Campground** (2727 W. Route 66, 928/774-7727, mid-March–Oct., $18 tents, $26 RVs w/hookup) is a half mile farther west with a pool, store, and deli.

Fort Tuthill County Campground (928/774-3464, May–Sept., $9 tents or RVs no hookups, $13 sites w/water and sewer) is five miles south of downtown off I-17 Exit 337 on the west side of the fairgrounds. It lacks showers, but offers hiking on a quarter-mile nature trail, the five-mile Soldiers Trail, and the Flagstaff Urban Trail System. Reservations, needed only on big weekends, cost an extra $5. **Black Bart's RV Park** (928/774-1912, $20 tent w/3-night limit, $22 RV w/hookups) is two miles east of downtown near I-40 Butler Avenue Exit 198. It may be the only campground in the state with an antique store! There's a good steak house next door.

Flagstaff KOA (5803 N. Hwy. 89, 928/526-9926 or 800/562-3524, $22 tent, $26–32 tent or RV w/hookups, $40 cabin) is 5 miles northeast of downtown on Route 66/U.S. Highway 89 or 1.1 miles north from I-40 Exit 201; turn west on Smoke Rise Drive at the light. Sites tend to be closely spaced, but the campground includes showers, laundry, playground, and a small store. A café serves inexpensive breakfasts in summer. Hikers can head up Mt. Elden right from the campground or stroll on the easy nature trail.

The adult **Greer's Pine Shadows** (7101 N. Hwy. 89, 928/526-4977, mid-April–mid-Oct., $19 w/hookups) accepts only self-contained RVs, as there are no restrooms or showers; it's 1.8 miles north of I-40. **J&H RV Park** (7901 N. Hwy. 89, 928/526-1829 or 800/243-5264, www.flagstaffrvparks.com, mid-April–mid-Oct., $23.50–29 RVs w/hookups) is an adult-oriented place with a hot tub, exercise room, showers, laundry, and a small store, three miles north of I-40 Exit 201. The owner enjoys humor, and he sells some of his little books.

Munds Park RV Resort (928/286-1309, April–Oct., $19 tent, $19–23.50 RV w/hookups) offers sites 17 miles south of Flagstaff just off I-17 Exit 322. **Ponderosa Forest RV Park & Campground** (928/635-0456 or 888/635-0456, $13 tents, $20 RVs w/hookups) includes showers, laundry, and a nearby store; it's north of I-40 Parks Exit 178, 17 miles west of Flagstaff and about halfway to Williams.

Established campgrounds in the Coconino National Forest lie southeast off Lake Mary Road and north off U.S. Highway 89; contact the Peaks Ranger Station (5075 N. Hwy. 89, Flagstaff, AZ 86004, 928/526-0866, www.fs.fed.us/r3/coconino).

Dispersed camping on Forest Service lands surrounding town is another option. The ponderosa pine forests offer lots of room but no facilities—just be sure you're at least two miles outside the city and not on private or state land. The Peaks and Mormon Lake Ranger District offices can make suggestions, supply a map showing closed areas, and sell the Coconino National Forest map that shows Forest Service land and the back roads. Freidlein Prairie, along Forest Road 522 off Snowbowl Road, has some designated dispersed campsites that are undeveloped and free; each of the sites has a brown vertical fiberglass post with a site number.

Carry water and be *very* careful with fire; in dry weather the Forest Service often prohibits fires in the woods and may even close some areas. Other rules require that you camp at least 200 feet from trails, lakes, streams, or wet meadows and at least one mile from established campgrounds. Because they're so fragile, alpine areas above 11,400 feet and all meadows are closed to camping.

FOOD

Flagstaff, for its size, offers an amazing number of places to eat. But then, it has a lot of hungry tourists and students to feed. Most restaurants cater to the eat-and-run crowd. You'll find the well-known chains and fast-food places on the main roads, but with a little effort you can discover some unique restaurants and cafés. Come downtown for atmosphere—old-fashioned home-style eateries abound.

You'll enjoy Flagstaff's clean mountain air while dining because of the city's nonsmoking ordinance. A few places, such as Monsoon on the Rim (downtown), Granny's Closet (S. Milton), and Buster's (S. Milton), have separate smoking and nonsmoking sections. Bars that serve food may be all smoking.

There are plenty of supermarkets in the shopping centers scattered around town. For fruits and veggies, visit **Flagstaff Farmers Market** (1901 N. 4th St., 928/774-4500, open daily) just off E. Route 66; backpackers will like the bulk foods and dried fruit section. **New Frontiers** (1000 S. Milton Rd., 928/774-5747, open daily) specializes in organic foods, and has a deli and bakery.

American and Southwestern

Downtown (North of the Tracks): Josephine's (503 N. Humphreys St., 928/779-3400, www.josephinesrestaurant.com, Mon.–Fri. plus Sat. in summer lunch, Mon.–Sat. dinner, $14–24) describes itself as a modern American bistro, and since the United States is a melting pot of many cultures, the menu reflects international influences. Popular choices include the New York strip steak, seared ahi tuna, and Mediterranean lamb meat loaf; there's at least one vegetarian item. The long wine list includes many available by the glass. Lunches of sandwiches, soups, and salads run $6.50–8.75. Depending on the weather, you may wish to sit near the fireplace inside or out on the front patio. The restaurant is in a 1911 craftsman bungalow of native malpais stone; reservations are recommended. **Charly's Pub and Grille** (in the old Weatherford Hotel at 23 N. Leroux St., 928/779-1919, daily lunch and dinner, $8–20) serves good American and Southwestern food.

Downtown (South of the Tracks): Beaver Street Brewery & Whistle Stop Café (11 S. Beaver St., 928/779-0079, daily lunch and dinner, $11–19) serves wood-fired pizza, sandwiches, salads, fondues, and nightly specials, along with a selection of local brews; there's a beer garden outside. For a romantic evening, try **Cottage Place** (126 W. Cottage Ave., 928/774-8431, www.cottageplace.com, Tues.–Sun. dinner, $21–31) with American and continental specialties in a 1909 bungalow; reservations are recommended.

South and West of Downtown: Dim lighting and old-fashioned furnishings set the mood at **Granny's Closet** (218 S. Milton Rd., just south of the railroad underpass, 928/774-8331, daily lunch and dinner, $8–22), which fixes steak and other meat dishes, seafood, and Italian cuisine; there's a sports bar for smokers. **Galaxy Diner** (931 W. Route 66, 928/774-2466, daily breakfast, lunch, and dinner, $8–15) features '50s music and movie-star decor with American classics such as sandwiches, platters, milkshakes, sodas, and sumptuous deserts; breakfasts are especially recommended and are served all day. **Woodlands Café** (1175 W. Route 66, 928/773-9118, daily breakfast, lunch, and dinner, $10–21) serves American food and some Southwestern and continental flavors at Radisson Woodlands Hotel.

South and west of downtown, you'll find popular chain restaurants in the Woodlands Village area and on adjacent S. Milton Road.

For more than 20 years, **Buster's** (1800 S. Milton Rd. in Green Tree Village, 928/774-5155, daily lunch and dinner, $14–25) has been turning out seafood, including an oyster bar, steaks, prime rib, and other meat dishes. The popular Chicken Sonoma has breast sautéed with artichoke hearts, tomatoes, mushrooms, and chardonnay. The restaurant is unusual for Flagstaff in having a separate smoking section.

Several miles south of town, **Jackson's Grill at the Springs** (928/213-9332, daily dinner, $15–60) has an idyllic setting in a meadow. The extensive menu includes steak, ribs, chicken, seafood, brick oven pizza, and salads, and there's a choice of more than 150 wines. You can dine in the main dining room, deck, patio, café, or lounge. Head south on Beulah Boulevard or I-17 to the Fort Tuthill/Airport Exit 337, then continue half a mile south on Highway 89A.

East of Downtown: Tucked away off the Business Route, **Brandy's Bakery & Restaurant** (1500 E Cedar Ave. #40, 928/779-2187, www.brandysrestaurant.com, daily breakfast and lunch, Tues.–Sat. dinner, $7–13) is worth the detour for its tasty and varied menu, plus baked items and espresso; art shows take place monthly. **Restaurante La Punta** (3050 E. Route 66, 928/527-9393, Mon.–Sat. lunch and dinner, $9–16) specializes in New Mexico cuisine.

Little America's **Western Gold Dining Room** (2515 E. Butler Ave., 928/779-7900, $25–35) serves a big brunch on Sunday, a buffet lunch Monday–Friday, and a choice of set-menu dinners nightly. **In the Pines Café** ($9.50–16.50) is open daily for breakfast, lunch, and dinner. **Black Bart's Steak House, Saloon, & Musical Revue** (2760 E. Butler Ave. near I-40 Exit 198, 928/779-3142, nightly dinner, $11–28) serves up steak, prime rib, baby back ribs, rack of lamb, chicken, shrimp, fish, veggie kabob, and some Italian dishes. Nightly specials appear, and there's a 12 and under menu. Singing waiters and waitresses entertain you.

Many locals feel it's worth the drive out to **Lupo's Horsemen Lodge** (8500 N. U.S. 89, 928/526-2655, www.horsemenlodge.com, $14–26), which fixes steak, ribs, chicken, trout, seafood, and vegetarian items; it's open for dinner nightly except Sunday (and Mon. in winter) on U.S. Highway 89, 3.6 miles north from I-40 Exit 201.

Cafés

Downtown (North of the Tracks): Café Espress (16 N. San Francisco St., 928/774-0541, daily breakfast and lunch, Tues.–Sun. dinner, $7–8) serves homemade natural foods, including many vegetarian items, coffees from the espresso bar, and baked goodies from the oven. **Kathy's** (7 N. San Francisco St., 928/774-1951, daily breakfast and lunch, Wed.–Sat. dinner, $5–6) is a cozy café with American standbys and a few exotic items such as Aussie burgers, tofu rolls, and Navajo tacos. **Downtown Diner** (7 E. Aspen Ave., 928/774-3492, daily breakfast, lunch, and dinner, $7–8) dishes out inexpensive American food; large photos of historic Flagstaff decorate the dining room.

Downtown (South of the Tracks): Macy's European Coffee House & Bakery (14 S. Beaver St., 928/774-2243, daily breakfast, lunch, and dinner, $5–7) offers a big selection of fresh-roasted coffee and an all-vegetarian menu of pasta dishes, sandwiches, soups, salads, quiches, and home-baked treats. **La Bellavia Sandwich Shoppe** (18 S. Beaver St., 928/774-8301, daily breakfast and lunch, $5–7) features an extensive breakfast menu, espresso, and creative sandwiches. **Pesto Brothers** (34 S. San Francisco St., 928/913-0775, Mon.–Sat. lunch, Thurs.–Sat. dinner, $8–14) offers a café and deli with antipasti, salads, pasta, fish, and meat dishes.

Morning Glory Café (115 S. San Francisco St., 928/774-3705, Tues.–Sat. lunch and Sat. late breakfast, $5–7) features hemp and many organic ingredients in a mostly vegetarian menu, including blue corn tamales, blue corn pancakes, ginger oatmeal cookies, and a variety of salads and soups.

South and West of Downtown: Mike and Ronda's (21 S. Milton Rd., 928/774-7008, daily breakfast and lunch, $5–10) pulls in the crowds with generous servings of low-priced American café fare; it's a great breakfast place, and nobody seems to mind the lack of decor. **The Crown Railroad Café** (2700 S. Woodlands Village Blvd. near Wal-Mart, 928/774-6775, daily breakfast, lunch, and dinner, $8–11) serves up popular American standbys, including a choice of 66 omelets; model trains entertain by circling the dining area.

Mexican

Downtown (North of the Tracks): Las Mañanitas (103 W. Birch Ave. and Beaver St., 928/226-7144, Mon.–Sat. breakfast, lunch, and dinner, $8–10) features specialties such as carne adobada (marinated pork) along with the usual Mexican favorites. **Kachina Downtown** (522 E. Route 66, 928/779-1944, daily late breakfast, lunch, and dinner, $8–18) presents Mexican, American, and Navajo food in a Spanish Colonial setting.

Downtown (South of the Tracks): Café Olé (119 S. San Francisco St., 928/774-8272, Tues.–Sat. dinner, $8–11) specializes in homemade Mexican dishes. **El Charro** (409 S. San Francisco St., 928/779-0552, Mon.–Sat. lunch and dinner, $6.50–14.50) is a popular Mexican café.

South and West of Downtown: Casa Bonita (1551 S. Milton Rd. in Sherwood Forest Shopping Center, 928/773-0065, daily lunch and dinner, $4–14) serves up fajitas, carne asada, tacos al carbon, camarones portuguesas (shrimp wrapped with bacon, cheese, and ham), and a variety of other dishes in a family atmosphere. **Garcia's** (1900 S. Milton Rd., 928/779-1960, daily lunch and dinner, $7–14) covers the Mexican favorites, including combos, fajitas, chimichangas, tacos, and enchiladas.

Italian and Mediterranean

Downtown (North of the Tracks): Pasto (19 E. Aspen Ave., 928/779-1937, daily lunch in summer, nightly dinner year-round, $11–22) serves Italian food, including vegetarian and wheat-free options, in a casual fine-dining atmosphere; reservations are recommended. **Mountain Oasis** (11 E. Aspen Ave., 928/214-9270, daily lunch and dinner, $8–16) has a tasty mix of Mediterranean, Southwestern, and international flavors with many vegetarian options.

East of Downtown: Mamma Luisa (2710 N. Steves Blvd., Kachina Square off E. Route 66, 928/526-6809, $8–16) has excellent Italian cuisine nightly for dinner; reservations are advised.

North of Downtown: The little **Dan's Italian Kitchen** (1850 N. Fort Valley Rd., 928/779-9349, daily lunch and dinner, $2–16) fixes good and inexpensive pasta dishes on the U.S. Highway 180 route to the Grand Canyon. Next door, **Late for the Train** (928/773-0100, daily) has a great variety of coffees plus sandwiches and baked goodies.

Indian

South and West of Downtown: Delhi Palace (2700 S. Woodlands Village Blvd. near Wal-Mart, 928/556-0019, daily lunch and dinner, $8–15) offers fine north Indian food; the lunch buffet is a great value. This is the restaurant where you're most likely to spot the author!

Chinese

Downtown (North of the Tracks): Monsoon on the Rim (6 E. Aspen Ave., 928/226-8844, daily lunch and dinner, $7–11) presents New Asian Cuisine and a sushi bar next to Heritage Square; seating options include the main dining room, some tables out front, and the Martini Bar (smoking).

South and West of Downtown: Hunan West (1302 S. Plaza Way, University Plaza off S. Milton Rd., 928/779-2229, Tues.–Sun. lunch and dinner, $6–15) features Mandarin along with many other styles of Chinese cuisine; specialties include crispy or fancy duck, sizzling rice seafood, and country-style sweet and sour pork. **Szechuan** (1451 S. Milton Rd. in Sherwood Forest Shopping Center, 928/774-8039, daily lunch and dinner, $7–12) offers spicy Szechuan along with other Chinese cuisines; popular dishes include General Tsao's chicken, noodle dishes, and crackling san shein (shrimp, beef, chicken, and vegetables sautéed in a mandarin sauce). The large buffet provides an outstanding selection of seafood, meat, and vegetarian items for both lunch and dinner daily.

East of Downtown: China Star (1802 E. Route 66, 928/774-8880, daily lunch and dinner, $6–8) has a large buffet every day, and you can order from the menu. **Golden Dragon Bowl** (2730 Lakin Dr. across from Kachina Square, 928/527-3238, daily lunch and dinner, $6–13) provides a lunch buffet option. In the Park Santa Fe Shopping Center, **Mandarin Gardens** (3518 E. Route 66, 928/526-5033, daily lunch and dinner, $7–12) serves a lunch buffet except on Sunday.

Thai

Downtown (North of the Tracks): Racha Thai (104 N. San Francisco St. in the Monte Vista Hotel, 928/774-3003, Tues.–Sat. lunch, Tues.–Sun. dinner, $8–13) offers flavorful Thai curries—including an unusual curry pot pie—on its long menu.

Downtown (South of the Tracks): Thai food devotees enjoy **Dara Thai Restaurant** (14 S. San Francisco St., 928/774-0047, Mon.–Sat. lunch and dinner, $8–13) for its fine selection of curries, seafood, meat, and veggie food.

Japanese

South and West of Downtown: Sakura Restaurant (1175 W. Route 66, 928/773-9118, www.sakuraflagstaff.com, Mon.–Sat. lunch, nightly dinner, $12–30) prepares Japanese teppanyaki steak, chicken, seafood, and a variety of combos in the Radisson Woodlands Hotel; the many sushi choices are also available for takeout.

Korean

Downtown (North of the Tracks): For good Korean food, it's the **Corea House** (115 E. Aspen Ave., 928/773-1122, www.coreahouse.net, daily lunch and dinner, $8–18) with tasty items like the *mandoo* (vegetable or meat pot stickers), *bindaedduk* (vegetable pancakes), *bulgogi* (marinated meat), and, of course, spicy kimchee (pickled cabbage or radish). The menu explains why the restaurant uses its unusual spelling.

Northern Arizona University

The Garden Terrace Dining Room (The Inn at NAU, S. San Francisco St., 928/523-1616, www.inn.nau.edu) serves a breakfast buffet daily and fine lunches Monday–Friday. On some Fridays, except in summer, chefs prepare a magnificent six-course set menu for dinner ($25); reservations are required.

University Union in the north-central campus offers a variety of fast-food eateries and Union Station, a large cafeteria.

INFORMATION

Visitor Center

The very helpful staff at the **Flagstaff Visitor Center** (1 E. Route 66, Flagstaff, AZ 86001, 928/774-9541 or 800/842-7293, www.flagstaffarizona.org) can answer your questions and tell you what's happening. The office, downtown in the Amtrak depot, is open in summer 9 A.M.–5 P.M. Sunday, 8 A.M.–7 P.M. Monday–Saturday; the rest of the year 9 A.M.–4 P.M. Sunday, 8 A.M.–6 P.M. Monday–Saturday. You can pick up literature in the lobby after hours. Other useful websites include www.flagstaffcentral.com for commercial and community services and www.flaglive.com with the latest on arts and entertainment.

Coconino National Forest

The **U.S. Forest Service** provides information and maps about camping, hiking, and road conditions in the Coconino National Forest surrounding Flagstaff at three offices in town and online at www.fs.fed.us/r3/coconino. You can also ask about visiting archaeological sites—the Coconino has more than 9,000 sites, the most of any national forest.

For detailed information on the Mt. Elden, Humphrey's Peak, and O'Leary Peak areas north of Flagstaff, contact the **Peaks Ranger Station** (5075 N. Hwy. 89, Flagstaff, AZ 86004, 928/526-0866, 7:30 A.M.–4:30 P.M. Mon.–Fri.); turn west .3 miles on Railhead Avenue from U.S. Highway 89 opposite the Flagstaff Mall. For the lake and forest country south of town, check with the **Mormon Lake Ranger Station** (4373

S. Lake Mary Rd., Flagstaff, AZ 86001, 928/774-1147, 7:30 A.M.–4:30 P.M. Mon.–Fri.).

The **Supervisor's Office** (1824 S. Thompson St., Flagstaff, AZ 86001, 928/527-3600, 7:30 A.M.–4:30 P.M. Mon.–Fri.) on the west side of town covers the entire forest; turn south on Thompson Street from W. Route 66 opposite the Maverik gas station.

Arizona Game and Fish Department

This office (3500 S. Lake Mary Rd., Flagstaff, AZ 86001, 928/774-5045, www.azgfd.com, 8 A.M.–5 P.M. Mon.–Fri.) provides fishing and hunting licenses and information.

State Trust Lands

If you'll be hiking or camping on these lands, you can purchase the required 12-month permit at the **Arizona State Land Department** (3650 Lake Mary Rd., Flagstaff, AZ 86001, 928/774-1425, www.land.state.az.us, 8 A.M.–5 P.M. Mon.–Fri.). Licensed anglers and hunters pursuing their activities don't need the permit.

Libraries

Looking for a good place to read up on Arizona or to keep dry on a rainy day? The attractive ski-lodge architecture of the downtown **Flagstaff City–Coconino County Public Library** (300 W. Aspen Ave., 928/779-7670, www.flagstaffpubliclibrary.org, 10 A.M.–9 P.M. Mon.–Thurs., 10 A.M.–7 P.M. Fri., 10 A.M.–6 P.M. Sat.) makes it an especially enjoyable spot. Many good regional books enrich the Arizona Collection. Exhibits by local artists and photographers change monthly. Only people with a library card can use the Internet computers for free, others pay a small charge. The smaller **East Flagstaff Community Library** (3000 N. 4th St., 928/774-8434, 1–5 P.M. Sun., 9 A.M.–9 P.M. Mon.–Thurs., 9 A.M.–5 P.M. Fri., 9 A.M.–1 P.M. Sat.) is on the southwest corner with Lockett Road.

NAU's **Cline Library** (928/523-6805, www.nau.edu/library, call for hours) carries many books and periodicals along with free Internet computers. Hikers can plan trips and copy maps in the Government Documents section. Upstairs, the **Special Collections and Archives Department** (928/523-5551, www.nau.edu/library, call for hours) contains an outstanding array of Arizona-related publications and photos; changing exhibits appear in the entranceway, and you can view thousands of images online.

The **Museum of Northern Arizona** (928/774-5211, ext. 256) has an excellent regional library in the Research Center across the highway from the museum; call for hours.

GETTING THERE AND AROUND

Tours

Open Road Tours (1 E. Route 66, 928/226-8060 or 877/226-8060, www.openroadtours.com) will show you around Flagstaff, the Grand Canyon, Antelope Canyon, Monument Valley, Petrified Forest/Meteor Crater, and Sedona. **American Dream Tours** (928/527-3369 or 888/203-1212, www.americandreamtours.com) specializes in Grand Canyon day tours; you can also join the tour in Williams or Tusayan. Local taxi companies arrange personalized Flagstaff and northern Arizona tours. Other local tour operators have brochures at the Visitor Center.

Car

A rental car allows more extensive sightseeing than does public transportation and costs less if several people get together. Rates fluctuate with supply and demand, competition, and the mood of the operators; call around for the best deals. See the Yellow Pages for agencies; you'll find offices in town and at the airport.

Bus

Mountain Line (928/779-6624, www.co.coconino.az.us/transit) serves most of the city and connects with NAU's Mountain Campus Transit; download a schedule or pick one up at the Flagstaff Visitor Center, public library, or at one of the Safeway stores in town.

Open Road Tours (1 E. Route 66, 928/226-8060 or 877/226-8060, www.openroadtours.com) offers a shuttle service north to the Grand Canyon National Park via Williams and Tusayan, and south to Phoenix's Sky Harbor Airport via Camp Verde, Cordes Junction, and Metro

Center. **Greyhound** (399 S. Malpais Lane, 928/774-4573 or 800/231-2222, www.greyhound.com) offers daily departures south to Phoenix and Sky Harbor Airport, east along I-40 to Winslow and Holbrook, and west to Williams and Kingman. Services also continue to Tucson, Los Angeles, Las Vegas, Albuquerque, and other destinations. The station lies just south of downtown off S. Milton Road.

Train

Amtrak (1 E. Route 66, 928/774-8679, 800/872-7245, www.amtrak.com) offers service on the Southwest Chief every evening for Los Angeles ($50–98 one-way), and every morning for Albuquerque ($47–92 one-way) and on to Chicago. The price depends on availability—book ahead or travel off-season for the lowest rates; round-trip tickets are double but there are also special Explore America fares.

Air

America West (800/235-9292, www.americawest.com) flies about five times daily to Phoenix for a stiff $229 each way, but advance purchases will be cheaper. Pulliam Field, Flagstaff's airport, lies five miles south of town off I-17 Exit 337.

East of Flagtaff

WALNUT CANYON NATIONAL MONUMENT

Good farmland, edible wild plants, and forests filled with game attracted the Sinagua to this pretty canyon more than 800 years ago. Ledges eroded out of the limestone cliffs provided shelter from rain and snow—the inhabitants merely had to build walls under the ready-made roofs. The clear waters of Walnut Creek flowed seasonally in the canyon bottom.

After occupying Walnut Canyon A.D. 1125–1250, the people moved on. Some Hopi clans trace their ancestors back to Sinagua at this site. More than 300 cliff dwellings remain; you can see and enter some along a loop trail. Another loop trail on the rim passes viewpoints, a pit-house site, and a two-room pueblo.

Visitor Center

A small museum (928/526-3367, www.nps.gov/waca, 9 A.M.–5 P.M. daily, usually extended in the warmer months, $5/person age 17 and up) displays pottery and other artifacts of the Sinagua culture. Exhibits show how the people farmed and how they used wild plants for baskets, sandals, mats, soap, food, and medicine. A map illustrates trading routes to other indigenous cultures. Staff offer interpretive programs and answer questions about the archaeology and natural history of Walnut Canyon. During the summer, they lead the Ledges Hike to cliff dwellings off the main trail, the Ranger Cabin Hike to a 1904 Forest Service cabin that once served as a visitors center for Walnut Canyon, and a Moonlight/Starlight walk that introduces archaeo-astronomy; call ahead for times and to make reservations for the hikes. A bookstore sells a wide selection of books, maps, and videos related to the monument and region.

The self-guided .9-mile **Island Trail** begins behind the visitors center. As it winds past 25 cliff dwellings, you begin to get a feeling of what it was like to live here. The paved path descends 185 feet with 240 steps, which you'll have to climb on the way out; allow 45–60 minutes. Because of the high elevation (6,690 feet), the trail isn't recommended for people with mobility, respiratory, or cardiovascular problems. The easy **Rim Trail** visits two scenic viewpoints, a pit-house site, and a small pueblo; signs describe plants and wildlife found here. Allow 20–30 minutes for the .75-mile loop, which is paved, level, and wheelchair accessible. Pets cannot go on trails.

Vegetation changes dramatically from the pinyon and juniper forests near the rim to the tall Douglas firs clinging to the canyon ledges. Black walnut and several other kinds of deciduous trees grow at the bottom. Rock layers will be familiar to Grand Canyon visitors. The lower 100 feet of Walnut Canyon is Coconino Sandstone, 265 million-year-old sand dunes that have turned to stone. The upper 300 feet is Kaibab Limestone, formed in a sea about 255 million years ago.

Walnut Canyon National Monument remains open all year except December 25, though snows can close the trails for short periods. Vehicles pulling cars and large trailers may have trouble negotiating the turnaround loop at the visitors center. You'll find picnic areas near the visitors center and on the drive in. From Flagstaff, head east seven miles on I-40 to Walnut Canyon Exit 204, then turn south three miles on a paved road.

Arizona Trail near Walnut Canyon

Hikers and mountain bikers enjoy forests, canyon scenery, and views of the San Francisco Peaks along this section of trail. A sign 2.5 miles in on the Walnut Canyon National Monument road points the way to a trailhead 1.7 miles to the west along a graded dirt road. From here the path heads southwest, crossing a side canyon of Walnut and paralleling the rim before dropping down into upper Walnut Canyon just west of Fisher Point in about six miles. A branch of Flagstaff's Urban Trail System joins here. In another mile you'll reach the junction for Sandy's Canyon Trail, which climbs the canyon to a trailhead near Lake Mary Road in .75 miles. The Arizona Trail curves to the southeast and continues four miles to Marshall Lake. Mountain bikers may need to walk the steep sections in the side canyon and on the descent into Walnut Canyon. The monument visitors center may have a map.

GRAND FALLS OF THE LITTLE COLORADO RIVER

In the spring, a thundering torrent of muddy brown water plunges 185 feet into the canyon of the Little Colorado River about 30 miles northeast of Flagstaff. The best time to see the spectacle is during March and April; in other months the river may dry up and yield nothing but an unimpressive trickle. High-clearance vehicles will be required for the dirt access roads, which should be avoided if muddy.

A lava flow from Merriam Crater, the large cinder cone 10 miles southwest, created the falls about 100,000 years ago. The tongue of lava filled the canyon, forcing the river out of its gorge, around the dam, and back over the rim into the original channel.

Grand Falls lies on the southwest corner of the Navajo Indian Reservation. From Flagstaff, take U.S. Highway 89 north 1.8 miles past Flagstaff Mall, turn right 8 miles on the Camp Townsend–Winona Road, then turn left onto Leupp Road. Follow Leupp Road northeast 13 miles, then turn north 10 miles on unpaved Indian Route 70 or turn north 10 miles on unpaved Indian Route 6910 between Mileposts 5 and 6, 7 miles farther east; the overlook is on a rocky road a half mile west of the main road. (If you come to the Little Colorado River ford, you've gone .4 miles too far.) The AAA Indian Country map will help in navigation, as there may not be signs on the unpaved roads. You'll see hues of the Painted Desert as the road descends to the river.

Other approaches: I-40 Winona Exit 211 (14 miles east of Flagstaff)—drive two miles on the Townsend–Winona Road, then turn right on Leupp Road to the Grand Falls turnoffs; I-40 Exit 245 (46 miles east of Flagstaff)—take Highway 99 to Leupp, then Leupp Road to the Grand Falls turnoffs. From Kykotsmovi, on the Hopi Indian Reservation, take paved Indian Route 2 southwest 49 miles to Leupp, then Leupp Road to the Grand Falls turnoffs.

The overlook has picnic tables; admission is free, though the Navajo Tribe asks you to help keep the area clean and leash your dogs so they won't disturb livestock. Also, don't go out in the streambed—mud makes the rocks very slippery and the strong currents have carried people over the falls to their deaths.

METEOR CRATER

A museum perched on the edge of Meteor Crater offers exhibits on meteorites, impact crater geology, space exploration, and astronomy (928/289-2362 or 800/289-5898, www.meteorcrater.com, 7 A.M.–7 P.M. daily in summer—Memorial Day to Labor Day—and 8 A.M.–5 P.M. daily the rest of the year, $12 adults, $11 ages 60+, $6 children

SUDDEN IMPACT

About 50,000 years ago, a blinding flash of light in the sky preceded an explosion on Earth equivalent to 20 million tons of TNT. A meteor of nickel-iron speeding along at around 40,000 miles an hour had smashed onto a plain east of where Flagstaff is today. The chunk of extraterrestrial rock, roughly 150 feet across and weighing several hundred thousand pounds, struck the Earth with such force that fragments were buried 3,000 feet underground. About 80 percent of the meteor vaporized upon impact, then precipitated back to earth. Shock waves killed every living thing in the area. Perhaps 5 percent of the meteor had worn away by the atmosphere on entry and another 5 percent was blasted out to rain down as fragments. An estimated 10 percent lies buried underground.

When the crater was first discovered in 1871, scientists thought it to be of volcanic origin. Philadelphia mining engineer Daniel Barringer, convinced that it was an impact crater, devoted the last 26 years of his life to finding the buried meteor. When drill holes in the crater floor missed the nickel-iron, he took a closer look at the rock layers and realized that the meteor had struck at an angle. He then started drilling on the southeast rim, where cores showed meteorite fragments, but a hard material jammed the drill bit at a depth of 1,376 feet as Barringer's money ran out.

Despite the failure to recover a rich mass of metal, his geologic studies added to the world's knowledge of impact structures. By 1929, the year of Barringer's death, the scientific community had finally come around to believing the crater to be of meteoric origin, the first one on Earth to be proved as such. Apollo astronauts learned about crater geology here, and they practiced travel on its lunar surface.

Though larger impact craters exist on our planet, none are so well preserved or spectacular. The giant pit measures 550 feet deep, almost 4,000 feet across, and 2.4 miles in circumference—enough room for 20 football fields.

© METEOR CRATER, ARIZONA

6–17). Paintings and a video portray meteors and the drama of Meteor Crater's formation. You can look closely at a hefty 1,406 lb. meteorite found nearby and see examples of other types of meteorites. Shatter-cones and shock metamorphism show what happens when rocks undergo powerful compression forces. Maps and photos illustrate additional impact craters on earth and other bodies of the solar system. Step out to the rim overlooks for views of the crater and surrounding countryside; telescopes and sight tubes help you see and identify features of the crater. In the front courtyard, the American Astronaut Wall of Fame honors those who have flown into space.

Staff at the privately owned Meteor Crater offer guided hour-long walks along a short section of the rim trail—weather permitting—at no extra charge; you'll need good walking shoes (no sandals or open-toed shoes), a hat, sunscreen, and water. The visitor center features a snack bar and a gift shop. No pets are permitted, but you may be able to leave yours in shade near the entrance. Meteor Crater is 40 miles east of downtown Flagstaff, or 20 miles west of Winslow; take I-40 Meteor Crater Exit 233, then head south 5.5 miles on a paved road.

Meteor Crater RV Park (928/289-4002 or 800/478-4002, $20 tents, $20–22 RV w/hookups) offers year-round camping with showers, laundry, and a convenience store/gas station. It's just off the I-40 exit for Meteor Crater.

The San Francisco Volcanic Field

Peaceful today, this 3,000-square-mile area of volcanic peaks, cinder cones, and lava flows presents some impressive landscapes and geology. Altogether, the field has more than 600 volcanoes. The majestic San Francisco Peaks, highest of all Arizona mountains, soar 5,000 feet above the surrounding plateau. Eruptions beginning between 1.4 million and 400,000 years ago created this giant stratovolcano, which may have stood 16,000 feet. The center later collapsed, perhaps in a violent Mt. St. Helens–style blast, forming a huge caldera, now known as the Inner Basin. During three Pleistocene ice ages, glaciers carved deep valleys on its slopes. Hundreds of cinder cones, of which Sunset Crater is the youngest, surround the Peaks. There's no reason to assume the San Francisco Volcanic Field is finished, either. The area has experienced volcanic activity interspersed with periods of calm during its long history. The first volcanoes in the field burst forth about six million years ago near present-day Williams. Later volcanoes sprung up progressively eastward, spreading 50 miles past Flagstaff to the Little Colorado River Valley, where the next eruption is likely to occur. On average, eruptions have occurred every 10,000 years, so another isn't "due" for a while, as the last one was less than 1,000 years ago.

Tribes of northern Arizona regard the San Francisco Peaks as a sacred place. The Hopi believe that the Peaks are the winter home of their kachina spirits and the source of clouds that bring rain for crops. The Peaks also occupy a prominent place in Navajo legends and ceremonies, representing one of the cardinal directions.

In 1984, the federal government set aside 18,963 acres of this venerable volcano for the Kachina Peaks Wilderness, selecting the name because of the importance of the site to the Hopi people. The Forest Service maintains a network of trails in the wilderness, and most of the volcanoes make good day-hike destinations. Cyclists may not ride here, even on the former roads, because of the wilderness designation. Foresters at the **Peaks Ranger Station** (5075 N. U.S. 89, Flagstaff, AZ 86004, 928/526-0866) offer maps and hiking information for this region. The book *Flagstaff Hikes* by Richard and Sherry Mangum lists many possibilities in the San Francisco Peaks area.

SUNSET CRATER VOLCANO NATIONAL MONUMENT

Sunset Crater, a beautiful black cinder cone tinged with yellows and oranges, rises 1,000 feet above jagged lava flows about 15 miles northeast of Flagstaff. Although more than 700 years have passed since the last eruptions, the landscape still presents a lunar appearance, with trees and plants struggling to grow.

Eruptions beginning in A.D. 1064 or 1065 sent indigenous people fleeing for safety. By 1110 activity had subsided enough to allow them to settle in the Wupatki Basin, 20 miles northeast of Sunset Crater. You can visit the remains of their communities and see a museum in Wupatki National Monument, reached via the Loop Road, one of the prettiest scenic drives in Arizona. Geologists continue working out the history of Sunset Crater. Some studies place the eruptions within a short period between 1040 and 1100; others suggest that lava flows and smaller ash eruptions continued from Sunset Crater possibly as late as 1280.

In the late 1920s, some Hollywood filmmakers thought Sunset Crater would make a great movie set. They planned to use dynamite to simulate an avalanche, but local citizens put a stop to their plans. Sunset Crater became a national monument in 1930. Before rangers prohibited climbing on Sunset Crater in 1973, hikers wore a deep gash in the soft cinder slopes. Most of the damage has been repaired, though you can still see faint scars. No off-trail hiking is permitted in the monument to protect both the landscape and the visitors.

The road and trails stay open all day; an admission fee of $3 per person over the age of 17 also includes entry to Wupatki National Monument. You can reach the monument's visitors

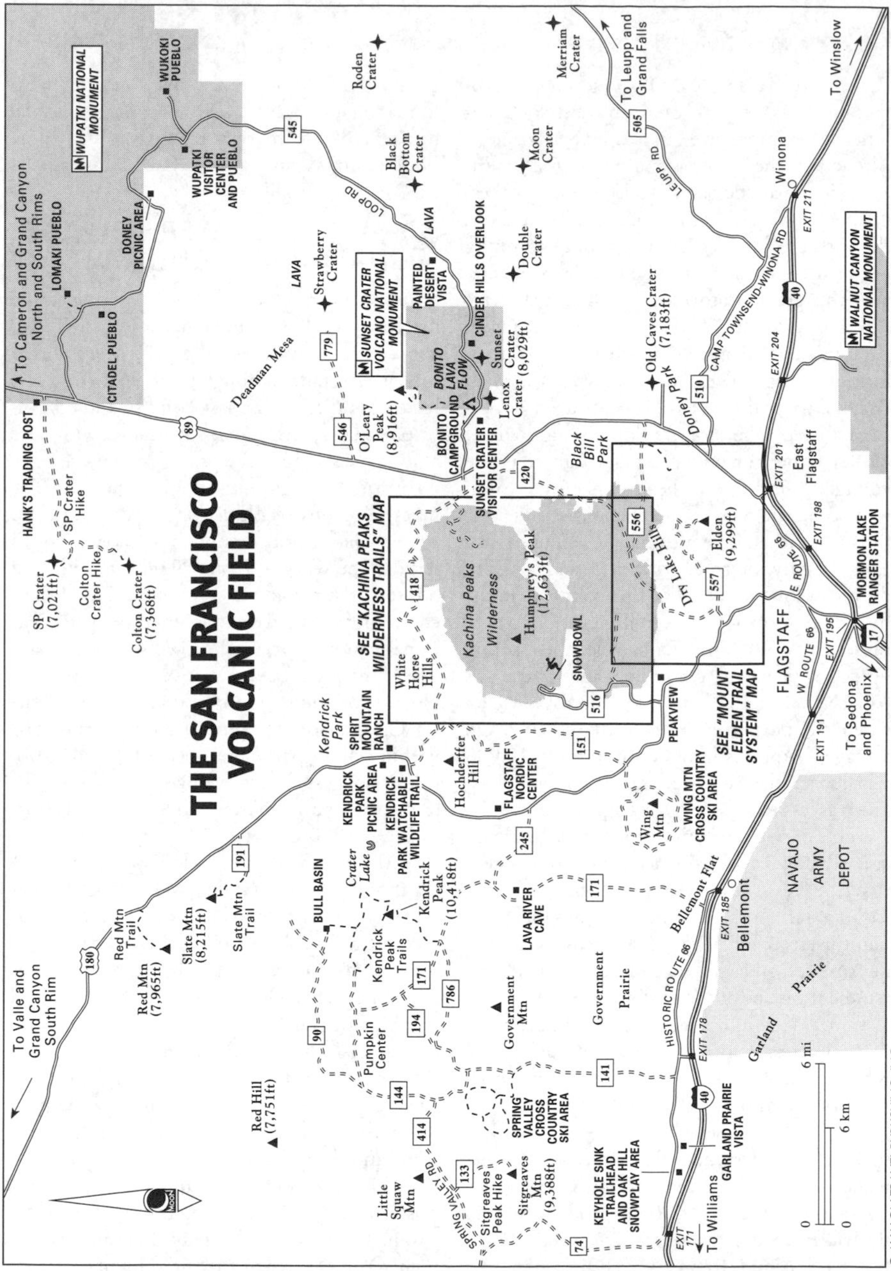
THE SAN FRANCISCO VOLCANIC FIELD
To Cameron and Grand Canyon North and South Rims
WUPATKI NATIONAL MONUMENT
WUKOKI PUEBLO
LOMAKI PUEBLO
CITADEL PUEBLO
DONEY PICNIC AREA
WUPATKI VISITOR CENTER AND PUEBLO
545
LOOP RD
Roden Crater
Merriam Crater
To Leupp and Grand Falls
505
LEUPP RD
To Winslow
Black Bottom Crater
Moon Crater
Winona
EXIT 211
LAVA
Strawberry Crater
SUNSET CRATER VOLCANO NATIONAL MONUMENT
PAINTED DESERT VISTA
CINDER HILLS OVERLOOK
Double Crater
CAMP TOWNSEND-WINONA RD
WALNUT CANYON NATIONAL MONUMENT
40
Deadman Mesa
779
BONITO LAVA FLOW
Sunset Crater (8,029ft)
Lenox Crater
Old Caves Crater (7,183ft)
Doney Park
510
EXIT 204
HANK'S TRADING POST
89
546
O'Leary Peak (8,916ft)
BONITO CAMPGROUND
SUNSET CRATER VISITOR CENTER
420
Black Bill Park
EXIT 201
East Flagstaff
SP Crater Hike
SP Crater (7,021ft)
Colton Crater Hike
Colton Crater (7,368ft)
SEE "KACHINA PEAKS WILDERNESS TRAILS" MAP
418
Kachina Peaks Wilderness
Humphrey's Peak (12,633ft)
556
Elden (9,299ft)
Dry Lake Hills
557
EXIT 198
66
E ROUTE
MORMON LAKE RANGER STATION
White Horse Hills
SNOWBOWL
516
PEAKVIEW
FLAGSTAFF
W ROUTE 66
EXIT 195
17
To Sedona and Phoenix
SEE "MOUNT ELDEN TRAIL SYSTEM" MAP
Kendrick Park
SPIRIT MOUNTAIN RANCH
KENDRICK PARK PICNIC AREA
KENDRICK PARK WATCHABLE WILDLIFE TRAIL
Hochderffer Hill
FLAGSTAFF NORDIC CENTER
151
Wing Mtn
WING MTN CROSS COUNTRY SKI AREA
EXIT 191
To Valle and Grand Canyon South Rim
180
Red Mtn Trail
Red Mtn (7,965ft)
Slate Mtn (8,215ft)
Slate Mtn Trail
191
BULL BASIN
Crater Lake
Kendrick Peak (10,418ft)
Kendrick Peak Trails
245
LAVA RIVER CAVE
171
Bellemont Flat
Bellemont
EXIT 185
NAVAJO ARMY DEPOT
90
194
786
Government Mtn
Government Prairie
HISTORIC ROUTE 66
Prairie
Garland
Red Hill (7,751ft)
Pumpkin Center
144
141
EXIT 178
414
SPRING VALLEY CROSS COUNTRY SKI AREA
GARLAND PRAIRIE VISTA
Little Squaw Mtn
SPRING VALLEY RD
133
Sitgreaves Peak Hike
Sitgreaves Mtn (9,388ft)
74
KEYHOLE SINK TRAILHEAD AND OAK HILL SNOWPLAY AREA
EXIT 171
To Williams
MOON
0 6 mi
0 6 km

THE SAN FRANCISCO VOLCANIC FIELD'S FOUR TYPES OF VOLCANOES

The San Francisco Peaks took the longest to form and rose the highest of any of its neighbors. It's a stratovolcano, in which alternating eruptions of cinders, lava, and other volcanic debris added layer upon layer, until a massive explosion on the north side caused a collapse, leaving a semicircle of peaks where the upper slopes once stood.

The next highest summits rose as highly viscous lava oozed out, creating steep-sided lava dome volcanoes such as Mt. Elden, Kendrick, Bill Williams, and more than 40 others.

Cinder cones, by far the most numerous, occurred when magma with large amounts of silicone dioxide gas rose to the surface. Powered by the high-pressure gas, foaming lava roared out the vent, solidified in the air, then rained down as cinders. Later in the eruption, when most of the gas had escaped the remaining lava became so dense that it could force its way out the base of the cinder cone, such as at Sunset and SP Craters.

Shield volcanoes, like those in Hawaii, form from layers of basalt that spread out relatively smoothly from the vent. The gentle slopes may not be impressive, but the lava caves left by subsurface lava rivers certainly are! You can enter a large one, Lava River Cave, south of Kendrick Peak.

center by driving north 12 miles from the Flagstaff Mall on U.S. Highway 89, then turning east 2 miles at the sign. This very scenic drive, known as the Loop Road, continues past Sunset Crater, drops down to pinyon-juniper country with views of the Painted Desert, crosses Wupatki National Monument, and then rejoins U.S. Highway 89 26 miles north of Flagstaff; the drive is 35 miles one-way and takes about an hour without stops.

You can experience the history of Sunset Crater at the visitors center (928/526-0502, www.nps.gov/sucr, 9 A.M.–5 P.M. daily, extended in summer, closed Dec. 25th). Video clips of recent eruptions elsewhere illustrate the fury that must have occurred here. An interactive computer program re-creates Sunset Crater's birth and growth. Mineral and lava specimens include some with corn casts—apparent offerings by local tribespeople during the eruption. Seismographs track your footsteps (great fun for the kids) and report on activity nearby and around the world.

Lenox Crater (elev. 7,240 feet) provides the opportunity to climb a cinder cone with a crater. It's a short, steep ascent of 280 feet, requiring 30–45 minutes for the one-mile round-trip to the rim and back. From the visitor center, drive about 1.3 miles east to the first pullout on the left.

The self-guided **Lava Flow Trail,** which begins 1.5 miles east of the visitors center, loops across the Bonito Lava Flow at the base of Sunset Crater; allow 30–60 minutes for the 1-mile walk, less for the paved .25-mile inner loop that's wheelchair accessible. A trail leaflet, available at the start of the trail and at the visitors center, explains geologic features and ecology. You'll see a miniature volcano, lava bubbles, squeeze-ups, and lava tubes that seem to have cooled only yesterday.

Cinder Hills Overlook offers a high vantage point on the northeast side of Sunset Crater, about five miles east of the visitors center. You'll see volcanoes in every direction and the colors of the Painted Desert to the north. The overlook is just south of the Loop Road near the east edge of the monument.

Painted Desert Vista is a bit lower, between Sunset Crater Volcano and Wupatki National Monuments, but still has fine views. Ponderosa pines mix with pinyon pines and juniper here. Picnic tables and a restroom are provided, but no water. You'll also find picnic tables near the visitors center and at the Lava Flow Trail.

Bonito Campground

In the ponderosa pines near the lava flow for which it's named, this national forest campground (928/527-1474 campground, 928/526-0866 Peaks Ranger Station) lies across the road from the monument's visitors center. Sites at the 6,900-foot elevation offer drinking water, flush toilets, grills, and fire rings (mid-April–mid-Oct., 10 A.M.–4 P.M., $15 1st vehicle, $6

2nd vehicle, and $5 day use). There's usually room. Interpretive programs run on weekend evenings in summer. Groups can reserve areas at nearby **O'Leary Group Campground** (877/444-6777, www.reserveusa.com).

Dispersed camping is allowed in other areas of the national forest such as along Forest Roads 420, 552, and 418 west of U.S. Highway 89; Forest Road 776 (can be dusty from ATVs) south of Sunset Crater; and Forest Road 150 (hot in summer) south of the road through Wupatki. Visitors center staff can make suggestions and sell you the Coconino Forest map.

O'Leary Peak

Weather permitting, the summit of this 8,916-foot lava-dome volcano provides outstanding views into Sunset Crater. From the turnoff a .25 miles west of the Sunset Crater visitors center, turn north .3 miles on Forest Road 545A at the O'Leary Group Campground sign to the trailhead. Follow the former road on foot or by mountain bike five miles one-way to the fire lookout tower at the top. The summit provides the best view of the colors of Sunset Crater and the Painted Desert beyond in late afternoon; the San Francisco Peaks look their best in the morning. No camping is allowed on O'Leary.

WUPATKI NATIONAL MONUMENT

Prehistoric farmers, identified as the Sinagua by archaeologists, settled in small groups near the San Francisco Peaks in about A.D. 600. They lived in partly underground pit houses and tilled the soil in those few areas with sufficient moisture to support corn and other crops. The eruption of Sunset Crater in A.D. 1064 or 1065 forced many to flee, but after about 1110, people returned and were joined by ancestral Puebloan people from northeastern Arizona. They settled 20 miles northeast of Sunset Crater in Wupatki Basin, which became the center of a group of cosmopolitan villages. A mix of cultural traits can be seen at Wupatki, including Kayenta Anasazi, Sinagua, Cohonina, and Hohokam. Large, multistoried pueblos replaced the brush shelters and pit houses of former times. Some villages seem defensively built; competition for scarce resources may have created friction or fostered cooperation.

During the 1200s, people began to leave the area. Archaeologists think the inhabitants migrated southward to the Verde Valley, eastward to Homolovi on the Little Colorado River, and northeastward to the Hopi mesas and Zuni villages. Hopi oral histories trace at least eight clans to the Wupatki area.

Seven of the best-preserved pueblos have road and trail access and are open daily from sunrise to sunset. All other sites and the monument's backcountry remain closed to visitors, except during the seasonal ranger-guided hikes to Crack-in-Rock. Visitors must stay on designated trails.

From Flagstaff, you can drive 12 miles north on U.S. Highway 89, then turn right and go 21 miles via Sunset Crater Volcano National Monument on the scenic Loop Road. Or take the northern turnoff from U.S. Highway 89 for the Loop Road, 26 miles north of Flagstaff, and head east 14 miles. The nearest motels and restaurants are in Flagstaff and Gray Mountain, the nearest camping is Bonito Campground. Hank's Trading Post offers groceries and snacks 1.2 miles north of the U.S. Highway 89–Wupatki junction.

Wupatki Pueblo

At its peak, Wupatki contained nearly 100 rooms and rose multiple stories. The Hopi name refers to "something long that has been cut or divided." A self-guided trail, beginning behind the visitors center, explains many of the features of Wupatki; pick up a trail brochure at the start.

You'll see pottery, tools, jewelry, and other artifacts of early cultures at the visitors center (928/679-2365, www.nps.gov/wupa, 9 A.M.–5 P.M. daily, extended hours in summer, closed Dec. 25th). You can buy regional books, posters, maps, and videos. Rangers may offer orientation talks and demonstrate prehistoric and modern crafts and activities.

A community room, where village meetings and ceremonies may have taken place, lies to one side of Wupatki. The ball court at the far end of the village may have been used for games or religious functions. It's one of several found in north-

© BILL WEIR

Wupatki Pueblo

ern Arizona, probably introduced by the Hohokam culture of the southern deserts. Archaeologists reconstructed the masonry ball court from wall remnants; the rest of Wupatki Pueblo is stabilized. A blowhole, 100 feet east of the ball court, may have had religious importance. A system of underground cracks connects to this natural surface opening; air blows out, rushes in, or does nothing at all, depending on atmospheric pressure. Researchers once tried to enter the system but couldn't get through the narrow passageways.

Wukoki Pueblo

Two or three families lived in this small pueblo, the best-preserved structure in the park, for perhaps three generations. You can step inside the rooms, one of which towers three stories and still has pieces of wood beam embedded in the walls. From the Wupatki visitors center, drive .25 miles toward Sunset Crater, then turn left 2.5 miles on a paved road.

Doney Picnic Area

Tables nestle in a juniper woodland between cinder cones about four miles northwest of the visitors center on the Loop Road; there's a restroom but no water. **Doney Mountain Trail** climbs gradually to a saddle in the Little Doney Craters, from which you can turn left to a lower overlook or right to a higher one, each about .4 miles one-way from the picnic area. Both forks pass small dwellings, probably used by the prehistoric people as field houses while tending nearby gardens. You'll enjoy a panorama of the Wupatki Basin, Painted Desert, and San Francisco Peaks. Interpretive signs explain area ecology and the exploits of prospector Ben Doney.

Citadel Pueblo

This fortresslike pueblo, perched atop a small volcanic butte nine miles northwest of the Wupatki visitors center, stood one or two stories high and contained about 30 rooms. From the top, look for some of the more than 10 other residences nearby (most of these are not open to visits). On the short path to the Citadel, you'll pass the pueblo of **Nalakihu,** Hopi for House Standing Outside the Village. Nalakihu consisted of two stories with 13 or 14 rooms.

Lomaki Pueblo

Lomaki (Hopi for Beautiful House) sits along a

small box canyon. Tree-ring dating of roof timbers indicates the occupants lived here about A.D. 1190–1240. The small two-story pueblo contained nine rooms. A .25-mile trail from the parking area also passes small dwellings beside Box Canyon. The turnoff for Lomaki lies northwest of Wupatki visitors center, .3 miles beyond Citadel on the opposite side of the road.

Crack-in-Rock Pueblo

Rangers lead overnight backpack trips to this area during April and October. Crack-in-Rock stands atop an easily defended mesa with sweeping views of the Little Colorado River and distant hills. You will see petroglyphs carved around the base of the mesa and on two nearby mesas, as well as many other pueblo sites. The 14-mile round-trip hike is moderately difficult and costs $50. Call or write for information at least two months in advance to Wupatki National Monument (HC 33, Box 444A #14, Flagstaff, AZ 86004, 928/679-2365).

MOUNT ELDEN TRAIL SYSTEM

To reach the summit of Mt. Elden, a 9,299-foot peak on the north edge of Flagstaff, you can hike any of several good trails or drive up a rough road. Wildflowers, a variety of forests, and panoramic views reward those who ascend even part way. A fire-lookout tower marks the summit. Climb the tower, if it's open, for the best views. On a clear day you'll see much of north-central Arizona: Oak Creek Canyon and Mormon Lake to the south; the Painted Desert to the east; Humphrey's Peak, Sunset Crater, and other volcanoes to the north; and Bill Williams Mountain to the west. Flagstaff lies directly below. An eruption of thick, sticky lava created Mt. Elden.

The hiking season runs May–October, a bit longer for the drier eastern slope. You'll need to carry water. To avoid the hair-raising experience of afternoon thunderstorms, set out early when hiking during July and August, the peak storm months. Allow at least half a day for a hike to the summit and back; elevation change is 1,300–2,400 feet, depending on the trailhead. Horseback riders and mountain bicyclists can use most of the trail system. Contact the Peaks Ranger Station (928/526-0866) for current trail information. The distances given below are one-way. Hikes are described clockwise, beginning on the east side.

Elden Lookout Trail #4

This 2.9-mile (one-way) trail seems easy at first, but then it becomes a steep and strenuous climb up the rocky east slope of Mt. Elden to the lookout tower, gaining 2,400 feet in elevation. To reach the Mt. Elden Trailhead (elev. 6,900 ft.), head east from downtown Flagstaff on Route 66, which becomes U.S. Highway 89, or take I-40 Exit 201 toward Page; the trailhead is on the left side of U.S. Highway 89, .3 miles north of the Peaks Ranger District turnoff. The grades and loose surface of this trail make it too hazardous for horse travel or mountain biking; neither is allowed.

Fatman's Loop Trail #25

The moderate two-mile loop has a few short steep sections. You'll pass volcanic rock formations (one that hikers have to squeeze through) and diverse plant life; elevation gain is 600 feet. Views take in parts of east Flagstaff and beyond. The loop begins from the lower part of Mt. Elden Lookout Trail; it's closed to horses.

Pipeline Trail #42

This easy 2.8-mile trail follows a gas pipeline right-of-way between the lower parts of Mt. Elden Lookout and Oldham Trails. You can see old lava flows on the south side of Mt. Elden and in the Elden Environmental Study Area. The Forest Service set aside the study area in the mid-1970s for school and environmental groups. Ponderosa pine and Gambel oak dominate the forest at the trail's 7,100- to 7,200-foot elevations.

Oldham Trail #1

Mt. Elden's longest trail at 5.5 miles, it begins at the north end of Buffalo Park (elev. 7,000 ft.) in Flagstaff and climbs gradually past boulder fields and cliffs on the west side of Mt. Elden. You cross Elden Lookout Road several times as the trail winds higher through forest and meadows to

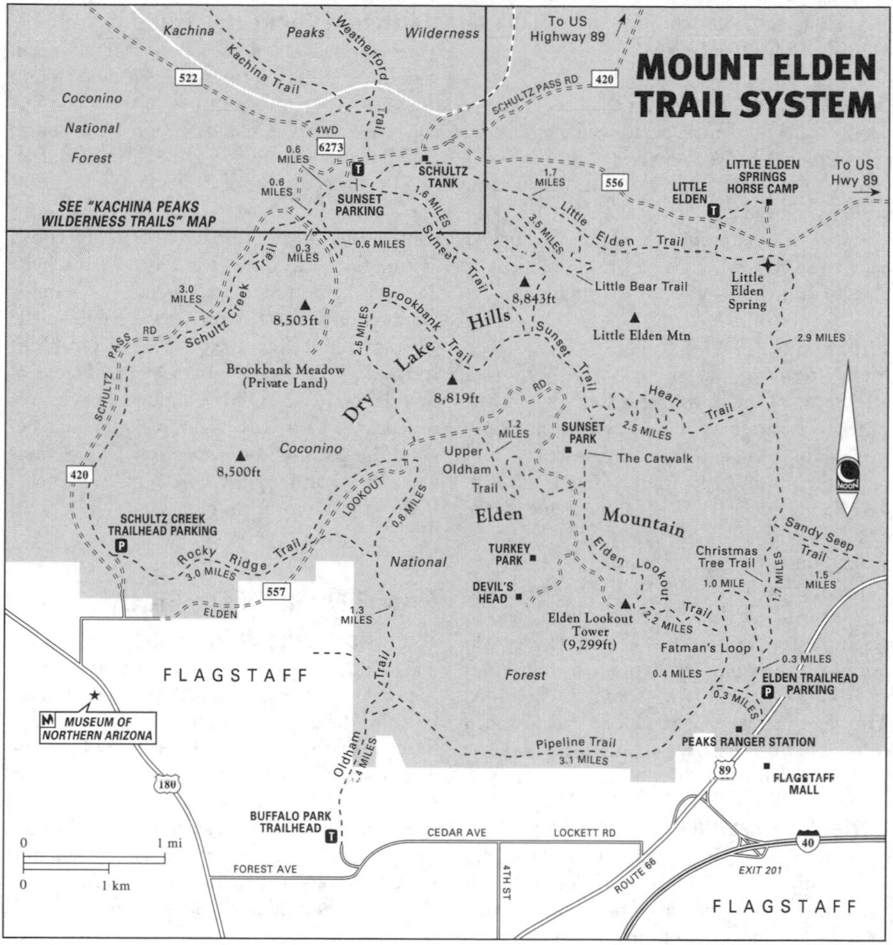

Oldham Park and on to Sunset Trail near the summit. The trail is moderately difficult and has an elevation gain of 2,000 feet.

Rocky Ridge Trail #153

Ponderosa pine, Gambel oak, alligator juniper, cliffrose, and yucca line this western approach to Mt. Elden. The easy trail begins from Schultz Creek Trailhead and connects with the Oldham and Brookbank Trails. Distance is 2.2 or 3 miles depending on which fork you take. Schultz Creek Trailhead lies a short way off Schultz Pass Road .8 miles in from U.S. Highway 180. Elevation change is only about 100 feet.

Brookbank Trail #2

This moderate 2.5-mile trail climbs north through a forested drainage to the edge of Brookbank Meadow, owned by the Navajo Tribe, then curves east to eventually meet Sunset Trail at a low saddle. Elevation gain is 1,000 feet. The trailhead (elev. 7,900 ft.) can be reached by hiking the Rocky Ridge or Oldham Trails or by driving a half mile in on Schultz Pass Road from

U.S. Highway 180, then turning 2.5 miles up Elden Lookout Road.

Schultz Creek Trail #152

This gentle 3.5-mile trail parallels an intermittent creek flowing between Sunset (elev. 8,000 ft.) and Schultz Creek (elev. 7,200 ft.) Trailheads. Sunset Trailhead is at Schultz Pass, 5.6 miles up Schultz Pass Road from U.S. Highway 180, and Schultz Creek Trailhead is a short way off Schultz Pass Road .8 miles in from U.S. Highway 180.

Sunset Trail #23

Alpine meadows and forests on the north side offer some of the most pleasant hiking on Mt. Elden. The four-mile trail climbs gradually through pine, fir, and aspen to Sunset Park and on to the summit; elevation gain is 1,300 feet. The Radio Fire of 1977 left scars visible on the east slope below. You can view the San Francisco Peaks, Sunset Crater, and Painted Desert.

Begin from the Sunset Trailhead (elev. 8,000 ft.), just west of Schultz Tank at Schultz Pass. To reach the trailhead, follow U.S. Highway 180 northwest three miles from downtown Flagstaff to Schultz Pass Road, then turn right 5.6 miles. This and the following Mt. Elden trails are open to people on horseback or mountain bike as well as on foot.

Little Bear Trail #112

This trail—steep in places—switchbacks 3.5 miles with a 1,000-foot elevation change between Little Elden Trail and Sunset Trail. See the map for the trailhead options.

Heart Trail #103

In a strenuous 2.5 miles, the trail switchbacks along a steep, rocky ridge within the area devastated by the 5,000-acre Radio Fire of June 1977. It connects Sandy Seep and Little Elden Trails with Sunset Trail at the saddle between Mt. Elden and Little Elden Mountain; elevation change is 1,300 feet. Local mountain bike enthusiasts have dubbed it "expert only." Experienced horseback riders can use the trail too. Seemingly desolate at first glance, the land is actually full of new growth and new life.

Northside Connector Trails

Three easy trails on the north side of Mt. Elden link with other trails to form a complete loop around the peak. They offer a variety of views and terrain—from the cool fir and pine forest of the north slope around the buttress of Little Elden Mountain, past the lower reaches of the Radio Fire area, and into dry ponderosa pine and Gambel oak of the east flank of Mt. Elden. **Little Elden Trail #69** curves around the north side of Mt. Elden from Schultz Tank to the bottom of Heart Trail in 4.7 miles. **Sandy Seep Trail #129** goes west 1.5 miles to the Christmas Tree Trail, then a bit farther to Heart and Little Elden Trails from a trailhead at the end of short Forest Road 9139; the turnoff is just north of Milepost 421 on U.S. Highway 89, .4 miles beyond the Townsend–Winona Road. **Christmas Tree Trail** connects the north end of Fatman's Loop with Sandy Seep, Heart, and Little Elden Trails in 1.7 miles one-way.

SAN FRANCISCO PEAKS

Kachina Peaks Wilderness

This wilderness area protects 18,960 acres on the Peaks. Its name reflects the religious importance of the area to the Hopi tribe. The Forest Service maintains a network of trails in the wilderness. Cyclists may not ride here, even on the former roads, because of the wilderness designation. Equestrians may not ride within the Inner Basin, as it's a watershed. For current hiking conditions, maps, and other trails, call the Peaks Ranger Station (928/526-0866).

Lamar Haines Memorial Wildlife Area

A small pond fed by two springs attracts birds and other wildlife. Ludwig Veit, for whom the springs are named, homesteaded here in 1892. Petroglyphs decorate nearby volcanic rocks. From the parking area, near Milepost 4.5 on the paved Snowbowl Road, walk through the gate and turn right .7 miles on an abandoned road. Lamar Haines (1927–1986) was active in education and conservation in the Flagstaff area.

Humphrey's Peak Trail #151

The alpine world on the roof of Arizona makes a

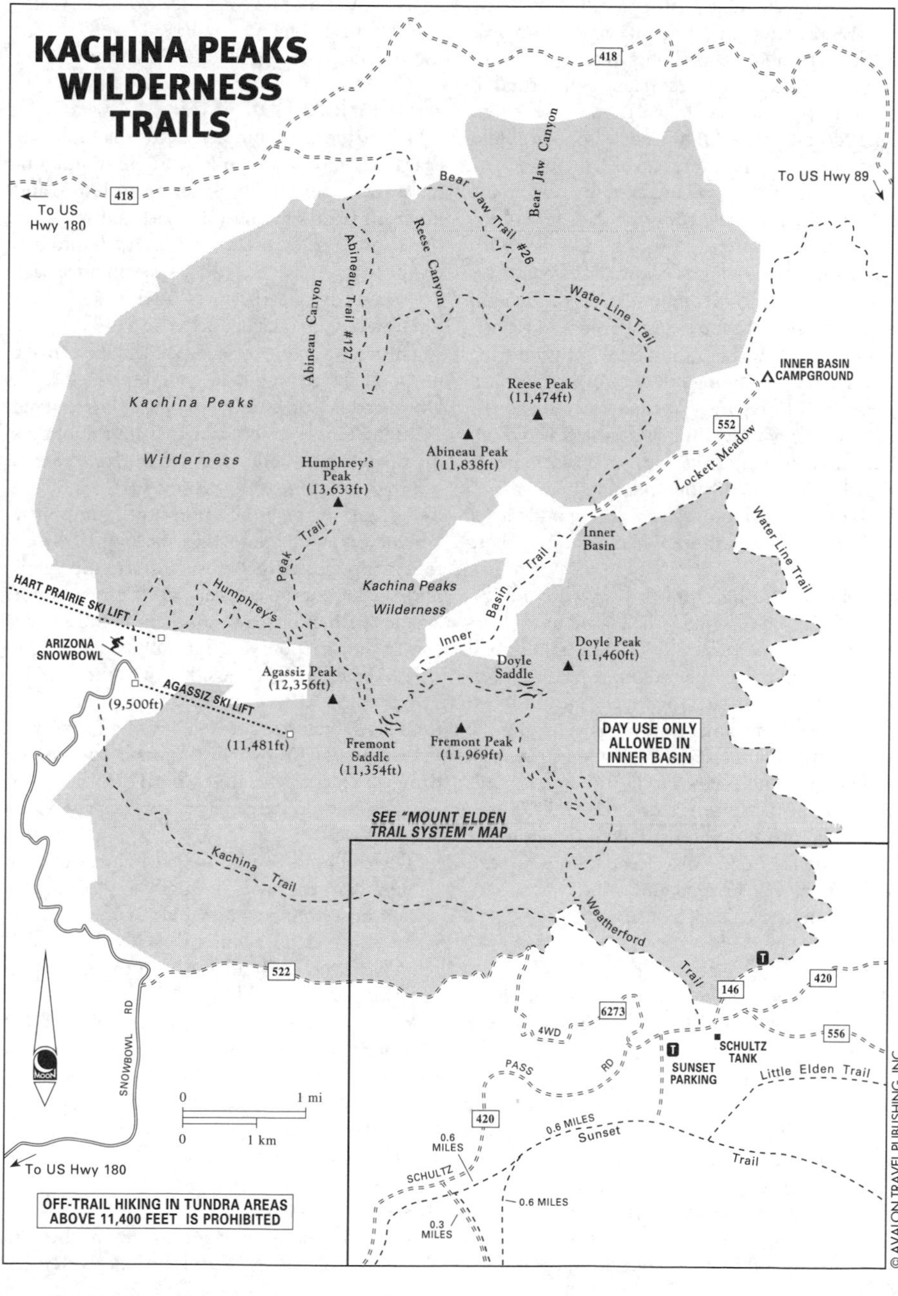
KACHINA PEAKS WILDERNESS TRAILS
418
To US Hwy 180
To US Hwy 89
Bear Jaw Canyon
Bear Jaw Trail #26
Reese Canyon
Abineau Trail #127
Abineau Canyon
Water Line Trail
INNER BASIN CAMPGROUND
552
Lockett Meadow
Reese Peak (11,474ft)
Abineau Peak (11,838ft)
Kachina Peaks
Wilderness
Humphrey's Peak (13,633ft)
Humphrey's Peak Trail
Inner Basin
Inner Basin Trail
Kachina Peaks Wilderness
HART PRAIRIE SKI LIFT
ARIZONA SNOWBOWL
Agassiz Peak (12,356ft)
AGASSIZ SKI LIFT
(9,500ft)
(11,481ft)
Doyle Saddle
Doyle Peak (11,460ft)
Fremont Saddle (11,354ft)
Fremont Peak (11,969ft)
DAY USE ONLY ALLOWED IN INNER BASIN
SEE "MOUNT ELDEN TRAIL SYSTEM" MAP
Kachina Trail
Weatherford Trail
522
SNOWBOWL RD
146
420
6273
4WD
556
SCHULTZ TANK
SUNSET PARKING
PASS RD
Little Elden Trail
0 1 mi
0 1 km
0.6 MILES
Sunset Trail
SCHULTZ
0.3 MILES
To US Hwy 180
OFF-TRAIL HIKING IN TUNDRA AREAS ABOVE 11,400 FEET IS PROHIBITED
© AVALON TRAVEL PUBLISHING, INC.

North-Central Arizona

challenging day-hike destination. Get an early start, as the strenuous nine-mile round-trip usually requires about eight hours to reach the summit and return. To protect fragile alpine tundra, the Forest Service asks hikers to stay on the designated trails above 11,400 feet. Also, don't build campfires or set up camps here.

Snow blocks the way much of the year, so the hiking season usually runs only late June–September. Come prepared for bad weather with good rain and wind gear. Snow and fierce winds can arrive any month of the year; getting caught in a storm near the top in just a T-shirt and shorts could be deadly. Lightning frequently zaps the peaks, especially during July and August, so you'll need to be prepared to turn back if storms threaten. In winter, winds and sub-zero cold can be extremely dangerous—only the most experienced groups should attempt a climb and they'll need to get a backcountry permit. Carry plenty of water; you'll need more when hiking at these high elevations.

The trail begins from the Snowbowl (elev. 9,500 ft.), contours under the Hart Prairie chairlift, then switchbacks up the mountain. You'll hike through dense forests of Engelmann spruce, corkbark fir, and quaking aspen. Near 11,400 feet, stunted Engelmann spruce and bristlecone pine cling precariously to the slopes. Higher still, only tiny alpine plants survive the fierce winds and long winters. At the saddle (elev. 11,800 ft.), turn left for Humphrey's Peak and follow the trail along the ridge. On a clear day you can see a lot of northern Arizona and some of southern Utah from the 12,633-foot summit.

Kachina Trail #150

This moderate trail on the southern slopes of Humphrey's Peak is five miles one-way. It's most easily done downhill by using a car shuttle. From the upper trailhead, on the south end of the lower Snowbowl parking lot (elev. 9,300 ft.), the Kachina winds east through spruce, fir, aspen, and ponderosa pine to meet the Weatherford Trail. You can reach the lower end of the Kachina Trail by driving 2.4 miles up the Snowbowl Road and turning right 4 miles on Forest Road 522 to its end (elev. 8,800 ft.), then continuing .4 miles on foot. Or you could continue down the Weatherford 2.4 miles to Schultz Pass (elev. 8,000 ft.) and the trailhead near Schultz Pass. Carry water.

Weatherford Trail #102

J. W. Weatherford completed this road into the Peaks in 1926, using only hand labor and animals. Cars could then sputter up to Doyle and Fremont Saddles. The toll road had few customers in the Depression years and fell into disrepair. Today, only hikers and those on horseback may travel the Weatherford Road, though livestock cannot be taken past Doyle Saddle.

The trail's gentle grade and excellent views make it a good choice for a family outing. You'll reach Doyle Saddle (elev. 10,800 ft.), which is marked Fremont Saddle on older maps, after about six miles. Here you'll enjoy views of the Inner Basin, summits, and surrounding countryside. Although it's possible to reach the summit of Humphrey's Peak on the Weatherford Trail, the long 19.4-mile round-trip discourages most climbers. Energetic hikers who've arranged a car shuttle can continue on the Weatherford Trail another 3.4 miles to its end at the junction with Humphrey's Trail, decide whether to make the side trip to the summit of Humphrey's Peak (about 2 miles round-trip from here), then descend 3.5 miles on Humphrey's Peak Trail to the Snowbowl. Another option is to drop down into the Inner Basin and Lockett Meadow on the Inner Basin Trail. Carry water and foul-weather gear.

The trailhead (elev. 8,000 ft.) is just east of Schultz Pass. Follow U.S. Highway 180 northwest 3 miles from downtown Flagstaff, then turn right 5.6 miles on Schultz Pass Road 420. Alternatively, you can head north 4.1 miles on U.S. Highway 89 from the Flagstaff Mall, turn west 5 miles on Forest Road 556, then turn left .4 miles on Forest Road 420. Still another approach is to follow Forest Road 420 for 8.8 miles from U.S. Highway 89; the turn is directly opposite the Sunset Crater turnoff, 12 miles north of the Flagstaff Mall.

Water Line Trail

Gentle grades and some good views of the San Francisco Volcanic Field and the Painted Desert are just two of the trail's attractions. The first nine miles from Schultz Pass to the Inner Basin skirt the Kachina Peaks Wilderness and are open to mountain bikers. Beyond the Inner Basin, the Water Line Trail enters the wilderness and continues another five miles, ending at the upper end of Abineau Trail (elev. 10,400 ft.). The lower trailhead (elev. 8,000 ft.) is .7 miles in on Forest Road 146, which turns off Forest Road 420 just .4 miles east of Schultz Pass.

Little Elden Springs Horse Camp

Designed especially for equestrians, it offers pull-through campsites with water, compost toilets, hitching posts, and ample room for horse trailers May–September. Sites (elev. 7,200 ft.) are $12 and can be reserved (877/444-6777, www.reserveusa.com). A handful of sites are first-come, first-served. Picnicking (10 A.M.–4 P.M.) costs $5. Anyone may stay here, but be prepared to camp among horses. An access trail leads to the Mt. Elden/Dry Lake Hills Trail system or you can head north five miles on Deer Hill Trail. From the Flagstaff Mall, go north 4.1 miles on U.S. Highway 89, turn west 2.1 miles on Forest Road 556, then north .3 miles at the sign.

Deer Hill Trail #99

This easy trail heads north five miles one-way from Little Elden Springs Horse Camp or Little Elden Springs trailhead, farther west on Forest Road 556. There's little elevation gain. The north trailhead is on Forest Road 420.

Inner Basin Campground and Hiking

The San Francisco Peaks surround a giant U-shaped valley known as the Inner Basin. It's a wonderful place to walk in summer among the aspen, fir, spruce, and wildflowers. At the entrance to the Inner Basin, **Lockett Meadow Campground** (elev. 8,600 ft.) lies in the aspen and conifers along the loop at road's end. Depending on weather, the season runs mid-May–mid-Oct.; there are vault toilets and an $8 fee, but no water; you can also use the sites for picnicking 10 A.M.–4 P.M. for $5. Designated day-use parking is free.

Inner Basin Trail offers wonderful hiking in the forest and a flower-filled meadow; it's a steady climb from Lockett Meadow and 3.8 miles one-way, ending at the Weatherford Trail. The first 1.5 miles follows a road through conifer and aspen forests to the Water Line Trail junction, where you have the options of turning left 9 miles for Schultz Pass Road or right 3 miles for the Abineau-Bear Paw Trail loop. Continuing on the Inner Basin Trail, you'll reach a long meadow and views of the surrounding peaks. If you still feel like some more climbing, continue to the far end of the meadow, where the trail enters conifers and steepens a bit on the ascent to the Weatherford Trail; turn left 100 feet on the Weatherford for a great panorama of the Inner Basin and the Painted Desert far beyond. You could climb Humphrey's Peak or, with a car shuttle, descend to Weatherford or Humphrey's Peak trailheads. Elevations range from 8,600 feet at Lockett Meadow to nearly 11,000 feet at the Weatherford Trail junction. The springs in the Inner Basin supply some of Flagstaff's water, but are covered and locked, so it's necessary to carry your own water. Aspen turn a magnificent gold in late September and early October. Because the Inner Basin is protected as a watershed and wilderness, there's no camping, bicycling, or livestock allowed.

From the Flagstaff Mall or I-40 Exit 201, drive north 12 miles on U.S. Highway 89 and turn left (west) onto Forest Road 420, opposite the Sunset Crater turnoff between Mileposts 430 and 431; be in the left lane in order to make the turn. Drive .6 miles on Forest Road 420, then turn right on Forest Road 552 and follow it 4.3 miles to Lockett Meadow. The unpaved road is steep and winding in places, so isn't suitable for low-clearance vehicles, large RVs, and vehicles pulling trailers.

Abineau and Bear Jaw Trails

These two trails climb about halfway up the north side of the San Francisco Peaks. On either path you'll enjoy cool forests of pine, fir, and aspen. Wildflowers grow in rocky alpine meadows near the top of Abineau Trail. Both trails start near Reese Tanks. Abineau Pipeline Trail, a dirt road closed to vehicles, connects the upper ends. With this road, Abineau and Bear Jaw make a good 6.5-mile hiking loop. Abineau is probably the prettier of the two, a good choice if you don't want to do the whole loop.

The trailhead lies on the opposite side of the Peaks from Flagstaff. Either take U.S. Highway 180, Forest Road 151 (second turnoff), and Forest Road 418 around the west side of the Peaks, or follow U.S. Highway 89, Forest Road 420, and Forest Road 418 around the east slopes; consult the Coconino Forest map. Beginning at Flagstaff, each drive is about 26 miles long one-way. A sign on Forest Road 418 marks the turnoff for the trailhead, 1.2 miles in on Forest Road 9123J. Park and walk up the trail to a T intersection: Abineau Trail goes to the right, Bear Jaw to the left. Signs and tree blazes mark both trails. Abineau Trail soon enters Abineau Canyon—actually more of a valley—and stays in it all the way to Water Line Trail, 2.5 miles away. You can retrace your steps or turn left 2.1 miles on the Water Line Trail and keep a sharp eye out for the upper end of Bear Jaw Trail, marked with a sign.

Bear Jaw Trail, two miles one-way, doesn't follow a valley at all—you have to be very careful to look for signs and tree blazes. Take special care near the bottom when following a road, because the trail later turns left away from the road; this turn is easy to miss. Allow 4–5 hours for the complete loop. You'll begin at 8,500 feet at the trailhead and reach 10,400 feet at the upper end of Abineau Trail. Carry water and raingear.

HIKING—NORTH OFF U.S. 89

Old Caves Crater

Ruins of a 70–80-room Sinagua pueblo sit atop the summit ridge of this volcano near Doney Park. Occupied about 1250–1300, it was the last large settlement of the culture before they migrated from this area. Did they choose this commanding location for the fine view or for defense? The archaeological record is silent.

The volcano holds some geological mysteries, too. Instead of the usual cinder cone with lava at its base, Old Caves Crater has its lava on the summit ridge. Furthermore, the lava formed room-like chambers called "bubbles." The Sinagua built their village above the bubbles, using them as rooms, then carved out storage alcoves and connecting passageways. The pueblo walls, built of unmortared stone, have largely fallen down, but you can see the underground chambers and shards of the Sinagua's plain pottery. Archaeologists found burials just below the pueblo and a ball court at the base of the volcano. Visitors must take care not to disturb the pueblo or remove anything from it.

Head north 5.5 miles on U.S. Highway 89 from I-40 Exit 201 to Silver Saddle Road, which has a traffic light between Mileposts 422 and 423, then turn right half a mile on to the marked trailhead, which will be on your left. Follow signs up to a trail junction on the summit ridge, then turn right to the pueblo. Take the other fork on the summit ridge to reach the highest point and a panorama of volcanoes to the north. The moderate hike is 1.2 miles one-way with a 430-foot elevation gain to the pueblo, then another 100 feet to the 7,183-foot summit.

Strawberry Crater Wilderness

Extrusions of slow-moving basaltic andesite formed this crater 50,000–100,000 years ago. Strawberry Crater's jagged features contrast with the much younger cinder cones nearby. Because the San Francisco Peaks form a rain shadow over this area, the crater receives only about seven inches of annual precipitation. Sparse vegetation of juniper, pinyon pine, cliffrose, and a few ponderosa pines cover the gently rolling terrain of cinders and lava. The 10,141-acre wilderness offers good cross-country hiking and a challenging climb to the crater summit. Prehistoric ruins lie within the area as well; artifacts must not be removed.

Strawberry Crater is northeast of Flagstaff between Sunset Crater Volcano and Wupatki National Monuments. The wilderness boundary lies just north of the Painted Desert Vista area on the road between the monuments, but it would be a long hike to reach the crater from here. You can drive much closer by going north about 16 miles from the Flagstaff Mall on U.S. Highway 89 to the bottom of a long grade, turning east 3.4 miles on Forest Road 546, then continuing 1.1 miles east on Forest Road 779 to a set of power lines near the wilderness boundary. An unmarked trail contours left around the crater to the inner basin, then follows a ridge to the summit, about two miles round-trip with a 500-foot elevation gain. You'll have a great panorama of the surrounding volcanoes and lava flows. Help preserve Strawberry Crater by not hiking on the steeper slopes; they're fragile and easily damaged.

SP Crater

This and nearby Colton Crater, about 14 miles due north of the San Francisco Peaks, offer interesting geology and good hiking. SP Crater's graceful shape and the black tongue of lava at its base resemble the contours of Sunset Crater. SP even features some reddish lava on its rim like its younger cousin. The near-perfect symmetry of this cinder cone has earned it photos in many geology textbooks.

Actually "SP" isn't the real name of this little volcano. Most likely prudish mapmakers turned red-faced when they heard what local cowboys called it. The cowboys saw the black spatter on the rim of the bowl-shaped crater and the leaking lava flow below, and figured the thing "looks just like a shit pot." The name stuck.

The climb is moderately difficult ascent of 800 feet to the rim. Any time of the year is all right for a hike as long as the weather is good. The Coconino Forest map or the 15-minute SP MTN topo map help in navigating the dirt roads, none of which are marked. From Flagstaff, drive 27 miles north on U.S. Highway 89 to Hank's Trading Post (Milepost 446). Or, from the Wupatki National Monument turnoff, go north 1.2 miles to the trading post. Turn left (west) 6.5 miles on the unmarked dirt road just south of the trading post. You can pick out SP, straight ahead, among the other volcanoes by its height and symmetry. Keep left where the road forks a half mile in. Six miles in—with SP Crater on your right and a large black water tank on your left—keep right at the fork, then look for a vehicle track on the right 100 yards farther. Take this track for a half mile and park. People four-wheeling beyond this point have made deep ruts on the slope.

Follow the track on foot to the grassy ridge top—SP Crater adjoins it on the right—then start up the black-cinder slope of SP itself. There's no real trail—it's one step up and two steps back on the loose sliding cinders. Perseverance will get you onto the rim for a close look at lava formations and a panoramic view of the San Francisco

© BILL WEIR

view of SP Crater from Colton Crater

Volcanic Field. Walking around the rim is rewarding, but descending into the 360-foot-deep crater is hazardous. The thick, blocky lava flow from SP's base extends 4.3 miles north and is about 70,000 years old.

Climbing Colton Crater

If you'd like to see another volcano or prefer an easier hike, visit nearby Colton Crater. Colton lies two miles due south of SP; take the other (left) fork near the black water tank on the road in, then go south two miles to an intersection with a road from the right. Park near here and head up the gentle slope to the rim, ascending about 300 feet. A gigantic explosion blew out the center of this volcano when hot basaltic magma met water-saturated rocks. Rock layers can be seen clearly. A baby red cinder cone, only 500 feet across, sits at the bottom of Colton Crater. It's an easy walk to the crater floor, actually 260 feet lower than the elevation outside the crater. Or you can walk around the rim through juniper and pinyon trees, climbing about 600 feet higher than the lowest part of the rim.

HIKING—NORTHWEST OFF U.S. 180

Kendrick Park Watchable Wildlife Trail

Two short loop trails and interpretive signs introduce the pronghorn, mule deer, and elk that you're likely to see in the large meadows nearby. The trailhead, 20 miles northwest of Flagstaff, has paved parking and a restroom; look for the sign between Mileposts 235 and 236. The quarter-mile loop is paved and nearly level through a ponderosa pine forest. You can branch off on a 1.5-mile loop that enters an aspen grove.

Slate Mountain

A well-graded trail provides good views in all directions. Kendrick Peak is to the south, the San Francisco Peaks to the southeast, and Red Mountain—with its distinctive red gash—just to the north. Trail markers label many trees and plants. Flowers line the way from spring through fall.

Early settlers mistook the fine-grained, light-gray rock of this mountain for slate. Geologists say it's rhyolite, a volcanic rock. Hiking time is about three hours for the five-mile round-trip; you'll ascend 850 feet. The 8,215-foot summit is a pleasant spot for a picnic. Hiking season runs May–October; carry water. To reach the trailhead, drive northwest 27 miles from Flagstaff on U.S. Highway 180, then turn west 2 miles on Forest Road 191, between Mileposts 242 and 243 on U.S. Highway 180. A sign marks the trailhead.

Red Mountain

Ever wanted to walk into the heart of a volcano? Then try Red Mountain. Unusual erosion has dissected the cinder cone from the summit straight down to its base. Walk through a little canyon between towers of black cinders to enter the volcano. A ladder helps you get up a six-foot-high stone wall, the only real climb. Ranchers built the wall for a stock pond, but cinders filled it in. Beyond the dam you'll enter a magical land of towering pinnacles and narrow canyons. This is a great place to explore; children will love it. Trees offer shade for a picnic.

Most of Red Mountain is soft volcanic tuff. Look for the rocks and minerals extruding from it: blocks and bombs of lava; small crystals of plagioclase feldspar, transparent, with striations; black, glassy pyroxene and hornblende; and volcanic dust, cinders, and lapilli (large cinders). Scientists estimate the age of the volcano at 740,000 years, but aren't sure how the huge amphitheater formed. Water erosion alone could not have carved out so much material in this arid land; lava flows or steam explosions might have had a hand in the unusual shape.

A lava flow covers part of Red Mountain's southwest side about 100 feet below the summit. To reach the top (elev. 7,965 ft.), take the trail back out of the crater and climb the gentle cinder slopes on the southeast side. You'll ascend about 1,000 feet.

Red Mountain is easy to reach; drive 33 miles northwest from Flagstaff on U.S. Highway 180—or 42 miles southeast from Grand Canyon National Park—to Milepost 247, then turn west .3 miles on a dirt road to the parking. Red Mountain lies 1.25 miles in on an easy trail with a 300-foot elevation gain.

HIKING—NORTHWEST OFF I-40

Kendrick Peak Wilderness

Although the San Francisco Peaks are higher, Kendrick Peak might well provide the better view—you get not only a splendid panorama of northern Arizona, but a view of the Peaks themselves. The Painted Desert, Hopi mesas, and far-distant Navajo Mountain lie to the northeast; the north rim of the Grand Canyon juts up to the north; Sitgreaves and Bill Williams mountains poke up to the west; Oak Creek Canyon and the Mazatzals lie to the south; and the magnificent San Francisco Peaks, surrounded by many smaller volcanoes, rise directly to the east. Three trails, ranging 8–11 miles in length round-trip, lead to Kendrick's 10,418-foot summit and fire-lookout tower. Hiking season lasts late June–September; longer on the southern Kendrick Trail. Carry water. The 15,000-acre Pumpkin Fire in 2000 burned much of the forest on Kendrick, including parts of the Pumpkin Trail and most of the Bull Basin Trail; they're not recommended due to fallen trees and difficulty in finding the way. Check with the Williams Ranger District office (928/635-5600) for current trail conditions.

The popular **Kendrick Trail #22** is the shortest, eight miles round-trip, and the least affected by the fire. Because it climbs the sunny southern slopes, you'll find it more likely to be open early or late in the season. A lookout cabin, equipped with a wood stove and three bare bunk beds, stands on the ridge a quarter mile below the summit. Hikers may use this little cabin, which has withstood the elements since 1912. To reach the trailhead (elev. 7,700 ft.), take I-40 Bellemont Exit 185 (10 miles west of Flagstaff), follow the frontage road 1 mile west, drive 12.5 miles north on Forest Road 171, then turn right 1 mile on a road marked Kendrick Trail. Alternatively, you can head northwest 14 miles on U.S. Highway 180 from Flagstaff to near Milepost 230, turn left 3 miles on Forest Road 245, turn right 3.1 miles on Forest Road 171, then right 1 mile at the sign for Kendrick Trail.

Lava River Cave

This well-preserved cave is about four miles south of Kendrick Peak. Red-hot lava broke through the ground near the San Francisco Peaks about 100,000 years ago, then moved westward across Hart and Government Prairies, reaching a thickness of more than 100 feet in places. As the outer layers of the smoking mass cooled, some of the fiery interior burst through a weak spot in the surface, partly draining the lava flow. This underground river of fire eventually cooled too.

Today, a collapsed ceiling reveals the passageway. No one knows the total length of this lava-tube cave, but about .7 miles are easily explored. The interior remains cool year-round, so a jacket or sweater is recommended. Keep an eye out for the ice that's often present just inside the entrance. Bring at least two flashlights to explore the cave, as it wouldn't be fun trying to feel your way out after your one-and-only light died.

The walls and ceiling form an amazingly symmetrical tunnel. The former lava river on the floor still displays all the ripple marks, cracks, and squeeze-ups of its last hours. There's only one main passageway, though a small loop branches off to the right about one-third of the way through and then rejoins the main channel. The main channel is large, with plenty of headroom, except for a section about two-thirds of the way through where you'll have to stoop.

To reach Lava River Cave, follow the directions to Kendrick Peak, but travel only 7.5 miles north on Forest Road 171, then turn right .3 miles on Forest Road 171B and walk another .2 miles. Alternatively, from Flagstaff you can head northwest 14 miles on U.S. Highway 180, turn left 3 miles on Forest Road 245, turn left 1 mile on Forest Road 171, then left on Forest Road 171B. The Coconino and Kaibab (Williams and Tusayan Districts) forest maps show the roads and cave, but may not identify the cave. A large ring of stones indicates the cave entrance.

Sitgreaves Mountain

Great views and beautiful forests make the 9,388-foot Sitgreaves summit an attractive destination. Reddish cinder cones, forested mountains, and vast grasslands stretch to the distant horizon.

Allow about four hours to hike the four miles to the top and back. Carry water. Hiking season for this northern approach lasts about May–October. The route follows a valley from the trailhead to the summit ridge, then turns right up the ridge to the highest point. No established trails or signs exist on Sitgreaves but none are needed—just stay in the valley until you reach the ridge. Be sure to descend via the same valley, unless you want a much longer hike! Walking is a bit easier if you keep to the right when going up—not so many fallen trees. Beautiful groves of aspen find this cool, moist, sheltered area to their liking.

Sitgreaves Mountain lies about seven miles north of I-40, about two-thirds of the way from Flagstaff to Williams. To find the trailhead you'll need either the Coconino or Kaibab (Williams and Tusayan districts) forest map. Take I-40 Pittman Valley Exit 171, go north seven miles on Forest Road 74 to its end, turn right and drive three miles on Forest Road 141 (Spring Valley Road), then look *really hard* on the right for a small road. The turnoff is very easy to miss and probably won't be marked. Map designations for the turnoff are T.23N., R.3E., sec. 13. You can drive your car in about one mile. When the road gives out, continue walking in the same direction up the valley.

Williams and Vicinity

WILLIAMS

Nestled west of Flagstaff among pine-forested hills and expansive meadows at an elevation of 6,780 feet, Williams proudly proclaims itself Gateway to the Grand Canyon. The town (pop. 2,800) offers a better choice of accommodations and restaurants at lower prices than those at the Grand Canyon, which lies just 58 miles north. The exceptionally well-preserved downtown recalls a bygone era when people moved at a slower pace and when Route 66 carried motorists across the West. In yet another reminder of the past, the popular Grand Canyon Railway puffs its way north to the Grand Canyon daily from the old station downtown.

Also, try not to miss the pretty country surrounding Williams—splendid Sycamore Canyon, tall volcanoes, small fishing lakes, forest drives, and hiking trails. Fans of Route 66 can drive segments of the old highway east of Williams and mountain bike two loops on old alignments west of town; the Visitor Information Center and the Forest Service office have brochures with maps.

History

Charles Rodgers, the first white settler here, started a cattle operation in 1878. The railroad town founded several years later took its name from Bill Williams Mountain just to the south. The mountain in turn honored mountain man Bill Williams, who roamed the West from 1825 until his death at the hands of Utes in 1849. He earned a reputation as a skilled marksman, trapper, trader, and guide—and, some say, as an accomplished horse thief, preacher of profane sermons, and prodigious drinker. An 8.5-foot statue of "Old Bill" stands in Monument Park at the west end of downtown.

Today the Bill Williams Mountain Men perpetuate his adventurous spirit. The group dons buckskin clothing and fur hats, stages a 180-mile horseback ride from Williams to Phoenix most years, and works to keep the history of the mountain men alive. The Buckskinners, a family-oriented group, puts on frontier-era garb for black-powder shoots.

A more recent period of Western history came to an end at Williams in October 1984, when I-40 bypassed the last section of old U.S. Route 66. A sentimental ceremony, complete with songwriter Bobby Troup of "Route 66" fame, marked the transition. The famous highway from Chicago to Los Angeles had carried many families to a new life in Arizona and California. Its replacement, I-40, now travels an unbroken 2,400-mile path from Durham, North Carolina, to Barstow, California. Local businesses suffered when traffic bypassed Williams, but have since bounced back as travelers stop in town to sample the history and hospitality.

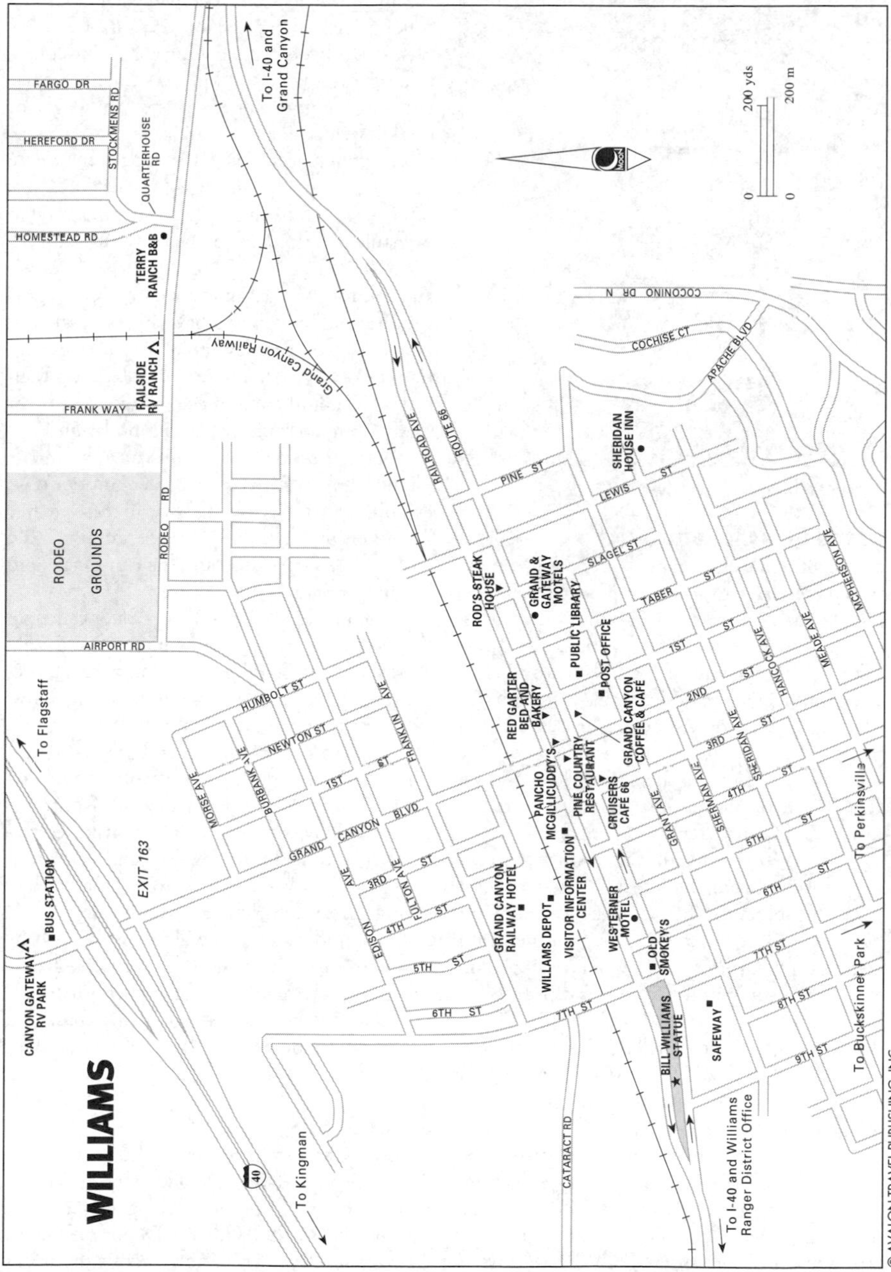

© AVALON TRAVEL PUBLISHING, INC.

North-Central Arizona

© BILL WEIR

Route 66 sign in downtown Williams

Grand Canyon Railway

Passenger trains first steamed out of Williams to the Grand Canyon's scenic splendor in 1901, replacing an expensive and arduous stagecoach ride. Railroad service ended with the last passenger train carrying just three customers in 1968, but it started anew after a 21-year hiatus. Once again, Canyon visitors can enjoy a relaxing ride through the forests and ranching country of northern Arizona to the historic log depot in Grand Canyon Village, just steps away from the rim. Grand Canyon Railway (800/THE-TRAIN or 800/843-8724, www.thetrain.com) runs steam locomotives from Memorial Day weekend through September, then vintage diesels the rest of the year. (If the train is too long for the steam engine to pull by itself, a diesel will be slipped in, too.) Trains run round-trip daily except December 24 and 25 from the 1908 Williams Depot downtown. The depot is half a mile south from I-40 Exit 163 on Grand Canyon Boulevard, or it can be reached via either of the other two I-40 Williams exits to downtown. Travelers in wheelchairs can access the depot and some of the train.

The restored 1923 Harriman coaches have reversible seats; round-trip fare is $58 for adults, $25 for kids age 2–16. You can also luxuriate in four additional categories: Club Class (same as coach but with a bar and complimentary morning coffee, juice, and pastries) for $79, $46 ages 2–16; First Class (oversized reclining chairs, air-conditioning, extra-large windows, continental breakfast, and afternoon appetizers and champagne or sparkling cider) for $116, $83 ages 2–16; Deluxe Observation Class (First Class with dome views; ages 11 and up only) for $137, $104 ages 11–16; or Luxury Parlor Car (First Class with seating in overstuffed divans and an open-air rear platform) for $147, $114 ages 2–16. One-way fares are available too. Add tax and park entry fee (let reservations staff know if you have a park pass). The Grand Canyon Railway also offers packages with train tickets, a room at the Grand Canyon Railway Hotel, and some meals, with options for Grand Canyon tours and accommodations.

Before the ride starts, you can take in the Grand Canyon Railway Museum, outdoor train exhibits, and a Wild West show; all these are free and open to the public. The depot also has a coffee bar, gift shop, and nearby Max and Thelma's restaurant.

Recommended check-in is 8 A.M. or earlier, in time to have breakfast, see the museum and Wild West show, and board the train for its 10 A.M. departure. The train arrives at Grand Canyon, across the street from El Tovar Hotel and canyon rim, about 12:15 P.M. Boarding time for the return trip is 3:15 P.M. for a 3:30 P.M. departure and 5:45 P.M. arrival back in Williams. South Rim tours are available at extra cost when you make reservations. The three hours at the Grand Canyon is enough for only a quick look, so you may wish to arrange to stay and ride back another day.

Once underway, you will be entertained by strolling musicians and Wild West characters. On the return trip you can expect a little excitement during a staged horseback chase and train robbery before "the law" catches up with the "outlaws."

Other Sights

Grand Canyon Railway Museum (7:30 A.M.–5:30 P.M. daily, free) illustrates local railroad history and a bit of ranching, logging, and mining. It's in the Williams Depot off Grand Canyon Boulevard, just north across the tracks from downtown. Near the depot, you're welcome to take a look at outdoor train exhibits and the morning Wild West show.

Stroll along **Route 66** downtown to soak up the atmosphere. The commercial buildings here remain much as they were decades ago. Many of the shops have restored interiors and selections of Native American work, antiques, or Route 66 memorabilia. Railroad Avenue also has some fine old structures.

You can see prehistoric Native American artifacts and exhibits of town history and forestry in the **Visitor Information Center** (200 W. Railroad Ave., 928/635-4061 or 800/863-0546, 8 A.M.–5 P.M. daily, to 6:30 P.M. daily in summer, free).

Events

Downtown rings to the sound of gunfire as cowboys stage shootouts every morning year-round at the train depot. Gunfights also break out on the streets every evening during summer. A band in Civil War–era garb plays tunes most evenings in summer. The Visitor Information Center will tell you the places and times of these events, all of which are free.

Rendezvous Days on Memorial Day weekend attracts the Buckskinners and Mountain Men to town for a black-powder shoot and a Saturday parade. Vintage war birds take to the skies above Valle for the **High Country War Birds Air Display** on the last weekend in June. Townsfolk celebrate **July 4th** with a parade and fireworks. Working cowboys show what they've learned in the **Cowpuncher's Reunion Rodeo** on the first weekend in August. A classic car show and a battle of the bands bring back the 1950s in the **Cool Country Cruise-In and Route 66 Festival** in mid-August. Top rodeo cowboys compete in the **PRCA Rodeo** on Labor Day weekend. **Mountain Village Holiday** runs from Thanksgiving to New Year's Day with arts and crafts and, on the first Saturday in December, a parade of lights.

Recreation

Buckskinner Park offers picnicking, hiking, and reservable group ramadas one mile south from Route 66 via 6th Street. **Buckskinner Trail #130** begins here and heads west to Clover Spring in .5 miles one-way and connects with the **Clover Spring Loop #46** for a total of 2 miles round-trip; it's a moderate hike with some hills. You can also hike the Clover Spring Loop and other trails from the Bill Williams Mountain Trailhead beside the Williams Ranger District Office. The Forest Service's four campgrounds offer picnicking options farther out from town; Dogtown has a free picnic area, but there's a $5 day-use fee if you use tables at any of the campgrounds.

Mountain Ranch Stables (behind the Quality Inn, 928/635-0706) offers a variety of trail rides from one hour to overnight, year-round; it's just south of I-40 Pittman Valley Exit 171, six miles east of Williams. **Stable in the Pines** (beside the Circle Pines KOA, 928/635-1930) has summer horseback riding; it's 3 miles east at I-40 Exit 167, then east .4 miles on the north frontage road.

Play golf on the rolling greens of the 18-hole **Elephant Rocks Golf Course** (928/635-4935, about mid-March–mid-Nov.). Go west on Railroad Avenue across I-40 (or take I-40 Exit 161 and head north), drive 1.5 miles, turn right at the entrance, and continue past natural boulders that resemble a herd of elephants.

Downhill-ski in winter at the small **Williams Ski Area** (4 miles south of town on Bill Williams Mountain, 928/635-9330), which offers a 2,000-foot poma lift (600 vertical feet), 700-foot rope tow for the beginners' slope, lessons, snack bar, rental shop, and ski shop. Full-day lift tickets cost $25 for adults and $20 for children and seniors. The season runs approximately mid-December to late March; call for conditions. Turn south 2.2 miles on 4th Street, then right at the sign.

Spring Valley Cross-Country Ski Trail has three loop possibilities of 6.5–8 miles each, rated easy to moderate; the season at the 7,480-foot-plus elevations runs winter to early spring. Spring Valley is 14 miles east to I-40 Parks Exit 178, then north 6 miles on Forest Road 141; Forest Service offices have a ski trail map. Undeveloped cross-country ski areas include Sevier Flat and Barney Flat on the way to Williams Ski Area and the White Horse Lake area.

Oak Hill Snowplay Area is eight miles east of town on I-40 to the Pittman Valley Road/Deer Farm Exit 171, then east 2.4 miles on Route 66 on the north side of I-40. Only inner tubes and other flexible materials may be used. Separate runs accommodate tubers and skiers.

ACCOMMODATIONS

Bed-and-Breakfasts

For a real sense of history, it's hard to beat the **Red Garter Bed and Bakery** (137 W. Railroad Ave., 928/635-1484 or 800/328-1484, www.redgarter.com, closed mid-Dec.–mid-Feb.), a restored 1897 Victorian romanesque building. The upstairs rooms of the former brothel all have private bath and include the Parlor ($85 d), Madam's Room ($100 d), Big Bertha's Room ($120 d), and Best Gal's Room ($120 d). Guests awaken to fresh-baked pastries for breakfast in the downstairs bakery, whose walls once echoed to the sounds of rowdy saloon customers. A Chinese chop house and opium den stood out back in the old days. Innkeeper John Holst has historic photos of the building, saloonkeeper, madam, and customers.

© BILL WEIR

A mannequin hangs out the window of a former brothel room in the Red Garter Bed & Bakery.

Sheridan House Inn (460 E. Sheridan Ave., 928/635-9441 or 888/635-9345, www.grandcanyonbedandbreakfast.com, $160–220 d) offers suites with private bath; rates include a gourmet breakfast, casual dinner, and many extras. **Legacies Bed & Breakfast** (450 S. 11th St., 928/653-4880 or 866/370-2288, www.legaciesbb.com, $125–165) offers luxury accommodations, each with a different theme, off a Great Room. All have private bath, and two offer fireplaces. An indoor hot tub is available, and hiking in the National Forest is just a short stroll away.

Mountain Country Lodge Bed & Breakfast (437 W. Route 66, 928/635-4341 or 800/973-6210, www.grandcanyon2.com, $48–92 d room, $146 suite) has nine themed rooms, all with private entrance and bath. The suite accommodates up to six people. Guests enjoy a full breakfast at the deli around the corner, which is open to the public Tuesday–Friday for lunch. **Canyon Country Inn** (442 W. Route 66, 928/635-2349 or 877/405-3280, $39–59 d) downtown offers homey rooms with private bath and continental breakfast. **Terry Ranch Bed & Breakfast** (701 Quarterhorse off Rodeo Dr., 928/635-4171 or 800/210-5908, www.terryranchbnb.com, $125–155 d) is a country Victorian log house with a veranda and rocking chairs. All rooms have private bath and a fireplace; one room features a whirlpool tub for two.

Hostel

Grand Canyon Red Lake Campground and Hostel (10 miles north on Highway 64 from I-40 Exit 165, near Milepost 194, 928/635-4753) is open all year with shared ($11/person) and private ($33 d) rooms, coin-operated showers, limited cooking facilities, a store, and tour booking. You can also camp here ($10 tents, $14 RVs w/hookups).

Under $50

Business Route I-40, between Exits 161 and 165, divides downtown into one-way streets—Route 66 eastbound and Railroad Avenue westbound. Grand Canyon Boulevard goes south from I-40

Exit 163 and meets these streets in the center of downtown. Most of the town's motels and restaurants lie along Route 66, formerly known as Bill Williams Avenue. Downtown offers the most atmosphere and the convenience of being able to walk to dining and shopping. Don't believe the old sign that still advertises rooms "from $3.50" on the 1892 Grand Canyon Hotel on Route 66—the hotel has been closed a while! The newest motels cluster near the three I-40 exits, with the exception of the top lodging in town, the Grand Canyon Railway Hotel downtown at the Williams Depot. The following summer rates will fluctuate depending on how busy the town is; expect to pay more if there's a major event going on. Most rates drop quite a bit in winter. Listings run west to east because that's the way you have to go on one-way Route 66.

Typical of the many no-frills independent motels along this street are the **Westerner Motel** (530 W. Route 66, 928/635-4312 or 800/385-8608, $40–52 d), **9 Arizona** (315 W. Route 66, 928/635-4552, $25–35 d), **Route 66 Inn** (128 E. Route 66, 928/635-4791 or 888/786-6956, $30–48 d), and **Royal American Inn** (134 E. Route 66, 928/635-9395, $35–45 d). If you'd like to stay in a restored 1936 motor court, the oldest in town, turn in to the **Grand Motel** (234 E. Route 66, 928/635-4601, $37–42 s, $40–49 d); the cozy rooms have a lot of charm. The **Gateway Motel** (219 E. Route 66), managed by the Grand Motel, is a more conventional motel across the street in the same price range.

$50–100

This category will get you newer accommodations with attractive Southwestern decor. Many offer swimming pools, a big attraction for families. **Days Inn** (2488 W. Route 66 near I-40 Exit 161, 928/635-4051 or 800/329-7466, $63 d room, $110–120 whirlpool tub suite) includes an indoor pool and hot tub just outside town; Denny's is next door. **Norris Best Value Inn** (1001 W. Route 66, 928/635-2202 or 800/496-2202, $55 s, $55–59 d) offers an outdoor pool and hot tub. **Grand Canyon Country Inn** (911 W. Route 66, 928/635-4045 or 866/635-4862, $40–90 d room, $130 suite) provides an indoor pool and hot tub. **Motel 6** (831 W. Route 66; 928/635-9000 or 800/466-8356; $46 s, $52 d weekdays; $56 s, $62 d Fri.–Sat.) has an indoor pool and hot tub. Across the street and a block closer to the town center, another **Motel 6** (710 W. Route 66; 928/635-4464 or 800/466-8356; $42 s, $48 d weekdays; $52 s, $58 d Fri.–Sat.) is a better deal if you don't need a pool or hot tub.

Turn north from downtown or south from I-40 Exit 163 for chain motels such as the **Howard Johnson Express Inn** (511 N. Grand Canyon Blvd., 928/635-9561 or 800/720-6614, $35–59 s, $49–89 d) with an indoor pool and hot tub and the **Holiday Inn** (950 N. Grand Canyon Blvd., 928/635-4114 or 800/465-4329, $89–119 d or $119–159 d for a suite) with an indoor pool, hot tub, and Doc Holliday's Steakhouse & Saloon (breakfast and dinner daily). Back downtown, **The Lodge on Route 66** (200 E. Route 66, 928/635-4534 or 877/563-4366, $89–179 d room, $229 suite) has brand-new interiors in a pueblo-style motor court; the rooms, some with fireplaces or kitchenettes, take their names from towns along Route 66.

If the country air is for you, then it's worth the drive out to **Quality Inn Mountain Ranch Resort** (7 miles east, just south of I-40 Exit 171, 928/635-2693 or 800/228-5151, $89–109 d) with a restaurant, an outdoor pool, hot tub, tennis, basketball, volleyball, and summer horseback riding in a beautiful forest and meadow setting. To really get away from it all, you can rent the **Spring Valley Cabin** ($50 up to 8 people) in the forest northeast of town from the Williams Ranger District office (928/635-2633); guests must bring their own bedding, then clean the cabin before departure.

$100–150

Best Western Inn of Williams (2600 W. Route 66 near I-40 Exit 161, 928/635-4400 or 800/635-4445, $99–129 d room, $139 suite) offers spacious Southwestern-style rooms and an outdoor pool and hot tub on a hillside just west of town. **Grand Canyon Railway Hotel** (235 N. Grand Canyon Blvd., 928/635-4010 or 800/843-8724, $129 d room, $179 suite) puts you close to the train, shopping, and other attractions of downtown. The distinctive architecture mirrors that of the nearby Williams Depot. Amenities include an indoor pool, hot tub, exercise room, pub, restaurant, and train/hotel packages. Up to eight guests can stay in the suites.

Commercial Campgrounds

Railside RV Ranch (877 Rodeo Rd., 928/635-4077 or 888/635-4077) offers showers and a store but lacks shade trees. As a bonus, you can watch the Grand Canyon Railway trains pass nearby. Rates run $19 tents (just a few sites available) and $24–26 RVs with hookups. It's on the northeast edge of town, yet convenient to both downtown and the highway to the Grand Canyon. From I-40 Exit 165, take the business route west toward town, then turn right on Rodeo Road; or from downtown, go north on Grand Canyon Boulevard, right on Edison Avenue, curve left on Airport Road, then right on Rodeo Road.

Canyon Gateway RV Park (Grand Canyon Blvd., just north of I-40 Exit 163, 928/635-2718 or 888/635-0329, www.grandcanyonrvparks.com, $10 tent or RV dry, $28 w/hookups) also has a location convenient to downtown and I-40. There's not much shade from the trees yet, but campers have showers and laundry.

Circle Pines KOA (3 miles east to I-40 Exit 167, then .5 miles east on the north frontage road, 928/635-2626 or 800/562-9379, $20–22 tents, $33–38 RVs w/hookups, $45–50 cabins) nestles in a ponderosa pine forest and has the prettiest setting of all the commercial campgrounds near Williams. Sites stay open all year; amenities include a store, showers, and laundry. A summertime café serves breakfast and lunch daily. You can amuse yourself with volleyball, badminton, basketball, minigolf, fun bikes, the game room, and an indoor pool and hot tub. In summer, the campground arranges evening movies, van tours to the Grand Canyon, and horseback riding.

In a juniper–pinyon pine woodland on the way to the Grand Canyon, **Grand Canyon KOA** (928/635-2307 or 800/562-5771, closed Nov.–Feb., $19 tents, $27–35 RVs w/hookups, $40–46 cabins) lies five miles north of Williams between Mileposts 190 and 191 on Highway 64. Guests enjoy an indoor pool and hot tub, store, game room, laundry, and showers. In summer, the campground offers breakfast and an evening barbecue cookout daily. **Grand Canyon Red Lake Campground and Hostel** (9 miles north on Highway 64, 928/635-4753, $10 tents, $14 RVs w/water and electric) is open all year with coin-operated showers, dump station, some cooking facilities, a store, and tour booking. A few large trees provide shade. **Ponderosa Forest RV Park & Campground** (928/635-0456 or 888/635-0456, tents $13, RVs $20 w/hookups) has year-round sites in the ponderosa pines with showers, laundry, and a nearby store. It's north of I-40 Parks Exit 178, 14 miles east of Williams and about halfway to Flagstaff.

Forest Service Campgrounds

The Williams Ranger District maintains four campgrounds, each beside a small fishing lake stocked with trout. Ponderosa pines shade the sites, which range in elevation from 6,600 to 7,100 feet. During the early-May to September or mid-October season, all have camp hosts, interpretive programs, drinking water, and dump stations (extra fee), but no showers. Kaibab and White Horse Lake offer paved roads. Cataract has an $8 fee and the others are $12; these fees are per site—you can have more than one vehicle. Kaibab, Dogtown, and White Horse Lake may stay open off-season without drinking water, fee, or camp host. Individuals and groups can reserve sites at Dogtown, and groups can reserve areas at Kaibab and White Horse Lake through 877/444-6777 or www.reserveusa.com. Boaters can use motors up to 8 hp on Cataract and Kaibab lakes, but only electric motors are allowed on the other lakes. Each lake has a boat ramp. Birds also know the trout are here—you'll likely see great blue herons perched motionless atop a stump or rock awaiting a meal. Osprey dive down from the heights to snatch their prey.

Dispersed camping is allowed throughout most of the forest except within half a mile of developed campgrounds, within .25 miles of surface water, or where you see a No Camping sign. Always be careful with fire, and heed posted restrictions.

Cataract Campground lies two miles northwest of town; head west on Railroad Avenue across I-40 to Country Club Drive (or take I-40 Exit 161 and go north), turn right one mile immediately after going under railroad tracks, turn left at the sign, then left into the entrance. **Kaibab Campground** is 3.5 miles northeast of town; drive east on Route 66 across I-40 (or turn north from I-40 Exit 165), go north .6 miles on AZ 64, then turn left 1 mile at the sign.

Dogtown Campground and several trails lie 7.5 miles southeast of town; drive 3.5 miles south on 4th Street, turn left 3 miles on Forest Road 140, then left 1.2 miles at the sign. **White Horse Lake Campground** lies 19 miles southeast near Sycamore Canyon; go 8 miles south on 4th Street, turn left on Forest Road 110, and follow signs. White Horse Lake Trail #33 goes around the east end of the lake, 1 mile one-way; you can branch off on Canyon Overlook Trail #70 to Sycamore Canyon in 2.5 miles round-trip. Winter visitors to the White Horse Lake area enjoy ice fishing, cross-country skiing, and snowmobiling.

FOOD

For good American food—and no smoking, despite the name—try **Old Smokey's** (624 W. Route 66, 928/635-1915, daily breakfast and lunch). **Pine Country Restaurant** (107 N. Grand Canyon Blvd., 928/635-9718, daily breakfast, lunch, and dinner) is a homey café in the center of town.

For Route 66 atmosphere, you can't beat **Cruisers Café 66** (233 W. Route 66, 928/635-2445, Sat.–Sun. lunch in summer, daily year-round dinner) with meat and vegetarian fajitas, steak, chicken, ribs, seafood, pasta dishes, and sandwiches. A barbecue fires up most evenings in the front patio, weather permitting. Bands perform on the patio some nights in summer.

Grand Canyon Coffee & Café (125 W. Route 66, 928/635-1255) fixes coffees, breakfasts, sandwiches, and some Asian specialties; may close weekends. The **Red Garter Bakery** (137 W. Railroad Ave., 928/635-1484) will tempt you with baked goods 7–11 A.M. and 4–8 P.M. daily.

Max and Thelma's (next to the depot, 928/635-8970, daily breakfast, lunch, and dinner) serves American food in a large hall popular with bus groups. You have the option of buffet or à la carte at each meal. Dinner entrées include prime rib, New York strip steak, baby back ribs, seafood, and pasta. It's named after the couple who brought the Grand Canyon Railway back to life.

Rod's Steak House (301 E. Route 66, 928/635-2671, Mon.–Sat. lunch and dinner) offers a Western-style atmosphere for good steak, seafood, and sandwiches. **Miss Kitty's Steakhouse and Saloon** (642 E. Route 66, 928/635-9161, daily dinner) serves up cowboy steak, ribs, seafood, and sandwiches in a spacious hall; musicians perform some evenings in summer.

Pancho McGillicuddy's Mexican Cantina (141 W. Railroad Ave., 928/635-4150, daily lunch in summer, daily dinner year-round) serves Mexican cuisine and a few American items in the colorfully decorated 1893 Cabinet Saloon building. The patio is popular in fine weather. Musicians perform daily on summer evenings and some weekends off season.

Pizza Factory (214 W. Route 66, 928/635-3009, daily lunch and dinner) turns out pizza, pasta, calzones, and sandwiches along with a small salad bar. **Indian Paradise** (412 N. Grand Canyon Blvd., 928/635-0800, daily lunch and dinner) serves north Indian cuisine in an elegant little dining room just north of downtown.

Safeway supermarket is at 637 W. Route 66.

INFORMATION AND SERVICES

Staff from both the Williams–Grand Canyon Chamber of Commerce and the Kaibab National Forest will assist you at the **Visitor Information Center** (200 W. Railroad Ave., Williams, AZ 86046, 928/635-4061 or 800/863-0546, www.williamschamber.com, 8 A.M.–5 P.M. daily, to 6:30 P.M. in summer). It's in a 1901 passenger train depot in the heart of downtown. The office serves so many travelers headed for the Grand Canyon that it stocks brochures and sells maps and books for that area too, as well as for the rest of Arizona.

Kaibab National Forest staff can tell you about backcountry drives, hiking, camping, fishing, and road conditions in the Williams area. Stop by the Visitor Information Center downtown or visit the **Williams Ranger District** office (742 S. Clover Rd., Williams, AZ 86046, 928/635-2633, www.fs.fed.us/r3/kai, 8 A.M.–5 P.M. Mon.–Fri.). From downtown, head west 1.5 miles on Railroad Avenue and turn left at the sign onto the frontage road just before I-40.

The **public library** (113 S. 1st St., 928/635-2263, closed Sun.–Mon.) offers Arizona books and Internet computers just south of Route 66. You'll find the **post office** across the street (120 S. 1st St.).

Tours and Transportation

If you'd like someone to show you the wonders of the Grand Canyon, try **Grand Canyon Van Tours** (Circle Pines KOA, 928/635-2626, summer only), **Marvelous Marv's Tours** (928/635-4948 or 800/655-4948, www.marvelousmarv.com), or **American Dream Tours** (928/527-3369 or 888/203-1212, www.americandreamtours.com).

Greyhound (1050 N. Grand Canyon Blvd., 928/635-0870 or 800/231-2222, www.greyhound.com) offers several east- and westbound departures daily from the stop at the Chevron station just north of I-40 Exit 163. **Amtrak** (800/872-7245, www.amtrak.com) trains stop at Williams Junction, three miles east of town; the Grand Canyon Railway Hotel offers a shuttle.

FARTHER AFIELD

Grand Canyon Deer Farm

You can walk among tame fallow deer and hand-feed them at this well-run petting zoo (928/635-4073 or 800/926-3337, $6.75 adults, $5.75 seniors 62+, $3.95 children 3–13). Arizona wildlife includes the fleet-of-hoof pronghorn and dexterous coatimundi. You'll also likely see reindeer, Sitka deer, miniature donkeys and horses, buffalo, llamas, pygmy goats, wallabies, marmosets, and talking birds. Peacocks strut across the grounds. Open daily except Thanksgiving and Christmas, the hours are seasonal: 8 A.M.–7 P.M. June–August, 9 A.M.–6 P.M. March–May and September–Oct, and 10 A.M.–5 P.M. November–February (weather permitting). Head eight miles east of Williams to I-40 Pittman Valley/Deer Farm Exit 171 (24 miles west from Flagstaff), turn north, then make a sharp left onto Deer Farm Road and follow it west for half a mile.

Historic Route 66

You can motor down the old highway for 22 miles one-way between Williams and Bellemont, 10 miles before Flagstaff. The scenic drive, part gravel, has signs and crosses Route 66's highest point—7,300 feet. A brochure from the Visitor Information Center in Williams describes the history and things to see along the way.

Bill Williams Mountain

Three hiking trails and a road lead to the summit of this 9,256-foot peak. Pine, oak, and juniper cover the lower slopes, and dense forests of aspen, fir, and spruce grow in protected valleys and at higher elevations. On a clear day, you'll enjoy views of the Grand Canyon to the north, San Francisco Peaks and many smaller volcanoes to the east, Sycamore Canyon and parts of the Verde Valley to the south, and vast rangelands to the west. If it's open, climb up the Forest Service lookout tower at the top for the best views. Hiking season lasts from about June to September; you should always carry water. Note that the entire Bill Williams Mountain watershed often closes in the dry months of early summer until the "monsoon" rains arrive.

Three trails lead to the heights, or you can drive up on an unpaved road (high-clearance vehicle needed). From downtown Williams head 4.7 miles south on 4th Street, then turn right 7 miles on Forest Road 111. The road closes in winter. With a car shuttle, you can go up one trail and down another, or hike a trail just in one direction.

The eight-mile-round-trip **Bill Williams Mountain Trail** climbs the north face of the mountain. You'll reach the road about a half mile from the summit; either continue on the trail across the road or turn up the road itself. The trailhead (elev. 6,900 ft.) is near the Williams Ranger District office, 1.5 miles west of town; from I-40, take Exit 161 toward Williams, then turn right (west) .7 miles on the frontage road.

The nine-mile-round-trip **Benham Trail** climbs the south and east slopes, crossing the road to the lookout tower several times. To reach the Benham Trailhead (elev. 7,265 ft.) from Williams, go south 3.5 miles on 4th Street, then turn right about .3 miles on Forest Road 140. The gentler grade of this trail makes it good for horseback riders as well as hikers; the trailhead has a corral and restroom.

The **Bixler Saddle Trail** climbs past majestic rock formations and good viewpoints on the west side of Bill Williams Mountain, then joins the Bill Williams Mountain Trail about half a mile from the top, six miles round-trip total to the summit. Take I-40 west from Williams to Devil Dog Road Exit 157, head south on Forest Road 108, which turns left after .5 miles, then right in another .4 miles; continue .1 miles, then look for Forest Road 45 on the left—it's easy to miss. Take this road and follow it 3.6 miles to its end at the Bixler Saddle Trailhead (elev. 7,700 ft.). The last bit requires a high-clearance vehicle; with a car you could park before the going gets too rough and walk. The Kaibab National Forest map (Williams District) will help to navigate the forest roads.

Keyhole Sink Trail

A pleasant stroll, also marked for cross-country skiers, leads through ponderosa pines to a seasonal pool in a little box canyon. Aspen, wildflowers, and lush grass thrive here; you're likely to see some birds, too. Prehistoric people left petroglyphs, estimated to be 1,000 years old, on the dark basaltic rock. The easy walk is about 1.2 miles round-trip with little elevation gain. To reach the trailhead, drive east on I-40 from Williams to Pittman Valley Exit 171, exit north, then head east 2.4 miles on Historic Route 66; parking is on the right at Oak Hill Snowplay Area, which features picnic tables, a warming shed, and toilets. The trailhead is north across the road. Coming from Flagstaff, you can take I-40 Parks Road Exit 178, turn north, then west 4.3 miles on Route 66. **Garland Prairie Vista Picnic Area** lies just 1.1 miles east of Oak Hill Snowplay Area.

Dogtown Trails

Dogtown Lake (elev. 7,100 ft.) offers a campground, picnic area, and good hiking. **Dogtown Lake Trail** makes a pleasant 1.8-mile stroll around the lake from the picnic area. **Davenport Hill Trail** begins near the boat ramp on the east side of the lake, follows Dogtown Wash, climbs to a bench, then switchbacks to the 7,805-foot summit. You'll pass through ponderosa pine, Douglas fir, white fir, and aspen forests with some good views. The trail is five miles round-trip and has an elevation gain of 700 feet. **Ponderosa Nature Trail** is an easy, level, one-mile loop that follows the first part of the Davenport Hill Trail; a brochure describes the forest environment at stops along the way. Dogtown Lake, named for the prairie dogs common in the Williams area, is 7.5 miles southeast of town; drive 3.5 miles south on 4th Street, turn left 3 miles on Forest Road 140, then left 1.2 miles at the sign. You can make a loop back to Williams by following signs on Forest Roads 140 and 141.

Sycamore Rim Trail

This 11-mile loop near upper Sycamore Canyon takes you past canyon viewpoints, seasonal waterfalls, lumber mill and railroad sites, lily ponds (good swimming), and pretty forest country. Stone cairns mark the trail. Trailheads lie southeast of Williams near the junction of Forest Roads 13 and 56, at the end of Forest Road 56, at Pomeroy Tanks off Forest Road 109, and at Sycamore Falls off Forest Road 109; see the Kaibab or Coconino National Forest maps. If you're in the mood for only a short hike, walk .3 miles south from the end of Forest Road 56 to an overlook of Sycamore Canyon. The Visitor Information Center downtown and the Williams Ranger District office have a map and trail description.

Overland Historic Trail

You can hike sections of this old trail that connected Antelope Springs (Flagstaff) with Fort Whipple near Prescott; 23 miles of the trail lie within the Kaibab National Forest. The Visitor Information Center and the Williams Ranger District office have information.

Sycamore Falls

Two waterfalls near White Horse Lake create a spectacle during spring runoff and after heavy rains. From the White Horse Lake entrance, head north 1.7 miles on Forest Road 109 to the trailhead, about 2 miles south of the junction with Forest Road 13. A small waterfall is visible in a canyon just to the right, but walk ahead and a bit to the left to see a larger one, 80–100 feet high.

Sycamore Point

You'll enjoy a breathtaking panorama of Sycamore Canyon from this overlook 23 miles southeast of Williams. Elk, deer, black bears, and other wildlife inhabit the wild and rugged wilderness below. From town, drive eight miles south on 4th Street, then turn left on Forest Road 110 and travel to its end, approximately 15 miles farther. The last five miles may be too rough for cars. No trails enter the canyon from this side, though you can spot a path going down the opposite side.

J.D. Dam

This pretty little reservoir lies .6 miles down Forest Road 105 from the Sycamore Point turnoff. A causeway leads out to the center. It's a catch-and-release trout lake, and there's good birding. Facilities are limited to a boat ramp and an outhouse. You could camp in the surrounding forest outside the fence.

Backroad Scenic Drive to Jerome via Perkinsville

Beginning as 4th Street in downtown Williams, this road heads south through the pine forests of the Mogollon Rim, drops down to the high-desert lands of the Verde Valley, crosses the Verde River at historic Perkinsville Ranch, then climbs rugged hills to the old mining town of Jerome. The first 25 miles is paved, followed by 27 miles of dirt. Though dusty and bumpy in spots, the route is usually OK in dry weather. No vehicle should attempt the unpaved section after winter snowstorms or heavy summer rains. Allow three hours for a one-way drive, more if you'd like to stop to admire the views. Stock up on gas and water before heading down this lonely road. The Prescott National Forest map covers the entire route.

For more of a challenge, you can drive the Great Western Trail from just east of Williams and join the main road north of Perkinsville. Small signs mark the Great Western Trail, some sections of which are way too rough for cars.

ASH FORK

The Flagstone Capital of the U.S.A., Ash Fork lies in high-desert grasslands at the junction of I-40 and Highway 89, 19 miles west of Williams and 50 miles north of Prescott. The town grew up around a railroad siding built near Ash Creek in 1882, where passengers and freight transferred to stagecoaches or wagons for Prescott and Phoenix. Ash Fork (pop. 650) now serves as a highway stop and center for ranching and sandstone quarrying. You'll see piles of flagstone along the road on the west side of town.

Accommodations

As in Williams, most of the businesses lie along two parallel one-way streets—Lewis Avenue for westbound traffic and Park Avenue for eastbound. Take I-40 Exits 144 or 146. Unlike Williams, the citizens here haven't been able to develop the town's Route 66 history, and nearly all of the travelers' facilities have closed. Still, you might enjoy a look at the old buildings downtown. **Ashfork Inn** (west of downtown near I-40 Exit 144, 928/637-2514, $22 s, $29 d) is the only motel worth looking at, and it's fairly basic.

Ash Fork Grand Canyon RV Park (783 Old Route 66, 928/637-2521, $9.50 tents, $18.50 RVs w/hookups, $18.50 cabins) provides a pool, store, and laundry, but showers cost $3 extra; turn south on 8th Street at the sign. **Hillside RV Park** (south frontage road near I-40 Exit 144, 928/637-2300) catches a lot of noise from I-40 and isn't as good a deal; $9 RVs no hookups, $25 w/hookups, plus $5/person for a shower; it also provides a store and laundry.

Food

You may wish to bring your own! There's just the **Picadilly Pizza & Subs** (next to the Chevron station just south of the I-40 Exit 144) on the west side of town and a smoky café on the east side. A park on Lewis Avenue has picnic tables.

SELIGMAN

Another old railroad town, Seligman (pop. 900) now relies more on ranching and tourists, and it has done a great job of playing up its Route 66 history. The first residents arrived in 1886 and called the place Prescott Junction, because a rail line branched south to Prescott. Though the Prescott line was later abandoned, the town survived. The present name honors brothers who owned the Hash Knife Cattle Company.

Route 66

When I-40 bypassed Seligman, many local businesspeople threw up their hands in despair, but not brothers Juan and Angel Degadillo. They organized a Route 66 association to promote the history and memories of Route 66 and, through dogged determination, succeeded. Juan operated his wacky Degadillo's Snow Cap for more than 50 years, before passing away in June 2004. You may meet Angel in the gift shop/visitors center/barbershop next door.

Seligman lies near the east end of the longest remaining section of Route 66. If coming from the east, you can join the historic highway at I-40 Crookton Road Exit 139, then motor over gently rolling hills for 17.5 miles into downtown. Or you can hop off I-40 at Exits 121 or 123. This former transcontinental highway takes a bit longer to drive across western Arizona, but it offers a change of pace and a glimpse of America's motoring past. It also gives access to the Havasupai and Hualapai reservations.

Accommodations

You have a fine choice of Route 66–era motels in the compact downtown. Don't expect frills such as swimming pools or wireless Internet! **Stagecoach 66 Motel** (639 E. Route 66, 928/422-3470, $30 s, $34 d) lies out on the east edge of town, but offers a pizza restaurant. Downtown, the **Aztec Motel** (312 E. Route 66, 928/422-3055, $27.50 s, $38.75–49.50 d) provides recently remodeled rooms around a courtyard. The 1932 **Deluxe Inn** (203 E. Route 66, 928/422-3244 or 800/823-0513, $31 s, $34 d) adds microwaves and fridges to its stone-fronted rooms, also facing a courtyard. **Canyon Lodge** (114 E. Route 66, 928/422-3255, $39 s, $43 d) also has microwaves and fridges, and it throws in coffeemakers and a continental breakfast. **Romney Motel/Supai Motel** (122 W. Route 66, 928/422-7666, $29 d) is the cheapest in town, but inspect the rooms first. **Historic Route 66 Motel** (500 W. Route 66, 928/422-3204, $47 s, $57 d) fronts a large parking lot on the west side of town.

Campgrounds

Seligman Route 66 KOA (just east of town, 928/422-0035 or 800/562-4017, $19 tent, $23.50–25 RV w/hookups, $33 cabin) features a swimming pool along with showers, laundry, and games.

Food

Get your malts, sodas, fast food, and maybe a joke or two at the colorful **Delgadillo's Snow Cap** (301 E. Route 66, 928/422-3291). Enjoy Patty's flavorful Thai-American home cooking at the **Mini Mart & Café** (223 E. Route 66,

© BILL WEIR

the late Juan Delgadillo with his trademark "slightly used napkins"

North-Central Arizona

928/422-0014, daily breakfast and lunch, Mon.–Sat. dinner). Patty's also offers a small grocery. The **Copper Cart Restaurant** (103 W. Route 66, 928/422-3241, daily breakfast and lunch, closes 4 P.M.) offers a varied American menu. **Meg's Coyote Pizza** (639 E. Route 66, 928/422-4697, closed Mon.) lies east of downtown. The two cafés on the west end of downtown lack nonsmoking sections, and aren't recommended. A small park in the center of town has picnic tables.

GRAND CANYON CAVERNS

Vast underground chambers and pretty cave features invite you to detour off old Route 66. The caverns (928/422-4565, www.grandcanyoncaverns.com) lie 25 miles northwest of Seligman, then 1 mile off the highway. A giant dinosaur stands guard in front. On 45-minute guided tours, you descend 210 feet by elevator and walk about .75 miles with some steps and inclines. The interior has been dry for millions of years and is now a comfortable 56°F year-round with a humidity of just 6 percent. Tours operate 8 A.M.–6 P.M. daily in the warmer months, then 9 A.M.–5 P.M. daily in winter (closed Dec. 25); admission is $13 adults, $10 children 4–12. Flashlight tours ($15 adults, $13 children) follow the same route, but offer an experience similar to what tourists had before 1962; call for times. Explorer tours ($45) take you on an adventurous route off the main trail and last about two hours, by reservation only.

At the caverns' entrance, you can see some cave exhibits, watch a video, peruse the gift shop, or visit the restaurant (open about the same hours as the tours). The nearby campground offers dry sites for tents and RVs ($12.50) and hookup sites ($18.50) including showers. **Grand Canyon Caverns Inn** (928/422-4565, $62 s, $72 d, less in winter) offers year-round accommodations near the turnoff on Route 66.

Lake and Rim Country

More than a dozen lakes dot the pine-forested plateau country southeast of Flagstaff. Hikers, birders, anglers, picnickers, and campers enjoy the quiet waters, rolling hills, and scenic canyons of the region. Animal life flourishes—you might spot elk, deer, turkey, maybe even bear. Abert's squirrels with long tufted ears scamper through the trees. Migratory waterfowl stop by the lakes, and you may see an osprey, and in winter, a bald eagle. The best times to see wildlife are early and late in the day. Rim-country temperatures remain comfortably cool even in midsummer, and showers fall almost daily on July and August afternoons.

Campsites often fill up during the peak summer months; you'll find less-crowded conditions early and late in the season, or at any time away from developed sites. Dispersed camping is available almost anywhere in any season within the national forests, though you're asked to avoid camping on meadows or within a quarter mile of springs, streams, stock tanks, or lakes. Boats are limited to those with electric motors on the smaller lakes and 8 hp gas motors on the larger ones; no restrictions apply on Upper Lake Mary.

MORMON LAKE RANGER DISTRICT

Two offices provide information about recreation and road conditions for this area. South of town, you can stop at the **Mormon Lake Ranger Station** (4373 S. Lake Mary Rd., 1.2 miles from Beulah Blvd., Flagstaff, AZ 86001, 928/774-1182, 7:30 A.M.–4:30 P.M. Mon.–Fri.). On the northeast side of town, swing by **Peaks Ranger Station** (5075 N. Hwy. 89, Flagstaff, AZ 86004, 928/526-0866, 7:30 A.M.–4:30 P.M. Mon.–Fri.). Both sell books and forest and topo maps. Online, check www.fs.fed.us/r3/coconino.

Canyon Vista Campground

Sites are in a mixed conifer, aspen, and oak forest at an elevation of 6,900 feet. The small campground has drinking water and a vault toilet, $12 during the mid-April–mid-October season. Picnicking (10 A.M.–4 P.M.) costs $5. Sandy's Canyon Trailhead at the north end of the campground leads into Walnut Canyon and the Arizona Trail. Follow Lake Mary Road for just over five miles, then turn left after crossing a cattle guard.

Lower and Upper Lake Mary

Beginning just eight miles from Flagstaff, these long, narrow reservoirs offer fishing, boating, and bird-watching. Walnut Creek, dammed to form these lakes, once continued down through Walnut Canyon past the many Sinagua ruins there. The Riordan brothers, who built the first reservoir early in the 20th century to supply water to their sawmill, named the lake for a daughter.

Lake Mary Road (County 3) parallels the shores of both lakes. From downtown Flagstaff, head south on Milton Road, turn right on Forest Meadows Street before the I-40 junction, turn left on Beulah Boulevard, then follow signs for Lake Mary Road. If you're driving north on I-17, take Exit 339 just before the I-40 junction.

Lower Lake Mary varies greatly in size, depending on rainfall and water needs. **Lower Lake Mary Boating and Picnicking Area,** near the dam, offers tables, grills, ramadas, and a place to hand-launch boats. Anglers catch mostly northern pike. The turnoff is between Mileposts 337 and 338.

Water-skiers zip across Upper Lake Mary in summer—it's one of the few lakes in this part of Arizona long and deep enough for the sport. Fishers pull catfish, northern pike, walleye, sunfish, and bluegill from the waters. **Lake Mary Boat Landing** features picnic tables, grills, ramadas, and a paved boat ramp; it's on Lake Mary Road .8 miles past the dam, between Mileposts 334 and 335. **Lake Mary Narrows Picnic Area,** on Lake Mary Road 1.5 miles farther uplake between Mileposts 331 and 332, features a fishing area with wheelchair access, tables, grills, ramadas, and a paved boat ramp.

Lakeview Campground (elev. 6,900 ft.) provides camping near the Narrows of Upper Lake Mary May–mid-October. Some sites are too small for trailers, but all have tent pads. You can walk to the water on a half-mile trail. The $12 fee includes drinking water and vault toilets; picnicking (10 A.M.–4 P.M.) is $5. It lies on the opposite side of the highway from the lake, 14 miles southeast of Flagstaff at Milepost 331

Sandy's Canyon Trail

This easy 1.5-mile round-trip trail features canyon, forest, and mountain views, with the option to continue on the Arizona Trail. Local rock climbers tackle the cliffs visible from the first few hundred feet of the trail. The path follows the rim of Walnut Canyon a short way, drops down Sandy's Canyon, then follows the floor of Walnut Canyon to a junction with the Arizona Trail in about three-quarters of a mile. Here you can turn southeast about four miles to Marshall Lake or north one mile to Fisher Point, then continue toward the trailhead near Walnut Canyon National Monument, another six miles. Another trail near Fisher Point branches northwest toward Flagstaff and its Urban Trail System. Sandy's Canyon Trailhead is reached 5.5 miles down Lake Mary Road from Highway 89A, then left .2 miles just past the second cattle guard. During winter you can park off the road near the locked gate and walk to the trailhead.

Marshall Lake

This small trout lake and its primitive boat ramp lie north of Upper Lake Mary. Head nine miles down Lake Mary Road from Flagstaff to the signed Marshall Lake turnoff, between Upper and Lower Lake Mary, then turn left three miles to the lake.

Ashurst Lake and Campgrounds

Anglers pursue rainbow trout while windsurfers slice through the water on this small lake. Two campgrounds, both with water, vault toilets, and a $10 fee, sit beside the lake—**Ashurst Campground** on the west shore and **Forked Pine** on the east. The season at this 7,000-foot elevation runs May–mid-October. Picnicking (10 A.M.–4 P.M.) costs $5. On the way in you'll pass the **Ashurst Dispersed Camping Area,** no water or fee. There's a boat ramp near the entrance to Ashurst Campground. From Flagstaff, travel southeast 18 miles on Lake Mary Road, then turn left 4 miles on paved Forest Road 82E (between Mileposts 326 and 327). **Coconino Reservoir,** one mile south of

Ashurst Lake on a dirt road, also has a good reputation for rainbow trout.

Pine Grove Campground

This large campground ($15) provides drinking water, coin-operated showers, flush toilets, dump station, paved roads, and summertime interpretive programs; picnicking (10 A.M.–4 P.M.) is $5. The camp host sells ice and firewood. About half of the sites can be reserved (877/444-6777, www.reserveusa.com), a good idea for summer weekends. The season at the 6,800-foot elevation is May–mid-October. Although not on a lake, the campground is within a few miles of Upper Lake Mary and Ashurst and Mormon Lakes. It lies opposite the turnoff for Ashurst Lake, 18 miles southeast of Flagstaff; turn west .8 miles on Forest Road 651 from Lake Mary Road.

Mormon Lake

Mormon settlers arrived on the shores of this lake in 1878 and started a dairy farm. Although Mormon is the largest natural lake in Arizona, the average depth is only 10 feet. The water level fluctuates; when it's low the lake is not much more than a marsh. Occasionally it dries up completely! Still, at times, anglers reel in sizable bullhead catfish and northern pike. Boats must be hand-carried to the water.

Lake Mary Road parallels the east shore and has a scenic viewpoint. The lodges, camping, and hiking areas lie along Mormon Lake Loop Road (Forest Road 90), which circles around the west side of the lake; the north turnoff is between Mileposts 323 and 324; south turnoff is between Mileposts 317 and 318. **Dairy Springs** and **Double Springs** campgrounds off this loop road both have drinking water, vault toilets, and a $10 fee; picnicking (10 A.M.–4 P.M.) costs $5. Half of the Dairy Springs sites and all those at **Dairy Springs Group Campground** can be reserved (877/444-6777; www.reserveusa.com). The season at this 7,000-foot elevation runs May–September. From Flagstaff, head southeast 20 miles on Lake Mary Road, then turn right 4 miles on Mormon Lake Loop Road to the Dairy Springs turnoff, or go 2 miles farther to the turnoff for Double Springs.

Lakeview Trail (2 miles round-trip) climbs to a viewpoint from Double Springs Campground. For a longer trip, start near Dairy Springs Campground and hike 1,500 feet above Mormon Lake on the six-mile round-trip **Mormon Mountain Trail;** you'll enjoy pretty forest country, though trees block views at the top. **Ledges Trail,** an easy one-mile round-trip hike from Dairy Springs Campground, runs out to a ledge overlooking the lake.

Cabins of **Montezuma Lodge** (928/354-2220, www.arizonamountainresort.com, mid-May–mid-Oct., $105 d weekdays, $125 d Fri.–Sat.) spread across 16 acres in the woods a quarter mile beyond Dairy Springs Campground.

Mormon Lake Lodge (928/774-0462 Flagstaff, 928/354-2227 local, www.mormonlakelodge.com), on the loop road at the south end of the lake, offers a variety of rooms and cabins ($45–145 for as many as seven persons), an RV park (May 15–Oct. 31, $24 RV w/hookups, $12 RV no hookups, $8 tent, $2 for showers), a Western-style steakhouse (daily breakfast, lunch, and dinner mid-May–mid-Oct., call for off-season weekend hours, $8–25), a saloon, grocery store with fishing and hunting supplies, and a gas station. Bands play weekends in summer at the saloon, which, like the steakhouse, is nonsmoking. You can rent mountain bikes and ATVs. **High Mountain Stables** (928/354-2359, www.highmountainstables.com, mid-May–mid-Oct.) near the lodge will take you out on horseback from one hour to all day or overnight; groups can arrange hay or wagon rides. When snow covers the land, hopefully about late December–March, the lodge provides cross-country ski trails, rentals, and lessons, along with snowmobile tours. A small **post office** is wedged between the lodge and store. **Munds Park,** 11 miles west of the Mormon Lake Loop Road via unpaved Forest Road 240, has a motel, RV park, restaurants, and a service station. You can also reach it at I-17 Exit 322, 18 miles south of Flagstaff.

Kinnikinick Lake and Campground

Rainbow and brown trout, with the occasional catfish, swim in this reservoir (elev. 7,000 ft.). Ponderosa and juniper trees and grasslands cover the gentle terrain around it. You're more likely to find solitude here, because the area lies off paved roads. The campground has drinking water, vault toilets, and a $10 fee May–September; picnicking (10 A.M.–4 P.M.) costs $5. Sites are open off-season without water, fee, or camp host. Anglers can use the gravel boat ramp and motors up to 8 hp. From Flagstaff, go southeast 25 miles on Lake Mary Road to just past Mormon Lake (between Mileposts 318 and 319), turn left 4.7 miles on Forest Road 125, then right 4.4 miles on Forest Road 82, following signs. Though unpaved, these forest roads are usually OK for cars. Be warned that Forest Road 82 from here south to Long Lake is extremely rough and rocky, requiring high-clearance vehicles, dry weather, and lots of time; it's not recommended.

MOGOLLON RIM RANGER DISTRICT

The cool ponderosa pine forests atop the Mogollon Rim here offer many opportunities for camping, fishing, hiking, and back-road travel. In winter, pullouts along Highway 87 and County 3 are plowed so people can play in the snow. The region centers on Clints Well, where County 3 meets Highway 87. A half mile south of this junction at Milepost 290 on Highway 87, **Happy Jack Information Center** (P.O. Box 19664, Happy Jack, AZ 86024, 928/477-2172, www.fs.fed.us/r3/coconino) provides recreation information and sells topo maps, forest maps, and regional books. It's open 9 A.M.–5 P.M. daily (with half an hour off for lunch) May–October; the rest of the year it's usually open Thursday–Monday 9 A.M.–4:30 P.M. and closed a half hour for lunch.

Foresters provide similar information at the **Blue Ridge Ranger Station** (HC 31, Box 300, Happy Jack, AZ 86024, 928/477-2255, 7:30 A.M.–4 P.M. Mon.–Fri.). From Clints Well, go northeast 9.5 miles on Highway 87 to the office on the right. From Winslow, head 43 miles southwest on Highway 87.

Stoneman Lake

Geologists have not decided whether the circular depression that holds this unusual lake is an old volcanic crater or a sinkhole. Although the lake can dry up during droughts, anglers have landed record yellow perch catches along with pike and sunfish. The lake has a picnic area and boat ramp but no campground. To reach Stoneman, either take the I-17 Stoneman Lake Exit 306 (34 miles south of Flagstaff) and go east nine miles on mostly unpaved Forest Road 213, or head south on Lake Mary Road eight miles past Mormon Lake, then turn west seven miles on Forest Road 213.

West Clear Creek Wilderness

The transparent waters of this year-round creek wind below pretty canyon walls on the way to the Verde River. Of the many canyons in the Mogollon Rim, West Clear Creek's has the greatest length—40 miles. Cross-bedded patterns of ancient sand dunes in Coconino Sandstone show clearly on the sheer cliffs. The creek offers excellent hiking, swimming, and fishing, though it may be difficult to entice the trout onto a hook. The warmer months are best for a visit to this canyon. There isn't much of a trail, so you'll be wading and swimming much of the time. In spring, snowmelt can raise the stream level too high for hiking, as can very heavy rains in any season. Water is always available from the creek; purify it first. Hikers should remember that trails out can be difficult to spot.

Maxwell Trail #37 and **Tramway Trail #32** lead into the upper reaches of West Clear Creek, from which you can also explore the tributaries of Willow and Clover Creeks. Each trail is less than a mile one-way and drops about 700 feet. To reach the trailheads, go 21 miles south of Mormon Lake on Lake Mary Road, then turn west and south on unpaved Forest Roads 81 and 81E, following signs and your map. Roads to the trailheads are rough and require high-clearance vehicles.

Adventurous hikers could spend a week traveling downstream to Bull Pen Ranch or Clear Creek Campground, though many deep pools, including one a quarter mile long, must be crossed. Allow plenty of time for a trek all the way through the canyon, as the rugged terrain and pools make for extremely slow going. Flotation vests are recommended for such trips because inflatable boats, tubes, and air mattresses are easily punctured. It's easy to forget to drink water in the cool depths, but one does need to drink a lot because of the exertions.

Clints Well

Natural springs here, a rarity in the region, have long been a stopping place for travelers. They were named for Clint Wingfield, an early pioneer. Lake Mary Road (County 3) meets Highway 87 at Clints Well; turn left for Winslow, right for Payson and Mesa. The small **Clints Well Campground** near the end of Lake Mary Road is free but lacks water. Turn a half mile south on Highway 87 from the junction for **Happy Jack Information Center, Long Valley Café** (American food daily breakfast, lunch, and dinner, $5–12), and a grocery store/service station. Two miles north of the junction on Lake Mary Road, **Happy Jack Lodge & RV Park** (928/477-2805 or 800/430-0385, www.happyjacklodge.com) offers cabins ($78 d–129 4 persons, some with kitchens), RV sites ($24 w/hookups), and tent camping ($12), along with showers ($3), laundry, a small store, and a dump station. A restaurant (Fri.–Sat. breakfast, lunch, and dinner, Sun. breakfast and lunch, may close in winter, $9–16) prepares American food.

Kehl Springs

Great views at the edge of the Mogollon Rim lie just a short walk away from this small campground; no fee or water. Aspen and oak trees put on a colorful display in autumn. From Clints Well, go southwest 3.3 miles on Highway 87, then turn left on Forest Road 147 to the Rim Road (see the Coconino Forest Map). These roads tend to be rough and dusty, but they should be okay for passenger vehicles in good weather.

Blue Ridge Reservoir

Hemmed in by the canyon walls of East Clear Creek, this skinny lake offers good trout fishing—best in spring and autumn—and great scenery. Trails lead to the water's edge, but steep terrain makes fishing easier from a boat. The popular **Rock Crossing Campground** nearby offers good views; it's open with water and an $8 fee from Memorial Day to Labor Day weekends. From Clints Well, head northeast five miles on Highway 87, turn right three miles on Forest Road 751 to the campground, then another three miles to the dam.

The smaller **Blue Ridge Campground** is open during the same season with the same fee; trailers are limited to 16 feet. From Clints Well, go northeast nine miles on Highway 87, then turn right one mile on Forest Road 138. Sections of **Moqui Group Area,** on Forest Road 138 before Blue Ridge Campground, can be reserved through Happy Jack Information Center. Anglers use Blue Ridge Campground as a base for Blue Ridge Reservoir, East Clear Creek, and Long Lake.

Long Lake

Catfish and northern pike are the fish most commonly pulled from this two-mile-long lake, but the waters harbor trout, bass, walleye, and panfish as well. You can camp in the area and use the primitive boat ramp; outhouses are the only facilities. Soldier Annex Lake and Soldier Lake lie to the west; electric motors only.

Turn northwest 3 miles on Forest Road 211 from Highway 87 near Blue Ridge Ranger Station, then head north 12 miles on Forest Road 82 to Long Lake. Or, from County 3, head 8 miles east on Forest Road 211, then turn north 12 miles on Forest Road 82. The turnoff for Soldier Annex Lake is a mile farther north, then left half a mile. The Coconino Forest map shows Forest Road 82 continuing another 12 miles to Kinnikinick Lake, but this section is extremely rough and makes for slow going.

Cabin Loop Trail System

This trail network connects three historic guard stations—General Springs, Pinchot, and Buck Springs—in a land of shallow canyons and forest ridges between Blue Ridge Reservoir and the Mogollon Rim. You could hike one of the segments with a car shuttle or make a variety of loops. An 8-mile segment of the **Arizona Trail** follows the trail system northeast from General Springs Trailhead, then turns north to Rock Crossing Campground.

Knoll Lake

A rocky island in the middle gives this lake its name. Knoll Lake is in Leonard Canyon, several miles north of the Mogollon Rim. There's a campground on a hill near the lake; sites have water and a $10 fee during the Memorial Day–Labor Day season. A road and hiking trail lead down to the boat ramp. Anglers come mostly to seek out rainbow trout. Getting here involves about 28 miles of dirt road from either Highway 87 or Woods Canyon Lake off Highway 260.

BLACK MESA RANGER DISTRICT

Foresters of the Black Mesa Ranger District of the Apache-Sitgreaves National Forest provide information and maps on recreation in the Mogollon Rim country from Chevelon Canyon to Black Canyon Lakes, including the very popular Rim Lakes Recreation Area. The **Mogollon Rim Visitor Center** offers an information desk, a few exhibits, and map sales at a handy location right on the rim at Al Fulton Point, opposite the Forest Road 300 turnoff from Highway 260; it's open 9 A.M.–4:30 P.M. daily from Memorial Day to Labor Day, but may close for lunch and on some weekdays depending on staffing. Step out on the back porch for a great panorama from the rim across wooded ridges extending all the way to Four Peaks near Phoenix. The first quarter mile of Forest Road 171 east of the visitor center has **picnic areas**—all with views; continue along the road for some designated dispersed camping sites. The visitor center is six miles west of Forest Lakes between Mileposts 282 and 283. From Payson, head 32 miles east on Highway 260 to just past where the highway tops out on the Mogollon Rim.

You can also stop by the **Black Mesa Ranger Station** (2748 Hwy. 260, P.O. Box 968, Overgaard, AZ 85933, 928/535-4481, www.fs.fed.us/r3/asnf, 8 A.M.–4:30 P.M. Mon.–Fri.) for recreation information on the Rim Country; it's two miles east of Heber on the south side of the highway between Mileposts 307 and 308.

Both offices have a pamphlet for the self-guided *Black Canyon . . . Journey Through Time Auto Tour* that describes prehistoric and historic sites along a 15.3-mile length of Forest Road 86 southwest of Heber.

A large part of the Rim Lakes Recreation Area has been set aside as a wildlife habitat area. Hikers, backpackers, cyclists, and equestrians are welcome here, but not motorized vehicles. The Mogollon Rim offers a great opportunity for seeing elk, deer, and other animals, especially in early morning and again in the evening. Take care not to be near the edge of the rim during summer thunderstorms, most likely in July and August, because it's said to be the second most lightning-struck place in the world.

Campgrounds fill on weekends from about the third week of June to Labor Day; you'll need to make a reservation or arrive by Friday morning to secure a spot. Groups can reserve sites at Woods Canyon, Spillway, Canyon Point, and Gentry campgrounds. Designated dispersed camping sites also help to accommodate the throngs of summer visitors. These areas are free, but lack water or facilities; look for them along sections of Forest Roads 237, 300, 169, 171, 195, 9350, and 9354. The forest roads east of Forest Lakes tend to be the least crowded for dispersed camping. Some people like autumn best—September and October generally have good weather and fishing, solitude, and aspen leaves turning to gold. Spring can be a fine time to visit as well.

ATVs may travel numbered forest roads only. Both vehicles and operators must be licensed for highway use.

Chevelon Crossing

This small campground overlooks Chevelon Creek many miles downstream from Woods Canyon Lake. The sites (elev. 6,200 ft.) remain open most of the year with no water or fee. Parking is tight and small vehicles will fit best. Try fishing for rainbow trout in the large pools upstream. Three routes lead to this remote campground. Forest Road 504 is the usual way in; turn off Highway 260 one mile west of Heber. You could also take Highway 99 south from Winslow and turn left on Forest Road 504, or take Forest Road 169 north from Forest Road

300 (the Rim Road; closed in winter) west of Woods Canyon Lake.

Chevelon Canyon Lake

This long, skinny reservoir lies 12 miles upstream from Chevelon Crossing via Forest Roads 169 and 169B. See the Apache-Sitgreaves Forest map for other ways of getting here. The lake offers trophy fishing for rainbow and brown trout; anglers must use artificial lures and observe size and catch limits. With 208 surface acres, this is one of the larger lakes on the Mogollon Rim. There's a primitive campground (elev. 6,400 ft., no water or fee) near the north shore.

Bear Canyon Lake

Anglers enjoy fishing with artificial lures or bait on this trout lake. The shore is steep and tree-covered, so it's easier to use boats for fishing, though you'll have to lug them to the water. There's a campground (no water or fee) near the north end. From Woods Canyon Lake, travel west 10 miles on Forest Road 300 (the Rim Road), then turn north and drive 2.5 miles on Forest Road 89.

Woods Canyon Lake

This popular lake was one of the first of seven created on the rim. Camp at either Aspen Campground ($12) or Spillway Campground ($14) near the lakeshore; both have drinking water and a season of about May–mid-September. Call to reserve a site (877/444-6777, www.reserveusa.com). A store that stays open into autumn has groceries, boat rentals, and motors (only electrics are permitted here). On summer weekends, staff lead walks and offer evening programs. **Rocky Point Picnic Area** ($5) on the south side of the lake is open for day use only. **Woods Canyon Nature Trail** makes a half-mile loop here. From Highway 260, near the edge of the Mogollon Rim, turn northwest five miles on paved Forest Roads 300 and 105.

Rim Top Trailhead and Snowplay Area

A large parking area, just .1s mile in from Highway 260 on Forest Road 300, provides access to General Crook Trail 611, Rim Lakes Vista Trail, and the 235 Road Bike Trail. In winter, it's plowed so visitors can enjoy the snow (no sleds or tubing).

Rim Lakes Vista Trail

This easy trail follows the rim for three miles with some fine views between Rim and Mogollon Campgrounds, both off Forest Road 300; elevation is 7,500 feet. **Military Sinkhole Trail** drops west and south 2.25 miles from Rim Lakes Vista Trail to Two-Sixty Trailhead and the Highline National Recreation Trail; you'll find the upper trailhead 1.9 miles in from Highway 260 on Forest Road 300 and the Two-Sixty Trailhead 27 miles east of Payson just off Highway 260.

Mountain Bike Trails

Cyclists enjoy **Willow Springs Loop,** an 8.1-mile series of forest roads in a wildlife habitat area signed for nonmotorized use. It's northeast of Willow Springs Lake; from Highway 260, go a half mile north on Forest Road 237 to the trailhead at the junction with Forest Road 236. The **235 Road Bike Trail,** west of Willow Springs Lake, heads north about four miles (one-way) into the wildlife habitat area. Both trails are at an elevation of about 7,600 feet.

Rim Road—Forest Road 300

This scenic road follows the Mogollon Rim between Highway 260 and Highway 87 for 51 miles. Most of it is dirt, passable by cautiously driven cars. Allow 3–4 hours one-way. Slow speeds are necessary because of hazardous washboard sections. Attractions include rim views, pretty forest scenes, and wildlife sightings. You'll also see effects of the 1990 Dude Fire. The eastern section lies within the Rim Lake Recreation Area, where one must use designated campsites. Dispersed camping is allowed along the western part of the drive, which is in the Coconino National Forest.

Willow Springs Lake

Anglers catch mostly rainbow trout in this U-shaped lake. There's a boat ramp but no campground. You can camp in designated dispersed areas nearby or at **Sinkhole Campground,** which has water and a $8 fee from mid-May to late October. From Highway 260, about 1 mile east of

Forest Road 300 (Rim Road) junction and 4 miles west of Canyon Point Campground, turn in a half mile on Forest Road 149 to Sinkhole Campground, then continue 3.5 miles to Willow Springs Lake. **Rim, Crook,** and **Mogollon Campgrounds** lie along Forest Road 300, beginning .8 miles in from Highway 260; all are open mid-May–late October with water and a $8 fee.

Canyon Point Campground

This large, easily accessible campground has drinking water, showers, a dump station, and some quad sites mid-May–late September; reserve through 877/444-6777 or www.reserveusa.com. Sites without hookups cost $14. Loop A has electric hookups at $16. Naturalists offer interpretive programs on summer weekends. **Sinkhole Trail** begins from Loop B and leads to a sinkhole, one mile round-trip. Canyon Point Campground lies just off Highway 260, five miles east of the Forest Road 300 (Rim Road) junction.

Forest Lakes Touring Center

This year-round recreation center (928/535-4047) provides cabins ($70–125 d weekdays, $78–150 d Fri.–Sat. and holidays) and an RV park, but offers only long-term sites during summer (May–Sept.). In winter, cross-country skiers come to glide over approximately 30 miles of marked and groomed trails and skating lanes atop the Mogollon Rim; trail passes cost $8. You can also arrange rentals, lessons, and tours. Forest Lakes Touring Center is in the village of Forest Lakes on Highway 260 near Milepost 288, 6 miles east of the Forest Road 300 (Rim Road) turnoff or 36 miles east of Payson.

A nearby store sells groceries, camping gear, and fishing supplies. Heber, 15 miles east, and Overgaard just beyond, have a few motels and cafés.

Black Canyon Lake

This small trout lake doesn't have a campground, but **Black Canyon Rim** and **Gentry** campgrounds lie within a few miles. Black Canyon Rim has water and an $8 fee mid-May–late September. Gentry has no water or fee, but sites can be reserved for families or groups (800/280-2267). Both stay open all year when not blocked by snow. From Canyon Point Campground, go east 4.5 miles on Highway 260, turn right 2.5 miles on Forest Road 300, then turn left three miles on Forest Road 86 to Black Canyon Lake.

Heber and Overgaard

These small towns stretch out along Highway 260. Both have cafés, stores, and a few RV parks. Heber offers the **Best Western Sawmill Inn** (1877 Hwy. 260, 928/535-5053 or 800/372-9564, $62 d weekdays, $69 d Fri.–Sat.), with an exercise room, and the modest **Canyon View Motel** (1842 Hwy. 260, 928/535-4598, $40 s, $45 d weekdays, $45 s, $50 d Fri.–Sat.). **Black Mesa Ranger Station** is also in Overgaard.

Buffalo Museum of America

Art and memorabilia celebrate this magnificent animal in a large collection (2269 Hwy. 260, just east of Overgaard, 928/535-4141, 10 A.M.–4 P.M. Sun., Mon., and Thurs., 10 A.M.–5 P.M. Fri.–Sat., may close in winter, $5 adult, $3 children). Inside you'll see an amazing variety of many examples of pop art, paintings, and sculpture that depict the buffalo. Besides life-sized stuffed figures of adults and calves, there's a buffalo prop from the movie *Dances with Wolves*—producers had to replicate the violent buffalo hunts without harming a single animal. Old photos and illustrations depict the colorful life of Buffalo Bill, along with his gloves and Sharps rifle. Plains Indian exhibits display elaborate ceremonial costumes.

Look for the group of large Western-style buildings of the Bison Ranch development on the south side of the highway near Overgaard. Bison Ranch (928/535-9545, www.bisonranch.net) also has trail and carriage rides, dining, shopping, and cabin rentals.

Below the Rim

PAYSON

Payson (elev. 5,000 feet) stands at almost the exact center of Arizona. The sheer cliffs of the Mogollon Rim tower 2,000 feet above to the north. Forested mountains lie in all directions and provide many opportunities for outdoor recreation. Hikers can explore the Mazatzal Wilderness to the southwest, Hellsgate Wilderness to the east, and Sierra Ancha and Salome Wildernesses to the southeast. Trout-filled streams and stocked reservoirs lure anglers to the water. Hunters come in season to bag elk, deer, turkey, and other game. Payson (pop. 15,000) boasts a few sights of its own, and makes a good base for exploring the surrounding countryside.

History

It wasn't the cool climate and beautiful scenery that attracted Payson's first settlers, but the glitter of gold. Miners set up camp in 1881, though ranching and lumbering soon reigned as the most rewarding occupations. A fort provided protection against Apache raids in the precarious early years.

The town's name honors Senator Louis Edwin Payson, who had nothing to do with the community and never came here. Frank C. Hise, former postmaster, assigned the name to repay a political favor.

Novelist Zane Grey fell in love with the canyons, towering forests, and expansive views of the Rim Country. He built a lodge at the foot of the Rim in 1920, then stayed often over the next nine years, enjoying the wilderness while working on novels about the American West. His hunting expeditions secured both ideas for stories and trophies for his walls. The devastating Dude Fire burned the lodge in 1990, but you can see a reconstruction of it along with exhibits of Zane Grey's life and books at the Rim Country Museum in Payson.

Rim Country Museum

Visiting and permanent exhibits (928/474-3483, www.rimcountrymuseums.org, noon–4 P.M. Wed.–Sun. $3 adults, $2.50 seniors, $2 students 12–18) take you from the days of the earliest peoples of the region to the Apache conflicts, timber and mining operations, agriculture, and pioneer entertainment. A blacksmith shop and a 1908 kitchen portray aspects of life in early Payson. The display on Zane Grey, who produced 131 novels, has some of his books and personal belongings. The museum complex includes Payson's 1930s forest ranger's station, a 1930s forest ranger's residence (now the Museum Store and ticket office), a replica of the two-story Herron Hotel (the main exhibit hall), and the upper section of the Mt. Ord Firetower. A replica of Zane Grey's cabin may be open by the time you visit. The Museum Store sells books on local and Arizona history as well as gift items. You can picnic on the tables outside or frolic in the adjacent Green Valley Park's playground and lake (electric motors OK). From Highway 87, turn west one mile on Main Street (at the chamber of commerce), turn right on Green Valley Parkway, then take the next left into the parking lot.

Museum of Rim Country Archaeology

The collection (510 W. Main St., 938/468-1128, noon–4 P.M. Wed.–Sun. $3 adults, $2.50 seniors, $2 students 12–18) displays tools, jewelry, and other prehistoric artifacts from the area along with exhibits on trade routes and archaeological techniques. A gift shop sells local crafts.

Entertainment and Events

Sawmill Theatres (201 W. Main St., 928/468-7535) plays current flicks. Music concerts and art festivals enliven the town during the warmer months; the chamber and newspaper listings tell what's on.

There a number of local annual events. The **PRCA Spring Rodeo** rides in May. Pine has an **arts & crafts festival** on Memorial Day weekend. **Rim Country Classic Car Show** rolls in April. **Strawberry Festival** in the town of Strawberry, makes merry with entertainment and arts and crafts in June two weekends after Memorial Day. Pine usually celebrates **July Fourth** on the weekend before, while Payson's entertainment and fireworks take place on the July 4. The world's oldest **Continuous Rodeo** (since 1884), dance, and parade arrive on the third weekend of August. **Rim Country Western Heritage Festival** brings in cowboy poets and Western artisans on October. Pine also has an **arts & crafts festival** on Labor Day weekend. The **Old-time Fiddlers' Contest** plays on the last weekend of September. **Swiss Village Christmas Lighting** adds a glow on the Friday after Thanksgiving. Pine has its **Tree Lighting** on the first of December.

Recreation

You'll find a swimming pool, tennis courts, ball fields, and picnic grounds in **Rumsey Park** (N. McLane Rd., 928/474-2774 pool, 928/474-5242 Parks & Recreation); from the junction of Beeline and Highway 260, go west on Longhorn Road, then turn right a half mile on McLane Road. **Green Valley Park,** one mile west on Main Street, offers a fishing lake, picnic areas, playground, and the Rim Country Museum.

Play golf on the 18-hole **Payson Golf Course** (1504 W. Country Club, 928/474-2273), which lies west of Green Valley Park. Head out on horseback from **Kohl's Ranch Lodge** (17 miles east on Hwy. 260, 928/478-4211 or 800/331-5645).

Accommodations

You can choose from motels in town or secluded cabins in the surrounding forests. Make reservations for the weekend rush in summer, when you'll have to pay the highest prices. The summer rates listed here will come down in winter.

$50–100: Options south of the highway junction include the **Holiday Inn Express** (206 S. Beeline Hwy., 928/472-7484 or 800/465-4329, $70 d weekdays, $90 d Fri.–Sat. and up) with a pool and hot tub, **Budget Inn & Suites** (302 S. Beeline Hwy., 928/474-2201 or 800/474-2201, $44–189 d) with fireplaces and hot tubs in some rooms, **Best Value Inn** (811 S. Beeline Hwy., 928/474-2283 or 888/315-2378, $50 d weekdays, $80 d Fri.–Sat.), **Motel 6** (101 W. Phoenix St. and S. Beeline Hwy., 928/474-4526 or 800/466-8356, $46 s, $52 d weekdays, $60 s, $66 d Fri.–Sat.), and **Paysonglo Lodge** (1005 S. Beeline Hwy., 928/474-2382 or 800/772-9766, $65–75 d ($80–92 Fri.–Sat.) including some fireplaces, a pool, and hot tub.

North of downtown, you can stay at the **Best Western Payson Inn** (801 N. Beeline Hwy., 928/474-3241 or 800/247-9477, $59–89 d weekdays, $79–149 d Fri.–Sat.), which offers fireplaces, pool, hot tub, and a two-bedroom apartment. The **Majestic Mountain Inn** (602 E. Hwy. 260, 928/474-0185 or 800/408-2442, www.majesticmountaininn.com, $65–99 d weekdays, $99–150 d Fri.–Sat.) has a pool and a choice of standard, deluxe (with a fireplace), and luxury rooms (fireplace and 2-person spa). The pueblo-styled **Comfort Inn** (809 E. Hwy. 260, 928/474-5241 or 800/888-9828, $49–89 d weekdays, $69–149 d Fri.–Sat. rooms, $89–149 d weekdays, $89–189 d suites) offers a pool and hot tub; suites include fireplaces and private hot tubs.

Christopher Creek Lodge (23 miles east of Payson, 928/478-4300, www.cclodge.com) offers motel rooms ($43 d weekdays, $53 d Thurs.–Sat.) and cabins with fireplaces ($90–106 d) in the resort village of Christopher Creek. Nearby you'll find cabins with fireplaces at **Creekside Cabins** (928/478-4557, $60 d weekdays, $80 d Fri.–Sat.), which also has a steakhouse and **Grey Hackle Lodge** (928/478-4392, www.greyhacklelodge.com, $60–110 d). **Mountain Meadows Cabins** (928/478-4415, www.mountainmeadows.com, $90–130 d) all have fireplaces and kitchens; some include a hot tub; head east from Christopher Creek on Highway 260, then turn two miles east down Colcord Road.

$100 and up: Kohl's Ranch Lodge (17 miles east of Payson, 928/478-4211 or 800/331-5645, $120–135 d studios, $140–150 d studio w/fireplace, $230–1,200 cabins w/fireplace) features an impressive A-frame lobby, restaurant, pool, exercise room, and riding stables beside Tonto Creek; most units include a kitchenette or kitchen and all of the cabins have a fireplace.

Forest Service Campgrounds

The Payson Ranger District office (928/474-7900) of the Tonto National Forest provides recreation information. Reservations for individual sites at Houston Mesa and the horse camp and for all of the district's group areas can be made with National Recreation Reservation Service (877/444-6777, www.reserveusa.com).

Houston Mesa Campground, only 1.5 miles north of town, has water, coin showers, a half-mile interpretive trail, and a dump station for $15; take Highway 87 north, then turn right .2 miles on Houston Mesa Road; the main campground is on the left. **Houston Mesa Horse Camp** ($12) across the road is just for people with horses. Both campgrounds may close in winter. There are also two group reservation areas and a trailhead for Houston Mesa Trail nearby.

Ponderosa Campground, 12 miles east of Payson on the south side of Highway 260, is open year-round with water and a dump station for $12; there's a group campground across the highway. **Upper Tonto Creek Campground,** 15 miles east of Payson, then 1 mile north up Forest Road 289, is open with water and a $10 fee mid-April–October. People also camp in undeveloped sites along Forest Road 289 between Highway 87 and the turnoff for Upper Tonto Creek Campground; all of these will be on your left; no water or fee, but there's a toilet. **Horton Picnic Area** has free day-use across the bridge just beyond the turnoff. **Christopher Creek Campground,** 19 miles east of Payson on the south side of Highway 260, provides water with a $12 fee mid-April–October. **Christopher Creek Picnic Area** ($5) and a group reservation area are nearby. **Sharp Creek Campground,** 26 miles east of Payson on the south side of Highway 260, has water and a $15 fee mid-April–October; tenters have a loop just for them; short trails lead to Sharp and Hunter Creeks, which attract wildlife but don't have enough water for fishing.

East Verde River Complex offers primitive camping in a series of recreation areas that begins about five miles in on Houston Mesa Road/Forest Road 199; none have water or fee. **Flowing Springs Recreation Site,** also part of the East Verde River Complex, is the only one with a toilet; head about five miles north of Payson on Highway 87, then turn right .8 miles on Forest Road 272. Many areas of the Tonto National Forest can be used for dispersed camping (no facilities or fee); for example, you can look for a spot off Control and Houston Mesa Roads below the Rim and off Forest Road 300 atop the Rim.

Commercial RV Parks

Payson Campground and RV Resort (808 E. Hwy. 260, 928/472-2267, $15 tent or RV no hookups, $25 RV w/hookups) has a hilltop setting one mile east from the highway junction; guests have a pool, recreation room, Internet access, showers, laundry, and a dump station. **Oxbow Estates RV Park** (3 miles south on the Beeline Hwy., 928/474-2042, $19 tent, $23 RV w/hookups) offers Internet access, showers, laundry, and a dump station. **Lamplighter RV Resort** (3.5 miles east on Hwy. 260, 928/474-5048, $25 RV w/hookups) caters to seniors and has a rec room, showers, and laundry.

Food

Dinner reservations will come in handy on Friday and Saturday at many restaurants. **Cucina Paradiso** (512 N. Beeline Hwy., 928/468-6500, Tues.–Sun. lunch and dinner, $11–18) prepares popular Italian dishes along with hot sandwiches and wood-fired pizza; the wine list offers Italian and California vintages. The **Country Kitchen** (210 E. Hwy. 260, 928/474-1332, $8–13), **Tiny's Family Restaurant** (600 E. Hwy. 260, 928/474-5429, $6–15), and the old-fashioned **Beeline Café** (815 S. Beeline Hwy., 928/474-9960, $5–11) feature home-style cooking daily for breakfast, lunch, and dinner.

Sesame Inn (203 E. Hwy. 260 near Safeway, 928/472-6888, daily lunch and dinner, $6–12) serves Mandarin, Hunan, Szechwan, and other styles of Chinese food. **Fiesta Mexicana** (911 S. Beeline Hwy., 928/468-0709, daily lunch and dinner, $8–14.50) offers a long menu of combos, meat and seafood dishes, enchiladas, and burritos. **Mazatzal Casino** (928/474-6044 or 800/777-7529) has gambling and a restaurant half a mile south of Payson on the Beeline Highway.

The Western-style **Zane Grey Steakhouse & Saloon** (17 miles east of Payson at Kohl's Ranch Resort, 928/478-4211, daily breakfast, lunch, and dinner, $11.50–25) rustles up ribs, a big hit with many visitors, as well as steaks, chicken, trout, seafood, and vegetarian dishes; there's a wine list, too. **Creekside Steakhouse** (23 miles east of Payson in Christopher Creek, 928/478-4557, daily breakfast, lunch, and dinner, $8–25) has a fine selection of steaks along with other meat dishes, trout, seafood, and some vegetarian items.

Bashas's and **Safeway** supermarkets lie on opposite sides of Highway 260 near the junction with the Beeline Highway, and **Wal-Mart Supercenter** lies one block north on the Beeline Highway.

Information and Services

The **Rim Country Regional Chamber of Commerce** (P.O. Box 1380, Payson, AZ 85547, 928/474-4515 or 800/672-9766, www.rimcountrychamber.com, 8 A.M.–5 P.M. Mon.–Fri., 10 A.M.–2 P.M. Sat.–Sun.) sits on the northwest corner of Beeline Highway and Main Street.

Payson Ranger District (1009 E. Hwy. 260, Payson, AZ 85541, 928/474-7900, www.fs.fed.us/r3/tonto, 8 A.M.–5 P.M. Mon.–Fri., also some Sat. in summer) has outdoor recreation information for the surrounding forests, Mogollon Rim, Mazatzals, and other scenic areas; you can purchase books and maps.

The spacious **Payson Public Library** (328 N. McLane Rd., 928/474-9260) has Arizona and Western collections and a children's room, but only Gila County residents get free Internet access. It's next to Rumsey Park northwest of downtown; you can head west on Longhorn Road from the highway junction, turn right on McLane Road, then left at the sign for the park.

Jackalope (234 E. Hwy. 260, 928/474-7081) sells both new and used books near Bashas'. **Wal-Mart Supercenter** (300 N. Beeline Hwy., 928/474-0029) has camping, fishing, and hunting supplies along with a supermarket.

The **post office** (100 W. Frontier St., 928/474-2972) is on the west side of Beeline Highway, one block north of the chamber office. **Payson Regional Medical Center** (807 S. Ponderosa St., 928/474-3222, www.paysonhospital.com) is one block east of the chamber of commerce office.

Getting There

White Mountain Passenger Lines (106 E. Bonita St., one long block south of the highway junction at Payson Packaging, 928/474-5260 or 866/255-4819, www.wmlines.com) runs buses Monday–Saturday between Phoenix and Show Low.

VICINITY OF PAYSON

Shoofly Village

A quarter-mile interpretive trail winds through scant ruins of this prehistoric settlement northeast of town. Occupied 1000–1250, it had a stone wall encircling courtyards, plazas, and about 80 rooms. Part of the trail has been paved for easy access. A pleasant picnic area lies nearby. From Highway 87 on the north edge of Payson, turn northeast three miles on Houston Mesa Road (keep right at the fork about 2 miles in), then turn right at the sign to a parking area.

Tonto Natural Bridge State Park

Deposits left by mineral springs have created the world's largest natural travertine bridge—and it's still growing! The springs flow as they have for many thousands of years, making the massive arch even larger and watering lush vegetation. You might not even realize you're standing on top when you arrive—the bridge measures 400 feet in width, 183 feet in height, and spans a canyon 150 feet wide. Graceful travertine formations underneath look like those inside a limestone cave. A small waterfall cascades over the top of the arch, forming jewel-like droplets of water that sparkle in the sun and create pretty rainbows. The park (928/476-4202, $3/person age 14+) is open 8 A.M.–7 P.M. daily from Memorial to Labor Day weekends, 9 A.M.–5 P.M. daily November–March, and 8 A.M.–6 P.M. daily the rest of the year; closed Christmas. From Payson, go 11 miles north on Highway 87, then turn left three miles on a paved road at the sign. The last 1.5 miles are steep and winding; it's recommended that vehicles and trailers over 16 feet use the parking lot at the top of the grade.

You can admire both sides of the bridge from viewpoints at the top and from trails in the

view through Tonto Natural Bridge

canyon. Wheelchair users can reach three of the viewpoints. On **Waterfall Trail,** you descend steps part way down the canyon to a spring-fed waterfall for a close-up look at travertine formations and some caves; the trail is only 300 feet long one-way. **Gowan Loop Trail** drops 200 feet in elevation to an observation platform at the lower end of the bridge, where you can admire the waterfall and explore the inside of the bridge's vast tunnel-like interior; the trail continues across Pine Creek and ascends the far canyon wall, then loops back across the top of the bridge in about half a mile. The short and steep **Anna Mae Trail** has some loose rock on a descent to the canyon floor just upstream from the bridge. **Pine Creek Trail** descends to the creek above the bridge; markers along the boulder-strewn creekbed show the way down to the bridge; rim to bridge is about half a mile.

Adventurous hikers can rock scramble over huge boulders on a route through the bridge, most easily done in the upstream direction between Gowan Loop and Anna Mae or Pine Creek Trails; high water may occasionally prevent access. For safety and preservation of the environment, park staff ask that you don't enter caves, climb on moss or cliffs, and don't go under the waterfall; there's no swimming or wading inside the bridge. Visitors often see javelina on the park grounds. Pets cannot go on the trails, but they're OK on a leash atop the bridge.

Picnic areas in this pretty forested valley make fine spots for lunch; groups can reserve day-use ramadas. Interpretive programs are offered on some days. A gift shop in the lodge sells books on the region. Groups can arrange tours and overnight accommodations.

Pine

This little town lies 15 miles north of Payson amid pine-forested hills. **Pine-Strawberry Museum** (928/467-3547, www.pinestrawhs.org) has good pioneer exhibits in a 1917 former Latter-Day Saints church beside the Community Center; it's open 1–4 P.M. Sunday and 10 A.M.–4 P.M. Monday–Saturday from May 15 to October 15, then 10 A.M.–2 P.M. Monday–Saturday the rest of the year. The **post office** lies across from the museum. Pine has a few trailer parks that may accept overnighters. Pine-Strawberry Arts & Crafts Guild sponsors **arts and craft festivals** in Pine on the weekends of Memorial Day, July 4, and Labor Day.

The Randall House restaurant (3821 N. Hwy. 87, 928/476-4077, Wed.–Sun. breakfast and lunch, $5–8) has a home-like setting and dates back to 1881; a guest cottage next door costs $125 d including breakfast. **Pine Haven Bed & Breakfast** (928/476-3809, www.pinehavenaz.com, $95–125 d including tax) has a different theme for each room, all with private bath. **Rimside Grill & Cabins** (3270 N. Hwy. 87 on the south side of Pine at MP 267, 928/476-3349 Fri.–Sun. breakfast, Wed.–Sun. lunch and dinner, call for winter hours, $8–14) serves American food in the dining room and on the deck and patio; there's often weekend entertainment in summer; the small cabin costs $85 d and the large one with kitchen is $125–150.

Strawberry

This tiny village sits just below the Mogollon

Rim, 19 miles north of Payson. Wild strawberries used to grow here, but nowadays they're hard to find. The **Strawberry Festival** in June has entertainment, crafts, and strawberries.

Turn west 1.5 miles on Fossil Springs Road at Strawberry Lodge to see Arizona's oldest **schoolhouse** (928/476-3097, 10 A.M.–4 P.M. Sat. and noon–4 P.M. Sun.); pioneers built the one-room log structure in 1885. The very scenic **Fossil Springs Road** continues west and descends a long grade to Fossil Creek, connects with an access road to Childs on the Verde River, then joins Highway 260 near Camp Verde; high-clearance vehicles do best on this largely unpaved road.

The more expensive rooms in **Strawberry Lodge** (Fossil Creek Rd. and Hwy. 87, 928/476-3333, $50–70 d) include fireplaces and balconies; an American restaurant serves breakfast, lunch, and dinner daily ($8–16). **Cabins on Strawberry Hill** (5306 Hwy. 87, 928/476-4252 local or 480/575-7866 Phoenix area, www.azcabins.com, $140 d) have kitchenettes and wood-burning stoves. Each room has its own personality in the **Windmill Corner Inn** (5075 Hwy. 87, 928/476-3064, $63 d weekdays, $78–93 d Fri.–Sat.). **Giuseppe's** (5076 Hwy. 87, 928/476-3355, Fri.–Sun. lunch, Wed.–Sun. dinner, $10–24) serves fine Italian cuisine including steaks, seafood, and pizza.

Tonto Creek Hatchery

Rainbow, brook, cutthroat, and sometimes Apache trout grow up at this hatchery (daily 8 A.M.–4 P.M., 928/478-4200) just below the Mogollon Rim. Visitors can take the interpretive walk, learn about the life cycle of trout, peer into the incubator and production rooms, and view fingerlings and catchable trout in outdoor raceways. A show pond has large fish that you can feed. Trout in the raceways shouldn't be touched or fed because of the danger of spreading diseases. From Payson, head east 17 miles on Highway 260 to Kohl's Ranch Lodge, then turn north 4.2 miles on Forest Road 289 at the sign.

Rancho Tonto Catch-A-Trout (928/478-0002) offers fishing in a pond at an old homestead 2.1 miles in on Forest Road 289, then right .2 miles. You must pay for what you catch. An attractive pine-log guest house ($200 weekdays, $250 Fri.–Sat.) has three bedrooms and can accommodate up to nine people.

Highline National Recreation Area

Highline Trail weaves in and out for 51 miles beneath the cliffs of the Mogollon Rim. Settlers built the trail in the 1800s to link their ranches and homesteads. Today hikers, horseback riders, and mountain bicyclists use the many interconnecting trails for a wide variety of journeys.

Pine Trailhead, at the west end, lies 15 miles north of Payson just off Highway 87. Two-Sixty Trailhead marks the east end, 27 miles east of Payson just off Highway 260. You can also reach the Highline from four other trailheads, from trails descending the Mogollon Rim above, and from valleys below. You can see effects of the 1990 Dude Fire on the central section. The Tonto National Forest *Highline Trails Guide* offers a map and brief trail descriptions; pick it up at Forest Service offices or the Payson Chamber of Commerce.

Mazatzal Wilderness

Native Americans knew this vast country of desert and mountains as Mazatzal (Land of the Deer). The name still fits, as only scattered ruins tell of the tribes, pioneers, and miners who passed this way. The wilderness covers over 252,500 acres beginning 8 miles west of Payson and extending 30 miles south. Climate zones range from the Lower Sonoran Desert, with saguaro and palo verde (2,200–4,000 ft.); up through the dry grasslands, oaks, pinyons, and junipers of the Upper Sonoran Desert (4,000–7,000 ft.); to the Transition Zone, with ponderosa pines and a few pockets of firs on the upper slopes (7,000–7,900 ft.). You might meet deer, javelina, black bear, or even a mountain lion. Hikers in this big country should be self-sufficient with maps, compass, and water; you can't rely on springs and streams in the summer. The 2004 Willow Fire burned more than half of the wilderness and damaged many trails, so check with the Payson Ranger District Office (928/474-7900) for current conditions.

YOUNG AND VICINITY

Remote and off the tourist track, Young is one of Arizona's last cow towns. To get here you must drive largely unpaved roads. Approximate travel times are one hour and 25 minutes from Payson and one hour and 45 minutes from Globe. From the north, take Highway 260 to near Milepost 284 atop the Mogollon Rim, about 33 miles east of Payson, then turn south 24 miles on Forest Road 512; the first 20 miles are dirt road. From the south near Roosevelt Lake, take Highway 188 from Roosevelt or Globe to the junction with Highway 288, then turn north 47 miles; the last 34 miles are dirt. All of these are best avoided after winter snows or heavy rains. Highway 288 has the apt designation "From the Desert to the Tall Pines National Scenic Byway."

In the late 1800s one of Arizona's bloodiest and most savage feuds took place in Pleasant Valley, between Young and the Rim. The trouble started when the Tewksbury clan gave protection to a band of sheep brought into the area in 1887. Cattle owners led by the Graham clan couldn't stand "woollies" and attacked, killing a Navajo sheepherder and destroying or driving away the animals. The Tewksburys retaliated, and the war was on. The fighting didn't end until every Graham had been killed. All efforts by the law to restore order failed; at least 30 people died during the five years of terror. History buffs can visit many of the battle sites near Young. The cemetery near Young Baptist Church, a half mile east of Moon's Saloon, contains marked graves belonging to five members of the Graham clan: Harry Middleton, Al Rose, Charles Blevin, William Graham, and John Graham.

Historians still debate details of the feud. Accounts of the tragedy are given in *A Little War of Our Own* by Don Dedera, *Arizona's Dark and Bloody Ground* by Earle Forrest, and *Globe, Arizona* by Clara Woody and Milton Schwartz. Zane Grey dramatized the events in his novel *To the Last Man.* Grey obtained his material during hunting trips in Pleasant Valley.

Today, a very independent breed of people inhabits Young. These folks, many retired, don't like authority or development. Even the Forest Service—Young's largest employer—represents too much government for some of them.

On the Road

Young's social life revolves around the **Antlers Café** on the south side of town and **Alice's Cantina** on the north side; both serve food, but you won't find a nonsmoking section. **Pleasant Valley Days** lets loose with a parade, entertainment, equestrian events, and arts and crafts on the third weekend in July.

Pleasant Valley Inn (928/462-3593, $55 s, $67 d) has fireplaces, fridges, and microwaves in the rooms. **Valley View Cabins** (928/462-3422, $45 d) offers rentals with kitchens on the south edge of town.

The **post office** is in the northeast part of town. **Pleasant Valley Medical Center** (928/462-3435) provides limited services on some days. There's also a grocery store and gas station in town.

For fishing, hiking, and camping information, contact the Tonto National Forest's **Pleasant Valley Ranger District Office** (P.O. Box 450, Young, AZ 85554, 928/462-4300, www.fs.fed.us/r3/tonto, 7:45–11:45 A.M. and 12:30–4:30 P.M. Mon.–Fri., and Sat. in summer); a sign marks the turnoff on the south side of town.

North of Young

The unfortunate Navajo sheepherder who fell as the first victim of the Pleasant Valley War is buried north of Young. A white cross, pile of stones, and sign mark the spot; from the main road (Forest Road 512), 4 miles north of Young and 20 miles south of Highway 260, turn west nearly 1 mile on Forest Road 200.

Alderwood Campground (elev. 5,200 ft.; no water or fee) is beside Haigler Creek six miles in on Forest Road 200 from Forest Road 512, then west half a mile on Forest Road 200A. **Haigler Canyon Recreation Site** (elev. 5,250 feet; no water or fee) has camping and fishing (trout April–Aug.); it's nine miles in on Forest Road 200 from Forest Road 512; you can also approach it from the north via Highway 260 and Forest Roads 291 and 200.

Valentine Ridge Campground (elev. 6,600 ft.; no water or fee) lies 18 miles north of Young or 6 miles south of Highway 260 via Forest Road 512, then 2 miles east on Forest Road 188. **Colcord Ridge Recreation Site** (no water or fee) is just east on Forest Road 33 from Forest Road 512, about 3 miles south of Highway 260 or 21 miles north of Young. **Airplane Flat Campground** (elev. 6,600 ft.; no water or fee) is about four miles farther in on Forest Road 33. **Upper Canyon Creek Recreation Site** (elev. 6,600 ft.; no water or fee) and **Canyon Creek Hatchery** lie just below the Rim; follow Forest Road 33 in five miles. The fish hatchery features a self-guided tour, open 8 A.M.–4 P.M. daily. Anglers can fish in Canyon Creek for rainbow and brown trout; check local fishing regulations.

Colcord Lookout (elev. 7,513 ft.) offers a sweeping panorama of the Young area and the Mogollon Rim; the tower is open about May–October; turn west three miles on Forest Road 291 from Forest Road 512 (opposite the Forest Road 33 turnoff).

South of Young

McFadden Peak has a road up to its lookout tower; turn west about one mile on Forest Road 561 from Highway 288, 16 miles south of Young

Groups can contact the Pleasant Valley Ranger District office to reserve **Reynolds Creek Group Site** (elev. 5,200 ft.), 19 miles south of Young, for day or overnight use. It's a good base for exploring the Salome and the Sierra Ancha Wilderness Areas and a worthwhile spot in itself for enjoying the pretty creek and wildlife; there's a fee but no potable water.

Workman Creek Waterfalls plunge 200 feet in a canyon south of Young; to get there, go south 21 miles on Highway 288, then turn left 3.2 miles on Forest Road 487 at the sign for Workman Creek Recreation Area, Sierra Ancha Wilderness; the turnoff is between Mileposts 284 and 285. A gate 2.6 miles in is closed December 15–March 31. The last quarter mile may be too rough for cars. On the way to the falls, you'll pass primitive campsites at **Creeksite, Cascade** and **Falls Recreation Sites,** no water or fee. This pretty canyon supports dense stands of Douglas fir and white fir, as well as smaller numbers of Arizona sycamore and the relatively rare Arizona maple.

Forest Road 487 continues 3.7 miles past the falls through pine forests, aspen groves, and meadows to the lookout tower atop Aztec Peak (7,748 ft.); you can get here with a high-clearance vehicle, mountain bike, or on foot. The tower, when open, provides great panoramas of the Sierra Anchas, Roosevelt Lake, Four Peaks, the Mazatzals, and many other features of central Arizona. **Abbey's Way Trail #151** also climbs to the top of Aztec Peak (800 ft. in 2 miles one-way); the trailhead is on the left .6 miles past the falls. **Parker Creek Trail #160** is on the right side of the road 1 mile past the falls; it goes southwest 3.4 miles to Highway 288, dropping 2,100 feet. The **Rim Trail #139** begins a short way down Parker Creek Trail and curves east and north 7.6 miles to Edwards Spring with good views. Most of the hike lies within the Sierra Ancha Wilderness. It makes an easy outing, with only a 500-foot elevation gain.

Coon Creek Trail #254 also branches off Parker Creek Trail for a 4.4-mile, 2,400-foot descent south along Coon Creek to a trailhead at the end of Forest Road 189. **Moody Point Trail #140** begins on the right 2.2 miles past the falls on Forest Road 487; it connects with the Rim Trail and continues east all the way across the Sierra Ancha Wilderness to Cherry Creek (which may be too high to cross when it's in flood) and Forest Road 203; this challenging trail is 8.6 miles long and drops 4,200 feet.

You can find many places for dispersed camping along Forest Road 487 above the falls, but only the established recreation areas can be used below the falls. Hikers can cool off in the **"tubs,"** natural pools in Workman Creek; from the Workman Creek bridge on Highway 288, follow the trail downstream 250 yards. **Rose Creek Campground** (elev. 5,400 ft.) enjoys a beautiful forest setting beside a creek 23 miles south of Young; no drinking water or fee. The turnoff from Highway 288 is between Mileposts 282 and 283.

Wilderness Areas

The 20,850-acre **Sierra Ancha Wilderness** lies 15 miles south of Young and 36 miles north of Globe. Lack of good roads and rugged terrain discourage most visitors—box canyons and sheer cliffs make travel difficult. Elevations range from 3,200 to 7,800 feet. Spring-fed creeks in the eastern portion of the wilderness have carved several short but deep box canyons, including Pueblo, Cold Springs, and Devil's Chasm. Prehistoric Salado built cliff dwellings in these canyons, then departed.

Forest Road 203 (Cherry Creek Rd.) loops around the east side of the Sierra Anchas, providing views into the spectacular canyons. You need a 4WD vehicle for this trip; the northern part of the road is particularly rough. Allow 3.5 hours for the drive. Forest Road 487 and other roads off Highway 288 provide access to trailheads in the high country of the west side. For hiking information and a wilderness map, contact the Forest Service in Young (928/462-4300) or in Phoenix (602/225-5200).

Salome Wilderness, between Young and Roosevelt Lake, protects 18,530 acres of the Salome and lower Workman Creek watersheds. Perennial waters hold trout and provide a rich riparian habitat for wildlife. The upper end and the higher slopes (elev. 6,543 ft.) support pinyon pine and juniper and some Douglas fir and ponderosa pine; the 5.3-mile **Hell's Hole Trail #284** begins at Highway 288 at the Reynold's Trailhead, 19 miles south of Young, and ends at Hell's Hole on Workman Creek in the upper part of the canyon. The lower end of the wilderness (elev. 2,500 ft.) has some saguaro, ocotillo, and chaparral; the two-mile-long **Jug Trail #61** connects Forest Road 60, north of Roosevelt Lake, with the lower end of Salome Creek.

Hellsgate Wilderness, between Young and Payson, preserves 36,780 acres of the watersheds of Tonto, Haigler, Marsh, and Houston Creeks. Sheer cliffs rising above the confluence of Tonto and Haigler Creeks form Hell's Gate; there's good fishing here but only the most adventurous anglers make it in on the steep, difficult **Hellsgate Trail #37,** which descends into Hell's Gate from both rims. The north trailhead is reached from Payson via Highway 260 and Forest Roads 405A and 893, then it's a six-mile hike to the creeks. Hikers with 4WD vehicles can drive to the south trailhead via Forest Roads 129 and 133; from there it's a 2.5-mile hike in. The trail can get very hot in summer; carry plenty of water.

Sedona

Monoliths of vivid red sandstone, seemingly cast adrift from the Mogollon Rim, create a magical setting for the Red Rock Country surrounding Sedona. Oak Creek, which carved much of this landscape, glides gracefully through town.

The prehistoric Hohokam and Sinagua tribes tilled the soil along Oak Creek for corn, beans, and squash long before white people came. American settlers first arrived in the late 1800s to farm and run cattle in the valley. The town dates from 1902, when Theodore Schnebly opened a post office, naming it for his wife, Sedona. In the same year, Schnebly also built a wagon road up the rim to haul vegetables and fruit to Flagstaff and lumber back to Sedona; the journey took about 11 hours each way.

From a tiny agricultural community 40 years ago, Sedona has developed into a major art center, resort, and spiritual retreat. The present area population of more than 17,000 includes many retired people, artists, and nature lovers.

Planning a Visit

Sunny skies and pleasant temperatures prevail here. At an elevation of 4,500 feet, Sedona avoids the extremes of both low desert and high mountains. The community centers around the Highway 89A–Highway 179 junction, referred to as the Y, 28 miles south of Flagstaff. Uptown Sedona lies north of the Y on Highway 89A, which continues on through Oak Creek Canyon. West Sedona stretches out west of the Y along Highway 89A, which goes to Cottonwood. Highway 179 branches off at the Y and goes south to the Village of Oak Creek and on to I-17.

In addition to the surrounding scenery, Sedona's attractions include outstanding art galleries, elegant restaurants, and luxurious resorts.

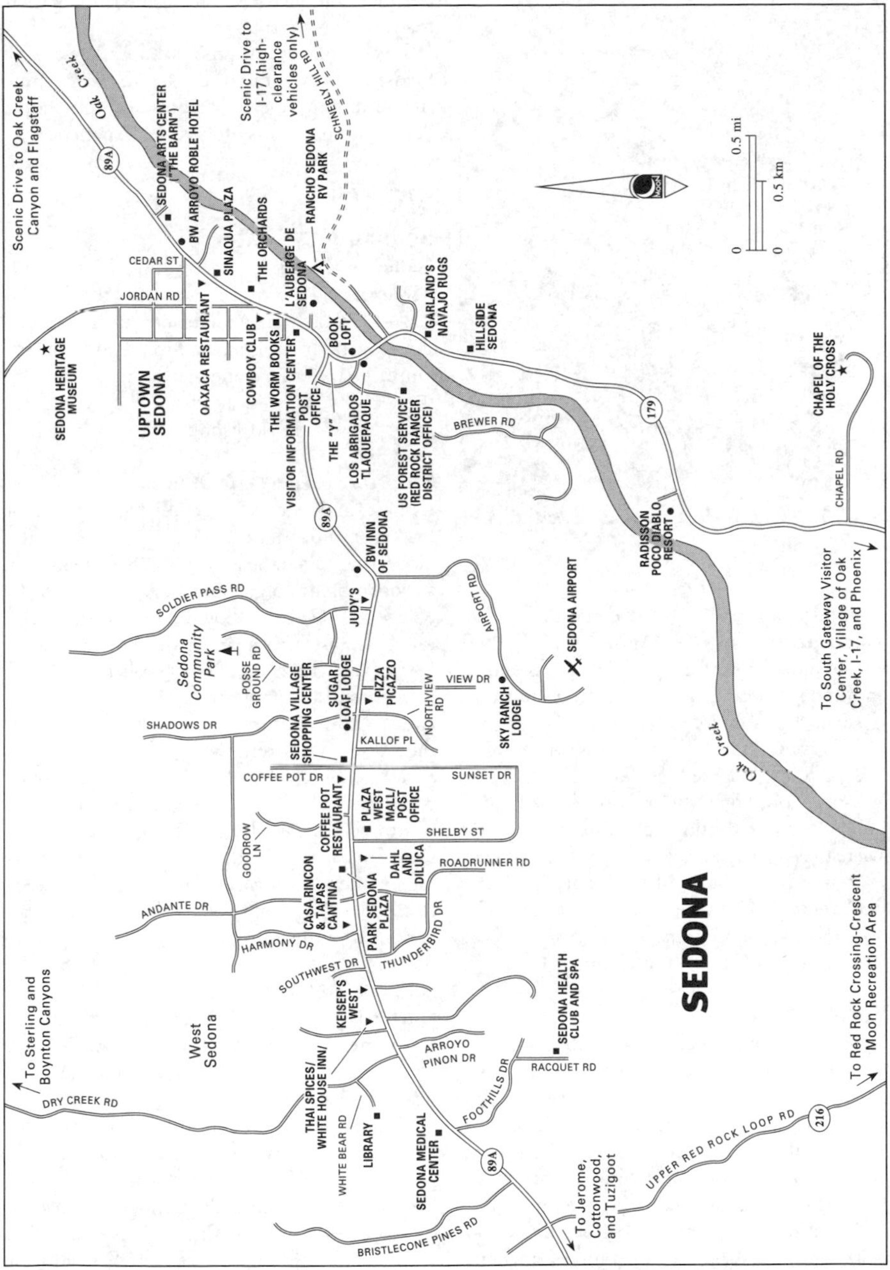
SEDONA
UPTOWN SEDONA
West Sedona
Scenic Drive to Oak Creek Canyon and Flagstaff
Scenic Drive to I-17 (high-clearance vehicles only)
To Sterling and Boynton Canyons
To Jerome, Cottonwood, and Tuzigoot
To Red Rock Crossing-Crescent Moon Recreation Area
To South Gateway Visitor Center, Village of Oak Creek, I-17, and Phoenix
Oak Creek
89A
179
216
SEDONA HERITAGE MUSEUM
SEDONA ARTS CENTER ("THE BARN")
BW ARROYO ROBLE HOTEL
SINAQUA PLAZA
THE ORCHARDS
RANCHO SEDONA RV PARK
SCHNEBLY HILL RD
CEDAR ST
JORDAN RD
OAXACA RESTAURANT
COWBOY CLUB
THE WORM BOOKS
L'AUBERGE DE SEDONA
VISITOR INFORMATION CENTER
POST OFFICE
BOOK LOFT
THE "Y"
LOS ABRIGADOS TLAQUEPAQUE
GARLAND'S NAVAJO RUGS
HILLSIDE SEDONA
US FOREST SERVICE (RED ROCK RANGER DISTRICT OFFICE)
BREWER RD
CHAPEL OF THE HOLY CROSS
CHAPEL RD
RADISSON POCO DIABLO RESORT
BW INN OF SEDONA
JUDY'S
SOLDIER PASS RD
AIRPORT RD
SEDONA AIRPORT
Sedona Community Park
POSSE GROUND RD
SEDONA VILLAGE SHOPPING CENTER
SUGAR LOAF LODGE
PIZZA PICAZZO
VIEW DR
NORTHVIEW RD
SKY RANCH LODGE
SHADOWS DR
KALLOF PL
COFFEE POT DR
SUNSET DR
COFFEE POT RESTAURANT
PLAZA WEST MALL/ POST OFFICE
SHELBY ST
GOODROW LN
CASA RINCON & TAPAS CANTINA
DAHL AND DILUCA
ROADRUNNER RD
ANDANTE DR
PARK SEDONA PLAZA
THUNDERBIRD DR
HARMONY DR
SOUTHWEST DR
KEISER'S WEST
SEDONA HEALTH CLUB AND SPA
ARROYO PINON DR
RACQUET RD
THAI SPICES/ WHITE HOUSE INN/
DRY CREEK RD
WHITE BEAR RD
LIBRARY
SEDONA MEDICAL CENTER
FOOTHILLS DR
UPPER RED ROCK LOOP RD
BRISTLECONE PINES RD
0 0.5 mi
0 0.5 km

© BILL WEIR

Loy Canyon Trail

Fountains and tree-shaded courtyards grace **Tlaquepaque** (t'lah-kay-PAH-kay), a re-created village famed for its art galleries, crafts shops, and fine restaurants. It's named for a suburb of Guadalajara, Mexico.

Hikers head for wilderness areas surrounding Sedona to explore the West Fork of Oak Creek, Wilson Mountain, Munds Mountain, Pumphouse Wash, and hundreds of other areas. Be aware that time-shares and other companies pose as tourist information offices; that's not their first job, so it's best to head for the Gateway Visitor Information Centers and the Sedona–Oak Creek Canyon Chamber of Commerce.

Vortexes

New Age adherents believe that strong spiritual energies concentrate here in vortexes, or psychic-energy points. In the early 1980s, Page Bryant and her otherworldly guide, Albion, identified seven vortexes in the Sedona area. Prominent among them are Bell Rock and Airport Mesa, from which "electric energy" flows to invigorate and inspire visitors, and Red Rock Crossing/Cathedral Rock, bearer of calming "magnetic energy." You may see altars or medicine wheels made of rocks at the sites.

If you'd like to learn more about these energy fields, drop by some of the town's many spiritual and New Age bookstores and gift shops. Some tour operators offer vortex experiences.

SIGHTS

Sedona Arts Center

Galleries (N. Hwy. 89A at Art Barn Road, 928/282-3865, www.sedonaartscenter.com, 10 A.M.–4 P.M. daily, free) on the north edge of town showcase both emerging and well-known artists. Shows change every one or two months. A gift shop sells work by local artists. The Center also offers classes and workshops.

Sedona Heritage Museum

Exhibits in the house and apple-packing shed of the 1930 Jordan farmstead take you back to the pioneering days of Sedona (928/282-7038, www.sedonamuseum.org, about 11 A.M.–3 P.M. daily, $3 age 12+). The Cowboy Room showcases early ranchers and their gear. In the Movie History Room, you'll learn about moviemakers who came to the Red Rock Country as early as the 1920s and the films they made here. Other sections of the museum illustrate work of the U.S. Forest Service and home life. An apple-sorting machine, which still runs, and other equipment lie in nearby sheds. Take Jordan Road north .6 miles from Highway 89A, then turn left into the parking lot after crossing a bridge. A short trail leads to the buildings; travelers with disabilities can park next to the museum.

Airport Mesa

You'll enjoy great views and some short hikes at this vortex site right in the middle of Sedona. The Saddle Loop Trails begin from the trailhead on the left, halfway up Airport Road. A 600-foot trail to Overlook Point climbs 105 feet and connects with the Coconino and Yavapai loops, which total .7 miles for all the segments; there's a map at the trailhead. Continue by road to the top of Airport Mesa for a fine viewpoint on the right. From the Y, head west one mile on Highway 89A, then turn left a half mile up Airport Road.

Chapel of the Holy Cross

The chapel's unusual architecture incorporates a giant cross and presents a striking sight atop a sandstone ridge. Inside, there's a commanding view south toward Bell Rock. A gift shop is downstairs. You're welcome to visit 9 A.M.–5 P.M. daily; donations welcome. Drive three miles south on Highway 179 from Highway 89A, then turn left three-quarters of a mile on Chapel Road.

ENTERTAINMENT, EVENTS, AND RECREATION

Sedona SuperVue Theater (6601 Hwy. 179, 928/284-3214, www.supervue.com) presents a giant-screen movie, *Sedona, the Spirit of Wonder,* a fine introduction to the area with some great aerial photography. Another film is usually shown, too. Look for the theater behind the factory stores in the Village of Oak Creek. Current movies play at the six-screen **Harkins** (2081 W. Hwy. 89A, 928/282-0222).

Events

The Sedona–Oak Creek Canyon Chamber of Commerce (928/282-7722 or 800/288-7336, www.visitsedona.com) is your best source for the latest information. Spring starts off with the **Sedona International Film Festival** (www.sedonafilmfestival.com), usually on the first weekend in March. Sedona goes green for the **St. Patrick's Day Parade** on March 17 or the nearest Saturday. **Chamber Music Sedona** (www.chambermusicsedona.org) attracts musicians from all over the world for 10 days in May; concerts also take place during the September–April season. More than 70 artists exhibit in the **Art and Sculpture Walk** (www.sedonaartscenter.com) in May. Sedona's best chefs offer samples of their food and wine in **Sedona Taste** on the first Sunday in June. Actors present the Bard's plays in **Shakespeare Sedona** (www.shakespearesedona.com) in July. Fireworks light the sky on the **Fourth of July.**

On Labor Day weekend in September, listen to classical music at the **Red Rocks Music Festival** (www.redrocksmusicfestival.com). **Fiesta del Tlaquepaque** (www.tlaq.com) entertains with mariachi bands, Mexican dances, food, arts, and crafts on the second Saturday of September. **Jazz on the Rocks Festival** (www.sedonajazz.com) plays on the fourth Saturday of September. The **Sedona Arts Festival** (www.sedonaartsfestival.org) presents entertainment, arts and crafts, and food, usually on the second weekend of October.

Los Abrigados shows off more than a million lights in the **Red Rock Fantasy of Lights** from the day after Thanksgiving until early January. The **Bed & Breakfast Guild Holiday Tour** in mid-December welcomes visitors with festive decorations and refreshments. More than 6,000 candle-lit luminarias brighten Tlaquepaque in the **Festival of Lights** (www.tlaq.com) on the second Saturday of December.

Recreation

In town, you'll find picnic tables, a playground, ball fields, and outdoor pool at **Sedona Community Park** (525 Posse Ground Road, .3 miles north of Hwy. 89A, 928/282-0112 or 282-7098). The **Sedona Racquet Club & Spa** (100 Racquet Road, 928/282-4197, www.srcs.us) offers tennis courts, a year-round pool, whirlpool tubs, fitness room, aerobics room, restaurant, and day spa. Go 3.8 miles west on Highway 89A from the Y, head south on Foothills Drive, then right on Racquet Road.

Radisson Poco Diablo Resort (2 miles south of the Y on Hwy. 179, 928/282-7333) features tennis courts (call and ask for the tennis shop to make reservations) and a nine-hole golf course. **Oak Creek Country Club** (690 Bell Rock Blvd., 928/284-1660) offers an 18-hole golf course in the Village of Oak Creek; from the Y, head south 6.5 miles on Highway 179, turn right on Bell Rock Road, then it's half a mile on the right. **Sedona Golf Resort** (35 Ridge Trail Dr., 928/284-9355) also has an 18-hole course open to the public on the south side of the Village of Oak Creek; head about 7 miles south on Highway 179, then turn right on Ridge Trail Drive. **Canyon Mesa Country Club** (500 Jacks Canyon Rd., 928/284-0036) offers a nine-hole course in the Village of Oak Creek; take

Highway 179 south 6.8 miles from the Y, then turn left about half a mile on Jacks Canyon Road. **Verde Santa Fe Golf Course** (928/634-5454) is an 18-hole course in Cornville, 15 miles west of town off Highway 89A.

Anglers can pull rainbow trout from Oak Creek. **Rainbow Trout Farm** (3 miles north of Sedona in Oak Creek Canyon, 928/282-5799, open daily) offers easier fishing for a fee, though you must pay for what you catch. Equipment is available and no license is needed.

Trail Horse Adventures (928/282-7252 or 800/723-3538, www.trailhorseadventures.com) offers a wide variety of trail rides and pack trips year-round in the Red Rock Country around Sedona. The stables are five miles southwest of town off lower Red Rock Loop Road.

SHOPPING

Art Galleries

As an art center, what Sedona lacks in size, it makes up for in quality. Its 40 art galleries display an impressive range of original art. Southwestern themes run through much of the work, in colors, forms, Native American motifs, and cowboy legends. Most of the art galleries lie along the first half mile of Highway 179 south of the Y; others can be found in Uptown Sedona along the first half mile of Highway 89A north of the Y.

Fountains, sycamore-shaded courtyards, and Spanish-colonial architecture create a delightful atmosphere at **Tlaquepaque** (.3 miles south on Hwy. 179 from Hwy. 89A, 928/282-4838, www.tlaq.com), an enjoyable starting point for a trip into Sedona's art world. A bit farther south, **Garland's Navajo Rugs** (411 Hwy. 179, 928/282-4070) has an especially fine selection. A couple of blocks farther, **Hillside Sedona** (671 Hwy. 179) offers galleries and restaurants in an attractive shopping area decorated with sculpture. In Uptown Sedona, **Sinagua Plaza** (320 N. Hwy. 89A) has galleries and dining.

Bookstores

The Worm Books & Music (207 N. Hwy. 89A, 928/282-3471) carries an excellent selection of regional, New Age, and general reading, plus topo maps and audio tapes. **The Book Loft** (175 Hwy. 179, 928/282-5173) sells mostly used books along with new regional and children's titles.

The Center for the New Age (341 Hwy. 179, 928/282-2085, www.sedonanewagecenter.com) offers books, local event information, vortex tours, astrological reports, aura photos, and other services and treatments.

Outdoor Gear

Sedona Sports (Creekside Plaza at 251 Hwy. 179, 928/282-1317) has outdoor recreation gear and maps and rents mountain bikes, binoculars, and fishing poles. **Canyon Outfitters** (2701 W. Hwy. 89A, 928/282-5293) carries a large selection of supplies for hiking, backpacking, and climbing. **Mountain Bike Heaven** (1695 W. Hwy. 89A, 928/282-1312) sells and rents mountain bikes and offers parts and repairs.

Factory Outlets

Oak Creek Factory Outlets (6601 S. Hwy. 179 in the Village of Oak Creek, 928/284-2150 or 888/545-7227) features brand-name bargains and a giant-screen movie theater.

ACCOMMODATIONS

You have a choice of about 30 bed and breakfast inns, many motels, and a variety of resorts in the area. Sedona–Oak Creek Canyon Chamber of Commerce (928/282-7722, www.visitsedona.com) provides information on places to stay.

Make reservations if you're coming to Sedona for a weekend during the March–November peak season, when the popular places can fill up fast. Rates listed here apply to the main season, though they can go higher on holidays and lower in the heat of summer. Categories are based on weekend double occupancy. Prices may drop 10–25 percent or so in winter. Travelers on a low budget may prefer to stay in the Camp Verde and Cottonwood areas to the south or in Flagstaff to the north.

Bed-and-Breakfasts

A Touch of Sedona Bed and Breakfast (595 Jordan Rd. in Uptown Sedona, 928/282-6462 or

800/600-6462, www.touchsedona.com, $145–195 d) offers rooms, one with a kitchen and all with a fireplace, plus hot tubs; the owner likes to spoil her guests! Nearby **Apple Orchard Inn** (656 Jordan Rd., 928/282-5328 or 800/663-6968, www.appleorchardbb.com, $135–230 d) has a different Old West theme for each room. Some rooms have fireplaces and most have patios and jetted tubs.

Casa Sedona (55 Hozoni Dr. in West Sedona, 928/282-2938 or 800/525-3756, www.casasedona.com, $165–270 d) offers a "cowboy to lace" range of rooms, each with a fireplace, plus hot tubs. Also in West Sedona, **Lantern Light Inn Bed & Breakfast** (3085 W. Hwy. 89A, 928/282-3419 or 877/275-4973, www.lanternlightinn.com) offers rooms—two have fireplaces—with an elegant country French decor ($125–185 d); a separate guesthouse is great for families ($295). **An Old West Bed and Breakfast** (65 Piki Dr. in West Sedona, 928/204-2737 or 800/801-2737, www.territorialhousebb.com, $125–215 d) offers Western hospitality and d3cor with a common room, hot tub, bicycles, and some fireplaces. **Boots & Saddles Bed & Breakfast** (2900 Hopi Dr. in West Sedona, 928/282-1944 or 800/201-1944, www.oldwestbb.com, $165–245 d) offers Southwestern rooms, all with whirlpool tubs, and some with a fireplace, patio, or balcony; there's a hot tub in the garden.

Stoneflower Bed & Breakfast (70 Chavez Ranch Rd., 928/282-2977 or 800/338-2334, www.stoneflower.com, $95 d) has an outdoor whirlpool tub in a scenic setting near Red Rock Crossing. Almost a mile from the Y junction, **The Inn on Oak Creek** (556 Hwy. 179, 928/282-7896 or 800/499-7896, www.sedona-inn.com, $190–285 d) offers rooms, each with a different outdoor theme, plus fireplaces and whirlpool tubs; some rooms have private decks overlooking Oak Creek. South in the Village of Oak Creek, **The Penrose B&B** (250 Red Butte Dr., 928/284-3030 or 888/678-3030, www.thepenrose.com, $205–240 d) has great views of the Red Rock Country from the rooms, each of which has a porch or balcony. **Adobe Village Graham Inn** (150 Canyon Circle Dr. in the Village of Oak Creek, 928/284-1425 or 800/228-1425, www.sedonasfinest.com) features a different theme for each unit. Standard rooms, all with fireplaces and jetted tubs, go for $189–558 d. Casitas, each with a fireplace and a whirlpool tub, run $359–449 d. Guests have the use of a pool, hot tub, and bicycles.

Canyon Villa Bed & Breakfast Inn (125 Canyon Circle Dr. in the Village of Oak Creek, 928/284-1226 or 800/453-1166, www.canyonvilla.com, $189–279 d) features great views, along with a pool, in a Spanish mission building. Each room has a different decor; some have a fireplace, and all have a patio or balcony.

$50–100

Star Motel (295 Jordan Rd. in Uptown Sedona, 928/282-3641, $60–70 d and up) offers rooms and two kitchenettes. **Iris Garden Inn** (390 Jordan Rd., 928/282-2552 or 800/321-8988, www.irisgardeninn.com, $59–125 d weekdays, $74–125 d Fri.–Sat.) has a garden and patio. **A Touch of the Southwest Suites** (410 Jordan Rd., 928/282-4747 or 800/309-7883, www.atouchofthesouthwest.com, $79–135 d) offers mostly suites with kitchens. **Rose Tree Inn** (376 Cedar St., 928/282-2065 or 888/282-2065, www.rosetreeinn.com, $85–135 d) has some kitchens, some fireplaces, and a hot tub. **Matterhorn Lodge** (230 Apple Ave., 928/282-7176 or 800/372-8207, www.matterhornlodge.com, $119–129 d) provides good views in Uptown Sedona along with a pool and spa; each motel unit has a patio or balcony. **La Vista Motel** (500 N. Hwy. 89A, 928/282-7301 or 800/896-7301, $60–80 d weekdays, $70–90 d Fri.–Sat.) offers a variety of rooms, including kitchenettes, at the north end of town.

Cedars Resort on Oak Creek (20 W. Hwy. 89A, 928/282-7010 or 800/874-2072, $89–129 d) has a pool, hot tub, views, and creek access. Atop Airport Mesa, **Sky Ranch Lodge** (Airport Rd., 928/282-6400 or 888/708-6400, www.skyranchlodge.com, $75–159 d rooms, $189 d cottages) sits high above town; you'll enjoy great views from some units, plus fireplaces, kitchenettes, and a pool. **Sugar Loaf Lodge** (1870 W. Hwy. 89A, 928/282-9451 or 877/282-0632, $50 d weekdays, $65 d Fri.–Sat.) has a pool and hot tub along with some of the lowest rates in town. **White House Inn** (2986 W. Hwy. 89A, 928/282-6680, $42 s, $46 d weekdays, $52 s, $56 d Fri.–Sat.) is low priced and has some kitchenettes. **Sedona Motel** (218 Hwy. 179, 928/282-7187, $70–100 d) lies one block south of Highway 89A.

Down in the Village of Oak Creek, **La Quinta Inns & Suites** (6176 Hwy. 179, 928/284-0711 or 800/531-5900, $79–109 d rooms, $99–159 d suites) includes a deluxe continental breakfast, pool, and hot tub. **Desert Quail Inn** (6626 Hwy. 179, 928/284-1433 or 800/385-0927, $89–159 d) offers a pool and Southwestern decor; some rooms have fireplaces and Jacuzzis.

Lo Lo Mai Springs (928/634-4700, www.lolomai.com, $55–125 d and up) has cabins—all with kitchens—along Oak Creek southwest of town. The 26-acre grounds have shade trees, a pool, hot tub, playground, and volleyball and basketball courts. Head west 10 miles on Highway 89A, turn left 1.7 miles on Page Springs Road/Yavapai County 50, then left at the sign.

$100–150

Los Abrigados Lodge (280 N. Hwy. 89A, 928/282-7125 or 800/542-8484, www.ilxresorts.com) has a pool and some fireplaces. Standard rooms go for $119 d, deluxe studios with a view and fireplace are $139 d, and suites run $169 d. Guests of **Best Western Arroyo Roble Hotel** (400 N. Hwy. 89A, 928/282-4001 or 800/773-3662, www.bestwesternsedona.com, $119–319 d rooms, $319 d creekside villas) have the use of its health club, with indoor and outdoor pools and hot tubs, a sauna, exercise room, and tennis.

Best Western Inn of Sedona (1200 W. Hwy. 89A, opposite the Airport Road turnoff, 928/282-3072 or 800/292-6344, $159 d, $179 d with fireplace) offers terraced rooms—most with views—along with a deluxe continental breakfast, pool, hot tub, and exercise room. **Hampton Inn** (1800 W. Hwy. 89A, 928/282-4700 or 800/426-7866, $129 d weekdays, $139 Fri.–Sat.) provides a deluxe continental breakfast, pool, and hot tub. **Super 8 Motel** (2545 W. Hwy. 89A, 928/282-1533 or 800/858-7245, $79–109 d weekdays, $99–119 d Fri.–Sat.) includes a restaurant and pool. **Days Inn** (2991 W. Hwy. 89A, 928/282-9166 or 800/329-7466, $85 d weekdays, $110 d Fri.–Sat. rooms, add $25 for suites) offers a pool and hot tub. **Southwest Inn at Sedona** (3250 W. Hwy. 89A, 928/282-3344 or 800/483-7422, $159–199 d rooms, $219 d suites) features fireplaces, a pool, and hot tub.

A half-mile south from Highway 89A, **Comfort Inn** (725 Hwy. 179, 928/282-3132 or 800/424-6423, $69–170 d weekdays, $109–170 d Fri.–Sat.) offers a pool and hot tub. Just beyond, **King's Ransom Quality Inn** (771 Hwy. 179, 928/282-7151 or 800/846-6164, $109–170 d) has a restaurant, pool, and hot tub.

In the Village of Oak Creek, **Bell Rock Inn & Suites** (6246 Hwy. 179, 928/282-4161 or 800/881-7625, $99–159 d rooms) features two pools, two hot tubs, a restaurant, and a sports lounge. Nearby **Kokopelli Inn** (6465 Hwy. 179, 928/284-1100 or 888/733-5656, $79–109 d weekdays, $99–159 d Fri.–Sat.) has a pool.

Resorts

The French country inn **L'Auberge de Sedona** (301 L'Auberge Lane, off N. Hwy. 89A .25 miles north of the Y, 928/282-1661 or 800/272-6777 res. only, www.lauberge.com) provides a romantic getaway in a wooded setting beside Oak Creek. You have a choice of cottages ($429–595 d), lodge rooms and suites ($169–375 d), and, on the hill, the Orchards rooms and suites ($105–225 d). Guests enjoy a pool, hot tub, and three dining options, including L'Auberge Restaurant, which serves some of the finest food in Arizona.

Also in Uptown Sedona, **Amara Creekside Resort** (310 N. Hwy. 89A, 928/282-4828 or 866/455-6610, www.amararesort.com, $179–339 d rooms, $389–429 d suites) presents a variety of contemporary rooms and suites, all with a patio or balcony and some with whirlpool bath. Guests enjoy the creek, canyon views, a pool, hot tub, exercise room, and a fine American/Southwestern restaurant.

Next to Tlaquepaque, one block south on Highway 179 from the Y, **Los Abrigados** (160 Portal Lane, 928/282-1777 or 800/521-3131, www.ilxresorts.com, $225–395 d suites, $1,500 two-bedroom house) includes three restaurants, exercise equipment, a sauna, pools, whirlpools, tennis courts, 18-hole miniature golf, a virtual golf center, and the Sedona Spa, which provides treatment and fitness programs.

Radisson Poco Diablo Resort (2 miles south on Hwy. 179 from the Y, 928/282-7333 or 800/333-3333, www.radissonsedona.com, $99–299 d) features a nine-hole executive golf course, tennis center, fitness center, pools, hot tubs, and a restaurant near Oak Creek. Some rooms include fireplaces and whirlpool tubs.

Northwest of Sedona: The **Enchantment Resort** (928/282-2900 or 800/826-4180, www.enchantmentresort.com, $295–395 d casita, $395–1075 d suite) lies in a delightful setting at the mouth of Boynton Canyon. The Southwestern-style suites and casitas all have private decks and many also include fireplaces and kitchens. Guests can take advantage of the spa facilities, indoor and outdoor pools, tennis courts, children's camp, and restaurants—all amid splendid canyon scenery. A destination spa, Mii amo (journey or passage), on the resort grounds provides many types of therapies and activities along with rooms, suites, and a restaurant. From the Y, head west 3.1 miles on W. Highway 89A, then turn right 5 miles on Dry Creek Road, following signs on paved roads.

Oak Creek Canyon: These nestle in the woods along Oak Creek. Distances are from the north edge of Sedona.

Red Rock Lodge (just north of town at 901 N. Hwy. 89A, 928/282-3591, www.redrocklodge.com, $49–175 d) has a fireplace in some rooms. **Briar Patch Inn** (2.6 miles north at 3190 N. Hwy. 89A, 928/282-2342 or 888/809-3030, www.briarpatchinn.com, $179–345 d) features cabins with private patios on nine acres beside the creek; most have wood-burning fireplaces and some have kitchens; breakfast is included—TV and phones are not.

Oak Creek Terrace Resort (4 miles north at 4548 N. Hwy. 89A, 928/282-3562 or 800/224-2229, www.oakcreekterrace.com, $82–225 d) gives you a choice of motel rooms, bungalows, or a cabin. Some units include kitchenettes, fireplaces, or hot tubs. **Slide Rock Lodge** (6 miles north at 6401 N. Hwy. 89A, 928/282-3531, www.sliderocklodge.com, $79–125 d) is just half a mile south of Slide Rock State Park. Rooms, some with wood-burning fireplaces, have a knotty pine decor but no phones or TVs. Sterling Pass Trail begins nearby.

Garland's Oak Creek Lodge (7.7 miles north at 8067 N. Hwy. 89A, 928/282-3343, www.garlandslodge.com, $140–175 s, $200–235 d) offers small log cabins overlooking the creek and larger cabins with wood-burning fireplaces farther back. Repeat visitors to this idyllic spot often book all of the cabins, but you may get in after a cancellation, especially on weekdays. Rates include breakfast, afternoon tea, and dinner; there's a two-night minimum. The dining room, also open to the public by reservation, serves outstanding food. The lodge closes on Sundays at noon—no dinners or overnight guests—and reopens Monday at 3 P.M. Its season runs from late March or early April to mid-November.

Junipine Resort (8 miles north at 8351 N. Hwy. 89A, 928/282-3375 or 800/742-7463, www.junipine.com, $170–320 d weekdays, $210–355 d Fri.–Sat.) features a kitchen and two fireplaces in each unit; some also have hot tubs and a view. The resort's café serves Southwestern and continental cuisine. Hikers can follow creek-side trails or head up to the rim.

Forest Houses Resort (8.9 miles north at 9275 N. Hwy. 89A, 928/282-2999, www.foresthousesresort.com, $80–140 d) lies across a narrow ford. Each house has distinctive stonework and rough-sawn wood, along with a kitchen and either a fireplace or wood-burning stove, a deck or patio, but no TVs. The larger units will appeal to families. Trails lead along the creek and climb up to the rim. There's a four-night minimum stay in summer, two nights other times, and it's closed January 1–mid-March.

Don Hoel's Cabins (9.1 miles north at 9440 N. Hwy. 89A, 928/282-3560 or 800/292-4635, www.hoels.com, $100–135 d) offers cozy cabins—no two alike—with kitchens. Only the common Parlor Room has TV. Hoel's Indian Shop, across the highway and north a bit, offers Native American work.

Forest Service Campgrounds

You'll find the prettiest spots in Oak Creek

Canyon off Highway 89A. You can make reservations for some sites at Cave Springs and Pine Flat (877/444-6777, www.reserveusa.com). Otherwise you'll need to arrive by Friday morning or even Thursday to find a weekend spot at any of the campgrounds. All have a $16 fee, plus $7 for a second vehicle. None provide hookups, but Cave Springs offers coin showers. Trailers and large RVs (up to 36 ft.) should head for Cave Springs or Pine Flat Campgrounds.

Manzanita Campground, 5.6 miles north of Sedona on the right, is open year-round and is often the first to fill up. **Bootlegger Campground,** 8.4 miles north of town on the left, is small—only 10 sites—and lacks drinking water, but some people prefer it; it closes November–mid-April. **Cave Springs Campground,** 11.1 miles north, lies west across the creek and has the most secluded setting; it also closes November–mid-April. **Pine Flat Campground,** one mile farther, has loops on both sides of the highway; it closes mid-November–March. **Chavez Group Campground** lies at the south edge of town off Highway 179, just beyond Radisson Poco Diablo Resort. Sites are available by reservation only (877/444-6777, www.reserveusa.com).

Oak Creek Canyon and most of the Red Rock Country are restricted to established campground use. Backpackers can camp in wilderness areas if they go at least one mile in from the wilderness boundary. The Forest Service in Sedona (928/282-4119, www.fs.fed.us/r3/coconino) can advise on both established and dispersed camping.

RV Parks

Hawkeye RV Park (40 Art Barn Rd. in Uptown Sedona, 928/282-2222, $17 tents, $22.50–$27.50 RVs w/hookups) offers year-round sites with showers, laundry, and access to Oak Creek; the campground may close soon, so it's a good idea to call ahead. The other RV parks in town also stay open year-round, but don't accept tents.

Rancho Sedona RV Park (928/282-7255 or 888/641-4261) offers shaded sites beside Oak Creek with showers, laundry, store, and phone/Internet connections ($29 w/water & electric, $36.50 w/full hookups, $40 for the adult quiet area, $55 for full-service sites close to the creek). From the Y, head south a half-mile on Highway 179, turn left on Schnebly Hill Road, then left on Bear Wallow Lane.

Lo Lo Mai Springs (928/634-4700, www.lolomai.com) has tent sites ($25 s, $30 d), RV sites ($30–40 w/hookups), and cabins ($55–125 d and up) along Oak Creek southwest of town. The 26-acre grounds have shade trees, showers, a pool, hot tub, playground, and volleyball and basketball courts. Head west 10 miles on Highway 89A, turn left 1.7 miles on Page Springs Road/Yavapai County 50, then left at the sign.

The nearby Verde Valley offers additional places to camp year-round.

FOOD

Resort Dining

L'Auberge de Sedona (301 L'Auberge Lane, off N. Hwy. 89A one quarter mile north of the Y, 928/282-1667, www.lauberge.com) prepares outstanding French cuisine in an elegant setting. Open daily for breakfast ($15–20) and lunch ($20–25) at the Terrace on the Creek. In the evening, you dine indoors (or on the terrace in summer) with a choice of dinner entrées ($30–40), a tasting menu ($75), and tasting menu with wine pairings ($120). Reservations should be made for dinner, but aren't needed for breakfast and lunch. Evening dress code is business casual.

The Orchards Bar & Grill (254 N. Hwy. 89A, 928/282-7200, daily breakfast, lunch, and dinner, $13–21) prepares creative regional American fare—chicken, ribs, fish, pasta, pizza, and sandwiches—using fresh ingredients. **Gallery on Oak Creek Restaurant** (310 N. Hwy. 89A, 928/282-4828 or 866/455-6610, www.amararesort.com, daily breakfast, lunch, and dinner, $17–30) at the Amara Creekside Resort serves creative American and Southwestern food. Artwork decorates the interior. You'll have a view of the red rocks from both the indoor and patio dining areas.

Steak & Sticks (Los Abrigados, 160 Portal Lane, 928/204-7849, Wed.–Mon. dinner, $14–30) features steaks, lamb, chicken, fish, and Sedona's only billiard club. **Joey Bistro** (Los Abrigados Resort, 160 Portal Lane, .2 miles south on Hwy. 179 from Hwy. 89A, 928/204-5639, daily dinner, may close Wed. Feb.–May, $9–26) offers tempting Italian pasta, meat, and seafood dishes. **T. Carl's** (Radisson Poco Diablo Resort, 2 miles south on Hwy. 179 from Hwy. 89A, 928/282-7333, ext. 235, daily breakfast, lunch, and dinner, $17–26) offers an extensive menu of Southwestern and continental dishes. There's a Sunday buffet for $20. The restaurant is named after Sedona Schnebly's husband.

Yavapai Restaurant (Enchantment Resort, 525 Boynton Canyon Rd. off Dry Creek Rd., 928/204-6000, daily breakfast, lunch, and dinner, $23–38) serves fine American and Southwest cuisine. You can dine inside or out on the terrace and take in beautiful canyon views. On Sundays, you can enjoy a jazz buffet brunch for $34.50. Reservations should be made for all meals.

Garland's Oak Creek Lodge (7.7 miles north of Sedona on Hwy. 89A, 928/282-3343, $30–38) prepares memorable American regional cuisine for breakfast and the four-course dinner during the April–mid-November season; reservations required. **Junipine Café** (Junipine Resort, 8 miles north of Sedona on Hwy. 89A, 928/282-7406, daily breakfast, lunch, and dinner, may close some days in winter, $10–18) serves continental and Southwestern fare.

American

Cowboy Club (241 N. Hwy. 89A in Uptown Sedona, 928/282-4200, daily lunch and dinner, $14–33) features "high desert cuisine" of Western-style steak, ribs, chicken, and fish) for dinner, as well as lighter fare for lunch. **Canyon Breeze** (300 N. Hwy. 89A in Uptown Sedona, 928/282-2112, daily breakfast, lunch, and dinner, $6–10) has great views of Red Rock country from the deck out back, along with such popular fare as sandwiches, pizza, fajitas, and tacos.

Judi's Restaurant (40 Soldier Pass Rd., 928/282-4449, Mon.–Sat. lunch and daily dinner, $11–22.50) is a long-running dining spot that's popular with the locals. You can choose from many seafood and meat dishes, a few pasta entrées, plus Judi's famous deserts. Judi's husband, Larry, is in the restaurant business too—he runs Keiser's West.

Shugrue's Hillside Grill (Hillside Sedona at 671 Hwy. 179, 928/282-5300, daily lunch and dinner, $19–48) prepares seafood, such as the signature flame-broiled shrimp scampi, along with pasta and meat dishes.

Sedona Airport Restaurant (928/282-3576, daily breakfast, lunch, and dinner, $11–22) offers creative dining while you watch the planes come and go atop Airport Mesa. It's especially good for breakfast. Follow Airport Road to its end from W. Highway 89A.

Heartline Café (1610 W. Hwy. 89A, 928/282-0785, daily lunch and dinner, $15–27) serves meat, seafood, and vegetarian items "with a twist." **Coffee Pot Restaurant** (2050 W. Hwy. 89A, 928/282-6626, daily breakfast and lunch, $3.50–11) has both indoor and patio dining. The menu features 101 varieties of omelets; kids may go for #101 with peanut butter, jelly, and banana.

Keiser's West (2920 W. Hwy. 89A, 928/204-2088, daily breakfast, lunch, and dinner, but no dinner Sun., $7.50–19) cooks up great breakfasts and also draws the crowds for its steak, seafood, pasta, barbecue, and Mexican entrées.

In the Village of Oak Creek, **Desert Flour Bakery & Bistro** (Castle Rock Plaza, 6446 Hwy. 179, 928/284-4633, daily breakfast and lunch, Wed.–Sat. for dinner, $9.50–14) prepares wood-fired pizza and such entrées as steak and salmon along with specialty breads, baked goodies, sandwiches, and salads.

Continental

René at Tlaquepaque (Tlaquepaque, .3 miles south on Hwy. 179 from Hwy. 89A, 928/282-9225, daily lunch and dinner, $20–36) serves outstanding continental cuisine in an elegant dining room and on Patio Azul. Specialties include Colorado rack of lamb, roast duck with sun-dried cherry sauce, seitan tofu Wellington, and flambé deserts.

The Hideaway (Country Square shopping center on Hwy. 179, .2 miles south of Hwy. 89A, 928/282-4204, daily lunch and dinner, $10–12.50) serves sandwiches for lunch and fine Italian food for dinner. There's a lounge upstairs and the main dining room below. Decks on both levels overlook Oak Creek and are very popular with diners.

Dahl and DiLuca Ristorante Italiano (2321 W. Hwy. 89A, across from Safeway, 928/282-5219, nightly dinner, $11–28) features a chef from Rome who prepares northern Italian cuisine such as the popular veal and fettuccine cioppino dishes. Diners enjoy live music and a choice of indoor and patio seating. **Pizza Picazzo** (1855 W. Hwy. 89A, 928/282-4140, daily lunch and dinner, $12.50–23.50) serves award-winning gourmet pizza.

Cucina Rústica (Tequa Plaza, 928/284-3010, nightly dinner, $16–26) in front of the Hilton in the Village of Oak Creek offers superb Mediterranean cuisine. The romantic dining rooms, two with fireplaces, seem right out of a European castle. On summer evenings, many diners enjoy being outside on the patios. The menu changes frequently but always features veal and fresh fish; you can even order takeout.

Pago's Pizzeria & Italian Cuisine (Castle Rock Plaza in the Village of Oak Creek, 928/284-1939, daily lunch and dinner, $10–18) fixes chicken, veal, seafood, pasta, calzone, pizza, and subs.

Mexican

El Rincon Restaurante Mexicano (Tlaquepaque, 928/282-4648, daily lunch and dinner, $4–15) serves excellent food, including fruit chimichangas and Navajo pizza, with indoor and shaded patio seating.

Javelina Cantina (671 Hwy. 179 in Hillside Sedona, 928/203-9514, daily lunch and dinner, $11–17) prepares a variety of popular standbys and new specialties, including fish tacos, chili rellenos, and fajitas.

Casa Rincon & Tapas Cantina (2620 W. Hwy. 89A, 928/282-4849, daily lunch and dinner, $4–21.50) features Southwestern and Mexican cuisine including such favorites as fajitas and grilled Oak Creek trout. Bands or entertainers perform most nights.

Asian

India Palace (1910 W. Hwy. 89A in Bashas's Shopping Center, 928/204-2300, daily lunch and dinner, $8–15) uses wonderful spices in a north India style. There's a good-value buffet option at lunch, and a choice of entrées and set meals at dinner. Also in Bashas's Shopping Center, **Peking Inn** (928/282-3118, daily lunch and dinner, $7–15) serves Mandarin, Szechuan, and other Chinese cuisines. Both lunch and dinner have buffet and à la carte options.

Takashi Japanese Restaurant (465 Jordan Rd. in Uptown Sedona, 928/282-2334, Tues.–Fri. lunch, Tues.–Sun. dinner, $18–24) serves a variety of Japanese styles and sushi. **Thai Spices** (2986 W. Hwy. 89A, 928/282-0599, Mon.–Sat. lunch and dinner, $6–12.50) cooks flavorful fresh Thai food and offers many vegetarian items. It's next to the White House Inn.

Mandarin House (6486 Hwy. 179 in Village of Oak Creek, 928/284-9088, daily lunch and dinner $6–23) offers Mandarin, Hunan, and Szechuan cuisines. **Sasaki Japanese Restaurant** (65 Bell Rock Blvd. in the Village of Oak Creek, 928/284-1757, daily dinner, $13.50–45) features a large menu.

INFORMATION AND SERVICES

Gateway Visitor Information Centers

Both Sedona–Oak Creek Canyon Chamber of Commerce and Coconino National Forest people staff the information desk of **Uptown Gateway** (P.O. Box 478, Sedona, AZ 86339, 928/282-7722 or 800/288-7336, www.visitsedona.com). Hours are 9 A.M.–3 P.M. Sunday, 8:30 A.M.–5 P.M. Monday–Saturday; winter hours (Nov.–March) run 9 A.M.–5 P.M. Monday–Saturday It's at the corner of N. Highway 89A and Forest Road, a block north of the Y.

If you're coming in on Highway 179 from I-17, the **South Gateway** will be on your left in the Tequa Plaza as you enter the Village of Oak Creek; it's set back a block from the highway. Both chamber (928/284-9582) and Forest Service (928/284-5324) people offer information here 8:30 A.M.–5 P.M. daily, except that the chamber office closes at 3 P.M. on Sunday.

Oak Creek Vista serves as the **North Gateway** (8 A.M.–5 P.M. daily except when blocked by snow), well worth a stop for the view if you're coming on Highway 89A from Flagstaff. This is the smallest visitors center, and focuses mostly on recreation in the national forest; you can purchase books and maps. Oak Creek Vista is 12 miles south of Flagstaff and 15.3 miles north of Sedona.

Oak Creek Visitor Center (928/203-0624, 8 A.M.–4:30 P.M. daily) offers recreation information, fishing licenses, maps, and some books under the trees at the south end of Indian Gardens, 3.5 miles north of Sedona on Highway 89A.

Coconino National Forest

The **Red Rock Ranger District** (250 Brewer Road, P.O. Box 300, Sedona, AZ 86339, 928/282-4119, www.fs.fed.us/r3/coconino, 8 A.M.–4:30 P.M. Mon.–Fri.) supplies information on camping, hiking, Native American ruins, backroad drives, and road conditions in the national forest surrounding Sedona. You can also purchase regional maps and books. In 2006 or 2007, the office will be moving to a new location, possibly on Hwy. 179 near the Woods Canyon Trailhead.

Library

Sedona Public Library (3250 White Bear Rd., 928/282-7714, www.sedonalibrary.org) is open noon–5 P.M. Sunday, 10 A.M.–8 P.M. Monday and Wednesday, 10 A.M.–6 P.M. Tuesday and Thursday, and 10 A.M.–5 P.M. Friday–Saturday; head west 3.1 miles on Highway 89A from the Y, turn north on Dry Creek Road, then make the first left on White Bear Road.

Services

The main **post office** (928/282-3511) is on Highway 89A just west of the Y; another is in West Sedona at 2081 W. Highway 89A on the southwest corner with Sunset Drive. **Sedona Medical Center** (3700 W. Hwy. 89A, 928/204-3000) is on the west edge of town. The nearest hospital is 19 miles southwest of Sedona at the **Verde Valley Medical Center** (269 S. Candy Lane in Cottonwood, 928/634-2251, www.nahealth.com).

GETTING THERE

Shuttles

The **Sedona–Phoenix Shuttle** (928/282-2066 or 800/448-7988 in Arizona, www.sedona-phoenix-shuttle.com), travels about eight times daily south to Camp Verde, Cottonwood, and Sky Harbor Airport ($40 one-way, $75 round-trip). The shuttle leaves from Super 8 Motel on W. Highway 89A in Sedona and from Bell Rock Inn in the Village of Oak Creek. **Ace Xpress Shuttle Service** (928/639-3357 Cottonwood or 800/336-2239, www.acexpress-shuttle.com) provides door-to-door service from Sedona and the Verde Valley to Sky Harbor Airport ($51 one-way, $84 round-trip).

GETTING AROUND

For a taxi, call **Bob's Taxi Service** (928/282-1234). Rental cars are available at the airport and in town. **Farabee Jeep Rental** (3009 W. 89A, 928/282-8700) will put you in the driver's seat and make suggestions for exploring local back roads.

Ground Tours

Sedona Trolley (276 W. Hwy. 89A, 928/282-5980, www.sedonatrolley.com) provides two 55-minute tours of town and the surrounding area; the chamber offices have a schedule.

© BILL WEIR

The challenging Broken Arrow Trail, navigated by Pink Jeep Tours, thrills riders with its steep grades and red rock scenery.

© BILL WEIR

Sedona on a Red Rock Bi-Plane tour

Many companies offer jeep trips into Sedona's rugged and spectacular backcountry. You have a choice of relatively gentle rides or serious four-wheeling, though drivers take it slow and easy on the rough sections. Kids under 12 or so get a discount. **Pink Jeep Tours** (204 N. Hwy. 89A, 928/282-5000 or 800/873-3662, www.pinkjeep.com) has been taking visitors around for more than 45 years. Their scenic, prehistoric ruin, rock art, and hiking trips cost $40–95 for 1.5–4 hours. **A Day in the West** (252 N. Hwy. 89A, 928/282-4320 or 800/973-3662, www.adayinthewest.com) offers a variety of scenic trips including a one- or two-hour jaunt up an old wagon road to a viewpoint for $28–45, a 1.5-hour tour on the popular Broken Arrow Trail for $50, and the 4.5- to 5-hour Western Experience that combines a Jeep tour, horseback ride, and cookout for $130. **Sedona Red Rock Jeep Tours** (270 N. Hwy. 89A, 928/282-6826 or 800/848-7728, www.redrockjeep.com) offers 1.5- to 3.5-hour scenic trips for $39–99, 3- to 4.5-hour archaeology tours for $79–135, 2.25-hour vortex experiences for $192, and a variety of horseback rides for $54–99. **Adventure Company** (Tlaquepaque, 928/204-1973 or 877/281-6622, www.sedonajeeptours.com) runs a variety of scenic and vortex trips of 1–2.75 hours that cost $35–65. Or, if you'd rather drive, the company will put you behind the wheel of a Jeep Wrangler on a tag-along tour and guide you via two-way radio, 2.5 hours costs $95, 4 hours is $125.

Earth Wisdom Jeep Tours (293 N. Hwy. 89A, 928/282-4714 or 800/482-4714, www.earthwisdomtours.com) presents scenic, sacred wheel, vortex, ruin, hiking, and horseback trips along with facts on Indian lore, spirituality, and nature. Excursions run 2–6 hours and cost $48–135. **Spirit Steps Tours** (928/282-4562 or 800/728-4562, www.spiritsteps.org) has a spiritual emphasis on vortex trips (3–4.5 hours), Native American ruin excursions (3–8 hours), and other programs ($20/hour/person).

Air Tours

These provide amazing perspectives of the Sedona area. **Red Rock Bi-Plane Tours/Sky Safari** (airport tour terminal, 928/204-5939 or 888/866-7433, www.sedonaairtours.com) offers exciting rides in a Waco open-cockpit biplane and less expensive rides in a Cessna; flights range from a 15-minute loop ($60 for the bi-plane, $39 in a Cessna) to a 45-minute grand tour ($149 bi-plane, $79 Cessna).

AeroSedona (airport main terminal, 928/282-7768, www.aerosedona.com) will show you the scenery from a Cessna on tours of 15–45 minutes ($35–90). **Sedona Sky Treks** (airport main terminal, 928/282-6628, www.skytreks.com) heads out to the Grand Canyon and Monument Valley on a variety of tours, some with ground excursions. The shortest Grand Canyon flight takes two hours and costs $165.

Arizona Helicopter Adventures (airport main terminal, 928/282-0904 or 800/282-5141, www.azheli.com) offers 12- to 35-minute tours of the Sedona area for $58–138 and a 2.5-hour ride all the way to the Grand Canyon for $630.

Fly high in a balloon with **AeroZona Balloon Company** (928/282-1499, www.azballoon.com), **Sky High Balloon Adventures** (928/204-1395 or 800/551-7597, www.skyhighballoons.com), **Northern Light Balloon Expeditions** (928/282-2274 or 800/230-6222, www.northernlightballoon.com), or **Red Rock Balloon Adventures** (928/284-0040 or 800/258-3754, www.redrockballoons.com).

Red Rock Country

Gorgeous scenery of rock and forest surrounds Sedona on all sides. Approaches to Sedona on Highway 179 or the even more dramatic Schnebly Hill Road (unpaved), both from I-17, inspire awe. The drive along Oak Creek Canyon north of town is one of the most scenic in the state. Back roads branch off from Sedona in many directions, but most of these are rough and require a high-clearance vehicle. Hikers have the most options. Two wilderness areas of pinnacles, mesas, and canyons begin at the edge of town—Munds Mountain Wilderness has 18,150 acres to the southeast and Red Rock/Secret Mountain Wilderness protects 43,950 acres to the northwest. Sedona's famous red rocks belong to the Schnebly Hill Formation, composed of ancient coastal deposits.

Red Rock Passes

Most of this land lies in the Red Rock Ranger District of the Coconino National Forest. To improve and maintain roads and trails, the Forest Service requires visitors to display one of the Golden Passes (or a National Parks pass w/hologram) or to purchase a Red Rock Pass to park anywhere in the forest near Sedona, except at one of the concession-operated day-use areas or campgrounds, which have separate fees. You don't need a pass if you stop and stay close and within sight of your vehicle to admire the scenery. The passes are available at gateway visitor information centers, from vending machines on some back roads, from the Forest Service, and from some local shops and resorts. You can purchase daily ($5), weekly ($15), and annual passes ($20 or $40). The $40 annual pass includes unlimited entries for day use at the concession-operated Grasshopper Point, Banjo Bill, Call of the Canyon, and Crescent Moon areas; Golden Age and Golden Access cardholders get a 50 percent discount on this pass. You can find out more about the passes at www.redrockcountry.org. The two state parks near Sedona have separate admissions and are not part of the Red Rock Pass program.

Hiking

Rugged canyons, delicate natural arches, and solitude await those who venture into the backcountry, much of which has changed little since prehistoric times. Hiking possibilities are virtually limitless—you can venture out on easy day hikes or chart a weeklong trek. The Red Rock Ranger District has 80–90 trails with plans to double that number. Vehicle break-ins have been a problem at trailheads, so you'll want to remove all valuables.

Spring and autumn offer the most pleasant temperatures, but hiking is possible all year. Summer visitors can avoid the 100°F-plus desert temperatures by starting early or heading for the

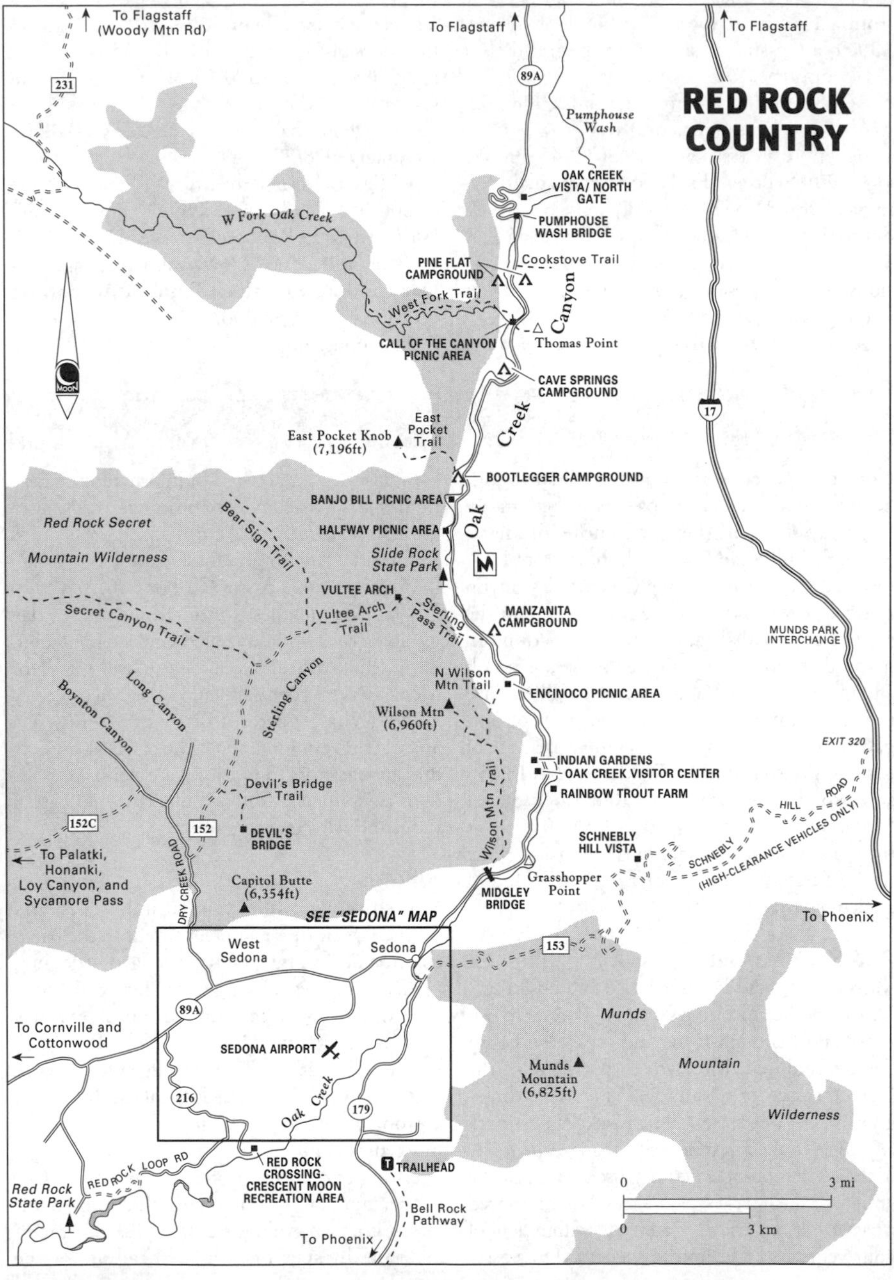
RED ROCK COUNTRY
To Flagstaff (Woody Mtn Rd)
To Flagstaff
To Flagstaff
231
89A
Pumphouse Wash
OAK CREEK VISTA/ NORTH GATE
PUMPHOUSE WASH BRIDGE
W Fork Oak Creek
PINE FLAT CAMPGROUND
Cookstove Trail
West Fork Trail
Oak Creek Canyon
CALL OF THE CANYON PICNIC AREA
Thomas Point
CAVE SPRINGS CAMPGROUND
17
East Pocket Knob (7,196ft)
East Pocket Trail
BOOTLEGGER CAMPGROUND
BANJO BILL PICNIC AREA
HALFWAY PICNIC AREA
Red Rock Secret Mountain Wilderness
Bear Sign Trail
Slide Rock State Park
VULTEE ARCH
Vultee Arch Trail
Sterling Pass Trail
MANZANITA CAMPGROUND
Secret Canyon Trail
MUNDS PARK INTERCHANGE
N Wilson Mtn Trail
ENCINOCO PICNIC AREA
Long Canyon
Boynton Canyon
Sterling Canyon
Wilson Mtn (6,960ft)
EXIT 320
INDIAN GARDENS
OAK CREEK VISITOR CENTER
RAINBOW TROUT FARM
Wilson Mtn Trail
Devil's Bridge Trail
152C
152
DEVIL'S BRIDGE
SCHNEBLY HILL VISTA
SCHNEBLY HILL ROAD (HIGH-CLEARANCE VEHICLES ONLY)
To Palatki, Honanki, Loy Canyon, and Sycamore Pass
DRY CREEK ROAD
Capitol Butte (6,354ft)
Grasshopper Point
MIDGLEY BRIDGE
SEE "SEDONA" MAP
To Phoenix
West Sedona
Sedona
153
89A
Munds Mountain Wilderness
To Cornville and Cottonwood
SEDONA AIRPORT
Munds Mountain (6,825ft)
216
Oak Creek
179
RED ROCK LOOP RD
RED ROCK CROSSING-CRESCENT MOON RECREATION AREA
TRAILHEAD
Red Rock State Park
Bell Rock Pathway
To Phoenix
0
3 mi
0
3 km

high country; winter hikers keep to the desert and canyon areas when snow blocks trails in the ponderosa pine forests above.

For information on backcountry travel, contact the U.S Forest Service office in Sedona (250 Brewer Road, 928/282-4119), or one of the gateway visitor information centers. The Coconino Forest map shows back roads and many trails. Also, consult *Sedona Hikes* by Richard and Sherry Mangum.

Mountain Biking

Cyclists cannot ride in the wilderness areas, but they have many trails to explore elsewhere. The Forest Service offers handouts on places to ride and sells maps. Popular areas include Brins Mesa northwest of town, Little Horse Trail (can be a loop with the Broken Arrow Trail) southeast of town, Mystic Trail (from Little Horse Trailhead, then north), Deadman's Pass Trail in Boynton Canyon, and Bell Rock Pathway off Highway 179 between Sedona and the Village of Oak Creek. Cathedral Bike Loop follows mostly unpaved roads in a 6.5-mile loop via Red Rock Crossing and Red Rock State Park (entry fee required), which has a map handout; note that there's no bridge at Red Rock Crossing, where the creek can be too high to cross during spring runoff. Most Sedona cycling is rated beginner to intermediate.

OAK CREEK CANYON

Take Highway 89A north from Sedona for a beautiful scenic drive past dramatic rock features, dense forests, and the sparkling creek. Picnic areas, hiking trails, and campgrounds along the way invite travelers to stop. Grasshopper Point and Slide Rock State Park offer natural swimming holes in Oak Creek. Secluded lodges

COURTESY OF SEDONA CHAMBER OF COMMERCE

Cyclists enjoy one of the many scenic trails around Sedona.

and cabins in Oak Creek provide accommodations. At the head of the canyon, 13 miles from Sedona, the highway climbs 700 feet in 2.3 miles of sharp switchbacks to Oak Creek Vista, a scenic viewpoint overlooking Oak Creek Canyon and Pumphouse Wash. The highway continues on to I-17 and Flagstaff, where you could also start the drive. In autumn (mid-Oct.–mid-November), multicolored leaves add to the rich hues of the sculptured canyon walls.

The beauty of Oak Creek Canyon attracts large crowds on summer weekends, when the highway becomes very crowded, parking can be impossible at popular stops, and campgrounds fill to the brim. Weekdays and off-season travel will be much easier, but if you can come only on a weekend, it's still worth doing. An early start will put you ahead of the pack and score a parking spot.

Wilson Mountain Trail #10

Energetic hikers will enjoy this climb from the bottom of Oak Creek Canyon to the top of Wilson Mountain. A stiff 2,300-foot ascent is followed by a long, level stretch extending to the north edge of the flat-topped mountain. Total trail length is 5.6 miles round-trip, or 4 miles if you turn around where the trail levels off on the summit plateau.

Two very different trails, Wilson Mountain #10 and North Wilson #123, start from the bottom (elev. 4,600 ft.), meet partway up on First Bench, then continue as one trail to the top. Wilson Mountain Trail begins at the north end of Midgley Bridge, 1.3 miles north of Sedona, and switchbacks through Arizona cypress, juniper, pinyon pine, agave, yucca, and other sun-loving plants. Higher up, manzanita, scrub live oak, and other chaparral-zone plants become more common. North Wilson Trail, on the other hand, climbs steeply through a cool canyon filled with tall ponderosa pine and Douglas fir; look for the trailhead on Highway 89A just north of the Encinoso Picnic Area, 4.6 miles north of town.

A stone cairn marks the junction of the trails at First Bench. This large level area dates from long ago, when a piece of Wilson Mountain's summit slid part way down the mountain. More climbing takes you to the rim of Wilson Mountain; keep right where the trail forks and follow the path north to some spectacular viewpoints. From the northernmost overlook, you can see tiny Vultee Arch far below across Sterling Canyon. Beyond, on the horizon, stand the San Francisco Peaks. Small meadows and forests of ponderosa pine and Gambel oak cover the large expanse of Wilson's summit. Carry 2–3 quarts of water.

Wilson Canyon and Mountain get their names from Richard Wilson, a bear hunter who lost a battle with a grizzly in June 1885. Wilson's bear gun was undergoing repairs on the day he spotted grizzly tracks in Oak Creek Canyon, but he set out after the bear anyway, toting a smaller rifle. Nine days later, horsemen found Wilson's badly mauled body up what's now Wilson Canyon. You can hike about 1.5 miles up the canyon from Midgley Bridge. The Huckaby Trail goes down the canyon from Midgley Bridge, crosses Oak Creek, follows an old wagon road through the valley, and connects with lower Schnebly Hill Road.

Grasshopper Point

This natural swimming hole in Oak Creek lies on the right 1.8 miles north of town. A $5 ($7 summer) parking fee is charged at the gate. Bring your own drinking water and perhaps a picnic. Hikers can follow Huckaby Trail downstream to the lower Schnebly Hill Road or go upstream on Allens Bend Trail and connect with Casner Canyon Trail, which climbs to upper Schnebly Hill Road.

Rainbow Trout Farm

Anglers will find the easiest fishing for rainbow trout on the right across Oak Creek, three miles north of Sedona (928/282-5799). Equipment is available and no license is needed, but you must pay for what you catch; it's open daily.

Indian Gardens and Oak Creek Visitor Center

A marker outlines the history of this spot, 3.5 miles north of town. Oak Creek Visitor Center, tucked under trees on the left, offers recreation information, fishing licenses, maps, and some books. To the north, a store and deli has tables in the patio in back. Garland's Indian Jewelry offers a large selection of Native American work.

Encinoso Picnic Area

Tables with drinking water on the left, 4.6 miles from town, offer a rest from travels. You can stop by year-round; a Red Rock Pass is needed to park.

Manzanita Campground

Turn right down the hillside to the sites beside Oak Creek, 5.6 miles north of town. It's open all year with water and a $16 fee. Sterling Pass Trail #46 begins on the other side of the highway and climbs the west rim.

Sterling Pass Trail #46

A hike to Sterling Pass (elev. 5,960 ft.) from Oak Creek Canyon provides fine views; you can continue down the other side to Vultee Arch. Begin from the west side of Highway 89A, 5.6 miles north of Sedona; the trailhead (elev. 4,840 ft.) lies a short way south of Slide Rock Lodge and 300 feet north of Manzanita Campground. The trail ascends through a small canyon to the pass, then drops 500 feet into Sterling Canyon to join Vultee Arch Trail; it's 3.3 miles round-trip to the pass or 5.2 miles round-trip to Vultee Arch. This approach to the arch avoids the bumpy drive on Forest Road 152.

Slide Rock State Park

Natural chutes and swimming holes at this park in Oak Creek Canyon, 6.4 miles north of Sedona, provide a great way to cool off in summer. Year-round attractions on the 43 acres include a short trail along cliffs above the creek, picnic spots, and a historic apple orchard. On the walk to the swim area, you'll see the orchard, farm machinery, old tourist cabins, packing shed, and farmhouse. Slide Rock Market serves snacks daily, then weekends in winter. You can purchase the park's apples from late August to October. Birds like the area, too, and the park has a checklist. Slide Rock State Park (928/282-3034) is open all year for day use only, $10 per vehicle (up to four people), $1 for each additional passenger and for walk-ins or cyclists. The parking lot fills nearly every day Memorial Day–Labor Day, and you may have to wait for a spot.

Some people like to wear jeans for sliding down the rock chutes, as the ride can be hard on the seat. Pets and glass containers may not go to the swim area. For safety, Oak Creek water is tested every day and the report is posted; you can also check the Water Quality Hotline (602/542-0202 Phoenix). Occasionally bacteria levels go too high and the swim area may close for the day.

Halfway Picnic Area

Tables lie on a shelf above Oak Creek, 7.3 miles north of town on the left. Open all year; you'll need a Red Rock Pass.

Banjo Bill Picnic Area

Located 7.7 miles north of town on the left, the area has water and a $5 ($7 summer) parking fee; it's closed in winter.

Bootlegger Campground

Though lacking water and close to the highway, this spot is a favorite of some campers. It lies on a shelf above the creek on the left, 8.4 miles north of town, and costs $16. The season runs April 15–October 31.

A. B. Young Trail #100

This well-graded but strenuous trail climbs out of Oak Creek Canyon to East Pocket Mesa, north of Wilson Mountain. The trail makes more than 30 switchbacks to reach the ponderosa pine-forested rim, a 1,600-foot climb and 3.2-mile round-trip. From the rim, the trail climbs gently to East Pocket Knob Lookout Tower, another .8 miles and 400 feet higher. You'll enjoy excellent views of Oak Creek Canyon on the way up, from the rim, and atop the lookout tower (open during the fire season in summer).

The trailhead (elev. 5,200 ft.) lies across Oak Creek behind Bootlegger Campground, just north of Milepost 383 on Highway 89A, 8.4 miles north of Sedona. Wade or hop stones across the creek—though don't cross if it's flooded—to a dirt road paralleling the bank, then look for a sign to the well-used trail climbing the slope. After leaving the woodlands along Oak Creek, the trail ascends through chaparral. Allow 3–4 hours and carry 1–2 quarts of water. Cattle ranchers built this trail in the 1880s to bring herds to pasture. The Civilian Conservation Corps under A. B. Young (hence the name) improved it in the 1930s.

Call of the Canyon Picnic Area and West Fork Trail #108

Sheer canyon walls, luxuriant vegetation, and a beautiful clear stream make a hike along West Fork an exceptionally beautiful experience. This major tributary of Oak Creek inspired Novelist Zane Grey's book *Call of the Canyon.* A nearly level trail extends about three miles up through the narrow canyon and crosses the stream many times; usually you can hop across on stones. Beyond the three-mile point, the canyon narrows and you'll have to start wading. Carry water and plenty of film. Because of the quantity and diversity of plant and animal species here, the lower six miles of the canyon has been designated a Research Natural Area, and hikers shouldn't build fires or camp here.

Turn left 10 miles north of Sedona, between Mileposts 384 and 385, for the picnic area and trailhead parking, which costs $5 ($7 summer). Try to arrive early, as there's often a wait for parking by midday. The tables are in an old apple orchard planted by the Thomas family who homesteaded here in the 1880s; bring your own water. After crossing Oak Creek on a bridge, you'll pass the ruins of Mayhews Lodge, built in the early 1900s and burned in 1980, before turning up West Fork.

Although most visitors come for a leisurely day hike, strong hikers can travel the entire 14-mile length of West Fork in one day. It helps to get an early start and arrange a car shuttle. Those making the full trip should start at the upstream trailhead, where Forest Road 231 (Woody Mountain Rd.) crosses West Fork. Woody Mountain Road begins as a turnoff from W. Route 66 in Flagstaff. From the upper trailhead, the first six miles is usually dry, followed by a series of deep pools that may require swimming. Avoid hiking in the canyon after heavy rains or if storms threaten. The rough terrain, fallen trees, and deep pools make backpacking difficult, so most people do the trip as a long day hike.

From the picnic area you can also hike **Thomas Point Trail #142** up the east rim of Oak Creek Canyon. This strenuous trail climbs 900 feet with fine views in two miles round-trip. At the top, follow cairns left to Thomas Point and a panorama of the San Francisco Peaks and upper Oak Creek Canyon.

Oak Creek Canyon Campgrounds

Cave Springs Forest Campground, 11.1 miles up the canyon and to the left, may be the prettiest of the Oak Creek campgrounds. The sites lie in the forest well away from the highway. You can look inside the small cave, where a spring supplies the campground's water. The season runs April 15–October 31 and there's a $16 fee. Campers have a store and coin showers. Some sites can be reserved (877/444-6777, www.reserveusa.com).

Pineflat Campground is 12.1 miles from Sedona on both sides of the highway. Ponderosa pines, Douglas fir, oaks, and sycamores provide shade. The season runs April 1–November 15 with water and a $16 fee. You can also reserve some sites (877/444-6777, www.reserveusa.com). Hikers can get a workout and some views on the climb to the east rim on **Cookstove Trail #143.** It's 1.5 miles round-trip and a 1,000-foot climb. The trailhead is on the east side of the highway just north of the campground.

Oak Creek Vista and North Gateway Visitor Center

On your right at the top of the climb out of Oak Creek Canyon, this overlook (elev. 6,419 ft.) has splendid views down the length of the canyon. Pumphouse Wash lies directly below. A little visitor center, sponsored by the Arizona Natural History Association, is open daily except winter, weather permitting, with recreation information on the Coconino National Forest and sales of books and maps. Native Americans display jewelry and other crafts for sale nearby. Oak Creek Vista is 15.3 miles north of Sedona and 12 miles south of Flagstaff. Parking here is free and you don't need a Red Rock Pass.

Griffith Spring Trail

If you feel like a short ramble under the ponderosa pines between Oak Creek Vista and Flagstaff, this one-mile loop trail will give you a chance to stretch your legs. It's on the east side of Highway 89A between Mileposts 396 and 397, 2.5 miles south of the Coconino County Fairgrounds turnoff. From the trailhead, which has a picnic table and an outhouse, follow the gravel path down a gentle slope to the loop, which passes a small canyon.

SCHNEBLY HILL ROAD

You'll enjoy some of the best views in the area along this bumpy back road that descends the Mogollon Rim east of Sedona. It's the most spectacular approach to Sedona, but is too rocky for cars—high clearance vehicles are needed. If you'd rather have someone else do the driving, sign up for a tour with one of the companies in Uptown Sedona.

The drive is about 12 miles one-way and is closed in winter. Take I-17 Exit 320 for the descent. To climb out from Sedona, turn off Highway 179 at the sign a half mile south of the Y. Allow plenty of time for the many curves and views. At about the halfway point, Schnebly Hill Vista features a spectacular panorama. The Red Rock Ranger District Office in Sedona (928/282-4119) can advise on road conditions.

BELL ROCK PATHWAY

This 3.7-mile (one-way) trail passes along the base of Bell Rock south of Sedona; elevation change is 200 feet. Both trailheads lie just east of Highway 179. The north trailhead, also used to reach Little Horse Trail, is near Milepost 310, just south of the Back O'Beyond/Indian Cliffs junction. The south trailhead is just north of the Village of Oak Creek. **Courthouse Butte Loop** begins .6 miles in from the south trailhead and goes around this butte in six miles; elevation gain is 400 feet.

WEST OF SEDONA

Crescent Moon Ranch/ Red Rock Crossing

Photographers and moviemakers have long admired this spot for its beautiful view of Cathedral Rock reflected in the waters of Oak Creek. Visitors also enjoy a swim in the creek or a picnic. Buildings and a working waterwheel of Crescent Moon Ranch add some history. Open daily with a $5 ($7 summer) parking fee. From the Y in Sedona, head west 4.2 miles on Highway 89A, turn left 1.8 miles on Upper Red Rock Loop Road, then left .9 miles on Chavez Ranch Road.

Red Rock State Park

Nature lovers come to walk the trails and picnic beside Oak Creek southwest of Sedona (928/282-6907, www.azstateparks.com, $6/vehicle up to 4 persons, $1 each additional person or cyclist). Bird-watching is good, with 150 species identified; ask for a list. Drop in at the visitor center to see exhibits on the diverse plants and wildlife; staff answer questions, tell of upcoming events, and sell books. You can join nature walks, bird walks, moonlight walks (April–Oct.), and First Sunday programs; call ahead or check the website for times.

Seven short hiking trails wind through lush riparian areas or up into the surrounding pinyon pine-juniper plant community. All of the trails interconnect with many loop possibilities. Smoke Trail, the shortest, follows the shore of Oak Creek in a .4-mile round-trip from the visitor center. Eagles Nest Trail crosses the creek to a scenic viewpoint in a 1.9-mile loop with a climb of 300 feet; the trail takes its name from a Disney movie filmed here. The House of Apache Fire atop a ridge has distinctive architecture and stonework patterned after Hopi pueblos; construction started in 1947 and never really finished, though the house served as a retreat center in the early 1970s. You can hike up to the house and read about its history. Mountain bikers can ride the 6.5-mile Cathedral Bike Loop from the park on mostly unpaved roads, some closed to motorists; there's a ford at Red Rock Crossing. A handout available at the park shows the way.

COURTESY OF SEDONA CHAMBER OF COMMERCE

picture-perfect Red Rock Crossing

To protect the fragile riparian area, no swimming, wading, or pets are allowed; some areas may be closed to protect wildlife. From the Y in Sedona, head west 5.5 miles on Highway 89A, turn left (south) 3 miles on Lower Red Rock Loop Road, then turn right .8 miles into the park to the visitor center. You can also drive via Upper Red Rock Loop Road—2 miles of pavement followed by 1.2 miles of bumpy dirt road.

Page Springs Hatchery

Meet the trout on a self-guided tour, open 7 A.M.–3:45 P.M. daily. They hatch at Sterling Springs, near the head of Oak Creek Canyon, then come here when they're three inches long. After a stay of 8–9 months, the trout reach a length of 8–10 inches and are ready to be released. A show pond contains large specimens. Warm-water fish, including threatened and endangered species, live in separate pools. The visitor center (928/634-4805) has exhibits on native fish of Oak Creek, sport fish, and fisheries management. **Page Springs North Wildlife Viewing Area** offers a short nature walk and birding from the parking area. From the Y in Sedona, head southwest 11 miles on Highway 89A to between Mileposts 362 and 363, then turn left 3.2 miles on Page Springs Road/Yavapai County 50.

Nearby **Bubbling Ponds Hatchery** raises native and exotic warm-water species, but the hatchery is not well marked and it's difficult to see the fish because either they are too small or the water is too murky. Birders wander through the **Bubbling Ponds Wildlife Viewing Area;** parking is just off Page Springs Road/Yavapai County 50, .8 miles past the Lo Lo Mai turnoff and .7 miles before Page Springs Fish Hatchery.

Devil's Bridge Trail #120

From the trailhead (elev. 4,600 ft.), a well-graded path climbs steadily through juniper, pinyon pine, Arizona cypress, and manzanita to the base of a long natural arch. You can't see the bridge until you're almost there, but when you arrive, the majestic sweep of the arch and fine views of distant canyons and mountains reward your effort. The 1.8-mile round-trip hike gains 400 feet in elevation. You can also follow a trail to the top of the arch.

Devil's Bridge lies northwest of Sedona on the other side of a ridge. From the Y in Sedona, head west 3.1 miles on Highway 89A, turn right 2 miles on paved Dry Creek Road (Forest Road 152C), then turn right and go 1.3 miles on the bumpy dirt Forest Road 152. Cautiously driven cars may be able to negotiate this road in dry weather; check with the Forest Service.

Vultee Arch Trail #22

This hike follows Sterling Canyon upstream to a small natural bridge visible in the sandstone to the north. Though the canyon is dry most of the year, Arizona cypress, sycamore, ponderosa pine, and other trees and plants find it to their liking. From the trailhead (elev. 4,800 ft.), you'll climb 400 feet on the 3.2-mile round-trip trail. Carry water, especially on hot days. The arch and a bronze plaque at the end of the trail commemorate aircraft designer Gerard Vultee and his wife Sylvia, who died when their plane hit East Pocket Mesa during a snowstorm on January 29, 1938. The trailhead for Vultee Arch lies at the end of Forest Road 152; follow the directions for Devil's Bridge Trail, then continue three miles past that turnoff to road's end.

Palatki and Honanki Ruins

Prehistoric Sinagua built these cliff dwellings, the largest pueblos in the Sedona Red Rocks area. Later, these early architects moved on, possibly to Tuzigoot and other sites along the Verde River and Oak Creek. Take great care not to touch the fragile rock art or ruins. For either site, you'll need a Red Rock Pass.

Palatki is Hopi for Red House. You'll need to call (928/282-3854) for a reservation before coming out; a visitors center/bookshop provides information and drinking water. The two pueblos date from 1150–1300 and once housed 30–50 people. Look on the alcove walls for pictographs that possibly represent clans. Red Cliffs, on a separate trail to the west, contains much more rock art and there's often a volunteer here to explain the different styles and time periods of the artwork. Pictographs and a few petroglyphs at the site have been attributed to the Archaic period (3,000–8,000 years ago), Southern Sinagua (A.D. 900–1300), Yavapai or Apache (1583–1875), and Anglo pioneers.

Honanki (Hopi for Bear House), below Loy Butte, is open 9:30 A.M.–4 P.M. daily. The pueblo, built between 1130 and 1280, once had as many as 72 rooms. You'll find rock art here, too.

From the Y in Sedona, head west 9.2 miles on Highway 89A to a group of mailboxes between Mileposts 364 and 365, turn right (north) 5 miles on Red Canyon Road, then continue north 1.6 miles on Forest Road 795 to its end at Palatki. The rougher but more scenic route follows Highway 89A west 3.2 miles from the Y, turns right (north) about 6 miles on Dry Creek Road (Forest Road 152C), which curves west to Forest Road 525, where you turn right, then right again on Forest Road 795 to Palatki. For Honanki, return to the junction of Forest Roads 525 and 795, then follow Forest Road 525 northwest four miles; you may need a high-clearance vehicle for this last stretch. The gateway visitors centers and the Forest Service office in Sedona (928/282-4119) have a handout on the ruins and sell the Coconino Forest map.

Sycamore Canyon Wilderness

Imagine Oak Creek Canyon without the highway, resorts, and campgrounds. That's Sycamore Canyon, a twisting slash in the earth 21 miles long and as wide as 7 miles. As the crow flies, Sycamore Canyon lies about 15 miles west of Oak Creek Canyon. A wilderness designation protects the canyon, so only hikers and horseback riders may descend to its depths. Several trails wind down to Sycamore Creek, mostly from the east side, but not a single road. Motorists can enjoy the sweeping view from Sycamore Point on the west rim, approached from Williams.

Sycamore Canyon Wilderness is under the jurisdiction of the Coconino, Kaibab, and Prescott National Forests. The gateway visitors centers and the Forest Service office in Sedona (928/282-4119) are your best sources of information for trail conditions, trailhead access, and water sources.

SOUTHEAST OF SEDONA

Heading southeast of Sedona, you'll eventually leave the famous Red Rock Country, but not the spectacular scenery. The pine-forested Mogollon Rim and its narrow canyons harbor many beautiful spots. The gateway visitors centers and the Forest Service office in Sedona (928/282-4119) can tell you about recreation in this area.

V-Bar-V Ranch Petroglyph Site

The 13 panels near Beaver Creek hold more than one thousand petroglyphs. Archaeologists think that the Sinagua created them during the end of their stay in the region. A volunteer at the site will point out and explain some of the symbols on the cliff face. You can visit only 9:30 A.M.–4 P.M. Friday–Monday; gates close at 3:30 P.M. Bring a Red Rock Pass to get in.

From Sedona, head south 15 miles on Highway 179 to the I-17 overpass (Exit 298) and continue straight on paved Forest Road 618 another 2.4 miles; turn right at the sign just past the Beaver Creek bridge. An easy one-third-mile walk takes you to the rock art.

Wet Beaver Creek Wilderness

Sycamore, cottonwood, ash, alder, Arizona walnut, and wildflowers grow along the pretty creek here. Yet, a short way from the water, the prickly pear cactus, agave, Utah juniper, and pinyon pine of the high desert take over. You might see mule or white-tailed deer, ringtail cat, coyote, javelina, Gambel's quail, red-tailed hawk, bald eagle, and great blue heron. Keep an eye out for rattlesnakes and poison ivy. Verde trout, some brown and rainbow, and suckers live in the creek, though most people find fishing conditions poor. Hikers enjoy trails along the lower creek, climbs to the Mogollon Rim, and difficult routes through the upper canyons. The many swimming holes in Wet Beaver Creek offer cool comfort in summer. Hiking in the lower canyon can be pleasant year-round.

To reach the 6,700-acre wilderness, take I-17 Sedona Exit 298, turn southeast two miles on Forest Road 618, then turn left a quarter mile at the sign to **Bell Trail #13.** Elevations range from 3,820 feet at the trailhead to 6,500 feet atop the Mogollon Rim. The first two miles of trail follow an old jeep road into the canyon, where the way narrows to a footpath. **Apache Maid Trail #15** begins at this point, climbing steeply out of the canyon to the north, then continuing at a moderate grade to Forest Road 620 near Apache Maid Mountain. This route is 9.5 miles one-way and gains 2,380 feet in elevation. The Bell Trail continues upstream another mile past pretty pools to Bell Crossing, where it crosses the creek and climbs out to the east to Roundup Basin and Forest Road 214 near Five Mile Pass; you'll cover 10.8 miles one-way and gain 2,450 feet in elevation.

The Crack, a deep pool 150 feet upstream from Bell Crossing, makes a good turnaround point for a leisurely day hike. Please don't camp here, as the area gets heavy use. Adventurous hikers can continue upstream if they're willing to swim through many deep pools of cold, clear water; bring some flotation devices, especially if toting a camera or pack. Experienced hikers can also enter the upper canyon via Waldroup, Jacks, or Brady canyons. These routes involve some brush and descents on small cliff faces. Beaver Creek and unpalatable stock tanks are the only sources of water, so it's best to bring your own. Topo maps are a must for off-trail travel and the sometimes-faint trails on the Mogollon Rim.

Fossil Springs Wilderness

Springs southeast of Camp Verde gush forth more than a million gallons of heavily mineralized water per hour at a constant 72°F, supporting a lush riparian environment. Swimming holes offer a cooling plunge in summer. The 11,550-acre wilderness protects the scenic beauty and abundant wildlife of Fossil Creek and some of its tributaries. Objects in the water may get a coating of calcium, hence the name Fossil Springs. Today the springs gush forth near the creekbed, but you can see ancient deposits of travertine on the cliffs above. Elevations range from 4,250 feet at the springs to 6,800 feet on the Mogollon Rim. Three trails lead to Fossil Springs, and you could arrange a car shuttle to avoid retracing your steps.

Beginning in 1909, a dam and flume below the springs fed the Childs hydroelectric plant. The system expanded with the addition of the Irving hydro station nearby on the Verde River in 1916. These historic generating stations originally supplied Jerome's mines, then Phoenix with much of their electrical needs. Environmental groups recently forced the plants to shut down, so that Fossil Creek can once again return to the canyon bottom. Some parts of the Irving station and flume will be preserved, but most of the structures will be removed.

You can descend **Fossil Springs Trail #18** from the east rim, dropping 1,280 feet in four miles on a former wagon road; when you reach the creekbed, turn left a short way to the springs. Loose rock makes hiking a challenge, but you'll enjoy fine views most of the way. The trailhead is 4.8 miles west from Strawberry via Fossil Springs Road (Forest Road 708). You'll pass the Strawberry Schoolhouse in 1.5 miles, then run out of pavement at the edge of Strawberry; look for the trailhead sign on the right.

A hike on **Flume Road Trail #154** from the Irving Trailhead offers the easiest way in. The trail crosses the creek, climbs steeply .5 miles to the Flume Road, then follows the road upcanyon 3.5 miles to the springs; elevation gain is 440 feet. Both hikers and bicyclists can follow the road, but cyclists must park before the wilderness boundary, just before the springs. Note that the Flume Road Trail may be closed for periods over the next several years during dismantling of the flume; check first with the Red Rock Ranger District (928/282-4119). The Irving Trailhead is at the bottom of a long descent on Fossil Springs Road, 9.7 miles from Strawberry. Alternatively, you can drive from Camp Verde by heading east 7 miles on Highway 260, then turning right 16.5 miles on Fossil Springs Road; this remote scenic drive winds through beautiful desert hills but is too rough for cars.

Mail Trail #84 descends from the north rim, dropping 1,300 feet in 3.1 miles; trailhead is 13 miles east on Highway 260 from the West Clear Creek bridge, then right on Forest Road 9247B to Mail Trail Tank #2 (high-clearance vehicle needed).

Verde Hot Springs

Two pools, one warm and one hot, lie on the west bank of the Verde River in the Tonto National Forest. They attract hot-springs enthusiasts willing to make the drive and hike to this remote spot. A resort once operated here, but only the baths and piles of rubble remain; yellow stains on the cliffs above the river mark past thermal activity. Visitors irregularly clean the baths at this clothing-optional site, so it's best to use caution before jumping in.

You can approach the trailhead on unpaved Fossil Springs Road (Forest Road 708) either from Camp Verde or from Strawberry, north of Payson. This road may be passable by cautiously driven cars, though high-clearance vehicles do best. From Camp Verde, take Highway 260 east 7 miles, turn right 14 miles on Fossil Springs Road, then right 6.5 miles to the Verde River. From Highway 87 in Strawberry, you can head west 12.5 miles on Fossil Springs Road, then turn left 6.5 miles at the sign for the Verde River. On the last 6.5 miles, you'll climb high into the hills, pass a turnoff for Stehr's Lake and a scenic 4WD route to Ike's Backbone, then descend to Childs Dispersed Recreation Area on the riverbank at road's end; the last quarter mile may be too rough for cars.

There's an outhouse and primitive camping at this heavily used site. Lovers of solitude will do better to camp elsewhere. A five-day stay limit applies. Because it's a family area, no nudity is permitted here. A one-mile trail heads upriver past the Childs Power Plant site and climbs to a road that goes upriver. When the road descends to river level, look for a place to ford the Verde River, then follow the trail downriver a few hundred yards to the hot springs. Don't count on finding signs for the last part of the hike. All of these roads in the Fossil Creek and Verde River areas lead through magnificent scenery, worthwhile drives even if you don't come for the hot springs.

Along the Verde River

Below the cream- and red-colored cliffs of the Mogollon Rim, the Verde River brings life to a broad desert valley. Spanish explorers named the river *verde* (green) for the luxuriant growth that lines its banks. The waters come from narrow canyons of Oak Creek, Wet and Dry Beaver creeks, West Clear Creek, Sycamore Creek, and other streams.

Prehistoric tribes camped in the area, finding a great variety of wild plant food and game between the 3,000-foot elevation of the lower valley and the rim country 4,000 feet higher. About A.D. 600–700, Native American groups began cultivating the Verde Valley, taking advantage of the fine climate, fertile land, and abundant water. Trade and contacts with the Hohokam culture to the south also aided development of the region. Hohokam people probably migrated into the Verde Valley too, though archaeologists can't determine whether early farming communities were actually Hohokam or simply influenced by their culture. Verde inhabitants learned to make pottery, grow cotton, weave cloth, and build ball courts.

The Sinagua people arrived from what is now the Flagstaff area between A.D. 1125 and 1200, gradually absorbing the local cultures. Villages then started to consolidate. Large, multistoried pueblos replaced the small pit houses of earlier times. Two of these pueblos, Montezuma Castle and Tuzigoot, have become national monuments. Archaeologists don't know why, but the Verde Valley population departed by 1425. The elaborate Hohokam culture, based in the Gila and Salt River Valleys to the south, also disappeared about this time. Perhaps some of the Sinagua migrated northeast, eventually joining the Hopi and Zuni pueblos.

Early Spanish explorers, arriving a century and a half later, found small bands of nomadic Tonto Apache and Yavapai roaming the valley. In language and culture, the Tonto Apache are related to the Apache and Navajo tribes to the east, while the Yavapai share cultural traits with the Hualapai and Havasupai to the northwest.

Anglos and Mexicans poured into the valley during a gold rush at the Hassayampa River and Lynx Creek in 1863. Farmers and ranchers followed, taking for themselves the best agricultural land along the Verde. The displaced tribes attacked the settlements but failed to drive off the newcomers. Soon the army arrived, building Camp Lincoln, later christened Fort Verde. General George Crook eventually subdued local tribes through clever campaigning and the enlistment of Apache scouts.

Tonto Apache and Yavapai received the Rio Verde Reservation in 1873, but the federal government took it away two years later, ordering the displaced tribes to proceed to the San Carlos Reservation, 150 miles away. In the cold February of 1875, they started the two-week journey on foot; of the 1,451 who began the trek, at least 90 died from exposure, were killed by infighting, or escaped.

Early in the 20th century, some Apache and Yavapai received permission to return to their Verde River homelands. What were once thousands of Native Americans occupying millions of acres now number less than 1,000 people on a few remnants of their former lands on the Camp Verde, Prescott, and Fort McDowell reservations.

Meanwhile, Anglo farmers in the Verde Valley prospered. Cottonwood, founded in 1879, became the valley's main trading center. Copper mining succeeded on a large scale at Jerome, which sprang to life high on a mountainside in 1882. Mine company officials built a giant smelter below Jerome in 1910 and laid out the town of Clarkdale. Depletion of the ore bodies in the early 1950s, however, forced many residents of Jerome and Clarkdale to seek jobs elsewhere. Today the Verde Valley thrives due to industry, farming, and popularity with tourists and retirees.

CAMP VERDE AND VICINITY

Early in 1865, 19 men set out from Prescott to start a farming settlement in the Verde Valley. They knew the mining camps around Arizona's new capital at Prescott would pay well for fresh

COURTESY OF THE SHARLOT HALL MUSEUM

hydraulic mining on Lynx Creek near today's Prescott Valley, ca. 1890

food. The eager farmers chose land where West Clear Creek joins the Verde, about five miles downstream from the modern town of Camp Verde. After the farmers had planted fields, dug an irrigation system, and built a fort, raiding tribes destroyed much of the crops and livestock. Army troops marched in and built Camp Lincoln, one mile north of the present town site. Because some people thought that too many place names then commemorated the former president, the army later changed the post's name to Camp Verde.

Native American hostilities kept the cavalry and infantry busy during the late 1860s and early 1870s. The infantry built a road, later known as the General Crook Trail, west to Fort Whipple (near Prescott) and east along the Mogollon Rim to Fort Apache. In 1871 the post moved one mile south to its current location, where more than 20 buildings lined up beside a parade field. An 1882 battle at Big Dry Wash marked the last large engagement between soldiers and Native Americans in Arizona. Having served its purpose, Fort Verde closed in 1891.

Today exhibits and the four surviving fort buildings at Fort Verde State Historic Park give a feeling of what life was like for the enlisted men, officers, and women who lived here. Other attractions near town include the multistoried cliff dwelling of Montezuma Castle, the unusual lake at Montezuma Well, wilderness areas, and the Verde River.

Fort Verde State Historic Park

Like most forts of the period, Fort Verde served as a supply post and staging area for army patrols. It never had a protective wall, nor did Native Americans ever attack it. Today, a 12-acre park (928/567-3275, 8 A.M.–5 P.M. daily, $2 adults, $1 ages 7–13) preserves the administration building, commanding officer's house, bachelors' quarters, doctor's quarters, and the old parade ground. A gift shop sells history books. From Main Street in downtown Camp Verde (2 miles east of I-17 Exit 287), turn east one block on Hollamon Street.

Begin your visit at the adobe administration building, used by General George Crook during the winter campaign of 1872–1873 that largely ended Native American raids in the region. Exhibits recall the soldiers and their families, Apache army scouts, settlers, and prospectors who came through here more than 100 years ago. You'll see old photos, maps, letters, rifles,

THE BALD EAGLE

Like many humans, the bald eagle *(Haliaeetus leucocephalus)* prefers fast food and a home near waterways. Fish make up over half its diet, supplemented with small mammals, birds, and some carrion.

The Second Continental Congress designated this bird as a national symbol in 1782 and Congress gave it official protection in 1940, but by the early 1970s biologists could find only seven pairs in Arizona. Populations have come back now that DDT has been eliminated and nesting sites protected.

Southern bald eagles live in central and northwest areas of Arizona and nest in the central part. Eagles may be either year-round residents or winter visitors who nest elsewhere, most often in the Pacific Northwest. Their yellow eyes have vision thought to be eight times sharper than ours. White feathers cover the head and tail of adults, with brown over the rest of the body. Youngsters have dark-brown feathers with some white on the underside, so they are sometimes mistaken for golden eagles, Arizona's only other eagle species. Both sexes look alike except for size; adult males weigh 8–9 pounds, while females weigh 10–14. They hold their wings—which span up to 7.5 feet—horizontally when soaring, unlike the uptilted wings of vultures and golden eagles.

Breeding pairs look for a tall tree or cliff site with good visibility, protection from wind, and a nearby source of fish; nests average 6–8 feet across. Resident eagles breed in January and February, so that the young won't be subject to heat stress. The mother lays two or three white eggs, which hatch in about 35 days. Both parents attend to the incubation and feeding of the eaglets. After 11 weeks the babies can fly, then after several more weeks they can live on their own. Because raising eaglets is such delicate business—frightened parents can break eggs or stay away from the nest too long—known breeding areas are closed to the public December 1–June 30. It's best to view with binoculars from a quarter of a mile away or more. Good places to sight bald eagles include Lake Pleasant, Bartlett Lake, the Salt and Verde Rivers, the Coolidge area, and Alamo Lake.

uniforms, saddles, and Native American artifacts. The three adobe buildings of Officers' Row have been restored and furnished as they were in the 1880s. Cavalry, infantry, and Indian scout reenactments take place during Fort Verde Days on the second weekend in October and a few other times during the year.

Montezuma Castle National Monument

This towering cliff dwelling so impressed early visitors that they mistakenly believed followers of the famous Aztec ruler had built it. Actually, this pueblo had been neither a castle nor part of Montezuma's empire. Sinagua built it in the 12th and 13th centuries, toward the end of their stay in the Verde Valley. The five-story stone and mortar structure contains 20 rooms, once occupied by about 35 people. It's tucked back under a cliff 100 feet above Beaver Creek. The overhang shielded the village from rain, snow, and the hot summer sun but allowed the winter sun's low-angle rays to warm the dwellings. The ruins are well preserved but too fragile to be entered, so you must view them from below. An even larger pueblo, Castle A, once stood against the base of the cliff; it had six stories and about 45 rooms, but little remains today. A level, paved one-third-mile trail loops below Montezuma Castle to the foundations of this second ruin.

The visitors center (928/567-3322, www.nps.gov/moca, 8 A.M.–5 P.M. daily, extended in summer, $3/person age 17 and up) has exhibits of artifacts and the everyday life of the Sinagua. Ask at the information desk to see the photo album of the cliff dwelling's interior. Related books, videos, and maps are sold. Giant Arizona sycamore trees shade a picnic area beside the river. Take I-17 Exit 289 and follow signs two miles; from Camp Verde, drive north three miles on Montezuma Castle Road, then turn right two miles at the sign.

Montezuma Well

This natural sinkhole, 11 miles northeast of Montezuma Castle, attracts visitors both for its scenic beauty as a desert oasis and for its prehistoric

Montezuma Castle

ruins. The Sinagua built pueblos here between A.D. 1125 and 1400, using lake water to irrigate their crops. Parts of their villages and irrigation canals can still be seen. The sinkhole measures 470 feet across and is only partly filled by a 55-foot-deep lake. Signs describe some of the plants and animals that dwell in the clear water. You may see turtles swimming in the lake but no fish, as the carbon dioxide level is too high for them.

A one-third-mile, self-guiding loop trail climbs to the rim, where a short trail winds down to the lake and to ruins sheltered in a cave. The main trail continues along the rim past a pueblo site and a large rectangular structure, which may have been a kiva, before beginning its descent to an ancient irrigation ditch. A short side trail to the left leads to the outlet where the lake drains into the ditch as it has since Sinagua times. Modern farmers continue to use the water, which flows at 1,100 gallons per minute. The main trail returns you to the parking area.

On the drive in, a tree-shaded picnic area and a prehistoric canal segment are down the road to the right a half mile before Montezuma Well. In another quarter mile on the main road, you can stop on the left to see a pit house exhibit. Timbers that once held up the walls and roof have long since rotted away, but distinct outlines remain of the supporting poles, walls, entrance, and fire pit.

Montezuma's Well is part of Montezuma Castle National Monument and is open during the same hours, but there's no admission charge here. From Camp Verde or Montezuma Castle, take I-17 north to Exit 293 and follow signs five miles; another approach begins at I-17 Sedona Exit 298, turns east, then south three miles on a gravel road.

Out of Africa Wildlife Park

This unusual animal park (928/567-2840, www.outofafricapark.com) features big cats from all over the world in both near-natural habitats and shows. In the very popular Tiger Splash show, the tigers dive into a large pool with their human friends in pursuit of balloons and toys. Wolves, hyenas, lions, reptiles, and birds appear in other demonstrations. Safari expeditions take you into the bush to see free-roaming wildlife such as giraffes, zebra, wildebeest, sable, and gemsbok.

Facilities include a playground, places to eat, and gift shops. A variety of shows runs through the day, so you'll get the most out of a visit with an early start. Formerly in the Phoenix area, the park has recently moved to a 104 acre site off Highway 260, three miles northwest from I-17 Exit 287. Call or check the website for directions and hours.

Events

The **Pecan & Wine Festival** in February features products from Arizona wineries, jazz, and an antique show. **Armed Forces Day** on the third weekend of May commemorates the History of the Soldier through all eras of American history with encampments and drills at Fort Verde State Historic Park. The July 4 **Independence Day Celebration** has family activities and fireworks. **Verde Valley Pow Wow,** sponsored by Cliff Castle Casino in July, presents Native American dance and drumming. The **Cornfest** marks the beginning of the harvest season in July with food, entertainment, arts, and crafts. **Pioneer Days** in September puts on a mule show, tractor pull, gun & knife show, country music concerts, and a chuckwagon dinner. **Fort Verde Days,** on the second weekend in October, brings back the old days with cavalry parades and drills, a barbecue, roping events, arts and crafts shows, games, and a dance.

Recreation

Play **golf** at Beaver Creek's 18-hole course (928/567-4487) at Lake Montezuma, near Montezuma Well.

Accommodations

$50–100: B's B&B (94 Coppinger St., 928/567-1988, bbb@wildapache.net, $50 s, 60 d) offers bed and breakfast with views and private baths in a home near Fort Verde State Park.

Three motels lie off Highway 260 (Finnie Flat Rd.) just east of I-17 Exit 287. **Super 8 Motel** (928/567-2622 or 800/800-8000, $50–55 s, $57–64 d) offers an indoor pool and hot tub. **Days Inn & Suites** (928/567-3700 or 800/747-9011, $72–79.50 d, $83–86 d suite) has an outdoor pool and hot tub. **Comfort Inn** (928/567-9000 or 866/302-2300, about $64 d) provides an outdoor pool and hot tub.

The Lodge at Cliff Castle Casino (just east of I-17 Exit 289, 928/567-6611 or 800/524-6343, www.cliffcastle.com, $74 d weekdays, $79 Fri.–Sat.) features luxury accommodations, restaurants, a casino, tours, trail rides, pool, and a hot tub; it's three miles from downtown on Middle Verde Road and opposite the turnoff for Montezuma Castle.

Over $100: Hacienda de la Mariposa (3875 Stagecoach Rd., 928/567-1490 or 888/520-9095, www.lamariposa-az.com, $195–205 d) is a bed & breakfast resort with large rooms in a Santa Fe–style building. The pretty setting on five acres along Beaver Creek is only a mile from Montezuma Castle.

Luna Vista Bed & Breakfast (928/567-4788 or 800/611-4788, www.LunaVistaBandB.com, $150–235 d) offers luxurious suites with pool, hot tub, and private patios in the countryside near Lake Montezuma, off I-17 Exit 293. Your horse can stay nearby in the stables.

Campgrounds

These normally stay open all year in the Verde Valley's mild climate. **Distant Drums RV Resort** (583 W. Middle Verde Rd., just northwest off I-17 Exit 289, 928/554-0444 or 877/577-5507, www.distantdrumsrvresort.com, $30 RV w/hookups) features large sites and a host of amenities including pool, hot tub, exercise room, store, and showers. The adult **Trails End RV Park** (983 Finnie Flats Rd., 928/567-0100, $22 RV/w hookups) includes showers and laundry; it's between downtown and I-17 Exit 287. The adult **Zane Grey RV Park** (928/567-4320 or 800/235-0608, www.zanegreyrvpark.com, $20 RV w/hookups) has showers and laundry in a rural setting; look for it on the left seven miles southeast on Highway 260, just beyond the West Clear Creek bridge.

Two campgrounds on national forest land (Red Rock Ranger District, 928/282-4119, www.fs.fed.us/r3/coconino) have drinking water all year and a $12 fee, but no showers or hookups. **Clear Creek Campground** is six miles southeast on Highway 260, then left just before West Clear Creek bridge. **Beaver Creek Campground** lies to the northeast; take I-17 north to Sedona Exit 298, then turn southeast 2.3 miles on Forest Road 618; or you can turn north on Forest Road 618 from Highway 260 at a junction west of the West Clear Creek bridge.

Food

Ming House (238 S. Main St. downtown in Fort Verde Plaza, 928/567-9488, daily lunch and dinner, $6–12) serves a variety of Chinese food and offers good buffets. **Rio Verde Restaurant** (south edge of town at 77 S. Access Rd., 928/567-9966, daily lunch and dinner, $7–14) cooks up Mexican and some American food. **Sister's and Co. Café** (Outpost Mall on Finnie Flats Rd., 928/567-0351, $6–9.50) serves American fare daily for breakfast, lunch, and dinner. **Bashas'** supermarket is also in the Outpost Mall.

The Ranch House (Beaver Creek Golf Course at Lake Montezuma, 928/567-4492, daily breakfast, lunch, and dinner, $9–19) has a large menu including dinner specialties of steak, prime rib, and seafood. **La Fonda Mexican Restaurant**

(928/567-3500, Tues.–Sat. lunch and dinner, $6–10) lies about four miles outside town on Finnie Flats Road (AZ 260) toward Cottonwood; go west 2 miles past I-17, then turn right .1 mile on Horseshoe Bend Drive.

Information and Services

Staff at the **Camp Verde Chamber of Commerce** (downtown at 385 S. Main and Hollamon Sts., Camp Verde, AZ 86322, 928/567-9294, www.campverde.org, 8 A.M.–4 P.M. Mon.–Fri. and sometimes Sat. in summer) will tell you about area sights and services, including Forest Service recreation opportunities. The city's website (www.cvaz.org) has event and recreation information. The **post office** lies just west of downtown on Finnie Flats Road.

Prescott National Forest's **Verde Ranger District Office** (P.O. Box 670, Camp Verde, AZ 86322, 928/567-4121, www.fs.fed.us/r3/Prescott, 8 A.M.–4:30 P.M. Mon.–Fri.) provides information on running the Verde River, wilderness areas, camping, hiking, and road conditions for the lands south and west of town. It's on Highway 260 just southeast of town.

Native Visions (Lodge at Cliff Castle, 928/567-3035) offers van tours to Montezuma Castle, Montezuma Well, and Tuzigoot plus horseback rides through nearby hills.

VERDE RANGER DISTRICT

Beasley Flat

Visitors enjoy pretty scenery, a picnic area, nature trail, and river access on the bank of the Verde River at Beasley Flat. The nature trail extends half a mile along the riverbank in the recreation area with viewpoints and river access trails; the lower section has a paved loop. From downtown Camp Verde, head south on Main Street about half a mile, turn right 8.5 miles on Salt Mine Road/Forest Road 574, then left 2 miles on unpaved Forest Road 529. Fishers can also access the river six miles in on Salt Mine Road. From I-17, you can take Exit 285 and go east 1.8 miles toward Camp Verde, turn right .5 miles on Oasis Road, right 7.4 miles on Salt Mine Road/Forest Road 574, then left 2 miles on unpaved Forest Road 529. No camping or motorized boats are permitted. Prescott National Forest offices have a map handout.

River Running on the Verde

Experienced boaters in kayaks or rafts can venture downriver 59 miles from Camp Verde to Sheep Bridge near Horseshoe Reservoir. You're likely to see wildlife and well-preserved prehistoric ruins along the way. An area of shoreline is closed December–April to protect a bald eagle nesting site. The main river-running season lasts January–early April during spring runoff, but inflatable kayaks can sometimes negotiate the shallow waters off-season. The ice-cold water in winter and spring necessitates use of full or partial wetsuits. With time for rest stops and scouting rapids, rafts typically average two miles per hour.

The wildest water flows between Beasley Flat and Childs. Canoeists often experience trouble negotiating the rapids here, winding up with smashed boats. Unless you really know what you're doing, it's best to avoid the potentially dangerous conditions below Beasley Flat.

Shuttle services may be available—ask at the Camp Verde Chamber of Commerce. The Verde Ranger District offers a *River Runners Guide to the Verde River* and can let you know if any companies offer rafting tours.

Cedar Bench Wilderness

Three trails cross the 16,000-acre wilderness, which extends along the Verde Rim as high as 6,678 feet and drops to a section of the Verde River at 2,800 feet in a remote area south of Camp Verde. Backcountry travelers can reach trailheads at the lower elevations off Forest Road 574 near Beasley Flat and from the rim via Dugas Road from I-17 Exit 268. Utah and alligator juniper, which the pioneers mistakenly called "cedars," grow at the higher elevations and in some canyons along with pinyon pine and Gambel oak. Chaparral covers much of the lower slopes. The Prescott, Tonto, and Coconino Forest maps show the back roads. The Verde Ranger District Office near Camp Verde provides information on road conditions and trails.

Pine Mountain Wilderness

Pine Mountain (6,814 ft.) crowns part of the Verde Rim south of Cedar Bench Wilderness and Camp Verde. The 20,100-acre Pine Mountain Wilderness offers solitude and natural beauty far from towns and highways. Forests of majestic ponderosa pine, pinyon pine and juniper woodlands, and chaparral cover the rough terrain. The rugged eastern side drops to an elevation of 3,800 feet in the Verde Valley. You might see mule or white-tailed deer, javelina, bear, or mountain lion.

To reach the trailhead, take I-17 Dugas Road Exit 268—18 miles south of Camp Verde and 6 miles north of Cordes Junction—then head southeast 18 miles on dirt Forest Road 68 to Salt Flat, a quarter mile before Nelson Place, an abandoned homestead. This road is best attempted in cars only in good weather.

You can hike a 9.6-mile round-trip loop to the top of Pine Mountain on Nelson Trail #159, Pine Mountain Trail #14, Verde Rim Trail #161, and Willow Springs Trail #12. Allow six hours and carry water. Elevation gain is about 1,600 feet. Other loop hikes in the area can be done too. Consult the Prescott, Tonto, or Coconino forest maps and the 7.5-minute Tule Mesa topo map. The Verde Ranger District Office near Camp Verde can advise on road and trail conditions.

COTTONWOOD

Named for the trees along the Verde River, Cottonwood provides a handy base for visiting the old mining town of Jerome, prehistoric ruins at Tuzigoot, wildlife areas, and the other attractions of the Verde Valley. The town is 14 miles northwest of Camp Verde, 17 miles southwest of Sedona, and 41 miles northeast across Mingus Mountain from Prescott.

Cottonwood has a split personality between the original Old Town and the strip development along the new section of Highway 89A that bypasses it. Old Town has the most personality, as you would expect, and is worth a visit; take Historic 89A from either Cottonwood or Clarkdale. Staff at the **Cottonwood Information Center** (928/634-9468, closed Sun.) in Old Town's 1929 jail will tell you about local history and services; a trail to the Verde River begins here.

Clarkdale, two miles northwest of Cottonwood, still has the look of a company town. From 1912 it housed officials and workers of the smelter that operated nearby. Although a lot of residents lost their jobs when the smelter shut down in 1952, others were glad to be rid of its heavy black smoke. You'll see the giant dome and other structures of the Phoenix Cement Company, which supplied the cement used in building Glen Canyon Dam on the Colorado River.

Clemenceau Heritage Museum

The Verde Historical Society operates this museum (corner of Willard St. and Mingus Ave., 928/634-2868, 9 A.M.–noon Wed. and 11 A.M.–3 P.M. Fri.–Sun., donations welcome) in the 1923–1924 Clemenceau School Building. The imaginative displays include a vintage classroom and permanent and rotating exhibits on local history. The model train room illustrates seven historic Verde Valley lines. Outside, you can see the restored 1921 Bank of Clemenceau. A gift shop sells books and souvenirs. The museum sponsors a Crafts American Style art show on the second Saturday of February and a Zeke Taylor Bar-B-Que on the second Saturday of November.

Dead Horse Ranch State Park

Visitors enjoy picnicking, camping, hiking, and fishing year-round at this park (928/634-5283) beside the Verde River. Giant cottonwoods shade the riverbanks and the three lagoons. Birders enjoy sightings year-round, especially along the Verde River Greenway Trail near the river and from a viewing platform at Tavasci Marsh, 1.5 miles northwest of the park. The Verde Valley Birding Festival (www.birdyverde.org) takes place in the park on the last weekend in April.

Hikers, mountain bikers, and equestrians enjoy the 40-mile trail network that extends out across neighboring national forest lands. Mountain bikers and hikers can make a seven-mile loop on Raptor Hill, Thumper, and Lime Kiln Trails, the latter once part of an old route between Sedona and Jerome. This intermediate ride, which connects with other trails, takes

© BILL WEIR

a quiet morning at the East Lagoon

about 1.5 hours on a mountain bike or 3.5 hours on foot.

The river and lagoons harbor trout in winter in addition to year-round largemouth bass, catfish, and bluegill; fly fishermen use a riverside trail upstream from the River Day Use Area. The lower (east) lagoon has a dock and boat ramp; you can take a boat out in this and the middle lagoons, but without motors or sails. Fish-cleaning stations are nearby.

The campgrounds offer showers and both dry and hookup sites. Tenters have a loop just for them in the upper part of the North Campground; the sites have fine views of the Verde Valley, but no shade trees. Equestrians can arrange to camp with their horses (ask in advance). On spring and autumn weekends all sites may fill and it's best to arrive early; you can call to check availability, but family sites are first-come, first-served. Groups can reserve their own areas. Cabins may be available by late 2005. A dump station is just inside the park entrance. Day use costs $5 per vehicle, campsites for tents or RVs run $12–$15 with no hookups, $19–22 with water and electric. From Main Street in Cottonwood, turn north on 10th Street and follow signs .9 miles.

Tuzigoot National Monument

Sinagua built and lived in this hilltop pueblo from the early 1100s to the early 1400s. Tuzigoot (TOO-zee-goot) stood two stories and contained about 77 ground-floor and perhaps 15 second-story rooms. At its peak in the late 1300s, the pueblo housed 225 people. The large size of the ruin may be the result of a drought in the 1200s, which forced many dry-land farmers to resettle at Tuzigoot and other villages near the Verde River. Most rooms lacked doorways—a ladder through a hatchway in the roof permitted entry. The original roofs, now gone, had pine and sycamore beams covered by willow branches and sealed with mud. While excavating the site in 1933–1934, University of Arizona researchers found a wide variety of artifacts, including grave offerings for 408 burials.

The Apache name Tuzigoot originally referred to nearby Peck's Lake and meant Crooked Water; people liked the word because it had a nice ring to it, so they gave the name to this site. Take Broadway, the old road running between Cottonwood and Clarkdale, then turn east 1.3 miles on Tuzigoot Road to the ruins.

A visitors center (928/634-5564, www.nps.gov/tuzi, 8 A.M.–5 P.M. daily, extended to 8 A.M.–7 P.M. daily Memorial Day–Labor Day, $3/person age 17+) next to the ruins displays some of the archaeological finds, including stone axes and tools, projectile points, pottery, turquoise and shell jewelry, and religious objects. Other exhibits illustrate what's known about Sinagua agriculture, weaving, building techniques, and burials. A room replica shows how a living area at Tuzigoot might have looked.

Outside, a quarter-mile trail loops through the maze of ruins; it's paved but too steep for wheelchairs. You can climb up to a second-story lookout at the summit for a panorama. The paved and level **Tavasci Marsh Overlook Trail** also begins just outside the visitors center and goes out to a viewpoint with good birding in .3 miles one-way.

Verde Canyon Railroad

Travelers embark at the Clarkdale station for a leisurely journey upstream into the beautiful Verde River Canyon (300 N. Broadway, Clarkdale, AZ 86324, 928/639-0010 or 800/293-7245, www.verdecanyonrr.com). A guide narrates the history and points out some of the historic ranches, wildlife, and geologic features. Bald eagles can often be seen nesting in spring; golden eagles, hawks, and blue herons may be sighted, too. The ride lasts about four hours round-trip, with turnaround at the historic railway buildings in Perkinsville. Vintage diesel engines pull comfortable, climate-controlled cars. If the weather's fine, you can stroll out to the open cars for the best panoramas. A café/grill at the station serves lunch, which you can have on the picnic tables outside or take on the train. A few snack items can be purchased on board; first-class includes hot and cold hors d'oeuvres. A small railroad museum (free) in the station exhibits historic photos and artifacts. A gift shop sells souvenirs. From Cottonwood, head north on Main Street, which becomes Broadway; if coming from Jerome, follow signs for Clarkdale and the railroad.

Tickets for coach class cost $40 adults, $36 seniors 65 and older, and $25 children under 12; first-class has plush, more spacious seating at $60 (all ages). Trains run 2–6 days a week depending on season—spring and autumn have the most departures. Special excursions include the Starlight Tours, which run on Saturday evenings near the full moon in the warmer months. Wheelchair users have access to the station and train.

Lower Sycamore Canyon

About four miles west of town, **Parsons Trail #144** drops into the mouth of Sycamore Canyon and winds upstream past lush foliage and towering cottonwood trees to Parsons Spring, 3.7 miles one-way with a 300-foot elevation change. Shorter hikes can be just as enjoyable as you admire the canyon walls, sparkling water, wildflowers, and birds. The trail makes six crossings of Sycamore Creek, which are easy except during spring runoff or after storms. You could also continue far up the canyon beyond the springs on a multiday trip. Another possibility is to hike Packard Trail #66, which connects the west rim with the creek, meeting where the Parsons Trail first joins the canyon bottom. Note that no camping is allowed in the lower canyon—you must proceed beyond Parson Spring. Nearly the entire canyon lies within the Sycamore Canyon Wilderness (see the description in the *West of Sedona* section).

From Cottonwood or Clarkdale, follow directions toward Tuzigoot National Monument across the Verde River, then turn left on Sycamore Canyon Road and follow it about nine miles past the abandoned mansion, once used by the Clark family, and the smokestack of the former Arizona Power Company. Most of this road is unpaved but possible for cars in dry weather.

Entertainment and Events

Blazin' M Ranch (928/634-0334 or 800/937-8643, www.blazinm.com) serves up a chuckwagon supper followed by a Western stage show with cowboy songs and humor. Other attractions include an old-time photo studio, train and horse rides, and a shooting gallery. Don't

COURTESY OF BLAZIN M RANCH

The Blazin' M Cowboys put on a great show.

miss the Wood 'N' West Gallery of animated wooden figures in dioramas that portray historic and humorous Old West scenes. The gate opens at 5 P.M. Wednesday–Saturday for outdoor activities, 6:30 P.M. for dinner of barbecued beef or chicken or a vegetarian option, then the show starts at 7:30 P.M.; closed January and August. Dinner and show cost $22 for adults, $13 for lil' wranglers 12 and under. Reservations are recommended, especially for a vegetarian dinner. Take 10th Street past the Dead Horse Ranch State Park entrance and follow signs.

Major annual events include the **Verde Valley Gem and Mineral Show** in late March and **Verde Valley Birding Festival** (www.birdyverde.org) on the last weekend in April. The **Antique Auto, Cycle & Aeroplane Show** and **Cinco de Mayo Sizzlin' Salsa Sunday** both occur on the first weekend in May, and the **Verde Valley Fair** in early May. The **Fourth of July Celebration,** of course, is in July. You'll find **Verde River Days** (environmental programs) on the last Saturday in September and a **Christmas Parade** in early December.

Recreation

Garrison Park (928/634-7468) near the corner of E. Mingus Avenue and 6th Street offers tennis courts and a summertime swimming pool. **Riverside Park,** near the turnoff for Deadhorse Ranch State Park, has picnic tables, playground, ball fields, and a skate park. The 18-hole **Verde Santa Fe Golf Course** (928/634-5454) is five miles northeast of town on Highway 89A.

Accommodations

Little Daisy Motel (34 S. Main St., 928/634-7865, $48–52 d) offers some kitchenettes. **Pines Motel** (920 S. Camino Real off S. Main St., 928/634-9975 or 800/483-9618, $49 s, $59 d, add $5 weekends) has a pool. **View Motel** (818 S. Main/Hwy. 89A, 928/634-7581, $46–48 s, $60 d room, $60 s, $60–65 d kitchenettes) offers a pool and hot tub up on a hillside.

Budget Inn & Suites (1089 S. AZ 260 near the junction with Hwy. 89A, 928/634-3678 or 888/720-1719, $45–89 s, $49–99 d) has well-equipped rooms. **Quality Inn** (301 W. Hwy. 89A, 928/634-4207 or 800/228-5151, $65–69 d, $69–79 d weekends) has a restaurant, pool, and hot tub. The **Best Western Cottonwood Inn** (993 S. Main St. on the corner of Hwy. 89A and Hwy. 260, 928/634-5575 or 800/350-0025, $55–82 d standard, $99 d deluxe) also features a restaurant, pool, and hot tub.

Flying Eagle Country Bed & Breakfast (2700 Windmill Lane in Clarkdale, 928/634-0211, $110 d) has fine views of the Verde Valley from its hillside setting; guests have a full breakfast, hot tub, and private bath.

Campgrounds

Dead Horse Ranch State Park and RV parks offer year-round camping with showers. **Turquoise Triangle RV Park** (2501 E. Hwy. 89A, 928/634-5294 or 888/994-7275, $22 RV w/hookups) is 1.5 blocks east of the junction with Highway 260. **Rio Verde RV Park** (3420 E. Hwy. 89A, 928/634-5990, $15 tent, $25 RV w/hookups) lies one mile east from the junction with Highway 260.

Food

In the dimly lit interior of **Nic's Italian Steak & Crab House** (925 N. Main St. in Old Town Cottonwood, 928/634-9626, nightly dinner, $10–29), chefs prepare tasty seafood, Tuscan-style grilled steaks, ribs, chicken, veal, and pasta; no reservations taken. Artwork decorates **Old Town Café** (1025 N. Main in Old Town Cottonwood, 928/634-5980, Tues.–Sat. breakfast and lunch, $6–7.50), which has an espresso bar, pastries, soups, salads, and sandwiches.

La Carreta (2181 E. Hwy. 89A, just east of the junction with Hwy. 260, 928/649-2845, daily lunch and dinner, $7–13) prepares Mexican cuisine. **Su Casa** (1000 S. Main St. in Clarkdale, 928/634-2771, daily lunch and dinner, $6–11) is a south-of-the-border café with a good selection of fajitas, asada dishes, and vegetarian items.

Mai Thai on Main (157 S. Main St., 928/649-2999, daily lunch and dinner, $7.50–11) fixes flavorful teriyaki, stir fries, noodle dishes, curries, and salads. **Golden Dragon** (1675 N. Cottonwood St. in Sawmill Square Shopping Center, 928/634-0588, daily lunch and dinner, $7–15) features Mandarin and Szechwan cuisine with a choice of menu or buffet offerings. **Ming House** (888 S. Main St., 928/639-2885, daily lunch and dinner, $6–12) prepares Hunan, Szechwan, and Cantonese food, also with a buffet option.

You can buy groceries at **Fry's** (Wal-Mart Shopping Center), **Safeway** (Sawmill Square Shopping Center), and **Food City** (Verde Valley Plaza). **Mount Hope Foods Naturally** is at 853 S. Main Street.

Information and Services

People at the **Cottonwood Chamber of Commerce** (1010 S. Main St., Cottonwood, AZ 86326, 928/634-7593, http://chamber.verdevalley.com, 9 A.M.–5 P.M. daily except holidays) will tell you about the sights, events, and facilities in the area. The office is in an adobe-style building conveniently located at the intersection of Highway 89A and Highway 260. **Cottonwood Public Library** (100 S. 6th St., 928/634-7559, closed Sun.) is between Highway 89A and Mingus Avenue.

The **post office** is at 700 E. Mingus Avenue. **Verde Valley Medical Center** (269 S. Candy Lane, 928/634-2251, www.verdevalleymedicalcenter.com) provides medical services and a regional physician directory.

Getting There

The **Sedona–Phoenix Shuttle** (928/282-2066 or 800/448-7988, $40 one-way, $75 round-trip) operates about eight times daily between Sedona and Phoenix Sky Harbor Airport with a stop at the Best Western Inn at Cottonwood. **Ace Xpress Shuttle Service** (928/639-3357 or 800/336-2239, www.acexpressshuttle.com, $51 one-way, $84 round-trip) provides door-to-door service from Sedona and the Verde Valley to Sky Harbor Airport.

JEROME

Jerome, clinging to the slopes of Cleopatra Hill above the Verde Valley, may have Arizona's most unusual layout and history. For more than 70 years the town's booming mines produced copper, gold, and silver. Most residents departed after 1953 when the mines closed, but Jerome has come back to life with museums, art galleries, antique shops, and restaurants. Old-fashioned buildings—some restored, others abandoned—add to the atmosphere. Walking Jerome's winding streets is like touring a museum of early-20th-century American architecture.

Expansive views across the Verde Valley take in Sedona's Red Rock Country, Sycamore Canyon, the Mogollon Rim, and the distant San Francisco Peaks. Three very different museums will introduce you to the human and mining history of the area.

History

Prehistoric tribes came to dig brilliant blue azurite and other copper minerals for use as paint and jewelry. Spanish explorers, shown the diggings by Native American guides, failed to see any worth in the place. In 1876, several American prospectors staked claims to the rich copper deposits, but they lacked the resources to develop them. Eugene Jerome, a wealthy lawyer and financier, smelled a profit and offered financial backing to those who would mine the ore. A surveyor laying out the town site named it in honor of the Jerome family, though Eugene himself never visited the area.

From the time the United Verde Copper Company began operating in 1882, the town's economy went on a wild roller-coaster ride dependent on copper prices. Mines closed for brief periods, then reopened. So many saloons, gambling dens, and brothels thrived in Jerome that a New York newspaper called it the "wickedest town in the West." Fires roared through the frame houses and businesses three times between 1897 and 1899, yet Jerome rose again each time, eventually becoming Arizona's fifth-largest city. Underground blasting and fault slippage shook the earth so much that some buildings keeled over and banks refused to take the average Jerome house or business as collateral. The town's famous sliding jail took off across the street and down the hillside, where it still lies today.

The community enjoyed its greatest prosperity during the Roaring '20s, when the population hit 15,000. The stock market crash and ensuing Depression spelled disaster for the copper industry; mines and smelter shut down and the population plummeted to less than 5,000. World War II brought Jerome's last period of prosperity before the mines closed for good in 1953. Many people thought Jerome would become a ghost town when the population shrank to only 50 souls. But, beginning in the late 1960s, artists, shop owners, tourists, retirees, and others rediscovered Jerome's unique character and setting.

Exploring Jerome

A walk around downtown will turn up lots of history and art. You'll get some good exercise too, as there's little level ground. Locals use stairways as a shortcut to get from one part of this vertical town to another, and you can also. The two one-way streets, Main and Hull, in the center of Jerome make a good walking loop. Plaques on some of the buildings tell about their colorful history. When you need a break, pop into a café or have a picnic at one of the shaded tables across Hull Avenue from the visitors center. Carriage rides provide another option for sightseeing; they start near the visitors center.

In the upper part of town, visit the unusual 1894 **Holy Family Church,** a large brick building just above the switchback. While many old Jerome structures have a pressed-metal ceiling, this church has decorative metal panels on the walls as well. It's no longer used for services, but is normally open daily for visitors. You can read about its history inside and admire the statues and other artwork.

Jerome State Historic Park

The Douglas Mansion, built in 1916 by James "Rawhide Jimmy" Douglas, tops a hill overlooking the Little Daisy Mine. Today, the old adobe-brick mansion (928/634-5381, 8 A.M.–5 P.M. daily, $3 adults, $2 ages 7–13) brims with Jerome mining lore. A video presentation portrays the many changes Jerome has seen. Old photos and artifacts introduce the miners and describe community life. An assay office, mining tools, and mineral displays show how the workers extracted metals from the earth. You can get a feel for what lies below in the three-dimensional model of Jerome's mineshafts, underground work areas, and geologic features. The elegant Douglas library looks much as it did when Rawhide Jimmy lived here.

COURTESY OF JEROME STATE PARK

a look inside the United Verde Mine's power room in 1911

At the viewpoints outside, signs identify many of Jerome's historic buildings. Walk around the mansion to see a giant stamp mill and the more primitive *arrastre* (drag-stone mill) and Chilean wheels once used to pulverize ore, plus other mining gear. Old vehicles rest in the carriage house. A small picnic area beside the mansion offers expansive views of the Verde Valley. Turn off Highway 89A at Milepost 345 at the lower end of Jerome (8 miles west of Cottonwood), then follow the paved road one mile.

Jerome Historical Society Mine Museum

Exhibits in an 1899 building that once housed a fashion salon now illustrate Jerome's development with paintings, photos, stock certificates, mining tools, and ore samples. A gift shop sells books about Jerome's fascinating history. The museum (928/634-5477, 9 A.M.–4:30 P.M. daily, $1 adults, free for children under 12) is downtown at the corner of Main Street and Jerome Avenue; look for the two large half-wheels.

Gold King Mine & Ghost Town

If you've ever wanted to poke around a ghost town, or if you're fascinated by old machinery, you'll enjoy this collection (928/634-0053, www.goldkingmine.net, 9 A.M.–5 P.M. daily, $4 adults, $3 seniors 62–74, $2 children 6–12). The mine and the town of Haynes came to life here in 1890–1914, when miners dug a 1,200-foot-deep shaft to extract a modest amount of gold and silver. Among the hoists, pumps, engines, five-stamp mill, and ore cars, look for the prospect tunnel, a blacksmith shop, a schoolhouse, and an assay office. For a small fee, you can see and hear "Big Bertha" run; it's a three-cylinder, 10,154-cubic-inch engine that once powered a mine; the flywheel alone weighs 13,000 pounds! A small petting zoo attracts the kids. You can watch an antique sawmill in operation daily. More than 100 trucks and other historic vehicles line the streets. Many are Studebakers, including a 1902 electric that still runs. An antique truck and equipment show takes place here in May on the weekend before Mother's Day, and there's a VW bus show in mid-September.

Enter through the gift shop, which sells mining memorabilia and other souvenirs. From the upper switchback on Highway 89A in downtown Jerome, turn northwest and drive one mile on Perkinsville Road. On the way you'll pass a large open-pit mine on the left, where Jerome's smelter stood at the beginning of the 20th century.

Perkinsville Road

This scenic back road drops from Jerome to the Verde River at the historic Perkinsville Ranch, then climbs into the ponderosa pine forests of the Mogollon Rim and on to downtown Williams. The first 27 miles are dirt, followed by 25 of pavement. Cars may be able to negotiate the road—bumpy and dusty in places—in dry weather. All vehicles should avoid the route after winter snowstorms or heavy summer rains. Allow at least three hours for a one-way drive, or more to stop for views, hikes, or a picnic. Stock up on gas and supplies, as none are available along the way. Turn northwest onto Perkinsville Road at the upper switchback in Jerome.

Mingus Mountain

The high country seven miles southwest of Jerome offers many camping, hiking, and back-road driving possibilities. Contact the Prescott National Forest offices in Prescott and near Camp Verde for recreation information. **Summit Picnic Area** (free), at the 7,023-foot pass on Highway 89A between Jerome and Prescott, offers tables, paved parking, and restrooms. In winter, this spot transforms into **Summit Snowplay,** where visitors glide along on innertubes and plastic dishes, but not on sleds; there's a $5 per vehicle parking fee.

Also at this pass, turn north a half mile on a paved road for **Potato Patch Campground,** which offers pull-through RV sites with electricity and water in B Loop for $15, and nonhookup sites farther back in the forest at Loop A for $10; the season runs May–September. On the way in, you'll pass a trailhead on the left for the Woodchute Wilderness.

The turnoff for **Mingus Mountain Campground** is on the other side of the highway at the pass; head in three miles on unpaved Forest Road 104; sites are open about May–September, with a $6 fee but no drinking water. Groups can reserve nearby **Playground** (877/444-6777 or www.reserveusa.com). Besides these developed campgrounds, you can also find many undeveloped places off the forest roads.

The small, 5,700-acre **Woodchute Wilderness** protects the gentle slopes of Woodchute Mountain (7,834 ft.), about 10 miles west of Jerome. Woodchute Trail heads north to the summit from a trailhead near Potato Patch Campground.

Entertainment and Events

For entertainment, locals hang out in the Spirit Room of the **Connor Hotel** and at **Paul & Jerry's Saloon,** both on upper Main Street. The **Jerome Home Tour,** on the third weekend of May, visits historic houses and buildings not normally open to the public. A **Garden and Patio Tour** runs in June. The Gold King Mine & Ghost town hosts its **Antique Truck and Equipment Show** on the weekend before Mother's Day in May and a **VW Bus Show** in mid-September. Jerome celebrates **Miners' Days/Spook Weekend** with miners' competitions, mariachi bands, and street vendors on the third weekend of October.

Shopping

Shops up and down Main Street and Hull Avenue display a wide variety of artwork, crafts, antiques, jewelry, and clothing. The one most likely to put a smile on your face is the 1890 **House of Joy** at 416 Hull Avenue. A bordello from 1912 to 1946, it later became a very popular restaurant. People had to make reservations far in advance to sample the culinary excellence, and chef/owner John Dempsey had the satisfaction of turning down President Nixon when all the tables had been booked. After three decades of serving food, John and his wife Mary semiretired and turned the building into a one-of-a-kind gift shop. Step inside to admire the brothel decor and the original ceiling. Prints of bygone "ladies" and other collectibles fill the cozy rooms.

A few doors downhill, **Jerome Artists Cooperative Gallery** (502 Main St., 928/639-4276, www.jeromeartistscoop.com) exhibits works by about 40 artists in the 1917 Hotel Jerome at the lower end of the one-way section. The **Old Mingus Art Center** houses galleries in former school buildings at the lower end of town. Of these, **Anderson/Mandette Studio** (928/634-3438, www.anderson-mandette.com, 11 A.M.–6 P.M. daily) has by far the largest collection on display.

Accommodations

Jerome's hotels and bed and breakfasts offer character and great views; make reservations for weekends. **Jerome Grand Hotel** (928/634-8200 or 888/817-6788, www.jeromegrandhotel.com) features a commanding panorama, comfortable lodging, and fine dining in the upper part of town. After opening in 1927 as the United Verde Hospital, then closing in 1950, the building lay dormant until an extensive renovation converted it to the hotel in 1996. All rooms have private bath and run $95 d for a standard, $120 d for a balcony, $160 d for connecting rooms, and $215 d for a suite. It's at the top of narrow Hill Street, which turns up opposite Jerome Palace's Haunted Hamburger.

The Surgeon's House (at the base of Hill St., 928/639-1452 or 800/639-1452, $100–150 d) has bed and breakfast rooms, all with private bath and three with views; the mining company built it in 1916 for the chief surgeon. The 1898 **Connor Hotel** (164 Main St., 928/634-5006 or 800/523-3554, www.connorhotel.com, $90–115 d) is the only original Jerome hotel still in business; all rooms have private bath.

The circa 1899 **Inn at Jerome** (309 Main St., 928/634-5094 or 800/634-5094, www.innatjerome.com, $55–85 d) features Victorian-style rooms—two with private bath—and a full breakfast. **Ghost City Inn** (541 Main St., 928/634-4678 or 888/634-4678, www.ghostcityinn.com, $90–135 d) occupies an 1898 Victorian boardinghouse filled with antiques; all rooms have private bath and there's a hot tub. **Cottage Inn** (747 East Ave., 928/634-0701, $75 d with breakfast) dates from 1904 and has 1940s decor.

Campgrounds

Besides Dead Horse Ranch State Park and the RV parks in Cottonwood, you can head seven miles up Highway 89A to the cool forests of Mingus Mountain.

Food

The Asylum (Jerome Grand Hotel, up Hill St. opposite the Haunted Hamburger, 928/639-3197, www.theasylum.biz, daily lunch and dinner, $17–28) prepares American cuisine and offers a long list of wines, some available by the glass. **Jerome Palace's Haunted Hamburger** (410 N. Clark St./AZ 89A, 928/634-0554, daily lunch and dinner, $12–16) features steak, prime rib, pasta, and sandwiches on the upper side of town. You can dine indoors or on the patio, which has great views.

Jerome Brewery (111 Main St., 928/639-8477, daily lunch and dinner, $7–10) offers several of their brews plus a long list of tasty appetizers, pizzas, gourmet sandwiches, and salads. **English Kitchen** (119 Jerome Ave., 928/634-2132, Tues.–Sun. breakfast and lunch, $3.50–8.50) is the oldest restaurant in Arizona; you can read about Chinese immigrant Charley Hong who established it in 1899. The patio has views.

Jerome Grill (309 Main St., 928/634-5094, daily breakfast and lunch, $6–9.50) serves American and Southwestern food. **Red Rooster Café** (363 Main St., 928/634-7087, daily lunch, $6–8) serves tasty quiches, sandwiches, soups, salads, and desserts in the building that housed Arizona's first Safeway. **Flatiron Café** (at the fork in the lower part of town where Hwy. 89A divides, 928/634-2733, may close Thurs., $6.50–8.50) serves breakfast, sandwiches, baked goods, fancy coffees, salads, and other refreshments in the morning and afternoon; there's a patio across Main Street.

Information and Services

Jerome Chamber of Commerce (310 Hull Ave., Drawer K, Jerome, AZ 86331, 928/634-2900, http://jerome.chamber.com) has information on sights and services in town; hours depend on staffing. It's near the sliding jail just past the large parking lots on the uphill section of Highway 89A. Jerome Community Park across the street has some tree-shaded picnic tables. **Jerome Public Library** (601 Clark St./Hwy. 89A, 928/639-0574) is in the upper part of town in the 1924 Clark Street Elementary School building. The **post office** is at 120 Main Street.

Prescott and Vicinity

That's *Prescutt,* pardner. The mile-high town rests in a mountain basin ringed by the pine-forested Bradshaws, towering Thumb Butte, the jumbled mass of Granite Mountain, boulder-strewn Granite Dells, and the vast grasslands of Chino and Lonesome Valleys. Downtown, the Doric-columned courthouse sits in a spacious grassy plaza surrounded by tall elm trees. The equestrian statue in front of the courthouse commemorates the spirit of William "Buckey" O'Neill, newspaperman, sheriff, mayor, adventurer, and Spanish-American War hero. Buckey led a company of Theodore Roosevelt's Rough Riders in Cuba, where an enemy bullet cut him down.

The Palace and a few other bars on Montezuma Street opposite the courthouse carry on the tradition of "Whiskey Row," where more than 20 saloons roared full-blast day and night in the late 1800s and early 1900s. The Sharlot Hall Museum, two blocks west, preserves Prescott's past with early buildings and excellent historical collections. On the other side of downtown, the Smoki (SMOKE-eye) Museum displays a wealth of artifacts from Native American cultures. About 100 Yavapai live in the Prescott area, mostly on a 1,400-acre reservation just north of town.

Though small, Prescott (pop. 36,000) contains several art galleries, an active artists' community, two colleges, and an aeronautical university. Just outside town, you can explore the area's forests, fishing lakes, mountains, and ghost towns.

History

Unlike most Western towns, which haphazardly boomed into existence, Prescott sprang from a

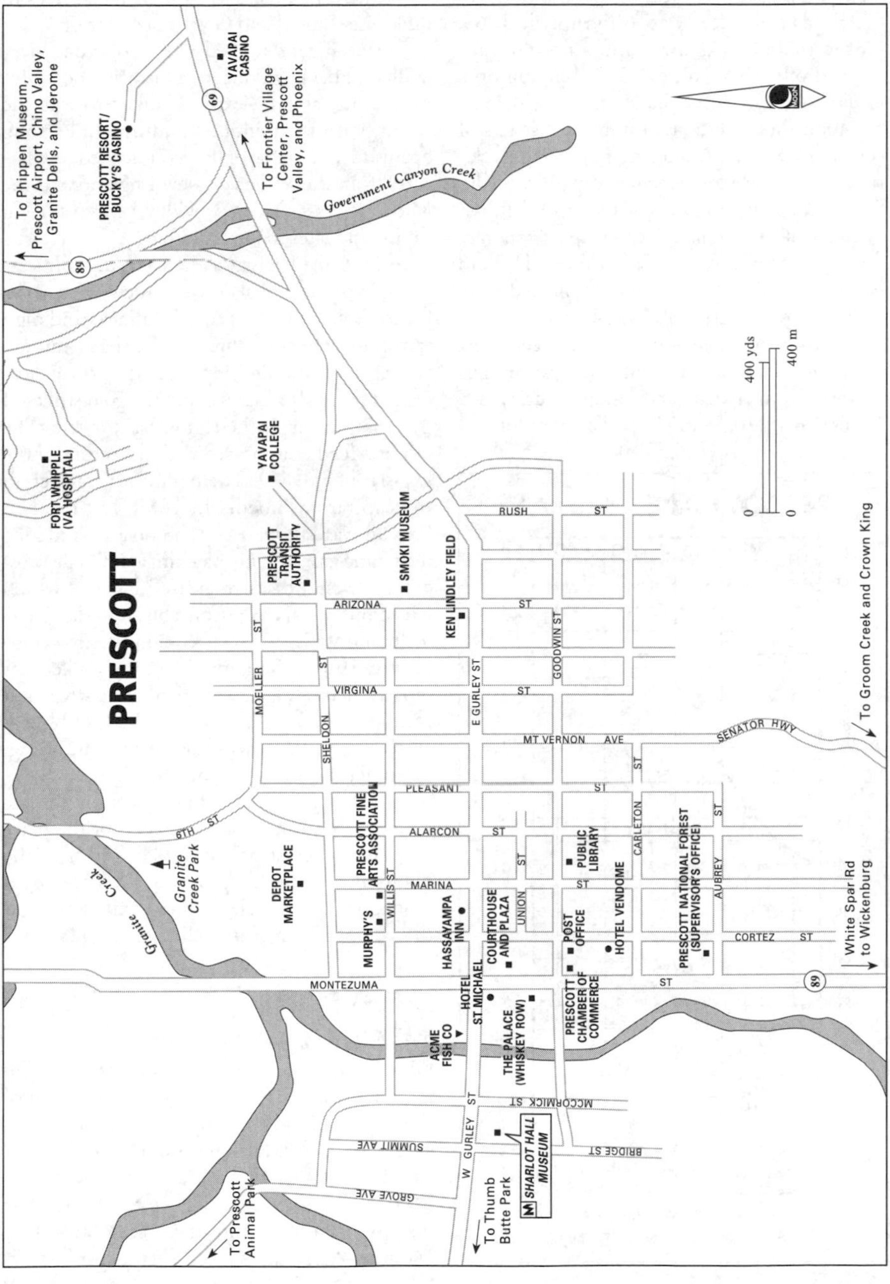

PRESCOTT

To Phippen Museum, Prescott Airport, Chino Valley, Granite Dells, and Jerome

YAVAPAI CASINO

PRESCOTT RESORT/ BUCKY'S CASINO

To Frontier Village Center, Prescott Valley, and Phoenix

Government Canyon Creek

FORT WHIPPLE (VA HOSPITAL)

YAVAPAI COLLEGE

PRESCOTT TRANSIT AUTHORITY

SMOKI MUSEUM

KEN LINDLEY FIELD

RUSH ST

ARIZONA

MOELLER ST

VIRGINA

SHELDON ST

E GURLEY ST

GOODWIN ST

MT VERNON AVE

SENATOR HWY

6TH ST

PLEASANT ST

CARLETON

To Groom Creek and Crown King

PRESCOTT FINE ARTS ASSOCIATION

ALARCON ST

PUBLIC LIBRARY

DEPOT MARKETPLACE

Granite Creek Park

MARINA

WILLIS ST

COURTHOUSE AND PLAZA

UNION ST

PRESCOTT NATIONAL FOREST (SUPERVISOR'S OFFICE)

AUBREY ST

MURPHY'S

HASSAYAMPA INN

POST OFFICE

HOTEL VENDOME

CORTEZ ST

White Spar Rd to Wickenburg

MONTEZUMA

HOTEL ST MICHAEL

PRESCOTT CHAMBER OF COMMERCE

ACME FISH CO

THE PALACE (WHISKEY ROW)

McCORMICK ST

BRIDGE ST

SUMMIT AVE

W GURLEY ST

SHARLOT HALL MUSEUM

GROVE AVE

To Prescott Animal Park

To Thumb Butte Park

400 yds

400 m

0

0

North-Central Arizona

© AVALON TRAVEL PUBLISHING, INC.

plan. Soon after Congress carved the territory of Arizona from New Mexico Territory in 1863, Governor John Goodwin and a party of appointed officials set off from Washington on a tour of the area. Their arduous three-month journey took them to the rich mineral districts of central Arizona, a promising new region relatively free of the Confederate sympathizers who lived in the southern towns of Tucson and Tubac.

Goodwin and his party first set up a temporary capital at Fort Whipple in Chino Valley. Then, to be closer to mining activities and timbered land, both the government and the fort moved 17 miles south to a site along Granite Creek. Fort Whipple served as the center for campaigns against Tonto Apache and Yavapai during the 1860s and 1870s. Sentries stood on alert for Native American attacks as workers felled trees to build the Capitol and Governor's Mansion.

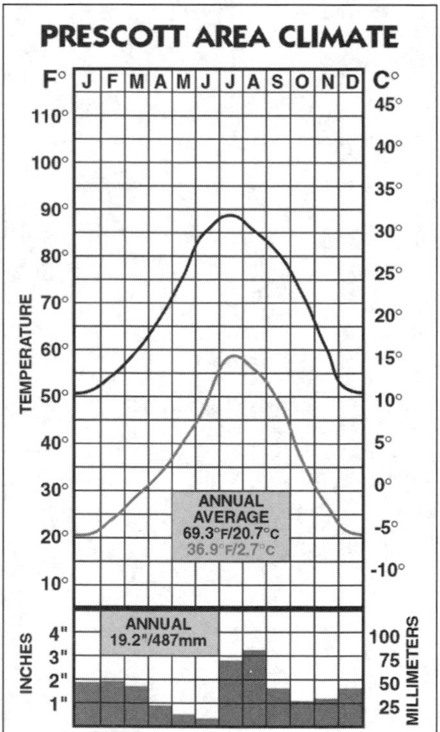

Early citizens named the settlement after William Hickling Prescott, a historian noted for his writings about Mexico. Unlike towns to the south, with their adobe buildings and strong Spanish-Mexican flavor, Prescott derived its character from the settlers of New England and the Midwest. Vast forests provided timber for log cabins and later frame buildings.

In 1867 the Legislature had a change of heart and moved the capital down to Tucson. Prescott's future looked bleak, as Apache attacks and high transportation costs threatened further mining and agricultural development. However, improved mining techniques and the gold strikes of the 1870s brought the region back to life. The outlook further improved with the return of the Legislature in 1877. The politicians transferred the capital to Phoenix in 1889, but by then Prescott was a thriving city and no longer needed the politicians. Mining, ranching, and trade prospered. Even a disastrous fire in 1900, which wiped out much of Prescott's business district—including Whiskey Row—couldn't destroy community spirit. Undaunted, the saloonkeepers moved their salvaged stock across the street and continued to serve libations as the fires blazed. Within days the townsfolk began rebuilding, creating the downtown you see today.

Agriculture and a bit of mining continue in the Prescott area, but it's the character of the place that charms most people. You'll find it in the many historic buildings lining Prescott's tree-shaded streets, the clean pine-scented air, and the agreeable four-season climate.

SIGHTS

Sharlot Hall Museum

Nine buildings make up this superb historical museum (415 W. Gurley St., two blocks west of the plaza, 928/445-3122, www.sharlot.org, $5 ages 19 and up). Summer hours (May–Sept.) run 10 A.M.–2 P.M. Sunday, 10 A.M.–5 P.M. Monday–Saturday; during the rest of the year it's closed Sunday and open 10 A.M.–4 P.M. Monday–Saturday. Check for upcoming liv-

ARIZONA'S DOOMSDAY CAPITAL

Although it's well known that Prescott had served as the first capital of Arizona, the mile-high city could have been the final capital. On September 21, 1961, at the height of cold-war hysteria, the *Arizona Republic* reported that state civil defense leaders had chosen Prescott to be the emergency capital if disaster struck. A three-inch-thick survival plan spelled out the details of how the state government would respond after a nuclear war. Prescott and Yavapai County, because they had no "priority targets," seemed the perfect refuge in case Phoenix had to be evacuated.

If the worst nightmares had come to pass, the National Guard Armory on Prescott's Gurley Street would have become the civil defense control center. State officials would set up shop on the west side of town, and federal departments on the east. State legislators were to meet in the three-story Elks Building, across from the Hassayampa Hotel, with representatives in the Elks Theater and senators in the Elks Club auditorium. Prescott Junior High would be transformed into the capitol. Members of the Arizona Supreme Court were to huddle in the Yavapai County Courthouse basement.

With a massive influx of refugees expected from other parts of Arizona and even the West Coast, the plans dictated that nonessential state agencies be suspended and their staff moved over to the ghost town of Jerome. In a last pitch for survival if Prescott had to be abandoned, the old Douglas mansion in Jerome was to be the state control center. And finally, the miles of tunnels beneath the old mining town could have sheltered many thousands of people if radioactive clouds swept in over the hills. One can imagine that metal drums of stale water and boxes of moldy biscuits still lie deep underground in Jerome's abandoned mines.

ing history programs, lectures, festivals, and theater productions.

You could start with a visit to the **Museum Center,** which offers a display illustrating the life of Sharlot Hall, temporary exhibits, and the Museum Archives (noon–4 P.M. Tues.–Fri., 10 A.M.–2 P.M. Sat.). Sharlot Hall, who founded the museum in 1927, was herself a pioneer—she arrived in Arizona by wagon in 1882 at the tender age of 12, then developed a keen interest in the land and people here. From 1909 to 1911 Sharlot served as the territory's first historian, traveling Arizona's primitive roads to collect information and stories firsthand. She also shared her impressions in stories and poems.

The two-story **Governor's Mansion,** built from logs on this site in 1864, might today seem too primitive to qualify as a mansion, but in those days most people lived in tents or lean-tos. In the beginning, Governor John Goodwin and Territorial Secretary Richard McCormick occupied opposite ends of the building. The territorial Legislature may have met here while awaiting completion of the Capitol. The mansion has been restored and furnished as it was during the early years. Outside, the **rose garden** commemorates outstanding Arizona women of the territorial years.

Exhibits inside the **Sharlot Hall Building** recreate military life at Fort Whipple and recall early ranches, mining operations, frontier saloons and stores, home life, and Prescott heroes. One room houses the exhibit *The Baskets Keep Talking: The Continuing Story of the Yavapai-Prescott Indian Tribe.*

Fort Misery, Arizona's oldest wooden structure, dates from 1863–1864 when it served as a general store. Judge John Howard lived here in the 1890s, and one story relates that the hospitable judge was such a bad cook that guests received "misery" at suppertime. The cabin appears as it did when he lived in it. The **Schoolhouse** is a replica of the territory's first public school, built near Granite Creek in 1867. The little **Ranch House** represents those of pioneers in the Prescott area.

The 1875 **Frémont House** contains furnishings typical of a well-to-do family of the late 1870s. Its wood-plank construction shows a considerable advance over the Governor's Mansion built just 11 years earlier. John C. Frémont, Arizona's fifth territorial governor, rented the

BUCKEY O'NEILL

William Owen O'Neill (1860–1898) came to Arizona in 1879, lured by Govenor John C. Frémont's promotion of the territory. After first visiting Tombstone and Phoenix, O'Neill arrived in Prescott, where he worked as court reporter, editor of the *Miner,* editor and publisher of the *Hoof and Horn,* probate judge, school superintendent, sheriff, tax assessor, author, onyx quarry operator, militia commander, volunteer fireman, and mayor. O'Neill got his nickname Buckey for "bucking the tiger" in faro, whose game cards had tigers on their backs.

When the Spanish-American War broke out in 1898, this popular figure petitioned Governor McCord for permission to raise "one thousand Arizona cowboys" to fight in Cuba. Although only 170 men came from Arizona, recruits from other western states and territories joined the group. Newspapers christened the volunteers the "Rough Riders." Displaying his courage below Kettle Hill in Cuba, Buckey reportedly said, "the Spanish bullet is not molded that will kill me"—just before being fatally shot by a sniper on July 1, 1898.

house 1878–1881. He had earned fame as an explorer of the West, but he failed in Arizona politics. Frémont didn't care for Prescott's climate and spent long periods back East or in Tucson. Public pressure forced his resignation after three years in office.

Admire the details of the 1877 late-Victorian **Bashford House** and step inside to see a few exhibits and a large gift shop that sells crafts and Arizona history books. Exhibits in the **Transportation Building** include Sharlot Hall's 1927 Durant Star Four auto, a stagecoach, wagons, sleighs, and bicycles.

Smoki Museum

From a split-twig figure of 4,000 years ago to the beautiful baskets and pottery of contemporary tribes, this collection (147 N. Arizona St., one block north of E. Gurley St., 928/445-1230, www.smokimuseum.org, $4 adults, $3 seniors over 65, $2 students, free for children 12 and under) preserves a wide variety of Southwest Native American artifacts. It's open 1–4 P.M. Sunday, 10 A.M.–4 P.M. Monday–Saturday, but is closed Tuesday–Thursday January–March. Much of the pottery and many of the stone tools come from prehistoric pit houses excavated in nearby Chino Valley. Paintings and sketches by Kate Cory illustrate Native American life; she lived with the Hopi from 1905 to 1912 and helped design the pueblo-style stone museum building, which opened in 1935. Finely crafted baskets show the skills of Apache, Yavapai, Hualapai, and Havasupai tribes. Some Hopi kachinas are on display too.

Former Senator Barry Goldwater, who belonged to the Smoki, donated many of the museum's items. Kids have a touch table and can try their hand at grinding corn. Guest artist and lecture programs occasionally take place. Researchers can arrange to use the library. A gift shop offers books along with jewelry and other arts and crafts made by Native American and Latin American artisans.

Anglo members of the community organized the Smoki "tribe" in 1921 to raise funds for the annual Frontier Days Rodeo by performing Native American dances. The presentations became very elaborate with a cast and crew in the hundreds. Although criticized by some Native American groups, the Smoki took a serious interest in Native American rituals, dance, and artifacts. The Smoki danced last in 1990 and disbanded in 2001.

Phippen Museum

Changing exhibits by outstanding artists celebrate Western fine art at this museum (4701 N. Hwy. 89, 928/778-1385, www.phippenartmuseum.org, 1–4 P.M. Sun., 10 A.M.–4 P.M. Tues.–Sat., $3 adults, $2 seniors and students, free for children 12 and under). Look for the ranch-style building on the right six miles north of Prescott. Shows change every three months, and you might see either established or promising new artists. The well-liked Western artist George Phippen (1915–1966)

George Phippen in his Skull Valley studio

helped establish the Cowboy Artists of America and served as its first president. You can watch videos on request and use the small library. A museum store sells artwork, jewelry, crafts, and cards. On Memorial Day weekend, the museum sponsors a big Western art show at Courthouse Plaza.

Heritage Park Zoo

Meet denizens of the Southwest, exotic creatures, and farm animals at this small but growing zoo (6 miles north of downtown on Heritage Park Rd., just south off Willow Creek Rd., 928/778-4242, www.heritageparkzoo.org, $5 adults, $4 seniors 65+, $2 children 3–12). Hours are 9 A.M.–5 P.M. daily May–October and 10 A.M.–4 P.M. daily November–April. Celebrities include Abbey the mountain lion, Shikar the Bengal tiger, Inca the black jaguar, and Shash the friendly black bear. Others that you'll meet include ring-tailed lemur, llamas, coatimundi, Mexican wolf, pronghorn, and collared peccary. Birds and reptiles are represented too, and the tarantulas have their own grotto. The zoo offers a picnic area, playground, and gift shop. Zoo by Moonlight takes place on full-moon nights May–September. Groups can arrange tours.

Fort Whipple

This army fort dates from 1863 and honors Brigadier General Amiel Weeks Whipple, who served with the Army Corps of Topographical Engineers until his death in the Civil War. The post played a major role during the Indian wars and was maintained until 1912. Ten years later it took on its present role as a Veterans Administration hospital. Many of the military buildings, including the barracks and officers' quarters, date from around 1900. You're welcome to visit the hospital grounds, though there's no museum or visitors center. Fort Whipple lies on the northeast edge of town off Highway 89.

ENTERTAINMENT AND EVENTS

The **Prescott Fine Arts Association** sponsors an art gallery and gift shop plus a program of plays, musicals, concerts, and family theater in the 1895 Sacred Heart Church at the corner of Marina and Willis Streets. The gallery and gift shop are open noon–4 P.M. Sunday and 10 A.M.–3 P.M. Tuesday–Saturday; shows change about every six weeks. The box office (208 N. Marina St., 928/445-3286, www.pfaa.net, 10 A.M.–3 P.M. Mon.–Sat.) is next door.

Yavapai College (1100 E. Sheldon St., 928/445-7300, www.yc.edu) presents a variety of plays, concerts, and other events in Performance Hall, on the left as you enter the campus. **Yavapai College Art Gallery** (in the same building, 928/776-2031, 10 A.M.–3 P.M. Mon.–Sat.) puts on exhibits by college, community, and national artists; new shows appear about every six weeks. Walk around Performance Hall to see contemporary art in the Sculpture Garden.

Two smoky 24-hour casinos sit on the east edge of town off Highway 69 just east of the Highway 89 junction. **Bucky's Casino** (1500 Hwy. 69, 928/776-5695 or 800/SLOTS-44) is on the hill in the Prescott Resort. The **Yavapai Casino** (1501 Hwy. 69, 928/445-5767or 800/SLOTS-44) is across the highway.

Events

There's something happening every summer night on the **Courthouse Plaza** (928/777-1122)—could be a concert, dance, or speech. **Softball** fans can catch a game in summer—Prescott bills itself as the Softball Capital of the World; contact Parks and Recreation (928/445-5291, www.cityofprescott.net).

Horses race May–September at **Yavapai Downs** (10401 Hwy. 89A, 928/775-8000 Prescott Valley, 602/257-9233 Phoenix, www.yavapaidownsatpv.com). From Prescott, head north on Highway 89, then turn right 8.5 miles on Highway 89A; from Prescott Valley, turn north on Glassford Hill Road, then right on Highway 89A.

On Memorial Day weekend, **Phippen Museum Western Art Show & Sale** brings about 160 artists to Courthouse Plaza. **Prescott Off Street Festival** has arts and crafts nearby on the same weekend.

Three events run on the first weekend of June: **Sharlot Hall Folk Arts Fair** celebrates pioneer skills with costumed participants demonstrating blacksmithing, woodworking, spinning, weaving, churning, and cowboy cooking. **Prescott Valley Days** features a parade, carnival, horse racing, car show, games, entertainment, and dancing. Down-home musicians pick and sing for the **Bluegrass Festival.** In mid-June, **Territorial Days** presents an arts and crafts show.

Around the July 4 holiday, **Frontier Days** (800/358-1888, www.worldsoldestrodeo.com) draws spectators from all over Arizona and beyond for the "World's Oldest Rodeo," in which cowboys have pitted themselves against livestock since 1888. You can also see a huge parade, western art show, entertainment, dances, and fireworks. Events begin in late June and last nearly a week; the parade runs about two hours and is held on a Saturday. On the second full weekend in July, Sharlot Hall Museum hosts the **Indian Art Market** with a variety of art, dances, and demonstrations.

On the third weekend of August, the **Arizona Cowboy Poets Gathering** celebrates the stories and songs of the cowboy life. On the third Saturday in September, **Sharlot Hall Museum Book Festival** brings a wide variety of authors to town. Also in September, look for the **Faire on the Square Arts & Crafts Show** and the **Yavapai County Fair.**

The first weekend of October sees both the **Folk Music Festival** and the **Fallfest in the Park Arts & Crafts Show.** The year winds up with **Arizona's Christmas City** events, including the Courthouse Christmas Lighting and Christmas Parade on the first Saturday in December, followed by the Acker Musical Showcase on the following Friday evening.

SHOPPING

The vast **Frontier Village Center** offers ethnic and chain restaurants and many stores a half mile east on Highway 69. Antiques enthusiasts will find shops in the two blocks of Cortez Street north of Courthouse Plaza.

The **Worm Bookstore** (128 S. Montezuma St., 928/445-0361) offers both new and used books, including many regional titles; topo and other maps are sold too. **Granite Mountain Outfitters** (320 W. Gurley St., 928/776-4949) offers outdoor equipment and supplies, as does **Popular Outdoor Outfitters** (1841 E. Hwy. 69 in Frontier Village Center, 928/445-2430).

RECREATION

The **YMCA** (750 Whipple St., 928/445-7221) has three year-round indoor pools, one mainly for lap swimming, one for diving, and one with a 150-foot water slide. Or swim at the indoor **Yavapai College pool** (1100 E. Sheldon St., 928/776-2175); ask for directions at the visitor center on your right as you enter campus. Play **tennis** at Yavapai College, at Prescott High School (on Ruth St.), or next to Ken Lindley Field (E. Gurley and Arizona Sts.).

Twenty-three miles to the north, **Summit Snowplay** offers wintertime fun in the snow at the 7,023-foot pass on Highway 89A between Prescott and Jerome. Innertubes and plastic dishes can be used, but no sleds. The site has paved parking, toilets, and a $5 per vehicle fee. In summer it's open as the **Summit Picnic Area** (no fee).

Golfers play on the 36-hole course at **Antelope Hills Golf Course** (8 miles north of town on Hwy. 89, 928/776-7888 or 800/972-6818) next to the airport. The town of Dewey, 14 miles east on Highway 69, offers two 18-hole golf courses: **Prescott Golf & Country Club** (928/772-8984 or 800/717-7274, www.prescottgolf.net) and **Quailwood Greens Golf Course** (928/772-0130).

Granite Mountain Stables (northwest of town off Williamson Valley Rd., 928/771-9551) offers hourly, all-day, moonlight, and overnight rides year-round, plus lessons.

ACCOMMODATIONS

Prescott offers a fine selection of places to stay, though few have rooms under $50 in summer. Be sure to make reservations for weekends during the warmer months, when desert dwellers come here to escape the heat. Book far in advance for Frontier Days, held around July 4, and expect to pay more. The following summer rates usually drop in winter. Categories are based on the cost of weekend (Fri.–Sat. nights) double occupancy.

Inns and Bed-and-Breakfasts

Dolls & Roses Bed and Breakfast (109 N. Pleasant St., 928/776-9291 or 800/924-0883, www.dollsandroses-bb.com, $99–109 d) offers rooms in an 1883 Victorian house just three blocks from Courthouse Square. **Pleasant Street Inn** (142 S. Pleasant St. at Goodwin, 928/445-4774 or 877/226-7128, www.pleasantbandb.com, $105–150 d) offers bed and breakfast with a variety of rooms and suites in an English traditional style. **Prescott Country Inn Bed and Breakfast** (503 S. Montezuma St., 928/445-7991 or 888/757-0015, www.prescottcountryinn.com, $59–99 d weekdays, $79–129 d Fri.–Sat.) provides rooms, suites, and cottages with country decor and a continental breakfast. **Prescott Pines Inn** (901 White Spar Rd./Hwy. 89, 928/445-7270 or 800/541-5374, www.prescottpinesinn.com) on the south edge of town offers "country Victorian" rooms for $65–109 d and a three-bedroom chalet for $269; breakfast is extra.

Near Watson Lake, **Log Cabin Bed and Breakfast** (928/778-0442 or 888/778-0442, www.prescottlogcabin.com, $109–159 d) is a modern log building with decks and hot tub. **Lynx Creek Farm Bed and Breakfast** (928/778-9573 or 888/778-9573, www.vacationlodging.com, $85–200 d), in the hills five miles east of town, features rooms and cabins with a small pool, hot tubs, an organic orchard and garden, and farm animals.

Historic Hotels

The massive **Hotel St. Michael** (205 W. Gurley St. at Montezuma, 928/776-1999 or 800/678-3757, www.hotelstmichael.net) opened as the Hotel Burke in 1891, but had to be rebuilt after the great fire wiped out Whiskey Row in 1900. Rooms, all with private bath, go for $49–79 d and suites are $89 d; add $10 to prices on weekends. Each guest receives a cooked-to-order breakfast. Caffé St. Michael at the hotel offers breakfast, lunch, and dinner daily.

Prescott's grand hotel when it opened in 1927, the **Hassayampa Inn** (122 E. Gurley St.,

928/778-9434 or 800/322-1927, www.hassayampainn.com) has been beautifully restored. The plush lobby features a painted ceiling, old piano, and other antiques. All rooms have private baths and are standard ($99–159 d), classic ($109–189 d), suite ($159–229 d), or Jacuzzi suite ($169–299 d). The hotel's Peacock Room offers elegant dining.

On a leafy lane just a block from the Courthouse Plaza, **Hotel Vendome** (230 S. Cortez St., 928/776-0900 or 888/468-3583, www.vendomehotel.com) is a small inn dating from 1917. The attractively restored rooms include private baths for $119 d room, $159 two-bedroom suite (up to 4 persons); subtract $40 on weekdays.

$50–100

Just east of downtown, the very pleasant **Best Western Prescottonian Motel** (1317 E. Gurley St., 928/445-3096 or 800/937-8376, $85–95 d weekdays, $95–105 d Fri.–Sat., offers a cooked-to-order breakfast, restaurant, pool, and hot tub. More basic choices nearby include the old-fashioned 1947 motor court **Apache Motel** (1130 E. Gurley St., 928/445-1422, $30 s, $40 d weekdays, $50 s, $60 d Fri.–Sat.) and the **Colony Inn** (1225 E. Gurley St., 928/445-7057 or 866/243-7285, $39–49 d weekdays, $45–65 d Fri.–Sat.), which has a pool. Also in this area are two chains, sitting side by side, **Motel 6** (1111 E. Sheldon St., 928/776-0160 or 800/466-8356, $40 s, $46 d weekdays, $57 s, $63 d Fri.–Sat.) with a small pool and **Super 8 Motel** (1105 E. Sheldon St., 928/776-1282 or 800/800-8000, $55 s, $60 d weekdays, $70 s, $75 d Fri.–Sat., $90 d suite) also with a pool. **Wheel Inn Motel** (333 S. Montezuma St., 928/778-7346 or 800/717-0902, $49–59 d weekdays, $69–79 d Fri.–Sat.) is a small, simple place just south of downtown.

Continuing south on Montezuma Street/White Spar Road/Highway 89 from downtown you'll see the large **Prescott Sierra Inn** (809 White Spar Rd., 928/445-1250 or 800/513-2014, $39–55 d weekdays, $49–79 d Fri.–Sat.) with a choice of economy, deluxe, and kitchenette units, some with a fireplace; amenities include a pool, hot tub, and the nearby Juniper Restaurant. Surrounded by ponderosa pines at the south edge of town, **Comfort Inn** (1290 White Spar Rd., 928/778-5770 or 800/889-9774, $86 d weekdays, $90 and up Fri.–Sat.) offers a hot tub; the Pine Cone Inn restaurant is across the highway.

$100 and Up

Guests enjoy great views atop the hill at **Prescott Resort Conference Center & Casino** (1500 Hwy. 69, 928/776-1666 or 800/967-4637, www.prescottresort.com, $89–145 d room, $99–165 d suite), which provides a fine-dining restaurant, an indoor/outdoor pool, whirlpool tub, sauna, fitness room, racquetball, and tennis; Western art adorns the lobby and hallways. **Forest Villas Hotel** (3645 Lee Circle, 4 miles east of downtown off Hwy. 69, 928/717-1200 or 800/223-3449, www.forestvillas.com, $95–208 d weekdays, $109–208 d Fri.–Sat.) offers balconies, views, breakfast, fitness center, and an outdoor pool and hot tub.

Forest Service Campgrounds

The Prescott National Forest (928/771-4700, www.fs.fed.us/r3/prescott) offers **dispersed campsites** in the Prescott Basin area near town. Each site has a marker, fire ring, and place to camp, but no water, toilets, or fees. Pick up a map from the Forest Service, Prescott Chamber of Commerce, or the website for locations. These are the only places within the Prescott Basin boundary that are open to dispersed camping.

White Spar Campground (2.5 miles south of downtown on Hwy. 89, $10) has drinking water but no showers or hookups; one loop stays open in winter, when water may or may not be available. **Lower Wolf Creek Campground** (9 miles south of town, $6) is open mid-May–mid-November but lacks water; go south 7.5 miles on Senator Highway/Forest Road 52, then turn west 1 mile on Forest Road 97. Or head south four miles on Highway 89 from Prescott, then turn east five miles on Forest Road 97. Groups can reserve **Upper Wolf Creek Campground** (877/444-6777, www.reserveusa.com).

You and your horse can stay at **Groom Creek Horsecamp** (6.5 miles south from town on Senator Highway/Forest Road 52), which offers family sites ($10) and a group reservation area

(Bradshaw Ranger District, 928/443-8000) with water May 1–October 31. Nearby, the popular **Groom Creek Loop Trail #307** makes an 8.7-mile loop through ponderosa pine forests to Spruce Mountain.

Southeast of Prescott, **Lynx Lake** and nearby **Hilltop Campgrounds** sit above a pretty lake containing trout and catfish. Lynx sites are open April 1–November 15; Hilltop is open May 1–September 30; both have drinking water and a $10 fee. Picnickers may use tables at a vista point on the north end of the lake and near the boat ramp at the south end for $2. To reach Lynx Lake, head east four miles on Highway 69 from town, then turn south 2.5 miles on Walker Road/Lynx Lake Road; Hilltop Campground is one mile farther. Lynx Lake Store (928/778-0720, closed Mon.) rents rowboats, paddleboats, and canoes at the north end of the lake.

Yavapai Campground (northwest of town near the base of Granite Mountain, $10) stays open all year with water; from W. Gurley Street, turn northwest and drive 4.3 miles on Grove Avenue, Miller Valley Road, and Iron Springs Road, then turn north and proceed 3.5 miles on Forest Road 374. Groups can reserve **Granite Group Camp** (877/444-6777, www.reserveusa.com).

In ponderosa pines near the village of Cherry, **Powell Springs Campground** (free) stays open all year; there's usually spring water, but it's safest to bring your own. From the turnoff on Highway 169 (25 miles east of Prescott and 5.5 miles west of I-17 Exit 278), turn north 4.5 miles on Forest Road 372/Cherry Road; see a highway or forest map. Forest Road 372 is a winding gravel road with good scenery, especially where it winds high above the canyon south of Cherry. You can also drive in from the Verde Valley; take I-17 Exit 287, go northwest 2.8 miles on Highway 260, then turn left (south) and drive 12.6 miles on Cherry Road.

Other Campgrounds

Watson Lake Park (4 miles north of town on Hwy. 89, 928/771-5841, $10 tents or RVs) overlooks the picturesque Granite Dells, but the campground is open only Friday–Saturday nights from Memorial Day to Labor Day; showers are available to campers. Day use at the park is free, and it's open daily year-round. Just north of Watson Lake Park, only RVers can stay at **Point of Rocks RV Campground** (3025 N. Hwy. 89, 928/445-9018, $20 RV w/hookups); it's open all year with showers, laundry, and a tiny store. **Willow Lake RV and Camping Resort** (5 miles north of town off Willow Creek Rd., 928/445-6311 or 800/940-2845, $14 tent, $20 RV w/hookups) features a swimming pool, fishing, store, and showers within walking distance of Willow Lake.

FOOD

American and Continental

Downtown: Murphy's (201 N. Cortez St., 928/445-4044, daily lunch and dinner, $11–30) serves steak, prime rib, chicken, seafood, sandwiches, and other dishes, many mesquite grilled, in an old mercantile building dating from 1890. Dim lighting, antiques, and greenery add to the romantic setting. On Sunday, you can order eggs Benedict and other brunch specialties. The daily sunset menu features reduced prices 4–5:30 P.M.

129 1/2 An American Jazz Grille (129-1/2 N. Cortez St., 928/443-9292, http://129andahalf.com, Tues.–Sat. dinner, $10–23) offers fine dining of steak, seafood, and pasta to the sounds of live jazz; reservations recommended. **The Office** (128 N. Cortez St., 928/445-1211, daily lunch and dinner, $7–15) features tasty Southwestern cuisine such as stacked enchiladas, fish tacos, and fajita salads. The sports bar interior has been held over from the previous business! The nonsmoking Board Room dining area is in back.

Chef Linda Rose presides over the fine dining at **The Rose Restaurant** (234 S. Cortez St., 928/777-8308, Wed.–Sun. dinner, $16–31). The northern Italian fare is cooked to order, and includes such favorites as cherry brandied duck, roasted rack of Colorado lamb, and vealinda. Diners have both indoor and outdoor seating at the early-20th-century Victorian cottage.

Zuma's Woodfire Café (124 N. Montezuma St., 928/541-1400, daily lunch and dinner, $9–22) has attractive Southwestern decor and a patio for gourmet pizza, pasta, meat, seafood, sandwiches, and salads. **The Palace** (120 S. Montezuma St.,

928/541-1996, www.historicpalace.com, daily lunch and dinner, $11–27) serves up steak, prime rib, seafood, and pasta dinners in a magnificent old building in the heart of Whiskey Row. The separate bar area has an 1880s Brunswick bar that patrons carried across to safety in the plaza during the fire of 1900. A honky-tonk pianist hits the ivories on Sundays, country and cowboy bands play Friday–Saturday nights, and dinner theaters are offered every other Monday. **Caffé St. Michael** (100 S. Montezuma St. at Gurley St., 928/778-2500, daily breakfast, lunch, and dinner, $10–16) on Whiskey Row offers a variety of meat, seafood, and pasta dishes along with espresso in an attractive historic setting.

The Hassayampa Inn's **Peacock Room** (122 E. Gurley St., 928/778-9434, ext. 104, daily breakfast, lunch, and dinner, $14–28) offers a luxurious old-fashioned atmosphere for a varied menu of American and continental specialties. Crab cakes feature on all of the menus, and the eggs Sardou (poached with spinach and artichoke topped by hollandaise sauce) is a popular breakfast option. Salads are so huge that diners often share one. The Hometown Dinner Hour runs 5–6 P.M. and costs $14.

Plaza Café (106 W. Gurley St., 928/445-3234, daily breakfast and lunch, $5.50–8.50) offers breakfasts, sandwiches, and salads across from the plaza. **Prescott Brewing Company** (130 W. Gurley St., 928/771-2795, daily lunch and dinner, $7–18) crafts its own beers and serves up a varied menu of tasty snacks, pizza, steak, fajitas, fish, salads, and vegetarian items across from the plaza.

Acme Fish Co. (220 W. Gurley St., 928/541-0221, Tues.–Sat. lunch and dinner, $7–19) prepares "food to cheer the sole" in cheerful dining rooms. Patrons often go for the fish and chips, but you can also order the daily catch, steak, pasta, or sandwiches. **Gurley Street Grille** (230 W. Gurley St., 928/445-3388, daily lunch and dinner, $6.50–18) serves upscale grilled specialties, burgers, pasta, pizza, and sandwiches in a 1901 commercial building. **Prescott Natural Foods Market** (330 W. Gurley St., 928/778-5875, daily) offers a deli café and grocery.

Other Areas: On the hill at the Prescott Resort, **Thumb Butte Dining Room** (1500 Hwy. 69, 928/776-1666, ext. 693, daily breakfast, lunch, and dinner plus a Sunday brunch buffet, $15–35) offers views and fine dining; the dinner menu includes steak, chicken, veal, seafood, and pasta.

La Bruzza's Italian Ristorante (1480 Iron Springs Rd., 928/778-1757, Tues.–Sat. dinner, $6–15) serves great food in a family restaurant northwest of downtown. Choices include tortellini, gnocchi, eggplant parmesan, and chicken milanese; no beer or wine is served but you can bring your own.

Papa's Italian Restaurant (1124 White Spar Rd., 928/776-4880, Tues.–Fri. lunch and dinner, Sat. dinner, $7–14) prepares Sicilian and some northern Italian cuisine. **Pine Cone Inn Supper Club** (1245 White Spar Rd., 928/445-2970, Wed.–Sun. dinner, $10–23) serves steak, seafood, and other American favorites; musicians play old-fashioned music.

Mexican

El Charro (120 N. Montezuma St., 928/445-7130, daily lunch and dinner, $6.50–13.50) is a simple café.

Asian

Thai House Cafe (230 N. Cortez St., 928/777-0041, Tues.–Fri. lunch and Tues.–Sat. dinner, $7.50–13) cooks flavorful meat and tofu dishes. **Chi's Cuisine** (114 N. Cortez St., 928/778-5390, Tues.–Fri. lunch and Tues.–Sat. dinner, $8–20) is a little downtown café with Chinese and Thai food. **Canton Dragon** (377 N. Montezuma St. in Depot Marketplace, 928/771-8118, daily lunch and dinner, $6.25–16.50) has over 100 choices in Cantonese, Szechuan, or Mandarin styles.

Fujiyama (1781 E. Hwy. 69 in Frontier Village Center, 928/776-8659, Tues.–Sun. lunch and dinner, closed last Sun. of the month, $10–14) offers Japanese food with a sushi bar. **Taj Mahal Restaurant** (1781 E. Hwy. 69 in Frontier Village Center, 928/445-5752, daily lunch and dinner, $7–15) features north Indian dining. There's a buffet option daily for lunch and a vegetarian buffet for Wednesday dinner.

INFORMATION AND SERVICES

Opposite the Courthouse Plaza, you can get a wealth of visitor information at the **Prescott Chamber of Commerce** (117 W. Goodwin St., P.O. Box 1147, Prescott, AZ 86302, 928/445-2000 or 800/266-7534, www.prescott.org, 9 A.M.–5 P.M. Mon.–Fri. and 10 A.M.–2 P.M. Sat.–Sun.). After hours, you can pick up literature just outside the door. The chamber sells a walking tour of downtown and a Prescott Driving Tour. The website www.visit-prescott.com also has event and visitor information.

The **Prescott National Forest** (344 S. Cortez St., Prescott, AZ 86303, 928/443-8000, www.fs.fed.us/r3/prescott, 8 A.M.–4:30 P.M. Mon.–Fri.) has recreation information for the area, including the Bradshaw District; much of the camping and hiking literature is also available at the Prescott Chamber of Commerce office.

Prescott's excellent **public library** (215 E. Goodwin St., 928/777-1500, www.prescottlib.lib.az.us, 1–5 P.M. Sun., 9 A.M.–5:30 P.M. Mon., 9 A.M.–9 P.M. Tues.–Thurs., and 9 A.M.–5:30 P.M. Fri.–Sat.) includes a Southwest collection and Internet access. **Yavapai College** (1100 E. Sheldon St., 928/776-2260 circulation, 928/776-2261 reference, www.yc.edu) also has a fine library, open daily during school terms, then Monday–Friday in summer.

The main **post office** is at 442 Miller Valley Road; the downtown branch sits on the corner of Goodwin and Cortez, across from Courthouse Plaza. **Yavapai Regional Medical Center** (1003 Willow Creek Rd., 928/445-2700 or 877/843-9762, www.yrmc.org) provides hospital services.

GETTING THERE AND AROUND

On **Prescott Historical Tours** (928/445-4567), Melissa Ruffner dresses in a Victorian costume when she leads visitors around the original Prescott town site; you'll need to make a reservation. Check with the chamber office for free walking tours, usually Friday–Sunday.

Buses of the **Prescott Transit Authority** (820 E. Sheldon St., 928/445-5470 or 800/445-7978, www.prescotttransit.com) head for Phoenix's Greyhound bus station and to Sky Harbor Airport about every hour during the day. **Shuttle U** (1505 W. Gurley St., 928/772-6114 or 800/304-6114, www.shuttleu.com) will also take you to Sky Harbor Airport; it goes about 11 times daily.

VICINITY OF PRESCOTT

Granite Dells

Massive boulders of ancient rock have weathered into delicately balanced forms and fanciful shapes, reflected in the surface of Watson Lake. Ruins and artifacts indicate that Native Americans used to live here. The scenic Dells offer a great place for boating, picnicking, or a stroll. Rock climbers tackle the challenging granite formations. Watson Lake Park, four miles north of town on Highway 89, offers year-round day use and summer weekend camping.

Prescott Peavine National Recreation Trail

This rails-to-trails path crosses Granite Dells on the east side of Watson Lake. Hikers, cyclists, and equestrians head down the nearly level, packed-gravel trail, which is 4.15 miles one-way and connects with several other trails. From Highway 89 at MP 315, turn east .3 miles on Prescott Lakes Parkway, then turn left .1 mile to the trailhead. Currently the trail ends at former Highway 89A, but eventually it may connect with Chino Valley's Peavine Trail.

Thumb Butte Trail

This popular loop hike begins just west of town and climbs Thumb Butte Saddle (6,300 ft.) for good views of Prescott and the surrounding countryside. The trail winds through a valley of dense ponderosa pine, then crosses windswept ridges where pinyon, juniper, oak, and prickly pear grow. A spur trail leads to a vista point with a panorama of the city, Granite Dells, Chino Valley, and countless mountains, including the distant San Francisco Peaks.

Reaching the fractured granite summit of Thumb Butte is hazardous and not recommended. The trail itself is a moderate outing of two miles round-trip with an elevation gain of

600 feet, taking about two hours. Signs identify many of the plants along the way and explain the forest ecosystem. Hiking season runs year-round except after winter snowstorms.

From downtown, head west 3.5 miles on Gurley Street and Thumb Butte Road to Thumb Butte Park; the trail is on the left side of the road and parking on the right (there's a $2 parking fee unless you have a Golden pass or National Parks pass w/hologram). Picnic tables, restrooms, and seasonal drinking water are nearby.

Granite Mountain Wilderness

On a day trip, hikers can explore the rugged Granite Mountain Wilderness and enjoy fine views from an overlook at an elevation of 7,185 feet. Rock climbers come to challenge the granite cliffs, which offer a nearly complete range of difficulties, but check first for seasonal closures. Five trails allow many hiking combinations, but only **Granite Mountain Trail #261** climbs to the top. This trail ascends gently 1.3 miles to a trail junction at Blair Pass, then turns right and switchbacks 1.3 miles to a saddle on Granite Mountain; from here the trail turns southeast, climbing another mile to a viewpoint. Ponderosa pines grow at the trailhead and on top of Granite Mountain, though much of the trail passes through manzanita, mountain mahogany, pinyon, agave, and other plants of the chaparral.

Average hiking time for the 7.5-mile round-trip hike is six hours. It's a moderately difficult trip with an elevation gain of 1,500 feet; carry water. It's open all year except when blocked by snow. Forest Service offices sell a Granite Mountain Wilderness map; you can also use the Iron Springs and Jerome Canyon 7.5-minute topos. From W. Gurley Street in Prescott, drive northwest 4.3 miles on Grove Avenue, Miller Valley Road, and Iron Springs Road, then turn right and travel 5 miles on Forest Road 374 past the campground and lake turnoffs. The trailhead has a $2 parking fee unless you have a Golden pass or National Parks pass with hologram.

Chino Valley Ranger District

This section of the Prescott National Forest lies northwest of town beyond Granite Basin Wilderness. It lacks developed sites, but it does have hiking trails, two wilderness areas, and good opportunities to spot wildlife. Except in hunting season, you're likely to have this country to yourself. Granite Knob (6,632 ft.) dominates **Apache Creek Wilderness.** pinyon pine, juniper, and chaparral cover most of the land with some ponderosa pine in the southwest corner.

Juniper Mesa Wilderness has cliffs on the south side of the mesa and some canyons on the north. Ponderosa pine, Arizona white oak, and alligator juniper grow in the canyons and on ridge tops, while pinyon pine, juniper, and chaparral cover the south slope; elevations run 5,650–7,050 feet. Prescott National Forest offices sell a map that covers both wilderness areas. **Chino Ranger District Office** (735 Hwy. 89 N, P.O. Box 485, Chino Valley, AZ 86323, 928/636-2200, www.fs.fed.us/r3/prescott, 8 A.M.–4:30 P.M. Mon.–Fri.) is north of Prescott in Chino Valley.

Bradshaw Mountains

Scenic drives and dozens of trails wind through this rugged range south of Prescott. You can get trail descriptions, maps, and back-road information from the Prescott National Forest office.

The **Senator Highway** weaves atop the Bradshaw Mountains between Prescott and Crown King with many fine views and some historic sites along the way. Despite the road's name, you'll need a high-clearance vehicle past the Groom Creek area. Head south from downtown on Mt. Vernon Avenue and continue straight on the Senator Highway, also marked as Forest Road 52.

Spruce Mountain has views, a lookout tower, and a picnic area at its 7,700-foot summit. From Prescott, turn south 5.5 miles on Mt. Vernon Avenue/Senator Highway/Forest Road 52, then turn left 4 miles up Forest Road 52A (not suited for RVs or trailers). **Groom Creek Trail #307** makes an 8.7-mile loop between here and Groom Creek Horsecamp.

Probably the most unusual trail is the 1,200-foot **Groom Creek School Nature Trail,** built by the Sunrise Lions Club of Prescott especially for blind people. Trail pamphlets explain natural features and processes. The trail lies just past the village of Groom Creek, six miles south of town on Mt. Vernon Avenue/Senator Highway/Forest Road 52.

An 1880s **charcoal kiln,** made of fitted granite blocks, once served precious-metal smelters in the Walker area. From Prescott, head east 4 miles on Highway 69, turn south 6.5 miles on Walker Road/Lynx Lake Road/Forest Road 197 to Walker, turn left on Big Bug Mesa Road/Forest Road 670 just north of Walker Fire Station, and follow signs .8 miles to parking—then it's a three-minute walk to the kiln.

Stagecoach passengers in the 19th century stopped at **Palace Station** on their way between Prescott and Peck's Mine. The station lies 11 miles south of Prescott on Mt. Vernon Avenue/Senator Highway/Forest Road 52. The rustic structure is now used as a residence and isn't open to the public, but you can view the exterior.

Crown King and Vicinity

Old mines, ghost towns, and wilderness surround this rustic village 55 miles southeast of Prescott via the Senator Highway. Prospectors discovered gold at the Crown King Mine in the 1870s, but mine owners had to wait until the late 1880s before the ore could be processed profitably. A branch line of the Prescott and Eastern Railroad reached the site in 1904. Legal battles closed mine operations in the early 1900s, and today the mining camp attracts retired people and serves as an escape from summer heat. The Crown King Saloon dates back to 1898, when it was built at Oro Belle camp, five miles southwest. Pack mules later hauled the structure piece by piece to Crown King.

Rough roads discourage the average tourist, but the region can be explored with maps, determination, and a high-clearance vehicle. The easiest way in is from Cleator on Forest Road 259, reached from the I-17 Bumble Bee or Cordes Exits. You'll follow the twisting path of the old railroad on the drive up; cautiously driven passenger vehicles can make it OK. With a high-clearance vehicle, you can approach Crown King on the very scenic Senator Highway (Forest Road 52) across the rugged Bradshaws from Prescott. Another route follows Pine Flat Road (Forest Road 177) from Mayer into the Bradshaws, then turns south on the Senator Highway. The Prescott National Forest map, sold at Forest Service offices, shows back roads and most trails.

Bradshaw Mountain Guest Ranch (928/632-4477, www.crownking.com, $85 d suites, $120–150 d cabins) is on the left as you turn into Crown King; guests enjoy the gardens, barbecue pits, and continental breakfast delivered to their door. You can also stay near Crown King at **Bear Creek Cabins** (928/632-5035 or 899-2031, $80 up to four persons) and **Cedar Roost** (928/632-5564, $65–105 d weekdays, $75–115 d Fri.–Sat.).

For atmosphere and great American food, try **The Mill** (928/632-7133, Fri.–Sun. lunch and dinner, and Sun. breakfast). Inside, the huge Gladiator Stamp Mill, built in 1893 and moved here from a site two miles away, now forms the centerpiece of the restaurant along with other materials salvaged from old buildings. The entrance is opposite the turnoff for Crown King. In Crown King, you can eat at the saloon or at a restaurant across the street, both open daily.

The general store sells groceries and has a post office. The staff at Crown King Work Center, up the hill from town, can tell you about trails and roads; they're mostly local people who know the area well. *Arizona Ghost Towns and Mining Camps* by Philip Varney contains good information on this historic and very scenic part of Arizona.

Horsethief Basin Recreation Area, seven miles to the southeast, offers camping in the Prescott National Forest. Hazlett Hollow Campground (elev. 6,000 ft.) is open May–October with water and a $6 fee. On the way you'll pass near 3.5-acre **Horsethief Lake,** a reservoir used for boating (electric motors OK) and fishing; no swimming or camping. Groups can reserve **Turney Gulch Campground** (877/444-6777, www.reserveusa.com), which has water. **Castle Creek Wilderness,** east of the campgrounds, has very steep and rocky terrain with vegetation ranging from chaparral to ponderosa pine.

Bloody Basin Road

Drivers with high-clearance vehicles can leave the crowds behind on this 60-mile scenic back road through the Tonto National Forest, connecting I-17 Bloody Basin/Crown King Exit

259 with Carefree and Cave Creek north of Phoenix. You'll enjoy views of the Mazatzals, rugged high-desert hill country, and wooded canyons. In Bloody Basin, 26 miles from I-17, a very bumpy side road goes southeast 12 miles to the Verde River and Sheep Bridge, where hikers can head into the Mazatzal Wilderness. Primitive camping is possible almost anywhere in Tonto National Forest, or you can stop at Seven Springs, CCC, or Cave Creek campgrounds near the south end of the drive.

Arcosanti

This unique experiment of visionary Italian architect Paolo Soleri slowly rises in the high-desert country 34 miles southeast of Prescott and 65 miles north of Phoenix. The public is welcome to visit this project—the first of its kind. A visitor center (HC 74, Box 4136, Mayer, AZ 86333, 928/632-7135, www.arcosanti.org, 9 A.M.–5 P.M. daily except major holidays, the visitor center is free) has a model of Arcosanti, architectural exhibits, and books by and about Soleri. The famous Cosanti bronze and clay windbells sold here make attractive gifts and help finance the project. To see the rest of the site you'll need to sign up for a guided tour, which lasts 50 minutes and departs on the hour, with the first at 10 A.M. and the last at 4 P.M., $8 adults, free for 17 and under. From I-17, take Cordes Junction Exit 262, follow signs 2.5 miles on an unpaved road.

A former student of Frank Lloyd Wright, Soleri envisions three-dimensional cities that will foster community spirit—now lost in many urban areas. Instead of today's sprawling metropolitan areas, Soleri suggests that cities grow vertically, leaving surrounding land in its natural state. Instead of long commutes, residents will take an elevator and short walks between home, work, and shopping; the time saved can then be devoted to enjoying life and socializing with neighbors. Soleri calls his revolutionary concepts "arcology," a joining of architecture and ecology. His strangely shaped buildings at Arcosanti make efficient use of the sun's energy. The south-facing apses, for example, allow winter sunlight to enter for warmth, yet they shade the interior during summer.

Construction began in 1970 and progresses slowly as funds come in. The current population of 70–85 can rise considerably during summer when the number of workers increases. Soleri typically spends three days a week here and the rest at Cosanti, the facility he designed in Scottsdale. Currently in the first of three phases, Arcosanti will house about 5,000 people upon completion, yet it will take up only five percent as much land as a conventional town. Greenhouses will provide both food and heating, while using only a fraction of the water normally needed for agriculture.

A café and bakery serve snacks and meals. The Visitors Trail leads across a small canyon to a viewpoint of the project. Arcosanti staff regularly schedule concerts, usually preceded by dinner and often followed by a light and sound show projected onto the mesa across the canyon. Seminars and workshops allow those interested to participate in construction.

Guest rooms (928/632-6217) are $20 s, $25 d ($30 with private bath), and $75 for the Sky Suite, which has two bedrooms and a kitchen. You'll need to make reservations and arrive between 9 A.M. and 5 P.M.

Near the interchange you'll find **Cordes Junction Motel & RV Park** (928/632-5186, $35 s, $41 d rooms, $22 RV w/hookups) as well as a small diner that serves breakfast and lunch.

The Grand Canyon and the Arizona Strip

Note: Please see front color map **Grand Canyon.**

This is a land of time. Massive cliffs reveal limestone composed of animals who lived in long-departed seas, sandstone formed of ancient desert sand dunes, and shale made of silt from now-vanished rivers and shores. Volcanic eruptions deposited layers of ash, cinders, and lava. Deeper into the Canyon lie the roots of mountain ranges, whose peaks towered over a primitive land two billion years ago. Time continues to flow with the cycles of the plants and animals that live here, and with the erosive forces of water and wind ever widening and deepening the Canyon chasm.

Two mighty but opposing forces—the uplifting of the massive Colorado Plateau and the vigorous downcutting by the Colorado River—

© BILL WEIR

Must-Sees

Look for the M icon to find the sights and activities you can't miss and the M icon for the best dining and lodging.

The Rim Trail invites you to stroll to many delightful Canyon views and historic buildings in the South Rim's Grand Canyon Village area (page 415).

Hermit Road leads west eight miles from Grand Canyon Village to new Canyon perspectives and the atmospheric stone building, Hermit's Rest. The Rim Trail parallels Hermit Road so that you can hike as much as you please, then take the Hermit's Rest Shuttle the rest of the way (page 419).

Desert View Drive heads east 25 miles from Grand Canyon Village past fine Canyon overlooks, a prehistoric pueblo, and another wonderful stone building, the Desert View Watchtower (page 421).

South Kaibab Trail Day Hikes will give you a feel for what it's like to be inside the Grand Canyon. After the initial descent, the trail ventures out along Cedar Ridge with sweeping panoramas. You can also join a ranger-led interpretive hike to Cedar Ridge (page 425).

Havasupai Indian Reservation contains a world of enchanting waterfalls and blue-green travertine pools deep within Havasu Canyon. Getting here takes effort, as there's no road into the canyon! You can hike or arrange for a horse or mule to carry you into this Shangri-La (page 436).

created the awe-inspiring Grand Canyon and its many tributaries. Neither pictures nor words can fully describe the sight. You have to experience the Canyon by traveling along the rim, descending into its depths, riding the waves of the Colorado River, and watching the continuous show of colors and patterns as the sun moves across the sky.

The Canyon's grandeur stretches for 277 miles across northern Arizona; it's up to 18 miles wide—10 miles on average—and one mile deep. Roads provide access to developed areas and viewpoints on both rims, while trails allow hikers and mules to descend precipitous cliffs to the Colorado River. Yet much of the park remains remote and is rarely visited by humans.

Most people head first to the South Rim, entering at either the South Entrance Station near Grand Canyon Village or the East Entrance Station near Desert View; a 25-mile scenic drive along the rim connects these two entrances. The South Rim features great views, a full range of accommodations and restaurants, and easy access—

Bright Angel Point feels like the end of the world, with sheer drop-offs on either side and a memorable view down the long Bright Angel Canyon to the Inner Gorge and the South Rim beyond (page 454).

Cape Royal Scenic Drive swings through beautiful conifer and aspen forests to the North Rim's highest viewpoint at Point Imperial, and to one of its most sweeping above a great bend in the Colorado River at Cape Royal. Short hiking trails, a prehistoric pueblo, and a variety of other viewpoints make for a great day's outing (page 455).

North Kaibab Trail Day Hikes will give you a taste of one of the Canyon's most exciting trails as you descend and traverse sheer cliffs (page 456).

Point Sublime on the North Rim lives up to its name with what may be the most memorable panorama in the Grand Canyon (page 462).

Toroweap has dizzying views of the Colorado River from cliffs nearly 3,000 feet high at the end of a long unpaved road on the North Rim (page 465).

Pipe Spring National Monument offers an experience of life on a ranch straight out of the Old West (page 475).

© BILL WEIR

Mt. Hayden rises from the depths east of Point Imperial

it's just 58 miles north of I-40 from Williams and roads and most facilities stay open all year. Attractions include the views and historic buildings at Grand Canyon Village, as well as scenic drives on Hermit Road to Hermits Rest (8 miles), and Desert View Drive to Desert View (25 miles). Some remarkable architecture lines the South Rim, including a series of unique stone structures designed by Mary Colter. The South Rim also features most of the Canyon's easily accessible viewpoints and trails. It's not surprising then, that large crowds of visitors are the main drawback of this part of the Canyon. Park staff have long-range plans to relieve the congestion by adding more shuttles, bike paths, and foot trails.

Only about one in ten visitors makes it to the North Rim, but if you're in that lucky monority you'll be rewarded with pristine forests, rolling meadows, splendid wildflower displays, and superb panoramas. Viewpoints here stand some 1,300 feet higher than those at the South Rim and provide a dramatically different perspective

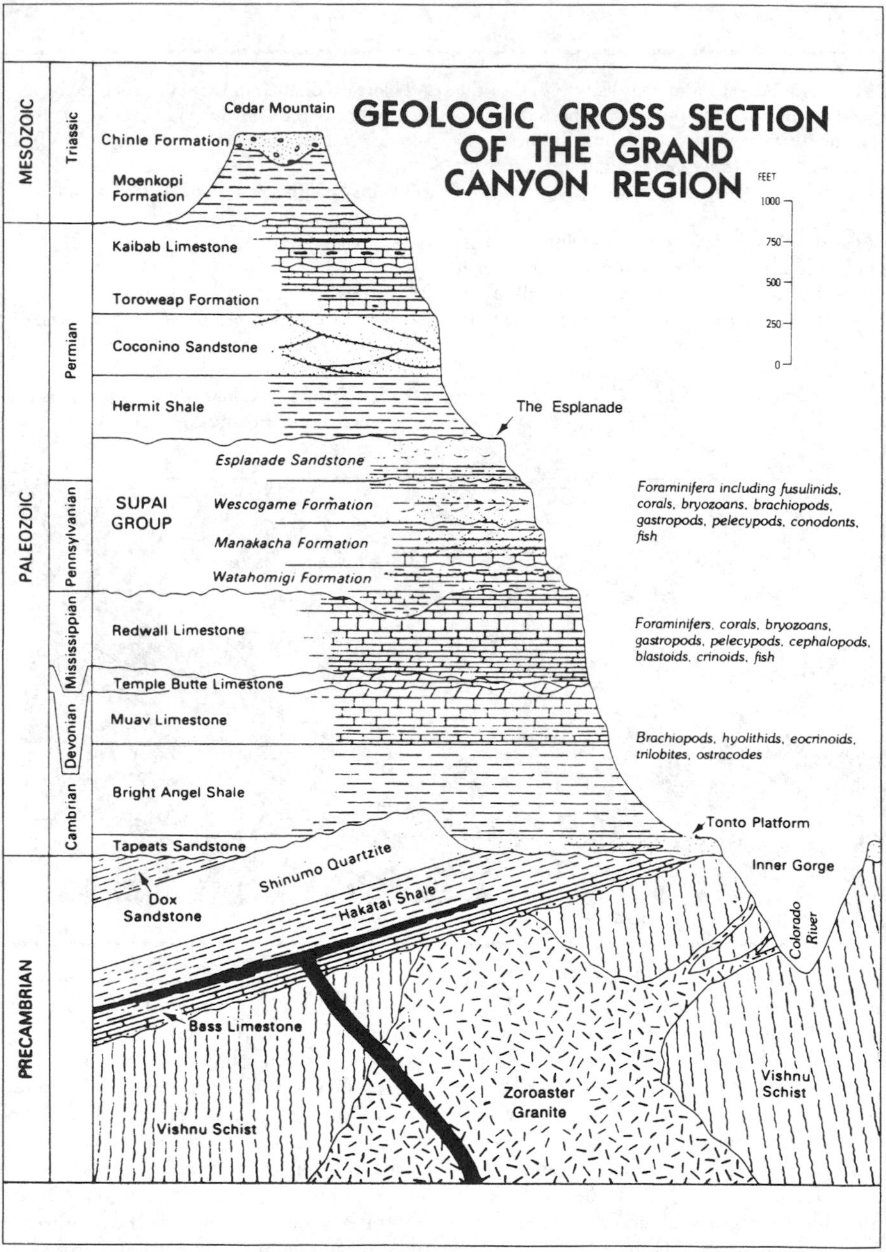
GEOLOGIC CROSS SECTION OF THE GRAND CANYON REGION
FEET
1000
750
500
250
0
MESOZOIC
Triassic
PALEOZOIC
Permian
Pennsylvanian
Mississippian
Devonian
Cambrian
PRECAMBRIAN
Cedar Mountain
Chinle Formation
Moenkopi Formation
Kaibab Limestone
Toroweap Formation
Coconino Sandstone
Hermit Shale
The Esplanade
Esplanade Sandstone
SUPAI GROUP
Wescogame Formation
Manakacha Formation
Watahomigi Formation
Foraminifera including fusulinids, corals, bryozoans, brachiopods, gastropods, pelecypods, conodonts, fish
Redwall Limestone
Foraminifers, corals, bryozoans, gastropods, pelecypods, cephalopods, blastoids, crinoids, fish
Temple Butte Limestone
Muav Limestone
Brachiopods, hyolithids, eocrinoids, trilobites, ostracodes
Bright Angel Shale
Tonto Platform
Tapeats Sandstone
Shinumo Quartzite
Inner Gorge
Dox Sandstone
Hakatai Shale
Colorado River
Bass Limestone
Zoroaster Granite
Vishnu Schist
Vishnu Schist
EDWIN D. MCKEE, U.S. GEOLOGIC SURVEY PROFESSIONAL PAPER 1173; G.P.O., 1982

The Grand Canyon

CANYON ROCKS

With 94 types of rock discovered in the Grand Canyon, how can you remember even the major formations? All you have to do is keep in mind the mnemonic, "Know the canyon history. See rocks made by time very slowly." From top to bottom,

Know	Kaibab Limestone
the	Toroweap Formation
canyon	Coconino Sandstone
history.	Hermit Shale
See	Supai Group
rocks	Redwall Limestone
made	Muav Limestone
by	Bright Angel Shale
time	Tapeats Sandstone
very slowly.	Vishnu Schist

of the Canyon. The North Rim area offers lodging, dining, and camping facilities similar to the South Rim's, though on a smaller scale; because of harsh winters, facilities at the North Rim operate only from mid-May to mid-October, though the road remains open until the arrival of the first big winter storm. Although the rims stand just 10 miles apart, motorists on the South Rim must drive 215 miles and about five hours via Cameron and Jacob Lake to get here.

Adventurous travelers on the North Rim willing to tackle 61 miles of dirt road (each way, and impassable when wet) can head west to Toroweap Overlook. This perch sits a dizzying 3,000 feet directly above the Colorado River—one of the Canyon's most spectacular viewpoints. There aren't any facilities other than the road and a primitive campground, so bring all your supplies, including water. Low elevations of 4,500–5,000 feet allow access most of the year.

Lonely and vast, the Arizona Strip lies north of the Colorado River. This land of forests, desert grasslands, mountains, and canyons covers 14,000 square miles, but supports only 3,200 people. The Grand Canyon presents a formidable barrier between them and the rest of the state; all highway traffic has to follow a circuitous route around the mighty chasm. To cover 140 miles as the crow flies, residents of Moccasin in the Arizona Strip must drive 357 miles to the Mohave County seat at Kingman, detouring through Utah and Nevada before reentering Arizona at Hoover Dam.

PLANNING YOUR TIME

Grand Canyon Village on the South Rim offers rooms and cabins, some right on the rim and others back in the forest. Dining choices include simple cafeterias, family restaurants, or the elegant dining room at El Tovar. The small town of Tusayan nine miles south of Grand Canyon Village also has a range of places to stay and eat, but there's the disadvantage that you may face long lines at the entrance station when you return to the park. Neither place has inexpensive accommodations, so low-budget travelers might consider camping or staying in Williams or Flagstaff. The only lodge on the North Rim, at Bright Angel Point, offers cabins and basic motel rooms; they're heavily booked, so you definitely need a reservation. If you don't mind the commute, two lodges north outside the park have rooms and cabins; you'll need reservations at

FORMATION OF THE GRAND CANYON

Geologists have a difficult time pinpointing the age of the Canyon itself, though it is far younger than even the most recent rock layers—those on the rim, which are about 270 million years old. These rocks lay near sea level 70 million years ago, when the Earth's crust began a slow uplift. Some time later the ancestral Colorado River settled on its present course and began to carve the Canyon.

The big question is when! Too much of the geologic record is missing to provide a conclusive answer. Studies of river deposits have led to conflicting theories of the birth date of the Grand Canyon: any time between 5 million and 70 million years ago, although many geologists support an age of 5–6 million years. Even the direction of the ancestral Colorado is in dispute—some geologists think that the Little Colorado and upper Colorado once drained northward; a look at a map of Marble Canyon supports this view, because the tributaries suggest a tilt of the land to the north. Or perhaps the Colorado River followed its present course but in the opposite direction, later to be reversed by tilting of the Colorado Plateau. Other theories suggest that the Colorado and Little Colorado flowed southward either into a giant lake or into the Rio Grande to the Gulf of Mexico. A second, younger river could have carved the lower Grand Canyon and eventually captured the upper river near the present junction of the Colorado and Little Colorado Rivers. Or perhaps the lake had filled to overflowing from other sources, then broken through and carved the Little Colorado and Colorado Rivers in a catastrophic flood about 5 million years ago. Still other geologists stick with John Wesley Powell's theory that the Colorado has always followed its present course after the uplift began. The problem with this idea is that no river deposits older than 5 million years have been found near the lower end of the Grand Canyon.

Regardless of how the Grand Canyon did form, gradual uplift continued, giving the waters a steeper gradient and thus greater power. Today, the South Rim reaches elevations of 7,000–7,500 feet, while the North Rim towers more than 8,800 feet high. The Colorado River drops through the Canyon at an average gradient of 7.8 feet per mile, 25 times that of the lower Mississippi.

these places as well. Camping is your only low-budget option for the North Rim. Farther north, the towns of Page, Fredonia, and nearby Kanab make useful bases for the Arizona Strip.

The highlights of each rim could be seen in a day. Longer stays will give you more time to soak in the Canyon's details, do some hiking or mule rides, and take in ranger programs. Backpacking trips and river running expeditions, both of which require advance planning, will give you memories for a lifetime.

Grand Canyon Village on the South Rim has very good transport connections and a choice of shuttles and tours to get around. Your own vehicle will give you more flexibility, though searching for a parking spot sometimes takes effort. Bright Angel Point on the North Rim can be reached via shuttle from the South Rim, but you really need your own transportation to visit nearby points of interest such as the Cape Royal Scenic Drive. A high-clearance 4WD vehicle will help you explore the remote backcountry of the Arizona Strip.

Climate

In one long day, a hiker can travel from the cold fir and aspen forests of the North Rim to the hot cactus country of the Canyon bottom—a climate change equal to that between Canada and Mexico. In the Inner Gorge (elev. 2,480 feet at Phantom Ranch), summer temperatures soar, with average highs over 100°F; the thermometer commonly tops 115°F in early July. Spring and autumn offer pleasantly warm weather and are the best times to visit. Winter down by the river can be fine, too; even in January, days warm up to the 50s or low 60s and freezes are rare. Only 9.4 inches of precipitation makes it to the bottom in an average year; snow and rain often evaporate completely while falling through the mile of warm Canyon air.

The South Rim enjoys pleasant weather most

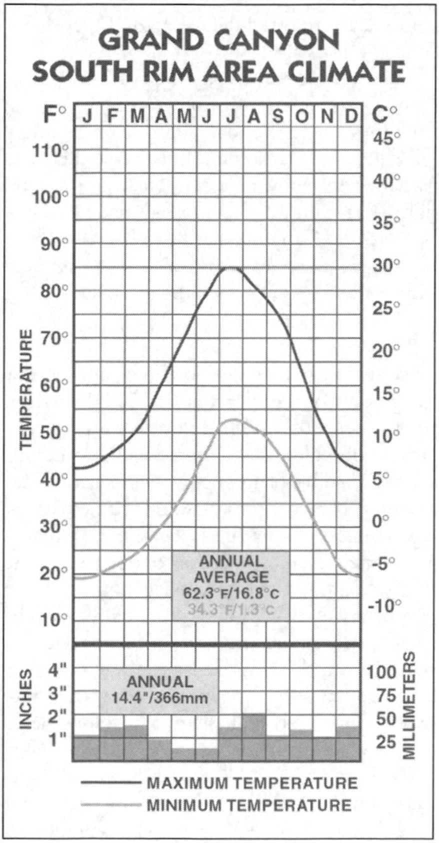

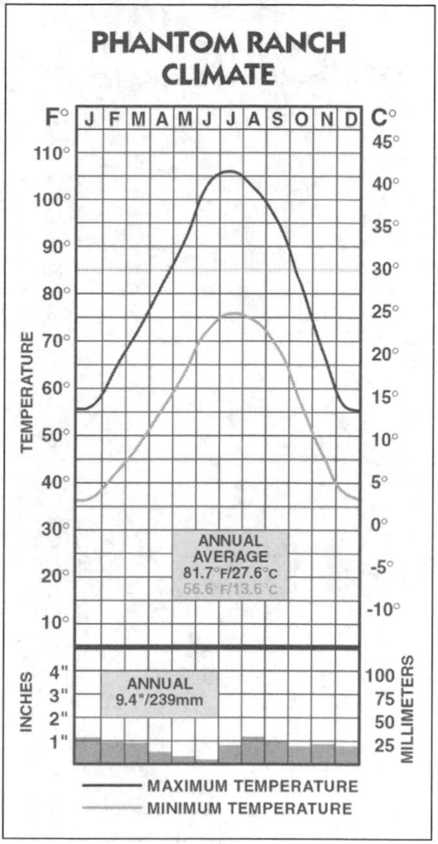

AVALON PUBLISHING

of the year. Summer highs reach the mid-80s, cooling during winter to highs in the upper 30s and lower 40s. Winter campers need warm sleeping bags to combat frosty nights when temperatures plunge into the teens. Yearly precipitation at the South Rim's Grand Canyon Village (elev. 6,950 feet) is 14.4 inches, with snow accumulations seldom exceeding two feet.

Although averaging only 1,300 feet higher, the North Rim in the Bright Angel Point area really gets socked in by winter storms. Snow piles up to depths of 6–10 feet in an average season, and the National Park Service doesn't even try to keep the roads open there from early November to mid-May. Summers can be a joy in the cool, fresh air; highs then run in the 60s and 70s. Bright Angel Ranger Station (elev. 8,400 feet) on the North Rim receives 25.6 inches of annual precipitation.

Most moisture falls during the winter and late summer. Spectacular afternoon thunderstorms build up mid-July to mid-September, soaking one spot in the Canyon and leaving another bone dry only a short distance away. The storms put on a great show from the rim viewpoints, but you should take cover if lightning gets close (less than 30 seconds between the flash and the thunder) and especially if the hair on your head stands on end or if you smell ozone. As in mountain areas, the Grand Canyon's weather can change rapidly. Always carry water and rain gear when heading down a trail.

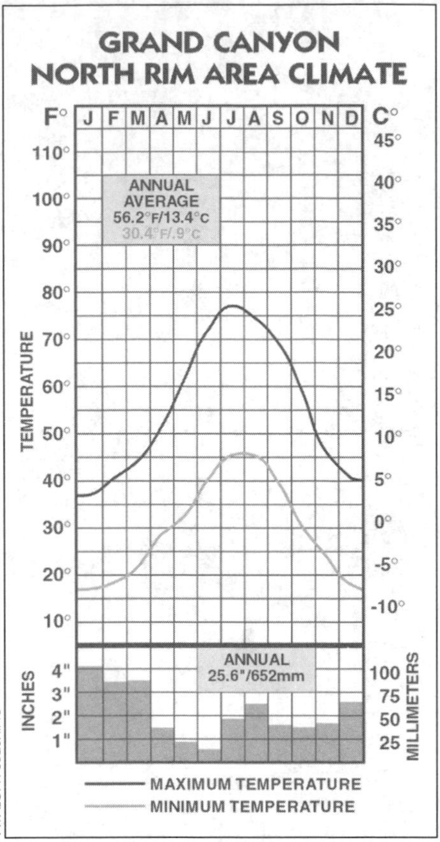

AVALON PUBLISHING

Flora and Fauna

The endless variations of elevation, exposure, and moisture allow for an astonishing range of plant and animal communities. The Canyon also acts as a barrier to many nonflying creatures who live on just one side of the Colorado River or only in the Inner Gorge.

Some mammals evolved into separate subspecies on each rim. The Abert's squirrel, though common in the Southwest, lives only on the South Rim within the park. This squirrel has tufted ears and a body and tail that are mostly gray with white undersides. The shy Kaibab squirrel, easily identified by an all-white tail and tufted ears, lives only on the North Rim. It probably evolved from Abert's squirrels that crossed the Colorado River thousands of years ago.

Common ravens fly at all elevations in the Canyon and in every season. You may wonder how they manage under the hot summer sun with their jet-black color, but the feathers are actually very shiny, reflecting much of the sunlight. The California condor has made a comeback to the Canyon, thanks to breeding and release programs. You may see them using their nine-foot wingspan to ride the thermals.

History

Ancestors of today's Pueblo tribes came to the Grand Canyon area in about A.D. 500. Like their predecessors, they hunted deer, bighorn sheep, jackrabbits, and other animals, while gathering such wild edible plant as pinyon and agave. The ancestral Puebloans also fashioned fine baskets and sandals. At their peak, between 1050 and 1150, they grew crops, crafted pottery, and lived in above-ground masonry villages. Toward the end of this period, drought hit the region. By 1150 nearly all the ancestral Puebloans had departed from the Grand Canyon, abandoning their thousands of sites. It's likely that their migrations eventually took them to the Hopi mesas and New Mexican pueblos.

While the ancestral Puebloans kept mostly to the east half of the Grand Canyon (east of today's Grand Canyon Village), another group of hunter-gatherers and farmers, the Cohonina, lived downstream between A.D. 600 and 1150. They adopted many of the agricultural and building techniques and crafts of their neighbors to the east. In 1300, the Cerbat, probable ancestors of the modern Havasupai and Hualapai, migrated onto the Grand Canyon's South Rim from the west. They lived in caves or brush shelters and ranged as far upstream as the Little Colorado River in search of game and wild plants. The Cerbat also planted crops in areas of fertile soil or near permanent springs. It's possible that the Cerbat had cultural ties with the earlier Cohonina.

Paiute living north of the Grand Canyon made seasonal trips to the North Rim, occasionally clashing with the Cerbat. The Paiute lived in brush shelters and relied almost entirely on hunting and gathering. Hopi knew of the Grand Canyon too; they came on religious pilgrimages to collect salt or to trade with the Havasupai.

In 1540, when Francisco Vásquez de Coronado led an expedition in search of the Seven Cities of Cíbola, Hopi villagers told a detachment of soldiers about a great canyon to the west. Hopi guides later took a party of Coronado's men, led by García López de Cárdenas, to the South Rim but kept secret the routes into the depths. The immensity of the Grand Canyon impressed the Spaniards, who failed in their attempt to find a way to the river. Franciscan priest Francisco Tomás Garcés, looking for souls to save, visited the Havasupai and Hualapai in 1776 and was well received. Historians credit Garcés with naming the Río Colorado (Red River).

James Ohio Pattie and other white fur trappers probably encountered the Grand Canyon in the late 1820s, but they provided only sketchy accounts of their visits. Lieutenant Joseph Ives led the first real exploration of the Colorado River. He chugged 350 miles by steamboat upstream from the river's mouth in 1857–1858 before crashing into a rock in Black Canyon. The party then continued overland to the Diamond Creek area in the western Grand Canyon. Ives thought the region worthless and doubted that people would come again.

Most of the Canyon remained a dark and forbidding unknown until Major John Wesley Powell bravely led a boat expedition through the chasm in 1869. On this trip, and on a second journey in 1871–1872, he and his men made detailed drawings and took notes on geology, flora, fauna, and prehistoric ruins. Powell recorded his experiences, now published as *The Exploration of the Colorado River and Its Canyons.*

After about 1880, prospectors entered the Grand Canyon to search for gold, silver, lead, copper, and asbestos deposits. In 1883, stagecoaches began bringing tourists to the Canyon at Diamond Creek, where J. H. Farlee opened a four-room hotel the following year. Prospectors Peter Berry, Ralph Cameron, and Niles Cameron built the Grandview Hotel in 1895 at Grandview Point and led tourists down a trail to Horseshoe Mesa. Other prospectors, such as John Hance and William Bass, also found guiding visitors more profitable than mining. Tourism began on a large scale soon after the railroad reached the South Rim in 1901. The Fred Harvey Company bought Bright Angel Lodge (a predecessor of today's Bright Angel Lodge), built the luxurious El Tovar Hotel, and took over from the smaller operators.

As the Canyon became better known, President Theodore Roosevelt and others pushed for greater federal protection. First a forest reserve in 1893, the Grand Canyon became a national monument in 1908 and a national park in 1919. The park's size doubled in 1975 when legislation extended the boundaries west to Grand Wash and northeast nearly to Lees Ferry. Grand Canyon National Park now includes 1,904 square miles and receives about five million visitors annually.

Park Practicalities

The park collects an admission fee of $20 per private vehicle ($10 per pedestrian or bicyclist) that's good for seven days at the south and east entrances of the South Rim and at the main entrance of the North Rim. You'll get a colorful park map and a copy of *The Guide* newspaper, which lists programs and sightseeing suggestions. Once you're in the park, visitors centers, exhibits, programs, and day hiking are free. Budget travelers can save money by stocking up on gas, groceries, and camping supplies at Flagstaff, Williams, or other towns away from the Canyon; prices at Tusayan and within the park can run substantially higher.

The Grand Canyon offers too much to see in one day—you'll probably wish to spend one or more nights in the area. In Grand Canyon Village you can stay at lodges right on the rim or a short walk back in the woods. The town of Tusayan, just outside the park nine miles south of Grand Canyon Village, provides additional places to stay. And farther south, the towns of Flagstaff and Williams offer a large selection of accommodations at lower prices; also, the little community of Valle on the way has two motels. All of these places also offer RV parks and tent sites.

You can obtain helpful trip-planning literature before your arrival by writing to the park (P.O. Box 129, Grand Canyon, AZ 86023) or visiting the official **website** www.nps.gov/grca, which provides a great deal of information, including news, visiting tips, hiking possibilities, and river-running opportunities. The **automated switchboard** (928/638-7888) connects with all park offices and offers recorded information, including a weather forecast; **hearing-impaired** callers use the TDD number (928/638-7804).

Groups can arrange to have weddings, get-togethers, and memorials at secluded spots on both rims; contact the park for details.

Safety

Theft has become a problem at the Canyon—be sure to hide valuables or keep them with you. Also check that car windows are all the way up and doors locked when you leave the vehicle. Park rangers patrol the park, serving as law enforcement officers and firefighters; see them if you have difficulties.

Beggars will almost certainly approach you at the overlooks, hoping for a handout. Squirrels and chipmunks are the most notorious offenders, and the occasional raven may hop over too. Just say no, as human food can be addictive for wildlife and may cause them to lose their ability to feed themselves. Also, feeding animals is against park regulations and will make National Park Service people *very* unhappy! In addition, a surprising number of people are bitten by the begging rock squirrels.

The South Rim

You'll find lots to see and do on this side of Grand Canyon National Park. Scenic drives and rim trails parallel the rim for long distances, providing countless inspiring panoramas of the depths. And if you decide to head down into the Canyon itself, half a dozen trails will take you there. Historic structures atop the rim have lots of character and some offer exhibits. Ranger programs through the day and in the evening inform and entertain. When it's time to take a break from sightseeing, you'll find many lodging, camping, dining, and shopping options.

Highways provide year-round access to the South Rim at two entrances. The main South Entrance Station near Grand Canyon Village lies just an hour north of I-40 at Williams via Highway 64 or 1.5 hours northwest of Flagstaff via U.S. Highway 180 and Highway 64. If you can arrive here before 8 A.M., you'll be glad you did. You'll not only save a possible hour or two of waiting in line, but you'll likely get a parking spot at Mather Point for the short stroll to Canyon View Information Plaza's orientation panels and information desk. Try to avoid arriving at the South Entrance mid-day (11 A.M.–1 P.M.) or late afternoon, as they're the busiest times. The largest crowds converge during the Easter, Memorial Day, and July 4th holidays.

The East Entrance Station near Desert View is about 1.5 hours north of Flagstaff via U.S. Highway 89 and Highway 64. If you're driving a loop out of Flagstaff or Williams, it's easiest to arrive at the East Entrance (lines tend to be shorter here), see the South Rim, and exit at the South Entrance.

GRAND CANYON VILLAGE

Parking may be your first thought upon arrival, but don't believe those horror stories! *The Guide* newspaper given at entrance stations shows the main parking areas, where you'll have a far better chance of snagging a spot than at the very crowded Mather Point, Yavapai Point, and Bright Angel Lodge areas. Once you've found a space, you can walk or take the free Village Shuttle to get around. Drivers with large rigs should head for Lot E near the Backcountry Information Center for day visits or to their campground if staying overnight.

Walking, especially on the very scenic Rim Trail, is the most enjoyable way of seeing the sights here.

Cycling is another option, though it's restricted to roads and bike paths. A few segments of the Greenway Trail, designed for non-motorized travel, have been completed in the Village, and the branch from Tusayan is in the works.

DRIVING RIM TO RIM

Although 215 miles and about five hours may seem long to cover just 10 raven-flying miles, the drive passes an incredible variety of scenery. From Grand Canyon Village on the South Rim, you'll first head east along the Desert View Drive with its many viewpoints of the Grand Canyon. Then, at 16.5 and 21.7 miles past Desert View, you'll come to overlooks into the sheer-walled Little Colorado River Canyon; they're also a good place to buy Navajo crafts directly from the families who made them.

Cameron Trading Post, a mile north of the Highway 64–U.S. Highway 89 highway junction, is a great place to take a break for a meal; the motel and Native American gallery here are very good as well. North from Cameron, the colors of the Painted Desert glow softly all around. At the Tuba City junction, dinosaur fans may wish to detour five miles east on U.S. Highway 160 to see tracks just north of the highway.

Continuing north on U.S. Highway 89 through Navajo lands, the long line of the Echo Cliffs rises high on the east before you turn onto U.S. Highway 89A and drop down to Navajo Bridge across the Colorado River. It's worth stopping at either end of the bridge to walk across the old span here and admire Marble Canyon. Lees Ferry and Lonely Dell Ranch lie about five miles north, allowing you to take in some history and see a bit of Glen Canyon.

The highway then skirts the base of the well-named Vermilion Cliffs before starting the long climb up to the pine-forested Kaibab Plateau; a viewpoint on the left shortly after the climb begins has a panorama of the Vermilion Cliffs, which blaze in fiery red at sunset. Three small motels with restaurants stand beside the highway below the cliffs. At Jacob Lake, which has a lodge, campground, RV park, restaurant, and a visitors center, turn south 45 miles on Highway 67, a beautiful forest and meadow drive that heads straight for Bright Angel Point on the North Rim.

Canyon View Information Plaza

This visitors center complex, a 300-yard stroll south of Mather Point, makes a good place to start your visit. Because it's designed as part of the public transportation system, there's no parking here. You can take the Village Shuttle, walk via the Rim Trail, or cycle via the Greenway. The Village Shuttle stops on the west side of the Plaza and the Kaibab Trail Shuttle on the east side. Despite the name, there's no view here—you have to walk over to Mather Point to see the Canyon.

Large outdoor panels have maps, sightseeing destinations, hiking possibilities, lodging, campgrounds, and other helpful information. You can also check listings of ranger-guided rim walks, Canyon hikes, talks, family activities, photography workshops, and evening presentations. Outdoor exhibits are available for viewing at all hours. Step inside the Visitor Center (928/638-7888, www.nps.gov/grca, 8 A.M.–5 P.M. daily, until 6 P.M. summer) for the information desk and some exhibits. Kids 4–14 can sign up for the Junior Ranger Program, which is also available at Yavapai Observation Station and Tusayan Museum.

The Grand Canyon Association's **Books & More,** on the south side of the Plaza, features a great selection of Canyon-related books, including ones for kids, plus topological maps, posters, videos, slides, and postcards.

Rim Trail

People of all ages enjoy a walk along this scenic trail, which offers views from many different vantage points and connects the main points of interest in the Grand Canyon Village area. Pick up brochures for the trail at the Visitor Center or along the trail. Shuttle buses stop at both ends of the trail and at many places along the way.

The popular 2.5-mile section east from Bright Angel Lodge to Mather Point is paved and nearly level, taking 45–90 minutes each way. You'll pass El Tovar Hotel, Hopi House, and Yavapai Observation Station in addition to many viewpoints. At Mather Point, you can take a short stroll south to Canyon View Information Plaza or continue

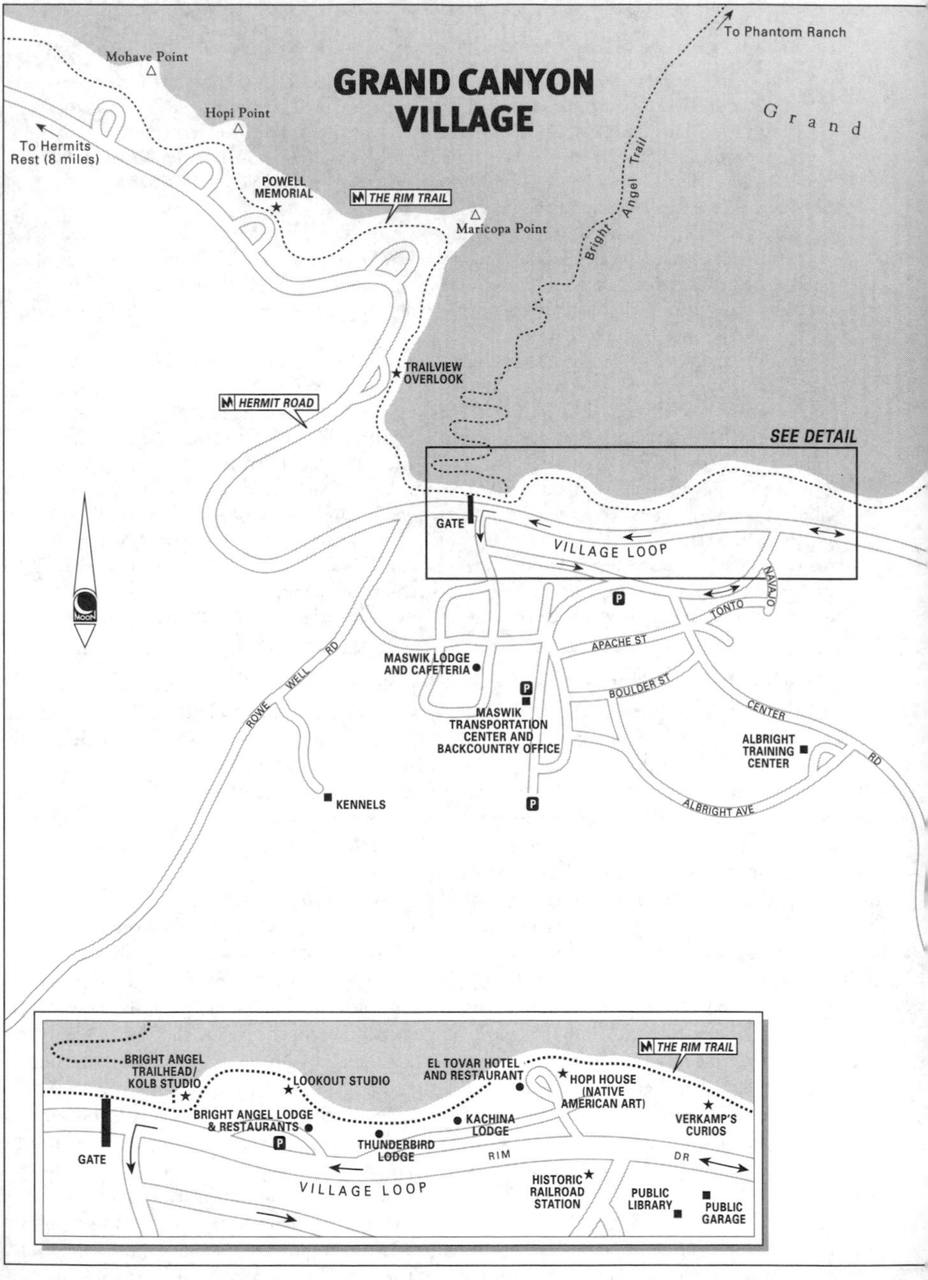

GRAND CANYON VILLAGE
To Phantom Ranch
Grand
Mohave Point
Hopi Point
To Hermits Rest (8 miles)
POWELL MEMORIAL
THE RIM TRAIL
Maricopa Point
Bright Angel Trail
TRAILVIEW OVERLOOK
HERMIT ROAD
SEE DETAIL
GATE
VILLAGE LOOP
NAVAJO
TONTO
APACHE ST
MASWIK LODGE AND CAFETERIA
ROWE WELL RD
BOULDER ST
CENTER RD
MASWIK TRANSPORTATION CENTER AND BACKCOUNTRY OFFICE
ALBRIGHT TRAINING CENTER
KENNELS
ALBRIGHT AVE
MOON
BRIGHT ANGEL TRAILHEAD/ KOLB STUDIO
LOOKOUT STUDIO
EL TOVAR HOTEL AND RESTAURANT
HOPI HOUSE (NATIVE AMERICAN ART)
THE RIM TRAIL
VERKAMP'S CURIOS
BRIGHT ANGEL LODGE & RESTAURANTS
KACHINA LODGE
THUNDERBIRD LODGE
GATE
RIM DR
VILLAGE LOOP
HISTORIC RAILROAD STATION
PUBLIC LIBRARY
PUBLIC GARAGE

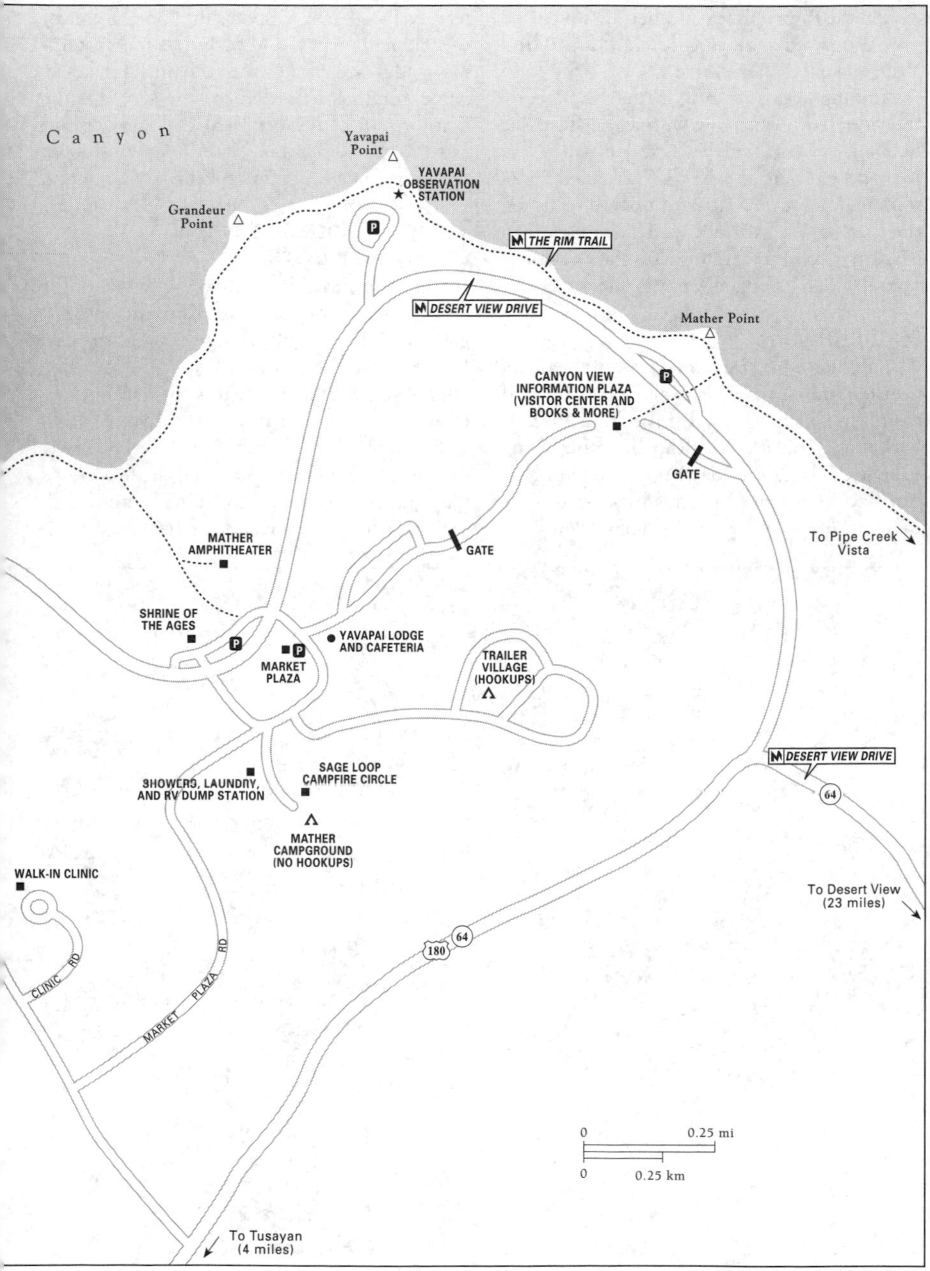

Canyon

Yavapai
Point △

★ YAVAPAI
OBSERVATION
STATION

Grandeur
Point △

P

M̄ THE RIM TRAIL

M̄ DESERT VIEW DRIVE

Mather Point △

CANYON VIEW
INFORMATION PLAZA
(VISITOR CENTER AND
BOOKS & MORE) ■

P

GATE

To Pipe Creek
Vista

MATHER
AMPHITHEATER
■

GATE

SHRINE OF
THE AGES
■

P ■ P

MARKET
PLAZA

● YAVAPAI LODGE
AND CAFETERIA

TRAILER
VILLAGE
(HOOKUPS)
Λ

M̄ DESERT VIEW DRIVE

64

SHOWERS, LAUNDRY, ■
AND RV DUMP STATION

SAGE LOOP
CAMPFIRE CIRCLE
■

Λ

MATHER
CAMPGROUND
(NO HOOKUPS)

WALK-IN CLINIC
■

To Desert View
(23 miles)

CLINIC RD

MARKET PLAZA RD

180 64

0 0.25 mi

0 0.25 km

To Tusayan
(4 miles)

N

The Grand Canyon

© AVALON TRAVEL PUBLISHING, INC.

east on the Rim Trail for another 1.3 miles one-way, also paved and nearly level, to Pipe Creek Vista on Desert View Drive.

Heading west from Bright Angel Lodge, the trail is paved but narrow with some steep sections and stairs to Trailview Overlook, then level to Maricopa Point, a total of 1.4 miles and 30–60 minutes one-way. A narrow, unpaved section of the Rim Trail continues west 6.7 miles from Maricopa Point to Hermits Rest, at the end of Hermit Road, taking 3–4 hours one-way.

Mather Point

The panorama here is the first view of the Grand Canyon for many visitors. Walk north 300 yards from the Canyon View Information Plaza or walk east 2.5 miles on the Rim Trail from Grand Canyon Village. You may be able to park here, but finding a space requires luck or an early morning arrival. Below Mather Point (elev. 7,120 feet) lie Pipe Creek Canyon, the Inner Gorge of the Colorado River, and countless buttes, temples, and points eroded from the rims. It takes its name from Stephen Mather, who served as the first director of the National Park Service and was in office when the Grand Canyon joined the national park system on February 26, 1919.

Yavapai Point and Yavapai Observation Station

Set on the brink of the Canyon with one of the best panoramas on the South Rim, this spot is a great place to take in the sunrises and sunsets. Panels inside the station (8 A.M.–5 P.M. daily, until 8 P.M. in summer) identify the many buttes, temples, points, and tributary canyons. You'll see the trail out to Plateau Point, Bright Angel Trail winding down to the river, the footbridge spanning the river at the base of the South Kaibab Trail, Boaters Beach (look for parked rafts), Phan-

A cloud inversion "fills" the Grand Canyon at Mather Point, December 1977.

tom Ranch, and Bright Angel Canyon. Besides the views, you can examine geology exhibits and browse the bookstore. Parking is difficult here—it's best to walk here along the Rim Trail or catch the Village Shuttle.

Verkamp's Curios

Just east past Hopi House, this venerable institution is worth a look for Native American crafts and Canyon souvenirs. John Verkamp found business too slow in his first attempt at a curio shop out of a tent in 1898, but he returned in 1905 and built on the present site. The family continues to run the business.

Hopi House

Architect Mary Colter patterned this unusual building, opened in 1905, after pueblo structures in the Hopi village of Old Oraibi. It has a stone and adobe exterior, thatched ceilings, and corner fireplaces. Hopi helped in the construction, lived on the upper floors, plied their crafts, displayed their work, and performed nightly dances. Today Hopi House (928/638-3458 gallery, free) has an outstanding collection of Native American art and crafts for sale. Both floors have a wide variety, but climb to the upper floor to see the best work. It's near the Canyon rim just east of El Tovar Hotel, and open 8 A.M.–8 P.M. daily in summer and 9 A.M.–5 P.M. daily in winter.

El Tovar Hotel

Architect Charles Wittlesey designed the 1905 log-and-stone building as a cross between a Swiss chalet and a Norwegian hunting lodge. Despite the remote location, many people of the time hailed it as the most luxurious hotel west of the Mississippi. Mary Colter had a hand in the interior design. Step inside the lobby to get a feel for this old hotel. You might enjoy a meal here too.

Bright Angel Lodge

A popular gathering point for Canyon visitors, this 1935 lodge has a lot of character. Besides the lobby, be sure to see the Bright Angel History Room (free) with displays about the "Harvey girls" and early tourism. Mary Colter designed the "geological fireplace" with the same rock layers as in the Canyon itself. Also step into the coffeehouse/lounge to check out murals by Hopi artist Fred Kabotie; commissioned in 1958, one of them pokes fun at tourists and another at Hopis doing a poor imitation of a Navajo dance. Outside on the Canyon rim behind the lodge, you can often see an endangered California condor making good use of its nine-foot wingspan.

Lookout Studio

The inspiration and materials for this 1914 Mary Colter building came from the Grand Canyon itself. Early visitors could relax by the fireplace in the lounge, purchase souvenirs and postcards in the art room, or gaze into the Canyon depths with a high-power telescope. It's open today with a gift shop and viewing platform. The studio stands on the Canyon's edge, just west of Bright Angel Lodge.

Kolb Studio

Perched on the rim near Lookout Studio and the Bright Angel Trailhead, this 1904 building began as the photography studio of the Kolb brothers. Emery Kolb expanded and operated it until his death in 1976 at the age of 95, enthralling Canyon visitors with movies he and his brother Ellsworth took on a 1911–1912 river-running expedition. The auditorium where Emery showed his long-running film now hosts visiting art exhibits. You can see some of the Kolb brothers' old photos and movie clips in an exhibit or purchase the show on DVD or VHS at the Grand Canyon Association's bookstore here. The studio (928/638-2771, free) is open 8 A.M.–5 P.M. daily, extended to 7 P.M. in summer.

HERMIT ROAD

The Santa Fe Railroad constructed this eight-mile-long road from Grand Canyon Village west to Hermits Rest in 1912. Stops along the way allow you to walk to the rim and enjoy the views. Highlights include a superb overlook of the Bright Angel Trail from Trailview, the copper and uranium Orphan Mine from Maricopa Point, great views and a historic marker at Powell Memorial, the Colorado River from Hopi and Mohave Points, the 3,000-foot sheer drop of the Abyss, and from Pima Point, views of Granite Rapid and the foundations of an old hotel below. Your map will help identify Canyon features: Bright Angel Trail switchbacking down to the grove of trees at Indian Garden, Plateau Point at the end of a short trail from Indian Garden, Bright Angel Canyon on the far side of the river, the many majestic temples rising out of the depths, and the rapids of the Colorado River.

Hermits Rest

The imaginative stone building here marks the westernmost viewpoint and end of the drive. Mary Colter designed the structure and its Great Fireplace according to what she thought a hermit might like. Hermits Rest offers a snack bar, gift shop, drinking water, and restrooms. A free shuttle bus runs the length of the drive except in winter, when you can take your own vehicle. Bicyclists enjoy this ride too, and they aren't affected by the shuttle-season ban on cars. Because Hermit Road is so narrow, cyclists need to pull off and dismount when large vehicles wish to pass.

If you've walked to Hermits Rest on the Rim Trail, you'll probably want to rest too. Louis Boucher, the Hermit, came to the Canyon in 1891 and stayed 21 years; he lived at Dripping Springs and constructed the Boucher Trail to his mining claims in Boucher Canyon.

MARY COLTER, ARCHITECT OF THE SOUTHWEST

In the male-dominated world of early-20th-century architecture, Mary Colter (1869–1958) succeeded in designing many of the Grand Canyon National Park's most notable structures. After Colter's father died in 1886, her mother gave her permission to attend the California School of Design in San Francisco and learn skills to support the remaining family members. Upon graduation, Colter moved to St. Paul, Minnesota, and began teaching mechanical drawing. She later applied for work with the Fred Harvey Company and, in 1901, obtained a contract to decorate the Indian Building, a new museum and sales gallery of Native American crafts between the Alvarado Hotel and the railroad depot in Albuquerque, New Mexico. Her association with the Fred Harvey Company ultimately spanned more than 40 years.

Colter's keen interest and research in Native American architecture led to a remarkable series of buildings along the Grand Canyon's South Rim, beginning with the Hopi House that opened in 1905. She used Southwestern themes and simple designs with careful attention to detail—interiors had to have just the right colors and furnishings, for example. So much thought went into the design of the buildings that each tells a story about its history or setting. Colter gave the stone Lookout Studio (opened in 1914), perched on the Canyon rim, a jagged roof that blends into the scenery. In the same year she completed Hermits Rest at the end of Hermit Road; its Great Fireplace and cozy interior give it the look of a place that a hermit prospector would inhabit. She sought the "lived-in look" and even had workmen smear soot on the new fireplace to enhance the atmosphere. Colter's work also extended to the bottom of the Grand Canyon, where in 1922 she designed the stone lodge and four cabins of Phantom Ranch. In 1932 she finished the Desert View Watchtower, using a variety of prehistoric and mod-

Mary Colter shows blueprints to Mrs. Ickes, wife of the secretary of the interior, in 1935.

DESERT VIEW DRIVE

Outstanding overlooks line this 25-mile drive from Grand Canyon Village east to Desert View. Grandview Point has an especially fine panorama, plus an exciting hiking trail. Other major viewpoints on the way to Desert View include Yaki Point, Moran Point, and Lipan Point. At Lipan, by looking both up- and down-canyon, you can see the entire geologic sequence of the Canyon.

Yaki Point and South Kaibab Trailhead

The turnoff is two miles east of Mather Point, but visitors must take a shuttle service to these destinations from Canyon View Information Plaza, except in winter, when private cars are allowed. Bicycling is another option. Hikers can get an early start by taking a special year-round shuttle from Bright Angel Lodge and the Backcountry Information Center directly to the South Kaibab Trailhead. From Yaki Point, at road's end, you can see much of the central Grand Canyon. The South Kaibab Trail snakes its way along Cedar Ridge below.

Grandview Point

Many people consider this aptly named point one of the best. It's 12 miles east of Grand Canyon Village, then .8 miles north. Sweeping

ern Native American themes; it's the most intriguing of her buildings. After settling on a watchtower patterned after those of the Four Corners region, Colter wrote, "First and most important was to design a building that would . . . create no discordant note against the time-eroded walls of this promontory." She not only designed the 1935 Bright Angel Lodge, intended to provide accommodations for tourists with moderate incomes, but also incorporated into it the 1890s Buckey O'Neill Cabin and Red Horse Station. Without her interest in these historic structures, they would have been torn down. She also designed the unusual geologic fireplace in the lodge's History Room.

La Posada Hotel, which opened in 1930 beside the railroad tracks in downtown Winslow, might be her most exotic commission—a fantasy of arches, halls, and gardens in a Spanish Colonial Revival style. La Posada nearly suffered demolition, the fate of the Alvarado Hotel, but it has been saved and restored; Winslow visitors are welcome to tour the public areas. Train travelers at Union Station in Los Angeles, built in 1939, can admire an interior design that brings a Southwestern flavor to the geometry of art deco. Colter enjoyed her professional life—she never married and was reportedly rarely at home. Only in recent times has the public taken note of Colter's work. Perhaps her position as "house architect" on a relatively small number of major buildings, some in remote areas, led to her relative obscurity. That's changed now, with books, exhibits, and documentaries appearing about her life. Five Colter structures have become National Historic Landmarks.

Hopi artist Fred Kabotie worked with Mary Colter on the Desert View Watchtower's interior artwork.

© GRAND CANYON NATIONAL PARK (NEG#8307)

panoramas take in much of the Grand Canyon from this commanding site above Horseshoe Mesa. The vastness and intricacies of the Canyon show themselves especially well here.

Historic Walk to the Grandview Hotel Site

If you'd like to seek out a bit of history, or just get away from the crowds for a while, it's possible to walk out to the site of the Grandview Hotel, one of the first on the South Rim. There's little left, just some old pipes, broken glass, and a cistern, but the view is still grand. From the Grandview Point turnoff, drive east .5 miles on the highway to an unsigned pullout on the north side, just before Milepost 251, and park. Walk east about half a mile along an old road, now open only to foot traffic, then wander over to the rim. If you continue along the rim a bit farther east you'll come to a pair of small reservoirs.

Grandview Lookout Tower

Some of the prettiest country of the Kaibab National Forest surrounds the lookout. For a panorama of the region, climb the 80-foot steel tower, built by the Civilian Conservation Corps in 1936. Turn south at the sign for Arizona Trail between Mileposts 252 and 253, two miles east of the Grandview Point turnoff, and proceed 1.3 miles on a dirt road to the tower. You can also drive east 15 miles on unpaved Forest Road 302 from the south edge of Tusayan. The Kaibab Forest Map (Tusayan District) shows the way in. Mountain bikers can follow trails from Tusayan to Grandview Lookout—a 16-mile trip one-way; the trailhead is on the west side of Highway 64, just north of Tusayan.

The historic **Hull Cabin** and outbuildings, two miles from the lookout by bumpy dirt road, once belonged to a sheep ranch. You're welcome to visit the grounds.

Tusayan Museum and Ruin

Ancestral Puebloans built this village in A.D. 1185–1190, according to tree-ring dating, then stayed 25–30 years before migrating elsewhere. Up to 30 people lived here, contending with poor soil, little rainfall, and scarce drinking water. Archaeologists who excavated part of the site in 1930 named it Tusayan, a Spanish term for Hopi territory. It's just south of Desert View Drive, 22 miles east of Grand Canyon Village and 3 miles before Desert View.

A small museum (928/638-2305, 9 A.M.–5 P.M. daily, closed some days in winter) introduces the ancestral Pueblo people and displays artifacts that they left behind. Illustrations show the village as it may have looked when occupied. You'll also see some split-twig figures made by archaic cultures. Other exhibits introduce modern tribes of the region. Related books can be purchased.

Outside, a .1-mile paved trail loops around the plaza and ruins of living quarters, storage rooms, and two kivas. A short side trail leads to an area that may have been used for growing crops. You can also take a guided tour; check *The Guide* for times. The trail stays open during daylight hours, weather permitting.

Desert View

This overlook at the east end of Desert View Drive presents a stunning view. Although the surrounding pinyon pines and junipers suggest a lower elevation, this is one of the highest spots on the South Rim. Far to the east lies the multihued Painted Desert that gave the viewpoint its name. Below, to the north, the Colorado River comes out of Marble Canyon, then curves west through the main part of the Grand Canyon.

The Fred Harvey Company built the 70-foot **Desert View Watchtower** in 1932, using stone around a steel frame. Architect Mary Colter incorporated elements from both prehistoric and modern tribes of the Four Corners region in designing the tower. It's not intended to be a replica of any particular watchtower, but rather an interpretation of Southwestern cultures. A leaflet describes the artwork and background of the watchtower. You enter through a room shaped like a Navajo hogan with a traditional log ceiling. Follow the stairs up through the tower's four levels. A snake altar lies in the center of the Hopi Room on the first floor. The large circular wall painting depicts the snake legend. Look around for the wedding scene, gods, and other Hopi symbols. Out on the adjacent terrace, you can view the Canyon through "reflectoscopes," which deepen the colors of the rock layers. Continue up to the second and third levels for a close look at replicas of Southwest petroglyphs. Finally, on the fourth level, you can gaze out windows from the highest viewpoint on the South Rim—7,522 feet.

The hogan-like entrance of the Watchtower has a gift shop. Nearby, you'll find a small information center/bookstore (9 A.M.–5 P.M. daily), another gift shop, snack bar (opens for breakfast at 8 A.M.), picnic tables, general store (groceries and outdoor supplies), and a service station. The large parking area has separate sections for cars, RVs, and buses.

A short road leads to **Desert View Campground** ($10), which offers sites in a pinyon pine–and-juniper woodland from mid-May to the end of October, weather permitting. The campground has drinking water but lacks hookups; no reservations are taken.

Vicinity of Desert View

Highway 64 continues east 33 miles from Desert View to U.S. Highway 89 and Cameron. Sheer 800-foot cliffs drop to the riverbed from two overlooks of the **Little Colorado River Canyon** on the Navajo Reservation. The first overlook, 16.5 miles from Desert View, requires a half-mile walk out to the best viewpoints. The second overlook, 5.2 miles farther east, has just a short walk to the views, plus a large market of Native American jewelry, pottery, and other crafts. Each turnoff is marked with a Scenic View sign.

Cape Solitude, directly above the confluence of the Little Colorado and Colorado Rivers, lives up to its name and features amazing views of both canyons. Adventurous drivers with 4WD can take back roads on the Navajo Reservation to the park boundary (tribal permit needed), then walk the last 6.7 miles. Unless the Little Colorado is in flood, you'll see turquoise-blue waters from mineral-rich springs in its canyon. Hikers can reach **Blue Springs** on a very rough route, about 1.5 miles one-way, with an elevation change of 2,100 feet; it's on the Navajo Reservation (tribal permit required) and approached on 4WD roads from Desert View via Cedar Mountain or from the Kaibab National Forest farther east. The Little Colorado offers a challenging hiking route between Cameron and the Colorado River; conditions constantly change, and it should be avoided when in flood. Hiking books describe some of these routes. You may find a ranger knowledgeable in these areas; ask around at Desert View, Tusayan Ruin, and the Backcountry Information Center. (See *Cameron* in the *Navajo and Hopi Country* chapter, for details on obtaining Navajo tribal permits to explore this remote country.)

VALLE

U.S. Highway 180 from Flagstaff meets Highway 64 from Williams at this junction 28 miles south of Grand Canyon Village. The tiny community (pronounced "Valley") has an excellent aviation museum, a simple theme park based on the *Flintstones* cartoon, two motels, a campground, convenience stores, gift shops, and gas stations.

Planes of Fame Air Museum

Outstanding aircraft of the past reside in this collection (Grand Canyon Valle Airport, south side of town, 928/635-1000, www.planesoffame.org, 9 A.M.–5 P.M. daily, to 6 P.M. in summer, $6 adults, $2 kids 5–11). It's affiliated with the Planes of Fame Air Museum based in Chino, California, so some planes rotate between the two locations or may be on tour.

During the Korean War, General Douglas MacArthur flew aboard the Lockheed Constellation C-121A named *Bataan,*" which has been beautifully restored and opened for tours ($3 extra). A 1928 Ford Trimotor, said to have been a personal aircraft of Henry Ford, still flies; this type of plane was used in early tourist flights over the Grand Canyon. You'll see replicas of a few famous WWI aircraft. WWII highlights include a Fuji Ohka 11 piloted suicide rocket, a Messerschmitt Bf 109G Gustav fighter plane, and an early P-51A Mustang. Newer fighters represent the dawn of the jet age. Some homebuilts and other light aircraft, a Link Trainer Model C-3 ("the sweat box"), and a timeline of women in aviation round out the collection. Around the last weekend in June, the museum sponsors the **High Country Warbirds Fly-In** with flybys of vintage aircraft.

The nearby airport terminal has a free display of antique autos and trucks, which you can see 7 A.M.–5:30 P.M. daily.

Flintstones Bedrock City

Fans of the cartoon series *The Flintstones* may enjoy walking around this life-size town (928/635-2600, 6 A.M.–8 P.M. daily in summer, 7 A.M.–4 P.M. daily in winter, $5 ages two and up). It has the houses of Fred and Barney and their families, businesses, dinosaur statues (one is a kids' slide), a little ride through a "volcano," and a theater where the cartoons play. The park is open year-round, but the volcano ride and theater don't run in winter. There's also a campground and a snack bar.

HIKING

Some of the Inner Canyon trails offer excellent day hiking in their upper sections. Or you can choose from a handful of easier trails atop the rim. You don't need a permit for any of these as long as they're done as a day hike. Water and sun protection are two of the keys to happiness when hiking. Also, allow twice as much time to climb back out as you spent descending! Summer heat bakes the Inner Canyon, so it's best to time your hiking for early or late in the day and take a siesta in a shady spot when the sun is at its fiercest. In winter, you'll find instep crampons useful if snow or ice covers the trails. Rangers warn, like a mantra, not to try to hike to the river and back in one day. Such a trip can be deadly in the warmer months, and is utterly exhausting the rest of the year.

Rim Trail

- Distance: 11.9 miles one-way
- Duration: 5–7 hours one-way
- Elevation Change: 480 feet
- Rating: Easy to Moderate
- Trailheads: Pipe Creek Vista on Desert View Drive and Hermits Rest on Hermit Road

You'll enjoy fine views all along the way. Most people walk short sections in the Grand Canyon Village area, but you could hike the trail's entire length and make a day of it. Shuttles connect each end of the trail with Grand Canyon Village. The eastern section between Pipe Creek Vista and Bright Angel Lodge is paved and nearly level for its 3.8-mile length. West from Bright Angel Lodge, the trail narrows and has some steep sections and stairs; the pavement runs out at Maricopa Point after 1.4 miles, then it's another 6.7 miles to Hermits Rest.

Bright Angel Trail Day Hike to Indian Garden

- Distance: 9.2 miles round-trip
- Duration: 6–9 hours round-trip
- Elevation Change: 3,060 feet
- Rating: Strenuous
- Trailhead: just west of Bright Angel Lodge in Grand Canyon Village

This well-graded trail is one of the few to have drinking water along its length; be sure to carry water for the dry stretches, however. Indian Garden, where Havasupai once farmed, has a ranger station, shaded picnic tables, year-round water, toilet, and a campground.

For a shorter hike, Mile-and-a-Half Resthouse offers a shade shelter, seasonal water, toilet, and emergency phone; the 3-mile round-trip drops 1,131 feet and takes 2–4 hours. Or you could continue to Three Mile Resthouse, which provides a shade shelter with seasonal water and emergency phone; it's 6 miles round-trip with a 2,112-foot descent and takes 4–6 hours.

Plateau Point, perched 1,300 feet directly above the swirling Colorado River, has a wonderful 360-degree panorama of the Canyon. From Indian Garden, follow a gentle side trail across the shadeless Tonto Platform to the point. This very strenuous day hike from the rim is 12.2 miles round-trip, with an elevation change of 3,195 feet; allow 8–12 hours.

Hermit Trail Day Hike to Santa Maria Spring

- Distance: 5 miles round-trip
- Duration: 5–8 hours round-trip

- Elevation Change: 1,680 feet
- Rating: Moderate
- Trailhead: just beyond Hermits Rest at the west end of Hermit Road

You'll get a very different perspective of the Grand Canyon from the Hermit, which switchbacks into a major tributary canyon. Santa Maria Spring is a cool spot with a stone shelter and toilet. Carry water for the entire trip as this spring and Dripping Springs offer only a tiny flow, which needs treating.

If you'd like a shorter hike, consider turning around at Waldron Basin, 3 miles and 2–4 hours round-trip, with an elevation change of 1,240 feet.

Also in the area, Dripping Springs adds moisture to a shady alcove that's 7 miles and 6–9 hours round-trip. Descend the Hermit Trail for 2 miles, dropping 1,440 feet, then turn left 1.5 miles on Dripping Springs Trail, climbing 400 feet. Keep left where the Boucher Trail turns north from Dripping Springs Trail.

South Kaibab Trail Day Hike to Cedar Ridge

- Distance: 3 miles round-trip
- Duration: 2–4 hours round-trip
- Elevation Change: 1,140 feet
- Rating: Moderate
- Trailhead: near Yaki Point off Desert View Drive

Cedar Ridge features great panoramas. You can go on your own or join a ranger-led hike. There's no drinking water on this trail; bring extra, as you may well wish to go farther than you had planned!

Ooh Aah Point will give you an introduction to the South Kaibab in 1.5 miles and 1–2 hours round-trip, with an elevation change of 780 feet.

For a greater challenge, you can continue past Cedar Ridge to Skeleton Point, a 6-mile, 4–6-hour round-trip, with an elevation change of 2,040 feet; be sure to get a very early start in summer.

Strong hikers enjoy continuing down to the Tonto Trail (4.4 miles from the rim), turning left 4.1 miles on the gently rolling Tonto to Indian Garden, then heading 4.6 miles up the Bright Angel Trail. Elevation change is about 3,000 feet. In summer, the Tonto Trail gets very hot, but a crack-of-dawn start will get you to the oasis at Indian Garden before the worst of the heat hits. The park's shuttles connect the trailheads for this 13.1-mile hike.

Grandview Trail Day Hike to Horseshoe Mesa

- Distance: 6 miles round-trip
- Duration: 6–9 hours round-trip
- Elevation Change: 2,500 feet
- Rating: Strenuous
- Trailhead: Grandview Point off Desert View Drive

Miners improved an old Indian route in 1892 so they could bring out high-grade copper ore from Horseshoe Mesa. Mining ceased in 1907, but mine shafts, machinery, and ruins of buildings remain. Be sure to carry plenty of water and pace yourself for the stiff climb back to the rim.

To get a feel for this steep trail and its fine views, you can head down to Coconino Saddle, a 1.5-mile round-trip, with a 1,600-foot drop; allow 1–2 hours.

Vishnu Trail

- Distance: 1.1-mile loop
- Duration: 1–2 hours
- Elevation Change: nearly level
- Rating: Easy
- Trailhead: Grandview Lookout Tower off Desert View Drive

You'll escape the crowds on this trail in the Kaibab National Forest. It's a good choice for families. From Grandview Lookout Tower, the trail goes northeast, then loops back via the Arizona Trail. A spur trail leads to Grand Canyon viewpoints.

Arizona Trail in the Kaibab's Tusayan Ranger District

- Distance: 24.2 miles one-way
- Duration: varies
- Elevation Change: 1,200 feet
- Rating: Easy to Moderate
- Trailhead: Grandview Lookout Tower off Desert View Drive

Whether you're setting out for a few hours or a few months, the Arizona Trail offers scenic hiking and mountain biking. The first mile southeast from Grandview Lookout Tower has interpretive signs about mistletoe. The trail heads generally south and downhill in three segments from the lookout to the south boundary of the Tusayan Ranger District. The 9.4-mile Coconino Rim Trail segment follows the top of 500-foot cliffs southeast of Grandview Lookout, expect some steep sections and switchbacks; views of the Painted Desert appear after about three miles. The mostly level 8.3-mile Russell Wash segment farther south crosses the transition from ponderosa forest in the north to pinyon pine and juniper in the south. The 4.6-mile Moqui Stage segment follows the old stagecoach route, used 1892–1901, from Moqui Stage Station to the south forest boundary.

Red Butte Trail

- Distance: 2.4 miles round-trip
- Duration: 1.5 hours up, 1 hour down
- Elevation Change: 866 feet
- Rating: Moderate
- Trailhead: From Tusayan, head south nine miles on Highway 64 to between Mileposts 226 and 227, then turn east 4.3 miles on Forest Roads 305, 340, and 340A. From the south, you can take Highway 64 to Milepost 224, then turn east 2.7 miles on Forest Roads 320, 340, and 340A to the trailhead. The Kaibab Forest map (Williams and Tusayan Districts) shows these roads.

Few people know about this mountain south of Tusayan, despite the good trail and fine views. It's a remnant of the red-colored Moenkopi Formation, protected from erosion by a thick lava cap. Atop the 7,326-foot summit, you can visit the lookout tower for the best 360-degree panorama. The large meadows just to the north hosted the Grand Canyon's original airport; a bit farther north stands the green tower of a uranium mine, currently inactive due to low ore prices. A long section of the North Rim rises farther to the north, Grandview Lookout Tower can just be seen on the wooded ridge to the northeast, and the San Francisco Peaks and Volcanic Field lie to the south. As on all trails in the Southwest, keep an eye out for rattlesnakes.

CROSS-COUNTRY SKIING

During the snow season beginning about late December, the Forest Service grooms trails from a trailhead .3 miles north of Grandview Lookout Tower off Desert View Drive.

MOUNTAIN BIKING

Arizona Trail

The best single-track with Canyon views lies along the Arizona Trail near Grandview Lookout Tower. Forest roads intersect the Arizona Trail allowing a variety of loops. For example, you can make a 14.6-mile loop from Grandview Lookout Tower on the Coconino Rim segment of the Arizona Trail and Forest Road 310 that parallels it.

Tusayan Bike Trails

These four interconnected trails begin from a trailhead on the west side of Highway 64 between the park's south entrance and Tusayan. Trail #1 makes a three-mile loop, taking about half an hour. Trail #2 is an eight-mile loop lasting just over an hour. Trail #3 is a nine-mile loop requiring about an hour and a half. Trail #4 branches off Trail #3 and continues east to Grandview Lookout Tower, 16 miles one-way from the Tusayan Trailhead.

MULE RIDES

Sure-footed mules have carried prospectors and tourists in and out of the Canyon for more than a century. These large animals, a crossbred from female horses and male donkeys, depart daily year-round on day and overnight trips. Although easier than hiking, a mule ride should still be considered strenuous—you need to be able to sit in the saddle for long hours and control your mount. These trips are definitely not for those afraid of heights or large animals.

Day trips proceed down the Bright Angel Trail to Indian Garden and out to Plateau Point, a spectacular overlook directly above the river; the 12-mile, seven-hour round-trip costs $132.88 per person. On the overnight trip you follow the Bright Angel Trail all the way to the river, cross a suspension bridge to Phantom Ranch, spend the night in a cabin, then come out the next day via the South Kaibab Trail. Prices with lodging and meals runs $360.58 for one person, $641.57 for two, and $292.80 for each additional person. Three-day, two-night trips offered November–March give you a full day at the bottom of the Canyon and cost $507.05 for one person, $854.92 for two, and $371.50 for each additional person. Mules also carry hikers' overnight gear to Phantom Ranch, $53.80 each way (30-pound limit). All these rates include tax.

Reservations should be made 9–12 months (up to 23 months) in advance for summer and holidays. Also be sure to claim your reservation at least one hour before departure. Without a reservation, get on the waiting list and there's a chance you'll make the trip, especially off-season; register in person between 6 and 10 A.M. the day before you want to go.

For information and reservations less than two days in advance, call the Bright Angel Lodge Transportation Desk (928/638-3283). To make reservations more than two days in advance, contact Xanterra Parks & Resorts (14001 E. Iliff Ave., Suite 600, Aurora, CO 80014, 888/297-2757 or 303/297-2757, www.grandcanyonlodges.com).

Enforced requirements for riders include good health, weight 200 pounds (91 kg) or less, fluency in English, and a height of at least four feet seven inches (138 cm). No pregnant women are allowed. A broad-rimmed hat, tied under the chin, long pants, a long-sleeved shirt, and sturdy shoes (no open-toed footwear) are necessary. Don't bring bags, purses, canteen, or backpacks, but you can carry a camera or binoculars. A bota (water bag), which ties on the saddle horn, is supplied.

TRAIL RIDES

Apache Stables (928/638-2891, www.apachestables.com) offers mule and horse rides through the Kaibab National Forest for one hour ($30.50), two hours ($55.50), and all the way to the South Rim and back in four hours ($95.50). Campfire trips ($40.50) ride out and take a wagon back, or you can take the wagon both ways ($12.50); bring your own food. Riding season runs spring to autumn depending on the weather. Reservations are recommended two weeks ahead in summer or two days the rest of the year—though last-minute openings are possible. The stables are one mile north of Tusayan.

TOURS

Bus Tours

These excursions (Box 699, Grand Canyon, AZ 86023, 928/638-3283, www.grandcanyonlodges.com) will show you the sights of the South Rim and present the Canyon's history, geology, wildlife, and architecture. **Hermits Rest Tour** (two hours, $16.25) visits viewpoints on Hermit Road. **Desert View Tour** (just under four hours, $28.50) travels along Desert View Drive. Begin or end the day with **sunrise** or **sunset** tours (1.5 hours, $12.25 each). Children under 16 go free with a paying adult. You can purchase the Desert View Tour with any other excursion for $35 and take the tours on separate days if you wish.

Railroad Express ($49 adult, $29 children 16 and under) drives you to Williams early in the morning to catch the train ride back to Grand Canyon Village; note that the train trip doesn't provide Canyon views. A **raft** trip (12 hours, $115 adult, $64 age 12 and under) runs the smooth-flowing Colorado River in Glen Canyon from the dam to Lees Ferry mid-March–early November; the tour also includes highlights along Desert View Drive and in the Navajo Reservation. Tours in the park leave daily (twice a day in summer for the Hermits Rest and Desert View tours). Lodge transportation desks sell tickets.

Backroad Tours

Grand Canyon Jeep Tours & Safaris (Tusayan, 928/638-5337 or 800/320-5337, www.grandcanyonjeeptours.com, March–Oct.) visits backcountry historic and scenic spots in the Kaibab National Forest and the Grand Canyon. The two-hour Canyon Pines Tour departs mid-day for $48 adult ($35 age 12 and under). The three-hour Grand Sunset Tour goes late in the afternoon—a good time to spot wildlife—and includes a stop to watch the sunset for $59 ($45 age 12 and under). The Indian Cave Paintings

Tour visits a site with petroglyphs and pictographs in the Kaibab National Forest for $40 adult ($30 age 12 and younger).

Study Tours

Grand Canyon Field Institute (Box 399, Grand Canyon, AZ 86023, 928/638-2485, www.grandcanyon.org/fieldinstitute) leads small groups to explore the Grand Canyon with day hikes, backpacking, river-running trips, van tours, and classroom instruction. You can pick up a schedule at the Grand Canyon Association bookstores in the park.

Air Tours

Flights over the Canyon provide breathtaking views and a look at some of the park's remote areas. About 40 scenic flight companies operate helicopters or fixed-wing aircraft here, mostly out of Las Vegas. The 50,000-plus flights a year sometimes detract from the wilderness experience of backcountry users—Tusayan's airport is one of the busiest in the state. However, restrictions on flight routes and elevations help minimize the noise.

Scenic flights depart all year from the Tusayan Airport area. Helicopters fly near rim-level and offer the novelty of their takeoffs and landings, but they cost much more. Fixed-wing aircraft fly about 1,000 feet higher and provide more airtime for your dollar; they also offer better children's discounts. Air Grand Canyon departs from the main terminal, while Grand Canyon Airlines and the helicopter companies fly from separate terminals nearby.

Grand Canyon Airlines (928/638-2407 or 800/528-2413, www.grandcanyonairlines.com) started flying here in 1927 with Ford Trimotors. Today the company uses high-wing, twin-engine planes on a 45- to 55-minute loop over the South Rim, Little Colorado River, and back over the North Rim ($79 adult, $49 children under 12). Planes leave from just north of the main terminal.

Air Grand Canyon (928/638-2686 or 800/247-4726, www.airgrandcanyon.com) flies high-wing Cessnas with a choice of a 30- to 40-minute flight over the eastern Canyon ($79 adult, $47 children 12 and under), a 50- to 60-minute loop over the eastern Canyon and North Rim ($95 adult, $52 children 12 and under), a 90- to 100-minute grand tour of the Grand and Marble Canyons to Lake Powell ($186 adult, $100 children 12 and under), a three-hour trip to Monument Valley and Lake Powell ($278 adult, $256 children 12 and under), and an all-day excursion with a flight to Page, smooth-water river trip to Lees Ferry, then by road back to the Grand Canyon ($260 adult, $240 children 12 and under). A full-day, combination flying and rafting tour to the lower Grand Canyon can be arranged with two days' notice ($595 per person).

Papillon Grand Canyon Helicopters (928/638-2419 or 800/528-2418, www.papillon.com) flies across the Canyon to the North Rim (25–30 minutes, $115 adult, $95 children 2–11) and over the eastern Grand Canyon and North Rim (45–50 minutes, $175 adult, $155 children 2–11). You can also arrange to land at Supai village in Havasu Canyon and visit the waterfalls on day and overnight excursions. Helicopters fly from a site north of the main terminal and across the street; a gift shop and photo lab are here.

Grand Canyon Helicopters (928/638-2764 or 800/541-4537, www.grandcanyonhelicoptersaz.com) heads across the Canyon to the North Rim (25–30 minutes, $135 adult, $115 children 2–12) and a loop over the eastern Grand Canyon and North Rim (40–50 minutes, $195 adult, $175 children 2–12) from the hill just east of the main terminal.

AirStar Helicopters (928/638-2622 or 800/962-3869, www.airstar.com) will take you across the Canyon to the North Rim and back (25–30 minutes, $99), around the eastern Grand Canyon (40–45 minutes, $145), and over both the eastern and North Rim areas (50–55 minutes, $165) from the hill just east of the main terminal.

ACCOMMODATIONS

The Grand Canyon offers too much to see in one day. In Grand Canyon Village you can stay right on the rim at Bright Angel Lodge, Thunderbird Lodge, Kachina Lodge, or El Tovar Hotel. Maswik and Yavapai lodges, in the woods about two blocks back from the rim, also offer rooms.

VISITING GRAND CANYON NATIONAL PARK ON A SHOESTRING

The steep prices charged for park admission and services can be daunting, yet the Grand Canyon can easily be seen for little more than a song. Getting a small group together will slice costs on the entry, camping, and lodging. A $50 National Parks pass will give unlimited entry to the park and all other National Park Service areas in the country for 12 months, a much better deal than forking out $20 every seven days to visit the Grand Canyon.

You can camp free in the Kaibab National Forest that adjoins both the South and North Rims, though you'll need your own wheels to do this. Backpackers and cyclists can stay in cheap walk-in campgrounds at both rims. The cafeterias at Yavapai and Maswik Lodges in Grand Canyon Village offer good deals, or you can fix your own meals. And the best things—the views, sunsets, day hikes, and interpretive programs—are free.

All of these may fill up from early April through October. The town of Tusayan, outside the park nine miles south of Grand Canyon Village, provides additional places to stay. Although last-minute rooms may be available, reservations 6–23 months in advance will give you the best choice.

Grand Canyon Village

Xanterra Parks & Resorts (14001 E. Iliff Ave., Suite 600, Aurora, CO 80014, 888/297-2757 or 303/297-2757 advance reservations, 928/638-2631 same-day reservations, fax 303/297-3175, www.grandcanyonlodges.com) operates all the lodges here, as well as Phantom Ranch at the bottom of the Canyon and the motel and cabins at the North Rim's Bright Angel Point. All lodge rooms, restaurants, bars, and public areas are totally smoke-free. Pets cannot stay in rooms, but there's a kennel available.

One of the grand old hotels of the West, **El Tovar** has offered the Canyon's finest accommodations and dining since 1905. This national historic landmark offers rooms—no two alike—with modern conveniences, yet it retains an old-fashioned lodge ambience. Guests enjoy a restaurant, concierge service, lounge, and gift shops. Of the 12 suites, 4 have Canyon views. Room rates run $123 for a standard double up to $175 for a deluxe and $225–285 for a suite.

Kachina and **Thunderbird Lodges,** on the rim between El Tovar and Bright Angel Lodge, offer modern rooms for $115 d back side or $125 d canyon side.

The rustic 1935 **Bright Angel Lodge** sits on the rim a short distance from the Bright Angel trailhead. Hikers and other visitors gather in the lobby, patio, restaurants, and lounge of this popular place. Rates for historic cabins run $84 d, rim cabins $105 d, and rim cabins with fireplace $127 d. The Buckey O'Neill Suite dates from the early 1890s and is one of the oldest structures in the park; it costs $241. Rooms in the lodge cost $49 with sink only, $55 with toilet, and $67 d with toilet and shower or tub; other facilities are down the hall. The **Bright Angel History Room** displays memorabilia from early tourist days and a "geological fireplace" in which Canyon rocks have been laid in the proper stratigraphic sequence. A series of murals in the Bright Angel Coffee House/Lounge by Hopi artist Fred Kabotie includes some humorous scenes. The transportation desk in the lobby organizes mule trips, bus tours, and Phantom Ranch accommodations.

Maswik Lodge, two blocks south of Bright Angel Lodge, has a cafeteria. In the south section, cozy cabins go for $64 d (closed in winter) and basic rooms for $77 d, and in the south section, larger, nicer rooms are $119 d. **Yavapai Lodge,** one mile east of Bright Angel Lodge near Market Plaza, offers modern rooms for $91 d in the west section and slightly better rooms for $103 d in the east section; there's also a cafeteria here. The lodge may close for part of the winter but opens during the holidays.

Tusayan

Motels, restaurants, an RV park/campground, an IMAX theater, and other tourist services line the highway in this compact town nine miles south of Grand Canyon Village. They're all well marked. Prices run on the high side for accommodations, though they drop in winter or any time business is slow.

$50–100: Seven Mile Lodge (928/638-2291, $75 d in summer, closed Jan.) offers basic rooms. No reservations are taken, so you may need to arrive by early afternoon to get a room during summer.

$100–200: Rodeway Inn/Red Feather Lodge (928/638-2414, 800/538-2345, or 800/228-2000 Rodeway reservations, www.redfeatherlodge.com) gives you a choice of standard rooms at $79–119 d in the older motel-style annex and deluxe rooms at $99–129 d in the newer hotel building. Amenities include an outdoor pool, hot tub, fitness room, and an adjacent restaurant. Pet owners can bring their furry friends along—this is the only lodging near the South Rim to accept them.

Grand Canyon Quality Inn & Suites (928/638-2673 or 800/228-5151, www.grandcanyonqualityinn.com) features a very attractive Southwestern decor. Inside the huge central atrium, you'll find the restaurant, Wintergarten Lounge, and an 18-foot hot tub. A gift shop lies off the lobby, and the pool and another hot tub are outside. Standard rooms are $118–139 d and suites go for $189 d from April to October 15.

Best Western Grand Canyon Squire Inn (928/638-2681 or 800/622-6966, www.grandcanyonsquire.com) claims to be the only resort near the Grand Canyon. Rooms cost $140 d standard/traditional, $159 d deluxe, and the few suites are $175–225 d. The Inn has two restaurants and a lounge near the front desk. The pool and tennis courts are just outside. Head downstairs for the exercise room and its indoor hot tub and sauna. Also downstairs, the Family Fun Center provides a bowling alley, pool tables, and video arcade. Saguaro Sports Bar & Grill across the hallway serves snacks and fast food. Also, there's a beauty salon and, of course, a gift shop. Cowboy exhibits and Western art decorate the lobby and other public areas.

Holiday Inn Express (928/638-3000, 888/538-5353, or 800/465-4329, www.grandcanyon.hiexpress.com) offers large modern rooms for $139 d in summer along with an indoor pool and hot tub. A nearby building has one-bedroom suites at $159 d, a kids' suite for $199, and two-bedroom suites for $225; there's an indoor hot tub, too.

Styled as a Western lodge, **The Grand Hotel** (928/638-3333 or 888/634-7263, www.grandcanyongrandhotel.com) presents a dinner theater with Native American programs and cowboy songs, a restaurant, and an indoor pool and hot tub; rooms go for $149 d ($159 with a balcony) in summer. Some guests prefer the street side to watch the sunsets, other people like the forest view in back.

Valle

You'll pass through this tiny town 28 miles south of Grand Canyon Village if you're taking the direct routes from Williams or Flagstaff. **Grand Canyon Inn** (928/635-9203 or 800/635-9203, $49–69 d) has a restaurant, outdoor pool, and a gift shop, but the restaurant may close part of the winter. The office also rents rooms in the **Grand Canyon Motel** ($79 d) across the highway. Reservations are recommended on summer weekends.

CAMPGROUNDS

Grand Canyon Village

Campgrounds tend to be crowded in the warmer months and it's strongly recommended to have a reservation from mid-March to October; otherwise, try to arrive before noon to look for a site. RVers have a dump station near the entrance to Mather Campground. Rangers enforce the "No camping outside designated sites" policy with stiff fines. Camping inside the Canyon or in backcountry areas atop the rim requires a permit from the Backcountry Information Center.

Mather Campground (800/365-2267 advance reservations, 928/638-7888 same day, http://reservations.nps.gov, $15) welcomes both tenters and RVers year-round with drinking water but no hookups. Family sites have a limit of six people, three tents, and two vehicles. A Golden Age or Access pass gets you in at half price. Reservations are a good idea most of the year, and can be made for family and group sites. If you're willing to brave the cold weather of December–February, all sites are first-come, first-served and cost $10. Backpackers and bicyclists have a walk-in area for $4 per person, no reservations needed; it has space even when the campground sign says Full. Coin-operated showers, laundry, and ice lie a short walk away at Camper Services near the campground entrance. You can attend campfire programs during the warmer months.

Just east of Mather Campground, **Trailer Village** ($24 RVs w/hookups) stays open all year. Reservations two months in advance are highly recommended from the week before Easter to the end of October and on any holiday; you can make them with Xanterra Parks & Resorts (14001 E. Iliff Ave., Suite 600, Aurora, CO 80014, 888/297-2757 or 303/297-2757 advance reservations, 928/638-2631 same-day reservations, fax 303/297-3175, www.grandcanyonlodges.com). When making reservations, you can request a site for your size rig or even a space suitable for tenting. Coin-operated showers, laundry, and ice at Camper Services are within walking distance.

Desert View

This campground, just inside the East Entrance Station 25 miles east of Grand Canyon Village, has sites in a pinyon pine–and-juniper woodland with drinking water but no hookups. It's open mid-May–October, weather permitting, for $10; no reservations taken.

Tusayan

Grand Canyon Camper Village (928/638-2887 or 877/638-2887, $20 tents or RVs no hookups, $36–46 w/hookups) offers coin showers and a playground. You can stay in a tepee ($25) during the warmer months. RVs have lots of space to maneuver, while tenters can pitch among the trees on a hill in the back. Reservations can be made only for the hookup sites, though spaces are usually available. The campground may close in winter.

Ten X Campground (May–Sept., $10), in the ponderosa pines of the Kaibab National Forest, has drinking water but no hookups or showers; there's usually room. Amphitheater programs take place weekend evenings. From Tusayan, go south two miles (between Mileposts 233 and 234), then turn east a quarter mile. Group sites nearby can be reserved; ask at the Tusayan Ranger Station (928/638-2443).

Dispersed camping off the unpaved roads in the Kaibab National Forest south of the park is another possibility—just practice no-trace camping, carry your own drinking water and a shovel, and stay at least a quarter mile from the nearest paved road and any surface water. Staff at the Tusayan Ranger Station, on the right one mile north of Tusayan, can suggest areas for dispersed camping. Be sure to heed posted fire restrictions—campfires and charcoal fires are often prohibited during the dry months of early summer. The Kaibab Forest map (Williams and Tusayan Districts) shows the back roads.

Valle

Flintstones Bedrock City (928/635-2600, $12 tents or RVs, $16 w/hookups) provides a campground 28 miles south of Grand Canyon Village on Highway 64. The theme park also offers a store, snack bar, coin showers, and laundry. Sites lack charm and are exposed to the winds. Open year-round, but no water hookups in winter.

FOOD

Grand Canyon Village

El Tovar Hotel (928/638-2526 ext. 6432, daily breakfast, lunch, and dinner, $18–26) offers elegant continental and American dining. Be sure to make reservations for dinner, though late seatings are often available. To get your choice of time and seating near a window, it's best to reserve ahead. Hotel guests can reserve up to 6 months in advance, non–hotel guests up to 30 days in advance. You can enjoy the ambiance at lower rates for breakfast ($8–12) and lunch ($10–15); no reservations are taken for these. If you're having lunch here, try to arrive early, as it's a popular destination for the railway passengers who arrive around noon.

In Bright Angel Lodge, the informal **Bright Angel Restaurant** (928/638-2526 ext. 6189, daily breakfast, lunch, and dinner, $8–12) has popular American food, including Southwestern items such as fajitas, plus limited Canyon views. The adjacent **Arizona Room** (928/638-2526 ext. 6296, daily lunch March–Oct. $8–12, daily dinner March–Dec., $11–24) features very fast lunchtime service for barbecue entrées, sandwiches, and salads, then a dinner menu of New York strip, prime rib, trout or wild salmon, and some Southwestern specialties. Large picture windows give everyone a view of the Canyon. Both restaurants offer a few vegetarian items. Neither place takes reservations, but there's an efficient waiting system; you're given a pager that announces when your table is ready. Sunset is the peak time; you can get in more easily by arriving earlier or later. **Bright Angel Coffee** in the lounge of Bright Angel Lodge will start your morning with java and pastries. For a quick sandwich, ice cream, or other snack, swing by **Bright Angel Fountain** on the Canyon rim behind Bright Angel Lodge; it's closed in the winter.

Maswik Lodge, two blocks south of Bright Angel Lodge, and **Yavapai Lodge,** one mile east of Bright Angel Lodge near Market Plaza, have large cafeterias open daily for breakfast, lunch, and dinner at relatively low prices.

Canyon Village Marketplace in Market Plaza has a supermarket and a deli counter with tables. You can also buy groceries at general stores in Desert View and Tusayan.

Tusayan

The spacious atrium and greenery in the **Grand Canyon Quality Inn & Suites'** restaurant (928/638-2673, daily breakfast, lunch, and dinner, $10–22) provide an enjoyable setting. Diners have a choice of à la carte or a buffet at each meal. Entrées include steaks, fish, wienerschnitzel, and Navajo tacos. The large selection of salads and fruit in the buffets will appeal to vegetarians; non-vegetarians will appreciate steak and seafood on the menu as well as a variety of meat dishes in the buffet.

In the Grand Hotel, **Canyon Star** (928/638-3333, daily breakfast, lunch, and dinner, $15–26) presents a dinner theater with Native American programs and cowboy songs; there's a buffet for breakfast and lunch.

Café Tusayan (928/638-2151, daily breakfast, lunch, and dinner, $6–20) serves American favorites next to the Red Feather Lodge. Dinner highlights include steak, prime rib, and fish; you can pick up a box lunch with a bit of advance notice.

Grand Canyon Squire Inn (928/638-2681) features the Coronado Room (nightly dinner, $15–25) for fine dining on steak, barbecued ribs, prime rib, fish, pasta, and some Southwestern and vegetarian items. The Canyon Room serves breakfast and lunch (buffet available in summer) and a daily summertime dinner buffet ($17). Downstairs, the Saguaro Sports Bar & Grill fixes pizza, sandwiches, and snacks.

The Western-style **Steakhouse** (928/638-2780, daily lunch in summer, daily dinner year-round, $7–26) serves up steak, chicken, shrimp, and even a few veggie options; you can also dine on the deck.

We Cook Pizza & Pasta (928/638-2278, daily lunch and dinner, $7–20) offers pizza, pasta, calzones, and sandwiches; it's self-service with indoor picnic-table seating. In the Grand Canyon Village Shops across from the IMAX, **Sophie's Mexican Kitchen** (928/638-1105, daily lunch and dinner, $3–10) is a colorful little café serving fajitas, tacos, chili rellenos, and other popular south-of-the-border fare. Nearby, **Jennifer's Bakery & Coffeehouse** (928/638-3433, daily breakfast, lunch, and dinner, $4.50–10) brews many styles of coffee and has a tempting array of sandwiches and pastries; you can surf the Internet as you sip. There's a fast-food court in the Grand Canyon IMAX Theater complex.

Valle

Grand Canyon Inn's restaurant (28 miles south of Grand Canyon Village, 928/635-9203, daily breakfast, lunch, and dinner, may close in winter, $12–17) cooks up steak, ribs, chicken, trout, and other American standbys.

INFORMATION

Canyon View Information Plaza

Drop by for a quick overview of things to see and do in the park; it's reached by the park shuttles or a 300-yard walk south of Mather Point. Step inside the Visitor Center for the information desk, open 8 A.M.–6 P.M. daily. The outdoor information panels are always available.

At the entrance stations, you'll receive a free copy of *The Guide* newspaper, which lists the latest visitor information on sightseeing, hiking, programs, places to stay and eat, and other visitor services. You can also obtain this information on the park's excellent website, www.nps.gov/grca. The park's mailing address is Box 129, Grand Canyon, AZ 86023. The **automated switchboard** (928/638-7888) provides visitor information, weather forecasts, and connects to all park offices if you're patient.

Grand Canyon and Arizona tourist information is available in Tusayan at the IMAX theater and in Valle at the Planes of Fame Air Museum.

Backcountry Information Center

For trail information and backcountry camping permits, drop by this office (Maswik Transportation Center, 928/638-7875, 8 A.M.–noon and 1–5 P.M. daily). Call 1–5 P.M. to speak with someone in person. For day hikes, which don't need a permit, you can also get trail information at Canyon View Information Plaza.

Kaibab National Forest

Though often overshadowed by Grand Canyon National Park, the Kaibab offers many recreation opportunities. For handouts on scenic drives, hiking, mountain biking, cross-country skiing, and historic sites, stop by the **Tusayan Ranger Station** (Box 3088, Tusayan, AZ 86023, 928/638-2443, www.fs.fed.us/r3/kai, 8 A.M.–4:30 P.M. Mon.–Fri.). It's in the Tusayan Administrative Site just outside the South Entrance Station. Staff can provide directions for hiking the Red Butte Trail, the prominent butte 12 miles south of Tusayan, as well as the Arizona Trail just south of the park. If sufficient snows arrive in winter, cross-country skiers can glide along loops near Grandview Lookout. The Kaibab National Forest map for the Tusayan District shows the trails and back roads.

Internet Resources

A "virtual tour" on the park's informative website www.nps.gov/grca will give you ideas of things to do on your visit. The Unofficial Grand Canyon National Park Home Page www.kaibab.org is also a good source. The commercial site www.thecanyon.com offers an introduction to the park, with listings of services and links to surrounding towns.

Getting online in the park is easy but costly at Internet kiosks found in many of the lodges. Jennifer's in Tusayan is an Internet café. Grand Canyon Community Library offers cheaper access, though is likely to be booked up.

Grand Canyon Community Library

This small collection (928/638-2718, noon–5 P.M. Mon.–Fri., 9 A.M.–1 P.M. Sat.) resides in an old schoolhouse tucked behind the garage and general office for the lodges in Grand Canyon Village; turn up Navajo Street, then turn left at the sign; don't worry about warnings that the street is just for residents. You'll find general and Southwestern reading along with periodicals. For a fee, you can use an Internet-connected computer, copy machine, or fax.

SERVICES

Entertainment

Rangers present **evening programs** (see listings in *The Guide* for times and places); you can find out the day's topics at the panels outside the Visitor Center or by calling 928/638-7888. Chamber music comes to the Grand Canyon in September during the **Grand Canyon Music Festival,** held at Shrine of the Ages auditorium.

Grand Canyon IMAX Theatre (Tusayan, 928/638-2468/2203, $10 adults, $7 kids 6–12) projects an impressive movie, *The Grand Canyon—The Hidden Secrets,* on a 70-foot screen with six-track stereo sound. The spectacular photography of the 34-minute presentation portrays prehistoric tribes, explorers, wildlife, river-running, and flying. Shows take place on the half hour 8:30 A.M.–8:30 P.M. daily March–October, then 10:30 A.M.–6:30 P.M. daily in winter. Look for the replicas of Major Powell's boats that were used in the movie. Services include fast-food restaurants, gift shops, an ATM, and tourist information.

Bright Angel Lodge's lounge offers live bands some days in spring and autumn. You'll also find lounges at El Tovar and Maswik lodges, though these don't normally provide entertainment.

Shopping

Grand Canyon Association (www.grandcanyon.org) has excellent selections of regional books, children's books, topo maps, posters, and videos in its shops at Canyon View Information Plaza, Kolb Studio, Yavapai Observation Station, Tusayan Ruin, and Desert View. **Canyon Village Marketplace** at Market Plaza in Grand Canyon Village and general stores at Tusayan and Desert View sell groceries, camping and hiking supplies, clothing, books, maps, souvenirs, and film. Canyon Village Marketplace is the largest and offers outdoor gear rentals and some repairs. There's a gift shop almost everywhere you turn in the developed areas of the South Rim! El Tovar, other lodges, most motels, helicopter terminals, and the airport have them. **Hopi House,** the pueblo replica just east of El Tovar, has an impressive array of Native American crafts and art from the Southwest; it's worth a visit to see both the architecture—interior and exterior—and the high-quality merchandise, especially upstairs. A bit farther east, **Verkamp's Curios** sells Native American crafts and other souvenirs. **Lookout Studio,** on the rim's edge near Bright Angel Lodge, features curios and books in a picturesque stone building. Other places to shop in the park include Hermits Rest and Desert View Watchtower, at opposite ends of the South Rim drives.

Pets

The **Grand Canyon Kennel** (near Maswik Lodge, 928/638-0534) houses animal friends who won't be permitted in the park lodges, on shuttle buses, or on the Inner Canyon trails; reservations are suggested. Pets on a leash (six-foot maximum) may walk the rim trails in developed areas. Rodeway Inn/Red Feather Lodge in Tusayan is the only place near the South Rim to accept pets. Service animals may be allowed below the rim with a permit from the Backcountry Information Center.

Other Services

Backpackers can stow their bags with the bellhop in the Bright Angel Lodge lobby. The **post office** (Market Plaza, 928/638-2512, 9 A.M.–4:30 P.M. Mon.–Fri., 11 A.M.–3 P.M. Sat.) has stamp machines in the lobby that are available after hours. **Bank One** (928/638-2437 or 800/226-5663) next door has a 24-hour ATM; it cannot change foreign currency or cash out-of-town checks. Another **post office** is in the general store at Tusayan. You'll also find an ATM here and at the IMAX theater across the highway. **Print film processing** is offered at Canyon Village Marketplace and several places in Tusayan. **Mobile phone** coverage is spotty at the Grand Canyon, and cannot be relied upon, especially below the rims. **Grand Canyon Garage** (928/638-2225, 638-2631 ext. 6502 after hours) fixes ailing cars and provides 24-hour emergency service. **Walk-In Medical Care** (928/638-2551, closed Sun.) offers medical services. For a dentist, call 928/638-2395. To summon an ambulance, or for other emergencies, dial 911.

Visitors with special needs should contact the park in advance and ask for the *Accessibility Guide.* Also check the park's website and *The Guide* for accessible facilities and activities. Hearing-impaired callers can use the TDD number (928/638-7804) for park information.

Camper Services provides coin-operated showers and laundry—both a welcome sight to any traveler who's been a long time on the road or trail—near the entrance to Mather Campground. Outside near Camper Services, you'll find a dump station and a faucet where you can fill your water jugs. Another water faucet is just above the Bright Angel Trailhead.

GETTING THERE AND AROUND

Shuttle Services

The park offers free shuttle services to reduce traffic congestion. Look for the schedules in *The*

Guide newspaper, free at entrance stations and information desks. Hermit Road and the Yaki Point/South Kaibab Trailhead road are closed to private vehicles except in winter (Dec.–Feb.), but travelers with disabilities can obtain a permit at the Visitor Center to drive their own vehicles.

The **Village Shuttle** connects Canyon View Information Plaza, Yavapai Observation Station, campgrounds, lodges, shops, and offices of Grand Canyon Village; buses operate daily year-round about every 15–30 minutes from early morning to late at night. The route takes about one hour round-trip.

The **Hermits Rest Shuttle** leaves from a transfer station just west of Bright Angel Lodge and goes to Hermits Rest with stops at overlooks along the way; it operates daily every 15–30 minutes from an hour before sunrise to an hour after sunset. The trip out and back takes 75 minutes if you don't get off. This shuttle doesn't run December–February, at which time the road is open to private vehicles.

The **Kaibab Trail Shuttle** connects Canyon View Information Plaza with the South Kaibab Trailhead, Yaki Point, and Pipe Creek Vista from one hour before sunrise to one hour after sunset every 15–30 minutes daily year-round; the round-trip takes 30 minutes. A **Hikers Express** departs 2–3 times daily in the early morning year-round for the South Kaibab Trailhead from the Bright Angel Lodge and the Backcountry Information Center.

Trans-Canyon Shuttle (928/638-2820, mid-May–mid-Oct., $65 one-way, $110 round-trip) offers daily round-trip van service between the South and North Rims; it departs from the Grand Canyon Lodge on the North Rim at 7 A.M. and arrives at Bright Angel Lodge on the South Rim by noon; the return trip leaves the South Rim at 1:30 P.M. and arrives at the North Rim by 6:30 P.M.

Taxi and Auto Rentals

Transportation Dispatch (928/638-2822) and **Grand Canyon Coaches** (928/638-0821) provide taxi services in the Tusayan and Grand Canyon Village areas and go out to some trailheads. **Enterprise Rent-a-Car** (928/774-9407 Flagstaff or 800/736-8222) will deliver or pick up a car at the Tusayan airport for an extra $150 each way.

Bus

Open Road Tours (928/226-8060 Flagstaff or 877/226-8060, www.openroadtours.com) offers a shuttle service from Flagstaff via Williams and Tusayan. The company also provides area tours and scheduled service to Phoenix's Sky Harbor Airport.

Train

Grand Canyon Railway (800/843-8724, www.thetrain.com) will transport you in vintage railway cars from downtown Williams to the 1909 log depot in Grand Canyon Village in the morning, then return in the afternoon.

Trains run daily except December 24 and 25. Steam engines lead the way in summer, then diesels are used the rest of the year. (See the *Williams* section of the *Flagstaff* chapter for the many dining and entertainment options provided.) Transportation desks in the lodges have a tour that combines a bus to Williams with the train back to the Grand Canyon.

Air

The airport just southwest of Tusayan offers scheduled flights, fixed-wing scenic tours, and a gift shop.

Scenic Airlines (928/638-2617 Grand Canyon, 702/638-3300 Las Vegas, or 800/634-6801, www.scenic.com) flies Twin Otters from North Las Vegas Airport at least twice a day year-round and offers tour packages. Fares run $141 one-way, $282 round-trip.

Air Vegas Airlines (928/638-9351 Grand Canyon, 702/736-3599 Las Vegas, or 800/255-7474, www.airvegas.com) provides both scheduled and tour flights four or five times daily all year in small, twin-engine, turbo-prop planes from North Las Vegas Airport. Tickets are $139 one-way, $278 round-trip; you can also sign up for one of the many tours out of Las Vegas.

Havasupai and Hualapai Indian Reservations

A map shows how little of the South Rim actually lies within the park! The lands of the Havasupai and Hualapai tribes hold beautiful side canyons, spectacular overlooks, and even a scenic drive to the bottom of the Grand Canyon.

THE HAVASUPAI INDIAN RESERVATION

The towering cliffs of Havasu Canyon enclose a land of blue-green waters, breathtaking waterfalls, and lush vegetation. Havasu Creek rushes through the canyon past the village of Supai before beginning its wild cascade down to the Colorado River. The canyon and its creek, about 35 air miles northwest of Grand Canyon Village, belong to the Havasupai. (*Havasu* means "blue water," and *pai* means "people.")

Getting There

The tribe wisely decided against allowing road construction in the canyon, so most residents and tourists enter by mule, horse, or foot. Helicopters provide another option, though the noisy machines seem out of place here.

The eight-mile trail from Hualapai Hilltop to Supai is the usual way in. From Seligman on I-40, take Highway 66 northwest for 28 miles (to between Mileposts 110 and 111), then turn right and go 63 miles on paved Indian Route 18 to Hualapai Hilltop. If coming from the west, take Highway 66 northeast out of Kingman for 60 miles, then turn left and drive the 63 miles. Stock up with supplies before leaving Highway 66, as no gas, water, or stores are available after the turnoff. The road to Hualapai Hilltop climbs into forests of ponderosa pine that give way to pinyon and juniper, then desert grasslands close to the rim. Parking areas and stables mark road's end. Maps show dirt-road shortcuts to Hualapai Hilltop, but they suffer from poor signs and rough surfaces.

Permits and Fees

You *must* have reservations, whether staying in the lodge or camping. Try to make them far ahead, especially for holidays, weekends, March–June, and September–November; you can use a Visa or MasterCard. When you arrive at Supai, stop to register and pay the $20 entrance fee. The tribe asks you to leave pets, alcohol, and firearms at home.

If you're staying at the lodge, make room and horse reservations through the staff there. Campers make reservations with Havasupai Tourist Enterprise (P.O. Box 160, Supai, AZ 86435, 928/448-2121 or 928/448-2141, www.havasupaitribe.com) and pay $10 per person per night. To preserve the canyon floor, no fires or charcoal are allowed, so bring a stove if you plan to cook. Camping outside the established campground is prohibited.

Hiking In

From Hualapai Hilltop (elev. 5,200 feet), the trail descends at a moderate grade into Hualapai Canyon for the first 1.5 miles, then levels off slightly for the remaining 6.5 miles to Supai village (elev. 3,200 feet). About 1.5 miles before the village, the trail joins the sparkling waters of Havasu Canyon. Try to get an early start from Hualapai Hilltop, especially in the warmer months—you'll wish to avoid the heat of the day in summer when temperatures soar past 100°F! Take a couple quarts of drinking water. Good hiking boots help on the rough, rocky stretches of trail. You'll get the most out of a visit with at least two nights in the canyon. Day hikes from the rim to the waterfalls aren't practical—the distance and climb are too much for even strong hikers.

Riding In

If you'd rather ride than walk, local families will take you and your gear on horses or mules from the parking lot at Hualapai Hilltop to Supai ($70 one-way or $120 round-trip) or all the way to the campground ($75 each way), 2.75 miles farther. One animal can carry about four packs (duffel bags are best) not exceeding 130 pounds total. A sightseeing ride from Supai to the falls and back can be arranged with the lodge. You should make reservations a couple of weeks in advance and pay a 50 percent deposit. Campers make arrangements through Havasupai Tourist Enterprise, lodge guests through the lodge. Also call two weeks before arrival to make sure your animal is available. Visitors may bring their own horses if they take along feed and pay a $20 trail fee.

The Waterfalls

Three cascades plunge over cliffs of the Redwall Limestone within a distance of just two miles. You'll first come to 75-foot-high **Navajo Falls,** which has several widely spaced branches 1.5 miles downstream from Supai. It's named after a 19th-century Havasupai tribal chief kidnapped by Navajo as an infant. Not until he grew to manhood did he learn of his true origin and return to the Havasupai.

A bit farther, spectacular **Havasu Falls** drops 100 feet into a beautiful turquoise-colored pool rimmed by travertine deposits. Clear, inviting waters make this a perfect spot for swimming or picnicking.

Awe-inspiring **Mooney Falls** plummets 196 feet into a colorful pool one mile beyond Havasu Falls. The Havasupai named this most sacred of waterfalls Mother of the Waters. The present name is that of a prospector who died here in 1880. When assistants lowered Daniel Mooney down the cliffs next to the falls, the rope jammed and Mooney hung helpless as the rope frayed and broke. He fell to his death on the rocks below, but 10 months passed before his companions could make their way down to reach and bury the travertine-encrusted body. A rough trail beside the falls descends along the same route hacked through the travertine in those months after Mooney's death. You'll pass through two tunnels and then ease down with the aid of chains and iron stakes. At the bottom—as soon as your knees stop shaking—you can enjoy a picnic or swim in the large pool. Miners extracting silver, lead, zinc, and vanadium drilled the holes that you see high on the canyon walls.

Beaver Falls, two miles downstream from Mooney, makes a good day hike from the campground or Supai. You'll pass countless inviting travertine pools and small cascades, of which Beaver Falls is the largest. The trail, rough in places, crosses the creek three times, climbs high up a cliff, then descends and crosses a fourth time below Beaver Falls. The trail continues downstream four more miles along Havasu Creek to the Colorado River. Travel fast and light if going to the river, as camping is prohibited below Mooney Falls. Photographing the falls can be a challenge; the best time to snap them in full sunlight is in May, June, and July.

Accommodations, Food, and Services

Havasupai Lodge (P.O. Box 159, Supai, AZ 86435, 928/448-2111, www.havasupaitribe.com, $75 s, $80 d, $8 each additional person) in Supai village offers non-smoking rooms with air-conditioning, two double beds, and private bath. The spartan rooms lack phones or TVs, but you probably won't miss them. Obtain the required reservations in advance; six weeks is recommended—six months at the most popular times.

The nearby **café** serves breakfast, lunch, and dinner daily, though it closes about 5 P.M. in winter. Try the Indian taco—red beans, beef, cheese, onion, and lettuce on fry bread. Ice cream prices are high, though not so bad when you consider what it takes to bring the frozen dessert to such a remote area. A **store** across the street, open daily, sells meat, groceries, and cold drinks. Bring cash for the café and store.

Send your postcard home via pack train—with a postmark to prove it! The **post office** next to the store is open weekdays. A **health clinic** in Supai provides emergency medical care.

Havasu Campground

Most visitors prefer to camp, listening to the sounds of the canyon and enjoying the brilliant display of stars in the nighttime sky. Havasu Campground begins a quarter mile below Havasu Falls (or 10.75 miles from Hualapai Hilltop) and provides drinking water from a faucet, picnic tables, and pit toilets. Most people don't realize that the campground extends three-quarters of a mile along Havasu Creek to the brink of Mooney Falls. You'll enjoy more solitude if you walk to the far end. Theft is a problem in the campground, so don't leave valuables in your tent or lying around.

THE HUALAPAI INDIAN RESERVATION

The Hualapai (Pine Tree People) live on nearly one million acres along the South Rim, downstream from the Havasupai. Visitors can experience a scenic drive into the Grand Canyon at Diamond Creek, spectacular viewpoints of the lower Grand Canyon from Grand Canyon West, and one-day Colorado River rafting trips.

Peach Springs

This community 54 miles northeast of Kingman on Highway 66 is the only town on the reservation. Peach Springs offers neither charm nor anything to see, but it does have a good motel and restaurant. **Hualapai Lodge** (900 Route 66, Peach Springs, AZ 86434, 928/769-2230 or 888/255-9550, www.grandcanyonresort.com, $80 s, $90 d, less in winter) provides comfortable rooms and a restaurant that serves breakfast, lunch, and dinner daily. Be sure to make room reservations during the popular April–October season.

In the lodge, you can obtain permits to drive the Diamond Creek Road and information on Grand Canyon West and Grand Canyon river-running. A grocery store and post office lie across the highway and a few doors west. Craft vendors may set up in the park across from the lodge.

Diamond Creek Road

You'll enjoy fine views on this 21-mile gravel road, the only road access to the river within the Grand Canyon. It turns off Highway 66 opposite the Hualapai Lodge and descends gently to the Colorado River. Most of the way follows the normally dry Peach Springs Canyon, then in the last few miles sparkling Diamond Creek. Diamond Peak (3,512 feet), with its "faceted" sides comes into view about half way down. Except for river-runners, who use the road to take out or put in boats, few people visit this spot. Yet the very first organized groups of tourists to the Canyon arrived at Diamond Creek in 1883. A hotel built here and used 1884–1889 was the first in the Grand Canyon.

If the weather has been dry for several days, cautiously driven cars can traverse the road. Storms, most common in July and August, may wash out sections and close the road or necessitate a high-clearance vehicle. A camping area near the Colorado River has a few picnic tables and some outhouses. Another campground is 1.2 miles before the river near the junction of Diamond and Peach Springs Canyons. Before turning down Diamond Creek Road, you must stop at the Hualapai Lodge to obtain permits. Sightseeing costs $6.42 per person (age 6 and over) for day use. Camping is $10.70 per night per person and includes the sightseeing fee. Fishing and hiking require additional permits at $8.56 each per person per day. Hikers can make only short trips in designated areas; ask a ranger first. Spring and autumn have the most pleasant temperatures at this 1,900-foot elevation; it's very hot in summer, but winter can be OK.

River-Running

Hualapai River Runners (P.O. Box 246, Peach Springs, AZ 86434, 928/769-2219 or 888/216-0076, www.grandcanyonresort.com) will take you on a one-day motorized-raft trip down the lower Grand Canyon from Diamond Creek, lift you out by helicopter to the rim at Grand Canyon West, then return you by road to Peach Springs, for $265. This is the only company to offer a day trip within the Grand Canyon. Rates during the March–October season cover food, waterproof bag for personal gear, and transportation from Peach Springs.

Grand Canyon West

This airport and tourist center in the remote northwest corner of the reservation receives many scenic flights out of Las Vegas, and it's also possible to drive here. Once you arrive, the Hualapai tribe offers a 4.5-mile bus tour along the rim of the western Grand Canyon to Guano Point, where you can enjoy a great panorama. The Colorado River lies nearly 4,000 feet directly below. Terraced cliffs rise even higher on the North Rim. The Canyon remains grand to the end, as you'll see. The Grand Wash Cliffs, which lie just out of sight downstream, mark the west end of both the Grand Canyon and the Colorado

© BILL WEIR

view down the lower Grand Canyon from Guano Point

Plateau. One of the steel towers used in a guano mining operation still stands on the point, and another tower is visible below. The towers supported a tram that transported guano from a bat cave located across the river. The tour also makes a short stop at an overlook of Eagle Point, an exceptionally long and narrow neck of land extending out into the Canyon.

Cost for the bus tour and a barbecue lunch at Guano Point runs $39.59 for adults, $28.89 for children 6–13; the lunch includes enough vegetables to satisfy most vegetarians, too. Tours depart frequently year-round and last about two hours; the first is at 9 A.M. and the last about 4:30 P.M.; no reservations are needed. For more excitement, you can take a helicopter ride to the bottom of the Canyon, hop into a motorized raft for a short river tour, then fly back—all for $149.30 or $160.40 w/the Guano Point tour. Hummer and ATV tours may be available too. Tickets, Quartermaster Point permits, and a gift shop are in the terminal building at the Grand Canyon West airport. It's a good idea to call ahead and allow plenty of time, because this is such a long drive out. Contact the Hualapai Lodge for information. Several fixed-wing and helicopter companies offer tours from Las Vegas; check with operators there for the many options.

While at Grand Canyon West, you can also enjoy a visit on your own to **Quartermaster Point** to see another outstanding panorama of the Grand Canyon. A quarter-mile trail from road's end leads down to the best views at the top of sheer cliffs. Quartermaster Canyon lies to your right, and Burnt Canyon is across the river. Twin Point stands above Burnt Canyon. Farther up-canyon, Kelly Point extends even farther out from the North Rim. You can also picnic at Quartermaster Point; the spot has a few tables and an outhouse. First, obtain a permit from the Grand Canyon West Terminal, $15 per person (free if you also take a tour). The turnoff is one mile before the Grand Canyon West Terminal, then 2.3 miles from the sign to the rim. Plans are in the works for a visitors center and campground at Quartermaster Point.

Getting to Grand Canyon West is also an adventure. Allow at least two hours one-way for any of the four driving routes, which allow loop possibilities, or you can fly from Las Vegas. Buck and Doe Road stays within the reservation all the way. This dirt road can be rough—ask about road conditions before you leave. When it's wet, even 4WD vehicles should avoid it. Buck and Doe turns north from Highway 66 between Mileposts 100 and 101, 2.7 miles west of Peach Springs; follow it 50 miles to the end, then turn right on paved Diamond Bar Road and go 4.3 miles. Antares Road, also dirt but likely to be better graded, turns north off Highway 66 farther west from Peach Springs, between Mileposts 74 and 75; take it 33 miles, turn right on paved Pearce Ferry Road and go 7 miles, then turn right on Diamond Bar Road and continue 21 miles. The first 14.4 miles on Diamond Bar Road is dirt but very scenic; you pass Joshua trees and enter a canyon through the Grand Wash Cliffs. Another back-road route involves heading north 40 miles on Stockton Hill Road from Kingman, then right on Pearce Ferry Road for 7.1 miles and right on Diamond Bar Road for 21 miles. The best road approaches from the west; take U.S. Highway 93 from Kingman or Las Vegas to paved Pearce Ferry Road, near Milepost 42, follow it 29 miles east, then turn right and go 21 miles on Diamond Bar Road. There are plans to pave all of Diamond Bar Road by the end of 2005.

Grand Canyon West Ranch (702/736-8787 or 800/359-8727, www.grandcanyonwestranch.com, $199 d, $269 4 persons) provides rustic cabins, Western dining, horseback riding, cattle drives, and wagon rides on a historic ranch off Diamond Bar Road, seven miles east of the Pearce Ferry Road junction. Helicopter flights from Las Vegas can be arranged too.

The Inner Canyon

The wonders of the Canyon reveal themselves best to those who enter its depths. Just being at the bottom of the Canyon is a delight, whether you're riding atop the waves, strolling between the convoluted walls of an unnamed side canyon, or enjoying life at camp. Experiencing the Canyon by river with some side hikes might be the single best way to see and appreciate the grandeur and beauty here.

One of the world's greatest adventures, the river voyage through the Grand Canyon provides both the excitement of roaring rapids and the tranquility of gliding in silent passages. Many beautifully sculptured side canyons, some with lush vegetation, can be easily reached only from the river.

Within the Grand Canyon, the Colorado River flows 277 miles, drops 2,200 feet, and thunders through 70 major rapids. Although explorers of the 19th century feared this section of the river, rendering it in dark and gloomy drawings, boating in the Canyon has become safe and enjoyable. It allows you to visit some of the grandest and most remote corners of the river system. Boating parties stop frequently to explore the twisting side canyons, old mining camps, and prehistoric ruins along the way.

Just remember that the Inner Canyon is a wilderness area, subject to temperature extremes, flash floods, rockslides, and other natural hazards. You can have a successful trip in the Canyon only by taking enough food, water, and other supplies.

HIKING

Always carry—and drink—water. All too often, people walk merrily down a trail without a canteen and then suffer terribly on the climb out. Only the Bright Angel and North Kaibab Trails have sources of treated water. In summer, carry one quart or liter of water for each hour of hiking; half a quart per hour should be enough in the cooler months. Electrolyte-replacement drinks may be helpful too. If hiking in the hot months (May–Sept.), it's a good idea to find a shady spot from 10 A.M. to 4 P.M. while the Canyon bakes under the sun.

Canyon trails offer little shade—you'll need a hat, sunglasses, and sunscreen. Footgear should have good traction for the steep trails; lightweight boots work well. During winter and early spring,

FUN ON THE TRAIL CHECKLIST

- In summer, it's well worthwhile to hit the trail at first light, before 7 A.M. at the latest. Or start after 4 P.M.; a lightweight flashlight provides the option of hiking after dark.
- Water and sun protection will come in handy even on short hikes, as the grand scenery will try to draw you in farther than you'd planned!
- Keep your body humming with frequent water and food (carbohydrate) breaks. All water and no food can lead to water intoxication—a dangerous condition caused by low electrolytes.
- Rangers recommend one gallon of water for an eight-hour hike in hot weather. Drinking water *before* you get thirsty will prevent the 10–20 percent loss of efficiency caused by even slight dehydration.
- If it's hot, try soaking your clothing in water for refreshing coolness.
- An easy pace allows the body to function more efficiently and feel better.
- Kicking back and putting your legs up for a 5–7-minute break once or twice an hour will refresh your leg muscles.
- It's best to ignore that temptation to try a rim-to-river-to-rim hike unless you're sure you can do it *and* the weather is cool.
- The Canyon Rule is to allow one third of the time and energy for the descent and the rest for the climb back up.
- Wind and rain can cause hypothermia even in summer, so raingear can save the day year-round.
- Traveling light increases the fun; food and water should be the heaviest items. You might be able to replace a heavy tent with a tarp and ground sheet, a heavy sleeping bag with a lightweight blanket, and the Walkman with the sounds of the Canyon.
- Rangers will be happy to advise you on your trip plans and possible difficulties that may lie ahead.

instep crampons—metal plates with small spikes—greatly improve footing on icy trails at the higher elevations. Rain gear will keep you dry during rainstorms; ponchos, on the other hand, provide poor protection against wind-driven rain. Be careful when rock-scrambling—soft and fractured rocks dominate in the Canyon. Don't swim in the Colorado River—its cold waters and swift currents are simply too dangerous.

Zones

Backcountry areas of the Grand Canyon have been divided into zones to give hikers an idea of what conditions to expect.

Corridor Zone trails receive regular maintenance and have signs, emergency phones, toilets, and easy trailhead access. They're the best choice for first-time visitors, because someone will likely be around to help in case of difficulty. Drinking water is available at some places along the way, but ask before setting out. Because water sources may be hours apart, you should still carry water. Camping is permitted only in established campgrounds.

Threshold Zone areas receive less maintenance and have fewer signs; you'll need to know where sources of water are and purify the water before drinking. The more heavily used areas have designated camping sites. Most trailheads are reached by dirt roads.

Primitive Zone hiking requires route-finding and Canyon experience, because you'll see only the occasional sign. The long distances between water make this zone best in autumn through spring. Trails and routes receive no maintenance—you could encounter difficult or hazardous conditions. Some trailheads require a 4WD vehicle for access.

Wild Zone routes should be tackled only by highly experienced Canyon hikers who can find their way on indistinct or nonexistent routes. Water may be unavailable or scarce, so this zone is best suited for the cooler months.

Information and Permits

Rangers are the best source of up-to-the-minute information for trails and permit procedures. On the South Rim, the **Backcountry Information Center** at Maswik Transportation Center is open 8 A.M.–noon and 1–5 P.M. daily all year. Staff answer the **Backcountry Information Line** (928/638-7875) Monday–Friday 1–5 P.M. except holidays. The **North Rim Backcountry**

Office is open 8 A.M.–noon and 1–5 P.M. daily May 15–late October, weather permitting. Bookstores in the park sell hiking guides and topo maps. (Also see *Suggested Reading* at the back of this book.

You'll need a permit for all overnight camping trips in the backcountry, but not for day hikes or stays at Phantom Ranch. Permits can be requested from the Backcountry Information Center in person, by mail (P.O. Box 129, Grand Canyon, AZ 86023), or by fax (928/638-2125). Ask for the *Backcountry Trip Planner,* which includes regulations, a map, and a permit request form, or obtain the information on the Web at www.nps.gov/grca.

Each permit costs a nonrefundable $10 plus $5 per person per night. If you plan on doing a lot of trips, the 12-month Frequent Hiker membership of $25 will let you purchase permits for just the $5 per person per night. The National Park Service limits the number of campers in each section of the Canyon to provide visitors with a quality wilderness experience and to protect the land from overuse. Try to submit your choices early, especially for holidays and the popular months of March to May. Requests are accepted up to four months in advance, starting with the first day of the month of that four-month period. Small groups—less than 6 people—have a greater chance of getting a permit; 11 is the maximum group size.

Permits can sometimes be obtained from rangers on duty at Tuweep, Meadview, and Lees Ferry Ranger Stations. However, these rangers are often hard to find because their patrol duties have priority. Pipe Spring National Monument can issue last-minute permits for some areas if space is available. Do not depend on obtaining a permit as a walk-in.

If you do arrive without a permit, show up at the Backcountry Information Center by 8 A.M. to find out what's available or to get on a waiting list. If you're flexible and have extra days, there's a good chance of getting into the Canyon.

Other Areas

Not all of the Grand Canyon lies within the park. Contact the Havasupai to hike Havasu Canyon, famous for its waterfalls, travertine pools, and blue-green waters. The Hualapai have the only road access to the bottom of the Grand Canyon via Diamond Creek with some day-hike possibilities. Many remote canyons, trailheads, and awesome viewpoints of the North Rim lie on lands of the Kaibab National Forest, Bureau of Land Management, and Lake Mead National Recreation Area.

CORRIDOR TRAILS

National Park Service rangers recommend that first-time visitors try one of the trails in the Corridor Zone to get the feel of Canyon hiking. These trails are wide and well marked. Rangers and other hikers will be close by in case you run into problems.

Camping along Corridor trails is restricted to established sites at Indian Garden, Bright Angel, and Cottonwood. Mice and other small varmints at these campgrounds have voracious appetites for campers' food—keep yours in the steel boxes provided or risk losing it.

Bright Angel Trail

- Distance: 9.3 miles one-way
- Duration: 5–6 hours down, 7–8 hours up
- Elevation Change: 4,460 feet
- Rating: Strenuous
- Trailhead: just west of Bright Angel Lodge in Grand Canyon Village

Havasupai used this route from the South Rim to reach their fields and the spring at Indian Garden. Prospectors widened the trail in 1890, later extending it to the Colorado River. Now it's the best-graded and most popular trail into the Canyon. Resthouses 1.5 and 3 miles below the rim contain emergency telephones and usually offer water from May 1 to September 30. Pipeline breaks commonly occur, so it's best to confirm at the Visitor Center or Backcountry Information Center that water is available. One-way distances from the top are 4.6 miles to Indian Garden (campground, water, and ranger station), 7.7 miles to the Colorado River, 9.3 miles to Bright Angel Creek (campground, water, ranger station), and 9.6 miles to Phantom Ranch.

ARIZONA TRAIL: THE GRAND CANYON SECTION

This part of the Arizona Trail presents one of the biggest challenges for trail users. Besides the deep descent into the chasm and long climb out the other side, hikers must plan ahead to obtain the required backcountry permit or to make a reservation at Phantom Ranch. The rim-to-rim distance is just too great to hike and enjoy in one day. If you don't get a permit or reservation ahead of time, you can show up at the Backcountry Information Office for a camping permit or at the Bright Angel Lodge Transportation Desk for a Phantom Ranch bed and hope that space is available. Obtaining a last-minute permit or reservation may delay transcanyon hikers for several days.

Bicyclists face a long detour. Not even the most experienced mountain biker will be permitted to ride down any of the trails into the Canyon because of dangers to the cyclist and other trail users. Also, the National Park Service won't allow cyclists to carry their bikes across the Canyon on pack frames, because the wide load could knock hikers off the trail. So cyclists will have to follow the same route as cars—adding more than 200 miles to the trip. Cyclists planning to camp on the Navajo Nation should obtain permission from the local landowner first.

The Arizona Trail reaches Grandview Lookout Tower from the south. (This area has some good day hiking, too.) The Arizona Trail turns west to Tusayan, then north to Grand Canyon Village to join the 9.3-mile Bright Angel Trail. One could also hike the short distance from Grandview Lookout to Grandview Trailhead, then take the Grandview, Tonto, and either South Kaibab or Bright Angel Trails down to the Colorado River. From the Colorado, North Kaibab Trail climbs 14 miles to the top of the North Rim. From here the Arizona Trail parallels the main road north to the North Entrance Station, then heads northeast to East Rim Viewpoint and on north to the Utah border at Stateline Trailhead, which has a tiny campground.

You can get the latest trail information for the Kaibab National Forest's South Rim area from the **Tusayan Ranger Station** (Box 3088, Tusayan, AZ 86023, 928/638-2443, www.fs.fed.us/r3/kai, 8 A.M.–4:30 P.M. Mon.–Fri.) in the Tusayan Administrative Site just outside the South Entrance Station. Over on the North Rim, contact the Kaibab National Forest's **North Kaibab Ranger District** (430 S. Main St., P.O. Box 248, Fredonia, AZ 86022, 928/643-7395, www.fs.fed.us/r3/kai, 8 A.M.–5 P.M. Mon.–Fri.) or the **Kaibab Plateau Visitor Center** (HC 64, Highway 67/U.S. Highway 89A, Jacob Lake, 928/643-7298, www.fs.fed.us/r3/kai, 8 A.M.–5 P.M. daily about May 15–Oct. 31, then weekends to mid-Dec.).

South Kaibab Trail

- Distance: 6.8 miles one-way
- Duration: 4–5 hours down, 6–8 hours up
- Elevation Change: 4,860 feet
- Rating: Strenuous
- Trailhead: Yaki Point, 4.5 miles by shuttle east of Grand Canyon Village

Hikers enjoy sweeping views up and down the Canyon on this trail. From the trailhead, the South Kaibab drops steeply, following Cedar Ridge toward the river and Bright Angel Creek. There's an emergency telephone at the Tipoff, 4.4 miles below the rim, where the trail begins to descend into the Inner Gorge.

Lack of shade and water and the steep grade make this trail especially difficult in summer. Only very strong hikers can make it all the way from rim to river and back in one day, and they're likely to find the trip grueling. During summer, however, this is dangerous for *anyone* and strongly discouraged.

River Trail

- Distance: 1.7 miles one-way
- Duration: one hour each way
- Elevation Change: nearly level
- Rating: Easy
- Trailhead: bottoms of the Bright Angel and South Kaibab Trails

This short connector trail parallels the river's

south shore in the twisted rocks of the Inner Gorge. Two suspension bridges cross the Colorado River toward Bright Angel Creek.

North Kaibab Trail

- Distance: 14.2 miles one-way
- Duration: 8–9 hours down, 10–12 hours up
- Elevation Change: 5,850 feet
- Rating: Strenuous
- Trailhead: two miles north of Grand Canyon Lodge

Few other Canyon trails compare in the number of interesting side trips and variety of scenery. Hikers on this trail start in the cool forests of the North Rim, descend through the woods into Roaring Springs Canyon, then follow rushing Bright Angel Creek all the way to the Colorado River. Snows close the road from as early as October until mid-May, but you can reach the lower end of the North Kaibab at Bright Angel Campground year-round from the South Rim. A long section of trail between the North Rim and Roaring Springs has been cut into sheer cliffs; waterfalls cascade over the rock face in spring and after rains. You can take a break at the picnic area near Roaring Springs, 4.7 miles and 3,050 feet below the North Rim; water is available from May to September.

Cottonwood Campground, 6.8 miles below the rim, is a good stopping point for the night or a base for day trips—it has a ranger station and May–September it has drinking water; winter campers must obtain and purify water from the creek. **Ribbon Falls,** nestled in a side canyon 1.5 miles from Cottonwood Campground, pours into a miniature paradise of travertine and lush greenery. **The Transept,** a canyon just upstream and across the creek, offers good exploring too.

From Cottonwood Campground, the North Kaibab Trail continues downstream along Bright Angel Creek, entering the dark, contorted schists and other rocks of the ancient Vishnu Group. Near the bottom you'll walk through Phantom Ranch then Bright Angel Campground. Although strong hikers can descend the trail in one day, this isn't recommended; you'll enjoy the trail's attractions far more over two days. Climbing out should definitely be attempted only over two days. Anglers often meet with success in pulling rainbow trout from Bright Angel Creek, especially in winter.

Phantom Ranch

Rustic buildings along Bright Angel Creek at the bottom of the Canyon offer dormitory beds ($27), cabins ($74 d, $11 each extra person up to 4), meals ($12.64 breakfast, $7.94 box lunch, $17.62 stew dinner, $28.14 steak dinner), drinks, snacks, and souvenirs. You must make reservations for accommodations and meals with transportation desks in the lodges or contact Xanterra Parks & Resorts (14001 E. Iliff Ave., Suite 600, Aurora, CO 80014, 888/297-2757 or 303/297-2757 in advance, 928/638-3283 same or next day, www.grandcanyonlodges.com). Reservations can be difficult to get, but you can make them up to 23 months in advance. Be careful not to miss a meal—no refunds are given! If you'd rather not carry your pack, mules are available for $53.80 each way (30-pound limit). Mules will carry you, too. (See *Mule Rides* in the *South Rim* section.)

SOUTH RIM—THRESHOLD, PRIMITIVE, AND WILD ZONES

Trails and routes in these zones lead to some beautiful corners of the park, offering solitude and new Canyon perspectives. Hikers here must be self-reliant—know where water sources are, how to use map and compass, and how to handle emergencies. Most trails follow prehistoric Indian routes or game trails that miners improved in the late 1800s. Conditions vary widely: Some trails are in excellent condition, while others are dangerous or require careful map reading. Hermit and Grandview get some maintenance, and other trails may receive attention. Hermit Trail, Hermit and Granite Rapids, Horseshoe Mesa, and parts of the Tonto Trail have designated camping areas, which you're required to use.

The Canyon offers thousands of possible routes for the experienced hiker. The late Harvey Butchart, master of Canyon off-trail hiking, described many routes. (See the *Suggested Reading* chapter.) Staff at the Backcountry Information Center will suggest interesting routes as well, and they'll give you an idea of current conditions. You'll no doubt come up with route ideas of your own while hiking through the Canyon and studying maps.

Just keep in mind that much of the Canyon's exposed rock is soft or fractured—a handhold or foothold can easily break off. The Colorado River presents a major barrier, as the water is too cold, wide, and full of treacherous currents to swim.

The following trails and routes are listed from west to east.

Tonto Trail

- Distance: 92 miles one-way
- Duration: Hikers rarely attempt the entire trail, but use it as a connector for loop trips.
- Elevation Change: minimal
- Rating: Easy to Strenuous
- Trailhead: access east end from bottom of New Hance Trail; west end from six miles down South Bass Trail

Canyon views change continually along this trail as it follows the contours of the Tonto Platform, winding in and out of countless canyons and sometimes revealing spectacular panoramas from the edge of the Inner Gorge. The Tonto connects most of the trails below the South Rim between the mouth of Red Canyon at Hance Rapid and Garnet Canyon far downstream. Average elevation on the gently rolling trail is 3,000 feet. You might lose it occasionally, but with attention to rock cairns and the map, you'll soon find it again. The sun bears down relentlessly in summer, when it's best to hike elsewhere.

South Bass Trail

- Distance: 8 miles one-way
- Duration: 5 hours down, 9 hours up
- Elevation Change: 4,400 feet
- Rating: Strenuous
- Trailhead: four miles north of Pasture Wash Ranger Station

William Bass learned about this route from the Havasupai in the 1880s, then used it to start a small tourism operation. Bass also built a trail up to the North Rim, crossing the river by boat and later in a cage suspended from a cable. No crossing exists today. The South Bass Trail is generally in good condition and easy to follow. It drops to the Esplanade, a broad terrace, then down to the river, the first reliable source of water. You'll need a high-clearance vehicle to reach the trailhead; ask at the Backcountry Information Center for directions. Havasupai may charge a fee for crossing a bit of their land on the way to the trailhead.

Boucher Trail

- Distance: 10 miles one-way from Hermit Trailhead to Boucher Creek
- Duration: 7–8 hours down, 9–10 hours up
- Elevation Change: 4,300 feet
- Rating: Very Strenuous
- Trailhead: Hermit Trailhead, eight miles west of Grand Canyon Village

Louis Boucher, the Hermit, came to the Canyon in 1891 and mined copper along the creek that bears his name until 1912. Steep terrain and rockslides can make the trail difficult—it's best left to experienced hikers with light packs. Take Hermit and Dripping Springs Trails to Boucher Trail, which winds along the base of the Hermit Shale, high above the west side of Hermit Canyon, with excellent views. You'll reach Tonto Trail just before Boucher Creek. The route down the creek to Boucher Rapid on the Colorado River is an easy 1.5 miles. The Boucher, Tonto, and Hermit Trails make a fine three- or four-day loop hike. Boucher and Hermit Creeks have water year-round.

Hermit Trail

- Distance: 8.5 miles one-way to Hermit Rapid
- Duration: 5–6 hours down, 8–10 hours up
- Elevation Change: 4,300 feet
- Rating: Strenuous
- Trailhead: eight miles west of Grand Canyon Village

Built for tourists in 1912 by the Santa Fe Railroad, most of Hermit Trail is in good condition; the few places covered by rockslides can easily be crossed. The trail begins just beyond Hermits Rest, at the end of Hermit Road. Water is available at Santa Maria Spring (2.5 miles one-way) and Hermit Creek (7 miles one-way). A sign on the Tonto Trail points the way down to Hermit Creek, which you can follow for an easy 1.5 miles to Hermit Rapid on the Colorado River. Rangers recommend that you not attempt the entire rim-to-river distance in one day. Backpackers may drive their own vehicle to the trailhead, even during the shuttle season.

Hermit Trail also connects with Waldron, Dripping Springs, and Tonto Trails. The 22.5-mile Hermit Loop hike, which follows the Hermit, Tonto, and Bright Angel Trails, is quite popular. You can find water on this loop year-round at Monument Creek and Indian Garden. Hikers can easily walk down the bed of Monument Creek to Granite Rapid, 1.5 miles one-way.

Grandview Trail

- Distance: 3 miles one-way
- Duration: 2–3 hours down, 4–6 hours up
- Elevation Change: 2,500 feet
- Rating: Strenuous
- Trailhead: Grandview Point

Day-hikers frequently use this steep but scenic trail to Horseshoe Mesa from Grandview Point. (See the description in the *Desert View Drive* section of the *South Rim*.) Three trails descend from Horseshoe Mesa to the Tonto Trail. A loop hike down to the Tonto Trail via Cottonwood Creek, east on the Tonto, then up via Miners Spring is a 13-mile, 3–4-day trip.

New Hance Trail

- Distance: 8 miles one-way
- Duration: 6 hours down, 8–9 hours up
- Elevation Change: 4,400 feet
- Rating: Very Strenuous
- Trailhead: off Desert View Drive, one mile southwest of the Moran Point turnoff

John Hance, one of the first prospectors to take up the tourist business, built this trail down Red Canyon in 1895. Suited for more experienced hikers, the trail—with poor footing in places—descends steeply to the river at Hance Rapid. Most of the trail is easy to follow, especially when you're descending. No reliable water is available before the river. Obtain directions from a ranger for the unmarked trailhead.

Escalante Route

- Distance: 15 miles one-way
- Duration: 2 days each way
- Elevation Change: 120 feet
- Rating: Very Strenuous
- Trailheads: bottoms of New Hance and Tanner Trails

The Tonto Trail's east end gives out at Hance Rapid, but you can continue upstream to Tanner Rapid and the Tanner Trail. Cairns mark the way, but expect rough terrain and a difficult time finding the route in some sections. The Colorado River, easily accessible only at the ends of the route, provides the only reliable source of water. The route is somewhat easier to hike in the downstream direction, Tanner to Hance.

Tanner Trail

- Distance: 10 miles one-way
- Duration: 5–7 hours down, 8–10 hours up
- Elevation Change: 4,700 feet
- Rating: Very Strenuous
- Trailhead: Lipan Point, off Desert View Drive

Seth Tanner improved this Indian trail in the 1880s to reach his copper and silver mines along the Colorado River. Although in good condition and easy to follow, the Tanner Trail is long and dry. It should be attempted only in the cooler months. Hikers often cache water partway down for the return trip.

Beamer Trail

- Distance: 9 miles one-way
- Duration: 1 day each way
- Elevation Change: minimal
- Rating: Strenuous
- Trailhead: bottom of Tanner Trail

This slim path begins at Tanner Canyon Rapid and follows the river four miles upstream to Palisades Creek, a good camping spot, then climbs to a high terrace for the remaining five miles to the Little Colorado River confluence. No camping is allowed within a half mile of the confluence.

NORTH RIM—THRESHOLD, PRIMITIVE, AND WILD ZONES

Whitmore Wash Trail

- Distance: .75 miles one-way
- Duration: .5 hours down, 1 hour up
- Elevation Change: 850 feet

- Rating: Moderate
- Trailhead: Follow County 5 and other dirt roads on the Arizona Strip from Toroweap, Fredonia, Colorado City, or St. George to the four-way intersection at Mt. Trumbull Schoolhouse, turn south 1.8 miles on BLM Road 257, then bear left 21.7 miles on BLM Road 1045 to its end.

Although little known or used, this trail offers the park's easiest hike from trailhead to river. The trick is in reaching the trailhead! You'll need a high-clearance 4WD vehicle and lots of time: The last 7.5 miles are rough, as the road crosses lava flows from Mt. Emma. This lava acts as a ramp for the road to descend deep into the Grand Canyon. The trail appears to drop off the rim where the road ends, but that's not the real trailhead. Instead, climb up above the barbed-wire fence to the trail.

The trail switchbacks, then skirts the base of a massive cliff of columnar basalt before ending on a sandy beach. Remnants of ancient lava dams can be seen on both sides of the river. A small trail near the bottom leads a half mile downstream to Whitmore Rapid and lower Whitmore Canyon, which you can explore for about a half mile upstream.

Lava Falls Route

- Distance: 1.5 miles one-way
- Duration: 2 hours down, 3–6 hours up
- Elevation Change: 2,500 feet
- Rating: Very Strenuous
- Trailhead: From Toroweap Overlook, backtrack on the road 2.8 miles and look for a dirt track on the left (3.5 miles south of Tuweep Ranger Station); follow it 2.5 miles across normally dry Toroweap Lake and around the west side of Vulcan's Throne. The route is too rough for cars and impassable for any vehicle when the lake contains water.

Cairns mark the way down a lunar landscape of volcanic lava. Although the route is short, it's considered difficult because of steep grades and poor footing. Summer temperatures get *dangerously* hot—elevation at the river is only 1,700 feet. Adventurous hikers will find it a good challenge in the cooler months. Bring more water than you think you'll need.

From the trailhead, the route descends to a hill of red cinders about two-thirds of the way down; the last part of the descent follows a steep gully. Barrel cacti thrive on the dark, twisted rock. The Colorado River explodes in a fury of foam and waves at Lava Falls, .3 miles downstream. Camping is allowed along the river with a permit.

Tuckup Trail

- Distance: more than 60 miles one-way
- Duration: up to you
- Elevation Change: minimal
- Rating: Strenuous
- Trailhead: just east of the Toroweap Overlook road, 4.7 miles south of the ranger station and 1.6 miles north of the overlook

Experienced Canyon hikers looking for solitude and expansive vistas can try this faint trail. It follows the Esplanade of the North Rim between the Toroweap Point area and 150 Mile Canyon. Back roads lead to trailheads near these two areas and to upper Tuckup Canyon, about the halfway point on the trail.

You can wander off on a variety of jaunts in this remote area. Hikers have followed the Tuckup Trail to Cottonwood Canyon, descended Cottonwood and Tuckup Canyons to the Colorado River (rope needed), hiked the shore downstream to Lava Falls Route, and climbed back up to Toroweap in a week or so of travel. Springs of varying reliability may provide water along the Tuckup Trail. Talk with rangers knowledgeable about the area for trailhead, spring, and hiking conditions.

Bill Hall and Thunder River Trails

- Distance: 12.5 miles one-way from Bill Hall Trailhead to Tapeats Rapid
- Duration: 7 hours down to Tapeats Creek, 9 hours down to Tapeats Rapid, nearly double that up
- Elevation Change: 5,050 feet to Tapeats Rapid
- Rating: Very Strenuous
- Trailhead: Reach the trailheads by turning west on Forest Road 22 from Highway 67 in De Motte Park, .8 miles south of the North Rim Store and 17.5 miles north of

Bright Angel Point; consult a Kaibab National Forest map (North Kaibab Ranger District). It's about 35 miles of dirt road and an hour and a half from Highway 67 to either trailhead. Cars can negotiate the roads in good weather, but winter snows bury this high country from about mid-November to mid-May.

Two trails descend from the North Rim: Thunder River Trail from the end of Forest Road 232 (just past Indian Hollow Campground) and Bill Hall Trail from the east side of Monument Point at the end of Forest Road 292A. The Bill Hall Trail saves five miles of walking but the steep grade can be slippery and hard on the knees. Both trails drop to the Esplanade, where the Bill Hall Trail merges with the Thunder River Trail. The Esplanade could be used for dry camping, and you may wish to cache some water here for the climb back out. Thunder River Trail then switchbacks down to Surprise Valley (about eight miles from the Bill Hall Trailhead), a giant piece of the rim that long ago slumped thousands of feet to its present position. The valley turns into an oven in summer and lacks water.

In another 1.5 miles, Thunder River Trail goes east across Surprise Valley and drops to the wonderfully cool and shaded oasis at Thunder River, your first source of water. The water blasts out of a cave in the Muav Limestone, cascades a half mile, then enters Tapeats Creek. It's not only the world's shortest river but suffers the humiliation of being a tributary to a creek!

The trail follows the river the half mile to Tapeats Creek, which, except at high water, can be followed 2.5 miles upstream to its source in a cave. The Colorado River is a 2.5-mile hike downstream along Tapeats Creek from Thunder River. If the creek runs too deep to cross, you can stay on a west-side trail all the way to the Colorado. Cottonwood trees, willows, and other cool greenery grace the banks of Thunder River and Tapeats Creek. Upper Tapeats Campsite is just below the Thunder River–Tapeats Creek confluence; Lower Tapeats Campsite lies downstream near the Colorado River. Good fishing attracts anglers to Tapeats Creek and perhaps did long ago—prehistoric Cohonina left ruins here.

Deer Creek Trail from Thunder River Trail

- Distance: 11 miles one way to the Colorado River at Deer Creek Falls
- Duration: 8 hours down to the Colorado River at Deer Creek Falls; nearly double that up
- Elevation Change: 5,100 feet
- Rating: Very Strenuous
- Trailhead: take Bill Hall or Thunder River Trail to Surprise Valley

Deer Creek Trail, marked by a large cairn in Surprise Valley, splits off to the west from Thunder River Trail and drops about 1.5 miles to Deer Creek (Dutton) Spring, another cave system from which a waterfall gushes. You can hike up to the falls for a closer look or take the path that goes higher and behind the falls. The creekside trail winds down one mile past some remarkable Tapeats narrows to Deer Creek Falls, which plummets more than 100 feet onto the banks of the Colorado River. The last bit of trail drops to the base of Deer Creek Falls; watch out for poison ivy on this section. Campsites lie along Deer Creek between Deer Creek Springs and the head of the narrows. Deer Creek Springs, 9.5 miles in, is the first water source.

North Bass Trail

- Distance: 14 miles one-way
- Duration: 8–10 hours down, nearly double that up
- Elevation Change: 5,300 feet
- Rating: Very Strenuous
- Trailhead: Swamp Point can be reached by high-clearance vehicle from Highway 67 in DeMotte Park via Forest Roads 22, 270, 223, 268, 268B, and Swamp Point Road. You'll need the current Kaibab Forest map, as old ones may not show these roads correctly. The drive from DeMotte Park to Swamp Point takes nearly two hours due to the roughness of Swamp Point Road.

Best suited for experienced hikers, this long and faint trail drops from Swamp Point on the North Rim to Muav Saddle, where there's a 1925 National Park Service cabin. The trail makes a sharp left toward Muav Springs, drops steeply to White Creek in Muav Canyon, follows a long bypass to a safe descent through the Redwall Limestone, winds down White Creek to Shinumo Creek, continues to Bass Camp, then cuts over a ridge to the left and drops down to a beach on the Colorado River. The trail reaches the Colorado about .3 miles below where the South Bass Trail comes down on the other side. A waterfall blocks travel down Shinumo Creek just before the river, which is why the trail climbs over the ridge. The Muav and Shinumo drainages create their own canyon worlds—you're not really exposed to the Grand Canyon until you climb the ridge near trail's end.

Once at the Colorado River, you can loop back to Bass Camp on another trail that begins at the downstream end of the beach and crosses over to lower Shinumo Creek, which you can then follow upstream back to Bass Camp and the North Bass Trail. Many routes off the North Bass Trail invite exploration, such as the Redwall Narrows of White Creek above the trail junction, Shinumo Creek drainage above White Creek, and Burro Canyon.

Muav Saddle Springs offers water just off the trail. White Creek has intermittent water above and below the Redwall. Shinumo Creek's abundant flow supports some small trout. Shinumo can be difficult to cross in spring and after summer storms; at other times you can hop across on rocks.

Powell Plateau Trail

- Distance: 1.5 miles one-way
- Duration: 1.5 hours each way
- Elevation Change: 100 feet
- Rating: Moderate
- Trailhead: Swamp Point

A good trail from Swamp Point connects this isolated "island" that lies within the vast reaches of the Grand Canyon. Once part of the North Rim, Powell Plateau has been almost completely severed from the rim by erosion, except for the Muav Saddle connection. The trail drops 800 feet to Muav Saddle on the North Bass Trail, then continues straight across the saddle and up 900 feet on another set of switchbacks to a ponderosa pine forest on Powell Plateau. Here the trail fades out. Many places on the seven-mile-long plateau offer outstanding views. Travel is cross-country, so you'll need a map and compass; expect to do some bushwhacking.

The easiest viewpoint to reach lies to the northwest; just follow the north edge of the plateau (no trail) to a large rock cairn about one mile from where the trail from Swamp Point tops out on the plateau. Dutton Point lies on the southeast edge of the plateau; hike along the east rim to reach it. You can camp on Powell Plateau with a backcountry permit; all water must be carried in from the trailhead or Muav Saddle Springs.

Clear Creek Trail

- Distance: 9 miles one-way
- Duration: 5 hours each way
- Elevation Change: 1,100 feet
- Rating: Strenuous
- Trailhead: .3 miles north of Phantom Ranch

This trail is the North Rim's counterpart to the Tonto Trail. Clear Creek Trail climbs 1,500 feet to the Tonto Platform, which it follows, winding in and out of canyons until dropping at the last possible place into Clear Creek. Carry water—there's no source before Clear Creek—and be prepared for very hot weather in summer. The best camping sites lie scattered among the cottonwood trees where the trail meets the creek.

Day hikers enjoy the first mile or so of Clear Creek Trail for its scenic views of the river and Inner Gorge. Once you arrive at Clear Creek, it's well worth spending a day or two for exploration of the area. The route to **Cheyava Falls,** the highest waterfall in the Canyon, takes 6–8 hours round-trip up the long northeast fork of Clear Creek. Cheyava Falls puts on an impressive show only in spring and after heavy rains. Other arms of the creek offer good hiking as well. The canyon that branches east about a half mile downstream from the end of Clear Creek Trail cuts through a narrow canyon of quartzite. You can also walk along Clear Creek to the Colorado River, a 5–7-hour round-trip hike through contorted granite and schist. The 10-foot-high waterfall a half mile from the river is bypassed by clambering around to the right.

Nankoweap Trail

- Distance: 14 miles one-way
- Duration: 8–9 hours down, 12–14 hours up
- Elevation Change: 4,800 feet from Saddle Mountain saddle, 6,000 feet from the upper trailhead, 4,000 feet from the lower trailhead
- Rating: Very Strenuous
- Trailheads: The Nankoweap Trail actually begins at Saddle Mountain saddle (2.4 raven-flying miles northeast of Point Imperial) in the Saddle Mountain Wilderness. To get here, start at either end of Saddle Mountain/Nankoweap Trail #57. You can hike three miles one-way from the lower trailhead at the south end of House Rock Buffalo Ranch Road 8910 (south from U.S. Highway 89A) or 2.7 miles one-way from near the end of Forest Road 610 (east off Highway 67). Both access roads are dirt, passable by cars in dry weather, but House Rock Buffalo Ranch Road 8910 lies 2,000 feet lower at an elevation of 6,800 feet, and it's less likely to be snowed in.

If you're experienced at Canyon hiking, and if you don't mind tiptoeing on the brink of sheer cliffs, this trail will open up a large section of the park for your exploration. The Nankoweap Trail drops several hundred feet from Saddle Mountain saddle, then runs along the contours of a ledge all the way to Tilted Mesa before descending to Nankoweap Creek. Careful route-finding is needed between Tilted Mesa and the creek. Nankoweap Creek, 10 miles from the trailhead, is the first source of water; you may want to cache water part way down for your return. The remaining four miles to the river is easy. Allow at least four days for a round-trip journey.

Running the Colorado River

A do-it-yourself river trip through the Grand Canyon requires a large commitment in time, whitewater experience, equipment, expense, and permit procedures. About one-third of river runners tackle these hurdles and obtain a noncommercial river-trip permit from the park. The easier option, taken by most, simply involves setting aside the time for the trip and paying a river company to handle the many details.

YOUR OPTIONS

Boats

Both oar-powered and motor-powered craft run the river. Motor-powered rafts can zip through the entire Canyon in six days, or zoom from Lees Ferry to Phantom Ranch in two days. The oar-powered boat trips take half again as much time but provide a quieter and more natural experience. On these smaller boats, passengers have the advantage of being able to talk easily with the crew and one another. Whether in a little or a big rig, you can be assured that the crew will work hard to provide a safe and enjoyable trip.

All but two of the tour companies use rafts of various sizes; the exceptions are Grand Canyon Dories and Grand Canyon Expeditions, which employ sturdy, hard-shelled dories with upturned ends. The dories ride high in the water as they dance through the waves. They're small—16–18 feet—with one person at the oars and just four passengers. Only the most skilled boaters can handle dories because, unlike rafts, they can't bounce off rocks without damage.

Small rafts typically measure 18 feet and carry four or five passengers plus one crew member to do the rowing. Some companies provide a paddle raft option—a small raft in which everyone has a paddle! The guide sits at the stern to steer and give instructions, but it's up to the passengers to succeed in running each rapid.

The motor-powered rigs can be 30 feet long or more and have pontoon outriggers for extra stability. A small outboard motor near the stern provides steering and speed. Some people dislike the use of motors in a wilderness, but these boats do allow more people to run the Colorado than would be possible if everyone went in non-motorized rigs.

Routes

Most tours put in at Lees Ferry, just upstream

from the park, and end downstream at Diamond Creek or beyond the Grand Canyon at Lake Mead. You can also travel just half the distance by joining or leaving the rafts at Phantom Ranch, which requires a hike or mule trip to get in or out. You can leave or join a tour in the lower section of river by helicopter from or to Hualapai land near Whitmore Wash, below Lava Falls. If you'd like just a taste of river-running, try a one-day, smooth-water trip from Glen Canyon Dam to Lees Ferry, just above Grand Canyon National Park, with **Wilderness River Adventures** based in Page. Or you can visit the lowermost part of the Grand Canyon and run a few rapids on a one-day trip with **Hualapai River Runners,** based in Peach Springs.

A typical commercial oar trip takes 12–15 days from Lees Ferry to Diamond Creek, covering 226 miles. The upper 87.5 miles takes five or six days from Lees Ferry to Phantom Ranch, the lower 138.5 miles requires eight or nine days from Phantom Ranch to Diamond Creek. Continuing to Lake Mead adds just a day or two. Equivalent motorized trips typically run eight days from Lees Ferry to Diamond Creek or Lake Mead, with three or four days from Lees Ferry to Phantom Ranch and four or five days from Phantom Ranch to Diamond Creek or Lake Mead.

Those preferring shorter trips can end a trip or begin a two- or three-day run in the lowermost Grand Canyon at Whitmore Wash. Although a trail from the North Rim ends here, river parties use helicopters between the river (on Hualapai land) and the Bar 10 guest ranch, where small planes shuttle people to Las Vegas or other destinations.

Other combinations are available, too. Extra days may be added to some trips for hiking or layovers, especially early or late in the season. Expect to pay about $250 per day; discounts may be available for groups, children under 14, early booking, and off-season journeys.

If you have children in tow, check for minimum age requirements. Sometimes these are left up to the passenger; some operators set a minimum age ranging 8–16 years. Most trips depart from Flagstaff, Page, St. George, or Las Vegas. Meals, camping gear, waterproof bags, and land transportation are usually included in the price. Experienced kayakers can tag along with many tours, paying a lower rate.

Seasons

The river-running season is normally April–October. When you choose to go makes a big difference in the river experience. Most people go during summer, because that's when they take their vacations. The Canyon gets very hot then, but a splash of river water will always be cooling. Hiking at this time is limited to shady side canyons with water. Spring—April to early June—offers many advantages. The redbud trees and many other plants bloom in beautiful colors, hiking weather is nearly perfect, days get longer, trip operators often add a couple of extra days for long hikes or layovers, and it's much easier to get a reservation for a trip. The downside is the possibility of cold weather, even sleet—which the author woke up to one April morning in the upper Canyon! Some boaters think that early June offers the best weather for a boat trip, though hiking can get hot then. Autumn brings shorter days, along with cooler temperatures. The Canyon is quieter after mid-September, when all the motorized rigs have left the river. Heavy-duty rain gear with sweaters underneath can keep spring and autumn boaters warm during cool spells.

Rafting the Lower Grand Canyon

This last section, beginning at Diamond Creek, offers beautiful Canyon scenery and some rapids. You can get on a trip here much more easily than in the upper Canyon, either with Hualapai River Runners or on your own. The park's River Permits Office gives free permits for up to two private parties (16 people maximum in each) per day. River runners will need to pay for a Hualapai permit to use the Diamond Creek Road access or to hike or camp on the south shore. The lower canyon bakes in summer, so spring, autumn, or even winter offer better weather for exploring side canyons.

Boating into the Lower Grand Canyon from Lake Mead

Boats—but not personal watercraft—may go up as far as Separation Canyon (Mile 240 on the river) from Lake Mead National Recreation Area without a permit. You can even canoe or kayak in this section of the Grand Canyon by arranging a powerboat to carry the boats from Lake Mead to Separation Canyon. Primitive camping is allowed on the park's north shore in this section, though high lake levels can flood all the spots. Check with the River Permits Office to see if you need a permit for shore camping. To camp inland, you'll need a backcountry permit. The Hualapai require a permit to hike or camp on their lands—the south shore.

Private River Trips

The first step is to read Grand Canyon National Park's regulations and procedures! Obtain them from the **River Permits Office** (Box 129, Grand Canyon, AZ 86023, 928/638-7884 or 800/959-9164, www.nps.gov/grca). The best time to reach someone in person is 8 A.M.–noon on weekdays. Step Two—getting the permit—will be the hard part. The River Permits Office has worked out a system for applications that's as fair as possible to everyone.

RIVER COMPANIES

The following companies offer a wide variety of trips through the Canyon, ranging from one-day introductions to adventurous 21-day expeditions. For the latest list, ask at the visitors center or contact the River Permits Office. The Internet works best because you get not only a list, but also links to the companies, which have colorful and informative sites. Try to make reservations six months to a year in advance. It's possible to get on a trip with short notice, especially if there are just a few in your group and you're going early or late in the season. Travel service **Rivers and Oceans** (12620 N. Copeland Lane, Flagstaff, AZ 86004, 928/526-4575 or 800/473-4576, www.rivers-oceans.com) specializes in river trips and will supply information about companies, make reservations, and let you know about last-minute openings.

All of the companies put in at Lees Ferry except for Wilderness River Adventure's day trips, which start from Glen Canyon Dam, and Hualapai River Runners trips, which begin at Diamond Creek in the lower Grand Canyon. Many of the other companies offer partial trips that let you start or leave from Phantom Ranch or Whitmore Wash.

Arizona Raft Adventures (4050 E. Huntington Dr., Flagstaff, AZ 86004, 928/526-8200 or 800/786-7238, www.azraft.com) goes to Diamond Creek on 12–15-day oar ($2,700–3,000) and 8- or 10-day motorized trips ($1,950–2,300), most with the option of ending or starting at Phantom Ranch. Paddle raft trips go too, either in combination with oar-powered rafts or all by themselves.

Arizona River Runners (Box 47788, Phoenix, AZ 85068-7788, 602/867-4866 or 800/477-7238, www.raftarizona.com) offers a 13-day oar trip to Diamond Creek ($2,685) with an option to end or start at Phantom Ranch and an 8-day motorized run to Lake Mead ($1,910) with the option to leave or join at Whitmore Wash.

Canyoneers (Box 2997, Flagstaff, AZ 86003, 928/526-0924 or 800/525-0924, www.canyoneers.com) rows 12-day oar trips ($2,700) and runs 7-day motorized trips ($1,770–1,800) to Lake Mead; both provide the option of ending or starting at Phantom Ranch.

Canyon Explorations/Expeditions (Box 310, Flagstaff, AZ 86002, 928/774-4559 or 800/654-0723, www.canyonexplorations.com) uses oar boats on runs to Diamond Creek of 13–16 days ($2,725–3,350). Paddle rafts always come along too, and some trips are all paddle rafts. Inflatable kayaks accompany the oar boats as well. Some departures have a Phantom Ranch exit/entry option.

Colorado River & Trail Expeditions (Box 57575, Salt Lake City, UT 84157-0575, 801/261-1789 or 800/253-7328, www.crateinc.com) goes by oar-powered raft ($2,650) to Diamond Creek in 11 days and by motorized rafts ($1,925) to Lake Mead in 8 or 9 days; a paddle raft goes along with the oar trips. You can leave or join at Phantom Ranch on the 9- and 11-day trips.

Diamond River Adventures (Box 1316, Page, AZ 86040, 928/645-8866 or 800/343-3121, www.diamondriver.com) offers 12-day oar trips ($2,480) and 8-day motorized trips ($1,580) to Diamond Creek with options of leaving or joining at Phantom Ranch or Whitmore Wash.

Grand Canyon Dories (Box 216, Altaville,

CA 95221, 209/736-0811 or 800/877-3679, www.grandcanyondories.com) features dories on 16-day trips ($4,234–4,314) to Diamond Creek; 19- and 21-day dory trips ($4,314–4,934) run in spring and autumn to Lake Mead. You can join or leave the trips at Phantom Ranch or Whitmore Wash.

Grand Canyon Expeditions (Box O, Kanab, UT 84741, 435/644-2691 or 800/544-2691, www.gcex.com) runs dories on 14-day trips to Lake Mead ($2,995); motorized rafts do this run in 8 days ($2,095). All trips go straight through without any passenger exchanges.

Hatch River Expeditions (Box 1200, Vernal, UT 84078, 435/789-3813 or 800/433-8966, www.hatchriverexpeditions.com) runs motorized rafts to Whitmore Wash in six and a half days ($1,850) with the option to leave or join at Phantom Ranch.

Hualapai River Runners (P.O. Box 246, Peach Springs, AZ 86434, 928/769-2219 or 888/216-0076, www.grandcanyonresort.com) will take you on a one-day motorized-raft trip down the lower Grand Canyon from Diamond Creek, lift you out by helicopter to the rim at Grand Canyon West, then return you by road to Peach Springs for $265. This is the only company to offer a day trip within the Grand Canyon. Rates during the March–October season cover food, waterproof bag for personal gear, and transportation from Peach Springs.

Moki Mac River Expeditions (Box 71242, Salt Lake City, UT 84171, 801/268-6667 or 800/284-7280, www.mokimac.com) heads down to Lake Mead on 14-day oar trips ($3,130) with an option to end or begin from Phantom Ranch and 8-day motorized raft trips ($2,083) without a passenger exchange.

O.A.R.S. (Box 67, Angels Camp, CA 95222, 209/736-4677 or 800/346-6277, www.oars.com) offers oar rafts to Diamond Creek in 13 or 14 days ($3,607–3,827) and 15- and 17-day runs all the way to Lake Mead ($4,013–4,238) with options to leave or join at Phantom Ranch (and Whitmore Wash, for the Lake Mead trips).

Outdoors Unlimited (6900 Townsend Winona Rd., Flagstaff, AZ 86004, 928/526-4511 or 800/637-7238, www.outdoorsunlimited.com) goes to Lake Mead in oar rafts in 13 days ($2,793) and 15 days (spring and autumn only, $3,129) with an option to leave or join at Phantom Ranch; a paddle raft comes along too, and some trips are all paddle rafts.

Tour West (Box 333, Orem, UT 84059, 801/225-0755 or 800/453-9107, www.twriver.com) runs oar rafts to Whitmore Wash in 12 days ($2,655) without any passenger exchanges; paddle rafts can be added on request. Motorized rafts go to Lake Mead ($2,100) with the option to join or leave at Whitmore Wash.

Western River Expeditions (7258 Racquet Club Dr., Salt Lake City, UT 84121, 801/942-6669 or 800/453-7450, www.westernriver.com) has motorized rafts going to Lake Mead in eight days ($3,000) with a passenger exchange at Whitmore Wash.

Wilderness River Adventures (Box 717, Page, AZ 86040, 928/645-3296 or 800/992-8022, www.riveradventures.com) heads for Whitmore Wash on 12-day oar trips ($2,980) with the option to end or start at Phantom Ranch. Motorized trips take 6–8 days to Whitmore Wash ($1,815–2,370) and can be joined or left at Phantom Ranch. The company also offers a half-day trip from Glen Canyon Dam to Lees Ferry on smooth water.

The North Rim

The North Rim offers an experience very different from that of the South Rim. Elevations around 1,300 feet higher result in lower temperatures and nearly 60 percent more precipitation. Rain and snowmelt have cut deeply into the North Rim so that it is now about twice as far back from the Colorado River as the South Rim. Dramatic vistas from the north inspired early explorers to choose names like Point Sublime, Cape Royal, Angel's Window, and Point Imperial.

Even away from the viewpoints, the North Rim displays great beauty. Spruce, fir, pine, and aspen forests thrive in the cool air. Wildflowers bloom in blazes of color in the meadows and along the roadsides. Aspens turn to gold from the last week of September to mid-October.

You'll find visitor facilities and major trailheads near Bright Angel Point, a 45-mile drive south on Highway 67 from Jacob Lake in the far north of Arizona. The road to Bright Angel Point opens in mid-May, then closes after the first big winter storm, which can happen any time from October into December.

In winter, a deep blanket of snow covers the Kaibab Plateau's rolling meadow and forest country. The snow cover typically reaches a depth of 4–10 feet; cross-country skiers and snowshoers find the conditions ideal. The park itself has no facilities open on the North Rim in winter; you can camp here, however, with a permit from the Backcountry Information Center.

BRIGHT ANGEL POINT AND VICINITY

Bright Angel Point

You'll get a North Rim edition of *The Guide* at the entrance station on the drive in. Park at the end of the road, near Grand Canyon Lodge, and follow the paved foot trail to the tip of Bright Angel Point, an easy half-mile round-trip walk taking about 30 minutes. Shells and other fossils can be spotted in the outcrop of Kaibab limestone on your right, just after a stone causeway. Roaring Springs Canyon on the left and Transept Canyon on the right join the long Bright Angel Canyon far below. John Wesley Powell's 1869 expedition camped at the mouth of this canyon, and Powell later gave the name Bright Angel Creek to its crystal-clear waters. Listen for Roaring Springs coming out of the depths on the left and you'll see where the springs shoot out of the cliff. A pumping station at the base supplies drinking water to both North and South Rims. Roaring Springs makes a good day-hike or mule-ride destination via the North Kaibab Trail. The volcanic summits on the horizon to the south are, from left to right, O'Leary, San Francisco Peaks, Kendrick, and Sitgreaves. Red Butte, on the right and closer, preserves a remnant of the Moenkopi Formation under a lava cap.

Grand Canyon Lodge

The grand old lodge of logs and stone dates from 1937. The patio, Sun Room, dining room, and lobby all make popular gathering places. Many North Rim visitors get their first breathtaking view of the Canyon through the massive windows of the Sun Room; in a corner you'll see a bronze statue of the famous burro "Brighty of the Grand Canyon," along with photos and stories about him. Rub his nose for good luck.

Mule Rides

You can ride trails along the rim or head partway down the North Kaibab Trail. No overnight trips are offered. Rim rides cost $30 for one hour to $55 for a half-day (minimum age seven); half-day trips down the North Kaibab Trail to the tunnel run $55 (minimum age eight), and full-day rides to Roaring Springs are $105 including lunch (minimum age 12). Requirements for riders are similar to those for South Rim trips, including proper riding attire (long pants and wide-brimmed hat), good health, fluency in English, and weight not over 200 pounds (91 kg) for the North Kaibab or 220 pounds (100 kg) for the rim rides. Call ahead or make reservations with the mule rides desk in the Grand Canyon Lodge lobby (928/638-9875 lodge, 435/679-8665 res-

SILENCE IN THE CANYON

Wilderness can provide a refuge from the ever-busier worlds that we create. Just being out in the canyons turns out to be a delightful experience. Part of this delight seems to come from the space and the silence, which then reflects back on our own minds. "Preserving the power of presence," as Jack Turner terms it in his book, *The Abstract Wild,* is far more complex than just looking after the biodiversity. Rather than believing that presence is something that we can add on to make the wilderness whole, he states that "the loss of aura and presence is the main reason we are losing so much of the natural world." Turner thinks that by viewing wilderness as amusement and resource, we lose sight of the magic and sacred nature of it.

In the Grand Canyon, this value of presence or silence has come under assault from a steady stream of aircraft circling over the heart of the Canyon. No local topic has become as heated or difficult to resolve. Pilots and passengers enjoy flying so much that they refuse to consider a ban on flights, yet proponents of presence will not be satisfied until the skies over the park become silent. Congress first addressed the noise problem in 1987, banning nonemergency flights below the rims and requiring the designation of flight-free zones. The current compromise of restricted flight paths reduces the noise over some parts of the park, but it comes far short of the tranquility that early tourists to the park must have experienced. Only public opinion, expressed to representatives in Congress and to the Grand Canyon National Park administration, will determine how much natural silence the Canyon will offer to future visitors.

idence, www.canyonrides.com). Rates include a shuttle from the lodge to the trailhead.

CAPE ROYAL SCENIC DRIVE

This paved road begins three miles north of the Grand Canyon Lodge and leads to some of the North Rim's most spectacular viewpoints. You could easily spend a full day taking in the overlooks and hiking the short trails. Bring water and food for a picnic, as no supplies are available on the drive. Driving distance from Grand Canyon Lodge to Point Imperial is 11 miles one-way and from the lodge to Cape Royal is 23 miles one-way.

Once past the turnoff for Point Imperial, the drive follows the east side of the Walhalla Plateau. You can hike on unmarked former roads to many fine vistas, which you'll likely have all to yourself. Most of the plateau is open to camping with a backcountry permit, though you'll have to walk a quarter-mile in from the Cape Royal Road. Staff at the North Rim Backcountry Office can make suggestions and issue backcountry camping permits.

Point Imperial

Here at an elevation of 8,803 feet, you'll be standing on the Grand Canyon's highest vantage point reachable by road. You'll see Nankoweap Creek below, Vermilion Cliffs on the horizon to the north, rounded Navajo Mountain on the horizon in Utah to the northeast, the Painted Desert far to the east, and the Little Colorado River Canyon to the southeast. To get here, follow Cape Royal Road 5.3 miles, then turn left and go 2.7 miles. Picnic tables and restrooms lie under the trees.

Vista Encantada

Continue along the twisting Cape Royal Road past a trailhead for the Ken Patrick Trail and little Greenland Lake onto the Walhalla Plateau and this viewpoint. Picnic tables make it a good lunch spot. The view northeast provides another perspective of the vast Nankoweap drainage and beyond. Drive a little farther south to **Roosevelt Point,** where you'll find a .2-mile loop trail from the start of the parking area leading to an overlook with a fine view.

Walhalla Overlook and Walhalla Glades Pueblo

After enjoying the views at the overlook, cross the road and follow a 100-yard trail to the prehistoric pueblo. These ancestral Puebloans, known to archaeologists as Kayenta Anasazi, farmed at least 100 sites on the Walhalla Plateau, mostly near the rim, where warm air currents extended the growing season. The villagers occupied this pueblo (elev. 8,000 feet) about A.D. 1050–1150, probably using it just in summer, then retreating to Unkar Delta (visible from Walhalla Overlook) after the harvests.

Cape Royal and Angels Window

At road's end, a level paved trail continues south .3 miles from the parking lot to Cape Royal (elev. 7,865 feet) and a fantastic panorama. It's the southernmost viewpoint of the North Rim in this part of the Grand Canyon. Trailside signs identify plants growing on the high, arid ridge. On the way you'll see Angels Window, a massive natural arch; a short side trail leads out to the top of it. At Cape Royal, signs point out Freya Castle to the southeast, Vishnu Temple and the distant San Francisco Peaks to the south, and a branch of Clear Creek Canyon and flat-topped Wotans Throne to the southwest.

HIKING

Transept Trail

- Distance: 3 miles round-trip
- Duration: 1.5 hours round-trip
- Elevation Change: nearly level
- Rating: Easy
- Trailheads: Grand Canyon Lodge and North Rim Campground

This trail winds along The Transept's rim. You can make a 3.2-mile loop by continuing on the Transept Trail a half mile past the campground to the Bridle Trail near the entrance to the administration area, then following the Bridle Trail back south to the Grand Canyon Lodge.

Bridle Trail

- Distance: 1.5-mile one-way
- Duration: 30–45 minutes
- Elevation Change: nearly level
- Rating: Easy
- Trailheads: Bright Angel Lodge and North Kaibab Trailhead

This handy connector trail parallels the road. It's also open to cyclists and leashed pets.

Arizona Trail

- Distance: 10 miles one-way
- Duration: about 5 hours
- Elevation Change: nearly level
- Rating: Easy
- Trailhead: North Kaibab Trailhead

This segment parallels the road between the North Kaibab Trailhead and the park's north boundary. Like the Bridle Trail, it's open to bicycles and leashed pets.

North Kaibab Trail Day Hike to Roaring Springs

- Distance: 10 miles round-trip
- Duration: 7–8 hours round-trip
- Elevation Change: 3,055 feet
- Rating: Strenuous
- Trailhead: North Kaibab Trailhead

A picnic area near Roaring Springs makes a good destination for ambitious day hikers; there's usually seasonal water.

A much easier option, Coconino Overlook affords a view into the depths of Roaring Springs Canyon from ledges atop the Coconino Sandstone; the 1.5-mile round-trip drops only 500 feet from the rim and takes about an hour. Or you could continue down switchbacks in the Coconino Sandstone to Supai Tunnel, 3.6 miles and 3–4 hours round-trip; elevation change is 1,415 feet; there may be seasonal water.

Ken Patrick Trail

- Distance: 10 miles one-way
- Duration: about 6 hours one-way
- Elevation Change: 560 feet
- Rating: Moderate
- Trailheads: Point Imperial and North Kaibab Trailhead

You'll enjoy forest scenery and views across the headwaters of Nankoweap Creek on this trail, best done with a car shuttle starting at Point Imperial so that you'll be hiking mostly downhill. For a shorter hike, you could follow the first three miles along the rim from Point Imperial, then return the same way. The trail is named for Ken Patrick, who worked as a ranger on the North Rim for several seasons in the early 1970s. He was shot and killed by escaped convicts while on duty at California's Point Reyes National Seashore in 1973.

Uncle Jim Trail

- Distance: 4 miles round-trip
- Duration: 2–3 hours round-trip
- Elevation Change: 80 feet
- Rating: Moderate
- Trailhead: North Kaibab Trailhead

The first half mile follows the Ken Patrick Trail, then the Uncle Jim turns southeast to make a loop around Uncle Jim Point. Views from the point include Roaring Springs Canyon and North Kaibab Trail. The trail's namesake, James "Uncle Jim" Owens, served as the Grand Canyon Game Reserve's first warden from 1906 until establishment of the national park.

Widforss Trail

- Distance: 10 miles round-trip
- Duration: about 6 hours round-trip
- Elevation Change: 180 feet
- Rating: Moderate
- Trailhead: From Grand Canyon Lodge, go north 2.7 miles on the highway, then turn left and go one mile on the Point Sublime Road; the turnoff is .3 miles south of the Cape Royal Road junction.

Gently rolling terrain, fine Canyon views, and a variety of forest types attract hikers to the Widforss Trail. From the edge of a meadow, the trail climbs a bit, skirts the head of The Transept, then leads through ponderosa pines to an overlook near Widforss Point. You're likely to see mule deer. Many people enjoy going just part way. There's a trail guide available.

Haunted Canyon lies at trail's end, flanked by The Colonnade on the right and Manu Temple, Buddha Temple, and Schellbach Butte on the left; beyond lie countless more temples, towers, canyons, and the cliffs of the South Rim. The trail and point honor Swedish artist Gunnar Widforss, who painted the national parks of the West between 1921 and 1934.

Point Imperial Trail

- Distance: 4 miles round-trip
- Duration: about 2 hours round-trip
- Elevation Change: nearly level
- Rating: Easy
- Trailhead: Point Imperial

The trail parallels the rim to the northern park boundary, where you could continue a short distance to the Saddle Mountain Trailhead. You'll cross areas burned in the 2000 Outlet Fire

Cape Final

- Distance: 4 miles round-trip
- Duration: 2–2.5 hours round-trip
- Elevation Change: 150 feet
- Rating: Easy
- Trailhead: Look for a small unpaved parking area on the east side of the road, 5.5 miles past Roosevelt Point and 1 mile before Walhalla Overlook.

The trail follows gently rolling terrain through the ponderosa pines east of the Cape Royal Road. You'll pass several overlooks on the way, but it's worth continuing to the grand finale above Unkar Creek Canyon at Cape Final.

Cliff Spring Trail

- Distance: 1 mile round-trip
- Duration: 1 hour round-trip
- Elevation Change: 200 feet
- Rating: Easy
- Trailhead: Begin from a small pullout on a curve of Cape Royal Road, 1.1 miles past Walhalla Overlook and .3 miles before Cape Royal parking area.

You'll enjoy pretty scenery on this trail, which winds down a forested ravine past a small prehistoric ruin to the spring under an overhang. Canyon walls open up impressively as you near the spring. It's possible to continue on a rougher trail another half mile for more canyon views.

North Rim Practicalities

The road from Jacob Lake to the North Rim may be open earlier in spring and later in autumn than the Grand Canyon Lodge, restaurants, gas station, and campground. Depending on weather, it closes in October, November, or December. A sign at Jacob Lake near the turnoff for the North Rim lists the services available. If you're looking for a room in summer, be sure to make reservations as far in advance as possible, as every lodge on the Kaibab Plateau will likely be full! Alternatives are to stay to the west in Fredonia or Kanab, or to the east in the lodges along U.S. Highway 89A or in Page, but these are long commutes. In autumn, you have a chance of getting in on short notice.

BRIGHT ANGEL POINT

Accommodations and Campgrounds

Grand Canyon Lodge, near Bright Angel Point, offers the only accommodations within the park on the North Rim. Lodging, all nonsmoking, comes in four types: Western Cabins (duplexes and quads with full bath, 2 queen beds, gas fireplace, and a porch, $111 d, $121 d w/view), two-bedroom Pioneer Cabins (shower, 1 double and 3 single beds, $101 4 persons), Frontier Cabins (duplexes with shower, one double and one single bed, $92 d), and motel rooms (shower and one queen bed, $91 d). Four of the Western Cabins feature views of Bright Angel Canyon. The season runs mid-May–mid-October; advance reservations are highly recommended. Contact Xanterra (14001 E. Iliff Ave., Suite 600, Aurora, CO 80014, 888/297-2757 or 303/297-2757 for advance reservations, 928/638-2611 for same-day reservations, fax 303/297-3175, www.grandcanyonnorthrim.com).

North Rim Campground (1.5 miles north and west of Grand Canyon Lodge, 800/365-2267, http://reservations.nps.gov, mid-May–mid-Oct., $15) lies in ponderosa pines and aspen at an elevation of 8,320 feet. There's drinking water but no hookups; after mid-October it stays open without water or fee. Be sure to make reservations, as the campground fills nearly every day; family and group sites can be reserved up to three months ahead. Four rim sites have views at a higher cost. Backpackers and bicyclists can camp at a walk-in area for $4 per person. Coin-operated showers, a laundry, store, and ice are available nearby.

Backcountry Camping

You're welcome to camp on much of the North Rim by obtaining a backcountry permit and following the park rules. It's usually easy to obtain a permit, even on the same day, from the North Rim Backcountry Office. Car camping is allowed at Point Sublime, Fire Point, and Swamp Point. Other areas, for which you must walk at least one-quarter mile in from the road, include Cape Final and other destinations on the Walhalla Plateau, Thompson Canyon/Point Imperial Trail, and Tiyo Point.

Food

Enormous picture windows let in the Canyon views at the **Grand Canyon Lodge's** rustic dining room (928/638-2611, daily breakfast, lunch, and dinner mid-May–mid-Oct., $13–23). The dinner menu includes steak, prime rib, pork, chicken, trout, salmon, and pasta, along with a wine list. Reservations will be needed for dinner, and can be made up to 60 days in advance. Both breakfast and lunch are first-come, first-served. Lunches ($7–11) provide lighter fare, or you can order a sack lunch with an hour's notice. Breakfasts have a buffet option.

The cafeteria-style **Deli in the Pines** (daily breakfast, lunch, and dinner) at the lodge offers faster service and lower prices but no atmosphere; you may wish to order takeout and picnic outside. The **Coffee Saloon** in the lodge serves up coffee and pastries early in the morning, then transforms to the **Rough Rider Saloon** with more potent beverages the rest of the day; exhibits commemorate Teddy Roosevelt.

Services

You'll find the **post office** (8 A.M.–4 P.M. Mon.–

Fri., 10 A.M.–2 P.M. Sat.) and a **gift shop** in Grand Canyon Lodge. Turn in toward the campground for the **service station, showers, laundry,** and the rustic log **general store** which stocks camping supplies, groceries, and sandwiches. **Water** is available in season at the North Kaibab Trailhead, campground entrance, and at the lodge's ice machines; off-season, the only place to get water is at the administration center, a quarter mile north of the campground turnoff.

Pets

Leashed animals can stretch their legs on the Bridle Trail between the Grand Canyon Lodge and North Kaibab Trailhead and along the Arizona Trail. They're not allowed in the lodge or on other trails, which is a big problem because there's no kennel on the North Rim. Pets may stay in campgrounds and at Jacob Lake Inn.

Information

The **North Rim Visitor Center** (928/638-7864, 8 A.M.–6 P.M. daily) near the lodge has an information desk, book sales, and a few exhibits. See your copy of *The Guide* for times of nature walks, talks, and children's programs. Kids 4–14 can take part in Junior Ranger activities. You can use the park's automated switchboard (928/638-7888) for recorded weather forecasts and visitor information, as well as to reach any office. Online, visit www.nps.gov/grca.

Obtain overnight camping permits and trail information from the **Backcountry Information Center** (Box 129, Grand Canyon, AZ 86023) on the South Rim or at the **North Rim Backcountry Office** (8 A.M.–noon and 1–5 P.M. daily May 15–Oct. 31, weather permitting) in the administrative area a quarter mile north of the campground turnoff.

Getting There and Around

A **Hiker Shuttle** goes to the North Kaibab trailhead early in the morning from Grand Canyon Lodge; make advance reservations at the lodge's front desk. **Trans-Canyon Shuttle** (928/638-2820, mid-May–mid-Oct., $65 one-way, $110 round-trip) offers daily round-trip van service between the North and South Rims; it departs from Grand Canyon Lodge at 7 A.M. and arrives at Bright Angel Lodge on the South Rim by noon; the return trip leaves the South Rim at 1:30 P.M. and arrives at the North Rim by 6:30 P.M.

NORTH OF THE PARK

Accommodations, Campgrounds, and Services

Kaibab Lodge (928/638-2389, www.kaibablodge.com, mid-May–mid-Oct., $95–150 d) offers a variety of rustic and modern cabins beside a large meadow at an elevation of 8,770 feet. It lies just west of Highway 67, 18.5 miles north of Bright Angel Point and 26 miles south of Jacob Lake. The restaurant serves breakfast and dinner ($6–19) daily and can fix a sack lunch. Be sure to make room reservations, though none are needed for dining. Across the highway, **North Rim Country Store** sells groceries, bottled water, camping and auto supplies, and gas and diesel from about May 15 to late October. **Water** is in short supply on most of the Kaibab Plateau! You can fill up your water jugs for free at Jacob Lake Campground or in the park, but nowhere in between.

De Motte Park Campground (just south of Kaibab Lodge, mid-May–mid-Oct., $12) has a beautiful setting in an aspen and mixed-conifer forest at an elevation of 8,760 feet; it provides drinking water and interpretive programs, but no showers or hookups. Try to arrive before noon for the best chance of getting a space—no reservations are taken.

Jacob Lake Inn (45 miles north of the North Rim at the junction of Highway 67 and U.S. Highway 89A, 928/643-7232, www.jacoblake.com) stays open all year with basic motel rooms ($91 d–$106 four persons), cabins ($72 d–$119 six persons), restaurant (American food, daily breakfast, lunch, and dinner, $13–17), grocery store, Native American crafts shop, and a service station. Navajo rugs and paintings decorate the dining area

Jacob Lake Campground (928/643-7770, mid-May–mid-Nov., $12) has sites in the ponderosa pines at an elevation of 7,920 feet, with drinking water but no hookups or showers;

there's usually room. Sites may be available later in the year, with no water or fee. Campers enjoy summer interpretive programs and nearby hiking trails. You can picnic here 10 A.M.–4 P.M. for $3. Head west .1 mile on U.S. Highway 89A from Highway 67, then turn right at the sign. Only groups can reserve sites with Recreation Resource Management (928/204-1698, www.camprrm.com).

In the ponderosa pines overlooking tiny Jacob Lake, **Kaibab Camper Village** (928/643-7804 or 800/525-0924 reservations, May 15–Oct. 15) provides tent spaces and dry RV sites for $12, sites with hookups for $22, and a bunkhouse at $65 d, $75 three people, $85 four people. Tent sites are usually available, though RVers should make reservations or arrive by noon. The campground has coin showers (also available to the public) and sells ice, firewood, and a few groceries. Head south .3 miles on Highway 67 from U.S. Highway 89A, then turn west .7 miles.

Allen's Outfitters (435/644-8150 or 435/691-3680) offers trail rides of one and two hours in the forest, half- and full-day trips to overlooks, and pack trips from about mid-May to early September from its stables .3 miles south on Highway 67 from U.S. Highway 89A and year-round in Kanab.

Information

Staff at the Forest Service's **Kaibab Plateau Visitor Center** (Jacob Lake, 928/643-7298, www.fs.fed.us/r3/kai, 8 A.M.–5 P.M. daily about May 15–Oct. 31, then weekends to mid-Dec.) provide information on the many viewpoints, trails, campgrounds, and historic sites in the Kaibab National Forest along the North Rim. Exhibits include a 3D model of the Grand Canyon and wildlife displays. You can purchase books and maps.

The Kaibab Plateau and Vicinity

Some visitors, after seeing the Bright Angel Point and Cape Royal area, ask what else there is to do. The answer is the rest of the Kaibab Plateau! Lofty viewpoints of the Grand Canyon, hiking trails, and back-road drives can keep you enthralled for days. Most viewpoints and other attractions lie in the Kaibab National Forest. Although nearly all forest roads are unpaved, cautiously driven cars can negotiate many of them in dry weather.

THE EASTERN KAIBAB PLATEAU

Jacob Lake

High in the pine forests at an elevation of 7,925 feet, this tiny village offers useful services and a bit of history. The nearby lake, actually just a pond, is named for Mormon missionary and explorer Jacob Hamblin. Jacob Lake Inn, the Kaibab Plateau Visitor Center, and Jacob Lake Campground lie near the Highway 67 turnoff for the Grand Canyon North Rim.

The 1910 **Jacob Lake Ranger Station,** one of the oldest in the Forest Service, overlooks the lake. It's occasionally open, and you can peer into the window at other times to see the no-frills interior of the two-room cabin. From U.S. Highway 89A, head south .3 miles on Highway 67, turn right .7 miles on Forest Road 461, then turn left .2 miles on Forest Road 282.

Jacob Lake Lookout offers views of plateaus and mountains in Utah to the north; it's one mile south on Highway 67, between Mileposts 580 and 581, from U.S. Highway 89A. **Dry Park Lookout** features great views from a 125-foot tower southwest of Jacob Lake. These and other lookouts, all shown on the Kaibab National Forest map, welcome visitors when they're staffed.

Between Jacob Lake and Fredonia, **Le Fevre Overlook** has a fine panorama of the Grand Staircase to the north; you can see Kanab nestled below the Vermilion Cliffs. The pullout, stone shelter, and restrooms lie on the north side of U.S. Highway 89A between Mileposts 590 and 591.

East Rim Viewpoint

A paved trail leads 300 yards from the parking area to the east edge of the Kaibab Plateau (elev.

8,800 feet), where you can take in the expansive vistas across the Marble Canyon area. It's also a great place to enjoy sunrises and sunsets enhanced by colors reflecting off the distant Vermilion Cliffs and Painted Desert. Camping isn't permitted within .5 miles of the viewpoint, but good places for primitive camping lie in the conifer and aspen forests nearby. From Highway 67 in De Motte Park (.8 miles south of the North Rim Country Store), turn east 4.2 miles on Forest Road 611. Cars and small RVs can easily travel the gravel road in good weather.

Another fine panorama lies farther north at the end of Forest Road 611, just 6.9 miles from Highway 67 (keep right at the fork 6.5 miles in; the last .4 miles is too rough for cars); walk a few hundred feet beyond road's end for the views. Still farther north, **Dog Point** also features a fine view; head east 1.3 miles on Forest Road 611 from Highway 67, then turn left (north) 7.2 miles on Forest Road 610 to its end; keep right at the fork 6.4 miles in.

Hikers can follow **Arizona Trail #101** along the rim or descend into North Canyon in the Saddle Mountain Wilderness from East Rim Overlook. **East Rim Trail #7** descends from a trailhead just north of the overlook, and **North Canyon Trail #4** descends from the rim 1.5 miles south. Together, these three trails make a loop of about six miles into the valley below. North Canyon Trail #4 continues down North Canyon to House Rock Valley, a total of seven miles one-way.

Marble Viewpoint

This overlook, southeast of East Rim Viewpoint, provides another perspective of Saddle Mountain Wilderness, Marble Canyon, Vermilion Cliffs and beyond. From Highway 67 in De Motte Park (.8 miles south of the North Rim Country Store), turn east 1.3 miles on Forest Road 611, right 6.7 miles on Forest Road 610, then left 4.6 miles on Forest Road 219 to its end. No camping is allowed within .5 miles of the viewpoint.

Saddle Mountain Trailhead

The drive out Forest Road 610 is worthwhile for the spectacular views of the Marble Canyon, Nankoweap, and House Rock Valley areas. From the trailhead (elev. 8,800 feet), **Saddle Mountain/Nankoweap Trail #57** drops several hundred feet to some good viewpoints. The trail continues to the Saddle Mountain saddle, 2.7 miles one-way; a good day-hike destination and the start of the challenging **Nankoweap Trail** to the Colorado River. From the saddle, Trail #57 continues north three miles down to Road 8910 in House Rock Valley (elev. 6,800 feet).

From the Highway 67 turnoff in De Motte Park, .8 miles south of the North Rim Country Store, head east 1.3 miles on Forest Road 611, then turn right and go 12 miles on Forest Road 610 to the trailhead. Cautiously driven cars should be able to do this in dry weather. The **Point Imperial Trail** begins on the right, .2 miles before Saddle Mountain Trailhead; it follows a former fire road 2 miles one-way through the forest to Point Imperial. The national park border is just south of Forest Road 611, so do not camp here without a backcountry permit. The Kaibab National Forest has many spots suitable for dispersed camping.

Although not shown on the Kaibab National Forest map, the road continues 1.4 miles past Saddle Mountain Trailhead to another great viewpoint of Marble Canyon, House Rock Valley, and far beyond. Use a high-clearance vehicle or hike in.

Saddle Mountain Wilderness

This 40,610-acre wilderness includes part of the densely forested Kaibab Plateau, along with sheer cliffs and narrow canyons that drop to House Rock Valley. Mountain lions and mule deer roam the area. North Canyon Wash is noted for its pure strain of native Apache trout. Saddle Mountain (elev. 8,424 feet), visible from Point Imperial, stands at the south end of the wilderness. Saddle Mountain/Nankoweap and North Canyon Trails cross the wilderness from the Kaibab Plateau to House Rock Valley.

HOUSE ROCK VALLEY

Despite its name, this land of gently rolling hills, grasslands, and pinyon and juniper woodlands is actually a plateau. It lies below the cliffs of the

Kaibab Plateau to the west and extends to the brink of Marble Canyon on the east. The well-named Vermilion Cliffs form the north boundary. About 100 **buffalo** roam freely across the 67,000 acres of House Rock Valley and up onto the Kaibab Plateau; you're most likely to see them in summer, least likely during hunting season in autumn. Viewpoints provide intimate views of Marble Canyon.

Adventurous hikers can follow trails from House Rock Valley down to the Colorado River via South Canyon and the Saddle Mountain/Nankoweap Trails. **North Canyon Trail #4** connects House Rock Valley with the East Rim Viewpoint area atop the Kaibab Plateau in seven miles one-way.

The turnoff for House Rock Valley Road 8910 is between Mileposts 559 and 560 on Highway 89A, 20 miles east of Jacob Lake and 21.5 miles west of Marble Canyon Lodge. Cars can usually travel unpaved Road 8910 in dry weather, but side roads may require a high-clearance vehicle.

Kaibab Plateau–House Rock Valley Scenic Drive

This adventure on Forest Roads 213 and 220 connects the Kaibab Plateau with House Rock Valley. You'll need a high-clearance 4WD vehicle for the steep and winding sections. Turn off Highway 67 just north of Milepost 602, about three miles north of the North Rim Country Store. Forest Road 213 crosses **Arizona Trail #101** 2.6 miles in. Seven miles in from Highway 67, Forest Road 213 begins the descent on short switchbacks. It skirts the north edge of Saddle Mountain Wilderness before ending after 8.6 miles at the East Side Game Road (Forest Road 220). Turn right and continue 8.5 miles down to House Rock Valley, following Tater Canyon part of the way to a T-junction with Road 8910, 17 miles south of U.S. Highway 89A. Turn left here for U.S. Highway 89A or turn right for Marble Canyon overlooks and Saddle Mountain Trailhead.

Buck Farm Overlook

You can drive right to the brink of Marble Canyon at this overlook (elev. 5,500 feet). Follow Road 8910 south 23.5 miles from U.S. Highway 89A to where it begins a loop; take the left fork east 2 miles, then turn left 3 miles on bumpy Forest Road 445H to its end. Buck Farm Canyon and Royal Arches can be seen below to the right. Tatahatso Point lies directly across the river.

Triple Alcoves Overlook

This viewpoint provides a very different panorama. Continue 2.5 miles south on Road 8910 from the Forest Road 445H junction to the trailhead sign on the left, then hike east .5 miles across Saddle Mountain Wilderness to the overlook.

Saddle Mountain Trailhead

At the south end of the Road 8910 loop, three miles past the Triple Alcoves trailhead, **Saddle Mountain/Nankoweap Trail #57** climbs three miles to the Saddle Mountain saddle, a fine day-hike destination. Here you can turn down the difficult **Nankoweap Trail** to the Colorado River or continue up Trail #57 another 2.7 miles to the Kaibab Plateau. In winter, when Highway 67 is closed, Road 8910 and this trail offer an alternative way to reach the North Rim.

THE WESTERN KAIBAB PLATEAU

Point Sublime

This well-named overlook, west of Bright Angel Point and southeast of Fire Point, lies at the end of a 17-mile dirt road negotiable by high-clearance vehicles or mountain bicycles, on horseback, or on foot. Point Sublime extends far into the Grand Canyon for awesome views. You can scan a great length of both North and South Rims and spot a section of Colorado River. The South Rim can be traced from below Bass Canyon upcanyon nearly to Desert View. Binoculars help you to see parts of the Tonto, Hermit, and South Kaibab Trails, along with Grand Canyon Village and Hermits Rest. On the North Rim, the Powell Plateau lies to the northwest, Confucius and Mencius Temples to the southeast, and Tiyo Point and Cape Royal to the east—truly sublime. Closer in, cliffs drop into the Tuna Creek drainage. Point Sublime is a great place to camp, but you'll need a backcountry permit to do so.

The route is bumpy and not always passable; check at the North Rim Backcountry Office or the North Rim Visitor Center. From Grand Canyon Lodge, near Bright Angel Point, go north 2.7 miles on Highway 67, then turn left on the unpaved Point Sublime Road (high-clearance vehicle needed) past the Widforss and Tiyo Point trailheads to Point Sublime. You can also follow roads from the Kaibab National Forest: Head west 2 miles on Forest Road 22 from the Highway 67 turnoff in De Motte Park (.8 miles south of the North Rim Country Store), turn south 2 miles on Forest Road 270, turn west 6 miles on Forest Road 223, then south 1.5 miles on Forest Roads 268 and 268B to the park boundary, where the road becomes rougher on the last 15 miles to Point Sublime. Keep left at the junction .2 miles inside the park (the right fork goes to Swamp Point), then keep right past the junctions for Kanabownits Lookout and the road to Highway 67. The Kaibab National Forest map (North Kaibab District) is essential for navigating these back roads.

Tiyo Point has been closed to vehicles, but you can hike in or go by horseback. Turn south 6.3 miles from Point Sublime Road at a large meadow, 4.2 miles in from Highway 67.

Fire Point

The panorama here takes in Tapeats Amphitheater, Steamboat Mountain, and Powell Plateau; Great Thumb Mesa lies across the river. Walk 100 feet out on the rocks for an even better look. A fine stand of ponderosa pine grows on the point. Carefully driven cars can negotiate the roads in good weather.

Turn west 2 miles on Forest Road 22 from Highway 67 in De Motte Park (.8 miles south of the North Rim Country Store), head south 2 miles on Forest Road 270, then turn west 13 miles on Forest Road 223 to its end. The last mile is within Grand Canyon National Park and will probably be rough.

Timp, North Timp, and Parissawampitts Point

Walk about one-third mile out on Timp Point from the parking area for the best panoramas and to see Thunder River emerge from the north wall of Tapeats Canyon and drop in two large cascades amid lush cottonwoods. You can also spot the trail that climbs from Thunder River to the top of the cliffs and over into Surprise Valley. Binoculars give the best view. Nearby North Timp and Parissawampitts Points also provide good perspectives.

Rainbow Rim Trail #10 follows the convoluted rim between Timp and Parissawampitts for 18 miles one-way. Mountain bikers can make many pleasant loops on this trail and on forest roads in the area. Forest Road 250 connects roads to these points, though it requires a high-clearance vehicle or a mountain bike. Cars can reach Timp Point (elev. 7,600 feet) in good weather by turning off Highway 67 at DeMotte Park (.8 miles south of the North Rim Store on AZ 67), then following Forest Roads 22, 270, 222, 206, and 271. Forest Road 271A branches to North Timp Point from 271. Parissawampitts Point may also be okay for cars; take Forest Roads 22, 270, 222, 206, then 214 to its end.

Crazy Jug Point

This point features great views and good access roads at an elevation of 7,500 feet. pinyon pine, cliff rose, and some ponderosa grow here. A walk of a few hundred feet from the parking area leads to the overlook. The Colorado River comes out from behind the Powell Plateau, wraps around Great Thumb Mesa, then winds far downstream. Dark, forested volcanoes of Mt. Trumbull and the rest of the Uinkaret Mountains rise to the west. Directly below are Crazy Jug Canyon, Tapeats Amphitheater, and other parts of the Tapeats Creek drainage. The lineup of Fence, Locust, North Timp, Timp, and Fire Points marks the Kaibab Plateau to the southeast. Forest Road 22 provides access either from the east edge of Fredonia (U.S. 89A between Mileposts 607 and 608) or from DeMotte Park (.8 miles south of the North Rim Store on AZ 67), then you'll follow Forest Roads 425 and 292B. Cars can do this trip in dry weather.

Monument Point and Bill Hall Trailhead

From road's end (elev. 7,050 feet), **Bill Hall Trail** climbs west up along the rim nearly a mile, past pinyon pine, juniper, and lots of cliff rose and wildflowers before plunging steeply to the Thunder River Trail. (See the *Inner Canyon* section for a description of the hike to Thunder River and Deer Creek Falls.) The ridge just above the trail has a sweeping panorama up Tapeats Canyon and down the Grand Canyon. Near the trailhead area, you'll see the effects of the Bridger Burn of 1996. This fire affected 54,000 acres—a large portion of the western Kaibab Plateau. Follow directions for Crazy Jug Point up to the junction half a mile before the point, then keep straight 1.7 miles on Forest Road 292A; it's okay for cars in dry weather.

Indian Hollow and Thunder River Trailhead

A tiny campground with an outhouse and tables lies .4 miles before the end of Forest Road 232 at an elevation of 6,300 feet. Ponderosa pine start to thin out closer to the rim, where pinyon pine, juniper, and Gambel oak predominate. At the rim, a short walk from road's end, you'll have a view of the Deer Creek drainage of the Grand Canyon. Great Thumb Mesa lies directly across to the south. The full length of the Powell Plateau presents itself to the southeast. Downcanyon, Mt. Sinyala stands near the mouth of Havasu Canyon.

Thunder River Trail drops steeply from the rim for the first few hundred yards, then follows the canyon contours west half a mile to a break in the cliffs, a good day-hike destination. (See the *Inner Canyon* section for a description of the hike to Thunder River and Deer Creek Falls.) From Forest Road 425, turn west on Forest Road 232 to its end. Cautiously driven cars might be able to make it; check with Kaibab National Forest staff.

Sowats Point

This viewpoint and trailhead overlook Jumpup Canyon at an elevation of 6,200 feet. **Jumpup-Nail Trail #8** descends into the depths here, six miles and a drop of 2,000 feet—steep in places—to **Ranger Trail #41** in Kanab Creek Wilderness. You can start on the same roads as those to Crazy Jug Point, but turn east on Forest Road 233 to its end. High-clearance vehicles will be needed for the last several miles.

Jumpup Point

An amazing canyon panorama greets the rare visitor who ventures out along the rough road on this long point in the western Kaibab Plateau. Five miles before the end of the point, the vast Jumpup Canyon appears on the left, along with its tributaries Sowats Canyon and Indian Hollow. Much of this canyon country lies in Kanab Creek Wilderness, which almost completely surrounds Jumpup Point. Although there's no trail access to the canyons from here, Ranger Trail can be seen far below where it's joined by Jumpup-Nail Trail, which descends from Sowats Point across to the east. You might spot bighorn sheep on one of the precarious ledges.

At road's end, a short walk reveals more views. Lower Kanab Canyon and the Grand Canyon seem almost lost in the vastness. Kanab Canyon and the broad Hack Canyon lie to the west. Mt. Trumbull stands as the highest of the volcanoes across Kanab Canyon. The summit of Mt. Logan, identified by its cliff profile, is just to the left and farther back. Vermilion Cliffs and other high points of Utah lie to the northwest and north.

Sparse pinyon pine, juniper, sage, and cactus of the high desert cover the point at an elevation of 5,650 feet. The Kaibab National Forest map (North Kaibab District) shows the ways in. From Jacob Lake, go south .3 miles on Highway 67, turn west on Forest Road 461, and take Forest Roads 462, 22, 423, 235, 423, then 201 to its end. Forest Road 22 provides access from either the east edge of Fredonia (U.S. 89A between Mileposts 607 and 608) or DeMotte Park (.8 miles south of the North Rim Store on AZ 67), then you'll follow Forest Roads 423, 235, 423, and 201. A high-clearance vehicle will be needed for the rocky sections of the last 10 miles of road. Mountain bikers enjoy this ride too.

Kanab Creek Wilderness

Kanab Creek has the largest canyon system in the Grand Canyon's North Rim, with headwaters

THE EXPLORATION OF THE COLORADO RIVER AND ITS CANYONS

Kanab Creek

100 miles north on the Paunsaugunt Plateau in Utah. The wilderness area protects 77,100 acres along the Kanab and its tributaries. Springs in Kanab Canyon nourish large cottonwood trees and lush growths of desert willow, tamarisk, maidenhair fern, and grass. The easy-to-moderate, 17-mile **Ranger Trail** wraps around the base of Jumpup Point in the heart of the wilderness. You can reach it on the west side via the easy 21.5-mile **Snake Gulch–Kanab Creek Trail #59,** as well as from Kanab or Hack Canyons. On the east side, Jumpup Cabin Trailhead and the difficult six-mile **Jumpup-Nail Trail #8** provide access. You'll need a Grand Canyon backcountry permit to camp in Kanab Canyon below the junction with Jumpup Canyon. Hack Canyon and a bit of the wilderness lie on BLM land; the office in Kanab, Utah, has information on trailhead access and hiking. Other trailheads lie in the Kaibab National Forest; contact the Fredonia or Kaibab Plateau Visitor Center offices for road and trail information.

Toroweap and the Western Arizona Strip

TOROWEAP

This remote area of the North Rim lies between Kanab Canyon to the east and the Pine Mountains (Uinkaret Mountains) to the west. An overlook (elev. 4,552 feet) provides awesome Canyon views from sheer cliffs nearly 3,000 feet high above the river. Toroweap, also known as Tuweap or Tuweep, lies 140 road miles west of the developed North Rim area of Bright Angel Point. You'll enjoy the amazing views, hiking, and solitude.

Although the area is in Grand Canyon National Park, no entry or campground fees were charged at press time. Obtain hiking information, backcountry permits, and emergency help at the Tuweep Ranger Station, open all year though the ranger does take a few days off now and then. There's an emergency phone here. If you'll need a backcountry permit, it's safer to obtain it beforehand, though you could try for a last-minute permit here or at Pipe Spring National Monument.

Between 1.2 million and 30,000 years ago, lava eruptions built about 60 volcanic cones here, even forming dams across the Colorado River. One of the dams towered nearly 2,000 feet, but the river washed it away long ago. pinyon pine, juniper, cactus, and small flowering plants cover the plateau. Watch for rattlesnakes. Hikers can enjoy many easy rambles near the rim, a difficult descent to the river near Lava Falls, a scramble up Vulcan's Throne, or multiday trips on the Tuckup Trail.

Toroweap Overlook

The views begin at road's end, where sheer cliffs drop to the Colorado River. **Mount Sinyala,** a butte 25 miles east of the overlook, marks the mouth of Havasu Canyon. Most of the Havasupai who live on the reservation dwell in Supai village, nine miles up Havasu Canyon. The **Hualapai Indian Reservation** lies directly across the Colorado River from the overlook. **Vulcan's Anvil,** also known as Vulcan's Forge or Thor's

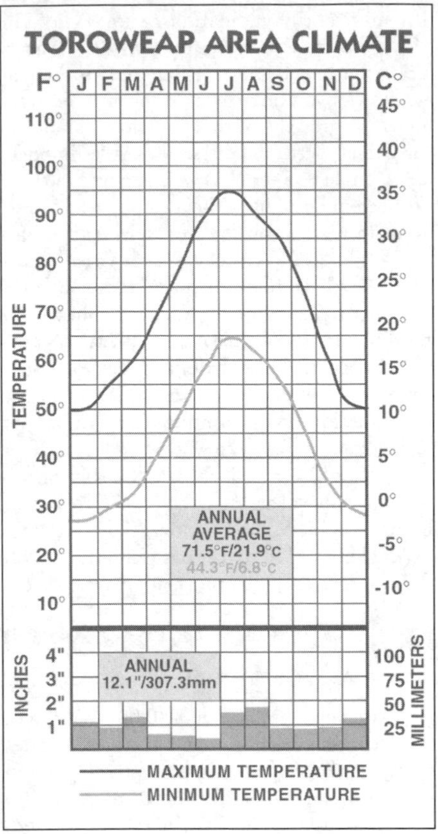

Hammer, rises in the middle of the river directly below. This 50-foot-high lava neck is all that remains of an extinct lava vent.

Lava Falls, visible 1.5 miles downstream, roars with a vengeance. You can see it from a point just one-eighth mile to the right from the overlook. Debris from Prospect Canyon on the South Rim forms the rapids, perhaps the roughest water in the Grand Canyon. Water flowing 8,000–20,000 cubic feet per second drops abruptly, then explodes into foam and spray. River-runners commonly rate these rapids a 10-plus on a scale of 1–10. You can reach Lava Falls on a very steep and strenuous hike, not recommended in summer. (See the *Inner Canyon* section.)

Saddle Horse Canyon Trail

The trailhead for this easy hike lies beside the main road, 5.7 miles south of the ranger station. The path heads east to a Colorado River overlook, then north with views of wonderfully weathered rock near Saddle Horse Canyon; it's about 1.6 miles round-trip.

Esplanade Loop Trail

This 2.9-mile hiking trail begins at the campground 5.4 miles south of the ranger station.

Vulcan's Throne

The 600-foot-high rounded cinder cone west of the overlook is one of the youngest volcanoes in the area. There's no trail, but you can hike to the top in about 1.5 miles round-trip; it's most easily reached by road via normally dry Toroweap Lake.

Toroweap Campground

Backed by low cliffs and overlooking small canyons, this small campground is 5.4 miles past the ranger station and .9 miles before the overlook at the end of the road. A couple of campsites may be available at the overlook, too. There's no water, camping charge, or permit needed for the established sites. Each site has an eight-person, two-vehicle limit; no reservations are accepted. If all campsites are full, you must obtain the expensive backcountry permit for other areas in the park or simply drive north and find an undeveloped spot on BLM land. Bring lots of water, extra food, and camping gear.

Getting There

Three roads lead into the area. The most popular one begins at Highway 389, 9 miles west of Fredonia; turn south 40 miles on County 109 at the sign for Toroweap 61; continue straight 7 miles on County 5, and straight 14 miles on County 115. These dirt roads are usually in good condition when dry, but have washboard sections. Watch for livestock and take it slow through washes and cattleguards. The last few miles are slow and rocky, but careful drivers should make it. The Tuweep Ranger

Station is on the left, 6.3 miles before the overlook. Beyond the ranger station, Toroweap Point (elev. 6,393 feet) towers on the left; dumpy Vulcan's Throne (elev. 5,102 feet) sits on the right.

You can also drive to Toroweap on a 90-mile dirt road from St. George (BLM Road 1069 and County 5 for 76 miles, then right 14 miles on County 115) or a 58-mile road from Colorado City (County 5 for 44 miles, then continue straight 14 miles on County 115). Avoid driving these roads after heavy rain or snow, especially the route from Colorado City. Snows usually block the road from St. George between October and May. Water, food, and gas are not available in this country. Bring a map—the BLM's Arizona Strip one is best—as signs may be missing at some junctions.

THE WESTERN ARIZONA STRIP

Highlights of this remote land west of the Toroweap area include Grand Canyon viewpoints, lofty volcanoes, and seldom-visited canyons. On a journey across this region, you'll experience everything from cool ponderosa pine forests to extremely arid Mohave Desert. The **Grand Canyon–Parashant National Monument** (www.nps.gov/para) protects more than one million acres here and many areas also have a wilderness designation.

History

Archaeologists have found evidence of hunter-gatherers, dating back more than 11,000 years. Ancestral Puebloans followed much later and may be ancestors of the Southern Paiute who

THE DESERT TORTOISE

A threatened species, the desert tortoise *(Gopherus agassizii)* survives the harsh climate of western Arizona by burrowing underground for about 95 percent of its lifetime. Here it escapes the 140°F surface temperatures in summer and the freezes of winter. It also seeks out catchment basins, where it will lie waiting when the rare rains seem likely. A tortoise's bladder can store a cup of liquid for later use, and they've been known to expel the bladder's contents at intruders. Wastes are excreted in a nearly dry form. Tortoises can withstand dehydration, then increase their weight 43 percent by drinking after a storm. Growth and sexual maturity depend much on availability of food and moisture. Several growth rings may appear each year. The female reaches maturity when about 7–8 inches long (mid-carapace), perhaps at 15 years of age. Mating peaks in late summer/early autumn, though egg laying won't take place until May or June, when tortoises lay 2–3 batches of 2–9 eggs. Babies emerge 3–4 months later. Oddly, experiments have shown that eggs incubated at 79–87°F turn out to be all males, at 88–91°F all females.

The tortoise's diet includes grasses, herbs, flowers, and new cactus growth. Males may fight each other for territory until one flees or gets flipped onto its back. If the defeated rival cannot right itself, it will die in the sun. Because the tortoise needs sand or gravel to burrow into, you're most likely to see one in washes and canyon bottoms. Life span may be 70 years or more. The male has a longer protruding plate (used in jousting matches) under its neck; he may be as much as 14 inches long and weigh up to 20 pounds. The female is a bit smaller. Laws forbid disturbing or collecting a wild tortoise, but habitat loss and "kidnappers" have left their future in doubt. The western box turtle *(Terrapene ornata)*, sometimes confused with the desert tortoise, is much smaller at about five inches long and has distinctive light and dark striping on its shell.

BOB RACE

The Grand Canyon

live in the region today. The prairie here showed little promise at first—the ground proved nearly impossible to plow and lacked water for irrigation. Determined Mormons began ranching in the 1860s, despite the constant isolation and occasional Navajo raids. They built Winsor Castle, a fortified ranch, in 1870 as a base for a large, church-owned cattle herd. Mormons also founded the towns of Fredonia, Short Creek (now Colorado City), and Littlefield.

Some of these settlers had fled Utah to escape federal laws prohibiting polygamy. About 3,000 members of an excommunicated polygamous Mormon sect still live in Colorado City and neighboring Hildale, Utah. (Note the huge size of "family" houses here!) Federal and state officials raided Colorado City several times, most recently in 1953, when 27 arrests were made—those charged received one year of probation. Since then, government policy has been mostly "live and let live," but state officials continue to worry about how to deal with allegations of teenage girls being forced to marry older men in the close-knit community.

Exploring the Western Arizona Strip

High-clearance 4WD vehicles are recommended in this remote and rugged land. Cautiously driven 2WD vehicles can negotiate roads to the Trumbull and Toroweap areas in dry weather from St. George, Colorado City, and Fredonia. Parts of these roads are so smooth that one can drive at high speeds, often too fast to spot that washout or rough cattle guard! Drivers of 2WD vehicles need to take extra care not to become stuck on steep, sandy, or washed-out roads.

All visitors must respect the remote location, lack of water, and absence of facilities. Note that mobile phones usually don't work here. Be sure to carry camping gear, extra food and water, tools, two spare tires, and a first-aid kit. Distances can be great—you may wish to carry extra gas. Some roads shown on maps may be very difficult, hazardous, or completely closed. Major junctions have signs and most roads also have a number, which helps with navigation. Some critical intersections lack signs, however, so it's highly recommended to have the BLM's Arizona Strip Visitor Map and to make frequent reference to it. Leave an itinerary with a reliable person in case you don't emerge on time. Some people live seasonally on the Arizona Strip, but you cannot count on being able to find anyone in case of trouble. Ranchers run cattle on the strip, so gates should be left as you found them. Drivers need to keep an eye out for endangered desert tortoises that may wander across the road in the Mohave Desert, west of the Grand Wash Cliffs and the Virgin Mountains.

Mountain Biking

Riders can do exciting trips in the mountains and out to Grand Canyon viewpoints. Marked trails for cyclists include the **Dutchman Trail,** an "easy" 9-mile loop near Little Black Mountain south of St. George and the "more difficult" 8.5-mile **Sunshine Loop** southeast of St. George.

Information

For travel information on the western Arizona Strip, contact the **Interagency Visitor Center** (345 E. Riverside Dr., St. George, UT 84790, 435/688-3246, www.az.blm.gov). It's open 7:45 A.M.–5 P.M. Monday–Friday, the best times for reaching someone with first-hand travel experience, and 9 A.M.–5 P.M. Saturdays and holidays. Take I-15 Bluff Street Exit 6 and turn southeast one-third mile on Riverside Drive; the office is on your left. This is also the home of the Arizona Strip Interpretive Association (ASIA), which has a good bookshop here.

The BLM's Arizona Strip Visitor Map shows topography, roads with numbers, and land ownership, all at a 1:168,960 scale. The more detailed USGS 1:100,000- and 1:24,000-scale topo maps will be handy for hikers.

SIGHTS

Hack Canyon

This tributary of Kanab Canyon northeast of Toroweap offers both great scenery—you'll feel like you're in the Grand Canyon—and access to the Kanab Creek Wilderness. The road was very rough at last report in 2004; check for current conditions. The turnoff from County 109 is 30 miles southwest of Fredonia and 38 miles north of Toroweap. Head east on BLM Road 1123 and you'll see the headwall of Hack Canyon on the left after 1.1 miles. The road drops in and follows the normally dry canyon bottom with ever higher and grander walls on each side. You'll reach the wilderness boundary and road's end at 9.7 miles from County 109.

A trail continues into the wilderness toward Kanab Canyon, 5 miles one-way, where you could turn downstream another 10.5 miles to the mouth of Jumpup Canyon or 16 miles to the Colorado River; a backcountry permit is needed to camp below Jumpup Canyon. Black Willow Spring, a short distance down the trail on your right in Hack Canyon, is one of the rare sources of water here.

Kanab Point

A great expanse of canyon falls away below your feet from this perch overlooking the confluence of the Kanab and Grand Canyons. Few people know about this lonely spot, yet it's one of the best Grand Canyon viewpoints. The drive out takes some care with navigation, as not all the junctions may have signs. You'll need the BLM's Arizona Strip Visitor Map, a high-clearance vehicle, and dry weather. The turnoff from County 109 is 4.7 miles south of the Hack Canyon junction, 34 miles southwest of Fredonia, and 34 miles north of Toroweap. Head east on BLM Road 1058, keep right at a fork 7.5 miles in, turn right at a fork 10.1 miles in (the wider left fork goes to an uranium mine), turn left at a T-junction 16.4 miles in, and continue .8 miles to the national park boundary; you'll reach Kanab Point in another 4 miles, for a total of 21.2 miles one-way from County 109. At the rim, the best panoramas of the Grand Canyon are .2 miles to the right, and the best ones of Kanab Canyon lie .3 miles to the left. To camp at the Point, you'll need a backcountry camping permit.

Nampaweap Rock Art Site

Archaic, ancestral Puebloan, and Paiute tribes have chipped thousands of glyphs into boulders near Mt. Trumbull, northwest of Toroweap. *Nampaweap* means "foot canyon" in Paiute, per-

© BILL WEIR

Nampaweap Rock Art Site

haps referring to its being on a travel corridor dating back to prehistoric times. Head west 3.7 miles on County Road 5 from the junction with Toroweap Road (or go east 3.5 miles from the Mt. Trumbull Trailhead), turn south 1.1 miles on BLM Road 1028 toward the private Arkansas Ranch, turn east into the parking area, and then walk .75 miles to the head of a small canyon. The rock art is on the canyon's north side.

Mount Trumbull Wilderness

Forests cover the basalt-rock slopes of Mt. Trumbull (8,028 feet), the centerpiece of this 7,900-acre wilderness located northwest of Toroweap. Oak, pinyon pine, and juniper woodlands grow on the lower slopes; ponderosa pine, Gambel oak, and some aspen cover the higher and more protected areas. Kaibab squirrels, introduced in the early 1970s, flourish in the forests. You might see or hear a turkey, too. The 5.4-mile round-trip climb to the summit makes an enjoyable forest ramble with some views through the trees. From the marked trailhead at an elevation of 6,500 feet on the southwest side of Mt. Trumbull, the wide path climbs around to the south side, with some good views across Toroweap Valley, the Grand Canyon, and the San Francisco Peaks. The trail then turns north and becomes faint, but cairns show the way to the summit, marked by a survey tower and some viewpoints. You can reach the trailhead by County Road 5 from Toroweap, Fredonia, Colorado City, or St. George; you'll know that you're close when ponderosa pines appear. The buildings and trailers across the field belong to a BLM site; if staff are in, they may be able to help with local information.

John Wesley Powell named Mt. Trumbull and nearby Mt. Logan after U.S. senators. Mormon pioneers built a steam-powered sawmill just west of the trailhead in 1870 to supply timbers for the St. George Temple. A historic marker describes the sawmill operation, and you can explore the site for the scant remnants. Water from Nixon Spring, higher on the slopes, once supplied the sawmill. A faucet near the road between the historic site and trailhead usually has water from the spring—a welcome sight for travelers in this arid land. Be sure to treat the water, as it doesn't meet drinking standards.

Mount Logan Wilderness

Scenic features of this 14,600-acre volcanic region include Mt. Logan (7,866 feet), other parts of the Uinkaret Mountains, and a large natural amphitheater known as Hell's Hole. Geology, forests, and wildlife resemble those of Mt. Trumbull, a short distance to the northeast. A road climbs the east side of Mt. Logan to within a half mile of the summit; the rest of the way is an easy walk—just continue north along the side of the ridge. At the top you can peer into the vast depths of Hell's Hole, a steep canyon of red and white rock. The sweeping panorama takes in much of the Arizona Strip and beyond to mountains in Nevada and Utah. Trees block the views to the south.

From County 5, just southeast of the Mt. Trumbull trailhead, turn southwest 4.2 miles on BLM Road 1044, then right 2.2 miles on BLM Road 1064 until it becomes rough and steep at its end. Many fine spots suitable for camping lie along the roads in ponderosa pines.

A rough 4WD road follows a corridor through the wilderness, from which hikers can turn south onto the old Slide Mountain Road (closed to vehicles) or enter Hell's Hole from below. You'll need to follow a map closely, as none of these destinations have signs; roads also branch off to other unmarked areas, adding to the navigational challenge. Loose rock and erosion of the corridor road require a high-clearance 4WD; it's slow going, but the road continues all the way down to the Whitmore Wash Road 1045, one mile north of the Bar 10 Ranch.

Mt. Trumbull School

Homesteaders arrived in this remote valley about 1917 to farm and raise livestock. Population peaked at 200–250 in the 1930s, when a drier climate forced residents to switch their livelihood from crops to cattle and sheep. People gradually drifted away until the last full-time resident departed in 1984. Abandoned houses stand empty, along with some houses that are inhabited seasonally. No trespassing is allowed on private lands, but you can get some good photos from the main roads. Dedicated teachers taught at the remote one-room schoolhouse from 1922 until the bell rang for its last class in 1968. Photo and document exhibits inside show what life was like here. Donations are appreciated.

Whitmore Wash Road

Lava flows from Mt. Emma in the Uinkaret Mountains form a ramp on which you can drive a high-clearance, 4WD vehicle deep into the Grand Canyon, though the last part of the drive is very rough. A short trail at road's end leads down to the Colorado River. (See the *Whitmore Wash Trail* section of the *Inner Canyon* section for directions and trail information.)

Bar 10 Ranch (P.O. Box 910088, St. George, UT 84791-0088, 435/628-4010 or 800/582-4139, www.bar10.com) lies along this road 80 miles from St. George and about 9 miles before the rim. It offers miles of open country and cowboy-style meals along with informal Western hospitality. Activities include horseback riding, pack trips, hiking, scenic flights, river trips, ATV tours, and entertainment. Many visitors spend a day here when shuttling in or out from a river trip by helicopter and flying by small plane to Las Vegas or other destinations. You can also drive (high-clearance vehicles recommended) or fly in. Reservations are required for the Bar 10, which stays open all year.

Whitmore Point

Spectacular views of the Grand Canyon, Parashant Canyon, Mt. Logan, and the Uinkaret Mountains greet those who head out to this 5,500-foot-high perch. Volcanoes and massive lava flows between here and the Toroweap area to the east can be seen clearly. There are plenty of good places to camp, with no permit needed.

From Mt. Trumbull Schoolhouse, head west then south 22.2 miles on BLM Road 1063. Some junctions have signs, but you'll need to refer frequently to a map. At 9.9 miles in, a jeep road to the right heads down Trail Canyon to Parashant Canyon, a good area for adventurous hikers. Continue straight (south) for Whitmore Point. As with most roads on the Arizona Strip, conditions get rougher as you come closer to the Grand Canyon, and a high-clearance vehicle is necessary.

Grand Wash Cliffs Wilderness

Grand Wash Cliffs mark the west edge of the Colorado Plateau and the end of the Grand Canyon. The wilderness encloses 36,300 acres along a 12-mile section of the cliffs in an extremely remote portion of Arizona. Desert bighorn sheep and raptors live in the high country; desert tortoises forage lower down. **Grand Wash Bench Trail,** a 10-mile gated road, follows a bench between the upper (1,800 ft.) and lower (1,600 ft.) cliffs; trailheads are on the north and south wilderness boundaries. Hikers can also wander cross-country to the cliffs from BLM Road 1061 along the west boundary of the wilderness.

An exceptionally scenic 4WD road through Hidden Canyon crosses the Grand Wash Cliffs north of the wilderness. From the eastern turnoff from County 5, 11.5 miles north of Mt. Trumbull Schoolhouse and 46 miles south of St. George, follow County Road 103 southwest 16.6 miles, then turn right on BLM Road 1003 at the sign for Hidden Canyon. Small canyon cliffs appear four miles in, then become higher and higher as the road winds downstream along the canyon floor, repeatedly crisscrossing the normally dry streambed. Juniper and pinyon pine on the Shivwits Plateau in the upper canyon give way to Joshua trees in the desert country below. After about 20 miles, you leave the canyons. BLM Road 1061 turns south for the west face of the Grand Wash Cliffs Wilderness. Numerous sandy washes require a high-clearance 4WD vehicle for Hidden Canyon and for most roads in the Grand Wash Cliffs area.

Mount Dellenbaugh

This small volcano atop the Shivwits Plateau offers a great panorama of the Arizona Strip. Vast forests of juniper and pinyon and ponderosa pine spread across the plateau. A long line of cliffs marks the Grand Canyon to the south. Beyond rise the Hualapai Mountains near Kingman. You can see other mountain ranges in Arizona, Nevada, and Utah as well. The mountain is named for Frederick Dellenbaugh, who served as artist and assistant topographer on Major Powell's second river expedition through the Grand Canyon in 1871–1872.

From Mt. Trumbull Schoolhouse, go north 11.5 miles on County 5, then turn southwest 42 miles on County 103, following signs. From St. George, Utah, it's 46 miles to the junction, then 42 miles to Mt. Dellenbaugh. The last five miles can be negotiated only when dry; high-clearance vehicles are recommended. The trailhead lies just past the NPS's Shivwits Ranger Station; follow an old jeep road, now closed to motor vehicles. The trail is an easy four miles round-trip, climbing 900 feet to the 7,072-foot summit.

Twin Point

Beautiful views from this overlook take in the lower Grand Canyon, Surprise Canyon, Burnt Canyon, and Sanup Plateau. Follow County 103 south 37 miles from County 5, keep straight where the road to Mt. Dellenbaugh turns left, and continue south. At a fork five miles farther, you can detour right one mile to an overlook of upper Burnt Canyon, perhaps named for the colorful yellow and red rock layers. The main road continues south 2.7 miles, then skirts the west rim of Burnt Canyon, offering many fine views. Just before the road ends, 14 miles from the Mt. Dellenbaugh junction, it forks left for Twin Point and right for a trailhead to Sanup Plateau. Ranchers run cattle down this trail for winter grazing. Twin Point offers plenty of places to camp, and no permit is needed.

Kelly Point

Located east of Twin Point, this point extends much farther south than any other on the North Rim. Road conditions have so deteriorated that as of 2004 the route is extremely rough, rocky, and slow—figure 5 mph on the last 20 miles. Getting here can be more like an expedition than a casual sightseeing jaunt—Twin Point has similar views, without the hardships for you and your vehicle. If you're determined and well prepared, follow County Road 103 past Mt. Dellenbaugh and continue south to road's end.

Paiute Wilderness

This 84,700-acre wilderness lies south of I-15 and the Virgin River in the northwest corner of Arizona. The jagged Virgin Mountains harbor a wide variety of plant and animal life between desert country at 2,400 feet and conifer forests surrounding 8,012-foot Mt. Bangs.

Several hiking trails wind through the rugged terrain. Cougar Spring Trailhead at the wilderness boundary provides the easiest route to the summit. Follow an old road up one mile through the wilderness to a saddle, then turn left one more mile up another old road toward the top. When the road ends, you'll need to bushwhack through some chaparral (wear long pants and look for cairns) and rock scramble the last quarter mile to the top; the climb takes about 4.5 hours round-trip. Despite the high elevations, only a few pines grow on the upper slopes; you'll see mostly manzanita, Gambel oak, and some hedgehog and prickly pear cactus. Surrounding ridges do have forests.

Other hiking options from Cougar Spring Trailhead area include the ridge north of Mt. Bangs and the 15-mile one-way **Sullivan Trail.** The Sullivan crosses the wilderness from Cougar Spring Trailhead or Black Rock Road to the Virgin River via Atkin Spring and Sullivan Canyon; expect some rough and poorly defined sections. The lower trailhead lies 1.5 miles downstream and across the Virgin River from Virgin River Canyon Recreation Area, near I-15, 20 miles southwest of St. George; check the depth of the Virgin River carefully and turn back if it's too high to cross safely.

Hikers have a choice of approaching Cougar Spring Trailhead from the east via Black Rock Road (#1004), a pretty route through ponderosa pines on Black Mountain (good camping and a few picnic tables); from the south via Lime Kiln Canyon (#242) and other roads; or from the west on the very steep Elbow Canyon Road (#299; best driven downhill).

From St. George, take the I-15 Bloomington Exit 4, head east 1.8 miles (becomes Brigham Road), turn south 3.8 miles on River Road to the Arizona border and continue south another 20 miles on Quail Hill Road (#1069), turn right 25 miles on Black Rock Road (#1004), then right .5 miles to the trailhead.

If coming from Toroweap, take County 5 to Mt. Trumbull Schoolhouse, turn north 40 miles on County 5, then left 25 miles on Black Rock Road (#1004) and right .5 miles to the trailhead. If you're feeling adventurous and have a high-clearance 4WD vehicle, Elbow Canyon Road (#299) is an option—head west from the trailhead, climb a bit to a pass, then plummet down the rough road to the desert plains below. Loose rock makes this drive much easier going downhill. Mesquite is about 18 miles from the trailhead. Lots of other very scenic roads head toward the Virgin Mountains too; see the Arizona Strip Visitor Map.

From Mesquite, Nevada, turn south .9 miles on Riverside Road, (just east of Oasis Casino), then turn left onto Lime Kiln Canyon Road 242 (just after crossing the Virgin River bridge). After .9 miles you'll see the road to Elbow Canyon on the left, but keep straight 16 miles for Lime Kiln Canyon, go over a pass, and descend past some pretty red sandstone outcroppings, then turn left 22 miles on BLM Road 1041 to Cougar Spring Trailhead.

Littlefield and Beaver Dam

These two farming communities lie near the Virgin River on opposite sides of I-15 in Arizona's extreme northwest corner. Turn north .6 miles from Beaver Dam Exit 8 for **Hamilton Ranch Golf Resort** (928/347-5111 or 866/626-5006, www.hamiltonranchgolf.com), a historic hotel and former movie-star retreat on old Highway 91. The restaurant ($7–12) serves breakfast and lunch daily year-round and dinner daily during the cooler months. Golfers play on an 18-hole course. A gas station/grocery store is nearby. Mesquite, Nevada, offers motels, restaurants, supermarkets, and glitter just eight miles west on I-15.

Beaver Dam Mountains Wilderness

This 19,600-acre wilderness includes alluvial plains and the rugged mountains north of I-15 in extreme northwestern Arizona and part of adjacent Utah. Desert bighorn sheep, desert tortoises, raptors, the endangered woundfin minnow, Joshua trees, and several rare plant species live here. There are no trails, but you can hike cross-country through the beautiful Joshua tree forest and explore canyons. Unpaved BLM Road 1005, 10 miles long, follows a corridor through the wilderness, providing easy access. The east end begins at I-15 Cedar Pocket Exit 18, opposite the Virgin River Recreation Area, 20 miles southwest of St. George. The west end (no sign) turns off between Mileposts 14 and 15 of Highway 91, 5.5 miles north of I-15 Beaver Dam Exit 8.

Virgin River Canyon Recreation Area

Picnic areas ($2) and campsites ($8) overlook the Virgin River at this scenic spot just south of I-15 Cedar Pocket Exit 18. It's open year-round with water, grills, flush toilets, and some shade ramadas, but no showers or hookups; the gate closes at 9 P.M. Expect hot weather in summer at this 2,260-foot elevation. Groups can reserve day-use and camping areas with the BLM's Arizona Strip office in St. George (435/688-3200). A .2-mile nature trail leads to hilltop views, where interpretive signs explain the unusual geology of the canyon at this transition between the Colorado Plateau and the Basin and Range Province; trailhead parking is on the left where the picnic and campground roads divide. Other trails drop from the picnic and camping areas to the river.

Beaver Dam Mountains

River-Running on the Virgin

Experienced white-water boaters prepared for changing conditions can tackle the Virgin River. A minimum of about 1,000 cubic feet per second (cfs) is needed, which doesn't occur every year; spring, and especially May, offers the best chance of sufficient flow. No permits are needed. The Interagency Visitor Center in St. George can advise on river travel and possibly on local boat rentals and shuttle services. River-runners can put in at the Man of War Road bridge in Bloomington, just south of St. George. Take-out can be at the last I-15 bridge or farther down on slow water near the Arizona town of Beaver Dam.

Little Black Mountain Petroglyph Site

Impressive groups of rock art, some believed to have calendar functions, cover boulders at the base of this mesa just south into Arizona from St. George. Archaeologists have discovered more than 500 individual designs. A short trail winds past the petroglyphs, where signs describe some of their features. From St. George, take the I-15 Bloomington Exit 4, head east 1.8 miles (becomes Brigham Road), turn south 3.8 miles on River Road to the Arizona border and continue south .4 miles on unpaved Quail Hill Road (#1069), turn east 4.5 miles to a T-junction (there's a gate on the way), then left into the parking area, which has a picnic table and outhouse.

Cottonwood Point Wilderness

This 6,860-acre wilderness contains jagged pinnacles, wooded canyons, and part of the multicolored 1,000-foot-high Vermilion Cliffs. Springs and seeps in the main canyon east of Cottonwood Point support a world of greenery surrounded by desert. The wilderness lies on the Utah border near Colorado City, west of Fredonia. Dirt roads from Highway 389 and Colorado City provide access; check with the BLM for trailhead directions.

FREDONIA

Though just a tiny town, Fredonia (pop. 1,220) is the largest community on the Arizona Strip. Mormon polygamists, seeking refuge from federal agents, settled here in 1885. They first called the place Hardscrabble but later chose the name Fredonia, perhaps a contraction of the words *freedom* and *doña* (Spanish for wife). Kanab, seven miles north in Utah, offers a much larger selection of accommodations, restaurants, shopping, and recreation.

The town's modest motels lie along Main Street (U.S. 89A). **Grand Canyon Motel** (175 S. Main St., 928/643-7646, $30–35 d) stays open year-round; there's no extra charge for tax or kitchenettes. Lying across the street from each other are the tiny **Ship Rock Motel** (337 S. Main St., 928/643-7355, $30–37 d) and **Blue Sage Motel & RV** (330 S. Main St., 928/643-7125, $35–40 d, $15 RV w/hookups); both places close in winter. Pine furnishings decorate rooms of the **Crazy Jug Motel** (465 S. Main St., 928/643-7752, $40–50 d); RV spaces cost $15 and include showers; tenters can stay here for $4.35/person.

For Mexican and American food, dine at **Nedra's Café** (165 N. Main St., 928/643-7591, daily breakfast, lunch, and dinner in summer, then closed Mon. the rest of the year, $6–13); popular entrées include carnitas (roast pork) and chicken chimichangas with white creamy jalapeño sauce. The **Crazy Jug Restaurant** (467 S. Main St., 928/643-7712, daily breakfast, lunch, and dinner, closed in winter, $5–15) serves American food. A couple of convenience stores in town offer groceries.

The **post office** (85 N. Main St.) is in the center of town. A **city park** on 2nd East has picnic tables, a playground, and a pool; turn east three blocks on Brown or Hortt from Main Street. The **public library** (130 N. Main St., 928/643-7137) has Internet computers.

The **Fredonia Welcome Center** (900 N. Main St., P.O. Box 217, Fredonia, AZ 86022, 928/643-7777, 9 A.M.–5 P.M. Mon.–Sat., closed winter) offers information about area attractions and services; there's a rest area here also.

Folks at the **North Kaibab Ranger District** (430 S. Main St., P.O. Box 248, Fredonia, AZ 86022, 928/643-7395, www.fs.fed.us/r3/kai, 8 A.M.–5 P.M. Mon.–Fri.) will tell you about hiking, Grand Canyon viewpoints, and the back roads of the national forest north of the Grand Canyon.

After hours, you can pick up information inside the vestibule. The Kaibab National Forest map (North Kaibab Ranger District) sold here is a must for exploring the Kaibab Plateau.

PIPE SPRING NATIONAL MONUMENT

Excellent exhibits at this early Mormon ranch, southwest of Fredonia, provide a look into Paiute and frontier life. The abundant water here first attracted prehistoric Basket Maker and Pueblo tribes, who settled nearby more than 1,000 years ago, then moved on. Paiutes, who believe they're related to these people, arrived later and now live on the surrounding Kaibab-Paiute Indian Reservation; in earlier times, they spent summers on the Kaibab Plateau and winters near Pipe Spring.

Mormons found the spring in 1858 and began ranching five years later, despite Navajo raiders who occasionally stole stock and were suspected of having killed two Mormon men who pursued them. Raids ended after 1870 when Mormons and Navajo signed a treaty. Mormon leader Brigham Young then decided to move the church's southern Utah cattle herd to Pipe Spring. A pair of two-story stone houses went up with walls connecting the ends to form a protected courtyard; workers added gun ports just in case, but the settlement was never attacked.

© BILL WEIR

the parlor in Winsor Castle

The structure became known as Winsor Castle—the ranch superintendent, Anson P. Winsor, possessed a regal bearing and was thought to be related to the English royal family. Winsor built up a sizable herd of cattle and horses and oversaw farming and the ranch dairy.

A telegraph office—the first in Arizona—opened in 1871, bringing the rest of the world closer. Eventually, so many newlyweds passed through after marriage in the St. George Temple that the road past Pipe Spring became known as the Honeymoon Trail. In the 1880s, the Mormon Church came under increasing assault from the U.S. government, primarily over the practice of polygamy. Fearing that the feds would soon seize church property, the church sold Winsor Castle to a non-Mormon in 1895.

President Harding proclaimed Pipe Spring a national monument in 1923 "as a memorial of Western pioneer life." Today, National Park Service staff keep the frontier spirit alive by maintaining the ranch much as it was in the 1870s. Activities such as gardening, weaving, spinning, quilt making, cheese making, and butter churning still take place, albeit on a smaller scale. Guided tours of Winsor Castle depart frequently, and explain how people lived here in the early days. On your own, you can explore the gardens, cowboy shacks, and traditional Paiute *kahn* (shelters). Demonstrations of Paiute food and crafts, along with other special programs, take place mainly on summer mornings and on weekends in spring and autumn. The half-mile-loop **Ridge Trail** climbs the hill behind the ranch to a viewpoint, where signs describe the history and geology of the area. Paiute guides offer a walking tour to a nearby rock art site for a fee; call ahead on a weekday to the tribal office (928/643-7245). Pipe Spring National Monument lies north off Highway 389, 14 miles southwest of Fredonia.

Visitors Center

Exhibits (928/643-7105, www.nps.gov/pisp, 8 A.M.–5 P.M. daily, extended in summer, $4 age 17 up) illustrate Paiute history and culture, as well as introduce the pioneers and cowboys who spent time here. A gift shop has a good selection of regional books, maps, and Southwestern Native American arts and crafts. Hikers may be able to obtain last-minute backcountry permits for the Grand Canyon National Park, a useful service for some North Rim destinations.

Campground and Services

Just northeast of the monument, the Paiute tribe operates a bargain-priced campground (928/643-7245 tribal office, $5 tent, $10 RV w/hookups). It's open year-round with showers, which are also available to non-campers for a small fee. Register with the campground host, gas station, or tribal office. There's a gas station/convenience store at the highway turnoff. The nearest restaurants and motels are in Fredonia and Kanab.

Page and the Northeastern Arizona Strip

PAGE

Until 1957, only sand and desert vegetation lay atop Manson Mesa (elev. 4,300 feet) in far northern Arizona, where Page now sits. That's when workers converged to build one of the largest construction projects ever undertaken—Glen Canyon Dam. The concrete structure gradually grew to a height of 710 feet, creating a lake covering 250 square miles with a shoreline of nearly 2,000 miles.

Prefabricated metal buildings for barracks, dining hall, and offices sprouted on the mesa. Trailers rolled in, one serving as a bank, another as a school. Newly planted grass and trees brought a touch of green to the desert. The remote spot gradually turned into a modern town with schools, businesses, and churches. Page (pop. 9,500), named by the Bureau of Reclamation for one of its commissioners, is the largest community close to Lake Powell and offers travelers a variety of places to stay and eat.

With the Arizona Strip to the west, Glen Canyon National Recreation Area to the north, and the Navajo Reservation to the east and south, Page makes a handy base for visiting all of these areas. The town overlooks Lake Powell and Glen Canyon Dam. The extensive services of Lake Powell Resorts & Marinas lie just six miles away at Wahweap.

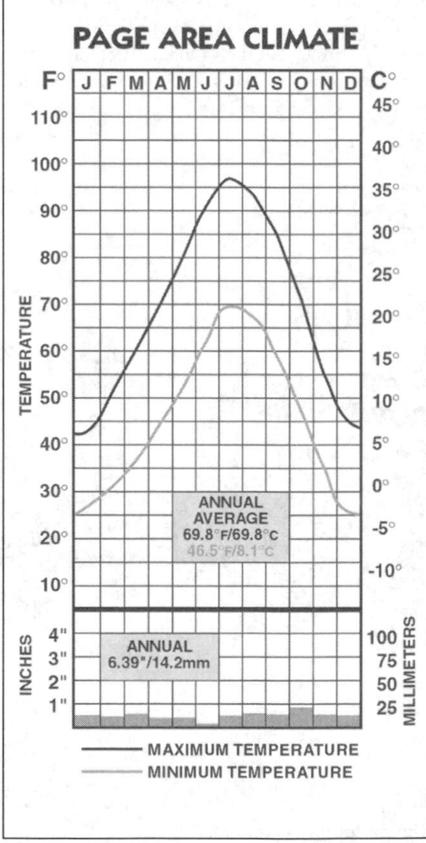

AVALON PUBLISHING

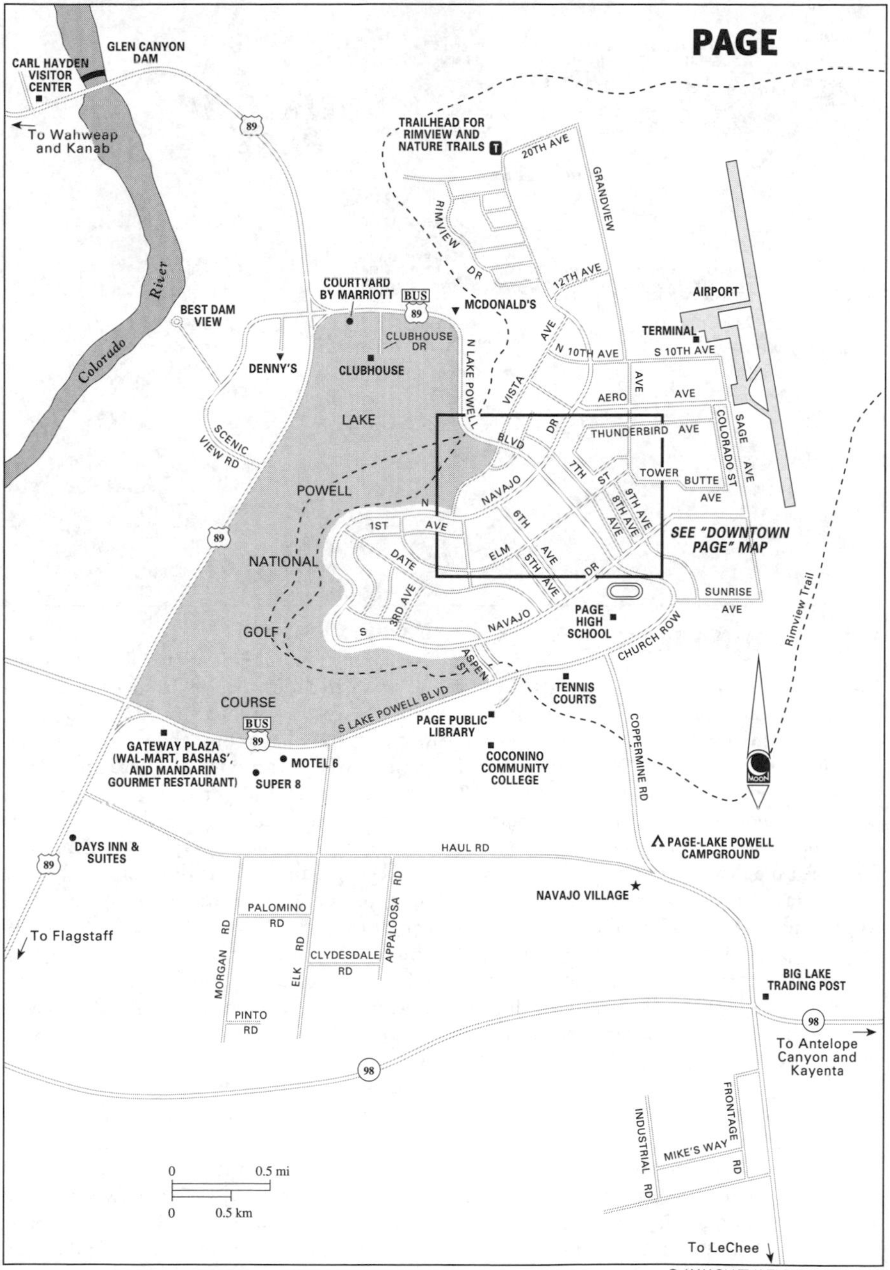
PAGE
GLEN CANYON DAM
CARL HAYDEN VISITOR CENTER
To Wahweap and Kanab
Colorado River
TRAILHEAD FOR RIMVIEW AND NATURE TRAILS
20TH AVE
GRANDVIEW
RIMVIEW DR
12TH AVE
COURTYARD BY MARRIOTT
BEST DAM VIEW
MCDONALD'S
AIRPORT
TERMINAL
CLUBHOUSE DR
CLUBHOUSE
DENNY'S
N LAKE POWELL
VISTA AVE
N 10TH AVE
S 10TH AVE
AERO AVE
LAKE POWELL NATIONAL GOLF COURSE
SCENIC VIEW RD
BLVD
DR
THUNDERBIRD AVE
COLORADO ST
SAGE AVE
7TH ST
TOWER BUTTE AVE
NAVAJO
9TH AVE
8TH AVE
6TH AVE
1ST AVE
SEE "DOWNTOWN PAGE" MAP
DATE
ELM
5TH AVE
DR
3RD AVE
SUNRISE AVE
NAVAJO
PAGE HIGH SCHOOL
CHURCH ROW
Rimview Trail
ASPEN ST
TENNIS COURTS
S LAKE POWELL BLVD
PAGE PUBLIC LIBRARY
COPPERMINE RD
GATEWAY PLAZA (WAL-MART, BASHAS', AND MANDARIN GOURMET RESTAURANT)
MOTEL 6
SUPER 8
COCONINO COMMUNITY COLLEGE
DAYS INN & SUITES
HAUL RD
PAGE-LAKE POWELL CAMPGROUND
NAVAJO VILLAGE
PALOMINO RD
APPALOOSA RD
To Flagstaff
MORGAN RD
ELK RD
CLYDESDALE RD
BIG LAKE TRADING POST
PINTO RD
To Antelope Canyon and Kayenta
INDUSTRIAL RD
FRONTAGE RD
MIKE'S WAY
0 0.5 mi
0 0.5 km
To LeChee

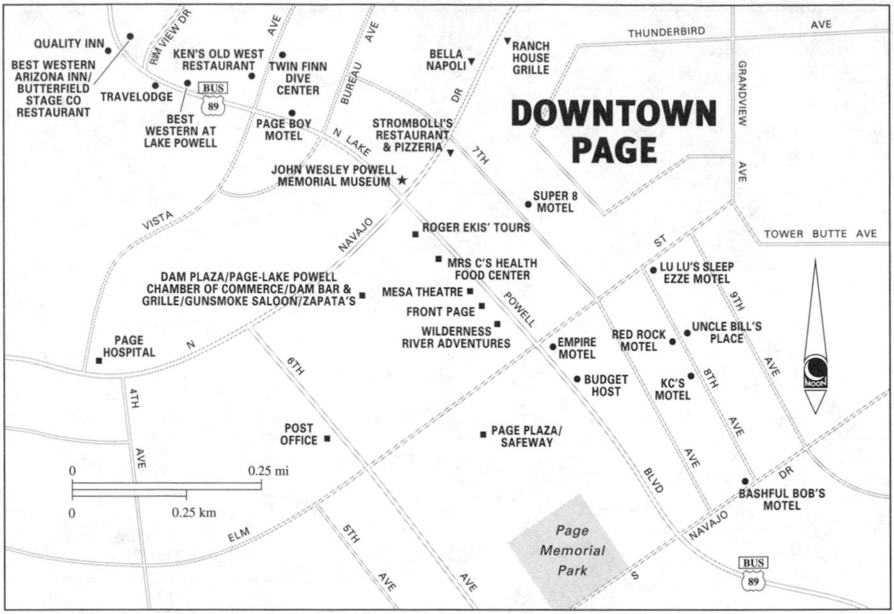

SIGHTS AND HIKES

Powell Museum

This varied collection (6 N. Lake Powell Blvd., 928/645-9496 or 888/597-6873, www.powellmuseum.org, 9 A.M.–5 P.M. Mon.–Fri., call for weekend hours, closed mid-Dec.–mid-Feb., $3 adults, $2 seniors 62+, $1 kids 5–12) honors scientist and explorer John Wesley Powell. In 1869 Powell led the first expedition down the Green and Colorado River canyons, then ran the rivers a second time in 1871–1872. It was he who named the most splendid section the Grand Canyon.

Old drawings and photographs illustrate Powell's life and voyages. Fossil and mineral displays interpret the thick geologic sections revealed by the canyons of the Colorado River system. Other exhibits contain pottery, baskets, weapons, and tools of Southwestern tribes, as well as memorabilia of early river runners, Page's early days, and Glen Canyon Dam. You can watch related videos on request. Regional books, videos, and posters are for sale. Staff offer travel info and can book Lake Powell boat tours, float trips, Antelope Canyon tours, and scenic flights.

Navajo Village

Navajo offer cultural programs about their beliefs and traditional skills from April to October at this living museum (928/660-0304, www.navajo-village.com). The four-hour program **An Evening with the Navajo** begins with demonstrations of cooking, weaving, and silversmithing, along with explanations of the sweat lodge and the two types of hogans here. You'll enjoy a dinner of traditional foods, watch song and dance performances, and listen to campfire stories. Cost is $50 adults and $35 children 6–13, plus tax. You can also sign up for a shorter evening program. Page–Lake Powell Chamber of Commerce and the Powell Museum also sell tickets.

The Best Dam View

An excellent panorama of Glen Canyon Dam and the Colorado River can be enjoyed just west of town. It's reached via Scenic View Road behind Denny's Restaurant off U.S. Highway 89; turn west at the junction of U.S. Highway 89 and N. Lake Powell Boulevard or west beside the Glen Canyon N.R.A. headquarters building and turn

arch in Lower Antelope Canyon

at the sign for Scenic Overlook. A short trail leads down to the best viewpoint.

Rimview Trail

An eight-mile trail for walkers, joggers, and cyclists encircles Page with many views of the surrounding desert and Lake Powell. The unpaved route generally follows the edge of the mesa and has some sandy and rocky sections that will challenge novice bike riders. If you find yourself more than 30 vertical feet below the mesa rim, you're off the trail. You can pick up a map from the Chamber of Commerce. A popular starting point is at the short nature-trail loop near Lake View School at N. Navajo Drive and 20th Avenue in the northern part of town.

Antelope Canyon

You'll see photos around town of the beautifully convoluted rock in this canyon, so narrow in places that you have to squeeze through. Sunshine reflects off the smooth Navajo Sandstone to create extraordinary light and colors that entrance visitors. Light beams reach the floor of upper Antelope only at midday May–August. Photographers need to bring a tripod to help capture the infinite colors, shapes, and patterns. Check the weather forecast before heading out, as slot canyons are deadly during a flash flood.

Antelope Canyon has a wider upper section known as "Corkscrew" that's exceptionally user-friendly—it's an easy walk on the sandy floor all the way through. The narrower lower section has ladders and requires a bit of scrambling. The shallow wash in between that you see from the highway gives no hint of the marvels up- or downstream. Both sections can easily be reached from Page by driving south on Coppermine Road or east on Highway 98 to the junction at Big Lake Trading Post, then continuing east one mile on Highway 98 toward the power plant. Turn right into the parking area for the upper canyon, or turn left half a mile on paved Antelope Point Road for the lower canyon. You'll pay $6 for a tribal entry permit—good for all sections—plus shuttle or entry fees. Sightseers can tour either section easily in an hour; photographers will probably wish to spend more time. The upper section has a $15 shuttle charge for the 3.5-mile drive to the trailhead and a one-hour guided visit; no walk-ins or private drive-ins are permitted. The cost increases to $25 for a two-hour photographer tour; a two-hour stay limit may apply. The lower canyon can be visited on guided or self-guided walks for $12.50 plus the $6 park fee. Children pay less. Guided excursions from Page to upper Antelope tend to be more convenient and cost only slightly more.

Rattlesnake Canyon, located near upper Antelope, also has beautiful narrow passages. It's reserved for photographers, who pay $25 for the first hour and $5 each additional hour. The upper Antelope ticket office provides a shuttle service.

The upper canyon ticket booth is usually open 8 A.M.–5 P.M. daily April–Oct., then about 9 A.M.–3 P.M. daily in winter. The lower canyon closes by 4 P.M. Note that these hours are the same as Page, which does not go on Daylight Savings Time. Try to avoid coming late in the day as the canyons may close early if business is slow. For information and off-season access, call the Antelope Canyon Navajo Tribal Park (928/698-2808) in LeChee, four miles south of Page. Both the upper canyon ticket booth and the LeChee office issue Rainbow Bridge hiking permits.

Horseshoe Bend Overlook

The Colorado River makes a sharp bend below this spectacular viewpoint. Look for the parking area just west of U.S. Highway 89, .2 miles south of Milepost 545; it's 2.5 miles south of Page's Gateway Plaza. A three-quarter-mile trail (one-way) leads from the parking, over a sandy ridge, to the overlook. Photographers will find a wide-angle lens useful for taking in the whole scene. Late mornings have good light for pictures; afternoons can be dramatic if the sky is filled with clouds.

PRACTICALITIES

Entertainment and Events

Catch movies at **Mesa Theatre** (42 S. Lake Powell Blvd., 928/645-9565). Fishing tournaments run March–September on the lake; contact Wahweap Marina. An Easter Sunrise Service takes place beside the lake at Wahweap. John Wesley Powell Days presents storytelling, art and photo contests, and a hilarious dry-land boat race in summer, usually in June.

On July 4th, there's a parade and fireworks.

© BILL WEIR

Horseshoe Bend

Mr. Burfel's Softball Tournament plays in September. On the Saturday before Halloween, see a huge jack-o-lantern display and a crafts show. In mid-November, Page–Lake Powell Balloon Regatta takes to the air and stages a balloon glow Saturday evening. In December, the Here Comes Santa Parade marks the holiday season in Page. The Wahweap Festival of Lights Parade on Lake Powell glides by on the first Saturday in December.

Shopping and Services

Blair's Trading Post (626 N. Navajo Dr., 928/645-3008 or 800/644-3008, www.blairstradingpost.com) has the feel of an old-style trading post. Ask to see the old Native American works and mementos of the family's trading business in the exhibit rooms upstairs.

DigitalLANDS (36 S. Lake Powell Blvd., 928/645-2241) provides an Internet café with technical support; you can download and copy digital photos to CD-ROM here. **Foto Quick** (644 Elm St., 928/645-5360) can take care of almost any digital, print, or E6 slide need, and customers get free Internet time.

The **post office** (44 6th Ave. 928/645-2571) and **Page Hospital** (501 N. Navajo Dr. and Vista Ave., 928/645-2424) are both near downtown.

Recreation

City of Page Memorial Park provides tables, playground, and greenery off S. Navajo Drive in the center of town.

Play **tennis** at the courts on S. Lake Powell Boulevard. **Lake Powell National Golf Course** (928/645-2023) offers a year-round, 18-hole championship course that wraps around the west side of the mesa; turn on Clubhouse Drive adjacent to the Courtyard by Marriott. **Twin Finn Diving Center** (811 Vista Ave., 928/645-3114, www.twinfinn.com) provides a variety of diving classes and rentals, plus kayak rentals and tours.

Accommodations

All Page motels lie on or near Lake Powell Boulevard, a 3.25-mile semicircle that branches off U.S. Highway 89. Page can be a busy place in summer, so it's a good idea to call ahead for reservations then. The summer rates listed here drop in winter (Nov.–March); expect to pay extra for views of the lake. Wahweap offers resort accommodations nearby at Lake Powell. (See the *Glen Canyon National Recreation Area* section.)

Under $50

The 8th Avenue apartments lie in Page's "historic district," a quiet residential area two blocks off Lake Powell Boulevard. They date from 1958–1959, and were built to house supervisors and foremen for the dam.

Lu Lu's Sleep EZZE Motel (105 8th Ave., 928/608-0273 or 800/553-6211, lulus@canyoncountry.net, $49–59 d) features some of the most luxurious rooms on this street. **Red Rock Motel** (114 8th Ave., 928/645-0062, www.redrockmotel.com, $39 s, $49 d) offers rooms, some with kitchens, plus two- and three-bedroom suites; all have private baths.

Uncle Bill's Place (117 8th Ave., 928/645-1224 or 888/359-0945, www.canyon-country.com/unclebill) has a worldwide reputation for the exceptional hospitality provided by Uncle Bill and his wife Françoise. Guests also enjoy the quiet garden and barbecue patio in back. Each unit includes a kitchen. You have a choice of apartments with shared bath and kitchen ($36 s, $39 d) or private one-bedroom ($49–69 up to 4 people), two-bedrooms ($89 up to 5), and three-bedrooms ($119 up to 6).

KC's Motel (126 8th Ave., 928/645-2947, www.kcmotel.com) offers rooms for $35–39 d and two-bedroom units for $49–69 d, all with private bath. You'll meet KC, the dog who runs the place, as well as his owner, Dick. **Bashful Bob's Motel** (around the corner at 750 S. Navajo Dr., 928/645-3919, www.bashfulbobsmotel.com, $32 s, $39 d and up) offers mostly two-bedroom apartments, all with kitchens.

$50–100

Courtyard by Marriott (600 Clubhouse Dr., 928/645-5000 or 800/851-3855, $69–99 d) offers views, restaurant, pool, hot tub, exercise room, and an adjacent 18-hole golf course.

Best Western Arizona Inn (716 Rim View Dr. and N. Lake Powell Blvd., 928/645-2466 or 800/826-2718, $89 d, $99 d lake view) provides fine views, pool, fitness room, and an adjacent restaurant. **Best Western at Lake Powell** (208 N. Lake Powell Blvd., 928/645-5988 or 888/794-2888, $89–99 d) has mountain views, pool, hot tub, and an exercise room.

Travelodge (207 N. Lake Powell Blvd., 928/645-2451 or 800/578-7878, $60–70 d) offers a pool and some three-bedroom suites ($155) that can accommodate up to eight people. The town's first motel, the recently remodeled **Page Boy Motel** (150 N. Lake Powell Blvd., 928/645-2416, $55 d) includes a pool.

South from downtown, you'll find **Motel 6** (637 S. Lake Powell Blvd., 928/645-5888 or 800/466-8356, $54 s, $60 d) with a pool. Next door, **Super 8** (649 S. Lake Powell Blvd., 928/645-5858 or 800/800-8000, $80 d) also offers a pool.

Lake Powell Days Inn & Suites (961 Hwy. 89, 928/645-2800 or 877/525-3769, $69–94 d) lies on the south edge of town beside U.S. Highway 89 with a pool and hot tub; some rooms have balconies. **Canyon Colors Bed & Breakfast** (225 S. Navajo Dr., 928/645-5979 or 800/536-2530, www.canyoncolors.com, $75–95 d) provides fireplaces, pool, and a patio with gas grill.

Campgrounds

Page–Lake Powell Campground (.7 miles southeast of downtown at 849 S. Coppermine Rd., 928/645-3374, $17 tents, $22–28 RVs w/hookups) has an indoor pool and hot tub, store, laundry, and showers; non-guests may use the showers or dump station for a small fee. Another campground and an RV park are in the Wahweap area.

Food

Ken's Old West (718 Vista Ave., 928/645-5160, daily dinner, closed Sun.–Wed. in winter, $10–23) serves up steaks, prime rib, chicken, and seafood in a Western setting; bands perform most nights in summer, and there's a patio out back. **Dam Bar & Grille** (644 N. Navajo Dr. in the Dam Plaza, 928/645-2161, Mon.–Sat. summer lunch, daily year-round dinner, $9–25) fixes steak, barbecue, seafood, pasta, and sandwiches; it also has a patio and a sports bar. Memorabilia and photos of the dam, lake, and boating decorate the spacious interior. The adjacent **Gunsmoke Saloon** (928/645-1888, Tues.–Sat. evenings) features billiards and dancing with a variety of music in a Western setting. Also next door, **Beans Gourmet Coffee** (open daily, but closes noon on Sun.) energizes with java and snacks. **Ranch House Grille** (819 N. Navajo Dr., 928/645-1420, daily breakfast and lunch, $5–10) is a great place for breakfast, served all day.

Picture windows frame a view of Lake Powell and the Vermilion Cliffs at the **Butterfield Stage Co. Restaurant** (704 Rim View Dr., 928/645-2467, daily breakfast, lunch, and dinner, $9–26) next to the Best Western Arizona Inn. You can dine on steak, prime rib, seafood, and other popular American food inside or on the large patio; either makes a great place to watch the sunset.

At the Courtyard by Marriott, **Pepper's Restaurant** (600 Clubhouse Dr., 928/645-5000, daily breakfast, lunch, and dinner, $10–20) prepares American and continental cuisine with a Southwestern touch; it offers buffets at breakfast year-round and at lunch on summer weekdays.

Italian paintings set the scene for dining at **Bella Napoli** (810 N. Navajo Dr., 928/645-2706, Mon.–Fri. lunch, Mon.–Sat. dinner, $10–28) which serves a fine selection of pasta, pizza, seafood, steak, chicken, and veal dishes; you have a choice of indoor or patio seating. The informal **Strombolli's Restaurant & Pizzeria** (711 N. Navajo Dr., 928/645-2605, daily lunch and dinner, closed Nov.–Feb., $8–18) provides a choice of indoor seating or an outdoor deck—a popular gathering spot for boaters in the summer.

Fiesta Mexicana (125 S. Lake Powell Blvd., 928/645-4082, daily lunch and dinner, $9–17) offers a variety of Mexican food, including many seafood dishes, in a vibrant dining room. **Zapata's** (614 N. Navajo Dr. in the Dam Plaza, 928/645-9006, daily lunch and dinner, $8–20) specializes in Sonoran cuisine; there's a patio in front.

For Chinese cuisine, try **Mandarin Gourmet Restaurant** (Gateway Plaza #683, 928/645-5516, daily lunch and dinner, $8–25); there's a buffet option for lunch and occasionally for dinner.

You can buy groceries at **Safeway** (Page Plaza), **Bashas'** (Gateway Plaza), and **Mrs. C's Health Food Center** (34 S. Lake Powell Blvd.).

Information

Centrally located in the Dam Plaza, the **Page–Lake Powell Chamber of Commerce** (644 N. Navajo Dr., Box 727, Page, AZ 86040, 928/645-2741 or 888/261-7243, www.pagelakepowellchamber.org) offers information about area sights and services, and can book lake and river tours, Antelope Canyon tours, and scenic flights. It's open 8 A.M.–6 P.M. Monday–Saturday April–September, then 9 A.M.–5 P.M. Monday–Friday the rest of the year.

The semicircular **Page Public Library** (479 S. Lake Powell Blvd., 928/645-4270, 10 A.M.–8 P.M. Mon.–Thurs., 10 A.M.–5 P.M. Fri.–Sat.) rises impressively from the mesa rim with fine views; it has an Arizona/Native American collection and Internet computers, but non–card holders must pay a fee to get online.

Front Page (48 S. Lake Powell Blvd., 928/645-5333) has regional titles, general reading, office supplies, and Antelope Canyon tours.

Getting There and Around

Great Lakes Airlines (www.greatlakesav.com) operates daily scheduled flights south to Phoenix and northeast to Denver; make reservations with United Airlines (800/241-6522) or Frontier (800/432-1359). **America West Express** (800/235-9292) flies to Phoenix.

Grand Circle Shuttle (928/645-6806, www.grandcircleshuttle.com) provides a taxi service around town and regional transport within a 300-mile radius. Wahweap Lodge operates **Page Shuttle** (928/645-2433) to Page and the airport. Most area motels also provide transportation for guests to and from the airport. **Buggy Rent-a-Car** (12 N. Lake Powell Blvd., 928/645-9347) has all sorts of vehicles. **Avis** (928/645-2024 or 800/522-2847) and **Enterprise** (928/645-1449 or 800/736-8222) offer cars at the airport.

Tours

You can obtain information and make reservations for many area tours through the Page–Lake Powell Chamber of Commerce and the Powell Museum.

Overland Canyon Tours (18 N. Lake Powell Blvd., 928/608-4072) heads to upper Antelope Canyon; a six-hour photographic tour visits "Canyon X," a relatively unknown and uncrowded slot canyon. **Roger Ekis' Antelope Canyon Tours** (22 S. Lake Powell Blvd., 928/645-9102 or 435/675-9109, www.antelopecanyon.com) goes to upper Antelope Canyon except in winter. **Grand Circle Adventures** (48 S. Lake Powell Blvd. in Front Page, 928/645-5594, www.antelopeslotcanyontours.com) will take you to upper Antelope year-round. **Antelope Canyon Adventures** (104 S. Lake Powell Blvd., 928/645-5501 or 866/645-5501, www.jeeptour.com) offers regular and photographers' tours to upper Antelope year-round.

Wilderness River Adventures (50 S. Lake Powell Blvd., 928/645-3279 or 800/528-6154) offers raft trips down the Colorado River from just below Glen Canyon Dam to Lees Ferry, traveling over 15 miles of smooth-flowing water through the beautiful canyon of Navajo Sandstone. You'll stop to inspect some fine petroglyphs, and you're likely to see condors, blue herons, ducks, and other birds. Half-day trips leave once or twice daily March–October, weather permitting, for $62 adults, $52 children 12 and under.

Westwind (928/645-2494, 800/245-8668, www.westwindairtours.com) takes to the air in single-engine Cessnas to Rainbow Bridge (40 min., $94), the Grand Canyon (90 min., $162), Monument Valley (90 min., $162, $200 w/ground tour), and a Grand Canyon–Monument Valley tour (3 hours, $250, $285 with a ground tour), all with a two-person minimum. **Boat tours** to Rainbow Bridge and other destinations leave from nearby Wahweap.

GLEN CANYON NATIONAL RECREATION AREA

Surrounded by spectacular canyon country, Lake Powell forms the centerpiece of this vast 1.25 million-acre recreation area. Just a handful of roads approach the lake, so it's best to explore this unique land of water and rock by boat or on foot. As big as the lake is, it comprises only 13 percent of Glen Canyon National Recreation Area. The recreation area also includes a beautiful remnant of Glen Canyon between Glen Canyon

THE DROUGHT

In 2004, the Colorado Basin had entered its worst drought in 98 years of recorded history. Lake Powell stood at less than half its storage of just five years before. Lake Mead had dropped to about half its capacity. The Colorado River now flows once again in what were once the upper reservoirs. Former islands have become peninsulas, and upper-lake recreation areas such as Hite on Lake Powell and South Cove on Lake Mead no longer have water access. Forests on the Colorado Plateau, though drought-resistant, have become more vulnerable to bark beetle and other insect infestations. At least one scientist has proclaimed this a 500-year drought.

Dam and Lees Ferry and reminders of pioneer life at Lees Ferry and nearby Lonely Dell Ranch.

Rainbow Bridge National Monument—50 miles uplake from the dam—protects the world's largest natural bridge. You can reach it on boat tours from Wahweap, by your own boat, or by hiking in on spectacular trails.

Lake Powell

Of all the artificial lakes in the United States, only Lake Mead, farther downstream, has a greater water-storage capacity. When full, Lake Powell boasts a shoreline of 1,960 miles—greater than the west coast of the continental United States—and enough water to cover the state of Pennsylvania a foot deep! Bays and coves offer nearly limitless opportunities for exploration by boaters. Only the southern part lies in Arizona, where you'll find Glen Canyon Dam, Wahweap's resort and marina, Antelope and Navajo Canyons, and the lower parts of Labyrinth, Face, and West Canyons. Lake Powell's surface elevation fluctuates an average of 20–30 feet through the year (fluctuation has reached nearly 100 feet), peaking in July; it reaches 3,700 feet when full.

Unusually low lake levels in recent years have greatly affected the appearance of the lake. Marinas have had to adapt by extending boat ramps and repositioning docks. Hite, the farthest uplake marina, no longer had water access as of mid-2004. On the positive side, beaches and side canyons have reappeared for the first time in 30 years. Check with the marinas or at the Carl Hayden Visitor Center for current lake conditions.

Carl Hayden Visitor Center and Dam Tours

Perched beside the dam, the Carl Hayden Visitor Center (P.O. Box 1507, Page, AZ 86040, 928/608-6404, www.nps.gov/glca, 8 A.M.–7 P.M. daily in summer, 8 A.M.–5 P.M. daily the rest of the year) offers tours of the dam, exhibits, and an information desk for the Glen Canyon National Recreation Area. Photos, paintings, and video programs illustrate construction of the dam and introduce the recreation area. A giant relief map helps you visualize the rugged terrain surrounding the lake; look closely and you'll spot Rainbow Bridge. Guided one-hour tours visit the top of the dam, the tunnels, the generating room, and the transformer platform—call for times; no purses or bags may be taken on the tours nor are there storage lockers. Senator Carl Hayden, the visitors center's namesake, was a major backer of water development in the West, and served as an Arizona member of Congress 1912–1969, a record 57 consecutive years.

Staff operate an information desk where you can find out about boating, fishing, camping, hiking, and interpretive programs in the immense Glen Canyon National Recreation Area. The Glen Canyon Natural History Association (www.glencanyonassociation.org) sells a wide variety of regional books.

Glen Canyon Dam

Construction workers labored 1956–1964 to build this giant concrete structure. It stands 710 feet high above bedrock, the top measuring 1,560 feet across. Its thickness ranges from 300 feet at the base to just 25 feet at the top. As part of the Upper Colorado River Storage Project, the dam provides water storage (its main purpose), hydroelectricity, flood control, and recreation on Lake Powell. Eight giant turbine generators churn out more than 1.3 million kilowatts at 13,800 volts. Vertigo victims shouldn't look down when driving across Glen Canyon Bridge, just down-

© BILL WEIR

Glen Canyon Dam from the Colorado River

stream of the dam. The cold green waters of the Colorado River emerge 700 feet below.

Conservationists deplore the loss of remote and beautiful Glen Canyon, buried today beneath Lake Powell, and call for the removal of the dam. That's very unlikely in the near future, so for now, only words, pictures, and memories remind us of Glen Canyon's lost wonders.

Entry Fees

Visits to developed areas cost $10 per vehicle or $3 per cyclist or hiker for seven days—free if you have a National Parks Pass, Golden Eagle, Golden Age, or Golden Access card. The annual pass to the recreation area runs $20. A seven-day permit for motorized boats is $10, then $4 for each additional one on the same trailer; an annual boat pass runs $20. Admission to the Carl Hayden Visitor Center is free.

Recreation at Lake Powell

Boating: If you don't have your own craft, Wahweap and Bullfrog marinas will rent you a boat for touring, fishing, skiing, or houseboating. Boat tours visit Rainbow Bridge and other destinations from Wahweap Marina. Sailboats find the steadiest breezes in Wahweap, Padre, Halls, and Bullfrog Bays, where spring winds average 15–20 knots. Kayaks and canoes can be used in the more protected areas. All boaters need to be alert for approaching storms that bring wind gusts which can exceed 60 mph. Waves on open expanses of the lake are sometimes steeper than ocean waves and can exceed six feet from trough to crest. Marinas and bookstores sell Lake Powell navigation maps. The National Park Service provides public boat ramps and ranger offices at most of the marinas. National Park Service publications detail not only the recreation opportunities, but also the dangers to be aware of.

Fishing: You'll need an Arizona fishing license for the southern five miles of Lake Powell and a Utah license for the rest. Get licenses and information from marinas or from sporting goods stores in Page. Anglers can catch bass (largemouth, smallmouth, and striped), walleye, channel catfish, black crappie, and bluegill sunfish. Trout swim in the cool waters of the Colorado River below the dam; special regulations apply here. Anglers need to be able to identify the river's four endangered fish and release them.

Hiking: You can choose between easy day trips or long wilderness backpack treks. The canyons of the Escalante in Utah rate among America's premier hiking areas. Other good areas within or adjacent to Glen Canyon N.R.A. include Rainbow Bridge National Monument, Paria Canyon, Dark Canyon, and Grand Gulch. (The first two are described later in this chapter; see *Moon Handbooks Utah* for Dark Canyon and Grand Gulch, as well as Escalante.) National Park Service staff at the Carl Hayden Visitor Center (928/608-6404) and the Bullfrog Visitor Center (435/684-7420, closed in winter) can suggest trips and supply trail descriptions. Several guidebooks to Lake Powell offer detailed hiking, camping, and boating information. Most of the canyon country near Lake Powell remains wild and little explored—hiking possibilities are limitless. Be sure to carry plenty of water.

Mountain Biking: Cyclists can head out on many back roads. The visitors centers have lists of possibilities.

Scuba: Divers can visit the canyon cliffs and rock sculptures beneath the surface. Visibility runs 30–40 feet in late August–November, the best season, and there's less boat traffic then. In other seasons, visibility can drop to 10–20 feet.

Climate

Summer, when temperatures can rise to more than 100°F, is the busiest season for swimming, boating, and waterskiing. Spring and autumn are the best times to enjoy the backcountry and to fish. Winter temperatures drop to highs in the 40s and 50s, with freezing nights and the possibility of snow. Lake surface temperatures range from a comfortable 80°F in August to a chilly 45°F in January. Chinook winds can blow day and night February–May. Thunderstorms in late summer bring strong, gusting winds with widely scattered rain showers. Annual precipitation averages about seven inches.

Packing It Out

Much of the revenue from the fees has gone toward improving water quality and cleaning up the shore. Visitors can help by packing out all trash. Also, anyone camping within one quarter mile of the lake must have a container for solid human wastes, unless a toilet is available on the beach or on your own boat. Plastic bags, with the exception of NPS-approved waste bag containment systems, may not be used for this purpose. Camps need to be within 200 yards of a toilet, even at the primitive camping areas, such as Lone Rock, Upper Bullfrog, Stanton Creek, Farley Canyon, and Dirty Devil River. Ask at the Carl Hayden Visitor Center for locations of floating restrooms/pump-outs/dump stations and land-based dump stations.

Marinas

Lake Powell Resorts & Marinas (2233 W. Dunlap Ave., Phoenix, AZ 85021, 800/528-6154, 602/277-8888 greater Phoenix, or fax 602/331-5258, www.lakepowell.com) operates accommodations, RV parks, restaurants, marina services, boat rentals, and boat tours. Reservations are recommended, especially in summer. To make reservations seven days or fewer in advance, contact each marina or resort directly. The company provides services at Wahweap (928/645-2433) in Arizona and at Bullfrog (435/684-3000) and nearby Halls Crossing (435/684-7000) in Utah. A ferry (435/684-3000) crosses the lake between Bullfrog and Halls Crossing, saving a long detour by road. Farther uplake, Hite (435/684-2278) has accommodations, but no water access as of mid-2004 due to low lake levels. All the marinas stay open year-round; you can avoid crowds and peak prices by arriving in autumn, winter, or spring. Private or chartered aircraft can fly to Page Airport, Bullfrog's small airstrip, and Halls Crossing's large airstrip.

Another company is currently developing a resort and marina at Antelope Point on Navajo land in Arizona.

Wahweap

The name means Bitter Water in the Ute language. Wahweap lies seven miles northwest of Page; turn right on Lake Shore Drive .7 miles past the visitor center.

Lake Powell Resort offers several types of rooms—many with lake views—at $119 d

($139 d lake view) summer, less in winter; guests enjoy swimming pools and the exercise room. The lodge's fine-dining restaurant, the Rainbow Room (928/645-1162, daily breakfast, lunch, and dinner) features a panoramic view; in summer there's live entertainment and dancing. Buffets may be available in summer for breakfast and lunch. Bené Pizza serves pizza, sandwiches, and smoothies daily in summer near the boat ramp entrance. The boat tour desk and a large gift shop lie just off the lobby.

An **RV park** ($27) north and west of the lodge provides hookups, store, coin showers, laundry, and use of the resort's pools and exercise room. **Wahweap Campground** (mid-March–Oct., $15) just to the north has drinking water but no showers or hookups; no reservations taken. Campers may use the pay showers and laundry at the RV park. **Interpretive programs** are given here most summer evenings. Turnoffs for the RV park, campground, picnic area, and a fish-cleaning station lie between Lake Powell Resort and Stateline, 1.3 miles northwest of the resort. Beyond the Stateline area, you'll come to the picturesque **Coves Day-Use Area,** set on low white bluffs overlooking the lake and a few beaches. You'll find boat ramps just south of the lodge and across the Utah border at Stateline.

The resort offers a variety of **lake tours** (928/645-1070 same week, 800/528-6154 more than seven days ahead) ranging from an hour-long paddlewheel cruise around Wahweap Bay ($13) to a 7.5-hour trip to Rainbow Bridge, 50 miles away ($99). The other tours are a 90-minute Antelope Canyon cruise ($28), 3-hour Navajo Tapestry tour to Navajo and Antelope Canyons ($49), and a 2.5-hour dinner cruise ($61). Children 3–12 get a discount except on the dinner cruise. **Boat rentals** at Stateline include kayaks, personal watercraft, fishing boats, runabout, patio boats, and a variety of houseboats. You can also rent water skis and water toys.

Vicinity of Wahweap

Lone Rock in Utah, six miles northwest of Wahweap off U.S. Highway 89, is a primitive recreation area on the shore; there are outhouses but no drinking water, and the cost is $6/vehicle. **Boat camping** along the lakeshore is a great option for people with their own craft; you must carry a portable toilet and be more than one mile from developed areas.

Antelope Point offers a boat ramp, docks, and beach access southeast of Wahweap on the other side of Page. Plans are in the works to develop a full-service resort, but as of mid-2004 only houseboats were offered; you can check with Antelope Point Marina (602/952-0114 resort, 800/255-5561 houseboat rentals, www.azmarinas.com). From the junction of Coppermine Road and Highway 98 south of Page, turn east 1 mile on Highway 98, then turn left 5.5 miles on Antelope Point Road to the boat ramp and docks at road's end. Turn right .3 miles just before the boat ramp for beach access.

RAINBOW BRIDGE NATIONAL MONUMENT

Rainbow Bridge forms a graceful span 290 feet high and 275 feet wide; the Capitol building in Washington, D.C., would fit neatly underneath. The easiest way to reach Rainbow Bridge is by boat tour on Lake Powell from Wahweap Marina.

The more adventurous can hike to the bridge from the unmarked Cha Canyon Trailhead (just north across the Arizona–Utah border on the east side of Navajo Mountain) in 17.5 miles each way or from the Rainbow Lodge ruins (just south of the Arizona–Utah border on the west side of Navajo Mountain) in 13 miles each way. The rugged trails wind through highly scenic canyons, meet in Bridge Canyon, then continue two miles to the bridge. Hikers must be experienced and self-sufficient. The best times to go are April–early June, September, and October. Winter cold and snow discourage visitors, and summer is hot and can bring hazardous flash floods. Because the trails are unmaintained and poorly marked, hikers need to use topo maps. The Carl Hayden Visitor Center has trail notes and trailhead directions for the hikes and sells topo maps. Also see the monument's website, www.nps.gov/rabr.

The National Park Service cannot issue hiking permits to Rainbow Bridge. Obtain the required tribal permits from Cameron Visitor Center (P.O.

Rainbow Bridge

Box 459, Cameron, AZ 86020, 928/679-2303, fax 928/679-2330) or from the Navajo Parks and Recreation Department (P.O. Box 2520, Window Rock, AZ 86515, 928/871-6647, www.navajonationparks.org). Both offices are open 8 A.M.–5 P.M. Monday–Friday; the Cameron office may extend its hours 7 A.M.–6 P.M. daily in summer. In the Page area, permits are available at the upper Antelope Canyon ticket booth and the Antelope Canyon Navajo Tribal Park office (4 miles south of Page in LeChee, 928/698-2808).

LEES FERRY

The Colorado River cuts one gorge after another as it crosses the high plateaus of southern Utah and northern Arizona. Travelers found the river a dangerous and difficult barrier until well into the 20th century. A break in the cliffs above Marble Canyon provided one of the few places where a road could be built to the water's edge. Until 1929, when Navajo Bridge finally spanned the canyon, vehicles and passengers had to cross by ferry. Zane Grey expressed his thoughts about this crossing—Lees Ferry—in *The Last of the Plainsmen* (1908):

I saw the constricted rapids, where the Colorado took its plunge into the box-like head of the Grand Canyon of Arizona; and the deep, reverberating boom of the river, at flood height, was a fearful thing to hear. I could not repress a shudder at the thought of crossing above that rapid.

The Dominguez-Escalante Expedition tried to cross at what's now known as Lees Ferry in 1776, but without success. The river proved too cold and wide to swim safely, and winds frustrated attempts to raft across. The Spaniards traveled 40 miles upriver into present-day Utah before finding a safe ford.

About 100 years later, Mormon leaders determined the Lees Ferry crossing to be the most convenient route for expanding Mormon settlements from Utah into Arizona. Jacob Hamblin led a failed rafting attempt in 1860, but he returned four years later and made it safely across.

Although Hamblin first recognized the value of

NAVAJO BRIDGE— THE OLD AND THE NEW

A new, wider bridge for traffic has replaced the old Navajo Bridge across Marble Canyon. The old bridge, just upstream from the new one, is admired for its design and beauty, and has been preserved as a pedestrian bridge. Now you can enjoy a walk 470 feet above the water on the old bridge's 834-foot length. (Do not throw anything off the bridge, as even a small object can pick up lethal velocity from such a height and hurt boaters below.)

A 1930s stone shelter built by the Civilian Conservation Corps and the **Navajo Bridge Interpretive Center** (8 A.M.–5 P.M. daily mid-April–mid-Nov.) stand just west of the bridges. Indoor and outdoor exhibits illustrate the history and construction details of both bridges. Inside the interpretive center, you'll find local travel information for the Grand Canyon and Glen Canyon National Recreation Area, including nearby Lees Ferry. There's also a large selection of regional books, maps, posters, videos, and music. Navajo sell crafts on the old bridge's east end. Both ends of the old bridge have parking.

© BILL WEIR

In this view from Navajo Bridge, rafters take a break before heading into the Grand Canyon.

this crossing, it now bears the name of John D. Lee, a colorful character who gained notoriety in the 1857 Mountain Meadows Massacre. One account of this unfortunate chain of events relates that Paiute, allied to the Mormons, attacked an unfriendly wagon train; Lee and fellow Mormons then joined in the fighting until all but the small children, too young to tell the story, lay dead.

When a federal investigation some years later uncovered Mormon complicity in the slaughter, the Mormon Church leaders, seeking to move Lee out of sight, asked him to start a regular ferry service on the Colorado River. This he did in 1872. One of Lee's wives remarked on seeing the isolated spot, "Oh, what a lonely dell," and thus Lonely Dell became the name of their ranch. Lee managed to succeed with the ferry service despite boat accidents and sometimes hostile Navajo, but eventually his past caught up with him. In 1877, authorities took Lee back to Mountain Meadows, where a firing squad and casket awaited.

Miners and farmers came to try their luck along the Colorado River and its tributaries. Charles Spencer, manager of the American Placer Company, brought in sluicing machinery, an amalgamator, and drilling equipment. In 1910 his company tried using mule trains to pack coal from Warm Creek Canyon, 15 miles upstream. When the mules proved inadequate, company financiers shipped a 92-foot steamboat in sections from San Francisco. The boat, the *Charles H. Spencer,* proved underpowered and was used only five times. The boiler, decking, and hull can still be seen at low water on the shore upstream from Lees Ferry Fort. Although Spencer's efforts to extract fine gold particles proved futile, he persisted in his prospecting here as late as 1965 and made an unsuccessful attempt to develop a rhenium mine.

The ferry service continued after Lee's departure, though fatal accidents occurred from time to time. The last run took place in June 1928, while the bridge was being built six miles downstream. The ferry operator lost control in strong currents and the boat capsized; all three people aboard and a Model-T were lost, putting an end to 55 years of ferryboating. Navajo Bridge opened in January 1929, an event hailed by the Flagstaff *Coconino Sun* as the "Biggest News in Southwest History." Standing 470 feet above the Colorado River, it was the world's highest steel arch bridge at the time. No longer did travelers have to face a dangerous ferry crossing or detour 800 miles to reach the other side.

Information and Getting There

The Lees Ferry area and the canyon upstream belong to the Glen Canyon National Recreation Area. Grand Canyon National Park begins just downstream. Rangers of the National Park Service administer both areas. **Navajo Bridge Interpretive Center** (closed in winter) near the highway turnoff is the handiest source of information for Lees Ferry. The **ranger station** (on the left .4 miles after the campground turnoff, 928/355-2234) offers boating, fishing, and hiking information and sells some books and maps, but it is open irregular hours.

Entry fees for Glen Canyon National Recreation Area, which can be paid at a self-service station a half mile from U.S. Highway 89A, cost $10 per vehicle or $3 per cyclist or hiker for seven days; admission is free if you have a National Parks Pass, Golden Eagle, Golden Age, or Golden Access card.

A paved road to Lees Ferry turns north from U.S. Highway 89A just west of Navajo Bridge. Follow the road in 5.1 miles and turn left .2 miles for Lonely Dell Ranch Historic District or continue .7 miles on the main road to its end for Lees Ferry Historic District. A self-guided tour booklet, available on site as well as at the Navajo Bridge Interpretive Center and Carl Hayden Visitor Center, gives the history of the historic districts.

Lonely Dell Ranch

A log cabin thought to have been built by Lee, with root cellar, blacksmith shop, ranch house, orchards, and cemetery, survive at Lonely Dell Ranch, a short distance up the Paria River. A walking tour of the site is about one mile round-trip. Shade trees provide a respite from summer heat, and tables invite a picnic. Day hikers can head up the **Paria Canyon Trail** from here, but overnight trips should begin at the upper trailhead in Utah.

Lees Ferry

Historic buildings on the Colorado River include Lees Ferry Fort (built in 1874 to protect settlers from possible Indian attack, but used as a trading post, residence, then a mess hall), a small stone post office (in use 1913–1923), and structures occupied by the American Placer Company and the U.S. Geological Survey. The boiler, one of four used by Spencer's unsuccessful placer operation, was abandoned in 1912. A little farther upstream you'll pass the submerged wreck of Spencer's steamboat.

From 1872 to 1899 ferries used the area above Lees Ferry Fort to cross in high and medium water; they crossed below the Paria confluence in low water. In 1899 a cable strung across the river upstream made life easier for the ferrymen. A walk through the main historic district is about one mile round-trip, or two miles round-trip if you go all the way to the upper ferry site, now marked by the ruins of ferrymen's stone houses and a remnant of the cable. It's possible to continue about a half mile farther on trails used by anglers.

Spencer Trail

Energetic hikers climb this unmaintained trail for fine views of Marble Canyon from the rim 1,700 feet above the river. The ingeniously planned route switchbacks up sheer ledges from just beyond Spencer's boiler. It's a moderately difficult hike to the top, three miles round-trip; you should get a very early start in summer and carry plenty of water.

Cathedral Wash Route

This two-mile round-trip hike follows a narrow canyon to a beach at Cathedral Rapid. Park at the second pullout, overlooking the wash, on the road to Lees Ferry, 1.4 miles in from U.S. Highway 89A and 3 miles before the campground.

Fishing and Boating

Rainbow trout flourish in the cold, clear waters released from Lake Powell through Glen Canyon Dam. Special fishing regulations apply here and are posted. Anglers should be able to identify and must return to the river any of the endangered native fish—the Colorado pikeminnow, bonytail chub, humpback chub, and razorback sucker. There's a fish-cleaning station and parking area on the left just before the launch areas. At road's end, you'll reach a paved upriver launch site used by boaters headed toward Glen Canyon Dam; Grand Canyon river-running groups use the unpaved downriver launch area. Powerboats can travel 14.5 miles up Glen Canyon almost to the dam. The National Park Service recommends a boat with a minimum 10 hp motor to negotiate the swift currents. Boating below Lees Ferry is prohibited without a permit from Grand Canyon National Park.

Campground

The sites at Lees Ferry Campground cost $10 and have drinking water, shaded tables, and small trees but no hookups or showers; there's usually space available. Campers can use showers and laundry facilities beside Marble Canyon Lodge. From U.S. Highway 89A, take Lees Ferry Road in 4.4 miles and turn left at the sign. A dump station is on the right, .4 miles past the campground turnoff.

You can use the plentiful campsites along the Colorado River above Lees Ferry. These sites lack piped water but are free. Remember to purify river water before drinking and pack out what you pack in.

BELOW THE VERMILION CLIFFS

These sheer cliffs, a striking red, appear to burst into flame at sunrise and sunset. The cliffs dominate the northern horizon for many miles; a pullout on U.S. Highway 89A, 30 miles west of Marble Canyon and 11 miles east of Jacob Lake, offers the best view. John Wesley Powell described them as "a long bank of purple cliffs plowed from the horizon high into the heavens."

Marble Canyon Lodge

The 1926 lodge (928/355-2225 or 800/726-1789) is on U.S. Highway 89A at the turnoff for Lees Ferry. You can stay in motel rooms ($54 s, $64–70 d), a cottage ($86 with 4 beds), or two-bedroom apartments ($134). The restaurant (daily breakfast, lunch, and dinner, $10–22) serves American food. Other services include a store (Native American crafts, regional books, and supplies for camping, river-running, and fishing), post office, laundry, coin showers, gas station, convenience store, and a paved airstrip. Major John Wesley Powell named the nearby section of Colorado River canyon for its smooth, marblelike appearance.

THE EXPLORATION OF THE COLORADO RIVER AND ITS CANYONS

the heart of Marble Canyon

Marble Canyon Outfitters (928/355-2245 or 800/533-7339, www.mcg-leesferry.com) offers guided trips and a shop for anglers.

Lees Ferry Lodge at Vermilion Cliffs

The lodge (928/355-2231 or 800/451-2231, www.leesferrylodge.com, $47 s, $53 d and up) offers motel rooms, two-bedroom units, and an American restaurant (daily breakfast, lunch, and dinner, $10–23). It's on U.S. Highway

The Grand Canyon

89A, 3 miles west of Marble Canyon and 38 miles east of Jacob Lake.

Ambassador Guide Services (800/256-7596, www.ambassadorguides.com) provides guides and a fly shop for anglers.

Badger Canyon–Marble Canyon Overlook

A dirt road leads to the edge of precipitous cliffs where these two canyons meet. The cold waters of the Colorado glide below. You may see river runners bouncing through Badger Creek Rapid or camped on the shore. Jackass Canyon meets Marble Canyon on the opposite side. There's no sign for the turnoff on U.S. Highway 89A, but it's on the left just .1 mile southwest (toward Jacob Lake) from Lees Ferry Lodge. Go through a gate and continue two miles to road's end. On the way you'll have views of Badger Canyon. Endangered cacti live here, so keep to the existing road and pullouts when driving or camping.

Cliff Dweller's Lodge

About 1890, Anglo traders built an unusual trading post underneath a giant boulder. You can still see the old buildings beside the modern establishment. The lodge (928/355-2228 or 800/433-2543, $60–70 d, less in winter) has an American restaurant with a shaded patio (daily breakfast, lunch, and dinner, $12–26), a small store, and a gas station. It's on U.S. Highway 89A, 9 miles west of Marble Canyon and 32 miles east of Jacob Lake.

Lee's Ferry Anglers Guides & Fly Shop (928/355-2261 or 800/962-9755, www.leesferry.com) has fishing guides and supplies.

San Bartolome Historic Site

Markers tell the story of the Dominguez-Escalante Expedition, which camped near here in 1776. Returning from a failed attempt to reach Monterey, California, the group struggled to find a route through the forbidding terrain to Santa Fe. Signs mark the site on the north side of U.S. Highway 89A between Mileposts 557 and 558, about midway between Marble Canyon and Jacob Lake.

PARIA CANYON—VERMILION CLIFFS NATIONAL MONUMENT

The wild and twisting canyons of the Paria River and its tributaries offer a memorable adventure for experienced hikers. Silt-laden waters have sculpted the colorful canyon walls, revealing 200 million years of geologic history. You enter the 2,000-foot-deep gorge of the Paria in southern Utah, then hike 38 miles downstream to Lees Ferry in Arizona, where the Paria empties into the Colorado River. Besides the canyons, this 110,000-acre wilderness area protects colorful cliffs, giant natural amphitheaters, sandstone arches, and parts of the Paria Plateau. On top of the plateau, wonderful swirling patterns in sandstone hills, known as the Coyote Buttes, enthrall visitors. The 2,000-foot-high, rosy-hued Vermilion Cliffs meet the mouth of Paria Canyon at Lees Ferry. The river's name, sometimes spelled Pahreah, is Paiute for "muddy water."

© BILL WEIR

the Narrows inside Paria Canyon

History

Ancient petroglyphs and campsites indicate that ancestral Puebloan people traveled the Paria more than 700 years ago. They hunted mule deer and bighorn sheep while using the broad lower end of the canyon to grow corn, beans, and squash.

The Dominguez-Escalante Expedition, the first white people to see the Paria, stopped at its mouth in 1776. After John Lee began his Colorado River ferry service in 1872, he and others farmed the lower Paria Canyon. Though outlaws used it and prospectors came in search of gold, uranium, and other minerals, much of the Paria Canyon remained little visited.

The Arizona Wilderness Act in 1984 designated Paria Canyon a wilderness, together with parts of the Paria Plateau and Vermilion Cliffs. In 2000, the Arizona portion of the wilderness and surrounding lands became the 294,000-acre Vermilion Cliffs National Monument.

Hiking

You can hike Paria Canyon in four days, though it's better to have five or six because there are many river crossings, and you'll want to take side trips up some of the tributary canyons. The trip is considered moderately difficult. Hikers should have enough backpacking experience to be self-sufficient, as help may lie days away. Flash floods can race through the canyon, especially July–September. Rangers will advise you if they think danger exists, but they no longer close the canyon when storms threaten. The upper end contains narrow passages, particularly between Miles 4.2 and 9. Rangers suggest all hikers obtain up-to-date weather information. For safety in case of flood, one should register at White House, Buckskin, Wire Pass, or Lees Ferry Trailheads when entering or leaving the canyons.

All visitors need to take special care to minimize impact on this beautiful canyon. Check the BLM Visitor Use Regulations before you go. Rules include no campfires or dogs in the Paria and its tributaries, a pack-in/pack-out policy (including toilet paper!), and a latrine location at least 200 feet away from the river and campsites when not in the narrows. Ask about disposable waste bags to keep the Paria Narrows even cleaner. Hiking parties may not exceed 10 people.

The best times to travel along the Paria are mid-March–June and late September–November. May, especially Memorial Day weekend, is the most popular time. Winter hikers often complain of painfully cold feet. Wear shoes suitable for frequent wading; light fabric and leather boots or jungle boots work better than heavy leather hiking boots.

You can draw good drinking water from springs along the way—see the BLM's book *Hiker's Guide to Paria Canyon.* It's best not to use river water because of the high silt content and contamination. Normally the river flows only ankle deep, but can rise to waist-deep levels in the spring or after rainy spells. During thunderstorms, water can roar up to 20 feet deep in the Paria Narrows and Buckskin and Wire Pass Canyons, so heed weather warnings. Floods usually subside within 12 hours. Quicksand, most prevalent after flooding, is more a nuisance than a danger—rarely more than knee deep. Many hikers carry a walking stick for probing the opaque waters before crossing. Conditions can change dramatically after a flood, especially in the narrow sections of Paria, Buckskin, and Wire Pass canyons, so it's best to get the latest advice from BLM staff.

Permits and Information

Backpackers need to apply in advance for a permit that costs $5 per person per day. Day hikers simply pay $5 each at any of the trailheads for a pass that's good for all three canyons—Paria, Buckskin, and Wire Pass. Backpacking permits, Coyote Buttes permits, weather forecasts, and up-to-date information are available from BLM staff at the Paria Contact Station in Utah, 30 miles northwest of Page on U.S. Highway 89 near Milepost 21, on the south side of the highway just east of the Paria River. The station is open 8:30 A.M.–4:15P.M. daily (Daylight Savings Time!) about mid-March–mid-November. Hikers can get drinking water at a faucet in front and see the current weather forecast.

You can check Paria and Coyote Buttes dates by phone and obtain permits by mail by contacting the **Arizona Strip Interpretive Association** (345

E. Riverside Dr., St. George, UT 84790, 435/688-3246). Information and off-season permits are available from the **Kanab Field Office** (318 N. 100 East, Kanab, Utah 84741, 435/644-4600, 7:45 A.M.–4:30 P.M. Mon.–Fri.). The website www.az.blm.gov/paria issues permits. The BLM's *Hiker's Guide to Paria Canyon* book ($8) has detailed maps and information.

Trailheads and Shuttle Services

Most hikers start from White House Trailhead, which lies two miles south of Paria Contact Station on a dirt road near an old homestead site called White House Ruins, of which only rubble remains. You can camp here (pit toilets and picnic tables) for a $5 fee. The exit trailhead is at Lonely Dell Ranch near Lees Ferry, 44 miles southwest of Page via U.S. Highways 89 and 89A; vehicles can be left at the 14-day parking area.

The hike requires a 150-mile round-trip car shuttle. You can make arrangements for others to do it for you, using either your car or theirs. For a list of shuttle services, check the website or ask at the Arizona Strip Interpretive Association, Paria Contact Station, or Kanab Field Office.

Paria Canyon Adventure Ranch (928/660-2674, www.pariacampground.com) offers camping ($7.50/person) and hostel beds ($12/person) year-round; rates include showers, which are available to the public for a small fee. Two-hour trail rides to nearby canyons run April–October. The turnoff is between Mileposts 21 and 22, just .6 miles west across the Paria River from the Paria Contact Station; on the way you'll pass a restaurant that serves dinner on Fridays and Saturdays.

Wrather Canyon Arch

One of Arizona's largest natural arches lies about one mile up this side canyon off Paria Canyon. The massive structure has a 200-foot span. Veer right (southwest) at Mile 20.6 on the Paria hike. The mouth of Wrather Canyon, which is easily missed, and other points along the Paria are unmarked; you need to follow your map. No camping is allowed in this canyon.

Buckskin Gulch

This amazing Paria tributary—said to be the world's longest slot canyon—features convoluted walls hundreds of feet high, yet narrows to as little as four feet in width. In some places the walls block out so much light that it feels as if you're walking in a cave. Be *very* careful to avoid times of flash floods. Hiking can be strenuous, with rough terrain, deep pools of water, and log and rock jams that sometimes require the use of ropes.

You can descend into Buckskin from two trailheads, Buckskin and Wire Pass, both approached by a dirt road passable for cars in dry weather. The hike from Buckskin trailhead to the Paria River is 16.3 miles one-way and takes 6–8 or more hours. From Wire Pass Trailhead it's 1.7 miles to Buckskin Gulch, then 11.8 miles to the Paria. You can climb out to a safe camping place on a hazardous route—extremely hazardous if you're not an experienced climber—about halfway down Buckskin Gulch; this way out should not be counted on as an escape route. Carry enough water to last until you reach the mouth of Buckskin Gulch.

Wire Pass and upper Buckskin Canyons make a great day-hike loop—you can follow Buckskin 4.5 miles from its trailhead to the confluence of Wire Pass Canyon, then turn 1.7 miles up Wire Pass; you could then walk, do a car shuttle, or hitch the 4 miles by road back to Buckskin Trailhead. The Buckskin Narrows begin 3.5 miles down, and you may wish to continue below the confluence to see more of this enchanting canyon. Wire Pass Canyon, which is even narrower in spots than Buckskin, may have some difficult spots. Look for petroglyphs on the right at the lower end of Wire Pass Canyon.

To reach these trailheads, go five miles west on U.S. Highway 89 from Paria Contact Station to the unmarked House Rock Valley Road (#700) between Mileposts 25 and 26, then turn south 4.5 miles to Buckskin or another 4 miles for Wire Pass. The Arizona border is just 1.2 miles farther, where you'll find the north end of the Arizona Trail and a tiny campground (no water) at Stateline Trailhead. House Rock Valley Road, marked in Arizona as Road 1065, continues 20 miles south to U.S. Highway 89A between Mileposts 565 and 566, near where the highway begins its climb to the Kaibab Plateau. At a pullout

2.9 miles before U.S. Highway 89A, you can look up to the condor release site atop the Vermilion Cliffs, clearly marked by white deposits of condor poop.

Coyote Buttes

The secret is out about this colorful swirling sandstone atop the Paria Plateau! You've probably seen photos of these wonderful features, but not directions on how to reach them. The buttes lie mostly in Arizona south of Wire Pass Canyon and have been divided into Coyote Buttes North and Coyote Buttes South. The famous Wave formation is in the north, so that region is the most popular. Once you get the required permit, BLM staff will give you a map and directions to the Wave. You may find cairns marking part of the way, but no signs. Even if you get permits by mail, it's worth dropping by the Paria Contact Station for directions. The Wave is about six miles round-trip and takes half a day, though there's more to see in the area. Photographers will find a wide-angle lens useful for taking in the sweep of the curved rock. Both north and south areas have countless beauty spots to discover, so it's worth making a full day of it and carrying food and lots of water.

© BILL WEIR

the Wave

The BLM issues the required permits for Coyote Buttes, which are day-use only; there's a $5 per person fee, and permit procedures are the same as for the Paria River. No dogs are allowed. Permits sell out far ahead in spring and autumn—the best times to visit. If you don't have a permit but your schedule is flexible, try for a next-day walk-in permit—check the procedure with BLM staff. In summer you can often get a walk-in permit, though a crack-of-dawn departure will be needed to get in and out before the temperatures hit 100°F or so.

Only a few people may visit each area per day because the Navajo Sandstone rock here is so fragile. It can break if climbed on—causing damage to both the scenery and hikers' bones—so it's important to stay on existing hiking routes and use soft-soled footwear. Hikers need to carry water and keep an eye out for rattlesnakes. Lightning storms occur most often in late summer but can appear at any time of year.

Trailhead access is off House Rock Valley Road. You can reach Coyote Buttes North from Wire Pass Trailhead or the more difficult Notch Access, about two miles south of Wire Pass Trailhead. Coyote Buttes South requires 4WD for Paw Hole Access, 2.6 miles in, and Cottonwood Cove Access farther back; deep sand may make these areas impassable during summer. You could walk to Paw Hole but it would be a tough slog. BLM staff can advise on road conditions.

The Toadstools

An easy hike of about a mile round-trip leads to these fanciful rock formations. From the Paria Contact Station, drive east 1.5 miles on U.S. Highway 89 and look for the unmarked parking on the north side where power lines turn away from the highway between Mileposts 19 and 20. Go through the pedestrian gate and follow footprints up the valley to red and white balanced rocks; more can be seen if you continue around to the left. No permits or fees are needed.

Navajo and Hopi Country

Multihued desert hills, broad mesas, soaring buttes, vast treeless plains, and massive mountains give an impression of boundless space. All of northeastern Arizona lies atop the Colorado Plateau, which averages 4,500–7,000 feet in elevation. Several pine-forested ranges rise above the desert near Arizona's borders with Utah and New Mexico. Navajo Mountain, just across the border in Utah, stands as the highest peak in the area at 10,388 feet. Nearby you'll find Rainbow Bridge, the world's highest natural stone span over water. Monument Valley's sheer-walled spires evoke awe farther east. The beautiful canyons in Navajo and Canyon de Chelly National Monuments shelter some of the Southwest's best-preserved prehistoric dwellings.

Ancient cultural traditions of Native Americans—ways of life that have survived to the

Must-Sees

Look for 🅼 to find the sights and activities you can't miss and 🅽 for the best dining and lodging.

🅼 **Navajo National Monument** holds three large prehistoric cliff dwellings that are amazingly well preserved, and you can hike to two of them (page 507).

🅼 **Monument Valley Navajo Tribal Park** inspires awe with its enchanting and iconic landscape (page 510).

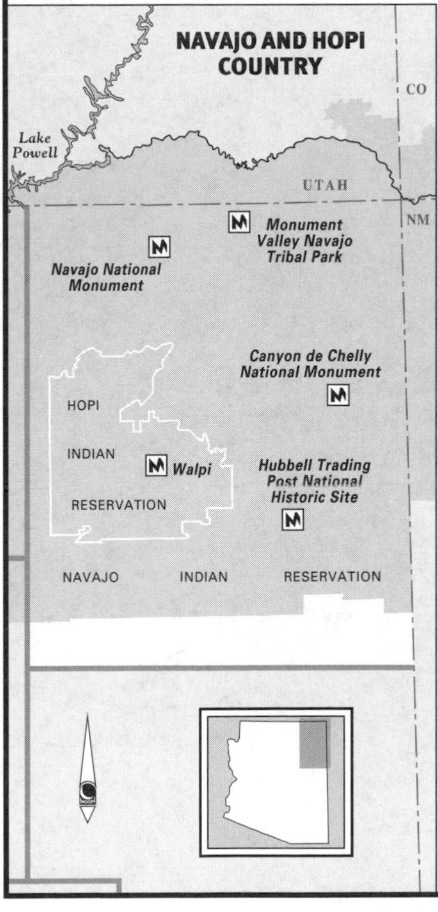

🅼 **Canyon de Chelly National Monument** enchants with exceptionally beautiful canyons, many prehistoric cliff dwellings, and a glimpse of traditional Navajo life (page 512).

🅼 **Hubbell Trading Post National Historic Site** is an authentic 19th-century trading post still in use and full of old baskets, Navajo rugs, kachina dolls, hardware, and groceries. Guided tours of trader John Lorenzo Hubbell's house tell about life here during the early days (page 522).

🅼 **Walpi** and other centuries-old Hopi villages seem to grow out of the mesa tops. Guided tours of Walpi tell about traditional life here (page 528).

© BILL WEIR

Antelope House Ruin

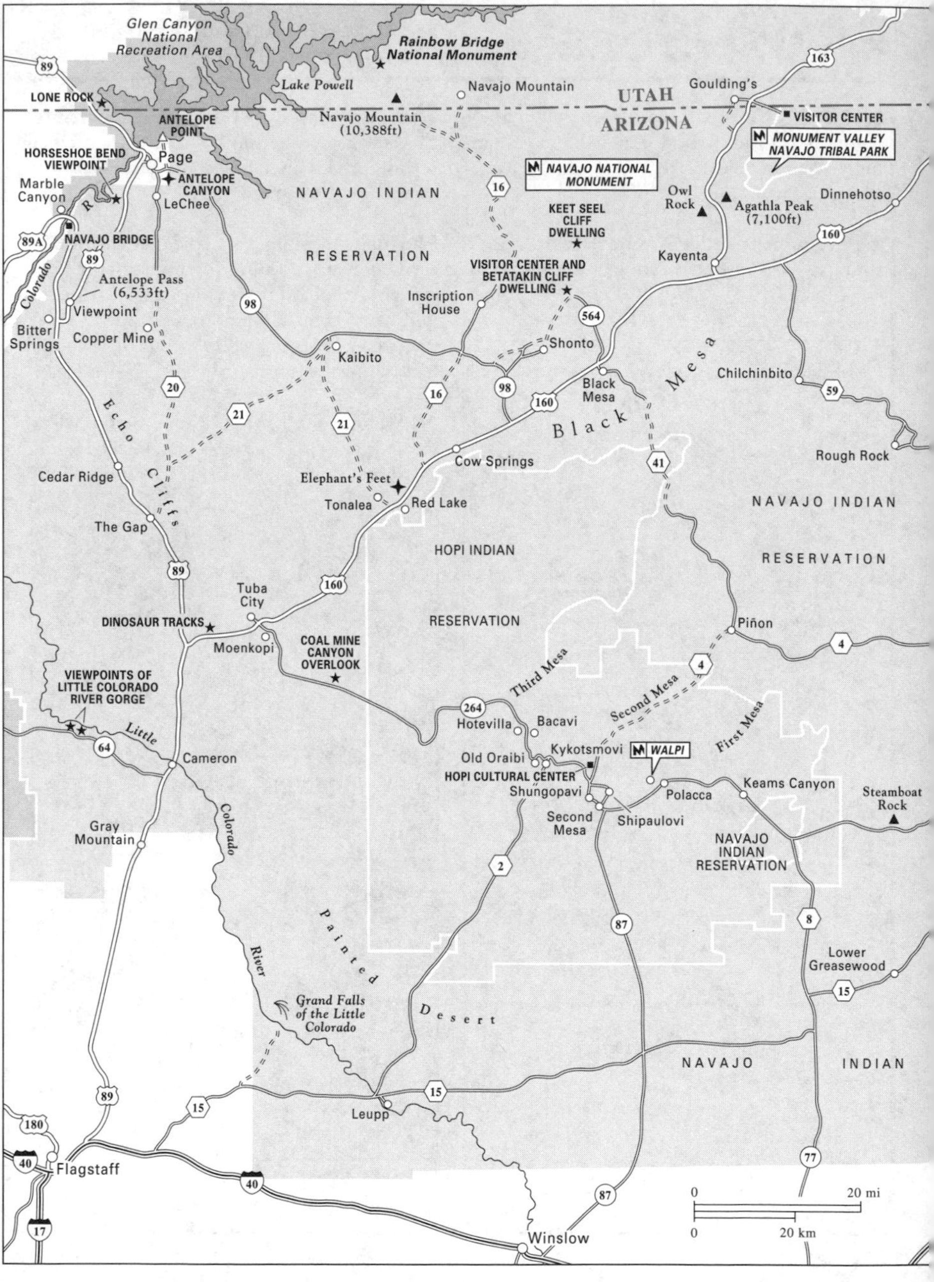

Glen Canyon National Recreation Area
Rainbow Bridge National Monument
Lake Powell
Navajo Mountain
Navajo Mountain (10,388ft)
UTAH
ARIZONA
Goulding's
VISITOR CENTER
MONUMENT VALLEY NAVAJO TRIBAL PARK
LONE ROCK
ANTELOPE POINT
Page
HORSESHOE BEND VIEWPOINT
ANTELOPE CANYON
Marble Canyon
LeChee
NAVAJO NATIONAL MONUMENT
NAVAJO INDIAN RESERVATION
KEET SEEL CLIFF DWELLING
Owl Rock
Agathla Peak (7,100ft)
Dinnehotso
Kayenta
NAVAJO BRIDGE
Colorado
Antelope Pass (6,533ft)
Viewpoint
Bitter Springs
Copper Mine
VISITOR CENTER AND BETATAKIN CLIFF DWELLING
Inscription House
Kaibito
Shonto
Black Mesa
Chilchinbito
Echo Cliffs
Cedar Ridge
Cow Springs
Rough Rock
Elephant's Feet
Tonalea
Red Lake
The Gap
HOPI INDIAN RESERVATION
NAVAJO INDIAN RESERVATION
Tuba City
DINOSAUR TRACKS
Moenkopi
COAL MINE CANYON OVERLOOK
Piñon
VIEWPOINTS OF LITTLE COLORADO RIVER GORGE
Third Mesa
Second Mesa
First Mesa
Little Colorado River
Cameron
Hotevilla
Bacavi
Old Oraibi
Kykotsmovi
WALPI
HOPI CULTURAL CENTER
Shungopavi
Polacca
Keams Canyon
Steamboat Rock
Second Mesa
Shipaulovi
Gray Mountain
NAVAJO INDIAN RESERVATION
Painted Desert
Lower Greasewood
Grand Falls of the Little Colorado
NAVAJO INDIAN
Leupp
Flagstaff
Winslow
0 20 mi
0 20 km
89
89A
163
160
16
98
564
20
21
59
41
4
264
64
2
87
8
15
180
40
17
77

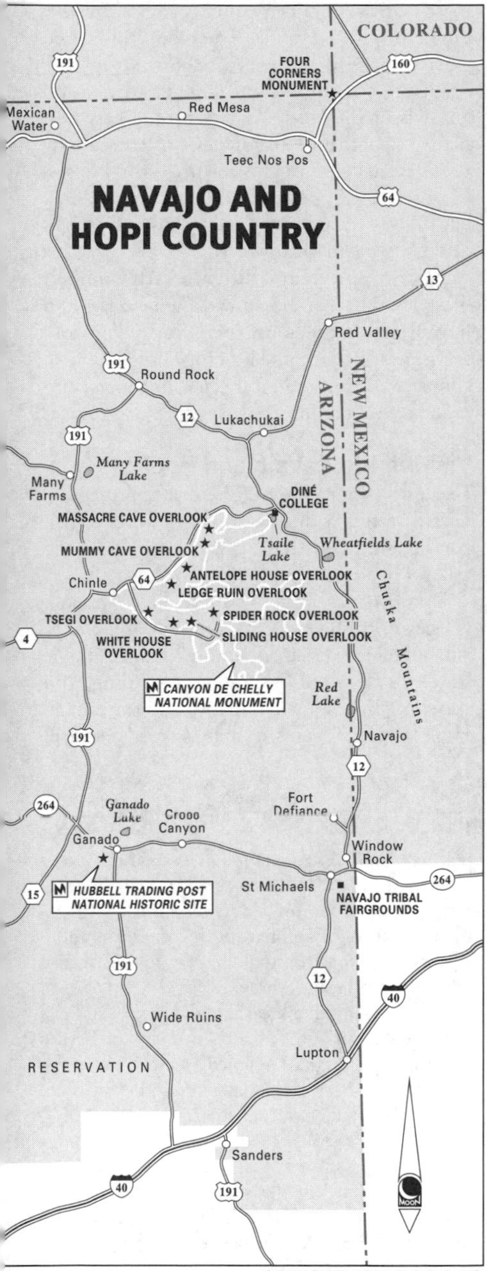

present—make this region a special place. The hardworking Hopi have lived here longest. Ruins, occupied by their ancestors as long ago as 1,500 years, lie scattered over much of northeastern Arizona and adjacent states. The once warlike and greatly feared Navajo, who call themselves Diné, came relatively late, perhaps 500–700 years ago.

Navajo and Hopi differ greatly in their lifestyles. The Navajo spread their houses and hogans across the countryside, often far from the nearest neighbor, while the Hopi usually live in compact villages, even if this means a long commute to fields or jobs. Today, Navajo and Hopi welcome visitors who respect tribal customs and laws. Here you'll have an opportunity to glimpse unique ways of life in a land of rare beauty.

PLANNING YOUR TIME

The region's sights fit well into a loop drive of a week or more. You'll enjoy not only the destinations, but also the beautiful wide-open landscapes along the way. Highlights on the Navajo lands include the majestic buttes and spires of Monument Valley, and the prehistoric cliff dwellings within the two national monuments of Navajo and Canyon de Chelly. Museums at the Navajo capital of Window Rock and farther north at Tsaile provide an insight into the tribe's culture. On the Hopi lands, be sure to visit the atmospheric traditional village of Walpi atop First Mesa, and the museum at the Hopi Cultural Center on Second Mesa. If you can time your visit for a weekend, you might be fortunate enough to experience a traditional dance, but these events are not always open to the public. Public transport is too limited for touring the region, so you'll need your own wheels.

Expect warm to hot summers and moderate to cold winters. Spring and autumn are the ideal times to visit, especially for hiking, though winds in March and April can kick up dust and sand. Afternoon thunderstorms frequently build up from early July to early September. Showers usually pass quickly, but flash floods pose a danger in canyons.

HISTORY

Indian Reservations

In 1878 the federal government began ceding to the Navajo land that has since grown into a giant reservation, spreading from northeastern Arizona into adjacent New Mexico and Utah. The Navajo Nation, with more than 250,000 members, is the largest Native American tribe in the country. In 1882 the federal government also recognized the Hopi's age-old land rights and began setting aside land for them. Approximately 10,000 Hopi live today on a reservation completely surrounded by Navajo land. Government officials have redrawn the reservation boundaries of the Navajo and Hopi many times, never to the satisfaction of both parties. In 1978, congressional and court decisions settled a major land dispute between the two tribes in favor of the Hopi. The victorious Hopi regained part of the territory previously designated for joint use, but largely settled by Navajo. To the Hopi this was long-overdue justice, while the Navajo called it The Second Long Walk.

NAVAJO AND HOPI CULTURES

White people have always had difficulty understanding Arizona's tribes, perhaps because these Native American cultures emphasize very different spiritual values. The Hopi and Navajo exist in accord with nature, not struggling against it, adapting to the climate, plants, and animals of the land. Yet when outsiders visit Native American villages, they often see only the material side of the culture—the houses, livestock, dress, pottery, and other crafts. One has to look deeper to gain even a small insight into Native American ways.

Navajo and Hopi differ greatly in their lifestyles. The Navajo spread their houses and hogans across the countryside, often far from the nearest neighbor. The Hopi usually live in compact villages, even if this means a long commute to fields or jobs.

Visiting the Navajo and Hopi

Learning about Native American cultures can reward visitors with new insights. It's easy to visit Navajo and Hopi lands; the tribes ask guests to follow only a few simple rules.

Hordes of eager photographers besieged Hopi villages from the late 1800s to the early 1900s, when the Hopi cried "No more!" And that's the way it is now—photography, recording, and sketching by visitors are *strictly* forbidden in all Hopi villages. Even the sight of a camera will

NAVAJO CODE TALKERS

The idea of using the Navajo language as a code for the military came to Philip Johnson, a son of missionaries to the Navajo. He convinced the U.S. Marines of the potential by assembling a group of Navajo and quickly passing coded messages back and forth. Recruiting began in May 1942 with a pilot program of 29 Navajo for the Pacific Theater. Success led to calls for more recruits and about 400 had qualified by the conclusion of World War II.

The code used 211 Navajo words—increased to 411 by war's end—for common military terms, plus a code word for each letter of the alphabet. The code talkers knew, for example, that *besh-lo* (iron fish) meant "submarine." Navajo servicemen had to memorize the code and be ready for communications at all times and in all conditions. They participated in grueling amphibious assaults and jungle combat in such places as GuadacanalGuadalcanal, Tarawa, Iwo Jima, and Okinawa. Adding to the dangers of combat, both Americans and Japanese sometimes mistook the Navajo, with their dark skin, for Japanese.

The code proved unbreakable and gave an added element of surprise for the American forces. Even after the war, the code remained a secret. Not until 1969 did the Marines declassify it and allow the Navajo code talkers to tell the full story. All received Congressional medals in 2001. You can learn more in books such as the Japanese author/photographer Kenji Kawano's *Warriors Navajo Code,* a very personal account with portraits and thoughts of the code talkers.

THE EXPLORATION OF THE COLORADO RIVER AND ITS CANYONS

Navajo sweathouse, late 1800s

upset some tribal members. The Navajo are more easygoing about photos, but you should always ask first and expect to pay a posing fee.

Reservation land, though held in trust by the government, is private property; obtain permission before leaving the roadways or designated recreational areas. Don't remove anything—a few feathers tied to a bush may make a tempting souvenir, but they're of great religious importance to the person who put them there. Normal good manners, respect, and observance of posted regulations will make your visit pleasurable for both you and your hosts. Alcohol and drugs have become a threat to tribal ways, so it's important for visitors not to bring either onto the reservations. When driving, keep an eye out for livestock and wildlife wandering across the road, as much of the land is open range.

You might enjoy tuning into local radio stations to hear favorite music and languages of the tribes. Hopi Radio KUYI at 88.1 FM has a large following for its traditional and contemporary Native American and other styles of music.

Ceremonies

Religion forms a vital part of both Navajo and Hopi cultures. Most Navajo ceremonies deal with healing. If someone is sick, the family calls in a healer who uses sand paintings, chants, and dancing to effect a cure. These events, often held late at night, aren't publicized. If you're driving at night and see large bonfires outside a house, it's likely there's a healing ceremony going on, but don't go over unless invited.

The Hopi have an elaborate, almost year-round schedule of dances in their village plazas and kivas (partly underground ceremonial rooms). Some ceremonies, such as those in the kivas, are closed to outsiders, but others may be open to the public. Nearly all Hopi dances serve as prayers for rain, fertile crops, and harmony. Men perform the kachina dances, and while they're dancing they *are* kachinas. The elaborate and brilliant masks, the ankle bells, the drums and chanting—all invite the attention of the kachinas, supernatural spirits who bring rain and blessings. At the end of the line of dancers, you might see boys who are learning the ritual; dance

Hopi method of dressing the hair

steps must be performed precisely. When watching, remember that this is a religious service. Dress respectfully, keep clear of the performers, be quiet, and don't ask questions. Villagers will not tolerate any breaking of the rules, such as taking photos or making sketches. Sometimes *all* visitors will be asked to leave if one misbehaves! Each village organizes its own dances, but does not advertise them. Word gets around, however, and people at the Hopi Cultural Center or the Cultural Preservation Office may know of the dances. Hopi ceremonies generally take place on the weekends. See the Hopi Calendar for an outline of the kachina and social dances.

PRACTICALITIES

Accommodations and Food

Motels in the widely scattered towns can quickly fill up in the summer tourist season, so reservations are a very good idea. Expect to pay more because there's so little competition. Accommodations in towns just outside the reservations—in Flagstaff, Winslow, Holbrook, Page, or Gallup—are generally a much better value. Campgrounds are likely to have space and you'll save a lot of money, but only a few have hookups.

Navajo and Hopi enjoy American, Mexican, and Chinese dishes as well as the ever-present fast foods. Try the Navajo or Hopi taco, a flat fry bread smothered with lettuce, ground beef, beans, tomatoes, chilies, and cheese. The Hopi Cultural Center restaurant on Second Mesa has many local specialties, but chances are the Hopi family at the next table will be munching on hamburgers and fries! No alcohol is sold or permitted on the Navajo and Hopi reservations; you won't find much nightlife, either.

Navajo Recreation and Permits

Navajo lands feature spectacular canyon and mountain scenery that can be explored by experienced hikers and 4WD enthusiasts. Remember that trails and back roads may not have signs and can be treacherous after rains. Hiking and 4WD guidebooks are your best sources of information. Tribal offices may have some backcountry information, and they can advise on any closed areas. Be sure to obtain permits for hiking or camping. Pets can come along only if on a leash at all times, because livestock roam much of the land. If parking in a remote area, it's best to ask permission to park at a residence and pay a small fee.

The main office of the **Navajo Parks & Recreation Department** (P.O. Box 2520, Window Rock, AZ 86515, 928/871-6647, www.navajonationparks.org, 8 A.M.–5 P.M. Mon.–Fri.) is just north of the Navajo Museum, Library, and Visitor Center. In the western Navajo Nation, which contains most of the popular backcountry areas, contact the **Cameron Visitor Center** (P.O. Box 459, Cameron, AZ 86020, 928/679-2303) at the U.S. Highway 89–Highway 64 junction in Cameron; it's usually open 7 A.M.–6 P.M. daily in summer, then 8 A.M.–5 P.M. Monday–Friday the rest of the year. Other places for permits include Upper Antelope Canyon and LeChee (928/698-2808) near Page, and Monument Valley Navajo Tribal Park (435/727-5872). Backcountry permits cost $5 per person per day and $5 per person

SHOPPING FOR NATIVE AMERICAN ARTS AND CRAFTS

The strength of the Navajo and Hopi cultures appears in their excellent arts and crafts. Trading posts and Native American crafts shops on and off the reservations offer large selections. You'll also have the opportunity to buy directly from the maker. Navajo sell from roadside stands, most numerous on the highways to Grand Canyon National Park. Hopi usually sell directly from their village homes. To learn about Native American art, drop in at the Heard Museum in Phoenix or the Museum of Northern Arizona in Flagstaff. Books—available in trading posts, bookstores, and libraries—describe crafts and what to look for when buying (See the *Suggested Reading* chapter.)

The best work commands high prices, but it can be a fine memento of a visit to Native American lands. Tribespeople know what their crafts are worth, so bargaining is not normally done. Competition, especially among Navajo at their roadside stands, can make for some very low prices, however. Discounts often mark the end of the tourist season in September and October.

The Navajo have long earned fame for silver jewelry and woven rugs; you'll also see their stonework, pottery, basketry, and sand paintings. Craftsmen learned to work silver from Mexicans in the 19th century, then gradually developed distinctive Navajo styles, such as the squash-blossom necklace with its horseshoe-shaped pendant. Silversmiths also turn out bracelets, rings, concha belts, buckles, and bolo ties. The Navajo are especially fond of turquoise, which appears in much of their work. Navajo once wove fine blankets using wool from sheep obtained from the Spanish and weaving skills learned from pueblo Indians, but factory-made blankets in the late 19th century nearly ended the market for handwoven ones. At the suggestion of trader John Lorenzo Hubbell, weavers switched to a heavier cloth for use as rugs, which became extremely popular. Rugs have evolved into more than a dozen regional styles and may be made from hand-spun and -dyed yarn or less expensive commercial yarn. Navajo once used sand paintings only in ceremonies but now also produce the distinctive designs and colors for the tourist trade.

The Hopi carve exotic kachina dolls from cottonwood roots and create jewelry, pottery, and basketry. The kachina dolls originally followed simple designs and served to educate children about Hopi religion. With the rising interest from outsiders, the Hopi began to carve more elaborate and realistic figures from the diverse Hopi pantheon. The dolls include clowns (painted with black and white stripes and often holding watermelon slices), animal-like forms, solemn masked figures, and fearsome ogres. Much thought and symbolism go into a Hopi carving, so even though its price is high, the doll will be good value. (Some Navajo have cashed in on the kachina-doll trade, but the Hopi may tell you that the Navajo don't really know about the kachina religion. Navajo dolls tend to have more fur, fiercer features, and lower prices.) Hopi silversmiths most often fashion inlay work using traditional symbols. The inlay is made from two sheets of silver, one with a design cut out, sandwiched together. This style, now a Hopi trademark, is seen in earrings, bracelets, rings, bolo ties, and belt buckles. The Hopi also turn out beautiful pottery and baskets, as they have for many centuries.

Artists of both tribes create attractive paintings, prints, and sculpture with Native American motifs.

per night for camping. Obtain permits in person or allow two weeks for processing by mail.

Fishing, hunting, and boating on the Navajo Nation require tribal permits from **Navajo Fish and Wildlife** (P.O. Box 1480, Window Rock, AZ 86515, 928/871-6451 or 871-6452, www.navajofishandwildlife.org, 8 A.M.–5 P.M. Mon.–Fri.), which is on the right, shortly before you reach Window Rock Monument. Staff can tell you of fishing conditions and which stores sell permits. Of the 14 lakes on the reservation that are stocked with fish, the most popular are the trout lakes Wheatfields and Tsaile in eastern Arizona and Asaayi and Whiskey nearby in New Mexico. State game and fish agencies have no jurisdiction here; you need only tribal permits.

Hopi Recreation and Permits

The Hopi generally don't allow outsiders to hike, fish, or hunt. You may be able to visit backcountry areas with a guide. Ask at the Tsakurshovi shop (1.5 miles east of the Hopi Cultural Center, 928/734-2478) or at the Hopi Cultural Center (928/734-2401), both atop Second Mesa.

Information

Not always easy to get! Motels, shops, and trading posts can be helpful; tribal police know regulations and road conditions. Try the museums run by the Navajo at Window Rock and Tsaile and by the Hopi on Second Mesa. Local newspapers report on politics, sports, and social events, but not religious ceremonies.

Navajo: Window Rock, the Navajo Nation capital, has the tribe's main tourist and recreation offices. Check the information desk at the Navajo Museum, Library, and Visitor Center in town, or contact the **Navajo Nation Tourism Department** (P.O. Box 663, Window Rock, AZ 86515, 928/871-6436, www.explorenavajo.com).

Hopi: The **Hopi Cultural Center** (P.O. Box 67, Second Mesa, AZ 86043, 928/734-2401, www.hopiculturalcenter.com) and **Cultural Preservation Office** (1 mile south of Highway 264 in the Tribal Headquarters building, P.O. Box 123, Kykotsmovi, AZ 86039, 928/734-3613) can answer visitors' questions and may know of upcoming dances open to the public.

What Time Is It?

This must be the question most frequently asked by reservation visitors! While the Navajo Nation and most of the United States go on Daylight Savings Time from early April to late October, the rest of Arizona stays on Mountain Standard Time. Keep in mind the time difference on Navajo land during DST or you'll always be one hour late; an easy way to remember is that the reservation follows the same time as its New Mexico and Utah sections. The Hopi, who rarely agree with the Navajo on anything, choose to stay on Mountain Standard Time.

Getting Around

Your own transportation is by far the most convenient, but tours of Navajo country do leave from major centers. **Navajo Transit System** (928/729-4002, www.navajotransitsystem.com) offers bus service across the Navajo and Hopi lands.

Navajo Country

CAMERON

Built in 1916 overlooking the Little Colorado River, **Cameron Trading Post** (928/679-2231 or 800/338-7385, www.camerontrading-post.com) commemorates Ralph Cameron, Arizona's last territorial delegate before statehood. The trading post's extensive services and strategic location near the Grand Canyon make it a popular stopping point in western Navajo country. Cameron Lodge ($89–99 d rooms, $149–179 suites, less in winter) offers attractive Southwest-style rooms, some with a balcony. A terraced garden adds refreshing greenery and flowers. An RV park ($15 w/hookups, no tents, no showers) lies across the highway.

Antique furnishings and Navajo rugs decorate the excellent restaurant (daily breakfast, lunch, and dinner, $8–18). Diners enjoy views of the Little Colorado Canyon, and they can choose from many American dishes plus some Mexican and Navajo items—try the Navajo taco in meat or vegetarian versions. The huge gift shop in the main building has a Navajo rug section where you may see a weaver at work. If you're interested in museum-quality Native American crafts and art, don't miss the separate gallery in a stone building out front; ask to see the upstairs rooms, too. The trading post also includes a grocery store, post office, and a service station. It's on the west side of U.S. Highway 89, one mile north of the junction with Highway 64 and 54 miles north of Flagstaff.

For Navajo Nation information and recreation permits drop by the **Cameron Visitor Center** (U.S. 89–AZ 64 junction, P.O. Box 459, Cameron, AZ 86020, 928/679-2303, fax 928/679-2330); it's open about 7 A.M.–6 P.M. daily May–September, then 8 A.M.–5 P.M. Monday–Friday the rest of the year. **Navajo Arts & Crafts Enterprise** (928/679-2244) next door offers a fine selection of Native American crafts. An **RV park** across U.S. Highway 89 is open all year with sites for tents ($8.50) and RVs ($16.50 w/hookups) as well as showers ($2), laundry, deli, and a store; check in at Simpson's Market (928/679-2532). The nearby **Trading Post** sells Native American crafts and supplies.

Vicinity of Cameron

You'll see colorful hills of the **Painted Desert** north and east of Cameron. To the west, the high, sheer walls of the **Little Colorado River Canyon** make an impressive sight. Viewpoints are 9 and 14 miles west of Cameron on Highway 64, about halfway to Desert View in Grand Canyon National Park. You'll also have a chance to shop for Navajo jewelry at the roadside stands in the Cameron area on U.S. Highway 89 and Highway 64.

At Gray Mountain, 10 miles south of Cameron on U.S. Highway 89, you can stay at the motel rooms of the **Anasazi Inn** (928/679-2214, $49–79 d, less in winter). The restaurant (across the highway, daily breakfast, lunch, and dinner, $7–14) cooks up American and Mexican items plus Navajo tacos. The adjacent Gray Mountain Trading Post sells Native American arts and crafts.

Backcountry Areas

Experienced hikers can explore remote and beautiful areas in the western Navajo lands. The Cameron Visitor Center sells the required permits and has some information; hiking guidebooks have more detailed descriptions. Navajo permits can also be obtained from staff at the Navajo Parks and Recreation office in Window Rock. If you'll also be camping in Grand Canyon National Park, get hold of permits from the Backcountry Information Center there.

Navigating the unmarked back roads to many of the trailheads may require as much map-reading skill as hiking the routes does. When it's not in flood, you can hike along the Little Colorado River all the way from Cameron down to the Colorado River in the Grand Canyon, though deep pools, quicksand, and flash floods can make the way difficult. The Little Colorado Canyon can also be entered via the Blue Springs Trail, Hopi Trail Crossing, and Hopi Salt Trail, all very challenging and only for knowledgeable canyon hikers. Marble Canyon has difficult rim-to-river routes at Eminence Break, Shinumo Wash, Salt Water Wash, and Jackass Canyon. Northeast near the Arizona–Utah border, Rainbow Bridge rates as one of the best hiking destinations on the Colorado Plateau.

TUBA CITY

This administrative and trade center for the western Navajo commemorates Chief Tuuvi of the Hopi tribe. He had converted to the Mormon religion and invited members to settle here. Mormons founded a settlement in 1877, but could not gain clear title to the land, and the U.S. Indian Agency took it over in 1903. The town (pop. 7,612, elev. 4,936 feet) is a handy stop for travelers, with several places to stay and some good restaurants. Attractive stone buildings in an oasis of green lawns and shade trees lie just north of the commercial district. Tuba City Trading Post, the first of these old structures, is worth a visit both for its unusual architecture and for the arts and crafts inside.

Sights Nearby

Dinosaur tracks left by several different species lie preserved in sandstone 5.5 miles west of Tuba City off U.S. Highway 160, about midway between Tuba City and U.S. Highway 89. The turnoff is on the north side of the highway between Mileposts 316 and 317, marked by signs for Dinosaur Tracks and Moenave. Navajo sell jewelry from stalls here. A guide will probably offer his services for a small tip, but you can find the several pathway sites on your own—look for the stone-lined paths to them.

Elephant's Feet, a pair of distinctive sandstone pillars, stand near Red Lake, 23 miles northeast of Tuba City on U.S. Highway 160 near Milepost 345.

Accommodations

Under $50: Greyhills Inn (928/283-4450 or 283-6271, ext. 142) provides one of the few inexpensive places to stay in the Navajo Nation; students of Greyhills High School operate the inn as part of a training program. Rates for rooms—all nonsmoking and with shared bath—are $39 s plus $5 for each additional person; people with hostel cards can stay for only $22 s, $30 d. Guests have use of a kitchen and a TV lounge. You can make the recommended reservations by phone or mail with the Hotel Management Program (Greyhills High School, P.O. Box 160, Tuba City, AZ 86045). From the junction of U.S. Highway 160 and Highway 264, go east .5 miles on U.S. Highway 160 to just past the pedestrian overpass, turn left, and follow the signs.

$50–100: Diné Inn Motel (928/283-6107, $60 s, $65–75 d) offers basic rooms—all nonsmoking—on the north side of U.S. Highway 160, one block east of the Highway 264 junction.

Over $100: Quality Inn Navajo Nation (928/283-4545 or 800/644-8383, www.qualityinnnavajonation.com, $95 s, $110 d, less in winter) sits in the center of town behind Tuba Trading Post, one mile north of the highway junction. The comfortable rooms have a Southwest decor; guests can use a free Internet computer.

Camping

The Quality Inn's **RV park** ($12 tents, $20 RV w/hookups) offers shade trees, showers, and laundry.

Food

The octagonal **Hogan Restaurant** (next to Quality Inn, 928/283-5260, daily breakfast, lunch, and dinner, $6–14) serves Navajo tacos, steaks, seafood, pasta, and Mexican dishes along with a salad bar; there's a lunchtime buffet. A half block to the east, **Kate's Café** (928/283-6773, daily breakfast, lunch, and dinner, $8–13) cooks up American and pasta dishes. The little **Tuuvi Café** (U.S. 160–AZ 264 junction, 928/283-6767, daily breakfast, lunch, and dinner, $5–13) prepares American food and Tuuvi tacos.

The Toh Nanees Dizi Shopping Center, a half mile east on U.S. Highway 160 from the highway junction, has the Chinese **Szechuan Restaurant** (928/283-5807, daily lunch and dinner, lunch buffet on weekdays, $6–8), **Pizza Edge** (928/283-

5938, Mon.–Sat. lunch and dinner, $4–16), and **Bashas'** supermarket and deli.

Shopping and Services

The unusually shaped **Tuba City Trading Post** in the center of town offers Native American arts and crafts. The stone structure dates to 1870 and the two-story octagon was added in 1920. **Van Trading Co.** (1.5 miles west of town on U.S. 160) sells Native American work, including dead-pawn jewelry, groceries, and most everything else.

The **post office** is east .5 miles on U.S. Highway 160 from the highway junction to just past the pedestrian overpass, then left. **Tuba City Public Library** (928/283-5856, closed Fri.–Sat.) offers an Arizona collection, general reading, and Internet computers in an old stone building across from the Quality Inn.

NAVAJO NATIONAL MONUMENT

Three spectacular prehistoric cliff dwellings, last occupied about 700 years ago, lie within scenic canyons in northern Navajo country. The ancestral Puebloan people who once lived here probably have descendants in present-day Hopi villages. Navajo families later settled in the area and named the canyons and ruins. Of the three sites, Betatakin is the most accessible; you can see it from a viewpoint near the visitors center or join a ranger-led hike into the dwelling.

Keet Seel, a 16-mile round-trip hike to the northeast, is the largest and best-preserved cliff dwelling in Arizona. Inscription House, to the west, is the smallest of the three ruins and is closed to the public.

You can reach the monument's headquarters and visitors center by following U.S. Highway 160 northeast 52 miles from Tuba City—or southwest 22 miles from Kayenta—then turning north 9 miles on Highway 564 at Black Mesa Junction. Tsegi Overlook, on the right just after you enter the monument, provides a fine introduction to the canyon country here.

Visitors Center

The ancestral Puebloan people left many questions behind when they abandoned this area. You can learn what is known about these people and ponder the mysteries at the visitors center (HC 71, Box 3, Tonalea, AZ 86044-9704, 928/672-2700, www.nps.gov/nava, 8 A.M.–5 P.M. daily, possibly extended in summer; closed Thanksgiving, Christmas, and New Year's Day). Exhibits of prehistoric pottery and other artifacts attempt to piece together what life was like for the early peoples. An excellent 25-minute video on the Hisatsinom ("people of long ago," the Hopi name for ancestral Puebloan people) and a 20-minute Betatakin tour video are shown on request. Rangers answer questions and sell books and maps. A bulletin board lists campfire programs and ranger-led walks. Navajo often demonstrate their arts and crafts in or near the visitors center. A gift shop offers Navajo work. You can peek into an old-style Navajo forked-stick hogan and see a sweathouse and wagon behind the visitors center. There's a picnic area across the parking area. Mosquitoes can be pesky at times—campers and hikers should have some repellent handy.

The easy, paved **Sandal Trail** begins behind the visitors center and winds through a pinyon-juniper woodland to Betatakin Point Overlook, which has a good view of the ruins across the canyon. The trail is one mile round-trip and drops 160 feet to the viewpoint. Signs along the way identify native plants and describe how Native Americans used them.

Aspen Trail branches off to the left 400 feet down Sandal Trail, then drops 300 feet with some steps into the head of Betatakin Canyon, .8 miles round-trip. The trail offers pretty scenery along the way and a view of the quaking aspen, Douglas fir, water birch, and red-osier dogwood trees on the canyon floor below; there's no ruin view or access from this trail.

Visiting Betatakin

Betatakin—Navajo for Ledge House—lies tucked in a natural alcove that measures 452 feet high, 370 feet across, and 135 feet deep. It contains 135 rooms and one kiva. Inhabitants built and abandoned the entire village within two generations, between A.D. 1260 and 1300.

You may hike here only with rangers, who lead daily four-hour tours in summer and occasionally off-season. Groups are limited to 25 people, first come, first served. Starting at the trailhead, one mile from the visitors center, the five-mile round-trip trail is primitive and drops 700 feet, then winds up a canyon to the cliff dwelling. Rangers warn of rock-fall danger in the alcove, so some visitors prefer to view the pueblo from outside. Thin air—the trailhead elevation is 7,300 feet—can make the hike very tiring. People with heart, respiratory, or mobility problems shouldn't attempt it.

Visiting Keet Seel

This isolated cliff dwelling is one of the best preserved in the Southwest. Keet Seel—Navajo for Broken Pottery—has 160 rooms and four kivas. The ruins look as though they were abandoned just a few years back, not seven long centuries ago. The site, 16 miles round-trip by trail, is open in summer. A permit is required, and there's a limit of 20 people per day. Visitors should make reservations two months ahead, though last-minute spots may be available. To pick up your permit, you must attend a scheduled trail orientation the afternoon before (recommended so that you can get an early start the next day) or in the morning. Remember that you're in Daylight Savings Time territory.

The trail descends 1,000 feet from Tsegi Point to the canyon bottom, travels downstream a short distance, then heads upstream into Keet Seel Canyon with a 400-foot elevation gain. You may have to do some wading. Carry water, as livestock pollute the streams. Visitors can enter the site only with a ranger, who is stationed nearby. There's a primitive campground (free, one-night limit) near Keet Seel; spring water, which needs treating, may be available. Strong hikers can do the round-trip in a day, though spending a night here makes for an easier, more relaxing visit. Ask for the Keet Seel Hiking Information sheet.

© BILL WEIR

A ranger-led hike leads down along sculpted canyon walls to Betatakin cliff dwelling.

© BILL WEIR

Keet Seel cliff dwelling

Campgrounds and Services

The free **Sunset View Campground** lies near the visitors center in a pinyon-juniper woodland; you can stay year-round but water is on only from about mid-May to mid-October. **Canyon View Campground,** one mile away, offers views, tables, outhouses, and group reservation sites, but no water or pavement; it closes in winter. There's nearly always room for campers; no reservations taken except for groups. Campfire programs may run in summer. Expect cold and likelihood of snow November–mid-March.

Anasazi Inn (18 miles away on the road to Kayenta, 928/697-3793, $79–99 d, less in winter) provides basic accommodations. The little café here is open daily for breakfast, lunch, and dinner.

Black Mesa Shopping Center, nine miles south of the visitors center at the junction of Highway 564 and U.S. Highway 160, has the closest grocery store and service station. The road south from here goes to the coal mines of the Peabody Coal Company, a major employer of the Navajo.

KAYENTA

The "Gateway to Monument Valley" has a population of 7,549 in a bleak, windswept valley (elev. 5,660 feet). Its name is loosely derived from the Navajo word *teehindeeh* (bog hole), as there were once shallow lakes here. Kayenta makes a handy stop for travelers in northern Navajo country, with good motels, a basic RV park, several restaurants, and shopping.

Drop by the Burger King on U.S. Highway 160 west of the highway junction to see **Navajo Code Talkers** exhibits. Next door, the **Navajo Cultural Center** has traditional forked-stick and octagonal hogans, a sweathouse, and a shade house.

Accommodations and Camping

$50–100: Roland's Navajoland Tours (U.S. 163, .5 miles north of U.S. 160, 928/697-3524, $60–70 d) provides a small bed and breakfast, plus Monument Valley tours. **Hampton Inn** (U.S. 160, west of the highway junction, 928/697-3170 or 800/426-7866, $93–124 d in summer) offers spacious rooms along with a restaurant, gift shop, and an outdoor pool.

$100–150: Best Western Wetherill Inn (U.S. 163, one mile north of U.S. 160, 928/697-3231 or 800/528-1234, $108 d in summer) has an indoor pool and a gift shop. Its name honors John Wetherill, an early trader and rancher in the region who discovered Betatakin, Mesa Verde, and other major ancestral Puebloan sites. **Holiday Inn** (U.S. 160 opposite the turnoff for Monument Valley, 928/697-3221 or 800/465-4329, $139 d in summer) provides a restaurant, gift shop, tours, and an outdoor pool.

Linville's Coin-Op Laundry (U.S. 163 in town, 928/697-3738) offers basic RV spaces for $10 w/hookups. Showers are also available to noncampers for a small fee.

Food

Hampton Inn's **Reuben Heflin Restaurant** (928/697-3170, daily dinner, $8–26) serves American, Southwestern, and Navajo food. Holiday Inn's **Wagon Wheel Restaurant** (928/697-3221, daily breakfast, lunch, and dinner, $9–20) prepares American and Southwestern dishes plus Navajo tacos; there's a breakfast buffet in season. The popular little **Amigo Café** (.2 miles north on U.S. 163 from the highway junction, 928/697-8448, Mon.–Sat. breakfast, lunch, and dinner, $5–13) fixes Mexican and American food. **Golden Sands Café** (near the Wetherill Inn, 928/697-3684, daily breakfast, lunch, and dinner, $7–15) offers American items.

Teehindeeh Shopping Center near the highway junction has a **Bashas'** supermarket and deli. Next door, the **Pizza Edge** (928/697-8427, Mon.–Sat. lunch and dinner, $4–16) dishes out pizza, calzones, and subs.

Shopping and Services

Navajo Arts & Crafts Enterprise (just east of the highway junction, 928/697-8611) has a good selection. Gift shops in each of the motels sell Native American arts and crafts. The **post office** is off U.S. Highway 163 just north of the shopping center.

MONUMENT VALLEY NAVAJO TRIBAL PARK

Sheer-walled mesas, buttes, and pinnacles stand majestically in this otherworldly landscape. Changing colors and shifting shadows across the rock faces and rippled sand dunes add to the feeling of enchantment. Agathla Peak and some lesser summits, roots of ancient volcanoes, rise in the southern part of the valley; their dark rock contrasts with the pale yellow sandstone monuments. The desert valley lies at an elevation of 5,564 feet and receives an annual precipitation of only 8.5 inches.

In 1863–1864, when Kit Carson was ravaging Canyon de Chelly and rounding up Navajo, Chief Hoskinini led his people to the safety and freedom of Monument Valley. Merrick Butte and Mitchell Mesa commemorate two miners who discovered rich silver deposits on their first trip to the valley in 1880. When they returned, both men reportedly met their deaths at the hands of Paiutes. Hollywood movies made the splendor of Monument Valley known to the outside world. *Stagecoach,* filmed here by John Ford in 1938, began a long series of movies, television shows, and commercials shot in the valley that continues to this day; warriors from John Wayne to Susan Sarandon have ridden across these sands.

Visitors Center

Perched on the rim of the heart of Monument Valley, the visitors center (435/727-5872, www.navajonationparks.org) provides an information desk, exhibits, restaurant, gift shop, and booths where you can sign up for tours; it's open 6 A.M.–8 P.M. daily in summer and 8 A.M.–5 P.M. daily the rest of the year; closed Thanksgiving Day afternoon and Christmas.

Visitors pay a $5/person fee (free ages 9 and under) to enter the tribal park. Staff can issue permits for hiking and camping in the Rainbow Bridge and San Juan River areas. From Kayenta, head north 24 miles on U.S. Highway 163 to just past the Utah border, then turn right 3.7 miles. Navajo sell crafts and food from little shops near the highway turnoff.

The View Restaurant (daily breakfast, lunch, and dinner, $8–10) in the upper level of the visitors center serves a variety of food to munch while you gaze across the famous landscape. A large gift shop next to the restaurant sells Native American arts and crafts. You can picnic at a viewpoint .4 miles north of the visitors center or near the entrance to Mitten View Campground.

Monument Valley Drive

This 17-mile, self-guided scenic drive begins at the visitors center and loops through the middle of the valley. Overlooks along the way provide sweeping vistas. The dirt road is normally OK if you drive cautiously, but don't attempt it with RVs over 27 feet or extremely low-clearance vehicles. Avoid stopping and becoming stuck in the loose sand that sometimes blows across the road. Allow 1.5 hours for the drive. No hiking or driving is permitted off the marked route. Only the visitors center and campground have water, so you'll probably want to bring some along. Entry to the drive closes half an hour before the visitors center does, and you must be out before dark.

Wildcat Trail

You can get a good feel for Monument Valley

© BILL WEIR

The setting sun peeks through West Mitten.

on this 3.2-mile loop around the West Mitten. It's the only hike in the park that you can do without a guide. The trail—foot travel only—begins from the picnic area .4 miles north of the visitors center, then drops down from the rim. Cairns and a few signs mark the way. It's open the same hours as Monument Valley Drive.

Valley Tours

Navajo guides at the visitors center offer tours year-round. The shortest trips last 1.5 hours and cover places on the self-guided route. Longer trips of 2.5 or 3.5 hours visit hogans, cliff dwellings, and petroglyphs in areas beyond the self-guided drive. Horseback rides from stables near the visitors center can easily be arranged, lasting 1.5 hours to all day; overnight trips are available too. Hiking tours can last from a few hours to a day or more.

Reservations aren't needed on day tours. If you'd like to do an overnight trip, it's best to call ahead and bring your own food and camping gear. **Totem Pole Tours** (435/727-3313) offers driving trips, photography tours, trail rides, and hiking, including cookouts and overnights. **Homeland Tours/Monument Valley Horseback Trailrides** (435/727-3466, www.cas-biz.com/homelandtours) can take you on a variety of back-road drives, trail rides, or hikes. **Roland's Navajoland Tours** (928/697-3524) offers many backcountry drives, photography tours, and hiking trips. **Simpson's Trailhandler Tours** (435/727-3362, www.trailhandlertours.com) runs driving, photography, and hiking tours, plus a hogan overnight cultural experience. **Dineh Trail Rides** (435/678-2960) heads out on trips from a half hour to overnight. **Sacred Monument Tours** (435/727-3218, www.monumentvalley.net) leads driving, horseback, hiking, and photography tours from a booth on the right just before Goulding's. **Navajo Country Guided Trail Rides** (just south of Milepost 403 on U.S. 163 near Agathla Peak, 435/727-3210, www.a-aa.com/trailride) can take you on rides from half an hour to overnight.

Accommodations and Food

Sites at **Mitten View Campground** near the visitors center have great views, though campers may have to contend with winds in this exposed location. The cost is $10, with coin-operated showers from early April to mid-October. No hookups are available, but there's a fill and dump station. Off-season the rate drops to $5, and you can use restrooms next to the visitors center. Primitive camping may also be possible at the Wildcat Trailhead .4 miles north of the visitors center, though the camping fee is likely to be the same. Goulding's Lodge offers the nearest motel, RV park, and supermarket. You'll also find motels at Kayenta in Arizona and at Mexican Hat and Bluff in Utah.

Visit the **Hogan Bed & Breakfast** (U.S. 163 between Mileposts 415 and 416, 1.6 miles south of the Monument Valley turnoff, 928/265-5382, $20/person or $25/person w/bedding) is open all year; the family also arranges 4WD, horseback, and hiking tours. **Country of Many Hogan Bed & Breakfast** (928/283-4125, $145 d in summer, less in winter), about halfway between

Monument Valley and Kayenta, offers accommodations in hogans. Dinner, camping, sweat lodge, horseback rides, hiking tours, and driving trips can be arranged at extra cost.

Goulding's Lodge and Trading Post

In 1924, Harry Goulding and his wife, Mike, opened a trading post at this scenic spot and ran it for more than 40 years. It's just north of the Arizona–Utah border and 1.5 miles west of the U.S. Highway 163 Monument Valley turnoff. The 1928 stone trading post is now the **Goulding's Museum,** full of prehistoric and modern Native American artifacts, movie photos, period rooms, and Goulding family memorabilia. It's open daily (on request in winter) and donations are appreciated; a leaflet available for purchase provides additional background on the exhibits. Nearby, a cabin built for John Wayne in *She Wore a Yellow Ribbon* has exhibits from the movie. Also nearby, the multimedia show *Earth Spirit* portrays the region.

Goulding's Lodge (P.O. Box 360001, Monument Valley, UT 84536, 435/727-3231 or 800/874-0902, www.gouldings.com) provides large modern rooms with balconies at $165 d June 1–October 15, dropping to $67 d by midwinter. Guests enjoy views, in-room movies, and an indoor pool. The **Stagecoach Dining Room** (daily breakfast, lunch, and dinner, $8–20) offers such American favorites as steak, chicken, pork chops, fish, pasta, stir-fry dishes, sandwiches, and a salad bar. Local specialties include fry bread and Navajo tacos.

The large gift shop sells high-quality Native American work plus souvenirs and books. Nearby on the main road, you'll find a convenience store with a fast-food counter, a gas station, and a laundry. Goulding's Grocery across the road is a good supermarket. An airstrip also lies nearby.

Goulding's Monument Valley Campground (435/727-3235 or 800/874-0902, March 15–Oct. 31, $16 tents, $26 RVs w/hookups) offers a pretty canyon setting one mile west of the lodge turnoff. Campers have an indoor pool, showers, laundry, convenience store/gift shop, tours, and a shuttle service to the lodge. Just before the campground, you'll pass a hospital and mission founded by the Seventh-Day Adventist Church.

Navajo guides narrate Monument Valley tours, which operate year-round at $35 for 2.5 hours, $40 for 3.5 hours, $58 for 5.5 hours, and $70 full day with lunch; children under 8 pay less. You can also experience Monument Valley on a full-moon tour, $35; call for dates and times. Pickup is available at both the lodge and the campground.

Oljato Trading Post

A sign near Goulding's Grocery points the way 11 miles northwest to this old-style trading post, established in 1921. Besides the canned goods and household items, you can see Navajo arts and crafts plus some historic exhibits.

FOUR CORNERS MONUMENT

An inlaid concrete slab marks the place where Utah, Colorado, New Mexico, and Arizona meet. This is the only spot in the United States where you can put your finger on four states at once. It's said that more than 2,000 people a day stop at the marker in the summer. Average stay? About 7–10 minutes. On the other hand, five national parks and 18 national monuments lie within a 150-mile radius of this point. Navajo, and occasionally Ute and Pueblo, set up craft and refreshment booths in summer. Navajo Parks and Recreation collects a small fee during the tourist season.

CANYON DE CHELLY NATIONAL MONUMENT

Spectacular canyons here shelter prehistoric cliff dwellings and traditional Navajo life in eastern Navajo country. Sheer sandstone walls rise as high as 1,000 feet, giving the canyons a fortresslike appearance. The 26-mile-long Canyon de Chelly (pronounced d'SHAY) and adjoining 35-mile-long Canyon del Muerto join a few miles upstream from the visitors center. Rim elevations range from 5,500 feet at the visitors center to 7,000 feet at the end of the scenic drives. Allow at least a full day to see some of the monument's 83,840 acres. April–October is the best time to visit. Winter brings cold weather and a chance of snow. Afternoon thunderstorms arrive almost daily in late summer, creating thousands of waterfalls that cascade over the rims, stopping when the skies clear.

The small, spread-out town of Chinle, just west of Canyon de Chelly National Monument, takes its name from a Navajo word meaning "where the water flows out," as the Rio de Chelly emerges from its canyon here.

The First Peoples

Nomadic tribes roamed these canyons more than 2,000 years ago, collecting wild foods and hunting game. Little remains of these early visitors, who must have found welcome shelter from the elements in the natural rock overhangs of the canyons. The ancestral Puebloan people (Anasazi in the Navajo language) made their first appearance about A.D. 1, living in alcoves during the winter and brush shelters in summer. By A.D. 500 they had begun cultivating permanent fields of corn, squash, and beans and fashioning pottery. Villagers lived at that time in year-round pit houses—partly underground structures roofed with sticks and mud.

© BILL WEIR

White House Ruin

Around A.D. 700 the population began to build above-ground cliff houses of stone. These pueblos (Spanish for "villages") also contained underground ceremonial rooms, known as kivas, used for social and religious purposes. Most of the cliff houses now visible in Canyon de Chelly date from A.D. 1100–1300, when an estimated 1,000 people occupied the many small villages. At the end of this period the ancestral Puebloan people migrated from these canyons and from other large population centers. Archaeologists speculate that possible causes include floods, drought, overpopulation, and soil erosion.

It's likely that some of these people moved to the Hopi mesas, as Hopi religion, traditions, and farming practices have many similarities with those of the Canyon de Chelly cliff dwellers. During the next 400 years, Hopi farmers sometimes used the canyons during the growing season, but they returned to the mesas after each harvest.

The Navajo Arrive

First entering Canyon de Chelly about A.D. 1700, the Navajo found it ideal for farming and as a base for raiding nearby Native American and Spanish settlements. In 1805, however, even the steep canyon walls proved inadequate refuge when the Spanish launched a punitive expedition; soldiers reported killing 115 Navajo, including 90 warriors, at what's now known as Massacre Cave. The Navajo identified the dead as mostly women, children, and old men. During the Mexican era, raids took place in both directions; the Navajo sought food and livestock, while Mexicans kidnapped women and children to serve as slaves.

Contact with white settlers also went badly—they encroached on Navajo land, and U.S. soldiers proved deceitful. Conflict came to an end in the winter of 1863–1864, when Colonel Kit Carson led detachments of the U.S. Cavalry into the canyons. The army destroyed the tribe's livestock, fruit trees, and food stores and captured as many Navajo as possible. The starving survivors had no choice but to surrender and be herded onto a desolate reservation in eastern New Mexico. After this infamous Long Walk, and four miserable years there, they were permitted to return to their beloved canyons in 1868.

Today, Navajo continue farming and grazing sheep on the canyon floors. You can see their distinctive round hogans next to the fields. More than 50 families live in the canyons, but most spend winters on the canyon rims, returning to their fields after the spring floods have subsided.

Visitors Center

Exhibits reveal Native American history from the archaic period (before A.D. 1) to the present, with many fine artifacts. Video programs provide additional insights into the peoples who have lived here, as do regional books available for purchase. A silversmith is often at work creating jewelry. Just outside, the Plant Walk identifies local flora and describes how the Navajo used them; borrow or purchase the leaflet from the visitors center. You can also step into a Navajo hogan nearby. A bulletin board lists scheduled talks, campfire programs, and hikes. The visitors center (P.O. Box 588, Chinle, AZ 86503, 928/674-5500, www.nps.gov/cach) is open 8 A.M.–6 P.M. daily in summer, then 8 A.M.–5 P.M. daily the rest of the year.

Canyons de Chelly and del Muerto

A paved scenic rim drive with viewpoints along each canyon lets you gaze into the depths; binoculars come in handy to see the ruins and other features. Each rim drive takes about two hours. For additional perspectives, you can travel inside the canyons by 4WD vehicle, horseback, or foot.

Except on the self-guided White House Ruin Trail, you may enter the canyons only with an authorized Navajo guide or monument ranger. This rule is strictly enforced to protect the ruins and the privacy of families living in the canyons. All land belongs to the Navajo people; the National Park Service administers policies only within monument boundaries.

Vehicles are occasionally broken into at overlooks. Thieves look for cash, cameras, camcorders, computers, and other valuables, which you'll want to store out of sight. Also be sure that windows are fully up and doors locked.

Hiking

If you have a guide, you can hike almost anywhere. Navajos will usually be waiting near the visitors center to accompany you on canyon trips; they can suggest routes depending on your interests and available time. Rangers at the visitors center can help make arrangements and issue the necessary permit. Comfortable walking shoes, water, insect repellent, and a hat will come in handy.

Expect to do some wading. In fact, under the hot summer sun with red rocks all around, you may insist on it—the cool water and the shade of the trees are irresistible. Autumn can bring especially good hiking weather, with comfortable temperatures and the spectacle of cottonwoods turning to gold. Guides charge $15 per hour for up to 15 people with a three-hour minimum. Overnight trips are possible, with additional charges by the guide and landowner of a negotiable $60–100.

Rangers occasionally lead half-day hikes in the lower canyon from late May to the end of September. These are free, but check departure time the day before—hikes leave promptly.

Canyon Driving Tours

Tours leave Thunderbird Lodge daily at 9 A.M. and 2 P.M. during the busy season and visit both canyons. In winter, you should call ahead to make sure trips are scheduled; there's a minimum of eight passengers. The popular trips run a half day ($40 adults, $30 children 12 and under) or full day ($65 adults and children, includes lunch). You'll enjoy unobstructed views from the back of an open truck that stops frequently for photography and viewing of ruins. Half-day trips typically head up Canyon del Muerto to Antelope House Ruin and up Canyon de Chelly to White House Ruin. Full-day excursions can go much farther up each canyon—as far as Mummy Cave in Canyon del Muerto and Spider Rock in Canyon de Chelly.

You can arrange private and group trips with **De Chelly Tours** (928/674-3772, www.dechellytours.com), **Canyon de Chelly Jeep Tours** (928/674-5433, www.canyondechellytours.com), and **Tseyi Jeep Tours** (928/674-3262, www.tseyijeeptour.com). You can also take your own 4WD vehicle into the canyons with a guide and permit arranged at the visitors center. The guide fee for up to five vehicles is $15 per hour with a three-hour minimum.

Horseback Riding

Justin's Horse Rentals (P.O. Box 881, Chinle, AZ 86503, 928/674-5678) will put you in the saddle for rides of two hours to several days; cost is $10 per hour for each rider and $15 per hour for the guide (one per group). The stables are down the dirt road opposite the Thunderbird Lodge/Cottonwood Campground turnoff.

Totsonii Ranch (P.O. Box 434, Chinle, AZ 86503, 928/755-6209, www.totsoniiranch.com) offers guided horse rides at $10 per hour per person plus $15 per hour for the guide. Popular trips include a viewpoint (2 hours), down the Bat Trail to Spider Rock and back (4 hours), out to Three Turkey Ruin (4 hours), and all the way to the mouth of the canyon (all day); overnight trips can be arranged too. The ranch is 1.6 miles down a dirt road off the South Rim Drive of Canyon de Chelly; keep straight where the drive turns left for Spider Rock Overlook.

You can also ride your own horse by arranging board and feed at one of the stables near the park and hiring an authorized Navajo guide.

Accommodations

Under $50: Many Farms Inn (Many Farms, 928/781-6362, $30 1–4 people) offers rooms with two beds and shared baths as part of a school training program. Guests can use the coffee room, TV lounge, and laundry. The office is open daily June–July, then Monday–Thursday the rest of the year. It's 17 miles north of Chinle in the small community of Many Farms on the way to Monument Valley and Four Corners. From the junction of U.S. Highway 191 and Indian Route 59, go north .7 miles on U.S. Highway 191, turn left .7 miles at the Many Farms High School sign, then turn right .3 miles.

$100–150: Thunderbird Lodge (928/674-5841/5842 or 800/679-2473, www.tbirdlodge.com, $97 s, $101 d April–Oct.) has an attractive setting amid lawns and shade trees a half mile south of the visitors center. The cafeteria, large gift shop, and tours here are a big hit with many visitors. The lodge began as a trading post for the Navajo in 1902, then expanded to accommodate tourists. **Holiday Inn** (928/674-5000 or 800/465-4329, $129 d March–Oct.) is just west of the visitors center; guests enjoy a restaurant, outdoor pool, gift shop, and tours. **Best Western Canyon de Chelly Inn** (928/674-5875 or 800/327-0354, www.canyondechelly.com, $99 d May–Oct.) lies 2.5 miles west of the visitors center in the town of Chinle, with a restaurant, indoor pool, wireless Internet, and a gift shop.

Camping

Cottonwood Campground, between the visitors center and Thunderbird Lodge, offers pleasant sites among large cottonwood trees. It's free and open all year, with water available only April–October; no showers or hookups are available, though there is a dump station. Rangers present campfire programs some nights from late May to the end of September. The campground usually has space; reservations are accepted only for group tent sites. Cottonwood trees also shade a **picnic area** near the campground entrance; water is available except in winter.

You can escape the crowds at **Spider Rock Campground** (928/674-8261 or 877/910-2267, http://home.earthlink.net/~spiderrock). It's set in a pinyon-juniper woodland 10 miles from the visitors center and half a mile before the Spider Rock turnoff on the South Rim Drive. Tents and small rigs cost $10; RV spaces run $15 but include water fill and dump. You can also rent a hogan for $25 and up. Water and solar showers cost extra. The owner offers day and overnight hikes to Spider Rock and other destinations.

Food

Thunderbird Lodge's cafeteria (daily breakfast, lunch, and dinner, $10–19) is a good choice for informal dining; at dinner you can order steaks, chicken, pork chops, shrimp, or lighter fare such as a Navajo taco; Navajo rugs decorate the walls. At the Holiday Inn, **Garcia's Restaurant** (daily breakfast, lunch, and dinner, $8–19) has a very attractive Southwestern decor and a dinner menu of steaks, trout, and Southwestern dishes. In high season, there's a breakfast buffet and a salad bar; in winter only breakfast and dinner are served. Canyon de Chelly Inn's **Junction Restaurant**

(daily breakfast, lunch, and dinner, $6–17) serves American, Chinese, and Navajo dishes plus pizza; breakfast is available all day.

Tseyi Shopping Center (U.S. 191 just north of the junction with Indian Route 7) has a **Pizza Edge** (928/674-3366, Mon.–Sat. lunch and dinner, $4–16) and a **Bashas'** supermarket and deli. Several fast-food places are nearby.

Shopping and Services

Navajo Arts & Crafts Enterprise (928/674-5338) sits opposite the Canyon de Chelly turnoff from U.S. Highway 191 in Chinle. Gift shops in the three lodges display Native American work. The **post office** and a **laundry** are in Tseyi Shopping Center. Campers can get **showers** on weekdays at the Chinle Chapter House, 1.4 miles toward town from the visitors center.

SOUTH RIM DRIVE OF CANYON DE CHELLY

All pullouts and turns are on the left. Distances include mileage between turnoffs and overlooks. Allow at least two hours for the drive. Parked vehicles should be locked and valuables removed.

Mile 0: Visitors Center

The nearby canyon walls stand only about 30 feet high where the Rio de Chelly enters Chinle Wash.

Mile 2: Tunnel Canyon Overlook

The canyon is about 275 feet deep here. Guides sometimes lead short hikes down the trail in this side canyon. Don't go hiking without a ranger or Navajo guide.

Mile 2.3: Tsegi Overlook

You'll see a Navajo hogan and farm below. *Tsegi* is the Navajo word for "rock canyon," which the Spanish pronounced "de chegui." American usage changed it to "de chelly."

Mile 3.7: Junction Overlook

Canyon del Muerto, across the canyon floor, joins Canyon de Chelly here. The sheer walls stand 400 feet high. Look for two cliff dwellings of ancestral Puebloan people. First Ruin is located in the cliff at the far side of the canyon to the left. The pueblo has 10 rooms and two kivas, and dates from the late 11th to late 13th centuries. Junction Ruin, with 15 rooms and one kiva, lies across and to the right, near where the two canyons join. These dwellings, like most others in the monument, face south to catch the sun's warmth in winter.

Mile 5.9: White House Overlook

Canyon walls rise about 550 feet at this point. White House Ruin, on the far side, is one of the largest in the monument. The name comes from the original white plaster on the walls in the upper section, which you can see from the overlook. Parts of 60 rooms and four kivas remain in the upper and lower sections, though there may have been 80 rooms before floodwaters carried away some of the lower section. As many as 12 ancestral Puebloan families may have lived in this village about 1060–1275.

White House Ruin Trail continues down from the overlook and crosses the canyon floor to give you a close look at the site. Allow two hours for the 2.5-mile round-trip; bring water but no pets. This is the only hike in the canyon permitted without a guide, but you must stay on the trail. You can buy a pamphlet describing it at the visitors center. Many trails connect the rim with the canyon bottom, but few are as easy as this one. The Navajo often used it to move sheep.

Mile 12: Sliding House Overlook

These ruins, perched on a narrow ledge across the canyon, are well named. The people who constructed the village on this sloping ledge tried to brace rooms with retaining walls. Natural depressions at the overlook collect water and are still sometimes used by the Navajo.

Mile 19.6: Face Rock Overlook

Small cliff dwellings sit high on the rock face opposite the viewpoint. Though the rooms look impossible to reach, the ancestral Puebloan people chipped handholds and toeholds into the rock.

Mile 20.6: Spider Rock Overlook

The South Rim Drive ends where rock walls

plummet 1,000 feet from the rim to the canyon floor. Follow the 200-yard paved trail for the view of Spider Rock, the highest of the twin spires. It rises 800 sheer feet from the bottom of Canyon de Chelly. One story relates how newly arrived Navajo found an old woman in the canyon who taught them how to weave. She's now known as Spider Woman, a Navajo deity who makes her home atop Spider Rock.

You can see tiny cliff dwellings in the canyon walls if you look hard enough. Monument Canyon comes in around to the right. Black Rock Butte (7,622 ft.), on the horizon, is the weathered heart of an extinct volcano.

NORTH RIM DRIVE OF CANYON DEL MUERTO

All turnoffs are on the right. Distances include mileage between turnoffs and overlooks. Allow at least two hours for the drive. Parked vehicles should be locked and valuables removed.

Mile 0: Visitors Center

Cross the nearby Rio de Chelly bridge and continue northeast on Indian Route 64.

Mile 5.9: Ledge Ruin Overlook

The ruin, set in an opening 100 feet above the canyon floor, dates from 1050–1275 and has 29 rooms, including two kivas, in a two-story structure. Walk south a short way to another overlook and a view downcanyon; a solitary kiva is visible high in the cliff face. A toe-and-handhold trail connects it with other rooms in a separate alcove to the west.

Mile 10: Antelope House Overlook

Keep right at the fork on the quarter-mile walk to the viewpoint. Antelope House Ruin had 91 rooms and a four-story building. The village layout is clear—from the overlook you gaze almost straight down on it. The round outlines are kivas. The square rooms were for living or storage. Floods have damaged some of the rooms, perhaps while the ancestral Puebloan people still lived there. Residents abandoned the site about 1260. Its name comes from paintings of pronghorn antelope, some believed to be the work of a Navajo artist in the 1830s.

The Tomb of the Weaver sits across from Antelope House in a small alcove 50 feet above the canyon floor. Here, in the 1920s, archaeologists found the burial site of an old man. The well-preserved body had been wrapped in a blanket made from what appeared to be golden eagle feathers. A cotton blanket and cotton yarn topped with a spindle whorl were enclosed.

From a viewpoint a short walk east from Antelope House Overlook, you can spot Navajo Fortress, the sandstone butte across the canyon. When danger threatened, the Navajo climbed up the east side using log poles as ladders. They pulled in the uppermost logs and pelted attackers with a hail of rocks. Navajo used this natural fortress from the time of the Spanish until the Kit Carson campaign.

Mile 18.7: Mummy Cave Overlook

Archaeologists in the late 1800s named this large cliff dwelling for two mummies found in the talus slope below. Canyon del Muerto (Spanish for Canyon of the Dead) reportedly also took its name from this find. Mummy Cave Ruin sits within two separate overhangs several hundred feet above the canyon floor. The largest section is on the east (to the left), with 50 rooms and three kivas; the west cave contains 20 rooms. Between these sections is a ledge with seven rooms, including a three-story tower of unknown purpose. The finely crafted tower dates from about A.D. 1284; archaeologists think it was built by people from Mesa Verde in Colorado.

Mile 20.6: Massacre Cave Overlook

The North Rim Drive ends here. In 1805, Antonio de Narbona led an expedition of Spanish soldiers and allied Native Americans to these canyons. A group of fleeing Navajo managed to scale the nearly 1,000 feet to this overhang. Narbona's troops, however, ascended to the rim overlooking the cave and fired down. Narbona's account listed 115 Navajo killed and 33 taken captive.

From Yucca Cave Overlook nearby, you can see a cave with at least four rooms and a kiva. A small cave to the left was used for food storage; a toe-and-handhold trail connected the two alcoves.

EAST OF CANYON DE CHELLY NATIONAL MONUMENT

Diné College (Tsaile Campus)

In 1957, recognizing the need for college education, the Navajo established a scholarship fund. Students had to leave the reservation to pursue their education, however, and the cultural gap between the Navajo and the outside world proved so great that many students dropped out. So in 1969 the tribe created Navajo Community College, later renamed Diné College. Students used temporary facilities at Many Farms, Arizona, until 1973, when campuses opened at Tsaile and at Shiprock, New Mexico. Students can choose from courses in many Navajo and Native American subjects—crafts, language, politics, music, dance, herbology, and holistic healing. The colleges offer vocational training and adult education too. The Tsaile campus (928/724-6630, www.dinecollege.edu) lies 23 miles east of the Canyon de Chelly visitors center and 54 miles north of Window Rock.

The unusual campus layout resulted from Navajo elders and healers working together with architects. Because important Navajo activities take place within a circle, the campus grounds and many of the buildings took on that shape. If you know your way around a hogan, you'll find it easy getting around campus: The library is tucked in where the medicine bundle is kept during a ceremony, the cooking area (dining hall) lies in the center, sleeping (dormitories) is centered in the west, the teaching area (classrooms) occupies the south, and the recreation area (student union and gym) is in the north. The central campus entrance, marked by the glass-walled Ned A. Hatathli Center, faces east to the rising sun.

The **Hatathli Museum** (928/724-6654, 8 A.M.–5 P.M. Mon.–Fri., donation requested) claims to be the "first true Native American museum." Managed entirely by tribespeople, the collection occupies the third and fourth floors of the hogan-shaped Hatathli Center. Exhibits display art and interpret the cultures of prehistoric peoples as well as Navajo and other modern tribes. Ned Hatathli was the first Navajo manager of the tribal Arts and Crafts guild and a Tribal Council member.

You're welcome to stroll the campus. From the first floor of the Hatathli Center, walk west out the back and the college library will be ahead on the left and the cafeteria ahead on the right. Both the library and the bookstore (just north of the cafeteria) have many Navajo-related titles.

Chuska Mountains

These colorful mountains in Arizona's northeast corner may remind you of Sedona with the sculpted red rocks below and white rocks above. A very scenic drive crosses the range, providing a shortcut to New Mexico. It's paved, but isn't maintained in winter. From the highway junction at Tsaile, head north seven miles on Indian Route N12, then turn right on Indian Route N13; there may be no sign at the junction, but it's beside a gas station between Mileposts 83 and 84. Over the next five miles you'll pass through the spread-out town of Lukachukai, then begin a steep ascent, entering forests of ponderosa pine and Douglas fir. Atop a ridge, after four miles of climbing, you'll pass some aspen groves and views into New Mexico. On the descent, the spires of Shiprock and its radiating volcanic dikes come into view. The highway ends at U.S. Highway 491 in New Mexico, where you can turn north to the town of Shiprock or south past its volcanic namesake toward Gallup.

Wheatfields Lake

This mountain lake lies surrounded by a ponderosa forest at an elevation of 7,300 feet, between Mileposts 64 and 65 on Indian Route N12, 10 miles south of Tsaile and 44 miles north of Window Rock. The rugged Chuska Mountains rise to the east. Trout swim in the waters. There's a badly trashed campground across the highway; bring your own water. Camping, fishing, and boating require Navajo permits. In fine weather, you'll enjoy views of colorful cliffs and forested mountains on a scenic drive through this area. Although paved, Indian Route N12 isn't recommended in winter.

Navajo, New Mexico

Trees from the extensive woodlands that surround the town of Navajo supply the town's large sawmill. A supermarket sells groceries and tribal fishing permits. Nearby **Red Lake,** named for the color of its aquatic vegetation, has catfish. Navajo is 17 miles north of Window Rock on Route 12, on the way to Wheatfields Lake, Tsaile, and Canyon de Chelly. **Asaayi Lake,** 11 miles northeast in New Mexico, offers trout fishing, nonmotorized boating, and camping (closed winter, $10 day use, $15 overnight, not suitable for RVs). Whiskey Lake is farther east, also on dirt roads, and has trout.

WINDOW ROCK AND VICINITY

In the early 1930s, Tseghahodzani, The Rock With a Hole in It, so impressed Commissioner of Indian Affairs John Collier that he chose the site for a Navajo administration center. The octagonal Navajo Council Chambers, representing a great ceremonial hogan, went up, and Window Rock became the capital of the Navajo Nation. Tribal Council delegates meet here to decide on reservation policies and regulations.

Window Rock is a small but growing town (area pop. about 8,000) at an elevation of 6,750 feet close to the New Mexico border. Besides the Council Chambers and offices, the town contains a very good museum, a small zoo, two parks, a motel, and a shopping center. Window Rock's commercial center is at the junction of Highway 264 and Indian Route N12.

© BILL WEIR

Window Rock

Navajo Museum, Library, and Visitors Center

Massive wood pillars of this impressive building soar to the central skylight high above. The entrance opens to the east, like the traditional log hogan in front. It's on the north side of Highway 264 in Tse Bonito Tribal Park, a half mile east of Window Rock Shopping Center. The park also offers some shaded picnic tables. The Navajo camped on this site in 1864 on The Long Walk to eastern New Mexico.

Spacious museum galleries (928/871-7941) present excellent historical and art exhibits from the permanent collection and visiting shows. The library (928/871-6376 or 871-6526) offers a Native American Collection, a Special Collections room, general reading, and Internet computers. A gift shop sells Native American arts and crafts along with books and souvenirs. Staff at the information desk (P.O. Box 663, Window Rock, AZ 86515, 928/871-6436, www.explorenavajo.com) in the lobby answer questions and provide Navajo and Arizona travel literature. The museum, library, gift shop, and information desk all stay open 8 A.M.–5 P.M. Monday and Saturday, and 8 A.M.–8 P.M. Tuesday–Friday. There's also an indoor theater and large outdoor amphitheater.

Navajo Nation Zoological and Botanical Park

Set beneath towering sandstone pinnacles known as The Haystacks, the collection (928/871-6573, 8 A.M.–5 P.M. daily) offers a close look at wild and domestic animals of the Navajo lands. Rattlesnakes and other small creatures inhabit the orientation building near the entrance. Wild creatures include the golden eagle, red-tailed hawk, elk, coyote, black bear, cougar, and bobcat. Domestic breeds include the Navajo churro sheep, which has a double fleece and often four horns. Prairie dogs, free of restricting cages, run almost everywhere. The park lies just northeast of the museum.

Window Rock Monument & Navajo Veteran's Memorial Park

This beautiful spot shaded by juniper trees lies at the foot of Window Rock. The "window" is a great hole, averaging 47 feet across, in a sandstone ridge. Loose stones just below the hole mark the site of a prehistoric pueblo. You're not allowed to climb up to the hole, though a trail around to the left passes through wonderfully sculptured hills. The park has picnic tables, water, and restrooms for day-use only. The Navajo Veteran's Memorial Park honors warriors from all eras of war and peace. Head north .5 miles on Indian Route N12 from Highway 264, turn right at the light and head .5 miles in, passing the Council Chambers on your left just before the park.

Navajo Nation Council Chambers

The Council meets at least four times a year within the circular walls here; you can watch the bilingual proceedings from the visitor seating. At other times, 12 standing committees of the Council carry out legislative work. You can step inside 8 A.M.–noon and 1–5 P.M. Monday–Friday to see colorful murals that depict Navajo history. For more information, call the Council Chambers (928/871-6417) or Council Delegates (928/871-6380) or see the website www.navajo.org. Drive north .5 miles on Indian Route N12 from Highway 264, turn right at the light, then take the left fork .4 miles in.

St. Michael Mission

In 1898, Franciscan friars established this mission to serve the Navajo. You can visit the original mission building, now a **historical museum** (928/871-4171, 9 A.M.–5 P.M. daily Memorial Day–Labor Day; groups can visit at other times by appointment, free). St. Michael Mission is 2.9 miles west of Window Rock Shopping Center on Highway 264, then .2 miles south on Mission Road at the sign. Exhibits in the stone building re-create the early mission days with a chapel and missionary room, then interpret Native American culture and the work of the early missionaries. A gift shop sells regional books, cards, and posters. The mission's large stone church dates from 1937, when it replaced an earlier adobe structure; it's usually open during the day. A circular chapel behind the parking area has an earthen floor and a 16-foot woodcarving, *The Redemption of Humanity* or *American Pieta* by a German artist. The carving shows a dead Native American being lowered from a teepee tarp to a woman in mourning, with two attendants.

Fort Defiance

Permanent springs in a nearby canyon attracted the Navajo, who named the area Tsehotsoi, Meadow between the Rocks. Colonel Edwin Vose Sumner had another name in mind in September 1851, when, in defiance of the Navajo, he established a fort on an overlooking hillside. Though the Navajo nearly overran Fort Defiance in 1860, the army successfully repelled a series of attacks before abandoning the fort during the Civil War. In 1863–1864, Colonel Kit Carson set up headquarters at the fort while rounding up and moving the Navajo. After the Navajo returned, destitute, in 1868, Navajo Agency offices issued them sheep and supplies here. The first school on the reservation opened in 1869, and the first regular medical service arrived in 1880. The old fort is gone now, but the town remains an administrative center with a hospital, schools, and Bureau of Indian Affairs offices.

Events

The **Fourth of July Celebration** brings a PRCA rodeo to town along with Navajo music, dancing, arts, and crafts. The **Navajo Nation Fair** (P.O. Box 2370, Window Rock, AZ 86515, 928/871-6647, www.navajonationfair.com) runs on the Wednesday–Sunday after Labor Day in September. Said to be the largest Native American fair, this five-day festival offers a mixture of traditional and modern attractions, including song and dance, a parade, agricultural shows, food, crafts, concerts, rodeo, and the crowning of Miss Navajo.

Accommodations and Camping

Quality Inn Navajo Nation Capital (48 W. AZ 264, 928/871-4108 or 800/662-6189, www.navajonationinn.com, $63 s, $68 d) features Navajo-style rooms, a restaurant, and a business center just east of the shopping center. **Navajoland Days Inn** (3.4 miles west in St. Michael at 392 W. AZ 264, 928/871-5690 or 800/329-7466, $70–80 d, $90 d minisuite) offers an indoor pool, hot tub, sauna, and an exercise room.

Window Rock doesn't have any place to camp, but you can drive 7 miles north on Indian Route N12 to **JWJ RV Park and Campground** (Fort Defiance, 928/729-5917, $20 RV w/hookups, $10 tent), which has a clubhouse and showers; it's on the east side of the highway. Assayi Lake in New Mexico (17 miles north to Navajo, then 11 miles northeast) is another option.

Food

The Quality Inn Navajo Nation Capital's **Diné Restaurant** (928/871-4108, daily breakfast, lunch, and dinner, $6–13) serves a varied menu of American, Navajo, and Mexican food, but closes at 6 P.M. on weekends. **China West Buffet** (Window Rock Shopping Center, 928/871-5622, Mon.–Fri. lunch and dinner, $5.41) has buffet only. **Denny's** (3.4 miles west in St. Michael next to the Days Inn, 928/871-2067, daily breakfast, lunch, and dinner, $7–14) serves American favorites. None of these restaurants have much to offer for vegetarians. There's a supermarket in the shopping center, and **Bashas'** supermarket and deli lies just to the west on Highway 264.

Shopping and Services

Navajo Arts & Crafts Enterprise (near the junction of Highway 264 and Indian Route 12, 928/871-4090) sells Navajo paintings, rugs, jewelry, jewelry-making supplies, and crafts. **Cool Runnings** (north side of Highway 264 in St. Michael, .1 miles east of Mission Rd., 928/871-5600, www.coolrunningsmusic.com) offers a large selection of music, plus crafts, craft and religious supplies, and T-shirts; it caters mainly to Navajo and has a very different atmosphere from the usual souvenir shop. **Post offices** are on a hill behind the Quality Inn and at the St. Michael Mission turnoff.

Information

The helpful **Navajo Nation Tourism Department** and the **public library** are in the Navajo Museum, Library, and Visitors Center.

For hiking and camping information and permits on Navajo lands, contact the **Navajo Parks and Recreation Department** (P.O. Box 2520, Window Rock, AZ 86515, 928/871-6647, www.navajonationparks.org, 8 A.M.–5 P.M. Mon.–Fri.), just north of the museum. Fishing and hunting on the Navajo Nation require tribal permits from **Navajo Fish and Wildlife** (P.O. Box 1480, Window Rock, AZ 86515, 928/871-6451 or 871-6452, www.navajofishandwildlife.org, 8 A.M.–5 P.M. Mon.–Fri.), on the right shortly before Window Rock Monument. Arizona Game and Fish has no jurisdiction over the reservation—you need only tribal permits.

Getting Around

Navajo Transit System (928/729-4002, www.navajotransitsystem.com) connects Window Rock with many communities on the Navajo and Hopi Reservations.

GANADO

The Spanish called this place Pueblo Colorado (Colored House) after a nearby ruin left by ancestral Puebloan people. The name later changed to Ganado to honor one of the great Navajo chiefs, Ganado Mucho, or Big Water Clansman, a signer of the treaty of June 1868 that returned the Navajo lands. A Presbyterian mission founded here in 1901 provided the Navajo with a school and hospital. The school grew into the two-year College of Ganado, whose buildings are now used as a hospital. Hubbell Trading Post, Arizona's most famous, comes straight out of the Old West. Ganado is on Highway 264,

30 miles west of Window Rock, 44 miles east of Keams Canyon, and 36 miles south of Chinle. The eastern Navajo town lacks accommodations and reliable restaurants, but there's a grocery store open daily.

HUBBELL TRADING POST NATIONAL HISTORIC SITE

John Lorenzo Hubbell began trading in 1876, a difficult time for the Navajo, who were still recovering from their traumatic internment at Fort Sumner. Born in New Mexico, Hubbell had already learned some Navajo culture and language by the time he set up shop. Money rarely exchanged hands during transactions; Navajo brought in blankets or jewelry and received credit. They would then select desired items, such as coffee, flour, sugar, cloth, and harnesses. If the Navajo had credit left after buying supplies, they generally preferred silver or turquoise to money. Those bringing wool or sheep to the trading post usually received cash, however.

Hubbell distinguished himself by his honesty and appreciation of the Navajo. His insistence on excellence in weaving and silverwork led to better prices for Navajo craftspeople. The trading post helped bridge the Anglo and Native American cultures, as Navajo often called on Hubbell to explain government programs and to write letters to officials explaining their concerns.

Visitors Center, Hubbell's House, and Trading Post

Hubbell Trading Post (south side of AZ 264, 1 mile west of Ganado, 928/755-3475, www.nps.gov/hutr, 8 A.M.–6 P.M. daily June–Sept., 8 A.M.–5 P.M. daily the rest of the year) is the real thing. Weavers (usually women) often demonstrate their skills in the visitors center, which also has an excellent bookstore with many titles about Native American history, art, and culture. You can try your hand at weaving a rug on the visitor loom with the instructions provided, and see if it's as easy as it looks!

Guides offer free scheduled tours of Hubbell's house and you can take a self-guided tour of the grounds and barn. The house contains superb rugs, paintings, baskets, and other crafts collected by Hubbell before his death in 1930 and by the Hubbell family thereafter.

The trading post still operates much as it always has, offering high-quality crafts or most anything else. Canned and yard goods pack the shelves, glass cases display pocket knives and other small items, horse collars and harnesses hang from the ceiling, and Navajo still drop in with items for trade. Check out the Native American baskets and other old artifacts on the ceilings and walls of the jewelry and rug rooms. A tree-shaded picnic area lies next to the visitors center. Major auctions of works by Navajo and Hopi artists take place in May and August.

Hopi Country

For centuries the Hopi people have made their homes in villages atop three narrow mesas, fingerlike extensions running south from Black Mesa. Early European visitors dubbed these extensions—from east to west—First Mesa, Second Mesa, and Third Mesa. Highway 264 skirts First Mesa and crosses over Second and Third Mesas on the way to Tuba City from Window Rock.

The mesas are supplied with water from reliable springs and have provided the Hopi with protection from enemies, as the 600-foot cliffs discouraged assailants. Hardworking farmers, the Hopi are usually peaceable and independent. They keep in close touch with nature and have developed a rich ceremonial life, seeking to maintain balance and harmony with their surroundings and one another. Villages remain largely autonomous even today. The Hopi Tribal Council serves mainly as a liaison between villages and agencies of the federal and state governments.

Visiting Hopi Villages

The Hopi tend to be very private people, though they do welcome visitors to their lands. Policies may vary from village to village and are often posted. All villages *strictly* prohibit such

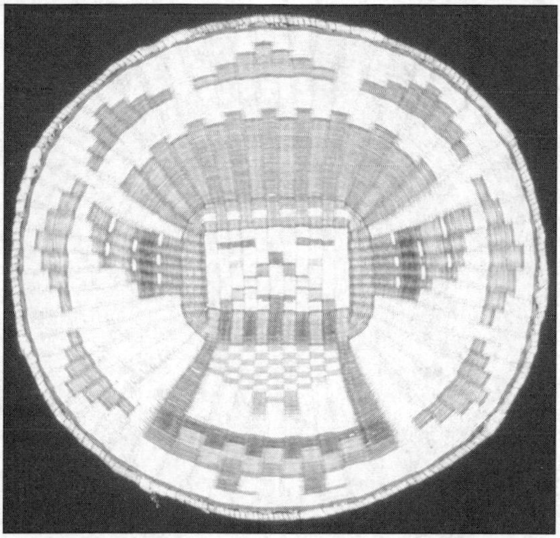

COURTESY OF THE HEARD MUSEUM

Supai Kachina on a Hopi wicker basket, late 1800s

disturbing activities as photography, sketching, and recording. To give residents their privacy, try to visit only between 8 A.M. and 5 P.M. and keep to the main streets and plazas. The village of Walpi asks that visitors enter only with an authorized Hopi guide.

The best time to visit a village is during a ceremony open to the public. Please remember that these are important religious rituals and that you are a guest. Some ceremonies have been placed off limits because of visitors' lack of respect. Check with the village having a dance to make sure that visitors are welcome. If so, you'll be allowed to experience Hopi culture. Dances take place in plazas on many weekends.

Information

To learn about upcoming dances open to the public, try contacting the Hopi Cultural Center (P.O. Box 67, Second Mesa, AZ 86043, 928/734-2401, www.hopiculturalcenter.com) and the Cultural Preservation Office (1 mile south of AZ 264 in the Tribal Headquarters building, P.O. Box 123, Kykotsmovi, AZ 86039, 928/734-3613). The village names in this section are given their common spelling, seen on most maps and signs, with the Hopi spelling in parentheses.

Tours

Guides can take you to petroglyphs and other historic sites, as well as introduce you to Hopi culture. Ask at the Tsakurshovi shop (between the Shungopavi turnoff and Hopi Cultural Center) or at the Hopi Cultural Center. On a tour with Gary Tso of the **Left-Handed Hunter Tour Company** (928/734-2567, lhhunter58@hotmail.com), you'll learn about Hopi culture while visiting artists, Old Oraibi, and a major petroglyph site.

KEAMS CANYON

This easternmost community on the Hopi Reservation is not a Hopi village, but an administrative town with various U.S. government agencies. The settlement lies at the mouth of a scenic wooded canyon named after Thomas Keam, who built a trading post here in 1875. From the town, the canyon winds northeast for about eight miles; the first three-mile stretch has a road. Kit Carson engraved his name on Inscription Rock, on the left about two miles in from Highway 264. You'll pass a picturesque Catholic church, then some pleasant picnic spots on the way in.

Practicalities

Keams Canyon Shopping Center, on Highway 264 just west of the Keams Canyon turnoff, offers a café, art gallery, grocery store, ice cream parlor, and service station. Keams Canyon Café (928/738-2296, Mon.–Fri. breakfast, lunch, and dinner, Sat. breakfast and lunch, $9–15) serves American, Mexican, and Native American dishes, plus pizza. McGee's Indian Art Gallery (928/738-2295, www.hopiart.com) has a fine selection of Native American arts and crafts as well as books and souvenirs.

Awatovi

Beginning as a small village in the 12th century, Awatovi (ah-WAHT-o-vee) had become an important Hopi town by 1540, when Spanish explorers from Coronado's expedition arrived.

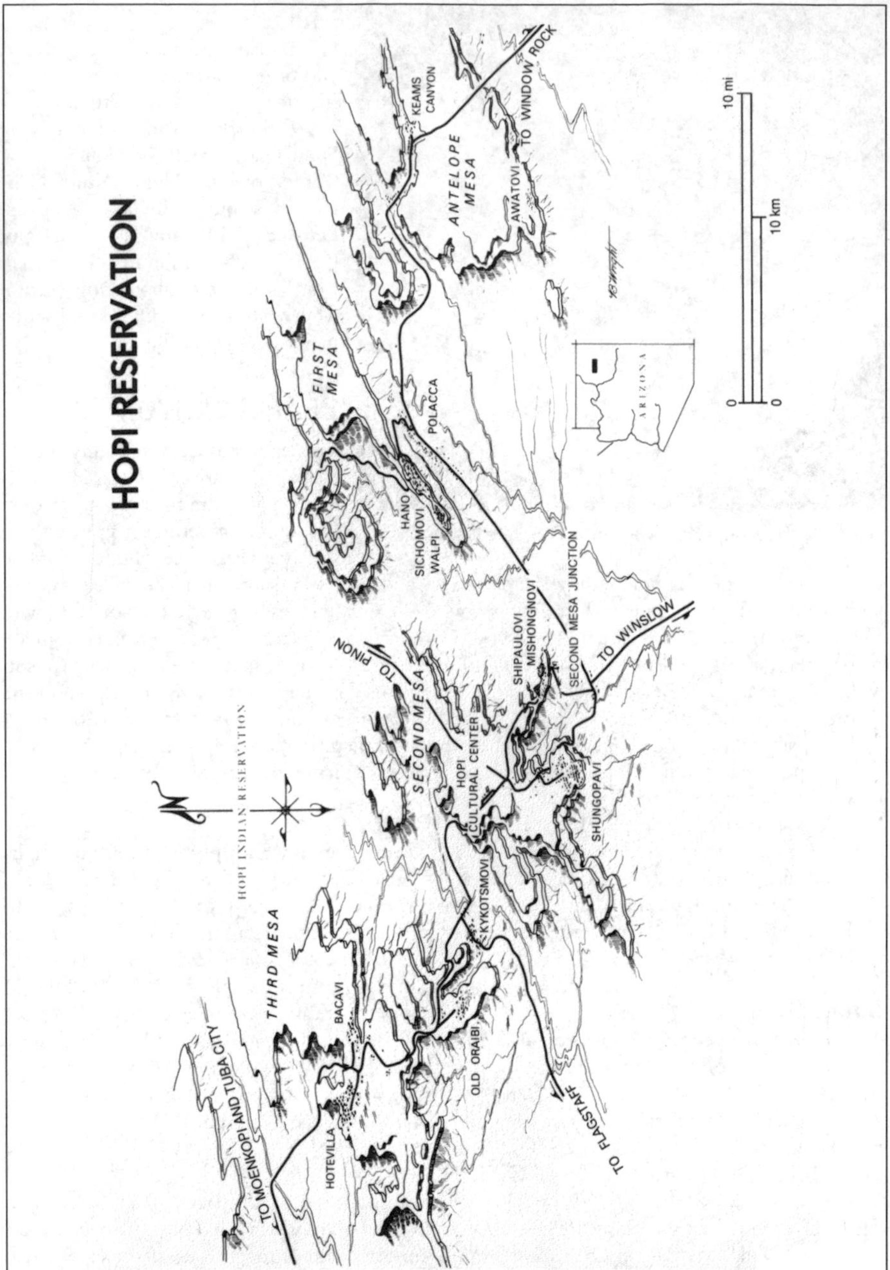
HOPI RESERVATION
HOPI INDIAN RESERVATION
N
TO MOENKOPI AND TUBA CITY
THIRD MESA
HOTEVILLA
BACAVI
OLD ORAIBI
KYKOTSMOVI
HOPI CULTURAL CENTER
SECOND MESA
TO PINON
SHUNGOPAVI
SHIPAULOVI
MISHONGNOVI
SECOND MESA JUNCTION
TO WINSLOW
TO FLAGSTAFF
WALPI
SICHOMOVI
HANO
FIRST MESA
POLACCA
ANTELOPE MESA
AWATOVI
KEAMS CANYON
TO WINDOW ROCK
ARIZONA
0
10 mi
0
10 km

THE EXPLORATION OF THE COLORADO RIVER AND ITS CANYONS

praying for rain, late 1800s

Franciscan friars in 1629 built a large church and friary using Hopi labor. Their mission lasted until 1680, when Hopi villagers, fearing that their culture would be destroyed by Christianity, joined their New Mexico Pueblo neighbors in successfully overthrowing Spanish rule, wrecking the Awatovi church, and killing most of the priests.

Spaniards re-established the mission in 1700, but other Hopi villages became so angered by this continued alien influence that they banded together and destroyed Awatovi. Of the 800 inhabitants, almost all the men were massacred and the women and children removed to other Hopi villages. Spanish troops retaliated a year later with little effect. Further missionary efforts among the Hopi proved futile. Only ghosts live at Awatovi today—it was never resettled. The ruin sprawls across 23 acres on the southwest tip of Antelope Mesa, with piles of rubble as high as 30 feet. The site is usually closed to the public.

FIRST MESA

Polacca

With an increasing population, some Hopi have built houses in settlements below the mesas, as at Polacca (po-LAH-kah). Still, if you ask residents of Polacca where they're from, they'll likely name one of the three villages on the mesa above. Polacca stretches for about a mile along the highway, but offers little of interest. Thrilling views, however, lie atop First Mesa, reached by a paved road that climbs steeply for 1.3 miles to Sichomovi on the crest. If you have a trailer or large vehicle, you must park it in Polacca or at parking areas .6 miles and 1 mile up.

Hano (Hanoki)

The first village you reach *looks* Hopi but is really a settlement of the Tewa, a Pueblo tribe from the Rio Grande region to the east. Fleeing from the Spanish after an unsuccessful revolt in 1696, a number of Tewa sought refuge here. Hopi leaders agreed, on the condition that the Tewa act as guardians of the access path to the mesa. Despite living close to the Hopi for so long, the Tewa have retained their own language and ceremonies. Hano's fascinating history is detailed in Edward P. Dozier's *A Tewa Indian Community in Arizona,* available in libraries.

HOPI KACHINAS AND CALENDAR

Kachinas appear to the Hopi from the winter solstice on December 21 until mid-July. They dance and sing in unison, symbolizing the harmony of good thought and deed, harmony required for rain to fall and for a balanced life. The rest of the year the kachinas remain in their home in the San Francisco Peaks.

A kachina can take three forms: a powerful unseen spirit, a dancer filled with the spirit, or a wooden figure representing the spirit. Kachina dancers are always male, even when the spirit is female. The men may present gifts of kachina figures to women and children during the dances. Each village sponsors its own ceremonies.

HOPI CALENDAR

Wuwuchim and Soyala (November–December)
These months symbolize the time of creation of the world. The villages tend to be quiet, as Hopi spend time in silence, prayer, and meditation.

Wuwuchim, a tribal initiation ceremony, marks the start of the ceremonial calendar year. Young men are initiated into adulthood, joining one of four ceremonial societies. Which society a man joins depends on his sponsor. Upon acceptance, the initiate receives instruction in Hopi creation beliefs. He's presented with a new name, and his childhood name is never used again. Only the Shungopavi village performs the entire Wuwuchim ceremony, and not every year. Other villages engage in parts of the Wuwuchim.

The Soyala Kachina appears from the west in the winter solstice ceremony, marking the beginning of the kachina season. As the days get longer, the Hopi begin planning the upcoming planting season; fertility is a major concern in the ceremony.

Buffalo Dances (January)
Men, women, and children perform these social dances in the plazas. They deal with fertility, especially the need for winter moisture in the form of snow.

Powamuya, the Bean Dance (February)
Bean sprouts are grown in a kiva as part of a 16-day ceremony. On the final day, kachina dancers form a long parade through the village. Children of about 10 years are initiated into kachina societies during the Powamuya. Ogre kachinas appear on First and Second mesas.

Kiva Dances (March)
A second set of nighttime kiva dances consists of *anktioni* (repeat dances).

Plaza Dances (April, May, and June)
The kachina dancers perform in all-day ceremonies lasting from sunrise to sunset, with breaks between dances. The group, and the people watching, concentrate in a community prayer calling on the spirits to bring rain for the growing crops.

Niman, the Home Dance (July)
At the summer solstice on June 21, the plaza dances end and preparations begin for the Going Home ceremony. In this rite, the last of the season, kachina dancers present the first green corn ears, then dance for rain to hasten growth of the remaining crops. Their spiritual work done, the kachinas return to their mountain home.

Snake, Flute, and Butterfly Dances (August)
The Snake and Flute ceremonies, held in alternate years, represent the clan groups who perform them in the interests of a good harvest and prosperity. The Snake Dance, usually closed to non-Hopi, takes place in even-numbered years at Shungopavi and Hotevilla and in odd-numbered years at Mishongnovi. The snakes, often poisonous rattlers, act as messengers to the spirits.

The Flute Ceremony takes place in odd-numbered years at Shungopavi and Walpi.

The Butterfly Dance, a social dance performed mainly by children, takes place in all villages. It also celebrates the harvest.

Women's Society Dances (September, October, and early November)
Held in the plazas, these ceremonies celebrate the harvest with wishes for health and prosperity. Chaos reigns during the Basket Dances; female dancers throw out baskets and other valuables to the audience, who engage in a mad free-for-all to grab the prizes. They mark the end of the ceremonial year.

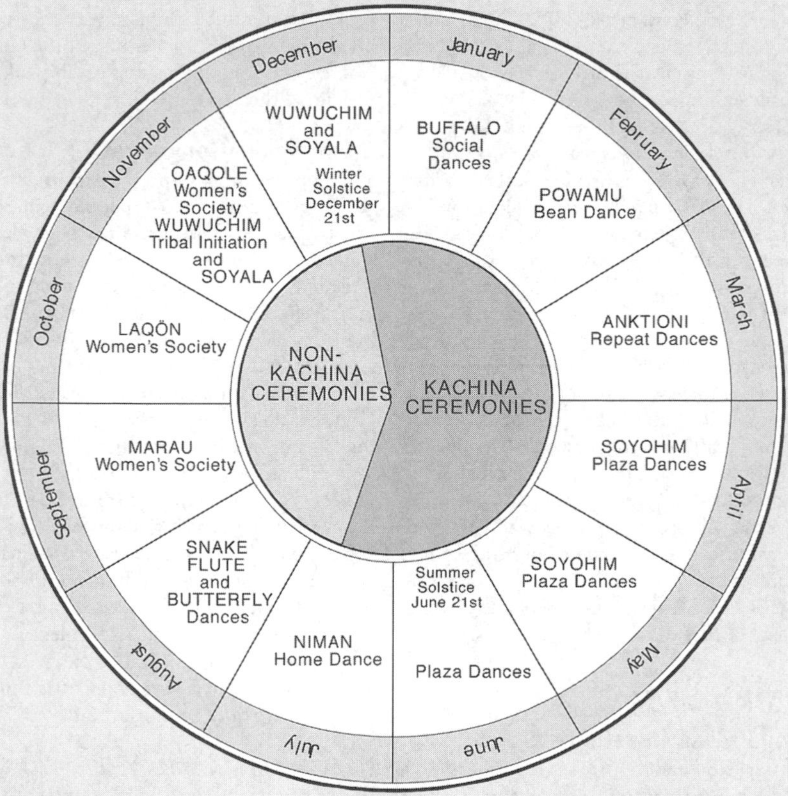

BOB RACE

Sichomovi (Sitsomovi)

To the visitor, Hano and the Hopi village of Sichomovi (see-CHO-mo-vee) appear as one, but residents know exactly where the dividing line is. Both Tewa and Hopi live here.

Walpi (Waalpi)

One of the most inspiring places in Arizona, Walpi (WAHL-pee) stands surrounded by sky and distant horizons. Ancient houses of yellow stone appear to grow from the mesa itself. A highlight for many visitors, Walpi dates from the 13th century and is renowned for its ceremonial dances and crafts.

Because this traditional village is small and its occupants sensitive, visitors may enter only with an authorized Hopi guide. One-hour walking tours (928/737-2262 Ponsi Hall, 928/737-2670 Community Development office, $8 adult, $5 youth 6–17) leave Ponsi Hall in Sichomovi 9:30 A.M.–5 P.M. daily in summer and 10 A.M.–3 P.M. daily the rest of the year. Note that the last tour leaves one hour before closing. Tours may not run on weekends and holidays, so it's best to call ahead before making a special trip out. Turn off Highway 264 near Milepost 392 at the First Mesa Village signed.

Walking from Sichomovi, you'll watch the mesa narrow to just 15 feet before widening again at Walpi. Unlike most other Hopi villages, Walpi lacks electricity and running water. Residents have to walk back toward Sichomovi to get water or to wash. Look for bowl-shaped depressions once used to collect rainwater. Precipitous foot trails and ruins of old defenses and buildings cling to the mesa slopes far below.

Signs outside houses in Walpi and the other First Mesa villages let you know where to shop. Usually men carve the kachina dolls and women fashion the pottery. Although most kachina dances at First Mesa remain closed to the public, you may be able to attend social dances.

SECOND MESA

Second Mesa (Junction)

Highways 264 and 87 meet at the foot of Second Mesa, 7 miles west of Polacca and 60 miles north of Winslow. **LKD's Diner** (928/737-2717, Mon.–Sat. lunch and dinner) serves Hopi tacos and tostadas, Mexican food, and burgers. **Hopi Fine Arts–Alph Secakuku** gallery sells arts and crafts. You'll also find a post office and supermarket here. **Honani Crafts Gallery** is .5 miles west at the turnoff for Shipaulovi and Mishongnovi villages.

Shipaulovi (Supawlavi) and Mishongnovi (Musangnuvi)

These villages are close neighbors on an eastern projection of Second Mesa. Dances often take place. You reach Shipaulovi (shih-PAW-lo-vee) and Mishongnovi (mih-SHONG-no-vee) by a short paved road that climbs steeply from Highway 264, a half mile west of the intersection with Highway 87, or by a mesa-top road (also paved, but not to be confused with the pinyon–Hard Rock Road) .3 miles east of the Cultural Center. Mishongnovi is east of Shipaulovi, at the end of the mesa.

Shungopavi (Songoopavi)

Shungopavi (shong-O-po-vee or shih-MO-pah-vee) is the largest (pop. 742) of the three Second Mesa villages. A sign near the village entrance states that dances are closed to non-Indians, though that's not always the case—you can ask in the village. **Dawa's Art and Crafts** on the road into the village sells locally made work. More galleries lie between the village turnoff and the Cultural Center. Shungopavi is .8 miles south off Highway 264, midway between the Hopi Cultural Center and the junction with Highway 87.

Joseph and Janice Day at **Tsakurshovi** (928/734-2478) provide a treasure trove of information about visiting and shopping in the Hopi lands; you'll also find an excellent array of kachinas, basketry, music, and other art in their little shop on the north side of the highway, .4 miles west of the Shungopavi turnoff and 1.5 miles east of the Hopi Cultural Center. A bit farther west on the highway, **Hopi Silver Arts and Crafts** and **Iskasopu Gallery** offer good selections.

Hopi Cultural Center

Both visitors and local Hopi enjoy coming to this excellent pueblo-style museum/motel/restaurant/gift shop complex. It's on the west side of Second Mesa, just before the road plunges down on the way to Third Mesa.

The museum (928/734-6650, www.hopiculturalcenter.com, $3 adults, $1 children 13 and under) displays fine exhibits of Hopi culture and crafts along with many historic photos. It's open 8 A.M.–5 P.M. Monday–Friday, 9 A.M.–3 P.M. Saturday and Sunday, but is closed weekends from about late October to late March. There's a small gift shop just inside the entrance, and you can often purchase traditional *piki* bread. (To learn more of Hopi mythology and customs, dig into off-reservation sources such as the Special Collections at Northern Arizona University or the Museum of Northern Arizona libraries, both in Flagstaff.)

The motel (P.O. Box 67, Second Mesa, AZ 86043, 928/734-2401, www.hopiculturalcenter.com, $90 s weekdays, $95 s Fri.–Sat., $5 each additional person) provides all-nonsmoking rooms with Hopi decor; rates drop $30 in winter. Reservations are highly recommended, as it's a long drive to the next motel. A free picnic area and campground lie next door among the juniper trees. There's no water or hookups, but you can use the restrooms in the Cultural Center.

The restaurant (daily breakfast, lunch, and dinner, $7–13) prepares good Hopi, American, Mexican, and pizza dishes. This is your big chance to try *paatupsuki* (pinto bean and hominy soup), or maybe some *noqkwivi* (traditional stew of lamb and hominy), or a breakfast of blue pancakes made of Hopi corn. Not to be outdone by Navajo neighbors, the restaurant serves a Hopi taco (with beef) and a Hopi tostada (vegetarian).

Hopi Arts & Crafts (928/734-2463, closed Sat.–Sun.) offers a variety of traditional work and a small exhibit with examples of early Hopi silver jewelry; it's just a short walk across the picnic/camping area. You may also see artwork for sale in a gallery at the Hopi Cultural Center and displayed by vendors on tables outside.

For a shortcut to Chinle and Canyon de Chelly, turn north off Highway 264 beside the Cultural Center to Pinyon Trading Post, 26 miles (mostly rough and only partly paved), then turn east 42 miles on paved roads.

THIRD MESA

Kykotsmovi (Kiqötsmovi)

The name means Mound of Ruined Houses. Hopi from Old Oraibi (o-RYE-bee) founded this settlement near a spring at the base of Third Mesa. Peach trees add greenery to the town. Kykotsmovi (kee-KEUTS-mo-vee), also known as New Oraibi, has offices of the Hopi Tribal Council.

The **Cultural Preservation Office** (P.O. Box 123, Kykotsmovi, AZ 86039, 928/734-3613, 8 A.M.–5 P.M. Mon.–Fri.) provides information for visitors to the Hopi Indian Reservation at its office in the Tribal Headquarters building, one mile south of Highway 264. **Kykotsmovi Village Store** in town sells groceries and fixes pizza, subs, and snacks. **Quotskuyva Fine Arts & Gifts** is on the Leupp Road between Mileposts 46 and 47, 1.2 miles south of Highway 264.

You can stop for a picnic along Highway 264 at Oraibi Wash, .8 miles east of the Kykotsmovi turnoff and across the bridge, or the Pumpkin Seed Hill overlook 1.2 miles west of the turnoff on the climb to Old Oraibi; both of these sites lie just north of the highway. Indian Route 2, leading south from Kykotsmovi to Leupp (pronounced loop), is paved and the shortest way to Flagstaff. You can either take the main road .5 miles west of the Kykotsmovi turnoff, or drive through the village, then turn right on the Leupp Road.

Old Oraibi (Orayvi)

This dusty pueblo perched on the edge of Third Mesa dates from 1150 and is probably the oldest continuously inhabited community in the United States.

The 20th century was difficult for this ancient village. In 1900 it ranked as one of the largest Hopi settlements, with a population of more than 800, but dissension caused many to leave. The first major dispute occurred in 1906 between two chiefs, You-ke-oma and Tawa-quap-tewa. Instead of letting fly with bullets and arrows, the leaders staged a "push-of-war" contest. A line was cut into the mesa and the two groups stood on either side. They pushed against each other as hard as they could until Tawa-quap-tewa's group crossed the line and won. You-ke-oma, the loser, left with his faction to establish Hotevilla four miles away. This event was recorded a quarter-mile north of Oraibi with the line and inscription: "Well, it have to be done this way now, that when you pass this LINE it will be DONE, Sept. 8, 1906." A bear paw cut in the rock is the symbol of Tawa-quap-tewa and his Bear Clan, while a skull represents You-ke-oma and his Skeleton Clan. Other residents split off to join New Oraibi at the foot of the mesa.

A ruin near Old Oraibi on the south end of the mesa is all that remains of a church built in 1901 by the Mennonite minister H. R. Voth. Most villagers disliked having it so close to their homes and were no doubt relieved when lightning destroyed the church in 1942. It's closed to the public but you can see the ruin from the village.

Old Oraibi lies two miles west of Kykotsmovi. Avoid driving through the village and stirring up dust; park outside—or next to **Hamana So-o's Arts & Crafts**—and walk. You can shop for Hopi arts and crafts here and at galleries nearby on the highway. Villagers may offer items for sale from their homes.

Hotevilla (Hot'vela)

Founded in 1906 after the split from Old Oraibi, Hotevilla (HOAT-vih-lah) got off to a shaky start. Federal officials demanded that the group move back to Old Oraibi so their children could attend school there. Twenty-five men agreed to return with their families, despite continued bad feelings. About 53 others refused to leave Hotevilla and were jailed for 90 days while their children were forcibly removed to a Keams Canyon boarding school. That winter the women and infants fended for themselves, with little food and inadequate shelter. In the following year the men returned, building better houses and planting crops. Exasperated authorities continued to haul You-ke-oma off to jail for his lack of cooperation and refusal to send village children to school. In 1912, government officials invited the chief to Washington for a meeting with President Taft, but the meeting didn't soften You-ke-oma's stance. Today the village is known for its dances, basketry, and other crafts. The turnoff for Hotevilla is 3.7 miles northwest of Old Oraibi and 46 miles southeast of Tuba City.

Bacavi (Paaqavi)

The You-ke-oma loyalists who returned to Old Oraibi under federal pressure continued to clash with the people of Tawa-quap-tewa. At one point, when two of the returning women died in quick succession, cries of witchcraft went up. Finally, in November 1909, tensions became unbearable. Members of the unwelcome group packed their bags once more and settled at a new site called Bacavi (BAH-kah-vee) Spring. The name means "jointed reed," after a plant found at the spring. Bacavi lies on the opposite side of the highway from Hotevilla.

Coal Mine Canyon

Hoodoos and crenulated cliffs of red, white, and gray rocks present a striking sight from the overlook. You may experience vertigo as you peer into the precipitous depths. Take care near the edge as the rock layers are very brittle. Hopi have long obtained coal from the seam just below the rim. A trail descends into the canyon, but you'll need a Navajo tribal permit to hike it. This very scenic spot has picnic tables and lies 30 miles northwest of Bacavi and 16 miles southeast of Tuba City on Highway 264. Look for a windmill and the Coal Mine Mesa Rodeo Ground on the north side of the highway (no signs) between Mileposts 337 and 338, then turn in across the cattle guard and follow the dirt road, which may be too rough for cars, .5 miles to the rim.

Moenkopi (Munqapi)

This Hopi village lies two miles southeast of Tuba City. Chief Tuba (c. 1810–1887) of Oraibi, 48 miles southeast, founded Moenkopi (The Place of Running Water) in the 1870s. Mormons constructed a woolen mill in 1879 with plans to use local labor, but the Hopi disliked working with machinery and the project failed. Moenkopi has two sections—only the upper village participates in the Hopi Tribal Council; the more conservative lower village does not. Water from springs irrigates the fields here, an advantage not enjoyed by other Hopi villages.

Eastern Arizona

Eastern Arizona will surprise you. Instead of arid desert country, you'll find 2,000 square miles of forested peaks, placid lakes, and sparkling streams in the White Mountains at the heart of the region. The region's natural beauty makes it a wonderful retreat from the hectic pace of urban areas. This is a place to relax and enjoy the outdoors, and some visitors spend the entire summer doing just that. You'll find excellent opportunities for hiking, horseback riding, fishing, and winter sports.

For a wildly scenic drive in the high country, explore the Coronado Trail between Clifton and Springerville. Slow and winding, the route offers almost unlimited picnicking, hiking, and camping possibilities. To the west, another highway presents a different thrill. As you drive along southwest of Show Low, the road suddenly begins to descend into a magnificent chasm; it's the Salt River Canyon, a smaller but equally colorful version of the Grand Canyon.

Traveling north from the White Mountains the scenery changes from mountain firs and pines, to junipers and vast rangelands, then to the multihued, barren hills of the Painted Desert. Here you'll see a "forest" millions of years old whose colorful logs now rest in Petrified Forest National Park.

Southward from the White Mountains, the

Must-Sees

Look for M to find the sights and activities you can't miss and M for the best dining and lodging.

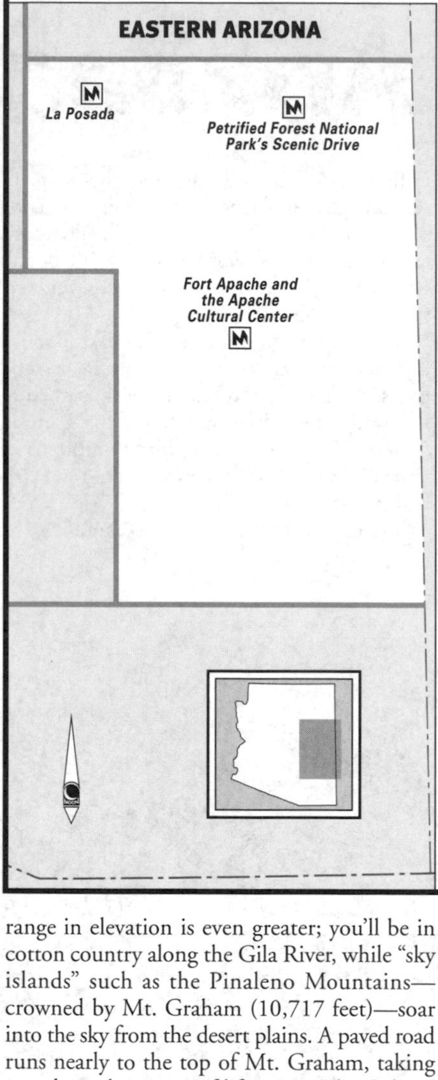

COURTESY OF THE OLD TRAILS MUSEUM, WINSLOW

Interior of Winslow's famed Harvey House, La Posada, in 1930. It included the busy newsstand in the background.

La Posada in Winslow wasn't just a hotel, but a re-creation of a grand hacienda. When movie stars and others arrived after the 1930 opening, they felt as if they were guests of an 18th-century Spanish don. Today you can experience the same effect on a stroll through the arched passageways, ballroom, gardens, and other public areas (page 534).

Petrified Forest National Park's Scenic Drive winds past fallen trees hundreds of million years old that have turned to colorful stone. Short trails lead to prehistoric pueblos—one made of petrified logs—and vistas of the Painted Desert (page 543).

Fort Apache and the Apache Cultural Center has well-preserved 19th-century fort buildings on Officers' Row and a good museum of White Mountain Apache culture and crafts (page 557).

range in elevation is even greater; you'll be in cotton country along the Gila River, while "sky islands" such as the Pinaleno Mountains—crowned by Mt. Graham (10,717 feet)—soar into the sky from the desert plains. A paved road runs nearly to the top of Mt. Graham, taking you through a range of life zones. The Galiuro Mountains to the west form a rugged wilderness with several peaks over 7,000 feet. Perennial streams add beauty to desert canyons in such places as Aravaipa Canyon Wilderness west of Safford and the Gila Box Riparian National Conservation Area east of town.

PLANNING YOUR TIME

Holbrook, in the north, is the logical base for a visit to Petrified Forest National Park. All of the towns in the White Mountains have places to stay and eat, but Greer offers the prettiest setting

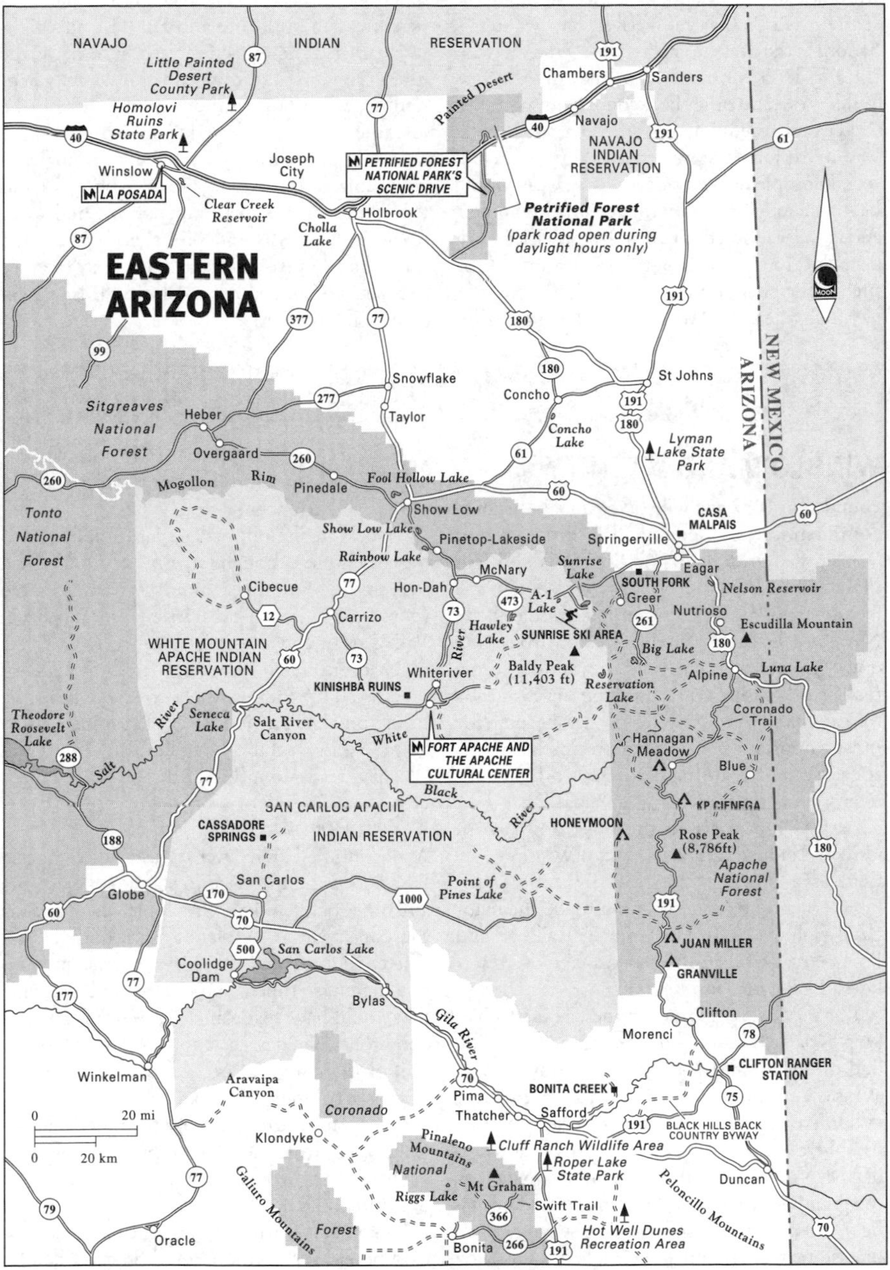

Eastern Arizona

with meadows and dense forests surrounding the sparkling Little Colorado River. Farther south, Safford is the best choice for the scenic drive up the Pinaleno Mountains, a hike in Aravaipa Wilderness, and other backcountry forays.

Leisurely scenic drives are perhaps the best way to explore Eastern Arizona—you can put together some driving fine loops. A week would be long enough to enjoy the region's highlights. Along the way you can take in history, science, or art at local museums, or stop to visit one of the prehistoric pueblo sites.

Much of eastern Arizona lies at elevations of 6,000–8,500 feet, where average summer temperatures run in the 60s and 70s (°F), and highs rarely exceed the mid-80s. Early summer is the driest time of year. From mid-July to early September, afternoon thunderstorms drench the forests almost daily, delivering about one-third of the area's approximately 15 inches of annual precipitation. Winter brings heavy snowfalls and low temperatures in the teens, but highs can reach the mid-40s and skiers enjoy the often bright and sunny winter days. You may even see some anglers out chopping holes in the lake ice in search of elusive trout.

The High Desert

WINSLOW AND VICINITY

Founded in 1882 as a railroad terminal, the town commemorates General Edward Francis Winslow, president of the St. Louis and San Francisco Railroad that was associated with the Atlantic and Pacific line running through here. Navajos called the place Beeshsinil (iron lying down). Ranchers turned the community into a major stock-raising center and shipping point. By the early 20th century, Winslow had become the most important community in northern Arizona. Route 66, formed in 1926 to help connect Chicago with the West Coast, brought America's motorists to the busy downtown. Charles Lindbergh came to design Winslow Airfield as a midway stop for flights between Chicago and Los Angeles, then made the inaugural flight in 1930. The Santa Fe Railroad and Fred Harvey Company opened a fabulous resort hotel, La Posada, also in 1930.

But alas, by the 1970s commercial flights had long bypassed the airfield, passenger train traffic had dried up, and I-40 bypassed downtown. Winslow lay tattered and nearly forgotten. Now visitors have started to discover the history and atmosphere of the old town. La Posada, nearly lost, has been dusted off, restored, and reopened as the grand Southwest hotel it once was. The airfield and a piece of Route 66 also survive, as do prehistoric ruins nearby in Homolovi Ruins State Park. The Old Trails Museum downtown portrays Winslow's colorful history with many old photos and artifacts.

Trade and the railroad remain important to the community, though tourism, trucking, and a state prison boost the economy as well. Winslow (pop. 9,475) lies in the Little Colorado River Valley at an elevation of 4,880 feet. Travelers find it a convenient stopover: Meteor Crater is 25 miles west, the Hopi and Navajo reservations lie to the north, Petrified Forest National Park is 50 miles east, and the Mogollon Rim forest and lake country is 40 miles south.

La Posada

Almost immediately after its 1930 opening, La Posada became *the* place to stay for movie stars and other rich and famous people who came for a relaxing getaway in splendid surroundings. Architect Mary Colter let loose her imagination, creating not so much a hotel as a grand hacienda that would have made an 18th-century Spanish don proud. She designed and oversaw construction of the magnificent arches, acres of exotic gardens, a ballroom, antiques "from their travels," and rustic furniture "made by the ranch hands." Colter considered it her masterpiece. People staying here felt as though they were personal guests of the fictional don.

La Posada turned out to be the last great railroad hotel built in the United States. The De-

COURTESY OF THE OLD TRAILS MUSEUM, WINSLOW

Canyon Diablo, about midway between Winslow and Flagstaff, held up track laying from December 1881 until the first train gingerly crossed this bridge in July 1882.

pression hurt business in the 1930s, then the post-war decline of the railroads forced the hotel to close in 1957. The Santa Fe Railroad converted some of it to offices. The building might have been torn down had not some people discovered this "lost treasure" and set to work restoring it. Now, after 40 years of lying dormant, La Posada once again welcomes guests with its spacious halls, dining area, lounge, and guestrooms. Patios and libraries invite guests to sit down and relax. A gift shop sells Southwestern items including Native American work, Mimbreño ware (with prehistoric designs), and books. You're welcome to drop by 7 A.M.–10 P.M. daily and take a self-guided walking tour of the grand public areas. With advance notice, the Winslow Harvey Girls offer guided tours. The hotel is online at www.laposada.org.

Old Trails Museum

This fun little museum (212 Kinsley Ave., 928/289-5861, 1–5 P.M. Tues.–Sat., closed Wed. Nov.–Feb., donations welcome) reveals life in the Winslow area from Stone Age to modern times. Popular exhibits include Homolovi pottery, railroad memorabilia, La Posada and Harvey Girls displays, Route 66 history, territorial doctors, and the moonshine still used by Italian immigrant Frank Ianni from the 1920s to the 1980s. You may see clothing worn by stage actress Norma Deane (1897–1926), a local girl who made it big in the theater, was engaged to famed star Victor Jory, then died on a visit home while trying to cross a flooded wash. The collection is downtown in a 1921 commercial building. You can purchase historic Winslow calendars and regional books.

The Corner

"Take it Easy," a hit single recorded by The Eagles in the early 1970s, inspired the little park near the museum with the lines "Standin' on a corner in Winslow, Arizona, such a fine sight to see. It's a girl, my Lord, in a flatbed Ford, slowin' down to take a look at me." Look for the statue and mural at the northwest corner of Route 66 (2nd St.) and Kinsley Avenue.

Brigham City

In 1876 Mormon pioneers arrived to establish this new settlement on the Little Colorado. They had been called by their church to provide a new place for members to live and work. The colonists' early optimism for the farming potential of bottomland along the Little Colorado soon faded as floods washed away dams and irrigation systems. Fear of Native American attacks caused residents to protect their community with walls 200 feet long and 7 feet high. Although never attacked, settlers abandoned Brigham City in 1881 because of the irrigation difficulties. It's slowly being reconstructed on a site just northeast of Winslow; ask at the chamber of commerce office. Old Trails Museum has a model of the settlement.

Homolovi Ruins State Park

Ancestral Puebloans lived in pit houses and later at six pueblo villages near present-day Winslow about A.D. 600–1390. The inhabitants, it's believed, then moved north to the Hopi mesas. Oral traditions passed down through generations of Hopi relate how ancestors emerged from a world beneath the present one and migrated in stages to their present home. Clan elders guided the migrations through revelations from dreams and meditations. The Hopi consider these ruins sacred and still leave *pahos* (prayer feathers) here for the spirits. Site visitors mustn't take or disturb anything; federal and state laws prohibit removal of artifacts. Even the tiniest pot shard must be left in place to preserve the sacred character of the sites.

The name Homolovi (Place of the Little Hills) applies to all sites in the Winslow area. Serious archaeological studies began only in 1984; you're welcome to watch the archaeologists when they're working here. The **visitors center** makes a good place to start with its exhibits, videos (shown on request), and information desk; you can purchase Hopi crafts and books on Native Americans. Staff offer workshops on crafts, gardening, archaeology, wildlife, and storytelling. Archaeology Day in July features tours and arts and crafts demonstrations. A pit house village site lies behind the visitors center, but the shallow depressions can hardly be seen.

A sign at the visitors center parking area points the way toward **Sunset Cemetery,** a 0.8-mile - round-trip walk. Lot Smith founded Sunset in 1876 beside the Little Colorado River, though floods and droughts forced abandonment of the Mormon settlement 11 years later.

The park (928/289-4106, $4/vehicle up to 4 people) is open sunrise to sunset daily; visitors center hours run 8 A.M.–5 P.M. daily except Christmas. Take I-40 Exit 257 for Highway 87, just east of Winslow, go north 1.3 miles to the park entrance, then turn left 2.1 miles to the visitors center; on the way in you'll pass the turnoff for the campground and Homolovi I on the left, then the Homolovi II turnoff on the right just before the visitors center.

The **campground** has tent pads, showers, dump station, and water and electric hookups for $10 ($15 if you use hookups) including park admission; there's a discount for weekly stays. Water hookups are available only mid-April–mid-October. The campground usually has room; no reservations are taken. You can walk to the visitors center on a 1.2-mile one-way trail.

Homolovi II is the largest site and forms the main section of the state park. Though badly weathered, the ruins show what a prehistoric site looks like before extensive excavation or reconstruction. A short loop trail, suitable for wheelchairs, leads along the top of a mesa past the ruins. Signs interpret and describe the village. Ancestral pueblo people occupied it 1250–1390 with a population as high as 3,000. The village comprised more than 1,200 rooms arranged around three plazas and probably stood two or three stories high. A group of five rooms in the West Plaza and a kiva in the Central Plaza have been excavated and stabilized to show the original floor plans. The village served as a major trade center and staging area for northward migrations. Waters of the Little Colorado River below attracted game and nourished crops and wild plant foods.

The trailhead for Homolovi II is 3.1 miles north of the visitors center on a paved road; a few picnic tables lie along the way in. You can also stop at the Tsu 'vö Loop Trail, a half-mile interpretive loop between twin buttes; a trail leaflet helps you locate petroglyphs and other features beside the trail.

Homolovi I, a pueblo of over 1,000 rooms near the Colorado River, takes some imagina-

© BILL WEIR

sifting through the diggings at Homolovi I, Homolovi Ruins State Park

tion because you can see only outlines of the walls. Follow the paved road 1.5 miles, then walk along a short dirt trail to reach it.

Homolovi III and IV lie west across the Little Colorado River from Homolovi II. Homolovi IV may be visited and has some fine petroglyphs; stop first at the visitors center to obtain directions. There's nothing to see at Homolovi III; the ruins have been buried to protect them from erosion.

Little Painted Desert County Park

Enjoy the views and beautiful sunsets from this park, 13 miles northeast of Winslow on Highway 87 (I-40 Exit 257). Facilities include a scenic rim viewpoint overlooking colorful desert hills, a hiking trail, and picnic tables.

McHood Park

Situated on both banks of Clear Creek Reservoir, McHood (928/289-4792 city offices) features swimming, boating, fishing, picnicking, and camping. Anglers catch trout, bass, and catfish. Boaters may use the launch ramp and head 2.5 miles upstream into a scenic canyon with 200-foot cliffs; look for petroglyphs. The area has good bird-watching too. The park stays open all year, no drinking water, hookups, or fee.

From Winslow, head south 1.3 miles on Highway 87, then left 4.7 miles on Highway 99 to the park. Turn left before the reservoir bridge to reach the shaded picnic tables overlooking the lake, swimming area, campground, and boat ramp or continue across the bridge and turn left to the day-use area with shaded picnic tables, playground, and group ramadas.

Entertainment and Events

Bands play Saturday evenings in summer at The Corner. Fireworks and local entertainers help celebrate **July 4th. Standin' on the Corner Celebration** on the first weekend in October offers music, arts and crafts, and classic cars. The **Christmas Parade** starts off the holiday season on the third Saturday in November.

Recreation

Winslow City Park (corner of Colorado Ave. and Cherry St., 928/289-5714 parks and recreation) has a year-round indoor pool (928/289-4543), summertime outdoor pool (928/289-4592), tennis and racquetball courts, ball fields, weight rooms, and sports programs.

Accommodations

Winslow has a good selection of motels, which can be very good values. You'll find them along old Route 66 (Business I-40) between I-40 Exits 252 and 255 and on North Park Drive near I-40 Exit 253. The I-40 business route splits downtown into Route 66/2nd Street (eastbound) and 3rd Street (westbound).

Under $50: Winslow Inn (701 W. 3rd St., 928/289-9389, $34 s, $36 d) and **Motel 10** (725 W. 3rd St., 928/289-3211 or 800/675-7478, $33 s, $36 d incl. tax) provide the basics.

$50–100: Econo Lodge (1706 N. Park Dr., just south of I-40 Exit 253, 928/289-4687 or

800/553-2666, $50 s, $70 d) includes an outdoor pool. The distinctively styled **Best Western Adobe Inn** (1701 N. Park Dr., just south of I-40 Exit 253, 928/289-4638 or 800/937-8376, $79 s, $84 d) offers an indoor pool, hot tub, and restaurant. **Travelodge** (1914 W. 3rd St., 928/289-4611 or 800/578-7878, $45 s, $50–52 d) has a pool. **Super 8 Motel** (1916 W. 3rd St., 928/289-4606 or 800/800-8000, $49 s, $63–65 d) just has rooms. **Days Inn** (2035 W. Hwy. 66 near I-40 Exit 252, 928/289-1010 or 800/329-7466, $65 d) sports an indoor pool and hot tub.

$100–150: Holiday Inn Express (Transcon Lane, just north off I-40 Exit 255, 928/289-2960 or 800/465-4329, $99 s, $109 d) features an indoor pool and hot tub.

La Posada (303 E. 2nd St., 928/289-4366, www.laposada.org, $89 d room, $109 d with a balcony or hot tub, $120–179 d suites) once again welcomes guests to its distinctive rooms and spacious halls decorated with art and hand-crafted furniture. All rooms have private baths, which was a rarity back in 1930. The Turquoise Room restaurant has some of the best food in northern Arizona. Amtrak passengers have only a short stroll to the hotel doors. There's a gift shop too.

Campgrounds

Freddie's RV Park (928/289-3201, $15.50 RV w/hookups) is just north of I-40 Exit 255 on the east side of town. Homolovi Ruins State Park offers sites with hookups in a far more natural setting.

Food

Named for the private dining car on the Santa Fe Super Chief, La Posada's **Turquoise Room** (928/289-2888, daily breakfast, lunch, and dinner, $16–27) serves retro–Fred Harvey and contemporary Southwestern cuisine. In the late 1800s and early 1900s, Fred Harvey restaurants served the region's best meals. Specialties popular back then included baked egg dishes, which you'll find on the breakfast menu. Dinners, for which you should make reservations, feature a changing selection of steak, prime rib, lamb, chicken, seafood, and pasta. The signature soup is corn on one side and bean on the other, with a signature on top! The Martini Lounge lies just off the dining room.

Seattle Grind (106 E. 2nd St., 928/289-2859, daily) offers a long list of coffees and teas plus pastries in a historic building near The Corner. **Entre Restaurant** (1919 W. 2nd St., 928/289-2141, daily lunch and dinner, $8–11) offers Chinese and American fare; there's also a lunch buffet on weekdays. **Sue's Place Family Restaurant** (723 W. 3rd St., 928/289-1234, Mon.–Sat. breakfast and lunch, Mon.–Fri. dinner, $6.50–9) has American favorites such as chicken fried steak and some Mexican items. On the east edge of town, just north off I-40 Exit 255, you can dine at **China Inn** (928/289-2086, Mon.–Sat. lunch and daily dinner, $7.25–14). Look for chain and truck-stop restaurants just north of I-40 Exit 253 off N. Park Drive. **Bashas'** and **Safeway** supermarkets are one block south of I-40 Exit 253 off N. Park Drive.

Information, Shopping, and Services

The **Winslow Chamber of Commerce** (P.O. Box 460, Winslow, AZ 86047, 928/289-2434, http://winslowarizona.org, 8 A.M.–5 P.M. Mon.–Fri.) provides maps and information on area sights and facilities. Call for current location.

For Native American art and crafts, drop in at the historic **Hubbell Trading Post** (523 W. 2nd St., 928/289-3986) to see work by the Arizona Indian Arts Cooperative.

The **public library** (420 W. Gillmore St., 928/289-4982), one block west from N. Park Drive, has a good collection of books on Arizona and the Southwest; it's open 10 A.M.–5 P.M. Tuesday and Friday, 10 A.M.–7 P.M. Wednesday and Thursday, and 11 A.M.–4 P.M. Saturday. The **post office** (223 N. Williamson Ave., 928/289-2131) is downtown between Route 66 and 3rd Street. **Winslow Memorial Hospital** (1501 Williamson Ave., 928/289-4691) is north of downtown.

Getting There

Amtrak (800/872-7245) offers rail service from La Posada, but there's no agent in town. **Greyhound** buses (2201 N. Park Dr., 928/289-9531, 800/231-2222) stop at the Super American Truck Stop off N. Park Drive just north of I-40 Exit 253.

Joseph City

Mormons established the farming community of Allen's Camp in 1876 under great difficulty. Attempts to dam the Little Colorado for irrigation failed repeatedly, leaving crops to wither away. Although four other Mormon settlements along the Little Colorado were abandoned, this town, renamed Joseph City, persevered. It is the oldest Anglo community in Navajo County.

HOLBROOK

When the railroad reached this site in 1881, Eastern investors recognized the surrounding rangelands as prime cattle country and wasted no time in seeking grazing rights. Within two years, the Aztec Land and Cattle Company based near Joseph City ran 60,000 head of cattle. The Aztec, better known as the Hashknife outfit after the shape of its brand, became the third-largest cattle empire in the United States. Its cowboys worked the longhorns across one million acres. On holidays, the cowpokes rode into Holbrook with guns blazing, looking for a good time. Rustling and poor management troubled the Hashknife operation until it shut down about 1900, but Holbrook (pop. about 5,000) remains a ranching center. Travelers often use Holbrook as a base for visiting the nearby Petrified Forest National Park and the Navajo and Hopi lands.

Navajo County Museum

You can relive some of the area's Wild West history in the 1898 former county courthouse downtown (100 E. Arizona St. and Navajo Blvd., 928/524-6558 or 800/524-2459, 8 A.M.–5 P.M. Mon.–Fri. and 8 A.M.–4 P.M. Sat.–Sun., donations welcome). The Holbrook Chamber of Commerce office is here too, with the same telephone numbers, but it closes on weekends. Period rooms and artifacts trace the changes from the prehistoric era through lawless frontier days to modern times. Head upstairs to see the courtroom, with its decorative metal ceiling, and some restored offices. Don't miss the dungeon-like jail downstairs.

International Petrified Forest and the Museum of the Americas

Several attractions invite a stop at this private museum (3 miles east at I-40 Exit 292, 928/524-9178 or 888/830-6682, 8 A.M.–5 P.M. daily, $5/vehicle). The large museum shows the artistry of both regional and Meso-American prehistoric cultures. A two-room reconstructed pueblo from Four-Mile Ruin (1100–1375), located southwest of Snowflake, stands in the middle of the museum. You'll see superb figurines and pottery, along with jewelry, tools, and other finds. A fossil display has some huge dinosaur bones, eggs, and dung. The unusual green petrified wood gets its color from chromium. Life-size dinosaurs will interest the kids. A large gift shop offers petrified wood and other souvenirs. A four-mile loop drive leads past a small herd of buffalo and colorful hills covered with large petrified logs.

Events

Pow-wow–style **Native American Dances** take place every week nightly during June and July on the lawn next to the old courthouse; check with the chamber for the schedule and times. The **Hashknife Pony Express** hits the trail every year in late January, when riders carry the mail from Holbrook to Scottsdale. You can send a letter along, too, by affixing the usual postage and marking the lower left corner "Via Pony Express." Enclose it in a second envelope and send it to Postmaster, Holbrook, AZ 86025. Fireworks and "the state's best barbecue" mark **July 4th. Old West Days** in August features Old West reenactors, Bucket of Blood foot and bicycle races, arts and crafts exhibits, a quilt show, music, and dancing. The **Navajo County Fair** runs in September. Townspeople decorate a room full of trees for the **Festival of Trees** on Thursday–Saturday of the first weekend of December. A nighttime **Christmas Parade of Lights** brightens downtown on the first Saturday in December.

Shopping

Although it's strictly forbidden to remove anything from Petrified Forest National Park, you can shop in Holbrook for samples of the strange wood-turned-stone that have come from private lands. Polished specimens run from a few dollars into the tens of thousands. Turquoise, geodes, and other treasures are available as well. **Jim Gray's Petrified Wood Co.** has an enormous selection just south of town at the junction of U.S. Highway 180 on the way to the south entrance of Petrified Forest National Park; look for huge petrified logs surrounding the store; you can watch cutting and polishing of the wood in the saw shop.

Recreation

Hunt Park features a picnic area, playground, outdoor swimming pool (928/524-3331), and tennis courts; turn east on Florida Street from Navajo Boulevard. The nine-hole **Hidden Cove Golf Course** (928/524-3097) lies about three miles west of town; take I-40 Exit 283 and turn north on Golf Course Road.

Accommodations

Holbrook offers many motels, some at bargain prices, along W. Hopi Drive and Navajo Boulevard. The two streets meet downtown, where their numbering begins; W. Hopi Drive heads west to I-40 Exit 285; Navajo Boulevard goes north to I-40 Exit 286, then curves east back to I-40 at Exit 289.

Under $50: The **Wigwam Motel** (811 W. Hopi Dr., 928/524-3048, www.wigwamgazette.info, $42 one bed, $48 two beds incl. tax) stands out as a Route 66 icon and favorite of both kids and adults. Dating from the late 1940s, the wigwams are both comfy and cozy and have original hickory furniture. All are nonsmoking. A small museum of Native American artifacts and petrified wood is off the lobby, and you can admire the many classic cars parked outside.

Others in the category include **Budget Inn Motel** (602 Navajo Blvd., 928/524-6263, $26 s, $30 d), **Best Inn** (2211 Navajo Blvd., 928/524-2654, $39 s, $42 d), **Sahara Inn** (2402 Navajo Blvd., 928/524-6298, $20 s, $24 d), **Relax Inn** (2418 Navajo Blvd., 928/524-6815, $23 s, $28 d), and **Ramada Limited** (2608 Navajo Blvd., 928/524-2566 or 800/272-6232, $35 s, $43 d), featuring an indoor pool and hot tub.

$50–100: Choices in this category include **Best Western Adobe Inn** (615 W. Hopi Dr., 928/524-3948 or 800/937-8376, $62 d) with a pool, **Holiday Inn Express** (1308 Navajo Blvd., 928/524-1466 or 800/465-4329, $89 d) with an indoor pool and hot tub, **Super 8** (1989 Navajo Blvd., 928/524-2871 or 800/800-8000, $52 s, $52–58 d) with a pool and hot tub, **Best Western Arizonian** (2508 Navajo Blvd., 928/524-2611 or 800/937-8376, $66 s, $73 d) with a pool, **Econo Lodge** (2596 Navajo Blvd., 928/524-1448 or 800/424-6423, $45 s, $50 d) with a pool, **Days Inn** (2601 Navajo Blvd., 928/524-6949 or 800/329-7466, $54 s, $64 d) with an indoor pool and hot tub, and **Comfort Inn** (2602 Navajo Blvd., 928/524-6131 or 800/424-6423, $70 s, $75 d) with a pool.

Campgrounds

OK RV Park (just north of I-40 Exit 286 at the corner of Roadrunner and Buzzard, 928/524-3226, $10 s, $13.50 d tent or RV no hookups, $23–26 w/hookups incl. tax) is open all year with showers and a laundry. The **KOA** (102 Hermosa, just off Navajo Blvd., 928/524-6689, $19 tent or RV no hookups, $23–30 RV w/hookups, $36 cabins) provides pancake breakfasts, cowboy cookouts, and a pool in the warmer months, and a store, game room, playground, showers, and laundry year-round; take I-40 Exit 286 or 289.

Cholla Lake County Park (928/288-3717), 10 miles west of Holbrook near a power plant, offers picnicking, camping, fishing, water-skiing, windsurfing, and swimming. Anglers pull largemouth bass, catfish, and sunfish from the 360-acre lake. A swimming area and fishing dock are wheelchair accessible. Day-use fee is $3 ($2 for county residents). Year-round camping includes showers, and costs $10 per night or $14 with water and electric; take I-40 Exit 277 and follow signs for about a mile.

Food

Mesa Italiana Restaurant (2318 Navajo Blvd., 928/524-6696, Mon.–Fri. lunch and daily dinner, $8.50–19) prepares fine Italian cuisine with veal, chicken, shrimp, pasta, and pizza; there's a wine list too. You can also order steaks and ribs from the American menu. Although the exterior looks plain, you'll find tasty food and fragrant aromas in the attractive interior. **Mesa Grill & Sports Bar** (928/524-6697, daily dinner) next door has the same menus but is smoky.

Very few of Holbrook's other restaurants offer a nonsmoking section. Two places that do are **Mr. Maestas** (502 Navajo Blvd., 928/524-6000, $5–14) and **El Rancho Restaurant** (867 Navajo Blvd., 928/524-3332, $2.50–13); both serve American and Mexican food and are open daily for breakfast, lunch, and dinner, though El Rancho closes on Monday.

Many popular fast-food places line Navajo Boulevard northeast of downtown. **Safeway** supermarket is at 702 W. Hopi Drive.

Information and Services

The helpful **Holbrook Chamber of Commerce** (100 E. Arizona St. at Navajo Blvd., Holbrook, AZ 86025, 928/524-6558 or 800/524-2459, www.ci.holbrook.az.us, 8 A.M.–5 P.M. Mon.–Fri.) offers both local and statewide literature in the old county courthouse along with Navajo County Museum historical exhibits. Also downtown is the **public library** (451 N. First Ave., 928/524-3732, 10 A.M.–5 P.M. Mon., 10 A.M.–7 P.M. Tues.–Thurs., 1–5 P.M. Fri., and 10 A.M.–2 P.M. Sat.). The **post office** (216 E. Hopi Dr., 928/524-3311) is also near downtown.

Getting There

Greyhound buses (101 Mission Lane and Navajo Blvd., 928/524-3832 or 800/231-2222) stop at Circle-K.

Petrified Forest National Park

Like the Grand Canyon, Petrified Forest National Park is an open book to the earth's past. The park lies in the Painted Desert, whose colorful hills provide a world-famous resource of petrified wood and related fossils. Layers of the Chinle—a widespread geologic formation delicately tinted with reds, grays, oranges, and whites—have eroded to reveal remains of life from 225 million years ago frozen in stone. Rivers in that period carried fallen trees, some of which towered almost 200 feet high, onto the floodplains. Waterborne minerals transformed the logs to stone, replacing wood cells and filling the spaces between with brightly colored quartz and jasper crystals. This now-arid land would be unrecognizable today to its ancient inhabitants: primitive fish, massive amphibians, and fearsome reptiles.

Some of the strange animals that once crawled and swam here became fossils, now on display in park exhibits, though the trees have traditionally attracted the most attention. In the late 1800s, collectors carted away vast quantities of petrified wood logs for souvenirs or dynamited the stone trees to retrieve their crystals. This loss led to a battle for preservation, won in 1906 when President Theodore Roosevelt signed a bill establishing the Petrified Forest National Monument. A 1958 act of Congress, followed by acquisition of new lands, changed the status of the land to a national park in 1962.

Research continues today to unravel the mysteries of how early life developed here all those millions of years ago. Archaeologists attempt to trace the early human history of the park, which extends back about 10,000 years to nomadic groups, some of whom later settled in pueblo farming communities before moving on about 1400.

Flora and Fauna

A surprising amount of life exists today in the park, despite the meager nine-inch annual rainfall and lack of permanent water. Evening primrose, Indian paintbrush, mariposa lily, sunflowers, and other plants bloom when they receive sufficient moisture. Snakeweed and rabbitbrush are common and especially conspicuous in autumn when their bright yellow blooms cover the hills throughout the park. Other plants you're likely to see include buckwheat—a shrub that turns orange-brown in autumn—and saltbush, named for the tiny salt crystals formed on its leaves to conserve moisture.

Lizards often sun themselves atop petrified logs, but snakes will probably sense you before you see them; the western rattlesnake is the only poisonous species found here, and it's seldom encountered. The collared lizard may attain a length of 14 inches and sometimes sports bright yellow and green shades along with its signature black-and-white neck band. Also commonly seen, the plateau striped whiptail lizard's sleek body has black-and-white stripes and a bluish tail. Most bird species found in the park visit only during spring and autumn while migrating between north and south. Hardy residents that you're likely to sight any time include ravens, rock wrens, and horned larks. Prairie dogs, black-tailed jackrabbits, and desert cottontails are often sighted, but pronghorn, coyotes, and bobcats also live here. The visitors center and museum offer checklists for birds and other animals.

The Three Sections

The southern section—the original national monument—features some of the finest petrified wood in the world. The central section contains the greatest number of prehistoric Native American sites. During their stay about A.D. 300–1400, the ancestral pueblo people progressed from seminomadic hunters and gatherers to farmers who lived in permanent pueblos and likely had a complex ceremonial life. Scientists examining the numerous petroglyphs have discovered some that function as solar calendars.

The northern section of the park has many viewpoints of the Painted Desert, famed for its landscape of ever-changing colors—the effect of the sun playing on hills stained by iron, manganese, and other minerals. Colors are most vivid early and late in the day, fading toward noon. Added in 1932, this northern section is the largest part of the park.

Visiting the Park

Sightseeing in the park can be enjoyable at any time of year; just protect yourself from the sun in the warmer months. You can begin the paved 28.6-mile scenic drive through the park at either end. If eastbound, you'll save miles by using the south entrance off U.S. Highway 180 from Holbrook, then continuing east on I-40 from the north entrance after visiting the park. If westbound, the north entrance offers shorter access. The drive takes 45 minutes non-stop; the average visit runs about two hours, but you could easily spend all day by visiting each stop and doing some short hikes.

The park is open 8 A.M.–5 P.M. daily except Christmas, with extended hours likely in the summer and shoulder seasons. Winter snow or ice storms occasionally close the road. Start early if you'd like to enjoy all of the walks, views, and exhibits. Pets can come along if they're leashed and don't go into buildings or off paved surfaces. Admission, good for seven days, is $10 per vehicle ($5 per visitor by motorcycle, bicycle, or foot); free with a National Parks, Golden Eagle, Golden Age, or Golden Access pass. For more information, contact Park Headquarters (P.O. Box 2217, Petrified Forest, AZ 86028, 928/524-6228, www.nps.gov/pefo).

The visitors center near the north entrance and the museum near the south entrance offer exhibits illustrating park geology, fossils, ecology, and human history. They also sell books, videos, postcards, posters, and maps. A list of the day's talks and walks will be posted. You can also talk with staff, pick up a bird list and leaflets on special topics, and obtain backcountry permits. Don't remove any petrified wood or other objects from the park—officials have a zero-tolerance policy toward thieves. Rangers estimate that tons of petrified forest would be lost every year if visitors were to pocket even tiny illicit souvenirs.

Services

The park has no campgrounds or lodging, though two gift shops just outside the south entrance offer primitive camping. Holbrook to the west of the park has the most extensive accommodations in the area. Picnic fixings come in handy. There's a cafeteria near the north entrance and a snack bar across from Rainbow Forest Museum inside the south entrance. Only the developed areas have water; you'll probably want to carry something to drink. Shops sell souvenirs outside the park near the south entrance, inside the park at the Rainbow Forest complex, and next to the visitors center at the north entrance station. Shops are the place to obtain petrified wood souvenirs, as the wood comes from private land outside the park boundaries.

Backcountry Travel

The wilderness remains relatively undiscovered—only one in a thousand park visitors strays more than a short distance from pavement. You're free to roam across the landscape and make your own discoveries. Few trails exist, but natural landmarks help guide you. Carry water and wear a hat for protection from the sun. Topo maps will be handy as the wilderness lacks signs. Rangers can give advice, suggest places to see, provide directions, and offer a hiking leaflet. They also issue the free permits required for overnight trips.

Campsites must be within the wilderness and at least one mile from the road. Even if you're planning only a long day hike, it's a good idea to discuss your plans with a ranger. Riding horses and pack animals is permitted, with a limit of six animals per party; carry feed and water. All backcountry users should note rules against campfires, pets, and firearms.

Painted Desert Wilderness in the north contains 43,020 acres of colorful mesas, buttes, and badlands. You can visit Native American sites and petroglyphs. Onyx Bridge, a 50-foot-long petrified tree in the Black Forest, about four miles round-trip, is a good destination. Pilot Rock (elev. 6,295 ft.), about seven miles northwest of the trailhead, stands as the highest point in the park. Kachina Point Trailhead provides access behind Painted Desert Inn.

SCENIC DRIVE

The author likes to drive from south to north, as described here, then catch the late afternoon colors over the Painted Desert, but you can drive in either direction.

Mile 0.1

At the turnoff from U.S. Highway 180 for the park's south entrance, **Petrified Forest Museum Gift Shop** (928/524-3470) and **Crystal Forest Museum and Gift Shop** (928/524-3500) stand on opposite sides of the road. Although neither place is connected with the park, both exhibit dazzling collections of polished petrified wood, including giant log cross-sections and carvings. You can buy most pieces, along with unpolished petrified wood and other minerals, rocks, fossils, and Native American crafts. Both shops allow primitive camping for tents and RVs; electric hookups are an optional $10 (free with $50 purchase).

Mile 0.2

At the **South Entrance Station,** a ranger collects fees and gives out park brochures. If you've brought in unpolished wood or other objects, ask the ranger to mark or bag them to avoid any misunderstandings about the source. It's against the law to take *anything* from the park.

Mile 2.4

On entering the **Rainbow Forest Museum,** you're likely to be greeted by the cast of a huge skeleton. It might be a ferocious phytosaur, a large crocodile-like reptile that lurked in the forests and swamps here during the Triassic period 225 million years ago, or a placerias, a two- to three-ton reptile that roamed in herds during the same time. The skeletons and other exhibits provide a look at the strange environment of cycads, ferns, fish, amphibians, reptiles, and other early life that existed then. Rangers provide information and backcountry permits. You can purchase books, videos, posters, postcards, and maps. A Conscience Wood exhibit contains stolen petrified wood, returned with apologetic and remorseful letters.

The **Giant Logs Trail** begins behind the museum, winding in a .4-mile loop past monster-sized logs—a rainbow of reds, yellows, grays, whites, blacks, pinks, and oranges. Old Faithful is 35 feet long and weighs an estimated 44 tons. **Fred Harvey's Rainbow Gift Shop and Fountain** offers Native American crafts, souvenirs, and a snack bar across the road from the museum. There's a picnic area nearby.

Mile 2.5

The trailhead for **Long Logs Trail** (1.6 miles round-trip) and **Agate House Trail** (2 miles round-trip) is across the bridge from the Rainbow

Forest Museum area; a hike on both trails is three miles round-trip. Each offers a good opportunity to look closely at ancient trees. The jumble of logs on the Long Logs Trail may have been a logjam buried in mud, sand, and volcanic ash. Many logs measure more than 100 feet long. Prehistoric tribes built the unusual Agate House entirely with chunks of colorful petrified wood. One of its seven rooms has been reconstructed to show their original size.

Mile 8.1

Crystal Forest Loop Trail has some of the prettiest and most concentrated petrified wood in the park along its paved three-quarter-mile path.

Mile 9.9

A turnoff for **Jasper Forest** leads a half mile to parking. The overlook provides great views to the west and north. Below lie pieces of petrified wood eroded from the hillsides.

Mile 10.1

Erosion carved out a gully beneath **Agate Bridge,** a large log, leaving a bridge. In years past, a Hashknife cowboy rode his horse across the log on a $10 bet. Rangers won't let you do this today—it's unsafe. Because of cracking, the log was braced with a concrete beam in 1917.

Mile 12.9

At the **Blue Mesa** turnoff, follow the side road about three miles to a series of panoramic overlooks atop the mesa. A one-mile-loop interpretive trail provides a good introduction to the Chinle Formation and its badlands topography.

Mile 14.5

The Tepees—symmetrical, cone-shaped hills—are visible from the pullout.

Mile 16.5

Newspaper Rock displays an impressive collection of ancient petroglyphs across the face of a huge sandstone boulder. The drawings have not been interpreted, but they seem to represent animals and spiritual figures. Bring binoculars to better examine the artwork or use the free telescopes.

Mile 17.4

At **Puerco Pueblo,** you can see the foundations of a one-story pueblo with about 100 rooms and a kiva built around a rectangular plaza. Before A.D. 1100, local Native Americans lived in small scattered settlements. The building of larger pueblos, such as Puerco, indicates a change to an agricultural lifestyle requiring greater cooperation of efforts. The broad, meandering Puerco River provided reliable water all year, and its flood plain had rich soil for farming. The river also attracted birds, pronghorn, and other game. Archaeologists believe that this site was occupied between 1250 and 1400. The last occupants appear to have packed up and left peaceably, perhaps over a period of years.

Many fine petroglyphs cover the boulders below the village. Though more scattered, they're comparable with the petroglyphs at Newspaper Rock. One of the Puerco petroglyphs marks the summer solstice. About 14 other sites with solar markings have been discovered in the park. Help protect the site by remaining on the trail.

Mile 17.7

The **Puerco River,** which you cross on a bridge north of the pueblo, was far different when Native Americans lived here. Records indicate that cottonwood trees grew along the floodplain as late as the 19th century. Ranchers took advantage of the abundant grasslands in the late 1880s, but drought in 1891–1894 dried up the grass, and gross overstocking destroyed the range. Runoff carried high concentrations of salts into the river, killing less salt-resistant plants. Floods have taken their toll, scouring and widening the river and leaving loads of silt in their wake. Now the river is dry much of the year.

The railroad tracks that you cross on the bridge are a reminder of how the Petrified Forest first gained national attention. Early travelers disembarked at the nearby Adamana Station, now abandoned, to visit the "trees turned to stone."

Mile 23.6 to Mile 26.0

If you're coming from the south, **Lacey Point Overlook** is the first of a series of Painted Desert viewpoints. **Whipple Point Overlook** commemorates one of the first white people to visit the Petrified Forest—Lieutenant A. W. Whipple, who arrived in 1853. At **Nizhoni Point Overlook,** the hillside below may appear to be covered with shards of glass. These are natural pieces of selenite gypsum, a very soft mineral you can scratch with your fingernail. **Pintado Point Overlook** sits atop a volcanic lava flow, which covers the entire rim and protects the underlying softer Chinle Formation from erosion. **Chinde Point Overlook and Picnic Area** has restrooms in the summer months.

Mile 26.2

Herbert Lore built the original **Painted Desert Inn** with Native American labor and local materials in 1924. Travelers bumping their way across Arizona on Route 66 stopped for meals and shopped for Native American crafts. After the National Park Service bought the inn and surrounding land in 1936, Civilian Conservation Corps workers rebuilt and enlarged the structure in a pueblo style. It served as a park concession and information station, but the six sleeping rooms were not used after WWII. Hopi artist Fred Kabotie painted the murals in the 1940s. Also look for the carved beams, handmade furniture, metal lamps, and decorated skylights created by the Civilian Conservation Corps.

Head downstairs to see the old bar room; continue outside and around to the left to peer into the cozy rooms, which still have their washbasins and corner fireplaces. The inn closed when the Painted Desert Visitor Center opened in 1962, and the old building faced demolition, but people recognized its unique Southwestern architecture—a mixture of Spanish and Native American pueblo styles—and saved it.

Now a national historic landmark restored to its 1940s appearance, Painted Desert Inn contains rotating historical and cultural exhibits (9 A.M.–5 P.M. daily, extended hours possible in summer). A bookstore sells regional books, posters, and crafts.

Kachina Point Overlook and the trailhead for **Painted Desert Wilderness** (Onyx Bridge, Black Forest, and so on) are behind the inn. You can follow the easy **Rim Trail** between here and Tawa Point Overlook .6 miles one-way.

Tawa Point Overlook offers a Painted Desert panorama and a trailhead for the Rim Trail to Kachina Point. **Tiponi Point Overlook** is your last (or first) overlook of the Painted Desert on the drive.

Mile 28.1

Painted Desert Visitor Center and **North Entrance Station** mark the north end of the drive near I-40 Exit 311. A 20-minute movie, shown on the hour and half-hour, illustrates the park's features and describes the formation of petrified wood. A few exhibits have plant and animal fossils. Staff will answer your questions and issue backcountry permits. **Fred Harvey Painted Desert Oasis** has a cafeteria, curio shop, and gas station.

South of Holbrook

SNOWFLAKE AND TAYLOR

Heading south from Holbrook, you'll notice the gradual transition from sparsely vegetated desert plains to grasslands and juniper woodlands near the twin towns of Snowflake and Taylor, then the pinyon and ponderosa pines at Show Low, Lakeside, and Pinetop. Mormon settlers established Snowflake in 1878 and built a solid community that thrives to this day. The town's name refers not to the weather, but to a traveling Mormon official, Erastus Snow, and the leader of the settlement, William Flake. The Snowflake Monument south across the street from the chamber office depicts the meeting of these two men. The wide streets and numbering system around the central church follow the Mormons' City of Zion plan.

Citizens take great interest in their pioneer heritage. A *Historic District Brochure* lists and maps more than 50 structures built in the late 1800s and early 1900s. You can see these on a self-guided or guided tour (the latter takes you inside some buildings not otherwise open).

Arizona's second Mormon temple opened west of town in 2002; although not open to the public, you can view the exterior. It's easy to get around town once you've become accustomed to the street naming system, which counts out in the four directions from the junction of Main Street (AZ 77) and Center.

Mormons also founded Taylor, just to the south, in 1881, and named it after a church president.

Stinson Pioneer Museum

The two adobe buildings, later joined, that form the museum date from about 1873 and are the oldest in Snowflake. William Flake purchased them along with the valley from cattleman James Stinson to establish the Mormon community. The first settlers held church meetings, school, and court here. Exhibits show many aspects of pioneer life. Silver Creek Forge in back has a working blacksmith shop that may be in operation when you visit. The museum is open year-round on your left, one block east of Main Street on 1st Street North (928/536-4881, 10 A.M.–4 P.M. Tues.–Sat., donations welcome).

The guided **Historic Home Tour** begins here and visits the interiors of the 1895 James M. Flake Home, 1860s William J. Flake cabin, 1893 John Freeman Home, and 1906 Jesse N. Smith Home.; other structures are also described on the tour, but you don't go inside. A self-guided tour leaflet is available too, if you'd like to explore on your own.

Events

Taylor's **Fourth of July Celebration and Rodeo** rides on the Friday and Saturday closest to the 4th. **Snowflake Pioneer Days Celebration** honors the founding anniversaries of both Salt Lake City and Snowflake on the Thursday–Saturday closest to July 24; highlights include a rodeo, parade, arts and crafts, a barbecue, fireworks, and a dance. **Taylor Sweet Corn Festival** on Labor Day weekend celebrates with a parade, arts and crafts, classic car show, and, of course, plenty of corn. The **12 Days of Christmas** begin on December 1 with a town and Christmas tree lighting.

Recreation

Snowflake has a large city park and a swimming pool on N. Main Street. **Snowflake Golf Course** (90 N. Country Club Dr., 3 miles west of downtown on AZ 277, 928/536-7233) offers 27 holes year-round.

Accommodations and Food

You can stay in an 1890 pioneer house at the **Osmer D. Heritage Inn B&B** (161 N. Main St., 928/536-3322 or 866/486-5947, www.heritage-inn.net, $65–120 d); each room has a different antique decor and private bath. **Cedar Motel** (39 S. Main St., 928/536-3249, $40–60 d) is also downtown and has some kitchenettes. **Comfort Inn** (2055 S. Main St., 928/536-3888 or 877/505-3888, $79 d regular, $99 d family, $109 d w/hot tub) features an indoor pool, hot tub, and an exercise room at the south edge of town. **Silver Creek Inn** (825 N. Main St. in Taylor, 928/536-2600 or 888/246-5440, $70 d) is just south of Snowflake and has a hot tub.

Amelia's Garden (305 S. Main St., 928/536-2046, Mon.–Sat. lunch, $4.50–6) offers tasty Mexican food, a variety of sandwiches, salads, and soups in an attractive house on the south side of downtown; you can pick up organic and natural foods in the grocery section. **La Cocina de Eva** (201 N. Main St., 928/536-7683, Mon.–Sat. late breakfast, lunch, and dinner, $3–11) serves fajitas, carnitas (roast pork), fish tacos, and many other popular Mexican items.

Information

The **Snowflake-Taylor Chamber of Commerce** (110 N. Main St., Snowflake, AZ 85937, 928/536-4331, 9 A.M.–4 P.M. Mon.–Fri.) in the 1893 John Freeman House has maps of the historic district and information about the places open to the public. It's on the corner of Main Street and 1st Street North, beside a supermarket and across from the church.

Getting There

White Mountain Passenger Lines (NAPA Auto Parts at 821 S. Main St., 928/536-4251 or 866/255-4819, www.wmlines.com) goes Monday–

Saturday to Show Low, Heber, Payson, Mesa, and Phoenix.

SHOW LOW

With so many recreation opportunities in the nearby Mogollon Rim country and White Mountains, Show Low has become an important year-round resort. Attractions include scenic drives, hiking, camping, horseback riding, golf, trout fishing, and skiing. The town of 9,200 (more than double that in summer) sits on the pine-forested Mogollon Rim at an elevation of about 6,400 feet.

Show Low got its name from a poker game played in 1876. Corydon Cooley, a noted Indian scout, and his partner, Marion Clark, established a 100,000-acre ranch here in 1870, but found the place wasn't big enough for both of them. Agreeing to settle their differences with a game of cards, they sat down at Cooley's kitchen table for a game of seven up. The two played through the night until finally Clark said, "Show low and you win." Cooley pulled out an unbeatable deuce of clubs and took the ranch.

Several years later, Mormons bought the property, and their church now occupies the gaming site. Show Low's main street took its name, Deuce of Clubs, from the winning card.

Show Low Historical Society Museum

Native American artifacts, old photos, post office, kitchen, and changing exhibits tell the town's story at this museum (541 E. Deuce of Clubs, 928/532-7115, 11 A.M.–3 P.M. Tues.–Sat. April–Oct., donations welcome). Visits can also be arranged by appointment (phone numbers are on the door). A gift shop sells handicrafts.

Fool Hollow Recreation Area

The 140-acre, U-shaped lake contains trout, smallmouth and largemouth bass, catfish, northern pike, bluegill, and a few walleye in this year-round multiagency park (3 miles northwest of Show Low, 928/537-3680). Ponderosa pines and junipers surround the cool waters at an elevation of 6,300 feet. East and west shores have boat ramps fish-cleaning stations. Boaters can use motors up to 10 hp. A 1.7-mile trail along the south shore connects the two boat ramp areas. The campground, which fills on many summer weekends, has sites with and without hookups, showers, and a dump station. Group day-use areas can be reserved. Camping fees run $15 tent or RV with no hookups, $20 at sites with hookups. Day use costs $6 per vehicle, $1 per pedestrian or bicyclist. Interpretive programs take place on Saturday evenings in summer. Kids have playgrounds in both the day-use and camping areas. Take Highway 260 west almost two miles, turn right on Old Linden Road and follow the signs one mile.

Show Low Lake

Known for its walleye, the lake also contains channel catfish, trout, smallmouth bass, and bluegill. Fishers have a boat ramp and can use motors to 10 hp. The Navajo County campground (5 miles south of Show Low, 928/537-4126, $12–14 no hookups, $18 w/electricity) on the lake's west side is open year-round with water, showers ($3), and a playground; groups can reserve ramadas. Picnicking in the campground costs $2. The store, open May–September, offers supplies and rents fishing boats. Go south four miles on Highway 260, then turn east 1.3 miles onto Show Low Lake Road at Wal-Mart.

Pintail Lake

A natural volcanic depression filled with treated wastewater attracts waterfowl and other wildlife north of Show Low. Artificial islands serve as nesting sites. Go north 3.5 miles on Highway 77 from the east edge of town, then turn right .4 miles on Pintail Lake Road (between Mileposts 345 and 346). A paved .3-mile trail (wheelchair accessible) leads to a viewing blind. A side trail leads to another viewing platform.

Entertainment and Events

Enjoy movies at **WME Show Low** (1850 S. White Mountain Rd., 928/367-7469), one mile south on Highway 260. **Thunder Raceway** (4701 E. Deuce of Clubs, 928/537-1111) offers a variety of automotive racing March–October.

Show Low Days in June puts on an arts and crafts fair along with a classic car show in the city park. Show Low celebrates **July Fourth**

with a parade and fireworks. In December, the town hosts an **Electric Parade** and dresses up in bright lights to celebrate the holidays. Softball tournaments and other events take place throughout the year; consult the Show Low Chamber of Commerce.

Recreation

The **city park** (951 W. Deuce of Clubs, 928/532-4130 Family Aquatic Center, 928/532-4140 Show Low Parks and Recreation) offers a year-round program of activities, an indoor swimming pool, picnic areas with ramadas, a playground, and tennis, basketball, softball, racquetball, and volleyball courts.

Play golf at the 18-hole **Show Low Golf Club** (860 N. 36th Dr., near the intersection of AZ 260 and Old Linden Rd. on the west side of town, 928/537-4564) or at the 18-hole **Silver Creek Golf Club** (White Mountain Lakes, 5 miles east on U.S. 60, then 7.5 miles north on Bourdon Ranch Rd., 928/537-2744).

Accommodations

Show Low has a good selection of chain and independent motels along Deuce of Clubs. The summer rates given usually come down a bit in winter. **Kiva Motel** (261 E. Deuce of Clubs, 928/537-4542, $42 s, $45 d) offers a hot tub and sauna. **Best Western Paint Pony Lodge** (581 W. Deuce of Clubs, 928/537-5773 or 800/937-8376, $70–80 d) includes breakfast. **Days Inn** (480 W. Deuce of Clubs, 928/537-4356 or 800/329-7466, $66 s, $71 d) has a restaurant and a year-round hydrojet pool. **Holiday Inn Express** (151 W. Deuce of Clubs, 928/537-5115 or 800/465-4329, $100 d) offers an indoor pool and hot tub. **KC Motel** (60 W. Deuce of Clubs, 928/537-4433 or 800/531-7152, $45–69 d) has Victorian decor along with a hot tub.

Campgrounds

Both tenters and RVers can camp at Fool's Hollow Lake and Show Low Lake, which are also the best choices for families. The RV and mobile home parks in the area cater to seniors and include **Waltner's RV Resort** (4 miles south on AZ 260, left half a mile on Show Low Lake Rd., then left to 4800 S. 28th St., 928/537-4611, open May 1–Oct. 15, $28 RV w/hookups and tax) and **Rim Crest RV Resort** (4.4 miles south on AZ 260, 928/537-4660, open April 15–Oct. 15, $20 RV w/hookups).

Food

Look for restaurants along Deuce of Clubs and south on Highway 260. **High in the Pines Deli** (1191 E. Hall St., 928/537-1453, Mon.–Sat. breakfast and lunch, $6–11) is a European-style coffeehouse with a wide range of sandwiches along with salads, soups, deserts, and some breakfast items; head two blocks south on White Mountain Boulevard from the highway junction, then turn right one block on Hall.

Branding Iron Steak House (1251 E. Deuce of Clubs, 928/537-5151, daily lunch and dinner, $8–37) offers prime rib and seafood as well as a lineup of steaks. **Licano's Mexican Food & Steakhouse** (573 W. Deuce of Clubs, 928/537-8220, daily lunch and dinner, $9–25) serves a variety of Mexican food, steaks, other meat dishes, and seafood.

Dine Chinese at **Asia Garden Restaurant** (59 W. Deuce of Clubs, 928/537-9333, Tues.–Sun. lunch and dinner, $7–11) and the buffet-only **China Moon Buffet** (4 miles south on AZ 260 at 4817 S. White Mountain Rd., 928/537-8828, Mon.–Sat. lunch and dinner, about $6).

Information and Services

Folks will tell you about accommodations and other services at the **Show Low Regional Chamber of Commerce** (81 E. Deuce of Clubs, Show Low, AZ 85901, 928/537-2326 or 888/746-9569, www.showlowchamberofcommerce.com, 9 A.M.–5 P.M. Mon.–Fri. and 9 A.M.–3 P.M. Sat.–Sun.); it's in a shopping center on the southeast corner of Deuce of Clubs and Central Avenue. The **public library** (180 N. 9th St., 928/532-4070, closed Sun.) now has a larger facility at this new location.

The **post office** (191 W. Deuce of Clubs, 928/537-4588) is near the center of town. **Navapache Regional Medical Center** (2200 E. Show Low Lake Rd., 928/537-4375) lies next to Wal-Mart, four miles south of Show Low on Highway 260 on the way to Pinetop-Lakeside.

Getting There and Around

Airline service may be available—check with the chamber of commerce. **White Mountain Passenger Lines** (1041 E. Hall St., 928/537-4539 or 866/255-4819, www.wmlines.com) offers bus service Monday–Saturday from Show Low to Snowflake, Heber, Payson, Mesa, and Phoenix. **Four Seasons Bus Connection** (928/537-0627, closed Sun.) serves local routes in the Show Low and Pinetop-Lakeside areas and goes to Hon-Dah.

PINETOP-LAKESIDE

The name well describes the pine forests and lakes at this site near the edge of the Mogollon Rim, some eight miles southeast of Show Low. In 1880, Mormon pioneers named their new community Fairview, but they renamed it Lakeside upon the completion of Rainbow Lake. Several smaller lakes have been added since, until the area now seems to consist as much of water as of land. Soldiers undertaking the long climb up the Mogollon Rim from Fort Apache in the 1870s often stopped to rest at a place they christened Pinetop; Mormon ranchers founded a settlement there in 1878.

Lakeside (elev. 6,745 ft.) on the north and Pinetop (elev. 7,279 ft.) just to the southeast have incorporated as Pinetop-Lakeside, a major recreational center dotted with innumerable summer cabins and resorts. The year-round population of 8,000 jumps to 30,000 in summer.

Mogollon Rim Overlook and Nature Trail

An easy one-mile walk, wheelchair-accessible, offers great views of forested valleys and ridges. Signs describe the area's forests, medicinal plants, and history. The trailhead lies just west of Highway 260, three miles north of the Lakeside Ranger Station. Or, from Show Low, head south 5.5 miles on Highway 260 from Deuce of Clubs.

Big Springs Environmental Study Area

A pleasant half-mile nature trail winds through a variety of wildlife habitats. The easy trail offers interpretive signs, though it can be muddy after rain or snow. Turn south half a mile on Woodland Road from Highway 260, then look for the parking area on the left.

Rainbow Lake

This 80-acre reservoir in Lakeside just west of Highway 260 is stocked with rainbow trout, brown trout, and some smallmouth bass and catfish. You can fish from the shore near the dam or rent a boat; the lake has an 8 -hp motor limit. Nearby Lakeside Campground ($10) is open May–October; you can reserve sites (877/444-6777, www.reserveusa.com).

Scott Reservoir

A slightly smaller fishing lake of 70 acres, Scott lies about three miles northeast of Pinetop-Lakeside. Take Porter Mountain Road (turnoff is one block south of Lakeside Ranger Station) east and north 1.4 miles, turn east .6 miles, then right to the reservoir. It offers a boat ramp and a small campground with no drinking water or fee. Only electric motors are permitted.

Woodland Lake

This 18-acre lake has rainbow and brown trout and some largemouth bass, catfish, and green sunfish; electric boat motors are OK. Woodland Lake Park offers picnicking, several trails, a fishing pier, boat ramp, tennis courts, volleyball, softball, and playgrounds, but no camping. Groups can reserve ramadas with Pinetop-Lakeside Parks and Recreation (928/368-6700). Trails circle the lake (1 mile) and go to other destinations. From White Mountain Boulevard/Highway 260, turn in about a half mile on Woodland Lake Road at the Chevron Station.

White Mountain Trail System

Eleven loops, many interconnected, wind through the forests in the Pinetop-Lakeside area. They total about 180 miles and are open to hikers, mountain bikers, and equestrians. In winter, cross-country skiers can glide down the paths. Drop by the Lakeside Ranger Station for maps and trail descriptions. The Pinetop-Lakeside Chamber of Commerce also may have this material.

Entertainment and Events

Enjoy movies at **Lakeside Cinema** (20 E. White Mountain Blvd., 928/367-7469). The **White Mountain Native American Art Festival** in July attracts Native Americans from all over the Southwest for dances, music, art, crafts, demonstrations, and food. August brings the **White Mountain Bluegrass Music Festival.** The **Fall Festival** on the last full weekend of September features an arts and crafts show and other presentations to mark the end of summer.

Recreation

You can go horseback riding in summer with **Porter Mountain Stables** (4048 Porter Mountain Rd., 928/368-5306) and **Pinetop Lakes Equestrian Center** (Bucksprings Rd. near the Pinetop Country Club, 928/369-1000). Play golf on the 18-hole executive course at **Pinetop Lakes Golf & Country Club** (one-quarter mile east on Bucksprings Rd. from White Mountain Blvd., 928/369-4531, open April–Oct.).

Accommodations

In this, the largest resort area in the White Mountains, you have a choice of many motels, cottages, cabins, and bed and breakfasts, all nestled in cool pine forests. Rates tend to run higher on summer weekends, when reservations are a good idea. The Pinetop-Lakeside Chamber of Commerce maintains a longer list of places to stay and can help you find what you're looking for.

Under $50: In Lakeside, **Bear's Paw Motel** (4229 Valley Lane, 928/368-5231, $37 d weekdays, $47 d Fri.–Sat.) has kitchenettes for $8 extra. **Forest House Motel** (2990 W. White Mountain Blvd., 928/368-6628 or 888/440-2220, $39 d weekdays, $48 d Fri.–Sat.) has a variety of rooms, some with kitchenettes.

In Pinetop, **Pinetop Lodge** (593 E. White Mountain Blvd., 928/367-3510, $35–65 d weekdays, $45–75 d Fri.–Sat.) offers a choice of rooms, some with kitchenettes and fireplaces. **Blue Ridge Motel and Cabins** (2012 E. White Mountain Blvd., 928/367-0758) has rooms ($39 d weekdays and $45 d Fri.–Sat.), small cabins with kitchenettes ($50 d), and large cabins with fireplaces and kitchenettes ($72 d).

$50–100: In Lakeside, **Lake of the Woods Resort** (2244 W. White Mountain Blvd, 928/368-5353, $90–105 d) is a great place for families. It features cabins, all with kitchens and fireplaces, and a private lake, boats, two hot tubs, and a sauna. **Lazy Oaks Resort** (1075 Larson Rd., 928/368-6203, www.lazyoaks.com, $69–85 d one bedroom, $101–126 4 persons two bedrooms) has a lakeside setting for its cabins, all with kitchenettes and fireplaces.

In Pinetop, **Northwoods Resort** (165 E. White Mountain Blvd., 928/367-2966 or 800/813-2966, www.northwoodsaz.com, $99 d studio, $119 d one bedroom, $149 two bedroom) offers cabins, all with kitchens and fireplaces and some with jetted tubs. **Whispering Pines Resort** (237 E. White Mountain Blvd., 928/367-4386 or 800/840-3867, www.whisperingpinesaz.com, $83–130 d) features one-, two-, and three-bedroom cabins with kitchenettes and fireplaces; some have spa tubs. **Best Western Inn of Pinetop** (404 E. White Mountain Blvd., 928/367-6667 or 800/937-8376, approximately $69 d weekdays, $119 d Fri.–Sat.) has a hot tub. **Buck Springs Resort** (6036 Buck Springs Rd., 928/369-3554 or 800/339-1909, www.buckspringsresort.com, $85 d one bedroom, $185 6 persons three bedrooms) features cottages with kitchens and fireplaces. **Mountain Haven Inn** (1120 E. White Mountain Blvd., 928/367-2101 or 888/854-9815, $54–119 d rooms, $135–200 cabins) has all nonsmoking units, some with fireplaces and kitchenettes. **Nine Pines Motel** (2089 E. White Mountain Blvd., 928/367-2999 or 888/597-4637, www.9pines.com, $48–75 d weekdays, $60–85 d Fri.–Sat.) features rustic pine-log furniture and has some fireplaces.

Campgrounds

Tenters and RVers can stay in the ponderosa pine forests at **Lakeside Campground** (across from the Lakeside Ranger Station, 928/368-5111 Lakeside Ranger Station, $10 May–Oct.); there's usually room. **Scott Reservoir** has a small campground three miles northeast of Lakeside on Forest Road 45 via Porter Mountain Road; the turnoff from Highway 260 is one block south of the Lakeside Ranger Station. No drinking water or charge; it often fills in summer. **Show Low Lake** has a good campground four miles north of Lakeside.

Los Burros Campground east of town lies in meadow and ponderosa pine country at an elevation of 8,000 feet; the nearby Los Burros Ranger Station and barn date from 1910; there's a campground host but no water or fee; head east 19 miles on U.S. Highway 60 from Show Low, then turn south 11 miles on Mt. Vernon Road/Forest Road 224, or go northeast 7.5 miles on Mt. Vernon Road/Forest Road 224 from Highway 260 at McNary. Another possibility is to head for the woods—you can camp free almost anywhere in the Sitgreaves National Forest. People at the Lakeside Ranger Station can suggest areas.

RV parks include **Rainbow Forest RV Park** (3720 Rainbow Lake Dr., 928/368-5286, $22 RV w/hookups) and the adult **Ponderosa RV Resort** (1666 Ponderosa Lane, 928/368-6989, open April 15–Oct. 15, $21 RV w/hookups).

Food

Restaurants are surprisingly good for such a small community. Festive lights and ornaments decorate the **Christmas Tree** (455 N. Woodland Rd., 928/367-3107, Wed.–Sun. dinner, $10–20), where you can dine on such favorites as chicken and dumplings, barbecued ribs, and beef stroganoff. **Charlie Clark's Steakhouse** (1701 E. White Mountain Blvd., 928/367-4900, daily dinner, $10–40) features steaks, of course, along with a great selection of seafood and some pasta dishes.

For Mexican dining, head over to **El Rancho** (1523 E. White Mountain Blvd., 928/367-4557, daily lunch and dinner, $8–15.50). The **Lotus Garden** (984 E. White Mountain Blvd., 928/367-2568, daily lunch and dinner, $6.25–20) serves Szechuan, Hunan, and other Chinese cuisines.

Information

Pinetop-Lakeside Chamber of Commerce (102-C W. White Mountain Blvd., P.O. Box 4220, Pinetop, AZ 85935, 928/367-4290 or 800/573-4031, www.pinetoplakesidechamber.com) provides the latest information on sights and services, including the national forest lands and the town of Greer. The office is centrally located next to Safeway on the main highway. It's open 9 A.M.–5 P.M. weekdays, 9 A.M.–1 P.M. weekends in summer, then 9 A.M.–4 P.M. weekdays the rest of the year.

Staff at the **Lakeside Ranger Station** (2022 W. White Mountain Blvd., Lakeside, AZ 85929, 928/368-5111, www.fs.fed.us/r3/asnf, 8 A.M.–4:30 P.M. Mon.–Fri.) will share information on camping, hiking, driving, and fishing in Apache-Sitgreaves National Forests. The office is across the highway from Lakeside Campground. **Arizona Game and Fish** (2878 E. White Mountain Blvd., Pinetop, AZ 85935, 928/367-4281, www.azgfd.com, 8 A.M.–5 P.M. Mon.–Fri.) provides wildlife information and sells fishing and hunting licenses and boating registrations.

Services

Post offices are at 712 E. White Mountain Boulevard., (928/367-4756), in the Pinetop part of town, and at 1815 W. Jackson Lane (one block off White Mountain Blvd., 928/368-6686), in the Lakeside part. Several shops along the highway sell and rent **skiing and snowboarding equipment** in season.

Larson Memorial Library (1595 W. Johnson Lane in Lakeside, 928/368-6688, closed Sun.) is near the corner of White Mountain Boulevard and Woodland Road.

Getting There and Around

White Mountain Passenger Lines (866/255-4819, www.wmlines.com) has bus connections with Heber, Payson, Mesa, and Phoenix. **Four Seasons Bus Connection** (928/537-0627, closed Sun.) serves Show Low, Pinetop-Lakeside, and Hon-Dah.

White Mountain Apache Reservation

Some of Arizona's best outdoor recreation can be found on the White Mountain Apache Reservation, which spans more than 1.6 million acres. You have choices among many campsites, fishing streams, lakes, ski runs, and hiking trails. Far-sighted planning and development by the White Mountain Apache resulted in the high-quality recreation available today. Though tribal permits are required for almost any activity, costs are reasonable. You don't need state licenses for fishing, boating, or hunting—just the tribal permits. Some areas, such as the summit of sacred Baldy Peak, are closed. Kinishba is the only prehistoric site that you may visit.

RECREATION

Sightseeing, Camping, and Skiing

You'll need a $6 vehicle permit for a picnic or sightseeing stop on the reservation unless you've already obtained a tribal permit for camping, fishing, or other recreational activity; hikers, cyclists, or bus passengers pay $3 each. Camping facilities are basic, usually just picnic tables, fireplaces, and toilets, though some campsites offer drinking water. Backpacking is permitted in certain areas with the proper permit. Camping fees ($8 per vehicle per night, or $175 per vehicle for 30 days) must be paid in advance; hikers, cyclists, and bus passengers pay $3 each. A back road crosses into the San Carlos Apache Reservation at Black River Crossing, but you need special-use permits from both tribes to use it.

Sunrise Park Resort Ski Area, with its many downhill runs, attracts ski enthusiasts in winter. Sunrise also offers snowboarding, cross-country skiing, and tubing. The tribe prohibits ATVs, horseback riding (except with authorized concessions), and swimming (except at hotels) everywhere on the reservation.

Boating and River Running

If you use a boat, you'll need a permit for it—$5 per day or $25 yearly for lake use. Sunrise is the only lake where gas motors (10 hp limit) are allowed; everywhere else you're limited to electrics.

Kayakers and rafters can enjoy a section of the Salt River Canyon, usually best run during the winter snowmelt March–May. River runners

APACHE TRADITIONS AND CRAFTS

Driving through the Apache homeland, you might think their culture is gone—you see members of the tribe living in modern houses, frequenting the shopping centers, and working at regular jobs. But the Apache continue to use their own language and preserve the old traditions. Boys still study under medicine men to learn the prayers, rituals, and medicinal plants used in healing ceremonies. And elaborate coming-of-age ceremonies still mark the passage of young women into adulthood. Known as Sunrise Dances, these rites usually take place on weekends during summer; check local papers for dates or ask at the cultural centers or tribal offices in Whiteriver and San Carlos. Buckskin dresses, worn by women before the introduction of calico, are occasionally seen at Sunrise Dances.

Frequently on the move in pre-reservation days, the Apache had only a few, utilitarian crafts. They still make some of their creations today—baskets, cradleboards, and beadwork. Attractive designs in beadwork decorate necklaces, bolo ties, and other adornments. Woodcarvers fashion realistic dolls depicting the dance movements of the Apache Spirit Dancers. Craftspeople on the San Carlos Reservation set peridot (a transparent yellow-green gemstone) in bolo ties, necklaces, earrings, and other jewelry. Look for all these at the cultural centers on the reservations.

COURTESY OF THE HEARD MUSEUM

Apache basket, early 1900s

doing the Salt River must obtain the proper permit, available at Salt River Canyon Trading Post on U.S. Highway 60, and have a suitable boat (no open canoes) and equipment.

Fishing and Hunting

The reservation includes 400 miles of mountain streams and more than 25 lakes. Anglers can go out year-round; ice fishing is popular on lakes not closed for the winter. The waters are stocked with trout from Alchesay and Williams Creek National Fish Hatcheries.

Fishing licenses cost $6 per day or $65 per calendar year. Children ages 10–14 pay $3 per day or $32 for the year; children under 10 fish free but must be with an adult holding a fishing permit. An agreement with the San Carlos Apache Tribe honors the fishing permits from either tribe along both banks of the Black and Salt rivers where the reservations meet; a special-use permit is required. Certain lakes require special permits and can be rented by groups. You can arrange a guide for fishing or hunting trips; ask for names at Hon-Dah Ski and Outdoor Sport.

Plentiful big and small game roam the reservation. The tribe has established regular hunting seasons for elk, mountain lion, javelina, and pronghorn. You'll need a guide for hunting elk, lion, bear, and pronghorn—also lots of money. The guided hunts can run more than $1,000 a day, but participants report a high success rate. Smaller animals and birds are more easily bagged and don't require a guide.

Rodeos

The Apache enjoy participating in and attending rodeos, which take place on many weekends through the warmer months. The **Tribal Fair and Rodeo** on Labor Day weekend is the major annual event. Rodeos, powwows, and other area events are listed in the local paper, the *Fort Apache Scout.*

Information

Staff at **Hon-Dah Ski and Outdoor Sport** (787 AZ 260, Pinetop-Lakeside, AZ 85935, 928/369-7669 or 877/226-4868), three miles south of Pinetop, are the best source of information for recreation on the reservation; you can also obtain permits here. It's open daily year-round on the east side of the Hon-Dah Casino complex. You can also obtain information directly from the **Game and Fish Department** (next to the White Mountain Apache Motel in Whiteriver, P.O. Box 220, Whiteriver, AZ 85941, 928/338-4385). The free annual newsletter, *White Mountain Apache Tribe Outdoor Recreation Regulations,* can be picked up at these two places and at many area businesses and tourist offices. Other year-round places for permits on the reservation are Sunrise General Store/Sports Center and Salt River Canyon Trading Post. In summer, you can also secure permits at Horseshoe Lake, Reservation Lake, and Hawley Lake. Off-reservation sources include Pinetop Sporting Goods in Pinetop, K-Mart in Show Low, Western Drug in Springerville, and Tempe Marine in Chandler.

Watch for logging trucks on the reservation's many back roads. Some roads may be too rough for cars, especially after rain or snow. Staff at the Hon-Dah Ski and Outdoor Sport store or at Game and Fish can advise on current conditions. Most road junctions have signs, but it's a

APACHE RESERVATION LIFE

Attempts over the years by the Spanish, the Mexicans, and finally the Americans to exterminate the Apache caused the tribes to retaliate with a murderous vengeance. By 1870, the U.S. government finally realized that a military solution just wouldn't work. The federal government then initiated a "Peace Policy," which placed all Native Americans on reservations and taught them to farm and raise livestock. The San Carlos Reservation, created in 1871 just south of the White Mountains, became home for various tribes—Mohave, Yavapai, Yuma, and several different groups of Apache.

Officials thought tribes would be easier to control if centralized on one reservation, but their plan may actually have extended the Apache wars. Quarrels developed between the different groups, attempts at farming fared poorly, and government agents frequently cheated the tribespeople. Geronimo and other war chiefs fled the reservation at times to lead raids against settlements in southern Arizona and northern Mexico. By the time Geronimo surrendered in 1886, the federal government recognized that the San Carlos Reservation had failed and removed all tribes except the San Carlos Apache. Meanwhile, many of the White Mountain and Cibecue Apache had succeeded in holding onto part of their own territory to the north, which became a reservation in 1897.

In 1918, a ranching program issued five head of cattle each to 80 Apache families. Although the program nearly failed, the herds on the Fort Apache Reservation eventually grew to 20,000 by 1931. Still, it wasn't until 1936 that white people finally removed the last of their own cattle from the reservations. Recognizing the recreational value of their lands, in the 1950s the White Mountain Apache began to build access roads, reservoirs, campgrounds, marinas, motels, restaurants, and a ski resort. They also own and operate a large lumber industry. During this development, the tribe has preserved their land's great natural beauty. San Carlos Apache have provided visitors facilities on their lands as well, though on a smaller scale.

good idea to consult a map in finding your way around the back roads.

The Apache and the federal government disagree on the name of the reservation; government officials tend to call it Fort Apache, while the Apache understandably prefer White Mountain Apache.

HON-DAH

The Apache name for this travelers' center means Be My Guest. It's 19 miles north of Whiteriver and three miles south of Pinetop at the intersection of Highways 260 and 73. **Hon-Dah Resort Hotel** (928/369-0299 or 800/929-8744, www.hon-dah.com) offers a hotel, restaurants, RV park, store/information center, gas station/convenience store, and casino. Hotel guests have use of a year-round pool, hot tub, and sauna. Rates for rooms run $89 d weekdays, $109 d Friday–Saturday; suites are $150 d weekdays, $180 d Friday–Saturday; reservations are recommended in summer. Timbers Lounge puts on entertainment Tuesday–Saturday.

Practicalities

Hon-Dah RV Park (across AZ 73 from the hotel, 928/369-7400 or 800/929-8744 ext. 7400, $21 w/hookups) offers year-round sites with showers, laundry, recreation room, phones, satellite TV, and store, but does not accept tents. Reservations are a good idea in summer and winter.

Indian Pine Restaurant (928/369-7552, daily breakfast, lunch, and dinner, $7–18) offers mostly American dining from a buffet and menu at each meal; dinner buffets feature seafood on Friday and prime rib on Saturday. The adjacent **Timbers Lounge** hosts a big Sunday brunch and presents live entertainment Tuesday–Sunday evenings.

Hon-Dah Ski and Outdoor Sport (928/369-7669 or 877/226-4868) provides information for recreation on the reservation and sells permits, sporting goods, and clothing. Open daily year-round on the east side of the Hon-Dah

Casino complex; in winter, it offers a full-service ski and snowboard shop.

HON-DAH TO SUNRISE LAKE AREA

McNary

Though there's not much to see, this old lumber town has an unusual history. Back in 1916, an energetic Flagstaff businessman named Tom Pollock chose the spot for a new lumber enterprise. Leasing the land from the Apache, he ran a railroad line in and named the place Cooley, after Corydon E. Cooley of the famous Show Low card game.

Meanwhile, 1,000 miles east in McNary, Louisiana, the W. M. Cady Lumber Co. was quickly running out of timbered land. So in 1924 Cady bought out Pollock's Apache Lumber Company and moved practically the whole town westward to Cooley. Renamed McNary, the town became known for its harmonious mixture of blacks, whites, Latinos, and Native Americans. When fire destroyed the sawmill in 1979, owners rebuilt 40 miles east near Eagar.

Hawley Lake

Trout swim in the waters of this 260-acre lake; in winter you can fish through the ice. Constructed in 1957, this was the first lake on the reservation designed for recreation. Services include a boat dock with rentals, service station/grocery store (928/335-7511), campground ($8) and RV park ($25); the store sells permits for fishing, camping, and other activities. The lodge (928/369-1753,) offers rooms ($65–250) and cabins ($109–159) from mid-May to the end of September.

From Highway 260, 11.3 miles east of Hon-Dah, turn south 11 miles on Highway 473; the first nine miles are paved. Despite the 8,200-foot elevation, the road is kept open year-round.

You'll need a special permit to fish at **Earl Park Lake** (47 acres), a half mile southeast of Hawley Lake.

Horseshoe Lake

You can fish on this 121-acre lake (elev. 8,100 ft.) for rainbow, brown, and brook trout. The boat dock and store (928/521-2613) provides information, camping and fishing supplies, boat rentals, and permits from mid-May to mid-September. In winter the road is cleared for ice anglers. Go 13.5 miles east of Hon-Dah on Highway 260, turn south at the sign, and follow the road one mile across the dam to the south side of the lake.

Sunrise Lake

Anglers prize this 891-acre lake (elev. 9,200 ft.) for its large brook trout. This is the only lake on the reservation where you can use gas motors, though limited to 10 hp. **Sunrise Marina** (behind the lodge, 928/735-7669, ext. 2155) offers boat and fishing-pole rentals, a paved boat ramp, and a few fishing supplies in summer.

Sunrise Park Lodge (928/735-7669 or 800/772-7669, $59 d standard, $79 d deluxe, $99 d spa suite in summer) features a restaurant (breakfast, lunch, and dinner daily), indoor pool, indoor and outdoor hot tubs, a sauna, and a volleyball area. The lodge closes for about six weeks at the end of the ski season in April, reopens for summer visitors Memorial Day to mid-September, then closes again until the ski season starts. From Highway 260, 20 miles east of Hon-Dah or 18 miles west of Springerville, turn south 3.5 miles on Highway 273 to the hotel.

Scenic Lift Rides (10 A.M.–4 P.M. Sat.–Sun.; $10 adult, $5 age 12 and under) at the ski area take you to the heights from about May 20 to October 10. Mountain bikes and snowboards can be rented at the Sports Shop located at the ski lift.

Sunrise General Store/Sports Center (on the highway a half mile south of the lodge, 928/735-7335) sells groceries, permits, and gas. Nearby **Blue Sky Stables** (928/735-7454) offers guided rides, hay rides, cookouts, and winter sleigh rides. An **RV campground** ($9) across the road from the store has electric hookups. **Sunrise Campground** ($8) is also nearby, on the left just after turning onto the Sunrise Ski Area road.

Sunrise Park Resort Ski Area

This cluster of three peaks—Sunrise, Apache, and Cyclone Circle—boasts more than 65 ski runs winding through pine and aspen forests of the White Mountains. The resort (P.O. Box 217,

McNary, AZ 85930, 928/735-7669 or 800/772-7669, www.sunriseskipark.com) offers great family skiing, with about 40 percent beginner, 40 percent intermediate, and 20 percent advanced terrain. A combination of one high-speed quad, two regular quads, four triples, one double, and two surface lifts keeps lines short. Snowmaking machines add to the natural snowpack for a season lasting late November–mid-April. Sunrise also offers a snowboard park, Nordic trails system, tubing hill, and horse-drawn sleigh rides.

Lift rates are $41 full day ($24 juniors 12 and under), $33 half day ($19 juniors 12 and under), $20 seniors 65–69, and free seniors 70+. A season pass costs $600 ($375 juniors 12 and under) but drops to $425 ($300 juniors) if you buy it early. The resort offers group and private lessons, rentals, sales, and repairs. Child-care services feature indoor and outdoor activities for children ages 3–6 and babysitting for infants up to age 2.

Sunrise Ski Area offers package deals and family plans that include room and lift tickets. Room-only rates run $68–195 d, jumping to $124–295 d during the holiday season (mid-December–early January) and on some Fridays, Saturdays, and holidays.

Shuttle buses connect Sunrise Park Lodge with the ski lifts and a day lodge about every 15 minutes. Accommodations are tight during the ski season, and many skiers stay at Greer (15 miles to the east), Springerville (22 miles east), or Pinetop-Lakeside (30 miles west).

Sunrise General Store/Sports Center (on the highway a half mile south of the lodge, 928/735-7335) offers rentals of cross-country skis and snowshoes, cross-country ski lessons, and a nearby network of trails for cross-country skiing and snowshoeing.

Reservation Lake

This 280-acre lake, the second largest on the reservation, offers good fishing for rainbow, brown, and brook trout. Cool forests of aspen, fir, and spruce grow at the 9,000-foot elevation. A marina (928/521-7458) offers rental boats, supplies, and permits late May–early September. Several campgrounds surround the lake.

The easiest way in is from the north: from Hon-Dah, take Highway 260 east 20 miles to Highway 273, head southeast on Highway 273 for 14 miles, turn south 10 miles on Forest Road 116, then turn right a half mile and cross a cattleguard to the lake. From Fort Apache, drive 46 miles east on Indian Routes Y-70 and Y-20 or take Y-55 and Y-20.

SOUTH OF HON-DAH

Alchesay and Williams Creek National Fish Hatcheries

These hatcheries keep the streams and lakes of the reservation stocked with trout. Williams Creek receives eggs from four or five species of trout, then raises the hatchlings to sportfishing size; large brood trout inhabit the raceways. Alchesay specializes in raising small native, rainbow, brown, and cutthroat trout of 6–8 inches. Visitors are welcome to view exhibits and stroll along a self-guided tour on 7 A.M.–3:30 P.M. weekdays at both hatcheries; closed holidays. Alchesay also has a picnic area.

The turnoff for Alchesay Hatchery is 4 miles north of Whiteriver between Mileposts 342 and 343 of Highway 73; a paved road with signs heads northeast along the White River 4.6 miles to the site. Roads to Williams Creek Hatchery turn off 13 miles north of Whiteriver, between Mileposts 351 and 352, and 15 miles north of Whiteriver (4 miles south of Hon-Dah) between Mileposts 353 and 354; follow signs 9 miles in on gravel roads.

WHITERIVER

The administrative center of the White Mountain Apache lies south of Hon-Dah in a valley at 5,000 feet, surrounded by high forested hills. It's easy to confuse the name of the town with that of the river flowing beside it, but the town is spelled as one word. Whiteriver has a motel, restaurant, shopping center, Indian Health Service Hospital, and tribal offices.

Practicalities

White Mountain Apache Motel (928/338-4927, $55 d) is just south of the shopping center. The motel's restaurant (daily breakfast, lunch, and dinner, $7.50–18) offers American food and pizza. You can obtain information and permits next door at the tribal **Game and Fish Department** (P.O. Box 220, Whiteriver, AZ 85941, 928/338-4385, 8 A.M.–noon and 1–5 P.M. Mon.–Fri.). **White Mountain Apache Shopping Center,** just south of the town center, includes a supermarket, stores, and post office.

Fort Apache and the Apache Cultural Center

In 1869, Major John Green selected this site near the confluence of the north and east forks of the White River as a supply base for troops in the field. Although the White Mountain Apache proved friendly, army officers thought it wise to keep an eye on them, meanwhile preventing white settlers from encroaching on Native American land.

Originally established as Fort Ord in 1870, the post's name changed to Camp Mogollon, then to Camp Thomas, and finally to Camp Apache—all within one year! Troops and Apache scouts rode out to subdue rebellious Apache in the Tonto Basin (1872–1873), and then to fight Victorio (1879) and Geronimo (1881–1886).

Alchesay, the most prominent Apache scout, became known for his honesty and dedication to both his people and the army. He helped put down rebellions of hostile tribes and assisted General Crook in making peace with Geronimo in 1886. Fort Apache saw its last major action during the Mexican Campaign (1916–1917). In 1922, the U.S. Indian Service converted the fort to a boarding school, naming it in honor of President Theodore Roosevelt. Most of the first students were Navajo, though local Apache enrolled later. About 100 students now attend the school.

Many venerable buildings still stand along officers' row. At the west end you can enter the first commanding officer's quarters, built of logs in 1871 and used by General Crook; it's open 8 A.M.–5 P.M. weekdays with exhibits about the fort's scouts and soldiers. The final and grandest commanding officer's quarters dates from 1892—it's built of stone, and sports a central tower. The adjutant's office near the east end of officers' row was built of adobe in 1876.

To learn about Apache history and culture, drop into the nearby **Apache Cultural Center** (928/338-4625, www.wmat.nsn.us, 8 A.M.–5 P.M. Mon.–Fri., and Sat. in summer, $5 adults, $3 seniors 65+ and students 7–17). Look for the conical roof. Museum exhibits interpret Apache culture and display fine examples of tribal crafts. The museum shop sells locally made baskets, cradleboards, and beadwork along with jewelry by other tribes, music, and books. Go southwest about 5 miles on the highway from the motel in Whiteriver, turn .7 miles left across the river, then left at the sign.

ARIZONA DEPARTMENT OF LIBRARY, ARCHIVES AND PUBLIC RECORDS, HISTORY AND ARCHIVES DIVISION, PHOENIX, #98-5851

When the Warm Springs Apache were moved in 1877 to San Carlos, across the river from the White Mountain reservation, Chief Victorio and a small band escaped. He led a campaign against Americans and Mexicans in 1879–1880, killing nearly 1,000 people before being shot by a Mexican bounty hunter.

Kinishba Ruins

Kinishba is Apache for Brown House. Prehistoric tribes built two large pueblos and smaller buildings here between 1232 and 1320. The mixed population came from areas of the Little Colorado, central Gila, and Salt Rivers. Residents abandoned the village about 1350, possibly because of insufficient water.

A University of Arizona team excavated the ruins from 1931 to 1939 and found 14 types of pottery and a great wealth of shell jewelry scattered

In the late 1930s, University of Arizona Archaeologist Byron Cummings excavated and partially reconstructed Kinishba, hoping it would become a national monument.

© BILL WEIR

across more than 700 rooms. Only one of the large structures has survived. Because it has not been stabilized, you may not enter, but you can view the ruins by walking a one-third-mile loop trail through the site. Before coming out, check in at the Apache Cultural Center and obtain a trail leaflet, which is the only permit that you need. From the Apache Cultural Center, return to the highway and turn left (west) 1.9 miles, then turn right at the sign on a dirt road; the ruins are 2 miles in (keep left at the fork 1.7 miles in).

WEST OF WHITERIVER

Cibecue

This small town in the western part of the reservation serves as the center for the Cibecue Apache, a group distinct from the White Mountain and San Carlos Apache. For administrative purposes though, the Cibecue area is considered part of the White Mountain Reservation. Visitors can enjoy camping and good fishing for rainbow and brown trout in the upper 15 miles of nearby Cibecue Creek. The first fishing and camping spots lie five miles north of town on a dirt road paralleling the creek. Elevations average about 6,000 feet. You need a special-use permit to drive past the town. To reach Cibecue, turn northwest on Indian Route 12 from U.S. Highway 60, eight miles south of Carrizo.

In the winter of 1880, a Cibecue medicine man named Noch-ay-del-klinne began preaching a new religion that predicted the expulsion of all white people. He soon gathered an enthusiastic following, worrying officers at Fort Apache. In August 1881, officers dispatched troops and 23 Apache scouts to arrest the medicine man. Fighting broke out upon their arrival at Cibecue, and Noch-ay-del-klinne was killed. The scouts then mutinied, joining the attack on the troops. Angry Apache pursued the survivors the entire 40 miles back to the fort. Captain Hentig and six other soldiers died in what's believed to be the only revolt by Apache scouts in their 75 years with the army.

Salt River Canyon

Father Eusebio Francisco Kino visited this colorful canyon in 1698, naming it Salado for the salt springs in the area. There are great views of the canyon from U.S. Highway 60 as the highway swoops down to a bridge 48 miles southwest of Show Low. You can explore further by driving on the dirt road that parallels the river. This route is highly scenic, with towering cliffs above and the river below. Take the turnoff just north of the highway bridge until you come to a fork. At the fork, you can turn left and drive under the bridge a half mile upriver to **Apache Falls,** or bear right four miles on the road downstream to Cibecue Creek. The road is rough in spots but passable for cautious motorists.

The desert country here at 3,000 feet contrasts sharply with the White Mountains, a short drive north. Saguaro cacti grow on the slopes to the right past the ford on Cibecue Creek. Don't cross if the water is fast-flowing and muddy.

The Salt Banks, three miles past Cibecue

© BILL WEIR

The Apache regard the Salt Banks beside the Salt River as sacred, so no visits are permitted, but you can see them on a raft trip.

Creek, are a long series of salt springs that have deposited massive travertine formations. Minerals and algae color the springs orange, red, and dark green. This site has long been sacred to the Apache, who draw salt here and perform religious ceremonies. It's closed to the public.

Past the Salt Banks, the road begins a steep climb, becoming too rough for cars. The White Mountain Apache have established several primitive campsites (no drinking water) along the Salt River between the highway bridge and Cibecue Creek. You can hike up the creek about .75 miles to a waterfall, but only guided trips can go canyoneering above this point. Salt River Canyon Trading Post, near the highway bridge, stocks supplies and permits. Anglers on the Salt River catch mostly channel catfish and some smallmouth bass and bluegill.

The Low Desert

SAN CARLOS APACHE RESERVATION

The San Carlos Reservation offers scenery for every season: cool pine forests in the northeast, grasslands and wooded ridges in the center, and cactus-studded desert in the southwest. In winter you'll probably want to stick to the low country around San Carlos Lake, then head for the hills in summer. The Black and Salt Rivers form a natural boundary with the White Mountain Apache Indian Reservation to the north. Much of the land is fine cattle-grazing country and supports large tribal herds. You can reach San Carlos Lake and Seneca Lake by paved highways, but roads to other recreation areas may be too rough for cars, especially after rains or snowmelt.

Events

Look for Apache dances, crafts, foods, and

cowboys showing off their riding skills at the **Bylas Rodeo** in April and at the **Veteran's Memorial Fair and Rodeo** on Veteran's Day weekend in November. **Traditional dances** are held during the summer; call the tribal office (928/475-2361) or Cultural Center (928/475-2894) for dates and places. The **Sunrise Ceremony,** marking the coming-of-age of young women, occurs most frequently, usually on summer weekends.

Recreation

Campsites are usually open all year. Recreation permits must be bought beforehand. In summer, observe fire restrictions.

Fishing is the big attraction for most visitors—San Carlos Lake is known as Arizona's hottest bass spot. Farther north you can catch trout, catfish, or bass in Point of Pines Lake, Seneca Lake, Dry Lake, and the Black River.

Gasoline motors can be used at San Carlos and Talkalai Lakes; at other lakes you're restricted to a single electric motor. The tribe doesn't allow ATVs or river-running; the White Mountain Apache, however, do allow river-running on the Salt River from their shore.

Hunters can pursue big and small game with the appropriate licenses. Certain areas of the reservation may be open only to tribal members. Some hunts require licensed guides.

Permits and Information

You need a recreation permit ($7/day) to camp, picnic, hike, or venture onto back roads unless you have a fishing, hunting, or special-use permit. Family permits include parents and kids 18 and under. Visitors to the Black and Salt Rivers or Bear Wallow Creek must have a special permit. One-day permits are good for 24 hours from midnight to midnight. No permit is needed for driving through on U.S. Highway 60, U.S. Highway 70, Road 800 to San Carlos, or Road 500 to Coolidge Dam.

Fishing licenses cost $7 per day or $75 per calendar year; they are free for children under 12 with a permit-holding adult. Obtain the Black and Salt River permit instead if you'll be fishing in those rivers or Bear Wallow Creek; it costs $20 per day for ages 12 and up, but it isn't needed for kids under 12. Boat permits are $3 per day or $30 per calendar year; a combined fishing and boat permit runs $100 for a calendar year. Permits can also be purchased at other locations in the area; ask for a list.

For permits and the latest regulations, facilities, fees, and road conditions, contact the **San Carlos Recreation and Wildlife Department** (P.O. Box 97, San Carlos, AZ 85550, 928/475-2343 or 888/475-2344, www.sancarlosrecreationandwildlife.com, 8 A.M.–4:30 P.M. Mon.–Fri. and 7 A.M.–3 P.M. Sat.). It's near the corner of Moon Base Road and U.S. Highway 70 between Mileposts 272 and 273, 1.5 miles east of the Highway 170 junction for San Carlos.

San Carlos

This small community is very much a government town. Rows of office buildings and apartments line the main street. Here you'll find most tribal offices, the post office, grocery store, San Carlos Café, and a service station. It's four miles north of U.S. Highway 70 on Highway 170, or you can take Road 800 from just east of Apache Gold Casino.

Shops sell Apache crafts such as baskets, beadwork, cradle boards, and peridot jewelry. Peridot is a deep yellow-green, transparent mineral; the cut stones, sold mounted or loose, resemble emeralds. Check for crafts at the **Cultural Center** on U.S. Highway 70, just east of the Highway 170 junction, and at **Apache Gold Casino** on U.S. Highway 70, seven miles east of Globe.

Apache Cultural Center

The San Carlos Apache tell their history from their creation to the present, using stories, photos, and dioramas. A gift shop sells books, paintings, and Apache crafts such as jewelry, beadwork, baskets, cradleboards, and woodcarvings of crown dancers. The center (928/475-2894, 9 A.M.–5 P.M. Mon.–Fri., $3 adult, $1.50 seniors, $1 kids, free under 12) is just east on U.S. Highway 70 from the Highway 170 junction, near Milepost 272.

San Carlos Lake

The 19,500-acre lake, when full, measures 23

miles long by 2 miles wide, making it the largest lake lying completely within Arizona. Though famed mostly for its prolific bass population, the waters have produced state-record specimens of flathead catfish, crappie, and bluegill. People come year-round despite the hot summers at the 2,425-foot elevation. Pullouts atop the 880-foot-high Coolidge Dam, dedicated by President Coolidge himself in 1930, allow you to view the dam and the canyon below.

San Carlos Lake Store (9.5 miles south of U.S. 70/Peridot and 2 miles north of the dam, 928/475-2756) provides information, fishing supplies, groceries, snacks, and gasoline; it's open daily. A small RV park lies across the parking lot ($15 w/hookups). A paved road just north of the store leads one mile down to **Soda Canyon Point Campground** (views, tables, and water) and a nearby boat ramp. Other campgrounds lie on both the north and south sides of the lake.

Other Recreational Areas

Talkalai Lake: The waters have given up some sizable largemouth bass, flathead and channel catfish, crappie, and bluegill. Gas motors up to 15 hp are permitted. The lake and campground (no drinking water) lie about three miles north of the town of San Carlos. It's named for Chief Talkalai, who served as an Indian scout with the army and helped capture Geronimo.

Cassadore Springs: This small picnic area and campground offers spring water about 12 miles north of the town of San Carlos.

Point of Pines: The 35-acre trout lake and campground (no drinking water) are in the eastern part of the reservation. From U.S. Highway 70, 5 miles east of the San Carlos turnoff, head northeast 55 miles on Indian Route 1000 to the campground; all but the last few miles are paved.

Seneca Park: Anglers catch trout, catfish, and largemouth bass in 27-acre Seneca Lake. The lake and campground (no drinking water) are in the northwest corner of the reservation just off U.S. Highway 60/Highway 77, 33 miles north of Globe and 5 miles south of the Salt River Canyon bridge.

Best Western Apache Gold Hotel & Casino

This tourist development lies on U.S. Highway 70 at the west edge of the San Carlos Apache lands, 12 miles west of San Carlos and 7 miles east of Globe. The hotel (928/475-7600 or 800/272-2438, $59 d weekdays, $79 d Fri.–Sat., $99–109 d whirlpool tub rooms) offers an 18-hole golf course, pool, hot tub, and sauna. The nearby RV park has sites in a sea of asphalt ($17 w/hookups). Restaurants fail to provide nonsmoking sections and aren't recommended.

SAFFORD

Surrounded by the rugged Pinaleno, Gila, and Peloncillo mountain ranges, Safford (elev. 2,900 ft.) lies in the broad Gila River Valley. Hohokam, Mogollon, and Anasazi sites in the valley date from about 300 B.C.–A.D. 1200. The Apache arrived about 1700 and managed to discourage European settlers until 1874. In that year four Civil War veterans founded a town named after Anson P. Safford, territorial Arizona's third governor. Five years later, Mormon settlers arrived to farm the valley, founding Smithville, later renamed Pima. Mormons also settled in the towns of Thatcher, Central, Eden, Graham, and Bryce.

Though small, Safford (pop. 9,500) serves as the Graham County seat and as the main retail and service center for a large area of southeastern Arizona. Cotton, especially in Pima, is king, but the irrigated bottomland also supports wheat, barley, alfalfa, and other crops.

Visitor highlights include Discovery Park

© BILL WEIR

harvesting desert cotton

(science exhibits), the Graham County and Pima historical museums, the scenic Mt. Graham Drive into the 10,000-foot-plus Pinaleno Mountains (hiking, fishing, and camping), Aravaipa and Bonita Canyons (wildlife and scenery along a perennial stream), and the Galiuro Wilderness (for adventurous hikers).

Discovery Park

Safford's science center continues to develop on 200 acres at the south end of town. Exhibits in the **Gov Aker Observatory** (928/428-6260, www.discoverypark.com, 6–10 P.M. Fri. and 4–10 P.M. Sat., $5 youth 13+, $3 ages 6–12) illustrate the history of astronomy from early concepts of the universe to cutting-edge research. Videos and interactive exhibits explain the workings of telescopes and the nature of the waves received from space. The shuttlecraft *Polaris* motion simulator ($6) "departs" for tours of the solar system. You can view surroundings by day through the world's largest camera obscura, and by night with a 20-inch astronomical telescope. A gift shop sells posters and science toys. New mining and agriculture museums may be completed by the time of your visit.

Outdoors, you can hop on a train ($1) for a narrated ride through the extensive park grounds until dusk. A wildlife area, reached by trail or train, has a wetlands with bird blinds. Tours of the Mt. Graham International Observatory are available about mid-May to mid-November and require advance reservations. From U.S. Highway 70 on the west side of town, take 20th Avenue 2.4 miles south to the entrance; or, from U.S. Highway 191 south of Safford, turn west on Discovery Park Boulevard to 20th Avenue, then turn left.

Graham County Historical Museum

Native American artifacts in the Prehistory Room include pottery and stone tools from early residents. As you continue through the rooms, you'll see displays of pioneer home life and ranching, school and community. Other galleries display vintage clothing and a doll collection. The museum (3430 Hwy. 70 in Thatcher, 928/348-0470, 10 A.M.–4 P.M. Mon., Tues., and Sat., free) is in the 1917 Thatcher Public School building just west of Safford; park on 4th Street.

Cotton Gin Tours

All that cotton in Graham County fields comes to two cotton gins in the Safford area. Both offer tours during the ginning season, from early October through December and sometimes into January. Call in advance to **Safford Valley Cotton Growers Co-op** (120 E. 9th St. off U.S. 191 in Safford, 928/428-0714) or **Glenbar Gin** (9845 W. U.S. 70, just west of Pima, 928/485-9255).

Events

The **Old-Time Fiddlers Contest** livens up February. **Horse racing** takes off at the county fairgrounds on the last weekend of March and the first weekend of April. **Cinco de Mayo** is celebrated on the weekend nearest May 5 with a parade and entertainment. **Pioneer Day** rolls out with a parade, barbecue, and entertainment on the weekend nearest July 24; the event rotates among Safford, Thatcher, and Pima.

Cowpunchers describe their feelings in the **Cowboy Poet Roundup** in September. The **Graham County Fair** features entertainment, local agricultural accomplishments, and crafts in October. You can shop at the **Cowboy Christmas Arts and Crafts Festival** on the weekend after Thanksgiving.

Recreation

You'll find an outdoor public **swimming pool** (1111 Thatcher Blvd., 928/348-1394, Memorial Day–Labor Day) in Firth Park behind the chamber of commerce. **Tennis** players can use the lighted courts at Graham County Park (2 miles south on U.S. 191) and at the junior high school (520 11th St.). **Graham County Park** also offers racquetball, basketball, ball fields, a jogging track, and picnicking; all but the track are lit for night use. Play golf year-round at the 18-hole **Mount Graham Golf Course** (4 miles southwest of town, 928/348-3140); turn south on 20th Avenue and follow signs. **Swings & Things Sports Park** (520 E. Hwy. 70, 928/348-8333) features a 36-hole miniature golf course and a driving range.

Feeling run-down with too many aches and pains? Then take the waters at **Essence of Tranquility** (5 miles south of Safford at 6074 S. Lebanon Loop Rd., 928/428-9312); turn west off U.S. Highway 191 on Lebanon or Cactus Roads. Massage and other treatments can be arranged, and visitors may stay in a teepee or their own tent.

Accommodations

Safford's motels line U.S. Highway 70, also marked on the west side of town as Thatcher Boulevard and on the east side as 5th Street. Each motel includes air-conditioning and most also have a swimming pool—you may want both in summer, when highs push 100°F!

Bed & Breakfast: For an experience of the Old West, check into the 1890 **Olney House Bed & Breakfast** (1104 Central Ave., 928/428-5118 or 800/814-5118, www.olneyhouse.com, $65–85 d). The three bedrooms in the house have a shared bath. There are also two cottages out back. The wealthy cattleman who built the house kept an eye on the town from the balcony, and you can too.

Under $50: Check out **Tour Rest Motel** (110 5th St., 928/428-3881, $28 s, $32 d), **Budget Inn** (1215 Thatcher Blvd., 928/428-7850, $30 s, $32 d) with a pool, and **Econo Lodge** (225 E. Hwy. 70, 928/348-0011 or 800/553-2666, $42 s, $46 d) with a pool and hot tub.

$50–100: Best Western Desert Inn (1391 Thatcher Blvd., 928/428-0521 or 800/528-1234, $59 s, $65–70 d, $80 d minisuite) offers a pool and restaurant. **Comfort Inn** (1578 Thatcher Blvd., 928/428-5851 or 800/424-6423, $62 s, $69 d) also has a pool and restaurant. **Day's Inn** (520 E. Hwy. 70, 928/428-5000 or 800/329-7466, $55 s, $75 d) includes a breakfast buffet, pool, and hot tub.

$100–150: Quality Inn & Suites (420 E. Hwy. 70, 928/428-3200 or 800/272-6232, $90 s, $120 d, add $15 for rooms with hot tubs, $130–165 d suites) features an indoor pool, indoor hydrotherapy pool, outdoor hot tub, saunas, batting cages, driving range, and a 36-hole miniature golf course. Some rooms have balconies and views of the Gila Mountains.

Teepees and Campgrounds

Essence of Tranquility (928/428-9312 or 877/895-6810) features hot spring mineral baths, teepee rentals ($20–80 depending on size), and tent camping ($10/person), including use of baths, recreation room, kitchen, and showers. Health treatments can be arranged too. From Safford, head south about five miles on U.S. Highway 191, turn right (west) on Lebanon Road, then left (south) where the road curves to 6074 S. Lebanon Loop Road.

RVers can stay at **Sunrise Village Mobile Home Park** (900 E. Hollywood Rd., 928/428-1895, $20 w/hookups) with a pool and hot tub, **Tower Mobile Park** (1.5 miles east at 2056 E. U.S. 70, 928/428-6997, $18 w/hookups), and the adult **Lexington Pines RV Resort** (1535 Thatcher Blvd., 928/428-7570, $19 w/hookups) with an exercise room and a hot tub.

Food

The **Branding Iron** (2.5 miles north of downtown, 928/428-7427, Mon.–Sat. dinner, $10–20) serves up steak, seafood, chicken, and sandwiches with a great view of the valley; reservations are a good idea on weekends. Go north on 8th Avenue, left on Safford-Bryce Road at the fork, then turn right up Branding Iron Lane. **Brick's Steakhouse** (4367 S. Hwy. 191, 928/348-8111, Mon.–Sat. lunch and dinner, $5–17) has a family atmosphere. The steaks, Southwest chicken, and seafood dishes are big hits; breakfast may be served on weekends. **Manor House Restaurant** (415 E. Hwy. 70, across from the Quality Inn, 928/428-7148, daily breakfast, lunch, and dinner, $7–17) has a Western decor for both American and Mexican food, including New York steaks, prime rib, ribs, seafood and a salad bar. Chefs offer buffets on weekends for breakfast and Monday–Saturday for lunch; the owners aim to please and include an adjacent saloon, banquet rooms, and a florist.

Dine Mexican at **Casa Mañana** (corner of U.S. 70 and 1st Ave., 928/428-3170, Mon.–Sat. lunch and dinner, $2–9.50); the chili relleno with onion sauce is a specialty. Favorites at **El Charro** (601 Main St., 928/428-4134, Mon.–Sat. lunch and dinner, $2–11) include the fajitas, chimichangas, and Mexican pizza. Nearby **Chalo's La Casa Reynoso** (611 6th Ave., 928/348-9889, daily lunch and dinner, $2–15) serves up steaks, fajitas, chimichangas, Navajo tacos, enchiladas, and combos; there's a sunroom in back.

Jumbo Chinese Restaurant (817 Thatcher Blvd., 928/428-2888, Mon.–Sat. lunch and dinner, $5.50–11) offers Cantonese and Szechuan cuisine; there's a lunch buffet. **Super Wok** (1275 Thatcher Blvd., 928/348-9452, daily lunch and dinner, $5.50–12.50) serves Chinese food "Safford Style" and prepares an all-day buffet. **China Taste** (1385 Thatcher Blvd., 928/348-3336, daily lunch and dinner, $6–13) features "New York-style" Chinese food in a large all-day buffet and on the menu.

You'll find shopping centers, supermarkets, chain restaurants, and fast-food places west of downtown on U.S. Highway 70.

Information

The very helpful **Graham County Chamber of Commerce** (1111 Thatcher Blvd., Safford, AZ 85546, 928/428-2511 or 888/837-1841, www.graham-chamber.com or www.visitgrahamcounty.com, 8 A.M.–5 P.M. Mon.–Fri. and 10 A.M.–2 P.M. Sat.) is on U.S. Highway 70 just west of downtown. An exhibit room has a detailed diorama of 11,000 years ago when humans first arrived in the Southwest, a diorama of a pueblo village circa A.D. 1400, photos and telescope models of Mt. Graham International Observatory, and displays on local cotton, mining and minerals, recreation, and prehistoric Native American finds. A rest area with picnic tables lies just outside and there's a public swimming pool out back.

The Coronado National Forest's **Safford Ranger Station** (711 14th Ave., Safford, AZ 85546, 928/428-4150, www.fs.fed.us/r3/coronado, 8 A.M.–4:30 P.M. Mon.–Fri.) has travel and recreation information on Mt. Graham Scenic Drive in the Pinaleno Mountains, the Galiuro Wilderness, and the lesser-known wildernesses of Santa Teresa and Winchester.

The **Bureau of Land Management** office (711 14th Ave., Safford, AZ 85546, 928/348-4400, www.az.blm.gov, 7:45 A.M.–4:15 P.M. Mon.–Fri.) provides information on many backcountry areas around Safford, including Aravaipa Canyon (for which you'll need a permit). Rockhounds can pick up brochures about collecting in the Black Hills (between Safford and Clifton) and Round Mountain (south of Duncan) areas.

The **public library** (808 7th Ave., 928/428-1531, closed Sun.) has an Arizona collection and a gift shop. The **Alumni Library** (northwest corner of Church St. and College Ave. in Thatcher, 928/428-8304) at Eastern Arizona College includes a media center.

Services

The **post office** (504 S. 5th Ave., 928/428-0220) is downtown just south of U.S. Highway 70. **Mount Graham Regional Medical Center** (1600 S. 20th Ave., 928/348-4000, www.mt-graham.org) lies southwest of downtown. **Gila Outdoor** (408 Main St., 928/348-0710, www.gilaoutdoor.com) offers topo maps, book, supplies, and clothing downtown.

Getting There and Around

Greyhound (1910 Thatcher Blvd., 928/428-2150) buses stop a couple of times a day in each direction on their cross-country routes. Check with the chamber of commerce for outdoor adventure tour operators.

VICINITY OF SAFFORD

Eastern Arizona Museum and Historical Society

You can learn about the Native Americans and pioneers of the area from this large collection (Pima, 9 miles west of Safford on U.S. 70, 928/485-9400 or 928/485-3032, 2–4 P.M. Wed.–Fri., 1–5 P.M. Sat., free) in a 1915 bank and town hall building. Visits can be arranged at other times too.

Cluff Ranch Wildlife Area

The Arizona Game and Fish Department maintains the 788-acre Cluff Ranch (928/485-9430) as a wildlife and recreation area. Birding is good and you're almost sure to see some free-roaming deer or javelina. Strips of grain crops are planted for wildlife. Streams from Mt. Graham fill two or three ponds and support lush riparian vegetation. Anglers catch trout in winter and largemouth bass, channel catfish, crappie, and bluegill year-round. Boats—oar, sail, or electric—can be used. Visitors may do primitive camping at the ponds; there's a vault toilet near Pond Three.

From U.S. Highway 70 in Pima, 9 miles west of Safford, turn south 1.5 miles on Main Street; the road curves west and becomes Cottonwood Road; continue another .4 miles, then turn south 4.5 miles on Cluff Ranch Road.

Roper Lake State Park

The shores of this pretty lake offer camping, picnicking, swimming, and fishing. A walking path leads out to the island, a day-use area with grass, shade trees, and a beach. Anglers can launch boats (electric motors OK) and try for trout (in winter), catfish, bass, bluegill, and crappie; a boat ramp is on the east side of the lake. Hedonists can relax in the hot tub, fed by a natural spring. Mariah Mesa Nature Trail begins near the hot tub and makes a half-mile loop up the mesa with good views; a trail leaflet and numbered posts identify desert plants. The park (6 miles south of Safford off U.S. 191, 928/428-6760, $6 day use, $12 camping, $19 w/water and electric, $35 cabin up to 6 people) stays open all year and provides showers and a dump station. There's usually room, though hookup sites can fill in winter; only groups can reserve areas. The visitors center offers a gift shop, laptop jack, and free loaner fishing rods.

Warm water from an artesian spring feeds **Dankworth Ponds Unit,** a day-use area that also offers good picnicking, fishing, and hiking. A 1.75-mile round-trip trail winds along the pond, crosses riparian areas and a mesquite bosque, climbs a little mesa to replicas of Native American dwellings, then continues to a dry wash. Admission fees cover both units of the Roper Lake State Park; Dankworth lies 2.7 miles farther south on U.S. Highway 191 (.7 miles south of the Swift Trail junction).

Mount Graham Drive and the Pinaleno Mountains

Mount Graham (10,720 ft.) in the Pinaleno Mountains soars nearly 8,000 feet above Safford—the greatest vertical rise of any mountain in Arizona. Visitors enjoy the views, cool breezes, hiking, picnicking, camping, and fishing. A gate just past Shannon Campground closes during the snow season of November 15 to around April 15 or later.

A good road, the 35-mile-long **Swift Trail Parkway (AZ 366),** ascends the eastern slopes through a remarkable range of vegetation and animal life. Starting among cactus, creosote bush, and mesquite of the upper Sonoran Desert, you'll soon arrive at pygmy forests of juniper, oak, and pinyon pine. Higher on the twisting road, you'll enter dense forests of ponderosa pine, Douglas fir, aspen, and white fir. Thick stands of Engelmann spruce dominate the highest ridges. The Mt. Graham red squirrel, Mt. Graham pocket gopher, white-bellied vole, and Rusby's mountain fleabane (a wild daisy) are found only in the Pinaleno Mountains.

Fire-lookout towers on two peaks offer superb views. **Heliograph Peak** (elev. 10,028 ft.) offers one of the best panoramas in the region; on a clear day you can see most of southeastern Arizona. The 2.2-mile road to the lookout is gated, but you can walk up it or take Arcadia Trail #328 1 mile from Shannon Campground, then turn up Heliograph Trail #328A 1 mile. The army built a heliograph station here in 1886 that used mirrors and sunlight to relay messages to troops. **Columbine Visitor Information Station,** at mile 29 on the Swift Trail, is in an old CCC building that once housed forest workers and firefighters; it may be open in summer.

Webb Peak (elev. 10,086 ft.) offers a better view of the Gila River Valley and surrounding mountains; you can reach the summit by going up 1 mile on Web Peak Trail #345 from Columbine public corrals, by walking on a 1.7-mile gated road, or by making a loop on both. You can stop for a picnic along the way at **Noon Creek** (7 miles up; elev. 5,200 ft.), **Round the Mountain** (7.5 miles; elev. 5,300 ft.; also has corrals and popular trailhead), **Wet Canyon** (10 miles; elev. 6,100 ft.), or **Clark Peak Trailhead** (36 miles; elev. 9,000 ft.). There's no water or charge at these places, but you would have to pay if picnicking at a campground.

If you're driving Highway 266 south of Mt. Graham, you could stop at **Stockton Pass Picnic Area** (free), which offers views and water at an elevation of 5,600 feet. To get there, head south 17 miles from Safford on U.S. Highway 191, then turn right (southwest) 12 miles on Highway 266; it's also the lower trailhead for the Shake Trail #309, which descends from the Pinelenos.

Six developed campgrounds have drinking water and a $10 fee mid-May–October. Campground elevations range from 6,700 feet at Arcadia to 9,300 feet at Soldier Creek. Anglers can camp and try for trout in Riggs Lake, near the end of the Swift Trail. Equestrians can use corrals, trails, camping, and parking at Round the Mountain, Cunningham, Columbine, and Clark Peak Trailhead. Round the Mountain may have stock water; Columbine offers both drinking and stock water.

To reach the start of the drive, go 7 miles south from Safford on U.S. Highway 191, or 26 miles north from I-10, and turn west at the sign. The first 21 miles is paved, followed by 14 miles of gravel to Clark Peak trailhead. This last section of road is gated November 15–April 15 because of snow and the need to protect the red squirrel habitat. The drive from Safford and back takes about 4.5 hours; be sure to stock up on gas and supplies before leaving town.

The Safford Ranger Station has an auto tour on the features of the Swift Trail, maps of the Coronado National Forest (Pinaleno Range), and information sheets on picnic areas, campgrounds, and trails. Hikers can choose among many trails but should be prepared for steep sections; ask about conditions, as fires have damaged some trails.

Mt. Graham International Observatory includes the 1.8-meter (71-inch) Vatican Advanced Technology Telescope, the 10-meter (394-inch) Heinrich Hertz Submillimeter Radio Telescope, and the Large Binocular Telescope, which uses two 8.4-meter (331-inch) mirrors to achieve the light-gathering ability of an 11.8-meter (465-inch) and the resolution of a 23-meter (906-inch) instrument. Tours are available through Discovery Park. Protecting red squirrel habitat is a major concern—and controversy—in the development of the telescope site. High Peak, the summit of Mt. Graham, is closed to protect the red squirrel.

Aravaipa Canyon Wilderness

A jewel in the desert, Aravaipa Canyon is renowned for its scenery and variety of wildlife. The waters of Aravaipa Creek flow all year, a rare occurrence in the desert, providing an oasis for birds and other animals. Giant cottonwood, ash, sycamore, and willow trees shade the canyon floor. Rocky hillsides, dotted with saguaro cactus and other desert plants, lie only a few steps from the lush vegetation along the creek. Birders have sighted about 200 species in the canyon, including bald eagle and peregrine falcon. Mule and white-tailed deer, javelina, and coatimundi frequent the area; you might even see a mountain lion or bighorn sheep. Remember to keep an eye out for any of several species of rattlesnakes.

Although there's no established trail, hiking is easy to moderate along the gravel creekbed. Tributary canyons invite side trips—Hell Hole Canyon is especially enchanting. You'll be wading frequently across the creek, so wear tennis shoes or other shoes that can get wet. Grassy terraces make inviting campsites.

To visit the 11-mile canyon—even for day-hikes—you must get a permit from the BLM office in Safford. You can make reservations online or by phone or mail up to 13 weeks in advance; spring and autumn weekends are especially popular; be sure to cancel if you or any of your party won't be coming. Only 50 people per day are permitted in the canyon, and there's a two-night (three-day) stay limit. Hikers have a 10-person group size limit. Horseback riders are welcome, but on overnight trips they must camp with their horses on the uplands above the riparian canyon; each group is limited to five animals. Pets are prohibited. Visitors must sign in at one of the trailheads and pay a fee of $5 per person per day.

Trailheads, though only 11 trail miles apart, are separated by 160 driving miles. The East Trailhead requires a high-clearance vehicle for the half dozen or so stream crossings; it's reached by Klondyke Road (turn off U.S. 70 about 15 miles northwest of Safford between Mileposts 313 and 314) or Fort Grant Road (turn off U.S. 191 19 miles south of Safford or 17 miles north of I-10's Willcox Exit 336).

A ranger is stationed in Klondyke, a settlement 10 miles before the trailhead. Two veteran Yukon prospectors established Klondyke in the early 1900s. **Klondyke Country Store & Lodge** (928/828-3335 or 877/728-3335, www.klondykestore.com) offers groceries, camping supplies, and a small lodge; it may close in summer and some days mid-week. **Fourmile Campground** nearby has drinking water year-round and a $5 fee; turn left in Klondyke at the sign. With 4WD, you can also camp along Turkey Creek Canyon (no facilities or fee), a pretty tributary of Aravaipa Creek near the East Trailhead.

The West Trailhead is much closer to Phoenix (120 miles) and Tucson (70 miles). A ranger station is located at Brandenburg, three miles before the trailhead. There's no camping at the trailhead. From the junction on Highway 77 near Milepost 124, about 11 miles south of Winkelman, turn east 12 miles on Aravaipa Road to the trailhead.

Bonita Creek

This perennial stream flows through a pretty canyon in the Gila Mountains, about 25 miles northeast of Safford. Primitive roads provide access to the creek; one road follows the riparian canyon for about two miles. Summer flash floods can take out the road, which has many stream crossings, so it's a good idea to first check conditions and routes with the BLM office.

You may spot prehistoric cliff dwellings—most served as granaries—in the canyon, but they are too fragile and footing on the steep hillsides too precarious to approach closely. Birding and hiking are best on weekdays. You can camp almost anywhere except at the mouth—just keep well above the washes to avoid being surprised by a flash flood.

From Safford, travel east about five miles on U.S. Highway 70 to the town of Solomon, then turn left (north) seven miles on Sanchez Road. At the sign for Gila Box Riparian National Conservation-area, turn left 2.5 miles on a graded dirt road to the west entry sign and continue, following signs for Bonita Creek. Other roads lead north to the trailhead for Lee Trail, a midway access point in Bonita Creek, and to Red Knolls Road, which crosses upper Bonita Creek.

A restored pioneer cabin from the 1920s marks the junction of Bonita Creek and the Gila River. There's also a wildlife-viewing platform. **Riverview Campground** nearby is open year-round with water, shade ramadas, and a $5 fee. **Flying W Group Day Use Area** is in the area, too.

The lower 15 miles of Bonita Creek and a 23-mile section of the Gila River are protected as the **Gila Box Riparian National Conservation Area.** Stop by the BLM in Safford for a brochure that includes a detailed map of the roads and facilities in the Conservation Area.

Safford–Morenci Trail

Pioneer ranchers and farmers built this trail in about 1874 to haul their products to the booming mines of the Morenci area. The trail fell into disuse with the advent of the automobile during the early 1900s. Today it receives little use and is often difficult to follow—you'll need topo maps and a compass.

Hikers and horseback riders enjoy the variety of desert and riparian environments along the way. The trail is 14 miles one-way with elevations ranging 3,700–6,200 feet. Bonita Creek, crossed about midway, makes a good camping spot; creek water must be treated before drinking. Roads to both the west and east trailheads may require 4WD vehicles in wet weather. Contact the BLM office in Safford for more information.

Hot Well Dunes Recreation Area

Sand dunes and hot tubs attract visitors to this remote 2,000-acre recreation area southeast of Safford. Off-road vehicle enthusiasts ride the dunes. Campsites offer a place to stay. Entry fee is $3 per vehicle or $30 for an annual permit. Drillers seeking oil in the 1920s hit hot water, which flows at more than 250 gallons per minute at a temperature of 106°F. From Safford, you can head east 7 miles on U.S. Highway 70, then turn south (between Mileposts 347 and 348) 25 miles on Haekel Road. Or drive 17 miles south from Safford on U.S. Highway 191, turn east (near Milepost 105) 12 miles on Tanque Road, then right 8 miles on Haekel Road. From Bowie on I-10 (Exits 362 or 366), turn north two miles on Central Avenue, turn right eight miles on Fan Road; then turn left nine miles on Haekel Road. The BLM office in Safford has information on the area.

Black Hills Back Country Byway

You can take this 21-mile scenic drive in dry weather. A high-clearance vehicle is best, though cautiously driven cars may be able to make it, too. Start from U.S. Highway 191, either east of Safford at Milepost 139 or south of Clifton at Milepost 160. At each end of the drive you'll find a National Back Country Byway kiosk with historical and road information. A BLM brochure describes history, geology, and natural resources at various points along the drive. Visitors with long trailers or RVs should leave them at the information kiosks.

The Black Hills make up the northern end of the Peloncillo Mountains, a volcanic range with alluvial sand and gravel on its flanks. Both ends of the byway begin on the sand and gravel, then climb into volcanic rock in the higher, central part of the drive. Lava flows consist of dark gray and gray brown andesite, rhyolite, and dacite interlayered with multicolored ash from both windblown falls and ash flows. Ash deposits range in color from red or yellow to gray.

The low sections of the drive pass through a desert scrub plant community with much creosote. Animals include diamondback rattlesnakes, whiptail lizards, kangaroo rats, and various species of raptors. Higher elevations include desert grasslands populated by Gambel's quail. Juniper, pinyon pine, and oaks grow along the highest section of the drive. Here you may see mule deer, javelinas, black-tailed rattlesnakes, and migratory birds.

Canyon Overlook Picnic Area lies 7.2 miles in from the southwest end at a high point overlooking the Gila River Canyon. At 17.1 miles from the southwest end, you'll find Old Safford Bridge Picnic Area on the north side of the 1918 bridge. **Owl Canyon Campground,** located on a cliff overlooking the river northeast of the bridge, offers sites with shade ramadas; there's a fee of $5, but no drinking water. Dispersed camping is allowed along the Byway except in riparian areas near the bridge.

Floating the Gila River

Boaters enjoy the solitude, sheer cliffs, and abundant bird life on this 23-mile trip through the Gila Box Riparian National Conservation Area northeast of Safford. You may also see bighorn sheep, beaver, and other wildlife. The Gila River runs year-round, but flow volume and season determine river-running conditions. January–April has the highest flows but very cold water. Levels usually drop in May and June, then pick up again after the July–September rains. Autumn can be fine with cooler temperatures and the cottonwoods turning to gold.

At low flows of 150–500 cfs, conditions are excellent for beginners, who can take inflatable kayaks; boats may have to be pulled through short shallow sections. Flows of 500–1,500 cfs allow rafts up to 14 feet as well as canoes and hard and inflatable kayaks. At 1,500–3,500 cfs, 12-foot and larger rafts do well; conditions are more challenging for kayaks (both hard and inflatable). Flows of 3,500–6,000 cfs require experienced rafters and very experienced kayakers for the Class II and III rapids and debris in the water. Only very experienced rafters with rafts 14 feet or larger should go at 6,000–10,000 cfs, when swift currents create many Class III rapids. Above 10,000 cfs, the river becomes hazardous, and running it is not recommended.

Put in is on the south side of the Old Safford Bridge on the Black Hills Back Country Byway. Take out is south of Riverview Campground or at Dry Canyon Boat Takeout, both northeast of Safford. The required river permits ($3/person) are available from a self-service pay station at the launch site. The BLM office in Safford can advise on flows, access, and availability of commercial trips. You can also obtain flows online at http://water.usgs.gov/realtime.html.

The Coronado Trail

Seeking treasures of the legendary Seven Cities of Cíbola, in 1540 Francisco Vásquez de Coronado and his men struggled through the rugged mountains of eastern Arizona. Though the Spaniard's quest failed, the name of this scenic highway recalls his effort. You'll discover the area's real wealth on a drive over Coronado's old route—rugged mountains covered with majestic forests rolling in blue waves towards the horizon. The blazing gold of aspen in autumn is matched only by the dazzling display of wildflowers in summer. The 123 miles of paved highway between Clifton and Springerville twist over country little changed from Coronado's time. When exploring this region, hikers, anglers, and cross-country skiers will find themselves far from the crowds. You may spot some of the Mexican wolves released between Clifton and Alpine. They're about the size of German shepherds—larger and heavier than coyotes. A few backcountry areas frequented by the wolves may be closed. Forest Service offices and the website http://mexicanwolf.fws.gov have information on the wolf program.

The Apache-Sitgreaves National Forests map shows many scenic backcountry loop possibilities. Allow enough time for the journey through this high country—even a nonstop highway drive requires 3.5 hours. With some 460 curves between Morenci and Alpine, this route certainly isn't suitable for those in a hurry. And you'll probably want to stop often to enjoy the views and maybe have a picnic. Drivers should stock up on groceries and gas before attempting the 89 miles from Morenci to Alpine; there are no towns along this stretch, though Hannagan Meadow Lodge has a small store/gas station.

Winter snows can close the highway from just north of Morenci to Alpine between mid-December and mid-March, though the section from Springerville to Alpine remains open. Miles of fine cross-country ski trails attract winter visitors to the forests near Alpine and Hannagan Meadow.

CLIFTON AND MORENCI

Coronado's expedition marched through this area in 1540, unaware of the gold and abundant copper ore lying deep within these hills. Mexican miners discovered gold in 1867 and began small-scale placer operations. As the gold played out, Eastern prospectors took an interest in the copper deposits. They registered claims and by 1872 had staked out the town of Clifton. The nearby mining towns of Joy's Camp (later renamed Morenci) and Metcalf also date to this time. Miners faced great difficulties at first, as the nearest railhead was far away in Colorado and frequent Apache raids interrupted work.

In 1878, Arizona's first railroad connected the smelter in Clifton with the Longfellow Mine at Metcalf, nine miles north. Mules pulled the empty ore cars uphill to the mine; on the way down, the mules got a free ride. Three tiny locomotives, one on display in Clifton, later replaced the mules. Miners worked underground during the first six decades; in 1937, after a five-year Depression-era hiatus, all mining shifted to the surface, where it continues today.

Both Metcalf and old Morenci are gone now—Metcalf abandoned and destroyed, and old Morenci quarried away. The new Morenci has a modern appearance but lacks the character of an old mining town. Clifton, the Greenlee County seat, still has its old buildings and lots of character. The imposing 1911 yellow brick courthouse stands in the south part of town. Booze joints and brothels, where desperados engaged in frequent shootouts, once lined Chase Creek Street. Today the street is quiet and the old jail empty, but Clifton remains one of Arizona's more historically distinctive towns. Clifton also claims fame as the birthplace of the Apache warrior Geronimo.

Sights

Clifton's old jail, close to the old train depot/chamber of commerce, was built in 1881 by blasting and hacking a hole into the hillside. The jail's first occupant turned out to be the man

COURTESY OF THE GREENLEE COUNTY HISTORICAL SOCIETY

Compare present-day Clifton with this view taken about 1912. Chase Creek Street is in the right foreground; the highway now runs where the locomotive shed in the foreground once stood.

who built it, Margarito Verala. After doing a fine job on the construction, Verala received his pay, got drunk on mescal, and proceeded to shoot up the town. You're welcome to step inside the gloomy interior. The 1880s Copper Head locomotive of the old Coronado Railroad rests next to the jail. Local artists exhibit at the **Art Depot** (928/865-3467) in the old depot.

Chase Creek Street parallels U.S. Highway 191 on the opposite side of the creek. Strolling along it, you can imagine how the scene once looked—when the boisterous miners of old came looking for a good time. To see exhibits and artifacts of the old days, drop into the **Greenlee County Historical Society Museum** (317 Chase Creek St., 928/865-3115, 2–4:30 P.M. Tues., Thurs., and Sat. or by appointment, donations welcome). A large model (ca. 1915) shows the ore deposits and mines of the area. The telephone switchboard and a beautiful cherrywood fireplace mantle come from the old Morenci Hotel. Murals from the early 1900s have humorous folk art. Local history books sold here tell fascinating stories.

Events

Horse races run in late March or early April at the fairgrounds in Duncan. Clifton celebrates **Cinco de Mayo** on the weekend nearest May 5. The **Greenlee County Fair and Rodeo** entertains during September in Duncan. A **Parade of Lights** brightens Clifton in early December.

Recreation

Cool off in the outdoor **swimming pool** (928/865-2003) near the plaza in Morenci. Play golf at the nine-hole **Greenlee Country Club** course (928/687-1099) in York Valley, 12 miles southeast of Clifton via U.S. Highway 191 and Highway 75.

Accommodations, Campgrounds, and Food

Rode Inn Motel (186 S. Coronado Blvd., 928/865-4536, $45 s, $50 d) is in south Clifton. **Morenci Motel** (928/865-4111, $59 d) lies six miles up the highway from Clifton and has a restaurant. The municipal **North Clifton RV Park** (928/865-4146 or 866/996-2787, $10 tent, $15–19 RV w/hookups) lies next to a large city park; turn off the highway on Zorilla Street, one block north of the depot, then turn left .5 miles on Frisco Avenue.

Clifton has several smoky cafés along the highway. Another option is a picnic—you'll find tables just off U.S. Highway 191 in Clifton south of the San Francisco River bridge and at a park just north of the Rode Inn. The **Morenci Motel's restaurant** (928/865-4111, lunch and dinner most days, $5–12) offers American and Mexican dining. **Golden City Chinese Restaurant** (928/865-5941, Mon.–Sat. lunch and dinner, $7–10), **R&R Pizza Express** (928/865-2200, Mon.–Sat. lunch and dinner, $4–13), and a **Dairy Queen** lie across the street in Morenci Plaza.

Stock up on groceries at **Bashas'** in the shopping plaza, especially if headed north, as no supplies or gas are available for the next 67 miles to Hannagan Meadow.

Information and Services

In Clifton's 1913 train depot, the **Greenlee County Chamber of Commerce** (P.O. Box 1237, Clifton, AZ 85533, 928/865-3313) provides information on the history, sights, and facilities of the area; hours depend on volunteer staffing. You can see old photos of Morenci, taken before it disappeared, and of Clifton in its busier days. Rockhounds can obtain directions to several agate digs.

For hiking and camping information on the south half of the Coronado Trail, see the Forest Service's **Clifton Ranger District** office (9 miles south of Clifton at Three Way, 397240 AZ 75, Duncan, AZ 85534, 928/687-1301/1314, 8 A.M.–4:30 P.M. Mon.–Fri.).

Clifton's **public library** (101 School St., 928/865-2461, open Mon.–Fri.) is across from the county courthouse. Morenci's **public library** (928/865-2775, open Mon.–Sat.) is in the shopping plaza. **Post offices** are at N. Coronado Blvd. in Clifton and in the shopping plaza in Morenci. **Morenci Healthcare Center** (Coronado Blvd. and Burro Alley, 928/865-4511) provides medical services.

SIDE TRIPS FROM CLIFTON

Mule Creek Road

Highway 78 winds into the pinyon-juniper forests of the Big Lue Mountains east of town and continues into New Mexico. Ponderosa pine and oak grow at the higher elevations near the campgrounds. Begin at the Three Way junction nine miles south of town. You can stay at **Black Jack Campground** (elev. 6,300 ft.) about 11 miles in and at **Coal Creek Campground** (elev. 5,900 ft.) 5 miles farther. These small campgrounds can usually be reached year-round; no water or fee.

San Francisco River Scenic Drive

Forest Road 212 winds from Clifton east up along the San Francisco River past ranches, old mines, and canyon scenery to Evans Point. Cars can travel at least a few miles and high-clearance 4WD vehicles can go farther. Head up Frisco Avenue on the west side of the river, cross the river on a concrete bridge, and continue upstream. Staff at the Clifton Ranger District office and Greenlee County Chamber of Commerce can advise you on this and other backcountry drives and hikes.

BELOW THE MOGOLLON RIM

Morenci Mine Overlook

From this high vantage point, 10 miles north of Clifton, you can gaze into one of the biggest man-made holes in the world. Giant 210-ton trucks look like toys laboring to haul copper ore out of the ever-deepening pit. On the drive up from Clifton (elev. 3,502 ft.) and modern Morenci (elev. 4,080 ft.), you'll pass a giant smelter (now closed), concentrators (also closed), and a solvent extraction/electrowinning plant. Tours may be offered; ask at the Morenci Motel (928/865-4111).

Granville Campground and Cherry Lodge Picnic Area

Both of these places nestle in a wooded canyon at an elevation of 6,800 feet and make pleasant stops. The camp and picnic sites are free and open all year; they lie on opposite sides of the road, about 20 miles north of Clifton between Mileposts 178 and 179.

Honeymoon Campground

As its name suggests, this is a secluded spot at the end of the 22-mile dirt Upper Eagle Creek Road. Elevation is 5,400 feet. No drinking water or fee. You can fish for trout in Eagle Creek, stocked from May to September. Turn west onto Forest Road 217 near Milepost 188 of the Coronado Trail. Many of the ranches along the way date back to the late 1800s.

Juan Miller Campgrounds

The season runs year-round when not blocked by snow at the upper (elev. 5,800 ft.) and lower (5,700 ft.) campgrounds; no drinking water or fee. Head east one mile from the Coronado Trail on Forest Road 475. The turnoff is near Milepost 189, 33 miles north of Clifton and 35 miles south of Blue Vista. Forest Road 475 continues east to Blue River, another 15 miles, passing many small canyons and ridges good for day hiking.

Rose Peak

At an elevation of 8,786 feet, Rose Peak offers great views north to the Mogollon Rim, east and southeast to the Blue River area and far into New Mexico, south to the Pinalenos, and west across the Apache reservations. It's also a good place for bird-watching. The turnoff lies near Milepost 207, about 51 miles north of Clifton and 17 miles south of Blue Vista. You can reach the forest lookout tower on a .5-mile trail or a 1.4 mile road (high-clearance vehicle needed); the gate is usually locked except during the fire season.

Strayhorse Campground

This free campground at an elevation of 7,600 feet is 64 miles north of Clifton and 4 miles and 1,600 feet below Blue Vista; turnoff is near Milepost 221. **Raspberry Creek Trail #35** leads east to Blue River in the Blue Range Primitive Area. **Highline Trail #47** goes west 14.5 miles, linking with several other trails; trails in this area, west of Strayhorse Campground, tend to be harder to follow.

ATOP THE MOGOLLON RIM

Blue Vista Overlook

In clear weather you can see countless ridges rolling away to the horizon from this 9,184-foot vantage point. Signs identify many of the mountain ranges, including Mt. Graham (elev. 10,717 ft.), the highest peak of the Pinaleno Range, 70 miles to the south. A short trail through the mixed conifer forest goes farther out on the ridge, though trees obscure the views.

The overlook sits at the very edge of the Mogollon Rim, 68 miles north of Clifton and seven miles south of Hannagan Meadow. Turn .3 miles southwest at the sign to paved parking, picnic tables, an outhouse, and wheelchair-accessible views.

Bear Wallow Wilderness

This area west of the Coronado Trail contains 11,000 acres, including what's thought to be the largest stand of virgin ponderosa pine in the Southwest. **Bear Wallow Trail #63** follows Bear Wallow Creek downstream through the wilderness west to the San Carlos Indian Reservation boundary, 7.6 miles one-way; elevations range from 8,700 feet at the trailhead to 6,700 feet at the reservation boundary. You can hike on the reservation with a Black and Salt River permit from the San Carlos Apache tribe.

Two shorter trails drop down to the trail and creek from the north. **Reno Trail #62** (1.9 miles one-way) meets Bear Wallow Trail at Mile 2.6; **Gobbler Point Trail #59** (2.7 miles one-way) meets Bear Wallow Trail at Mile 7.1. Reach upper trailheads from Forest Road 25, which turns off U.S. Highway 191 opposite the road for K. P. Cienega Campground. Foresters at the Alpine Ranger District office have trail descriptions and can advise on current conditions.

K. P. Cienega Campground

Sites in this idyllic spot overlook a large meadow

(*cienega* is Spanish for meadow) and a sparkling stream, though recent fires have burned some of the surrounding ridges; there's no water or charge. From the Coronado Trail 2 miles north of Blue Vista Overlook and five miles south of Hannagan Meadow, turn east 1.5 miles on a dirt road to the campground. On the way, you'll pass the trailhead for **K. P. Trail #70,** which heads into the Blue Range Primitive Area.

HANNAGAN MEADOW AND VICINITY

Splendid forests of aspen, spruce, and fir surround the tiny village of Hannagan Meadow (elev. 9,100 ft.), 22 miles south of Alpine. A network of trails offers some great hiking; several trails also lead into the adjacent Blue Range Primitive Area. Here, in areas relatively unknown, you'll find some of the best cross-country skiing and snowmobiling in all of Arizona. The road from Alpine is normally open in winter, though storms occasionally shut it down for a few days.

Hannagan Meadow Campground and Trails

This national forest campground .3 miles south of the lodge on the highway stays open mid-May–mid-September; no drinking water or fee. You can hike from the campground, if staying there, or from the Ackre Lake–Fish Creek Trailhead just to the south. The **Ackre Lake Trail** heads to Ackre Lake, 3.5 miles, and to remote areas of the Blue Range Primitive Area. **Fish Creek Trail** follows the creek all the way from Ackre Lake to the Black River, about 12 miles one-way.

Hannagan Meadow Lodge

The cozy rooms and rustic cabins at this remote lodge (HC 61, P.O. Box 335, Alpine, AZ 85920, 928/339-4370, www.hannaganmeadow.com) offer comfortable year-round accommodations, all with private bath. Rooms and suites in the lodge run $60–100 d, and log cabins go at $80–125 for up to four people. The lodge dining room (breakfast daily, lunch Fri.–Sat., and dinner daily, $10–17) serves dinners of steak, prime rib, chicken, trout, salmon, and pasta. A small gas station/store sits next door. You can rent mountain bikes and cross-country skis.

Winter Sports

Cross-country skiers in the Hannagan Meadow area can glide along four marked trails totaling about 27 km (16.7 miles) during the late November–late March season. The Alpine Ranger District office and Hannagan Meadow Lodge have maps. A snowmobile trail starts from the north end of the lodge area.

BLUE RANGE PRIMITIVE AREA

This rugged wilderness country lies south of Alpine along the Arizona–New Mexico border. The south-flowing Blue River, fed by several perennial streams, neatly divides the primitive area. The Mogollon Rim, with high cliffs forming the south boundary of the Colorado Plateau, crosses the area from west to east. Geologic uplifting and downcutting have created spectacular rock formations and rough, steep canyons. Elevations range from 9,100 feet near Hannagan Meadow to 4,500 feet in the lower Blue River.

Hiking down from the rim, you'll find spruce, fir, and ponderosa pine forests giving way to pinyon pine and juniper. Wildlife includes Rocky Mountain elk, Coues white-tailed deer, mule deer, black bear, mountain lion, Mexican wolf, javelina, and bobcat. You may also see such rare and endangered birds as the southern bald eagle, spotted owl, American peregrine falcon, aplomado falcon, Arizona woodpecker, black-eared bushtit, and olive warbler. The upper Blue River and some of its tributaries harbor small numbers of trout.

You have many day-hike and backpack options; check with the Forest Service office in Alpine for maps, trail descriptions, and the latest conditions (fires have damaged some areas). The best times to go are April–early July and September–late October. Violent thunderstorms lash the mountains in July and August. Snow covers much of the land from November to March. You can hike from trailheads along the Coronado Trail/U.S. Highway 191 on the west and Blue Road/Forest Road 281 and Red Hill

Road/Forest Road 567 on the north; other trailheads lie to the east in New Mexico.

ALPINE

This high mountain valley (elev. 8,046 ft.), surrounded by extensive woodlands, attracted Mormon settlers who settled in 1879. They named their town Frisco for the nearby San Francisco River, but, inspired by the mountain setting, they later renamed it Alpine. Alpine (pop. 600) is an excellent base for hiking, mountain biking, fishing, hunting, horseback riding, golfing, scenic drives, and—in winter—cross-country skiing, sledding, and snowmobiling.

Events

Bush Valley Craft Fair takes place on Memorial Day weekend in May. Worms strain for the finish line in **Worm Races and Parade** on the second full weekend in July. Classic cars glitter in the **Cool August Nights** at Tal-Wi-Wi Lodge on the first Saturday. The **CASI Chili Cookoff** spices up August on the third Saturday. Shop early in the **Bush Valley Christmas Bazaar** on Labor Day weekend.

Recreation

You can **ride horses** at Sprucedale Ranch. Cross-country skiers roam the groomed trails northwest of town in Williams Valley or south of town at Hannagan Meadow. See how far you can hit a golf ball through the thin mountain air at **Alpine Country Club** (928/339-4944), which offers an 18-hole course and a restaurant April 15–October 15; head east three miles on U.S. Highway 180, then turn south two miles and follow signs.

Accommodations

Places tend to fill up on summer weekends, when you'll need reservations. **Mountain Hi Lodge** (928/339-4311) provides rooms at $46 d weekdays, $53 d Friday–Saturday, and kitchenettes at $56–78 d weekdays, $61–78 d Friday–Saturday on Main Street.

Alpine Cabins (just east on U.S. 180 from the highway junction, 928/339-4440, closed mid-Dec.–March, $55 up to four persons) has a variety of kitchenettes. **Coronado Trail Cabins & RV** (.5 miles south of town on U.S. Hwy 191, 928/339-4772) has cabins with kitchenettes about April–December at $55–69 d; RV spaces are open April–October and cost $23 w/hookups. **Sportsman's Lodge** (U.S. 191 just north of the highway junction, 928/339-4576 or 888/202-1033) offers motel rooms for $50 d and kitchenettes for $75 d.

Tal-Wi-Wi Lodge (3 miles north of Alpine, 928/339-4319 or 800/476-2695, www.talwiwilodge.com) has a seasonal restaurant and year-round rooms at $69 d, $79 d with fireplace, $89 d with hot tub, $99 d with fireplace and hot tub. **Sprucedale Ranch** (P.O. Box 880, Eagar, AZ 85925, 928/333-4984, www.sprucedaleranch.com) offers accommodations at a working cattle and horse ranch at an elevation of 7,400 feet. Minimum stays are six days at $475 adult with a reduced rate for children. From Alpine, drive 14 miles south on U.S. Highway 191, turn right nine miles on Forest Road 26, then right one mile on Forest Road 24 to the ranch turnoff.

Campgrounds

Alpine Divide Campground is set in a forest of ponderosa pine and Gambel oak four miles north of Alpine. It offers sites with drinking water about mid-May–mid-September, for $7. The rest of the year, camping is on a pack-in/pack-out basis and free.

Luna Lake Campground lies near the north shore of this 75-acre lake amid meadows and ponderosa pine forests near the New Mexico border; it's open with drinking water mid-May–mid-September and costs $8; family and group sites can be reserved (877/444-6777, www.reserveusa.com). Head east four miles from Alpine on U.S. Highway 180, then turn left 1.5 miles. Mountain bikers hit the dirt on the **Luna Lake Loop,** whose 2.5- and 8-mile circuits begin on the right just before the campground. On the south shore just off the highway, you'll find a free picnic area with shaded tables, a fishing dock, and a boat ramp. Nearby, a year-round store offers bait, tackle, and boat rentals. Anglers go after trout in all four seasons—even through the ice in winter. Birders flock to the west shore to see a heron rookery in May–June; bald eagles nest as early as January and fledge between May and early July.

Coronado Trail Cabins & RV (.5 miles south of town on U.S. 191, 928/339-4772, $23 RV w/hookups) is open about April–October. **Outpost RV & Trailer Park** (on U.S. 180 near Luna Lake, 928/339-4854, $15 RV w/hookups) has sites for self-contained units April 15–October 15. **Alpine Village RV Park** (U.S. 180 in Alpine, 928/339-1841) offers sites year-round ($5 for tents, $18 for RVs w/hookups); showers cost an extra $4 per person. **Meadow View RV Park** (one block north of the junction of U.S. 191 and U.S. 180 in Alpine, 928/339-1850, $20 RV w/hookups) is open year-round for self-contained rigs.

Food

High Country Buffet and Lollypop Shoppe (just east on U.S. 180 from the highway junction in town, daily breakfast, lunch, and dinner, $10) has themed buffets for lunch and dinner and sometimes for breakfast along with homemade ice cream and other sweet treats; call for hours in winter. Across the street, **Bear Wallow Café** (928/339-4310, daily breakfast, lunch, and dinner, $6–20) serves American food, but can be smoky. **Tal-Wi-Wi Lodge** (3 miles north of Alpine, 928/339-4319, $6–16) serves breakfast on weekends and dinner Thursday–Saturday from May to late November. The **Alpine Country Club's** restaurant (928/339-4944) serves a brunch on Sunday, lunch Tuesday–Saturday, and dinner Friday–Saturday from April 15 to October 15; head east three miles on U.S. Highway 180, then turn south and follow signs about two miles. **Alpine Country Store** sells groceries on U.S. Highway 180 in town.

Information and Services

For a list of accommodations and services, contact the **Alpine Chamber of Commerce** (P.O. Box 410, Alpine, AZ 85920, 928/339-4330 answering machine, www.alpinearizona.com). People at the Apache-Sitgreaves National Forests' **Alpine Ranger District** office (U.S. 191 in town, P.O. Box 469, Alpine, AZ 85920, 928/339-4384, 8 A.M.–4:30 P.M. Mon.–Fri.) provide information on scenic drives, fishing, hiking, mountain biking, camping, and cross-country ski trails. The district covers the north half of the Coronado Trail, including Escudilla Mountain and most of the Blue Range Primitive Area. You can also obtain local tourist information and purchase books and maps. The TDD number for those with hearing impairments is 928/339-4566.

Alpine's **public library** (928/339-4925) is .4 miles east on U.S. Highway 180 from the highway junction. The **post office** is on U.S. Highway 191 just north of the highway junction. The **Tackle Shop and Sports Center** (928/339-4338) has groceries, fishing and hunting supplies, and cross-country ski rentals near the highway junction.

VICINITY OF ALPINE

The **East and West Forks of the Black River** west of town have fishing, hiking, and campgrounds; continue west for Big Lake, Crescent Lake, and other recreation areas.

Blue River-Red Hill Scenic Loop

On this backcountry drive you'll roll by the Blue River, remote ranches, and rugged hill country. The Forest Service maintains two small campgrounds along the way—Upper Blue, with spring water, and Blue Crossing. Both lie near the Blue River at an elevation of 6,200 feet; no charge.

From Alpine, head east three miles on U.S. Highway 180 and turn south on Forest Road 281 (Blue Road). After 10 miles you'll reach the Blue River; follow it downstream 9 miles to the junction with Forest Road 567 (Red Hill Road). A river ford here can be impassable in high water. Red Hill Road twists and climbs out of the valley, following ridges with good views, to U.S. Highway 191, 14 miles south of Alpine. If driving in the other direction, you'll find the Red Hill Road turnoff between Mileposts 239 and 240 on U.S. Highway 191. The forest roads are gravel and should be OK in dry weather for cautious drivers. Ask at the Alpine Ranger District office for more information on this and other scenic drives in the area.

Hikers may want to try **Red Hill Trail #56;** this 7.6-mile trail follows a jeep track to the Blue Range Primitive Area, descends along ridges via Red Hill (elev. 7,714 ft.), drops into Bush Creek, and follows it to Tutt Creek. **Tutt Creek Trail #105** connects the lower end of Red Hill Trail with Red Hill Road, .8 miles to the east. The upper trailhead (elev. 8,000 ft.) is on Forest Road 567 one mile east of U.S. Highway 191; the lower trailhead (5,800 ft.) is on Forest Road 567 a half mile before the Blue River.

Mountain Biking

The Apache-Sitgreaves National Forests offer many good areas for mountain biking. Marked trails in the Alpine District include upper (8 miles) and lower (2.5 miles) loops near Luna Lake, Georges Lake near Alpine (4.5 miles, 7.5 miles without shuttle), Terry Flat Loop (6 miles) at Escudilla Mountain, Hannagan Meadow Loop (5.5 miles) south of Alpine, and Williams Valley (5 miles) northwest of Alpine.

Escudilla Mountain and Wilderness

In 1540, Coronado spotted the 10,912-foot summit of this ancient volcano; perhaps a homesick member of his expedition named the mountain after an *escudilla,* a soup bowl used in his native Spain.

In 1951 a disastrous fire burned the forests on the entire north face of Escudilla. Aspen trees then took over where mighty conifers once stood, the normal sequence after a mountain fire. Raspberries, snowberries, currants, elderberries, strawberries, and gooseberries now flourish here too. The forests of spruce, fir, and pine on top escaped the fire; lower down you'll find surviving woodlands of aspen, Rocky Mountain maple, ponderosa pine, and Gambel oak. Elk, deer, black bear, and smaller animals roam the hillsides. Escudilla was once grizzly country, but the last one was killed by the 1930s.

Now a wilderness area of 5,200 acres, Escudilla offers excellent hiking. Outstanding views from the fire lookout—the highest in Arizona—reward those who make the climb. The actual summit (10,912 ft.)—Arizona's third highest—lies a half mile to the north and 36 feet higher, but trees there completely block the views.

Escudilla National Recreation Trail, a well-graded, 3.3-mile trail from Terry Flat (elev. 9,600 ft.), ascends to Escudilla Lookout through aspen, meadows, and conifers. The old Government Trail originally began at Hulsey Lake and, though shown on some maps, it's no longer maintained and isn't recommended.

From U.S. Highway 191 between Mileposts 420 and 421, about 6 miles north of Alpine and 21 miles south of Springerville, turn east 4.6 miles on Forest Road 56 to Terry Flat Loop, then take the left fork .4 miles to the trailhead. **Terry Flat Loop** is a worthwhile destination in itself—the six-mile dirt road encircles Terry Flat Meadow with many fine views of Escudilla Mountain. Cautious drivers can usually make the trip with cars in dry weather. Families enjoy outings and trout fishing at **Hulsey Lake,** about two miles in on Forest Road 56; small boats can be carried and hand launched.

Nelson Reservoir

Rainbow, brown, and brook trout live in this 60-acre lake surrounded by a woodland of pinyon pine and juniper. It's just west of U.S. Highway 191, 11 miles north of Alpine and 10 miles south of Springerville. Restrooms, a paved boat ramp, and handicapped fishing station are provided at the north end; no fires or camping. Winter visitors can fish through the ice.

Sipe White Mountain Wildlife Area

Elk, mule deer, pronghorn, and turkey roam the rolling hills and meadows southwest of Springerville. Waterfowl and other birds drop by the lakes. A visitors center (928/333-4518 residence) has exhibits and a few picnic tables; it's usually open 8 A.M.–5 P.M. Wednesday–Sunday from Memorial Day to Labor Day. You're welcome to hike or horseback ride during daylight hours. The elk population peaks at about 1,000 during the September–October rut season, when the males bugle and compete with each other, and the females meow; sunrise and sunset are the best times to see and hear the elk in action. Rudd Creek Pueblo, a short walk from the visitors center, dates to about 1225–1300 when ancestral Pueblo people used the 50 masonry rooms and two great kivas. From U.S. Highway 191 at Milepost 405 near the crest of a ridge, about five miles south of downtown Springerville, turn south five miles on a gravel road.

Springerville and Vicinity

SPRINGERVILLE AND EAGAR

Since Henry Springer's trading post opened in 1879, Springerville has grown into an important trade, ranching, and lumbering center. Today it's a handy stop for travelers. Springerville and the adjacent town of Eagar lie in Round Valley beside the Little Colorado River at an elevation of 6,965 feet. Rolling grass-covered hills surround the valley.

The *Madonna of the Trail,* an 18-foot statue in Springerville, commemorates the hardy pioneer women of yesteryear. You can't miss the giant dome of the Round Valley Ensphere in Eagar; this multipurpose building has a total floor area of 189,000 square feet, unusually large for such a small community. It is said to be the only domed high school football field in the country.

Casa Malpais

Believed to have been a major trade and ceremonial center, this prehistoric ruin built between A.D. 1260 and 1440 by the Mogollon people contains some unusual features. Huge cracks—more than 100—under the site served as ceremonial and burial chambers, referred to as "catacombs" by some archaeologists. The masonry pueblo at Casa Malpais (House of the Badlands) rose two and three stories with more than 120 rooms. The Great Kiva, square in the Mogollon style, measures 55 by 62 feet; archaeologists think it once had a roof. Other features at the site include rock art, masonry stairways, and an oval wall enclosing what may have been an astronomical observatory. The village sits on a series of terraces at the edge of a large lava flow, just north of present-day Springerville.

Tours, the only way to enter the ruins, last about 1.5 hours and involve 1.5 miles of walking and a 250-foot climb; bring water and a hat in summer. You may see excavations in progress during the warmer months. Because of their sacred nature, the underground chambers are closed to the public.

Before going out to the site, meet at the museum (318 E. Main St., 928/333-5375, 8 A.M.–4 P.M. daily) in downtown Springerville; tours usually leave at 9 A.M., 11 A.M., and 2 P.M. in good weather; additional tours may be added in summer. The museum offers good exhibits of local finds along with a fine selection of regional books. There's no charge to see the exhibits here; tours cost $7 for adults, $5 for seniors 55+ and students.

Renee Cushman Art Collection

Renee Cushman willed her valuable collection of European art and furniture, which ranges from Renaissance to early 20th century, to the Church of Latter-Day Saints in Springerville (150 N. Aldrice Burk, 1.5 blocks off Main Street). Call 928/333-4514 for an appointment to see the collection, which is housed in three rooms.

Events

The community celebrates **July 4th** with a parade, rodeo, barbecue, dance, and fireworks. **Eagar Daze,** the first weekend in August, features a talent show, games, barbecue, and a dance. A **Christmas Lights Parade** is held on the first Saturday in December.

Shopping

Stuart Books (319 E. Main St. in Springerville, 928/333-2031) offers new and used books. Pick up fishing, hunting, and camping supplies in Springerville at **Western Drug and General Store** (105 E. Main St., 928/333-4321) or at **Sport Shack** (329 E. Main St., 928/333-2222). Over in Eagar, the **Sweat Shop** (42 N. Main St.,

928/333-2950) sells sporting goods and rents mountain bicycles and cross-country skis.

Recreation

Springerville Park offers shaded picnic tables and a playground near the White Mountain Historical Society Park; turn south three blocks on Zuni from Main. Old buildings of the historical park are open some days, ask at the chamber office. Eagar has the indoor **Round Valley Swimming Pool** (116 N. Eagar St., 928/333-2238, closed in winter).

Accommodations

Under $50: White Mountain Motel (333 E. Main St., 928/333-5482, $29 s, $34 d rooms, $35–45 d kitchenettes) offers simple lodging. **Reed's Motor Lodge** (514 E. Main St., 928/333-4323 or 800/814-6451, www.k5reeds.com) provides a variety of rooms at $36–45 s, $41.50–52.50 d, and $59.50–82.50 d suites; the hosts have an art gallery and decorate some rooms with works by regional artists; guided hike and horse tours can be arranged.

$50–100: El Jo Motor Inn (435 E. Main St., 928/333-4314, $45 s, $50 d and up) has the basics. **Rode Inn** (242 E. Main St., 928/333-4365 or 877/220-6553, $55 s, $65 d weekdays, $65 s, $75 d Fri.–Sat., $145 d suites) offers deluxe lodgings. In Eagar you can stay at the **Best Western Sunrise Inn** (128 N. Main St., 928/333-2540 or 800/528-1234, $70 d), which has a sauna and exercise room. Also in Eagar, **Paisley Corner Bed and Breakfast** (287 N. Main St., 928/333-4665, $75–95 d) has rooms with private bath in a 1910 house.

Campgrounds

Casa Malpais Campground (1 mile northwest on U.S. 60, 928/333-4632, $10 tent or $16 RV w/hookups) has showers, laundry, and a small store. Nearby Becker Lake offers trout fishing. **Bear Paw RV Park** (425 E. Central Ave. in Eagar, 928/333-4650, $16.25 RV w/hookups) is open all year for self-contained rigs.

Food

For American and Mexican food in Springerville, try **Booga Red's Restaurant & Cantina** (521 E. Main St., 928/333-2640, daily breakfast, lunch, and dinner, $7–16). **Safire Restaurant** (411 E. Main St., 928/333-4512, daily breakfast, lunch, and dinner, $5–18) fixes American and a few Mexican items nearby. Locals also dine at **Coyote Creek Steakhouse** (corner of E. Hwy. 60 at D St., 928/333-4023, daily dinner, $9–25) for steaks and other American cuisine; head east on U.S. Highway 60 and continue .6 miles past the U.S. Highway 191 junction. **Java Blues** (341 E. Main St., 928/333-5282, daily, about $6) is a colorful coffeehouse serving everything from espresso to Italian sodas along with sandwiches, salads, quiches, and pastries. **Round Valley Plaza** (just south of downtown Springerville on S. Mountain Ave.) has a supermarket and other stores.

Information and Services

Staff at the **Springerville-Eagar Regional Chamber of Commerce** (318 E. Main St., P.O. Box 31, Springerville, AZ 85938, 928/333-2123, www.springerville-eagar.com, 9 A.M.–4 P.M. daily) in downtown Springerville can tell you about the area and services.

For maps and the latest information on recreation and road conditions in the Apache-Sitgreaves National Forests, visit either of the two U.S. Forest Service offices on S. Mountain Avenue. The **Springerville Ranger District Office** (165 S. Mountain Ave., just north of Round Valley Plaza, P.O. Box 760, Springerville, AZ 85938, 928/333-4372, 7:30 A.M.–4:30 P.M. Mon.–Fri.) has specific information on Big Lake, Mt. Baldy, Greer, South Fork, and other areas of the district. The **Supervisor's Office** (309 S. Mountain Ave., just south of Round Valley Plaza, P.O. Box 640, Springerville, AZ 85938, 928/333-4301, 7:30 A.M.–4:30 P.M. Mon.–Fri.) has general information on the Apache-Sitgreaves National Forests.

Round Valley Public Library (367 N. Main St. in Eagar Plaza, 928/333-4694, open Mon.–Sat.) is behind the Dairy Queen in Eagar. **White Mountain Regional Medical Center** (118 S. Mountain Ave., 928/333-4368) is in downtown Springerville.

SOUTH FORK

An entertaining museum, a campground, and cabins lie in the meadows and forests along the South Fork of the Little Colorado River. Turn south on Apache Co. 4124 from Highway 260 between Mileposts 390 and 391, about five miles west of Springerville/Eagar.

Little House Museum

On a tour through a series of buildings at X Diamond Ranch, including a cabin and a granary dating from the 1890s, your guide uses photos and heirlooms to tell stories of the pioneers. Working nickelodeons and other music machines from the past provide little interludes. The 90-minute tours (928/333-2286, www.xdiamondranch.com, $7 adults, $3 children) go year-round by reservation only.

The X Diamond Ranch also offers log cabins ($105–165 d), trail rides, rock-art tours (hiking or horseback), archaeology programs, and private fishing access (catch-and-release; fishing equipment can be rented). Turn in 2.4 miles on Apache Co. 4124, then right .7 miles at the sign.

South Fork Campground

Campsites ($6) in the ponderosa pines lie along both sides of the stream at an elevation of 7,520 feet. They're open with water mid-May–end of October. Turn south 2.8 miles on Apache Co. 4124 to road's end. You can hike farther upstream on South Fork Trail #97 from the campground.

GREER

This little town sits in a pretty valley high in the White Mountains at 8,500 feet. Settlers first arrived in 1879, then later named their community for Americus Vespucius Greer, a prominent Mormon pioneer.

Today Greer comes to life in the summer, when visitors enjoy fishing, forest walks, and the cool mountain air. Winter is also a busy season—snow worshippers flock to the slopes of nearby Sunrise Ski Area or put on their skinny skis to glide along the miles of marked cross-country ski trails just outside town. The quietest times are mid-April–early May, when the first signs of spring appear, and autumn, when days are crisp and aspens turn gold. Greer lies 15 miles east of Sunrise Ski Area, 16 miles west of Springerville and 225 miles northeast of Phoenix. From the junction on Highway 260, turn south five miles on Highway 373.

Butterfly Lodge Museum

This 1913 cabin recalls the extraordinarily colorful lives of two inhabitants. James Willard Schultz (1859–1947) came west in his youth, married a Blackfoot maiden, then later became a noted explorer, storyteller, archaeologist, Native American–rights advocate, and popular author. He wrote 37 adventure books, beginning with *My Life as an Indian.* Schultz set three books in Arizona, where he got to know the Hopi, Navajo, and Apache tribes. Although an outsider to the close-knit Mormon village of Greer, he enjoyed life at his cabin and hunting trips in the wilderness. His son, Lone Wolf (Hart Merriam Schultz, 1882–1970), also roamed the West before receiving encouragement from artist Thomas Moran in 1906 to take formal art training. Lone Wolf enjoyed great success by the 1920s with his Western paintings and sculpture.

Exhibits in the restored cabin tell about their lives and families. You'll also see writings of the father and artwork of the son. A gift shop sells articles, cards, and books, including *On the Road to Nowhere: A History of Greer, Arizona 1879–1979,* by the museum's curator, Karen M. Applewhite. The museum (928/735-7514, 10 A.M.–5 P.M. Fri.–Sun. Memorial Day–Labor Day weekends, $2 adults, $1 ages 12–17) is half a mile south of the Circle B Market, then east at the sign.

Recreation

You can fish for trout in the waters of the Little Colorado River in and near town and in the **Greer Lakes,** three small reservoirs offering boating (electric motors OK) and picnicking north of town; turn east off Highway 373 opposite Hoyer Campground.

Butler Canyon Trail (cross-country ski trail in winter) is a one-mile, self-guided nature trail just north of town; turn east .1 mile off Highway

373 at the sign for Montlure Camp and Nature Trail, .7 miles south of Circle B Market.

Cross-country skiers enjoy a variety of loop trails in the woods northwest of town from **Squirrel Spring Recreation Area** (west side of Hwy. 373 about halfway to Greer) and **Pole Knoll Recreation Area** (south side of Hwy. 260 just east of Milepost 383); each trailhead has picnic tables and an outhouse. Aspen Trail (1.4 miles one-way, "easiest") connects the two areas. You could also hike the ski trails in the warmer months. Elevations in the ponderosa pine and aspen forests range 8,900–9,500 feet. Obtain ski-trail maps from local businesses or from the **Springerville Ranger District** office (928/333-4372) in Springerville.

Railroad Trail turns south from Highway 260 at Milepost 379 near the White Mountain Apache Reservation border and winds across meadows and forest to Big Lake in 21 miles one-way. There's an outhouse at the trailhead. Snowmobilers may use the trail in winter.

Accommodations

Greer resorts offer lodge rooms and rustic cabins; most cabins have kitchens and cozy fireplaces.

Under $50: Circle B Motel (928/735-7540, $49 d) lies next to the market of the same name on the way into town. **Molly Butler Lodge** (in town, 928/735-7226, www.mollybutlerlodge.com, $55 d and $70 d), established in 1910, is the oldest guest lodge in Arizona; it's open year-round and has a restaurant.

$50–100: Greer Mountain Resort (2.7 miles north of town, 928/735-7560, www.greermountainresort.com) offers apartments ($75 d), cabins ($100 d and $135 d), and a restaurant (daily breakfast and lunch). **The Aspens** (928/735-7232, $85–105 d) has cabins. **Snowy Mountain Inn** (3 miles north of town, 928/735-7576 or 888/766-9971, www.snowymountaininn.com, $150–180 cabins, $275–350 houses) has a restaurant (Fri–Sat. dinner), fishing pond, and hot tubs.

White Mountain Lodge (928/735-7568 or 888/493-7568, www.wmlodge.com) offers rooms ($85–145 d) with breakfast and private baths in an 1892 farmhouse, plus cabins ($95–225 d); the Little Colorado River and a beaver pond in back have fishing. **Cattle Kate's Lodge** (928/735-7744, $75–85 d rooms, $125 d suites) includes a full breakfast and offers a fishing pond and a seasonal restaurant.

Over $100: Greer Lodge & Spa (928/735-7216 or 866/826-8262, www.greerlodgeaz.com, $125–185 d weekdays, $150–220 d Fri.–Sat. lodge rooms, $160–295 cabins) features luxurious accommodations, a restaurant, and a private trout pond. The award-winning **Red Setter Inn & Cottages** (928/735-7441 or 888/994-7337, www.redsetterinn.com) features rooms in a log lodge ($150–210 d), small cottages ($265 d), and a four-bedroom housekeeping cabin ($600 per night); all guests enjoy a full breakfast.

Campgrounds

You'll pass the two national forest campgrounds of **Benny Creek** ($8) and **Rolfe C. Hoyer** ($14) on the way in to Greer. Both lie under ponderosa pines at an elevation of about 8,250 feet with water about mid-May–end of September. Hoyer Campground is larger with a nature trail, showers, and dump station. Sites at both campgrounds can be reserved (877/444-6777, www.reserveusa.com).

Food

Molly Butler Lodge (928/735-7226, daily lunch in summer and for dinner year-round, $11–27) features prime rib along with steaks, chicken, trout, and seafood; the dining rooms have fine views of the valley. **Greer Mountain Resort Café** (928/735-7560, daily breakfast and lunch, $5.50–7.50) is 2.7 miles north of town.

At river's edge, the **Greer Lodge & Spa** (928/735-7217, daily breakfast, lunch, and dinner, $9–19) offers decks and large picture windows that let you to take in the meadow and lake views while dining on such entrées as beef filet, chicken, kebabs, and pizza; musicians perform most evenings.

Services and Information

Circle B Market (928/735-7540) offers groceries, fishing gear, camping supplies, boat rentals, and cross-country ski rentals. For tourist information, you can visit the Springerville-Eagar Regional Chamber of Commerce office (www.springerville-eagar.com) in Springerville and check the Greer Business Association's website (www.greerarizona.com).

MOUNT BALDY WILDERNESS

The pristine forests and alpine meadows of 11,590-foot Mt. Baldy present a fine opportunity to visit a subalpine vegetation zone. You'll see magnificent forests untouched by commercial logging. Engelmann and blue spruce dominate, but quaking aspen, white fir, corkbark fir, Douglas fir, southwestern white pine, and ponderosa pine also cover the slopes. You might catch a glimpse of elk, mule or white-tailed deer, black bear, beaver, wild turkey, blue grouse, or other wildlife. Mount Baldy is an extinct volcano eight or nine million years old, worn down by three periods of glaciation.

Trails

West Fork #94 and **East Fork #95** trails follow the respective branches of the Little Colorado River on the northeast slopes of Mt. Baldy. Each trail is 6.5 miles long; they meet on the grassy summit ridge. The summit is another mile away, but the last half mile of trail crosses White Mountain Apache land, which is closed to outsiders. The Apache vigorously enforce this closure—errant hikers have been arrested, and their gear confiscated—so don't try to sneak in! Apache make pilgrimages to this sacred peak.

Hiking season stretches June–October, but plan to be off the ridges in early afternoon in July and August to avoid thunderstorms. The trailheads, about four miles apart by road, are easily reached from Sunrise, Big Lake, or Greer. In fact, both trails also go north to Greer, about five miles away.

The West Fork Trailhead (elev. 9,240 ft.) lies just outside the wilderness boundary at the end of Forest Road 113J, a half mile in from Highway 273. The East Fork Trailhead (elev. 9,400 ft.) begins near the Phelps Cabin site, .2 miles in from Highway 273. An all-day or overnight loop hike uses a 3.3-mile connecting trail that joins the lower ends of West Fork and East Fork trails. This trail, which may not appear on maps, goes from the West Fork Trail (.3 miles up from the trailhead) to the Phelps Cabin site area.

Horseback riders are welcome on the trails, too. They'll appreciate the corrals at **Gabaldon Campground,** which offers basic camping—no water, tables, or fee—in spruce trees off Highway 273, just east of Phelps Trailhead. Trail #95 connects the campground and trailhead. The season runs about June–September at this 9,400-foot elevation.

Anglers catch brook, rainbow, and a few native cutthroat trout in the creeks. The Forest Service asks visitors to limit hiking and riding groups to 12 people and camping groups to 6. Forest Service offices sell a topo map of Mt. Baldy Wilderness.

BIG LAKE

Rolling mountain meadows and forested hills of spruce and fir surround this pretty lake. Top-rated for trout by many anglers, Big Lake (575 acres) boasts a marina, campgrounds, hiking trails, and a riding stable. The marina offers rental boats, motors, fishing supplies, gas, and groceries from late April/early May to mid-November. A fish-cleaning station lies across the parking lot, and a public boat ramp is a short drive away.

Nearby **Crescent Lake** (197 acres) features trout fishing and a smaller marina—boat rentals and snacks—but no campgrounds. The Forest Service operates a visitors center on the main road between the two lakes; check out the naturalist programs, displays, books, and maps.

At Big Lake you have a choice of four campgrounds: **Rainbow** ($12–14), **Grayling** ($12), **Brookchar** ($10), and **Cutthroat** ($10). All have drinking water. Both RVers and tenters can stay at Rainbow and Grayling, but only tents are allowed at Brookchar and Cutthroat. Showers and a dump station are available. Camping season with water lasts mid-May–mid-September; Grayling, Brookchar, and Cutthroat stay open mid-April–Thanksgiving if weather permits. Expect cool nights at the 9,100-foot elevation even in midsummer. Reserve campsites at 877/444-6777 or www.reserveusa.com.

Big Lake lies about 20 miles south of Highway 260 via paved Highway 261 and Highway 273; the turnoff is at Milepost 393, 7 miles east of the Greer junction and 3 miles west of Springerville. The Apache-Sitgreaves Forests map shows other ways in.

Vicinity of Big Lake

Mountain bikers can enjoy the marked **Indian Springs Trail #627,** a 7.5-mile loop south of Big Lake; the 3-mile (one-way) **West Fork Destination Trail** branches off the loop to the West Fork of the Black River. There are many other fine rides on the forest roads as well.

Lee Valley Lake (35 acres) contains brook trout—best early and late in the season—and great scenery at an elevation of 9,400 feet near Mt. Baldy Wilderness; it's off Highway 273 between Big Lake and Sunrise. **Winn Campground** sits at the end of Forest Road 554, two miles in from Highway 273. Greer, Lee Valley Lake, Sunrise Lake, Big Lake, and Crescent Lake all lie within a 10-mile radius. Camping season at the 9,320-foot elevation runs mid-May–end of September; sites have drinking water and an $12 fee; they and **Winn Group** can be reserved (877/444-6777, www.reserveusa.com).

The **East Fork of the Black River** offers fishing for rainbow trout. Stay at **Diamond Rock, Aspen,** or **Buffalo Crossing campgrounds** (all free); drinking water at Diamond Rock only. The season runs early May–end of October. The area is 9 miles southeast of Big Lake and 10–14 miles southwest of Alpine.

The **West Fork of the Black River** has fishing for rainbow and brown trout. **West Fork Campground** beside the stream is free but lacks drinking water. An eight-mile hike leads downstream from Forest Road 116 to West Fork Campground. The Apache-Sitgreaves National Forests map shows back roads in the area.

NORTH OF SPRINGERVILLE

Wenima Wildlife Area

This riparian corridor stretches nearly two miles along the Little Colorado River. A picnic table under the trees marks the trailhead for the 2.5-mile-round-trip Beavertail Trail that turns left downstream and the 1-mile-round-trip Powerhouse Trail that winds upstream from just over the bridge. From the U.S. Highway 191–U.S. Highway 60 junction 3 miles northwest of Springerville, turn north .1 miles on U.S. Highway 191, then turn east 1.4 miles on Hooper Ranch Road.

Lyman Lake State Park

Rain and snowmelt from the White Mountains flow down the Little Colorado River and fill this 1,500-acre lake. Juniper trees and other high-desert vegetation grow in the wide valley at an elevation of 6,000 feet. Though it's cold here in winter, anglers come year-round to try for channel catfish, largemouth bass, and walleye. Lyman Lake is large enough for sailing and waterskiing, and has no motor restrictions. Water skiers test their skills in a ski slalom course near the dam. Anglers enjoy a section of the west end designated as a no-wake area.

The park (928/337-4441, $5 day use, $12 camping, $19 w/hookups, $35–75 cabin or yurt) lies 17 miles north of Springerville and 10 miles south of St. Johns on U.S. Highway 180/191 between Mileposts 380 and 381, then east 1.3 miles. Petrified Forest National Park is just 53 miles away. The contact station has photos and artifacts of prehistoric Native American sites in the area, including Rattlesnake Point Pueblo.

From the first weekend in May to the last one in September, rangers lead 90-minute tours across the lake to the Ultimate Petroglyph Trail at 10 A.M. on Saturday and Sunday and one-hour tours to the Rattlesnake Point Pueblo at 2 P.M. on Saturday and Sunday; reservations recommended. You can also visit these sites on your own, but you'll need a boat to reach the start of the Ultimate Petroglyph Trail. Fireworks on July 4 light up the skies in a Fire Over the Water display. Water-ski tournaments for novices run on July 4 and Labor Day weekend.

An excellent year-round campground includes restrooms, showers, hookups, and a dump station. Boaters can also use undeveloped campsites on the shore. Campers should prepare for strong winds on the open terrain. You'll may see

© BILL WEIR

along Ultimate Petroglyph Trail, Lyman Lake State Park

Eastern Arizona

swallows nesting—they're the reason the campground has so few mosquitoes!

Two small peninsulas, with a protected swim area in between, jut into the lake from the campground and day-use areas. The neck of the north peninsula has a store, day-use area, group ramada area, two paved boat ramps, a boat dock, fishing pier, and 1.2 miles of hiking trails with views. The store offers groceries, snacks, and fishing supplies about April–October. A day-use area with a fish-cleaning station lies across the road.

Petroglyph panels and views on the south peninsula attract visitors to the pair of trail loops here, totaling 1.5 miles.

St. Johns

Spanish explorers named this spot on the Little Colorado River El Vadito (Little River Crossing). In 1871, Solomon Barth founded a settlement along the river with his brothers and some Mexican families, then moved six miles upstream to the present site the following year. Residents named the community San Juan after its first female resident, Señora Maria San Juan de Padilla de Baca. Postal authorities supposedly refused to accept a foreign name, so it was changed to Saint John, with an *s* added for phonetic effect. Mormon settlers arrived in 1879 from Utah. Today, St. Johns (pop. 3,700) serves as the Apache County seat, 27 miles north of Springerville and 44 miles southeast of Petrified Forest National Park.

You can learn more about the area's history and see pioneer and Native American artifacts in the **Apache County Museum** (180 W. Cleveland St., 928/337-4737, 8 A.M.–5 P.M. Mon.–Fri., closed holidays, donations welcome). Archaeological highlights unearthed in the area include tusks and a jaw from a mammoth and a leg bone from a giant camel. Out back, you'll find a petroglyph panel, jail, log cabin (c. 1882), adobe building reconstruction, and farm equipment. The **St. Johns Chamber of Commerce** (P.O. Box 929, St. Johns, AZ 85936, 928/337-2000, 8 A.M.–5 P.M. Mon.–Fri.) is in the museum.

St. Johns has a **Budget Inn** (75 E. Commercial St., 928/337-2990, $40 s, $40–46 d) and a

Days Inn (125 E. Commercial St., 928/337-4422 or 800/329-7466, $55 d). **El Camino** (277 White Mountain Dr., 928/337-4700, Mon.–Sat. lunch and dinner, $3–9) serves Mexican fare on the road to Springerville. **George's Place Too** (928/337-3425, daily dinner, $7–25) prepares steaks, seafood, and Italian cuisine one mile east on U.S. Highway 191 toward Sanders.

The **San Juan Fiesta** in mid-June celebrates with a parade, barbecue, dances, and games. A **July Fourth** festival features a barbecue, games, and fireworks. **Pioneer Day,** on the weekend nearest July 24, has a parade, rodeo, pageant, barbecue, and dances. The **Apache County Fair** in September presents exhibits and horse races. In mid-December, a large community choir forms a living Christmas tree.

The pleasant **city park** (2nd West and 2nd South) includes covered picnic tables, a playground, outdoor pool, and courts for tennis, volleyball, racquetball, and handball; from the museum, turn south two blocks on 2nd West. The **public library** (245 W. 1st South, 928/337-4405) has a Southwest collection and Internet access; from the museum go one block south, then turn right one block.

Kolhuwalawa

Arizona's 23rd Indian reservation was created in 1985, returning to the Zuni (ZOO-nee) their heaven. The Zuni believe these 1,400 acres, 14 miles north of St. Johns, to include the place where human spirits return after death. Anthropologists think that Zuni religious leaders have held sacred dances and ceremonies here since at least A.D. 900, when ancestors of the tribe began migrating from pueblos in Arizona to New Mexico.

The Zuni people, like the Hopi, still live in pueblos and maintain many of their old traditions. You can visit Zuni Pueblo, one of the fabled Seven Cities of Cíbola sought by Coronado in 1540. Zuni is in New Mexico, 58 miles northeast of St. Johns.

Concho Lake

Concho is stocked with trout. The adjacent **Concho Valley Country Club** (928/337-4644 golf shop, 800/658-8071 golf reservations) features an 18-hole golf course. **Concho Valley Motel** (928/337-2266, $40–50 d) has a restaurant open weekends for breakfast and daily for lunch May–October.

Know Arizona

The Land

GEOGRAPHY

Though geologically complex, overall the land surface of Arizona tilts slightly downward to the southwest. More than 90 percent of the state's drainage flows into the southwest corner via the Colorado River and its tributaries. By the time the river enters Mexico, it has descended to an elevation of only 70 feet. Mountain ranges rise in nearly every part of Arizona, but they achieve their greatest heights in the north-central and eastern sections. Humphrey's Peak, part of the San Francisco Peaks near Flagstaff, crowns the state at 12,633 feet. Geographers divide Arizona into the high Colorado Plateau Province of the north and the Basin and Range Province of the rest of the state. Average elevation statewide is about 4,000 feet. Measuring 335 miles wide and 390 miles long, Arizona is the sixth largest state in the country.

Colorado Plateau

This giant uplifted landmass in northern Arizona also extends across much of adjacent Utah, Colorado, and New Mexico. Rivers have cut deeply into the plateau, forming the Grand Canyon and other vast gorges. Volcanoes have broken through the surface and left hundreds of cinder cones, such as multicolored Sunset Crater. The most recent burst of volcanic activity in Arizona took place at Sunset Crater about 800 years ago. Most elevations on the plateau are between 5,000 and 8,000 feet. Sheer cliffs of the Mogollon (MUGGY-own) Rim drop to the desert, marking the plateau's south boundary. To the west, the plateau ends at Grand Wash Cliffs.

Basin and Range Province

Many ranges of fault-block mountains, formed by faulting and tilting of the earth's crust, poke through the desert plains of western, central, eastern, and southern Arizona. Several peaks rise above 9,000 feet, creating biological "islands" inhabited by cool-climate animals and plants. Tucson-area residents, for example, can leave the Sonoran Desert and within an hour reach the cool fir and aspen forests of Mt. Lemmon.

CLIMATE

During any season, some part of Arizona enjoys near-perfect weather. Sunny skies and low humidity prevail over the entire state most of the time. Average winter temperatures run in the 50s in the low desert and the 20s–30s in the mountains and high plateaus. Desert dwellers endure average temperatures in the 80s and 90s in summer, when high-country residents enjoy averages in the 70s. Parker, along the Colorado River, attained 127°F on July 7, 1905—the highest reading ever recorded in the state. Even on a normal summer day in the low desert, you can expect highs in the low 100s. Desert areas can experience swings of 40°F between day and night due to the dry air and the lack of moderating forests.

Precipitation

Rain and snowfall correspond roughly to elevation: The southwest corner receives less than 5 inches of precipitation annually, while the higher mountains and the Mogollon Rim get about 25 inches. Most falls either in winter as gentle rains and snow, or in summer as widely scattered thundershowers. Winter moisture comes mostly in December–March, revitalizing the desert; brilliant wildflower displays appear after a good wet season. Summer afternoon thunderclouds billow in towering formations from about mid-July to mid-September. The storms, though producing heavy rains, tend to be localized in areas less than three miles across. Summer thundershowers make up 60–70 percent of the annual precipitation in the low desert and about 45 percent on the Colorado Plateau.

Storm Hazards

Rainwater runs quickly off the rocky desert surfaces and into gullies and canyons. Flash floods can form and sweep away anything in their paths, including boulders, cars, and campsites. Take care not to camp or park in potential flash-flood areas. If you come to a section of flooded roadway, a common occurrence on desert roads after storms, just wait until the water goes down—usually within an hour or so. Summer lightning causes forest and brush fires, and it poses a danger to hikers foolish enough to climb mountains when storms threaten.

Flora and Fauna

LIFE ZONES

A wide variety of plant and animal life finds homes within Arizona's great range of elevations—more than 12,000 feet. Sensitive and endangered plant species receive protection from a state law that prohibits collecting or destroying most cacti and wildflowers without a permit from the landowner. Cacti need time to grow—a saguaro takes 50 years to mature—and cannot survive large-scale collecting. Some plants, such as the senita cactus and elephant tree, grow only in southern Arizona and Mexico.

© BILL WEIR

"He went that-a-way!"—a saguaro

Migratory birds often stop by the mountains and wetlands. The colorful parrotlike trogon bird and more than a dozen species of hummingbirds fly up from Mexico to spend their summers in the mountains of southeastern Arizona. Canada geese and other northern waterfowl settle in for the winter on rivers and lakes in the low desert.

To help simplify and understand the different environments of Arizona, some scientists use the Merriam system of life zones. Because plants rely on rainfall, which is determined largely by elevation, each life zone can be expected to occur within a certain range of elevations. The elevation ranges are not exact—south-facing mountain slopes receive more sun and lose more moisture to evaporation than north-facing slopes at the same level. Canyons and unusual rainfall patterns can also play havoc with classifications. Yet the life zones do provide a general idea of what kind of vegetation and animal life you can expect when traveling through the state.

Lower Sonoran Zone

Arizona's famed desert country of arid plains, barren mountains, and stately saguaro cacti covers about one-third of the state. The southern and western sections under 4,500 feet lie within this zone. The big cities and most of the state's population are here, too. With irrigation, farmers find the land good for growing vegetables, citrus, and cotton. Cacti thrive: You'll see prickly pear, cholla, and barrel, as well as the giant saguaro, whose white blossom is the state flower. Desert shrubs and small trees include the paloverde, ocotillo, creosote, mesquite, and ironwood. Flowering plants tend to bloom after either winter rains (the Sonoran or Mexican type) or summer showers (the Mojave or Californian type).

STRANGE CREATURES OF THE DESERT

Solpugid (sun spider)
This feisty predator (*Eremobates* spp.) has the largest jaws relative to its size of any animal in the world. Only about two inches long, the solpugid moves fast—its prey has little chance of escaping. The two tiny black eyes atop its head provide poor vision, so this arthropod navigates mostly by waving a pair of sticky arms, called pedipalps, in front. You're not likely to see the hairy, sand-colored beast because it's shy and often hunts at night; dusk is the best time to spot one. They live a solitary life, coming together only to mate. The male excretes seminal fluid on the ground, then transfers it with his pedipalps to the female, who buries her 50–200 eggs in the ground. She stays with the hatchlings, feeding them, until they're ready to fend for themselves. The solpugid doesn't have venom, but it shouldn't be handled on account of its powerful jaws. It's beneficial to us because it keeps down populations of ticks, mites, and other harmful arthropods.

Vinegaroon (whip scorpion)
The sharp claws and curved tail of this dark-brown to black arthropod (order Uropygi, *Mastigoproctus giganteus*) resemble those of a scorpion, but the creature lacks any means to inject venom. Instead, for defense, it can aim its whiplike tail with great accuracy and squirt concentrated acetic acid (vinegar) with a small amount of caprylic acid onto a predator. Caprylic acid enables the acetic acid to pass through the hard outer skin of other arthropods. The vinegaroon comes in about 100 species. Three or four pairs of eyes on the sides of its head supplement the two eyes on the front. The slender front pair of legs serve as feelers to navigate and to search out grasshoppers and other prey. Males secrete a sperm sac, which they may transfer to the female. The mother stays with her sac of up to 35 eggs until the offspring hatch, then carries them until they've grown large enough to survive on their own. Vinegaroons are shy and nocturnal, so you'll be lucky to see one. If you're sprayed by a vinegaroon, wash or rinse the area thoroughly with water.

Hercules beetle (rhinoceros or horned beetle)
The Hercules *(Dynastes granti)* is the largest—as long as three inches—of Arizona's horned beetles. The male brandishes two splendid black horns, one curving up from his prothorax (section behind the head) and the other downward from his head. The beetle with the biggest horns usually gets the females—though males rarely use the horns to do battle. The beautifully polished head and forewings are gray with brown spots and lines. When threatened, the beetle will squirt a brown substance from its abdomen and fly off with a noisy buzz.

Tarantula
About 30 species of these gentle giants (*Aphonopelma* spp., *Dugesiella* spp.) inhabit Arizona's deserts. Adults have a leg span of 2–4 inches, with dense fur on the legs and abdomen, and range in color from light- to dark-brown. They live in burrows, logs, or under debris, coming out at night to dine on small insects and spiders. Females stay close to home their entire lives—which can be up to 25 years. The males leave their burrows upon reaching sexual maturity at about 10 years, then wander in search of a mate, usually in June–August; this is when you're most likely to see tarantulas. The males die soon after mating; sometimes eaten by a female. After mating, females stay with their egg sac for six to seven weeks until the babies hatch; about a week later the youngsters leave their mother's burrow. Both ends of the spider can be hazardous to predators: The tarantula may rear up on its hind legs and bare its fangs, or stand on its front legs and use its other legs to hurl a cloud of barbed or poisonous hairs off its abdomen. Enemies include various birds, lizards, snakes, and even a wasp—the tarantula hawk—which paralyzes the spider, then lays eggs that hatch and feed on the body.

Though rare, tarantula bites should be allowed to bleed for a few minutes, then cleaned; the irritating hairs can be removed with tape.

RATTLESNAKES

Arizona is home to 11 species of rattlesnake (*Crotalus* spp.). They range in length from less than two feet to about five feet. All feed on small rodents and can live more that 20 years in the wild. Eggs stay within the mother's body until hatched. The newborn snakes need no maternal care; they have poison and the ability to strike just minutes after birth. Babies stay where they were born for the first 7–10 days until they shed their skin and gain their first rattle. These tiny rattlesnakes can be aggressive and deadly—they cannot make a rattle sound, are difficult to see, and haven't developed the ability to regulate how much venom they inject. A new rattle appears each time a snake sheds its skin—as often as three times a year for a rapidly growing youngster. The number of rattles doesn't accurately indicate the snake's age; the snakes grow at varying rates, and the rattles can break off over the reptile's lifetime.

Rattlesnakes belong in the backcountry—we can share their space by being watchful and respectful. They come out only when the air temperature is a comfortable 65–85°F, typically in the daytime during spring and autumn, and at night during summer. Like other creatures, rattlesnakes display different temperaments. Mojave rattlesnakes have a fiercer reputation than other species and may even pursue an intruder. Rattlers in the Grand Canyon and other parts of the Colorado Plateau seem relatively docile.

On rare occasions, a snake will strike without warning, but more often it will just rattle or ignore you completely. They tend to be very defensive, however, and will strike if someone steps on them or gets too close. If you find yourself uncomfortably near a rattlesnake, it's best to back off slowly; a quick movement could provoke a strike. Snakes can blend in remarkably well with the colors and patterns of their surroundings, so hikers must be alert to see them. More than once the author has been asked by someone coming from behind, "Hey, did you see that rattlesnake beside the trail?" "Rattlesnake?"

Who Gets Bitten?

According to Steven Curry, Associate Medical Director of the Samaritan Regional Poison Control Center in Phoenix, "The majority [of snakebite victims] are inebriated men, frequently unemployed, and almost universally tattooed." An estimated 80 percent of snakebite victims had been "messing around" with snakes.

Treatment

The only effective treatment for rattlesnake bites is an antivenin injection, available at a hospital. Identification of the species will help in the selection of the best antivenin. To give first aid: Calm and reassure the victim, remove jewelry before swelling begins, avoid movement of the affected part, keep the limb lower than the heart, wash with cold water to reduce infection risk, and get the person to a hospital as soon as possible. Despite what movie actors do, don't give any alcohol or drugs. Also, don't apply ice packs, make incisions, or use a tourniquet, as these may do more harm than good. Venom has a variety of effects, including damage to muscle tissue and the dangerous lowering of blood pressure that can damage major organs. On a happier note, many strikes are "dry bites" with no venom injected; these are more likely in brief, surprise encounters—yet another incentive not to tease snakes.

BOB RACE

Western diamondback rattlesnake

Most desert animals retreat to dens or burrows during the heat of the day, when ground temperatures can reach 150°F. Look for wildlife in early morning, evening, or at night: kangaroo rats, squirrels, mice, desert cottontail, black-tailed and antelope jackrabbits, spotted and striped skunks, gray and kit foxes, ringtail, javelina, bighorn sheep, coyote, and the extremely shy mountain lion. Common birds include the cactus wren (state bird of Arizona), Gambel's quail, Gila woodpecker, roadrunner, hawks, eagles, owls, and common raven. Sidewinder and western diamondback rattlesnakes are occasionally seen. The rare Gila monster, identified by a beadlike skin with black and yellow patterns, is the only poisonous lizard in the United States; it's slow and nonaggressive but has powerful jaws. Also watch out for poisonous invertebrates, especially the small slender scorpion—its sting is dangerous and can be fatal to children. Spiders and centipedes can also inflict painful bites. Careful campers check for unwanted guests in shoes and other items left outside.

Upper Sonoran Zone

This zone encompasses 4,500- to 6,500-foot elevations in central Arizona and in widely scattered areas throughout the rest of the state. Enough rain falls here to support grasslands or stunted woodlands of juniper, pinyon pine, and oak. Chaparral-type vegetation grows here too, forming a nearly impenetrable thicket of manzanita and other bushes. Many of the animals found in the Lower Sonoran Zone live here as well. You might also see black bear, desert mule deer, white-tailed deer, and the antelope-like pronghorn. Rattlesnakes and other reptiles like this zone best.

Transition Zone

The sweet-smelling ponderosa pines grow in this zone, at 6,500–8,000 feet, where much of the winter's precipitation comes as snow. Ponderosas cover many parts of the state, but their greatest expanse—the largest in the country—lies along the southern Colorado Plateau, from Williams in north-central Arizona eastward into New Mexico. Gambel oak, junipers, and Douglas fir commonly grow among the ponderosas.

Squirrels and chipmunks rely on the pinecones for food; other animal residents here include desert cottontail, black-tailed jackrabbit, spotted and striped skunks, red fox, coyote, mule deer, white-tailed deer, elk, black bear, and mountain lion. Wild turkey live in the woods, along with the Steller's jay, screech owl, hummingbirds, juncos, and common raven. Most of the snakes here—gopher, hognosed, and garter—are harmless, but you might also run across a western diamondback rattler.

Canadian Zone

Douglas firs dominate the cool, wet forests between 8,000 and 9,500 feet, mixed with Engelmann and blue spruce, white and subalpine

OLD-GROWTH FORESTS

Only 5 percent of Arizona's original forest remains. It survives in remote canyons and on a few mountains, some under federal protection. Scientists find the old-growth forests an amazingly complex interaction of life and decay. Hundreds of species of fungi, insects, birds, animals, and plants feed or protect one other in ways still being discovered. Much has also been learned about forest management from these old systems. Checks and balances in these forests limit damage of insect and mistletoe infestations, an advantage that managed forests of uniformly aged trees don't share.

Fires in the old growths burn cool and close to the ground and do little harm, because the shade from mature trees prevents excessive growth of brush and thickets of small trees; also, the branches of mature trees lie above the reach of most fires. Natural fires move through every 5–7 years, clearing the underbrush and fertilizing the soil with ash. Even in death, a large tree can stand 50 years, providing a home for generations of birds and insects. Foresters once removed these old snags as fire hazards, but now we know that many birds depend on them.

fir, and quaking aspen. Little sunlight penetrates the dense forests, where the trees function as their own windbreak. Grasses and wildflowers grow in lush meadows amid the forests. You'll find Canadian Zone forests on the Kaibab Plateau of the Grand Canyon's North Rim, the San Francisco Peaks, the White Mountains, and other high peaks. Look and listen for squirrels as they busily gather cones for the long winter. Deer and elk graze in this zone, but rarely higher.

Hudsonian Zone

Strong winds and a growing season of less than 120 days prevent trees from reaching their full size at elevations of 9,500–11,500 feet. Forests here receive twice as much snow as their neighbors in the Canadian Zone just below. Often gnarled and twisted, the dominant species are Engelmann and blue spruce, subalpine and corkbark fir, and bristlecone pine. This zone appears in Arizona only atop the highest mountains.

On a bright summer day, the trees, grasses, and tiny flowering alpine plants buzz with insects, rodents, and visiting birds. Come winter, most animals move to lower and more protected areas.

Alpine Zone

In Arizona, only the San Francisco Peaks exhibit this zone, which lies above about 11,500 feet, the upper limit of tree growth. Freezing temperatures and snow can blast the mountain slopes even in midsummer. About 80 species of plants, many also present in the North American Arctic, manage to survive on the Peaks despite the rocky soil, wind, and cold. One species of groundsel and a buttercup appear only here. Seasonal visitors include a dwarf shrew and three species of birds, the Lincoln and white-crowned sparrows and the water pipit.

History

PREHISTORIC PEOPLES

Paleo-Indians

Arizona's first people discovered this land more than 15,000 years ago. Spears in hand, tribespeople hunted bison, camel, horse, antelope, and mammoth. Smaller game and wild edible plants completed their diet. About 9000 B.C., when the climate grew drier and grasslands turned to desert, most of the large animals died off or left. Overhunting may have hastened their extinction.

Desert Culture Tradition

The early tribes survived these changes by relying on seeds, berries, and nuts collected from wild plants and by hunting smaller game such as pronghorn, deer, mountain sheep, and jackrabbit. Having acquired a precise knowledge of the land, the small bands of related families moved in seasonal migrations timed to coincide with the ripening of plants in each area. They traveled light, probably carrying baskets, animal skins, traps, snares, and stone tools. Most likely they sought shelter in caves or built small brush huts. Some Arizona tribes continued a similar nomadic lifestyle until the late 1800s.

Emergence of Distinct Cultures

Between 2000 and 500 B.C., cultivation skills came to the uplands of Arizona from Mexico. Groups planted corn and squash in the spring, continued their seasonal migration in search of wild food, then returned to harvest the fields in autumn. Agriculture became more important after about 500 B.C., when beans were introduced; the combination of beans, corn, and squash gave the people a nutritious, high-protein diet. The earliest pottery, for cooking beans and storing other foods and water, was developed at about the same time.

From about 100 B.C. to A.D. 500, as they devoted more time to farming, the tribes began building villages of partly underground pit houses near their fields. Regional farming cultures appeared: the Hohokam of the southern deserts, the Mogollon of the eastern uplands, and the ancestral Puebloans (Anasazi) of the Colorado Plateau in the north.

Growth and the Great Pueblos

Villages grew larger and more widespread as populations increased from A.D. 500 to 1100. Aboveground pueblo dwellings began to replace the old-style pit houses. Trade among the Southwest cultures and with those in Mexico brought new ideas for crafts, farming, and building, along with valued items such as copper bells, parrots (prized for their feathers), and seashells and turquoise for jewelry. Cotton cultivation and weaving skills also developed.

Major towns appeared between A.D. 900 and 1100, possibly serving as trade centers. Complex religious ceremonies, probably similar to those of the present-day Hopi, took place in kivas (ceremonial rooms) and village plazas in the uplands. Ball courts and platform mounds, most often found in the southern deserts, likely served both religious and secular purposes. Desert dwellers also dug elaborate irrigation networks in the valleys of the Salt and Gila Rivers.

Decline and Consolidation

People began to pack up and abandon, one by one, whole villages and regions throughout Arizona between 1100 and the arrival of the Spanish in 1540. Archaeologists attempt to explain the migrations with theories of drought, soil erosion, warfare, disease, and aggression of Apache and Navajo newcomers. Refugees swelled the populations of the remaining villages during this period; eventually, most of these places emptied, too.

Some ancestral Puebloans survived to become the modern Hopi in northeastern Arizona, but the Mogollon seem to have disappeared completely. Pima, likely descendents of the Hohokam, have legends of conflicts among the Hohokam that brought an end to that civilization.

The Athabaskan Migration

From western Canada, small bands of Athabaskan-speaking people slowly migrated to the Southwest. They arrived about 1300–1600 and established territories in the eastern half of present-day Arizona and adjacent New Mexico. Never a unified group, they followed a nomadic life of hunting, gathering, and raiding neighboring tribes. Some of the Athabaskans, later classified as Navajo on the Colorado Plateau and Apache farther south and east, learned agriculture and weaving from their pueblo neighbors.

SPANISH EXPLORATION AND RULE

The Conquistadors

Estévan, a Moorish slave of the viceroy of Mexico, became the first non–Native American to enter what is now Arizona. He arrived from the south in an advance party of Fray Marcos de Niza's 1539 expedition, sent by the viceroy to search for the supposedly treasure-laden Seven Cities of Cíbola.

The first of these "cities" that the party entered, a large Zuni pueblo in present-day New Mexico, proved disastrous for the explorers—they met their deaths at the hands of the villagers. Upon hearing the news, Fray Marcos dared view the pueblo only from a distance. Though he returned to Mexico empty-handed, his glowing accounts of a city of stone encouraged a new expedition led by Francisco Vásquez de Coronado.

Coronado departed from Mexico City in 1540 with 336 soldiers, almost 1,000 Native American allies, and 1,500 horses and mules. Instead of gold, the expedition found only houses of mud inhabited by hostile people. Despite hardships, Coronado explored the region for two years, traveling as far north as present-day Kansas. A detachment led by García López de Cárdenas visited the Hopi mesas and the Grand Canyon rim. Another officer of the expedition, Hernando de Alarcón, explored the mouth of the Colorado River in hopes of finding a water route to resupply Coronado. He found the task impossible.

Missions and Presidios

Nearly 100 years passed after Coronado's failed quest before the Spanish reentered Arizona. A few explorers and prospectors made brief visits, but Franciscan missionaries came to stay. They opened three missions near the Hopi villages and had some success in gaining converts, despite strong objections from traditional Hopi.

When pueblo villages in neighboring New Mexico revolted against the Spanish in 1680, the traditional Hopi joined in, killing the friars and many of their followers. Missionary efforts then shifted to southern Arizona, where the tireless Jesuit priest Eusebio Francisco Kino explored the new land and built missions from 1691 to 1711. Harsh treatment by later missionaries and land abuses by settlers caused the Pima tribes to revolt in 1751. The Spanish then instituted reforms and built a presidio at Tubac to prevent another outbreak. Similar harsh treatment by Spaniards at two missions on the lower Colorado River caused a revolt there in 1781; no attempt was made to reestablish them.

Arizonac

A fantastic silver strike during the Spanish era in 1736 drew thousands to an arroyo known to local Native Americans as Arizonac, where sheets of native silver weighing 25–50 pounds each were said to cover the ground. The exact location of this extraordinary find is uncertain, but it probably lay west of present-day Nogales. The boom soon ended, but a book published in 1850 in Spain recounted the amazing story. An American mine speculator picked up the tale and used it to publicize and sell mining shares. The name Arizonac, shortened to Arizona, became so well known that politicians later chose it for the entire territory. At least that's one theory of how Arizona got its name.

Mexican Takeover

This land had always existed on the far fringes of civilization, so politics and the Mexican fight for independence had little effect on Arizona. When three centuries of Spanish rule came to an end with Mexican independence in 1821, almost nothing changed. In the presidios, a new flag and an oath of loyalty to Mexico marked the transition. Isolation and hostile Apache continued to discourage settlement. Mission work declined as the Mexican government expelled many of the Spanish friars.

ARRIVAL OF THE ANGLOS

Mountain Men

Early in the 19th century, adventurous traders and trappers left the comforts of civilization in the eastern states to seek new lives in the West. In 1825, Sylvester Pattie and his son made the first known journey by Anglos to what is now Arizona. The younger Pattie later set down his adventures in *The Personal Narrative of James Ohio Pattie.* Although occasionally suffering attacks from hostile tribes, the Patties and later mountain men coexisted more or less peacefully with the Mexicans and Native Americans. When U.S. Army explorers and surveyors first visited Arizona in the 1840s and 1850s, they relied on mountain men to show them trails and water holes.

Arizona Enters the United States

Anglo traders did an increasingly large business in the Southwest after Mexican independence—their supply route from Missouri was far shorter and more profitable than the Mexicans' long haul from Mexico City. Arizona was of little importance in the Mexican War of 1847–1848, which was ignited by American desire for Texas and California, disputes over Mexico's debts, and Mexican indifference to a political solution. The 1848 Treaty of Guadalupe Hidalgo ceded to the United States not only Texas and California, but everything in between—including Arizona and New Mexico. As part of the vast New Mexican Territory, created by Congress in 1850, Arizona remained a backwater. The Gadsden Purchase added what's now southernmost Arizona in 1854.

New Trails

Most early visitors regarded Arizona as nothing but a place to cross on the way to California. The safest routes lay within the lands of the Gadsden Purchase, where Captain Philip Cooke built a wagon road during the Mexican War. Many '49ers, headed for gold strikes in California, used Cooke's road, better known as the Gila Trail. Hostile tribes and difficult mountain crossings discouraged travel farther north, even after

Lieutenant Edward Beale opened a rough wagon road across northern Arizona in 1857. Steamboat service on the lower Colorado River, beginning in 1852, brought cheaper and safer transportation to western Arizona.

Americans Settle In

As the California Gold Rush died down in the mid-1850s, prospectors turned eastward to Arizona. They made their first big find, a placer gold deposit, near the confluence of the Colorado River and Sacramento Wash in 1857. More strikes followed. For the first time, large numbers of people came to Arizona to seek their fortunes. Farmers and ranchers established themselves, cashing in on the market provided by the new mining camps and army posts.

Native American Troubles and the Civil War

Mountain men and government surveyors initially maintained good relations with local tribes, but this peace ended only a few years after first contact. Conflicts between white people and tribespeople over economic, religious, and political rights, and over land and water, led to loss of land and autonomy for the Native Americans. Both sides committed atrocities as each sought to drive out the other. Army forts provided a base for troops attempting to subdue the tribes as well as a refuge for travelers and settlers.

Most Arizonans initially sided with the Confederacy during the Civil War, but quickly switched when large numbers of federal troops arrived. The Battle of Picacho Pass, on April 15, 1862, was the most significant conflict of the Civil War this far west. Confederate forces killed Lieutenant James Barrett, leader of the Union detachment, and two privates. Aware that Union reinforcements would soon arrive, the Confederates retreated back down the Butterfield Road to Tucson and on toward Texas.

TERRITORIAL YEARS

Despite the wars and uncertainties of the early 1860s, Arizona emerged for the first time as a separate entity on February 24, 1863, when President Lincoln signed a bill establishing the Arizona Territory. Formerly, as part of New Mexico, Arizona had lacked both federal representation and law and order. In 1864, Governor John Goodwin and other appointed officials laid out Arizona's first capital at Prescott.

Continuing Troubles

Control of hostile tribes, especially the Apache and Navajo, proved to be the new territory's most serious problem. Although Arizona's Native Americans failed to drive out the newcomers, they did succeed in holding back development. Not until the great Apache leader Geronimo surrendered for the last time in 1886 did white residents of the territory feel safe.

Frontier Days End

The arrival of the railroads in the 1870s and 1880s and concurrent discoveries of rich copper deposits brought increasing prosperity. Ranching, farming, and logging grew in importance. By 1890 Arizona no longer needed most of its army forts. Only Fort Huachuca in southeastern Arizona survived as an active military post from the Indian wars to the present.

Mormon Settlement

Mormons in Utah, seeking new freedoms and opportunities, migrated south into Arizona. They first established Littlefield in the extreme northwest corner of Arizona in 1864. A flood washed out the community in 1867, but determined settlers rebuilt in 1877. Mormons developed other parts of the Arizona Strip in the far north and operated Lees Ferry across the Colorado River, just upstream from the Grand Canyon. From Lees Ferry, settlers headed as far south as St. David on the San Pedro River in Cochise County. Some settlements had to be abandoned due to land ownership problems, poor soil, or irrigation difficulties. Mormon towns prospering today include Springerville (founded 1871), Joseph City (1876), Mesa (1878), and Show Low (1890).

STATEHOOD AND MODERN ARIZONA

After years of political wrangling, President William H. Taft signed a proclamation admitting Arizona as the 48th state on Valentine's Day, February 14, 1912. Citizens turned out for parades and wild celebrations. In Phoenix, Governor-elect George W. P. Hunt led a triumphal procession to the Capitol. He had arrived in the territory in 1881 as an unemployed miner, then worked his way up to become a successful merchant, banker, territorial representative, and president of Arizona's Constitutional Convention. Hunt's support of labor, good roads, and other liberal causes won him seven terms in the governor's office.

Arizona lived up to its nickname, the Copper State, riding the good times when copper prices were high, as during WWI and the Roaring '20s, then suffering during economic depressions. The need for water, that all-important resource for farms and cities, also preoccupied citizens. New dams across the Gila, Salt, and Verde Rivers of central Arizona ensured the state's growth.

Claims on the Colorado River, however, led to a long-running feud with California and other thirsty states. Arizona pressed for its water rights from the early 1920s until 1944, even calling out the National Guard at one point to halt construction of Parker Dam, designed to supply water to Los Angeles. Wartime priorities finally forced the Arizona Legislature to make peace

STATE SYMBOLS

The seal portrays Arizona at statehood in 1912. It contains the Latin motto *Ditat Deus,* God Enriches. On the left, a quartz mill and a miner with pick and shovel symbolize the state's mining industry. Fields of cotton and citrus grow in fields on the right, irrigated by the reservoir and mountain watershed beyond. Cattle graze in the lower right. A rising sun represents Arizona's sunny climate.

The central star has a copper color, identifying Arizona as the United State's greatest copper producer. The red and yellow rays form a sunset, as this is a Western state, and have the colors of the Spanish flags brought to this land by Coronado in 1540; their number—13—commemorates the original American colonies. The solid-blue field of the lower half of the flag further links the state with the union.

THE FABULOUS FIVE

In 1998, women swept into all five top executive spots in Arizona's state government. Crowned the Fabulous Five by local newspapers, Jane Dee Hull won the governor's race, Betsey Bayless took Secretary of State, Janet Napolitano became Attorney General, Carol Springer the Treasurer, and Lisa Graham Keegan the Superintendent of Public Instruction. Never before had a state elected women to even the top two executive offices, let alone to all five! "This was not a backlash against men," stated Napolitano, "This was about qualified women running for office and winning."

In January 2003, Janet Napolitano took over the reins as governor and another woman, Janice K. Brewer, stepped into the number two spot—Secretary of State.

Women had earned important posts in Arizona government since the early days, when Sharlot Hall accepted the appointment of Territorial Historian in 1909. The challenges of Arizona politics during early statehood in 1915 didn't deter Rachel Allen Berry, who took her seat in the Arizona House of Representatives, and Frances Willard Munds, who became an Arizona State Senator. Both women were among the first in the nation to hold such posts. Women have gone to the top in the judicial branch, too. Sandra Day O'Connor, after rising to Arizona Senate Majority Leader, took on the job of Maricopa County Superior Court Judge, then served as an Arizona Court of Appeals Judge before becoming the first woman to be appointed to the U.S. Supreme Court in 1981.

and join the other river states in the Colorado River Compact.

WWII and the Postwar Boom

The pace of life quickened considerably during WWII, when Arizona devoted much of its land and resources to the war effort. The good flying weather convinced the Army Air Corps to build training bases here. Arizona deserts proved ideal for General Patton and other army officers to prepare their troops for coming battles. Aeronautical and other defense industries built factories, helping state manufacturing income to jump from $17 million in 1940 to $85 million just five years later. Several massive POW camps housed captured Germans and Italians. Japanese-Americans also endured internment; in fact, authorities herded so many Japanese into the Poston camp south of Parker that for a time it ranked as Arizona's third-largest city.

The war, and the air-conditioning that made low-desert summers bearable, changed the state forever. Many of the workers and armed forces people who passed through during the hectic war years returned to settle in Arizona. Even some of the German POWs, it's said, liked Arizona so well that they made their homes here. Much of the industry and many military bases remained as well. Retired people took a new interest in the state's sunny skies and warm winters. Whole towns, such as Sun City, rose just for the older set. Arizona has continued to grow and diversify, yet it retains its natural beauty and Old West heritage.

Tribes

NORTHERN ARIZONA

Havasupai

Long before the first white people arrived, this tribe farmed the fertile Havasu Canyon floor during the summer, then moved to the plateau after the harvest to gather abundant wild foods and firewood during winter. Spanish missionary Francisco Garcés visited the Havasupai in 1776, finding them a happy and industrious people. Though a peaceful group, they suffered the usual fate of American tribes—confinement to a tiny reservation while white people grabbed their lands. The Havasupai protested, but it wasn't until 1975 that the tribe's winter homelands were returned. Their reservation now spans 188,077 acres; most of the 500–600 tribal members on the reservation live in Supai village.

Supai lies 35 air miles northwest of Grand Canyon Village in Havasu Canyon, a major Grand Canyon tributary. The waterfalls, travertine pools, and greenery of the remote canyon have earned it fame as a Shangri-La.

Hualapai

The Pine Tree People once occupied a large area of northwestern Arizona. In language and culture, they're closely tied to the Havasupai and Yavapai tribes. Early Anglo visitors enjoyed friendly relations with the Hualapai, but land seizures and murders by the newcomers led to warfare. Army troops defeated the Hualapai and herded them south onto the Colorado River Reservation, where many died. Survivors fled back to their traditional lands, part of which later became the Hualapai Indian Reservation. Today about half of the 1,500 tribal members live on the 993,000-acre reservation, which includes much of the lower Grand Canyon's South Rim. Highlights for visitors include the spectacular viewpoints from the rim of the lowermost Grand Canyon, a drive into the Grand Canyon along Diamond Creek, and rafting trips on the Colorado River.

Peach Springs, a small town 54 miles northeast of Kingman on Highway 66, is the only one on the reservation. The road that descends to the Colorado River in the Grand Canyon begins here.

Paiute

A small band of Paiute lives on the Kaibab-Paiute Reservation, west of Fredonia in far northern Arizona. In earlier times they used this area as a winter home and spent summers in the forests of the Kaibab Plateau to the east. About 250 Paiute, who speak a Uto-Aztecan language, live on the reservation. The tribe arrived some time after A.D. 1300, though members believe themselves related to the ancestral Puebloans who had once lived on this land. The adjacent Pipe Spring National Monument preserves pioneer and tribal ways of life.

Navajo

The seminomadic Navajo, relatives of the Athabaskans of western Canada, wandered into the area east of the Grand Canyon between A.D. 1300 and 1600. This adaptable tribe learned agriculture, weaving, pottery, and other skills from its Puebloan neighbors and became skilled horsemen and sheepherders with livestock obtained from the Spanish. Their name comes from the Spanish term Apaches de Nabajó (Apaches of the cultivated fields).

The Navajo habit of raiding neighboring tribes—this time, white people—almost caused the tribe's downfall. In 1863–1864, the U.S. Army rounded up all the Navajo it could find and forced the survivors to make The Long Walk from Fort Defiance in eastern Arizona to a bleak camp at Fort Sumner in eastern New Mexico. This attempt at forced domestication failed dismally, and the Navajo were released four years later to return to their homeland. The colorful velveteen blouses and long, flowing skirts worn today by some Navajo women date back in style to this period; they're what U.S. Army wives were then wearing!

Hopi

Legends and long-abandoned pueblos indicate that the tribe has lived here for more than a thousand years. Old Oraibi, a Hopi village dating from at least A.D. 1150, is thought to be the oldest continuously inhabited settlement in the United States, and some Hopi identify even older village sites as the homes of their ancestors, whom they call Hisatsinom.

Spanish explorers entered the region in the 1500s, looking for gold and treasure, but they had to leave empty-handed. Desiring to save Hopi souls, Spanish friars arrived about 1630 and had some success until traditional Hopi leaders, fearing the loss of their own culture, joined with the New Mexico Pueblo tribes in a revolt against the Spanish in 1680. Hopi killed any foreigner unable to escape, massacred many of their own people who were Christians, and tore down the mission buildings. During the 1800s, American frontiersmen arrived seeking mineral wealth and fertile lands, but they met with disappointment. So the Hopi continued to farm in relative peace, raising crops of corn, squash, and beans.

Curious tourists overwhelm the tribe at times, but the Hopi welcome visitors who respect local culture and regulations. Highlights of a visit on the reservation include a trip to Walpi, a traditional stone village that seems to grow out of its spectacular ridge-top setting on First Mesa; the museum at the Cultural Center on Second Mesa; and the kachina and other dances performed on many weekends. (Only some dances are open to the public.)

WESTERN ARIZONA

Six tribes now live along the lower Colorado River between the Grand Canyon and the Gulf of California. The three Yuman-speaking tribes—Mohave, Quechan, and Cocopah—have occupied this land since prehistoric times. Uto-Aztecan-speaking Chemehuevi, followed by some Hopi and Navajo of northeastern Arizona, later joined them.

Mohave

Northernmost of the Yuman tribes, the Mohave formerly lived in loosely organized bands, uniting only for warfare or defense. They farmed the bottomlands, hunted, and gathered wild foods. Crafts included finely made baskets, pottery, and beadwork. Ceremonial dances and long funeral wakes played important roles in Mohave social life. Even today, the Mohave and Quechan cremate their dead—a rare practice among Native Americans.

Mohave live on the Fort Mohave Reservation near Needles, California, and in a larger group on the Colorado River Reservation near Parker, Arizona. You can learn more about the tribe and view their crafts at the tribal museum just south of Parker.

Chemehuevi

This group of Paiute once roamed the eastern Mohave Desert as hunting and gathering nomads. They settled in the Chemehuevi Valley of the Colorado River in the early 1800s, taking up the agricultural practices of their Mohave neighbors. The U.S. government granted the Chemehuevi a reservation in 1907, but Lake Havasu inundated much of their farmland in 1938. The tribe now lives on the Chemehuevi Reservation opposite Lake Havasu City and on the Colorado River Reservation.

Quechan

Formerly known as the Yuma, the tribe now prefers the name Quechan. In the 19th century, Quechan territory included much of the lower Colorado and about 25 miles of the Gila River Valley. The federal government trimmed their land considerably during the late 19th and early 20th centuries. Today the tribe lives in California on the Quechan Indian Reservation opposite Yuma, Arizona. You can visit their museum in a historic building of former Camp Yuma.

Cocopah

Before the arrival of white people, the Cocopah lived downstream from the Quechan in the Colorado River delta, once one of the most fertile areas of the Southwest. Like other Colorado River tribes, though, the people suffered greatly from European-introduced diseases. Today the Cocopah live on three tiny reservations south of Yuma and in Mexican villages in Sonora and Baja California.

CENTRAL ARIZONA

Pima and Maricopa

The Pima followed the prehistoric Hohokam, probably relatives with whom they had much in common. Living along the valleys of the Gila and Salt Rivers, the Pima used the farming methods of their predecessors but had many difficulties when white people built dams upstream early in the 20th century. Today the Pima farm, raise cattle, work in small industries, and create traditional handicrafts.

Maricopa tribespeople, who originally lived along the Colorado River, migrated up the Gila River to escape their aggressive Mohave and Yuma neighbors. Pima and Maricopa now share the Salt River Indian Reservation (east of Scottsdale) and Gila River Indian Reservation (southeast of Phoenix). You'll find tribal museums on each of the reservations.

Yavapai

The tribe shares cultural traits with the Hualapai and Havasupai to the north. Yavapai, along with

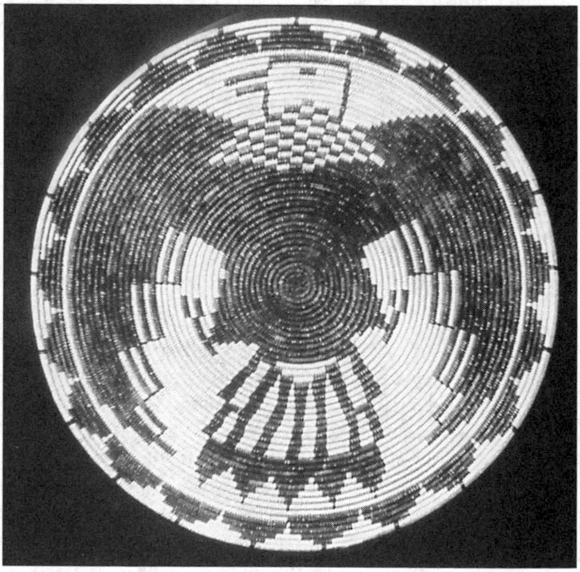

COURTESY OF THE HEARD MUSEUM

Yavapai coiled basket

Tonto Apache, received the Rio Verde Reservation in 1873, but the federal government took it away two years later, ordering the displaced Native Americans to proceed to the San Carlos Reservation, 150 miles away. In the cold February of 1875, they started the two-week journey on foot; of the 1,451 who began the trek, at least 90 died from exposure, were killed by infighting, or escaped.

Early in the 20th century, some Yavapai and Apache received permission to return to their Verde River homelands. What were once thousands of Native Americans occupying millions of acres now number less than 1,000 people on a few remnants of their former lands on the Camp Verde, Prescott, and Fort McDowell Reservations.

Apache

While most Apache in Arizona live in the eastern part of the state, some make their homes on several small reservations in north-central Arizona and with the Mohave on Fort McDowell Reservation northeast of Phoenix.

EASTERN ARIZONA

Apache

Groups are thought to have migrated from western Canada to the Southwest via the Great Plains, reaching Arizona in about the 16th century. Close relatives of the Navajo, the Apache have a similar language and customs. The early Apache lived a nomadic life—the men hunted game while the women gathered wild edible plants. They had few material possessions and probably lived in small conical huts covered with animal skins. Cultivation of corn, beans, and squash, learned from either the Pueblo or Navajo tribes, later supplemented hunting and gathering.

Horses obtained from the Spanish gave the Apache great mobility, and by the mid-18th century their raiding routes stretched from the Hopi mesas in the north to central Sonora in Mexico. Their predatory habits did not endear them to their neighbors—in fact, the name Apache may have come from a Zuni word for enemy.

The Apache vigorously defended their lands from encroaching settlers, and soon earned a reputation as the fiercest tribe in the Southwest. Though nothing could stop men hungry for gold and land, the Apache certainly tried. Apache resistance slowed the development of Arizona towns and industries until late in the 19th century.

Two large reservations provide homes for most tribal members. The White Mountain Apache Reservation spreads across a very scenic region of forests and lakes northeast of Phoenix. To the south, across the Salt and Black Rivers, the San

APACHE SCOUTS

Why did Apache with the U.S. Army fight other Apache? Western Apache bands in central Arizona felt little tribal identity with eastern (Chiricahua) bands of southeastern Arizona and adjacent New Mexico and Mexico. Apache rivalries made it easy for the army to recruit them.

As warriors, the Apache scouts took naturally to soldiering. They already knew their own methods of fighting, so they needed little formal training. Scouts enjoyed the prestige of having weapons and the freedom to travel, unlike their reservation-bound brethren. They realized that cooperation with the army and government officials provided a better alternative than risking deportation, which both the Navajo and the Chiricahua Apache suffered.

Pay provided another inducement—scouts received the equivalent of a regular soldier's pay and they could claim horses, mules, and equipment captured from renegade Apache. They also sought to pick up knowledge from the Anglo soldiers to share with their own society.

Apache could enlist for terms of 3, 6, or 12 months. They formed units of 250 men commanded by regular army officers and Apache noncommissioned officers.

Carlos Apache Reservation has both forest and desert country, including the large San Carlos Lake. Each tribe has a good cultural center/museum and offers visitors extensive outdoor recreation activities.

SOUTHERN ARIZONA

Tohono O'odham

The first white people couldn't believe that humans lived in such wild and parched desert, yet the Tohono O'odham (tah-HO-no AH-tomb) have thrived here for centuries. Close relatives of the Pima, the Tohono O'odham once occupied a vast section of the Sonoran Desert of southern Arizona and northern Mexico. Neighboring tribes called these desert dwellers Papago (Bean People), but the tribe prefers the more dignified term Tohono O'odham, meaning Desert People Who Have Emerged from the Earth. The Tohono O'odham believe that their tribe, like the plants and animals, belongs to the earth.

Originally, the Tohono O'odham maintained both winter and summer villages, staying near reliable springs in the winter, then moving to fields watered by summer thunderstorms. They gathered mesquite beans, agave, cactus fruit, acorns, and other edible plants and hunted rodents, rabbits, deer, and pronghorn. Their farms yielded native tepary beans, corn, and squash.

After the 1854 Gadsden Treaty split their land between Mexico and the United States, the Mexican Tohono O'odham population gradually withered away, absorbed into Mexican culture. Some families migrated into Arizona. Today only about 200 Tohono O'odham remain south of the border. In 1874, the U.S. government began setting aside land for the tribe in the 71,095-acre San Xavier Reservation. Tohono O'odham land now totals about 2.8 million acres—roughly the size of Connecticut. The second-largest reservation in the country, it stretches across much of southern Arizona and is home to more than 8,000 people.

The old ways have largely disappeared because of contact with modern technology. Today most Tohono O'odham, like everyone else in Arizona, live in standard houses and farm, ranch, or work for wages. Skilled basketmakers continue their ancient tradition, however. You'll see the attractive Tohono O'odham crafts in gift shops and in the visitors center at Kitt Peak.

Early Spanish missionaries gained many converts—the Roman Catholic Church has the largest following on the reservation, though Protestant churches have believers as well. Almost all villages have a small chapel.

Most Tohono O'odham are friendly, but the tribe has shown little interest in tourism. The vast reservation has hardly any visitor facilities and not a single motel, tourist office, or tribal museum. Two attractions, in addition to the desert scenery, make a visit worthwhile: the world-famous Kitt Peak Observatory and the Tohono O'odham All-Indian Rodeo and Fair, usually held on the first weekend of February.

Getting There and Around

Air

More than a dozen major airlines fly to Phoenix and Tucson. Fares and schedules tend to change frequently—a travel agent can help you find the best flights, or you can do it yourself on the Internet. Big-city newspapers usually run advertisements of discount fares and tours in their Sunday travel sections. Phoenix offers the most connections and generally the lowest fares. Sometimes you can get good deals to Tucson; if not, there's a shuttle bus service between the two cities. You'll have the best chance of getting low fares by planning a week or more ahead and staying over a Saturday night (or any night with Southwest Airlines); round-trip fares will almost always be a much better value than one-way, though changes may be costly.

Phoenix serves as the hub for nearly all flights within the state. Destinations from Phoenix's Sky Harbor Airport (PHX) include Page (PGA),

DRIVING TIPS

Summer heat puts an extra strain on both car and driver. Make sure the cooling system, engine oil, transmission fluid, fan belts, and tires are in top condition. Carry several gallons of water in case of breakdown or radiator trouble. Never leave children or pets in a parked car during warm weather—temperatures inside can cause fatal heatstroke in just minutes. Radiator caps must not be opened when the engine is hot, because the escaping steam can cause severe burns.

At times the desert has *too much* water—late-summer storms frequently flood low spots in the road. Wait for the water to go down, until you can see bottom, before crossing. If the car begins to hydroplane after a rainstorm, it's best to remove your foot from the accelerator, avoid braking, and keep the steering straight until the tires grip the road again. Drive in the "footsteps" of the car ahead, if you can.

Dust storms also tend to be short-lived but can completely block visibility. Treat them like dense fog: Pull completely off the road and stop, turning off your lights so as not to confuse other drivers.

Radio stations carry frequent updates when weather hazards exist. With a VHF radio (between 162.4 and 162.55 MHz), you can pick up continuous weather forecasts in the Flagstaff, Lake Powell, St. George, and Las Vegas areas.

If stranded in the backcountry, whether on the desert or in the mountains, stay with the vehicle unless you're *positive* of the way out; then leave a note detailing your route and departure time. Airplanes can easily spot a car—leave your hood and trunk up and tie a piece of cloth to the antenna—but a person trying to walk out is difficult to see. If you're stranded, emergency supplies can definitely help: blankets or sleeping bags, raingear, gloves, first-aid kit, tools, jumper cables, motor oil, shovel, rope, traction mats or chains, flashlight, flares, fire extinguisher, maps, water, food, and a can opener.

School crossings and buses require extra care. You must stop if someone is using a crosswalk. Crossings in use by school children have a 15 mph posted speed—police have ticketed drivers going 20 mph in them! When you see a school bus stopped with red lights flashing and a stop sign arm extended, you must stop in *both* directions until the lights and arm are turned off, unless there is a *physical* barrier dividing the roadway and you're traveling in the opposite direction.

Unless posted otherwise, speed limits are 15 mph when you're approaching a school crossing, 25 mph in business and residential districts, and 55 mph on open highways and city freeways. Some open highways may have limits as high as 65 mph, and some rural interstates as high as 75 mph. Although it's tempting to let loose on long, empty highways, they haven't all been designed for extreme speeds—a speeding car could top a small rise and suddenly find itself bearing down on a flock of sheep crossing the road. Deer, elk, and other stray animals can pose a danger too, especially at night.

You can make right turns from the right lane on a red light, unless prohibited by a sign, after coming to a complete stop and yielding to other traffic. Left turns on a red light can similarly be made if you're in the far left lane of a one-way street and turning onto another one-way street and there's no sign prohibiting the turn.

Reversible lanes in Phoenix and some other cities have signs designating the lane for certain hours: Through Traffic, Do Not Use, and Other times 2 way left.

Seat belts must be worn by all front-seat passengers. Child safety seats are required for those younger than five years or weighing less than 40 pounds.

Arizona has very strict laws against driving under the influence of drugs or drink. Penalties for the first offense include mandatory jail term, fine, license suspension, and screening, education, and/or treatment.

The *Arizona Driver License Manual* contains a good review of driving knowledge and road rules. It's available free in most large towns at the state Motor Vehicle Division office or you can download it from www.dot.state.az.us/mvd.

Flagstaff (FLG), Prescott (PRC), Kingman (IGM), Bullhead City (IFP), Lake Havasu City (HII), Yuma (YUM), Tucson (TUS), and Sierra Vista (FHU). The cost per mile of these short hops is high but you'll often enjoy excellent views.

America West (800/235-9292, www.americawest.com) uses the Phoenix airport as a hub and claims to have the most Arizona flights; it also flies from Tucson, but all flights go via Phoenix. **Southwest Airlines** (800/435-9792, www.southwest.com) offers many flights from Phoenix and some direct connections out of Tucson. Southwest has long been a leader in low-cost fares, and since its flights don't appear on flight reservation computers, you need to contact them directly.

Train

Amtrak (800/872-7245, www.amtrak.com) runs two luxury train lines across Arizona. On the northern route, the Southwest Chief runs daily in each direction between Los Angeles and Chicago, with stops in Arizona at Kingman, Williams Junction, Flagstaff, and Winslow. On the southern route, the Sunset Limited connects Los Angeles with Orlando, and stops in Yuma, Tucson, and Benson, but it runs only three times per week in each direction. Shuttle buses connect Phoenix with both trains.

Amtrak usually charges more than buses but has far roomier seating, as well as sleepers and dining cars. Fares depend upon availability—advance planning or off-season travel will get you the lowest prices. Travel agents outside North America sell USA rail passes (not for U.S. or Canadian citizens).

Bus

Greyhound (800/231-2222, www.greyhound.com) offers frequent service on its transcontinental bus routes across northern and southern Arizona and between Flagstaff and Phoenix. The company often offers special deals on bus passes and "one-way anywhere" tickets. Overseas residents may buy a Greyhound Ameripass at additional discounts outside North America.

Local bus services run in Phoenix, Tucson, Flagstaff, and other cities. Free shuttles serve part of the Grand Canyon National Park's South Rim. Always have exact change ready when taking local buses.

Car

Most people choose cars as the most convenient and economical way to get around; you can easily rent them in any sizable town in Arizona. Four-wheel-drive vehicles will be handy if you plan extensive travel on back roads. Phoenix and Tucson offer the largest selection, as well as RV and 4WD rentals. Nearby Las Vegas and Albuquerque can be convenient for car rentals too. It's worth shopping around not only for the best deal from different agencies, but also in different cities, as taxes form a large part of the rental cost.

Driveaways—autos scheduled for delivery to another city—can be worth looking into. If the auto's destination is a place you intend to visit, it can be like getting a free car rental. You have to be at least 21 years old and pay a refundable deposit of $75–150. There will be time and mileage limits. Ask for an economy car if you want the lowest driving costs. In a large city—Phoenix or Tucson in Arizona—look in the Yellow Pages under "Automobile Transporters and Driveaways."

Four-Wheeling

Back roads offer superb scenery in almost every part of Arizona. Joining a local club is a great way to get started. Books and literature offer tips on how to explore remote areas safely. The **Arizona State Association of 4 Wheel Drive Clubs** (P.O. Box 23904, Tempe, AZ 85285, 602/258-4294, www.asa4wdc.org) can direct you to clubs in the state.

The Great Western Trail (www.gwt.org) follows existing back roads between the Mexican border and Canada via Arizona, Utah, Wyoming, Montana, and Idaho. The 800-mile Arizona section crosses roughly the middle of the state, though some segments have yet to be completed.

Biking

To be fully alive to the land, skies, sounds, plants, and birds of Arizona, consider a bicycle tour.

THE ARIZONA TRAIL

The inspiration for a non-motorized trail across the entire state from Mexico to Utah came to Flagstaff teacher and hiker Dale Shewalter in the mid-1980s. Now his vision nears completion, thanks to government agencies and volunteers who have worked hard to make the 790-mile trail a reality.

The trail offers great hiking or riding opportunities, whether you're looking for a day's outing or a major adventure. It traverses some of the state's most scenic, historic, and biologically diverse areas and is open to hikers, cyclists, and equestrians—but not to motorized vehicles. Elevations range from a low of 1,700 feet at the Gila River to 9,600 feet in the San Francisco Peaks. In winter, cross-country skiers and snowshoers can take to the snow on some sections. Cyclists have alternate routes where needed to bypass the Grand Canyon and other wilderness areas that are closed to them.

If you want to travel the whole distance, a spring departure works well, because you can enjoy the cooler weather of the desert sections in the state's south and central regions, then hit ideal summer weather atop the plateaus in the north. You can follow progress of the trail—and find out how you can volunteer—by contacting the **Arizona Trail Association** (P.O. Box 36736, Phoenix, AZ 85067-6736, 602/252-4794, www.aztrail.org).

At the south end, the trail begins on the Mexican border in Coronado National Memorial, winds north to Montezuma Pass, then climbs into the Huachuca Mountains and Miller Peak Wilderness via the Crest Trail. The route drops down to the Parker Canyon Lake area and runs through the Canelo Hills to near Patagonia. It continues north through the Santa Rita, Rincon, Santa Catalina, and Superstition Mountains before descending to Roosevelt Lake near Tonto National Monument. The trail crosses Roosevelt Dam, then winds up into the Mazatzal Mountains in the heart of Arizona.

The sheer cliffs of the Mogollon Rim mark the next major climb, then the trail crosses East Clear Creek, Anderson Mesa, and upper Walnut Canyon. Here the trail heads for the mountains again, this time to volcanic Mt. Elden and the San Francisco Peaks—Arizona's highest. The Arizona Trail skirts the Peaks before turning northwest toward Grandview Lookout and the South Rim of the Grand Canyon. After crossing this great chasm, the trail skirts the Canyon's east rim with views across Marble Canyon and beyond. The trail crosses Highway 89A about two miles east of Jacob Lake, then continues north 12 miles through the forest to the Utah border and trail's end.

Cyclists can take forest roads around most of the wilderness areas, but they will have to do some highway stretches, too, most notably around the Grand Canyon via Navajo Bridge near Lees Ferry.

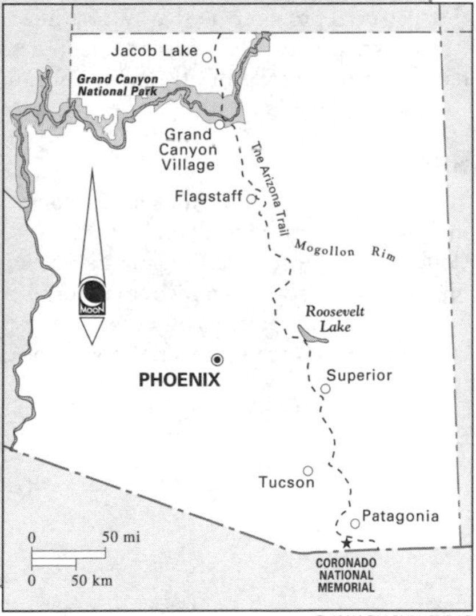

Gliding across the desert or topping out on a mountain pass are experiences beyond words. Some effort, a lightweight touring or mountain bicycle, and awareness of your surroundings are all that's required. Bookstores and bicycle shops sell publications on bicycle touring. As when hiking, always carry rain and wind gear and plenty of water. Also don't forget to wear a bicycling helmet.

Start with short rides if you're new to bicycle touring, then work up to longer cross-country trips. Learn to maintain and repair your steed, and you'll seldom have trouble on the road. An extra-low gear of 30 inches or less will take the strain out of long mountain grades. The performance of mountain bikes for touring can be improved by using road tires (no knobs) and handlebar extensions (for a variety of riding positions).

Mountain bikes, with their shocks, fat tires, and rugged construction, come into their own in the backcountry. The national forests offer some fine riding on roads and trails. County parks surrounding Phoenix have scenic desert trails designed especially for mountain bikers. Some other parks around the state offer riding possibilities as well. For a real adventure you can try the wide-open spaces of the Arizona Strip, though you'll probably need a 4WD vehicle to carry water here. Cyclists cannot ride in designated wilderness areas or off-road on National Park Service lands.

Hiking

You'll get the best feel for Arizona's canyons and mountains by visiting them on foot. The Grand Canyon offers the most challenging and extensive hiking in the state—a lifetime is too short to see everything here. Countless other canyons, especially in the Colorado Plateau of northern Arizona, also offer exceptionally scenic hiking opportunities. The state's many mountains can keep a hiker well entertained, too. You can climb most summits on a day hike.

Tours

See your travel agent or check travel websites for the latest on package tours to Arizona. Within the state, local operators offer everything from city tours to rafting trips through the Grand Canyon. Gray Line offers the largest selection of bus excursions, ranging from half a day to three days, out of Phoenix and Tucson. Smaller companies offer back-road trips to scenic spots inaccessible to regular vehicles; you'll find them in Phoenix, Tucson, Yuma, Sedona, Page, Monument Valley, and Canyon de Chelly. Flightseeing trips provide a birds-eye view of Sedona's Red Rock Country, the Grand Canyon, and other spectacular areas. The *Getting Around* sections in this book list some operators; also consult local chambers of commerce and visitors centers.

The nonprofit organization **Elderhostel** (11 Avenue de Lafayette, Boston, MA 02111-1746, 617/426-7788 or 877/426-8056, www.elderhostel.org) offers educational adventures for people 55 and over (spouses can be under 55). Many programs take place in Arizona, exploring archaeology, history, cultures, crafts, nature, and other topics. Participants join small groups for short-term studies and stay in simple accommodations, which helps keep costs low.

Grand Canyon Field Institute (Box 399, Grand Canyon, AZ 86023, 928/638-2485, www.grandcanyon.org/fieldinstitute) leads small groups on explorations of the Grand Canyon with day hikes, backpacking, river-running trips, van tours, and classroom instruction.

Health and Safety

In emergencies, dial 911 or use the emergency number listed on most telephones. Hospital emergency rooms offer the quickest help, but cost much more than a visit to a clinic or a doctor's office.

Hypothermia

Your greatest danger outdoors is one that can sneak up and kill with very little warning. Hypothermia, a lowering of the body's temperature below 95°F, causes disorientation, uncontrollable shivering, slurred speech, and drowsiness. The victim may not even realize what's wrong. Unless corrective action is taken immediately, hypothermia can lead to death. That's why hikers should travel with companions and always carry wind and rain protection; close-fitting raingear works better than ponchos.

If cold and tired, don't waste time. Seek shelter and build a fire; change into dry clothes and drink warm liquids. A victim not fully conscious should be warmed by skin-to-skin contact with another person in a sleeping bag. Try to keep the victim awake and drinking warm liquids.

Remember that temperatures can plummet rapidly in Arizona's dry climate—a drop of 40°F between day and night is common. Be especially careful at high elevations, where summer sunshine can quickly change into freezing rain or a blizzard.

Coping with Heat

We can take cues from desert wildlife on how best to live in a potentially hostile landscape. In summer, the early morning and evening have the most pleasant temperatures to be out and about. Photographers know that these times offer the best light for photography, too. When captivated by the grand scenery, it's easy to forget to drink enough water, but you'll be glad you did drink enough at the end of the day! For maximum efficiency, the body also needs food when hiking—snacks will increase your endurance.

Wilderness Checklist

- Before heading into the backcountry, check with a knowledgeable person about weather, water sources, fire danger, trail conditions, and regulations.
- Tell a reliable person where you're going and when you expect to return.
- Travel in small groups for the best experience; group size may also be regulated.
- Try not to camp on meadows, as the grass is easily trampled and killed.
- Avoid digging tent trenches or cutting vegetation.
- Use a camp stove to prevent marring the land.
- If you do make a campfire, a small one on mineral soil is best. A generous amount of water will extinguish the fire. Note that burying it can be catastrophic—dirt creates an oven, which can set roots on fire and start a forest fire.
- Camp at least 300 feet away from springs, creeks, and trails. State law prohibits camping within a quarter mile of a sole water source so that wildlife and stock won't be scared away.
- Wash away from streams and lakes.
- Don't drink untreated water in the wilderness, no matter how clean the water appears. It may contain the parasitic protozoan *Giardia lamblia,* which causes the unpleasant disease giardiasis. Boiling your water for several minutes will kill giardia as well as other bacterial or viral pathogens. Filtering and iodine treatments usually work, too, although they're not as reliable as boiling.
- Bring a trowel for personal sanitation and dig 4–6 inches deep. In desert areas it's best to bag and carry out toilet paper because the stuff lasts for years and years in a dry climate; backcountry visitors in the Grand Canyon and Paria Canyon *must* pack it out.
- Carry plenty of feed for horses and mules.
- Leave dogs at home; they foul campsites and disturb wildlife and other hikers. If you do bring one, please keep it under physical control at all times. They're not allowed in the backcountry of national parks.

GIARDIA

It can be tough to resist: You're hiking in a beautiful area by the banks of a crystal clear stream. The water in your canteen tastes stale, hot, and plastic; the nearby stream looks so inviting that you can't resist a cautious sip. It tastes delicious, clean, and cold, and for the rest of your hike you refresh yourself with water straight from the stream.

Days pass and you forget about drinking untreated water. Suddenly one evening after your meal you become terribly sick to your stomach. You develop an awful case of cramps and feel diarrhea beginning to set in. Food poisoning?

Well, it could be the effects of Giardia, a protozoan that has become common in even the remotest of mountain streams. Giardia is carried in animal or human waste that is deposited or washed into natural waters. When ingested, it begins to reproduce, causing a sickness that can become very serious and may require medical attention.

You can take precautions against Giardia with a variety of chemical purifying and filtering methods or by boiling water before drinking it. Directions for chemical and filtering methods need to be followed carefully to be effective against the protozoan in its cyst stage of life, when it encases itself in a hard shell. The most effective way to eliminate such threats is to boil all suspect water for a few minutes.

• Take home all your trash, so animals can't dig it up and scatter it.
• Help preserve Native American and historic ruins.
• A survival kit and small flashlight can make the difference if you're caught in a storm or are out longer than expected. A pocket-sized container can hold what you need for the three essentials: *fire building* (matches in waterproof container and candle), *shelter* (space blanket, knife, and rope), and *signaling* (mirror and whistle).
• If lost, *realize it,* then find shelter and stay in one place. If you're sure of a way to civilization and plan to walk out, leave a note of your departure time and planned route.

Information and Services

Arizona Office of Tourism

Located on the west side of downtown, the helpful office (1110 W. Washington Street, Suite 155, Phoenix, Arizona 85007, 602/364-3700 or 866/891-3640, fax 602/364-3702, www.arizonaguide.com, 8 A.M.–5 P.M. Mon.–Fri.) provides information on every region of the state. Local tourist offices also have the state literature.

Arizona Public Lands Information Center

This one-stop center in Phoenix (call for location, 602/417-9300 or, www.publiclands.org, 8:30 A.M.–4:30 P.M. Mon.–Fri.) should be able to meet all your needs for recreation information and permits on federal and state lands in Arizona. You can order publications and permits directly at 800/986-1151 or az_plic@blm.gov.

Arizona State Parks

The main office (1300 W. Washington, Phoenix, AZ 85007, 602/542-4174 or 800/285-3703, www.azstateparks.com, 8 A.M.–5 P.M. Mon.–Fri.) has an information desk and gift shop. Staff answer a Wildflower Hotline (602/542-4988) during office hours in spring.

State Trust Lands

Although not specifically intended for recreation, these lands have some backcountry areas that you may wish to explore. To do so, purchase a 12-month Recreation Permit for $15 per person or $20 per family. (Licensed fishers and hunters pursuing their activities are exempt, but need a permit if camping.) Permits can be obtained by mail or in person in Phoenix (602/542-4631), Tucson (520/628-5480), Flagstaff (928/774-1425), and the Arizona Public Lands Information Center in Phoenix (602/417-9300).

Maps

The *Benchmark Arizona Road & Recreation Atlas* covers the state with exceptionally beautiful and easy-to-read maps at a 1:400,000 scale; it's sold in stores. The *Guide to Indian Country* map published by the Automobile Club of Southern California provides superb coverage of the Four Corners region, including the Grand Canyon and the Navajo and Hopi Indian reservations; it's sold in stores, and AAA members can get it free from AAA offices. The 1:126,720-scale National Forest Service maps will be handy on many backcountry drives; Forest Service offices and stores sell them. For exploring the lonely Arizona Strip, the 1:168,960-scale *Arizona Strip District Visitor Map* will prove essential for navigation; it's published by the Bureau of Land Management and sold at their offices and in stores. Hikers and mountain bikers will appreciate the detailed U.S.G.S. topographic maps of the region, available in a variety of scales and formats from outdoors stores. You can also download topo maps free from Internet sites such as www.topo.zone.

Post Offices and Telephones

The U.S. Postal Service (800/275-8777, www.usps.gov) offices are open business hours Monday–Friday and sometimes shorter hours on Saturday.

Telephone numbers in northern and western Arizona uses the 928 area code. Phoenix, in the center of the state, has a 602 area code; Glendale and other cities to the west use 623; and Tempe, Scottsdale, Mesa, and other places to the east have 480. Tucson, Florence, and the rest of southeastern Arizona are in the 520 code. Use these when dialing 1+ or 0+ numbers inside as well as outside Arizona. To obtain a local number from Information, dial 1-411; for a number in another area code or another state, dial 1, the area code, then 555-1212; there's a fee for this service. Many airlines, auto rental firms, and motel chains have toll-free 800, 888, 877, or 866 numbers; if you don't have the number, just dial 800/555-1212 for information.

Prepaid telephone cards provide much lower costs for long-distance calls than plunking in coins or using a telephone company billing card; discount stores often have the lowest prices for the prepaid cards.

Time

Travelers in Arizona should remember that the state is on mountain standard time all year, except for the Navajo Reservation, which goes on daylight saving time—add one hour April–October—to conform with its Utah and New Mexico sections. Note that the Hopi Reservation, completely within Arizona and surrounded by the Navajo, stays on standard time year-round along with the rest of the state. In summer, Arizona runs on the same time as California and Nevada, and one hour behind Utah, Colorado, and New Mexico. In winter, Arizona is one hour ahead of California and Nevada, on the same time as Utah, Colorado, and New Mexico.

TIPS FOR FOREIGN TRAVELERS

Entering the United States

Canadians can enter without a visa, and Mexicans can apply for a card that permits visa-free crossings. Citizens of many developed countries can visit without a visa. Visit the website http://travel.state.gov for the regulations, lists of U.S. embassies and consulates, and application forms. If you don't have Internet access, simply check with your country's U.S. embassy or consulate for the application procedure.

Currency Exchange

Only Phoenix offers foreign currency exchange

within the state. Credit cards, especially Visa and MasterCard, are accepted at most businesses. ATMs in almost every town are the best way to get cash; the machines accept most credit and debit cards, but the latter usually have lower or no fees—ask at your home financial institution. Bring traveler's checks in U.S. dollars as a backup; they're widely accepted.

The Metric System

National Park Service literature uses both English and metric units, but otherwise the metric system sees little use in the United States. For help in converting between the two systems, consult the conversion table at the back of this book.

Electricity

Electric current in the U.S. is 110–120 volts, 60-cycles. Nearly all portable electronic devices have a universal power supply that will run on this voltage. Travel stores sell the adapter for the flat, two-pin-style U.S. plug; the Radio Shack chain is also a handy source of adapters in the United States. Electrical appliances manufactured for use in other countries may need a transformer, though it might be cheaper just to buy a new appliance after you arrive.

Suggested Reading

DESCRIPTION AND TRAVEL

Annerino, John. *Adventuring in Arizona.* Tucson: University of Arizona Press, 2003. True to its name, this excellent guide describes hiking trails, canyoneering adventures, climbing routes, river trips, and back-road driving tours through the state's most spectacular country. Includes history, ecology, geology, and travel tips.

Arizona Highways. 2039 W. Lewis Ave., Phoenix, AZ 85009, 602/712-2200 or 800/543-5432, www.arizonahighways.com. Published monthly, this outstanding magazine features superb color photography with articles on the state's history, people, places, wildlife, back roads, hiking, and humor. Arizona Highways also publishes many books on these themes, plus some large-format photography titles.

Babbitt, Bruce, ed. *Grand Canyon: An Anthology.* Flagstaff: Northland Publishing, 1978. Twenty-three authors from the days of the Spanish to the present relate their experiences of the Grand Canyon.

Broyles, Bill. *Our Sonoran Desert.* Tucson: Rio Nuevo Publishing, 2003. A passionate introduction with stunning color photography in a large format.

Casey, Robert L. *Journey to the High Southwest.* Chester, CT: Globe Pequot Press, 2000. The author presents travel experiences and advice for southern Utah and adjacent Arizona, New Mexico, and Colorado.

Cook, James E. *Arizona Landmarks.* Phoenix: Arizona Highways, 1985. Recent color photos combine with historic illustrations to illustrate Arizona's natural beauty and human history.

Cook, James E. *Travel Arizona: The Back Roads.* Phoenix: Arizona Highways, 1989. Twenty routes—on and off pavement—have descriptions with brilliant photography.

Greater Phoenix Explorer: Phoenix Official Visitors Guide. Greater Phoenix Convention & Visitors Bureau (50 N. 2nd St., Phoenix, AZ 85004, 602/254-6500 or 877/225-5749, www.visitphoenix.com). This free magazine, published twice a year, offers extensive listings of sights and practicalities for Phoenix and surrounding cities.

Green, Stewart. *Arizona Scenic Drives.* Helena, MT: Falcon Press, 1992. Twenty-nine scenic drives are described, with maps and camping information.

Kline, Bonnie, and others. *Grand Canyon Village & West Tour, Grand Canyon East Tour,* and *Sedona Red Rock Country.* Scottsdale: Waypoint Tours, 2004, www.waypointtours.com. Audio tours on CD or downloadable as MP3 files provide a professional narration at your command.

Leydet, Francois. *Time and the River Flowing: Grand Canyon.* New York: Sierra Club-Ballantine Books, 1968. Essays on and color photos of the Grand Canyon.

Mangum, Richard K., and Sherry G. Mangum. *Flagstaff Historic Walk: A Stroll Through Old Downtown.* Flagstaff: Hexagon Press, 2003. This handy pocket-sized book tells the story of early Flagstaff with many old photos. The authors lead occasional tours of downtown too; ask at the Flagstaff Visitor Center.

Mangum, Richard K., and Sherry G. Mangum. *Flagstaff Past & Present.* Flagstaff: Hexagon Press, 2003. This wonderfully designed album uses many charming photos to tell the story of this mountain town.

Mangum, Richard K., and Sherry G. Mangum. *Route 66 Across Arizona: A Comprehensive Two-Way Guide for Touring Route 66.* Flagstaff: Hexagon Press, 2001. Beautiful color photography illustrates the history and romance of the old highway. Maps and descriptions help you plan your own journey.

Martin, Don, and Betty Woo. *Arizona in Your Future: The Complete Relocation Guide for Job-Seekers, Retirees and Snowbirds.* Columbia, CA: Pinecone Press, 1998. This guide provides "essential data" on many of the state's cities.

Muench, David, and Lawrence W. Cheek. *David Muench's Arizona; Cherish the Land, Walk in Beauty.* Phoenix: Arizona Highways, 1997. More than 120 color photos reveal light, form, life, and ecology in a large-format book.

Muench, David, Frank Waters, and John C. Van Updyke. *Eternal Desert.* Phoenix: Arizona Highways, 1990. Color photography and text interpret the stone, wind, water, life, and tracings of ancient man on the desert; includes advice for travelers.

Mulford, Karen Surina. *Arizona's Historic Escapes.* Winston-Salem, NC: John F. Blair, 1997. The author has searched out 94 memorable places to stay throughout the state that have exceptional atmosphere and history. They include bed and breakfasts, historic hotels, inns, guest ranches, and resorts.

Rees, Lucy. *The Maze, A Desert Journey.* Tucson: The University of Arizona Press, 1996. A contemporary Welsh woman explores the wilderness of Arizona on horseback from the Verde Valley to the Hopi mesas.

Searcy, Paula. *Travel Arizona: The Scenic Byways.* Phoenix: Arizona Highways, 1997. Spectacular color photos entice readers on 22 drives through the state's history and scenery.

Tegler, Dorothy. *Retiring in Arizona: Your One-Stop Guide to Living, Loving and Lounging Under the Sun.* Fiesta Books, 1996. Full of facts to help you choose your area, then settle in.

Tucson Official Visitors Guide. Metropolitan Tucson Convention and Visitors Bureau (110 S. Church Ave., Suite 9100, Tucson, AZ 85701, 520/624-1817 or 800/638-8350, www.visittucson.org). An informative free magazine updated twice yearly.

Varney, Philip. *Arizona Ghost Towns and Mining Camps: A Travel Guide to History.* Phoenix: Arizona Highways, 1995. Explore the ruins of Arizona's boom-and-bust towns with this well-illustrated guide.

Wallace, Robert. *The Grand Canyon.* The American Wilderness Series. New York: Time-Life Books. A well-illustrated book covering the Canyon with excellent photography by Ernst Haas.

Whitney, Stephen. *A Field Guide to the Grand Canyon.* Seattle: Mountaineers Books, 1996. Excellent, well-illustrated guide to the Canyon's geology, early Native Americans, flowers, trees, birds, and animals. Most of the information also applies to other canyons on the Colorado Plateau. Includes practical advice for visiting and hiking in the Grand Canyon.

Writers' Program of the WPA. *Arizona: A State Guide.* Tucson: Hastings House, 1940, 1956. Reprinted in 1991 under the title *The WPA Guide to 1930's Arizona* by the University of Arizona Press. A classic guidebook that still makes good reading.

HIKING, BICYCLING, AND EQUESTRIAN

Abbott, Lon, and Terri Cook. *Hiking the Grand Canyon's Geology.* Seattle: The Mountaineers, 2004. The introduction vividly relates the geologic story told by the Grand Canyon, then each trail description provides practical advice on hiking and things to look for. GPS coordinates help find points of interest.

Adkison, Ron. *Hiking the Grand Canyon National Park.* Helena, MT: Falcon Press, 1997. Following a good introduction, the state's most popular trails are covered, with maps, detailed descriptions, and elevation profiles.

Aitchison, Stewart, and Bruce Grubbs. *Hiking Arizona.* Helena, MT: Falcon Press, 1996. One of the best all-around hiking guides to the state; the 102 hikes cover a wide variety of regions and terrain.

Annerino, John. *Hiking the Grand Canyon.* A Sierra Club Totebook. San Francisco: Sierra Club Books, 1993. Easily the most comprehensive guide to trails and routes within the Canyon. A long introduction provides background on geology, natural history, Native Americans, and hike planning. The large foldout topo map clearly shows trails and routes. River-runners will be pleased to find a section of trail descriptions beginning at the water's edge.

Annerino, John. *Outdoors in Arizona: A Guide to Hiking and Backpacking.* Phoenix: Arizona Highways, 1995. Spectacular color photos and detailed maps illustrate descriptions of 48 hikes.

Bennett, Sarah. *Mountain Biking Arizona.* Helena, MT: Falcon Press, 1996. This handy guide, illustrated with maps and photographs, describes many classic rides.

Blair, Gerry. *Rockhounding Arizona.* Helena, MT: Falcon Press, 1998. A guide to Arizona's natural wealth with descriptions, maps, and photographs of more than 70 of the state's best hunting sites for turquoise, gold, agates, garnet, crystals, and fossils.

Butchart, Harvey. *Grand Canyon Treks: 12,000 Miles Through the Grand Canyon.* Bishop, CA: Spotted Dog Press, 1998. This book combines the texts of legendary Grand Canyon hiker and explorer Harvey Butchart's three earlier guides, originally published in the 1970s and 1980s by La Siesta Press. It's a great source of ideas for off-trail hikes and climbs.

Carlson, Jack, and Elizabeth Stewart. *Hiking Guide to the Superstition Wilderness.* Tempe: Clear Creek Publishing, 1995. More than 50 hikes in the Superstition Wilderness are described with trail maps, difficulty rating, and history and legends of the Superstitions including the Lost Dutchman Mine.

Cowgill, Pete, and Eber Glendening. *Trail Guide to the Santa Catalina Mountains.* Tucson: Rainbow Expeditions, 1998. This handy guide describes trails and routes of this range north of Tucson.

Fletcher, Colin. *The Man Who Walked Through Time*. New York: Random House, 1989. Well-written adventure tale of Fletcher's two-month solo hike through the Grand Canyon. Fletcher was the first to travel its length within the park on foot.

Freeman, Roger, and Ethel Freeman. *Day Hikes and Trail Rides in and around Phoenix*. Baldwin Park, CA: Gem Guides Book Co., 2000. Detailed trail descriptions of the excellent hiking and horseback riding in the rugged Sonoran Desert surrounding Arizona's biggest city.

Ganci, Dave. *Hiking the Southwest: Arizona, New Mexico, and West Texas*. San Francisco: Sierra Club Books, 1983. A handy guide with a good introduction, practical hints, and information on a variety of trails.

Hancock, Jan. *Horse Trails in Arizona*. Phoenix: Golden West Publishers, 1994. Descriptions of 42 trails include location, length, elevations, water sources, corrals, and trailer parking.

Jones, Tom Lorang, and Jerry Sieve. *The Arizona Trail: The Complete Guide*. Englewood, CO: Westcliffe Publishers, 2004. Illustrated by many color photos, each section of the 750-mile trail includes detailed descriptions for both long-distance and day hikers. Maps and elevation profiles let you know what to expect.

Lucchitta, Ivo. *Hiking Arizona's Geology*. Seattle, WA: The Mountaineers Books. On any of the 41 hikes described here, you'll not only experience the fine scenery, but also learn how it all came to be. The introduction and illustrations clearly explain geologic terms and Arizona's rocks.

Kals, W.S. *Land Navigation Handbook*. San Francisco: Sierra Club Books, 1983. You'll be able to explore Arizona's vast backcountry with confidence after reading this book. The handy pocket-guide not only offers details on using map and compass, but tells how to navigate using the sun, the stars, and an altimeter.

Kelsey, Michael R. *Canyon Hiking Guide to the Colorado Plateau*. Provo, UT: Origin Books Sales, Inc., 1999. One of the best guides to hiking in the canyon country, with descriptions and maps for destinations in Arizona, Utah, and Colorado. Geologic cross-sections show the formations you'll walk through. The author uses the metric system, but the book is otherwise easy to follow.

Kelsey, Michael R. *Hiking and Exploring the Paria River*. Provo, UT: Origin Books Sales, Inc., 1998. The classic Paria Canyon hike, with information on nearby Bryce Canyon and other geologically colorful areas. Includes histories of John D. Lee, ghost towns, ranches, and mining.

Kiefer, Don R. *Hiking Arizona*. San Marino, CA: Golden West Publishers, 1991. Fifty hikes, many little known, with tips for safe and enjoyable hiking. The author has also written *Hiking Arizona II* (1993), *Hiking Central Arizona* (1996), *Hiking Northern Arizona* (1996), and *Hiking Southern Arizona* (1996).

Leavengood, Betty. *Tucson Hiking Guide*. Boulder: Pruett Publishing Co., 1997. A comprehensive guide to the hiking trails of the Tucson area.

Mangum, Richard K., and Sherry G. Mangum. *Flagstaff Hikes*. Flagstaff: Hexagon Press, 2001. This comprehensive guide describes 146 hiking trails surrounding Flagstaff and includes elevation charts.

Mangum, Richard K., and Sherry G. Mangum. *Sedona Hikes*. Flagstaff: Hexagon Press, 2004. A guide to 130 day-hikes and five vortex sites, with maps and directions.

Martin, Bob, and Dotty Martin. *Arizona's Mountains: A Hiking & Climbing Guide*.

Boulder: Pruett Publishing Co., 1991. A guide to hiking and climbing in Arizona; includes maps and charts.

Martin, Bob, and Dotty Martin. *Hiking Guide to the Santa Rita Mountains of Arizona.* Boulder: Pruett Publishing Co., 1986. This guide covers mountains and canyons south of Tucson with topo maps, charts, and 52 hike descriptions.

Mazel, David, and Robert Blake. *Southern Arizona Trails.* Berkeley: Wilderness Press, 1997. An excellent hiking guide to many of the designated wilderness areas in the central and southern parts of the state.

Ray, Cosmic. *Fat Tire Tales and Trails.* Flagstaff: Cosmic Ray, 2004. "Lots of way cool mountain-bike rides around Arizona . . . both summer and winter fun."

Sagi, G. J. *Fishing Arizona.* Phoenix: Golden West Publishers, 1992. Travel directions lead to 50 good fishing lakes with maps of the shorelines plus information about the types of fish found in each lake. The state record for each species is listed.

Stevenson, Jeffrey L. *Rim Country Mountain Biking.* Boulder, CO: Pruett Publishing, 1995. The 63 rides on the Mogollon Rim range from easy to technical; maps and elevation profiles show the way.

Thybony, Scott. *Official Guide to Hiking the Grand Canyon.* Grand Canyon: Grand Canyon Association, 2003. Introduction and guide to the best-known trails.

Warren, Scott S. *Exploring Arizona's Wild Areas: A Guide for Hikers, Backpackers, Climbers, Cross-Country Skiers, & Paddlers.* Seattle: The Mountaineers, 2002. Although the author covers only the designated wildernesses and the new national monuments, these will keep you busy for a long time.

Waterman, Laura, and Guy Waterman. *Backwoods Ethics: A Guide to Low-Impact Camping and Hiking.* Woodstock, VT: Countryman Press, 2003. Thoughtful commentaries on how hikers can explore the wilderness with minimal impact. Case histories dramatize the need to protect the environment.

RIVER-RUNNING AND BOATING

Abbey, Edward. *Down the River.* New York: E.P. Dutton, 1991. Abbey expresses joy and concern in a series of thoughtful, witty, and wide-ranging essays on the American West.

Belknap, Buzz. *Grand Canyon River Guide.* Westwater Books, 1990. Covers the 288 miles of Colorado River through Marble and Grand Canyons between Lees Ferry and Lake Mead.

Crumbo, Kim. *A River Runner's Guide to the History of the Grand Canyon.* Boulder: Johnson Books, 1981. Highly readable guide with a foreword by Edward Abbey.

Kelsey, Michael R. *Boater's Guide to Lake Powell.* Treasure Chest Publications, 1991. This comprehensive guide will help you explore the lake, whether traveling in a small inflatable raft, as the author did, or a more luxurious craft. Includes many maps, photos, and hiking descriptions.

Ryan, Kathleen Jo (photographer and producer). *Writing Down the River: Into the Heart of the Grand Canyon.* Flagstaff: Northland Publishing, 1998 and Grand Canyon: Grand Canyon Association, 2004. Fifteen of today's best women writers tell of their experiences in the Grand Canyon. Impressive color photos illustrate the pages.

Slingluff, Jim. *Verde River Recreation Guide.* San Marino, CA: Golden West Publishers, 1990. This guide covers river-running on the Verde and its tributaries with boating tips and natural history.

Stephens, Hal G., and Eugene M. Shoemaker. *In the Footsteps of John Wesley Powell: An Album of Comparative Photographs of the Green and Colorado Rivers, 1871–72 and 1968.* Boulder: Johnson Books and The Powell Society, 1987. Fascinating photo album of identical river views snapped nearly 100 years apart. Photos show how little—and how much—the forces of erosion, plants, and human beings have changed the Green and Colorado River Canyons. The text describes geologic features of each of the 110 pairs of photos. Maps show locations of camera stations. Out of print, but worth seeking out in a library.

Stevens, Larry. *The Colorado River in Grand Canyon: A Comprehensive Guide to Its Natural and Human History.* Flagstaff: Red Lake Books, 1998. The introduction and maps guide you from Lees Ferry to Lake Mead with descriptions of geology, Native American history, exploration, flora, and fauna.

HISTORY

Albano, Bob, ed. *Days of Destiny.* Phoenix: Arizona Highways Wild West Series, 1996. Twenty stories about lawmen and desperados and the twisting fates they met.

Chaput, Don. *Dr. Goodfellow, Physician to the Gunfighters, Scholar, and Bon Vivant.* Westernlore Press, 1996. The life of the doctor who lived in Tombstone during its wildest years and patched up Virgil Earp and other shooting victims.

Crampton, C. Gregory. *Standing Up Country.* Tucson: Rio Nuevo Publishers, 2000. Illustrated historical account of the Native Americans, explorers, outlaws, miners, settlers, and scientists who came to the canyon lands of Arizona and Utah.

Dellenbaugh, Frederick S. *A Canyon Voyage: A Narrative of the Second Powell Expedition Down the Green-Colorado River from Wyoming, and the Expeditions on Land, in the Years 1871 and 1872.* Tucson: University of Arizona Press, reprinted 1984. Dellenbaugh, artist and assistant topographer on the expedition, provides a spellbinding narrative.

Dimock, Brad. *Sunk Without a Sound.* Flagstaff: Fretwater Press, 2001. The tragic honeymoon of Glen and Bessie Hyde, who disappeared on a river trip in the Grand Canyon in 1928, remains one of the Canyon's most haunting mysteries. Here is the story of their disappearance along with possible reappearances. The author not only extensively researched the facts and theories, but recreated the Hydes' trip with a replica of their crude Idaho sweep scow that proved nearly uncontrollable in the rapids.

Farrell, Robert J., ed. *Manhunts & Massacres.* Phoenix: Arizona Highways Wild West Series, 1997. Eighteen true stories relate some of Arizona's most notorious holdups and massacres.

Farrell, Robert J., ed. *They Left Their Mark.* Phoenix: Arizona Highways Wild West Series, 1997. Sixteen stories of exceptional heroes and characters from Spanish explorer Juan Bautista de Anza to the quiet Pima soldier who helped raise the flag over Iwo Jima.

Faulk, Odie B. *Arizona: A Short History.* Norman, OK: University of Oklahoma Press, 1979. Popular account of Arizona from the first days of European exploration through the territorial years and statehood.

Fontana, Bernard L. *Entrada: The Legacy of Spain & Mexico in the United States.* Tucson: Southwest Parks and Monuments Assoc., 1994 The author guides the reader in text and photos to parks across the country where this legacy has been preserved.

Forrest, Earle R. *Arizona's Dark and Bloody Ground.* Tucson: University of Arizona Press, 1936, 1984. An account of the ruthless Pleasant Valley War between cattle and sheep ranchers.

Ghiglieri, Michael P. *First Through the Grand Canyon: The Secret Journals and Letters of the 1869 Crew Who Explored the Green and Colorado Rivers.* Flagstaff: Puma Press, 2003. It turns out that Major John Wesley Powell, who led the first expedition downriver through the Grand Canyon, didn't tell the full story! New research reveals some very different perspectives on one of the most famous river trips of all time.

Ghiglieri, Michael P., and Thomas M. Meyers. *Over the Edge: Death in Grand Canyon* Flagstaff: Puma Press, 2001. Gripping tales of tragedy, with lessons to be learned. The accounts also point out the fallacy of today's 911 mindset in expecting an instant rescue when things go wrong.

"The Heart of Ambos Nogales." *The Journal of Arizona History.* Vol. 17, No. 2 (Summer 1976): page 161. The story of Nogales.

Hughes, J. Donald. *In the House of Stone and Light.* Grand Canyon: Grand Canyon Association, 2003. This well-illustrated history of the Grand Canyon covers the time from the early Native Americans to the modern park.

Iverson, Peter J. *Barry Goldwater.* Norman, OK: University of Oklahoma Press, 1997. This biography focuses on the famous senator's influence on Arizona politics—still felt today—and how he can be understood as a man of his time and place.

Johnson, G. Wesley, Jr. *Phoenix: Valley of the Sun.* Continental Heritage Press, 1982. Excellent text and photos trace the development of Phoenix from the ancient Hohokam to the modern metropolis.

Lummis, Charles F. *Some Strange Corners of Our Country.* Tucson: University of Arizona Press, 1891, 1892, reprinted in 1989. Step back a century to visit the Southwest's Indian country, Grand Canyon, Petrified Forest, and Montezuma Castle.

Mitchell, John D. *Lost Mines of the Great Southwest.* Glorieta, NM: Rio Grande Press, 1933, 1984. Who isn't enthralled by legends of lost treasure? You'll reach for a pick and shovel after reading these.

Sheridan, Thomas E. *Arizona: A History.* Tucson: University of Arizona Press, 1995. This volume takes the reader from paleolithic times to the 1990s.

Sikorsky, Robert. *Quest for the Dutchman's Gold: The 100-Year Mystery; The Facts, Myths and Legends of the Lost Dutchman Mine and the Superstition Mountains.* San Marino, CA: Golden West, 1991. The history of the most famous lost mine of all.

Smith, Dean, and others. *Arizona Album: The Road to Statehood.* Phoenix: Arizona Highways, 1987. Meet Native Americans, politicians, lawmen, miners, women, gamblers, and sports enthusiasts in the years leading to statehood.

Summerhayes, Martha. *Vanished Arizona.* Lincoln: University of Nebraska Press, 1979. Reprint of 1911 Salem Press second edition. In 1874 a young New England woman marries an army officer, then they set off together for some of the wildest corners of the West. Her accounts bring frontier Arizona life into sharp focus.

Trimble, Marshall. *Arizona Adventure: Action-Packed True Tales of Early Arizona.* San Marino, CA: Golden West, 1994. Nineteen stories from Arizona's Old West.

Trimble, Marshall. *The Law of the Gun.* Phoenix: Arizona Highways Wild West Series, 1997. Trimble sets the record straight about gunfighters in the Old West, then relates stories about famous lawmen and villains.

Trimble, Marshall. *Roadside History of Arizona.* Missoula: Mountain Press Publishing Co., 1986. These fascinating tales, with many historic photos, have been organized by region and highway.

Wagoner, Jay J. *Arizona Territory 1863–1912: A Political History.* Tucson: University of Arizona Press, 1970. Excellent history of the territorial years.

ARCHAEOLOGY

Ambler, J. Richard. *The Anasazi: Prehistoric Peoples of the Four Corners Region.* Flagstaff: Museum of Northern Arizona, 1977, 1983. One of the best overviews of the ancestral pueblo people's history.

Andrews, John P., and Todd W. Bostwick. *Desert Farmers at the River's Edge: The Hohokam and Pueblo Grande.* Phoenix: Pueblo Grande Museum and Cultural Park, 1997. The authors trace this sophisticated prehistoric people from their origins, through their daily life in the Sonoran Desert, to the end of their civilization. The fine text has many illustrations.

Grant, Campbell. *Canyon de Chelly: Its People and Rock Art.* Tucson: University of Arizona Press, 1978. The author describes the geology, archaeology, and history of the canyons. Nearly half the well-illustrated text is devoted to a discussion of the wealth of petroglyphs and pictographs left by the ancestral pueblo people, Hopi, and Navajo.

Gregonis, Linda, and Karl Reinhard. *Hohokam Indians of the Tucson Basin.* Tucson: University of Arizona Press, 1979. Introduction to the prehistoric Hohokams.

Lister, Robert, and Florence Lister. *Those Who Came Before: Southwestern Archaeology in the National Park System.* Tucson: Southwest Parks & Monuments Assoc., 2000. A well-illustrated guide to the history, artifacts, and ruins of prehistoric Native American cultures in the Southwest. Includes descriptions of the parks and monuments that contain these sites today.

McGregor, John C. *Southwestern Archaeology.* Champaign: University of Illinois Press, 1982. If you're curious why archaeologists like their work and how they do it, this book presents the motivations and techniques of this special group of scientists. It also describes cultures and artifacts from the earliest known peoples to the present.

Noble, David Grant. *Ancient Ruins of the Southwest.* Flagstaff: Northland Publishing, 2000. A well-illustrated guide to the prehistoric ruins of Arizona, New Mexico, Colorado, and Utah.

Oppelt, Norman T. *Guide to Prehistoric Ruins of the Southwest.* Boulder: Pruett Publishing Co., 1989. An introduction to ancient cultures with descriptions of more than 200 sites in Arizona, New Mexico, Colorado, and Utah.

Patterson, Alex. *A Field Guide to Rock Art Symbols of the Greater Southwest.* Boulder: Johnson Books, 1992. A dictionary-style guide to petroglyphs and pictographs grouped by subject with many illustrations.

Roberts, David. *In Search of the Old Ones: Exploring the Anasazi World of the Southwest.* New York City: Touchstone Press, 1997. In his quest to understand prehistoric people, the author relates stories of early archaeological discoveries along with his own explorations in the Southwest. The book is unusual in that it's told from the perspective of a writer, not an archaeologist.

Viele, Catherine. *Voices in the Canyon.* Tucson: Southwest Parks and Monuments Assoc., 1980. Highly readable and well-illustrated book about the ancestral pueblo people and their villages of Betatakin, Keet Seel, and Inscription House.

ARIZONA TRIBES OF TODAY

Bassman, Theda, and Gene Balzer. *The Beauty of Navajo Jewelry.* Walnut, CA: Kiva Publishing, 2003. Each of the striking photographs has a description of the artist and the techniques used.

Courlander, Harold. *The Fourth World of the Hopis: The Epic Story of the Hopi tribe as Preserved in Their Legends & Traditions.* Albuquerque: University of New Mexico Press, 1987.

Day, Jonathan S. *Traditional Hopi Kachinas: A New Generation of Carvers.* Flagstaff: Northland Publishing, 2000. Jonathan Day provides a look into Hopi culture with cultural background, interviews with carvers, and 90 color photos. You'll learn the differences between kachina dolls made for collectors and traditional ones for ceremonial use.

Dedera, Don. *Navajo Rugs: How to Find, Evaluate, Buy and Care for Them.* Flagstaff: Northland Publishing, 1996. This handy book provides a history of Navajo weaving, including regional styles, plus practical advice on shopping for and care of rugs.

Dittert, Alfred, Jr., and Fred Plog. *Generations in Clay: Pueblo Pottery of the American Southwest.* Flagstaff: Northland Publishing, 1980. An introduction to the pottery of the Pueblo tribes, both prehistoric and modern. Well-illustrated with black-and-white and color photos.

Dyk, Walter (recorded by). *Left Handed Son of Old Man Hat: A Navajo Autobiography.* Lincoln: University of Nebraska Press, 1995, original copyright 1938. This Navajo relates his story of growing up in the late 1800s.

Fontana, Bernard. *Of Earth and Little Rain.* Tucson: University of Arizona Press, 1990. Essays and photos on life of the Tohono O'odham.

Gillmore, Frances, and Louisa Wetherill. *Traders to the Navajos.* Albuquerque: University of New Mexico Press, 1934, 1983. The Wetherills lived in and explored the Monument Valley region, trading with the Navajo. The authors tell stories about lost mines, early travelers, and the Navajo people.

Gilpin, Laura. *The Enduring Navaho.* Austin: University of Texas Press, 1994. Outstanding photography illustrates the Navajo people, their homes, land, ceremonies, crafts, tribal government, and trading posts.

Jacka, Lois Essary, and Jerry Jacka. *Art of the Hopi, Contemporary Journeys on Ancient Pathways.* Flagstaff: Northland Publishing, 1998. Beautiful color photos on almost every page of this large-format book show the skills, versatility, and variety of Hopi artists.

Kawano, Kenji. *Warriors: Navajo Code Talkers.* Flagstaff: Northland Publishing, 1991. The story of how a small group of Navajo Marines in the Pacific during World War II drew upon their language to create a code that could not be broken by the Japanese. Kenji, a Japanese himself, first came to the Navajo lands in 1971 and became the official photographer of the code talkers association 11 years later. His portraits of 75 surviving Navajo code talkers, taken informally at their homes, are accompanied by quotes of their experiences.

Locke, Raymond F. *The Book of the Navajo.* Los Angeles, CA: Mankind Publishing Co., 2002. The author recounts Navajo legends, art, culture, and history from early to modern times.

Luckert, Karl W. *Coyoteway: A Navajo Holyway Healing Ceremonial.* Tucson: The University of Arizona Press and Flagstaff: Museum of Northern Arizona Press, 1979. A rare look at an important Navajo ceremony. It requires nine days and involves chanting, fire-making, sand painting, and other rituals. Photos and chant translations provide a peek into intricate Navajo beliefs.

Page, Susanne, and Jake Page. *Hopi.* New York: Harry N. Abrams, Inc., 1994 and Abradale Press, 1994. The authors record Hopi spiritual life in text and large color photos, revealing aspects of everyday living, ceremonies, and sacred places rarely seen by outsiders.

Simmons, Leo, ed. *Sun Chief: The Autobiography of a Hopi Indian.* New Haven: Yale University Press, 1963. A Hopi tells of his experiences growing up in both the Hopi and Anglo worlds, then returning to traditional ways.

Suntracks, Larry Evers. *Hopi Photographers/Hopi Images.* Tucson: University of Arizona Press, 1983. The pages feature photography of the Hopi from 1880 to 1980, including historic photos by Anglos and modern work by Hopi photographers; photos appear in black-and-white and color.

Wright, Barton. *Clowns of the Hopi.* Flagstaff: Northland Publishing, 1994, and Walnut, CA: Kiva Publishing 2004. These characters amuse audiences while protecting traditions. The book provides explanations, including the deeper meanings of the clown's antics, with drawings and historic and modern photos.

Wright, Margaret. *Hopi Silver.* Albuquerque: University of New Mexico Press, 2003. Illustrated pages provide history and examples of Hopi silversmithing.

Yava, Albert. *Big Falling Snow.* Albuquerque: University of New Mexico Press, 1992. A Tewa-Hopi discusses the history and traditions of the Tewa and Hopi, including conflicts with missionaries and government officials who tried to Americanize the tribes.

Zolbrod, Paul G. *Diné bahanè: The Navajo Creation Story.* Albuquerque: University of New Mexico Press, 1988. Deities, people, and animals come to life in this translation of Navajo mythology.

NATURAL SCIENCES

Alcock, John. *In a Desert Garden: Love & Death Among the Insects.* New York: W.W. Norton, 1997. The author brings both the keen eye of a scientist and the light-hearted view of a gardener as he relates observations of the insect world at his home in the Sonoran Desert.

Barnes, F.A. *Canyon Country Geology.* Thompson Spring, UT: Arch Hunter Books, 2000. Geologic history and guide to rockhounding with an emphasis on southeastern Utah and adjacent Arizona.

Chronic, Halka. *Roadside Geology of Arizona.* Missoula: Mountain Press Publishing Co., 1986. This book—well-illustrated with photos, maps, and diagrams—has been organized along major highway routes. It also covers some national parks and national monuments.

Cunningham, Richard L. *50 Common Birds of the Southwest.* Tucson: Southwest Parks & Monuments Assoc., 1999. Each bird is represented by a color photo and description of migration, feeding, and nesting habits; the text includes Spanish and Latin names.

Desert Botanical Garden staff, and others. *Desert Wildflowers: A Guide for Identifying, Locating, and Enjoying Arizona Wildflowers and Cactus Blossoms.* Phoenix: Arizona Highways, 1997. Text and color photos take you through the seasons in the different desert regions of the state and provide practical advice for growing your own native plants at home.

Dodge, Natt N., and Jeanne R. Janish. *Flowers of the Southwest Deserts.* Tucson: Southwest Parks and Monuments Assoc., 1985. Desert plant and flower guide for elevations under 4,500 feet.

Doolittle, Jerome. *Canyons and Mesas.* The American Wilderness Series. New York: Time-Life Books, 1974. Text and photos give a feel for the ruggedly beautiful country of northern Arizona and adjacent Utah and Colorado.

Elmore, Francis H., and Jeanne R. Janish. *Shrubs and Trees of the Southwest Uplands.* Tucson: Southwest Parks and Monuments Assoc., 1976. Color-coded pages help locate plants and trees found above 4,500 feet.

Fischer, Pierre C. *70 Common Cacti of the Southwest.* Tucson: Southwest Parks & Monuments Assoc., 1989. A color photo and description accompany each species.

Gray, Mary Taylor. *Watchable Birds of the Southwest.* Missoula, MT: Mountain Press Publishing, 1995. Color pictures reveal 68 species in wetlands, open-country, and high-country habitats.

Halfpenny, James, and Elizabeth Biesiot. *A Field Guide: Mammal Tracking in North America.* Boulder: Johnson Books, 1988. No need to guess what animal passed by. This well-illustrated guide shows how to read the prints of creatures large and small. More determined detectives can peruse the intriguing scatology chapter.

Hare, Trevor. *Poisonous Dwellers of the Desert.* Tucson: Southwest Parks and Monuments Assoc., 1995. The text describes creatures to watch out for—poisonous insects, snakes, and the Gila monster—with advice on insecticides and bite treatment. Also listed are some nonvenomous animals often mistakenly thought to be poisonous.

Hodge, Carle. *All About Saguaros.* Phoenix: Arizona Highways, 1997. Text and color photos take you through the life of this huge cactus and relate how important it is to the Tohono O'odham and to wildlife.

Nations, Dale, and Edmund Stump. *Geology of Arizona.* Dubuque: Kendall/Hunt Publishing Co., 1997. Learn how time and geologic processes have formed the state's remarkable natural features. The book provides a comprehensive introduction to geology with good photos and illustrations.

Olin, George. *House in the Sun: A Natural History of the Sonoran Desert.* Tucson: Southwest Parks and Monuments Assoc., 1994. This guide, illustrated with many color photos, portrays the Sonoran Desert—why it exists and how life has adapted to it. The text also tells how *you* can adapt to the sometimes harsh conditions there, enjoying the desert in safety.

Olin, George, and Dale Thompson. *Mammals of the Southwest Deserts.* Tucson: Southwest Parks & Monuments Assoc., 1982. Black-and-white and color drawings help you to recognize these animals.

Peterson, Roger Tory. *A Field Guide to Western Birds.* Boston: Houghton Mifflin Co., 1998. Well-illustrated with drawings.

Phillips, Steven J. and Patricia Wentworth Comus. *A Natural History of the Sonoran Desert.* Tucson: Arizona-Sonora Desert Museum, Berkeley: University of California Press, 2000. This one-stop 628-page guide tells of the wonders of the Sonoran desert. Illustrated pages describe the geological setting and climate and provide a guide to the plants and wildlife that make their homes here.

Smith, Robert L. *Venomous Animals of Arizona.* Tucson: University of Arizona Press, 1982. Ever wonder about a scorpion's love life? Good descriptions of poisonous insects and animals, with medical notes.

Sweet, Muriel. *Common Edible and Useful Plants of the West.* Happy Camp, CA: Naturegraph Publishers, 1976. Nontechnical descriptions of plants and trees, giving their importance as food, medicines, and other uses. Most of these helpful plants were first discovered by Native Americans and later used by pioneer settlers.

SELECTED FICTION

Coleman, Jane Candia. *Doc Holliday's Woman.* Warner Books, 1995. Based on a true story of Kate Elder who rescued Doc from a hanging and saw him fight at the OK Corral. The author has also published books of Western poetry.

Coleman, Jane Candia. *Stories from Mesa Country.* Swallow Press/Ohio University Press, 1991. Fourteen short stories illustrate how people—especially women—of the old West dealt with their difficulties.

Grey, Zane. This prolific writer produced 131 novels, including many about Arizona. He built a cabin in the woods below the Mogollon Rim, and made frequent visits there during the 1920s. He enjoyed setting off on hunting trips to gather both trophies for his walls and stories for new books.

Ríos, Alberto Alvaro. *Pig Cookies and Other Stories.* Chronicle Books, 1995. Thirteen short stories bring a northern Mexican village to life; the author was born in Nogales, Arizona.

Taylor, Lawrence J., and Maeve Hickey. *The Road to Mexico.* Tucson: University of Arizona Press, 1997. An amusing account of a strange journey, with many cultural insights, from Tucson to Nogales and into Mexico.

Turner, Nancy E. *These Is My Words: The Diary of Sarah Agnes Prine 1881–1901 Arizona Territories.* ReganBooks, 1998. A novel about a woman growing up on the rough frontier.

Urrea, Luis Alberto. *In Search of Snow.* HarperCollins, 1994. A novel of a Don Quixote–like character and his pal who search for life and love in the Arizona desert in the mid-1950s.

Williams, Jeanne. *Home Mountain.* St. Martin's Paperbacks, 1990. A love story set on the east side of the Chiricahuas about a woman who followed her dreams to Arizona and met a fearless outlaw and a powerful ranger in the 1880s.

CHILDREN'S BOOKS

Blue, Martha and others. *Little Prankster Girl.* Flagstaff: Salina Bookshelf Inc., 2003. This story tells of a Navajo girl's determination to learn weaving and gain recognition from those around her. The text is in both English and Navajo.

Lowell, Susan, and Jim Harris. *The Three Little Javelinas.* Rising Moon, 1992. A Southwest version of the three little pigs story with wonderful illustrations. It's also available in a bilingual Spanish-English edition.

Moreillon, Judi, and Michael Chiago. *Sing Down the Rain.* Walnut, CA: Kiva Publishing, 1997. Poetic account of the Tohono O'odham's traditional life in the desert; with illustrations.

Skrepcinski, Denice, and others. *Cody Coyote Cooks.* Tricycle Press, 1996. A Southwest cookbook for kids with coyote tales and recipes that kids can follow.

REFERENCE

Benchmark Arizona Road & Recreation Atlas. Skokie, IL: Rand McNally, 2004. Exceptionally easy-to-read maps at 1:400,000 scale with GPS grids and both shaded landscape and color-coded land-ownership maps.

Walker, Henry P., and Don Bufkin. *Historical Atlas of Arizona.* Norman, OK: University of Oklahoma Press, 1986. Clear maps and concise text cover the geography, Native American tribes, exploration, and development of Arizona.

CUISINE

Fischer, Al, and Mildred Fischer. *Arizona Cook Book.* San Marino, CA: Golden West, 1983. A culinary guide to the state, including Native American, Western, and barbecue cuisine. Prepare your own cactus jelly and other delicacies.

Kavena, Juanita Tiger. *Hopi Cookery.* Tucson: University of Arizona Press, 1980. Learn how to make piki bread, fashion a yucca pie, fix squash and fresh corn casserole, and bake a prairie dog.

Mann, Betsey. *By Request: Most Wanted Recipes from Arizona's Favorite Restaurants.* Flagstaff: Northland Publishing, 1998. You can cook up some of the most popular dishes from the menus of neighborhood to five-star restaurants.

Internet Resources

Although a virtual visit to Arizona cannot replace the real thing, you'll find an enormous amount of helpful information on the Internet. Thousands of websites interlink to cover everything from the Grand Canyon's environmental issues to Scottsdale restaurant reviews. Up-to-the-minute weather and news reports lie at your fingertips 24 hours a day.

WHERE TO START

www.arizonahandbook.com
Drop by the author's website for the latest updates, Internet links, and photo galleries; it's an extension of this book and a way to put in your two cents worth.

Yahoo
www.yahoo.com
Yahoo will take you almost anywhere in Arizona with its well-organized offerings. Enter and select Regional U.S. States, then Arizona. From there you can select Cities or such topics as arts, community and culture, government, news, recreation and sports, and travel. Other search engines work well, too.

The Arizona Office of Tourism
www.arizonaguide.com
This online guide takes you to many corners of the state. **Arizona Web Hub** (www.azweb-hub.com) also has an extensive list by subject. **AZ Tourist Online** (www.aztourist.com) describes the travel scene with stories, news, dining reviews, and event listings.

Arizona Republic
www.azcentral.com
Although based in the Phoenix area, this site has excellent statewide coverage of news, weather, sports, business, entertainment, and travel.

Arizona Highways
www.arizonahighways.com
Arizona Highways offers some of the same beautiful photos, travel information, hike descriptions, and entertaining stories found in its magazine pages.

Desert USA
www.desertusa.com
If you're interested in learning about the desert, check for information on places to visit and the plants and animals you might meet there.

AZWilderness
www.azwilderness.com
Describes many trails along with articles, a forum, and a calendar. Also visit **AZventure in Hiking** (www.swlink.net/~ttidyman/hiking) for trails, links, clubs, and Grand Canyon information.

OUTSTANDING LOCAL SITES

Grand Canyon National Park
www.nps.gov/grca
The park has so many things to see and do that it's well worth visiting the official site.

Flagstaff Convention & Visitors Bureau
www.flagstaffarizona.org

In north-central Arizona, the Flagstaff Convention & Visitors Bureau will fill you in on the sights and services there.

Sedona-Oak Creek Chamber of Commerce
www.visitsedona.com

The Chamber of Commerce website takes you to the magical Red Rock Country south of Flagstaff.

Greater Phoenix Convention & Visitors Bureau
www.phoenixcvb.com

In south-central Arizona, the Greater Phoenix Convention & Visitors Bureau presents regional travel information.

Metropolitan Tucson Convention & Visitors Bureau
www.visittucson.org

Farther south, the Metropolitan Tucson Convention & Visitors Bureau has the latest on travel in and around the Old Pueblo.

Index

Astronomy

D

G

Ghost Towns

H

I

J

K

L

Mountain Biking

Prehistoric Sites

Scenic Drives

T

U

Acknowledgments

Many thanks to the hundreds of people who assisted in making the *Moon Handbooks Arizona* as complete and accurate as it is. I am especially indebted to my mother, Doris Weir, for editing the entire book—diligently rearranging words and commas to make the text easier and clearer to read. I've also been fortunate to have a fine crew at Avalon Travel Publishing who helped plan the new edition, edited the text, updated the maps, laid out the pages, and delivered the book into your hands.

The staff of the National Park Service, U.S. Forest Service, Bureau of Land Management, U.S. Fish and Wildlife Service, Arizona Game and Fish, and Arizona State Parks, whose high standards make Arizona such a wonderful place to visit, have been extremely helpful on my travels and in verifying the manuscript. Tourist offices—from the tiniest communities to those in the big cities—supplied valuable ideas, advice, and maps. Barton Wright's excellent drawing of the Hopi Reservation, which he kindly gave permission to use in earlier editions, appears again in the Hopi Country section.

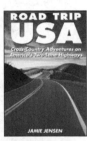

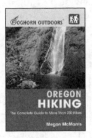

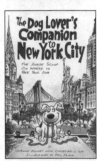

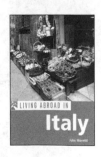

U.S.~Metric Conversion

1 inch	=	2.54 centimeters (cm)
1 foot	=	.304 meters (m)
1 yard	=	0.914 meters
1 mile	=	1.6093 kilometers (km)
1 km	=	.6214 miles
1 fathom	=	1.8288 m
1 chain	=	20.1168 m
1 furlong	=	201.168 m
1 acre	=	.4047 hectares
1 sq km	=	100 hectares
1 sq mile	=	2.59 square km
1 ounce	=	28.35 grams
1 pound	=	.4536 kilograms
1 short ton	=	.90718 metric ton
1 short ton	=	2000 pounds
1 long ton	=	1.016 metric tons
1 long ton	=	2240 pounds
1 metric ton	=	1000 kilograms
1 quart	=	.94635 liters
1 US gallon	=	3.7854 liters
1 Imperial gallon	=	4.5459 liters
1 nautical mile	=	1.852 km

To compute Celsius temperatures, subtract 32 from Fahrenheit and divide by 1.8. To go the other way, multiply Celsius by 1.8 and add 32.

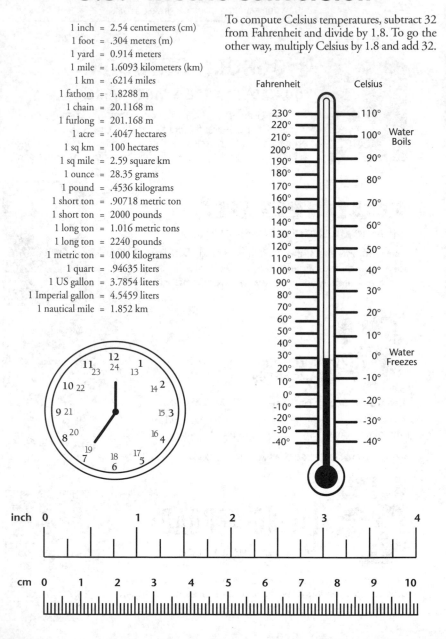

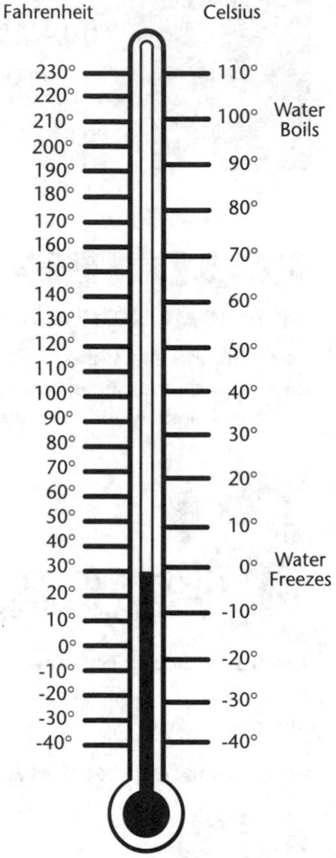

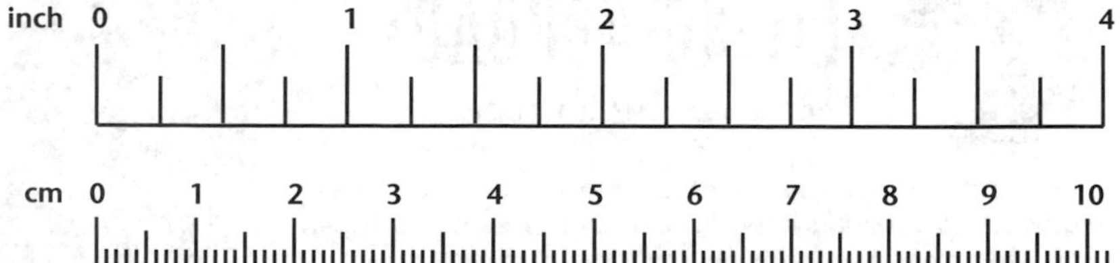

Keeping Current

Although we strive to produce the most up-to-date guidebook humanly possible, change is unavoidable. Between the time this book goes to print and the moment you read it, a handful of the businesses noted in these pages will undoubtedly change prices, move, or even close their doors forever. Other worthy attractions will open for the first time. If you have a favorite gem you'd like to see included in the next edition, or see anything that needs updating, clarification, or correction, please drop us a line. Send your comments via email to atpfeedback@avalonpub.com, or use the address below.

Moon Handbooks Arizona
Avalon Travel Publishing
1400 65th Street, Suite 250
Emeryville, CA 94608, USA
www.moon.com

Editor: Sabrina Young
Series Manager: Kevin McLain
Acquisitions Editor: Rebecca K. Browning
Copy Editor: Kate McKinley
Graphics Coordinator: Deb Dutcher
Production Coordinator: Amber Pirker
Cover Designer: Kari Gim
Interior Designer: Amber Pirker
Map Editors: Kat Smith, Kevin Anglin
Cartographers: Mike Morgenfeld, Kat Kalamaras, Suzanne Service
Indexer: Deana Shields

ISBN: 1-56691-689-5
ISSN: 1538-120X

Printing History
1st Edition—1986
9th Edition—April 2005
5 4 3 2 1

AVALON
publishing group incorporated

Avalon Travel Publishing
An Imprint of
Avalon Publishing Group, Inc.

Front cover photo: Cathedral Rock, Sedona, © Niebrugge Images

Printed in the U.S.A. by Worzalla